S0-BDG-296

## Themes and Writers Series

**G. Robert Carlsen**

General Editor

---

FOCUS
*Themes in Literature*

PERCEPTION
*Themes in Literature*

INSIGHTS
*Themes in Literature*

ENCOUNTERS
*Themes in Literature*

AMERICAN LITERATURE
*Themes and Writers*

BRITISH AND
WESTERN LITERATURE
*Themes and Writers*

# About the Editors of the Themes and Writers Series

**G. Robert Carlsen,** Professor of English and Professor of Education at the University of Iowa, has taught English in the public schools of Minneapolis and at the Universities of Minnesota, Colorado, Texas, Hawaii, and Iowa. He has served as a consultant in curriculum revision to a number of school systems in Texas, Iowa, Colorado, California, Oklahoma, and Virginia. For many years he was the book review editor of young people's books for the *English Journal* and was a coauthor of an edition of *Books for You.* Dr. Carlsen is a past president of the National Council of Teachers of English. He has written some seventy articles for professional journals and is coauthor of *The Brown-Carlsen Test of Listening Comprehension* and of the National Council of Social Studies' publication entitled *Social Understanding Through Literature.* He is also the author of *Books and the Teen-Age Reader.*

**Ruth Christoffer Carlsen** is a coauthor with Dr. Carlsen of several anthologies for young readers. She has also written successful juvenile books. Her research was of particular value in the development of the anthology series. As a coauthor with her husband she works on the development of anthology materials, in particular, for the texts *Perception* and *Encounters.*

**Anthony Tovatt** is Professor of English in Burris Laboratory School, Ball State University. He has been the director of an extended research study on the teaching of composition under the Program for English of the United States Office of Education. For eighteen years he edited the column "This World of English," which appeared regularly in *The English Journal.* Active over the years in the National Council of Teachers of English, he has made many contributions to materials that the NCTE has published and made available to classroom teachers. His articles have appeared in professional journals and his poetry has appeared in magazines and newspapers. Dr. Tovatt's colorful career began in a rural, one-room high school near a western Indian reservation where teachers before him had been intimidated by the students and beaten off before the school year ended. His stories of four happy years there read like some of Jesse Stuart's accounts of his early teaching experience.

**Patricia O. Tovatt** has taught English at both high school and junior high school levels in Colorado and Indiana. She works as a coauthor with her husband on the development of anthology materials, in particular for the texts *Focus* and *Insights.*

**Edgar H. Schuster,** Language Arts Coordinator for the Allentown (Pa.) School District, has taught English in both urban and suburban high schools in the Philadelphia area. He has also taught at the college level. He has written articles for many professional journals, including the *Clearing House,* the *English Journal,* and *Educational Leadership.* Dr. Schuster has been a Master Teacher at Harvard University and is a recipient of a Lindback Foundation Award for Distinguished Teaching. He is a coauthor of McGraw-Hill's *American English Today.*

**Miriam Gilbert,** Associate Professor of English at the University of Iowa, has taught English and American Literature at Iowa since 1969. Her primary work, both as a teacher and a director, has been with Shakespeare's plays. She has presented papers and led discussions on the teaching of Shakespeare, including two workshops for teachers at the Institute of Renaissance Students in Ashland, Oregon. At Iowa she has been a frequent teacher in the Literature Semester, a team-taught intensive survey course. Dr. Gilbert currently serves as Director of Undergraduate Studies in English at the University of Iowa.

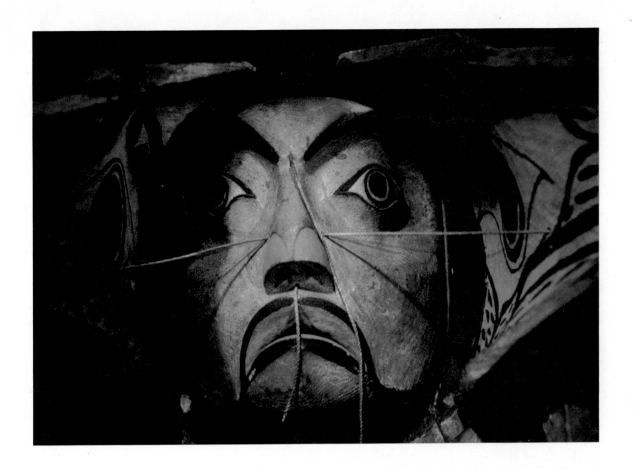

# ENCOUNTERS

*Third Edition*
THEMES IN LITERATURE

G. Robert Carlsen / Ruth Christoffer Carlsen

**Webster Division, McGraw-Hill Book Company**
New York, St. Louis, San Francisco, Dallas, Atlanta

## Special Acknowledgments

The Editors and the Publishers wish to thank Ms. Eleanor Wier, Secondary
Reading Consultant, Ferguson-Florissant School District, St. Louis, Missouri,
for her work in developing reading skills material for the program and
Mr. Lee Davis, English and Humanities Teacher, Sleepy Hollow High School,
Tarrytown, New York, for his work on the Galleries of Fine Arts and on the
development of related gallery and humanities activities for the program.

Editorial Development: John A. Rothermich
Editing and Styling: Linda Richmond
Design: James Darby
Production: Suzanne Cox
Permissions: Karen Sekiguchi

Photo Editor: Suzanne Volkman
Cover Photo: Esther Henderson/Photo Researchers

**Library of Congress Cataloging in Publication Data**

Carlsen, G   Robert, date   comp.
  Encounters.
  (Themes and writers series)
  Includes indexes.
  SUMMARY: A thematically arranged anthology of
poems, short stories, plays, and novellas for the
tenth-grade reader.
  1. Literature—Collections.  [1. Literature—
Collections]  I. Carlsen, Ruth Christoffer.
II. Title.
PZ5.C1828En   1979   808.8   77-28473
ISBN 0-07-009863-8

Copyright © 1979, 1973, 1967 by McGraw-Hill, Inc. All Rights Reserved.
Printed in the United States of America. No part of this publication
may be reproduced, stored in a retrieval system, or transmitted, in any
form or by any means, electronic, mechanical, photocopying, recording,
or otherwise, without the prior written permission of the publisher.

# Contents

## Brief Encounters

# Crosscurrents

# Private Moods

# Dreams

# People under Pressure

# Life's Ironies

Every man
who knows how to read
has it in his power to magnify himself,
to multiply the ways
in which he exists,
to make his life full, significant
and interesting.

ALDOUS HUXLEY

# BRIEF ENCOUNTERS

*The Parable
of the Good Samaritan*

*St. Luke* 10:30–37

A certain man went down from Jerusalem to Jericho, and fell among thieves, who stripped him of his raiment, and wounded him, and departed, leaving him half dead.

And by chance there came down a certain priest that way: and when he saw him, he passed by on the other side.

And likewise a Levite, when he was at the place, came and looked on him, and passed by on the other side.

But a certain Samaritan, as he journeyed, came where he was: and when he saw him, he had compassion on him; and went to him, and bound up his wounds, pouring in oil and wine, and set him on his own beast, and brought him to an inn, and took care of him.

And on the morrow when he departed, he took out two pence, and gave them to the host, and said unto him, Take care of him; and whatsoever thou spendest more, when I come again, I will repay thee.

Which now of these three, thinkest thou, was neighbor unto him that fell among the thieves?

The Good Samaritan, *Vincent Van Gogh. Kröller-Müller Museum, Otterlo*
*The great Dutch painter Van Gogh captures the climactic moment of this famous brief encounter.*

For almost two thousand years, people have read and remembered the parable of the Good Samaritan. Its simplicity testifies to the power of a tale well told. Here in a few words is a varied gallery of unexpected meetings filled with open or hidden conflicts. The brief encounter with the robbers ends disastrously for the traveler; the meeting with the priest changes the fate of neither; but the encounter with the Samaritan is a rewarding one. Hence, this one short tale explores varieties of brief encounters.

Meetings between strangers are always interesting. When such meetings take place between extraordinary people or in extraordinary circumstances, they acquire the power to fascinate us. Out of these meetings develop dramatic changes in people's lives —some tragic, some comic, some lasting, and some fleeting.

Since capable writers have an eye for change and for patterns in human existence, they are always interested in meetings that disrupt the calm, normal flow of life: the dramatic moment. Each meeting, no matter how casual, has some effect—good, bad, or callously indifferent—on the human character.

Theodore H. White in his book *The Mountain Road* gives an imaginative definition of this theme.

> You hold a block of metal in your hand. And it's solid. Yet within the metal there are molecules or atoms, all moving by laws of their own. Press a block of pure gold against a block of silver. When you separate them they seem unchanged. But a good physical chemist will show you that where they have been in contact invisible flecks of gold have wandered across the barrier of structure and buried themselves in the silver. And atoms of silver, somehow, in the structure of the gold.
>
> I think that when people are pressed close they act the same way. Part of you enters them, part of them enters you. Long after you forget the names and faces, they are still a part of you. Sometimes it is frightening to think that every person you have ever hated, or feared, or run away from is part of you. But so is every person you have ever learned from, every friend you ever had.

As you read the following selections, continually ask yourself questions about this theme: What meetings with other have changed your opinions or action? What are the forces that set someone for one person but against another?

That the strangers who meet one another in the pages of this section meet only briefly and under extraordinary circumstances throws a strong light on their actions. Each reveals himself or herself in attitudes that the ordinary routine of his or her life would normally conceal. For this reason, this theme is rich in sudden discoveries, surprising outcomes, dramatic choices.

If you were to ask a modern writer to retell the parable of the Good Samaritan in a modern setting, say, Mexico, and to tell the story from the victim's point of view, you might get a story like "Stopover in Querétaro." However, this personal narrative records an actual experience. See whether the author changes his attitude toward strangers as he is forced into close contact with people of a foreign land.

# Stopover in Querétaro

### JERROLD BEIM

Two years ago my family and I were driving to Mexico City on the Juarez highway.[1] We had a blowout and the car turned over. My wife, who was driving, and my daughter were killed instantly. One of my twin sons, Andy, suffered a severe concussion and had to be hospitalized in a town called Querétaro,[2] about ninety kilometers[3] from Mexico City. My other son, Seth, was uninjured but stunned by what had happened; and I had minor injuries and was in a state of shock.

Many people have said to me since: "Wasn't it awful that it had to happen in a strange country?" And I'll confess that at the time, staying at the hospital in Querétaro, I felt that I was at the end of the world, far from family or friends who could have been of help or comfort to me. But let me tell it as it happened.

Immediately after the accident we were surrounded by Mexicans, mostly country people in sombreros and *rebozos*,[4] and all, naturally, total strangers. But one man, in a business suit, was leading Seth and me to his car. In excellent English he explained that he had been behind us and had seen our car turn over. It was he who had summoned the police and ambulance from Querétaro, and now he was driving Seth and me to the hospital. The ambulance had sped ahead with Andy. The man told me his name was Juan Martinez.[5] He asked if I knew any Spanish, and when I told him I spoke only a little he assured me that he would stay with me until he saw we were getting proper care.

Querétaro was a sizable town, but it seemed primitive, and I doubted that we could get adequate medical attention. The sight of the hospital did not ease my anxiety. It was run by a Dr. Francisco Alcozer Pozo,[6] and did not even look like a hospital. The nurse who greeted us explained that the doctor lived on one side of the patio, and his mother lived on the opposite side. To the rear was the hospital itself, a row of little rooms opening off the patio. Seth and I were taken into one of these rooms. The nurse explained too rapidly for me to understand (Juan Martinez interpreted) that the doctor was busy with Andy.

Juan took Seth out to the patio while the nurse cleaned and bandaged the cut on my head. I glanced about the room and noticed that the paint on the walls was scaling, the furnishings were antiquated. I was overwhelmed by what had happened to my wife and daughter, and certain that in this God-forsaken place Andy would not receive the medical care he would need to survive.

Soon Juan returned with Seth and a man in a white coat.

"This is the doctor," Juan said. "Doctor Pozo."

---

1. This is the highway south from Ciudad Juárez \'sē·ū ᵃthath ᵃhwa·räs\ the Mexican city across the Rio Grande from El Paso, Texas.
2. Querétaro\kā ᵃrā·ta·rō\ the capital of its state, has a population of about 35,000.
3. kilometer\kǐ ᵃlǒ·mə·tər\ 3,280.8 ft., about three-fifths of a mile.
4. rebozo\rā ᵃbō·sō\ a long colorful scarf or drape worn by Mexican women.
5. Juan Martinez\hwan mar ᵃtē·nās\
6. Francisco Alcozer Pozo\fran ᵃsēs·kō al·kō ᵃsär ᵃpō·sō\

Copyright, July 1954, Curtis Publishing Company.
Reprinted by permission of McIntosh and Otis, Inc.

My spirit rallied slightly when I saw the doctor. He was tall and thin, and he had an intelligent face. In slow and not very good English he expressed his deep sympathy for all that had happened. He said he doubted that any of Andy's bones were broken—he'd have to wait for the X rays—but he was sure Andy had a severe concussion. The boy was still unconscious.

I wanted to send to Mexico City for a specialist at once. Doctor Pozo said he would do whatever I desired but he thought we should see the X rays first. He looked at the cut on my head, my finger, and then he examined Seth, who was sitting on the foot of the bed.

Suddenly from outside I heard voices that made my heart leap. They were definitely American!

"It must be *Señor* and *Señora*[7] MacKenzie," Doctor Pozo explained. "They are Americans who live here."

Americans here! They came in, an attractive man and woman, who apparently knew the doctor well. Doctor Pozo left me alone with them.

The MacKenzies had heard of the accident and had come at once to offer help. They said they were the only Americans in Querétaro, Mr. MacKenzie being the manager of a local gabardine factory. They assured me that Doctor Pozo was a very competent physician; but I felt that they would have to say that, under the circumstances.

Seth, apparently still stunned, sat silent on the bed.

"Let us take Seth home for the time being," Mrs. MacKenzie suggested. "We have a five-year-old boy who would love his company. At least, you won't have to worry about him."

Even though these people were complete strangers, Seth readily went with them. I think he was glad to get away from all the horrors of the past few hours.

There were scores of things I had to do. My family and my wife's family had to be notified, and the MacKenzies helped get them on the telephone which was just outside the room. My wife and I had always approved of cremation,

and the MacKenzies offered to make all the arrangements. When they finally left they promised to bring Seth back for a visit the next day.

It wasn't until they were gone that I realized Juan Martinez had disappeared. I rang for the nurse and made her understand that I was looking for the man who had brought me here. She said he had left the hospital. And I hadn't even had a chance to thank him for all he had done.

Later Doctor Pozo returned. Andy was still unconscious, and it was clearly evident that he had a severe concussion. I repeated that I wanted to call in a brain specialist from Mexico City, and Doctor Pozo put in the call. The specialist said that Andy could not be moved for weeks, and he didn't feel there was any point in his coming to Querétaro. It was obvious to him that Andy's progress depended on time and he said that Doctor Pozo could handle the situation as well as he. He suggested, however, that we keep him informed by telephone. I still wasn't satisfied. If Andy pulled through, I felt it would be only a matter of luck.

Doctor Pozo now turned to setting my dislocated finger. I remember fading from consciousness while it was being done and dreaming we were in the car again, on our way to Mexico City. Then I would come to and realize what had happened. Only heavy sedatives put me to sleep that night.

Another nurse was on duty in the morning. This one spoke a bit of English, and told me there was no change in Andy, but that a man was waiting to see me.

It was Juan Martinez. I greeted him like an old friend. Where had he disappeared to yesterday?

He had seen me with the Americans, and knew they would take care of me. But he had stayed overnight in Querétaro wanting to be of further help and hoping that maybe the little boy would be better. Now he had to get on to Mexico City.

---

7. **Señor**\sän ᴬyōr\ mister. **Señora**\sän ᴬyō·ra\ mistress.

I didn't know how to express my gratitude for all he had done. We exchanged addresses. I would look him up in Nogales.[8] We would be sure to see each other again.

I was lonelier than ever after Juan Martinez left. Only the telephone kept me bolstered through the day. Family and friends called, offering all kinds of help. It was decided that I should send Seth to his grandmother's while I remained with Andy.

Mrs. MacKenzie visited me during the day, too, bringing Seth, along with her own boy. The children had had a wonderful time together. Arrangements were made for Seth to be driven to Mexico City, then to go on to the United States by plane.

While Mrs. MacKenzie was there Doctor Pozo summoned me. Andy had regained consciousness. He stared at me with recognition, though not a sound came from his lips. Doctor Pozo said it might be weeks before he spoke.

Bidding good-by to Seth was hard. Though I knew the separation was only temporary, it emphasized how broken my family had become.

8. **Nogales**\sp. pron. nō ▲ga•läs\ evidently the Mexican town of about 14,000 across the border from the Arizona town of Nogales.

Late in the afternoon an unexpected call came through from my brother. He lived in San Francisco, but he had flown to Mexico City and was leaving for Querétaro in a few minutes.

His first words as he came in were, "We must have you removed to Mexico City at once!"

I explained why that couldn't be done. But it was wonderful having him with me. He spent the night in the hospital, and we sat up talking for hours.

For the next few days Andy's condition scarcely changed. Doctor Pozo drained fluid from the boy's spine and hinted that an operation might be necessary if he didn't begin to talk soon.

Doctor Pozo had suggested to my brother that I should leave Andy's bedside for a while, and explore the town. So one sunny morning we ventured outdoors. The hospital was located on a narrow, cobblestoned street and at the very next corner was a small-town Mexican market place, swarming with flies and filled with unappetizing food. My brother had come through this market on his arrival in Querétaro —that was why he had been so shocked. We walked until we reached the plaza, with its inevitable bandstand, and we sat on one of the benches under large shade trees. I felt myself being eyed by everyone who walked past.

"This town is off the usual tourist beat," I told my brother. "They're not accustomed to seeing Americans."

An old woman in a dark-blue shawl approached us.

"I guess she wants money," my brother said, digging into his pocket. But her hand wasn't out, and she was speaking to me. After she had repeated her words, I understood, and I fought to keep back the tears.

"She knows that I am the American who was in the accident," I told my brother, "and that my little boy is very sick. She is praying—for the souls of my wife and daughter—and for the recovery of my boy."

One afternoon just before my brother had to leave, I was sunning in the patio while he sat with Andy. Suddenly he came running toward me.

"I showed him a book and asked if he'd like me to read it to him—and he spoke. Just one word—'Yes'—but he spoke!"

We found the doctor and went to Andy's bedside. Yes—he spoke—just a word at a time, slowly, with effort, and only when asked something—but he spoke!

As I returned to the hospital after seeing my brother off, a cluster of ragged urchins was around the door. They looked at me and grinned.

"*El niño está hablando!*"[9] one of them said. They had heard the good news already. And one of the children held out a toy, a little horse carved of balsa wood and painted colorfully. "*Por el niño!*"[10]

One afternoon I ventured into a local hotel for lunch; I had waited until Andy had fallen asleep, and had left word where I would be. Soon after I was seated the waiter told me I was wanted on the telephone. I became alarmed, and as I lifted the phone it was a vast relief to hear the voice of an American—a man:

"You don't know me, sir, but I'm here with a group of American doctors visiting hospitals and clinics all over Mexico. I met Doctor Pozo this morning and he told me about your accident. I saw him perform an operation this morning, and I thought you would be interested in knowing that I consider him a very fine doctor and an excellent surgeon. Your son is in very good hands."

I apologized to Doctor Pozo for my lack of confidence. He said that it was only natural for a father to be anxious, especially one who had gone through all I had.

As the days went by Andy got constantly better. He was talking more and soon he was able to sit up in the sunny patio.

One afternoon Doctor Pozo said Andy could travel at the end of the week, if we would like

---

9. **El niño está hablando**\ĕl ▲nēn·yō ĕs ▲ta 'ha ▲blan-dō\ The boy is talking.
10. **Por el niño**\pōr ĕl ▲nēn·yō\ For the boy.

to move to Mexico City. Andy would have to be hospitalized for a while longer, but Doctor Pozo thought we would be more comfortable there.

I had a job to do before I left, one that I had put off for days. I had to decide what to do with my wife's and daughter's clothes. I spoke to Doctor Pozo and he suggested that I give the adult clothes to the clinic where they would be distributed to needy people, and the child's things to the orphanage. Doctor Pozo would take the things for the clinic, but he thought it would be nice if I went to the orphanage myself. It was in a building that once had been a private residence, and Doctor Pozo said it was an example of pure colonial architecture[11] that I ought to see.

It wasn't an easy mission, sorting my little girl's clothes and then carrying them to the orphanage. All the buildings along the street looked very much alike, with crumbling pink, blue or white walls; but the convent was easily distinguishable by its sturdy architecture and by the cross over the doorway. I rang the bell and managed to say to the old man who let me in, "Clothes for the children."

He led me into the most beautiful patio I have ever seen. A fountain played in an expanse of green lawn, and arches curved on the three walls of the house that enclosed it. The Mother Superior[12] in her long black robes came toward me. We conversed for a few moments, and then I started to leave.

"The children wish to thank you," she said, and motioned me into one of the interior rooms.

It was an immense, beautiful room, with shiny tile floors and a high, carved ceiling. It was sparsely furnished, but what there was looked like precious Spanish antiques. The Mother Superior disappeared for a moment, then returned leading a line of small girls in neat blue pinafores.

My daughter had been blue-eyed and flaxen-haired. These little girls were black-haired, with dark, shining eyes. I had been deprived of my daughter and these were children without fathers or mothers. I wanted to take every one in my arms. They thanked me for the clothes, in clear, piping voices, and then I left.

I remember being unable to go right back to the hospital. I sat in the plaza, getting control of myself, so that I could return to Andy. Then I noticed a tall, nice-looking man about my age, walking hesitantly toward me.

He sat down beside me. Was I the gentleman staying at the hospital with the little boy who had been hurt?

Yes, I was.

He owned that dry-goods store on the corner, he told me, nodding proudly toward it. I tried to convey that I thought it a fine-looking store. I couldn't bring myself to say that I wanted to be alone.

And then he explained why he had ventured to intrude on my privacy. He had seen me sitting here in the plaza and had wanted to talk to me many times. Because he felt a deep sympathy for me. A few years ago he and his family had started for Mexico City. His wife's parents lived there, and he used to take his wife and their three children to visit them once or twice a year. On that last trip, his car had been in an accident, too— a speeder had crashed into it. His wife and two of his children had been killed. And since then life for him had been an agony.

"Only now it is a little better. It is such an old proverb and it must sound foolish to you now, but time does help things. And time will help you, even though you still have much pain to live through."

I couldn't answer him. But suddenly I wasn't alone and I knew that really I had never been a stranger in Querétaro, nor was this such a foreign land. I was sitting beside someone who had been through the same ordeal. There were benches like this and people like us in every country of the world.

---

11. **colonial architecture,** the style of architecture in vogue when the American states and Mexico were colonies of Great Britain and Spain, respectively. It often blended sturdy strength with pleasant simplicity and graceful adornment.
12. **Mother Superior,** the title of the woman in charge of a convent.

It was about two days later that I left by hired car for Mexico City. Andy was settled comfortably in the back seat and I was beside the driver.

Doctor Pozo, the MacKenzies, the nurses, the servants—all had said good-by to us from the hospital door. Word had got around that we were leaving, and people of the town—men in sombreros, women in shawls, a man in the doorway of a dry-goods store—waved to us as we left Querétaro.

---

### I

#### TRACING A CHANGE OF ATTITUDE

Although a stopover is ordinarily a casual and unimportant interruption of a trip, this stopover is neither casual nor unimportant, for the lives of the Beim family are terribly and finally changed by the automobile accident. As Beim recovers from the shock of his loss, an equally profound change takes place in the mind of the writer. It is brought about directly by his encounters with the people of Querétaro. Here are some quotations from the story. What feelings and attitudes on the writer's part do they reveal? Trace a developing pattern from the first through the last.

1. " 'Wasn't it awful that it had to happen in a strange country?' "

2. "Americans here!"

3. "And I hadn't even had a chance to thank him for all he had done."

4. "An old woman . . . approached us. . . . She was 'praying—for the souls of my wife and daughter—and for the recovery of my boy.' "

5. "I apologized to Dr. Pozo for my lack of confidence. He said that it was only natural for a father to be anxious. . . ."

6. ". . . I wasn't alone and I knew that really I never had been a stranger in Querétaro, nor was this such a foreign land."

### II

#### IMPLICATIONS

Reading should always be a pleasure. Whether a story is light or serious, readers' enjoyment of it will be greater and their understanding more last-ing if they let it stimulate their own thinking. After most of the selections in this anthology, you will find general statements like the ones that follow. Their purpose is to ask you to evaluate what you have read in your own terms. They may be used as the basis of class discussions, of debates, or of brief written essays. And while they help you clarify and organize your reactions to the story, they will also sharpen your ability to express your own opinions more accurately.

1. Something inside us seems to make us distrust foreigners.

2. Tragedy tends to remove the barriers between strangers.

3. Although Jerrold Beim lost a great deal through the accident, he also gained something valuable through his encounters with the people of Querétaro.

### III

#### TECHNIQUES

"Stopover in Querétaro" is an informal essay, a short piece of prose written in everyday conversational language about one subject and its effects upon the writer. There are many kinds of essays, ranging, for instance, from a highly impersonal report of scientific research to such deeply personal accounts as this one. In an informal essay, writers reveal much about their own personalities as they describe their experiences.

1. What would you say are the most important character traits the author reveals in this essay? Compare your opinions with those of the rest of the class.

2. If this account had been written in the third person instead of the first person, what differences would it have made in your reactions to it?

3. From each of the following pairs of adjectives, choose the one that better describes the quality of this essay.

   **a.** down to earth    high-flown
   **b.** difficult    easy
   **c.** objective    subjective
   **d.** straightforward    devious
   **e.** emotional    unemotional
   **f.** restrained    unrestrained
   **g.** quiet    brassy

Do the seven adjectives you have selected completely describe the style of the essay? What others would you add?

Contests of courage and endurance
often produce strange results: respect, fear,
hate, admiration. In such contests,
winning or losing may well be a secondary issue.
What are the results of the meeting
between strangers in "The Grains of Paradise"?
Is it ever true that from defeat comes victory?

# The Grains
# of Paradise

## JAMES STREET

I do not like stories that suggest one thing and mean another and so, right off, I want you to know that the grains of paradise are the seeds of little hot peppers, very hot; and that this is a story about some fiery little peppers and some people in the village of Feliz,[1] which is down in Mexico's state of Tabasco and nine hundred miles from nowhere.

The hotel was on a corner when I was there years ago, and across the way was a church which was surrounded by a gray wall, and the wall was shared by bougainvillaea, buzzards and unmeasured time. It was mid-afternoon when I got out of the bus at the hotel. The bus was painted purple and yellow, and bore the name of Rosaura, painted in red. I am sure it was the name of the driver's sweetheart. In Feliz, everything was personalized.[2]

An Indian was sleeping by the doorway. And his ox team was sleeping, hitched to a two wheeled cart, and two or three dogs. Everything was sleeping. Nothing stirred in the high-mountain solitude of Feliz. The hotel was cool inside, and shadowy, and the clerk opened his eyes when he heard my steps and greeted me

sleepily in Spanish. I replied in Spanish, my very best, and that's pretty bad.

Quickly he was alert and spoke to me in English. His English was no better than my Spanish. He was smaller than I am, considerably smaller, and I am about average. His clothes were mussy, but his little black mustache was trim.

I signed the register, and he studied my signature and then he spoke it aloud, "Mr. Cordell Hoyle, Lystra, North Carolina."

For a second he hesitated, and looked up at me and down at my name, and I had the feeling he was going to ask me a question or make some comment, some pleasantry about the weather or the trip or maybe about American visitors. But he didn't. He asked me if I'd had lunch, and when I told him I hadn't, he said that the kitchen was closed, but that he'd arrange for me to have a snack after I'd washed up. Then he hissed, "Psst, psst," and a barefooted Indian came out of the shadows. The clerk told him to take my bags to Room No. 3.

It was a bowl-and-pitcher room[3] and was on the corner and had two windows. Out of one I could see the plaza of Feliz, empty at that hour and its trees drooping their somnolence. Out of the other I could see the church—the Church of the Tears of the Blessed Virgin—and beyond the church were the mountains, hovering high in desperate grandeur, heavy green for miles, then hazy blue into the sky.

It was these mountains that had brought me to Southern Mexico, down almost to where the country joins Guatemala. In those days I worked for the University of North Carolina's College of Agriculture and for months I had been in Tabasco and in the adjacent state of Chiapas,[4] looking for a certain variety of corn

---

1. **Feliz**\'fā 'lēs\ Tabasco\tə 'bäs·kō\ is in southern Mexico, southeast of Vera Cruz.
2. **personalize**\'pər·sə·nə 'laiz\ to endow with a personality, to give a name to and treat as a person.
3. **bowl-and-pitcher room**, one equipped with a wash basin and a water pitcher. The room (and perhaps the whole hotel) lacked modern plumbing.
4. **Chiapas**\'chya 'pas\ a state south of Tabasco and north and west of Guatemala.

Copyright 1955 by The Curtis Publishing Co. reprinted by permission of the Harold Matson Company, Inc.

to be used for experimental purposes. I had come to Feliz to rest a day or two before pulling out for home.

I washed the dust from my face and hands, and changed my shirt and went back to the lobby. The owner of the hotel was there. He was a paunchy man, glistening sweat, and his clothes were as disheveled as the clerk's, and his mustache was just as trim.

None of the Indians had mustaches, but the owner and the clerk were Ladinos[5] and their mustaches were evidence of this classification, which is economic and not racial. A Ladino is a townsman, an owner of property, a Christian who follows Latin ways. He wears shoes, and never sandals, and always the mustache. He may be part Indian, a mestizo,[6] but he is never all Indian.

The Indians profess Christianity, in a way, but really cling to their Mayan[7] faith. Some own property in town, but not many. There is a caste barrier between the Ladinos and the Indians, and, again, this is economic and not racial.

The clerk introduced me to the owner, whose name I do not remember, and he said that my lunch would be ready in a few minutes, and walked away. I leaned against the desk and lit a cigarette, and then I remembered my manners and offered one to the clerk. He accepted it gravely and with thanks.

"I have been in the United States," he said.

"Is that so? Where?"

" I went to school in the United States. For a year."

"Yes? Where?"

He looked at the ash of his cigarette and tapped it off. "In Mississippi." He glanced at me quickly, almost defiantly, as though he expected me to challenge him or laugh, or something.

"The university?" I asked. "Or Mississippi State?"

"No." He was not quite sure of himself, even timid, and I wondered what the to-do was about and why the hesitation, and then he said, "At a place you never heard of, I'm sure. At Hattiesburg,[8] Mississippi. There's a college there."

I laughed. "Hattiesburg! Well, now, whatta you know."

He drew back. "It is amusing?"

"No. Just cockeyed. Funny peculiar, not funny laughing. I married in Hattiesburg."

"You say." He was very serious.

"Yes, I say. My wife's from Hattiesburg. So you went to Mississippi Southern, huh?"

Have you ever seen gratitude and good will ooze from a man? No, "flow" is a better word. Have you ever seen a man so pleased that he just sort of melts, and grins? That's what this fellow did. He flipped away his cigarette, a sassy, cocky little flip, and propped his elbow on the register. "You went to Mississippi Southern?"

"No. But I know about it."

"Where is it?"

"In Hattiesburg. Like you said." I wasn't peeved, but maybe a little bit short because I couldn't figure out what he was getting at.

"Where in Hattiesburg?"

"Now look, mister. I don't follow you. Mississippi Southern is a college in the little city of Hattiesburg, and Hattiesburg is in Southern Mississippi. You go down—yes, you go down West Pine Street, past the post office, and make a bend to the right. That'll be Hardy Street. Then out Hardy Street, past a cemetery, and on out to the college. What's it all about?"

His smile was so bright and so warm that I began grinning, and then I laughed again, and so did he.

"I tell you." He reached out his hand and we shook. "My name is Tio Felipe Ignacio de Fuestes. The people here call me Tio."

---

5. **Ladinos**\lə ᵃdē·nōs\
6. **mestizo**\měsᵃtē·zō\ a half-breed, a person of mixed European and American-Indian ancestry.
7. **Mayan**\ᵃma·yən *or* ᵃmai·yən\ The Maya Indians of Central America showed a relatively high civilization when Columbus visited America.
8. **Hattiesburg** is in southeastern Mississippi between Laurel and Gulfport. The name of the college has been changed from Mississippi Southern to Southern Mississippi.

"Yes?" I knew I mustn't hurry him.

"This is not my village. I am of Mérida,[9] in Yucatán."

"Mérida, huh?"

"I was a tourist guide. To the ruins and places. I met a professor from Mississippi Southern and he got me in and helped me. He was Professor Johnson. You know him maybe—Professor Johnson?"

I said I didn't, and looked in toward the dining room, where an Indian girl was putting my lunch on a table. She wore a brightly colored blouse and her hand-woven skirt was tight around her thighs. She was barefooted and as graceful as a cat, and as noiseless.

The clerk came out from behind the desk and stood between me and the girl, and touched my arm to get my attention. "The people in this village will not believe I went to school in the United States."

"The devil you say. What's so strange about going to school in the United States? Lots of Mexicans do."

He shrugged that mean-anything gesture of Latins, the hands out and the shoulders rising. "Not to Hattiesburg, Mississippi, Mr. Hoyle. If I had told them New Orleans or Texas. Or Florida or California. But Hattiesburg, Mississippi ____" He shrugged again.

I knew exactly what he meant—exactly. Hattiesburg, Mississippi, just doesn't sound like a place where a man would go to college from a long ways off. Boston, yes. Chicago, New York, Atlanta—a dozen places, a hundred. But not Mississippi Southern in Hattiesburg. So I knew he was telling the truth. There was no reason for him to kid me and, besides, a four-flusher[10] never would have picked out Hattiesburg.

"The Ladinos think I have lied. To show off," he explained.

"Making like a big shot. I follow you now."

"The Indians don't care, or matter. But the Ladinos think I am a big mouth."

"And you want me to tell them that you really have been to school in the United States. O.K. I'll tell them."

"Only a few North Americans ever come to Feliz. From Los Angeles, New York—places like that. They have never heard of my college. Or of Hattiesburg. I ask them and they look at me and shake their heads, and the Ladinos laugh."

The Indian waitress had stepped back from my table and my lunch was ready, and so I told the fellow to send the scoffers to me and that I'd put them right, and I went into the dining room. A couple of greasy meat patties were on my plate, and some canned corn and shriveled tomatoes. In a land that dripped exotic fruits, a land of fine peppers and black beans, here I was getting lunch-wagon hamburgers. Anyway, the coffee was good.

I was thinking of enchiladas and avocados, of thin tortillas[11] spread with black-bean paste or mountain honey, and then the owner came in and pulled up a chair. He "Psst-psst'd" at the Indian girl and she brought him a cup of coffee. He sipped his brew noisily and wiped his mustache with his fingers.

"Tio ____" He nodded toward the lobby. "Tio in there tells me you have been in Mississippi."

"That's right. In Hattiesburg. I know about the college where he went."

He was not impressed and took another sip of coffee. "There is a hotel in this place?"

"Two or three, last time I was there." I was having fun, sort of like playing a quiz game. "The largest one was the Forrest Hotel."

Now he was impressed, but tried not to show it. Even so, he was persistent, "Tio says there is a railroad in this place."

"Three, last time I was there." I didn't like the owner particularly, and thought it was about time to dress him down. I figured him for a flabby little tyrant who probably had given

---

9. **Mérida**\sp. pron. ˄mā·rē·tha\ a city of about 100,000, is the capital of Yucatán. Yucatán\'yū·kə ˄tan\ is northeast of Tabasco.

10. **four-flusher**\'fôr ˄flə·shər\ a bluffer or impostor.

11. **enchilada**\ĕn·chĭ ˄la·da\ a roll of thin fried dough with a chopped meat filling. **avocado**\'a·və ˄ka·dō\ a pulpy green tropical vegetable eaten raw and often used in salads. **tortilla**\'tôr ˄tē·ya\ a very thin round, crisp, fried cake.

Tio a hard time. "Tell you something, mister." I pushed my empty cup away and lit a cigarette. "Your clerk says he has been to college in Hattiesburg, Mississippi. He has. I've got a hundred pesos to ten pesos that he has."

I have never seen a Latin American who wouldn't cover a bet if he had the slightest outside chance of winning.

"A hundred to ten," I repeated, and loud enough for the Indian waitress to hear.

The owner drained his cup and got up. "I never bet with strangers. Have some more coffee, Mr. Hoyle, but you will excuse me, please."

He left me and walked out into the afternoon, and I knew to spread the news that Tio really had been to college, like he said, and that he was willing to bet that it was so, and that he had a gringo[12] to back it up.

Tio waited until the boss was safely away, and came to my table and sat down, and the waitress brought him coffee without being told to do so. She smiled at him, a quick, sly little smile of triumph shared. "You have done me a gracious service, Mr. Hoyle." He offered me one of his own cigarettes and lit one for himself.

"That's more than you've done for me." I nodded toward the food that I hadn't touched. "Is this the sort of stuff you eat?"

Tio was surprised. "I thought you would approve. I told them about the hamburgers. In Hattiesburg—hamburgers. Day and night, hamburgers."

"In Mexico I like Mexican food. Good hot Mexican food, red-hot."

"Oh?" Tio was delighted and proud. "You say?"

"Sure, I say. Have you got any tortillas back there? And bean paste? And some hot peppers?"

Tio clapped his hands like a proprietor, and the waitress came running, and he spoke to her so rapidly that I caught none of it, and she, too, was proud and hurried back to the kitchen. Tio leaned back in his chair and blew smoke toward the ceiling, like a man suddenly sure of himself, like a bantam cockerel[13] that had found his

way around the barnyard. "It is the food of the land, my friend."

The tortillas were thin and the bean paste was spicy and without lumps. And there was a bottle of beer with a red rooster on the label. The peppers, however, weren't much. No authority. Long red peppers that had been dried so long that their kick was gone. I recognized them immediately as Ashanti, the dried fruit of *Piper clusii*.[14] I picked up one and tasted it, and to me it was almost bland.

"Be careful," Tio cautioned me. "They are hot."

"Hot? Those things?" I tossed the pepper back into the dish and took a long swallow of beer. "They are for children. For nursing children."

"They do not burn?" Tio's cigarette was almost to his fingers and he seemed not to notice it. "There is no sweat? No fire in the belly?"

"Listen, my friend." I picked up another of the peppers and tore it open and tasted the seeds, and they were mild. That is, to me they were mild. "I'm a hot-pepper man, Tio. And when I say hot-pepper man, I mean *hot*-pepper man."

"But they do not eat hot peppers in the United States. Here and there, yes. But hot peppers there are weak peppers here."

"I'm from here and there." I spread a tortilla thick with bean paste and smacked my delight. "I used to live in Louisiana and they have hot peppers in Louisiana. Little red devils with fire in their skin and hell in their seeds."

Tio clapped his hands again and spoke to the Indian girl, and she quickly was back with a little bowl of *furias*. Nice and fat and sort of a greenish yellow. They had been steeped in vinegar, though, and much of the sting was out. Still, they had some authority, unless you happen to be a hot-pepper man like me. I took two

---

12. **gringo**\ˈgrĭŋ·gō\ a foreigner to Mexico or Central America, especially U.S. citizens.

13. **bantam**\ˈbăn·təm\ **cockerel**\ˈkŏ·kə·rəl\ a miniature rooster, often having a bold disposition.

14. **Ashanti**\a ˈshan·tē\ **Piper clusii** is the scientific botanical designation.

13

of them in one bite, and the waitress actually gaped at me, and turned and ran back to the kitchen.

Tio was fascinated. "You do not sweat. Or grab for the beer. You do not even blow your breath out hard. This is a thing, my friend. Those are *furias*."

"For growing boys," I said.

The Indian girl had come back to the doorway of the dining room, and three or four other Indians were with her, and they were watching me. Tio waved his hand and she ran and fetched a bottle of beer for him.

"Bring two more," he said. "And one for Manuel in the kitchen, and one for Ricardo in the garden. For Pablo and Pedro." The boss was gone and he really was big-wheeling. "One over to Father Francisco. To little Father Diego and big Father Diego. A Rooster beer for all."

The hotel was as gay as a *cantina*.[15] The Indians beamed and the chef gave the waitress a pat when she passed by him. Tio went to the desk and took two cigars from the owner's private box, and we lit up.

Then he said, "So you like Mexican food. And hot peppers. You will come with me. I take you to the place of Hilario Villareal."

I was warm inside from the beer and peppers, and felt chipper for the first time in weeks, and he told one of the Indians to look after things and we went forth. The village was waking up and some of our hotel Indians were shooting off firecrackers over by the church gate.

"To arouse the saints from their siesta," Tio explained. "They think the saints should be up and about their jobs."

We crossed over to the plaza and walked around it twice. He was puffing his cigar and talking up a storm and making sure that everybody in the plaza saw us together. He led the way into a *cantina* and ordered two more beers. A radio was limping a scratchy melody, and Tio spoke up so all could hear, "In Feliz, not so much as a movie. In Hattiesburg, Mississippi —in Hattiesburg, where I went to college, talking pictures every night. And the baseball."

"You tell 'em, brother," I said. "In Hattiesburg, the football also. And hamburgers."

"You tell 'em, brother," he said.

We made another round of the plaza, in case somebody had missed us, and Tio was silent for a spell, a mighty short one. Then he glanced up at me and away, and said, "In Hattiesburg, my friends called me Chili. I didn't mind. In Mexico, chili is a pepper. In Hattiesburg, it is meat and beans and pepper powder. But they called me Chili. You know how it is up there. Always the nickname."

"Chili, huh? O.K., Chili. My friends call me Pete." I started laughing, "Goes back to when I was so high. Just a kid. Little boy." I don't know why I told him, just wanted to tell him. "Used to run around playing like I was a biddy,[16] a little chicken. Going 'Peep, peep.' My sister got to calling me Peep, and it got to be Pete. You know how it is."

He took off his hat and leaned against a tree and laughed. "O.K., Pete. Now we go to the place of Hilario Villareal. Me and you."

We walked on, and again he was silent, this time for several minutes. The beer was wearing off and I noticed that he was frowning.

At last he said, "About me going to college in the United States. I told you the Indians do not care, and do not matter. Well, Hilario Villareal is an Indian. He matters."

I knew that something was eating him and that he would tell me at his own time. Sure enough, we had walked almost another block and he picked up his story. "Hilario Villareal is the best pepper man in Feliz. He eats *furias* for breakfast. With beer."

"They'll wake you up all right," I said. "And put fire in your blood."

Tio's cigar was soggy and frayed and he threw it away. The exhilaration had gone out of him. "Hilario Villareal grows his own peppers and has a secret. He wet-rots[17] leaves for

---

15. **cantina**\\'kan ᵃtē·na\\ a small restaurant, often one with entertainment for evening trade.
16. **biddy**, a small hen.
17. **wet-rot**, to induce rotting under very moist conditions.

his plants and grows them on a south slope that is sheltered on three sides. And in the dry season he waters them from a bucket. I tell you to have respect for his peppers. His soil is very sour and his peppers are very hot."

It meant only that the Indian understood prevailing winds, that he used acid soil, humus[18] and controlled moisture. I was looking forward to a session at his table, to a bait of *tacos* and *tortas compuestas,* maybe with some real Capsicums, fresh from the bush and oozing their pungent piperine.[19]

"Hilario Villareal is very proud. He does not like Ladinos. Particularly, he does not like me. He thinks I am a big mouth."

"About Hattiesburg, huh?"

"Yes. He thinks I am a man of guile."

"What do you care?"

"Hilario Villareal has a daughter. Her name is Nena.[20]"

So that was it: A Ladino, an Indian girl and her father, who didn't like Ladinos. There was nothing for me to say, and besides, I was hungry. And then we were at Villareal's place. Like the hotel, it was on a corner and several Indians were loafing around the door, and we made our way inside, and there was Hilario Villareal, Indian-faced and grave and with all the dignity of the Mayan, the unchanged. And there was Nena. She and her father saw us come in, and her father glanced her way and she walked out, across the patio to the family's quarters. I didn't get a good look at her, but what I got was good.

Tio stepped to the counter and bought a little black cigar that was strong enough to do push-ups. I went over and sat at a table, and Tio said to the proprietor, "He is my friend. He has been to Hattiesburg, Mississippi, where I went to school, as you know."

Hilario did not even give him the courtesy of a reply. He was a heavy man, very heavy for an Indian, and although standing, he folded his hands across his stomach and looked disdainfully away from Tio. Several Indians drifted in and stood around, looking at me and at Tio, but mostly at me.

Then Hilario came over to my table, and I said, "My friend Tio tells me you have the best food in Feliz. And peppers."

"You like Mexican food?"

"Only if it is good."

He walked toward the kitchen, and I looked over at Tio and grinned, and then I looked around the place: the old calendars, a poster about a bullfight in Mexico City, and the clock that advertised an American soft drink.

Hilario was back much sooner than I expected, and I had an idea he wanted me to be through and both of us out of there. He had *tacos* and tortillas and honey. Also a little bowl of long peppers. They were *Pipers officinarum.* Tasty, but with about as much kick as ginger ale. The tacos were marvelous, however, and the tortillas were as thin as paper and the best I had ever eaten. I reached over and picked up one of the peppers and spoke slowly to Tio, so that they all could make out my words, "In Hattiesburg—in Hattiesburg, Mississippi, where you went to college, we eat these for dessert, eh, Chili?"

"Only children," he said, and tilted his cigar. "Sometimes old women who are sick, but always children."

"With sugar and cream." I tossed the pepper back into the bowl.

Hilario came to my table again and ate one of the peppers, smacking his lips in approval. Then he spoke to me, but did not look at me, "You like peppers?"

"Only if they are good."

It was Tio's cue, and he took it. He walked slowly, proudly, to my side and felt in his pocket and pulled out seventeen pesos. It wasn't much—only about $3.40—but I knew that it was all he had, and he put it on the table

---

18. **humus**\ᐟhyū·məs\ recently decayed leaf and other vegetable material in soil.

19. **tacos**\ᐟta·kōs\ tortilla rolls with meat filling. **tortas compuestas**\ᐟtōr·tas ˈkŏm·pu ᐟĕs·tas\ tarts of thin fried dough with a filling, often of fruit. **Capsicum**\ᐟkăp·sĭ·kəm\ a typical pepper fruit. **piperine**\ᐟpĭ·pə ˈrēn\ the chemical alkaloid that is the main component of pepper.

20. **Nena**\ᐟnā·na\

*"The Inn,"* Rene d'Harnoncourt. *Courtesy of the artist.*

and said, "My friend, Pete, is the best pepper man in Feliz."

Hilario glanced scornfully at the money, and with all the contempt of a dueling master who has been challenged by an insolent cove.[21] For a second, I thought he was going to ignore Tio's challenge. That could have led to trouble, and so I took out my wallet and counted out a hundred pesos and slipped them under Tio's wager.

"For a cushion," I said. "The confidence of my friend is worthy of a cushion."

The spectators, all Indians, looked from one to the other, and then hard at Hilario, and he turned his back to me and walked behind his counter and picked up a cigar box and counted the money that was in it. Apparently it wasn't

21. **cove**\kōv\ a slang expression more English than American to mean "fellow; chap."

16

enough, because he left us and, without haste, crossed his patio to the family quarters. Soon he was back, and with Nena.

She never looked up lest she meet the gaze of Tio, but went behind the counter and waited. Hilario put a hundred and seventeen pesos on the table and said, "My daughter will serve us."

I nodded and he sat down and Tio moved closer behind me. The Indians moved over behind Hilario. I pushed the tacos aside, but kept the tortillas in front of me.

"You must have bread with peppers?" Hilario asked.

"Never yet have I seen peppers so hot that I must reach for the bread."

"You sweat?" Hilario was laying down the rules.

"In the sun, yes. But never from peppers. With me, the peppers warm my blood, not my skin."

"You blow hard the breath?"

"No."

"Then you sip?"

"No. I nibble."

"I sip."

"That is fair."

I moved the tortillas closer to me, and Nena brought him a bottle of beer, and the rules were set. He could sip and I could nibble. But he must wait a full minute between pepper and beer, and I must wait a full minute between pepper and bread.

Nena brought out some spiced meat and two bowls of ground pepper. One of plain black pepper which is the dried fruit of *Piper nigrum*, picked green. This is the pepper of antiquity, of Malabar and Travancore.[22] This is the pepper that sent men venturing in the days of Solomon and Sheba.[23] Rome paid ransom to Alaric[24] in *Piper nigrum*. It is romantic, but tame. The other bowl contained white pepper, which is *Piper nigrum* prepared from the ripe fruits.

Hilario dipped a bit of meat into the black pepper and another into the white pepper and ate them. I crossed my arms and leaned back in my chair as though I had been given offense.

"No?" Hilario was surprised, and tried not to show it.

"No. Does the hospitality of Feliz offer pap[25] to a stranger?" I took fifty more pesos out of my wallet. "This is for the white pepper and the black pepper. I will not tease my tongue."

Hilario stared at me and some of the hauteur went out of him, and I felt a possibility of understanding between us, of friendship a far way off, but moving toward us. Slowly he reached into his pocket and took out more money and matched my ante.

Then he turned to Nena and said, "The cayennes.[26] Only the cayennes. We have here a man of mettle."

The girl ran across the patio and more Indians came into the place and ranged themselves alongside the counter and behind Hilario. Then Ladinos came in and stood by Tio and behind me. I don't know how the word got around so fast, but there they were: the mustached Ladinos and the Indians, each backing his own kind, for I had become associated with the Ladinos. The hotel owner was there, and he whispered to Tio and stepped to the table and counted out a hundred pesos and put them in front of me, and stepped back.

Hilario reached into his pocket again, but one of the Indians touched his arm. Then all the Indians gave money to the one and he matched the hotel owner's bet.

Nena came back in and she had a tray of peppers, each kind in little piles. Only cayennes,

---

22. **Malabar**\ˈmă·lə ˈbar\ a district in the southwest coast of India. **Travancore**\ˈtră·van ˈkōr\ a state in the western part of extreme south India.

23. **Solomon**, a Hebrew king, important in the Old Testament, noted for his wisdom and for his building the great temple of Jerusalem. **Sheba**\ˈshē·bə\ the Queen of Sheba, hearing of the temple and Solomon's fame, paid him a famous state call.

24. **Alaric**\ˈa·lə·rĭk\ the Visigoth who conquered and occupied Rome in A.D. 410. For a huge ransom he withdrew his armies from it.

25. **pap**\păp\ baby food.

26. **cayenne**\ˈkai·ĕn\ a strong, long, twisted red pepper.

the burning Capsicums. There are about thirty species of this delicacy, and she had six. There were green infernos and green terrors, yellow-jackets and yellow furies, red torrids and red frenzies.

Hilario selected one of the red frenzies and held it up for all to see. It was wrinkled near the stem; then fat and tapering to a point. He put the whole pepper in his mouth and chewed slowly. The Indian nodded solemnly, and as he chewed we both watched the clock, and when a minute had passed he reached for his beer and took a sip.

I pulled the tray close to me and fingered through the frenzies until I found two that suited me, both wrinkling their ripeness and then swelling fat into juice and skin and seeds. I held them up for Tio to approve and put both of them into my mouth. My lips stung and the lining of my mouth was hot quick and then prickling stings. I watched the clock through my minute of grace and took my nibble of tortilla.

The Ladinos crowded around Tio and patted him on the back; not me at all, but my sponsor. Then the hotel owner went among them and they gave him money and he receipted it and laid it on the table. The Indians matched it, digging deep this time because they did not have so much money as the Ladinos.

There was a quizzical look in Hilario's eyes. Maybe it was doubt. But, then, maybe it was admiration because I had taken two red frenzies, and without sweat, without the hard blowing of the breath.

We both took torrids, and this time I took only one. My lips had hardened to the sting, but my mouth was ridging inside. I puckered fast to draw saliva. Then the tingle was in my throat and deep down, but not yet to the belly. The tortilla helped some.

The bets were anted[27] again and the hotel owner called out that he was offering odds on me. "Seven to five," he called out. "On Mr. Hoyle. He is the friend of Tio, and Tio is my employee, and as all of you know"—he waved his arm in a broad gesture—"my employee

went to the school, to the college, in the United States. And Mr. Hoyle, who is my guest, knows the place. This is a truth, and I say seven to five."

There were no takers from among the Indians. They were shamefaced because they had no more money, and the Ladinos snickered. One of the Indians took off his jacket, a hand-woven garment of blue, embroidered with sacred pagan symbols. It was his most valued possession, and he walked to the table to put it there, but Hilario held out his hand and stopped him and shook his head.

Then Hilario spoke to me, ignoring the hotel owner and all the other Ladinos, "You have made your bets, Mr. Hoyle?"

"I have made my bets, Mr. Villareal."

He called his daughter, and she raised her eyes as she walked to him and seemed to be looking at him, but she was looking at Tio. The father spoke low to her, and I did not hear his words, but she nodded understanding and ran across the patio and returned with a little hide-covered box. Hilario counted out five hundred pesos—about a hundred dollars. A lot of money anywhere, a fortune in Feliz. "I take no odds," he said. "Cover the wager, gentlemen."

The Ladinos hesitated and Tio was embarrassed for them and jerked off his ring and threw it on the table. It was a gold band and worn and obviously old. Hilario picked it up and felt it and looked at it a long time, and handed it back to Tio. "I will not take a man's ring. It has memories. So have I. And now I have a new memory, the honor of knowing a man who has faith in a stranger."

The hotel owner motioned his friends into a huddle and they emptied their pockets and the owner counted out five hundred pesos and covered the bet. He held the rest of the money in his hand. Hilario pushed his box to the side of the table. I don't know if he had more money in there or not. I just knew they were not going to

---

27. **ante**\ˈăn·tē\ a poker stake put up before the deal to build the pot. Here, more bets were placed before the next round of the contest began.

bluff that fellow. If there was no more money, then there was his cantina and his house, and his land and the land of his friends.

Everything was set again and we chose our peppers—this time the yellow ones—greenish yellow, and hotter than the reds. I got by my first one and was on a yellow fury when I felt the sweat ooze out on the back of my neck, down under my collar. They couldn't see it. I was hurting, the numbing burn of piperine, which is a crystalline alkaloid that tightens the tissues like wet rawhide. Each minute got longer, and the tortillas didn't help much.

Next Hilario reached for the green ones—the busters. So did I, and the heat seared down to my belly, and I straightened quickly to stave off a cramp.

I made it through the terrors and the infernos, but Hilario was in visible agony. He was blowing hard the breath, and sweat was rolling from under his chin and down his neck. There was consternation among the Indians and jubilation among the Ladinos. Hilario spread his hands on the table, his fingers wide, and blinked at me and the tears flowed.

He managed to smile. "They are hot, sir."

"They are hot." I smiled too.

We had gone through the cayennes and I was hoping that the thing was over, and was willing, even anxious, to settle for a draw.

Hilario, though, took a deep gulp of beer and wiped his eyes and nodded to Nena. She hurried across the patio and came back with a little bowl, and in it were two little peppers. The Ladinos began jabbering excitedly and the Indians moved closer. Nena put the peppers on the table and I got a good look at them.

*Amomum melegueta!* I had never seen a whole one before. The spice trade calls them Guinea peppers. Such little nuggets launched armadas in the old days, sails from Spain and Portugal. Men died for those peppers as for gold and glory. They are the hottest things that grow and their seeds are praised as the grains of paradise.

Hilario studied me for my reaction, and then he said, "You have seen such before?"

"No. Only the seeds."

"They are the grains of paradise. I raise them."

"They are hot."

"You say. And I tell you, for I will be fair with you, I never before have eaten a whole one. At one time. Only the nibble."

"This will end it," I said.

"This will end it. I will wait two minutes for the sip."

"And I will wait two minutes for the bread."

We rested a spell, relaxing in an armistice, and I glanced over my shoulder to catch Tio's eye and to reassure him, but he was looking at Nena. Hilario loosened his collar and pulled his shirt wide open and reached out and picked up one of the peppers. I took the other. We put them in our mouths at the same time and began chewing. The heat jolted me. The roof of my mouth corroded and the tissues inside my cheeks contracted like burning cellophane. But I knew I was going to make it—I just knew it.

But Hilario was in contorted misery. His mouth was pinched and he was blowing hard, and then the sweat popped out of his forehead and the tears rolled out of his eyes. He was breathing deeply, like a man who had run a long race. I had him.

I heard the Ladinos muttering their boasts, their vaunts of triumph. I saw the Indians and the stricken looks on their faces. They had been beaten again. The mighty had crushed the humble. The meek must remain the downtrodden.

Then I did a crazy thing. I still don't know why, and don't ask me why. I had a minute to go and the heat inside me was wearing off. But I reached over and grabbed a tortilla. The Ladinos yelled out their astonishment and spluttered their wrath. The Indians looked from one to the other, and they could not believe they had won. Hilario was staring at me, probing deep for an explanation. Then he snatched his bottle of beer and drained it and swished the beer around in his mouth and spat and spat.

The Ladinos turned on Tio and berated him, and he seemed not to mind at all, only looking down at me and across the room at Nena and at the Indians. Then the Ladinos stomped out and left much of their money behind and much of their pride.

"It was too hot," I said to Tio.

"But it was almost over and he was blowing hard the breath."

"I was burning up inside, Chili. Maybe it didn't show, but I was burning up."

He said no more; only shrugged.

Hilario pushed back his chair. "There will be drinks. Beer for all and brandy for those who want it." He walked behind his counter and stood by Nena. "I will drink first, and to my daughter and to my daughter's man, Tio Felipe Ignacio de Fuestes. Only a good man is worthy of the friendship of such a man as Mr. Hoyle."

The Indians nodded their acceptance of the pronouncement and their approval of Tio. He walked from behind me and over to the counter and near Nena, and she raised her eyes from the floor and looked up at him and then down again. He helped Hilario open the beer. Some of the Indians took brandy and we all drank, and then Hilario said, "And now to Mr. Hoyle, who is not a stranger among us. If there is a favor we can do, we do it."

It came to me then. I don't care what has been written or what has been told before, it came to me for the first time, right then. Acid soil. Controlled moisture. A sheltered south slope and the grains of paradise. I had been offered a favor and I asked it: a few of the peppers to remember this day. Hilario was glad to give them to me. He put the *Amomum melegueta* in a paper bag, and I hung around only long enough for another round of drinks, and then I hurried to the hotel and packed. A bus left at twilight and I was on it, heading home.

The first year I planted them in a hothouse and nursed them through. The green nuggets and their seeds of gold. Then I had enough seed for a patch, and then enough seed for several acres. That's the way it started, and now I know of no place where you cannot buy my peppers or spices from the Hoyle Spice Company. I even ship peppers back to Tabasco, even to Feliz, for there is money in coals to Newcastle[28] if you do it right. I have never been back to Feliz or to Hattiesburg. I have never heard from Tio or from any of them.

Sometimes it bothers me that I let the Ladinos down. We were talking about it just the other day, sitting around my swimming pool. I told this story, and we got to talking about whether I'd done right or wrong. My wife said I'd done right because I'd got Tio and Nena together. Some of the others said I'd been downright noble because I'd sided with the Indians, who had been pushed around so much. A few said that my successful business was proof that I was right, that I was sharp, that I was clever.

However, three of my friends—the three I like best—said I'd done a lowdown thing, that I had patronized the humble and had thrown down those who had trusted me. The least I could do, they said, was to go back to Feliz and give them a clinic or a movie house, or something. Someday I might do it. I know such gifts are not deductible,[29] but all the same, I might do it. I just might.

---

I

BREAKING DOWN BARRIERS

People may be pitched together in a brief encounter and yet have no meeting of minds because a wall exists between them—a wall of prejudice, fear, hatred, distaste, or ignorance. A brief encounter has significance, especially if the wall is broken down. In "Stopover in Querétaro" the love and kindness of the Mexicans overcame the author's distrust. In this story it is the American who changes the attitudes of the Mexicans. What do you think are the qualities that destroy the barrier

28. **Newcastle**, a coal mining center on the northeast coast of England. "To carry coals to Newcastle" is to take a commodity to a place where it is already plentiful.
29. The author means that such gifts would not be deductible on a United States income tax return.

of distrust between the following characters: Pete and Tio, Pete and Hilario, Tio and Hilario?

In the following quotations who is the speaker? Who is the person spoken to or spoken about? What does each quotation tell you about the feelings between the two persons?

**1.** "His clothes were mussy, but his little black mustache was trim."

**2.** "Have you ever seen gratitude and good will ooze from a man?"

**3.** "I felt a possibility of understanding between us, of friendship a far way off, but moving toward us."

**4.** " '. . . And now I have a new memory, the honor of knowing a man who has faith in a stranger.' "

II

IMPLICATIONS

Which of the two judgments expressed in the following passage do you agree with? State your reasons. If you agree with neither and have a third interpretation, be sure to back up your opinion with evidence from the story.

"Some . . . said I'd been downright noble because I'd sided with the Indians, who had been pushed around so much. . . . Three of my friends . . . said I'd done a lowdown thing, that I had patronized the humble and thrown down those who had trusted me."

III

TECHNIQUES

In a sense, any story written exists in two places at the same time—on the printed page and in the reader's mind. On the printed page, the writer has ordered and arranged insights and impressions of people, places, and events into a meaningful pattern. The reader must first make an honest effort to grasp the writer's meaning and then test the insights and the pattern given by the writer against what the reader knows about life. Each reader must find in the story the meaning it has for her or him.

Throughout this book, you will study the various elements that experienced readers look for in different kinds of literature. As your skill in recognizing these elements increases, so will your ability to read, to appreciate, and to enjoy good literature. Three of the basic elements in every story are exposition, conflict, and climax. These are the elements which you will examine in the short stories in BRIEF ENCOUNTERS.

*Exposition*

When readers begin a short story, they instinctively look for the answers to four questions: Who are the people? Where are they? When is the story taking place? What is the basic situation, or starting point of the story? It is the writer's task to supply answers to these questions as quickly and naturally as possible. This material is called the *exposition* of the story. It does not necessarily all come in one block at the beginning. Sometimes clues are given through the dialogue, sometimes through the careful use of a single sentence here and there or even a single adjective or clause. In most nineteenth-century short stories, the writer often seemed to stop and say, "Now, reader, here are the things you need to know before getting into this story." In contemporary writing, the author usually tries to provide this information so quickly and casually that the reader is not conscious of it.

The first sentence of "The Grains of Paradise" gives you a clear idea of what kind of man the narrator is. By *not* giving you any information about dates or time, the author lets you know that the time could be either the past or the present. Time, therefore, is not a crucial element in the story.

Skim the first part of "The Grains of Paradise" and locate the passages where the author answers the following questions: Who are the characters? Where is the story taking place? What is the basic situation?

*Conflict*

Stories are built around a conflict, a struggle between two or more opposing forces. The writer establishes this conflict in such a way that the reader's curiosity is aroused and he or she reads on to find out how the conflict will come out. In some stories, the conflict exists between people— one person is pitted against another. In others, the conflict may develop between a person and a set of circumstances that threaten his or her security or a force of nature that threatens her or his life. And often, in the finest writing, the conflict is an inner one between two or more instincts, emotions, or values in one person. There is usually more than one conflict in a story, as in "The Grains of Paradise," but there is always one major conflict to which the others contribute.

There are at least three conflicts at work in "The Grains of Paradise." Two are between individuals, and one is between opposing groups. Name the persons involved in each conflict. Which, in your opinion, is the main conflict? Why?

*Climax*

Whatever the nature of the major conflict in a story, the two opposing forces inevitably progress to a point in the action when one must win and the other lose. This point at which the reader feels certain that the story must turn one way or another is the climax. It is the moment when "something's got to give" . . . when the conflict turns toward a solution.

This resolution is not necessarily the end of the story. A concluding section often explains the resolution and tells some of the effects it had or will have on the characters.

All three of the conflicts in "The Grains of Paradise" are brought together in the pepper-eating contest. What is the moment of climax in this contest, and how is each conflict resolved by the outcome of the contest? Would you say that the author made the resolution seem plausible? What reasons can you find for the decision that the narrator made? How did the decision lead to the resolution?

IV
WORDS

**A.** Context frequently supplies clues which permit you to infer the general meaning of an unfamiliar word. You probably can guess the general meaning of *antiquated* in the following sentence: "I glanced about the room and noticed that the paint on the walls was scaling, the furnishings *antiquated*." If you do not know what *antiquated* means, the fact of paint scaling tells you that it has something to do with the poor condition of the room. Look up *antiquated* in your dictionary. What special effect did the author achieve through the use of the word? In the following phrases and clauses, determine first from context the meaning of the italicized words and then check your meaning in the dictionary:

**1.** Only heavy *sedatives* put me to sleep that night.

**2.** A *cluster* of ragged *urchins* was around the door. One of the children held out a toy. . . .

**3.** . . . explained why he had ventured to *intrude* on my privacy.

**4.** . . . someone who had been through the same *ordeal.*

**5.** . . . made some comment, some *pleasantry* about the weather.

**6.** He was a paunchy man glistening sweat and his clothes were as *disheveled* as the clerk's, and his mustache was just as trim.

**7.** I could see the plaza, empty at that hour, and its trees drooping their *somnolence.*

**8.** At one point a character in "Grains of Paradise" "looked *disdainfully* away" and later he "glanced *scornfully* at the money." What is the difference in meaning between *disdain* and *scorn*?

**B.** In English words of two or more syllables are likely to be composed of either affixes and roots or of compound roots. An affix is a prefix like the *in-* in *inclose*, and *dis-* in *distrust*, or a suffix like the *-y* in *lucky*, the *-ish* in *bookish*. The part of a word to which a prefix or suffix is attached is called a root. Sometimes the root is an independent word—*close*, *trust*, *luck*, and *book* in the illustrations above. But sometimes the root has no independent existence without affixes, like the *-clude* of *conclude*, the *-flect* of *reflect*, the *-dict* of *diction*, the *-junct* of *juncture.*

Three very common roots, all of them from Latin, are *-fin*, meaning "limit, term, end" as in *define, final, infinite; -port-,* meaning "bear, carry" as in *transport, import,* and *porter;* and *-junct-,* meaning "join" as in *juncture, adjunct,* and *conjunction.* Watch for these and other roots in your reading. Use your dictionary to analyze the roots in the following words from "Stopover in Querétaro" and from "Grains of Paradise": *concussion, confess, adequate, opposite, sympathy, dislocated, intrude, solitude, profess, proprietor, pungent, confidence, spectator, associated, admiration, corrode, contract, contort.*

**C.** Though *tortilla* is a Spanish word, it is fairly familiar to speakers of American English. The reason for its familiarity is that it is a word that was borrowed from Spanish settlers during the early history of America. Other loan-words traceable to the Spanish colonists include: *mustang, corral, stampede, bronco, tamale, bonanza, desperado, vigilante, cafeteria, chaparral, rodeo, chili con carne, taco.*

Corsica is an island noted for its warm climate
and its hot-tempered people. They are a people
who live according to an ancient
and primitive code. One mellow autumn day,
two people are thrust together
under circumstances that test this code.

# Mateo Falcone

## PROSPER MÉRIMÉE

On leaving Porto-Vecchio[1] from the northwest and directing his steps towards the interior
of the island, the traveler will notice that the
land rises rapidly, and after three hours' walking over tortuous paths obstructed by great
masses of rock and sometimes cut by ravines, he
will find himself on the border of a great
maquis.[2] The maquis is the domain of the Corsican shepherds and of those who are at variance with justice. It must be known that, in
order to save himself the trouble of manuring
his field, the Corsican husbandman sets fire
to a piece of woodland. If the flames spread
farther than is necessary, so much the worse!
In any case he is certain of a good crop from
the land fertilized by the ashes of the trees
which grow upon it. He gathers only the heads
of his grain, leaving the straw, which it would
be unnecessary labor to cut. In the following
spring the roots that have remained in the earth
without being destroyed send up their tufts of
sprouts, which in a few years reach a height
of seven or eight feet. It is this kind of tangled
thicket that is called a maquis. They are made
up of different kinds of trees and shrubs, so
crowded and mingled together at the caprice
of nature that only with an ax in hand can a
man open a passage through them, and maquis
are frequently seen so thick and bushy that
the wild sheep themselves cannot penetrate
them.

If you have killed a man, go into the maquis
of Porto-Vecchio. With a good gun and plenty
of powder and balls, you can live there in
safety. Do not forget a brown cloak furnished
with a hood, which will serve you for both
cover and mattress. The shepherds will give
you chestnuts, milk and cheese, and you will
have nothing to fear from justice nor the relatives of the dead except when it is necessary for
you to descend to the city to replenish your
ammunition.

When I was in Corsica, Mateo Falcone had
his house half a league from this maquis. He
was rich enough for that country, living in
noble style—that is to say, doing nothing—on
the income from his flocks, which the shepherds, who are a kind of nomads, lead to pasture here and there on the mountains. When I
saw him, two years after the event that I am
about to relate, he appeared to me to be about
fifty years old or more. Picture to yourself a
man, small but robust, with curly hair, black as
jet, an aquiline nose, thin lips, large, restless
eyes, and a complexion the color of tanned
leather. His skill as a marksman was considered
extraordinary even in his country, where good
shots are so common. For example, Mateo
would never fire at a sheep with buckshot; but
at a hundred and twenty paces, he would drop
it with a ball in the head or shoulder, as he
chose. He used his arms as easily at night as
during the day. I was told this feat of his skill,
which will, perhaps seem impossible to those
who have not traveled in Corsica. A lighted
candle was placed at eighty paces, behind a
paper transparency about the size of a plate.
He would take aim, then the candle would be
extinguished, and, at the end of a moment,
in the most complete darkness, he would fire
and hit the paper three times out of four.

With such a transcendent accomplishment,
Mateo Falcone had acquired a great reputation. He was said to be as good a friend as he

---

1. **Porto-Vecchio**\ˈpȯr·tō ˈvĕk·yō\ a seaport town in
southeastern Corsica.
2. **maquis**\ˈma ˈkē\ a thick underbrush.

*A general view of Corte, isolated in the rugged mountains of central Corsica.*

was a dangerous enemy; accommodating and charitable, he lived at peace with all the world in the district of Porto-Vecchio. But it is said of him that in Corte,[3] where he had married his wife, he had disembarrassed himself very vigorously of a rival who was considered as redoubtable in war as in love; at least, a certain gun-shot which surprised this rival as he was shaving before a little mirror hung in his window was attributed to Mateo. The affair was smoothed over and Mateo was married. His wife Giuseppa had given him at first three daughters (which infuriated him), and finally a son, whom he named Fortunato, and who became the hope of his family, the inheritor of the name. The daughters were well married: their father could count at need on the poniards and carbines of his sons-in-law. The son was only ten years old, but he already gave promise of fine attributes.

On a certain day in autumn, Mateo set out at an early hour with his wife to visit one of his flocks in a clearing of the maquis. The little Fortunato wanted to go with them, but the clearing was too far away; moreover, it was necessary someone should stay to watch the house; therefore the father refused; it will be seen whether or not he had reason to repent.

He had been gone some hours, and the little Fortunato was tranquilly stretched out in the sun, looking at the blue mountains, and thinking that the next Sunday he was going to dine in the city with his uncle, the Caporal,[4] when he was suddenly interrupted in his meditations by the firing of a musket. He got up and turned to that side of the plain whence the noise came.

---

3. **Corte**\⁁kŏr•tā\ a town in central Corsica.
4. **Caporal**\⁁kä•pə 'ral\ foreman.

Other shots followed, fired at irregular intervals, and each time nearer; at last, in the path which led from the plain to Mateo's house, appeared a man wearing the pointed hat of the mountaineers, bearded, covered with rags, and dragging himself along with difficulty by the support of his gun. He had just received a wound in his thigh.

This man was an outlaw, who, having gone to the town by night to buy powder, had fallen on the way into an ambuscade of Corsican light-infantry. After a vigorous defense he was fortunate in making his retreat, closely followed and firing from rock to rock. But he was only a little in advance of the soldiers, and his wound prevented him from gaining the maquis before being overtaken.

He approached Fortunato and said: "You are the son of Mateo Falcone?"—"Yes."

"I am Gianetto Saupiero. I am followed by the yellow-collars.[5] Hide me; for I can go no farther."

"And what will my father say if I hide you without his permission?"

"He will say that you have done well."

"How do you know?"

"Hide me quickly; they are coming."

"Wait till my father gets back."

"How can I wait? Malediction! They will be here in five minutes. Come, hide me, or I will kill you."

Fortunato answered him with the utmost coolness:

"Your gun is empty, and there are no more cartridges in your belt."

"I have my stiletto."

"But can you run as fast as I can?"

He gave a leap and put himself out of reach.

"You are not the son of Mateo Falcone! Will you then let me be captured before your house?"

The child appeared moved.

"What will you give me if I hide you?" said he, coming nearer.

The outlaw felt in a leather pocket that hung from his belt, and took out a five-franc piece, which he had doubtless saved to buy ammuni-tion with. Fortunato smiled at the sight of the silver piece; he snatched it, and said to Gianetto:

"Fear nothing."

Immediately he made a great hole in a pile of hay that was near the house. Gianetto crouched down in it and the child covered him in such a way that he could breathe without it being possible to suspect that the hay concealed a man. He bethought himself further, and, with the subtlety of a tolerably ingenious savage, placed a cat and her kittens on the pile, that it might not appear to have been recently disturbed. Then, noticing the traces of blood on the path near the house, he covered them carefully with dust, and, that done, he again stretched himself out in the sun with the greatest tranquillity.

A few moments afterwards, six men in brown uniforms with yellow collars, and commanded by an Adjutant, were before Mateo's door. This Adjutant was a distant relative of Falcone's. (In Corsica the degrees of relationship are followed much further than elsewhere.) His name was Tiodoro Gamba; he was an active man, much dreaded by the outlaws, several of whom he had already entrapped.

"Good day, little cousin," said he, approaching Fortunato; "how tall you have grown. Have you seen a man go past here just now?"

"Oh! I am not yet so tall as you, my cousin," replied the child with a simple air.

"You soon will be. But haven't you seen a man go by here, tell me?"

"If I have seen a man go by?"

"Yes, a man with a pointed hat of black velvet, and a vest embroidered with red and yellow."

"A man with a pointed hat, and a vest embroidered with red and yellow?"

"Yes, answer quickly, and don't repeat my questions!"

"This morning the curé[6] passed before our

---

5. **yellow-collars,** regular Corsican soldiery.
6. **curé**\ˈkyū 'rā\ a parish priest.

door on his horse, Piero. He asked me how papa was, and I answered him—"

"Ah, you little scoundrel, you are playing sly! Tell me quickly which way Gianetto went? We are looking for him, and I am sure he took this path."

"Who knows?"

"Who knows? It is I who know that you have seen him."

"Can any one see who passes when they are asleep?"

"You were not asleep, rascal; the shooting woke you up."

"Then you believe, cousin, that your guns make so much noise? My father's carbine has the advantage of them."

"The devil take you, you cursed little scapegrace. I am certain that you have seen Gianetto. Perhaps, even, you have hidden him. Come, comrades, go into the house and see if our man is there. He could only go on one foot, and the knave has too much good sense to try to reach the maquis limping like that. Moreover, the bloody tracks stop here."

"And what will papa say?" asked Fortunato with a sneer. "What will he say if he knows that his house has been entered while he was away?"

"You rascal," said the Adjutant, taking him by the ear, "do you know that it only remains for me to make you change your tone? Perhaps you will speak differently after I have given you twenty blows with the flat of my sword."

Fortunato continued to sneer.

"My father is Mateo Falcone," said he with emphasis.

"You little scamp, you know very well that I can carry you off to Corte or to Bastia. I will make you lie in a dungeon, on straw, with your feet in shackles, and I will have you guillotined if you don't tell me where Gianetto is."

The child burst out laughing at this ridiculous menace. He repeated:

"My father is Mateo Falcone."

"Adjutant," said one of the soldiers in a low voice, "let us have no quarrels with Mateo."

Gamba appeared evidently embarrassed. He spoke in an undertone with the soldiers who had already visited the house. This was not a very long operation, for the cabin of a Corsican consists only of a single square room, furnished with a table, some benches, chests, housekeeping utensils and those of the chase. In the meantime, little Fortunato petted his cat and seemed to take a wicked enjoyment in the confusion of the soldiers and of his cousin.

One of the men approached the pile of hay. He saw the cat, and gave the pile a careless thrust with his bayonet, shrugging his shoulders as if he felt that his precaution was ridiculous. Nothing moved; the boy's face betrayed not the slightest emotion.

The Adjutant and his troop were cursing their luck. Already they were looking in the direction of the plain, as if disposed to return by the way they had come, when their chief, convinced that menaces would produce no impression on Falcone's son, determined to make a last effort, and try the effect of caresses and presents.

"My little cousin," said he, "you are a very wide-awake little fellow. You will get along. But you are playing a naughty game with me; and if I wasn't afraid of making trouble for my cousin, Mateo, the devil take me, but I would carry you off with me."

"Bah!"

"But when my cousin comes back I shall tell him about this, and he will whip you till the blood comes for having told such lies."

"You don't say so!"

"You will see. But hold on!—be a good boy and I will give you something."

"Cousin, let me give you some advice: if you wait much longer Gianetto will be in the maquis and it will take a smarter man than you to follow him."

The Adjutant took from his pocket a silver watch worth about ten crowns, and noticing that Fortunato's eyes sparkled at the sight of it, said, holding the watch by the end of its steel chain:

"Rascal! you would like to have such a watch as that hung around your neck, wouldn't you, and to walk in the streets of Porto-Vecchio proud as a peacock? People would ask you what time it was, and you would say: 'Look at my watch.'"

"When I am grown up, my uncle, the Caporal, will give me a watch."

"Yes; but your uncle's little boy has one already; not so fine as this either. But then, he is younger than you."

The child sighed.

"Well! Would you like this watch, little cousin?"

Fortunato, casting sidelong glances at the watch, resembled a cat that has been given a whole chicken. It feels that it is being made sport of, and does not dare to use its claws; from time to time it turns its eyes away so as not to be tempted, licking its jaws all the while, and has the appearance of saying to its master, "How cruel your joke is!"

However, the Adjutant seemed in earnest in offering his watch. Fortunato did not reach out his hand for it, but said with a bitter smile:

"Why do you make fun of me?"

"By heaven! I am not making fun of you. Only tell me where Gianetto is and the watch is yours."

Fortunato smiled incredulously, and fixing his black eyes on those of the Adjutant tried to read there the faith he ought to have had in his words.

"May I lose my epaulettes," cried the Adjutant, "if I do not give you the watch on this condition. These comrades are witnesses; I cannot deny it."

While speaking he gradually held the watch nearer till it almost touched the child's pale face, which plainly showed the struggle that was going on in his soul between covetousness and respect for hospitality. His breast swelled with emotion; he seemed about to suffocate. Meanwhile the watch was slowly swaying and turning, sometimes brushing against his cheek. Finally, his right hand was gradually stretched toward it; the ends of his fingers touched it; then its whole weight was in his hand, the Adjutant still keeping hold of the chain. The face

was light blue; the cases newly burnished. In the sunlight it seemed to be all on fire. The temptation was too great. Fortunato raised his left hand and pointed over his shoulder with his thumb at the hay against which he was reclining. The Adjutant understood him at once. He dropped the end of the chain and Fortunato felt himself the sole possessor of the watch. He sprang up with the agility of a deer and stood ten feet from the pile, which the soldiers began at once to overturn.

There was a movement in the hay, and a bloody man with a poniard in his hand appeared. He tried to rise to his feet, but his stiffened leg would not permit it and he fell. The Adjutant at once grappled with him and took away his stiletto. He was immediately secured, notwithstanding his resistance.

Gianetto, lying on the earth and bound like a fagot, turned his head towards Fortunato, who had approached.

"Son of—!" said he, with more contempt than anger.

The child threw him the silver piece which he had received, feeling that he no longer deserved it; but the outlaw paid no attention to the movement, and with great coolness said to the Adjutant:

"My dear Gamba, I cannot walk; you will be obliged to carry me to the city."

"Just now you could run faster than a buck," answered the cruel captor; "but be at rest. I am so pleased to have you that I would carry you a league on my back without fatigue. Besides, comrade, we are going to make a litter for you with your cloak and some branches, and at the Crespoli farm we shall find horses."

"Good," said the prisoner. "You will also put a little straw on your litter that I may be more comfortable."

While some of the soldiers were occupied in making a kind of stretcher out of some chestnut boughs and the rest were dressing Gianetto's wound, Mateo Falcone and his wife suddenly appeared at a turn in the path that led to the maquis. The woman was staggering under the weight of an enormous sack of chestnuts, while her husband was sauntering along, carrying one gun in his hands, while another was slung across his shoulders, for it is unworthy of a man to carry other burdens than his arms.

At the sight of the soldiers Mateo's first thought was that they had come to arrest him. But why this thought? Had he then some quarrels with justice? No. He enjoyed a good reputation. He was said to have a particularly good name, but he was a Corsican and a highlander, and there are few Corsican highlanders who, in scrutinizing their memory, cannot find some peccadillo, such as a gun-shot, dagger-thrust, or similar trifles. Mateo more than others had a clear conscience; for more than ten years he had not pointed his carbine at a man, but he was always prudent, and put himself into a position to make a good defense if necessary. "Wife," said he to Giuseppa, "put down the sack and hold yourself ready."

She obeyed at once. He gave her the gun that was slung across his shoulders, which would have bothered him, and, cocking the one he held in his hands, advanced slowly towards the house, walking among the trees that bordered the road, ready at the least hostile demonstration, to hide behind the largest, whence he could fire from under cover. His wife followed closely behind, holding his reserve weapon and his cartridge-box. The duty of a good housekeeper, in case of a fight, is to load her husband's carbines.

On the other side the Adjutant was greatly troubled to see Mateo advance in this manner, with cautious steps, his carbine raised, and his finger on the trigger.

"If by chance," thought he, "Mateo should be related to Gianetto, or if he should be his friend and wish to defend him, the contents of his two guns would arrive amongst us as certainly as a letter in the post; and if he should see me, notwithstanding the relationship!"

In this perplexity he took a bold step. It was to advance alone towards Mateo and tell him of the affair while accosting him as an old acquaintance, but the short space that separated him from Mateo seemed terribly long.

"Hello! old comrade," cried he. "How do you do, my good fellow? It is I, Gamba, your cousin."

Without answering a word, Mateo stopped, and in proportion as the other spoke, slowly raised the muzzle of his gun so that it was pointing upward when the Adjutant joined him.

"Good-day, brother," said the Adjutant, holding out his hand. "It is a long time since I have seen you."

"Good-day, brother."

"I stopped while passing, to say good-day to you and to cousin Pepa here. We have had a long journey to-day, but have no reason to complain, for we have captured a famous prize. We have just seized Gianetto Saupiero."

"God be praised!" cried Giuseppa. "He stole a milch goat from us last week."

These words reassured Gamba.

"Poor devil!" said Mateo, "He was hungry."

"The villain fought like a lion," continued the Adjutant, a little mortified. "He killed one of my soldiers, and not content with that, broke Caporal Chardon's arm; but that matters little, he is only a Frenchman. Then, too, he was so well hidden that the devil couldn't have found him. Without my little cousin, Fortunato, I should never have discovered him."

"Fortunato!" cried Mateo.

"Fortunato!" repeated Giuseppa.

"Yes, Gianetto was hidden under the hay-pile yonder, but my little cousin showed me the trick. I shall tell his uncle, the Caporal, that he may send him a fine present for his trouble. Both his name and yours will be in the report that I shall send to the Attorney-general."

"Malediction!" said Mateo in a low voice.

They had rejoined the detachment. Gianetto was already lying on the litter ready to set out. When he saw Mateo and Gamba in company he smiled a strange smile, then, turning his head towards the door of the house, he spat on the sill, saying:

"House of a traitor."

Only a man determined to die would dare pronounce the word traitor to Falcone. A good blow with the stiletto, which there would be no need of repeating, would have immediately paid the insult. However, Mateo made no other movement than to place his hand on his forehead like a man who is dazed.

Fortunato had gone into the house when his father arrived, but now he reappeared with a bowl of milk which he handed with downcast eyes to Gianetto.

"Get away from me!" cried the outlaw, in a loud voice. Then, turning to one of the soldiers, he said:

"Comrade, give me a drink."

The soldier placed his gourd in his hands, and the prisoner drank the water handed to him by a man with whom he had just exchanged bullets. He then asked them to tie his hands across his breast instead of behind his back.

"I like," said he, "to lie at my ease."

They hastened to satisfy him; then the Adjutant gave the signal to start, said adieu to Mateo, who did not respond, and descended with rapid steps towards the plain.

Nearly ten minutes elapsed before Mateo spoke. The child looked with restless eyes, now at his mother, now at his father, who was leaning on his gun and gazing at him with an expression of concentrated rage.

"You begin well," said Mateo at last with a calm voice, but frightful to one who knew the man.

"Oh, father," cried the boy, bursting into tears, and making a forward movement as if to throw himself on his knees. But Mateo cried, "Away from me!"

The little fellow stopped and sobbed, immovable, a few feet from his father.

Giuseppa drew near. She had just discovered the watch-chain, the end of which was hanging out of Fortunato's jacket.

"Who gave you that watch?" demanded she in a severe tone.

"My cousin, the Adjutant."

Falcone seized the watch and smashed it in a thousand pieces against a rock.

"Wife," said he, "is this my child?"

Giuseppa's cheeks turned a brick-red.

"What are you saying, Mateo? Do you know to whom you speak?"

"Very well, this child is the first of his race to commit treason."

Fortunato's sobs and gasps redoubled as Falcone kept his lynx-eyes upon him. Then he struck the earth with his gunstock, shouldered the weapon, and turned in the direction of the maquis, calling to Fortunato to follow. The boy obeyed. Giuseppa hastened after Mateo and seized his arm.

"He is your son," said she with a trembling voice, fastening her black eyes on those of her husband to read what was going on in his heart.

"Leave me alone," said Mateo. "I am his father."

Giuseppa embraced her son, and bursting into tears entered the house. She threw herself on her knees before an image of the Virgin and prayed ardently. In the meanwhile Falcone walked some two hundred paces along the path and only stopped when he reached a little ravine which he descended. He tried the earth with the butt-end of his carbine, and found it soft and easy to dig. The place seemed to be convenient for his design.

"Fortunato, go close to that big rock there."

The child did as he was commanded, then he kneeled.

"Say your prayers."

"Oh, father, father, do not kill me!"

"Say your prayers!" repeated Mateo in a terrible voice.

The boy, stammering and sobbing, recited the Pater and the Credo.[7] At the end of each prayer the father loudly answered, "Amen!"

"Are those all the prayers you know?"

"Oh! father, I know the Ave Maria[8] and the litany that my aunt taught me."

"It is very long, but no matter."

---

7. **Pater**\ˆpa·tär\ the Lord's Prayer. **Credo**\ˆkrē·dō\ an official profession of faith.
8. **Ave Maria**\ˆa·vä maˆrē·a\ a salutation and prayer to the Virgin Mary.

The child finished the litany in a scarcely audible tone.

"Are you finished?"

"Oh! my father, have mercy! Pardon me! I will never do so again. I will beg my cousin, the Caporal, to pardon Gianetto."

He was still speaking. Mateo raised his gun, and, taking aim, said:

"May God pardon you!"

The boy made a desperate effort to rise and grasp his father's knees, but there was not time. Mateo fired and Fortunato fell dead.

Without casting a glance on the body, Mateo returned to the house for a spade with which to bury his son. He had gone but a few steps when he met Giuseppa, who, alarmed by the shot, was hastening hither.

"What have you done?" cried she.

"Justice."

"Where is he?"

"In the ravine. I am going to bury him. He died a Christian. I shall have a mass said for him. Have my son-in-law, Tiodoro Bianchi, sent for to come and live with us."

---

## I

### AN ANCIENT CODE OF HONOR

The readers are left with a sense of shock when they finish "Mateo Falcone." This reaction occurs because they bring their own feelings and their own code of a more civilized and stable society to the situation. Only upon reflection do they come to see that the devastating outcome of all the circumstances that the writer has carefully presented is inevitable. The brief encounter that begins as a meeting between a man and a boy on a lazy autumn day changes forever the lives of all the people involved in it.

## II

### IMPLICATIONS

Consider and discuss this story in terms of the following questions:

**1.** What is the code that Mateo Falcone has set for his life?

**2.** Is this code the result of the conditions under which he lives or the result of the kind of person he is?

**3.** In what ways does Fortunato indicate that he is learning the ways of his father?

**4.** Is it an impulse of the moment that makes Mateo kill his son?

**5.** Actually, Mateo Falcone appears very briefly in the story; far more space is given to the other characters. Why then is the story called "Mateo Falcone"?

## III

### TECHNIQUES

"Mateo Falcone" has been referred to as a masterpiece. As Poe turned the short work of fiction into a distinctive literary form in America, so Mérimée, through this story, made the short story a polished work of art in France. He holds himself to a concise, objective portrayal of the actions of a small group of people. But the compressed record hits the reader's mind with great force.

*Exposition*

"Mateo Falcone" illustrates the handling of exposition as it was typically done a hundred years ago. How would you describe this method? Why is it effective for this story?

The setting which is part of the exposition is of particular importance in "Mateo Falcone." Imagine the story taking place in a city, and you will quickly see that such a setting would have been inappropriate. What effect does the kind of country they live in have on the lives of the characters? What qualities of the landscape are reflected in the characteristics of those who live there?

*Conflict*

The conflict in "Mateo Falcone" is an inner one occurring in both Fortunato's and Mateo's decisions. Both make a choice between their personal feelings and their adherence to the code of the maquis. Why does Fortunato decide the way he does? Why does Mateo decide he must kill his son?

*Climax*

At what point in the story does Mateo Falcone seem to determine what he must do? Does the reader suspect his decision at the time he makes it? Why?

Sometimes people we do not know may influence our feelings,
our thoughts, and our lives. In the following poems, six poets probe the effects
of brief encounters between strangers.

# *The Man He Killed*

Had he and I but met
By some old ancient inn,
We should have sat us down to wet
Right many a nipperkin![1]

But ranged[2] as infantry,    5
And staring face to face,
I shot at him as he at me,
And killed him in his place.

I shot him dead because—
Because he was my foe,    10
Just so: my foe of course he was;
That's clear enough; although

He thought he'd 'list,[3] perhaps,
Offhand like—just as I—
Was out of work—had sold his traps[4]—    15
No other reason why.

Yes; quaint and curious war is!
You shoot a fellow down
You'd treat if met where any bar is,
Or help to half-a-crown.[5]    20

THOMAS HARDY

---

1. **nipperkin**\ˈnĭ·pər ˈkĭn\ a cup or glass containing about half a cup.
2. **ranged**, arranged, ordered in ranks.
3. **'list**, enlist.
4. his **traps**, tools, equipment, whatever he used in his trade.
5. **half-a-crown** or half crown, a British coin worth two shillings and six-pence, about $0.35 in U.S. currency.

### HOW STRANGE
### AND CURIOUS WAR IS

Using the voice of a soldier, Hardy presents the troubled thoughts of one who has killed a stranger for no personal reason at all. The rambling, conversational tone of the poem makes the speaker seem warmly human and, in the process, underlines the inhumanity of his act. What were the man's feelings at the moment he met the enemy soldier? What disturbs him later about the encounter?

The third stanza of this poem does a masterful job of fitting the poetic form to the meaning. In the first line, as the soldier gropes for an explanation of his action, his inability to find a satisfactory answer is underscored when the rhythm and meaning are left hanging on "because—." The futility of his search is further emphasized in the second line by his hollow repetition of "because" followed hurriedly by the obvious, empty answer expressed in simple, single-syllable words. Then, pausing to reassure himself, the rush of repetition in the third line shows his relief at having found *an* answer. But the last word of the stanza breaks the established stanza pattern, indicating the doubt that has crept into his mind. Find other places in this poem where the form of the lines fits the meaning of the lines.

## In the Old House
### (A True Story)

House silent
grandchildren put to bed
she was drinking
a glass of sherry
among strewn building blocks          5
and woolly animals
by the sitting-room fire
when on the stairs she heard
patter of feet.

"Go back to bed!" she called          10
no answer
but the feet came on downstairs.
So, crossly,
out into the hall
there he came:                        15
down the stairs
no grandchild of hers—
about six
nightshirt
half asleep                           20
clutching his blanket
sucking his thumb

didn't say anything, went on
straight past her across the hall
into the kitchen, but when she followed  25
he was gone
never seen before or since.

Was it the presence of other children in the
    old house
that called him so briefly            30
from his deep
deep sleep?

JOAN AIKEN

From *The Skin Spinner's Poems* by Joan Aiken. Copyright ©
1976 by Joan Aiken. Reprinted by permission of The Viking
Press.

**AN ENCOUNTER WITH THE UNREAL**

Somewhere in the back of everyone's mind is
the feeling that ghosts, spirits, and witches do
exist. There are many people who claim to have
had encounters, always brief, with such phenom-
ena. Notice the ordinariness of the situation. What
do you think causes the ghost to appear? Notice
also the way the language is abbreviated—"House
silent" instead of "The house is silent." How does
this device sharpen the poem's effect?

# *The Alarm Clock*

Alarm clock
sure sound
loud
this mornin' . . .
remind me of the time   5
I sat down
in a drug store
with my
mind
away far off . . .   10
until the girl
and she was small
it seems to me
with yellow hair
a hangin'   15
smiled up and said
"I'm sorry but
we don't serve

you people
here"   20
and I woke up
quick
like I did this mornin'
when the
alarm   25
went off . . .
It don't do
to wake up
quick . . .

MARI EVANS

From *I Am A Black Woman*,
published by William Morrow
& Company, 1970, by per-
mission of the author.

## STRANGE ASSOCIATIONS

We all know the feeling of waking up suddenly, whether by the ring of an alarm clock or the terror of a bad dream. We react with a whole medley of feelings: shame, irritation, confusion. The day is off to a bad start. But there are sudden awakenings other than those from a sound sleep. What are some of these? What do you know about the speaker of this poem? Why did the alarm clock remind her of a brief encounter she had with a blonde girl? Did the encounter have any impact on the blonde girl?

We generally think that poetry uses more pattern in language than does prose. Pattern is achieved by the organized use of repetitions. It may be repeated beats (rhythm); repeated word sounds (rhyme); or repeated phrases. Contemporary poetry tends to discard the older kinds of repetition, but it still uses a pattern to hold it together and make it different from prose. Its repetitions are more like the irregular pounding of waves on the shore than the steady beat of a machine. Can you detect any repeated elements in "The Alarm Clock"?

# ◊ *Corner*

The cop slumps alertly on his motorcycle,
Supported by one leg like a leather stork.
His glance accuses me of loitering.
I can see his eyes moving like a fish
In the green depths of his green goggles.     5

His ease is fake. I can tell.
My ease is fake. And he can tell.
The fingers armored by his gloves
Splay and clench, itching to change something.
As if he were my enemy or my death,     10
I just standing there watching.

I spit out my gum which has gone stale.
I knock out a new cigarette—
Which is my bravery.
It is all imperceptible:     15
The way I shift my weight,
The way he creaks in his saddle.

The traffic is specific though constant.
The sun surrounds me, divides the street between us.
His crash helmet is whiter in the shade.     20
It is like a bull ring as they say it is just before the fighting.

I cannot back down. I am there.

Everything holds me back.
I am in danger of disappearing into the sunny dust.
My levis bake and my T shirt sweats.     25

My cigarette makes my eyes burn.
But I don't dare drop it.

Who made him my enemy?
Prince of coolness. King of fear.
Why do I lean here waiting?      30
Why does he lounge there watching?

I am becoming sunlight.
My hair is on fire. My boots run like tar.
I am hung-up by the bright air.

Something breaks through all of a sudden,      35
And he blasts off, quick as a craver,
Smug in his power; watching me watch.

RALPH POMEROY

Reprinted with permission of the Macmillan Company from *In the Financial District* by Ralph Pomeroy. Copyright © by Ralph Pomeroy, 1961.

## WHO MADE HIM MY ENEMY?

The stand-off in this poem is classic. Two people, separated by age, levels of authority, differing attitudes, and fear of the other meet in a brief encounter where nothing happens but everything does.

From the staccato style of the short lines ("His ease is fake. I can tell. / My ease is fake. And he can tell.") we immediately sense the tension between the two men. Find other lines that either heighten or describe the tension. Can you describe the police officer? The narrator? How can a person be a "Prince of coolness. King of fear"? Can you answer the narrator's question, "Who made him my enemy?" Are your answers any more satisfactory than the simple one of the soldier's found in Hardy's poem?

## To a Beautiful Girl Whose Name I Don't Know

All of a part of the people
experiencing the same hurt
that day we were told about
world hunger.
six hundred thirty-five dead every hour.          5
this is to you
the girl with the kind work boots.
turning to listen closer into the words
we accidentally touched
(your feet and my back)                           10
i remember you speaking in soft tones in back
    of me,
to a friend beside you—
interrupting only to say
i'm sorry.                                        15
actually, i think it was my fault
if it was, i'm glad
had i not touched you
we would never have shared a smile.

AUDREY BROOKS

"To a Beautiful Girl Whose Name I Don't Know" by Audrey Brooks, from *It Is the Poem Singing into Your Eyes* edited by Arnold Adoff. Copyright © 1971 by Arnold Adoff. Reprinted by permission of Harper & Row.

THE ACCIDENTAL TOUCHING

We maintain a little cocoon of space around us as we move in crowds of strangers. Only our friends have the freedom to reach through and touch us. What happens when a stranger accidentally breaks through this wispy barrier, as happens in this poem? What makes this a significant encounter for the speaker?

# *Faces*

People that I meet and pass
   In the city's broken roar,
Faces that I lose so soon
   And have never found before,

Do you know how much you tell                    5
   In the meeting of our eyes,
How ashamed I am, and sad
   To have pierced your poor disguise?

Secrets rushing without sound
   Crying from your hiding places—          10
Let me go, I cannot bear
   The sorrow of the passing faces.

—People in the restless street,
   Can it be, oh can it be
In the meeting of our eyes                        15
   That you know as much of me?

SARA TEASDALE

Reprinted with permission of The Macmillan Company from COLLECTED POEMS by Sara Teasdale. Copyright 1920 by The Macmillan Company, renewed 1948 by Mamie T. Wheless.

## DO WE ALL WEAR DISGUISES?

Sara Teasdale suggests that we all wear disguises, even when we feel, as in a crowded street, that nobody could be watching us. According to this poem, what is it that people try to hide from one another? What understanding does she gain of herself?

## IMPLICATIONS

Look at the following statements and see if the poems you have just read support or negate the idea presented.

**1.** People tend to wear masks no matter where they may be.

**2.** Each encounter leaves its own mark on those involved.

**3.** Not all wars are fought on the battlefield with live ammunition.

**4.** Both young and old people are vulnerable and easy to hurt in a brief encounter.

# Gallery

## BRIEF ENCOUNTERS

The unpredictable drama of the brief encounter,
like every theme of the human experience, has intrigued the artist
as well as the writer for countless ages.
Battle scenes, moments of conquest, brief, tense struggles
between individuals are all common in the art of every land.
Also richly pictured are those prized moments when individuals
meet on other ground and offer a helping hand,
or rejoice together, or drown their sorrows, or even when there is a
second of mutual awareness as lonely people pass in the night.
  This gallery gives a brief glimpse of the wide range
of paintings that tell in their own terms of line and color
the excitement and emotional stir created
by the theme of brief encounters.

The giant Goliath, in the well-known Bible story
of David's victory with a slingshot, expected his encounter
with the stripling shepherd boy to be brief and victorious.
Sheer contrast of the unexpected outcome and the overturning
of expected odds have made this brief encounter
a treasured story for thousands of years.
From the conquests of Charlemagne comes the ancient French
epic of *The Song of Roland*. It tells of the return
of Charlemagne's legions from Spain and of the heroic deeds
and death of the knight Roland. The original epic gave rise
to other tales, among them Ariosto's *Orlando Furioso*,
in which Roland fights with Rodomonte the Saracen King
of Algiers in an attempt to cross his bridge. Examine the details.
  Notice the contrast between the serenity of the landscape
and the brief turbulence of the struggling men in the foreground.

DAVID
WITH THE HEAD
OF GOLIATH
*Guido Reni*

THE COMBAT
BETWEEN ROLAND
AND RODOMONTE
*Dosso Dossi*
*Wadsworth Atheneum,*
*Hartford, Connecticut*

In 354 A.D., Martin was a young
and reluctant soldier
whose principles had already
led him to give away
everything he owned.
When he came upon a poor
shivering beggar, he had little
to contribute so he divided
the cloak he was wearing
and gave the beggar the
sheepskin lining.
Later, according to the legends
of St. Martin, Bishop of Tours,
he received a vision of Christ
wearing this lining
and blessing Martin
for his noble gesture.
Pondering the meaning
of this brief encounter
led Martin to seek baptism
in the early Christian church
and to dedicate his life
to its causes.

ST. MARTIN
AND THE BEGGAR
*El Greco*
*National Gallery of Art,*
*Washington, D.C.,*
*Widener Collection*

Like so many of Winslow Homer's paintings, this brief facing of soldiers from the Union and the Confederacy is full of the stuff of storytellers. The characters are presented in detail, caught in an instant of awareness —a "moment of truth."

PRISONERS
FROM THE FRONT
*Winslow Homer*

This brief encounter occurred on September 14, 1923, and is a matter of newspaper record and boxing history. Firpo was KO'd in two rounds!

DEMPSEY AND FIRPO
*George Bellows*
*1924, Oil, Collection of the Whitney Museum of American Art, New York*

So much for history. Alfred Maurer provides us with a more personal sort of encounter: Ourself with ourself. Maurer's cubist style shows the front, top, and sides of the subject simultaneously, which is an indication of the complicated problems *we* face when we face ourselves. Look in a mirror. Is what you see *all* of the self you will have to encounter in order to get through another day? Or are there other, intertwined sides to you that the mirror never reveals?

TWIN HEADS
*Alfred H. Maurer*
*Collection of Whitney Museum of American Art.*

FIGHT FOR THE
WATERHOLE
*Frederic
Remington*

Water was precious in the desert areas of the far West, as the frontier painter
Remington tells us vividly. This encounter could not be brief enough
for the embattled men. Note how the pale but intense colors give a sense
of the great dry heat of the desert bowl.

After lonely stretches of months or even years at sea,
the returning captains made the most of their brief encounters with their fellow
seamen. Judging from the events the self-taught American painter recorded
with fascination in the Dutch Guinea port of Surinam,
for many the merriment should have been much more brief.

SEA CAPTAINS
CAROUSING IN SURINAM
*John Greenwood*
*The St. Louis Art Museum*

NIGHT
HAWKS
*Edward Hopper*

In startling contrast to the roistering sea captains,
the city painter Edward Hopper has painted a stark
and touching scene: four people, not really meeting, in an
all-night cafe. As in Homer's paintings, we are conscious
of the tension of an untold story.

Is there something in human nature that makes one distrust strangers?

# One Ordinary Day, With Peanuts

## SHIRLEY JACKSON

Mr. John Philip Johnson shut his front door behind him and came down his front steps into the bright morning with a feeling that all was well with the world on this best of all days, and wasn't the sun warm and good, and didn't his shoes feel comfortable after the resoling, and he knew that he had undoubtedly chosen the precise very tie which belonged with the day and the sun and his comfortable feet, and, after all, wasn't the world just a wonderful place? In spite of the fact that he was a small man, and the tie was perhaps a shade vivid, Mr. Johnson irradiated this feeling of well-being as he came down the steps and onto the dirty sidewalk, and he smiled at people who passed him, and some of them even smiled back. He stopped at the newsstand on the corner and bought his paper, saying *"Good* morning" with real conviction to the man who sold him the paper and the two or three other people who were lucky enough to be buying papers when Mr. Johnson skipped up. He remembered to fill his pockets with candy and peanuts, and then he set out to get himself uptown. He stopped in a flower shop and bought a carnation for his buttonhole, and stopped almost immediately afterward to give the carnation to a small child in a carriage, who looked at him dumbly and smiled, and Mr. Johnson smiled, and the child's mother looked at Mr. Johnson for a minute and then smiled too.

When he had gone several blocks uptown, Mr. Johnson cut across the avenue and went along a side street, chosen at random; he did not follow the same route every morning, but preferred to pursue his eventful way in wide detours, more like a puppy than a man intent upon business. It happened this morning that halfway down the block a moving van was parked, and the furniture from an upstairs apartment stood half on the sidewalk, half on the steps, while an amused group of people loitered, examining the scratches on the tables and the worn spots on the chairs, and a harassed woman, trying to watch a young child and the movers and the furniture all at the same time, gave the clear impression of endeavoring to shelter her private life from the people staring at her belongings. Mr. Johnson stopped, and for a moment joined the crowd, and then he came forward and, touching his hat civilly, said, "Perhaps I can keep an eye on your little boy for you?"

The woman turned and glared at him distrustfully, and Mr. Johnson added hastily, "We'll sit right here on the steps." He beckoned to the little boy, who hesitated and then responded agreeably to Mr. Johnson's genial smile. Mr. Johnson brought out a handful of peanuts from his pocket and sat on the steps with the boy, who at first refused the peanuts on the grounds that his mother did not allow him to accept food from strangers; Mr. Johnson said that probably his mother had not intended peanuts to be included, since elephants at the circus ate them, and the boy considered, and then agreed solemnly. They sat on the steps cracking peanuts in a comradely fashion, and Mr. Johnson said, "So you're moving?"

"Yep," said the boy.

"Where you going?"

"Vermont."

"Nice place. Plenty of snow there. Maple

"One Ordinary Day With Peanuts" by Shirley Jackson. First published in *The Magazine of Fantasy and Science Fiction.* Copyright © 1955 by Shirley Jackson. Reprinted by permission of Brandt & Brandt.

sugar too; you like maple sugar?"

"Sure."

"Plenty of maple sugar in Vermont. You going to live on a farm?"

"Going to live with Grandpa."

"Grandpa like peanuts?"

"Sure."

"Ought to take him some," said Mr. Johnson, reaching smoothly into his pocket. "Just you and Mommy going?"

"Yep."

"Tell you what," Mr. Johnson said. "You take some peanuts to eat on the train."

The boy's mother, after glancing at them frequently, had seemingly decided that Mr. Johnson was trustworthy, because she had devoted herself wholeheartedly to seeing that the movers did not—what movers rarely do, but every housewife believes they will—crack a leg from her good table, or set a kitchen chair down on a lamp. Most of the furniture was loaded by now, and she was deep in that

45

nervous stage when she knew there was something she had forgotten to pack—hidden away in the back of a closet somewhere, or left at a neighbor's and forgotten, or on the clothesline—and was trying to remember under stress what it was.

"This all, lady?" the chief mover said, completing her dismay.

Uncertainly, she nodded.

"Want to go on the truck with the furniture, sonny?" the mover asked the boy, and laughed. The boy laughed too and said to Mr. Johnson, "I guess I'll have a good time at Vermont."

"Fine time," said Mr. Johnson, and stood up. "Have one more peanut before you go," he said to the boy.

The boy's mother said to Mr. Johnson, "Thank you so much; it was a great help to me."

"Nothing at all," said Mr. Johnson gallantly. "Where in Vermont are you going?"

The mother looked at the little boy accusingly, as though he had given away a secret of some importance, and said unwillingly, "Greenwich."

"Lovely town," said Mr. Johnson. He took out a card, and wrote a name on the back. "Very good friend of mine lives in Greenwich," he said. "Call on him for anything you need. His wife makes the best doughnuts in town," he added soberly to the little boy.

"Swell," said the little boy.

"Good-bye," said Mr. Johnson.

He went on, stepping happily with his new-shod feet, feeling the warm sun on his back and on the top of his head. Halfway down the block he met a stray dog and fed him a peanut.

At the corner, where another wide avenue faced him, Mr. Johnson decided to go on uptown again. Moving with comparative laziness, he was passed on either side by people hurrying and frowning, and people brushed past him going the other way, clattering along to get somewhere quickly. Mr. Johnson stopped on every corner and waited patiently for the light to change, and he stepped out of the way of anyone who seemed to be in any particular hurry, but one young lady came too fast for him, and crashed wildly into him when he stopped to pat a kitten which had run out onto the sidewalk from an apartment house and was now unable to get back through the rushing feet.

"Excuse me," said the young lady, trying frantically to pick up Mr. Johnson and hurry on at the same time. "Terribly sorry."

The kitten, regardless now of danger, raced back to its home. "Perfectly all right," said Mr. Johnson, adjusting himself carefully. "You seem to be in a hurry."

"Of course I'm in a hurry," said the young lady. "I'm late."

She was extremely cross and the frown between her eyes seemed well on its way to becoming permanent. She had obviously awakened late, because she had not spent any extra time in making herself look pretty, and her dress was plain and unadorned with collar or brooch, and her lipstick was noticeably crooked. She tried to brush past Mr. Johnson, but, risking her suspicious displeasure, he took her arm and said, "Please wait."

"Look," she said ominously, "I ran into you and your lawyer can see my lawyer and I will gladly pay all damages and all inconveniences suffered therefrom but please this minute let me go because I am late."

"Late for what?" said Mr. Johnson; he tried his winning smile on her but it did no more than keep her, he suspected, from knocking him down again.

"Late for work," she said between her teeth. "Late for my employment. I have a job and if I am late I lose exactly so much an hour and I cannot really afford what your pleasant conversation is costing me, be it ever so pleasant."

"I'll pay for it," said Mr. Johnson. Now these were magic words, not necessarily because they were true, or because she seriously expected Mr. Johnson to pay for anything, but because Mr. Johnson's flat statement, obviously innocent of irony, could not be, coming from

Mr. Johnson, anything but the statement of a responsible and truthful and respectable man.

"What do you mean?" she asked.

"I said that since I am obviously responsible for your being late I shall certainly pay for it."

"Don't be silly," she said, and for the first time the frown disappeared. "I wouldn't expect you to pay anything—a few minutes ago I was offering to pay you. Anyway," she added, almost smiling, "it was my fault."

"What happens if you don't go to work?"

She stared. "I don't get paid."

"Precisely," said Mr. Johnson.

"What do you mean, precisely? If I don't show up at the office exactly twenty minutes ago I lose a dollar and eighty cents an hour, or three cents a minute or . . . ." She thought. ". . . About a dime for the time I've spent talking to you."

Mr. Johnson laughed, and finally she laughed, too. "You're late already," he pointed out. "Will you give me another six cents worth?"

"I don't understand why."

"You'll see," Mr. Johnson promised. He led her over to the side of the walk, next to the buildings, and said, "Stand here," and went out into the rush of people going both ways. Selecting and considering, as one who must make a choice involving perhaps whole years of lives, he estimated the people going by. Once he almost moved, and then at the last minute thought better of it and drew back. Finally, from half a block away, he saw what he wanted, and moved out into the center of the traffic to intercept a young man, who was hurrying, and dressed as though he had awakened late, and frowning.

"Oof," said the young man, because Mr. Johnson had thought of no better way to intercept anyone than the one the young woman had unwittingly used upon him. "Where do you think you're going?" the young man demanded from the sidewalk.

"I want to speak to you," said Mr. Johnson ominously.

The young man got up nervously, dusting himself and eyeing Mr. Johnson. "What for?" he said. "What'd I do?"

"That's what bothers me most about people nowadays," Mr. Johnson complained broadly to the people passing. "No matter whether they've done anything or not, they always figure someone's after them. About what you're going to do," he told the young man.

"Listen," said the young man, trying to brush past him, "I'm late, and I don't have any time to listen. Here's a dime, now get going."

"Thank you," said Mr. Johnson, pocketing the dime. "Look," he said, "what happens if you stop running?"

"I'm late," said the young man, still trying to get past Mr. Johnson, who was unexpectedly clinging.

"How much do you make an hour?" Mr. Johnson demanded.

"A Communist, are you?" said the young man. "Now will you please let me—"

"No," said Mr. Johnson insistently, "how much?"

"Two fifty," said the young man. "And now will you—"

"You like adventure?"

The young man stared, and, staring, found himself caught and held by Mr. Johnson's genial smile; he almost smiled back and then repressed it and made an effort to tear away. "I got to hurry," he said.

"Mystery? Like surprises? Unusual and exciting events?"

"You selling something?"

"Sure," said Mr. Johnson. "You want to take a chance?"

The young man hesitated, looked longingly up the avenue toward what might have been his destination and then, when Mr. Johnson said "I'll pay for it" with his own peculiar convincing emphasis, turned and said, "Well, okay. But I got to see it first, what I'm buying."

Mr. Johnson, breathing hard, led the young man over to the side where the girl was standing; she had been watching with interest Mr. Johnson's capture of the young man and now, smiling timidly, she looked at Mr. Johnson as though prepared to be surprised at nothing.

Mr. Johnson reached into his pocket and took out his wallet. "Here," he said, and handed two bills to the girl. "This about equals your day's pay."

"But no," she said, surprised in spite of herself. "I mean, I couldn't."

"Please do not interrupt," Mr. Johnson told her. "And here," he said to the young man, "this will take care of you." The young man accepted the money dazedly, but said, "Probably counterfeit" to the young woman out of the side of his mouth. "Now," Mr. Johnson went on, disregarding the young man, "what is your name, miss?"

"Kent," she said helplessly. "Mildred Kent."

"Fine," said Mr. Johnson. "And you, sir?"

"Arthur Adams," said the young man stiffly.

"Splendid," said Mr. Johnson. "Now, Miss Kent, I would like you to meet Mr. Adams. Mr. Adams, Miss Kent."

Miss Kent stared, wet her lips nervously, made a gesture as though she might run, and said, "How do you do?"

Mr. Adams straightened his shoulders, scowled at Mr. Johnson, made a gesture as though he might run, and said, "How do you do?"

"Now this," said Mr. Johnson, taking several bills from his wallet, "should be enough for the day for both of you. I would suggest perhaps, Coney Island—although I personally am not fond of the place—or perhaps a nice lunch somewhere, and dancing, or a matinee, or even a movie, although take care to choose a really good one; there are so many bad movies these days. You might," he said, struck with an inspiration, "visit the Bronx Zoo, or the Planetarium. Anywhere, as a matter of fact," he concluded, "that you would like to go. Have a nice time."

As he started to move away, Arthur Adams, breaking from his dumbfounded stare, said, "But look here, mister, you can't do this. Why—how do you know—I mean, we don't even know—I mean, how do you know we won't

just take the money and not do what you said?"

"You've taken the money," Mr. Johnson said. "You don't have to follow any of my suggestions. You may know something you prefer to do—perhaps a museum, or something."

"But suppose I just run away with it and leave her here?"

"I know you won't," said Mr. Johnson gently, "because you remembered to ask me that. Good-bye," he added, and went on.

As he stepped up the street, conscious of the sun on his head and his good shoes, he heard from somewhere behind him the young man saying, "Look, you know you don't have to if you don't want to," and the girl saying, "But unless you don't want to . . ." Mr. Johnson smiled to himself and then thought that he better hurry along; when he wanted to he could move very quickly, and before the young woman had gotten around to saying, "Well, I will if you will," Mr. Johnson was several blocks away and had already stopped twice, once to help a lady lift several large packages into a taxi and once to hand a peanut to a sea gull. By this time he was in an area of large stores and many more people and he was buffeted constantly from either side by people hurrying and cross and late and sullen. Once he offered a peanut to a man who asked him for a dime, and once he offered a peanut to a bus driver who had stopped his bus at an intersection and had opened the window next to his seat and put out his head as though longing for fresh air and the comparative quiet of the traffic. The man wanting a dime took the peanut because Mr. Johnson had wrapped a dollar bill around it, but the bus driver took the peanut and asked ironically, "You want a transfer, Jack?"

On a busy corner Mr. Johnson encountered two young people—for one minute he thought they might be Mildred Kent and Arthur Adams—who were eagerly scanning a newspaper, their backs pressed against a storefront to avoid the people passing, their heads bent together. Mr. Johnson, whose curiosity was insatiable, leaned onto the storefront next to them and peeked over the man's shoulder; they were scanning the "Apartments Vacant" columns.

Mr. Johnson remembered the street where the woman and her little boy were going to Vermont and he tapped the man on the shoulder and said amiably, "Try down on West Seventeen. About the middle of the block, people moved out this morning."

"Say, what do you—" said the man, and then, seeing Mr. Johnson clearly, "Well, thanks. Where did you say?"

"West Seventeen," said Mr. Johnson. "About the middle of the block." He smiled again and said, "Good luck."

"Thanks," said the man.

"Thanks," said the girl, as they moved off.

"Good-bye," said Mr. Johnson.

He lunched alone in a pleasant restaurant, where the food was rich, and only Mr. Johnson's excellent digestion could encompass two whipped-cream-and-chocolate-and-rum-cake pastries for dessert. He had three cups of coffee, tipped the waiter largely, and went out into the street again into the wonderful sunlight, his shoes still comfortable and fresh on his feet. Outside he found a beggar staring into the windows of the restaurant he had left and, carefully looking through the money in his pocket, Mr. Johnson approached the beggar and pressed some coins and a couple of bills into his hand. "It's the price of the veal cutlet lunch plus tip," said Mr. Johnson. "Good-bye."

After his lunch he rested; he walked into the nearest park and fed peanuts to the pigeons. It was late afternoon by the time he was ready to start back downtown, and he had refereed two checker games and watched a small boy and girl whose mother had fallen asleep and awakened with surprise and fear which turned to amusement when she saw Mr. Johnson. He had given away almost all of his candy, and had fed all the rest of his peanuts to the pigeons, and it was time to go home. Although the late afternoon sun was pleasant, and his shoes were still entirely com-

fortable, he decided to take a taxi downtown.

He had a difficult time catching a taxi, because he gave up the first three or four empty ones to people who seemed to need them more; finally, however, he stood alone on the corner and—almost like netting a frisky fish—he hailed desperately until he succeeded in catching a cab which had been proceeding with haste uptown and seemed to draw in toward Mr. Johnson against its own will.

"Mister," the cab driver said as Mr. Johnson climbed in, "I figured you was an omen, like. I wasn't going to pick you up at all."

"Kind of you," said Mr. Johnson ambiguously.

"If I'd of let you go it would of cost me ten bucks," said the driver.

"Really?"

"Yeah," said the driver. "Guy just got out of the cab, he turned around and give me ten bucks, said take this and bet it in a hurry on a horse named Vulcan, right away."

"Vulcan?" said Mr. Johnson, horrified. "A fire sign on a Wednesday?"

"What?" said the driver. "Anyway, I said to myself if I got no fare between here and there I'd bet the ten, but if anyone looked like they needed the cab I'd take it as a omen and I'd take the ten home to the wife."

"You were very right," said Mr. Johnson heartily. "This is Wednesday, you would have lost your money. Monday, yes, or even Saturday. But never never never a fire sign on a Wednesday. Sunday would have been good, now."

"Vulcan don't run on Sunday," said the driver.

"You wait till another day," said Mr. Johnson. "Down this street, please, driver. I'll get off on the next corner."

"He TOLD me Vulcan, though," said the driver.

"I'll tell you," said Mr. Johnson, hesitating with the door of the cab half open. "You take that ten dollars and I'll give you another ten dollars to go with it, and you go right ahead and bet that money on any Thursday on any horse that has a name indicating . . . let me see, Thursday . . . well, grain. Or any growing food."

"Grain?" said the driver. "You mean a horse named, like, Wheat or something?"

"Certainly," said Mr. Johnson. "Or, as a matter of fact, to make it even easier, any horse whose name includes the letters C, R, L. Perfectly simple."

"Tall corn?" said the driver, a light in his eye. "You mean a horse named, like, Tall Corn?"

"Absolutely," said Mr. Johnson. "Here's your money."

"Tall Corn," said the driver. "Thank *you*, mister."

"Good-bye," said Mr. Johnson.

He was on his own corner and went straight up to his apartment. He let himself in and called "Hello?" and Mrs. Johnson answered from the kitchen, "Hello, dear, aren't you early?"

"Took a taxi home," Mr. Johnson said. "I remembered the cheesecake too. What's for dinner?"

Mrs. Johnson came out of the kitchen and kissed him; she was a comfortable woman, and smiling as Mr. Johnson smiled. "Hard day?" she asked.

"Not very," said Mr. Johnson, hanging his coat in the closet. "How about you?"

"So-so," she said. She stood in the kitchen doorway while he settled into his easy chair and took off his good shoes and took out the paper he had bought that morning. "Here and there," she said.

"I didn't do so badly," Mr. Johnson said. "Couple young people."

"Fine," she said. "I had a little nap this afternoon, took it easy most of the day. Went into a department store this morning and accused the woman next to me of shoplifting, and had the store detective pick her up. Sent three dogs to the pound—*you* know, the usual thing. Oh, and listen," she added, remembering.

"What?" asked Mr. Johnson.

"Well," she said, "I got onto a bus and asked the driver for a transfer, and when he helped someone else first I said that he was impertinent, and quarreled with him. And then I said why wasn't he in the army, and I said it loud enough for everyone to hear, and I took his number and I turned in a complaint. Probably got him fired."

"Fine," said Mr. Johnson. "But you do look tired. Want to change over tomorrow?"

"I *would* like to," she said. "I could do with a change."

"Right," said Mr. Johnson. "What's for dinner?"

"Veal cutlet."

"Had it for lunch," said Mr. Johnson.

---

I

## PLAYING A GAME

The skeptical reader probably cannot quite believe that Mr. Johnson is as good as he appears to be at the beginning of the story. Still, his actions are eccentric enough in themselves to keep the reader's interest. It comes as a shock to discover at the story's end that the Johnsons are playing a deliberate game which includes taking turns at the "good" and the "evil" role. Pretending to be what we are not is a deep desire in human beings: children play at being adults or pirates or cowboys and Indians. As adults we continue to play roles, but not quite so obviously or necessarily consciously.

## II

## IMPLICATIONS

How do you react to the following statements? Are they true, false or something in between?

**1.** People have desires to help and desires to hurt. The Johnsons have found a way to balance their positive and negative desires.

**2.** Most people are instantly suspicious of strangers in a brief encounter.

**3.** Deliberately playing this game of "brief encounters" as the Johnsons do is morally wrong.

## III

### TECHNIQUES

*Exposition*

As this story proceeds, the reader continues to be mystified by Mr. Johnson's actions and keeps looking for that important part of the exposition that will explain things. Where does this material come in the story? How did you react to this technique of retaining significant information about characters until the end of the story? If most short stories were written this way, would the impact be the same?

*Conflict and Climax*

There can be conflict between characters, within a character, or between a character and the environment. Are any of these present in "One Ordinary Day, With Peanuts"? What holds the interest of the readers? What questions do they have in their minds? Where is this resolved? Try skimming back through the story now that you know the outcome. Do the events take on more significance or less?

## IV

### WORDS

1. Having given Mildred and Arthur some money, Mr. Johnson suggests they take in a matinee or some other entertainment. Like a number of other English words, *matinee*, meaning "a dramatic or musical performance given usually in the afternoon," was borrowed from the French. Another word of French origin, *marquee* (from *marquise*) refers to the signboard over the entrance to the building where shows, including matinees, are given.

Borrowing words from the French language has a long history; it began, in fact, with the Norman victory over the English in 1066. After their victory the Normans (who were Frenchmen) made French the official language of the upper classes in England, while the lower classes maintained their native language. Many French words came into the English language at this time. In early America, the English-speaking colonists came into contact with French explorers and French settlements, and naturally there was mutual borrowing of words. And this borrowing of words continues to this day, although not at such a great rate as before.

Test your knowledge of the following French loan-words, and look up the meaning of those that you do not know: *connoisseur, picayune, bayou, cache, communique, bouillon, chaise longue, camouflage.*

2. When Mrs. Johnson said, "I had a little nap this afternoon, took it easy most of the day," no native speaker of English would have trouble understanding what she meant. But a foreigner just learning the language might be mystified by the expression "took it easy," for Mrs. Johnson was not literally "taking" anything. She was resting. This expression, which doesn't mean what the actual words say, is said to be *idiomatic*.

Idiomatic expressions are plentiful in English. Upon meeting someone, we say, "How do you do?" Here we clearly are not asking the person how to perform some act, but we are politely greeting him. And when a girl says that she and Johnny are "going together," she obviously doesn't mean that they are taking a trip; she is saying that they date on a more or less steady basis.

Can you explain why each of the following expressions is idiomatic: catch a cold; catch on (understand); foot the bill; look out!; make a date; look up a buddy; catch fire; strike up a conversation; wait on tables (in a restaurant); gave himself away (revealed his secret).

3. What was the color, would you imagine, of the carnation that Mr. Johnson bought for his buttonhole? It could have been red or pink or white. However, the carnation was originally thought of as being pink, or flesh colored; in fact, it gets its name from the Latin stem *carn-*, meaning "flesh."

It seems incredible that a delicate, beautiful flower like the carnation could be related to a repulsive term like *carnage*—but it is. During a holiday period, we bemoan the carnage on our highways; that is, we grieve because of the mass slaughter of human flesh in car accidents.

See whether you can answer these questions involving words derived from the *carn-* stem: How does a *carnivorous* animal differ from a *herbivorous* one? Why is the period (several weeks long) before Lent referred to as *carnival* season in New Orleans? What is meant by *reincarnation*?

&#9753; You are about to witness
a series of conversations between four
people. But it is up to you to determine
the where, what, who, when, why, and how.
You must be the costumer, the actors,
the set designer, the lighting technician,
and the director
in order to give this "brief encounter"
an actual performance in your mind.

# The Pen of My Aunt

## GORDON DAVIOT

## *Characters*

*Madame*
*Simone*
*Stranger*
*Corporal*

SCENE: *A French country house during the Occupation.*

*The lady of the house is seated in her draw-ingroom.*

SIMONE. (*Approaching*) Madame! Oh, ma-dame! Madame, have you———

MADAME. Simone.

SIMONE. Madame, have you seen what———

MADAME. Simone!

SIMONE. But madame———

MADAME. Simone, this may be an age of bar-barism, but I will have none of it inside the walls of this house.

SIMONE. But madame, there is a—there is a

MADAME. (*Silencing her*) Simone. France may be an occupied country, a ruined nation, and a conquered race, but we will keep, if you please, the usages of civilization.

SIMONE. Yes, madame.

"Pen of My Aunt" by Josephine Tey, reprinted from *Pen of My Aunt*, Peter Davies, Publishers. Reprinted by permission of David Higham Associates, Ltd.

MADAME. One thing we still possess, thank God; and that is good manners. The enemy never had it; and it is not something they can take from *us*.

SIMONE. No, madame.

MADAME. Go out of the room again. Open the door———

SIMONE. Oh, *madame*! I wanted to tell you ———

MADAME. ———open the door, shut it behind you—quietly—take two paces into the room, and say what you came to say. (SIMONE *goes hastily out, shutting the door. She re-appears, shuts the door behind her, takes two paces into the room, and waits.*) Yes, Simone?

SIMONE. I expect it is too late now; they will be here.

MADAME. Who will?

SIMONE. The soldiers who were coming up the avenue.

MADAME. After the last few months I should not have thought that soldiers coming up the avenue was a remarkable fact. It is no doubt a party with a billeting order.

SIMONE. (*Crossing to the window*) No, ma-dame, it is two soldiers in one of their little cars, with a civilian between them.

MADAME. Which civilian?

SIMONE. A stranger, madame.

MADAME. A stranger? Are the soldiers from the Combatant branch?

SIMONE. No, they are those beasts of Admin-istration. Look, they have stopped. They are getting out.

MADAME. (*At the window*) Yes, it is a stranger. Do you know him, Simone?

SIMONE. I have never set eyes on him before, madame.

MADAME. You would know if he belonged to the district?

SIMONE. Oh, madame, I know every man be-tween here and St. Estèphe.

MADAME. (*Dryly*) No doubt.

SIMONE. Oh, merciful God, they are coming up the steps.

MADAME. My good Simone, that is what the steps were put there for.

SIMONE. But they will ring the bell and I shall have to———

MADAME. And you will answer it and behave as if you had been trained by a butler and ten upper servants instead of being the charcoal-burner's daughter from over at Les Chênes. (*This is said encouragingly, not in unkindness.*) You will be very calm and correct———

SIMONE. Calm! Madame! With my inside turning over and over like a wheel at a fair!

MADAME. A good servant does not have an inside, merely an exterior. (*Comforting*) Be assured, my child. You have your place here; that is more than those creatures on our doorstep have. Let that hearten you———

SIMONE. Madame! They are not going to ring. They are coming straight in.

MADAME. (*Bitterly*) Yes. They have forgotten long ago what bells are for.

[*The door opens.*]

STRANGER. (*In a bright, confident, casual tone*) Ah, there you are, my dear aunt. I am so glad. Come in, my friend, come in. My dear aunt, this gentleman wants you to identify me.

MADAME. Identify you?

CORPORAL. We found this man wandering in the woods———

STRANGER. The corporal found it inexplicable that anyone should wander in a wood.

CORPORAL. And he had no papers on him———

STRANGER. And I rightly pointed out that if I carry all the papers one is supposed to these days, I am no good to God or man. If I put them in a hip pocket, I can't bend forward; if I put them in a front pocket, I can't bend at all.

CORPORAL. He said that he was your nephew, madame, but that did not seem to us very likely, so we brought him here.

[*There is the slightest pause;
just one moment of silence.*]

MADAME. But of course this is my nephew.

CORPORAL. He is?

MADAME. Certainly.

CORPORAL. He lives here?

MADAME. (*Assenting*) My nephew lives here.

CORPORAL. So! (*Recovering*) My apologies, madame. But you will admit that appearances were against the young gentleman.

MADAME. Alas, Corporal, my nephew belongs to a generation who delight in flouting appearances. It is what they call "expressing their personality," I understand.

CORPORAL. (*With contempt*) No doubt, madame.

MADAME. Convention is anathema to them, and there is no sin like conformity. Even a collar is an offense against their liberty, and a discipline not to be borne by free necks.

CORPORAL. Ah yes, madame. A little more discipline among your nephew's generation, and we might not be occupying your country today.

STRANGER. You think it was that collar of yours that conquered my country? You flatter yourself, Corporal. The only result of wearing a collar like that is varicose veins in the head.

MADAME. (*Repressive*) Please! My dear boy. Let us not descend to personalities.

STRANGER. The matter is not personal, my good aunt, but scientific. Wearing a collar like that retards the flow of fresh blood to the head, with the most disastrous consequences to the grey matter of the brain. The hypothetical grey matter. In fact, I have a theory———

CORPORAL. Monsieur, your theories do not interest me.

STRANGER. No? You do not find speculation interesting?

CORPORAL. In this world one judges by results.

STRANGER. (*After a slight pause of reflection*) I see. The collared conqueror sits in the high places, while the collarless conquered lies about in the woods. And who comes best out of that, would you say? Tell me,

54

Corporal, as man to man, do you never have a mad, secret desire to lie unbuttoned in a wood?

CORPORAL. I have only one desire, monsieur, and that is to see your papers.

STRANGER. (*Taken off guard and filling in time*) My papers?

MADAME. But is that necessary, Corporal? I have already told you that———

CORPORAL. I know that madame is a very good collaborator and in good standing———

MADAME. In that case———

CORPORAL. But when we begin an affair we like to finish it. I have asked to see monsieur's papers, and the matter will not be finished until I have seen them.

MADAME. You acknowledge that I am in "good standing," Corporal?

CORPORAL. So I have heard, madame.

MADAME. Then I must consider it a discourtesy on your part to demand my nephew's credentials.

CORPORAL. It is no reflection on madame. It is a matter of routine, nothing more.

STRANGER. (*Murmuring*) The great god Routine.

MADAME. To ask for his papers was routine; to insist on their production is discourtesy. I shall say so to your Commanding Officer.

CORPORAL. Very good, madame. In the meantime, I shall inspect your nephew's papers.

MADAME. And what if I———

STRANGER. (*Quietly*) You may as well give it up, my dear. You could as easily turn a steamroller. They have only one idea at a time. If the Corporal's heart is set on seeing my papers, he shall see them. (*Moving toward the door*) I left them in the pocket of my coat.

SIMONE. (*Unexpectedly, from the background*) Not in your *linen* coat?

STRANGER. (*Pausing*) Yes. Why?

SIMONE. (*With apparently growing anxiety*) Your *cream* linen coat? The one you were wearing yesterday?

STRANGER. Certainly.

SIMONE. Merciful Heaven! I sent it to the laundry!

STRANGER. To the laundry!

SIMONE. Yes, monsieur; this morning; in the basket.

STRANGER. (*In incredulous anger*) You sent my coat, *with my papers in the pocket,* to the laundry!

SIMONE. (*Defensive and combatant*) I didn't know monsieur's papers were in the pocket.

STRANGER. You didn't know! You didn't know that a packet of documents weighing half a ton were in the pocket. An identity card, a *laisser-passer,*[1] a food card, a drink card, an army discharge, a permission to wear civilian clothes, a permission to go farther than ten miles to the east, a permission to go more than ten miles to the west, a permission to———

SIMONE. (*Breaking in with spirit*) How was I to know the coat was heavy! I picked it up with the rest of the bundle that was lying on the floor.

STRANGER. (*Snapping her head off*) My coat was on the back of the chair.

SIMONE. It was on the floor.

STRANGER. On the back of the chair!

SIMONE. It was on the floor with your dirty shirt and your pajamas, and a towel and what not. I put my arms round the whole thing and then—woof! into the basket with them.

STRANGER. I tell you that coat was on the back of the chair. It was quite clean and was not going to the laundry for two weeks yet—if then. I hung it there myself, and———

MADAME. My dear boy, what does it matter? The damage is done now. In any case, they will find the papers when they unpack the basket, and return them tomorrow.

STRANGER. If someone doesn't steal them. There are a lot of people who would like to lay hold of a complete set of papers, believe me.

---

1. **laisser passer** \'le-sā pa-◆sā\ to allow to pass.

MADAME. (*Reassuring*) Oh, no. Old Fleureau is the soul of honesty. You have no need to worry about them. They will be back first thing tomorrow, you shall see; and then we shall have much pleasure in sending them to the Administration Office for the Corporal's inspection. Unless, of course, the Corporal insists on your personal appearance at the office.

CORPORAL. (*Cold and indignant*) I have seen monsieur. All that I want now is to see his papers.

STRANGER. You shall see them, Corporal, you shall see them. The whole half-ton of them. You may inspect them at your leisure. Provided, that is, that they come back from the laundry to which this idiot has consigned them.

MADAME. (*Again reassuring*) They will come back, never fear. And you must not blame Simone. She is a good child, and does her best.

SIMONE. (*With an air of belated virtue*) I am not one to pry into pockets.

MADAME. Simone, show the Corporal out, if you please.

SIMONE. (*Natural feeling overcoming her for a moment*) He knows the way out. (*Recovering*) Yes, madame.

MADAME. And Corporal, try to take your duties a little less literally in future. My countrymen appreciate the spirit rather than the letter.

CORPORAL. I have my instructions, madame, and I obey them. Good day, madame. Monsieur.

[*He goes, followed by* SIMONE—*door closes. There is a moment of silence.*]

STRANGER. For a good collaborator, that was a remarkably quick adoption.

MADAME. Sit down, young man. I will give you something to drink. I expect your knees are none too well.

STRANGER. My knees, madame, are pure gela-tine. As for my stomach, it seems to have disappeared.

MADAME. (*Offering him the drink she has poured out*) This will recall it, I hope.

STRANGER. You are not drinking, madame.

MADAME. Thank you, no.

STRANGER. Not with strangers. It is certainly no time to drink with strangers. Nevertheless, I drink the health of a collaborator. (*He drinks*) Tell me, madame, what will happen tomorrow when they find that you have no nephew?

MADAME. (*Surprised*) But of course I have a nephew. I tell lies, my friend; but not *silly* lies. My charming nephew has gone to Bonneval for the day. He finds country life dull.

STRANGER. Dull? This—this heaven?

MADAME. (*Dryly*) He likes to talk and here there is no audience. At Headquarters in Bonneval he finds the audience sympathetic.

STRANGER. (*Understanding the implication*) Ah.

MADAME. He believes in the Brotherhood of Man—if you can credit it.

STRANGER. After the last six months?

MADAME. His mother was American, so he has half the Balkans in his blood. To say nothing of Italy, Russia, and the Levant.

STRANGER. (*Half amused*) I see.

MADAME. A silly and worthless creature, but useful.

STRANGER. Useful?

MADAME. I—borrow his cloak.

STRANGER. I see.

MADAME. Tonight I shall borrow his identity papers, and tomorrow they will go to the office in St. Estèphe.

STRANGER. But—he will have to know.

MADAME. (*Placidly*) Oh, yes, he will know, of course.

STRANGER. And how will you persuade such an enthusiastic collaborator to deceive his friends?

MADAME. Oh, that is easy. He is my heir.

STRANGER. (*Amused*) Ah.

MADAME. He is, also, by the mercy of God, not

too unlike you, so that his photograph will not startle the Corporal too much tomorrow. Now tell me what you were doing in my wood.

STRANGER. Resting my feet—I am practically walking on my bones. And waiting for to-night.

MADAME. Where are you making for? (*As he does not answer immediately*) The coast? (*He nods*) That is four days away—five if your feet are bad.

STRANGER. I know it.

MADAME. Have you friends on the way?

STRANGER. I have friends at the coast, who will get me a boat. But no one between here and the sea.

MADAME. (*Rising*) I must consult my list of addresses. (*Pausing*) What was your service?

STRANGER. Army.

MADAME. Which Regiment?

STRANGER. The 79th.

MADAME. (*After the faintest pause*) And your Colonel's name?

STRANGER. Delavault was killed in the first week, and Martin took over.

MADAME. (*Going to her desk*) A "good collaborator" cannot be too careful. Now I can consult my notebook. A charming color, is it not? A lovely shade of red.

STRANGER. Yes—but what has a red quill pen to do with your notebook?—Ah, you write with it of course—stupid of me.

MADAME. Certainly I write with it—but it is also my notebook—look—I only need a hairpin—and then—so—out of my quill pen comes my notebook—a tiny piece of paper —but enough for a list of names.

STRANGER. You mean that you keep that list on

your desk? (*He sounds disapproving*)

MADAME. Where did you expect me to keep it, young man? In my corset? Did you ever try to get something out of your corset in a hurry? What would you advise as the ideal quality in a hiding-place for a list of names?

STRANGER. That the thing should be difficult to find, of course.

MADAME. Not at all. That it should be easily destroyed in emergency. It is too big for me to swallow—I suspect they do that only in books—and we have no fires to consume it, so I had to think of some other way. I did try to memorize the list, but what I could not be sure of remembering were those that —that had to be scored off. It would be fatal to send someone to an address that—that was no longer available. So I had to keep a written record.

STRANGER. And if you neither eat it nor burn it when the moment comes, how do you get rid of it?

MADAME. I could, of course, put a match to it, but scraps of freshly-burned paper on a desk take a great deal of explaining. If I ceased to be looked on with approval my usefulness would end. It is important there- fore that there should be no sign of anxiety on my part: no burned paper, no excuses to leave the room, no nods and becks and winks. I just sit here at my desk and go on with my letters. I tilt my nice big inkwell sideways for a moment and dip the pen into the deep ink at the side. The ink flows into the hollow of the quill, and all is blotted out. (*Consulting the list*) Let me see. It would be good if you could rest your feet for a day or so.

STRANGER. (*Ruefully*) It would.

MADAME. There is a farm just beyond the Marnay crossroads on the way to St. Estèphe ———(*She pauses to consider*)

STRANGER. St. Estèphe is the home of the single-minded Corporal. I don't want to run into him again.

MADAME. No, that might be awkward; but that farm of the Cherfils would be ideal. A good hiding-place, and food to spare, and fine people———

STRANGER. If your nephew is so friendly with the invader, how is it that the Corporal doesn't know him by sight?

MADAME. (*Absently*) The unit at St. Estèphe is a non-commissioned one.

STRANGER. Does the Brotherhood of Man ex- clude sergeants, then?

MADAME. Oh, definitely. Brotherhood does not really begin under field rank, I understand.

STRANGER. But the Corporal may still meet your nephew somewhere.

MADAME. That is a risk one must take. It is not a very grave one. They change the per- sonnel every few weeks, to prevent them becoming too acclimatized. And even if he met my nephew, he is unlikely to ask for the papers of so obviously well-to-do a citizen. If you could bear to go *back* a little———

STRANGER. Not a step! It would be like—like denying God. I have got so far, against all the odds, and I am not going a yard back. Not even to rest my feet!

MADAME. I understand; but it is a pity. It is a long way to the Cherfils farm—two miles east of the Marnay crossroads it is, on a little hill.

STRANGER. I'll get there; don't worry. If not tonight then tomorrow night. I am used to sleeping in the open by now.

MADAME. I wish we could have you here, but it is too dangerous. We are liable to be billeted on at any moment, without notice. However, we can give you a good meal, and a bath. We have no coal, so it will be one of those flat-tin-saucer baths. And if you want to be very kind to Simone you might have it somewhere in the kitchen regions and so save her carrying water upstairs.

STRANGER. But of course.

MADAME. Before the war I had a staff of twelve. Now I have Simone. I dust and Simone sweeps, and between us we keep the dirt at bay. She has no manners but a great heart, the child.

STRANGER. The heart of a lion.

MADAME. Before I put this back you might memorize these: Forty Avenue Foch, in Crest, the back entrance.

STRANGER. Forty Avenue Foch, the back entrance.

MADAME. You may find it difficult to get into Crest, by the way. It is a closed area. The pot boy at the Red Lion in Mans.

STRANGER. The pot boy.

MADAME. Denis the blacksmith at Laloupe. And the next night should take you to the sea and your friends. Are they safely in your mind?

STRANGER. Forty Avenue Foch in Crest; the pot boy at the Red Lion in Mans; and Denis the blacksmith at Laloupe. And to be careful getting into Crest.

MADAME. Good. Then I can close my notebook —or roll it up, I should say—then—it fits neatly, does it not? Now let us see about some food for you. Perhaps I could find you other clothes. Are these all you————

[*The* CORPORAL's *voice is heard mingled in fury with the still more furious tones of* SIMONE. *She is yelling: "Nothing of the sort, I tell you, nothing of the sort," but no words are clearly distinguishable in the angry row. The door is flung open, and the* CORPORAL *bursts in dragging a struggling* SIMONE *by the arm.*]

SIMONE. (*Screaming with rage and terror*) Let me go, you foul fiend, you murdering foreign creature, let me go. (*She tries to kick him*)

CORPORAL. (*At the same time*) Stop struggling, you lying deceitful little bit of no-good.

MADAME. Will someone explain this extraordinary————

CORPORAL. This creature————

MADAME. Take your hand from my servant's arm, Corporal. She is not going to run away.

CORPORAL. (*Reacting to the voice of authority and automatically complying*) Your precious

servant was overheard telling the gardener that she had never set eyes on this man.

SIMONE. I did not! Why should I say anything like that?

CORPORAL. With my own two ears I heard her, my own two ears. Will you kindly explain that to me if you can.

MADAME. You speak our language very well, Corporal, but perhaps you are not so quick to understand.

CORPORAL. I understand perfectly.

MADAME. What Simone was saying to the gardener, was no doubt what she was announcing to all and sundry at the pitch of her voice this morning.

CORPORAL. (*Unbelieving*) And what was that?

MADAME. That she *wished* she had never set eyes on my nephew.

CORPORAL. And why should she say that?

MADAME. My nephew, Corporal, has many charms, but tidiness is not one of them. As you may have deduced from the episode of the coat. He is apt to leave his room————

SIMONE. (*On her cue; in a burst of scornful rage*) Cigarette ends, pajamas, towels, bedclothes, books, papers—all over the floor like a *flood*. Every morning I tidy up, and in two hours it is as if a bomb had burst in the room.

STRANGER. (*Testily*) I told you already that I was sor————

SIMONE. (*Interrupting*) As if I had nothing else to do in this enormous house but wait on you.

STRANGER. Haven't I said that I————

SIMONE. And when I have climbed all the way up from the kitchen with your shaving water, you let it get cold; but will you shave in cold? Oh, no! I have to bring up another————

STRANGER. I didn't ask you to climb the damned stairs, did I?

SIMONE. And do I get a word of thanks for bringing it? Do I indeed? You say: "*Must you bring it in that hideous jug; it offends my eyes.*"

STRANGER. So it does offend my eyes!

MADAME. Enough, enough! We had enough of that this morning. You see, Corporal?

CORPORAL. I could have sworn——

MADAME. A natural mistake, perhaps. But I think you might have used a little more common sense in the matter. (*Coldly*) And a great deal more dignity. I don't like having my servants manhandled.

CORPORAL. She refused to come.

SIMONE. Accusing me of things I never said!

MADAME. However, now that you are here again you can make yourself useful. My nephew wants to go into Crest the day after tomorrow, and that requires a special pass. Perhaps you would make one out for him.

CORPORAL. But I——

MADAME. You have a little book of permits in your pocket, haven't you?

CORPORAL. Yes. I——

MADAME. Very well. Better make it valid for two days. He is always changing his mind.

CORPORAL. But it is not for me to grant a pass.

MADAME. You sign them, don't you?

CORPORAL. Yes, but only when someone tells me to.

MADAME. Very well, if it will help you, I tell you to.

CORPORAL. I mean, permission must be granted before a pass is issued.

MADAME. And have you any doubt that a permission will be granted to my nephew?

CORPORAL. No, of course not, madame.

MADAME. Then don't be absurd, Corporal. To be absurd twice in five minutes is too often. You may use my desk—and my own special pen. Isn't it a beautiful quill, Corporal?

CORPORAL. Thank you, madame, no. *We* Germans have come a long way from the geese.

MADAME. Yes?

CORPORAL. I prefer my fountain pen. It is a more efficient implement. (*He writes*) For the 15th and 16th. "Holder of identity card number"—What is the number of your identity, monsieur?

STRANGER. I have not the faintest idea.

CORPORAL. You do not know?

STRANGER. No. The only numbers I take an interest in are lottery numbers.

SIMONE. I know the number of monsieur's card.

MADAME. (*Afraid that she is going to invent one*) I don't think that likely, Simone.

SIMONE. (*Aware of what is in her mistress's mind, and reassuring her*) But I really *do* know, madame. It is the year I was born, with two "ones" after it. Many a time I have seen it on the outside of the card.

CORPORAL. It is good that someone knows.

SIMONE. It is—192411.

CORPORAL. 192411. (*He fills in the dates*)

MADAME. (*As he nears the end*) Are you going back to St. Estèphe now, Corporal?

CORPORAL. Yes, madame.

MADAME. Then perhaps you will give my nephew a lift as far as the Marnay crossroads.

CORPORAL. It is not permitted to take civilians as passengers.

STRANGER. But you took me here as a passenger.

CORPORAL. That was different.

MADAME. You mean that when you thought he was a miscreant[2] you took him in your car, but now that you know he is my nephew you refuse?

CORPORAL. When I brought him here it was on service business.

MADAME. (*Gently reasonable*) Corporal, I think you owe me something for your general lack of tact this afternoon. Would it to be too much to ask you to consider my nephew a miscreant for the next hour while you drive him as far as the Marnay crossroads?

CORPORAL. But ———

MADAME. Take him to the crossroads with you and I shall agree to forget your—your lack of efficiency. I am sure you are actually a very efficient person, and likely to be a sergeant any day now. We won't let a blunder or two stand in your way.

CORPORAL. If I am caught giving a lift to a civilian, I shall *never* be a sergeant.

MADAME. (*Still gentle*) If I report on your conduct this afternoon, tomorrow you will be a private.

CORPORAL. (*After a long pause*) Is monsieur ready to come now?

STRANGER. Quite ready.

CORPORAL. You will need a coat.

MADAME. Simone, get monsieur's coat from the cupboard in the hall. And when you have seen him off, come back here.

SIMONE. Yes, madame.

[*Exit* SIMONE.]

CORPORAL. Madame.

MADAME. Good day to you, Corporal.

[*Exit* CORPORAL.]

STRANGER. Your talent for blackmail is remarkable.

MADAME. The place has a yellow barn. You had better wait somewhere till evening, when the dogs are chained up.

STRANGER. I wish I had an aunt of your calibre. All mine are authorities on crochet.

MADAME. I could wish you were my nephew. Good luck, and be careful. Perhaps one day, you will come back, and dine with me, and tell me the rest of the tale.

[*The sound of a running engine comes from outside.*]

STRANGER. Two years today, perhaps?

MADAME. One year today.

---

2. **miscreant** \‸mis-krē-ənt\ one who behaves criminally or viciously.

STRANGER. (*Softly*) Who knows? (*He lifts her hand to his lips*) Thank you, and *au revoir*. (*Turning at the door*) Being sped on my way by the enemy is a happiness I had not anticipated. I shall never be able to repay you for that. (*He goes out. Offstage he says*) Ah, my coat—thank you, Simone.

[*Sound of car driving off.*]

[MADAME *pours out two glasses. As she finishes,* SIMONE *come in, shutting the door correctly behind her and taking two paces into the room.*]

SIMONE. You wanted me, madame?

MADAME. You will drink a glass of wine with me, Simone.

SIMONE. With you, madame!

MADAME. You are a good daughter of France and a good servant to me. We shall drink a toast together.

SIMONE. Yes, madame.

MADAME. (*Quietly*) To Freedom.

SIMONE. (*Repeating*) To Freedom. May I add a bit of my own, madame?

MADAME. Certainly.

SIMONE. (*With immense satisfaction*) And a very bad end to that Corporal!

CURTAIN

## I
### READING A PLAY

When you read this play, you probably brought to it the same reading habits that you use in reading a short story or novel. But reading a play is a completely different experience from reading other forms of literature. When authors write dialogue, they are imagining these words as being spoken by actors on a stage, not as being read silently. Both the characters and the audience are hearing the words for the first time. Everything people in the audience learn about who, what, where, when, why, and how, they learn from what they hear and see. But readers of a play must do even more. From the dialogue on the page they must create in their minds the appearances and the personalities of the characters, the appearance of the set, and so forth. This is why the headnote suggested that you would have to do, in your mind, everything from costuming the actors to directing the play. The production you create in your mind may be a very different one from that conceived by your classmate.

First, let's see how you each visualize the characters. There are some guidelines given in the dialogue, but generally these are only slight hints. Most of the image comes from your own mind. This means that there may be many different versions of how the characters look. None are either correct or incorrect; it is simply a matter of choice. As you answer the following questions, look back through the lines of the play to see if you can find any support for your ideas. Decide the following for each of the four characters (Madame, the Stranger, the Corporal, and Simone): (1) age, (2) height, (3) dress, (4) mannerisms, (5) intelligence, and (6) how he or she would behave in a quite different situation, such as buying groceries.

But a play is different from other literature in still another way. It is made up of a series of scenes. A scene does not necessarily mean a change of setting on the stage. When dramatists speak of a scene, they mean a change in characters present on the stage. Each time a character enters or leaves the stage, one scene is ended and another begins. Go through the play and find the scenes. There are eight of them. Two are very, very brief indeed. Each scene in itself is a miniature chunk of drama. Each has a climax, which is defined as the high point of action. Once you have identified the eight scenes, find the climax in each. When you act the play either in your mind or in front of the class, knowing the high point of each little dramatic incident will help you create a rising sense of tension and excitement that reaches its highest point at the climax of the whole play. This is the point when both the characters and audience learn how the situation is going to work out.

Reading a play is much like reading a sheet of music. Both the words and notes on a page are open to varied interpretations. This is what makes the reading of plays so exciting. The reader becomes a part of the creative act.

## II

### IMPLICATIONS

Consider and discuss your reactions to the following questions.

**1.** In this brief encounter you are instantly on the side of the Stranger and against the Corporal. Yet you actually know little about either person or the situation. Why does this happen?

**2.** What triggers Madame and Simone to play the roles of the aunt and aggrieved servant? How dangerous is this?

**3.** In beginning French language texts, one of the first phrases that used to be taught was *"la plume de ma tante"* (the pen of my aunt). Does knowing this add anything to your insight or enjoyment?

**4.** After brief encounters, we often replay in our minds what we should have said or done. How does this affect your enjoyment of this play?

## III

### TECHNIQUES

*Conflict*

Identify the conflict. Is it one between people, or is it created by a set of circumstances? What question in your mind is set in motion?

*Climax*

Find the point of climax in this play. What is your feeling when you reach this point?

### SUMMING UP

## *Brief Encounters*

### THEME

I think that when people are pressed close they act the same way. Part of you enters them, part of them enters you. Long after you forget the names and faces, they are still a part of you. Sometimes it is frightening to think that every person you have

ever hated, or feared, or run away from is part of you. But so is every person you have ever learned from, every friend you ever had."

—Theodore H. White

In daily life, people are thrown together in innumerable accidental situations. These meetings are neither planned nor permanent. The people involved separate and go their different ways. But in the momentary coming together something happens. The effects may be great or small, for good or bad, but whether it is recognized by the participants or not, an effect is there. Their lives have been changed.

### IMPLICATIONS

Now, before reading the novel *His Enemy, His Friend*, pull together your impressions of the short selections in BRIEF ENCOUNTERS by evaluating the following set of propositions. Consider as many of the selections you think the propositions apply to, before you form an opinion. The more evidence you can cite, the sounder your opinion will be.

**1.** Brief encounters seem to be accidents, but it is possible that they are part of a plan that we, as human beings, do not understand.

**2.** Beneath superficial differences, most people are alike in basic human traits and characteristics.

**3.** Whether a person is a friend or an enemy sometimes depends on circumstances outside one's own control.

**4.** Brief encounters may change the direction of one's life.

**5.** A person with a strong personal code of conduct is never at a loss in an unusual encounter. He or she never has any doubts about what his or her reactions should be.

**6.** In all of us, there lie hidden qualities that brief encounters may surprisingly bring out.

TECHNIQUES

*Conflict*

There are three major sources of conflicts: those between people, those between people and nature, and those between conflicting drives and needs within a person.

Which kinds of conflicts occur in the following: "The Grains of Paradise," "Mateo Falcone," and "The Pen of My Aunt"?

*Exposition*

Exposition is the information necessary to get the reader quickly into the story: the who, where, when, why, and what. The conflict or problem is the "what."

For the following selections, identify who is involved, where the action is taking place, what the historical time is, and the reason (why) for the conflict: "The Grains of Paradise," "Mateo Falcone," and "The Pen of My Aunt."

*Climax*

Climax comes at the moment when the conflict turns toward a solution. In some stories there is more than one conflict, and therefore there can be two climaxes. This is true in "The Grains of Paradise." What are the two climaxes?

Are there other selections in the unit where there are multiple conflicts and climaxes?

*Poetry*

The six poems you have read on pages 31 through 37 cover a variety of poetic styles. In a few words, characterize the style of each poem. Is it lofty, conversational, polished, rough? Show how each style is appropriate or inappropriate to the poem's subject matter. What experiences are similar to those in the prose selections? Which are different? How? What does poetry accomplish that prose does not?

*Essay*

"Stopover in Querétaro" is an essay rather than a short story. However, as an essay that recounts a personal experience, it is in many ways similar to a story. How do exposition, conflict, and climax function in this essay?

## Introduction to
## His Enemy, His Friend

Thomas Hardy's poem, "The Man He Killed," speculates about the strange quirk of fate in which the relationship between two people is determined by the circumstances under which they meet. *His Enemy, His Friend* is a further exploration of this quality of human life. How does a person become your enemy? How does another become your friend? Do you control the relationship or does it come about simply by the accident of being thrown together in a neighborhood or classroom? Is friendship determined by qualities you like or dislike in another person or is it perhaps a matter of psychological chemistry? Or are one's reactions determined by forces in the culture: the accident of your being born in a given country, a member of a given race, into a given religion? We all like to think that we are the masters of our fates, as a familiar English poem states. But are we? Do we really have control over who becomes our enemy and who becomes our friend?

John Tunis says that his story is about the conscience of a man. Conscience is the faculty of recognizing right from wrong in regard to one's own conduct. So conscience is a very personal thing. Individuals may recognize certain actions as right and have no sense of guilt in performing them. Other actions are considered wrong, and, though a person may go ahead and do them, she or he is uneasy or uncomfortable in the act. People who have no such guide for their actions, who act purely on the basis of a pain or pleasure scale, are deficient as human beings. Conscience may be a quality that is learned or imposed by one's culture. But in its finest sense it is a system of values that an individual has fought through and determined for himself or herself. It comes from an ability to get inside the skin of another person so that the world can be seen through that person's eyes, feeling her or his needs and understanding his or her rights. It comes from a realization of how one's own actions set up ripples that affect other people.

One of the continuing problems of human existence occurs when the individual's conscience conflicts with the demands of the culture. This is the theme of much great literature: of *Antigone*, one of the greatest of the ancient Greek plays, of *Hamlet*, perhaps the greatest play written in the English language. It is the problem of the conscientious objector in modern America and of many young adults who see some aspects of contemporary society as hypocritical.

This story of conscience you are about to read is laid in France during the German occupation of that country during World War II. The map is important to help you locate places and movements of characters. During the 1930s Hitler made his spectacular rise to power in Germany and for awhile lifted the Germans out of the hopelessness they had felt since World War I. France and Germany had a long, traditional history of enmity. When Germany was suddenly reinvigorated, France put all of its efforts into fortifying its common border with Germany. Much to France's surprise, Germany swept through Belgium around the end of the fortified defenses and overwhelmed the defenders. For the next four years France was governed by a puppet government of Frenchmen who were willing to collaborate with Germany, but the Germans continued to occupy the country. It was a time of great deprivation. Most young male Frenchmen were shipped east to Germany to serve almost as slave labor in the German war effort. The French Jews were systematically eliminated by being sent to German concentration camps. However, there was a strong underground organization of French patriots who resisted the conquerors. There were frequent incidents against the Germans.

As the war dragged along and the allied forces gained increasing strength, Hitler knew that the invasion of France would probably come from England. He therefore built a strong system of defenses along the French coast, actually extending them all the way to Norway. Natives in the coast villages lived in both great expectancy and dread of the coming assault. The invasion would throw out the hated Germans, but it would also probably bring devastation to the towns. The actual invasion began on June 6, 1944, at a spot on the Normandy coast called by the code name of Omaha Beach. From the details of geography given in the story, you must conclude that the setting of *His Enemy, His Friend* is a village on the French coast of the English Channel, north of the actual invasion area.

Before you start, it is also important to read the author's note about the story. Tunis writes:

. . . sport plays an important part in these pages. The sport dealt with is the game that Europeans call football. When played in the United States, it is association football, or soccer. Since my story is set abroad, I have used the term "football" throughout.

Unlike American football, which is half football and half basketball and neither the one nor the other, the European sport is based upon kicking and passing along the ground. No player save the goalkeeper may touch the ball with his hands. The game is played by eleven men on each side. No substitutions are permitted. There are two halves of forty-five minutes each, and the ball used is round, not oval as in American football. It is a game enormously popular with the young, and draws immense crowds all over the world.

# HIS ENEMY, HIS FRIEND

JOHN TUNIS

## Part I

Eve of Battle
June, 1944

### 1

The black-haired sergeant, in the gray-green uniform of the army of Adolf Hitler's Third Reich,[1] sat smoking his pipe on the stone steps of the house. Beside him was a boy of eight or nine in a faded polo shirt, a ragged pair of dark blue shorts, and sneakers so frayed that both his big toes stuck out of them.

The sergeant and the boy were discussing a subject that each considered important and their serious faces reflected this.

"Was that the time, Feldwebel[2] Hans, when you scored the only goal for Hamburg against Stuttgart?" asked the boy.

"Noooo . . ." responded the young soldier. "No, as I remember now," he went on in excellent French, "that was the year . . . ."

"I know, I know. Don't tell me," the boy cried, excitement in his voice. "I have an account in my scrapbook. Can I show you my scrapbook sometime, Feldwebel Hans? I can? I know; it was the year Hamburg was tied by the Racing Club of Paris, thanks to Bonvallet's last-minute goal. Am I right?"

"Right! Only actually I didn't play in that particular match. A bad knee. And bad luck, too. It was the spring before the war and that

knee kept me out of service for thirteen months. Psst . . . come here . . . here . . . ."

He snapped his fingers and held out one hand. A dog was coming toward them, a white and black, short-haired distant relative of a fox terrier. He was a kind of Grande Rue[3] dog, an animal born in the street, heaven knows where and when, a dog of most uncertain heritage. He approached with caution as the big man took the square pipe from his mouth and leaned forward encouragingly.

The dog edged nearer. One glance told you it was a long while since anyone had stroked him, given him a good meal, said a kind word to him. The sergeant reached out and kneaded the back of the animal's neck. Immediately the dog responded by coming in closer. Then he sat on his haunches, seemingly content, for once befriended.

Finally the German rose, knocked his pipe on the stone steps, and stretched. "Yes, of course you can show me your scrapbook. I'd be interested. Bring it along anytime in the afternoon. Well, we must get the morning report from the blockhouse. It hasn't come yet and the Herr Hauptmann[4] will be annoyed."

Together they walked down the Grande Rue, the main and only street of the village of Nogent-Plage,[5] the tawny-haired boy in the ragged shorts and the tall Feldwebel. The dog walked between them, his tail wagging.

Since it was a lovely morning in early June, the street was full of people. It seemed as though everyone they met greeted the sergeant. Old ladies in black carrying half-empty shopping bags, housewives with long loaves of grayish bread under their arms, children, espe-

---

1. **Reich**\raihk\ literally, empire. The Third Reich refers to the German government under Hitler from 1933–1945.
2. **Feldwebel**\⁀fĕlt 'vä·bĕl\ sergeant.
3. **Grande Rue**\⁀grand ⁀rü\ Grand Street, as common as our Main Street; Grande Rue dog, a stray dog.
4. **Herr Hauptmann**\⁀hĕr ⁀haupt 'man\ (Mr.) Captain. The German language uses Herr before such titles.
5. **Nogent-Plage**\nō 'zhənt ⁀plazh\ Nogent Beach, the name of the town.

Reprinted by permission of William Morrow & Company, Inc., Copyright © 1967 by Lucy R. Tunis.

cially the boys who invariably appeared when the *Feldwebel* was around, all wished him good day, addressing him as Colonel and speaking in German.

"*Guten Tag,*[6] *Herr Oberst.*[7] *Guten Tag . . . .*"

Although he had told them all a hundred times that he was not an *Oberst*, a colonel, but a *Feldwebel*, a sergeant, and a supply sergeant at that, he responded to their words with an old-fashioned courtesy, speaking in French as a rule, touching one finger to the brim of his stained forage cap in a most unsoldierly gesture, and wishing them good day in return.

"*Eh . . . bonjour,*[8] *Madame Dupont. Bonjour.*"

The old lady in the faded black dress bobbed and ducked her head. "*Guten Tag, Herr Oberst. Guten Tag . . . .*"

There it was once again! How often he had spelled it out for them, sometimes severely.

"*Nein, nein, bitte. Ich bin ein Feldwebel, ein Unteroffizier, nicht ein Oberst . . . .*"[9]

The people of the village simply smiled and went on addressing him as *Herr Oberst*.

At first he felt this was intentional. After all, with these tricky French one could never tell. Perhaps it was their cynical way of sneering at the fact that the son of a baron, from an old army family, should be merely a sergeant. Occasionally at night when he could not sleep due to the roar of the guns along the coast spattering antiaircraft fire into the heavens, he wondered whether the French were stubborn, stupid, or insolent. As time went on, however, he realized that to the people in Nogent-Plage he represented authority. For them he was a person to whom they could protest, appeal, with whom they could discuss their grievances. It was the *Feldwebel* who listened to their objections to what they felt were unfair regulations of the German High Command along the coast.

Occasionally these regulations were changed. More often they were just ignored by the sergeant and his superiors. It was easier that way. Hence he accepted the greetings of the vil-

lagers, and although the military rank they conferred upon him amused his men and not infrequently annoyed his commanding officer, there was little anyone could do with the stubborn French.

The only person who did not call him *Herr Oberst* was the boy in the ragged blue shorts. He felt immediately that the sergeant disliked this and always addressed him as Feldwebel Hans. Perhaps this was how the big German first noticed him. It drew them together; their passion for football cemented the bond.

That day, the fourteen hundredth and fifth day of the occupation of the village of Nogent-Plage by the Germans, a day that was to explode in such violence and change forever the lives of the boy, the *Feldwebel*, and everyone in town, began in calm and quiet. During the long months of the occupation, people in the village had passed and repassed the same troops for days without end. Often even their first names were known to the townsfolk— harsh sounding Teutonic[10] names such as Helmut, Gottfried, and Gerhardt. Over the years, many regiments had visited this hamlet by the sea, the men sunning themselves along the waterfront, or playing football under the direction of the *Feldwebel* on the hard, sandy beach below the cliff. Never was anyone else accorded recognition by the villagers. In fact, they often made fun of the other Germans, not infrequently to their faces. Of all the soldiers, only the Feldwebel Hans was a friend.

He was a friend above all to the boys of the village, because he was a former football player, and especially to young Jean-Paul Varin.[11] Wherever the sergeant went the boy attached himself, following from place to place, often with his pal, René Le Gallec,[12]

---

6. **Guten Tag**\\'gü·tən ᐃtagk\\ Good day.
7. **Oberst**\\ᐃō 'bĕrst\\ Colonel.
8. **bonjour**\\bōn 'zhur\\ Good day.
9. No, no, please. I am a sergeant, a non-commissioned officer, not a colonel.
10. **Teutonic**\\tü ᐃtan·ək\\ Germanic.
11. **Jean-Paul Varin**\\ᐃzha(n)ᐃpōl·və ᐃrä(n)\\
12. **René Le Gallec**\\rə ᐃnä·lə·gal ᐃlĕk\\

70

slightly older and also a *fervent*[13] of football. When the German sergeant played or coached his men, the two boys could not take their eyes off him. The younger, especially, watched with a furious intentness. Unconsciously even his body moved, swung, stopped short, riposted[14] as the big German athlete's did. In vain his mother rang the bell for dinner. You spoke to him and he did not hear. The boy watched, listened to the football talk, played and practiced, went so far as to learn German so that he would fully understand the soldiers talking. Football was his life, his passion, his existence. And the Feldwebel Hans was his god.

## ⚜ 2

Not only Jean-Paul Varin but all the good people of Nogent-Plage had definite feelings about the Feldwebel Hans. If one had to be occupied by the Germans, the villagers all agreed, it was better that he should be in town.

"Why, the *Herr Oberst* is the son of a baron, if his brother is killed in the Luftwaffe[1] he too will be a baron. Ah, say what you like, *monsieur,*[2] blood does tell. He's part of that old Schleswig-Holstein[3] aristocracy. You know what those people are like."

"How true, *madame,* how true! Besides, he is a man of the world, not merely an ace of the football. He plays the cello and appreciates the good wine of Bordeaux[4]—and the Normandy[5] cider too, yes indeed. Well, his mother was French, you know, from Sedan.[6] To my way of thinking, he might just as well have been French. *Yes,* I agree . . . ."

"*Eh bien,*[7] his mother was a De Mezière from Sedan. For me he is no militarist, but really a civilized type. He loves the children in town and they love him. Why, *monsieur,* he is their hero. That Varin boy follows him everywhere. You know the *Herr Oberst* was the great defensive back for Bayern of Munich. Once before the war he played for Germany, at the age of nineteen, too!"

"Yes indeed, the boys and girls love him. If I call my René, and he doesn't answer, I know he is watching the *Herr Oberst* coaching football."

"To be sure," interjected a fat woman. "I, for one, shan't forget either when the partisans[8] burned the bridge at Verville and that *Hauptmann* tried to take my husband off to Germany, last year. Ah, no, I told the *Herr Oberst.* Look, my husband was beside me in bed that awful night. He believed me. He even convinced the High Command. He has connections, you know."

Now the villagers were all talking at once.

"Ah, yes, only he could have done it. Why not? A supply sergeant, perhaps, but he understands and respects French culture and French civilization. Naturally, his mother was French. But yet after all, he is German . . . ."

"Yes, *monsieur,* most of these barbarians know neither France nor the French. Well, this man is no stony-faced Prussian[9] such as some we've had stationed in this town since 1940."

"Indeed, *madame,* I recall when the town had to be evacuated, remember, at the time of the big raid on Dieppe.[10] The *Herr Oberst* interceded for us with the *Kommandant*[11] at Caen,[12] you recall? Those who really lived here were permitted to stay. Oh, I am entirely in accord with you. We are truly fortunate to have him here in Nogent-Plage. Truly . . . ."

---

13. **fervent**\fər 'va(n)\ enthusiastic fan.
14. **riposted**\rĭ ˄pōs·təd\ quickly returned a thrust—a fencing term.

---

1. **Luftwaffe**\˄luft 'vaf·ə\ air force.
2. **monsieur**\mə 'syə\ Sir or Mister.
3. **Schleswig-Holstein,** a state in west Germany.
4. **Bordeaux,** a city and port in southwest France.
5. **Normandy,** region in northwest France.
6. **Sedan,** a city in northeast France.
7. **Eh bien**\ĕ 'byĕ(n)\ Oh, well.
8. **partisans,** a guerrilla band; here, the Underground.
9. **Prussian,** a despotic and ruthless individual.
10. **Dieppe**\dē 'ĕp\ port of northern France.
11. **Kommandant**\'kō·man ˄dant\ Commander.
12. **Caen**\ka(n)\ city in northwest France.

"Fortunate to have him," that was how the villagers felt about the Feldwebel Hans Joachim Wolfgang von und zu Kleinschrodt,[13] to give him his full name. And he was the one German soldier who seemed to be permanently stationed at Nogent-Plage, which after a while became a rest camp for troops from the Russian front. Usually a regiment or a battalion stayed only a few weeks or a month in this village on the Normandy coast. Then one wet, foggy morning the siren would blow. That piercing noise meant the end of peace and repose for those Germans. From work, from relaxation, from the football game on the beach coached by the *Feldwebel*, they hustled back to their billets,[14] fear in every heart. Early on in the war when Hitler's forces were winning from Crete to Norway and each month a different nation was gobbled up by the Greater Reich, the troops had left for the East singing and cheering.

Then the war was a glorious romp. But two winters in the snow outside Moscow changed this. Now they hardly spoke as they packed and made ready to depart. Sullenly they collected the regimental baggage, silently loaded the transport wagons. When the short, sharp whistle of the *Ober-Feldwebel*[15] rang out, they would line up along the Grande Rue dismally waiting inspection and the command to move off.

"*Achtung!*[16] Right face! Forward ... hup ... hup ...."

So, off in columns of four down the coastal road to entrain[17] for the East. Nowadays the villagers of Nogent-Plage made an event of this. They lined the streets, watching not without pleasure the grim faces of the soldiers, making sardonic[18] remarks the Germans could not understand.

"*Hein!*[19] They don't seem quite so happy to say good-by, do they?"

"Would you, my friend, with the Russian bear breathing down your neck?"

"Ah, but remember, they used to have nothing but motorized equipment. And all that new English matériel captured at Dunkerque.[20]

Remember, *madame?* That has worn out now. Look at those poor old horses. And the wagons falling apart ...."

No, the war was no longer glorious for the Germans. Troops of different regiments came and went, only the *Herr Oberst* remained. It was a corps decision to leave him at Nogent-Plage. He was valuable there because he had a quality few of his countrymen possessed. The villagers hated the occupying forces with a fierce Norman hatred, looking and longing for only one thing—the Allied invasion and freedom from German domination. The *Herr Oberst* knew this quite as well as anyone. Yet, thanks largely to him, order prevailed in the village. There were no shootings, no terrorist attacks, no raids as in other towns along the coast. So far as the Germans could tell, the villagers never tried to signal planes or ships. Never had a *Gauleiter*[21] been summoned from Berlin to restore order. In fact, the High Command at Caen had such a good opinion of Nogent-Plage that it considered awarding the town a medal for its correct attitude toward German troops.

Certainly nobody ever called the *Feldwebel* a keen soldier. He obeyed orders and did his duty. That was all. In private life he was a von und zu Kleinschrodt, younger son of an ancient Baltic military family famous in the history of his country. His father had been a Colonel of Uhlans[22] in the First World War. Brought up in the army tradition, he had, perhaps, had too much of it. Not only did the

---

13. **Hans Joachim Wolfgang von und zu Kleinschrodt** \hans 'yō·ə ˄hkĭm ˄vōlf·gaṅ·fōn·undt·tzū ˄klĭn 'shrōdt\
14. **billets**\˄bil·ətz\ quarters assigned to soldiers.
15. **Ober-Feldwebel,** sergeant-major, warrant officer class.
16. **Achtung**\ahk ˄tūṅ\ Attention!
17. **entrain,** take a train.
18. **sardonic**\sar ˄dan·ĭk\ bitter, mocking.
19. **Hein!** Ha!
20. **Dunkerque**\˄dən 'kərk\ seaport of northern France. It was the scene of the rescue under German fire of some 300,000 British soldiers by volunteer civilian boats.
21. **Gauleiter**\˄gau·lai·tər\ chief official of a political district under Nazi control.
22. **Uhlans**\˄ū·lənz\ Prussian light cavalry.

big, seemingly awkward young man look out of place in uniform beside his brisk, competent, Heil Hitlering[23] comrades, but the way he saluted, even his reports, left much to be desired. Many a commanding officer at Nogent-Plage had tried to reform him and given up the attempt. Because of his family and his connections he was no laughing stock —in fact, quite the reverse. Yet he was not entirely in favor with the High Command at Caen.

What attracted the people of Nogent-Plage to the *Feldwebel* was not merely his fame as an athlete, but his agreeable manner, so different from that of many of the Germans. Also there was his love of music. As he was an indifferent soldier, he was an indifferent musician and played the cello, to tell the truth, rather badly. However, he enjoyed playing with Georges Varin, the local schoolmaster and father of young Jean-Paul. Monsieur Varin was an equally bad violinist, but often, when the priest came to accompany them of an evening on the sadly inadequate piano, the three sat immersed in Bach and Beethoven until long after curfew. As a consequence, on those nights, the padre[24] was forced to stay with the schoolmaster until morning.

In the single *café* in town, the Bleu Marin, the German soldiers, playing the harmonica and singing as they drank their beer, were ignored by the French natives. But whenever the tiny bell on the door tinkled ever so slightly and the *Herr Oberst* entered, the fishermen at their *belote* game glanced up and nodded pleasantly. When the curfew sounded they picked up their cards, avoided the gaze of the harmonica players, and left, bidding the *Feldwebel* good night on the way out.

"*Guten Nacht*,[25] *Herr Oberst*," they said to him.

"*Eh . . . bon soir*,[26] *bon soir, messieurs*,"[27] he replied.

### ❧ 3

Nogent-Plage was like a sheltered spot in a storm. Yet during four long years, though the villagers were never in danger, they heard sounds all day and night that brought the war inside them. One was the endless clack-clack, clack-clack of hobnailed boots on concrete. You heard it in daylight, late at night after curfew, early in the black hours before dawn when the patrols stomped down the Grande Rue. You heard it and soon hated it more than anything else, because it brought the presence of German troops into your home and your heart.

Another familiar sound was the thromb-thromb of the motorized fishing vessels, indistinctly heard, indistinctly seen through the fog which so often covered the coast. Nogent-Plage was a fishing village, and the Germans permitted certain selected fishermen to go out three kilometers—no more—on Mondays and Thursdays. People in town could tell the day of the week by this sound. Naturally, when the vessels returned to the shingled beach below the cliff, a platoon of Germans was waiting to requisition (meaning grab off) their share of the catch. This share was anything up to sixty or seventy-five percent.

If you stood at a certain point on the cliff outside the village, or if you watched from a second-story window of Madame Dupont's house, you could make out the coastal road winding into the distance like a long black ribbon. To use it a Frenchman had to have a special permit, or *Ausweiss*,[1] from the German High Command in Caen.

The road, Route Nationale Number 40, twisted and turned, dipped and rose, as it followed the coast. From Nogent-Plage you could see it stretching for miles, empty of

---

23. **Heil Hitlering,** *Hail Hitler* was the salute and greeting used during the Nazi regime. *Heil Hitlering* in this context refers to soldiers who greeted other soldiers properly at all times.
24. **padre,** father; priest.
25. **Guten Nacht**\ˈgü·tən ˄nahkt\ good night (German).
26. **bon soir**\bōn ˈswȯir\ good evening (French).
27. **messieurs**\mē ˈsyə\ gentlemen; plural of *monsieur.*

---

1. **Ausweiss**\˄aus ˈvais\ permit.

traffic save for a few German army trucks. To travel upon it was, as the French said, "to make the *gymnastique*."[2] Indeed, it resembled an obstacle course, what with the sand from the dunes that had blown over it in places and the holes that had not been filled in since the start of the war four years before.

The whole region was bare and barren, especially in winter, and the winds harsh, cold, strong. They blew so fiercely that few trees survived, and on clear days one had an unobstructed view up and down the coast. The first thing you noticed was the big blockhouse just below the top of the cliff on which the village rested, then other blockhouses at intervals of a mile or so along the shore. They were all size, large and small, of gray concrete, which the Germans had forced the French to construct and pay for. These fortifications and others around the *Haupt Kämpflinie*,[3] the great warline, were Hitler's main defense against invasion from the sea.

Here and there along the coastal road were sentry boxes, six feet tall, with conical roofs. Each was large enough for two men and two machine guns. You could see their barrels sticking through the slits on each side. They served to check on traffic and also acted as lookouts over the ocean. Behind the road, away from the water, the dunes stretched for miles, bristling with stakes against parachutists and seeded with mines and booby traps.

To the pilots of the R.A.F. planes Nogent-Plage was a landmark: the first glimpse of enemy-held territory, the first sight of occupied France, the first shriek and whistle of antiaircraft fire, and, if it was night, the first tracer bullets rushing up in the dark. By day the surf crashing on the beach was the first thing they saw below as they roared in out of the mist. Then the rocky cliff above the sand, the village with its single street, and the black ribbon of road stretching away to left and right.

Nogent-Plage itself consisted of only a handful of brick and stone houses, with a gap here and there where a field of fire had been cleared for the guns of the blockhouse. Beyond, in back, was nothing save those endless dunes stretching away to the horizon.

The sand had been there when William the Conqueror set off in his small boats in 1066 to invade England, when Napoleon in 1803 stood on the cliff and looked across to the shores of Sussex, when Hitler on the same cliff in 1940 shook his fist at Britain, the endlessly moving sand was still there. At times the wind blew so fiercely it made one feel that the sand would eventually smother the tiny settlement on its rock jutting into the English Channel.

The German soldiers who garrisoned Nogent-Plage at the start of the war were giant six-footers who had awed the villagers. That had changed. Now the German troops were usually a dismal-looking lot. They were farmers' boys from Thuringia, stunted adolescents or weary old men. But this June morning the people of the town felt uneasy. For some weeks a new breed of German soldiers, a tough battery of Silesians, had been stationed in town. They were a motorized flak[4] unit, highly trained, efficient, equipped with light and heavy machine guns and antiaircraft weapons, continually marching up and down the single street in tight formation. They were shock troops and wanted everyone to know it. They appeared invincible. Their smartness, their discipline, even the way they saluted and their officers returned salutes were impressive.

Above everything, accompanying all comings and goings, was noise—the pound-pound of a hundred pairs of hobnailed boots in unison, the shouts of their noncoms,[5] the raucous calls on the loudspeakers.

*Machen Sie schnell*,[6] *schnell*, *schnell*, hup, hup . . . .

These men seemed forever on their toes, ready for anything, not war-weary troops rest-

---

2. **make the gymnastique,** perform athletic stunts.
3. **Haupt Kämpflinie**\haupt ˄kĕmp 'flĭn·ē\ main line of battle.
4. **flak,** antiaircraft fire.
5. **noncoms,** noncommissioned officers.
6. **Machen Sie schnell**\'mahk·ən·zē ˄shnĕl\ hurry.

ing after months on the icy plains of Russia. They were stationed in Nogent-Plage to kill and be killed. Quite evidently.

Uneasiness hung over the village that day. For one thing there was organized movement in the Bloch villa. This house had been taken by the occupying forces early in the war, because it belonged to a family of Jews long since dead, deported, or forgotten. It made an excellent headquarters in the center of town. Dispatch riders coated with dust dashed up, black leather briefcases under one arm. Engineers worked on the radio aerial on the roof. From the blockhouse came a sudden burst of fire.

Could all this mean, the villagers speculated, that the invasion was coming? That long-promised, long-awaited, long-hoped-for invasion, so often hinted at in the B.B.C.[7] broadcasts from London called by the natives, "The *Bibbice.*" Against all regulations, those Normans, proud, unbending in their attitude toward the occupiers, listened every day to the *Bibbice.* Once Monsieur Varin, the teacher who lived next door to the Bloch villa, had switched his radio on to the B.B.C. wavelength and sat waiting to turn the volume down before the news from London began. Unfortunately he fell asleep. Those first words woke him with a start.

*"Ici Londres . . . ."*[8]

With a bound he leaped across the room and shut the set off. But the Germans billeted in the next house, almost in the next room, must surely have heard it and reported it. He went to bed in a sweat of anguish, lying awake all night waiting for the hammering on the door that meant a German prison camp—or worse.

Nothing happened. The night patrols passed as usual. He heard the low, mechanical beat of their metal heels on the concrete, clack-clack, clack-clack. But no thunderous pounding on his door. The *Herr Oberst,* he guessed, knew what had happened and had arranged things so the German headquarters at Caen did not.

DISCUSSION FOR UNDERSTANDING

**1.** Who is Feldwebel Hans? Where is he stationed? What is his personal background?

**2.** What do the villagers think of the *Feldwebel?*

**3.** What are the reactions of his fellow officers toward him?

**4.** How does the young Jean-Paul Varin show his admiration for the *Feldwebel?*

**5.** How do the German soldiers now stationed in Nogent-Plage differ from the ones stationed there earlier?

**6.** Describe Nogent-Plage and the surrounding area.

**7.** What has made the townspeople uneasy on this day?

**8.** Jean-Paul Varin is still a child, yet how have his encounters with the *Feldwebel* had an effect on him?

### 4

The Feldwebel Hans, as the boy called him, sat on the stone steps of his billet in the pleasant spring sunshine. He rose and yawned. If the glorious *Reichswehr,*[1] the German army, didn't think much of him as a soldier, he, in turn, didn't think much of the *Reichswehr.* He was hardly passionate about roll calls, drilling, medals, uniforms, saluting, family tradition, army tradition, national tradition—all this seemed to mean little to him. He could easily have obtained a commission through his connections, but the officer corps with its caste feeling nauseated him. Once you get to be an officer, even a lieutenant, he always said, everyone below you suspects you.

Now, with the thin dog near him and the boy as usual at his side, he picked up a clipboard with papers attached, stuck his empty pipe in his pocket, and walked down the Grande Rue and past the sign *Juden Ver-*

---

7. **B.B.C.,** British Broadcasting Company.
8. **Ici Londres**\ē 'sē ▲lōnd(rə)\ London here, or, London calling (French).

---

1. **Reichswehr**\▲raihks·vär\

*boten*,[2] with the name of the general command officer underneath. The boy did not notice it. That sign banishing Jews had been there four years, which was forever to Jean-Paul Varin. It dated back so far he could not remember when it hadn't been there. His father, he well knew, hated it, but there it was, part of the town like the Grande Rue and the cliff on which the town stood and the ocean below.

Down the street they walked, the French boy and the German supply sergeant. Since they were invariably together, nobody took this as strange. The *Herr Oberst* this morning was hardly Hitler's ideal of a soldier of the Greater Reich. He wore a rather grubby tunic[3] and an ancient garrison cap.[4] If his bearing and general attitude did not express contentment, neither did he appear dissatisfied with his job. The boy beside him, he simply walked along greeting those who greeted him.

Clack-clack-clack-clack, his heels sounded on the concrete pavement. Not clack-clack, clack-clack, short, sharp, brutal, as those of most soldiers sounded, but leisurely, in a slow cadence. At the end of the village the sergeant and the boy reached the vacant lot beside the small church. The thin, lonely dog had scampered ahead and now was in the middle of the road, sitting and waiting. As often at this time of day, the Père Clement,[5] the village priest, was coaching René Le Gallec with a football, or *ballon*, as the French called it. The Feldwebel Hans liked the padre, who had been retired to this backwater when the Occupation submerged everyone. Still active at seventy, he especially enjoyed coaching the football players, for he had been a great athlete himself in his youth.

This morning Père Clement's soutane[6] was tied up around his waist with a coarse rope so he could run. This arrangement disclosed thick cotton underdrawers, heavy black-wool stockings reaching to his knees, and rough peasant boots, badly scuffed and scarred. The padre in his time at Nogent-Plage had developed many young football stars, and the Le Gallec boy

with whom he was practicing was the best of all. The *Herr Oberst* stood watching, sucking on his empty pipe, throwing in an occasional suggestion or word of advice. Finally he could no longer resist getting into it himself. Glancing up the street to make sure the new, fire-eating *Hauptmann* commanding the battery was engaged in his office, he yanked off his tunic, snapping a button in the process. The button bounced and rolled. He let it go, intending to pick it up later, placed his tunic on the grass, laid the clipboard beside it, and stepped forward.

Immediately something inside changed. Now he was in his world, in his element, master of himself. His big frame loose and coordinated, he controlled that round ball with his feet almost delicately, pushing a short stab over to the padre, taking it back, turning it across to the boy with an insolent accuracy beautiful to watch.

A spurt past the old man, a short step to the right to dodge the boy, then to the left to catch the pair off balance. All the time he was babying the ball until he had René and the Père Clement so confused that they were ducking first one way, then the other, totally unsure of themselves.

The boy in the blue shorts stood transfixed, his body moving as the *Feldwebel* moved, twisted, stopped, and ran. Two young women going past watched, fascinated.

"Ahhhh, ahhh . . ." they said in admiration. At Nogent-Plage, whenever the Feldwebel Hans played football with the boys a crowd gathered. If he was on the beach coaching the regimental team, a gang of the local lads always sat on the sea wall, commenting.

So this morning half a dozen younger boys

---

2. **Juden Verboten**\ˈyü·dən·fĕr ˈbō·tən\ Jews not allowed.
3. **tunic**, a long close-fitting jacket worn as part of a uniform.
4. **garrison cap**, wedge-shaped cap worn as part of a uniform.
5. **Père Clement**\ˈpār ˈklə ˈma(n)\
6. **soutane**\sü ˈtan\ cassock with buttons down the front.

suddenly appeared from nowhere the second he began to play. Now he was concentrating upon René's moves.

"No, no, not with the right foot, the left . . . . You must learn to pass equally well with either foot . . . . Don't shoot too soon . . . . Take your time, you have time . . . . Watch that ball . . . and keep your head down. Just watch the ball. Try to remember your teammates are all watching you. They will get it if your pass is a good one. Be careful, don't lift your head. That's better . . . lifting the head is always fatal."

He was no longer the casual *Feldwebel*. Now he had become a wonderful, moving, vibrant force, the great athlete, the virtuoso of ball control, master of himself and his well-coordinated body. When he took the ball to explain what he meant with a cross or a kick, he seemed almost to caress it.

One of the young women watching glanced up the street as she heard a door slam. She saw the new commanding officer step out of the Bloch villa, heard a clicking of heels that resounded down the Grande Rue, observed the sentries presenting arms. "*Herr Oberst,*" she said. "*Herr Oberst! Der Hauptmann kommt.*" The captain is coming.

The athlete stopped instantly, picked up his tunic, hastily put it on, and, reaching to the ground for his pipe and the clipboard, again became the nondescript *Feldwebel*. His garrison cap on one side of his head, he sauntered off toward the blockhouse for the morning report—now an hour overdue.

The dog rose and followed him. At that moment the *Feldwebel* noticed the little Deschamps girl in the middle of the road, about fifteen yards ahead. Evidently the child had strayed from home. There she stood, a target for passing military vehicles. He got down on one knee and called to her.

"*Hier Liebling.*"[7] Come here.

The child turned to look. She was adorable in her faded pink dress, the tiny skirt so short and shrunken from constant washings that it flared out from her thin legs. The big man held out his arms. It was not precisely the typical picture of a German soldier in France in the fifth year of the Occupation.

Instantly the child responded, toddling toward the *Feldwebel*, her arms also outstretched. Then the door of a house banged open, and the girl's mother rushed up to the *Feldwebel*. Knowing she did not understand German, he said in French, "She was in the middle of the street."

The woman took the child from him and began to scold her. Frightened, the little girl started to cry. Together they went into the house, leaving the Feldwebel Hans in the road, the stray dog at his side.

He walked briskly down the street toward the blockhouse, and as he did the dog again rose and followed along.

## 5

By noon a wind had arisen, bringing a chill from the water. The fog was burning off as it so frequently did at this time of the year. Superficially it was like every day in Nogent-Plage, but there were signs of things to come. Formations of large planes passed over the village all morning, roaring off into the interior. What did they portend? Were they the usual attacks on bridges, railroad yards, and airfields around Paris? Who could tell?

Georges Varin, the teacher, sat alone at a small iron table on the pavement before the Bleu Marin, chatting with Monsieur Lavigne[1] the proprietor, a heavy-set man of forty-five with a dirty white apron around his waist. On the table was a cup of bitter coffee made of acorns and heaven-knows-what, the result of wartime shortages.

"Another cup, Monsieur the Professor?" asked the *patron*.[2] Monsieur Varin was no more a professor than the Feldwebel Hans was a colonel, being only the village school-

---

7. Hier, Liebling\ˈhēr ˈlēb·li̇ŋ\ Come here, honey.

1. Lavigne\la ˈvēn(yə)\

2. patron\pa ˈtrō(n)\ proprietor.

master. However, everyone called him professor since he had studied two years in Paris and was an educated man, one to be treated with respect in the village. He was useful in various ways. For instance, he helped the farmers across the dunes who could neither read nor write by penning letters for them, in a script full of flourishes, to their sons in German prison camps.

Dark, small, stocky, and articulate, he used to wear glasses, for he was nearsighted. Unfortunately they had broken and as no new ones were obtainable, even in Caen or Rouen, he carried a pocket magnifying glass to read the communiques in the daily papers. Whenever he read his forehead wrinkled and his eyebrows rose.

Though accepted by everybody, Monsieur Varin was not popular with the right-thinking, church-going part of Nogent-Plage. He was a Marxist and regularly voted the Communist ticket, a fact he never concealed from anyone. Yet even those who disliked him and distrusted his political convictions respected him as a good Frenchman. Had he not fought three years in the First World War, been wounded and returned to combat? Again he had been called to the colors and served through the whole campaign of 1940 as a noncommissioned officer in a frontline unit.

All his life Georges Varin and his family had lived in Nogent-Plage. Early in the Occupation he became acquainted with the Feldwebel Hans. They respected each other and had a love of music in common. Slowly over the years they became friends. In times of trouble there had been instances when only the teacher through the Feldwebel Hans had managed to get German headquarters in Caen to listen to the protests of the villagers. Once Marcel Deschamps, the fisherman, had lost his bearings in a dense fog and against regulations did not reach shore until the next morning. Ordinarily he would have been imprisoned for this offense, but the Feldwebel Hans saved him so that he received a warning only.

Few villagers felt there was anything wrong between the schoolmaster and the German sergeant, or considered Monsieur Varin a collaborator and friend of the Nazis. Not only did he despise collaborators, he invariably spoke of Marshal Pétain, head of the French collaborationist regime, as "that old donkey." So Monsieur Varin, though not entirely popular, found his friendship with the Feldwebel accepted because it helped the town. In much the same way the Feldwebel was accepted by his superiors.

Because of his background and army connections, the Feldwebel talked freely and frankly to an old family friend, Major Kessler, Adjutant at Headquarters of the Northern Command. Usually Major Kessler was accessible to the Feldwebel on the telephone in a tight moment. The officer in charge of the garrison at Nogent-Plage knew this and obtained favors for himself through his subordinate, the sergeant. On the staff at Headquarters in Caen, they regarded von Kleinschrodt with amusement and indulgence.

"Yes, a strange chap, that von Kleinschrodt. Prefers to remain a Feldwebel when he could, of course, have a commission. I remember his father well at Verdun in 1917—a brave man. But this lad is different. Ah well, he saves us a lot of headaches by his knowledge of the people and the region. Nobody knows them better."

Thus each side and all concerned had something to gain by the arrangement, and the Germans officially ignored the sergeant's friendship with the schoolmaster, something irregular between enemies in time of war.

This morning while Monsieur Varin was sitting on the terrace of the Bleu Marin waiting for the arrival of the Feldwebel Hans, the widow Dupont passed by. Her late husband had actually fought in the Franco-Prussian War of 1870, and she was a little dried-up apple of a woman, weighing perhaps eighty pounds, bent and shrunk with age. She always nodded good morning to everyone she met as she proceeded along the Grande Rue. Her black string bag contained four carrots, a turnip, and an onion for her usual midday meal of soup, even now starting to simmer on the back of her stove at home. The moment she saw Monsieur Varin she stood still and beckoned to him.

Reluctantly he rose to meet her. The widow Dupont was celebrated in the village for buttonholing people, usually grasping the men by the lapel of their jackets. Also for her bad breath, a compound of garlic and red wine consumed twice a day for eighty years. Hence the teacher did not regard her approach with anticipation.

As ever, she came close to him, far too close, and seized the lapel of his jacket as if to keep him from edging off.

"Monsieur Varin," she said, "would you perhaps care to do a favor for me?"

"Willingly, *madame*," he replied, trying to disengage himself from her grasp. "Always a pleasure to be of use to you."

"*Ah, bon.*[3] One can always count upon you, Monsieur Varin. I wish I could say the same for others in this town. I mention no names— oh no, no names—but doubtless you are aware to whom I refer. Well, it is about my grandson. You may remember he was sent off to work in Germany when he became seventeen by the Fritz[4] in their forced-labor organization, the Todt[5] organization they called it. He worked in an airplane factory. Such a nice lad, too, respectful and honest, and a good Catholic besides, I assure you . . ."

"Yes, yes, *madame*." Impossible to bring her to the point, but at least he managed to move back slightly. He was awaiting not only the arrival of the Feldwebel Hans, but who knows perhaps a glass of that good German beer. "Yes, I remember Michel, a fine boy. What happened, Madame Dupont?"

She drew herself up. "Ah, *justement* nothing! You see each month he wrote me faithfully. I'm all he has left. Now for over two months—almost three, Monsieur Varin—nothing. You see he was working in that airplane factory at Altona, near Hamburg, I believe. The British have been bombing it now for

several weeks. So I wonder . . . would it be possible . . . do you think you could get me news of him?"

The teacher took out a worn black notebook with a small pencil attached. He wrote: "Dupont, Michel. Aged 17."

"Do you know his number?"

"Six . . . four . . . nine . . . three . . . one . . . zero."

He wrote it down. "Good, count upon me to do whatever is possible. Although I warn you it won't be easy with these fire-eaters that have come to town, these Silesians. But I'll talk to the Feldwebel Hans; he's always helpful. You know his brother is on Goering's staff. I'll try; I'll do my best."

Her aged, wrinkled face beamed. "Thank you, Monsieur Varin, thank you infinitely. I knew I could count upon your help. Ah, what would Nogent-Plage ever do without you? *Au 'voir!*"[6] And she weaved off downstreet, ducking and bobbing to everyone she met.

## 6

The schoolmaster replaced the black notebook in his pocket and resumed his seat at the iron table. Here we are, coming to a crisis in the war, and she wants news of her great-grandson, one of God knows how many foreigners forced to work for the Germans. Well, I suppose he is all she has.

At this moment the Feldwebel Hans, clipboard in his hand, strolled up. In warm weather the two often met at noon and the sergeant usually offered the teacher a glass of German beer, which was reserved by the *patron* of the *café* for the German soldiers who had to sign for it. The *Feldwebel*, wiping his face, sat down. The stray dog, still accompanying him, also sat down, panting.

"Hot, very hot," remarked the German. Then to the proprietor, "Two beers, please."

---

3. **bon**\bō(n)\ good.
4. **Fritz**, nickname for the Germans.
5. **Todt**\tōt\ Death.
6. **Au 'voir**, shortened form of *au revoir*\ō·rə ˄vwar\ good-bye.

Monsieur Lavigne wiped a corner of the table with his dirty white apron.

"*Merci*,"[1] said the teacher. "*Eh bien,* what's new today? Are we ready for the invasion?" At times he enjoyed needling the young German. "Your compatriots act as though they expected it this afternoon at the latest."

"*Ach*, these frontline furiosos,[2] they are impossible. Always drilling, shouting at each other, saluting. Frankly, my friend, I am skeptical about your invasion. Perhaps, yes . . . it is possible. But look at that blockhouse over there. Nothing can wreck it, nothing. You saw it built yourself. There are ten meters of solid concrete over those guns. Tell me, what shells could penetrate such a depth?" He took a large swallow of the beer.

Enjoying his own beer as a guest of the *Reichswehr* and one not permitted by German army regulations to drink it, Monsieur Varin did not care to contradict his host. But he did not hesitate to voice his doubt.

"*Ah, oui*, you may be right. But after all, my friend, things haven't been going too well for you people lately. One has only to look at the maps. They tell the story of what's happening over there on the Eastern front."

The *Feldwebel* did not wish to betray a lack of confidence before a Frenchman, so he said, "Ha-ha, ho-ho, let the English come. We are ready for them."

The teacher nodded, but he wondered. Daily he read between the lines of the censored Paris press and followed the maps with attention. As he often told the Père Clement when they were alone, those maps indicated plainly the extent of the impending disaster for the Germans.

It's coming, he told himself. I only want to be here to see it. And surely, he thought, it must come before long or it will be too late. After four years of occupation, of hardships and privation, tempers in the village were rising. That little girl who choked to death last month because no doctor could get through the coastal road. The thin legs of the boys and girls on the street. When you see your children

go to bed hungry night after night, well, a man will do anything.

And those strange warships spotted off the coast when the fog lifted suddenly one afternoon. What were they doing? Those massive flights of planes on their daily bombing runs from England. Were they pounding the enemy's lines of communications in preparation for an imminent invasion? Certainly the Germans were on the alert. Signs of crisis abounded. Nogent-Plage was obviously no longer a kind of convalescent area for battered troops. It had been transformed, by orders from Berlin, of course, into a frontline garrison, a pivotal point of the main coastal defense. That was plain. And the battalion of Silesians was here for one purpose. To repel an invasion on the beaches. Somehow the invasion must succeed.

"It must," said the teacher out loud.

## ✣ 7

The Hauptmann Seeler, new commanding officer of the garrison, sat at his desk in the Bloch villa. The windows overlooking the sea were boarded up and his only company was a photograph of Hitler. A thin sheet of paper was before him. It was typewritten, marked at the top: *Geheim.*[1] Secret. Below was a heading *Oberkommando Des Heeres.* From the Army High Command.

This document was about the invasion, which the *Abwehr,* Intelligence Department of the German General Staff, felt to be imminent. It outlined the steps being taken to repel the assault and detailed the disposition of troops and reserves in the neighborhood of Nogent-Plage. The Hauptmann Seeler was on the telephone. His voice was crisp, soldierly.

"*Ja*, Major Kessler, *ja. Jawohl . . . .*"[2]

"In an hour or more, *Hauptmann,* you will

---

1. **Merci**\mär ˄sē\ Thanks.
2. **furiosos**\˄fyur•e ˄ō•sōz\ enthusiasts.

---

1. **Geheim**\gĕ ˄haim\
2. **Jawohl**\ya ˄vōl\ yes indeed.

receive *Alarmstruppe*³ II. Do you understand?"

"*Ja, ja,* Major Kessler." Of course he understood. *Alarmstruppe* II was the order for the highest state of readiness against an invasion. The *Major* continued, "We know nothing for certain, *Hauptmann,* but there is a rumor well substantiated that the invasion fleet is at sea. Perhaps, who knows . . . ."

"I understand, *Major.*"

"Remember, Nogent-Plage is a pivotal position in the defense of the coast."

"*Jawohl, Herr Major.* We are ready; my troops are veterans. We won't be caught asleep."

"Good. *Heil* Hitler!" The *Major* rang off.

But the *Hauptmann* was perturbed. He rose and stalked the room. A former *Feldwebel,* promoted to commissioned rank on the field of battle in North Africa, he was a fussy, myopic little man with thick glasses, a strict disciplinarian who strutted with authority. He was also a brave officer, as the decorations from his campaigns in the desert showed.

The month before he had been sent in with his Silesians to take over and reorganize the defense of Nogent-Plage, but the situation he had found was worse than he had imagined. Until he arrived, nobody seemed alert and discipline was indifferent. Then there was that *Feldwebel.* The invasion imminent, the Fatherland in the very greatest peril, and what was he doing? Playing football with the boys, greeting civilians in the street. True, the town was quiet for the moment. Yet with all the terrorists about, one could never tell.

The *Hauptmann* trusted nobody and experience told him this was a wise attitude in war. Although his men all said the *Feldwebel* was a great football star, this nonsense must end. The captain, whose fattish body and thick glasses betrayed the fact that he could not run across the street or see a football unless it hit him in the face, was determined to maintain the discipline so essential in this moment of crisis.

Furiously he shuffled the papers on his desk. Paperwork was his soul, his goal, his be-all and end-all. As a sergeant he had been celebrated for his impeccable reports, always forwarded through channels, always on time. Large forms, legible, correctly indented, and sent along to a superior were in his belief the mark of a professional officer. Paperwork, he often told his men, was the other, seldom seen side of discipline.

As for that lazy *Feldwebel,* it made no difference if he was the greatest centre forward Germany ever had. We're at war. I'm in charge here and the troops and the townspeople had better realize it! The more he reflected about the *Feldwebel,* the more annoyed he became. That sloppy soldier's popularity with the troops and, worse still, the townsfolk was a cause of concern for the *Hauptmann.* Why, he thought, everyone knows that but for his family connections he would have been reduced to the ranks long ago.

In any event, it is my duty as his superior officer to report his inefficiency to the *Oberkommando* at Caen. Let them do as they wish. And they will have to do something after they hear from me. I shall make a point of telephoning this morning. But first I must have it out with him, Count *von und zu* Whatshisname. Utter nonsense, that title business. Four years now he has been enjoying himself in the safety of this charming seaside resort while I was up to my neck in sandstorms, fighting with Rommel⁴ in North Africa. And promoted from the ranks by the General Bayerlein himself!

He seized the telephone and called the blockhouse beyond the village. "*Unteroffizier Kleinschrodt,*" he said curtly.

The soldier at the other end of the line feeling tenseness in the voice of his commanding officer, informed him that the *Feldwebel* had left some minutes ago with the morning report.

"Which should have been on my desk when

---

3. **Alarmstruppe**\a ˈlärm ˈstrü·pə\ readiness signal.
4. **Rommel,** German field marshal, commander of the German forces in North Africa in World War II.

I came to this office at seven o'clock today," said the *Hauptmann.* "Punctuality is the first duty of the soldier."

Knowing the officer's passion for paperwork, the soldier at the blockhouse quickly agreed. The *Hauptmann* slammed down the phone without bothering to reply. He took the papers from his desk, put them into his safe, tried the handle to be sure it was locked, and rose. Straightening his tunic with a sharp tug, adjusting the angle of his cap, locking the door behind him, buttoning the key into the upper pocket of his blouse, he left the office and went out into the street.

The two sentries whirled to attention in unison, presenting arms. The *Hauptmann* flicked a glove carelessly to the visor of his cap in his best imitation of General Rommel. After the dimly lit office the sunlight from the sea dazzled him a moment. His first sight was the *café* almost opposite. What he observed enraged him.

There sat the lazy *Feldwebel,* smugly smoking his pipe and talking to a French civilian. Worse, as the *Hauptmann* noticed on approaching, the Frenchman was drinking beer against all army regulations. Obviously it was German beer. The *Hauptmann* also recognized the man, a teacher in town. He had been pointed out as a possible partisan, perhaps even someone who would transmit intelligence to the British.

The *Hauptmann* stalked across the street, anger flushing his face. The clack-clack of his heels had an ominous sound. Suddenly spotting his commanding officer approaching, the *Feldwebel* rose hastily, too hastily, stepping back squarely onto the dog's front paw. The animal yelped twice and skittered away and the *Feldwebel* lost his balance. He reached out and caught at the table, which overturned, and the two half-empty glasses of beer and the two beer bottles fell to the stone sidewalk. Then, retrieving his balance, he stood stiffly at attention, waiting for the storm to break. It broke with a thunderclap.

*"Was haben Sie,* Kleinschrodt?"[5] asked the

*Hauptmann,* ice in his voice. The Iron Cross (First Class) and the Knight's Cross (with a golden oak leaf) trembled on his chest as he spoke. To have to stand here with this lout, he thought. Me, with my decorations and four wound stripes on my sleeve!

But he stood there, saying nothing now, simply looking the *Feldwebel* up and down. As he did so his eye caught one of the bottles of beer on the ground, label up.

"Reserved for the *Wehrmacht,*"[6] it said.

The *Hauptmann* looked the *Feldwebel* over angrily. An ancient garrison cap with stained visor was on the back of his head, not over his eyes as regulations stipulated. His tunic was dirty. One button was missing. His shoes were unshined, no doubt from that stupid football he played with the village boys. As the *Hauptmann* stood contemplating this sorry figure of a noncommissioned officer in the army of our glorious *Führer,*[7] he reflected suddenly on those deadly battles in North Africa, where for over two years he had risked his life.

The injustice infuriated the *Hauptmann* and his dislike of the *Feldwebel* was so intense that he completely lost control of his temper. For the first time his voice rose.

"What's the matter with you?" he cried, reaching out and grabbing the *Feldwebel's* tunic where the button was missing. He gave it a strong yank and the other three buttons spattered onto the pavement. The tunic fell open and hung grotesquely from the broad shoulders of the younger man.

There he stood, a ridiculous-looking soldier, while the little *Hauptmann,* baring his teeth, spewed out a torrent of guttural abuse. Like all former noncommissioned officers, the *Hauptmann* was an expert in flaying the lower ranks. He did not raise his voice again, or shout, but his words were plain.

---

5. Literally, "What have you, Kleinschrodt?" He means, "What's the matter?"
6. **Wehrmacht**\ˈvär ˈmahkt\ German armed forces in World War II.
7. **Führer**\ˈfyu̇·rər\ literally, leader; the title applied to Hitler.

82

"You'll put away childish things, *Feldwebel. Kein Fussball. Verstehen Sie?*" No football. Understand?

And he had only begun. For a fact, this *Feldwebel* really did not know what war was, and the *Hauptmann* took pains to tell him so. Monsieur Varin, who had also risen, wanted intensely to leave, but this meant getting round the overturned table and attracting the attention of the *Hauptmann*. So he stood there while the abuse continued. Scornfully the little officer pointed down at the bottles, the glasses, and the spilled beer, now a wet spot on the pavement.

Sweat appeared on the *Feldwebel's* forehead. A drop rolled off his nose. Still the tirade continued, every syllable distinct. Monsieur Varin had served in two wars under officers of every social class, all grades and temperaments. Never had he listened to such humiliation of a fellow soldier. A nasty piece of work indeed, this *Hauptmann*, thought Monsieur Varin, listening. It was quite obvious, as the officer pointed to the overturned table, what was being said. Do this again and you will be reduced to the ranks.

"You call yourself a soldier, Kleinschrodt?" said the *Hauptmann*, utter contempt in his tone. It was a question needing no answer. "*Verstehen Sie? Verstehen Sie?*"

"*Ja, mein Hauptmann, jawohl.*"

The abuse went on for several minutes more, and then without warning the officer half turned and held out his hand across the upset table.

"*Papieren!*"[8]

It was a command. The teacher fumbled in his coat pocket and yanked out the *Ausweiss* that everyone in the Zone of the Armies was required to carry at all times.

The officer looked at it attentively, then inspected Monsieur Varin up and down. "*Schulmeister, nicht?*"[9]

The Frenchman nodded. Yes, a schoolmaster. He was tense and frightened, not knowing what was coming, but sure it would be unpleasant. Did it mean he would be arrested?

"*Kommunist, nicht wahr?*[10] In France all schoolmasters are Communists."

A sweeping accusation. But in France many teachers were indeed Leftists and quite a few were Communists. Monsieur Varin stood silently before the German officer, so youthful to him yet so old in battle years. For a few seconds the silence persisted. The teacher could have denied the accusation. What real proof was there? No, even though his life depended upon it, he could not forgo his deep beliefs. So he nodded.

"*Ja, Herr Hauptmann.* I am a Communist."

There he stood, expecting immediate arrest. Now the sweat appeared on the forehead of the Frenchman. Men had been sent to prison for less. But apparently, with this career soldier who obviously knew France, truth was best. The next question would be harder still, because he could never betray his heritage. The officer would ask him if he was a Jew, and one grandfather on his mother's side had been Jewish. As long as France was France and a nation, he was a Frenchman, but to the Germans, if they knew of that grandfather, he would be a Jew.

Surely the *Feldwebel*, with access to the records in the little town hall, knew all about his background, yet had never reported him. Nobody else in Nogent-Plage was aware of his ancestry, for his grandfather had long since died in Lyon.

The teacher stood waiting for the obvious question, but the bespectacled little officer kept silent. He turned, slapped his gloves in a gesture of contempt, and without bothering to return the salute of the *Feldwebel*, stalked down the street. Activity among the soldiers visibly increased as he passed.

Monsieur Varin discovered his legs were weak. He was trembling. Strange, he thought, feeling his heart bump, how the heat grows at noon on a spring day in Nogent-Plage.

---

8. **Papieren!**\pa ⁺pē·rən\ Your identification papers!
9. Schoolmaster, aren't you?
10. Communist, isn't that true?

1. What do you learn about Père Clement?

2. What sort of man is Georges Varin, the schoolteacher?

3. What kind of relationship does the *Feldwebel* have with the schoolteacher?

4. Why does the Hauptmann Seeler dislike the *Feldwebel*?

5. Describe the scene and action when the *Hauptmann* comes upon the *Feldwebel* at the inn.

6. What is the effect of this *brief encounter* on the schoolteacher; the *Hauptmann*; the *Feldwebel*?

## 8

It was afternoon. The farmer Marquet[1] sat on the plank seat of his old-fashioned cart, with wooden slats sloping outward at the top, filled with thick, oozy seaweed—fertilizer for his land. Years of harsh work had made him seem older than he was. But his horse, although thin like every living thing after four years of occupation, had a cared-for look.

The farmer's home was an ancient stone house in a hamlet called La Roye, beyond the dunes in back of town. His wife was long since dead, one son had been killed in the campaign of 1940, another, Pierre, was a prisoner of war in Germany. He lived alone and the people of Nogent-Plage considered him slightly mad, because he had a habit of talking to himself. Twice each year he took the long road around the dunes to the coast for fertilizer.

His only companion was his horse whose name was Sebastian. Why Sebastian? Nobody ever found out. But between them was a bond of affection. The animal seemed to understand his lonely master's needs. And the farmer cared more for the horse, perhaps, than anything save his land, for which he had the fierce possessiveness of the peasant. Between them they would manage to keep the soil nourished and the fields cultivated until the day when his boy would return from Germany.

Slowly the horse pulled the heavy load, up the hill, past the blockhouse, and into the village. Half a dozen young soldiers, stripped to the waist, torsos tanned, towels over their shoulders, picked their way down the cliff to the sea, carefully avoiding the mines and barbed wire. The old man watched with a passionate hatred. How much longer, he wondered, shall we have to look on these well-fed barbarians?

As the cart entered the village, the door of a house at which two sentries were stationed opened and a bespectacled officer stepped out. On his breast was a double row of campaign medals and the Iron Cross. His boots, which reached to his knees, shone in the sun. He walked briskly, shoulders back, every inch of his small frame an officer of the *Wehrmacht*. From the cart, the old man observed that his gaze went from right to left along the street— he missed nothing. On he moved, the Grande Rue now empty save for a few soldiers at the far end.

As the farmer watched he heard a sudden report, like a shot from a hunting rifle, not loud like an army weapon, being fired. At first he was not sure what had happened. To his amazement, one moment the officer was striding down the street, then he was stretched out on the pavement. As he crumpled, one arm fell behind in a peculiar gesture.

A siren went off. Soldiers rushed from a house, rifles at the ready. A tall, black-haired sergeant ran into the street as the siren kept screaming.

All around, soldiers appeared. By this time the farmer Marquet was near enough to see blood on the spotless tunic of the officer who lay, legs outstretched, on the pavement. Two medical corpsmen opened his blouse and listened to his heart.

The tall, black-haired man in charge was exploding orders, pointing first to one side of the street, then the other. A group of soldiers began working the left side. If the door of a

---

1. **Marquet**\mar 'kā\

house was locked, they pounded it in with rifle butts. From windows on the second floor, shutters opened and frightened faces of women appeared. The same words echoed back and forth.

"*Pas possible!*"[2]

"*Pas possible!*"

Who could have done such a thing? "Impossible! And here in Nogent-Plage!"

Suddenly the farmer Marquet's horse was stopped, and he was yanked roughly to the ground. Two helmeted young soldiers gripped him, two others searched him, but to his surprise did not ask for his *Ausweiss*. They merely hustled him across the road.

He tried to protest. "*Voila*,[3] I only happened to be in town for the moment. I came in from my farm at La Roye for a load of seaweed for fertilizer. *M'ssieurs* . . . for my land. I live . . . over there . . . back of the dunes . . . ."

Not understanding what he was saying and not caring, they pushed him along. Quite plainly they were taking him someplace. A strange and terrible fear seized him, not for himself but for his horse. The horse was being left behind, his only friend, all he had. The beast realized his master was leaving him and whinnied loudly. Then the farmer heard that familiar clop-clop as the horse attempted to follow.

"Sebastian! Sebastian!" he shouted, twisting halfway around in the grip of the soldiers.

The horse, pulling the heavy cart, fell farther and farther behind, the reins dragging on the pavement.

"Sebastian!" shrieked the farmer, realizing what was happening and where, in all probability, he was being taken. In utter despair he cried out, "Ah, who will take care of Sebastian when I am gone?"

## 9

The *Feldwebel* sank into the chair of the murdered officer. His cap was on the desk before him. He reflected grimly that he had rushed into the street at the sound of the shot without a cap, something the *Hauptmann* had never done in all his army life. Before the *Feldwebel* were the neat piles of orders— orders from field headquarters in Bayeux, orders from Division Headquarters in Caen, orders from the High Command in Berlin. Each pile was carefully clipped and filed chronologically, according to regulations.

He took up the telephone. "Major Kessler at Division Headquarters," he said to the operator in the blockhouse.

Replacing the phone he sank forward with his head in his hands. What idiot could have done this? So great was the misery of the Feldwebel Hans, so keen his understanding of what had happened and, more important, of what lay ahead, that a cry of agony burst from him there in the empty room: "*Ach, du Lieber Gott.*"[1]

The telephone rang. Immediately he straightened up, controlled himself. "This is the Feldwebel von Kleinschrodt."

"Good. Major Kessler here. Have your men been alerted, *Feldwebel*?"

"Indeed yes, *Major*. But I have bad news to report. The Hauptmann Seeler has just been shot by a terrorist."

"Shot? Impossible! I talked to him an hour ago . . . ."

"Yes, *Major*, it just happened. He was dead in the middle of the street when the men reached him."

"Have you found the assassin?"

"No, *Major*, not yet, but the men have sealed up the village and are making a house-to-house search. They will surely turn him up."

"He must be found, *must* be found, and made an example of. Execute him publicly. Let me talk to the Oberleutnant Schmidt."

"*Herr Major*, he is at the Defense School at Ostend."

---

2. **Pas possible!**\ˌpa 'pɔ ˈsēb(l)\ Not possible!
3. **Voilà**\vwa 'la\ Look; see here.

---

1. **Ach, du Lieber Gott**\ˈahk·dū ˈlē·bər·gɔt\ Oh, dear God.

"Well then, the *Leutnant*—what's his name? —Wirtig, isn't it?"

"Sir, he is on leave in Bremen."

"All leaves were cancelled as of yesterday. He should be back this afternoon. For the moment you are the senior officer there. To be sure, we will get another officer to you immediately, for with these terrorist raids up and down the coast Schmidt and Wirtig may have trouble returning. Let me see, perhaps the Leutnant Brandt from Blockhouse 242 . . . . No, that won't do, we need him for those big guns; he is a specialist. Let me see now. *Ach,* what a time for this to happen! That Polish chap, that Silesian in Blockhouse H98. No, he is a meteorologist and needed where he is. Well, we'll get someone to you as soon as possible. In the meantime, *Feldwebel,* until the criminal is found, six hostages should be taken into custody. Here"—he turned to someone in his office—"get me that folder on Nogent-Plage, Beckenbauer. We were discussing it with the Hauptmann Seeler a short while ago . . . . No, you didn't put it back. Ah, this is indeed a bad moment for a thing of this sort, and with two officers away . . . . Now, here it is. According to this, you have a teacher there named Martin. No, V-Varin, have you not? Right. Do you know the man?"

The *Feldwebel* froze. Faced with what lay ahead, he could not speak. The *Major* continued.

"Are you there, *Feldwebel?* Do you hear me? Those damned terrorists have been cutting wires all along the coast today. I say, are you there? Do you know this man? I can't hear you. Do you know him? It appears he is a Communist . . . ."

Finally the *Feldwebel* found his voice. "Yes, you are right, *Major.* I believe he is a Communist. But never active to my belief. I've known him three or four years now and—"

The other broke in. "They're all alike, all of them, these darned Communists. I've had a lot of experience with them; they don't care a bit for the land where they were born and raised. Moreover, this one is Jewish."

For a few seconds the *Feldwebel* was stunned. How, he wondered, had this ever reached Caen? "No one ever said he was Jewish, *Herr Major,*" he suggested tentatively.

"The records show it. I cannot understand how he was ever permitted to remain in that sensitive area all these years. Someone has blundered badly, and I intend to discover who it was. At any rate, get him now. Then there is another chap, man by the name of Lavigne. Runs the *café* on the Grande Rue." He read from a paper. "'A hangout for dubious characters.' So the report states. Here it is. 'To be watched. Owner was mixed up with terrorists at the time of the Dieppe raid in '42.' We suspect him also. Is there a priest in the village?"

This was too much. In the mind of the *Feldwebel* rose the picture of old Père Clement with his soutane tied up around his waist and those thick cotton underdrawers. "Why yes, *Major,* there is, but actually the local padre is old and inoffensive. Not at all the kind of person to give us any trouble . . . ."

"*Feldwebel,* we are making examples of these men. Was anyone taken at the time of the murder?"

"No, *Major,* that is . . . only an old farmer from the back country. He merely happened to be passing in his cart at the time. He knows nothing whatever . . . ."

"Yes, yes," interrupted the officer impatiently. "You miss the point. Get him. Or did he escape? Did you pick him up?"

"Yes, *Major,* we have him. Only, if you would permit, sir, I'd like to suggest . . . ."

"No comments necessary, *Feldwebel.* Just obey orders. We want six—the teacher, the *café* proprietor, the old farmer, the priest, a fisherman, a boy perhaps. Give them one hour in which to confess. If the culprit is not found and none of them confesses, make an example of them. Have them shot. As a warning, you understand, to other terrorists."

"Yes, *Major,* I quite understand."

"Good. Now for your personal information as you are in charge at Nogent-Plage temporarily. Terrorists have been at work up and down the coast since dawn. This line may be cut any minute. We have patrols out, but the bridge at Varengeville has been blown up and the highway below Dampart completely destroyed. Hence, as far as reinforcements are concerned, you are isolated for the time being. In fact, we are all isolated. Fécamp is isolated. So is Étretat. We are on our own, *Feldwebel.* Is that quite clear?"

"*Jawohl, Herr Major.*" It was only too clear. For the first time in his long years at Nogent-Plage the Feldwebel Hans felt the isolation and the loneliness and the danger. They were Germans in a hostile land, about to be attacked from the front and perhaps the rear. The *Major* went on.

"Meanwhile, do not forget. The defense rests in your hands. You are responsible."

"We are ready, sir," he replied resolutely. After all, perhaps a way out could be found. Perhaps, he thought, the invasion will intervene; perhaps they won't be shot.

The *Major* lowered his voice. "For your information, *Feldwebel,* we are advised that the invasion fleet is now in mid-Channel, making about six knots. Most likely they are planning an early-morning assault, hoping to be covered by this fog. It is thick here at present. And at such a moment! *Feldwebel,* only one thing counts. The Fatherland. Our country is in peril. The Greater Reich faces its most critical hour. Your first duty is to round up the six hostages. Unless the assassin of the Hauptmann Seeler is found within the hour, have a firing squad shoot them. Report to me as soon as you have them in custody. Remember, this is not a football game . . . ."

The *Feldwebel* started to say something, but the *Major* cut him short. "I repeat, Feldwebel von Kleinschrodt, this is not a football game. Understand? *Heil* Hitler."

He rang off. The *Feldwebel* rose from the desk. There was tragedy ahead. And he was in the middle of it. To shoot, to kill a friend. In a way, they were all friends. But they were also enemies of his country, and he was in charge at Nogent-Plage. He represented the

Third Reich for the moment. What choice did he have? He was responsible for the safety of his men. There were the orders.

"Corporal Eicke," he called out, yanking down his tunic with the same gesture the Hauptmann Seeler had used at the same desk just a little while ago.

First, of course, comes one's country.

## ⟨⟩ 10

The farmer Marquet half fell, half stumbled down the badly lit stairs. He picked himself up and looked around. He was in the cellar of the Bloch villa.

Opposite was a narrow, oblong, barred window through which came a dampness from the sea. He noticed a fog was collecting, for the wind had died away. On the other side of the stairs another small window gave onto a vacant lot where, he knew, the boys of the village practiced football. There was no glass in either window.

The earth floor of the cellar was moist. The place was filled with odds and ends left behind by the Jewish Bloch family when the war had burst upon them, driving them from Nogent-Plage. Where were they now? What woman had used that rusty sewing machine? What child had played with that faceless doll? Who had sat on that old wooden bench or those chairs without backs?

He slumped down on the bench. The thought of Sebastian with the load of seaweed standing patiently in the street above struck him with such a stabbing pain that he groaned aloud.

"Ah, Sebastian," he cried. "And my poor Pierre in Germany. He will never know what happened to his old father."

The door at the top of the cellar opened and light penetrated the gloom. He glanced up from his misery as Lavigne, in his dirty white apron, was shoved roughly downstairs. The *café* owner, a stout man, picked himself up, rubbing his hip.

"But," he shouted, "I tell you I had nothing

whatever to do with it. I was inside washing dishes. I was inside when the shot was fired. I had nothing to do with it." Then realizing that nobody was listening, he saw the futility of his protestations and shook his fist at the door above. "Ah, those *Fridolins*, those barbarians!"

The door opened again, and a German voice said, "*Unter . . . .*"[1]

Monsieur Varin, the teacher, was pushed down. Next came the Père Clement and young René Le Gallec, with whom he had been practicing football. The priest picked himself up as the door slammed and shouted, "But I had nothing to do with the shooting of the *Hauptmann*. I was playing football beside my church with this boy. The *Herr Oberst* knows I could have had nothing to do with it. He passed by, himself, but a short while before. He played with us. Ask the *Herr Oberst* . . . ."

The door opened once more and Marcel Deschamps, the fisherman, was hurled down. Then a helmeted soldier with a submachine gun stomped downstairs, followed by a corporal. The corporal went over to the teacher, sitting on the bench and rubbing the knee he had scraped during his tumble into the cellar.

"*Sprechen Sie Deutsch?*"[2] he asked.

"*Ja. Ich kann Deutsch sprechen.*"[3]

Then followed a torrent of guttural words, so fast that the teacher had trouble making them out. But he understood enough to put the sense of the remarks into French.

"This village is surrounded," he translated. "Every exit is guarded. Every house in town is being searched. But we have orders from Headquarters that if the murderer of the Hauptmann Seeler is not found—or none of you confesses to the murder—you will all be shot within one hour. These orders are from our *Kommandateur* at Caen."

The German corporal spun around and went up the stairs, followed at a respectful distance by the soldier. The door opened, then slammed shut. A key turned in the lock. Darkness and silence fell over the cellar.

Their eyes gradually became accustomed to the gloom. The farmer Marquet wept tears of despair. Monsieur Lavigne stalked in a rage up and down the dirt floor. The priest, hands extended, asked, "But who could have done such a thing? Surely it must have been somebody from outside the town."

"Yes, certainly, it must have been a stranger. Someone from Évreux, no doubt."

"They will find him soon, and we shall all be released, I am sure," said the Père Clement.

Only Monsieur Varin was thinking clearly enough at the moment to fit the pieces together. It took no genius to guess what had happened—and also what lay ahead. The Silesian shock troops sent in as a garrison, the cutting of bridges along the coast, the soldiers in battle dress—everything told him the invasion was imminent. Some young hothead must have felt this was a chance not to be missed, a chance to throw the garrison into confusion by killing its commanding officer and so to hurt the outfit at this critical instant in the war. To a rifleman firing through the blinds of a second-story window the Hauptmann Seeler was an easy target.

Ah, thought the teacher, those crazy young people, acting as young people so often do, without thinking of others, with no regard for what might happen to those of us left here in the village. Naturally the Germans would avenge the death of the *Hauptmann*. Anyone could have foretold that.

And what difference who the assassin was. If the slayer escapes, we six will be executed. He rose from the bench.

"Come, my friends, the *Feldwebel* is now in command here. He has helped us before, but even if he has authority we mustn't depend on him. He may know we are innocent, he will do all he can at Headquarters, but we must help ourselves. We must organize . . . ."

"Organize!" snorted Monsieur Lavigne.

---

1. **Unter,** Down; Get down there.
2. Do you speak German?
3. Yes, I can speak German.

"How can we organize locked in this cellar, with fifty minutes of life left?"

The teacher ignored his outburst. "Look, I have friends up the coast. Things have been happening, things that are the signal I anticipated. And see that fog coming in? What better weather for an invasion fleet to approach the coast? They plan these things, you know; they leave nothing to chance."

Suddenly René Le Gallec, who had been watching from the narrow window, shouted, "They're coming! I hear them! Listen!"

A rumble came from the sea. It grew louder, louder. Soon it turned into a massive roar. Together the men rushed to the window. There in the haze above the low-lying fogbank were planes, planes, more planes than they had ever seen before, so many that they seemed to blacken the sky.

The five men and the boy shouted, yelled, screamed, waved white handkerchiefs through the narrow, barred window, turned and embraced each other. Rescue! Deliverance! Release! Unquestionably those planes were headed straight for the Bloch villa. Already the antiaircraft batteries down the coast were sputtering, then the blockhouse just outside the town joined in. But the planes roared majestically on. Their sound was that of a thousand express trains, a thousand thunderstorms, drowning out the guns.

The invasion at last! Long-awaited, long-hoped-for! They were saved!

Now the planes were directly above, passing overhead, continuing on. None detached themselves to descend on Nogent-Plage. Whatever it meant, wherever they were going, it was no attack upon the garrison of the town. Soon the planes vanished from sight. The noise died away. The antiaircraft fire from the blockhouse stuttered and stopped. One by one, the men left the window. The Père Clement stood staring into space. The farmer sank back again on the bench. Young René Le Gallec crumpled to the floor as if hit by a blow.

The hostages heard the voice of the *Herr Oberst* up above, giving a harsh, crisp command. It seemed somehow out of character. It had an ominous sound. Then came the stomping of boots. Evidently they were reinforcing the guard outside the front door of the Bloch villa.

Below, in the cellar, five men and a boy faced death in forty-eight minutes.

## 11

When the Hauptmann Seeler had come to Nogent-Plage in the spring that year, he, like everyone else, was immediately attracted to the Feldwebel von Kleinschrodt. Old army family. Nobility. Celebrated German athlete. The *Hauptmann* was impressed. But not for long. He soon had the young man sized up and perceived that he lacked real soldierly qualities. He then tried his best to reform him as other commanding officers in Nogent-Plage had done, to help him live up to the great traditions of his heritage.

Often he used to stand the *Feldwebel* at attention and lecture him. "Kleinschrodt, your trouble is you are like the Americans. I know well the Americans. For nine years I was head porter at the Schweitzerhof in Dresden and met many of them. Americans want to be liked. They are almost pathetic in this childish desire to be liked. Actually, this is an infantile trait. Americans are children, young and old. It is why they do not make good soldiers. In North Africa we had no trouble with them at Kasserine. We have nothing to fear from them, nothing. They wish to be liked. That is agreeable, yes; it is better to be liked than disliked. Best of all is for a man to be respected. Respect is the basis for discipline—at home, in business, in the Army. Now you are greatly admired by the troops here and liked by the people of the village. But you are not respected. Never forget that soldiers, too, are children. They will never obey you unless they respect you."

These words the *Feldwebel* remembered, for he was finding the *Hauptmann* right about obedience and respect. As he sat at the desk which an hour before had belonged to the murdered man, as he checked the deployment of the troops—his troops for the moment—around the village, as he listened to the telephoned report of a sentry a mile from town, he was amazed at himself. He had assumed responsibility. He had become the senior officer of the garrison at Nogent-Plage.

No time to waste words. His voice was quite as crisp and curt over the phone, his tunic as spotless, as carefully hooked under the chin as that of the late *Hauptmann*. The invasion was at hand. It might come anywhere, any moment, surely by morning. Maybe right now advance elements were trying to land up the coast under cover of the fog. His duty was to his men, to his country, to the Third Reich. He felt attuned to it without thinking.

And the men? There was a change in their bearing toward him, a surprising deference as they knocked on the door or addressed him. A certain respect that was new had crept into everyone's voice. They seemed to be turning to him, leaning on him, trustfully, hopefully. That was as natural as it was for him to assume the duties and the responsibilities of command.

And yet, all this solved nothing. It is not easy to obey order when the orders are to have your friends shot; it is hard to issue orders when those orders mean a firing squad for your friends. Hanging over him was the thought of what lay ahead. When his mind was busy with other things it was all right. But the moment he stopped to think about it, revulsion took possession of him. Those men were his friends. That boy he had played football with. Obviously the teacher had Marxist leanings. Certainly, we had discussed them together. But brave. Loyal. A good Frenchman. How on earth can I kill a man like him? A veteran of two wars, already decorated upon the field of battle. For I'm the one who has to give the orders to fire. To watch them fall. To certify to their deaths. How can I do this? And that boy! A child really. My God . . . .

He rose and walked up and down the silent, empty room. The Le Gallec boy haunted him, devastated him, destroyed him. How could he? But he must obey orders.

A short, sharp knock at the door and the corporal entered to hand him a radio dispatch from Headquarters. It merely confirmed what the *Major* had told him, alerting all officers commanding troops that a landing, either a feint or the real thing, was expected along the Normandy coast late tonight or early tomorrow morning. He filed it carefully with the other orders.

The telephone rang, and the operator said, "The Major Kessler, *Herr Feldwebel*."

"Von Kleinschrodt? Is that you?" The anxious tone in the *Major's* voice was meaningful. Now the *Feldwebel* began to feel and appreciate the terrible responsibility of command. The *Major* was obviously full of the imminent crisis, obviously worried.

"*Ja*, Major Kessler."

"You were to report to me as soon as you secured those hostages. Have you done so?"

"Yes sir, I was about to call you. They have been apprehended as you ordered." In the back of the *Feldwebel's* mind the same question kept rising. How can I save them? Surely some way must be found.

"And have you discovered the murderer of the Hauptmann Seeler?"

"No, *Major*, not yet, but we are still . . . ."

"Good grief, man, how can he escape from a small village? Was the place surrounded? It was? Did you post sentries at all exits? Have you searched the houses thoroughly? Thoroughly, *Feldwebel?*" His tone was packed with exasperation. Plainly he was edgy. "Get him. It's important to teach these partisans a lesson. When they kill, Frenchmen must be killed. No nonsense about it."

"Quite, *Major*. My Silesians here are first-class troops. They have been through many partisan attacks in Poland and Russia. I have three search parties out under the most experienced noncoms. They will dig up the man. Just a question of time, I assure you."

"Good. If not, you understand, those six

French must be executed. You understand, do you not, *Feldwebel?*"

"Perfectly, sir. I only wondered . . . I only meant . . . . I do happen to know these six hostages. I can guarantee myself that none of them had a thing to do with the murder of the *Hauptmann.*"

The voice of the older man rose irritably. "*Hier haben Sie nicht mitzureden.*" That's none of your business. "*Feldwebel,* listen to me carefully. These men are an example to the populace. A warning, you might say. If they are all innocent, so much the better. The villagers along the coast must be impressed with the seriousness of the situation and know what measures we shall take if there is trouble. We have shot sixteen terrorists at Abbeville and are rounding up a dozen at Yvetot."

A pause, then the *Major* went on. "You may recall, *Feldwebel,* that in March a band of Italian partisans killed thirty-three of our SS men outside Rome?"

"Yes, *Herr Major.*"

"Then you also remember that we were forced to execute three hundred and thirty-five Italians, that is, slightly over ten Italians for every German. At Nogent-Plage we are moderate, only six for one German and an officer at that. We are being lenient, really. Are you there, *Feldwebel?*"

The annoyed voice at the other end persisted. "These lines are being cut constantly now. Did you get that Jewish fellow? What's his name? Are you still on the line? Do you hear me?"

"Yes, *Herr Major,* we got him. His name is Varin."

"And the priest, as I suggested?"

"The Père Clement. But truly, *Major,* he had nothing whatever to do with the killing of the Hauptmann Seeler. Actually he is almost eighty. That I would vouch for myself."

The *Major* paid no attention to the *Feldwebel's* comments. "And the *café* owner, probably a Communist also."

"His place is closed up. We have him."

"His name? I had it before, I think. We must have his name. Remember, you are to post a notice after the execution listing these Frenchmen by name and stating that any further sabotage or interference with German forces carrying out their duties will mean that twenty-five more hostages will be selected and dealt with in the same manner. Is that quite clear? Now the man's name . . . . Are you there, *Feldwebel?* Or are you perhaps dreaming of football? This is not a game. You are a soldier of the Greater Reich."

"Yes, *Major,* I am still on the line. The man's name is Charles Lavigne."

"Good! You realize, of course, that the situation is critical. Perhaps *the* most critical moment of the war. The Herr Generalfeldmarschall Rommel, under whom I had the honor of serving two years in North Africa, sent around a secret bulletin last week before he was wounded. He anticipated an attempt at a landing by the English and Americans about this period, with the moon full and the tide high. He urged us all in the strictest terms, *Feldwebel,* not to forget that we must defeat the invaders here, on the beaches. We cannot permit them to get a foothold inland where their superiority in the air will count. We must throw them back at all costs, von Kleinschrodt. You understand?"

"Yes, *Major,* I understand."

"You are in a key position. Your responsibility is therefore great. From that rock—I inspected it myself with the *Herr Generalfeldmarschall*—one can sweep the coast for several miles in each direction. We depend upon you. The Fatherland is in peril tonight; the invasion may burst on us any moment. Germany counts on all her sons, *Feldwebel,* especially those from an old and famous army family such as yours. Remember your father, who died gloriously on the field of battle, and your grandfather, the General von Kleinschrodt. Be worthy of them! Obey orders implicitly. Do not fail. Do you hear me?"

"Yes, *Major* . . . ."

"Good. Now if we cannot get an officer to you, then you must carry out the execution and post the proclamation. As soon as the assassin of the Hauptmann Seeler is found or the hostages shot, notify me at once by telephone. Yes, of course, if you find the partisan who committed the crime, you may release the hostages with a warning. But be sure to take pains to frighten them. I gave you one hour. How much time is left?"

The Feldwebel Hans looked carefully at his watch. "Thirty-nine minutes, *Major.*"

"Right! Let me have a report. And *Heil Hitler!*"

The Feldwebel Hans replaced the telephone and sat staring into the empty room. The face of every person in the cellar rose before him: Varin, Lavigne, the Père Clement, Marquet, Deschamps, and the boy. He couldn't even bear to say the boy's name to himself.

At least this much he could do. He pressed the buzzer on the desk. A corporal knocked and entered immediately, alert, attentive, keyed up. And deferential. Amazing how the man's whole bearing and attitude had changed in one hour.

He met the gaze of the soldier steadily.

"Here, Grossman. Take pencils and paper down to those people in the cellar. For messages . . . ." His voice shook ever so slightly, as he said, "They will understand."

Only too well, he thought. They will now realize that their friend the *Herr Oberst* has failed them. They are about to be shot. How could he? they will ask each other. Ah, all Germans are alike, each one will say. Underneath they are all Boches.[1] He is like all the rest; they are all the same, they will say.

The corporal took the pads and pencils, clicked his heels, and went out, shutting the door carefully. The *Feldwebel* put his head down on the desk and wept. He wept for the affection that was gone, the friendships that had failed, the trust that was no more. He cried for those six hostages, but most of all he cried for himself. Because for the first time in his life he saw so plainly and so well that there was no health in him.

12

Monsieur Lavigne, the *café* owner, and Monsieur Varin, the teacher, were quietly talking beside the small cellar window that gave onto the vacant lot adjoining the Bloch villa. Despite the commotion caused by the killing of the Hauptmann Seeler, half a dozen boys were playing football there as usual. One was Jean-Paul, the teacher's young son. Occasionally the ball bounced back off the brick wall of the Bloch villa.

The teacher, a shortish man, took a small wooden box and found he could see plainly through the window. A helmeted sentry with a fixed bayonet stalked back and forth before the house. Monsieur Varin looked at his watch. It was an old-fashioned timepiece, a thick, gold affair that once had belonged to his father and his grandfather. He treasured it and wore it attached to his trouser pocket by a worn leather strap. He soon discovered that the sentry walking back and forth in front of the house was out of sight of the cellar window for about twenty-one or twenty-two seconds, eleven going and eleven returning.

"Pssst . . . pssst . . . psst . . . Jean-Paul . . . Jean-Paul!"

The boy hearing his name, yet not sure where the sound of his father's voice came from, stood perplexed with the ball under one arm. Then he saw that face framed by the little cellar window.

"Papa . . . ."

"Sssh . . . don't look this way," cautioned the teacher. "Wait until the *Fridolin* gets past. Play! Kick that ball!"

The boy instantly obeyed. As soon as the sentry vanished from sight, he kicked the round balloon almost up to the window and leaned down.

"Papa!"

"Sssh, a message. I'm giving you a message

---

1. **Boches**\bȯsh\ German soldiers, a term of disparagement.

for Madame Borel, out on the road to Varenge-ville. Understand?"

The boy understood. He gulped. "*Ouai, ouai.*[1] I understand," he panted, now frightened at the sight of his father behind the barred window. He took the ball, whirled, kicked it high into the air and raced after it.

The sentry turned, stomped his heels, and went into his act. Except for the little cellar window which the man had failed to notice, all the windows of the Bloch villa giving onto the empty lot had been bricked up. Hence he paid little attention to the band of boys at play. As soon as he disappeared, Jean-Paul grabbed the ball, kicked it toward the window, ran after it, and knelt down to hear his father's instructions.

"Listen carefully. Go get your bicycle. And your fishing pole. Go to the end of town and tell the sentry if he stops you that you are going fishing. Then get to Madame Borel's house as soon as you can, and explain what has happened. That we have been taken by the Fritz."

The lad rushed away as Monsieur Varin stepped down from the wooden box. His face was wet with anxiety. Would the boy get through? Could Madame Borel summon help in time? Is the old truck available?

"Whoof! At least there is a chance. If they get here before the hour is up. How much left?"

"Thirty-six minutes."

"*Eh, juste!* If they get that old Berleit truck they used to derail the train at Montford. The sides are armored. This will take time. Also men and guns to tackle these Silesians. But boldness must pay off. With the old truck they can make it here in fifteen, eighteen minutes. Unless they run into a German patrol."

Everyone listened with attention. Nobody in that cellar had suspected that Monsieur Varin was so close to the Resistance, yet no one was greatly surprised. He seemed to assume leadership.

At this point the door above opened and a helmeted soldier entered, followed by another who stood at the top of the stairs watching with a gun. The first man handed each of the hostages a pencil and a pad of paper. No words were spoken. Nor were any necessary. Each one turned the pad over, examining it. The pads were blocks of old German army orders, blank on the back.

The soldiers left, relocking the cellar door, leaving the six looking down at those ominous squares of paper. Still nobody said a word. Nothing the *Herr Oberst* could have done would have been so utterly final.

"Ah—" A kind of sob came from young René Le Gallec, curled up on the dirt floor. "*Ah, mon père,*" he addressed the priest. "Once you said that someday I would be good enough to play for France. You should know; you played for France long ago. Now I shall never, never . . ." he cried.

"*Chut!*"[2] The priest leaned down and placed his hand on the shoulder of the boy. "Come, René, we are not lost yet. We are alive. They may send us to Germany, but we shall return. The *Fridolins* are beaten; they know it themselves. See, the *Herr Oberst* is now commanding the garrison. They cannot find an officer to relieve him!"

In a little while everyone except the farmer Marquet was writing. The teacher, crouched against the wall, had his pad on his knees. He wrote clumsily with the aid of his magnifying glass, forehead wrinkled, eyebrows raised in the air.

By ancestry I am at least partly a Jew, although not by religion, for in all honesty I have never attended any synagogue or professed any creed. Yet I feel neither pride nor shame in my origins; indeed I never think about them save in the presence of an anti-Semite, of whom there appear to be many in my beloved France today. First of all, I am a Frenchman. Second, a teacher of French youth. Third, a Marxist, something that, like my origin I have never attempted to conceal.

---

1. **Ouai**\wĕ\ yes.
2. **Chut!**\shũt\ Hush!

Why should I? My great great grandfather served as a soldier of Napoleon at Austerlitz. My grandfather was wounded in the Franco-Prussian War of 1870. I, myself, was twice wounded in the battles along the Somme in the campaigns of 1917 and 1918. I fought through the disaster of 1940. Because of this or because of my decorations—for the Germans like the French have a military tradition and a respect for soldiers, even their enemies—I have not been sent away from my home here in Nogent-Plage. Hence this France, from which today some of my compatriots would like to exile me, remains the land where my emotions are fixed, my being is centered. I have drunk her culture. I have done my best to defend her honor with my body, to help train her youth. I breathe fully only when in her climate. Next to my wife whom I adore, and my dear son Jean-Paul who is my pride and joy, I count my country as my nearest and dearest.

*Adieu La France,*
Georges Varin

Across the room, Marcel Deschamps the fisherman was kneeling before the priest. René Le Gallec waited his turn. The farmer Marquet, his head between his hands, sat motionless on the bench. He had written nothing and was muttering to himself.

For how can you write a letter of farewell to a horse named Sebastian?

## 13

René had made his confession, yet his blond head remained bowed. At last he looked up, still on his knees before the padre. There were tears in his eyes.

"My parents don't even know where I am. They think I went swimming. I told them I was going swimming with Michel." Then he voiced the thought of everyone in that cellar. "Why doesn't the *Herr Oberst* do something? Only this morning he told me I should use the left foot more. You remember, don't you, Père? He said I had an excellent left foot. Why doesn't he do something? Now he must be in

command here. He has always been good to the people of Nogent-Plage, always . . . ."

He broke down, sobbing, staggered by the brutal injustice of what had happened. Half an hour before he had been free, outside in the sunshine kicking his precious football, the one the *Herr Oberst* had obtained for him. Now he was locked up in the cellar of the Bloch villa, soon to be sentenced to a German prison camp for life. Or something worse, though he could not quite bring himself to believe the Germans would really shoot six innocent people.

Except for the farmer, the men stood talking in knots, Monsieur Lavigne and the teacher leaning against an iron stanchion, the fisherman saying something softly, all shaking a little. All thinking much the same thing. It simply can't be. Things aren't like this. We've never had anything like this before in Nogent-Plage, never. The *Herr Oberst* knows us all. He has worked miracles before. He got us out of trouble so often these past years. Surely he will today.

Their faith in the Feldwebel Hans was touching. Only the teacher was dubious. "You'll get out of this mess," he remarked to the *café* owner. "It will be all right for you, not for me. To the Germans, I am a Jew." He held out his hands in a little Gallic gesture of despair.

At this point they were interrupted by sudden noises overhead. A whistle blew shrilly. The boots of running soldiers above thudded on the floor. They heard the voice of the *Herr Oberst* shouting orders in that guttural German. His voice had changed. Now it was the tone of all the many officers who had garrisoned Nogent-Plage during those long years of occupation.

Far down the street a machine gun gave a stuttering bark, fell silent, barked once more. Monsieur Varin quickly reached the top of the wooden box beside the window. Jean-Paul and the other football players had scattered. Peering out, he could see about fifty feet of the Grande Rue.

The door at the top of the cellar stairs opened with a crash. A soldier stood there pointing a gun at the hostages below. *"Nicht bewegen! Nicht bewegen!"* he shouted. Don't move.

Nobody moved. Nobody had any intention of moving. All were far too frightened to move.

The teacher knew immediately what was happening. The Underground was mounting an attack on the Bloch villa in a desperate attempt to free the six prisoners. Unfortunately, the Germans directed by the Feldwebel Hans were ready. Upstairs they began firing out of the windows facing the street. A heavy truck roared past on the Grande Rue, firing in turn.

Below another machine gun went into action. Bullets bit into the walls of the Bloch villa, sending stone splinters flying. Windowpanes shattered, showering glass onto the pavement. Then came bursts of firing the teacher assumed to be from the rescue truck. Finally he heard it racing off in the direction of Varengeville.

The soldier at the head of the cellar stairs lowered his gun as the noise died away in the distance. The sound of the door closing and the key turning in the lock was painfully definitive. The teacher leaned as far as the little window allowed. He saw German troops moving up the street with the body of a French civilian on a stretcher, the arms of the dead man hanging over the sides. Soon two more bodies went by, then a badly wounded German limping along and assisted by two comrades.

The young football players, not entirely unaccustomed to the sound of machine guns in recent years, returned to the lot and stood watching the activity on the Grande Rue. There was too much commotion in the street for the Germans to pay any attention to them.

"Jean-Paul!"

The boy turned, startled. He grabbed the football from a comrade and kicked it toward the low cellar window, then trotted after it

casually. Meanwhile, Monsieur Varin hastily untied the worn leather strap of his watch from his belt and, taking it out of his pocket, tossed it through the barred window on the ground before his son. The boy leaning over for the football scooped up the watch in one deft movement and kicked the ball hard against the house, letting it rebound. His father stood admiring the quickness and ease of the boy's movement, so utterly free and natural, so unconscious, and watched him stuff the watch into his trouser pocket of the ragged blue shorts.

Pray God nobody was looking. Nobody was. The boy raced off home, down the street. At least he was safe. Monsieur Varin stepped down from the box.

*"Ahhhh,"* he said, shaking his head.

That futile rescue attempt had cost three lives and completely failed. *"Ahhhh!"* he exclaimed in despair. He leaned down and picked up the block of paper, with his small, precise writing, and slumped to the bench.

The farmer Marquet, his head in his hands, still sat motionless. Still he had written nothing.

## 14

The Chateau de Varennes on the outskirts of Normandy was a busy place that June day. As Headquarters of the Northern Command, it was the nerve center of the defense of the entire region. From a peak of the roof of the Chateau hung dozens of telephone wires that went off in every direction. Camouflaged Mercedes[1] deposited staff officers carrying black briefcases under one arm. Dispatch riders roared up on olive-drab motorcycles. Inside, in a larger corner apartment on the second floor that had once been an upstairs sitting room, two staff officers were in earnest consultation.

Behind a desk in this office sat the Baron General von Wenig, chief of staff of the North-

---

1. **Mercedes**\mər ˈsā·dēz\ a make of car.

ern Command. He was a strong, stocky man with close-cropped hair and a stretched-out mouth used to giving orders and having them instantly obeyed. He looked out through French windows at a cherry tree in blossom and the park beyond, where the grass was green in the spring sunshine.

"Ah, I see. You could do nothing with him."

"Nothing," answered the other man, also a general, tall, tanned, stalking the carpeted room. "Absolutely nothing. He seems to me to exist in a world of his own. However, as you know, it is difficult to talk on the telephone in times such as these. One doesn't dare speak openly with so many listening in. But he seems determined."

"He seems to me determined to die. I've heard medical men talk of a death wish. Now I begin to understand. Doesn't he realize, Klaus, that it is far better to die for one's country under English gunfire than to die from the bullets of a firing squad?"

The tall officer walking up and down nodded. He had a fine, intelligent face, sensitive yet strong. His hair was neatly brushed back from his forehead and this gave him a spare, well-groomed appearance. When he spoke, his eyes had a kind of irony in them, as though he had seen everything.

"Yes, naturally, he knows. He understands the army viewpoint. He must realize this has been done numberless times in the last war. But he cannot bring himself to shoot those six French."

"But Klaus, he knows the necessity for firmness in dealing with *franc-tireurs*.[2] They are enemies of his country. In short, they are murderers."

"True, but he claims they are simply men of the village."

"Makes no difference. They must be made an example of. Otherwise he is a traitor to the Army. Doesn't he see that? If we didn't take measures, we should have riots throughout our rear, with those British and Americans firing at us from the sea. This is the overriding consideration. He is disobeying the orders of a superior. There is only one thing to do." The seated man slammed his fist down on the desk.

"Heinrich, permit me. It isn't as easy as all that. This young man believes he is right."

"He believes what? What is right? Does he believe in a duty to the land of his birth? His father died for the Fatherland here in France. Does he believe in tradition? In family obligations? Does he, Klaus? His brother risks his life daily in the *Luftwaffe*, and this young man sits comfortably in a seaside village discussing right and wrong. Let us not waste time on the matter. You and I know that were it not for his connections at home, he would be behind bars right now. Tell me, who is replacing him at Nogent-Plage?"

"A certain Leutnant Rancke from Blockhouse 262B, about five miles east."

The man behind the desk half rose. "Not Rancke. R-A-N-C-K-E?" He broke into an agonized scream. "That fellow was attached to my division at Anzio last year. He is worthless, absolutely worthless! Quite incapable of making a decision on anything, even the smallest matter. What is the *Wehrmacht* coming to? Surely we are down to the dregs if we have to depend on the likes of Rancke! We cannot entrust even a small garrison such as Nogent-Plage to this idiot. Until that *Oberleutnant* gets back tomorrow from Ostend, we must find a replacement. Not Rancke. Meanwhile, as I see it, there is only one thing to do. You are taking over Wissant tomorrow from Straub, right? Then you must leave immediately, stop off and see von Kleinschrodt yourself, persuade him . . . ."

"*Jawohl, Herr General.*"

"At once. You are an older man, a career soldier, not only his family friend, but someone he trusts and respects. He knows you and takes your advice. I shall cancel the order for Rancke and get that man back from Ostend. You take over Nogent-Plage until he arrives."

"But suppose the boy refuses to carry out orders. Suppose he refuses to execute those Frenchmen."

2. **franc-tireurs**\\'fra(n)·tē 'rĕr\\ snipers.

"Then of course you must do it. He should be made to attend as a witness. Everything done strictly according to regulations, *General*. Leave him in command until his lieutenant returns. Then we must court-martial him, as soon that is, as we have repelled the invasion."

The General Froelicher, speeding along in the Mercedes on Route Nationale Number 40 glanced through the haze out to sea. It made him recall the big estate on the Baltic, and the Colonel von Kleinschrodt who had been his dearest friend and a comrade for three years in World War I. He did not like his mission in the least as he thought about the boy. A strange, quiet youth, different from the others, except that he liked football and, I must admit, always played it excellently. I remember once on a wild boar hunt on the family place, he was then about ten or twelve. By mistake somebody shot a stag. The animal dropped, but did not die. I recall he writhed on the ground until one of the beaters went up and killed him. As the blood poured from the stag's head, the boy took one look and fainted. Just like that . . . he fell to the ground . . . .

All the way to Nogent-Plage he thought and worried about the interview to come. Finally they drew up before the Bloch villa in Nogent-Plage. Outside in the Grande Rue, Madame Dupont was hobbling along, nodding and bobbing her head to the other women, the inevitable black string bag in her hand. Observing a vehicle approaching in a cloud of dust, she hastily stepped onto the sidewalk. With these young army drivers one was never safe.

The car stopped with a screaming of brakes. It was covered with a film of sand that could not obscure its high polish. A soldier jumped out and smartly held the rear door open, clicking his heels together. And an officer stepped onto the pavement.

He was tall, well-tanned, with fine features. There was a row of ribbons on his tunic. She recognized the Ritterkreuz and the Order Pour Le Merité, one of the highest combat decorations of the German Army. Somehow the aristocratic-looking officer and his whirlwind arrival reminded her of the white horses, the plumes and the gleaming breastplates of the Garde Republicaine of her youth.

Ah, she thought, what smartness, what discipline! No wonder we French could not withstand these people. Surely there is no Army like this. We had only ineffectual troops like Monsieur Varin and young Pierre Marquet, the farmer's son. A nice man, Monsieur Varin, to be sure, certainly, but careless in his dress. And actually, a Communist. He doesn't even conceal it, either.

The smart officer returned the salute of the soldier at the door of the car, saluted again with a glove in his hand as the sentries before the Bloch villa came to attention, and went inside.

In the office of the Hauptmann Seeler, the *Feldwebel* sat by himself where he had been sitting alone for over an hour. The clock on the wall of the silent room showed more than sixty minutes past time for the execution. The *Feldwebel* was more lonely than he had ever been in his life. This loneliness hurt. There was nobody to help, to talk with him, to advise or even disagree with him. The decision was all his. He, too, had heard the big car arriving. Since a car was an event in Nogent-Plage at the moment, it could mean only one thing. Someone from Headquarters had come to place him under arrest, perhaps bringing a replacement to command the garrison. They waste no time in the Army, he thought, as he caught the slamming of the car doors, the sound of the front door opening, the crisp clicking of the sentry's heels. An officer of importance, no doubt the Major Kessler himself. He was ready. The terrible uncertainty was over, the doubts and hesitations finished. The *Feldwebel* felt glad. Standing straight, he put on his cap, yanked down his tunic, and waited for whatever was to come.

A stomping of feet in the corridor. Then the orderly knocked and simultaneously threw open the office door. The *Feldwebel* felt the pride in his subordinate's tone as he announced the visitor. Not every *Feldwebel* was called upon by a staff officer. Let alone a general.

"The General Froelicher," affirmed the soldier, saluting and holding the door open stiffly, then quickly closing it.

The *Feldwebel* had expected anything but this. He was astonished, bewildered, but he, too, clicked his heels and saluted. The visitor came toward him, arms outstretched.

"My poor boy, my poor boy . . . ." He embraced the younger man. Suddenly a little of the aching and loneliness ceased. Someone cared.

"My boy, my boy . . . ." The visitor stepped back, holding him tightly by the forearm, looking into his eyes.

"Yes, my *General*." He was not far from tears, and the older man realized it and broke in.

"*General! General* indeed! I am still your godfather, am I not? I am still old Uncle Klaus. I had to see you, Hans. This is all so terrible."

He moved away, sat down, crossed his legs, showing an expensive pair of leather boots burnished with age and constant polishing. He took out a cigarette case of gold and extended it. "Have one. They are Turkish. Very good."

The *Feldwebel* refused politely. To have accepted would have been a kind of surrender at the start. However, he pushed a small china ashtray across the desk to his godfather. "You know, you cannot imagine what it means to see you at this moment, Uncle Klaus."

The general, elegant, poised, lit his cigarette with a gold lighter. "Of course. You need help. That is what godfathers are for, my boy. Now tell me. What is this all about? Frankly, I don't understand."

The *Feldwebel* started to talk. He desperately needed and indeed wanted to tell the whole story to this man he loved and respected, who knew him so well, who had been part of his existence since childhood. But it was difficult to begin. Although the Froelichers

were old family friends and neighbors back home along the Baltic Sea, they were traditional army people. How could the general be expected to understand? It would make no sense to him.

"You see, Uncle Klaus . . . . I don't quite know how to put it. I have been ordered to do something I cannot bring myself to do."

"Hans, my boy, I didn't come here this afternoon when we are all in such danger to deliver platitudes or preach a sermon. The situation we face is much too serious. I came to save you from yourself."

The younger man nodded. He looked at his godfather, using an old expression of his mother's. "*Um Gottes Willen.*"[3]

"All right. Now tell me everything. I know you have been ordered to execute six hostages. I realize you do not want to do it. But what makes you feel you are more important than the German Reich? Isn't that a bit egotistical?"

The face of the *Feldwebel* flushed. "I don't feel that way at all, Uncle Klaus, and you must know it. I am merely a noncommissioned officer who has never seen battle, the only soldier in Nogent-Plage who doesn't wear a row of combat ribbons on his chest. The *only one*. I am unimportant. I realize this. But, Uncle Klaus, I am me. What I am asked to do betrays myself."

"Hans, my boy, you know you are in the wrong, don't you now? To set your own opinion against that of your country at war? You must see that. You are not in contact with realities, my boy. These people are our enemies. We have occupied them with firmness, but correctly, and with politeness. We have even been lenient with them at times. Yet they still resist. They do not want us here. They hate us, Hans. Many good German soldiers in France and in Italy and Russia, too, have carried out equally distasteful orders. This is accepted military practice."

"I am well aware of that, Uncle Klaus. But

---

3. **Um Gottes Willen**\ʊm ˈgɔtəs ˈvĭ·lən\ God willing.

once again, I am me. They are other people. I am **Hans Joachim Wolfgang von und zu Kleinschrodt.** This disobedience of orders is the most difficult thing I ever did in all my life, believe me."

"Of course. Your gesture is a fine one. I respect it. I am a liberal. I can see your side as perhaps some of my colleagues would not. It does you great credit, Hans. But do you appreciate the consequences? You will most certainly be court-martialed for refusing to carry out a direct command. Nogent-Plage is in the front lines now. You cannot have an Army which obeys some orders and doesn't obey others. We obey all orders, the orders of our superiors, the orders of the *Führer.* If you go through with this, nothing I can do will save you. Nobody can save you. And you are one of the young Germans who should lead the Fatherland of tomorrow. Hans, my boy, we look to you to carry out our hopes for the future, to help govern Europe unified by the Greater Reich."

Suddenly his voice became weary. Now the general was no longer a trim, alert staff officer, but an aging, tired man who had carried the burden long years and was appealing to the next generation. The spark had left him. His eyes grew black with fatigue.

Feldwebel Hans moved his head as if in acquiescence. His eyes caught the clock on the wall. It was an hour and a half beyond the time set for the execution, and those six hostages still waited in the cellar.

"Let me say just one thing, my boy. In life, you will find that the things we long for beyond all others, the things we really desire most, are the things we cannot have. Life is that way, full of disappointments for us all. Believe me, nobody escapes this."

Again the young man seemed to acknowledge the words, to accept them, but he did not speak. Finally he looked at his godfather. "My uncle, I hardly know . . . I am not sure . . . . I am not conceited enough to be certain, but in my deep heart I feel it is wrong to kill these six men. It is worse than wrong; it is

evil. José Marti said once: 'He who witnesses a crime and does not protest, commits it himself.' "

Now the general was taken aback. "Who on earth is José Marti?"

"He was a Cuban."

"A Cuban!" A lesser breed, the scorn in the tone of the general plainly indicated.

"Yes, a Cuban revolutionary, a great patriot. He is a hero even today throughout South America. I believe he was killed by the Spaniards, I am not sure. Anyhow, he was telling us a truth, Uncle Klaus. By the way, have you ever read Rilke?"[4]

"No." The general felt slightly uncomfortable. He suddenly realized that his godson was in some ways older than himself. Truly this boy had matured. There was a new firmness about the mouth. It was not unimpressive. Here was a twenty-year-old standing up against the authority of the *Wehrmacht.* For a few seconds the general was caught up in admiration of his godson. Why, I was like him as a young man, he thought. I had faith. Whatever happened to me? Why did I never take a stand against Adolf Hitler? Or at least have the guts to resign my commission. Why did I sit back and accept it all as my friends and colleagues did, until we discovered he owned us entirely, and it was too late? Why?

Reluctantly he returned to the somber situation at hand. He pulled a paper from his pocket and took out glasses.

"Hans, my boy, this is a brutal thing we are doing. I agree. But war is brutal. Only by being brutal can we save the lives of the good German soldiers under your command. Sometimes, like yourself, I have doubts. Then I always come back to this, an activity report which I cut out and kept. It is Herr Himmler, then Gauleiter of Poland, speaking: 'If the local population from the Nazi point of view is hostile, racially inferior, or composed of criminal elements who attack German troops in the act of carrying out their duties, all those

---

4. **Rilke**\ˈrĭl·kə\ German poet, born in Prague.

suspected of supporting these terrorists are to be shot and the women and children deported.' Now we did this in the First World War to protect our troops; we did it here in France at Oradour, we did it at Lidice[5] in Czechoslovakia, and we did it many times in Poland. In Nogent-Plage I consider we have really been most lenient."

"But Uncle Klaus . . . ."

"Wait! Listen to me. It is past midafternoon. We may well have the invasion any minute, at any place along the coast. I speak to you, Hans, in the name of your father whom I so deeply loved. Think! Reflect! Obey your superiors."

"But don't you see. I cannot excuse myself by depositing my conscience with my superiors. Sometimes disobedience is not wrong. Believe me, Uncle Klaus, there are times when it is not wrong. To disobey when your whole being tells you to is obeying your conscience."

"Nonsense, my boy, nonsense! Suppose everyone did that? What kind of an Army would we have? Would we be here? Would we be on the Vistula? Would we hold everything from Narvik to Rome? What would happen to us if everyone acted as you are doing?"

"What everyone does is their concern. What I do is mine."

"Hans! For the last time, I beg you, no matter what you feel, no matter the rights and wrongs and your inner struggle which I respect, obey the orders of your superior officer. Were you not a von und zu Kleinschrodt, do you know what would happen to you?

"We would tie you to the rear of an army truck and invite you to run until you were so badly cut up you would collapse and give in. That is what we would do. You are betraying your family and your class."

The young man sat motionless behind the desk in misery. Although he loved his godfather and trusted him, although he was so close to him that he felt his presence deeply, he was still terribly alone. But he gave no sign of yielding. A tiny spiral of smoke rose from the ashtray as the cigarette burned out. There

was a sad, heavy silence. Neither man spoke.

Then the general rose, his chair scraping the floor. He pressed the buzzer on the desk. The orderly entered immediately, standing at attention before the general.

"Where are the six prisoners?"

"Downstairs, sir. In the cellar."

"Bring them up."

## 15

"Are you certain that your watch is at the hour?"

"No. But if it is wrong, the church clock is wrong also."

The only remaining watch belonged to the padre. There were twelve minutes left, then ten minutes, then five. At last the hour was up. The cellar door did not slam open with a crash. No helmeted soldiers came for them. What did it mean? The six looked at each other more easily.

"I feel sure the *Herr Oberst* has persuaded them to do nothing. He knows none of us played any part in the killing. I felt certain, I said so, remember? I said he would get us out . . . ."

Only the teacher was less sure. True, it was not like the Germans to be late, especially where death was concerned. Perhaps they had caught the murderer. If so, nobody would bother to tell them.

Half an hour passed. An hour. A little more than an hour. Above, telephones rang. Long discussions followed in German. After a while a car screamed to a stop on the Grande Rue outside. How strange, thought Monsieur Varin, that one's hearing becomes so acute at moments like this. He could hear men walking on the hard floor above and distinguish footsteps, the slow pacing of the *Feldwebel*, the quick, brisk steps of the orderlies. Clack-clack, clack-clack, clack - clack . . . clack - clack - clack - clack . . . . Then silence.

They waited, tired now, weary from fatigue

---

5. Lidice \ˈlĭ·dyĭ·tsē\ a village in Czechoslovakia destroyed by the Nazis in 1942 in reprisal for the assassination of a high Nazi official.

100

and anxiety and tension, drooping a little, all of them. They sat on the hard dirt floor, back against the stone wall, heads nodding.

At last the key turned in the lock and the cellar door flew open. At the top of the stairs stood a soldier with the usual submachine gun in his hands.

"*Hinaus!*"[1] He beckoned them up. Horrible sound, thought the teacher. A horrible sound and a horrible language. I always disliked it and I always will.

The hostages rose clumsily to their feet. They'll probably release us now. They have no evidence against us. The *Herr Oberst* knows we had nothing to do with the killing of the Hauptmann Seeler. Silently, meekly, they went up the stairs one by one. Just outside the cellar door stood the *Feldwebel* with a tall German officer, elegant in shiny boots, his chest covered with campaign ribbons and combat decorations. The hostages stared at them dully, drained now of all emotion.

The *Feldwebel* signaled a squad of soldiers and turned quickly away, unable to stand the look on those French faces, feeling their faith vanish as he gave the silent orders. The troops formed about them, half leading, half pushing the five men and the boy into the Grande Rue.

When the farmer Marquet, the first in line, was thrust outside, a wild shrieking arose. The prisoners stood for a few seconds blinking in the unaccustomed sunlight. All the women of Nogent-Plage, old and young, surrounded the steps of the Bloch villa in a semicircle. They were being held off by helmeted soldiers with bayonets attached to their rifles.

The women also were armed. They had brought brooms, shovels, pitchforks, and rakes. They brandished them before the soldiers, screaming as the hostages stepped hesitantly into the street.

"Marcel! Marcel! *Mon bien-aimé . . . .*"[2]

"Georges! Georges! *Suis ici . . . ici . . . .*"[3]

The wife of the fisherman tried to break through to her husband. A German soldier seized her and tossed her roughly to the pavement.

At this, like a kind of signal, the women attacked *en masse*. With their shovels and pitchforks, their rakes and brooms, they tried to break through the soldiers and reach the men and the boy. It was impossible for the *Feldwebel* standing on the steps of the Bloch villa to give the order to fire into the melee. To have done so would have meant the massacre of both townspeople and troops. For long seconds the street was in utter confusion.

Run! Run! Run! Run, you idiots, thought the *Feldwebel*, half hoping that the six would burst away in all directions. Surely a few would escape. But they were dazed so they did nothing. The *Feldwebel* blew a short blast on the whistle he had removed from his upper breast pocket, shouted crisp commands, and slowly the women were overpowered and forced back. Pitchforks were seized and tossed aside. The troops formed quickly about the prisoners and the column moved down the street. Only two, the Catholic and the Communist went with heads erect.

My God, thought the *Feldwebel*, I'm marching them to death. Just what I said I'd never do. How did I get here?

From the pleading women who stumbled along beside the column came sobs and screams. Impossible to think coherently, to act intelligently in that emotion. He glanced around.

The General Froelicher was bringing up the rear, there to see the sentence was carried out. He gave no orders, although the soldiers needed no orders. They had done it many times in other, distant lands.

"Charles! Charles!" shrieked the wife of the *café* owner. "Charles! *Regarde-moi*."[4]

"*Ah, mon fils*,"[5] cried the teacher, seeing his wife with the boy at her side. Jean-Paul had the white football under his arm. He was

---

1. **Hinaus!**\hĭn ▲aus\ Out!
2. **Mon bien-aimé**\mō(n)▲byĕn-ā 'mā\ My best beloved.
3. **Suis ici . . . ici**\swē·ē ▲sē·ē ▲sē\ Here I am . . . here.
4. **Regarde-moi**\rə ▲gard 'mwa\ Look at me.
5. **mon fils**\'mō(n) ▲fēs\ my son.

sobbing bitterly, tears on his face. *"Adieu, Jean-Paul. Adieu. Et toi, chérie . . . ."*[6]

No man, no woman was shouting to the farmer Marquet. Nor, indeed, did he expect anyone to. But the moment he had come out on the steps of the Bloch villa, his eyes searched the Grande Rue anxiously. What had become of Sebastian? Only a mangy dog trotting along beside the weeping women was now visible. The farmer knew what had happened. The villagers had led Sebastian away. No meat had been available in Nogent-Plage for a long time. They would shoot Sebastian at once.

The soldiers marched in cadence, their boots striking the concrete with that harsh sound. Suddenly Jean-Paul Varin burst away from his mother's arm and rushed up to the *Feldwebel* at the head of the column.

"Jean-Paul!" cried Madame Varin. "Jean-Paul."

Now he was attacking the big German, hitting him with clenched fists, kicking at his legs, weeping and shouting.

Instantly his mother was beside him, dragging him back to the sidewalk. Kneeling down, she held him tightly to her. He buried his head in her shoulder.

Quickly the column reached the end of the Grande Rue—and the low wall with its machine guns. A raging tide of women surrounded the troops, held back only by their bayonets.

Each hostage was blindfolded. They knew no hope at last. All illusions were gone. A quiet descended so deep you could hear the half slap, half crunch of the waves on the pebbly beach below. And the sobs of Jean-Paul tearing his body as he clung to the arms of his mother.

René Le Gallec next to the teacher reached out, groping for the hand of the older man. His anguished voice was plainly audible. "Will it hurt, Monsieur the Professor, will it hurt?"

And the reply of the man, distinct above the weeping that now swept the circle of waiting women. *"Non, mon petit,* it won't hurt. You

won't feel it." Then the teacher threw back his head and shouted with all his strength.

*"Vive La France."*[7]

The *Feldwebel* could stand it no longer. Then from behind came the voice of his godfather, composed, clear, crisp. *"Schiessen!"*[8]

*"Vive La . . . ."*

The rifles sounded in unison. They made a queer echo in the fog now approaching from the sea. Startled, the thin dog raced down the road, past the six crumpled figures on the sea wall, toward St.-Valéry in the distance.

---

### DISCUSSION FOR UNDERSTANDING

**1.** How do the following react to the killing of the *Hauptmann?* the villagers; the soldiers; the *Feldwebel;* the *Major* at division headquarters?

**2.** How are the hostages selected? How long does the *Feldwebel* have to find the assassin?

**3.** Why is the German command so set on this sudden, swift judgment?

**4.** What is Feldwebel Hans' dilemma?

**5.** What happens to the Underground's rescue attempt?

**6.** How do the hostages react to their imprisonment?

**7.** Why do the hostages not break and make a run for it when the women attack?

**8.** What is the effect of the General's brief encounter with the *Feldwebel?*

---

6. **Adieu. Et toi, chérie**\a ᴬdyə·ā ᴬtwa·shā ᐟrē\ Goodbye. And you too, dear.
7. **Vive La France**\ᴬvēv·la ᴬfra(n)s\ Long live France.
8. **Schiessen!**\ᴬshē-sən\ Fire!

# Part II

## Judgment at Rouen
## 1948

For most Americans, World War II did not begin until December 7, 1941, at Pearl Harbor. For the French it really began in early May, 1940, with the invasion of France, and the fighting was over in six weeks—almost as soon as it started. Then followed more than four years of occupation by a foreign army, of living under enemy rule.

After the end of the war came trials of various war criminals. Especially remembered are those at Nuremberg, which sentenced to death the most notorious of the Nazi leaders who had not emulated Hitler by taking their own lives: Frank, Frick, Streicher, von Ribbentrop, and others. Here for the first time was established the principal that made not states but individuals answerable to law for acts committed in war.

Less celebrated than the trials at Nuremberg were smaller trials in various lands where the people had suffered at the hands of Gestapo men, Storm Troopers, and even some German army officers. One of them, perhaps the most discussed all over France, was the trial of the Baron Hans Joachim Wolfgang von und zu Kleinschrodt.

It was held in Rouen, the city where Joan of Arc was burned to death by English troops in 1431. In 1499 a building was begun to house the Parliament of Normandy. Later it was turned over to the Law Courts and became the Palais de Justice.[1] Here, several years after the war, the baron was brought to justice for the shooting of six innocent French civilians on the afternoon of June 5, 1944, only hours before Nogent-Plage was stormed under cover of the guns of the British fleet and the *Feldwebel* with almost a hundred of his soldiers was taken prisoner by Canadian troops.

When his case was called he was offered either French or German counsel or, if he so desired, both. He asked for neither. His defense was that he had not shot the hostages or given the order to do so. The order was given by a superior officer, the General Klaus Froelicher, who had been in Nogent-Plage at the time.

Obviously the court found this hard to accept. The General Froelicher had later been killed leading an encircled division at the Battle of St.-Lô. Germans, everyone knew, were not in the habit of disobeying commands, and it was established that Headquarters had commanded the Feldwebel von Kleinschrodt to have the six hostages shot. Moreover, his signature was at the bottom of the proclamation issued to the townspeople after the execution.

The trial attracted attention in all of Europe because the defendant was a prominent athlete, celebrated for his football exploits. The proceedings were short and passionate. Witnesses, mostly inhabitants of Nogent-Plage, including several widows of the men who had been killed, testified against him. Their quiet bitterness was impressive. It was shown that a Hauptmann Seeler commanding the garrison at Nogent-Plage had been shot to death in the street on June 5, 1944, the day before the invasion of Normandy. The baron, then an ordinary *Feldwebel*, or noncommissioned officer, assumed command and was ordered to seize six hostages and confine them. This he did. Unless the murderer was discovered, he was to shoot the six within the hour.

Was there a superior officer present at the execution? One had come to town, yes. Madame Dupont and others had seen him arrive at the Bloch villa in a big Mercedes. But was he actually present when the six hostages were shot? Nobody was sure. After all, there had been all that swirling, screaming confusion when the women had attacked the German troops with pitchforks and rakes. And later, during the execution itself, all eyes had

---

1. **Palais de Justice**\pă ˈlä·də·zhūs ˈtēs\ Hall of Justice.

been on the condemned six. So if he was there, nobody could recall seeing him. And anyway it was the *Feldwebel,* at the head of the column, who had marched the men down with the firing squad, and presumably he had given the order for their death.

Because of the fame of the accused, public interest in the trial was great. Foreign as well as French journalists were present. One American correspondent, perhaps more imaginative than his colleagues, sent on to New York a vivid description of the baron as the Butcher of Nogent-Plage. The title stuck. So that was how all the witnesses and spectators in the high-vaulted fifteenth-century courtroom of the Palais de Justice at Rouen came to think of him.

A *hussier,* or bailiff, in knee breeches, stood up with a document in his hands. He read rapidly.

"Whereasontheafternoonof June fifth nineteenhundredandfortyfourtheaforesaid defendantcausedtodieatthehandsofafiring squadthefollowinginnocentFrenchcivilians RenéLeGallecGeorgesVarinCharlesLavigne LouisMarquetMarcelDeschampsandthePère ClementthereforeyouHansJoachimWolfgang vonundzuKleinschrodthavebeenconvictedof themurderoftheabovenamedsixFrenchmen. Thedefendantwillcomeforwardtobe sentenced."

The spectators half rose to watch the black-haired man stand and, with shoulders squared, step into the box. He was in civilian clothes, wearing a sports jacket with leather patches on the elbows that told of happier times. It fitted his muscular frame tightly because of its age, but still it became him. The witnesses, especially those women in black wearing black veils, watched with icy anger. Nothing could bring back their men.

The bearded judge with the little red-and-white cap upon his brow leaned forward.

"Has the defendant anything to say?"

The courtroom was quiet. Since the baron had hardly spoken in his defense except to deny his guilt, it hardly seemed likely that he would talk now. But after a moment he nodded.

Arms folded, he said, *"Hauptrichter,*[2] I have only this to say. I am not guilty of the charges. I did not pronounce the order to have the six hostages shot. In fact, I disobeyed that order. Had Germany won the war, I should have been court-martialed by my own countrymen and faced a firing squad myself."

A murmur ran through the courtroom. The bearded judge gavelled sharply for silence. The defendant resumed.

"No, I did not kill the hostages. I did not kill them because the order to do so offended my conscience. And when conscience and the state conflict, the conscience of a man must take precedence.

"But if I did not obey this order, I perhaps obeyed others I should not have obeyed. As my chiefs were wrong to obey the orders of a madman. We were all guilty, *nous étions tous des assassins.*[3] Hence we must pay the price. I am ready. But first, I wish to say this. Someday you French and"—here he looked at the row of correspondents—"you Americans, even you Americans who were victorious and therefore think such a thing is impossible, someday you may also murder, torture, drop bombs, and kill innocent people in the name of some cause or in the belief that you are somehow defending your country while fighting in a foreign land, as we did."

Once again the gavel sounded. The judge said, "The defendant will now be sentenced. Hans Joachim Wolfgang von und zu Kleinschrodt, acting for the Court of Cassation, I sentence you to ten years at hard labor. Sentence to begin immediately.

"The case is now ended. The court is dismissed."

---

2. **Hauptrichter**\ˈhaupt·rĭhk·tər\ Judge.
3. **nous étions tous des assassins**\'nü·zā 'tyō(n) ˈtü·dä·za·sa ˈsä(n)\ we were all murderers.

# Part III
## Soldier from the Wars Returning
### June, 1964

### 1

Germany came to a full stop that day. France also ground to a standstill. So did Scandinavia, the Low Countries, and lands far more distant from the ancient city of Rouen, where the contest was to be held.

Saturday afternoon is a busy time in Europe. Not that day. Factories everywhere shut long before the kickoff. Stores, shops, offices closed. Theaters emptied. Traffic subsided. Each metropolis suspended its normal activities.

The only crowded places were bars, *cafés, bistros, bierstubes, trattorie.*[1] People poured into them to watch the game on television. Twelve countries had requested the match live for their national networks. All Europe was aroused.

Why this excitement over a game of football? First, because it was more than a game. This contest pitted the Stade Rouennais, champions of France, against Bayern-Munich, champions of Germany. Hence it was a French-German contest, the first time since the end of the war that a team from across the Rhine was to play in a country which had suffered more than four years of occupation, deportation, and even starvation.

Everyone who knew football realized there would be a twelfth man on the field for France: the French crowd in the stands.

But chiefly the match was important because of two outstanding players. Who in all France could forget that the greatest of German goalkeepers was the man who had shot French hostages during the war and been tried in the very city of Rouen? And if the Munich team was led and inspired by its veteran captain and goalkeeper, the French also had their star. He was a young, nervous, magnificent forward named Jean-Paul Varin.

Everywhere in France he was called the *"comingman français."*

In cities, towns, and villages throughout the land, thousands of boys addressed a football the way Jean-Paul did. Young men of every age tried to run like him, shoot like him, pass like him. He was far better known than any politician or movie star. When you saw men with their heads together in a *café* or a train, they were not necessarily talking about business or politics. More likely they were discussing Jean-Paul Varin.

Now he would come up against the great German veteran. After the Feldwebel von Kleinschrodt had gotten out of prison, serving six years of his ten-year term, he had felt lost. His brother had been killed in action in the last week of the war. Many friends were also gone. Some were still in Russian prisoner-of-war camps. His mother was dead. His family vanished. The great estate on the Baltic was in ruins, devastated by the Russians, then occupied by the British. Finally one night the main house and other buildings caught fire and burned to the ground.

Where could he go? What could he do? He did the thing that came naturally, the thing he liked best of all—he turned to football. It was a poorish living, coaching junior teams in and around Hamburg. For several years he practiced continually, running to get his legs back. At first it was difficult for him to keep up with his boys when refereeing one of their matches. Gradually his legs returned. So did his form. Often he played goal. As goalie he could see the entire field, watch all the boys in action, coach them as they ran and passed. With a whistle around his neck he would blow twice to stop play and race out to correct their mistakes.

The boys learned. They liked the challenge of the man in the goal before them. They improved. Before long his teams began to win. They were noticed, and he became known as

---

1. English, French, German, and Italian words for bars and eating places.

the animator[2] of football among the youth of Germany.

After several years in which he kept attracting attention, the manager of Werder of Berlin had the idea of asking him to try out for the team. He did, playing superbly. As a goalkeeper his age—he was then thirty-eight—mattered less. True, he had slowed down, but in goal he was magnificent. He knew all the techniques of the attacker. His reflexes were still keen, his coordination perfect, and he could outlast anybody on the field. When he stepped in for Werder-Berlin the team won nineteen straight games.

Next he transferred to Bayern-Munich and helped them win a title with his superb play in goal. He soon became mentor and team leader. Within a few years he had twelve caps—that is, he had played twelve times for his native land in international competition. Once he traveled to London, where his defensive play won a game against West Ham, the English champions. By this time he was God the father of German sport.

Now, with his team, he was returning for the first time to France. The small stadium at Rouen was, of course, sold out. It normally held fewer than 20,000 people, and although 10,000 extra wooden seats had been added, hordes had to be turned away. A makeshift press box had been constructed for the dozens of sportswriters and radio and television reporters. They came from as far away as Oslo in the north and Rome in the south. Suddenly this sleepy city on the Seine had become the sporting capital of the entire continent. Dozens of commentators speaking every language in Europe appeared, all concentrating on that afternoon of football.

So wherever you happened to be that day you heard their rapid-fire commentary—across the street, from the *café* on the corner, from every open window and every open door.

In France and Germany middle-aged men stared at television screens, dreaming dreams of their youth. Young men and boys saw themselves on other fields for other teams: Rotweiss of Essen, Real of Madrid, Benficia of Lisbon. No other single event in the history of sport had ever before united so many millions in so many disparate lands.

Yet who could forget one salient fact? Certainly nobody present at the game, no one watching in France, was unaware that the father of young Jean-Paul Varin had been murdered by the Feldwebel von Kleinschrodt in a small Normandy village twenty years ago. Everyone knew that as a boy of seven or eight he had witnessed the killing of his father. There it was. There it remained in the hearts and minds of French men and women. Try as they would, and many honestly did try, they could not expunge the bitter memories of that June day. The story of the shooting had been brought out in the trial. It had burned into them all. You might try to thrust it aside, you might say it was ancient history, an incident of two decades ago, best forgotten. You might make an effort to ignore it.

The fact, however, was that the greatest goalkeeper in the history of German football was the hated symbol of French defeat. He was the Butcher of Nogent-Plage.

## 2

The German team arrived several days prior to the game and put up at a small hotel on the Seine nearly six miles from Rouen. Each morning before practice they went for a five-mile walk across country.

"Stamina, that's what football is all about," the baron said to them. "The team that is the freshest in the last five minutes usually wins. We took the league because we outlasted better teams. Look at me. I'm over forty, but I believe I could outlast some of you young chaps because I've still got my legs. You fellows with your Porsches and Karmann Ghias will lose the use of your legs someday."

They realized he was right. Had they not seen him run in a practice match when occa-

---

2. **animator,** promoter.

sionally he came forward on the field to coach the offense?

The afternoon before the day of the game he took each man out alone for a stroll in the countryside, discussing the tactics to be used, the makeup of the French team, how they should handle their adversaries, and especially what to do about Varin.

"We should allow Varin and the French to do the running. Let them play their game and hold them. Nothing is more discouraging than to play your best and not score. Then every few minutes you boys turn it on. When the opportunity arises, go. You can score goals, Sepp. Turn it on, suddenly, unexpectedly. These boys are dangerous here in Rouen before their own crowd, but they can be beaten."

Never did he mention his notoriety as the Butcher of Nogent-Plage, which would make the match so bitterly fought. He did not need to. His teammates were as aware of it as he was.

Early that evening, before dinner, a press conference was arranged in the dining room of the hotel. Television cameras pointed directly at the baron. On a table before him a dozen microphones had been placed to pick up his words. The journalists and commentators kept after him from every corner of the room, talking in four or five languages, some needling, others more understanding and less insistent. He replied evenly to each man, pausing a few seconds to think before responding, never permitting himself to be ruffled by the most hostile remarks. Even when a blond Dane asked whether he was pleased to be back in France again.

Those queries he did not care to answer he turned aside tactfully, discussing only matters pertinent to the game. His adroitness at handling this rather unfriendly group of newsmen made you appreciate his qualities. You could understand why he had been chosen to assume responsibility and lead his team into action. How, he was asked, would Germany defend against the marvelous French offense, which nobody to date had stopped?

He thought a moment and then replied slowly, "France is a nation of individualists. You would expect the French players to be a great team, of course they are. To win in their league they had to be. I saw them play last year at Dusseldorf—they are magnificent attackers, finely trained, skillful, never letting up. But, nevertheless, though they are a team of champions, they are also and primarily a team of individualists. By that I mean they sometimes ask a man to do it on his own. Now our tactics are somewhat different."

As he spoke, the room grew unnaturally quiet. Here was a football captain talking frankly, freely, and yet modestly about his opponents and the tactics he would use against them the following afternoon. His cool confidence was contagious. Reporters bent forward to catch every word. All present knew of whom he was thinking: Jean-Paul Varin, the greatest centre forward ever produced in France.

Then a small dark Italian spoke. His German was excellent, his tone unpleasant. "Do you fear Varin?"

A collective sigh, a sort of "aaahhh" rose. One reporter stopped midway in the act of lighting a cigarette. Another, who had stood up to rush away and file copy to meet an early deadline, quietly sat down again.

Surely this was too much. This was pushing him too far. This was unfair. The tall figure behind the table did not stir. But watching closely, you could see his right hand tighten around the stem of a microphone.

The newsmen waited for his answer. Would he explode in anger? Would he suggest that he had been tried, convicted, and imprisoned by the French for a crime he had not committed. Or would he ignore the question entirely?

For endless seconds he stood motionless. Then his mouth opened and in flawless Italian he replied. "We Germans greatly respect the French team and all their players. We do not fear anyone."

# 3

The football played abroad is a sport in which there is less violence than the football played in the United States. Names are taken by the referee, players are cautioned, but only occasionally is a man sent off the field for deliberate roughness. Since there is no substitution in European football, the loss of a player is a severe penalty because then a team must play with only ten men against eleven. To lose a goalkeeper or an important forward can be disastrous.

But if there is usually no great amount of violence on the field in games between top-class teams, violence persists in the stands. In Spain and Italy especially, the fans go crazy, and football riots are front-page news everywhere.

Recently a French sporting newspaper published an advertisement which read: "Monsieur Collet, the referee of the football match last Sunday between the Racing Club de Calais and the Stade Roubaisienne, wishes to thank the members of the Calais team for saving his life after the match." A joke? No, it happened. Football abroad is a serious affair. Many teams keep a car under the stadium during their games. The engine is running and a chauffeur sits at the wheel to rush the referee to safety if the home team loses.

Sometimes riots get out of hand. Fixtures in the stands are uprooted, rocks, bricks, and even seats have been torn loose and hurled onto the field. Players have been shot at during a contest. In the coalfields of Yorkshire in the North of England, they throw what is called a Barnsley snowball. This is a lump of coal covered with snow and hurled at an offending referee.

The day of the game at Rouen, a great broad river of people flowed through the turnstiles of the stadium. Young people, old people, poor people, rich people, people of all kinds and classes. Men in expensive Alpine hats, men in cloth caps and work clothes. Thousands of women and girls were there, for the game had breached the sex barrier be-cause of the attraction of the young football genius on the French side. Speculators were getting fifty dollars a ticket outside, and selling all they could obtain.

Many Germans carried huge banners of greeting from across the Rhine. *München Grüsst Frankreich. Berlin Grüsst Frankreich. Bremen Grüsst Frankreich.*[1]

Then outside the stadium came an explosion. A car had caught fire. Two men leaped from it and were lost in the crowd. Successive blasts rocked the car as one bunch of firecrackers after another went off. The fire was put out by the Rouen Fire Department—luckily on hand and waiting—and policemen, who then searched the parked vehicles. Many were filled with fireworks and other explosives, guns, even small cannon to celebrate the victory or perhaps menace the winners. These cars were seized and put under guard.

Inside, the chanting, cheering, and sometimes jeering crowd roared at everything. Hawkers passed through the stands selling programs, beer, and souvenirs, from T-shirts to ties and blazers with France or Germany embroidered on the pockets. At last the German team trotted single file onto the field. Thousands of horns blew triumphantly, thousands of Germans waved red-black-and-gold banners with drill-hall precision, left-right, left-right, left-right, all in unison.

"Hoi, hoi, hoi," they shouted. This was their team, the one that had shut out Torpedo Moscow for the first time. The noise from the stands beat down on the field like heavy surf pounding on sand or shale.

The Germans wore blue shorts and white jerseys. Then the French appeared in dark red jerseys and white shorts. Immediately thousands of tricolored flags sprang up on the opposite side, fluttering in a kind of irreverent pattern of color in the afternoon sunshine. All over the stands strangers addressed each other.

"There! That's Jules Garnier, Number four."

"That's Bonnet . . . ."

---

1. Munich (Berlin, Bremen) greets France.

"That's Laffont, six. With the bandage around his left knee. He was hurt against Lille, you know. They said he might not play."

"Which is Varin?"

"Varin! You've never seen Varin! He's Number two. That's him, the tall boy who looks like an angel."

"Ah, so that's Varin. We only saw him once on television. We're from Marseille."

"We've come all the way from Bordeaux. Ah, there's Rudy now."

The referee, in blue shorts, high blue stockings and a blue jersey, appeared below. He was Rudolph Stampfli, a former fullback for Zurich and once a Swiss international who spoke four languages. He was known as the best referee in all Europe, firm, decisive, noted for his quick decisions, and possessing a vast knowledge of the game.

The two captains conferred with him, the tall baron twitching the brim of his gray cap, that lucky cap he had saved since before the war and wore only in an international match. Garnier, the captain of France and the massive outside right who had competed fifteen times for his country, shook the hands of the Munich goalkeeper.

On the sidelines the two teams waited. The tension built up and up. The players longed for the game to start. After the opening rush downfield they would forget everything—the crowds, the shouts, the whistles—everything save that round balloon at their feet.

It'll be all right, each man told himself. I'll be fine as soon as play begins.

## 4

But it did not start. The band played "The Watch on the Rhine," the German national anthem. Then the "Marseillaise." Still the game did not start. Time passed. Seconds were minutes, minutes seemed as long as a day. The athletes did what athletes the world over do in such circumstances. They leaped high in the air, squatted and squatted again. They kicked their feet out and up. They bent over, twisting at the waist, to touch the ground on either side. Some walked around nervously, unable to stand still.

Nothing happened. From above, the French stands whistled and shouted. The delay was torture for everyone. The captains standing beside the stocky referee straightened up. But the ball stayed under the arm of Rudy Stampfli. The crowd all over now yelled for action.

"*Commencez!*"[1]

"*Anfangen!*"[2]

"Why don't they begin?"

"*Commencez! Commencez! COMMENCEZ!*"

It appeared that the jam at the entrance gates had been so great, the confusion in the stands so widespread, that many spectators had not yet found their seats and were blocking the aisles. Hence the kickoff was delayed. The wait seemed forever.

The referee looked at his watch. Six, seven minutes had passed. Eight. Nine. Ten.

His arm went up. He snapped his out-pointed hand toward the small circle at midfield. The whole stadium roared as the teams rushed out, eager for action. One Frenchman crossed himself as he stood poised for action, not for victory, no, but to acquit himself well that day.

Suddenly the whistle sounded. The start proved that this was no match for weak hearts. France kicked off and pushed the ball gently to Bonnet, a wing, who kicked it far ahead to the right, a pass beautifully spotted. Varin set off at full speed as though the ball were already there. Sepp Obermeyer, Uncle Sepp, the German veteran who had been assigned to mark Varin, was caught flat-footed by that amazing and effortless burst of speed. You had to play against the boy to appreciate him.

Here it was, the very first minute of the game and the famous French attack built around their young star centre forward, around ball control, around pace and more pace was taking over.

---

1. **Commencez!**\kɔ·ma(n) 'sā\ Begin! (French).
2. **Anfangen!**\ˈan·fang·gĕn\ Begin! (German).

"VarIN . . . Var . . . IN . . . Var . . . IN . . . Var . . . IN . . . ."

The cheers rose, burst into an unearthly roar as the tall Number 2, taking the ball back on the pass, snaked his way through the German defense, stopped short, twisted, curled the ball around his feet, raced ahead, evading the defensive backs. A dart, a dash, a stop, a pivot, a turn, a twist, and he was nearing the goal.

"*Regardez!* Look at that! *Allez, Jean-Paul, Allez!*[3] *ALLEZ FRANCEFRANCEFRANCE* . . . ."

In millions of homes all over the nation millions of men and women were screaming the same refrain. "*Allez! Allez,* Jean-Paul . . . ."

The crowd on the French side of the stadium went wild. They were in a frenzy as that red-shirted Number 2 bore down on the goal.

The huge knot of photographers behind the left goalpost steadied themselves, feet wide apart, straining forward, cameras at their eyes. Before the goal the tall German veteran waited coolly. He tugged at his cap, watching the French boy pass the ball to a teammate and receive it back. The baron was wise and knowledgeable. Better than anyone he knew the importance of his slightest move. He had to guess and guess correctly. Waiting just long enough, he raced out, bent low, and scooped the ball away as the Frenchman slammed into him and went flying over his shoulder to land with a crash on the turf. The shock of their collision could be heard all over the field.

The German was older, more solid, more inured to blows of this sort. Besides, anticipating the shock he had braced for the boy's onrush. Yet even he staggered from the impact before he could rise, straighten out, and kick the ball far down the field. The French player who had tumbled as though shot from the sky lay unconscious upon the turf. The whistle blew loudly.

For a moment there was silence in the stadium, a silence more violent than the roaring that had preceded it. Then a screaming chant

---

3. **Allez!**\a 'lā\ Come on! Go! (French).

rose from the French side. What had been in the back of their minds all afternoon now came out in a torrent of sound. It wasn't that the French—both present in the stadium and elsewhere watching—lived in the past. But that the past lived in them.

"Le Boucher! Le Boucher! Le Boucher!"[4]

## ◊ 5

The French stood and chanted. Now a shrill, derogatory whistling could be heard, too, mixed with boos. A brick arched up from the crowd and landed on the field. Another entangled itself in the nets of the goal, then another and another. Immediately armed policemen with riot guns appeared. They fanned out, facing the stands and scanning them from the edge of the field. They were tough cops in boots and helmets, ready to toss out anyone who disturbed play.

No more bricks were hurled, but the chanting and whistling continued. "Le Boucher! Le Boucher!"

Nothing more fell onto the field, but the shouting and whistling continued.

Players frequently know nothing and hear nothing the moment play begins. Often the baron had to be told which opponents had scored a goal on him. But this time it was hard for him not to recognize the name they were calling him. Every Frenchman and Frenchwoman in the stadium or watching on TV was sure that the baron had injured Varin on purpose.

*"Ah, quel sale type, quel salot!"*[1]

But then, everyone agreed, what would you expect? Those Germans just have to win at any cost, at any cost.

The long legs of the boy stretched out on the ground stirred ever so slightly, the first sign of returning consciousness. The baron walked over to see how he was, but the French players who had formed a circle around Jean-Paul, refused to step aside for him. Now the boy sat up, his head in his hands. Yves Robin, the French trainer, and

Garnier bent over him, slopping water on his face. They helped him up and he walked a few steps, plainly dizzy. There was a cut on the right side of his forehead. Blood ran down his cheek.

The crowd noticed it immediately. "Aaaahhh . . ." they cried. But what would you expect from the Butcher of Nogent-Plage?

The trainer gave the boy something from a bottle to drink and wound a bandage around his head. Jean-Paul raised his hands in protest, but the trainer, paying no attention, taped the bandage securely.

The baron leaned against a goalpost. He had in his time survived many on-field collisions, but this one had shaken him up, too. His body ached. He bent over, panting, then straightened up. The French stands jeered. However, he went to Varin and patted his shoulder. Jean-Paul nodded. He was all right.

His fans shrieked for a penalty kick. Even the captain of the French team stood protesting. But the referee shook his head. Varin jogged up and down to cheers from the stands. Finally he indicated that he was ready.

The referee placed the ball near midfield, and the game got under way again. For a while the play was negative, nervous, and uncertain. Because of the injury to their star the French momentarily lost their poise. The Germans at once seized their chance. Quick, direct, with passes short and sure, their game well coordinated and neat, they broke dangerously into French territory. Schroeder, their centre forward, shook loose, and after a series of passes had a great opportunity to the left of the goal, and young Helmut Herberger, the punch of the German team, crossed over, reached the ball, and drove it with all the force of his instep toward the goalie. Bosquier, the Frenchman, made a magnificent save at point-blank range. The ball, however, spun from his grasp.

---

4. **Le Boucher!**\lə·bū 'shā\ The Butcher.

---

1. Oh, what a rotten guy!

Big Schwartz, following up, kicked it again. Again Bosquier saved, diving at the ball just in time. The French stands were ecstatic.

Two great teams, two superb goalies.

As play progressed, Varin slowly regained his top form, and as he did the French side came to life, now attacking without mercy, using long, articulated passes. So perfect was their position play that a teammate was invariably reaching the ball on those passes at the exact moment. Their surge downfield was a joy to watch.

Even the Germans were impressed. So were the sportscasters. High on top of the stands a wooden platform had been constructed over supporting uprights—a precarious perch for cameramen and commentators. The little Italian television man from Milan who had been so rough with the baron at the press conference was speaking what seemed a thousand words a minute into his microphone. As Varin, taking and passing the balloon, bore down on the German goal, he screamed, "Ah, il furia francese . . . ."[2]

The French attack, especially that of Varin and the wingbacks, was built on speed and more speed and tinged with that Frenchiness of the French, containing all their national characteristics—dash, drive, cerebration. Whereas the Germans felt that ball control was vital at all times, the French took risks and brought them off. When the Germans obtained the balloon, they kept it until it could safely be passed to a teammate. Their passes were short, accurate. Yet, watching, one felt that there was power in their game, that they were a team that could explode at any time.

Of the two, France was seductive, artful; Germany stronger and more brutal. Never again did Obermeyer allow Varin to get loose. He kept continually at the heels of the French star, for he also was fast. And although France always seemed to be attacking, forever banging away at the German goal, the Germans' defense was so tight that after that first sortie it looked as if the home team was never going to score. The crowd watched, cheered, groaned as two national temperaments, two styles of play, unfolded below them. Millions all over Europe sat transfixed by their TV sets.

His youthful, dynamic energy fully regained, Varin dominated the field, perhaps even more noticeably because of the white bandage around his head, a kind of helmet of Navarre. If you don't learn football by the time you are ten years old, you never will. Jean-Paul Varin, the French centre forward, had learned it truly and well as a boy from the Père Clement, once an international competitor for France. He had learned it also by listening to and playing with the *Herr Oberst* or, as he called him, the Feldwebel Hans, now calmly awaiting his onslaught in the German goal.

## 6

Nobody can play truly inspired football in an empty arena. It was the roaring mass of the crowd that brought out the greatness of the teams and their stars. There were twenty-two players on the field, but the concentration of the stands was on two: the baron and Jean-Paul.

The struggle became a duel not between France and Germany, but between the veteran and the youngster. Often when the German had blocked a sudden thrust or caught a stinging kick, he would tease Varin by holding out the ball, then dodging a few steps, bouncing it a few times in the penalty box as he ran forward. Then would come a sly roll-out to a forward at one side or that great zooming kick, high, far back into French territory.

Thousands of local fans who had no tickets, but had come to the stadium hoping to pick up one at the last minute, stood patiently outside in the sunshine, willing merely to listen to the noise from within.

They could tell with exactitude whenever Jean-Paul was off and running by that surge of sound from the French stands, that rising roar: "*Allez*, Jean-Paul! *Allez! Allez! Allez!*"

---

2. Ah, the avenging Frenchman (Italian).

It would reach a frenzied pitch, a crescendo, as the boy neared the German goal, then subside into a vast, collective groan as the baron made another acrobatic catch, another desperate save, and the German stands cheered.

The two defenses were equally effective, but the French side had a diversity that their opponents lacked. They kept the home crowd up by the fluidity of their play. On the attack they pressed forward constantly, always assaulting the enemy goal. On the defense they contracted smoothly. The amazing accuracy of their passing was such that each man seemed to have eyes in the back of his head. They could send and receive a ground pass at full speed. Suddenly, without warning, would come that quick cross to a teammate, perhaps with his back to the German goal, who instantly whirled and shot.

But if the French were the more thrustful, tearing holes in the German defense at thirty yards out, still they could not score. That big panther in the goal, leaping from side to side, blocked everything.

He deftly deflected a stray shot over the crossbar, coolly punched another ball around the corner post, then dived to prevent a score on a low kick from Bonnet, the French winger. The Germans were technically superb. They were the epitome of controlled power. Yet over all was the baron, completely in command, vigilant, watching each man, calling crisply to his teammates as the play fluctuated up and down. He was the soul of the German side, the great tactician, the Rommel of football.

A truly magnificent player, even the French spectators agreed. But for him France would have scored and scored again as the forwards pressed the attack. In the sense that they were in German territory most of the time, the French were winning. They held the upper hand. But what good is it to dominate a game if you cannot score?

With a top-notch goalkeeper, even second-rate teams find it easy to defend—if, that is, they do nothing else. But the tactics of the Germans were by no means solely defensive. Strong, intelligent, they waited until the precise moment to strike—then struck hard. Their team had no offensive genius like Varin. But they had perfect ball control with short, accurate passes, unspectacular but impossible to intercept. It was football that demanded much of a man: patience, skill, and fitness. Especially fitness.

On the home team was that great centre forward of France, that boy with the white bandage around his head. Centre forward is one of the most important positions on a team. Rarely is it given to a youngster. But Jean-Paul Varin had an old football head on his young shoulders. He could move either way, pass with either foot. His control was so perfect that he was always able to do the unexpected: kick to the goal the instant an opportunity presented itself or pass to an unmarked teammate. Moreover, he had a peculiar trick of moving the ball up to an adversary, showing it to him, and then slipping away, almost magically, with the balloon still at his feet. There was an electric quality about his moves that communicated to his teammates and the crowd alike.

He was indeed *"guele d'ange,"* angel face, as the French called him.

There was a studied elegance, a kind of joy in his bearing on the field. Despite the injury he had suffered, he kept smiling. On the white bandage was a spreading reddish stain. He had a French fineness of feature that was seductive. Tall, frank, outrageously spoiled by nature, he was the boy that everyone wanted for a brother, that every woman would have liked for a husband or a son.

His character, too, made itself felt. You were attracted to him despite yourself. If you had never seen him play, you came to the field determined not to enthuse over Varin. In five minutes you were on your feet, shouting like everyone else: *"Allez,* Jean-Paul! *Allez! Allez!"*

Even the Germans applauded his skills, his moves on the field so marvelously thought out in advance.

"*Ein fussballwunderkind,*"[1] they said to each other.

"*Ja, ja, ein fussballwunderkind . . . ja, ja . . . .*"

The interchanging forward line of France, whirling, twisting, shifting, moving in a pattern to the exact spot on the field, kept passing the ball from one teammate to another. Sepp Obermeyer, who had been so completely fooled in the opening sequences of the game, now stuck to Varin unerringly.

As one German in the stands remarked to a friend, "Sepp stays with that Frenchman so closely he'll end up in their dressing room at half time."

Varin's function was to set up the goal, to create the opening for others as well as score himself. Sometimes he was the decoy forward, quite as important as the man with the ball. Then next time, with everyone expecting a pass, he would turn suddenly and strike himself. Often the Germans knew exactly what he was going to do—only they didn't know when.

On the field the referee blew his whistle for a German tripping and gave France a free kick from thirty yards out. His manner was firm and decisive. You could see he was a no-nonsense kind of referee.

The ball was beyond the penalty box. A wall of huge Germans stood before Garnier, the French captain, as he went back to kick. He tried hard to curve the ball around them and did so, but Borkowski, the big blond Silesian, knocked it away and the baron had no trouble reaching and holding it. That penalty could have been costly, he thought, as he rolled the balloon out to Otto Schoen, his winger at the left.

Play continued, chiefly about the German defensive zone. Suddenly the referee's whistle sounded again. It was half time. The game came to a halt. Neither side had scored. The players, shoulders hunched with fatigue and strain, bodies consumed by the fierce intensity of the struggle, slumped off to their dressing rooms.

The first forty-five minutes of the match had seemed to last forever. In another way, it seemed that only a few minutes ago they had all filed out onto the field, waiting for play to begin.

---

### DISCUSSION FOR UNDERSTANDING

**1.** How did von Kleinschrodt come to be the goalie on the championship Bayern-Munich football team?

**2.** How does the European game of football differ from the American version?

**3.** What indications are there that the situation at the game between the champions of Germany and France is tense—before the game? during play?

**4.** What is the difference in playing style between the French and German teams?

 **7**

Not much was said in the German dressing room between the halves. What was there to say? The players were too weary to talk. They sat on the benches, heads bowed, panting, speechless. Only the baron moved from one to the other, praising a stop made, a pass executed, a kick here, a thrust there, warning someone about a single careless moment of play. The men listened to their captain. Otto Schoen was the man who spoke up. The veteran winger raised his head. He saw the lines in the goalkeeper's face, recognized the tremendous responsibility that was on him. Rising, he put his arms around the baron.

"Hans, if you keeping playing like this, we can beat that team."

Time to resume play. They clattered across the wooden floor of the dressing room, down the long concrete corridor, and onto the field. Their appearance brought the German stands up. An ecstatic display of red-gold-and-black flags greeted them.

---

1. A football wonder child, superstar.

The second half began. The French pressure, sharp, incisive, continued. The baron's goalkeeping was still amazing. He was a cross between an acrobat and an octopus. Unerringly he sized up each play coming toward him, guessed where the ball was going to go even before it was kicked. His arms, his big hands, his long fingers seemed to attract every shot to his grasp. Now a hard one was knocked over the crossbar, now a cannonball drive at his ankles was cleanly stopped and held. Often the kick was going away from him, but he reached and saved them all.

In that saturated bombardment of the German goal it looked so easy. But that was his trademark, making those stops look easy.

Why, you said to yourself, watching from the stands, I could have held that one. I could have stopped that kick, held that ball. You forgot, unless you knew the game, his experience and that knack of anticipating each play. Above all you ignored his amazing reflexes, which contributed so much to his skill and to keeping Germany even with France as the second half moved along without a score.

Equally steady on the high ones just under the crossbar, the short, quick stabs from in close, or those long, hard kicks beyond the penalty box, he contained them all. The ball would come at him out of a melee of arms, legs, and feet, so hard it stung his hands. But he held it. Gradually the sportswriters, the television commentators in the makeshift press box, their field glasses to their eyes, began to realize the German goalie was extracting the poison from the French attack.

Still the waves of attackers in red jerseys bore down on the baron. Each time he held them off, cleared the goal, saved Germany. Each time the dagger of France was blunted. Once Robert Laffont, the French inside left, made a superb thrust. From a mix-up in the penalty box he cleared a kick low, hard to the corner. The French stands went wild for it seemed a sure score. Somehow the baron got across, stopped the balloon with outstretched hands, an impossible stab. It got

away from him and dribbled along the ground. Two French players were on the ball but he reached it first, quick as only the great player can be. Diving for it, he rolled over and over on the turf, the ball cradled in his stomach. Both sides cheered his great preventive football.

To make such a save is the mark of genius. A little while before the French were calling him a butcher. Now they applauded along with the exultant Germans. The French are like the rest of us. They wanted terribly to win that match. But, like the rest of us, they were not insensitive to talent when they saw it. What they were watching was football genius, and every French spectator knew it.

After a corner kick for France from which nothing resulted, Germany now moved to the attack alertly. France fell back, regrouped, ready, anxiously watching. For a moment the baron stood panting, weary, one arm outstretched against a goalpost. However, the swing of fortune was shortlived, the respite soon over. Following some infighting around the French goal, Varin stole the ball and was off, moving with those long, effortless strides across midfield and into enemy territory.

There it was, that quick, accurate flick to Bonnet, the burst of speed into open country ahead for the return. The young centre forward took a cross back, and the moment he stopped the ball made a sudden, unexpected flip to Carpentier, the inside right, just behind him. Again that roar rose: "France . . . France . . . France . . . ." Once more they threatened.

Carpentier charged in. Before the goal, Borkowski of Germany, one of the stoppers of the Munich defense, a great oak of a man, made a slashing slide tackle which jarred the ball loose. But in the full momentum of his drive the Frenchman was a truck with the brakes gone. What happened was partly, perhaps, resentment over the blow to Varin, but mostly explosive exasperation at the so-near-and-yet-so-far game that France had played all afternoon. Carpentier leaped into the air and collided with the baron.

When the French go in they go in hard. Away flew the gray cap the baron wore. He fell to the ground as the referee raced over, blowing his whistle and pointing to Carpentier.

First a hush. Then a half moan swept the German stands as they stared at their man stretched out on the ground. Without that goalie Germany would be helpless. Everyone knew it.

Each spectator seemed to have felt the shock of that collision. Along the German side of the stadium they watched anxiously. The unvoiced thought hung in the air: if he is finished, we're finished. We're through if the baron has to leave the game. Every eye focused upon the knot of men around the figure at the goal line. The baron writhed on the turf as the trainer bent over him. He twisted and turned. His knees came up slowly. You could see the agony on his face.

The men watched him solicitously. After a while they helped him up. He leaned over, straightened his body, staggered a little, shaken from his second blow of the afternoon. Cheers came from all over the stadium. He walked around unaided. The whole crowd burst into applause.

Once or twice he half stumbled as he took his place, jogging back and forth along the goal line. Then he washed his neck and face with cold water, toweled himself, picked up his cap, and went back into the goal. The German banners waved triumphantly.

This time the ball went to the far end with Germany getting a free kick. Otto Schoen stood ready. A free kick from close up is dangerous for the defense. Will it be a soft, lofted ball or a hard, swift kick? He kicked. The ball just cleared the crossbar above the goal. No score. A tremendous roar of joy exploded from French throats, an enormous groan from the German spectators.

Aching all over, holding on to one goalpost, the baron watched a play developing at the far end. He saw no crowd, heard nothing, felt nothing but the danger ahead. Every instant his eyes under the old gray cap were fixed on that white balloon moving toward him in a kind of inexorable pattern.

France was coming on the attack with Varin upon the ball. For a second he lost it in a welter of legs and feet at midfield. Then once again that graceful, moving athlete came up with the ball.

"Look out, Sepp! Watch that winger, Horst! Watch him! Watch him, WATCH HIM . . . ."

Now it's over to Varin . . . to Bonnet . . . stop him, Fritz, stop him . . . back to Varin . . . a cross to Garnier almost intercepted . . . no! Back to Varin, who is breaking through . . . .

The kick was low, hard, into the far corner of the goal. The baron jumped for it with all his great strength, his body parallel to the ground, touched the ball, missed it, and lay prone on the turf.

Pandemonium! Horns. Cheers. Red-white-and-blue flags aflame in the sunshine. Cheers. Shouts. Yells. France! France! France!

Jean-Paul turned and raced away, both arms high in the air. Skip-skip, leap-leap. He somersaulted on the grass in joy; as he came back he was surrounded by several teammates who hugged and kissed him. Others rushed up to embrace him. It was all his. After the shots missed, the kicks blocked, after those endless and hopeless assaults it was his own, his first goal in his first international match for France.

Can happiness be greater?

All the while the big German goalie lay flat on his stomach, pounding the turf in anguish with his bruised fists and knuckles. Helmut Herberger, the winger, young in years yet somehow old with insight and understanding, recognized the agony inside his captain. He raced over, knelt beside him, bent over and caressed the man's shoulders.

Finally the baron rose. The whistle of the referee sounded. Germany kicked off, a little push to the right. The game was practically over now, for only three minutes remained. The stadium was a cockpit of noise, nerves, passion. The thousands in the stands lived and died a hundred deaths. The delirious French shouted and screamed with joy. They even joined in as the baron coolly repulsed another thrust.

"Ah, let's admit it. He is a *brave type,* strong, stubborn. *Un maître,* a master. *Un vrai*[1] champion."

But up in the press box the old hands all said, "Watch out, France. The game isn't finished. Be careful. Any team that scores first and camps on a one-goal lead may find itself in trouble if it merely tries to defend."

## 8

France! France! France! France! A great, lusty, full-throated roar. The French felt victory ahead. It was over, done, almost through. Triumph was there for the taking.

Jules Garnier, the captain and winger, and every man on the French team knew, however, that the Germans were still dangerous. Perhaps they knew it even better than those experts shaking their heads from side to side in the press box. Because they had lived through many games won and lost in the final minutes. They had often felt the inconsequence of fate dealing them an unexpected blow or turning disaster into sudden victory.

Keep moving! Keep up the pressure, they urged each other. Whatever happens, don't let down now.

The soccer player needs the stamina of the long-distance runner, the reflexes of a boxer, and the concentration of a golfer. But it wasn't so easy after ninety minutes of attacking football. France had been setting the pace; now legs ached, feet were leaden. To run required an effort of will, to race down the field was torture. Every French forward had lost a little drive, a tiny part of his reflexes. But they did not give in or let up. Those red jerseys still pressed forward around the German goal.

As ever, the baron controlled the ball with that fluid beauty which was his alone. He seemed to wait until the last possible second before flinging his big frame at the white sphere. But he needed every inch of his height and every ounce of his power to reach those

kicks, those punches from the feet and heads of the French forwards. Now it was a shot diverted to one side, now a ball that ricocheted off his chest. The French gave him no respite. They realized to a man that another goal would put the game on ice. Yet they could not hammer through.

The contest was a football match no longer. It was war. It was nation against nation. It was those two eternal rivals, France and Germany. It was life and death in the afternoon. Play grew rougher as the seconds passed. Rough tactics begot rough tactics. Only one thing counted—victory before the final whistle blew.

"France! France! France!" chanted the French spectators in unison. Only a minute and a half to go now. The Germans, backs against the wall, still fought stubbornly and savagely. They could not match the consummate artistry of Jean-Paul Varin. They simply had no forward in his class. But they were still a team and team play counts. They remained solid players, unshaken by misfortune, refusing to accept defeat until the whistle blew.

A slow ball, a bobbler from thirty feet out, came bouncing irregularly toward the baron. He knew how often a mistimed shot can catch a goalie off balance. Carefully and deliberately he went down on one knee, watched the French forwards rushing toward him, then rose, stepped calmly aside, and booted the ball high in the air and far downfield.

There was a mix-up before the French goal. Bosquier cleared the ball, but it rolled over the line and Germany received a corner kick. Nobody scores anymore on corner kicks, and the French defense loomed high and powerful.

Schroeder's kick went up, came down. As it did, Otto Schoen, the German winger, crashed in like an American tackle blocking a punt. Short, square, Otto was the retriever, the uninspired but ever dependable man of the German team. He threw his compact frame into that wall of French defenders, squeezed through, and headed the ball at the goal.

---

1. **vrai**\vrā\ true.

A French back headed it away. A German headed it back in. A Frenchman leaped up, a German hit it with his forehead. Ping . . . ping . . . ping . . . ping . . . the ball never touched the ground.

Then Borkowski, the halfback, tall and powerful, leaped high in the air above everyone and caught it squarely on his blond, flat head. But the shot struck the crossbar, bounced back, bobbled dangerously along the ground before the goal. Three men were on it, but Sepp Obermeyer, following it up like a cat, was first. With one quick blow of his foot he hammered it home. The score was tied.

Pandemonium shook the German stands, a kind of collective madness. Thousands of red-black-and-gold flags gyrated in the sunshine. Thousands of Bavarian hunting horns echoed in the air. Thousands of voices roared out his name.

"Sepp . . . Sepp . . . Sepp . . . ."

Yes, and Otto, too, who started it, the man you never noticed on the field, the player you always took for granted, Otto, steady, unspectacular, always taking the weight off his teammates by his tackles and pass interceptions. Sepp had scored the goal, but it had been invented by Otto.

Sepp. Otto. The Germans in the stands cheered them, jumped up and down in jubilation, and their teammates embraced the two men.

The French stood silent. Less than a minute left in the final half. Now for the first time France felt the pressure. Big Garnier leaned over in exhaustion, utterly spent, shaking his head in agonized disappointment. Even young Varin felt like a coasting car, moving without the motor running. He was still dangerous, but worn down by his efforts all afternoon.

Here the soundness of the baron's tactics told. Now Germany, elated at having tied the score, began to control play with an insolent competence. The halfbacks, the bombers, sure-footed and disciplined, rolled into action, their passes accurate, their position play perfect, despite the chewed-up turf. Now the Germans were the ones who seemed to have eyes in the back of their heads, often sending the ball to a spot they could not see, knowing a teammate would be there at the exact moment to receive it.

The unbearable tension increased. The stands were in an absolute frenzy. Each second was charged with electricity. The game was a fraction of a minute from the end.

It all began so innocuously, so innocently. Horst Heppner came downfield with the ball and threaded a pass to Schwartz. Speed told, for the entire French defense was caught on the hop. A tiny mistake, a failure of anticipation or lack of concentration due to over-fatigue, a defender two feet behind instead of two feet ahead, and Germany was off.

Schwartz made a short, crisp pass to Heppner and received the ball back. Then, with the ball at his feet, he raced in a wide arc around two weary defenders. His speed was dazzling. Now he was in open territory and within twenty-five yards of the French net.

He sighted the goal and let go with his left foot. The ball was moving away from Bosquier, who made a desperate stab, rolling over and over on the ground as it shot past him.

An instant later the whistle blew. The game was over. Germany had won.

## 9

Down on the field one man stood out for everyone to see.

Big Jules Garnier, the French captain, never shaved before an important match. Now his face was black with beard. Sweat poured from his forehead. His red jersey was filthy and torn. Panting, exhausted, he rushed up to Rudy Stampfli, still immaculate in his blue shorts, pointing at Heppner and arguing with what breath he had left.

The French stands, silent, horror-struck after that unexpected goal, understood immediately. Suddenly everyone took up the refrain. *"Faute! Faute! FAUTE!"*[1]

---

1. **Faute!**\fōt\ Foul!

Obviously Garnier was claiming offside on the last play. The Frenchman towered over the stocky little Swiss. Two, three, four French players, all equally positive and vehement, surrounded the referee as he stood with the ball under one arm.

There he remained, listening impassively, holding his ground, feet apart. Finally he moved away, shaking his head firmly. Then someone caught his free arm and spun him around. He was face to face with Bosquier, the goalkeeper, a hot-headed Marseillais.

"*Nein . . . nein . . . nein . . . .*" Even from the press box you could see Rudy Stampfli's expression and the set of his jaw.

"*NEIN!*" There it was. The goal was good. No, there was no German offside on the play. The score stands. The game is over, done, lost, and won.

By this time French troops had swarmed all over the field and were encircling the German players to protect them from an ugly, menacing crowd that had poured down from the stands.

The enraged French fans, milling around on the turf shouted at the Germans and the referee. Good sense, fair play were not at the moment in them. To a man they honestly believed that France had been cheated.

Look, they cried to one another, what can you expect? Rudy is from Zurich. I don't trust the German-Swiss. Had he been from Geneva, from the Suisse Romande, things would have been different. You know, everyone claims he was a friend of the baron's family, that he knew the von Kleinschrodts before the war. Besides he often played against him. It's unfair. The referee should have been Dutch or English or Spanish or Portuguese or even a Macaroni.

Why anyone could see that German halfback was plainly offside on that pass. Otherwise Jules would have caught him and cut him down. France was robbed by that second goal.

Still Stampfli shook his head, pushing away the French players. Still the angry fans howled

at the Germans and hurled imprecations at the referee. Soldiers formed a tight ring around Stampfli and the victorious team and forced a passage through the mob. So into a tunnel under the stands they went, past the back of the stadium where in improvised cubbyholes sportswriters were dictating copy to Berlin, Madrid, or Rome.

"*Ne coupez pas, mademoiselle, ne coupez pas!*"[2] screamed an agonized voice.

"*Und dann . . . Varin . . . nein, nein. Varin . . . V-A-R-I-N.*"

"Final score: Germany two, France one. Yes, that's the final. Germany scored in the last second of the game."

The hot, sweaty, exhausted players and the Swiss referee, as emotionally drained as any of them, rushed by these reporters hard at work and were hustled over to a German bus that was standing and waiting, its engine running, a driver at the wheel.

Beside the bus was a row of police cars and army jeeps. Helmeted soldiers sat in each jeep, cradling tommy guns on their knees. The players' clothes, bags, and personal belongings had already been loaded, and one by one with Stampfli they filed aboard and sank into a seat. Soon the bus filled up. Behind it was a smaller vehicle, a Volkswagen minibus. Into it piled five players who could not get into the larger bus: the baron, Otto Schoen, Sepp Obermeyer, Helmut Herberger, and young Schroeder, the centre forward.

The troops formed a cordon around the two buses, letting nobody near. In three minutes they were off. All traffic was held up to let them get away. The buses swung out with their armed escort ahead and behind, crossed the Seine, and went down a long, straight avenue lined with poplar trees. For twenty minutes they rolled along at a good speed, the jeeps leading the way with honking horns, the police cars following. About fifteen miles from the city and well out into the countryside, they turned into a long driveway leading to a large

---

2. **Ne coupez pas!**\nə·kū·pā pa\ Don't cut me off!

hotel. Everybody climbed out. Clothes and bags were unloaded, and they all filed into the hotel where the manager passed out keys to rooms with baths on the upper floors.

An hour later they piled back into the buses and the caravan set out again. They had been told to avoid the main roads and take the coastal highway to the frontier. So they rode for an hour through the radiant spring countryside, and when they reached the sea the jeeps and police car honked several times, pulled over, turned around, and left.

Now the two buses went on alone, headed for Munich and its streets packed with thousands upon thousands of celebrating football fans.

## ⟨⟨◊⟩⟩ 10

The point of playing a game is to win. To fight hard, to play fairly, but to win. Otherwise, what on earth is the use? Defeat kills a great athlete. Defeat is numbing. It silences a dressing room after a game, renders everyone speechless. Defeat is humbling, obscene.

But victory is sweet. When you also play well in a game it is sweeter. Every man in that minibus from young Helmut Herberger to the veteran Otto Schoen had played a part in the triumph. Each one was elated. Each one had given his best. Had they not beaten a better team, stopped young Varin and held him to a single goal?

Inter of Milan couldn't do that! Nor Real of Madrid, either!

How quickly, when one wins, the aches and pains, the bone weariness, the bruises, and the hurts are forgotten. They sat there, not singing and cheering as their teammates were doing ahead in the larger bus, which was now almost lost on the horizon, but suffused in happiness. Each man savored the moments, remembering that pass, that stop, that last final team rush downfield. Yes, they were a team; they had played as a team, won as a team. As they had done all year in Germany against the rest of the league, as they had done against Torpedo Dynamo of Mos-

cow and Chelsea Bridge of London. The world was warm. The world always is when you want badly to win and finally do.

They rode in silence: dependable Otto, Sepp Obermeyer, with a bruise across his forehead, Helmut Herberger, Schroeder, the centre forward, his blond hair standing straight up after the shower he had taken in the hotel, and the baron, exhausted, slumped in his seat. They were happy, relaxed, anxious only to get out of France and reach home. The straight road led along the coast as far as they could see, winding up and along the dunes and cliffs and headlands in the distance. The larger bus by this time was so far ahead it had vanished. They were alone.

Soon they passed concrete blockhouses that once, long ago, had been part of Rommel's famous Atlantic wall. Some were now tilted upward at weird angles, their guns pointing harmlessly at the sky. Others were mounds of rubble. Still others were untouched, remaining exactly as they were when their garrisons filed out with hands behind heads in surrender twenty years before.

The players watched them slip past uneasily. This was a defeat they preferred to ignore.

They went up a hill. The sea was smooth and calm in the evening light of June. Then the minibus rolled into a village of one street, the children parting in the road to watch it go by. All at once the bus slowed, groaned, stopped dead.

The driver shook his head in exasperation. "Ah, that darn magneto again."

He opened the door, got down, and raised the hood in the rear. Immediately a crowd of youngsters gathered to watch. Behind the driver the players rose, stretched, and filed slowly into the street. The last man out was the baron. You could tell how stiff and sore he was by the careful way he left the bus, how he held the door handle as he descended.

Ernst, the driver, was now underneath the vehicle, and Sepp, who knew engines, was leaning down and talking to him. Just ahead, beside a low seawall, was a monument. The baron walked over and looked at it.

Nothing ornate, nothing overdone, the monument was neither elaborate nor expensive. It consisted of a slab of roughly hewn granite topped by a granite arm and fist rising into space. High above the water, it must have been visible far out at sea. Silhouetted against the sky, the stone fist held a sword broken just above the hilt.

On the slab was a metal plaque. Twenty years of moisture-laden fogs had weathered it so badly that it was barely legible. The baron bent down. With difficulty he made out names of those who had been his enemies, his friends.

Mort pour la France
June 5, 1944

Georges Varin, *Instituteur*
Le Père Clement, *Prêtre*
Charles Lavigne, *Gérant*
Louis Marquet, *Agriculteur*
Marcel Deschamps, *Pécheur*
René Le Gallec, *quinze ans, Étudiant*[1]

My God, thought the baron, this is Nogent-Plage! We're on the Grande Rue and it is the fifth of June!

## 11

Young Schroeder and Herberger joined him before the monument, leaning over to read the lettering on the plaque. What could it possibly mean to these boys? the baron wondered. They were but a few years old when it all happened, twenty years ago to the day.

The children of the village, openly curious, surrounded the strangers from the stranded bus. Once again the baron reflected, as he had so often in the past, on how appealing were the French youngsters. The boys wore shorts and striped jerseys, the girls checked dresses and wide-brimmed straw hats.

Like everyone else in the home town of Jean-Paul Varin, these children had spent the afternoon watching the game. Therefore, the

face of Otto Schoen, the crewcut of Sepp Obermeyer, above all the lined, handsome features of the baron were familiar to them.

One boy, bolder than the others, edged toward the big man and with up-turned face asked, "Are you Monsieur the Baron von Kleinschrodt?"

For a minute the man almost shook his head. Then looking down at the child, he realized the boy could have been the son of René Le Gallec, had René Le Gallec lived and played for France. The denial died away in his throat. At least he owed the truth to those six whose names were on the simple monument. So he nodded.

Elated, the boy shrieked, jumping up and down, "Laurent! Kiki! Jules! *Viens vite! Le Baron est à* Nogent-Plage."[1]

They came from nowhere, they scrambled up the cliff, they swarmed about him, thrusting bits of paper and grubby pencils at him. Others rushed from their houses to join the group. He stood there signing his name, hearing as he did that familiar half slap, half crunch of the waves on the pebbly beach below. It took him back to that distant June afternoon, that day which began in such calm and quiet and ended in such disaster for everyone concerned. Suddenly he felt a jab in his sore ribs. It was the more painful side, where he had fallen and perhaps injured himself. It hurt. He looked up angrily.

Before his face were the eyes of a madman. It was more than mere madness; there was ferocity in those eyes, a kind of animal savagery. The man had quite obviously not shaved for a week. His hair was long and matted. In his hands was a hunting rifle. It felt most uncomfortable against the baron's ribs.

The children immediately explained. "Ah, it's only Pierre. Crazy Pierre, Monsieur the Baron, don't take any notice of him."

---

1. The identifications are as follows: schoolmaster, priest, tavern keeper, farmer, fisherman, fifteen-year-old student.

---

1. Come quickly! The Baron is in Nogent-Beach.

"It's only Pierre Marquet. Don't worry . . . ."

"He was in prison camp five years. He's touched in the head . . . ."

So the demented son of old Louis Marquet stood there, holding a deadly weapon, and incredibly, as if the madman simply did not exist, the boys kept after the baron for his autograph. The baron was a famous football player, the same as Jean-Paul. They had heard their elders talk about him many times in connection with the killing of six hostages from the village during the war. But to the children, the hostages were merely names on a monument, whereas the baron was a living legend, someone everybody had watched that afternoon on TV, the incredible German goalkeeper.

Suddenly Crazy Pierre was joined by a biggish man, also with an insane look in his eyes. He, too, had a weapon, a tommy gun cradled in his arm.

The boys spoke up. "It's the Racleur. The fiddler. He was at Dachau[2] five years. He's mad, too."

Vaguely the baron remembered a village youth who had assaulted a German officer when he was picked up in a labor sweep at Verville. That was all. How strange he should remember.

A big, wild-faced woman joined the growing circle. Her straggly hair blew about in the wind. The baron had recognized her coming down the street. She carried a small pistol which once belonged to some German officer.

Her voice was grating, menacing. "So, you have returned! You have dared to come back!" She next addressed herself to what was now a sizable crowd of villagers, young and old, crying out that the *Herr Oberst* had pretended to be a friend and then butchered her only son, René. Her rapid French was much too fast for any of the Germans but the baron to follow. She was taking over and the crowd was with her, stirring uneasily at her words.

"Monsieur Le Boucher," she suddenly screamed. She motioned the baron ahead with her pistol. Crazy Pierre and the Racleur aped

her gesture with their weapons. He moved along with his teammates and the minibus driver beside him.

On both sides of the street the wooden shutters of second-story windows flew open with that whanging sound he recalled so well. Women leaned out to watch. *"Herr Oberst,"* they said, pointing at him. *"Herr Oberst."* They did not say it in a polite, pleasant fashion as they used to long ago. Now they mouthed the old familiar name in a brutal, savage way. The strange procession moved up the Grande Rue, followed by every child in town.

That house there was the home of the widow Dupont. She must be dead by now. She had a small white fox terrier, which stood outside yapping at everyone who passed. He never yapped at me; he knew I liked dogs. That's where the Bleu Marin used to be. I see they call it the Café des Mariniers now. The awning is yellow and the chairs outside are different. I always liked those old iron ones.

Schroeder, Herberger, Obermeyer, Schoen, and the driver looked at him. What's up? Where are they taking us? He had no idea, save that it was ridiculous. They must all be mad.

They paused before an unoccupied stone house. It was the Bloch villa.

Someone kicked roughly at the front door. It crashed open. They were all pushed inside by the insane French with their guns. The room on the right, he could dimly see, had been his headquarters. They were shoved down a flight of steps into the cellar, dark and dank, a dirty floor underfoot. This, he recalled, had been where those six hostages had huddled while he sat upstairs in the office so tormented and alone.

The five other Germans surrounded him, asking questions. What does it all mean? Who are these crazy people with guns? Did the end of the game upset them this much? Did

---

2. **Dachau**\ˈda·hkau\ a notorious Nazi concentration camp.

they take football that seriously? What's the matter with them? The baron's teammates knew, of course, that he was the so-called Butcher of Nogent-Plage. What they did not know was that this was Nogent-Plage. So what's going on, Herr Hans?

Footsteps echoed overhead. Then Madame Le Gallec's voice could be heard giving orders. She was obviously in command. But what was happening? The minutes seemed eternal. Just so, thought the baron, they must have seemed to those five Frenchmen and a boy in this same cellar twenty years before.

## 🎴 12

The little red Renault rolled along the back roads, following almost exactly the same course the two German buses had taken half an hour before. The packed crowd around the French dressing room had given Jean-Paul a tremendous ovation when he appeared, and the police had to wedge a path to his parked car. Now, out in the country, with his mother beside him, the bitterness of defeat still hung over his heart.

She knew how desperately he had wanted victory in that match and how badly he felt. So she said little at first. Then, as they spun along toward Nogent-Plage, as they drew farther and farther from the stadium, from the crowd and the noise and the scarred turf, above all from the black depression which had pervaded the dressing room, he began to answer briefly.

"Yes, to play well is satisfying. I did my best. But I was playing today for France. I was part of a team."

"The whole team played well. You deserved to win."

"Both teams played well; both deserved to win." There was a hardness, a bleakness about his voice. Unfortunately he was right. Both teams deserved to win and fate had not smiled upon France.

She tried to change the subject. "You know the thing that amazed me about him?" No need to explain to whom she referred. "He

seems so little changed. Prison and all the years since the war haven't greatly altered him. How did he look close up?"

"Like Gibraltar. Like the world's best goalie. Put him on our side, and we would have won by six to ten points. Not that Georges Bosquier isn't a good goalkeeper; he is, the best in France. But the baron today . . . well, I've never seen anything like it and nobody else has either."

She was silent for several miles. He was right; nobody had ever seen such a goalie in action before.

"You know, Jean-Paul, I've always felt all my life that there was something different about the Germans, even about the *Herr Oberst,* even before that day . . . . He . . . you see . . . they've been our enemies . . . ."

The young man shrugged his shoulders. "Oh, *Maman,* they are no different from ourselves. They want to win; they would always give anything to beat us. We too wanted to win; we gave everything to beat them and failed. As a boy I felt we would never do the things the Germans did to us during the war. Then came our colonial wars, in Vietnam and in Algeria. Oh, especially in Algeria. Tortures. Massacres. Cruelty. Dropping bombs on innocent villages. You see the point is that everyone loses control in a war. Sometimes in sport, too."

They were coming to the sea now, and it was calm in the June evening. Madame Varin started to protest. Surely this was going a bit far. She pointed out that the Algerian war was not the same as a World War.

"You must realize, Jean-Paul, Algeria was a *département*[1] of France. It had been so ever since 1830 . . . a long time, my boy."

He was tired, ravaged by defeat when victory had been so close he could taste it. Although he loved his mother and tried to be patient, he burst out. "Yes, of course I know. Did I not hear this repeated a hundred times in school, in books, in the newspapers! I know

---

1. **département,** province.

it all. I can say it by heart, like every French schoolboy. I learned about the army that landed at Sidi-Ferraud on June 14, 1830. About the Insurrection of 1871 and the creation of the new *département* of Algeria. I know it all. But what is the fact? The fact is that we invaded North Africa and colonized it. We subjugated the people . . . ."

"But Jean-Paul, surely Algeria is different. It had been French for over a hundred years. Even the Moslems were French citizens."

"Yes, they were French citizens, and they were allowed to serve in our armed forces and die for France. What other rights did they have? Algeria had been settled by French *colons*[2] for a hundred years . . . ."

"My boy, you forget the Marêchal Lyautey.[3] And how the Moslems prayed for him in their mosques during the war with the Riff and how they sobbed openly in the streets at his death. Ah, you are far too young to remember these things."

"*Maman, chère Maman,* I know about the *marêchal.* He built Morocco into a fruitful consumer for French products."

How stubborn he was, she thought, how exactly like his father with these strange ideas of Marxism and equality. "Jean-Paul, you forget that we poured money, French money, into North Africa, and lives too, thousands of them, some of our noblest and best, men who had the interests of the North Africans at heart."

"Spare me, *Maman,*" he said, fatigue in his voice. "True, we poured money into North Africa, but we took millions more from it. We . . . ."

His mother interrupted. "Look! What's that? Ahead, off to the right. It looks like a glow on the horizon. A fire, perhaps. Could it be in Nogent-Plage?"

He looked ahead. There was a slight glow in the distance over the cliffs. "Well, it could be. But most likely it is Varengeville. They're forever having fires there. We'll be able to tell when we get around the next headland."

He increased the little car's speed. They zipped along the empty coastal road toward the glow in the distance. Soon it became larger. Yes, it could be Nogent-Plage.

## 13

The whole town was in the Grande Rue as he pulled up with his mother in the red Renault. They almost dragged him from behind the wheel, raised him to their shoulders, carried him up the street past the smoldering ruin of the Volkswagen minibus, twisted and charred.

"Var . . . IN! Var . . . IN! Var . . . IN!"

He's ours. Ours, you understand, ours from Nogent-Plage. Win or lose, the greatest centre forward in all Europe, the best France has ever produced. Born right here in this village, too.

"Var . . . IN! Var . . . IN! Var . . . IN!"

At first the noise and excitement and the faces of the crowd confused Jean-Paul. What was it? What was happening? There was a smell of smoke in the air. In agitated tones a half-dozen voices shouted the explanation.

"They burned the bus, Jean-Paul. The bus that was carrying the Fritz back to Germany. The Germans cheated this afternoon at Rouen. They cheated . . . ."

"Crazy Pierre started it . . . ."

"He has the Germans locked up in the cellar of the Bloch villa, Jean-Paul . . . ."

Now he began to understand. Something evil was happening. The evil could be seen in those faces. Immediately he forced his way down from their shoulders as they crowded about, yelling and cheering, echoing the same cry that had resounded over the Stade Rouennais that afternoon.

"Var . . . IN! Var . . . IN! Var . . . IN!"

"But attention! Listen to me! Those German players . . . ."

"Oh they're under lock and key in that cellar. And their baron, too. Ah, let me tell you

---

2. **colons,** colonists.
3. **Lyautey**\ˈlyȯ ˈtā\ French marshal who was resident general of Morocco 1912–1916, 1917–1925.

the Feldwebel Hans is locked up in the cellar for a change. *Et comment!* We have him. Let him fry with the others."

"Jean-Paul, Madame Le Gallec and Pierre are going to burn the place to the ground . . . ."

"But you can't do that!"

"We will. We are doing it already. We are burning that foul building where such harm was done in Nogent-Plage. And the baron shot your father, didn't he? Didn't he? He murdered six people from this town. Then this afternoon the Germans cheated; that's why they won. France was the better team. Everyone knew it, everyone could see it . . . ."

Jean-Paul shoved, pushed, worked his way out of the embraces, the back slapping, toward the Bloch villa. Crazy Pierre was carrying hay on a pitchfork, evidently to supplement the fire that he and Madame Le Gallec had started, that now was beginning to blaze up in earnest. The boy knew the madman was capable of anything.

He fought through the crowd and stood facing them on the steps of the villa. It was easy to see the fever in their eyes. This was a mob, led in whole or in part by Crazy Pierre, and the mob was momentarily insane. He raised his hand and shouted at the top of his lungs, "Listen to me! Listen to me!"

Behind him he heard the crackle of old paint. He could smell the ancient wainscoting burning.

"Friends, neighbors, we must stop this insanity. We cannot . . . ."

"Jean-Paul, he killed your father," a woman screamed. "He murdered six of us."

"He shot my boy, René," Madame Le Gallec cried. "He shot your father, too."

For a second Jean-Paul realized this sickness was the same malady which had swept the French stands in Rouen that afternoon. "Look, my friends. Today I was hurt. I was sore, bruised, inside and out . . . ." Hurry, hurry, he thought to himself, in a few minutes it will be too late. "I also felt bitter towards those Germans. But we cannot take human lives. What would my father say, I ask you? He was a

humanist; he would have told us we cannot continue to cherish grudges. If we keep feeding on these hatreds handed down to us by our ancestors, our grandfathers and great grandfathers, where are we? Friends, what good are wars? Who ever won a war? Who ever profited from them in the end?"

Slowly the madness that hung over the mob seemed to diminish and even the anger in the faces lessened. He could feel the decent people on the far edges of the crowd asserting themselves. Why, Jean-Paul is right. We cannot murder these men. We must not let them die in the cellar.

"Friends! Marcel! Pierre! Yves, you knew my father. You, Madame Bonnet, you also knew him. Reflect! There were six French in that cellar twenty years ago. Now, in the same cellar, we have six Germans. Shall we do to them what they did to us? If so, how are we different from those who murdered my father? If we kill them, we are guilty of the same crime. Somehow, somewhere, we must break this evil chain and look on each other as human beings."

He seized the moment of their hesitation, turned abruptly, rushed at the door. Crazy Pierre barred the way. Jean-Paul gave him a body block, tore the rifle from his grasp, and threw it to the street. He rushed into the hallway. One thrust of his powerful right leg knocked a cellar door panel loose. There was sufficient space for the Germans to squeeze through.

"Quick! Quick, or the building will fall in on us all!"

"Here, Sepp, give me your hand."

Then he pulled Otto through and young Herberger, frightened and babbling something to him. Someone was beside him now, attacking the door with an axe. It cracked, splintered, burst apart. Another panting German stepped out and another. Last of all came the baron.

Through the smoke in the light of the blaze, the German recognized Varin and threw his arms around him.

"Jean-Paul, believe me! I did not give the order to fire. I did not kill your father."

He held the younger man tight. Varin in turn clasped him. He nodded. *"Oui, je sais, je sais,"* he said. I know. I know.

Once outside in the crisp sea air the Germans staggered about, limp and dazed, some trembling. But the dementia of the moment seemed to have passed. That evil atmosphere seemed to have vanished. Villagers were helping the German athletes and the minibus driver, supporting them, leading them away from the fire. A woman brought them water from a bucket.

Now, except for Crazy Pierre and the widow Le Gallec, who was still screaming about the Butcher of Nogent-Plage, everybody was quiet, chastened, frightened as they perceived how narrowly a tragedy had been averted. Inside the Bloch villa the flames hissed and roared, but hoses were now playing into the windows. The danger was past.

Jean-Paul and the baron had appeared on the steps with their arms around each other's shoulders. Now they stood across the street from the burning building, still with their arms around each other's shoulders. It was difficult to tell who was supporting whom.

Then quick, explicit, unmistakable came the sound of the shot. The baron's hand went up, clutching his temple. He spun around and tumbled to the pavement at Varin's feet.

"Ah . . ." a collective groan came from them all as Crazy Pierre raced down the Grande Rue, waving his rifle in the air.

There lay the man. Jean-Paul looked at the red puncture on his forehead from which the blood was pouring. He slipped down beside him weeping, beside the dead body of his enemy, his friend.

## I

## SOMEHOW, SOMEWHERE, WE MUST BREAK THIS EVIL CHAIN AND LOOK ON EACH OTHER AS HUMAN BEINGS!

So says Jean-Paul Varin as he stands on the steps of the burning villa and tries to reason with the townspeople who are intent on incinerating the six Germans in the cellar. His words, standing alone, express the moral of this story. The incidents have been carefully constructed to move toward this point. Great numbers of people have been thrown together in accidental encounters that have led to this moment. Their relationships have been colored, as the young man says, by hatreds handed down from grandfathers and great-grandfathers. Jean-Paul and Hans almost succeed in meeting on the basis of fellow human beings. But their relationship is frustrated by forces outside themselves: by barriers of nationality (even though Hans is half-French); by the assassination of the *Hauptmann* for which neither is responsible and the execution of the six hostages which neither can prevent. The continuing, inherited enmity that colors their relations is further illustrated by the football game. As the game nears its end, the players lose control of their feelings and seek brutal body contacts with their opponents. When the game ends, the French cannot accept the score as simply the whim of fate or the result of a supreme moment of endurance on the part of the rival athletes. Instead they insist that the Germans have cheated. So encounters throughout the book have shown evidence of inherited prejudices. Meeting people openly and frankly as fellow human beings is never quite possible . . . unless the chain can be broken. As a reader, could you accept these characters as people like yourself, or were your reactions colored by your inherited prejudices?

## II

### IMPLICATIONS

Consider the following quotations from the story. What do you think the story implies by the statement? How do you react from your own experiences?

1. "First, of course, comes one's country." (p. 87)

2. "Americans want to be liked. They are almost pathetic in this childish desire to be

liked . . . . It is why they do not make good soldiers." (p. 89)

**3.** "Best of all is for a man to be respected. Respect is the basis for discipline—at home, in business, in the Army." (p. 89)

**4.** "He who witnesses a crime and does not protest, commits it himself." (p. 99)

**5.** "I cannot excuse myself by depositing my conscience with my superiors . . . . What everyone does is their concern. What I do is mine." (p. 100)

**6.** "When conscience and the state conflict, the conscience of a man must take precedence." (p. 104)

**7.** "You cannot have an Army which obeys some orders and doesn't obey others. We obey all orders . . . ." (p. 99)

**8.** "Nobody can play truly inspired football in an empty arena." (p. 112)

**9.** "You see the point is that everyone loses control in a war. Sometimes in sport, too." (p. 123)

**10.** "The point of playing a game is to win. To fight hard, to play fairly, but to win. Otherwise, what on earth is the use?" (p. 120)

**11.** "Victory is sweet. When you also play well in a game it is sweeter." (p. 120)

### III
### TECHNIQUES

*Exposition*

Throughout this unit you have examined the way writers provide necessary background information to a story. This is called *exposition*. In general, the more naturally and unobtrusively this is done, the greater the literary craftsmanship of the writer. In older literature, writers were inclined almost to say, "Dear Reader, here are a few things you ought to know." So casually is the exposition inserted into *His Enemy, His Friend* that it may surprise you to look back on the story and see how much space it actually occupies. The first real incident of the book is the shooting of the German officer.

**1.** What things did you have to be told as background to that incident?

**2.** In which chapter does the shooting take place?

**3.** Is there anything in the chapters preceding the assassination that is not exposition?

*Conflict*

The conflict of the story is summed up in the title: *His Enemy, His Friend.*

**A.1.** How does the title define the problem of the *Feldwebel*?

**2.** How does the title define Jean-Paul's problem?

**B.** In addition to the central conflicts involving the two major characters in the story, there are several minor ones involving other people.

**1.** What is the conflict the teacher faces?

**2.** What is the conflict troubling Hans' godfather?

**3.** What is the *Hauptmann's* problem?

*Climax*

Each of the main conflicts has its own resolution or climax.

**1.** Where does Hans resolve his conflict?

**2.** Where does Jean-Paul resolve his conflict?

### IV
### WORDS

**A.** Like other national groups, Germans have contributed to American English. As early as 1683, there were German settlements in Pennsylvania, and by the middle of the nineteenth century German communities had sprung up in such cities as Detroit, New York, Cleveland, and Milwaukee. To these Germans and their descendants American English is indebted, in one way or another, for the following words: *stein, kindergarten, rathskeller, ouch, pretzel, pinochle, liverwurst, sauerkraut, delicatessen, pumpernickel, poker,* and *frankfurter.* Can you think of others?

**B.** In *His Enemy, His Friend*, the highly trained shock troops are referred to as a *motorized flak unit.* The word *flak* is derived from *Fliegerabwehrkanone,* which is German for "aircraft defense cannon." A word formed, as *flak* was, by combining the first letter or letters from several longer words, is called an *acronym.* Other examples of acronyms are *radar* (radio detection and ranging), *gestapo* (*Geheime Staats Polizei,* meaning "secret state police"), *laser* (light amplification by stimulated emission of radiation), and *sonar* (sound navigation ranging). From what words is each of the following acronyms formed: *scuba, AWOL, jeep, posh, loran, NASA,* and *quasars?*

**C.** Using contextual clues as well as your word analysis skills, see whether you can figure out the meaning of the italicized word in the following sentences from *His Enemy, His Friend:*

**1.** "Above everything, accompanying all comings and goings, was noise . . . the *raucous* calls on the loudspeakers."

**2.** "Stores, shops, offices closed. Theaters emptied. Traffic *subsided*."

**3.** "The soldiers marched in *cadence*, their boots striking the concrete with that harsh sound."

---

### BIOGRAPHICAL NOTES

## Jerrold Beim

Jerrold Beim (1910–1957) was an author of children's stories, essays, and short stories. When he was in the fourth grade, his teacher read aloud his story "The Life of a Christmas Seal" and then said, "Jerry, you ought to be a writer." He took her seriously. Unable to afford college, he worked in a bank and then as an advertising manager for a department store while he wrote on the side. Later he quit advertising because he wanted to write full time. After a period of little success, he began selling his work. In 1935, he married and after selling a story to *Cosmopolitan* he and his wife spent the proceeds on a car and took off for Mexico, staying two years. During this time, he wrote *The Burro That Had a Name*, a story for children; this started him on his career in the children's field. Strangely enough, the boy who survived the Mexican crash was later killed in an auto accident in the United States.

## James Street

James Street (1903–1954), Mississippi-born, was a reporter at age fifteen. At seventeen, he attended a seminary and served as a Baptist minister from 1923 to 1926 before returning to the newspaper field. In 1933, he moved to New York City and worked as a reporter for two New York papers. In 1937, he decided to try to earn his living by free-lance writing and produced novels, news and feature stories for newspapers, articles and short stories for magazines. He was a regular contributor to *Holiday* with his travel articles. Many of his novels concerned the South and its people. He died in Chapel Hill, North Carolina.

## Prosper Mérimée

Prosper Mérimée (1803–1870) achieved renown as a French novelist, archaeologist, and essayist, but his full power and mind is best demonstrated in a score of tales which he wrote over a period of 40 years. They range in length from the 150 pages of *Colomba* to a mere 12 in *L'Enlèvement de la Redoute*. As a group they are considered to be "novellas" ("little novels"). *Carmen*, which probed the character of gypsies, was later used as the libretto for an opera by Bizet; *Mateo Falcone* explored the subject of Corsican honor; *La Venus d'Ille* and *Lokis* were built on some grisly superstitions. Many critics consider his novellas as the finest nineteenth-century examples of their kind.

## Thomas Hardy

Thomas Hardy (1840–1928) had three careers in his lifetime. Born in Dorsetshire, England, he was educated at King's College, London. At sixteen he went to work for a church architect and even won a prize for one of his designs. When he was twenty-three, he began writing poems, though he continued his work as an architect for five more years. His next career was as a novelist. In general, he set these works in a section of England called Wessex and explored, through his characters' actions, the theme of the helplessness of man caught by fate. *Far from the Madding Crowd, The Return of the Native, The Mayor of Casterbridge, Tess of the D'Urbervilles* were highly successful novels that are still popular with readers today. *Jude, the Obscure,* published in 1896, was severely attacked by critics; the attacks so angered Hardy that he swore he would never write another novel. He turned then to poetry and achieved great recognition with his long poem, *The Dynasts,* an epic-drama chronicling England's struggle against Napoleon. He began to publish lyric poetry when he was seventy years old.

## Joan Aiken

Joan Aiken (1924–    ), born in Sussex, England, is a British citizen because her famous father, the poet Conrad Aiken, neglected to register her birth at the American embassy. In 1945 she married a British journalist, Ronald Brown, who died of TB in 1955. Finding herself widowed and with two young children to support, Ms. Aiken turned to writing to support herself. She has published eleven books for children and six for adults, ranging from *The Windscreen Weepers*, a science fiction novel for adults, to *A Necklace of Raindrops*, for the young reader. Her very first story was published when she was 17, and it was broadcast on the BBC *Children's Hour*. She says she writes to please herself and her children.

## Mari Evans

Mari Evans, a native of Toledo, Ohio, was a John Hay Whitney Fellow, 1965–66, and a consultant for the National Endowment of the Arts. Her poetry has been used extensively in textbooks and anthologies. Producer/Director of a weekly half-hour television series "The Black Experience," she is Writer-in-Residence and Assistant Professor in Black Literature at Indiana University, Bloomington. Her poetry volume *I Am A Black Woman* was published in 1970.

## Ralph Pomeroy

Ralph Pomeroy (1926–      ), was educated at the Art Institute of Chicago, the University of Illinois, and at the University of Chicago. His varied career has included work as a magazine editor, art gallery director, stage manager, and bartender. His most recent collection of poems, *In the Financial District*, was published in 1968.

## Sara Teasdale

Sara Teasdale (1884–1933) was a Missouri-born poet who was educated by tutors and in a private school. While still quite young, she toured Europe and the Near East and at one time was enthusiastically courted by the poet, Vachel Lindsay, whose overwhelming exuberance fascinated and frightened her. In 1914 she married Ernst Filsinger and moved to New York City. But she was essentially a lone spirit and the marriage ended in divorce. During her lifetime she published seven books of poetry, of which *Love Songs* (1917) won a special Pulitzer Prize. Her poetry, direct and almost barren of imagery and metaphor, strives to communicate a mood rather than to state universal truths. Her last years were spent in seclusion . . . almost friendless. She drowned in her bath in a New York apartment.

## Shirley Jackson

Shirley Jackson (1919–1965), novelist and short story writer, graduated from Syracuse University in 1940. One of her short stories, "The Lottery," which appeared in *The New Yorker*, established her as the master of the Gothic horror tale. Her works center on two types of writing: the humorous, in which the delights and turmoils of ordinary home life are made hilarious, and the horror story, in which abnormal behavior is made perilously ordinary. *Raising Demons* (1957) and *Life Among the Savages* (1953) represent the first type, and *We Have Always Lived in the Castle* (1962) is an example of the second. She once said she wrote because "it's the only chance I get to sit down," and that writing "gives me an excuse not to clean out closets."

## Gordon Daviot

Gordon Daviot (1897–1952) was a pseudonym of Elizabeth Mackintosh, British playwright and author. Brought up in Inverness, Scotland, she trained to be a physical education teacher and taught at various schools in England and Scotland. But before she could attain much stature in this field, she had to return home to care for her father. She then began writing, and her first short stories were accepted by the *English Review*. In 1929, Mackintosh wrote her first detective-story under the name of Gordon Daviot. She then began to study theater and wrote a number of plays. Now she began using the pseudonym Gordon Daviot for plays, and her great-grandmother's name, Josephine Tey, for her mystery stories. Her first popular mystery novel published in the United States was *Miss Pym Disposes*. In England, Mackintosh's reputation rests on her plays; in the United States, on her mystery novels.

## John Tunis

John Tunis (1889–1975) was born in Cambridge, Massachusetts, and graduated from Harvard University. He served in World War I in overseas service and later turned to sports writing for the *New York Evening Post*. His articles and stories have appeared in most popular American magazines in recent years, and he has authored nearly two dozen books for the teen-age reader, most of them with a sports-oriented theme. He is one of the most popular writers of this type of story in the country. Some of his works are: *Silence Over Dunkerque, Buddy and the Old Pro, The Kid Comes Back, Schoolboy Johnson, All-American,* and *Iron Duke*.

## The Parable
## of the Prodigal Son

*St. Luke* 15:11–24

There was a man who had two sons; and the younger of them said to his father, "Father, give me the share of property that falls to me." And he divided his living between them. Not many days later, the younger son gathered all he had and took his journey into a far country, and there he squandered his property in loose living. And when he had spent everything, a great famine arose in that country, and he began to be in want. So he went and joined himself to one of the citizens of that country, who sent him into his fields to feed swine. And he would gladly have fed on the pods that the swine ate; and no one gave him anything. But when he came to himself he said, "How many of my father's hired servants have bread enough and to spare, but I perish here with hunger! I will arise and go to my father, and I will say to him, Father I have sinned against heaven and before you; I am no longer worthy to be called your son; treat me as one of your hired servants."

And he arose and came to his father. But while he was yet at a distance, his father saw him and had compassion, and ran and embraced him and kissed him. And the son said to him, "Father, I have sinned against heaven and before you; I am no longer worthy to be called your son." But the father said to his servants, "Bring quickly the best robe and put it on him; and put a ring on his hand, and shoes on his feet; and bring the fatted calf and make merry; for this my son was dead, and is alive again; he was lost, and is found." And they began to make merry.

Now his elder son was in the field; and as he came and drew near to the house, he heard music and dancing. And he called one of the servants and asked what this meant. And he said to him, "Your brother has come, and your father has killed the fatted calf, because he has received him safe and sound." But he was angry and refused to go in. His father came out and entreated him, but he answered his father, "Lo, these many years I have served you, and I never disobeyed your command, yet you never gave me a kid, that I might make merry with my friends. But when this one of yours came, who has devoured your living with harlots, you killed for him the fatted calf!" And he said to him, "Son, you are always with me, and all that is mine is yours. It was fitting to make merry and be glad, for this your brother was dead, and is alive; he was lost, and is found."

# CROSSCURRENTS

Return of the Prodigal Son, *Rembrandt, National Gallery of Art, Washington, D.C.*
*Rembrandt made many remarkable etchings of Bible stories. Here*
*he suggests the crosscurrents present in this memorable moment of reunion.*

Conflicts are a writer's raw material. Because the ties that hold a family together are those of need and those of love, conflicts are nowhere more dramatic than within the family circle. The parable of the Prodigal Son suggests that family problems have not changed much in their basic patterns over the last 2,000 years. The son's departure with his inheritance is typical of a young person's desire to leave the family and strike out independently. Once out in the world and on his own, he squanders his money on riotous living. Finally, he turns homeward. There he is welcomed by his father with a lavish feast and an outpouring of love. Naturally, the reliable, hard-working older brother feels cheated and bitter.

Crosscurrents in family life is one of the oldest themes in literature. An ancient Egyptian tale relates the problems arising in a family from the presence of a mother-in-law. The *Ramayana* of India is an epic of family jealousy. Even such folk tales as "Cinderella," "Snow White," and "The Ugly Duckling" point up family conflicts. Similarly, all the stories that follow will explore this theme. You will see such conflicts leading to tragedy, as in D. H. Lawrence's "The Rocking-Horse Winner," and to happy and humorous outcomes, as in Mohr's "A Very Special Pet." Ray Bradbury's "The Veldt" uses the eerie techniques of science fiction to expose the age-old conflict between children and their parents.

In spite of the selfless love which should ideally guide the members of a family, each person grows up with his or her own personal desires, private sets of feelings and reactions, and individual goals. The conflicts that result when these individual desires, feelings, and goals collide are the writer's raw material in the following selections. Events that might seem trivial or harmless to a stranger may acquire, when passed through the magnifying glass of family relationships, the power to hurt deeply. But not all family crises are tragic ones, by any means. The exaggerated explosions that occur in families are matter as much for comedy as they are for grief.

Just what humor is, or why we are amused by certain things, has been the subject of much serious thought. One of the most inclusive explanations is that humor lies in the deviation from the expected or normal pattern of behavior. The mind expects one action and an unexpected action occurs. Such twists of the normal highlight the incongruous in life, the unsuitable, inappropriate, illogical.

In the stories that follow, you will have the opportunity to examine, from both the serious and the humorous viewpoint, situations that reflect the crosscurrents in life.

◆
A tragic accident! . . . Family members
freeze in shock . . . crosscurrents springing
from need and guilt emerge.

# The Stone Boy

### GINA BERRIAULT

Arnold drew his overalls and raveling
gray sweater over his naked body. In the
other narrow bed his brother Eugene went on
sleeping, undisturbed by the alarm clock's
rusty ring. Arnold, watching his brother sleeping, felt a peculiar dismay; he was nine, six
years younger than Eugie, and in their waking
hours it was he who was subordinate. To dispel emphatically his uneasy advantage over
his sleeping brother, he threw himself on the
hump of Eugie's body.

"Get up! Get up!" he cried.

Arnold felt his brother twist away and saw
the blankets lifted in a great wing, and, all in
an instant, he was lying on his back under the
covers with only his face showing, like a baby,
and Eugie was sprawled on top of him.

"Whassa matter with you?" asked Eugie in
sleepy anger, his face hanging close.

"Get up," Arnold repeated. "You said you'd
pick peas with me."

Stupidly, Eugie gazed around the room as
if to see if morning had come into it yet.
Arnold began to laugh derisively, making soft
snorting noises, and was thrown off the bed.
He got up from the floor and went down the
stairs, the laughter continuing, like hiccups,
against his will. But when he opened the staircase door and entered the parlor, he hunched
up his shoulders and was quiet because his
parents slept in the bedroom downstairs.

THE STONE BOY by Gina Berriault. First published in
*Mademoiselle.* Copyright 1957 by Gina Berriault. By permission of Toni Strassman, Agent.

Arnold lifted his .22-caliber rifle from the
rack on the kitchen wall. It was an old lever-
action Winchester that his father had given
him because nobody else used it any more. On
their way down to the garden he and Eugie
would go by the lake, and if there were any
ducks on it, he'd take a shot at them. Standing
on the stool before the cupboard, he searched
on the top shelf in the confusion of medicines
and ointments for man and beast and found a
small yellow box of .22 cartridges. Then he sat
down on the stool and began to load his gun.

It was cold in the kitchen so early, but later
in the day when his mother canned the peas,
the heat from the wood stove would be almost
unbearable. Yesterday she had finished preserving the huckleberries that the family had
picked along the mountain, and before that
she had canned all the cherries his father had
brought from the warehouse in Corinth. Sometimes on these summer days Arnold would
deliberately come out from the shade where
he was playing and make himself as uncomfortable as his mother was in the kitchen by
standing in the sun until the sweat ran down
his body.

Eugie came clomping down the stairs and
into the kitchen, his head drooping with
sleepiness. From his perch on the stool Arnold
watched Eugie slip on his green knit cap.
Eugie didn't really need a cap; he hadn't had
a haircut in a long time and his brown curls
grew thick and matted, close around his ears
and down his neck, tapering there to a small
whorl. Eugie passed his left hand through his
hair before he set his cap down with his right.
The very way he slipped his cap on was an
announcement of his status; almost everything
he did was a reminder that he was eldest—
first he, then Nora, then Arnold—and called
attention to how tall he was (almost as tall as
his father), how long his legs were, how small
he was in the hips, and what a neat dip above
his buttocks his thick-soled logger's boots
gave him. Arnold never tired of watching
Eugie offer silent praise unto himself. He won-

dered, as he sat enthralled, if when he got to be Eugie's age, he would still be undersized and his hair still straight.

Eugie eyed the gun. "Don't you know this ain't duck season?" he asked gruffly, as if he were the sheriff.

"No, I don't know," Arnold said with a snigger.

Eugie picked up the tin washtub for the peas, unbolted the door with his free hand, and kicked it open. Then, lifting the tub to his head, he went clomping down the back steps. Arnold followed, closing the door behind him.

The sky was faintly gray, almost white. The mountains behind the farm made the sun climb a long way to show itself. Several miles to the south, where the range opened up, hung an orange mist, but the valley in which the farm lay was still cold and colorless.

Eugie opened the gate to the yard, and the boys passed between the barn and the row of chicken houses, their feet stirring up the carpet of brown feathers dropped by the molting chickens. They paused before going down the slope to the lake. A fluky morning wind ran among the shocks of wheat that covered the slope. It sent a shimmer northward across the lake, gently moving the rushes that formed an island in the center. Killdeer, their white markings flashing, skimmed the water, crying their shrill sweet cry. And there at the south end of the lake were four wild ducks swimming out from the willows into open water.

Arnold followed Eugie down the slope, stealing, as his brother did, from one shock of wheat to another. Eugie paused before climbing through the wire fence that divided the wheat field from the marshy pasture around the lake. They were screened from the ducks by the willows along the lake's edge.

"If you hit your duck, you want me to go in after it?" Eugie said.

"If you want," Arnold said.

Eugie lowered his eyelids, leaving slits of mocking blue. You'd drown 'fore you got to it, them legs of yours are so puny," he said.

He shoved the tub under the fence and,

pressing down the center wire, climbed through into the pasture.

Arnold pressed down the bottom wire, thrust a leg through, and leaned forward to bring the other leg after. His rifle caught on the wire and he jerked at it. The air was rocked by the sound of the shot. Feeling foolish, he lifted his face, baring it to an expected shower of derision from his brother. But Eugie did not turn around. Instead, from his crouching position, he fell to his knees and then pitched forward onto his face. The ducks rose up crying from the lake, cleared the mountain background, and beat away northward across the pale sky.

Arnold squatted beside his brother. Eugie seemed to be climbing the earth, as if the earth ran up and down, and when he found he couldn't scale it, he lay still.

"Eugie?"

Then Arnold saw it, under the tendril of hair at the nape of the neck—a slow rising of bright blood. It had an obnoxious movement, like that of a parasite.

"Hey, Eugie," he said again. He was feeling the same discomfort he had felt when he had watched Eugie sleeping; his brother didn't know that he was lying face down in the pasture.

Again he said, "Hey, Eugie," an anxious nudge in his voice. But Eugie was as still as the morning about them.

Arnold set his rifle on the ground and stood up. He picked up the tub and, dragging it behind him, walked along by the willows to the garden fence and climbed through. He went down on his knees among the tangled vines. The pods were cold with the night, but his hands were strange to him, and not until some time had passed did he realize that the pods were numbing his fingers. He picked from the top of the vine first, then lifted the vine to look underneath for pods and then moved on to the next.

It was a warmth on his back, like a large hand laid firmly there, that made him raise his head. Way up on the slope, the gray farm-house was struck by the sun. While his head had been bent the land had grown bright around him.

When he got up, his legs were so stiff that he had to go down on his knees again to ease the pain. Then, walking sideways, he dragged the tub, half full of peas, up the slope.

The kitchen was warm now; a fire was roaring in the stove with a closed-up rushing sound. His mother was spooning eggs from a pot of boiling water and putting them into a bowl. Her short brown hair was uncombed and fell forward across her eyes as she bent her head. Nora was lifting a frying pan full of trout from the stove, holding the handle with a dish towel. His father had just come in from bringing the cows from the north pasture to the barn and was sitting on the stool, unbuttoning his red-plaid mackinaw.

"Did you boys fill the tub?" his mother asked.

"They ought of by now," his father said. "They went out of the house an hour ago. Eugie woke me up comin' downstairs. I heard you shootin'—did you get a duck?"

"No," Arnold said. They would want to know why Eugie wasn't coming in for breakfast, he thought. "Eugie's dead," he told them.

They stared at him. The pitch crackled in the stove.

"You kids playin' a joke?" his father asked.

"Where's Eugene?" his mother asked scold-ingly. She wanted, Arnold knew, to see his eyes, and when he had glanced at her, she put the bowl and spoon down on the stove and walked past him. His father stood up and went out the door after her. Nora followed them with little skipping steps, as if afraid to be left alone.

Arnold went into the barn, down along the foddering passage past the cows waiting to be milked, and climbed into the loft. After a few minutes he heard a terrifying sound coming toward the house. His parents and Nora were returning from the willows, and sounds sharp as knives were rising from his mother's breast and carrying over the sloping fields. In a short while he heard his father go down the back steps, slam the car door, and drive away.

Arnold lay still as a fugitive, listening to the cows eating close by. If his parents never called him, he thought, he would stay up in the loft forever, out of the way. In the night he would sneak down for a drink of water from the faucet over the trough and for whatever food they left for him by the barn.

The rattle of his father's car as it turned down the lane recalled him to the present. He heard voices of his Uncle Andy and Aunt Alice as they and his father went past the barn to the lake. He could feel the morning growing heavier with sun. Someone, probably Nora, had let the chickens out of their coops, and they were cackling in the yard.

After a while another car turned down the road off the highway. The car drew to a stop and he heard the voices of strange men. The men also went past the barn and down to the lake. The undertakers, whom his father must have phoned from Uncle Andy's house, had arrived from Corinth. Then he heard every-body come back and heard the car turn around and leave.

"Arnold!" It was his father calling from the yard.

He climbed down the ladder and went out into the sun, picking wisps of hay from his overalls.

Corinth, nine miles away, was the county seat. Arnold sat in the front seat of the old Ford between his father, who was driving, and Uncle Andy; no one spoke. Uncle Andy was his mother's brother, and he had been fond of Eugie because Eugie had resembled him. Andy had taken Eugie hunting and had given him a knife and a lot of things, and now Andy, his eyes narrowed, sat tall and still be-side Arnold.

Arnold's father parked the car before the courthouse. It was a two-story brick building with a lamp on each side of the bottom step.

They went up the wide stone steps, Arnold and his father going first, and entered the darkly paneled hallway. The shirt-sleeved man in the sheriff's office said that the sheriff was at Carlson's Parlor examining the Curwing boy.

Andy went off to get the sheriff while Arnold and his father waited on a bench in the corridor. Arnold felt his father watching him, and he lifted his eyes with painful casualness to the announcement, on the opposite wall, of the Corinth County Annual Rodeo and then to the clock with its loudly clucking pendulum. After he had come down from the loft, his father and Uncle Andy had stood in the yard with him and asked him to tell them everything, and he had explained to them how the gun had caught on the wire. But when they had asked him why he hadn't run back to the house to tell his parents, he had had no answer —all he could say was that he had gone down into the garden to pick the peas. His father had stared at him in a pale, puzzled way, and it was then that he had felt his father and the others set their cold turbulent silence against him. Arnold shifted on the bench, his only feeling a small one of compunction imposed by his father's eyes.

At a quarter past nine Andy and the sheriff came in. They all went into the sheriff's private office, and Arnold was sent forward to sit in the chair by the sheriff's desk; his father and Andy sat down on the bench against the wall.

The sheriff lumped down into his swivel chair and swung toward Arnold. He was an old man with white hair like wheat stubble. His restless green eyes made him seem not to be in his office but to be hurrying and bobbing around somewhere else.

"What did you say your name was?" the sheriff asked.

"Arnold," he replied, but he could not remember telling the sheriff his name before.

"Curwing?"

"Yes."

"What were you doing with a .22, Arnold?"

"It's mine," he said.

"Okay. What were you going to shoot?"

"Some ducks," he replied.

"Out of season?"

He nodded.

"That's bad," said the sheriff. "Were you and your brother good friends?"

What did he mean—good friends? Eugie was his brother. That was different from a friend, Arnold thought. A best friend was your own age, but Eugie was almost a man. Eugie had had a way of looking at him, slyly and mockingly and yet confidentially, that had summed up how they both felt about being brothers. Arnold had wanted to be with Eugie more than with anybody else, but he couldn't say they had been good friends.

"Did they ever quarrel?" the sheriff asked his father.

"Not that I know," his father replied. "It seemed to me that Arnold cared a lot for Eugie."

"Did you?" the sheriff asked Arnold.

If it seemed so to his father, then it was so. Arnold nodded.

"Were you mad at him this morning?"

"No."

"How did you happen to shoot him?"

"We was crawlin' through the fence."

"Yes?"

"An' the gun got caught on the wire."

"Seems the hammer must of caught," his father put in.

"All right, that's what happened," said the sheriff. "But what I want you to tell me is this, why didn't you go back to the house and tell your father right away? Why did you go and pick peas for an hour?"

Arnold gazed over his shoulder at his father, expecting his father to have an answer for this also. But his father's eyes, larger and even lighter blue than usual, were fixed upon him curiously. Arnold picked at a callus in his right palm. It seemed odd now that he had not run back to the house and wakened his father, but he could not remember why he had not. They were all waiting for him to answer.

"I come down to pick peas," he said.

"Didn't you think," asked the sheriff, stepping carefully from word to word, "that it was more important for you to go tell your parents what had happened?"

"The sun was gonna come up," Arnold said.

"What's that got to do with it?"

"It's better to pick peas while they're cool."

The sheriff swung away from him, laid both hands flat on his desk. "Well, all I can say is," he said across to Arnold's father and Uncle Andy, "he's either a moron or he's so reasonable that he's way ahead of us." He gave a challenging snort. "It's come to my notice that the most reasonable guys are mean ones. They don't feel nothing."

For a moment the three men sat still. Then the sheriff lifted his hand like a man taking an oath. "Take him home," he said.

Andy uncrossed his legs. "You don't want him?"

"Not now," replied the sheriff. "Maybe in a few years."

Arnold's father stood up. He held his hat against his chest. "The gun ain't his no more," he said wanly.

Arnold went first through the hallway, hearing behind him the heels of his father and Uncle Andy striking the floorboards. He went down the steps ahead of them and climbed into the back seat of the car. Andy paused as he was getting into the front seat and gazed back at Arnold, and Arnold saw that his uncle's eyes had absorbed the knowingness from the sheriff's eyes. Andy and his father and the sheriff had discovered what made him go down into the garden. It was because he was cruel, the sheriff had said, and didn't care about his brother. Was that the reason? Arnold lowered his eyelids meekly against his uncle's stare.

The rest of the day he did his tasks around the farm, keeping apart from the family. At evening when he saw his father stomp tiredly into the house, Arnold did not put down his hammer and leave the chicken coop he was

repairing. He was afraid that they did not want him to eat supper with them. But in a few minutes another fear that they would go to the trouble of calling him and that he would be made conspicuous by his tardiness made him follow his father into the house. As he went through the kitchen he saw the jars of peas standing in rows on the workbench, a reproach to him.

No one spoke at supper, and his mother, who sat next to him, leaned her head in her hand all through the meal, curving her fingers over her eyes so as not to see him. They were finishing their small, silent supper when the visitors began to arrive, knocking hard on the back door. The men were coming from their farms now that it was growing dark and they could not work any more.

Old Man Matthews, gray and stocky, came first, with his two sons, Orion, the elder, and Clint, who was Eugie's age. As the callers entered the parlor, where the family ate, Arnold sat down in a rocking chair. Even as he had been undecided before supper whether to remain outside or take his place at the table, he now thought that he should go upstairs, and yet he stayed to avoid being conspicuous by his absence. If he stayed, he thought, as he always stayed and listened when visitors came, they would see that he was only Arnold and not the person the sheriff thought he was. He sat with his arms crossed and his hands tucked into his armpits and did not lift his eyes.

The Matthews men had hardly settled down around the table, after Arnold's mother and Nora had cleared away the dishes, when another car rattled down the road and someone else rapped on the back door. This time it was Sullivan, a spare and sandy man, so nimble of gesture and expression that Arnold had never been able to catch more than a few of his meanings. Sullivan, in dusty jeans, sat down in the other rocker, shot out his skinny legs, and began to talk in his fast way, recalling everything that Eugene had ever said to him. The other men interrupted to tell of occasions they remembered, and after a time Clint's young voice, hoarse like Eugene's had been, broke in to tell about the time Eugene had beat him in a wrestling match.

Out in the kitchen the voices of Orion's wife and of Mrs. Sullivan mingled with Nora's voice but not, Arnold noticed, his mother's. Then dry little Mr. Cram came, leaving large Mrs. Cram in the kitchen, and there was no chair left for Mr. Cram to sit in. No one asked Arnold to get up, and he was unable to rise. He knew that the story had got around to them during the day about how he had gone and picked peas after he had shot his brother, and he knew that although they were talking only about Eugie, they were thinking about him, and if he got up, if he moved even his foot, they would all be alerted. Then Uncle Andy arrived and leaned his tall lanky body against the doorjamb, and there were two men standing.

Presently Arnold was aware that the talk had stopped. He knew without looking up that the men were watching him.

"Not a tear in his eye," said Andy, and Arnold knew that it was his uncle who had gestured the men to attention.

"He don't give a hoot, is that how it goes?" asked Sullivan, trippingly.

"He's a reasonable fellow," Andy explained. "That's what the sheriff said. It's us who ain't reasonable. If we'd of shot our brother, we'd of come runnin' back to the house, cryin' like a baby. Well, we'd of been unreasonable. What would of been the use of actin' like that? If your brother is shot dead, he's shot dead. What's the use of gettin' emotional about it? The thing to do is go down to the garden and pick peas. Am I right?"

The men around the room shifted their heavy, satisfying weight of unreasonableness.

Matthews' son Orion said: "If I'd of done what he done, Pa would've hung my pelt by the side of that big coyote's in the barn."

Arnold sat in the rocker until the last man had filed out. While his family was out in the kitchen, bidding the callers good night, and

the cars were driving away down the dirt lane to the highway, he picked up one of the kerosene lamps and slipped quickly up the stairs. In his room he undressed by lamplight, although he and Eugie had always undressed in the dark, and not until he was lying in his bed did he blow out the flame. He felt nothing, not any grief. There was only the same immense silence and crawling inside of him; it was the way the house and fields felt under a merciless sun.

He awoke suddenly. He knew that his father was out in the yard, closing the doors of the chicken houses so that the chickens could not roam out too early and fall prey to the coyotes that came down from the mountains at daybreak. The sound that had wakened him was the step of his father as he got up from the rocker and went down the back steps. And he knew that his mother was awake in her bed.

Throwing off the covers, he rose swiftly, went down the stairs and across the dark parlor to his parents' room. He rapped on the door.

"Mother?"

From the closed room her voice rose to him, a seeking and retreating voice. "Yes?"

"Mother?" he asked insistently. He had expected her to realize that he wanted to go down on his knees by her bed and tell her that Eugie was dead. She did not know it yet— nobody knew it—and yet she was sitting up in bed, waiting to be told, waiting for him to confirm her dread. He had expected her to tell him to come in, to allow him to dig his head into her blankets and tell her about the terror he had felt when he had knelt beside Eugie. He had come to clasp her in his arms and, in his terror, to pommel her breasts with his head. He put his hand upon the knob.

"Go back to bed, Arnold," she called sharply.

But he waited.

"Go back! Is night when you get afraid?"

At first he did not understand. Then, silently, he left the door and for a stricken moment stood by the rocker. Outside, everything was still. The fences, the shocks of wheat seen through the window before him were so still it was as if they moved and breathed in the daytime and had fallen silent with the lateness of the hour. It was a silence that seemed to observe his father, a figure moving alone around the yard, his lantern casting a circle of light by his feet. In a few minutes his father would enter the dark house, the lantern still lighting his way.

Arnold was suddenly aware that he was naked. He had thrown off his blankets and come down the stairs to tell his mother how he felt about Eugie, but she had refused to listen to him, and his nakedness had become unpardonable. At once he went back up the stairs, fleeing from his father's lantern.

At breakfast he kept his eyelids lowered as if to deny the humiliating night. Nora, sitting at his left, did not pass the pitcher of milk to him, and he did not ask for it. He would never again, he vowed, ask them for anything, and he ate his fried eggs and potatoes only because everybody ate meals—the cattle ate, and the cats; it was customary for everybody to eat.

"Nora, you gonna keep that pitcher for yourself?" his father asked.

Nora lowered her head unsurely.

"Pass it on to Arnold," his father said.

Nora put her hands in her lap.

His father picked up the metal pitcher and set it down at Arnold's plate.

Arnold, pretending to be deaf to the discord, did not glance up, but relief rained over his shoulders at the thought that his parents recognized him again. They must have lain awake after his father had come in from the yard: had they realized together why he had come down the stairs and knocked at their door?

"Bessie's missin' this morning," his father called out to his mother, who had gone into the kitchen. "She went up the mountain last night and had her calf, most likely. Some-

body's got to go up and find her 'fore the coyotes get the calf."

That had been Eugie's job, Arnold thought. Eugie would climb the cattle trails in search of a newborn calf and come down the mountain, carrying the calf across his back, with the cow running down along behind him, mooing in alarm.

Arnold ate the few more forkfuls of his breakfast, put his hands on the edge of the table, and pushed back his chair. If he went for the calf, he'd be away from the farm all morning. He could switch the cow down the mountain slowly, and the calf would run along at its mother's side.

When he passed through the kitchen, his mother was setting a kettle of water on the stove. "Where you going?" she asked awkwardly.

"Up to get the calf," he replied, averting his face.

"Arnold?"

At the door he paused reluctantly, his back to her, knowing that she was seeking him out, as his father was doing, and he called upon his pride to protect him from them.

"Was you knocking at my door last night?"

He looked over his shoulder at her, his eyes narrow and dry.

"What'd you want?" she asked humbly.

"I didn't want nothing," he said flatly.

Then he went out the door and down the back steps, his legs trembling from the fright his answer gave him.

---

### I

### HOW UNFATHOMABLE IS HUMAN NATURE?

The readers in this story know what is happening only through Arnold's view of the things people say and do. The boy cannot really explain why he does what he does. Neither can the readers, although they may have known a similar iciness in their own families under somewhat less drastic circumstances. Arnold is beset by complex reactions, both understanding and not understanding what he has done. He is not a monster, just a small boy who knows of no way to change the horrible situation and bring Eugie back to life. Neither can he find a way to rid himself of the blackness that has settled on him. Fumblingly, he tries many things: hiding in the hay loft, stubbornly sitting in the living room, leaving the lamp on while he undresses, going to his mother's room, refusing to ask that food be passed to him, setting out to find the cow. Why is it that human behavior and emotions are so incomprehensible, even in the family, where those involved should know one another best?

## II
### IMPLICATIONS

Consider the following statements and discuss them in the light of your reactions to the story and your own personal experiences. None of them is necessarily true or false.

**1.** The family would have treated Arnold differently if he had run back immediately and told his parents about the accident.

**2.** The story indicates that Arnold is jealous of Eugie.

**3.** Most children try to ignore accidents for which they are responsible.

**4.** It is normal for a family to be insensitive to the wrongdoer's inner agony.

**5.** Adults tend to treat children as if they were deaf and dumb, saying things about them and to them that are needlessly cruel.

**6.** It is the nature of people to want wrongdoers to demonstrate their guilt and their regret for their actions.

**7.** Arnold's picking the peas is a more rational action than reporting the accident.

## III
### TECHNIQUES

In BRIEF ENCOUNTERS, attention was focused on the writer's use of exposition, conflict, and climax. CROSSCURRENTS will consider characterization and plot.

### Characterization

Characterization refers to the writer's ability to picture an imaginary person so vividly that the reader feels the character is a real, live human being. Characterization may include a detailed physical description of a character; but, more important, it should build a feeling about the personality of the character so that the reader knows how that character reacts and feels and thinks. Human beings are not simple but complicated; hence, writers have the job of suggesting in a few deft strokes the inconsistencies, the desires, the longings, and the values that the characters possess. Writers may do this through direct statement, conversation, description of action, and by the reaction of one character to another.

In "The Stone Boy" everything is told from Arnold's point of view. Thus there is little direct reference to the kind of person he is. Yet the readers probably have the feeling that they know him intimately. What do you learn about him from the following.

**1.** His way of treating Eugie when he gets up in the morning.

**2.** His reaction to the fact that this is not duck hunting season.

**3.** His response when his father calls him down from the loft.

**4.** His sitting in the living room when the neighbors call.

**5.** His knocking on his mother's door at night.

**6.** His response the next day when his mother asks him if he knocked at her door in the night.

### Plot

Plot is the sequence of related actions in a story. Just as highway engineers plot a road from one city to the next, so authors must lay out their incidents leading from the beginning to the end of the story. As a blueprint of a road may be either richly detailed or the barest of outlines, so too a plot may be loaded with incidents or starkly limited to a few. A plot may go directly by the shortest route to the story's destination or it may go off on a detour.

A good writer makes events in a story occur plausibly. The action should flow naturally from the characters. If the author forces the characters into unlikely behavior in order to advance the plot, the story will seem artificial.

What events lead up to each of the following:

**1.** Arnold's killing of Eugie.

**2.** The family's actions on finding Eugie's body.

**3.** The neighbors' discussion of the accident.

Sometimes a story is so told
that the characters and the actions
seem real, yet the reader feels
that the author is driving at something
different from the surface meaning. The events
become symbols of a deeper significance.
"The Rocking-Horse Winner" is such a story,
for the actions on the surface,
interesting as they are, are really the means
to point up the irreconcilable crosscurrents
in a family's life.

# The Rocking-Horse Winner

### D. H. LAWRENCE

There was a woman who was beautiful, who started with all the advantages, yet she had no luck. She married for love, and the love turned to dust. She had bonny children, yet she felt they had been thrust upon her, and she could not love them. They looked at her coldly, as if they were finding fault with her. And hurriedly she felt she must cover up some fault in herself. Yet what it was that she must cover up she never knew. Nevertheless, when her children were present, she always felt the centre of her heart go hard. This troubled her, and in her manner she was all the more gentle and anxious for her children, as if she loved them very much. Only she herself knew that at the centre of her heart was a hard little place that could not feel love, no, not for anybody. Everybody else said of her: "She is such a good mother. She adores her children." Only she herself, and her children themselves, knew it was not so. They read it in each other's eyes.

There were a boy and two little girls. They lived in a pleasant house, with a garden, and they had discreet servants and felt themselves superior to any one in the neighbourhood.

Although they lived in style, they felt always an anxiety in the house. There was never enough money. The mother had a small income, and the father had a small income, but not nearly enough for the social position which they had to keep up. The father went into town to some office. But though he had good prospects, these prospects never materialized. There was always the grinding sense of the shortage of money, though the style was always kept up.

At last the mother said: "I will see if I can't make something." But she did not know where to begin. She racked her brains, and tried this thing and the other, but could not find anything successful. The failure made deep lines come into her face. Her children were growing up, they would have to go to school. There must be more money, there must be more money. The father, who was always very handsome and expensive in his tastes, seemed as if he never would be able to do anything worth doing. And the mother, who had a great belief in herself, did not succeed any better, and her tastes were just as expensive.

And so the house came to be haunted by the unspoken phrase: *There must be more money! There must be more money!* The children could hear it all the time, though nobody said it aloud. They heard it at Christmas, when the expensive and splendid toys filled the nursery. Behind the shining modern rocking-horse, behind the smart doll's-house, a voice would start whispering: "There *must* be more money! There *must* be more money!" And the children would stop playing, to listen for a moment. They would look into each other's eyes, to see if they had all heard. And each one saw in the eyes of the other two that they too had heard. "There *must* be more money! There *must* be more money!"

From THE COMPLETE SHORT STORIES OF D. H. LAWRENCE, Volume III. Copyright 1933 by the Estate of D. H. Lawrence, copyright © renewed 1961 by Angelo Ravagli and C. Montague Weekley, Executors of the Estate of Frieda Lawrence Ravagli. Reprinted by permission of The Viking Press, Inc.

It came whispering from the springs of the still-swaying rocking-horse, and even the horse, bending his wooden champing head, heard it. The big doll, sitting so pink and smirking in her new pram,[1] could hear it quite plainly, and seemed to be smirking all the more self-consciously because of it. The foolish puppy, too, that took the place of the teddy-bear, he was looking so extraordinarily foolish for no other reason but that he heard the secret whisper all over the house: "There *must* be more money!"

Yet nobody ever said it aloud. The whisper was everywhere, and therefore no one spoke it. Just as no one ever says: "We are breathing!" in spite of the fact that breath is coming and going all the time.

"Mother," said the boy Paul one day, "why don't we keep a car of our own? Why do we always use uncle's, or else a taxi?"

"Because we're the poor members of the family," said the mother.

"But why are we, mother?"

"Well—I suppose," she said slowly, and bitterly, "it's because your father has no luck."

The boy was silent for some time.

"Is luck money, mother?" he asked, rather timidly.

"No, Paul. Not quite. It's what causes you to have money."

"Oh!" said Paul vaguely. "I thought when Uncle Oscar said *filthy lucker*, it meant money."

"*Filthy lucre* does mean money," said the mother. "But it's lucre, not luck."

"Oh!" said the boy. "Then what *is* luck, mother?"

"It's what causes you to have money. If you're lucky you have money. That's why it's better to be born lucky than rich. If you're rich, you may lose your money. But if you're lucky, you will always get more money."

"Oh! Will you? And is father not lucky?"

"Very unlucky, I should say," she said bitterly.

The boy watched her with unsure eyes.

"Why?" he asked.

"I don't know. Nobody ever knows why one person is lucky and another unlucky."

"Don't they? Nobody at all? Does *nobody* know?"

"Perhaps God. But He never tells."

"He ought to, then. And aren't you lucky either, mother?"

"I can't be, if I married an unlucky husband."

"But by yourself, aren't you?"

"I used to think I was, before I married. Now I think I am very unlucky indeed."

"Why?"

"Well—never mind! Perhaps I'm not really," she said.

The child looked at her, to see if she meant it. But he saw by the lines of her mouth that she was only trying to hide something from him.

"Well, anyhow," he said stoutly, "I'm a lucky person."

"Why?" said his mother, with a sudden laugh.

He stared at her. He didn't even know why he had said it.

"God told me," he asserted, brazening it out.

"I hope He did, dear!" she said, again with a laugh, but rather bitter.

"He did, mother!"

"Excellent!" said the mother, using one of her husband's exclamations.

The boy saw she did not believe him; or, rather, that she paid no attention to his assertion. This angered him somewhat, and made him want to compel her attention.

He went off by himself, vaguely, in a childish way, seeking for the clue to "luck." Absorbed, taking no heed of other people, he went about with a sort of stealth, seeking inwardly for luck. He wanted luck, he wanted it, he wanted it. When the two girls were playing dolls in the nursery, he would sit on his big rocking-horse, charging madly into space, with a frenzy that made the little girls peer at him uneasily. Wildly the horse careered, the waving dark hair of the boy tossed, his eyes had a strange glare in them. The little girls dared not speak to him.

When he had ridden to the end of his mad little journey, he climbed down and stood in

---

1. **pram**\prăm\ a baby carriage or perambulator. (The word is mostly British rather than American.)

front of his rocking-horse, staring fixedly into its lowered face. Its red mouth was slightly open, its big eye was wide and glassy-bright.

"Now!" he would silently command the snorting steed. "Now, take me to where there is luck! Now take me!"

And he would slash the horse on the neck with the little whip he had asked Uncle Oscar for. He knew the horse could take him to where there was luck, if only he forced it. So he would mount again, and start on his furious ride, hoping at last to get there. He knew he could get there.

"You'll break your horse, Paul!" said the nurse.

"He's always riding like that! I wish he'd leave off!" said his elder sister Joan.

But he only glared down on them in silence. Nurse gave him up. She could make nothing of him. Anyhow he was growing beyond her.

One day his mother and his Uncle Oscar came in when he was on one of his furious rides. He did not speak to them.

"Hallo, you young jockey! Riding a winner?" said his uncle.

"Aren't you growing too big for a rocking-horse? You're not a very little boy any longer, you know," said his mother.

But Paul only gave a blue glare from his big, rather close-set eyes. He would speak to nobody when he was in full tilt. His mother watched him with an anxious expression on her face.

At last he suddenly stopped forcing his horse into the mechanical gallop, and slid down.

"Well, I got there!" he announced fiercely, his blue eyes still flaring, and his sturdy long legs straddling apart.

"Where did you get to?" asked his mother.

"Where I wanted to go," he flared back at her.

"That's right, son!" said Uncle Oscar. "Don't you stop till you get there. What's the horse's name?"

"He doesn't have a name," said the boy.

"Gets on without all right?" said the uncle.

"Well, he has different names. He was called Sansovino last week."

"Sansovino, eh? Won the Ascot.[2] How did you know his name?"

"He always talks about horse-races with Bassett," said Joan.

The uncle was delighted to find that his small nephew was posted with all the racing news. Bassett, the young gardener, who had been wounded in the left foot in the war and had got his present job through Oscar Cresswell, whose batman he had been, was a perfect blade[3] of the "turf." He lived in the racing events, and the small boy lived with him.

Oscar Cresswell got it all from Bassett.

"Master Paul comes and asks me, so I can't do more than tell him, sir," said Bassett, his face terribly serious, as if he were speaking of religious matters.

"And does he ever put anything on a horse he fancies?"

"Well—I don't want to give him away—he's a young sport, a fine sport, sir. Would you mind asking him yourself? He sort of takes a pleasure in it, and perhaps he'd feel I was giving him away, sir, if you don't mind."

Bassett was serious as a church.

The uncle went back to his nephew, and took him off for a ride in the car.

"Say, Paul, old man, do you ever put anything on a horse?" the uncle asked.

The boy watched the handsome man closely.

"Why, do you think I oughtn't to?" he parried.

"Not a bit of it! I thought perhaps you might give me a tip for the Lincoln."

The car sped on into the country, going down to Uncle Oscar's place in Hampshire.[4]

"Honour bright?" said the nephew.

"Honour bright, son!" said the uncle.

"Well, then, Daffodil."

---

2. **Ascot** \ˈas ˈkŏt\ a famous English horse race. Later this story mentions other famous English races, the **Lincoln**, the **Leger**, the **Grand National**, and the **Derby** \ˈdar·bē\.
3. **batman**, a British army officer's personal orderly and servant. **blade**, English and informal, means "lively young fellow, often a fan or devotee of something."
4. **Hampshire** \ˈhămp·shər\ a south-central shire, or county, in England.

*Bassett: "Master Paul would get me talking about racing events, spinning yarns."*

"Daffodil! I doubt it, sonny. What about Mirza?"

"I only know the winner," said the boy. "That's Daffodil."

"Daffodil, eh?"

There was a pause. Daffodil was an obscure horse comparatively.

"Uncle!"

"Yes, son?"

"You won't let it go any further, will you? I promised Bassett."

"Bassett be hanged, old man! What's he got to do with it?"

"We're partners. We've been partners from the first. Uncle, he lent me my first five shillings, which I lost. I promised him, honour bright, it was only between me and him; only you gave me that ten-shilling note I started winning with, so I thought you were lucky. You won't let it go further, will you?"

The boy gazed at his uncle from those big, hot, blue eyes, set rather close together. The uncle stirred and laughed uneasily.

"Right you are, son! I'll keep your tip private.

Daffodil, eh? How much are you putting on him?"

"All except twenty pounds," said the boy. "I keep that in reserve."

The uncle thought it a good joke.

"You keep twenty pounds in reserve, do you, you young romancer? What are you betting, then?"

"I'm betting three hundred," said the boy gravely. "But it's between you and me, Uncle Oscar! Honour bright?"

The uncle burst into a roar of laughter.

"It's between you and me all right, you young Nat Gould," he said, laughing. "But where's your three hundred?"

"Bassett keeps it for me. We're partners."

"You are, are you! And what is Bassett putting on Daffodil?"

"He won't go quite as high as I do, I expect. Perhaps he'll go a hundred and fifty."

"What, pennies?" laughed the uncle.

"Pounds," said the child, with a surprised look at his uncle. "Bassett keeps a bigger reserve than I do."

Between wonder and amusement Uncle Oscar was silent. He pursued the matter no further, but he determined to take his nephew with him to the Lincoln races.

"Now, son," he said, "I am putting twenty on Mirza, and I'll put five for you on any horse you fancy. What's your pick?"

"Daffodil, uncle."

"No, not the fiver[5] on Daffodil!"

"I should if it was my own fiver," said the child.

"Good! Good! Right you are! A fiver for me and a fiver for you on Daffodil."

The child had never been to a race-meeting before, and his eyes were blue fire. He pursed his mouth tight, and watched. A Frenchman just in front had put his money on Lancelot. Wild with excitement, he flayed his arms up and down, yelling *Lancelot! Lancelot!* in his French accent.

Daffodil came in first, Lancelot second, Mirza third. The child, flushed and with eyes blazing,

was curiously serene. His uncle brought him four five-pound notes, four to one.

"What am I to do with these?" he cried, waving them before the boy's eyes.

"I suppose we'll talk to Bassett," said the boy. "I expect I have fifteen hundred now; and twenty in reserve; and this twenty."

His uncle studied him for some moments.

"Look here, son!" he said. "You're not serious about Bassett and that fifteen hundred, are you?"

"Yes, I am. But it's between you and me, uncle. Honour bright!"

"Honour bright all right, son! But I must talk to Bassett."

"If you'd like to be a partner, uncle, with Bassett and me, we could all be partners. Only, you'd have to promise, honour bright, uncle, not to let it go beyond us three. Bassett and I are lucky, and you must be lucky, because it was your ten shillings I started winning with. . . ."

Uncle Oscar took both Bassett and Paul into Richmond Park for an afternoon, and there they talked.

"It's like this, you see, sir," Bassett said. "Master Paul would get me talking about racing events, spinning yarns, you know, sir. And he was always keen on knowing if I'd made or if I'd lost. It's about a year since, now, that I put five shillings on Blush of Dawn for him— and we lost. Then the luck turned, with that ten shillings he had from you that we put on Singhalese. And since that time, it's been pretty steady, all things considering. What do you say, Master Paul?"

"We're all right when we're sure," said Paul. "It's when we're not quite sure that we go down."

"Oh, but we're careful then," said Bassett.

"But when are you sure?" smiled Uncle Oscar.

"It's Master Paul, sir," said Bassett, in a secret, religious voice. "It's as if he had it from

---

5. **fiver**\ˈfai·vər\ English slang, a five-pound note.

heaven. Like Daffodil, now, for the Lincoln. That was as sure as eggs."

"Did you put anything on Daffodil?" asked Oscar Cresswell.

"Yes, sir. I made my bit."

"And my nephew?"

Bassett was obstinately silent, looking at Paul.

"I made twelve hundred, didn't I, Bassett? I told uncle I was putting three hundred on Daffodil."

"That's right," said Bassett, nodding.

"But where's the money?" asked the uncle.

"I keep it safe locked up, sir. Master Paul he can have it any minute he likes to ask for it."

"What, fifteen hundred pounds?"

"And twenty! And forty, that is, with the twenty he made on the course."

"It's amazing!" said the uncle.

"If Master Paul offers you to be partners, sir, I would, if I were you; if you'll excuse me," said Bassett.

Oscar Cresswell thought about it.

"I'll see the money," he said.

They drove home again, and sure enough, Bassett came round to the garden-house with fifteen hundred pounds in notes. The twenty pounds reserve was left with Joe Glee, in the Turf Commission deposit.

"You see, it's all right, uncle, when I'm *sure!* Then we go strong, for all we're worth. Don't we, Bassett?"

"We do that, Master Paul."

"And when are you sure?" said the uncle, laughing.

"Oh, well, sometimes I'm *absolutely* sure, like about Daffodil," said the boy; "and sometimes I have an idea; and sometimes I haven't even an idea, have I, Bassett? Then we're careful, because we mostly go down."

"You do, do you! And when you're sure, like about Daffodil, what makes you sure, sonny?"

"Oh, well, I don't know," said the boy uneasily. "I'm sure, you know, uncle; that's all."

"It's as if he had it from heaven, sir," Bassett reiterated.

"I should say so!" said the uncle.

But he became a partner. And when the Leger was coming on, Paul was "sure" about Lively Spark, which was a quite inconsiderable horse. The boy insisted on putting a thousand on the horse, Bassett went for five hundred, and Oscar Cresswell two hundred. Lively Spark came in first, and the betting had been ten to one against him. Paul had made ten thousand.

"You see," he said, "I was absolutely sure of him."

Even Oscar Cresswell had cleared two thousand.

"Look here, son," he said, "this sort of thing makes me nervous."

"It needn't, uncle! Perhaps I shan't be sure again for a long time."

"But what are you going to do with your money?" asked the uncle.

"Of course," said the boy, "I started it for mother. She said she had no luck, because father is unlucky, so I thought if I was lucky, it might stop whispering."

"What might stop whispering?"

"Our house. I *hate* our house for whispering."

"What does it whisper?"

"Why—why"—the boy fidgeted—"why, I don't know. But it's always short of money, you know, uncle."

"I know it, son, I know it."

"You know people send mother writs,[6] don't you, uncle?"

"I'm afraid I do," said the uncle.

"And then the house whispers, like people laughing at you behind your back. It's awful, that is! I thought if I was lucky . . ."

"You might stop it," added the uncle.

The boy watched him with big blue eyes that had an uncanny cold fire in them, and he said never a word.

"Well, then!" said the uncle. "What are we doing?"

"I shouldn't like mother to know I was lucky," said the boy.

"Why not, son?"

"She'd stop me."

---

6. **writ**\rĭt\ a court order to pay one's bills.

"I don't think she would."

"Oh!"—and the boy writhed in an odd way—"I don't want her to know, uncle."

"All right, son! We'll manage it without her knowing."

They managed it very easily. Paul, at the other's suggestion, handed over five thousand pounds to his uncle, who deposited it with the family lawyer, who was then to inform Paul's mother that a relative had put five thousand pounds into his hands, which sum was to be paid out a thousand pounds at a time, on the mother's birthday, for the next five years.

"So she'll have a birthday present of a thousand pounds for five successive years," said Uncle Oscar. "I hope it won't make it all the harder for her later."

Paul's mother had her birthday in November. The house had been "whispering" worse than ever lately, and, even in spite of his luck, Paul could not bear up against it. He was very anxious to see the effect of the birthday letter, telling his mother about the thousand pounds.

When there were no visitors, Paul now took his meals with his parents, as he was beyond the nursery control. His mother went into town nearly every day. She had discovered that she had an odd knack of sketching furs and dress materials, so she worked secretly in the studio of a friend who was the chief "artist" for the leading drapers.[7] She drew the figures of ladies in furs and ladies in silk and sequins for the newspaper advertisements. This young woman artist earned several thousand pounds a year, but Paul's mother only made several hundreds, and she was again dissatisfied. She so wanted to be first in something, and she did not succeed, even in making sketches for drapery advertisements.

She was down to breakfast on the morning of her birthday. Paul watched her face as she read her letters. He knew the lawyer's letter. As his mother read it, her face hardened and became more expressionless. Then a cold determined look came on her mouth. She hid the letter under the pile of others, and said not a word about it.

"Didn't you have anything nice in the post for your birthday, mother?" said Paul.

"Quite moderately nice," she said, her voice cold and absent.

She went away to town without saying more.

But in the afternoon Uncle Oscar appeared. He said Paul's mother had had a long interview with the lawyer, asking if the whole five thousand could be advanced at once, as she was in debt.

"What do you think, uncle?" said the boy.

"I leave it to you, son."

"Oh, let her have it, then! We can get some more with the other," said the boy.

"A bird in the hand is worth two in the bush, laddie!" said Uncle Oscar.

"But I'm sure to know for the Grand National; or the Lincolnshire; or else the Derby. I'm sure to know for one of them," said Paul.

So Uncle Oscar signed the agreement, and Paul's mother touched the whole five thousand. Then something very curious happened. The voices in the house suddenly went mad, like a chorus of frogs on a spring evening. There were certain new furnishings, and Paul had a tutor. He was really going to Eton,[8] his father's school, in the following autumn. There were flowers in the winter, and a blossoming of the luxury Paul's mother had been used to. And yet the voices in the house, behind the sprays of mimosa and almond blossoms, and from under the piles of iridescent cushions, simply trilled and screamed in a sort of ecstasy: "There must be more money! Oh-h-h, there must be more money. Oh, now now-w! Now-w-w-w—there must be more money!—more than ever! More than ever!"

It frightened Paul terribly. He studied away at his Latin and Greek with his tutors. But his intense hours were spent with Basset. The Grand National had gone by: he had not "known," and had lost a hundred pounds. Summer was at hand. He was in agony for the Lin-

---

7. **draper**\ˈdrā·pər\ chiefly British, a seller of clothes and dry goods.

8. **Eton**\ˈē·tən\ a very famous boys' school in England.

coln. But even for the Lincoln he didn't "know" and he lost fifty pounds. He became wild-eyed and strange, as if something were going to explode in him.

"Let it alone, son! Don't you bother about it!" urged Uncle Oscar. But it was as if the boy couldn't really hear what his uncle was saying.

"I've got to know for the Derby! I've got to know for the Derby!" the child reiterated, his big blue eyes blazing with a sort of madness.

His mother noticed how overwrought he was.

"You'd better go to the seaside. Wouldn't you like to go now to the seaside, instead of waiting? I think you'd better," she said, looking down at him anxiously, her heart curiously heavy because of him.

But the child lifted his uncanny blue eyes.

"I couldn't possibly go before the Derby, mother!" he said. "I couldn't possibly!"

"Why not?" she said, her voice becoming heavy when she was opposed. "Why not? You can still go from the seaside to see the Derby with your Uncle Oscar, if that's what you wish. No need for you to wait here. Besides, I think you care too much about these races. It's a bad sign. My family has been a gambling family, and you won't know till you grow up how much damage it has done. But it has done damage. I shall have to send Bassett away, and ask Uncle Oscar not to talk racing to you, unless you promise to be reasonable about it; go away to the seaside and forget it. You're all nerves!"

"I'll do what you like, mother, so long as you don't send me away till after the Derby," the boy said.

"Send you away from where? Just from this house?"

"Yes," he said, gazing at her.

"Why, you curious child, what makes you care about this house so much, suddenly? I never knew you loved it."

He gazed at her without speaking. He had a secret within a secret, something he had not divulged, even to Bassett or to his Uncle Oscar.

But his mother, after standing undecided and a little bit sullen for some moments, said:

"Very well, then! Don't go to the seaside till after the Derby, if you don't wish it. But promise me you won't let your nerves go to pieces. Promise you won't think so much about horse-racing and *events,* as you call them!"

"Oh, no," said the boy casually. "I won't think much about them, mother. You needn't worry. I wouldn't worry, mother, if I were you."

"If you were me and I were you," said his mother, "I wonder what we *should* do!"

"But you know you needn't worry, mother, don't you?" the boy repeated.

"I should be awfully glad to know it," she said wearily.

"Oh, well, you *can,* you know. I mean, you ought to know you needn't worry," he insisted.

"Ought I? Then I'll see about it," she said.

Paul's secret of secrets was his wooden horse, that which had no name. Since he was emancipated from a nurse and a nursery-governess, he had had his rocking-horse removed to his own bedroom at the top of the house.

"Surely, you're too big for a rocking-horse!" his mother had remonstrated.

"Well, you see, mother, till I can have a real horse, I like to have some sort of animal about," had been his quaint answer.

"Do you feel he keeps you company?" she laughed.

"Oh, yes! He's very good, he always keeps me company, when I'm there," said Paul.

So the horse, rather shabby, stood in an arrested prance in the boy's bedroom.

The Derby was drawing near, and the boy grew more and more tense. He hardly heard what was spoken to him, he was very frail, and his eyes were really uncanny. His mother had sudden seizures of uneasiness about him. Sometimes, for half-an-hour, she would feel a sudden anxiety about him that was almost anguish. She wanted to rush to him at once, and know he was safe.

Two nights before the Derby, she was at a big party in town, when one of her rushes of anxiety about her boy, her first-born, gripped her heart till she could hardly speak. She fought with the feeling, might and main, for she believed in common sense. But it was too strong. She had to leave the dance and go downstairs to telephone to the country. The children's nursery-governess was terribly surprised and startled at being rung up in the night.

"Are the children all right, Miss Wilmot?"

"Oh yes, they are quite all right."

"Master Paul? Is he all right?"

"He went to bed as right as a trivet.[9] Shall I run up and look at him?"

"No," said Paul's mother reluctantly. "No! Don't trouble. It's all right. Don't sit up. We shall be home fairly soon." She did not want her son's privacy intruded upon.

"Very good," said the governess.

It was about one o'clock when Paul's mother and father drove up to their house. All was still. Paul's mother went to her room and slipped off her white fur cloak. She had told her maid not to wait up for her. She heard her husband downstairs, mixing a whiskey-and-soda.

And then, because of the strange anxiety at her heart, she stole upstairs to her son's room. Noiselessly she went along the upper corridor. Was there a faint noise? What was it?

She stood, with arrested muscles, outside his door, listening. There was a strange, heavy, and yet not loud noise. Her heart stood still. It was a soundless noise, yet rushing and powerful. Something huge, in violent, hushed motion. What was it? What in God's name was it? She ought to know. She felt that she knew the noise. She knew what it was.

Yet she could not place it. She couldn't say what it was. And on and on it went, like a madness.

Softly, frozen with anxiety and fear, she turned the doorhandle.

The room was dark. Yet in the space near the window, she heard and saw something plunging to and fro. She gazed in fear and amazement.

Then suddenly she switched on the light, and saw her son, in his green pajamas, madly surging on the rocking-horse. The blaze of light suddenly lit him up, as he urged the wooden horse, and lit her up, as she stood, blonde, in her dress of pale green and crystal, in the doorway.

"Paul!" she cried. "Whatever are you doing?"

"It's Malabar!" he screamed, in a powerful, strange voice. "It's Malabar."

His eyes blazed at her for one strange and senseless second, as he ceased urging his wooden horse. Then he fell with a crash to the ground, and she, all her tormented motherhood flooding upon her, rushed to gather him up.

But he was unconscious, and unconscious he remained, with some brain-fever. He talked and tossed, and his mother sat stonily by his side.

"Malabar! It's Malabar! Bassett, Bassett, I know! It's Malabar!"

So the child cried, trying to get up and urge the rocking-horse that gave him his inspiration.

"What does he mean by Malabar?" asked the heart-frozen mother.

"I don't know," said the father stonily.

"What does he mean by Malabar?" she asked her brother Oscar.

"It's one of the horses running for the Derby," was the answer.

And, in spite of himself, Oscar Cresswell spoke to Bassett, and himself put a thousand on Malabar: at fourteen to one.

The third day of the illness was critical: they were waiting for a change. The boy, with his rather long, curly hair, was tossing ceaselessly on the pillow. He neither slept nor regained consciousness, and his eyes were like blue stones. His mother sat, feeling her heart had gone, turned actually into a stone.

In the evening, Oscar Cresswell did not come, but Bassett sent a message, saying could he come up for one moment, just one moment? Paul's mother was very angry at the intrusion, but on second thought she agreed. The boy was the same. Perhaps Bassett might bring him to consciousness.

The gardener, a shortish fellow with a little brown mustache, and sharp little brown eyes,

---

9. **trivet**\trĭ·vət\ a tripod, but here used idiomatically to mean "entirely all right."

tiptoed into the room, touched his imaginary cap to Paul's mother, and stole to the bedside, staring with glittering, smallish eyes, at the tossing, dying child.

"Master Paul!" he whispered. "Master Paul! Malabar come in first all right, a clean win. I did as you told me. You've made over seventy thousand pounds, you have; you've got over eighty thousand. Malabar came in all right, Master Paul."

"Malabar! Malabar! Did I say Malabar, mother? Did I say Malabar? Do you think I'm lucky, mother? I knew Malabar, didn't I? Over eighty thousand pounds! I call that lucky, don't you, mother? Over eighty thousand pounds! I knew, didn't I know I knew? Malabar came in all right. If I ride my horse till I'm sure, then I tell you, Bassett, you can go as high as you like. Did you go for all you were worth, Bassett?"

"I went a thousand on it, Master Paul."

"I never told you, mother, that if I can ride my horse, and *get there*, then I'm absolutely sure—oh, absolutely! Mother, did I ever tell you? I *am* lucky."

"No, you never did," said the mother.

But the boy died in the night.

And even as he lay dead, his mother heard her brother's voice saying to her: "Actually, Hester, you're eighty-odd thousand to the good and a poor devil of a son to the bad. But, poor devil, poor devil, he's best gone out of a life where he rides his rocking-horse to find a winner."

---

## I

### IS LUCK ENOUGH?

In this story, Lawrence takes a bitter woman, incapable of any real depth of feeling, and shows how her dissatisfaction and unhappiness permeate her family, represented here by Paul. She has faith in only one thing—luck. But even that is a bitter faith, for she believes that she herself has none. Although Paul's extraordinary luck at the races brings her a fortune, he really can do nothing to satisfy her. She and the family are on a rocking-horse riding harder and harder to nowhere.

## II

### IMPLICATIONS

"The Rocking-Horse Winner" is a story exceptionally rich in implications. The statements that follow touch on some of them. Remember that the purpose of these discussions is not that everyone should agree but that each should bring his or her own experience and thinking clearly to bear on the questions that are raised.

**1.** The mother communicates her anxieties to the children although she never mentions them directly.

**2.** Paul's desperate eagerness to help his mother is not natural.

**3.** Paul's mother is a person who is incapable of love, even of loving her own children.

**4.** In every society there are drones and workers . . . the mother represents the one segment and Paul the other.

**5.** Paul is "best gone out of a life where he rides his rocking-horse to find a winner."

## III

### TECHNIQUES

*Characterization*

Two methods of characterization are used in "The Rocking-Horse Winner." Reread the first four paragraphs. What details are given to establish the picture of the mother? Reread the first conversation between Paul and his mother and Paul's treatment of the rocking-horse immediately afterwards. How many impressions do you gather of Paul from what he says and from the way he treats his horse, even though no direct statements are made about him?

*Plot*

In modern short stories, writers are increasingly concerned with the relationship between character and incident. What happens is dependent on the kind of people that are involved. In what ways does the personality of the following characters determine what happens?

**a.** The mother
**b.** Bassett
**c.** Uncle Oscar

### IV
#### WORDS

**A. 1.** Writers often add force to their work through the use of carefully selected adverbs of manner, those that express the manner in which something is done as in these expressions: a curve that projected *giddily*, staring *fixedly*, grinned *inanely*. Find other expressive adverbs of manner in the selections you have read. Observe how the exact adverbs add consciousness. Instead of "it seems to me," writers may use "seemingly" to express doubt; or instead of "it was obvious," they use _____; instead of "with great speed," they may use _____.

**2.** A good writer, however, depends more upon vivid verbs; for many active, vivid verbs suggest manner as well as action. Compare: he went away with great speed; he went away speedily; he sped away. What general action is indicated by the italicized verbs below? What additional information is concentrated in the verb?

The light *glinted* merrily upon his horn-rimmed spectacles.

He *pitched* forward upon his face.

Arnold felt his brother *twist* away.

He *pursed* his mouth tight.

The boy *writhed* in an odd way.

His face *hardened* and became more expressionless.

He was *emancipated* from a nurse and a nursery-governess.

Paul's mother *slipped* off her white fur coat.

The gardener *tiptoed* into the room.

**B.** From context determine the meanings of the italicized words. Then check the meanings in your dictionary.

**1.** "They had *discreet* servants and felt themselves superior to everyone in the neighborhood."

**2.** "Wildly the rocking-horse *careened*."

**3.** "He would speak to nobody when he was in full *tilt*."

**4.** "He had a secret within a secret, something he had not *divulged*."

**C. 1.** Often forms of roots may vary because English has sometimes used one form of a Latin word for one series of English words, another form for another. In taking roots from Latin verbs, for instance, English has sometimes used present tense forms and sometimes past participle forms. Notice the following sets of roots: -*pend*-, -*pens*-, meaning "to hang," as in *suspend* and *suspense*; -*pon*-, -*pos*-, meaning "to place," as in *postpone* and *compose*; -*scrib*-, -*script*-, meaning "to write," as in *describe* and *description*; and -*string*-, -*strict*-, meaning "to pull or bind tight," as in *stringent* and *stricture*. In these roots the first form is from the present tense of the Latin verb, the second form the past participle. Analyze the following words into affixes and roots, with the aid of your dictionary: *recognize, defiant, vibration, solicitude, terrify, immense, tentative, inspect, perfect, intervene, appreciably, sufficient, annihilation, accumulation, illusion, commendable, protrude, unison, reject, prospect, assertion, obscure, inspiration.*

**2.** Find out from the etymologies in your dictionary whether the following pairs of words contain the same root: *convince, evince; terrify, terrestrial; protect, detect; definite, finally; complete, replete; immense, commensurate; museum, amuse; fervor, fervid; impulse, propulsion; recite, citation; exclamation, reclamation.*

Childhood is the age of innocence,
or could it be
that it is not as innocent as it seems?

# Snake in the Grass

## HELEN CRESSWELL

Robin could tell, right from the beginning, that he was going to enjoy the picnic. To begin with, Uncle Joe and Auntie Joy had brought him a present, a bugle.

He took a long, testing blow. The note went on and on and on—and on. He saw Auntie Joy shudder and his cousin Nigel put his hands to his ears. Nigel was twelve, and Robin hardly even came up to his shoulder.

"We'll be off now, " Uncle Joe said, climbing into his car. "See you there."

Robin got into the back seat of his father's car.

"It's lovely at Miller's Beck," his mother said. "You'll love it, Robin."

Robin did not reply. The picnic hamper was on the back seat, too, and he was trying to squint between the wickerwork to see what was in there. In the end he gave up squinting, and sniffed. Ham, was it? Tomatoes? Oranges, definitely, and was it—could it be—strawberries?

He sat back and began to practice the bugle. He kept playing the same three notes over and over again, and watched the back of his father's neck turning a dark red.

"D'ye *have* to play that thing now?" he growled at last. "We shall all end up in a ditch!"

"I'm only trying to learn it, Dad," said Robin.

Reprinted by permission of Lothrop, Lee & Shepard from *Strange Fish and Other Stories* edited by Leon Garfield. Copyright by William Morrow and Company, 1974; copyright by Helen Cresswell, 1973.

"I've always wanted a bugle."

An hour later, when they reached Miller's Beck, he had invented a tune that he really liked and had already played it about a hundred times. It was a kind of cross between Onward Christian Soldiers and My Old Man's a Dustman.

The minute the car stopped Robin got out and ran down to the stream. He pulled off his shoes and socks and paddled in. The water was icy cold and clear as tap water, running over stones and gravel and small boulders.

Robin began to paddle downstream after a piece of floating bark he wanted for a boat, when

"Ooooooooch!' he yelled. 'Owwwwch!"

A sharp pain ran through his foot. He balanced on one leg and lifted the hurt foot out of the water. He could see blood dripping from it.

"Ooooowh!" he yelled again "Help!"

He began to sway round and round on his good leg, like a spinning top winding down. He threw out his arms, yelled again and was down, flat on his bottom in the icy-beck.

"Robin," he heard his father scream. "Robin."

He sat where he was with the water above his waist and the hurt foot lifted above the water, still dripping blood. He couldn't even feel the foot any more. He just sat and stared at it as if it belonged to somebody else.

His father was pulling off his shoes and socks and next minute was splashing in beside him and had lifted him clean up out of the water. Robin clutched him hard and water squelched between them. Robin's elbow moved sharply and he heard his father's yell.

"Hey, my glasses."

Robin twisted his head and saw first that he was dripping blood all over his father's trousers, second that the bottoms of his father's trousers were in the water because he hadn't had time to roll them up, and third that lying at the bottom of the beck were his father's spectacles. Robin could see at a glance that they were broken—at least, one of the lenses was.

His father staggered blindly out of the water, smack into Uncle Joe who was hopping on the bank.

"Here! Take him!" he gasped.

Then Robin was in Uncle Joe's arms, dripping blood and water all over *him*, and was carried back up the slope with his mother and Auntie Joy dancing and exclaiming around them.

It was half an hour before the picnic could really begin. By then, Robin was sitting on one of the folding chairs with his foot resting on a cushion on the other chair. This meant that both his parents were sitting on the grass. Robin's foot was bandaged with his father's handkerchief and the blood had soaked right through it and had made a great stain on the yellow cushion. Robin's shorts were hanging over the car bumper where they were dripping onto Nigel's comic, Robin was wearing his swimming trunks and had his mother's new pink cardigan draped round his shoulders. There was blood on that, too.

"*Everyone's* got a bit of blood," he noted with satisfaction.

Admittedly, his father and Uncle Joe had come off worst. His father sat half on the rug and half off with his trousers dripping. He had to keep squinting about him and twisting his head round to see through the one remaining lens of his glasses. Robin kept staring at him, thinking how queer he looked with one small, squinting eye and one familiar large one behind the thick pebble lens. It made him look a different person—more a creature than a person, really, like something come up from under the sea.

"Are you comfy, dear?" asked his mother.

Robin nodded.

"Are you hungry?"

Robin nodded.

"Ravenous."

"Pass Robin a sandwich, Nigel" said Auntie Joy sharply. "Sitting there stuffing yourself!

And you'd better not have any more, till we see how many Robin wants. Bless his heart! Does he look pale to you, Myra?"

The picnic got better and better every minute. Robin had at least three times his share of strawberries and Auntie Joy made Nigel give Robin his bag of crisps because she caught him sticking out his tongue at Robin. Nigel went off in a huff and found his comic all over blood and the minute he tried to turn the first page, it tore right across.

"That hankey's nearly soaked," Robin said, watching Auntie Joy helping herself to the last of the strawberries. "I've never seen so much blood. You should have seen it dripping into the water. It turned the whole stream a sort of horrible streaky red."

Auntie Joy carried on spooning.

"If I'd been in the sea, I expect it'd have turned the whole *sea* red," Robin went on. "It was the thickest blood I ever saw. Sticky, thicky red blood—streams of it. Gallons. I bet it's killed all the fishes."

Auntie Joy gulped and bravely spooned out the remaining juice.

"I won't bleed to death, will I?" he went on. "Bleed and bleed and bleed till there isn't another drop of blood left in my whole body, and I'm dead. Just like an empty bag, I'd be."

Auntie Joy turned pale and put down her spoon.

"Just an empty bag of skin," repeated Robin thoughtfully. "That's what I'll be."

"Of course you won't, darling!" cried his mother.

"Well, this handkerchief certainly is bloody," said Robin. "There must've been a bucket of blood. A *bowlful* anyway!"

Auntie Joy pushed away her bowl of strawberries.

"I wonder what it could've been?" went on Robin. "That cut me, I mean."

"Glass!" his mother said. "It must have been. It's disgraceful, leaving broken glass lying about like that. Someone might have been crippled for life."

"Dad," said Robin, after a pause. At first his father did not hear. He had stretched out at full length and was peering closely at his newspaper with his one pebble eye.

"Dad!" His father looked up. "Dad, hadn't you better go and pick *your* glass up? From your specs, I mean? Somebody else might go and cut themselves."

"The child's right!" his mother cried. "Fancy the angel thinking of that! Off you go, George, and pick it up, straight away!"

Robin's father got up slowly. His trousers flapped wetly about his legs and his blood-stained shirt clung to him.

"And mind you pick up every little bit!" she called after him, "Don't you want those strawberries, Joy?"

She shook her head.

"Could you manage them, Robin?"

Robin could. He did. When he had finished, he licked the bowl.

Once the tea things were cleared away, everyone settled down. Auntie Joy was knitting a complicated lacy jacket that meant she had to keep counting under her breath. His mother read, Uncle Joe decided to wash his car, and his father was searching for the sports pages of his newspaper that had blown away while he was down at the beck picking up his broken spectacles. Nigel had a new model yacht and took it down to the stream. Robin watched him go. All *he* had was a sodden comic, and the bugle.

He played the bugle until the back of his father's neck was crimson again and Auntie Joy had twice lost count of her stitches and had to go right back to the beginning of the row again. For a change, he tried letting her get half way across a row and then, without warning, gave a deafening blast. She jumped, the needles jerked, and half the stitches came off.

After the third time, even that didn't seem funny any more. Robin swung his legs down and tested the bad foot. Surprisingly, it hardly hurt at all. He stood right up and took a few steps. His mother looked up.

"Robin!" she squealed. "Darling! What are you doing."

"It's all right, Mum," he said. "It doesn't hurt. It's stopped bleeding now. It looks worse than it is, the handkerchief being all bloody."

"I really think you should sit still," she said.

Robin took no notice and went limping down to the beck. Nigel was in midstream, turning his yacht. It was a beauty.

"Swap you it for my bugle," he said, after a time.

"What?" Nigel turned to face him. "You're crazy. Crazy little kid!"

"I'll swap," repeated Robin.

"Well, I *won't*." Nigel turned his back again.

Robin stayed where he was. Lying by his feet were Nigel's shoes, with the socks stuffed inside them. Gently, using the big toe of his bandaged foot, he edged them off the bank and into the water. They lay there, the shoes filled and the socks began to balloon and sway. Fascinated, Robin watched. At last the socks, with a final graceful swirl, drifted free of the shoes and began to float downstream.

Robin watched them out of sight. After that, there seemed nothing he could do. What *could* you do, with your foot all bandaged up? The picnic was going all to pieces.

He felt a little sting on his good leg and looked down in time to see a gnat making off. He swatted hard at it, and with a sudden inspiration clapped a hand to his leg, fell to his knees and let out a blood curdling howl.

"Robin!" He heard his mother scream. "Robin."

They were thundering down the slope towards him now, all of them, even Uncle Joe, wash leather in hand.

"Darling! what is it?"

"Snake!" gasped Robin, squeezing his leg tight with his fingers.

"Where?" cried Auntie Joy. He pointed up stream, towards the long grass. He noticed that her wool was wound round her waist and her knitting trailing behind her, both needles missing.

"Where did it *bite* you?" she cried.

Robin took his hands away from the leg. Where they had clutched it, the skin was red and in the middle of the crimson patch was the tiny prick made by the gnat.

"Oooooh!" He heard his mother give an odd, sighing moan and looked up in time to see that she was falling. His father leapt forward and caught her just in time and they both fell to the ground together.

"Biting the dust," thought Robin, watching them.

"Here!" cried Auntie Joy. "We'll have to suck the poison out!"

She dropped to her knees beside him, her hair awry and face flushed. Next minute she had her mouth to Robin's leg and was sucking it, with fierce, noisy sucks. He tried to jerk his leg away but she had it in an iron grip. At last she stopped sucking and turning her head aside spat fiercely right into the stream. It was almost worth having her suck, to see her spit.

"Carry him up to the car!" she gasped, scrambling up. "I must see to Myra!"

Uncle Joe picked him up for the second time that day and carried him away. Over his shoulder Robin could see the others bending over his mother, trying to lift her. Best of all, he could see Nigel beating round in the long grass with a stick while his boat, forgotten, sailed slowly off downstream.

"Gone," Robin thought. "Gone for ever."

Uncle Joe put him down in the driving seat of his own car.

"Be all right for a minute, old chap?" he asked.

Robin nodded.

"Have a mint." He fished one from his pocket. "Back in a minute. Better go and see if I can find that brute of a snake. Don't want

Nigel bitten."

Then he was gone. Robin stared through the windscreen towards the excited huddle by the bank. It seemed to him that everyone was having a good time except himself. There he sat, quite alone, scratching absently at the gnat bite.

Idly he looked about the inside of the car. Usually he wasn't allowed in. It was Uncle Joe's pride and joy. The dashboard glittered with knobs and dials. He twiddled one or two of them, and got the radio working, then a green light on, then a red, then the windscreen wipers working. He pushed the gearstick and it slotted smoothly into place. To his left, between the bucket seats, was the handbrake. He knew how to release it—his father had shown him.

The brake was rightly on, and it was a struggle. He was red in the face and panting by the time he sat upright again. The car was rolling forward, very gently, down the grassy slope, then gathering speed as it approached the beck.

By the time they saw him it was too late. The car lurched then bounced off the bank and into the water. It stopped, right in mid-stream.

Robin looked out and saw himself surrounded by water.

"The captain goes down with his ship!" he thought.

He saw his mother sit up, stare, then fall straight back again. He saw the others, wet, bloodstained and horrorstruck, advancing towards him.

With a sigh he let his hands fall from the wheel. It was the end of the picnic, he could see that. He wound down the window and put out a hand to wave. Instead, it met glass and warm flesh. He heard a splash and a tinkle. Level with the window, he saw his father's face. Now *both* his eyes were small and squinting. Small, squinting and murderous.

The picnic was definitely over.

## A FUN PICNIC, BUT NOT FOR ALL

What makes a good picnic? Robin thinks he is going to enjoy the picnic from the moment he is given the bugle. After he has cut his foot and the others give him more than his share of strawberries, he thinks the picnic is getting better and better. Once he has pushed Nigel's shoes and socks into the water, he feels there is nothing else to do and the picnic is going to pieces. When Uncle Joe leaves him in the car and goes back to hunt the snake, Robin thinks "everyone was having a good time except himself." As he sits in the car in the middle of the stream, he realizes "The picnic was definitely over." In Robin's mind, what are the makings of a good picnic?

### II

## IMPLICATIONS

From a careful reading of the story and your own experiences, form your opinion of the following statement's truth or falsity. There is not necessarily a right or wrong answer.

**1.** Robin deliberately sets out to get everyone's goat.

**2.** Robin is so self-centered that he has no concern over the effect of his actions on the others.

**3.** The reader secretly likes Robin.

**4.** Adults often see children as they *think* they are, not as they *really* are.

### III

## TECHNIQUES

*Characterization*

As you recall, authors may create their characters for the reader by using a variety of methods: what they say, what they do, what they think, what others say about them, and what they look like. Robin is the central character here. What information about him comes from each of the methods given? Which method is used most extensively?

*Plot*

Often, plots are built out of a pattern of recurring incidents, each one slightly more climactic than the last. This is sometimes called a "three times and out" pattern, even though there may not always be only three incidents. This pattern structure is the one used in "Snake in the Grass." What are the incidents? Do they move toward a climax?

♦ Two great branches of the creative art:
the storyteller and the gossip.

# Story of the Widow's Son

## MARY LAVIN

This is the story of a widow's son, but it is a story that has two endings.

There was once a widow, living in a small neglected village at the foot of a steep hill. She had only one son, but he was the meaning of her life. She lived for his sake. She wore herself out working for him. Every day she made a hundred sacrifices in order to keep him at a good school in the town, four miles away, because there was a better teacher there than the village dullard that had taught herself.

She made great plans for Packy, but she did not tell him about her plans. Instead she threatened him, day and night, that if he didn't turn out well, she would put him to work on the roads, or in the quarry under the hill.

But as the years went by, everyone in the village, and even Packy himself, could tell by the way she watched him out of sight in the morning, and watched to see him come into sight in the evening, that he was the beat of her heart, and that her gruff words were only a cover for her pride and her joy in him.

It was for Packy's sake that she walked for hours along the road, letting her cow graze the long acre of the wayside grass, in order to spare the few poor blades that pushed up

Reprinted by permission of the author.

through the stones in her own field. It was for his sake she walked back and forth to the town to sell a few cabbages as soon as ever they were fit. It was for his sake that she got up in the cold dawning hours to gather mushrooms that would take the place of foods that had to be bought with money. She bent her back daily to make every penny she could, and as often happens, she made more by industry, out of her few bald acres, than many of the farmers around her made out of their great bearded meadows. Out of the money she made by selling eggs alone, she paid for Packy's clothes and for the greater number of his books.

When Packy was fourteen, he was in the last class in the school, and the master had great hopes of his winning a scholarship to a big college in the city. He was getting to be a tall lad, and his features were beginning to take a strong cast. His character was strengthening too, under his mother's sharp tongue. The people of the village were beginning to give him the same respect they gave to the sons of the farmers who came from their fine colleges in the summer, with blue suits and bright ties. And whenever they spoke to the widow they praised him up to the skies.

One day in June, when the air was so heavy the scent that rose up from the grass was imprisoned under the low clouds and hung in the air, the widow was waiting at the gate for Packy. There had been no rain for some days and the hens and chickens were pecking irritably at the dry ground and wandering up and down the road in bewilderment.

A neighbor passed.

"Waiting for Packy?" said the neighbor, pleasantly, and he stood for a minute to take off his hat and wipe the sweat of the day from his face. He was an old man.

"It's a hot day!" he said. "It will be a hard push for Packy on that battered old bike of his. I wouldn't like to have to face into four miles on a day like this!"

"Packy would travel three times that distance if there was a book at the other end of the road!" said the widow, with the pride of those who cannot read more than a line or two without wearying.

The minutes went by slowly. The widow kept looking up at the sun.

"I suppose the heat is better than the rain!" she said, at last.

"The heat can do a lot of harm, too, though," said the neighbor, absent-mindedly, as he pulled a long blade of grass from between the stones of the wall and began to chew the end of it. "You could get sunstroke on a day like this!" He looked up at the sun. "The sun is a terror," he said. "It could cause you to drop down dead like a stone!"

The widow strained out further over the gate. She looked up the hill in the direction of the town.

"He will have a good cool breeze on his face coming down the hill, at any rate," she said.

The man looked up the hill. "That's true. On the hottest day of the year you would get a cool breeze coming down that hill on a bicycle. You would feel the air streaming past your cheeks like silk. And in the winter it's like two knives flashing to either side of you, and peeling off your skin like you'd peel the bark off a sally-rod!"[1] He chewed the grass meditatively. "That must be one the steepest hills in Ireland," he said. "That hill is a hill worthy of the name of a hill." He took the grass out of his mouth. "It's my belief," he said, earnestly looking at the widow—"it's my belief that that hill is to be found marked with a name in the Ordnance Survey map!"

"If that's the case," said the widow, "Packy will be able to tell you all about it. When it isn't a book he has in his hand it's a map."

"Is that so?" said the man. "That's interesting. A map is a great thing. A map is not an ordinary thing. It isn't everyone can make out a map."

The widow wasn't listening.

"I think I see Packy!" she said, and she opened the wooden gate and stepped out into the roadway.

At the top of the hill there was glitter of spokes as a bicycle came into sight. Then there was a flash of blue jersey as Packy came flying downward, gripping the handlebars of the bike, with his bright hair blown back from his forehead. The hill was so steep, and he came down so fast, that it seemed to the man and woman at the bottom of the hill that he was not moving at all, but that it was the bright trees and bushes, the bright ditches and wayside grasses that were streaming away to either side of him.

The hens and chickens clucked and squawked and ran along the road looking for a safe place in the ditches. They ran to either side with feminine fuss and chatter. Packy waved to his mother. He came nearer and nearer. They could see the freckles on his face.

"Shoo!" cried Packy, at the sqawking hens that had not yet left the roadway. They ran with their long necks straining forward.

"Shoo!" said Packy's mother, lifting her apron and flapping it in the air to frighten them out of his way.

It was only afterwards, when the harm was done, that the widow began to think that it might, perhaps, have been the flapping of her own apron that frightened the old clucking hen, and sent her flying out over the garden wall into the middle of the road.

The old hen appeared suddenly on top of the grassy ditch and looked with a distraught eye at the hens and chickens as they ran to right and left. Her own feathers began to stand out from her. She craned her neck forward and gave a distracted squawk, and fluttered down into the middle of the dusty road.

Packy jammed on the brakes. The widow screamed. There was a flurry of white feathers and a spurt of blood. The bicycle swerved and fell. Packy was thrown over the handlebars.

---

1. **sally-rod** \ˈsal-lē-rŏd\ a willow branch.

It was such a simple accident that, although the widow screamed, and although the old man looked around to see if there was help near, neither of them thought that Packy was very badly hurt, but when they ran over and lifted his head, and saw that he could not speak, they wiped the blood from his face and looked around, desperately, to measure the distance they would have to carry him.

It was only a few yards to the door of the cottage, but Packy was dead before they got him across the threshold.

"He's only in a weakness!" screamed the widow, and she urged the crowd that had gathered outside the door to do something for him. "Get a doctor!" she cried, pushing a young laborer towards the door. "Hurry! Hurry! The doctor will bring him around."

But the neighbors that kept coming in the door, quickly, from all sides, were crossing themselves, one after another, and falling on their knees, as soon as they laid eyes on the boy, stretched out flat on the bed, with the dust and dirt and the sweat marks of life on his dead face.

When at last the widow was convinced that her son was dead, the other women had to hold her down. She waved her arms and cried out loud, and wrestled to get free. She wanted to wring the neck of every hen in the yard.

"I'll kill every one of them. What good are they to me, now? All the hens in the world aren't worth one drop of human blood. That old clucking hen wasn't worth more than six shillings, at the very most. What is six shillings? Is it worth poor Packy's life?"

But after a time she stopped raving, and looked from one face to another.

"Why didn't he ride over the old hen?" she asked. "Why did he try to save an old hen that wasn't worth more than six shillings? Didn't he know he was worth more to his mother than an old hen that would be going into the pot one of these days? Why did he do it? Why did he put on the brakes going down one of the worst hills in the country?

Why? Why?"

The neighbors patted her arm.

"There now!" they said. "There now!" and that was all they could think of saying, and they said it over and over again. "There now! There now!"

And years afterwards, whenever the widow spoke of her son Packy to the neighbors who dropped in to keep her company for an hour or two, she always had the same question to ask—the same tireless question.

"Why did he put the price of an old clucking hen above the price of his own life?"

And the people always gave the same answer.

"There now!" they said, "There now!" And they sat as silently as the widow herself, looking into the fire.

But surely some of those neighbors must have been stirred to wonder what would have happened had Packy not yielded to his impulse of fear, and had, instead, ridden boldly over the old clucking hen? And surely some of them must have stared into the flames and pictured the scene of the accident again, altering a detail here and there as they did so, and giving the story a different end. For these people knew the widow, and they knew Packy, and when you know people well it is as easy to guess what they would say and do in certain circumstances as it is to remember what they actually did say and do in other circumstances. In fact it is sometimes easier to invent than to remember accurately, and were this not so two great branches of creative art would wither in an hour: the art of the storyteller and the art of the gossip. So, perhaps, if I try to tell you what I myself think might have happened had Packy killed that cackling old hen, you will not accuse me of abusing my privileges as a writer. After all, what I am about to tell you is no more of a fiction that what I have already told, and I lean no heavier now upon your credulity than, with your full consent, I did in the first instance.

And moreover, in many respects the new story is the same as the old.

It begins in the same way too. There is the widow grazing her cow by the wayside, and walking the long roads to the town, weighted down with sacks of cabbages that will pay for Packy's schooling. There she is, fussing over Packy in the mornings in case he would be late for school. There she is in the evening watching the battered clock on the dresser for the hour when he will appear on the top of the hill at his return. And there too, on a hot day in June, is the old laboring man coming up the road, and pausing to talk to her, as she stood at the door. There he is dragging a blade of grass from between the stones of the wall, and putting it between his teeth to chew, before he opens his mouth.

And when he opens his mouth at last it is to utter the same remark.

"Waiting for Packy?" said the old man, and then he took off his hat and wiped the sweat from his forehead. It will be remembered that he was an old man. "It's a hot day," he said.

"It's very hot," said the widow, looking anxiously up the hill. "It's a hot day to push a bicycle four miles along a bad road with the dust rising to choke you, and sun striking spikes off the handlebars!"

"The heat is better than the rain, all the same," said the old man.

"I suppose it is," said the widow. "All the same, there were days when Packy came home with the rain dried into his clothes so bad they stood up stiff like boards when he took them off. They stood up stiff like boards against the wall, for all the world as if he was still standing in them!"

"Is that so?" said the old man. "You may be sure he got a good petting on those days. There is no son like a widow's son. A ewe lamb!"

"Is it Packy?" said the widow, in disgust. "Packy never got a day's petting since the day he was born. I made up my mind from the first that I'd never make a soft one out of him."

The widow looked up the hill again, and set herself to raking the gravel outside the gate as if she were in the road for no other purpose. Then she gave another look up the hill.

"Here he is now!" she said, and she raised such a cloud of dust with the rake that they could hardly see the glitter of the bicycle spokes, and the flash of blue jersey as Packy came down the hill at a breakneck speed.

Nearer and nearer he came, faster and faster, waving his hand to the widow, shouting at the hens to leave the way!

The hens ran for the ditches, stretching their necks in gawky terror. And then, as the last hen squawked into the ditch, the way was clear for a moment before the whirling silver spokes.

Then, unexpectedly, up from nowhere it seemed, came an old clucking hen and, clucking despairingly, it stood for a moment on the top of the wall and then rose into the air with the clumsy flight of a ground fowl.

Packy stopped whistling. The widow screamed. Packy yelled and the widow flapped her apron. Then Packy swerved the bicycle, and a cloud of dust rose from the braked wheel.

For a minute it could not be seen what exactly had happened, but Packy put his foot down and dragged it along the ground in the dust till he brought the bicycle to a sharp stop. He threw the bicycle down with a clatter on the hard road and ran back. The widow could not bear to look. She threw her apron over her head.

"He's killed the clucking hen!" she said. "He's killed her! He's killed her!" and then she let the apron fall back into place, and began to run up the hill herself. The old man spat out the blade of grass that he had been chewing and ran after the woman.

"Did you kill it?" screamed the widow, and as she got near enough to see the blood and feathers she raised her arm over her head, and her first was clenched till the knuckles shone white. Packy cowered down over the carcass of the fowl and hunched up his shoulders as if to shield himself from a blow. His legs were spattered with blood, and the brown and white feathers of the dead hen were stuck to his hands, and stuck to his clothes, and they were strewn all over the road. Some of the short white inner feathers were still swirling with the dust in the air.

"I couldn't help it, Mother. I couldn't help it. I didn't see her till it was too late!"

The widow caught up the hen and examined it all over, holding it by the bone of the breast, and letting the long neck dangle. Then, catching it by the leg, she raised it suddenly above her head, and brought down the bleeding body on the boy's back, in blow after blow, spattering the blood all over his face and his hands, over his clothes and over the white dust of the road around him.

"How dare you lie to me!" she screamed, gaspingly, between the blows. "You saw the hen. I know you saw it. You stopped whistling! You called out! We were watching you. We saw." She turned upon the old man. "Isn't that right?" she demanded. "He saw the hen, didn't he? He saw it?"

"It looked that way," said the old man, uncertainly, his eye on the dangling fowl in the widow's hand.

"There you are!" said the widow. She threw the hen down on the road. "You saw the hen in front of you on the road, as plain as you see it now," she accused, "but you wouldn't stop to save it because you were in too big a hurry home to fill your belly! Isn't that so?"

"No, Mother. No! I saw her all right but it was too late to do anything."

"He admits now that he saw it," said the widow, turning and nodding triumphantly at the onlookers who had gathered at the sound of the shouting.

"I never denied seeing it!" said the boy, appealing to the onlookers as to his judges.

"He doesn't deny it!" screamed the widow. "He stands there as brazen as you like, and admits for all the world to hear that he saw

the hen as plain as the nose on his face, and he rode over it without a thought!"

"But what else could I do?" said the boy, throwing out his hand; appealing to the crowd now, and now appealing to the widow. "If I'd put on the brakes going down the hill at such a speed I would have been put over the handlebars!"

"And what harm would that have done you?" screamed the widow. "I often saw you taking a toss when you were wrestling with Jimmy Mack and I heard no complaints afterwards, although your elbows and knees would be running blood, and your face scraped like a gridiron!" She turned to the crowd. "That's as true as God. I often saw him come in with his nose spouting blood like a pump, and one eye closed as tight as the eye of a corpse. My hand was often stiff for a week from sopping out wet cloths to put poultices on him and try to bring his face back to rights again." She swung back to Packy again. "You're not afraid of a fall when you go climbing trees, are you? You're not afraid to go up on the roof after a cat, are you? Oh, there's more in this than you want me to know. I can see that. You killed that hen on purpose—that's what I believe! You're tired of going to school. You want to get out of going away to college. That's it! You think if you kill the few poor hens we have there will be no money in the box when the time comes to pay for books and classes. That's it!" Packy began to redden.

"It's late in the day for me to be thinking of things like that," he said. "It's long ago I should have started those tricks if that was the way I felt. But it's not true. I want to go to college. The reason I was coming down the hill so fast was to tell you that I got the scholarship. The teacher told me as I was leaving the schoolhouse. That's why I was pedaling so hard. That's why I was whistling. That's why I was waving my hand. Didn't you see me waving my hand from once I came in sight of the top of the hill?"

The widow's hands fell to her side. The

wind of words died down within her and left her flat and limp. She didn't know what to say. She could feel the neighbors staring at her. She wished that they were gone away about their business. She wanted to throw out her arms to the boy, to drag him against her heart and hug him like a small child. But she thought of how the crowd would look at each other and nod and snigger. A ewe lamb! She didn't want to satisfy them. If she gave in to her feelings now they would know how much she had been counting on his getting the scholarship. She wouldn't please them! She wouldn't satisfy them!

She looked at Packy, and when she saw him standing there before her, spattered with the furious feathers and the crude blood of the dead hen, she felt a fierce disappointment for the boy's own disappointment, and a fierce resentment against him for killing the hen on this day of all days, and spoiling the great news of his success.

Her mind was in confusion. She started at the blood on his face, and all at once it seemed as if the blood was a bad omen of the future that was for him. Disappointment, fear, resentment, and above all defiance, raised themselves within her like screeching animals. She looked from Packy to the onlookers.

"Scholarships! Scholarships!" she sneered, putting as much derision as she could into her voice and expression.

"I suppose you think you are a great fellow now? I suppose you think you are independent now? I suppose you think you can go off with yourself now, and look down on your poor slave of a mother who scraped and sweated for you with her cabbages and her hens? I suppose you think to yourself that it doesn't matter now whether the hens are alive or dead? Is that the way? Well, let me tell you this! You're not as independent as you think. The scholarship may pay for your books and your teacher's fees but who will pay for your clothes? Ah ha, you forgot that, didn't you?" She put her hands on her hips. Packy hung his

head. He no longer appealed to the gawking neighbors. They might have been able to save him from blows but he knew enough about life to know that no one could save him from shame.

The widow's heart burned at sight of his shamed face, as her heart burned with grief, but her temper too burned fiercer and fiercer, and she came to a point at which nothing could quell the blaze till it had burned itself out. "Who'll buy your suits?" she yelled. "Who'll buy your boots?" She paused to think of more humiliating accusations. "Who'll buy your breeches?" She paused again and her teeth bit against each other. What would wound deepest? What shame could she drag upon him? "Who'll buy your nightshirts or will you sleep in your skin?"

The neighbors laughed at that, and the tension was broken. The widow herself laughed. She held her sides and laughed, and as she laughed everything seemed to take on a newer and simpler significance. Things were not as bad as they seemed a moment before. She wanted Packy to laugh too. She looked at him. But as she looked at Packy her heart turned cold with a strange new fear.

"Get into the house!" she said, giving him a push ahead of her. She wanted him safe under her own roof. She wanted to get him away from the gaping neighbors. She hated them, man, woman and child. She felt that if they had not been there things would have been different. And she wanted to get away from the sight of the blood on the road. She wanted to mash a few potatoes and make a bit of potato cake for Packy. That would comfort him. He loved that.

Packy hardly touched the food. And even after he had washed and scrubbed himself there were stains of blood turning up in the most unexpected places: behind his ears, under his fingernails, inside the cuff of his sleeve.

"Put on your good clothes," said the widow, making a great effort to be gentle, but her manners had become as twisted and as hard as the branches of the trees across the road from her, and even the kindly offers she made sounded harsh. The boy sat on the chair in a slumped position that kept her nerves on edge and set up a further conflict of irritation and love in her heart. She hated to see him slumping there in the chair, not asking to go outside the door, but still she was uneasy whenever he as much as looked in the direction of the door. She felt safe while he was under the roof; inside the lintel under her eyes.

Next day she went in to wake him for school, but his room was empty; his bed had not been slept in, and when she ran out into the yard and called him everywhere there was no answer. She ran up and down. She called at the houses of the neighbors but he was not in any house. And she thought she could hear sniggering behind her in each house that she left, as she ran to another one. He wasn't in the village. He wasn't in the town. The master of the school said that she should let the police have a description of him. He said he never met a boy as sensitive as Packy. A boy like that took strange notions into his head from time to time.

The police did their best but there was no news of Packy that night. A few days later there was a letter saying that he was well. He asked his mother to notify the master that he would not be coming back, so that some other boy could claim the scholarship. He said that he would send the price of the hen as soon as he made some money.

Another letter in a few weeks said that he had got a job on a trawler, and that he would not be able to write very often but that he would put aside some of his pay every week and send it to his mother whenever he got into port. He said that he wanted to pay her back for all she had done for him. He gave no address. He kept his promise about the money but he never gave any address when he wrote. . . . And so the people may have let their thoughts run on, as they sat by the fire with the widow, many a night, listening to her complaining voice saying the same thing over and over. "Why did he put the price of an old hen above the price of his own life?" And it is possible that their version of the story has a certain element of truth about it too. Perhaps all our actions have this double quality about them; this possibility of alternative, and that it is only by careful watching and absolute sincerity, that we follow the path that is destined for us, and, no matter how tragic that may be, it is better than the tragedy we bring upon ourselves.

---

### I

### ARE THERE ALWAYS POSSIBLE ALTERNATIVES TO AN ACTION?

What if Packy had taken the alternative action and run over the hen? The neighbors construct the second ending as they dream by the fire. They know the widow well. They know how hard she has worked, what pride she takes in Packy's accomplishments, her fear of people thinking he is a ewe lamb, and her cover-up of any show of affection with gruff words on a sharp tongue. In the second version she has not changed at all. She is presented exactly as she is in the first. But the people also know her son well. He is gentle, sensitive, and unable to defend himself against his mother's nagging words. He is devastated by her accusations at his moment of triumph. In the last paragraph, as the widow once again says, "Why did he put the price of an old hen above the price of his own life?" you feel a sadness at her unhappiness and yet cannot help but wonder if the alternative action would have brought her more guilt and misery than her son's death.

### II

### IMPLICATIONS

What is your reaction to the following statements?

**1.** The story amuses the reader even though both endings are grim.

**2.** The "Story of the Widow's Son" is about a failure in communication between child and parent.

**3.** "Perhaps all our actions have this double quality about them; this possibility of alternative."

## TECHNIQUES

*Characterization*

In folk literature, characters are usually of the kind labeled "stock" characters. Given only a few details, the reader instantly recognizes what they are supposed to represent: the wicked stepmother, the handsome prince, the beautiful, virtuous heroine. Is the widow more than a stock character?

*Plot*

Here is a story with two separate endings. The plot line is the same in both versions up to the moment of Packy's decision to put on the brakes or to run over the hen. At this point the plot line moves in two different directions. The two are pulled back together in the last paragraph, where once again the widow is lamenting before the fire in a neighbor's home. Are the two plot lines equally plausible?

See if you can construct other alternative endings. Think what would have happened if the boy had been hurt only slightly or, perhaps, so badly that he was simply a vegetable. Or could his mother's attack cause him to behave as she says he does—lazily and thoughtlessly? Could he possibly have turned on her under the attack and shouted her down? Be sure you keep the widow as the same shrewish woman that she is in the first two endings.

♦
♦ To the children
of the Fernández family
Joncrofo, the skinny hen,
is more important than even their mother
had guessed. For the skinny hen
makes up for so many things.

# A Very Special Pet

### NICHOLASA MOHR

The Fernández family kept two pets in their small five-room apartment. One was a large female alley cat who was a good mouser when she wasn't in heat. She was very large and had a rich coat of grey fur with black stripes and a long bushy tail. Her eyes were yellow and she had long white whiskers. Her name was Maríalu.

If they would listen carefully to what Maríalu said, Mrs. Fernández assured the children, they would hear her calling her husband Raúl.

"Raúl . . . Raúl . . . this is Maríalu . . . Raúl . . . Raúl . . . this is Maríalu," the children would sing loudly. They all felt sorry for Maríalu, because no matter how long and hard she howled, or how many times she ran off, she could never find her real husband, Raúl.

The second pet was not really supposed to be a pet at all. She was a small, skinny white hen with a red crest and a yellow beak. Graciela and Eugenio Fernández had bought her two years ago, to provide them and their eight children with good fresh eggs.

Her name was Joncrofo, after Graciela Fernández's favorite Hollywood movie star, Joan

"A Very Special Pet" from *El Bronx Remembered* by Nicholasa Mohr. Copyright © 1975 by Nicholasa Mohr. Reprinted by permission of Harper & Row, Publishers, Inc.

Crawford. People would repeat the hen's name as she pronounced it, "Joncrofo la gallina."

Joncrofo la gallina lived in the kitchen. She had one foot tied with a very long piece of twine to one of the legs of the kitchen sink. The twine was long enough for Joncrofo to wander all over the kitchen and even to hop onto the large window with the fire escape. Under the sink Mrs. Fernández kept clean newspapers, water, and cornmeal for the hen, and a wooden box lined with some soft flannel cloth and packing straw. It was there that they hoped Joncrofo would lay her eggs. The little hen slept and rested there, but perhaps because she was nervous, she had never once laid an egg.

Graciela and Eugenio Fernández had come to the Bronx six years ago and moved into the small apartment. Except for a trip once before to the seaport city of Mayagüez in Puerto Rico, they had never left their tiny village in the mountains. To finance their voyage to New York, Mr. and Mrs. Fernández had sold their small plot of land, the little livestock they had, and their wooden cabin. The sale had provided the fare and expenses for them and their five children. Since then, three more children had been born. City life was foreign to them, and they had to learn everything, even how to get on a subway and travel. Graciela Fernández had been terribly frightened at first of the underground trains, traffic, and large crowds of people. Although she finally adjusted, she still confined herself to the apartment and seldom went out.

She would never complain; she would pray at the small altar she had set up in the kitchen, light her candles, and murmur that God would provide and not forget her and her family. She was proud of the fact that they did not have to ask for welfare or home relief, as so many other families did.

"Papi provides for us. We are lucky and we have to thank Jesus Christ," she would say, making the sign of the cross.

Eugenio Fernández had found a job as a porter in one of the large buildings in the garment center in Manhattan. He still held the same job, but he hoped to be promoted someday to freight-elevator operator. In the meantime, he sold newspapers and coffee on the side, ran errands for people in the building, and was always available for extra work. Still, the money he brought home was barely enough to support ten people.

"Someday I'm gonna get that job. I got my eye on it, and Mr. Friedlander, he likes me . . . so we gotta be patient. Besides the increase in salary, my God—I could do a million things on the side, and we could make a lotta money. Why I could. . . ." Mr. Fernández would tell his family this story several times a week.

"Oh, wow! Papi, we are gonna be rich when you get that job!" the children would shriek.

"Can we get a television when we get rich, Papi?" Pablito, the oldest boy, would ask. Nellie, Carmen, and Linda wanted a telephone.

"Everybody on the block got a telephone but us." Nellie, the oldest girl, would speak for them.

The younger children, William, Olgita, and Freddie, would request lots of toys and treats. Baby Nancy would smile and babble happily with everybody.

"We gonna get everything and we gonna leave El Bronx," Mr. Fernández would assure them. "We even gonna save enough to buy our farm in Puerto Rico—a big one! With lots of land, maybe a hundred acres, and a chiken house, pigs, goats, even a cow. We can plant coffee and some sugar, and have all the fruit trees—make a lotta money. Why I could. . . ." Mr. Fernández would pause and tell the children all about the wonderful food they could eat back home in his village. "All you need to get the farm is a good start."

"We gonna take Joncrofo, right?" the kids would ask. "And Maríalu? Her too?"

"Sure," Mr. Fernández would say goodnaturedly, "even Raúl, her husband, when she finds him, eh?" He would wink, laughing.

165

"And Joncrofo don't have to be tied up like a prisoner no more—she could run loose."

It was the dream of Graciela and Eugenio Fernández to go back to their village as owners of their own farm, with the faith that the land would provide for them.

This morning Mrs. Fernández sat in her kitchen, thinking that things were just not going well. Now that the holidays were coming and Christmas would soon be here, money was scarcer than ever and prices were higher than ever. Things had been hard for Eugenio Fernández; he was still working as a porter and lately had been sick with a bad throat. They had not saved one cent toward their farm. In fact, they still owed the dry-goods salesman for the kitchen curtains and two bedspreads; even insurance payments were long overdue. She wanted to find a job and help out, but there were still three small preschool children at home to care for. Lately, she had begun to worry; it was hard to put meat on the table.

Graciela Fernández sighed, looking about her small, clean kitchen, and caught sight of Joncrofo running frantically after a stray cockroach. The hen quickly jerked her neck and snapped up the insect with her beak. In spite of all the fumigation and daily scrubbing, it seemed there was always a cockroach or two in sight. Joncrofo was always searching for a tasty morsel—spiders, ants, even houseflies. She was quick and usually got her victim.

The little white hen had a wicked temper and would snap at anyone she felt was annoying her. Even Maríalu knew better; she had a permanent scar on her right ear as a result of Joncrofo's sharp yellow beak. Now the cat carefully kept her distance.

In spite of Joncrofo's cantankerous ways, the children loved her. They were proud of her because no one else on the block had such a pet. Whenever other children teased them about not having a television, the Fernández children would remind them that Joncrofo was a very special pet. Even Baby Nancy would laugh and clap when she saw Joncrofo rushing toward one of her tiny victims.

For some time now, Mrs. Fernández had given up any hope of Joncrofo producing eggs and had also accepted her as a house pet. She had tried everything: warm milk, fresh grass from the park, relining the wooden box. She had even consulted the spiritualist and followed the instructions faithfully, giving the little hen herbs to eat and reciting the prayers; and yet nothing ever worked. She had even tried to fatten her up, but the more Joncrofo ate, it seemed, the less she gained.

After thinking about it for several days, this morning Graciela Fernández reached her decision. Tonight, her husband would have good fresh chicken broth for his cold, and her children a full plate of rice with chicken. This silly hen was really no use alive to anyone, she concluded.

It had been six long years since Mrs. Fernández had killed a chicken, but she still remembered how. She was grateful that the older children were in school, and somehow she would find a way to keep the three younger ones at the other end of the apartment.

Very slowly she got up and found the kitchen cleaver. Feeling it with her thumb, she decided it should be sharper, and taking a flat stone, she carefully sharpened the edge as she planned the best way to finish off the hen.

It was still quite early. If she worked things right, she could be through by noontime and have supper ready before her husband got home. She would tell the children that Joncrofo flew away. Someone had untied the twine on her foot and when she opened the window to the fire escape to bring in the mop, Joncrofo flew out and disappeared. That's it, she said to herself, satisfied.

The cleaver was sharp enough and the small chopping block was set up on the kitchen sink. Mrs. Fernández bent down and looked Joncrofo right in the eye. The hen stared back without any fear or much interest. Good, thought Mrs. Fernández, and she walked back into the apartment where Olgita, Freddie, and Baby Nancy were playing.

"I'm going to clean the kitchen, and I don't want you to come inside. Understand?" The children looked at her and nodded. "I mean it—you stay here. If I catch you coming to the kitchen when I am cleaning, you get it with this," she said, holding out her hand with an open palm, gesturing as if she were spanking them. "Now, I'm going to put the chair across the kitchen entrance so that Baby Nancy can't come in. O.K.?" The children nodded again. Their mother very often put one of the kitchen chairs across the kitchen entrance so the baby could not come inside. "Now," she said, "you listen and you stay here!" The children began to play, interested only in their game.

Mrs. Fernández returned to the kitchen, smoothed down her hair, readjusted her apron, and rolled up her sleeves. She put one of the chairs across the threshold to block the entrance, then found a couple of extra rags and old newspapers.

"Joncrofo," she whispered and walked over to the hen. To her surprise, the hen ran under the sink and sat in her box. Mrs. Fernández bent down, but before she could grab her, Joncrofo jumped out of her box and slid behind one of the legs of the kitchen sink. She extended her hand and felt the hen's sharp beak nip one of her fingers. "Ave María!" she said, pulling away and putting the injured finger in her mouth. "O.K., you wanna play games. You dumb hen!"

She decided to untie the twine that was tied to the leg of the sink and then pull the hen toward her. Taking a large rag, she draped it over one hand and then, bending down once more, untied the twine and began to pull. Joncrofo resisted, and Mrs. Fernández pulled. Harder and harder she tugged and pulled, at the same time making sure she held the rag securely, so that she could protect herself against Joncrofo's sharp beak. Quickly she pulled, and with one fast jerk of the twine, the hen was up in the air. Quickly Mrs. Fer-

nández draped the rag over the hen. Frantically, Joncrofo began to cackle and jump, flapping her wings and snapping her beak. Mrs. Fernández found herself spinning as she struggled to hold on to Joncrofo, who kept wriggling and jumping. With great effort, Joncrofo got her head loose and sank her beak into Mrs. Fernández's arm. In an instant she released the hen.

Joncrofo ran around the kitchen cackling loudly, flapping her wings and ruffling her feathers. The hen kept an eye on Mrs. Fernández, who also watched her as she held on to her injured arm. White feathers were all over the kitchen; some still floated softly in the air.

Each time Mrs. Fernández went toward Joncrofo, she fled swiftly, cackling even louder and snapping wildly with her beak.

Mrs. Fernández remained still for a moment, then went over to the far end of the kitchen and grabbed a broom. Using the handle, she began to hit the hen, swatting her back and forth like a tennis ball. Joncrofo

167

kept running and trying to dodge the blows, but Mrs. Fernández kept landing the broom each time. The hen began to lose her footing, and Mrs. Fernández vigorously swung the broom, hitting the small white hen until her cackles became softer and softer. Not able to stand any longer, Joncrofo wobbled, moving with slow jerky movements, and dropped to the floor. Mrs. Fernández let go of the broom and rushed over to the hen. Grabbing her by the neck, she lifted her into the air and spun her around a few times, dropping her on the floor. Near exhaustion, Mrs. Fernández could hear her own heavy breathing.

"Mami . . . Mamita. What are you doing to Joncrofo?" Turning, she saw Olgita, Freddie, and Baby Nancy staring at her wide-eyed. "Ma . . . Mami . . . what are you doing to Joncrofo?" they shouted and began to cry. In her excitement, Mrs. Fernández had forgotten completely about the children and the noise the hen had made.

"Oooo . . . is she dead?" Olgita cried, pointing. "Is she dead?" She began to whine.

"You killed Joncrofo, Mami! You killed her. She's dead." Freddie joined his sister, sobbing loudly. Baby Nancy watched her brother and sister and began to cry too. Shrieking, she threw herself on the floor in a tantrum.

"You killed her! You're bad, Mami. You're bad," screamed Olgita.

"Joncrofo . . . I want Joncrofo. . . ." Freddie sobbed. "I'm gonna tell Papi," he screamed, choking the tears.

"Me too! I'm gonna tell too," cried Olgita. "I'm telling Nellie, and she'll tell her teacher on you," she yelled.

Mrs. Fernández watched her children as they stood looking in at her, barricaded by the chair. Then she looked down at the floor where Joncrofo lay, perfectly still. Walking over to the chair, she removed it from the entrance and before she could say anything, the children ran to the back of the apartment, still yelling and crying.

"Joncrofo. . . . We want Joncrofo. . . . You're bad . . . you're bad. . . ."

Mrs. Fernández felt completely helpless as she looked about her kitchen. What a mess! she thought. Things were overturned, and there were white feathers everywhere. Feeling the tears coming to her eyes, she sat down and began to cry quietly. What's the use now? She sighed and thought, I should have taken her to the butcher. He would have done it for a small fee. Oh, this life, she said to herself, wiping her eyes. Now my children hate me. She remembered that when she was just about Olgita's age she was already helping her mother kill chickens and never thought much about slaughtering animals for food.

Graciela Fernández took a deep breath and began to wonder what she would do with Joncrofo now that she was dead. No use cooking her. They won't eat her, she thought, shaking her head. As she contemplated what was to be done, she heard a low grunt. Joncrofo was still alive!

Mrs. Fernández reached under the sink and pulled out the wooden box. She put the large rag into the box and placed the hen inside. Quickly she went over to a cabinet and took out an eyedropper, filling it with water. Then she forced open Joncrofo's beak and dropped some water inside. She put a washcloth into lukewarm water and washed down the hen, smoothing her feathers.

"Joncrofo," she cooed softly, "cro . . . cro . . . Joncrofita," and stroked the hen gently. The hen was still breathing, but her eyes were closed. Mrs. Fernández went over to the cupboard and pulled out a small bottle of rum that Mr. Fernández saved only for special occasions and for guests. She gave some to Joncrofo. The hen opened her eyes and shook her head, emitting a croaking sound.

"What a good little hen," said Mrs. Fernández. "That's right, come on . . . come, wake up, and I'll give you something special. How about if I get you some nice dried corn? . . . Come on." She continued to pet the hen and talk sweetly to her. Slowly, Joncrofo opened her beak and tried to cackle, and again she made a croaking sound. Blinking her eyes, she sat up in her box, ruffled her feathers, and managed a low soft cackle.

"Is she gonna live, Mami?" Mrs. Fernández turned and saw Olgita, Freddie, and Baby Nancy standing beside her.

"Of course she's going to live. What did you think I did, kill her? Tsk, tsk . . . did you really think that? You are all very silly children," she said, and shook her finger at them. They stared back at her with bewilderment, not speaking. "All that screaming at me was not nice." She went on, "I was only trying to save her. Joncrofo got very sick, and see?" She held up the eyedropper. "I had to help her get well. I had to catch her in order to cure her. Understand?"

Olgita and Freddie looked at each other and then at their mother.

"When I saw that she was getting sick, I had to catch her. She was running all around, jumping and going crazy. Yes." Mrs. Fernández opened her eyes and pointed to her head, making a circular movement with her right index finger. "She went cuckoo! If I didn't stop her, Joncrofo would have really killed herself," she said earnestly. "So I gave her some medicine—and now. . . ."

"Is that why you got her drunk, Mami?" interrupted Olgita.

"What?" asked Mrs. Fernández.

"You gave her Papi's rum . . . in the eyedropper. We seen you," Freddie said. Olgita nodded.

"Well," Mrs. Fernández said, "that don't make her drunk. It . . . it . . . ah . . . just calms her down. Sometimes it's used like a medicine."

"And makes her happy again?" Olgita asked. "Like Papi? He always gets happy when he drinks some."

"Yes, that's right. You're right. To make Joncrofo happy again," Mrs. Fernández said.

"Why did she get sick, Mami, and go crazy?" asked Freddie.

"I don't know why. Those things just happen," Mrs. Fernández responded.

"Do them things happen on the farm in Puerto Rico?"

"That's right," she said. "Now let me be. I gotta finish cleaning here. Go on, go to the back of the house; take Baby Nancy . . . go on."

The children left the kitchen, and Mrs. Fernández barricaded the entrance once more. She picked up the box with Joncrofo, who sat quietly blinking, and shoved it under the sink. Then she put the cleaver and the chopping board away. Picking up the broom, she began to sweep the feathers and torn newspapers that were strewn all about the kitchen.

In the back of the apartment, where the children played, they could hear their mother singing a familiar song. It was about a beautiful island where the tall green palm trees swayed under a golden sky and the flowers were always in bloom.

---

### IMPLICATIONS

Consider the following statements. Do you agree or disagree?

**1.** The story strikes one as both funny and pathetic.

**2.** The crosscurrent is set in motion because Joncrofo means something different to the children from what she means to the mother.

**3.** Mrs. Fernàndez was foolishly intimidated by the children.

### TECHNIQUES

*Characterization*

The principal character is Mrs. Fernández. Think back through the story and see how many details you remember about her. Do these total up to a picture of a real person?

*Plot*

Plot grows out of character, as you have seen in "The Stone Boy" and in "The Rocking-Horse Winner." But, at times, plot helps develop the reader's picture of a character. Mrs. Fernández's concern for her hungry family makes her decide to kill the hen. But in turn, as she attempts the killing, what do you learn that you might not have otherwise known?

♦Divisive crosscurrents
between parents and their children
provide the dramatic base in the
next two poems.

# ♦*Souvenir de Londres*

M y parents quarrel in the neighbour room:—
"How did you sleep last night?" "I woke at four
To hear the wind that sulks along the floor
Blowing up dust like ashes from the tomb."

"I was awake at three." "I heard the moth          5
Breed perilous worms." "I wept
All night, watching you rest." "I never slept
Nor sleep at all." Thus ghastly they speak, both.

How can these sleep who eat upon their fear
And watch their dreadful love fade as it grows?   10
Their life flowers like an antique lover's rose
Set puff'd and spreading in the chemist's jar.

I am your son, and from bad dreams arise.
My sight is fixed with horror, as I pass
Before the transitory[1] glass                    15
And watch the fungus cover up my eyes.

STEPHEN SPENDER

---

1. **transitory**\\'trăn(t)s•ə ▲tōr•ē\\ of brief duration.

---

Copyright 1934 and renewed 1962 by Stephen Spender. Reprinted
from SELECTED POEMS, by Stephen Spender, by permission of
Random House, Inc.

---

A NIGHT EVALUATION OF PARENTS
The title of the poem you just read means
"Memory of London." And it also uses an experience common to most young people—that of overhearing their parents quarreling at night. The reaction of the speaker is one of horror. "How can these sleep?" he asks. What does he feel about his parents' relationship? What figure of speech is used to describe their life? Do you expect your marriage to be different?

# The Whipping

The old woman across the way
   is whipping the boy again
and shouting to the neighborhood
   her goodness and his wrongs.

Wildly he crashes through elephant ears,    5
   pleads in dusty zinnias,
while she in spite of crippling fat
   pursues and corners him.

She strikes and strikes the shrilly circling
   boy till the stick breaks    10
in her hand. His tears are rainy weather
   to woundlike memories:

My head gripped in bony vise
   of knees, the writhing struggle
to wrench free, the blows, the fear    15
   worse than blows that hateful

Words could bring, the face that I
   no longer knew or loved . . .
Well, it is over now, it is over,
   and the boy sobs in his room,    20

And the woman leans muttering against
   a tree, exhausted, purged—
avenged in part for lifelong hidings
   she has had to bear.

ROBERT HAYDEN

"The Whipping" by Robert Hayden from SELECTED POEMS. Copyright © 1966 by Robert Hayden. Reprinted by permission of October House Inc.

## NEW UNDERSTANDINGS

The writer in this poem has taken an experience common to most of us and has transformed it so that it gains a meaning we may not have seen before. Why is the woman really punishing the boy? Is the punishment of children usually motivated by such needs? Notice that the speaker says that the boy's tears start the flow of his own memories. What are these memories?

Two thousand years ago
the story of "The Prodigal Son"
told of conflicts between parents and children
that are still present in families today.
Is there any reason to assume that they will be
any different in families of the future?
Will more gadgets, more creature comforts,
more scientific "miracles" relieve the tensions
in a family? Ray Bradbury turns his ingenious
and imaginative mind to this problem
in "The Veldt." Though the reader
may be horrified and want to reject the events
in this tale, he is persuaded to believe them
by Bradbury's skill as a storyteller.

# The Veldt

### RAY BRADBURY

George, I wish you'd look at the nursery."

"What's wrong with it?"

"I don't know."

"Well, then."

"I just want you to look at it, is all, or call a psychologist in to look at it."

"What would a psychologist want with a nursery?"

"You know very well what he'd want." His wife paused in the middle of the kitchen and watched the stove busy humming to itself, making supper for four.

"It's just that the nursery is different now than it was."

"All right, let's have a look."

They walked down the hall of their soundproofed, Happylife Home, which had cost them thirty thousand dollars installed, this house which clothed and fed and rocked them to sleep and played and sang and was good to them. Their approach sensitized a switch some-

where and the nursery light flicked on when they came within ten feet of it. Similarly, behind them, in the halls, lights went on and off as they left them behind, with a soft automaticity.

"Well," said George Hadley.

They stood on the thatched floor of the nursery. It was forty feet across by forty feet long and thirty feet high; it had cost half again as much as the rest of the house. "But nothing's too good for our children," George had said.

The nursery was silent. It was empty as a jungle glade at hot high noon. The walls were blank and two dimensional. Now, as George and Lydia Hadley stood in the center of the room, the walls began to purr and recede into crystalline distance, it seemed, and presently an African veldt appeared, in three dimensions, on all sides, in color, reproduced to the final pebble and bit of straw. The ceiling above them became a deep sky with a hot yellow sun.

George Hadley felt the perspiration start on his brow.

"Let's get out of this sun," he said. "This is a little too real. But I don't see anything wrong."

"Wait a moment, you'll see," said his wife.

Now the odorophonics[1] were beginning to blow a wind of odor at the two people in the middle of the baked veldtland. The hot straw smell of lion grass, the cool green smell of the hidden water hole, the great rusty smell of animals, the smell of dust like a red paprika in the hot air. And now the sounds: the thump of distant antelope feet on grassy sod, the papery rustling of vultures. A shadow passed through the sky. The shadow flickered on George Hadley's upturned, sweating face.

"Filthy creatures," he heard his wife say.

"The vultures."

"You see, there are the lions, far over, that way. Now they're on their way to the water hole. They've just been eating," said Lydia. "I don't know what."

Copyright 1950 by Ray Bradbury. Reprinted by permission of the Harold Matson Company, Inc.

1. This story is of course a fantasy of the future. To make the future seem true the author has invented some new words like odorophonics\'ō·də·rə ᴸfŏ·nĭks\. This word would suggest devices intended to send out appropriate odors and sounds together.

"Some animal." George Hadley put his hand up to shield off the burning light from his squinted eyes. "A zebra or a baby giraffe, maybe."

"Are you sure?" His wife sounded peculiarly tense.

"No, it's a little late to be sure," he said, amused. "Nothing over there I can see but cleaned bone, and the vultures dropping for what's left."

"Did you hear that scream?" she asked.

"No."

"About a minute ago?"

"Sorry, no."

The lions were coming. And again George Hadley was filled with admiration for the mechanical genius who had conceived this room. A miracle of efficiency selling for an absurdly low price. Every home should have one. Oh, occasionally they frightened you with their clinical accuracy, they startled you, gave you a twinge, but most of the time what fun for everyone, not only your own son and daughter, but for yourself when you felt like a quick jaunt to a foreign land, a quick change of scenery. Well, here it was!

And here were the lions now, fifteen feet away, so real, so feverishly and startlingly real that you could feel the prickling fur on your hand, and your mouth was stuffed with the dusty upholstery smell of their heated pelts, and the yellow of them was in your eyes like the yellow of an exquisite French tapestry, the yellows of lions and summer grass, and the sound of the matted lion lungs exhaling on the silent noontide, and the smell of meat from the panting, dripping mouths.

The lions stood looking at George and Lydia Hadley with terrible green-yellow eyes.

"Watch out!" screamed Lydia.

The lions came running at them.

Lydia bolted and ran. Instinctively, George sprang after her. Outside, in the hall, with the door slammed, he was laughing and she was crying, and they both stood appalled at the other's reaction.

"George!"

"Lydia! Oh, my dear poor sweet Lydia!"

"They almost got us!"

"Walls, Lydia, remember; crystal walls, that's all they are. Oh, they look real, I must admit—Africa in your parlor—but it's all dimensional superreactionary, supersensitive color film and mental tape film behind glass screens. It's all odorophonics and sonics, Lydia. Here's my handkerchief."

"I'm afraid." She came to him and put her body against him and cried steadily. "Did you see? Did you feel? It's too real."

"Now, Lydia . . ."

"You've got to tell Wendy and Peter[2] not to read any more on Africa."

"Of course—of course." He patted her.

"Promise?"

"Sure."

"And lock the nursery for a few days until I get my nerves settled."

"You know how difficult Peter is about that. When I punished him a month ago by locking the nursery for even a few hours—the tantrum he threw! And Wendy too. They *live* for the nursery."

"It's got to be locked, that's all there is to it."

"All right." Reluctantly he locked the huge door. "You've been working too hard. You need a rest."

"I don't know—I don't know," she said, blowing her nose, sitting down in a chair that immediately began to rock and comfort her. "Maybe I don't have enough to do. Maybe I have time to think too much. Why don't we shut the whole house off for a few days and take a vacation?"

"You mean you want to fry my eggs for me?"

"Yes," she nodded.

"And darn my socks?"

"Yes." A frantic, watery-eyed nodding.

"And sweep the house?"

"Yes, yes—oh, yes!"

"But I thought that's why we bought this house, so we wouldn't have to do anything?"

---

2. There is irony in the choice of **Peter** and **Wendy** as the children's names. Children named Peter and Wendy are prominent in J. M. Barrie's *Peter Pan*, a totally different kind of story.

"That's just it. I feel like I don't belong here. The house is wife and mother now and nursemaid. Can I compete with an African veldt? Can I give a bath and scrub the children as efficiently or quickly as the automatic scrub bath can? I cannot. And it isn't just me. It's you. You've been awfully nervous lately."

"I suppose I have been smoking too much."

"You look as if you didn't know what to do with yourself in this house, either. You smoke a little more every morning and drink a little more every afternoon and need a little more sedative every night. You're beginning to feel unnecessary too."

"Am I?" He paused and tried to feel into himself to see what was really there.

"Oh, George!" She looked beyond him, at the nursery door. "Those lions can't get out of there, can they?"

He looked at the door and saw it tremble as if something had jumped against it from the other side.

"Of course not," he said.

At dinner they ate alone, for Wendy and Peter were at a special plastic carnival across town and had televised home to say they'd be late, to go ahead eating. So George Hadley, bemused, sat watching the dining-room table produce warm dishes of food from its mechanical interior.

"We forgot the ketchup," he said.

"Sorry," said a small voice within the table, and ketchup appeared.

As for the nursery, thought George Hadley, it won't hurt for the children to be locked out of it awhile. Too much of anything isn't good for anyone. And it was clearly indicated that the children had been spending a little too much time on Africa. That *sun*. He could feel it on his neck, still, like a hot paw. And the *lions*. And the smell of blood. Remarkable how the nursery caught the telepathic emanations of the children's minds and created life to fill their every desire. The children thought lions, and there were lions. The children thought zebras, and there were zebras. Sun—sun. Giraffes—giraffes. Death and death.

That *last*. He chewed tastelessly on the meat that the table had cut for him. Death thoughts. They were awfully young, Wendy and Peter, for death thoughts. Or, no, you were never too young, really. Long before you knew what death was you were wishing it on someone else. When you were two years old you were shooting people with cap pistols.

But this—the long, hot African veldt—the awful death in the jaws of a lion. And repeated again and again.

"Where are you going?"

He didn't answer Lydia. Preoccupied, he let the lights glow softly on ahead of him, extinguish behind him as he padded to the nursery door. He listened against it. Far away, a lion roared.

He unlocked the door and opened it. Just before he stepped inside, he heard a faraway scream. And then another roar from the lions, which subsided quickly.

He stepped into Africa. How many times in the last year had he opened this door and found Wonderland, Alice, the Mock Turtle, or Aladdin and his Magical Lamp, or Jack Pumpkinhead of Oz, or Dr. Doolittle, or the cow jumping over a very real-appearing moon—all the delightful contraptions of a make-believe world.[3] How often had he seen Pegasus[4] flying in the sky ceiling, or seen fountains of red fireworks, or heard angel voices singing. But now, this yellow hot Africa, this bake oven with murder in the heat. Perhaps Lydia was right. Perhaps they needed a little vacation from the fantasy which was growing a bit too real for ten-year-old children. It was all right to exercise one's mind with gymnastic fantasies, but when the lively child mind settled on one pattern . . .? It seemed that, at a distance, for the past month, he had heard lions roaring, and smelled their strong odor seeping as far away as his study door. But, being busy, he had paid it no attention.

George Hadley stood on the African grassland alone. The lions looked up from their feeding, watching him. The only flaw to the illusion was the open door through which he could see his wife, far down the dark hall, like a framed picture, eating her dinner abstractedly.

"Go away," he said to the lions.

They did not go.

He knew the principle of the room exactly. You sent out your thoughts. Whatever you thought would appear.

"Let's have Aladdin and his lamp," he snapped.

The veldtland remained; the lions remained.

"Come on, room! I demand Aladdin!" he said.

Nothing happened. The lions mumbled in their baked pelts.

"Aladdin!"

He went back to dinner. "The fool room's out of order," he said. "It won't respond."

"Or—"

"Or what?"

3. **Wonderland,** the background for the adventures of Alice in *Alice in Wonderland,* in which the **Mock Turtle** appears. **Aladdin and his Magical Lamp** figure in one of the well-known stories from the *Arabian Nights.* **Jack Pumpkinhead of Oz**\ŏz\ is a character in the Oz books by Frank Baum. **Dr. Doolittle** is another character in stories that children might be expected to enjoy.

4. **Pegasus**\ˈpĕ•gə•səs\ a winged horse that figures in the adventures of Bellerophon \bĕ ˈlā•rə•fən\ a Greek legendary hero.

"Or it can't respond," said Lydia, "because the children have thought about Africa and lions and killing so many days that the room's in a rut."

"Could be."

"Or Peter's set it to remain that way."

"Set it?"

"He may have got into the machinery and fixed something."

"Peter doesn't know machinery."

"He's a wise one for ten. That I.Q. of his—"

"Nevertheless—"

"Hello, Mom. Hello, Dad."

The Hadleys turned. Wendy and Peter were coming in the front door, cheeks like peppermint candy, eyes like bright blue agate marbles, a smell of ozone on their jumpers from their trip in the helicopter.[5]

"You're just in time for supper," said both parents.

"We're full of strawberry ice cream and hot dogs," said the children, holding hands. "But we'll sit and watch."

"Yes, come tell us about the nursery," said George Hadley.

The brother and sister blinked at him and then at each other. "Nursery?"

"All about Africa and everything," said the father with false joviality.

"I don't understand," said Peter.

"Your mother and I were just traveling through Africa with rod and reel; Tom Swift[6] and his Electric Lion," said George Hadley.

"There's no Africa in the nursery," said Peter simply.

"Oh, come now, Peter. We know better."

"I don't remember any Africa," said Peter to Wendy. "Do you?"

"No."

"Run see and come tell."

She obeyed.

"Wendy, come back here!" said George Hadley, but she was gone. The house lights followed her like a flock of fireflies. Too late, he realized he had forgotten to lock the nursery door after his last inspection.

"Wendy'll look and come tell us," said Peter.

"She doesn't have to tell *me*. I've seen it."

"I'm sure you're mistaken, Father."

"I'm not, Peter. Come along now."

But Wendy was back. "It's not Africa," she said breathlessly.

"We'll see about this," said George Hadley, and they all walked down the hall together and opened the nursery door.

There was a green, lovely forest, a lovely river, a purple mountain, high voices singing, and Rima,[7] lovely and mysterious, lurking in the trees with colorful flights of butterflies, like animated bouquets, lingering in her long hair. The African veldtland was gone. The lions were gone. Only Rima was here now, singing a song so beautiful that it brought tears to your eyes.

George Hadley looked in at the changed scene. "Go to bed," he said to the children.

They opened their mouths.

"You heard me," he said.

They went off to the air closet, where a wind sucked them like brown leaves up the flue to their slumber rooms.

George Hadley walked through the singing glade and picked up something that lay in the corner near where the lions had been. He walked slowly back to his wife.

"What is that?" she asked.

"An old wallet of mine," he said.

He showed it to her. The smell of hot grass was on it and the smell of a lion. There were drops of saliva on it, it had been chewed, and there were blood smears on both sides.

He closed the nursery door and locked it, tight.

In the middle of the night he was still awake and he knew his wife was awake. "Do you

5. Agate\ˈă·gət\ the material from which colored marbles are often made. Ozone\ˈō ′zōn\ a form of oxygen especially associated with fresh and bracing air.

6. Tom Swift, the hero of a long series of boys' books during the early decades of this century. Often his adventures were fantastic.

7. Rima\ˈrē·mə\ the forest heroine of *Green Mansions*, a romance by W. H. Hudson placed in Argentina.

think Wendy changed it?" she said at last, in the dark room.

"Of course."

"Made it from a veldt into a forest and put Rima there instead of lions?"

"Yes."

"Why?"

"I don't know. But it's staying locked until I find out."

"How did your wallet get there?"

"I don't know anything," he said, "except that I'm beginning to be sorry we bought that room for the children. If children are neurotic at all, a room like that—"

"It's supposed to help them work off their neuroses in a healthful way."

"I'm starting to wonder." He stared at the ceiling.

"We've given the children everything they ever wanted. Is this our reward—secrecy, disobedience?"

"Who was it said, 'Children are carpets, they should be stepped on occasionally'? We've never lifted a hand. They're insufferable—let's admit it. They come and go when they like; they treat us as if we were offspring. They're spoiled and we're spoiled."

"They've been acting funny ever since you forbade them to take the rocket to New York a few months ago."

"They're not old enough to do that alone, I explained."

"Nevertheless, I've noticed they've been decidedly cool toward us since."

"I think I'll have David McClean come tomorrow morning to have a look at Africa."

"But it's not Africa now, it's Green Mansions country and Rima."

"I have a feeling it'll be Africa again before then."

A moment later they heard the screams.

Two screams. Two people screaming from downstairs. And then a roar of lions.

"Wendy and Peter aren't in their rooms," said his wife.

He lay in his bed with his beating heart.

"No," he said. "They've broken into the nursery."

"Those screams—they sound familiar."

"Do they?"

"Yes, awfully."

And although their beds tried very hard, the two adults couldn't be rocked to sleep for another hour. A smell of cats was in the night air.

"Father?" said Peter.

"Yes."

Peter looked at his shoes. He never looked at his father any more, nor at his mother. "You aren't going to lock up the nursery for good, are you?"

"That all depends."

"On what?" snapped Peter.

"On you and your sister. If you intersperse this Africa with a little variety—oh, Sweden perhaps, or Denmark or China—"

"I thought we were free to play as we wished."

"You are, within reasonable bounds."

"What's wrong with Africa, Father?"

"Oh, so now you admit you have been conjuring up Africa, do you?"

"I wouldn't want the nursery locked up," said Peter coldly. "Ever."

"Matter of fact, we're thinking of turning the whole house off for about a month. Live sort of a carefree one-for-all existence."

"That sounds dreadful! Would I have to tie my own shoes instead of letting the shoe tier do it? And brush my own teeth and comb my hair and give myself a bath?"

"It would be fun for a change, don't you think?"

"No, it would be horrid. I didn't like it when you took out the picture painter last month."

"That's because I wanted you to learn to paint all by yourself, son."

"I don't want to do anything but look and listen and smell; what else *is* there to do?"

"All right, go play in Africa."

"Will you shut off the house sometime soon?"

"We're considering it."

"I don't think you'd better consider it any more, Father."

"I won't have any threats from my son!"

"Very well." And Peter strolled off to the nursery.

"Am I on time?" said David McClean.

"Breakfast?" asked George Hadley.

"Thanks, had some. What's the trouble?"

"David, you're a psychologist."

"I should hope so."

"Well, then, have a look at our nursery. You saw it a year ago when you dropped by; did you notice anything peculiar about it then?"

"Can't say I did; the usual violences, a tendency toward a slight paranoia here or there, usual in children because they feel persecuted by parents constantly, but, oh, really nothing."

They walked down the hall. "I locked the nursery up," explained the father, "and the children broke back into it during the night. I let them stay so they could form the patterns for you to see."

There was a terrible screaming from the nursery.

"There it is," said George Hadley. "See what you make of it."

They walked in on the children without rapping.

The screams had faded. The lions were feeding.

"Run outside a moment, children," said George Hadley. "No, don't change the mental combination. Leave the walls as they are. Get!"

With the children gone, the two men stood studying the lions clustered at a distance, eating with great relish whatever it was they had caught.

"I wish I knew what it was," said George Hadley. "Sometimes I can almost see. Do you think if I brought high-powered binoculars here and—"

David McClean laughed dryly. "Hardly." He turned to study all four walls. "How long has this been going on?"

"A little over a month."

"It certainly doesn't *feel* good."

"I want facts, not feelings."

"My dear George, a psychologist never saw a fact in his life. He only hears about feelings; vague things. This doesn't feel good, I tell you Trust my hunches and my instincts. I have a nose for something bad. This is very bad. My advice to you is to have the whole damn room torn down and your children brought to me every day during the next year for treatment."

"Is it that bad?"

"I'm afraid so. One of the original uses of these nurseries was so that we could study the patterns left on the walls by the child's mind, study at our leisure, and help the child. In this case, however, the room has become a channel toward—destructive thoughts, instead of a release away from them."

"Didn't you sense this before?"

"I sensed only that you had spoiled your children more than most. And now you're letting them down in some way. What way?"

"I wouldn't let them go to New York."

"What else?"

"I've taken a few machines from the house and threatened them, a month ago, with closing up the nursery unless they did their homework. I did close it for a few days to show I meant business."

"Ah, ha!"

"Does that mean anything?"

"Everything. Where before they had a Santa Claus now they have a Scrooge.[8] Children prefer Santas. You've let this room and this house replace you and your wife in your children's affections. This room is their mother and father, far more important in their lives than their real parents. And now you come along and want to shut it off. No wonder there's hatred here. You can feel it coming out of the sky. Feel that sun. George, you'll have to change your life. Like too many others, you've built it around creature comforts. Why, you'd

8. **Scrooge**\skrūj\ a character in Dickens' *Christmas Carol* who refused to feel the joy of the Christmas Season.

starve tomorrow if something went wrong in your kitchen. You wouldn't know how to tap an egg. Nevertheless, turn everything off. Start new. It'll take time. But we'll make good children out of bad in a year, wait and see."

"But won't the shock be too much for the children, shutting the room up abruptly, for good?"

"I don't want them going any deeper into this, that's all."

The lions were finished with their red feast.

The lions were standing on the edge of the clearing watching the two men.

"Now *I'm* feeling persecuted," said McClean. "Let's get out of here. I never have cared for these rooms. Make me nervous."

"The lions look real, don't they?" said George Hadley. "I don't suppose there's any way—"

"What?"

"—that they could *become* real?"

"Not that I know."

"Some flaw in the machinery, a tampering or something?"

"No."

They went to the door.

"I don't imagine the room will like being turned off," said the father.

"Nothing ever likes to die—even a room."

"I wonder if it hates me for wanting to switch it off?"

"Paranoia is thick around here today," said David McClean. "You can follow it like a spoor. Hello." He bent and picked up a bloody scarf. "This yours?"

"No," George Hadley's face was rigid. "It belongs to Lydia."

They went to the fuse box together and threw the switch that killed the nursery.

The two children were in hysterics. They screamed and pranced and threw things. They yelled and sobbed and swore and jumped at the furniture.

"You can't do that to the nursery, you can't!"

"Now, children."

The children flung themselves onto a couch, weeping.

"George," said Lydia Hadley, "turn on the nursery, just for a few moments. You can't be so abrupt."

"No."

"You can't be so cruel."

"Lydia, it's off, and it stays off. And the whole damn house dies as of here and now. The more I see of the mess we've put ourselves in, the more it sickens me. We've been contemplating our mechanical, electronic navels for too long. How we need a breath of honest air!"

And he marched about the house turning off the voice clocks, the stoves, the heaters, the shoe shiners, the shoe lacers, the body scrubbers and swabbers and massagers, and every other machine he could put his hand to.

The house was full of dead bodies, it seemed. It felt like a mechanical cemetery. So silent. None of the humming hidden energy of machines waiting to function at the tap of a button.

"Don't let them do it!" wailed Peter at the ceiling, as if he was talking to the house, the nursery. "Don't let Father kill everything." He turned to his father. "Oh, I hate you!"

"Insults won't get you anywhere."

"I wish you were dead!"

"We were, for a long while. Now we're going to really start living. Instead of being handled and massaged, we're going to *live*."

Wendy was still crying and Peter joined her again. "Just a moment, just one moment, just another moment of nursery," they wailed.

"Oh, George," said the wife, "it can't hurt."

"All right—all right, if they'll only just shut up. One minute, mind you, and then off forever."

"Daddy, Daddy, Daddy!" sang the children, smiling with wet faces.

"And then we're going on a vacation. David McClean is coming back in half an hour to help us move out and get to the airport. I'm going to dress. You turn the nursery on for a minute, Lydia, just a minute, mind you."

And the three of them went babbling off while he let himself be vacuumed upstairs through the air flue and set about dressing himself. A minute later Lydia appeared.

"I'll be glad when we get away," she sighed.

"Did you leave them in the nursery?"

"I wanted to dress, too. Oh, that horrid Africa. What can they see in it?"

"Well, in five minutes we'll be on our way to Iowa. Lord, how did we ever get in this house? What prompted us to buy a nightmare?"

"Pride, money, foolishness."

"I think we'd better get downstairs before those kids get engrossed with those damned beasts again."

Just then they heard the children calling, "Daddy, Mommy, come quick—quick!"

They went downstairs in the air flue and ran down the hall. The children were nowhere in sight. "Wendy? Peter!"

They ran into the nursery. The veldtland was empty save for the lions waiting, looking at them. "Peter, Wendy?"

The door slammed.

"Wendy, Peter!"

George Hadley and his wife whirled and ran back to the door.

"Open the door!" cried George Hadley, trying the knob. "Why, they've locked it from the outside! Peter!" He beat at the door. "Open up!"

He heard Peter's voice outside, against the door.

"Don't let them switch off the nursery and the house," he was saying.

Mr. and Mrs. George Hadley beat at the door. "Now, don't be ridiculous, children. It's time to go. Mr. McClean'll be here in a minute and . . ."

And then they heard the sounds.

The lions on three sides of them, in the yellow veldt grass, padding through the dry straw, rumbling and roaring in their throats.

The lions.

Mr. Hadley looked at his wife and they turned and looked back at the beasts edging slowly forward, crouching, tails stiff.

Mr. and Mrs. Hadley screamed.

And suddenly they realized why those other screams had sounded familiar.

"Well, here I am," said David McClean in the nursery doorway. "Oh, hello." He stared at the two children seated in the center of the open glade eating a little picnic lunch. Beyond them was the water hole and the yellow veldtland; above was the hot sun. He began to perspire. "Where are your father and mother?"

The children looked up and smiled. "Oh, they'll be here directly."

"Good, we must get going." At a distance Mr. McClean saw the lions fighting and clawing and then quieting down to feed in silence under the shady trees.

He squinted at the lions with his hand up to his eyes.

Now the lions were done feeding. They moved to the water hole to drink.

A shadow flicked over Mr. McClean's hot face. Many shadows flickered. The vultures were dropping down the blazing sky.

"A cup of tea?" asked Wendy in the silence.

---

I

MAKING THE IMAGINARY REAL

One problem in writing of the unknown is to make it seem possible and even ordinary to the reader. Bradbury uses many devices to accomplish this task. Principally, he writes as if you, the reader, already knew about the age with which he is dealing. He comments casually about the automatic shoe lacers, the lighting system, the air closet, and the playroom. But he combines enough familiar details with the strange so that the reader accepts the strange the same way he accepts the familiar.

II

IMPLICATIONS

1. Consider the following quotations from the story. Who is speaking in each? How do the attitudes expressed reveal the conflicts in the story?

a. "But nothing's too good for our children."

b. "They *live* for the nursery."

**c.** "I don't remember any Africa . . . do you?"

**d.** "I don't want to do anything but look and listen and smell, what else *is* there to do?"

**e.** "We've given the children everything they ever wanted. Is this our reward . . . secrecy, disobedience?"

**f.** "Too much of anything isn't good for anyone."

**g.** "Children are like carpets, they should be stepped on occasionally."

**2.** How do such statements serve as a bridge between the world of today and the world of the story?

**3.** What do you believe to be the cause of the violent crosscurrents between these children and their parents? Would the vacation have lessened their conflicts?

### III
### TECHNIQUES

*Characterization*

This story is almost devoid of characterization. Readers know that they are dealing with parents and their two children, but this is basically all the information that is given. Why isn't it necessary to know these four people better?

*Plot*

Why did Bradbury find it necessary to have the children off at the plastic carnival as the story opened? Later, why must he introduce the psychologist into the story? Notice that this story is divided into sections. What happens or what is said in the last three or four lines of each section that makes the reader aware of the deepening of the conflict?

### IV
### WORDS

**A.** From context determine the meaning of the italicized words:

**1.** "So George Hadley, *bemused*, sat watching the dining-room table produce warm dishes of food from its mechanical interior."

**2.** "Remarkable how the nursery caught the telepathic *emanations* of the children's minds."

**3.** "*Preoccupied*, he let the lights glow softly on ahead of him, extinguish behind him as he padded to the nursery door."

**4.** "The lions looked up from their feeding, watching him. The only flaw in the *illusion* was the open door through which he could see his wife . . . ."

**5.** "Oh, so you admit you have been *conjuring* up Africa, do you?"

**6.** ". . . a slight *paranoia*, usual in children because they feel persecuted by parents constantly."

**B. 1.** More very common roots include *-vert-*, *-vers-*, meaning "turn"; and *-vid-*, *-vis-*, meaning "to see, sight"; as in the words *convert* and *conversion*, *evident* and *vision*. Sometimes a common Latin root may appear in not only two but even three different forms. The root *-ced-*, as in *precede*, or *-ceed-*, as in *proceed*, or *-cess-*, as in *recession* or *procession*, is a good illustration. You can probably conclude that it may mean "go, pass" (although it has other uses, as in *cede* and *cession*, in which it means "to pass over or yield"). A Latin root meaning "to run, a running, a course" appears as *-cur-*, in *concur* or *occur*; *-curr-*, in *current* or *concurrent*; and *-curs-* in *cursory* or *precursor*.

**2.** Some common prefixes are *ab-* (or *a-* or *abs-*), meaning "off, away," and ad (or *ac-*, *af-*, *ag-*, *al-*, *an-*, *ap-*, *ar-*, *as-*, *at-*, depending on the following consonant), meaning "to, toward." How many words can you make up by joining these prefixes to the common roots that you have studied so far?

As soon as one person is joined by another,
crosscurrents of needs, ambitions, and purposes begin.
Writers have dramatized this aspect of the human condition
within their own medium of words. The painter
and the engraver visualize the same area of personal tension
within the confines of their canvases or their drawing boards.
Notice how the pictures in this gallery overlap in content
and then begin to set up crosscurrents of their own.

MY PARENTS
*Henry Koerner*

The old people on their lonely, separate roads in the autumn forest
very obviously speak of the divided channels of crosscurrents.
But it is interesting to learn that to the artist the picture, MY PARENTS,
was an attempt to reunite his beloved family,
which had been separated by death and the concentration camps
of World War II. The old people are his devoted parents,
forced apart in lonely old age but together now in the eye of the beholder.
The locket hanging from the tree in the foreground
pictures their children and completes the family group so irretrievably
washed apart by the crosscurrents of life in time of war.

PEASANTS INTERIOR
*Louis LeNain*

IN THE PARLOR
*Honoré Sharrer*

Family groups inevitably
contain crosscurrents, and through
the sensitive eye of the painter
these differing moods become
more obvious to the rest of us.

Look closely at the individuals
in the peasants group
from seventeenth-century France.
Who seems resentful?
Who full of hope?
Who may be in despair
and who appears determined?
Can you imagine something of
their lives from what you see here?

In the parlor there are
rather ordinary twentieth-century
Americans. The artist
is commenting on the quality
of life today. What do you
suppose her comment is?

FAMILY PICTURE    *Max Beckmann*
*1920, Oil on canvas, 25⅝ x 39¾"*
*Collection, The Museum of Modern Art, New York*
*Gift of Abby Aldrich Rockefeller*

Max Beckman, like Koerner,
suffered deeply from the disasters
of World War II and his view of life
became harsh and painful.
His picture of a family
uses the exaggerations
of a very modern style
as well as differing activities
and brooding expressions
to make his point
about the crosscurrents that may
exist within a single family.
What currents can you pick out
from this complex picture?

THE SICK CHILD
*Edvard Munch*

The pale but determined head
of the sick child
sets up a crosscurrent washing
over the fatigue and despair
of the mother. The emotional paths
of even the closest people
may not run a parallel course.

Saltimbanques are entertainers somewhat like the circus performers
you have seen in America. Picasso painted this picture
during his lovely rose and blue periods and the crosscurrents within it
may not be the first thing you see. But if you look closely
and with imagination you will pick up the same threads
that were woven into each of the other family pictures in this gallery.

185

PAST AND PRESENT, NO. 2
*Augustus Egg*
*Reproduced by courtesy*
*of the trustees of*
*The Tate Gallery, London*

SAMSON THREATENS
HIS FATHER-IN-LAW
*Rembrandt Van Rijn*

**M**ost of what you need to know
to guess at the nature
of the crosscurrents
in this sentimental
but once popular picture
is contained in the title,
PAST AND PRESENT.
Whatever has gone before
in this story-rich picture
looks different to each person,
"present" and "past."

**R**embrandt uses an incident
from the ancient Bible story
of the boisterous hero
Samson as a means
of portraying the crosscurrents
between a man
who feels himself ill-used
and his adversary.
The actual Bible story is
from episodes told
of Samson's early life.

Not all crosscurrents
are troubled ones.
The serene South Sea island people
pictured by Gauguin are,
in their separate ways,
setting up very gentle crosscurrents.

THE BIG TREE
*Paul Gauguin*

# Crosscurrents

Unlike friends, families are not of our own choosing. Each person inherits a family at birth. It is inevitable that people bound so closely together should be subject to controversies and conflicts as they express their feelings, hopes, ambitions, and beliefs. Because of the universality of the family experience, it is one of the most natural subjects for literature. And because the very essence of storytelling lies in problems and conflicts, family disputes have always been raw material for stories. As you have seen, writers treat such material sometimes with grim seriousness and sometimes with humor.

In the preceding group of selections, you have viewed crosscurrents arising in family living and have seen how there is more than one cause setting them in motion. Some crosscurrents were created by a lack of communication between members of the family. Others were created by indifference or self-centeredness. One was created by a family member's lust for money. But a basic cause of most crosscurrents, as shown in all the selections, is the difference in point of view between children and parents. The conflicts in such stories are heightened, and the reactions of the people are sharpened, because the participants are members of a family, not merely friends or chance acquaintances.

## IMPLICATIONS

1. Disturbances in families may spring from many causes. In which of the stories do you find evidence of conflicts or problems arising from the following.

   a. Indifference of one member of the family to another?

   b. Lack of communication?

   c. Self-centeredness of one or more family members?

   d. A difference in the goals or the desires among family members?

2. What are some of the basic emotions that you found involved in these stories about families?

3. To outsiders, the family unit may seem to have a definite personality which is different from the personalities of the individuals who make up the family. In a sentence or two, describe the families in the following stories. Then characterize the individuals in each family.

   a. "The Rocking-Horse Winner"

   b. "The Veldt"

## TECHNIQUES

*Characterization*

1. Think back through the stories in this section. Which characters are the most memorable? Are the most memorable characters for you the ones you would like best if you actually knew them? How do you explain your reaction?

2. What are the principal devices that writers use to characterize the people they create? Which writer made the most skillful use of these devices?

3. Is it possible to have a good story without fully developed characters?

*Plot*

1. What kinds of problems does a writer face in plotting a story?

2. Name some of the characteristics of a satisfying plot.

3. Cite examples of plots in these stories that are closely tied to characterization.

# The Diary of Anne Frank

## Introduction

ANN BIRSTEIN
*and*
ALFRED KAZIN

In March 1945, a young girl died in Bergen-Belsen,[1] unaware that she was leaving behind her a work that shed the first tiny human light on an episode in history that was unspeakably inhuman. She was a lovely girl, not quite sixteen when she died, with enormous dark gray eyes, a pretty little mouth, and a very brave heart. But like any awkward and self-conscious adolescent, she was weighed down by a sense of her shortcomings. She worried about her looks; she thought of herself as a coward, so often full of fear that she never realized how heroically she overcame it. Certainly, it would have been beyond her to imagine that the diary she kept for two years would have an impact on the entire world; how could it when the events of her lifetime were so enormous she could only seem puny by comparison? Her only real certainty was that she meant to be a writer anyway, and that her subject would have to be the world in which she found herself alive, no matter how terrible or even how unaccountably lovely her experiences in it might seem. For two years before her arrest she wrote all the time. She wrote while she was in hiding from the Nazis and could not take one step outdoors or in the daytime speak above a whisper. She wrote although the bombs came down so heavily at night that she fled for comfort into her father's bed. She wrote so steadily that by the time she was fifteen she had finished the equivalent of two books, one the *Diary*, the other a collection of short stories, essays, and reminiscences. As she said, with amazement at her own daring, she wrote because, "I want to go on living even after my death!" She has—reminding us that each of those millions who died in agony and despair, each of those victims whom the Nazis "exterminated" was, like Anne Frank, a separate and precious human spirit.

Of Anne Frank's actual life, as apart from her work, there is very little to tell; she did not live to see her sixteenth birthday. But because she had a great capacity for happiness, her life all in all was quite a happy one. She was born in Frankfurt, Germany, on June 12, 1929, to fairly wealthy Jewish parents, and she was lucky in her family, for although no one in her lifetime considered her unusual or profound, she was always able to count on a great deal of love and mutual respect in her home. She had a grandmother whom she adored and whom she refers to both in her diary and her stories as a "guardian angel," and an older sister, Margot, who was by everyone's account both beautiful and kind. With her mother she got on less well, though her complaints are largely just the usual ones of any growing girl. Actually, her mother taught Anne a great deal, especially lessons in charity. "No one ever becomes poor from giving," Mrs. Frank used to say, and Anne herself repeats this in her little essay called "Give." But it was her father Anne loved best, and with reason. He was and is a cultured man of great personal nobility and quiet courage, exactly the kind of father an adolescent girl could always turn to.

In 1933, when Hitler came to power, the Franks moved to Amsterdam, and though life soon closed in on them—the Franks, no longer wealthy, had to take in boarders; Holland was

---

From *The Works of Anne Frank.* Copyright © 1959 by Otto H. Frank. Reprinted by permission of Doubleday & Company, Inc.

1. **Bergen-Belsen,** a notorious Nazi concentration camp in southern Germany.

*The large house in the middle is the rear of the Anne Frank house. The fourth floor window was for two years Anne's only access to the outside world.*

invaded and capitulated to Germany; the Nazis issued strict anti-Jewish decrees; Anne had to leave the Montessori School, which she had loved, and go to the Jewish Lyceum—Anne remained the same humorous child she had always been. Lies Goosens, an old school friend in Amsterdam, who later saw Anne in Belsen, remembers her being considered a "problem child, very talkative"; by Mr. Frank's own tender confession, she never in life seemed so "deep" as she appeared in her diary. She was a vivid girl, but definitely not a prodigy. Ironically enough, the very vividness and intensity of the adolescent self-confrontation that was to make the *Diary* famous perhaps made Anne seem more conventional than she really was. The headmistress of the Montessori School in Amsterdam (now the Anne Frank School) remembers that Anne did not show any early promise, and that many of her pupils wrote with more imagination and feeling than did Anne.

When we read the accounts of those who had known Anne, we can see that although she had always been very distinct to them and often arresting, she had been seen only as a very young girl, and externally very much a girl of her own age. She had a passion for movie stars, whose pictures she collected, and for royalty—one of her main preoccupations was the difficulty of finding suitable husbands for Princess Elizabeth and Princess Margaret of Great Britain. She was a great talker, often an incessant one, as her family and teachers knew only too well, and her fondness for make-believe was such that she would bring a suitcase along even when she was just visiting for an hour next door. Anne giggled with her girl friends, was saucy and flirtatious with boys, played a lot of ping-pong, and consumed great quantities of ice cream afterward. She had a lovely thirteenth birthday with a party, home movies, flowers, and many presents, among them a small clothbound diary which Anne decided at once was "possibly the nicest of all." Then, a month after this birthday, life closed in on the Franks for good. On a hot July morning in 1942 they went into hiding, walking across Amsterdam in the pouring rain to a small group of rooms behind Mr. Frank's former offices. Here they and four others were to stay cooped up for more than two years, until the Dutch Green Police routed them out on August 4, 1944; and here Anne's diary, that nice present, was to grow and grow until, like all truly remarkable books, it finally outgrew its own author.

In a certain sense, however, it isn't fair to call the *Diary of a Young Girl* a diary at all, since from the very first it was more to her than a purely personal record of triumphs and defeats. Always she had toward her own experience the marvelous ambivalence of the born novelist, and immediately after claiming that "neither I—nor for that matter anyone else—will be interested in the unbosomings of a thirteen-year-old schoolgirl," on the very same page of her journal she has already chosen a literary form—the entries will be in the shape of letters to an imaginary girl named Kitty—

and embarked on a concise sketch, not only of her own life, but of general conditions in Holland. This same uncanny sense of an unseen audience, actually of posterity, prevails throughout her work. Scared out of her wits as she must have been when she went into hiding, one of the first things she writes about it is a detailed description of the hiding place and the bits and pieces of furnishings that went into it. When new people arrive, first the Van Daans and then Dussel, the dentist, she has them down on paper practically the minute they are through the door. With a writer's eye for how much is implied in the ordinary events of an ordinary day, she describes a typical morning, afternoon, and evening in the annexe; how they went to the toilet; where they slept; what they talked about while they peeled potatoes and shelled peas and stuffed sausages. She fell in love with the boy upstairs, yearned desperately for her first kiss, and in the breathless moment before it finally came broke into tears—which she described meticulously: "I sat pressed closely against him and felt a wave of emotion come over me, tears sprang into my eyes, the left one trickled onto his dungarees, the right one ran down my nose and also fell onto his dungarees. Did he notice? He made no move or sign to show that he did. . . . At half past eight I stood up and went to the window, where we always say good-by. . . . He came toward me, I flung my arms around his neck and gave him a kiss on his left cheek, and was about to kiss the other cheek, when my lips met his and we pressed them together."

To everything that happened to her, to everything that she felt, Anne gave a kind of permanence by transcribing it, and day after day she went on adding still another segment to the world she was creating. In the stories, where she chose her subjects, this world is not so real. But in her diary, where her subject chose her, its vividness and poignance are overwhelming. We can see them all: Mrs. Frank, always a little in the shadows, defending the upbringing of her children, or discussing with Mrs. Van Daan the best way to address servants; Mrs.

*Behind this bookcase are the stairs leading to the hideout. Through this passage Miep and Mr. Kraler funneled all the food, clothing, medicine, and news.*

Van Daan taking time out for a little flirtation with Dussel, the pompous old dentist, or else picking a fight with Mr. Van Daan ("But Putti . . . Mr. Frank always answers his wife, doesn't he?"); young, shy Peter Van Daan lying listlessly in his cluttered boy's room upstairs; Margot, always composed and gentle; Mr. Frank putting aside his beloved Dickens to settle a quarrel and put things right again; their Dutch protectors coming upstairs with their thoughtful little presents and their tantalizing whiffs of the outside world; and Anne, working out her genealogical tables, pasting up her pictures of movie stars, talking so much that everyone has to tell her to shut up—and then transforming herself into the ninth member, the one who retired to the little table so hard won from Mr. Dussel to bring the others to life.

What makes her achievement really amazing is how little, aside from her own natural gifts of observation and her sense of humor, she had to work with. Other people have countrysides and multitudes. For Anne, the one boy upstairs was love; a single chestnut tree seen from her window, nature; a patch of blue sky—heaven. No wonder that soon she began to think of her diary and some of her sketches as the basis for a book after the war. *Het Achterhuis* (The House Behind) she meant to call it—a perfect title for the first book of a young girl, suggesting mystery and suspense and excitement; she even had a list of pseudonyms for the people in it.

*The fourth floor window (shown on page 190) from the inside. To Anne the branches of the chestnut tree and the patch of sky became "nature" and "heaven."*

When life in "the house behind" finally came to an end with the raid of the Green Police, it is ironic that in their search for loot the Police overlooked the precious diary. But Dutch friends who had sustained the Franks during the two-year confinement found Anne's notebooks and hid them until she should return. Only the father returned—to learn that he alone was left and to be given his daughter's notebooks by Miep and Elli. The little books

must have seemed pathetic enough to Otto Frank when, after his own slow recovery to health, he returned to Amsterdam to learn, after agonizing inquiries, that his wife and two children were dead.

At first Mr. Frank had copies of the *Diary* privately circulated as a memorial to his family. It was a Dutch university professor who urged formal publication of the book, and with only very slight excisions by Mr. Frank, *Het Achterhuis* was published in Amsterdam by Contact Publishers, in June 1947. The book soon went through several editions. In 1950, it was published in Germany by the Heidelberg firm of Lambert Schneider. The first printing was 4,500 copies, and many booksellers were actually afraid to show it in their windows; but the book caught on rapidly, and the sales of the pocket edition, published by S. Fischer Verlag, total more than half a million. In 1950 it was published in France; in 1952, in England and the United States. By now the book has been translated into twenty-two languages, has been published in twenty countries, and has sold more than two and a half million copies. In the United States it had an enormous success in the Pocket Book edition and later was circulated by the Teen Age Book Club, the Book Find Club, and republished in the Modern Library. The book was serialized by an American newspaper syndicate, with a calculated audience of ten million readers, and millions more read it when it was condensed in *Omnibook* and *Compact* magazines. A German translation of the book has been used in the United States as a school reader.

The book had a second life when it was dramatized by Frances Goodrich and Albert Hackett and became one of the most successful enterprises of the contemporary theater. In the United States the play won all the principal theater awards, and has since been produced in over twenty countries. It was also made into a film, and now the story of Anne Frank has become perhaps the most celebrated document of a single human being's ordeal during World War II.

# THE DIARY OF ANNE FRANK

*Dramatized by*

FRANCES GOODRICH

*and*

ALBERT HACKETT

Based upon the book,
*Anne Frank: Diary of a Young Girl*

## Characters

(in order of appearance)

MR. FRANK
MIEP
MRS. VAN DAAN
MR. VAN DAAN
PETER VAN DAAN
MRS. FRANK
MARGOT FRANK
ANNE FRANK
MR. KRALER
MR. DUSSEL

*The time: During the years of World War II and immediately thereafter.*

*The place: Amsterdam.*

*There are two acts.*

Copyright 1954, 1956 as an unpublished work. Copyright © 1956 by Albert Hackett and Otto Frank. Reprinted by permission of Random House, Inc.

# Act One

### SCENE I

*The scene remains the same throughout the play. It is the top floor of a warehouse and office building in Amsterdam, Holland. The sharply peaked roof of the building is outlined against a sea of other rooftops, stretching away into the distance. Nearby is the belfry of a church tower, the Westertoren, whose carillon rings out the hours. Occasionally faint sounds float up from below: the voices of children playing in the street, the tramp of marching feet, a boat whistle from the canal.*

*The three rooms of the top floor and a small attic space above are exposed to our view. The largest of the rooms is in the center, with two small rooms, slightly raised, on either side. On the right is a bathroom, out of sight. A narrow steep flight of stairs at the back leads up to the attic. The rooms are sparsely furnished with a few chairs, cots, a table or two. The windows are painted over, or covered with makeshift blackout curtains.[1] In the main room there is a sink, a gas ring for cooking and a wood-burning stove for warmth.*

*The room on the left is hardly more than a closet. There is a skylight in the sloping ceiling. Directly under this room is a small steep stairwell, with steps leading down to a door. This is the only entrance from the building below. When the door is opened we see that it has been concealed on the outer side by a bookcase attached to it.*

*The curtain rises on a empty stage. It is late afternoon November, 1945.*

*The rooms are dusty, the curtains in rags. Chairs and tables are overturned.*

*The door at the foot of the small stairwell swings open.* MR. FRANK *comes up the steps*

---

1. **Blackout curtain,** a heavy dark curtain to prevent light from within from being seen.

*into view. He is a gentle, cultured European in his middle years. There is still a trace of a German accent in his speech.*

*He stands looking slowly around, making a supreme effort at self-control. He is weak, ill. His clothes are threadbare.*

*After a second he drops his rucksack on the couch and moves slowly about. He opens the door to one of the smaller rooms, and then abruptly closes it again, turning away. He goes to the window at the back, looking off at the Westertoren as its carillon strikes the hour of six, then he moves restlessly on.*

*From the street below we hear the sound of a barrel organ and children's voices at play. There is a many-colored scarf hanging from a nail.* MR. FRANK *takes it, putting it around his neck. As he starts back for his rucksack, his eye is caught by something lying on the floor. It is a woman's white glove. He holds it in his hand and suddenly all of his self-control is gone. He breaks down, crying.*

*We hear footsteps on the stairs.* MIEP[2] GIES *comes up, looking for* MR. FRANK. MIEP *is a Dutch girl of about twenty-two. She wears a coat and hat, ready to go home. She is pregnant. Her attitude toward* MR. FRANK *is protective, compassionate.*

MIEP. Are you all right, Mr. Frank?

MR. FRANK. (*Quickly controlling himself*) Yes, Miep, yes.

MIEP. Everyone in the office has gone home . . . It's after six. (*Then pleading*) Don't stay up here, Mr. Frank. What's the use of torturing yourself like this?

MR. FRANK. I've come to say good-bye . . . I'm leaving here, Miep.

MIEP. What do you mean? Where are you going? Where?

MR. FRANK. I don't know yet. I haven't decided.

MIEP. Mr. Frank, you can't leave here! This is your home! Amsterdam is your home. Your business is here, waiting for you . . . You're needed here . . . Now that the war is over, there are things that . . .

MR. FRANK. I can't stay in Amsterdam, Miep. It

has too many memories for me. Everywhere there's something . . . the house we lived in . . . the school . . . that street organ playing out there . . . I'm not the person you used to know, Miep. I'm a bitter old man. (*Breaking off*) Forgive me. I shouldn't speak to you like this . . . after all that you did for us . . . the suffering . . .

MIEP. No. No. It wasn't suffering. You can't say we suffered.

(*As she speaks, she straightens a chair which is overturned.*)

MR. FRANK. I know what you went through, you and Mr. Kraler. I'll remember it as long as I live. (*He gives one last look around*) Come, Miep.

(*He starts for the steps, then remembers his rucksack, going back to get it.*)

MIEP. (*Hurrying up to a cupboard*) Mr. Frank, did you see? There are some of your papers here. (*She brings a bundle of papers to him*) We found them in a heap of rubbish on the floor after . . . after you left.

MR. FRANK. Burn them.

(*He opens his rucksack to put the glove in it.*)

MIEP. But, Mr. Frank, there are letters, notes . . .

MR. FRANK. Burn them. All of them.

MIEP. Burn *this?*

(*She hands him a paperbound notebook.*)

MR. FRANK. (*Quietly*) Anne's diary. (*He opens the diary and begins to read*) "Monday, the sixth of July, nineteen forty-two." (*To* MIEP) Nineteen forty-two. Is it possible, Miep? . . . Only three years ago. (*As he continues his reading, he sits down on the couch*) "Dear Diary, since you and I are going to be great friends, I will start by telling you about myself. My name is Anne Frank. I am thirteen years old. I was born in Germany the twelfth of June, nineteen twenty-nine. As my family

---

2. **Miep**\mēp\.

194

is Jewish, we emigrated to Holland when Hitler came to power."

(*As* MR. FRANK *reads on, another voice joins his, as if coming from the air. It is* ANNE's *voice.*)

MR. FRANK AND ANNE. "My father started a business, importing spice and herbs. Things went well for us until nineteen forty. Then the war came, and the Dutch capitulation, followed by the arrival of the Germans. Then things got very bad for the Jews."

(MR. FRANK's *voice dies out.* ANNE's *voice continues alone. The lights dim slowly to darkness. The curtain falls on the scene.*)

ANNE's VOICE. You could not do this and you could not do that. They forced Father out of his business. We had to wear yellow stars. I had to turn in my bike. I couldn't go to a Dutch school any more. I couldn't go to the movies, or ride in an automobile, or even on a streetcar, and a million other things. But somehow we children still managed to have fun. Yesterday Father told me we were going into hiding. Where, he wouldn't say. At five o'clock this morning Mother woke me and told me to hurry and get dressed. I was to put on as many clothes as I could. It would look too suspicious if we walked along carrying suitcases. It wasn't until we were on our way that I learned where we were going. Our hiding place was to be upstairs in the building where Father used to have his business. Three other people were coming in *with* us . . . The Van Daans and their son Peter . . . *Father* knew the Van Daans but we had never met them . . .

(*During the last lines the curtain rises on the scene. The lights dim on.* ANNE's *voice fades out.*)

SCENE II

*It is early morning, July, 1942. The rooms are bare, as before, but they are now clean and orderly.*

MR. VAN DAAN, *a tall, portly man in his late forties, is in the main room, pacing up and down, nervously smoking a cigarette. His clothes and overcoat are expensive and well cut.*

MRS. VAN DAAN *sits on the couch, clutching her possessions, a hatbox, bags, etc. She is a pretty woman in her early forties. She wears a fur coat over her other clothes.*

PETER VAN DAAN *is standing at the window of the room on the right, looking down at the street below. He is a shy, awkward boy of sixteen. He wears a cap, a raincoat, and long Dutch trousers like "plus fours."[1] At his feet is a black case, a carrier for his cat.*

*The yellow Star of David[2] is conspicuous on all of their clothes.*

MRS. VAN DAAN. (*Rising, nervous, excited*) Something's happened to them! I know it!

MR. VAN DAAN. Now, Kerli!

MRS. VAN DAAN. Mr. Frank said they'd be here at seven o'clock. He said . . .

MR. VAN DAAN. They have two miles to walk. You can't expect . . .

MRS. VAN DAAN. They've been picked up. That's what's happened. They've been taken . . .

(MR. VAN DAAN *indicates that he hears someone coming.*)

MR. VAN DAAN. You see?

(PETER *takes up his carrier and his schoolbag, etc., and goes into the main room as* MR. FRANK *comes up the stairwell from below.* MR. FRANK *looks much younger now. His movements are brisk, his manner confident. He wears an overcoat and carries his hat and a small cardboard box. He crosses to the* VAN DAANS, *shaking hands with each of them.*)

MR. FRANK. Mrs. Van Daan, Mr. Van Daan, Peter. (*Then, in explanation of their late-*

---

1. **plus fours,** baggy, loose, knee breeches.
2. **Star of David,** a six-pointed star formed by two intersecting equilateral triangles. It is often a symbol of Judaism, and Jews under Hitler were forced to wear it.

*ness*) There were too many of the Green Police[3] on the streets . . . we had to take the long way around.

(*Up the steps come* MARGOT FRANK, MRS. FRANK, MIEP (*not pregnant now*) *and* MR. KRALER. *All of them carry bags, packages, and so forth. The Star of David is conspicuous on all of the* FRANKS' *clothing.* MARGOT *is eighteen, beautiful, quiet, shy.* MRS. FRANK *is a young mother, gently bred, reserved. She, like* MR. FRANK, *has a slight German accent.* MR. KRALER *is a Dutchman, dependable, kindly.*

*As* MR. KRALER *and* MIEP *go upstage to put down their parcels,* MRS. FRANK *turns back to call* ANNE.)

MRS. FRANK. Anne?

(ANNE *comes running up the stairs. She is thirteen, quick in her movements, interested in everything, mercurial in her emotions. She wears a cape, long wool socks and carries a schoolbag.*)

MR. FRANK. (*Introducing them*) My wife, Edith. Mr. and Mrs. Van Daan (MRS. FRANK *hurries over, shaking hands with them*) . . . their son, Peter . . . my daughters, Margot and Anne.

(ANNE *gives a polite little curtsy as she shakes* MR. VAN DAAN's *hand. Then she immediately starts off on a tour of investigation of her new home, going upstairs to the attic room.*

MIEP *and* MR. KRALER *are putting the various things they have brought on the shelves.*)

MR. KRALER. I'm sorry there is still so much confusion.

MR. FRANK. Please. Don't think of it. After all, we'll have plenty of leisure to arrange everything ourselves.

MIEP. (*To* MRS. FRANK) We put the stores of food you sent in here. Your drugs are here . . . soap, linen here.

MRS. FRANK. Thank you, Miep.

MIEP. I made up the beds . . . the way Mr. Frank

and Mr. Kraler said. (*She starts out*) Forgive me. I have to hurry. I've got to go to the other side of town to get some ration books for you.

MRS. VAN DAAN. Ration books? If they see our names on ration books, they'll know we're here.

MR. KRALER. There isn't any-thing . . . ⎫

MIEP. Don't worry. Your names won't be on them. (*As she hurries out*) I'll be up later. ⎬ *Together*

MR. FRANK. Thank you, Miep.

MRS. FRANK. (*To* MR. KRALER) It's illegal, then, the ration books? We've never done anything illegal.

MR. FRANK. We won't be living here exactly according to regulations.

(*As* MR. KRALER *reassures* MRS. FRANK, *he takes various small things, such as matches, soap, etc., from his pockets, handing them to her.*)

MR. KRALER. This isn't the black market,[4] Mrs. Frank. This is what we call the white market . . . helping all of the hundreds and hundreds who are hiding out in Amsterdam.

(*The carillon is heard playing the quarter-hour before eight.* MR. KRALER *looks at his watch.* ANNE *stops at the window as she comes down the stairs.*)

ANNE. It's the Westertoren!

MR. KRALER. I must go. I must be out of here and downstairs in the office before the workmen get here. (*He starts for the stairs leading out*) Miep, or I, or both of us, will be up each day to bring you food and news and find out what your needs are. Tomorrow I'll get you a better bolt for the door at the foot of the stairs. It needs a bolt that you can throw yourself and open only at our signal. (*To* MR. FRANK) Oh . . . You'll tell them about the noise?

---

3. **Green Police,** an auxiliary Dutch police force created to aid Nazi occupation forces.
4. A **black market** deals in illegal commodities or makes sales under illegal conditions.

MR. FRANK. I'll tell them.

MR. KRALER. Good-bye then for the moment. I'll come up again, after the workmen leave.

MR. FRANK. Good-bye, Mr. Kraler.

MRS. FRANK. (*Shaking his hand*) How can we thank you?

(*The others murmur their good-byes.*)

MR. KRALER. I never thought I'd live to see the day when a man like Mr. Frank would have to go into hiding. When you think—

(*He breaks off, going out.* MR. FRANK *follows him down the steps, bolting the door after him. In the interval before he returns,* PETER *goes over to* MARGOT, *shaking hands with her. As* MR. FRANK *comes back up the steps,* MRS. FRANK *questions him anxiously.*)

*The Franks and Van Daans have just arrived and are removing their extra clothes. They are in the common room in the center of the stage. The attic space is above.*

MRS. FRANK. What did he mean, about the noise?

MR. FRANK. First let us take off some of these clothes.

(*They all start to take off garment after garment. On each of their coats, sweaters, blouses, suits, dresses, is another yellow Star of David.* MR. *and* MRS. FRANK *are underdressed quite simply. The others wear several things, sweaters, extra dresses, bathrobes, aprons, nightgowns, etc.*)

MR. VAN DAAN. It's a wonder we weren't arrested, walking along the streets . . . Petronella with a fur coat in July . . . and that cat of Peter's crying all the way.

197

ANNE. (*As she is removing a pair of panties*) A cat?

MRS. FRANK. (*Shocked*) Anne, please!

ANNE. It's all right. I've got on three more.

(*She pulls off two more. Finally, as they have all removed their surplus clothes, they look to* MR. FRANK, *waiting for him to speak.*)

MR. FRANK. Now. About the noise. While the men are in the building below, we must have complete quiet. Every sound can be heard down there, not only in the workrooms, but in the offices too. The men come at about eight-thirty, and leave at about five-thirty. So, to be perfectly safe, from eight in the morning until six in the evening we must move only when it is necessary, and then in stockinged feet. We must not speak above a whisper. We must not run any water. We cannot use the sink, or even, forgive me, the w.c. The pipes go down through the workrooms. It would be heard. No trash . . . (MR. FRANK *stops abruptly as he hears the sound of marching feet from the street below. Everyone is motionless, paralyzed with fear.* MR. FRANK *goes quietly into the room on the right to look down out of the window.* ANNE *runs after him, peering out with him. The tramping feet pass without stopping. The tension is relieved.* MR. FRANK, *followed by* ANNE, *returns to the main room and resumes his instructions to the group*) . . . No trash must ever be thrown out which might reveal that someone is living up here . . . not even a potato paring. We must burn everything in the stove at night. This is the way we must live until it is over, if we are to survive.

(*There is silence for a second.*)

MRS. FRANK. Until it is over.

MR. FRANK. (*Reassuringly*) After six we can move about . . . we can talk and laugh and have our supper and read and play games . . . just as we would at home. (*He looks at his watch*) And now I think it would be wise if we all went to our rooms, and were settled before eight o'clock. Mrs. Van Daan, you and your husband will be upstairs. I regret that there's no place up there for Peter. But he will be here, near us. This will be our common room, where we'll meet to talk and eat and read, like one family.

MR. VAN DAAN. And where do you and Mrs. Frank sleep?

MR. FRANK. This room is also our bedroom.

MRS. VAN DAAN. That isn't right. We'll sleep here and you take the room upstairs. } *Together*

MR. VAN DAAN. It's your place.

MR. FRANK. Please. I've thought this out for weeks. It's the best arrangement. The only arrangement.

MRS. VAN DAAN. (*To* MR. FRANK) Never, never can we thank you. (*Then to* MRS. FRANK) I don't know what would have happened to us, if it hadn't been for Mr. Frank.

MR. FRANK. You don't know how your husband helped me when I came to this country . . . knowing no one . . . not able to speak the language. I can never repay him for that. (*Going to* VAN DAAN) May I help you with your things?

MR. VAN DAAN. No. No. (*To* MRS. VAN DAAN) Come along, *liefje*.[5]

MRS. VAN DAAN. You'll be all right, Peter? You're not afraid?

PETER. (*Embarrassed*) Please, Mother.

(*They start up the stairs to the attic room above.* MR. FRANK *turns to* MRS. FRANK.)

MR. FRANK. You too must have some rest, Edith. You didn't close your eyes last night. Nor you, Margot.

ANNE. I slept, Father. Wasn't that funny? I knew it was the last night in my own bed, and yet I slept soundly.

MR. FRANK. I'm glad, Anne. Now you'll be able to help me straighten things in here. (*To* MRS. FRANK *and* MARGOT) Come with me . . . You and Margot rest in this room for the time being.

---

5. liefje\ˈlēf·yə\ dear.

(*He picks up their clothes, starting for the room on the right.*)

MRS. FRANK. You're sure . . . ? I could help . . . And Anne hasn't had her milk . . .

MR. FRANK. I'll give it to her. (*To* ANNE *and* PETER) Anne, Peter . . . it's best that you take off your shoes now, before you forget.

(*He leads the way to the room, followed by* MARGOT.)

MRS. FRANK. You're sure you're not tired, Anne?

ANNE. I feel fine. I'm going to help Father.

MRS. FRANK. Peter, I'm glad you are to be with us.

PETER. Yes, Mrs. Frank.

(MRS. FRANK *goes to join* MR. FRANK *and* MARGOT.)

(*During the following scene* MR. FRANK *helps* MARGOT *and* MRS. FRANK *to hang up their clothes. Then he persuades them both to lie down and rest. The* VAN DAANS *in their room above settle themselves. In the main room* ANNE *and* PETER *remove their shoes.* PETER *takes his cat out of the carrier.*)

ANNE. What's your cat's name?

PETER. Mouschi.

ANNE. Mouschi! Mouschi! Mouschi! (*She picks up the cat, walking away with it. To* PETER) I love cats. I have one . . . a darling little cat. But they made me leave her behind. I left some food and a note for the neighbors to take care of her . . . I'm going to miss her terribly. What is yours? A him or a her?

PETER. He's a tom. He doesn't like strangers.

(*He takes the cat from her, putting it back in its carrier.*)

ANNE. (*Unabashed*) Then I'll have to stop being a stranger, won't I? Is he fixed?

PETER. (*Startled*) Huh?

ANNE. Did you have him fixed?

PETER. No.

ANNE. Oh, you ought to have him fixed—to keep him from—you know, fighting. Where did you go to school?

PETER. Jewish Secondary.

ANNE. But that's where Margot and I go! I never saw you around.

PETER. I used to see you . . . sometimes . . .

ANNE. You did?

PETER. . . . in the school yard. You were always in the middle of a bunch of kids.

(*He takes a penknife from his pocket.*)

ANNE. Why didn't you ever come over?

PETER. I'm sort of a lone wolf.

(*He starts to rip off his Star of David.*)

ANNE. What are you doing?

PETER. Taking it off.

ANNE. But you can't do that. They'll arrest you if you go out without your star.

(*He tosses his knife on the table.*)

PETER. Who's going out?

ANNE. Why, of course! You're right! Of course we don't need them any more. (*She picks up his knife and starts to take her star off*) I wonder what our friends will think when we don't show up today?

PETER. I didn't have any dates with anyone.

ANNE. Oh, I did. I had a date with Jopie to go and play ping-pong at her house. Do you know Jopie de Waal?

PETER. No.

ANNE. Jopie's my best friend. I wonder what she'll think when she telephones and there's no answer? . . . Probably she'll go over to the house . . . I wonder what she'll think . . . we left everything as if we'd suddenly been called away . . . breakfast dishes in the sink . . . beds not made . . . (*As she pulls off her star, the cloth underneath shows clearly the color and form of the star*) Look! It's still there! (PETER *goes over to the stove with his star*) What're you going to do with yours?

PETER. Burn it.

ANNE. (*She starts to throw hers in, and cannot*) It's funny, I can't throw mine away. I don't know why.

PETER. You can't throw . . . ? Something they branded you with . . . ? That they made you wear so they could spit on you?

ANNE. I know. I know. But after all, it *is* the Star of David, isn't it?

(*In the bedroom, right,* MARGOT *and* MRS. FRANK *are lying down.* MR. FRANK *starts quietly out.*)

PETER. Maybe it's different for a girl.

(MR. FRANK *comes into the main room.*)

MR. FRANK. Forgive me, Peter. Now let me see. We must find a bed for your cat. (*He goes to a cupboard*) I'm glad you brought your cat. Anne was feeling so badly about hers. (*Getting a used small washtub*) Here we are. Will it be comfortable in that?

PETER. (*Gathering up his things*) Thanks.

MR. FRANK. (*Opening the door of the room on the left*) And here is your room. But I warn you, Peter, you can't grow any more. Not an inch, or you'll have to sleep with your feet out of the skylight. Are you hungry?

PETER. No.

MR. FRANK. We have some bread and butter.

PETER. No, thank you.

MR. FRANK. You can have it for luncheon then. And tonight we will have a real supper . . . our first supper together.

PETER. Thanks. Thanks.

(*He goes into his room. During the following scene he arranges his possessions in his new room.*)

MR. FRANK. That's a nice boy, Peter.

ANNE. He's awfully shy, isn't he?

MR. FRANK. You'll like him, I know.

ANNE. I certainly hope so, since he's the only boy I'm likely to see for months and months.

(MR. FRANK *sits down, taking off his shoes.*)

MR. FRANK. Anneke,[6] there's a box there. Will you open it?

(*He indicates a carton on the couch.* ANNE *brings it to the center table. In the street below there is the sound of children playing.*)

ANNE. (*As she opens the carton*) You know the way I'm going to think of it here? I'm going to think of it as a boarding house. A very peculiar summer boarding house, like the one that we—(*She breaks off as she pulls out some photographs*) Father! My movie stars! I was wondering where they were! I was looking for them this morning . . . and Queen Wilhelmina![7] How wonderful!

MR. FRANK. There's something more. Go on. Look further.

(*He goes over to the sink, pouring a glass of milk from a thermos bottle.*)

ANNE. (*Pulling out a pasteboard-bound book*) A diary! (*She throws her arms around her father*) I've never had a diary. And I've always longed for one. (*She looks around the room*) Pencil, pencil, pencil, pencil. (*She starts down the stairs*) I'm going down to the office to get a pencil.

MR. FRANK. Anne! No!

(*He goes after her, catching her by the arm and pulling her back.*)

ANNE. (*Startled*) But there's no one in the building now.

MR. FRANK. It doesn't matter. I don't want you ever to go beyond that door.

ANNE. (*Sobered*) Never . . . ? Not even at night-time, when everyone is gone? Or on Sundays? Can't I go down to listen to the radio?

MR. FRANK. Never. I am sorry, Anneke. It isn't safe. No, you must never go beyond that door.

(*For the first time* ANNE *realizes what "going into hiding" means.*)

ANNE. I see.

MR. FRANK. It'll be hard, I know. But always remember this, Anneke. There are no walls, there are no bolts, no locks that anyone can put on your mind. Miep will bring us books. We will read history, poetry, mythology. (*He gives her the glass of milk*) Here's your milk. (*With his arm about her, they go over to the*

---

6. **Anneke**\ˈä·nə·kə\ little Anne.
7. **Wilhelmina**\ˈwǐl·hěl·ˈmē·na\ (1880–1962), Queen of the Netherlands from 1890 to 1948.

*couch, sitting down side by side*) As a matter of fact, between us, Anne, being here has certain advantages for you. For instance, you remember the battle you had with your mother the other day on the subject of overshoes? You said you'd rather die than wear overshoes? But in the end you had to wear them? Well now, you see, for as long as we are here you will never have to wear overshoes! Isn't that good? And the coat that you inherited from Margot, you won't have to wear that any more. And the piano! You won't have to practice on the piano. I tell you, this is going to be a fine life for you!

(ANNE's *panic is gone.* PETER *appears in the doorway of his room, with a saucer in his hand. He is carrying his cat.*)

PETER. I . . . I . . . I thought I'd better get some water for Mouschi before . . .

MR. FRANK. Of course.

(*As he starts toward the sink the carillon begins to chime the hour of eight. He tiptoes to the window at the back and looks down at the street below. He turns to* PETER, *indicating in pantomime that it is too late.* PETER *starts back for his room. He steps on a creaking board. The three of them are frozen for a minute in fear. As* PETER *starts away again,* ANNE *tiptoes over to him and pours some of the milk from her glass into the saucer for the cat.* PETER *squats on the floor, putting the milk before the cat.* MR. FRANK *gives* ANNE *his fountain pen, and then goes into the room at the right. For a second* ANNE *watches the cat, then she goes over to the center table, and opens her diary.*

*In the room at the right,* MRS. FRANK *has sat up quickly at the sound of the carillon.* MR. FRANK *comes in and sits down beside her on the settee, his arm comfortingly around her.*

*Upstairs, in the attic room,* MR. *and* MRS. VAN DAAN *have hung their clothes in the closet and are now seated on the iron bed.*

Mr. Frank: *"But always remember this, Anne. There are no walls, there are no bolts, no locks that anyone can put on your mind."*

MRS. VAN DAAN *leans back exhausted.* MR. VAN DAAN *fans her with a newspaper.*

ANNE *starts to write in her diary. The lights dim out, the curtain falls.*

*In the darkness* ANNE's *voice comes to us again, faintly at first, and then with growing strength.*),

ANNE'S VOICE. I expect I should be describing what it feels like to go into hiding. But I really don't know yet myself. I only know it's funny never to be able to go outdoors . . .

never to breathe fresh air . . . never to run and shout and jump. It's the silence in the nights that frightens me most. Every time I hear a creak in the house, or a step on the street outside, I'm sure they're coming for us. The days aren't so bad. At least we know that Miep and Mr. Kraler are down there below us in the office. Our protectors, we call them. I asked Father what would happen to them if the Nazis found out they were hiding us. Pim said that they would suffer the same fate that we would . . . Imagine! They know this, and yet when they come up here, they're always cheerful and gay as if there were nothing in the world to bother them . . . Friday, the twenty-first of August, nineteen forty-two. Today I'm going to tell you our general news. Mother is unbearable. She insists on treating me like a baby, which I loathe. Otherwise things are going better. The weather is . . .

(*As* ANNE'S *voice is fading out, the curtain rises on the scene.*)

SCENE III

*It is little after six o'clock in the evening, two months later.*
MARGOT *is in the bedroom at the right, studying.* MR. VAN DAAN *is lying down in the attic room above.*
*The rest of the "family" is in the main room.* ANNE *and* PETER *sit opposite each other at the center table, where they have been doing their lessons.* MRS. FRANK *is on the couch.* MRS. VAN DAAN *is seated with her fur coat, on which she has been sewing, in her lap. None of them are wearing their shoes.*
*Their eyes are on* MR. FRANK, *waiting for him to give them the signal which will release them from their day-long quiet.* MR. FRANK, *his shoes in his hand, stands looking down out of the window at the back, watching to be sure that all of the workmen have left the building below.*

*After a few seconds of motionless silence,* MR. FRANK *turns from the window.*

MR. FRANK. (*Quietly, to the group*) It's safe now. The last workman has left.

(*There is an immediate stir of relief.*)

ANNE. (*Her pent-up energy explodes*) WHEE!
MRS. FRANK. (*Startled, amused*) Anne!
MRS. VAN DAAN. I'm first for the w.c.

(*She hurries off to the bathroom.* MRS. FRANK *puts on her shoes and starts up to the sink to prepare supper.* ANNE *sneaks* PETER'S *shoes from under the table and hides them behind her back.* MR. FRANK *goes in to* MARGOT'S *room.*)

MR. FRANK. (*To* MARGOT) Six o'clock. School's over.

(MARGOT *gets up, stretching.* MR. FRANK *sits down to put on his shoes. In the main room* PETER *tries to find his.*)

PETER. (*To* ANNE) Have you seen my shoes?
ANNE. (*Innocently*) Your shoes?
PETER. You've taken them, haven't you?
ANNE. I don't know what you're talking about.
PETER. You're going to be sorry!
ANNE. Am I?

(PETER *goes after her.* ANNE, *with his shoes in her hand, runs from him, dodging behind her mother.*)

MRS. FRANK. (*Protesting*) Anne, dear!
PETER. Wait till I get you!
ANNE. I'm waiting! (PETER *makes a lunge for her. They both fall to the floor.* PETER *pins her down, wrestling with her to get the shoes*) Don't! Don't! Peter, stop it. Ouch!
MRS. FRANK. Anne! . . . Peter!

(*Suddenly* PETER *becomes self-conscious. He grabs his shoes roughly and starts for his room.*)

ANNE. (*Following him*) Peter, where are you going? Come dance with me.
PETER. I tell you I don't know how.
ANNE. I'll teach you.
PETER. I'm going to give Mouschi his dinner.

ANNE. Can I watch?

PETER. He doesn't like people around while he eats.

ANNE. Peter, please.

PETER. No!

(*He goes into his room.* ANNE *slams his door after him.*)

MRS. FRANK. Anne, dear, I think you shouldn't play like that with Peter. It's not dignified.

ANNE. Who cares if it's dignified? I don't want to be dignified.

(MR. FRANK *and* MARGOT *come from the room on the right.* MARGOT *goes to help her mother.* MR. FRANK *starts for the center table to correct* MARGOT's *school papers.*)

MRS. FRANK. (*To* ANNE) You complain that I don't treat you like a grownup. But when I do, you resent it.

ANNE. I only want some fun . . . someone to laugh and clown with . . . After you've sat still all day and hardly moved, you've got to have some fun. I don't know what's the matter with that boy.

MR. FRANK. He isn't used to girls. Give him a little time.

ANNE. Time? Isn't two months time? I could cry. (*Catching hold of* MARGOT) Come on, Margot . . . dance with me. Come on, please.

MARGOT. I have to help with supper.

ANNE. You know we're going to forget how to dance . . . When we get out we won't remember a thing.

(*She starts to sing and dance by herself.* MR. FRANK *takes her in his arms, waltzing with her.* MRS. VAN DAAN *comes in from the bathroom.*)

MRS. VAN DAAN. Next? (*She looks around as she starts putting on her shoes*) Where's Peter?

ANNE. (*As they are dancing*) Where would he be!

MRS. VAN DAAN. He hasn't finished his lessons, has he? His father'll kill him if he catches him in there with that cat and his work not done. (MR. FRANK *and* ANNE *finish their dance. They bow to each other with extravagant*

formality) Anne, get him out of there, will you?

ANNE. (*At* PETER's *door*) Peter? Peter?

PETER. (*Opening the door a crack*) What is it?

ANNE. Your mother says to come out.

PETER. I'm giving Mouschi his dinner.

MRS. VAN DAAN. You know what your father says.

(*She sits on the couch, sewing on the lining of her fur coat.*)

PETER. For heaven's sake, I haven't even looked at him since lunch.

MRS. VAN DAAN. I'm just telling you, that's all.

ANNE. I'll feed him.

PETER. I don't want you in there.

MRS. VAN DAAN. Peter!

PETER. (*To* ANNE) Then give him his dinner and come right out, you hear?

(*He comes back to the table.* ANNE *shuts the door of* PETER's *room after her and disappears behind the curtain covering his closet.*)

MRS. VAN DAAN. (*To* PETER) Now is that any way to talk to your little girl friend?

PETER. Mother . . . for heaven's sake . . . will you please stop saying that?

MRS. VAN DAAN. Look at him blush! Look at him!

PETER. Please! I'm not . . . anyway . . . let me alone, will you?

MRS. VAN DAAN. He acts like it was something to be ashamed of. It's nothing to be ashamed of, to have a little girl friend.

PETER. You're crazy. She's only thirteen.

MRS. VAN DAAN. So what? And you're sixteen. Just perfect. Your father's ten years older than I am. (*To* MR. FRANK) I warn you, Mr. Frank, if this war lasts much longer, we're going to be related and then . . .

MR. FRANK. *Mazeltov!*[1]

MRS. FRANK. (*Deliberately changing the conversation*) I wonder where Miep is. She's usually so prompt.

(*Suddenly everything else is forgotten as*

---

1. **mazeltov**\ˈmä·zəl ˈtäv\ congratulations.

*they hear the sound of an automobile coming to a screeching stop in the street below. They are tense, motionless in their terror. The car starts away. A wave of relief sweeps over them. They pick up their occupations again.* ANNE *flings open the door of* PETER'S *room, making a dramatic entrance. She is dressed in* PETER'S *clothes.* PETER *looks at her in fury. The others are amused.*)

ANNE. Good evening, everyone. Forgive me if I don't stay. (*She jumps up on a chair*) I have a friend waiting for me in there. My friend Tom. Tom Cat. Some people say that we look alike. But Tom has the most beautiful whiskers, and I have only a little fuzz. I am hoping . . . in time . . .

PETER. All right, Mrs. Quack Quack!

ANNE. (*Outraged—jumping down*) Peter!

PETER. I heard about you . . . How you talked so much in class they called you Mrs. Quack Quack. How Mr. Smitter made you write a composition . . . " 'Quack, quack,' said Mrs. Quack Quack."

ANNE. Well, go on. Tell them the rest. How it was so good he read it out loud to the class and then read it to all his other classes!

PETER. Quack! Quack! Quack . . . Quack . . . Quack . . .

(ANNE *pulls off the coat and trousers*)

ANNE. You are the most intolerable, insufferable boy I've ever met!

(*She throws the clothes down the stairwell.* PETER *goes down after them.*)

PETER. Quack, quack, quack!

MRS. VAN DAAN. (*To* ANNE) That's right, Anneke! Give it to him!

ANNE. With all the boys in the world . . . Why I had to get locked up with one like you! . . .

PETER. Quack, quack, quack, and from now on stay out of my room!

(*As* PETER *passes her,* ANNE *puts out her foot, tripping him. He picks himself up, and goes on into his room.*)

MRS. FRANK. (*Quietly*) Anne, dear . . . your hair. (*She feels* ANNE'S *forehead*) You're warm. Are you feeling all right?

ANNE. Please, Mother.

(*She goes over to the center table, slipping into her shoes.*)

MRS. FRANK. (*Following her*) You haven't a fever, have you?

ANNE. (*Pulling away*) No. No.

MRS. FRANK. You know we can't call a doctor here, ever. There's only one thing to do . . . watch carefully. Prevent an illness before it comes. Let me see your tongue.

ANNE. Mother, this is perfectly absurd.

MRS. FRANK. Anne, dear, don't be such a baby. Let me see your tongue.

(*As* ANNE *refuses,* MRS. FRANK *appeals to* MR. FRANK) Otto . . . ?

MR. FRANK. You hear your mother, Anne.

(ANNE *flicks out her tongue for a second, then turns away.*)

MRS. FRANK. Come on—open up! (*As* ANNE *opens her mouth very wide*) You seem all right . . . but perhaps an aspirin . . .

MRS. VAN DAAN. For heaven's sake, don't give that child any pills. I waited for fifteen minutes this morning for her to come out of the w.c.

ANNE. I was washing my hair!

MR. FRANK. I think there's nothing the matter with our Anne that a ride on her bike, or a visit with her friend Jopie de Waal wouldn't cure. Isn't that so, Anne?

(MR. VAN DAAN *comes down into the room. From outside we hear faint sounds of bombers going over and a burst of ack-ack.[2]*)

MR. VAN DAAN. Miep not come yet?

MRS. VAN DAAN. The workmen just left, a little while ago.

MR. VAN DAAN. What's for dinner tonight?

MRS. VAN DAAN. Beans.

---

2. **ack-ack**\\'ăk'ăk\\ antiaircraft fire.

MR. VAN DAAN. Not again!

MRS. VAN DAAN. Poor Putti! I know. But what can we do? That's all that Miep brought us.

(MR. VAN DAAN *starts to pace, his hands behind his back.* ANNE *follows behind him, imitating him.*)

ANNE. We are now in what is known as the "bean cycle." Beans boiled, beans en casserole, beans with strings, beans without strings . . .

(PETER *has come out of his room. He slides into his place at the table, becoming immediately absorbed in his studies.*)

MR. VAN DAAN. (*To* PETER) I saw you . . . in there, playing with your cat.

MRS. VAN DAAN. He just went in for a second, putting his coat away. He's been out here all the time, doing his lessons.

MR. FRANK. (*Looking up from the papers*) Anne, you got an excellent in your history paper today . . . and very good in Latin.

ANNE. (*Sitting beside him*) How about algebra?

MR. FRANK. I'll have to make a confession. Up until now I've managed to stay ahead of you in algebra. Today you caught up with me. We'll leave it to Margot to correct.

ANNE. Isn't algebra *vile*, Pim!

MR. FRANK. Vile!

MARGOT. (*To* MR. FRANK) How did I do?

ANNE. (*Getting up*) Excellent, excellent, excellent, excellent!

MR. FRANK. (*To* MARGOT) You should have used the subjunctive here . . .

MARGOT. Should I? . . . I thought . . . look here . . . I didn't use it here . . .

(*The two become absorbed in the papers.*)

ANNE. Mrs. Van Daan, may I try on your coat?

MRS. FRANK. No, Anne.

MRS. VAN DAAN. (*Giving it to* ANNE) It's all right . . . but careful with it. (ANNE *puts it on and struts with it*) My father gave me that the year before he died. He always bought the best that money could buy.

ANNE. Mrs. Van Daan, did you have a lot of boy friends before you were married?

MRS. FRANK. Anne, that's a personal question. It's not courteous to ask personal questions.

MRS. VAN DAAN. Oh I don't mind. (*To* ANNE) Our house was always swarming with boys. When I was a girl we had . . .

MR. VAN DAAN. Not again!

MRS. VAN DAAN. (*Good-humored*) Shut up! (*Without a pause, to* ANNE. MR. VAN DAAN *mimics* MRS. VAN DAAN, *speaking the first few words in unison with her*) One summer we had a big house in Hilversum. The boys came buzzing round like bees around a jam pot. And when I was sixteen! . . . We were wearing our skirts very short those days and I had good-looking legs. (*She pulls up her skirt, going to* MR. FRANK) I still have 'em. I may not be as pretty as I used to be, but I still have my legs. How about it, Mr. Frank?

MR. VAN DAAN. All right. All right. We see them.

MRS. VAN DAAN. I'm not asking you. I'm asking Mr. Frank.

PETER. Mother, for heaven's sake.

MRS. VAN DAAN. Oh, I embarrass you, do I? Well, I just hope the girl you marry has as good. (*Then to* ANNE) My father used to worry about me, with so many boys hanging round. He told me, if any of them gets fresh, you say to him . . . "Remember, Mr. So-and-So, remember I'm a lady."

ANNE. "Remember, Mr. So-and-So, remember I'm a lady."

(*She gives* MRS. VAN DAAN *her coat.*)

MR. VAN DAAN. Look at you, talking that way in front of her! Don't you know she puts it all down in that diary?

MRS. VAN DAAN. So, if she does? I'm only telling the truth!

(ANNE *stretches out, putting her ear to the floor, listening to what is going on below. The sound of the bombers fades away.*)

MRS. FRANK. (*Setting the table*) Would you mind, Peter, if I moved you over to the couch?

ANNE. (*Listening*) Miep must have the radio on.

(PETER *picks up his papers, going over to the couch beside* MRS. VAN DAAN.)

MR. VAN DAAN. (*Accusingly, to* PETER) Haven't you finished yet?

PETER. No.

MR. VAN DAAN. You ought to be ashamed of yourself.

PETER. All right. All right. I'm a dunce. I'm a hopeless case. Why do I go on?

MRS. VAN DAAN. You're not hopeless. Don't talk that way. It's just that you haven't anyone to help you, like the girls have. (*To* MR. FRANK) Maybe you could help him, Mr. Frank?

MR. FRANK. I'm sure that his father . . . ?

MR. VAN DAAN. Not me. I can't do anything with him. He won't listen to me. You go ahead . . . if you want.

MR. FRANK. (*Going to* PETER) What about it, Peter? Shall we make our school coeducational?

MRS. VAN DAAN. (*Kissing* MR. FRANK) You're an angel, Mr. Frank. An angel. I don't know why I didn't meet you before I met that one there. Here, sit down, Mr. Frank . . . (*She forces him down on the couch beside* PETER) Now, Peter, you listen to Mr. Frank.

MR. FRANK. It might be better for us to go into Peter's room.

(PETER *jumps up eagerly, leading the way.*)

MRS. VAN DAAN. That's right. You go in there, Peter. You listen to Mr. Frank. Mr. Frank is a highly educated man.

(*As* MR. FRANK *is about to follow* PETER *into his room,* MRS. FRANK *stops him and wipes the lipstick from his lips. Then she closes the door after them.*)

ANNE. (*On the floor, listening*) Shh! I can hear a man's voice talking.

MR. VAN DAAN. (*To* ANNE) Isn't it bad enough here without your sprawling all over the place?

(ANNE *sits up.*)

MRS. VAN DAAN. (*To* MR. VAN DAAN) If you didn't smoke so much, you wouldn't be so bad-tempered.

MR. VAN DAAN. Am I smoking? Do you see me smoking?

MRS. VAN DAAN. Don't tell me you've used up all those cigarettes.

MR. VAN DAAN. One package. Miep only brought me one package.

MRS. VAN DAAN. It's a filthy habit anyway. It's a good time to break yourself.

MR. VAN DAAN. Oh, stop it, please.

MRS. VAN DAAN. You're smoking up all our money. You know that, don't you?

MR. VAN DAAN. Will you shut up? (*During this,* MRS. FRANK *and* MARGOT *have studiously kept their eyes down. But* ANNE, *seated on the floor, has been following the discussion interestedly.* MR. VAN DAAN *turns to see her staring up at him*) And what are you staring at?

ANNE. I never heard grownups quarrel before. I thought only children quarreled.

MR. VAN DAAN. This isn't a quarrel! It's a discussion. And I never heard children so rude before.

ANNE. (*Rising, indignantly*) I, rude!

MR. VAN DAAN. Yes!

MRS. FRANK. (*Quickly*) Anne, will you get me my knitting? (ANNE *goes to get it*) I must remember, when Miep comes, to ask her to bring me some more wool.

MARGOT. (*Going to her room*) I need some hairpins and some soap. I made a list.

(*She goes into her bedroom to get the list.*)

MRS. FRANK. (*To* ANNE) Have you some library books for Miep when she comes?

ANNE. It's a wonder that Miep has a life of her own, the way we make her run errands for us. Please, Miep, get me some starch. Please take my hair out and have it cut. Tell me all the latest news, Miep. (*She goes over, kneeling on the couch beside* MRS. VAN DAAN) Did you know she was engaged? His name is Dirk, and Miep's afraid the Nazis will ship him off to Germany to work in one of their war plants. That's what they're doing with some of the young Dutchmen . . . they pick them up off the streets—

MR. VAN DAAN. (*Interrupting*) Don't you ever get tired of talking? Suppose you try keeping still for five minutes. Just five minutes.

(*He starts to pace again. Again* ANNE *follows him, mimicking him.* MRS. FRANK *jumps up and takes her by the arm up to the sink, and gives her a glass of milk.*)

MRS. FRANK. Come here, Anne. It's time for your glass of milk.

MR. VAN DAAN. Talk, talk, talk. I never heard such a child. Where is my . . . Every evening it's the same, talk, talk, talk. (*He looks around*) Where is my . . . ?

MRS. VAN DAAN. What're you looking for?

MR. VAN DAAN. My pipe. Have you seen my pipe?

MRS. VAN DAAN. What good's a pipe? You haven't got any tobacco.

MR. VAN DAAN. At least I'll have something to hold in my mouth! (*Opening* MARGOT's *bedroom door*) Margot, have you seen my pipe?

MARGOT. It was on the table last night.

(ANNE *puts her glass of milk on the table and picks up his pipe, hiding it behind her back.*)

MR. VAN DAAN. I know. I know. Anne, did you see my pipe? . . . Anne!

MRS. FRANK. Anne, Mr. Van Daan is speaking to you.

ANNE. Am I allowed to talk now?

MR. VAN DAAN. You're the most aggravating . . . The trouble with you is, you've been spoiled. What you need is a good old-fashioned spanking.

ANNE. (*Mimicking* MRS. VAN DAAN) "Remember, Mr. So-and-So, remember I'm a lady."

(*She thrusts the pipe into his mouth, then picks up her glass of milk.*)

MR. VAN DAAN. (*Restraining himself with difficulty*) Why aren't you nice and quiet like your sister Margot? Why do you have to show off all the time? Let me give you a little advice, young lady. Men don't like that kind of

thing in a girl. You know that? A man likes a girl who'll listen to him once in a while . . . a domestic girl, who'll keep her house shining for her husband . . . who loves to cook and sew and . . .

ANNE. I'd cut my throat first! I'd open my veins! I'm going to be remarkable! I'm going to Paris . . .

MR. VAN DAAN. (*Scoffingly*) Paris!

ANNE. . . . to study music and art.

MR. VAN DAAN. Yeah! Yeah!

ANNE. I'm going to be a famous dancer or singer . . . or something wonderful.

(*She makes a wide gesture, spilling the glass of milk on the fur coat in* MRS. VAN DAAN's *lap.* MARGOT *rushes quickly over with a towel.* ANNE *tries to brush the milk off with her skirt.*)

MRS. VAN DAAN. Now look what you've done . . . you clumsy little fool! My beautiful fur coat my father gave me . . .

ANNE. I'm so sorry.

MRS. VAN DAAN. What do you care? It isn't yours . . . So go on, ruin it! Do you know what that coat cost? Do you? And now look at it! Look at it!

ANNE. I'm very, very sorry.

MRS. VAN DAAN. I could kill you for this. I could just kill you!

(MRS. VAN DAAN *goes up the stairs, clutching the coat.* MR. VAN DAAN *starts after her.*)

MR. VAN DAAN. Petronella . . . *liefje! Liefje!* . . . Come back . . . the supper . . . come back!

MRS. FRANK. Anne, you must not behave in that way.

ANNE. It was an accident. Anyone can have an accident.

MRS. FRANK. I don't mean that. I mean the answering back. You must not answer back. They are our guests. We must always show the greatest courtesy to them. We're all living under terrible tension. (*She stops as* MARGOT *indicates that* VAN DAAN *can hear. When he is gone, she continues*) That's why we must control ourselves . . . You don't hear Margot getting into arguments with them, do you? Watch Margot. She's always courteous with them. Never familiar. She keeps her distance. And they respect her for it. Try to be like Margot.

ANNE. And have them walk all over me, the way they do her? No, thanks!

MRS. FRANK. I'm not afraid that anyone is going to walk all over you, Anne. I'm afraid for other people, that you'll walk on them. I don't know what happens to you, Anne. You are wild, self-willed. If I had ever talked to my mother as you talk to me . . .

ANNE. Things have changed. People aren't like that any more. "Yes, Mother." "No, Mother." "Anything you say, Mother." I've got to fight things out for myself! Make something of myself!

MRS. FRANK. It isn't necessary to fight to do it. Margot doesn't fight, and isn't she . . . ?

ANNE. (Violently rebellious) Margot! Margot! Margot! That's all I hear from everyone . . . how wonderful Margot is . . . "Why aren't you like Margot?"

MARGOT. (Protesting) Oh, come on, Anne, don't be so . . .

ANNE. (Paying no attention) Everything she does is right, and everything I do is wrong! I'm the goat around here! . . . You're all against me! . . . And you worst of all!

(She rushes off into her room and throws herself down on the settee, stifling her sobs. MRS. FRANK sighs and starts toward the stove.)

MRS. FRANK. (To MARGOT) Let's put the soup on the stove . . . if there's anyone who cares to eat. Margot, will you take the bread out? (MARGOT gets the bread from the cupboard) I don't know how we can go on living this way . . . I can't say a word to Anne . . . she flies at me . . .

MARGOT. You know Anne. In half an hour she'll be out here, laughing and joking.

MRS. FRANK. And . . . (She makes a motion upwards, indicating the VAN DAANS) . . . I told your father it wouldn't work . . . but no . . .

no . . . he had to ask them, he said . . . he owed it to him, he said. Well, he knows now that I was right! These quarrels! . . . This bickering!

MARGOT. (With a warning look) Shush. Shush.

(The buzzer for the door sounds. MRS. FRANK gasps, startled.)

MRS. FRANK. Every time I hear that sound, my heart stops!

MARGOT. (Starting for PETER's door) It's Miep. (She knocks at the door) Father?

(MR. FRANK comes quickly from PETER's room.)

MR. FRANK. Thank you, Margot. (As he goes down the steps to open the outer door) Has everyone his list?

MARGOT. I'll get my books. (Giving her mother a list) Here's your list. (MARGOT goes into her and ANNE's bedroom on the right. ANNE sits up, hiding her tears, as MARGOT comes in) Miep's here.

(MARGOT picks up her books and goes back. ANNE hurries over to the mirror, smoothing her hair.)

MR. VAN DAAN. (Coming down the stairs) Is it Miep?

MARGOT. Yes. Father's gone down to let her in.

MR. VAN DAAN. At last I'll have some cigarettes!

MRS. FRANK. (To MR. VAN DAAN) I can't tell you how unhappy I am about Mrs. Van Daan's coat. Anne should never have touched it.

MR. VAN DAAN. She'll be all right.

MRS. FRANK. Is there anything I can do?

MR. VAN DAAN. Don't worry.

(He turns to meet MIEP. But it is not MIEP who comes up the steps. It is MR. KRALER, followed by MR. FRANK. Their faces are grave. ANNE comes from the bedroom. PETER comes from his room.)

MRS. FRANK. Mr. Kraler!

MR. VAN DAAN. How are you, Mr. Kraler?

MARGOT. This is a surprise.

MRS. FRANK. When Mr. Kraler comes, the sun begins to shine.

MR. VAN DAAN. Miep is coming?

MR. KRALER. Not tonight.

(KRALER *goes to* MARGOT *and* MRS. FRANK *and* ANNE, *shaking hands with them.*)

MRS. FRANK. Wouldn't you like a cup of coffee? . . . Or, better still, will you have supper with us?

MR. FRANK. Mr. Kraler has something to talk over with us. Something has happened, he says, which demands an immediate decision.

MRS. FRANK. (*Fearful*) What is it?

(MR. KRALER *sits down on the couch. As he talks he takes bread, cabbages, milk, etc., from his briefcase, giving them to* MARGOT *and* ANNE *to put away.*)

MR. KRALER. Usually, when I come up here, I I try to bring you some bit of good news. What's the use of telling you the bad news when there's nothing that you can do about it? But today something has happened . . . Dirk . . . Miep's Dirk, you know, came to me just now. He tells me that he has a Jewish friend living near him. A dentist. He says he's in trouble. He begged me, could I do anything for this man? Could I find him a hiding place? . . . So I've come to you . . . I know it's a terrible thing to ask of you, living as you are, but would you take him in with you?

MR. FRANK. Of course we will.

MR. KRALER. (*Rising*) It'll be just for a night or two . . . until I find some other place. This happened so suddenly that I didn't know where to turn.

MR. FRANK. Where is he?

MR. KRALER. Downstairs in the office.

MR. FRANK. Good. Bring him up.

MR. KRALER. His name is Dussel . . . Jan Dussel.

MR. FRANK. Dussel . . . I think I know him.

MR. KRALER. I'll get him.

(*He goes quickly down the steps and out.* MR. FRANK *suddenly becomes conscious of the others.*)

MR. FRANK. Forgive me. I spoke without consulting you. But I knew you'd feel as I do.

MR. VAN DAAN. There's no reason for you to consult anyone. This is your place. You have a right to do exactly as you please. The only thing I feel . . . there's so little food as it is . . . and to take in another person . . .

(PETER *turns away, ashamed of his father.*)

MR. FRANK. We can stretch the food a little. It's only for a few days.

MR. VAN DAAN. You want to make a bet?

MRS. FRANK. I think it's fine to have him. But, Otto, where are you going to put him? Where?

PETER. He can have my bed. I can sleep on the floor. I wouldn't mind.

MR. FRANK. That's good of you, Peter. But your room's too small . . . even for *you.*

ANNE. I have a much better idea. I'll come in here with you and Mother, and Margot can take Peter's room and Peter can go in our room with Mr. Dussel.

MARGOT. That's right. We could do that.

MR. FRANK. No, Margot. You mustn't sleep in that room . . . neither you nor Anne. Mouschi has caught some rats in there. Peter's brave. He doesn't mind.

ANNE. Then how about *this?* I'll come in here with you and Mother, and Mr. Dussel can have my bed.

MRS. FRANK. No. No. *No!* Margot will come in here with us and he can have her bed. It's the only way. Margot, bring your things in here. Help her, Anne.

(MARGOT *hurries into her room to get her things.*)

ANNE. (*To her mother*) Why Margot? Why can't I come in here?

MRS. FRANK. Because it wouldn't be proper for Margot to sleep with a . . . Please, Anne. Don't argue. Please.

(ANNE *starts slowly away.*)

MR. FRANK. (*To* ANNE) You don't mind sharing your room with Mr. Dussel, do you, Anne?

ANNE. No. No, of course not.

MR. FRANK. Good. (ANNE *goes off into her bedroom, helping* MARGOT. MR. FRANK *starts to search in the cupboards*) Where's the cognac?

MRS. FRANK. It's there. But, Otto, I was saving it in case of illness.

MR. FRANK. I think we couldn't find a better time to use it. Peter, will you get five glasses for me?

(PETER *goes for the glasses.* MARGOT *comes out of her bedroom, carrying her possessions, which she hangs behind a curtain in the main room.* MR. FRANK *finds the cognac and pours it into the five glasses that* PETER *brings him.* MR. VAN DAAN *stands looking on sourly.* MRS. VAN DAAN *comes downstairs and looks around at all the bustle.*)

MRS. VAN DAAN. What's happening? What's going on?

MR. VAN DAAN. Someone's moving in with us.

MRS. VAN DAAN. In here? You're joking.

MARGOT. It's only for a night or two . . . until Mr. Kraler finds him another place.

MR. VAN DAAN. Yeah! Yeah!

(MR. FRANK *hurries over as* MR. KRALER *and* DUSSEL *come up.* DUSSEL *is a man in his late fifties, meticulous, finicky . . . bewildered now. He wears a raincoat. He carries a briefcase, stuffed full, and a small medicine case.*)

MR. FRANK. Come in, Mr. Dussel.

MR. KRALER. This is Mr. Frank.

DUSSEL. Mr. Otto Frank?

MR. FRANK. Yes. Let me take your things. (*He takes the hat and briefcase, but* DUSSEL *clings to his medicine case*) This is my wife Edith . . . Mr. and Mrs. Van Daan . . . their son, Peter . . . and my daughters, Margot and Anne.

(DUSSEL *shakes hands with everyone.*)

MR. KRALER. Thank you, Mr. Frank. Thank you all. Mr. Dussel, I leave you in good hands. Oh . . . Dirk's coat.

(DUSSEL *hurriedly takes off the raincoat, giving it to* MR. KRALER. *Underneath is his white dentist's jacket, with a yellow Star of David on it.*)

DUSSEL. (*To* MR. KRALER) What can I say to thank you . . . ?

MRS. FRANK. (*To* DUSSEL) Mr. Kraler and Miep . . . They're our life line. Without them we couldn't live.

MR. KRALER. Please. Please. You make us seem very heroic. It isn't that at all. We simply don't like the Nazis. (*To* MR. FRANK, *who offers him a drink*) No, thanks. (*Then going on*) We don't like their methods. We don't like . . .

MR. FRANK. (*Smiling*) I know. I know. "No one's going to tell us Dutchmen what to do with our damn Jews!"

MR. KRALER. (*To* DUSSEL) Pay no attention to Mr. Frank. I'll be up tomorrow to see that they're treating you right. (*To* MR. FRANK) Don't trouble to come down again. Peter will bolt the door after me, won't you, Peter?

PETER. Yes, sir.

MR. FRANK. Thank you, Peter. I'll do it.

MR. KRALER. Good night. Good night.

GROUP. Good night, Mr. Kraler.

We'll see you tomorrow, etc., etc.

(MR. KRALER *goes out with* MR. FRANK. MRS. FRANK *gives each one of the "grownups" a glass of cognac.*)

MRS. FRANK. Please, Mr. Dussel, sit down.

(MR. DUSSEL *sinks into a chair.* MRS. FRANK *gives him a glass of cognac.*)

DUSSEL. I'm dreaming. I know it. I can't believe my eyes. Mr. Otto Frank here! (*To* MRS. FRANK) You're not in Switzerland then? A woman told me . . . She said she'd gone to your house . . . the door was open, everything was in disorder, dishes in the sink. She said she found a piece of paper in the wastebasket with an address scribbled on it . . . an address in Zurich.[3] She said you must have escaped to Zurich.

ANNE. Father put that there purposely . . . just so people would think that very thing!

DUSSEL. And you've been *here* all the time?

3. **Zurich**\ˈzu̇·rĭk\ a city in Switzerland (which the Nazis did not control).

MRS. FRANK. All the time . . . ever since July.

(ANNE *speaks to her father as he comes back.*)

ANNE. It worked, Pim . . . the address you left! Mr. Dussel says that people believe we escaped to Switzerland.

MR. FRANK. I'm glad. . . . And now let's have a little drink to welcome Mr. Dussel. (*Before they can drink,* MR. DUSSEL *bolts his drink.* MR. FRANK *smiles and raises his glass*) To Mr. Dussel. Welcome. We're very honored to have you with us.

MRS. FRANK. To Mr. Dussel, welcome.

(*The* VAN DAANS *murmur a welcome. The "grownups" drink.*)

MRS. VAN DAAN. Um. That was good.

MR. VAN DAAN. Did Mr. Kraler warn you that you won't get much to eat here? You can imagine . . . three ration books among the seven of us . . . and now you make eight.

(PETER *walks away, humiliated. Outside a street organ is heard dimly.*)

DUSSEL. (*Rising*) Mr. Van Daan, you don't realize what is happening outside that you should warn me of a thing like that. You don't realize what's going on . . . (*As* MR. VAN DAAN *starts his characteristic pacing,* DUSSEL *turns to speak to the others*) Right here in Amsterdam every day hundreds of Jews disappear . . . They surround a block and search house by house. Children come home from school to find their parents gone. Hundreds are being deported . . . people that you and I know . . . the Hallensteins . . . the Wessels . . .

MRS. FRANK. (*In tears*) Oh, no. No!

DUSSEL. They get their call-up notice . . . come to the Jewish theatre on such and such a day and hour . . . bring only what you can carry in a rucksack. And if you refuse the call-up notice, then they come and drag you from your home and ship you off to Mauthausen.[4] The death camp!

MRS. FRANK. We didn't know that things had got so much worse.

DUSSEL. Forgive me for speaking so.

ANNE. (*Coming to* DUSSEL) Do you know the de Waals? . . . What's become of them? Their daughter Jopie and I are in the same class. Jopie's my best friend.

DUSSEL. They are gone.

ANNE. Gone?

DUSSEL. With all the others.

ANNE. Oh, no. Not Jopie!

(*She turns away, in tears.* MRS. FRANK *motions to* MARGOT *to comfort her.* MARGOT *goes to* ANNE, *putting her arms comfortingly around her.*)

MRS. VAN DAAN. There were some people called Wagner. They lived near us . . . ?

MR. FRANK. (*Interrupting, with a glance at* ANNE) I think we should put this off until later. We all have many questions we want to ask . . . But I'm sure that Mr. Dussel would like to get settled before supper.

DUSSEL. Thank you. I would. I brought very little with me.

MR. FRANK. (*Giving him his hat and briefcase*) I'm sorry we can't give you a room alone. But I hope you won't be too uncomfortable. We've had to make strict rules here . . . a schedule of hours . . . We'll tell you after supper. Anne, would you like to take Mr. Dussel to his room?

ANNE. (*Controlling her tears*) If you'll come with me, Mr. Dussel?

(*She starts for her room.*)

DUSSEL. (*Shaking hands with each in turn*) Forgive me if I haven't really expressed my gratitude to all of you. This has been such a shock to me. I'd always thought of myself as Dutch. I was born in Holland. My father was born in Holland, and my grandfather. And now . . . after all these years . . . (*He breaks off*) If you'll excuse me.

(DUSSEL *gives a little bow and hurries off after* ANNE. MR. FRANK *and the others are subdued.*)

---

4. **Mauthausen**\ˈmaut ˈhau·zən\ a Danube village in upper Austria, where a concentration camp was located.

ANNE. (*Turning on the light*) Well, here we are.

(DUSSEL *looks around the room. In the main room* MARGOT *speaks to her mother.*)

MARGOT. The news sounds pretty bad, doesn't it? It's so different from what Mr. Kraler tells us. Mr. Kraler says things are improving.

MR. VAN DAAN. I like it better the way Kraler tells it.

(*They resume their occupations, quietly.* PETER *goes off into his room. In* ANNE'S *room,* ANNE *turns to* DUSSEL.)

ANNE. You're going to share the room with me.

DUSSEL. I'm a man who's always lived alone. I haven't had to adjust myself to others. I hope you'll bear with me until I learn.

ANNE. Let me help you. (*She takes his briefcase*) Do you always live all alone? Have you no family at all?

DUSSEL. No one.

(*He opens his medicine case and spreads his bottles on the dressing table.*)

ANNE. How dreadful. You must be terribly lonely.

DUSSEL. I'm used to it.

ANNE. I don't think I could ever get used to it. Didn't you even have a pet? A cat, or a dog?

DUSSEL. I have an allergy for fur-bearing animals. They give me asthma.

ANNE. Oh, dear. Peter has a cat.

DUSSEL. Here? He has it here?

ANNE. Yes. But we hardly ever see it. He keeps it in his room all the time. I'm sure it will be all right.

DUSSEL. Let us hope so.

(*He takes some pills to fortify himself.*)

ANNE. That's Margot's bed, where you're going to sleep. I sleep on the sofa there. (*Indicating the clothes hooks on the wall*) We cleared these off for your things. (*She goes over to the window*) The best part about this room . . . you can look down and see a bit of the street and the canal. There's a houseboat . . . you can see the end of it . . . a bargeman lives there with his family . . . They have a

baby and he's just beginning to walk and I'm so afraid he's going to fall into the canal some day. I watch him. . . .

DUSSEL. (*Interrupting*) Your father spoke of a schedule.

ANNE. (*Coming away from the window*) Oh, yes. It's mostly about the times we have to be quiet. And times for the w.c. You can use it now if you like.

DUSSEL. (*Stiffly*) No, thank you.

ANNE. I suppose you think it's awful, my talking about a thing like that. But you don't know how important it can get to be, especially when you're frightened . . . About this room, the way Margot and I did . . . she had it to herself in the afternoons for studying, reading . . . lessons, you know . . . and I took the mornings. Would that be all right with you?

DUSSEL. I'm not at my best in the morning.

ANNE. You stay here in the mornings then. I'll take the room in the afternoons.

DUSSEL. Tell me, when you're in here, what happens to me? Where am I spending my time? In there, with all the people?

ANNE. Yes.

DUSSEL. I see. I see.

ANNE. We have supper at half past six.

DUSSEL. (*Going over to the sofa*) Then, if you don't mind . . . I like to lie down quietly for ten minutes before eating. I find it helps the digestion.

ANNE. Of course. I hope I'm not going to be too much of a bother to you. I seem to be able to get everyone's back up.

(DUSSEL *lies down on the sofa, curled up, his back to her.*)

DUSSEL. I always get along very well with children. My patients all bring their children to me, because they know I get on well with them. So don't you worry about that.

(ANNE *leans over him, taking his hand and shaking it gratefully.*)

ANNE. Thank you. Thank you, Mr. Dussel.

(*The lights dim to darkness. The curtain falls on the scene.* ANNE'S *voice comes to us faintly at first, and then with increasing power.*)

ANNE'S VOICE. . . . And yesterday I finished Cissy Van Marxvelt's latest book. I think she is a first-class writer. I shall definitely let my children read her. Monday the twenty-first of September, nineteen forty-two. Mr. Dussel and I had another battle yesterday. Yes, Mr. Dussel! According to him, nothing, I repeat . . . nothing, is right about me . . . my appearance, my character, my manners. While he was going on at me I thought . . . sometime I'll give you such a smack that you'll fly right up to the ceiling! Why is it that every grownup thinks he knows the way to bring up children? Particularly the grownups that never had any. I keep wishing that Peter was a girl instead of a boy. Then I would have someone to talk to. Margot's a darling, but she takes everything too seriously. To pause for a moment on the subject of Mrs. Van Daan. I must tell you that her attempts to flirt with father are getting her nowhere. Pim, thank goodness, won't play.

(*As she is saying the last lines, the curtain rises on the darkened scene.* ANNE'S *voice fades out.*)

### SCENE IV

*It is the middle of the night, several months later. The stage is dark except for a little light which comes through the skylight in* PETER'S *room.*

*Everyone is in bed.* MR. *and* MRS. FRANK *lie on the couch in the main room, which has been pulled out to serve as a make-shift double bed.*

MARGOT *is sleeping on a mattress on the floor in the main room, behind a curtain stretched across for privacy. The others are all in their accustomed rooms.*

*From outside we hear two drunken soldiers singing "Lili Marlene."[1] A girl's high giggle*

*is heard. The sound of running feet is heard coming closer and then fading in the distance. Throughout the scene there is the distant sound of airplanes passing overhead.*

*A match suddenly flares up in the attic. We dimly see* MR. VAN DAAN. *He is getting his bearings. He comes quickly down the stairs, and goes to the cupboard where the food is stored. Again the match flares up, and is as quickly blown out. The dim figure is seen to steal back up the stairs.*

*There is quiet for a second or two, broken only by the sound of airplanes, and running feet on the street below.*

*Suddenly, out of the silence and the dark, we hear* ANNE *scream.*

ANNE. (*Screaming*) No! No! Don't . . . don't take me!

(*She moans, tossing and crying in her sleep. The other people wake, terrified.* DUSSEL *sits up in bed, furious.*)

DUSSEL. Shush! Anne! Anne, for God's sake, shush!

ANNE. (*Still in her nightmare*) Save me! Save me!

(*She screams and screams.* DUSSEL *gets out of bed, going over to her, trying to wake her.*)

DUSSEL. For God's sake! Quiet! Quiet! You want someone to hear?

(*In the main room* MRS. FRANK *grabs a shawl and pulls it around her. She rushes in to* ANNE, *taking her in her arms.* MR. FRANK *hurriedly gets up, putting on his overcoat.* MARGOT *sits up, terrified.* PETER'S *light goes on in his room.*)

MRS. FRANK. (*To* ANNE, *in her room*) Hush, darling, hush. It's all right. It's all right. (*Over her shoulder to* DUSSEL) Will you be kind enough to turn on the light, Mr. Dussel? (*Back to* ANNE) It's nothing, my darling. It was just a dream.

---

1. **"Lili Marlene"**\ˈlē·lē ˈmär ˈlān\ a very popular song among German soldiers in World War II.

(DUSSEL *turns on the light in the bedroom.* MRS. FRANK *holds* ANNE *in her arms. Gradually* ANNE *comes out of her nightmare, still trembling with horror.* MR. FRANK *comes into the room, and goes quickly to the window, looking out to be sure that no one outside has heard* ANNE's *screams.* MRS. FRANK *holds* ANNE, *talking softly to her. In the main room* MARGOT *stands on a chair, turning on the center hanging lamp. A light goes on in the* VAN DAANS' *room overhead.* PETER *puts his robe on, coming out of his room.*)

DUSSEL. (*To* MRS. FRANK, *blowing his nose*) Something must be done about that child, Mrs. Frank. Yelling like that! Who knows but there's somebody on the streets? She's endangering all our lives.

MRS. FRANK. Anne, darling.

DUSSEL. Every night she twists and turns. I don't sleep. I spend half my night shushing her. And now it's nightmares!

(MARGOT *comes to the door of* ANNE's *room, followed by* PETER. MR. FRANK *goes to them, indicating that everything is all right.* PETER *takes* MARGOT *back.*)

MRS. FRANK. (*To* ANNE) You're here, safe, you see? Nothing has happened. (*To* DUSSEL) Please, Mr. Dussel, go back to bed. She'll be herself in a minute or two. Won't you, Anne?

DUSSEL. (*Picking up a book and a pillow*) Thank you, but I'm going to the w.c. The one place where there's peace!

(*He stalks out.* MR. VAN DAAN, *in underwear and trousers, comes down the stairs.*)

MR. VAN DAAN. (*To* DUSSEL) What is it? What happened?

DUSSEL. A nightmare. She was having a nightmare!

MR. VAN DAAN. I thought someone was murdering her.

DUSSEL. Unfortunately, no.

(*He goes into the bathroom.* MR. VAN DAAN *goes back up the stairs.* MR. FRANK, *in the main room, sends* PETER *back to his own bedroom.*)

MR. FRANK. Thank you, Peter. Go back to bed.

(PETER *goes back to his room.* MR. FRANK *follows him, turning out the light and looking out the window. Then he goes back to the main room, and gets up on a chair, turning out the center hanging lamp.*)

MRS. FRANK. (*To* ANNE) Would you like some water? (ANNE *shakes her head*) Was it a very bad dream? Perhaps if you told me . . . ?

ANNE. I'd rather not talk about it.

MRS. FRANK. Poor darling. Try to sleep then. I'll sit right here beside you until you fall asleep.

(*She brings a stool over, sitting there.*)

ANNE. You don't have to.

MRS. FRANK. But I'd like to stay with you . . . very much. Really.

ANNE. I'd rather you didn't.

MRS. FRANK. Good night, then. (*She leans down to kiss* ANNE. ANNE *throws her arm up over her face, turning away.* MRS. FRANK, *hiding her hurt, kisses* ANNE's *arm*) You'll be all right? There's nothing that you want?

ANNE. Will you please ask Father to come.

MRS. FRANK. (*After a second*) Of course, Anne dear. (*She hurries out into the other room.* MR. FRANK *comes to her as she comes in*) Sie verlangt nach Dir!

MR. FRANK. (*Sensing her hurt*) Edith, *Liebe, schau . . .*

MRS. FRANK. *Es macht nichts! Ich danke dem lieben Herrgott, dass sie sich wenigstens an Dich wendet, wenn sie Trost braucht! Geh hinein, Otto, sie ist ganz hysterisch vor Angst.* (*As* MR. FRANK *hesitates*) *Geh zu ihr.*[2] (*He looks at her for a second and then goes to get a cup of water for* ANNE. MRS. FRANK *sinks down on the bed, her face in her hands, trying to keep from sobbing aloud.* MARGOT

---

2. The German may be translated as follows: "She is asking for you." "Edith, dear one, look." "It does not matter. I thank the dear Lord that she at least thought of you if she was in doubt. Go in, Otto; she is entirely hysterical from anxiety. Go to her."

*comes over to her, putting her arms around her*) She wants nothing of me. She pulled away when I leaned down to kiss her.

MARGOT. It's a phase . . . You heard Father . . . Most girls go through it . . . they turn to their fathers at this age . . . they give all their love to their fathers.

MRS. FRANK. You weren't like this. You didn't shut me out.

MARGOT. She'll get over it . . .

(*She smooths the bed for* MRS. FRANK *and sits beside her a moment as* MRS. FRANK *lies down. In* ANNE'S *room* MR. FRANK *comes in, sitting down by* ANNE. ANNE *flings her arms around him, clinging to him. In the distance we hear the sound of ack-ack.*)

ANNE. Oh, Pim. I dreamed that they came to get us! The Green Police! They broke down the door and grabbed me and started to drag me out the way they did Jopie.

MR. FRANK. I want you to take this pill.

ANNE. What is it?

MR. FRANK. Something to quiet you.

(*She takes it and drinks the water. In the main room* MARGOT *turns out the light and goes back to her bed.*)

MR. FRANK. (*To* ANNE) Do you want me to read to you for a while?

ANNE. No. Just sit with me for a minute. Was I awful? Did I yell terribly loud? Do you think anyone outside could have heard?

MR. FRANK. No. No. Lie quietly now. Try to sleep.

ANNE. I'm a terrible coward. I'm so disappointed in myself. I think I've conquered my fear . . . I think I'm really grown-up . . . and then something happens . . . and I run to you like a baby . . . I love you, Father. I don't love anyone but you.

MR. FRANK. (*Reproachfully*) Anneke!

ANNE. It's true. I've been thinking about it for a long time. You're the only one I love.

MR. FRANK. It's fine to hear you tell me that you love me. But I'd be happier if you said you loved your mother as well . . . She needs your help so much . . . your love . . .

ANNE. We have nothing in common. She doesn't understand me. Whenever I try to explain my views on life to her she asks me if I'm constipated.

MR. FRANK. You hurt her very much just now. She's crying. She's in there crying.

ANNE. I can't help it. I only told the truth. I didn't want her here . . . (*Then, with sudden change*) Oh, Pim, I was horrible, wasn't I? And the worst of it is, I can stand off and look at myself doing it and know it's cruel and yet I can't stop doing it. What's the matter with me? Tell me. Don't say it's just a phase! Help me.

MR. FRANK. There is so little that we parents can do to help our children. We can only try to set a good example . . . point the way. The rest you must do yourself. You must build your own character.

ANNE. I'm trying. Really I am. Every night I think back over all of the things I did that day that were wrong . . . like putting the wet mop in Mr. Dussel's bed . . . and this thing now with Mother. I say to myself, that was wrong. I make up my mind, I'm never going to do that again. Never! Of course I may do something worse . . . but at least I'll never do *that* again! . . . I have a nicer side, Father . . . a sweeter, nicer side. But I'm scared to show it. I'm afraid that people are going to laugh at me if I'm serious. So the mean Anne comes to the outside and the good Anne stays on the inside, and I keep on trying to switch them around and have the good Anne outside and the bad Anne inside and be what I'd like to be . . . and might be . . . if only . . . only . . .

(*She is asleep.* MR. FRANK *watches her for a moment and then turns off the light, and starts out. The lights dim out. The curtain falls on the scene.* ANNE'S *voice is heard dimly at first, and then with growing strength.*)

ANNE'S VOICE. . . . The air raids are getting worse. They come over day and night. The noise is terrifying. Pim says it should be music to our ears. The more planes, the sooner will come the end of the war. Mrs. Van Daan pretends to be a fatalist. What will be, will be. But when the planes come over, who is the most frightened? No one else but Petronella! . . . Monday, the ninth of November, nineteen forty-two. Wonderful news! The Allies have landed in Africa. Pim says that we can look for an early finish to the war. Just for fun he asked each of us what was the first thing we wanted to do when we got out of here. Mrs. Van Daan longs to be home with her own things, her needle-point chairs, the Beckstein piano her father gave her . . . the best that money could buy. Peter would like to go to a movie. Mr. Dussel wants to get back to his dentist's drill. He's afraid he is losing his touch. For myself, there are so many things . . . to ride a bike again . . . to laugh till my belly aches . . . to have new clothes from the skin out . . . to have a hot tub filled to overflowing and wallow in it for hours . . . to be back in school with my friends . . .

(*As the last lines are being said, the curtain rises on the scene. The lights dim on as* ANNE's *voice fades away.*)

### SCENE V

*It is the first night of the Hanukkah[1] celebration.* MR. FRANK *is standing at the head of the table on which is the Menorah. He lights the Shamos, or servant candle, and holds it as he says the blessing. Seated listening is all of the "family," dressed in their best. The men wear hats,* PETER *wears his cap.*

MR. FRANK. (*Reading from a prayer book*) "Praised be Thou, oh Lord our God, Ruler of the universe, who has sanctified us with Thy commandments and bidden us kindle the Hanukkah lights. Praised be Thou, oh Lord our God, Ruler of the universe, who has wrought wondrous deliverances for our fathers in days of old. Praised be Thou, oh Lord our God, Ruler of the universe, that

Thou has given us life and sustenance and brought us to this happy season." (MR. FRANK *lights the one candle of the Menorah as he continues*) "We kindle this Hanukkah light to celebrate the great and wonderful deeds wrought through the zeal with which God filled the hearts of the heroic Maccabees,[2] two thousand years ago. They fought against indifference, against tyranny and oppression, and they restored our Temple to us. May these lights remind us that we should ever look to God, whence cometh our help." Amen. [Pronounced *O-mayn.*]

ALL. Amen.

(MR. FRANK *hands* MRS. FRANK *the prayer book.*)

MRS. FRANK. (*Reading*) "I lift up mine eyes unto the mountains, from whence cometh my help. My help cometh from the Lord who made heaven and earth. He will not suffer thy foot to be moved. He that keepeth thee will not slumber. He that keepeth Israel doth neither slumber nor sleep. The Lord is thy keeper. The Lord is thy shade upon thy right hand. The sun shall not smite thee by day, nor the moon by night. The Lord shall keep thee from all evil. He shall keep thy soul. The Lord shall guard thy going out and thy coming in, from this time forth and forevermore." Amen.

ALL. Amen.

(MRS. FRANK *puts down the prayer book and goes to get the food and wine.* MARGOT *helps her.* MR. FRANK *takes the men's hats and puts them aside.*)

DUSSEL. (*Rising*) That was very moving.

ANNE. (*Pulling him back*) It isn't over yet!

---

1. **Hanukkah**\ˈha·nə·kə\ an eight-day Jewish festival in remembrance of victories of the Maccabees. **Menorah**\mə ˈnō·rə\ a candlestick used in Hebrew Services, often with holders for seven candles. The **Shamos**\ˈsha·məs\ candle, one used to light the others. Men keep their hats on at many Jewish ceremonials.
2. **Maccabees**\ˈmă·kə·bēz\ Jewish patriots of the second and first centuries B.C.

MRS. VAN DAAN. Sit down! Sit down!

ANNE. There's a lot more, songs and presents.

DUSSEL. Presents?

MRS. FRANK. Not this year, unfortunately.

MRS. VAN DAAN. But always on Hanukkah everyone gives presents . . . everyone!

DUSSEL. Like our St. Nicholas' Day.

*(There is a chorus of "no's" from the group.)*

MRS. VAN DAAN. No! Not like St. Nicholas! What kind of a Jew are you that you don't know Hanukkah?

MRS. FRANK. (*As she brings the food*) I remember particularly the candles . . . First one, as we have tonight. Then the second night you light two candles, the next night three . . . and so on until you have eight candles burning. When there are eight candles it is truly beautiful.

MRS. VAN DAAN. And the potato pancakes.

MR. VAN DAAN. Don't talk about them!

MRS. VAN DAAN. I make the best *latkes*[3] you ever tasted!

MRS. FRANK. Invite us all next year . . . in your own home.

MR. FRANK. God willing!

MRS. VAN DAAN. God willing.

MARGOT. What I remember best is the presents we used to get when we were little . . . eight days of presents . . . and each day they got better and better.

MRS. FRANK. (*Sitting down*) We are all here, alive. That is present enough.

ANNE. No, it isn't. I've got something . . .

*(She rushes into her room, hurriedly puts on a little hat improvised from the lamp shade, grabs a satchel bulging with parcels and comes running back.)*

MRS. FRANK. What is it?

ANNE. Presents!

MRS. VAN DAAN. Presents!

DUSSEL. Look!

MR. VAN DAAN. What's she got on her head?

PETER. A lamp shade!

ANNE. (*She picks out one at random*) This is for

Margot. (*She hands it to* MARGOT, *pulling her to her feet*) Read it out loud.

MARGOT. (*Reading*)
"You have never lost your temper.
  You never will, I fear,
  You are so good.
  But if you should,
  Put all your cross words here."

*(She tears open the package)*

A new crossword puzzle book! Where did you get it?

ANNE. It isn't new. It's one that you've done. But I rubbed it all out, and if you wait a little and forget, you can do it all over again.

MARGOT. (*Sitting*) It's wonderful, Anne. Thank you. You'd never know it wasn't new.

*(From outside we hear the sound of a streetcar passing.)*

ANNE. (*With another gift*) Mrs. Van Daan.

MRS. VAN DAAN. (*Taking it*) This is awful . . . I haven't anything for anyone . . . I never thought . . .

MR. FRANK. This is all Anne's idea.

MRS. VAN DAAN. (*Holding up a bottle*) What is it?

ANNE. It's hair shampoo. I took all the odds and ends of soap and mixed them with the last of my toilet water.

MRS. VAN DAAN. Oh, Anneke!

ANNE. I wanted to write a poem for all of them, but I didn't have time. (*Offering a large box to* MR. VAN DAAN) Yours, Mr. Van Daan, is *really* something . . . something you want more than anything. (*As she waits for him to open it*) Look! Cigarettes!

MR. VAN DAAN. Cigarettes!

ANNE. Two of them! Pim found some old pipe tobacco in the pocket lining of his coat . . . and we made them . . . or rather, Pim did.

MRS. VAN DAAN. Let me see . . . Well, look at that! Light it, Putti! Light it.

*(*MR. VAN DAAN *hesitates.*)*

---

3. **latke**\ˈlät·kə\ a griddle cake, usually made of potatoes.

ANNE. It's tobacco, really it is! There's a little fluff in it, but not much.

(*Everyone watches intently as* MR. VAN DAAN *cautiously lights it. The cigarette flares up. Everyone laughs.*)

PETER. It works!

MRS. VAN DAAN. Look at him.

MR. VAN DAAN. (*Spluttering*) Thank you, Anne. Thank you.

(ANNE *rushes back to her satchel for another present.*)

ANNE. (*Handing her mother a piece of paper*) For Mother, Hanukkah greeting.

(*She pulls her mother to her feet.*)

MRS. FRANK. (*She reads*)
"Here's an I.O.U. that I promise to pay.
Ten hours of doing whatever you say.
Signed, Anne Frank."

(MRS. FRANK, *touched, takes* ANNE *in her arms, holding her close.*)

DUSSEL. (*To* ANNE) Ten hours of doing what you're told? *Anything* you're told?

ANNE. That's right.

DUSSEL. You wouldn't want to sell that, Mrs. Frank?

MRS. FRANK. Never! This is the most precious gift I've ever had!

(*She sits, showing her present to the others.* ANNE *hurries back to the satchel and pulls out a scarf, the scarf that* MR. FRANK *found in the first scene.*)

ANNE. (*Offering it to her father*) For Pim.

MR. FRANK. Anneke . . . I wasn't supposed to have a present!

(*He takes it, unfolding it and showing it to the others.*)

ANNE. It's a muffler . . . to put around your neck . . . like an ascot, you know. I made it myself out of odds and ends . . . I knitted it in the dark each night, after I'd gone to bed. I'm afraid it looks better in the dark!

MR. FRANK. (*Putting it on*) It's fine. It fits me perfectly. Thank you, Anneke.

(ANNE *hands* PETER *a ball of paper, with a string attached to it.*)

ANNE. That's for Mouschi.

PETER. (*Rising to bow*) On behalf of Mouschi, I thank you.

ANNE. (*Hesitant, handing him a gift*) And . . . this is yours . . . from Mrs. Quack Quack. (*As he holds it gingerly in his hands*) Well . . . open it . . . Aren't you going to open it?

PETER. I'm scared to. I know something's going to jump out and hit me.

ANNE. No. It's nothing like that, really.

MRS. VAN DAAN. (*As he is opening it*) What is it, Peter? Go on. Show it.

ANNE. (*Excitedly*) It's a safety razor!

DUSSEL. A what?

ANNE. A razor!

MRS. VAN DAAN. (*Looking at it*) You didn't make that out of odds and ends.

ANNE. (*To* PETER) Miep got it for me. It's not new. It's second-hand. But you really do need a razor now.

DUSSEL. For what?

ANNE. Look on his upper lip . . . you can see the beginning of a mustache.

DUSSEL. He wants to get rid of that? Put a little milk on it and let the cat lick it off.

PETER. (*Starting for his room*) Think you're funny, don't you.

DUSSEL. Look! He can't wait! He's going in to try it!

PETER. I'm going to give Mouschi his present!

(*He goes into his room, slamming the door behind him.*)

MR. VAN DAAN. (*Disgustedly*) Mouschi, Mouschi, Mouschi.

(*In the distance we hear a dog persistently barking.* ANNE *brings a gift to* DUSSEL.)

ANNE. And last but never least, my roommate, Mr. Dussel.

DUSSEL. For me? You have something for me?

(*He opens the small box she gives him.*)

ANNE. I made them myself.

DUSSEL. (*Puzzled*) Capsules! Two capsules!

ANNE. They're ear-plugs!

DUSSEL. Ear-plugs?

ANNE. To put in your ears so you won't hear me when I thrash around at night. I saw them advertised in a magazine. They're not real ones . . . I made them out of cotton and candle wax. Try them . . . See if they don't work . . . see if you can hear me talk . . .

DUSSEL. (*Putting them in his ears*) Wait now until I get them in . . . so.

ANNE. Are you ready?

DUSSEL. Huh?

ANNE. Are you ready?

DUSSEL. Good God! They've gone inside! I can't get them out! (*They laugh as* MR. DUSSEL *jumps about, trying to shake the plugs out of his ears. Finally he gets them out. Putting them away*) Thank you, Anne! Thank you!

MR. VAN DAAN. A real Hanuk-kah!

MRS. VAN DAAN. Wasn't it cute of her?

MRS. FRANK. I don't know when she did it.

MARGOT. I love my present.

⎫
⎬ *Together*
⎭

ANNE. (*Sitting at the table*) And now let's have the song, Father . . . please . . . (*To* DUSSEL) Have you heard the Hanukkah song, Mr. Dussel? The song is the whole thing! (*She sings*) "Oh, Hanukkah! Oh, Hanukkah! The sweet celebration . . ."

MR. FRANK. (*Quieting her*) I'm afraid, Anne, we shouldn't sing that song tonight. (*To* DUSSEL) It's a song of jubilation, of rejoicing. One is apt to become too enthusiastic.

ANNE. Oh, please, please. Let's sing the song. I promise not to shout!

MR. FRANK. Very well. But quietly now . . . I'll keep an eye on you and when . . .

(*As* ANNE *starts to sing, she is interrupted by* DUSSEL, *who is snorting and wheezing.*)

DUSSEL. (*Pointing to* PETER) You . . . You! (PETER *is coming from his bedroom, ostentatiously holding a bulge in his coat as if he were holding his cat, and dangling* ANNE'S *present be-fore it*) How many times . . . I told you . . . Out! Out!

MR. VAN DAAN. (*Going to* PETER) What's the matter with you? Haven't you any sense? Get that cat out of here.

PETER. (*Innocently*) Cat?

MR. VAN DAAN. You heard me. Get it out of here!

PETER. I have no cat.

(*Delighted with his joke, he opens his coat and pulls out a bath towel. The group at the table laugh, enjoying the joke.*)

DUSSEL. (*Still wheezing*) It doesn't need to be the cat . . . his clothes are enough . . . when he comes out of that room . . .

MR. VAN DAAN. Don't worry. You won't be bothered any more. We're getting rid of it.

DUSSEL. At last you listen to me.

(*He goes off into his bedroom.*)

MR. VAN DAAN. (*Calling after him*) I'm not doing it for you. That's all in your mind . . . all of it! (*He starts back to his place at the table*) I'm doing it because I'm sick of seeing that cat eat all our food.

PETER. That's not true! I only give him bones . . . scraps . . .

MR. VAN DAAN. Don't tell me! He gets fatter every day! Damn cat looks better than any of us. Out he goes tonight!

PETER. No! No!

ANNE. Mr. Van Daan, you can't do that! That's Peter's cat. Peter loves that cat.

MRS. FRANK. (*Quietly*) Anne.

PETER. (*To* MR. VAN DAAN) If he goes, I go.

MR. VAN DAAN. Go! Go!

MRS. VAN DAAN. You're not going and the cat's not going! Now please . . . this is Hanukkah . . . Hanukkah . . . this is the time to celebrate . . . What's the matter with all of you? Come on, Anne. Let's have the song.

ANNE. (*Singing*)

"Oh, Hanukkah! Oh, Hanukkah!
The sweet celebration."

MR. FRANK. (*Rising*) I think we should first blow out the candle . . . then we'll have something for tomorrow night.

MARGOT. But, Father, you're supposed to let it burn itself out.

MR. FRANK. I'm sure that God understands shortages. (*Before blowing it out*) "Praised be Thou, oh Lord our God, who has sustained us and permitted us to celebrate this joyous festival."

(*He is about to blow out the candle when suddenly there is a crash of something falling below. They all freeze in horror, motionless. For a few seconds there is complete silence.* MR. FRANK *slips off his shoes. The others noiselessly follow his example.* MR. FRANK *turns out a light near him. He motions to* PETER *to turn off the center lamp.* PETER *tries to reach it, realizes he cannot and gets up on a chair. Just as he is touching the lamp he loses his balance. The chair goes out from under him. He falls. The iron lamp shade crashes to the floor. There is a sound of feet below, running down the stairs.*)

MR. VAN DAAN. (*Under his breath*) God Almighty! (*The only light left comes from the Hanukkah candle.* DUSSEL *comes from his room.* MR. FRANK *creeps over to the stairwell and stands listening. The dog is heard barking excitedly*) Do you hear anything?

MR. FRANK. (*In a whisper*) No. I think they've gone.

MRS. VAN DAAN. It's the Green Police. They've found us.

MR. FRANK. If they had, they wouldn't have left. They'd be up here by now.

MRS. VAN DAAN. I know it's the Green Police. They've gone to get help. That's all. They'll be back!

MR. VAN DAAN. Or it may have been the Gestapo,[4] looking for papers . . .

MR. FRANK. (*Interrupting*) Or a thief, looking for money.

MRS. VAN DAAN. We've got to do something . . . Quick! Quick! Before they come back.

MR. VAN DAAN. There isn't anything to do. Just wait.

(MR. FRANK *holds up his hand for them to be quiet. He is listening intently. There is complete silence as they all strain to hear any sound from below. Suddenly* ANNE *begins to sway. With a low cry she falls to the floor in a faint.* MRS. FRANK *goes to her quickly, sitting beside her on the floor and taking her in her arms.*)

MRS. FRANK. Get some water, please! Get some water!

(MARGOT *starts for the sink.*)

MR. VAN DAAN. (*Grabbing* MARGOT) No! No! No one's going to run water!

MR. FRANK. If they've found us, they've found us. Get the water. (MARGOT *starts again for the sink.* MR. FRANK, *getting a flashlight*) I'm going down.

(MARGOT *rushes to him, clinging to him.* ANNE *struggles to consciousness.*)

MARGOT. No, Father, no! There may be someone there, waiting . . . It may be a trap!

MR. FRANK. This is Saturday. There is no way for us to know what has happened until Miep or Mr. Kraler comes on Monday morning. We cannot live with this uncertainty.

MARGOT. Don't go, Father!

MRS. FRANK. Hush, darling, hush. (MR. FRANK *slips quietly out, down the steps and out through the door below*) Margot! Stay close to me.

(MARGOT *goes to her mother.*)

MR. VAN DAAN. Shush! Shush!

(MRS. FRANK *whispers to* MARGOT *to get the water.* MARGOT *goes for it.*)

MRS. VAN DAAN. Putti, where's our money? Get our money. I hear you can buy the Green Police off, so much a head. Go upstairs quick! Get the money!

MR. VAN DAAN. Keep still!

MRS. VAN DAAN. (*Kneeling before him, pleading*) Do you want to be dragged off to a concentration camp? Are you going to stand

---

4. **Gestapo** \\'gĕs ▲ta·pō\\ the dreaded Nazi secret police.

there and wait for them to come up and get you? Do something, I tell you!

MR. VAN DAAN. (*Pushing her aside*) Will you keep still!

(*He goes over to the stairwell to listen. PETER goes to his mother, helping her up onto the sofa. There is a second of silence, then ANNE can stand it no longer.*)

ANNE. Someone go after Father! Make Father come back!

PETER. (*Starting for the door*) I'll go.

MR. VAN DAAN. Haven't you done enough?

(*He pushes PETER roughly away. In his anger against his father PETER grabs a chair as if to hit him with it, then puts it down, burying his face in his hands. MRS. FRANK begins to pray softly.*)

ANNE. Please, please, Mr. Van Daan. Get Father.

MR. VAN DAAN. Quiet! Quiet!

(*ANNE is shocked into silence. MRS. FRANK pulls her closer, holding her protectively in her arms.*)

MRS. FRANK. (*Softly, praying*) "I lift up mine eyes unto the mountains, from whence cometh my help. My help cometh from the Lord who made heaven and earth. He will not suffer thy foot to be moved . . . He that keepeth thee will not slumber . . ."

(*She stops as she hears someone coming. They all watch the door tensely. MR. FRANK comes quietly in. ANNE rushes to him, holding him tight.*)

MR. FRANK. It was a thief. That noise must have scared him away.

MRS. VAN DAAN. Thank God.

MR. FRANK. He took the cash box. And the radio. He ran away in such a hurry that he didn't stop to shut the street door. It was swinging wide open. (*A breath of relief sweeps over them*) I think it would be good to have some light.

MARGOT. Are you sure it's all right?

MR. FRANK. The danger has passed. (*MARGOT goes to light the small lamp*) Don't be so terrified, Anne. We're safe.

DUSSEL. Who says the danger has passed? Don't you realize we are in greater danger than ever?

MR. FRANK. Mr. Dussel, will you be still!

(*MR. FRANK takes ANNE back to the table, making her sit down with him, trying to calm her.*)

DUSSEL. (*Pointing to PETER*) Thanks to this clumsy fool, there's someone now who knows we're up here! Someone now knows we're up here, hiding!

MRS. VAN DAAN. (*Going to DUSSEL*) Someone knows we're here, yes. But who is the someone? A thief! A thief! You think a thief is going to go to the Green Police and say . . . I was robbing a place the other night and I heard a noise up over my head? You think a thief is going to do that?

DUSSEL. Yes. I think he will.

MRS. VAN DAAN. (*Hysterically*) You're crazy!

(*She stumbles back to her seat at the table. PETER follows protectively, pushing DUSSEL aside.*)

DUSSEL. I think some day he'll be caught and then he'll make a bargain with the Green Police . . . if they'll let him off, he'll tell them where some Jews are hiding!

(*He goes off into the bedroom. There is a second of appalled silence.*)

MR. VAN DAAN. He's right.

ANNE. Father, let's get out of here! We can't stay here now . . . Let's go . . .

MR. VAN DAAN. Go! Where?

MRS. FRANK. (*Sinking into her chair at the table*) Yes. Where?

MR. FRANK. (*Rising, to them all*) Have we lost all faith? All courage? A moment ago we thought that they'd come for us. We were sure it was the end. But it wasn't the end. We're alive, safe. (*MR. VAN DAAN goes to the table and sits. MR. FRANK prays*) "We thank Thee, oh Lord our God, that in Thy infinite mercy Thou hast again seen fit to spare us."

*(He blows out the candle, then turns to* ANNE*)* Come on, Anne. The song! Let's have the song! *(He starts to sing.* ANNE *finally starts falteringly to sing, as* MR. FRANK *urges her on. Her voice is hardly audible at first.)*

ANNE. *(Singing)*

"Oh, Hanukkah! Oh, Hanukkah!
The sweet . . . celebration . . ."

*(As she goes on singing, the others gradually join in, their voices still shaking with fear.* MRS. VAN DAAN *sobs as she sings.)*

GROUP.

"Around the feast . . . we . . . gather
In complete . . . jubilation . . .
Happiest of sea . . . sons
Now is here.
Many are the reasons for good cheer."

*(*DUSSEL *comes from the bedroom. He comes over to the table, standing beside* MARGOT, *listening to them as they sing.)*

"Together
We'll weather
Whatever tomorrow may bring."

*(As they sing on with growing courage, the lights start to dim)*

"So hear us rejoicing
And merrily voicing
The Hanukkah song that we sing.
Hoy!"

*(The lights are out. The curtain starts slowly to fall)*

"Hear us rejoicing
And merrily voicing
The Hanukkah song that we sing."

*(They are still singing, as the curtain falls.)*

*Curtain*

# Act Two

## SCENE I

*In the darkness we hear* ANNE'S *voice, again reading from the diary.*

ANNE'S VOICE. Saturday, the first of January, nineteen forty-four. Another new year has begun and we find ourselves still in our hiding place. We have been here now for one year, five months and twenty-five days. It seems that our life is at a standstill.

*The curtain rises on the scene. It is late afternoon. Everyone is bundled up against the cold. In the main room* MRS. FRANK *is taking down the laundry which is hung across the back.* MR. FRANK *sits in the chair down left, reading.* MARGOT *is lying on the couch with a blanket over her and the many-colored knitted scarf around her throat.* ANNE *is seated at the center table, writing in her diary.* PETER, MR. *and* MRS. VAN DAAN *and* DUSSEL *are all in their own rooms, reading or lying down.*

*As the lights dim on,* ANNE'S *voice continues, without a break.*

ANNE'S VOICE. We are all a little thinner. The Van Daans' "discussions" are as violent as ever. Mother still does not understand me. But then I don't understand her either. There is one great change, however. A change in myself. I read somewhere that girls of my age don't feel quite certain of themselves. That they become quiet within and begin to think of the miracle that is taking place in their bodies. I think that what is happening to me is so wonderful . . . not only what can be seen, but what is taking place inside. Each time it has happened I have a feeling that I have a sweet secret. *(We hear the chimes and then a hymn being played on the carillon outside)* And in spite of any pain, I long for the time when I shall feel that secret within me again.

*(The buzzer of the door below suddenly*

*sounds. Everyone is startled,* MR. FRANK *tiptoes cautiously to the top of the steps and listens. Again the buzzer sounds, in* MIEP's *V-for-Victory[1] signal.*)

MR. FRANK. It's Miep!

(*He goes quickly down the steps to unbolt the door.* MRS. FRANK *calls upstairs to the* VAN DAANS *and then to* PETER.)

MRS. FRANK. Wake up, everyone! Miep is here! (*ANNE quickly puts her diary away.* MARGOT *sits up, pulling the blanket around her shoulders.* MR. DUSSEL *sits on the edge of his bed, listening, disgruntled.* MIEP *comes up the steps, followed by* MR. KRALER. *They bring flowers, books, newspapers, etc.* ANNE *rushes to* MIEP, *throwing her arms affectionately around her*) Miep . . . *and Mr. Kraler . . .* What a delightful surprise!

MR. KRALER. We came to bring you New Year's greetings.

MRS. FRANK. You shouldn't . . . you should have at least one day to yourselves.

(*She goes quickly to the stove and brings down teacups and tea for all of them.*)

ANNE. Don't say that, it's so wonderful to see them! (*Sniffing at* MIEP's *coat*) I can smell the wind and the cold on your clothes.

MIEP. (*Giving her the flowers*) There you are. (*Then to* MARGOT, *feeling her forehead*) How are you, Margot? . . . Feeling any better?

MARGOT. I'm all right.

ANNE. We filled her full of every kind of pill so she won't cough and make a noise.

(*She runs into her room to put the flowers in water.* MR. *and* MRS. VAN DAAN *come from upstairs. Outside there is the sound of a band playing.*)

MRS. VAN DAAN. Well, hello, Miep. Mr. Kraler.

MR. KRALER. (*Giving a bouquet of flowers to* MRS. VAN DAAN) With my hope for peace in the New Year.

PETER. (*Anxiously*) Miep, have you seen Mouschi? Have you seen him anywhere around?

MIEP. I'm sorry, Peter. I asked everyone in the neighborhood had they seen a gray cat. But they said no.

(MRS. FRANK *gives* MIEP *a cup of tea.* MR. FRANK *comes up the steps, carrying a small cake on a plate.*)

MR. FRANK. Look what Miep's brought for us!

MRS. FRANK. (*Taking it*) A cake!

MR. VAN DAAN. A cake! (*He pinches* MIEP's *cheeks gaily and hurries up to the cupboard*) I'll get some plates.

(DUSSEL, *in his room, hastily puts a coat on and starts out to join the others.*)

MRS. FRANK. Thank you, Miepia. You shouldn't have done it. You must have used all of your sugar ration for weeks. (*Giving it to* MRS. VAN DAAN) It's beautiful, isn't it?

MRS. VAN DAAN. It's been ages since I even saw a cake. Not since you brought us one last year. (*Without looking at the cake, to* MIEP) Remember? Don't you remember, you gave us one on New Year's Day? Just this time last year? I'll never forget it because you had "Peace in nineteen forty-three" on it. (*She looks at the cake and reads*) "Peace in nineteen forty-four!"

MIEP. Well, it has to come sometime, you know. (*As* DUSSEL *comes from his room*) Hello, Mr. Dussel.

MR. KRALER. How are you?

MR. VAN DAAN. (*Bringing plates and a knife*) Here's the knife, *liefje.* Now, how many of us are there?

MIEP. None for me, thank you.

MR. FRANK. Oh, please. You must.

MIEP. I couldn't.

MR. VAN DAAN. Good! That leaves one . . . two . . . three . . . seven of us.

DUSSEL. Eight! Eight! It's the same number as it always is!

---

1. **V-for-Victory** signal, made often by the Allies and their European supporters in World War II, consists of three short notes and one long, the Morse code for the letter V. The first four notes of Beethoven's Fifth Symphony were sometimes used.

MR. VAN DAAN. I left Margot out. I take it for granted Margot won't eat any.

ANNE. Why wouldn't she!

MRS. FRANK. I think it won't harm her.

MR. VAN DAAN. All right! All right! I just didn't want her to start coughing again, that's all.

DUSSEL. And please, Mrs. Frank should cut the cake.

MR. VAN DAAN. What's the difference?

MRS. VAN DAAN. It's not Mrs. Frank's cake, is it, Miep? It's for all of us.

*Together*

DUSSEL. Mrs. Frank divides things better.

MRS. VAN DAAN. (*Going to* DUSSEL) What are you trying to say?

MR. VAN DAAN. Oh, come on! Stop wasting time!

*Together*

MRS. VAN DAAN. (*To* DUSSEL) Don't I always give everybody exactly the same? Don't I?

MR. VAN DAAN. Forget it, Kerli.

MRS. VAN DAAN. No. I want an answer! Don't I?

DUSSEL. Yes. Yes. Everybody gets exactly the same . . . except Mr. Van Daan always gets a little bit more.

(VAN DAAN *advances on* DUSSEL, *the knife still in his hand.*)

MR. VAN DAAN. That's a lie!

(DUSSEL *retreats before the onslaught of the* VAN DAANS.)

MR. FRANK. Please, please! (*Then to* MIEP) You see what a little sugar cake does to us? It goes right to our heads!

MR. VAN DAAN. (*Handing* MRS. FRANK *the knife*) Here you are, Mrs. Frank.

MRS. FRANK. Thank you. (*Then to* MIEP *as she goes to the table to cut the cake*) Are you sure you won't have some?

MIEP. (*Drinking her tea*) No, really, I have to go in a minute.

(*The sound of the band fades out in the distance.*)

PETER. (*To* MIEP) Maybe Mouschi went back to our house . . . they say that cats . . . Do you ever get over there . . . ? I mean . . . do you suppose you could . . .?

MIEP. I'll try, Peter. The first minute I get I'll try. But I'm afraid, with him gone a week . . .

DUSSEL. Make up your mind, already someone has had a nice big dinner from that cat!

(PETER *is furious, inarticulate. He starts toward* DUSSEL *as if to hit him.* MR. FRANK *stops him.* MRS. FRANK *speaks quickly to ease the situation.*)

MRS. FRANK. (*To* MIEP) This is delicious, Miep!

MRS. VAN DAAN. (*Eating hers*) Delicious!

MR. VAN DAAN. (*Finishing it in one gulp*) Dirk's in luck to get a girl who can bake like this!

MIEP. (*Putting down her empty teacup*) I have to run. Dirk's taking me to a party tonight.

ANNE. How heavenly! Remember now what everyone is wearing, and what you have to eat and everything, so you can tell us tomorrow.

MIEP. I'll give you a full report! Good-bye, everyone!

MR. VAN DAAN. (*To* MIEP) Just a minute. There's something I'd like you to do for me.

(*He hurries off up the stairs to his room.*)

MRS. VAN DAAN. (*Sharply*) Putti, where are you going? (*She rushes up the stairs after him, calling hysterically*) What do you want? Putti, what are you going to do?

MIEP. (*To* PETER) What's wrong?

PETER. (*His sympathy is with his mother*) Father says he's going to sell her fur coat. She's crazy about that old fur coat.

DUSSEL. Is it possible? Is it possible that anyone is so silly as to worry about a fur coat in times like this?

PETER. It's none of your darn business . . . and if you say one more thing . . . I'll, I'll take you and I'll . . . I mean it . . . I'll . . .

(*There is a piercing scream from* MRS. VAN DAAN *above. She grabs at the fur coat as* MR. VAN DAAN *is starting downstairs with it.*)

MRS. VAN DAAN. No! No! No! Don't you dare take that! You hear? It's mine! (*Downstairs*

PETER *turns away, embarrassed, miserable*)
My father gave me that! You didn't give it to
me. You have no right. Let go of it . . . you
hear?

(MR. VAN DAAN *pulls the coat from her
hands and hurries downstairs.* MRS. VAN
DAAN *sinks to the floor, sobbing. As* MR.
VAN DAAN *comes into the main room the
others look away, embarrassed for him.*)

MR. VAN DAAN. (*To* MR. KRALER) Just a little
—discussion over the advisability of selling
this coat. As I have often reminded Mrs. Van
Daan, it's very selfish of her to keep it when
people outside are in such desperate need of
clothing . . . (*He gives the coat to* MIEP) So
if you will please to sell it for us? It should
fetch a good price. And by the way, will you
get me cigarettes. I don't care what kind they
are . . . get all you can.

MIEP. It's terribly difficult to get them, Mr. Van
Daan. But I'll try. Good-bye.

(*She goes.* MR. FRANK *follows her down the
steps to bolt the door after her.* MRS. FRANK
*gives* MR. KRALER *a cup of tea.*)

MRS. FRANK. Are you sure you won't have some
cake, Mr. Kraler?

MR. KRALER. I'd better not.

MR. VAN DAAN. You're still feeling badly? What
does your doctor say?

MR. KRALER. I haven't been to him.

MRS. FRANK. Now, Mr. Kraler! . . .

MR. KRALER. (*Sitting at the table*) Oh, I tried.
But you can't get near a doctor these days
. . . they're so busy. After weeks I finally managed to get one on the telephone. I told him
I'd like an appointment . . . I wasn't feeling
very well. You know what he answers . . . over
the telephone . . . Stick out your tongue!
(*They laugh. He turns to* MR. FRANK *as* MR.
FRANK *comes back*) I have some contracts
here . . . I wonder if you'd look over them
with me . . .

MR. FRANK. (*Putting out his hand*) Of course.

MR. KRALER. (*He rises*) If we could go downstairs . . . (MR. FRANK *starts ahead,* MR. KRALER

*speaks to the others*) Will you forgive us? I
won't keep him but a minute.

(*He starts to follow* MR. FRANK *down the
steps.*)

MARGOT. (*With sudden foreboding*) What's
happened? Something's happened! Hasn't it,
Mr. Kraler?

(MR. KRALER *stops and comes back, trying
to reassure* MARGOT *with a pretense of
casualness.*)

MR. KRALER. No, really. I want your father's
advice . . .

MARGOT. Something's gone wrong! I know it!

MR. FRANK. (*Coming back, to* MR. KRALER) If
it's something that concerns us here, it's better that we all hear it.

MR. KRALER. (*Turning to him, quietly*) But . . .
the children . . . ?

MR. FRANK. What they'd imagine would be
worse than any reality.

(*As* MR. KRALER *speaks, they all listen with
intense apprehension.* MRS. VAN DAAN
*comes down the stairs and sits on the bot-
tom step.*)

MR. KRALER. It's a man in the storeroom . . . I
don't know whether or not you remember
him . . . Carl, about fifty, heavy-set, near-
sighted . . . He came with us just before you
left.

MR. FRANK. He was from Utrecht?

MR. KRALER. That's the man. A couple of weeks
ago, when I was in the storeroom, he closed
the door and asked me . . . how's Mr. Frank?
What do you hear from Mr. Frank? I told
him I only knew there was a rumor that you
were in Switzerland. He said he'd heard that
rumor too, but he thought I might know
something more. I didn't pay any attention
to it . . . but then a thing happened yesterday
. . . He'd brought some invoices to the office
for me to sign. As I was going through them,
I looked up. He was standing staring at the
bookcase . . . your bookcase. He said he
thought he remembered a door there . . .
Wasn't there a door there that used to go up

225

to the loft? Then he told me he wanted more money. Twenty guilders[2] more a week.

MR. VAN DAAN. Blackmail!

MR. FRANK. Twenty guilders? Very modest blackmail.

MR. VAN DAAN. That's just the beginning.

DUSSEL. (*Coming to* MR. FRANK) You know what I think? He was the thief who was down there that night. That's how he knows we're here.

MR. FRANK. (*To* MR. KRALER) How was it left? What did you tell him?

MR. KRALER. I said I had to think about it. What shall I do? Pay him the money? . . . Take a chance on firing him . . . or what? I don't know.

DUSSEL. (*Frantic*) Don't fire him! Pay him what he asks . . . keep him here where you can have your eye on him.

MR. FRANK. Is it so much that he's asking? What are they paying nowadays?

MR. KRALER. He could get it in a war plant. But this isn't a war plant. Mind you, I don't know if he really knows . . . or if he doesn't know.

MR. FRANK. Offer him half. Then we'll soon find out if it's blackmail or not.

DUSSEL. And if it is? We've got to pay it, haven't we? Anything he asks we've got to pay!

MR. FRANK. Let's decide that when the time comes.

MR. KRALER. This may be all my imagination. You get to a point, these days, where you suspect everyone and everything. Again and again . . . on some simple look or word, I've found myself . . .

(*The telephone rings in the office below.*)

MRS. VAN DAAN. (*Hurrying to* MR. KRALER) There's the telephone! What does that mean, the telephone ringing on a holiday?

MR. KRALER. That's my wife. I told her I had to go over some papers in my office . . . to call me there when she got out of church. (*He starts out*) I'll offer him half then. Good-bye . . . we'll hope for the best!

(*The group call their good-bye's half heartedly.* MR. FRANK *follows* MR. KRALER,

to bolt the door below. During the following scene, MR. FRANK comes back up and stands listening, disturbed.*)

DUSSEL. (*To* MR. VAN DAAN) You can thank your son for this . . . smashing the light! I tell you, it's just a question of time now.

(*He goes to the window at the back and stands looking out.*)

MARGOT. Sometimes I wish the end would come . . . whatever it is.

MRS. FRANK (*Shocked*) Margot!

(ANNE *goes to* MARGOT, *sitting beside her on the couch with her arms around her.*)

MARGOT. Then at least we'd know where we were.

MRS. FRANK. You should be ashamed of yourself! Talking that way! Think how lucky we are! Think of the thousands dying in the war, every day. Think of the people in concentration camps.

ANNE. (*Interrupting*) What's the good of that? What's the good of thinking of misery when you're already miserable? That's stupid!

MRS. FRANK. Anne!

(*As* ANNE *goes on raging at her mother,* MRS. FRANK *tries to break in, in an effort to quiet her.*)

ANNE. We're young, Margot and Peter and I! You grownups have had your chance! But look at us . . . If we begin thinking of all the horror in the world, we're lost! We're trying to hold onto some kind of ideals . . . when everything . . . ideals, hopes . . . everything, are being destroyed! It isn't our fault that the world is in such a mess! We weren't around when all this started! So don't try to take it out on us!

(*She rushes off to her room, slamming the door after her. She picks up a brush from the chest and hurls it to the floor. Then she*

---

2. **guilder**\ˈgĭl·dər\ a unit of currency in the Netherlands, worth approximately twenty-six cents.

*sits on the settee, trying to control her anger.*)

MR. VAN DAAN. She talks as if we started the war! Did we start the war?

(*He spots* ANNE'S *cake. As he starts to take it,* PETER *anticipates him.*)

PETER. She left her cake. (*He starts for* ANNE'S *room with the cake. There is silence in the main room.* MRS. VAN DAAN *goes up to her room, followed by* VAN DAAN. DUSSEL *stays looking out the window.* MR. FRANK *brings* MRS. FRANK *her cake. She eats it slowly, without relish.* MR. FRANK *takes his cake to* MAR-GOT *and sits quietly on the sofa beside her.* PETER *stands in the doorway of* ANNE'S *darkened room, looking at her, then makes a little movement to let her know he is there.* ANNE *sits up, quickly, trying to hide the signs of her tears.* PETER *holds out the cake to her.*) You left this.

ANNE. (*Dully*) Thanks.

(PETER *starts to go out, then comes back.*)

PETER. I thought you were fine just now. You know just how to talk to them. You know just how to say it. I'm no good . . . I never can think . . . especially when I'm mad . . . That Dussel . . . when he said that about Mouschi . . . someone eating him . . . all I could think is . . . I wanted to hit him. I wanted to give him such a . . . a . . . that he'd . . . That's what I used to do when there was an argument at school . . . That's the way I . . . but here . . . And an old man like that . . . it wouldn't be so good.

ANNE. You're making a big mistake about me. I do it all wrong. I say too much. I go too far. I hurt people's feelings . . .

(DUSSEL *leaves the window, going to his room.*)

PETER. I think you're just fine . . . What I want to say . . . if it wasn't for you around here, I don't know. What I mean . . .

(PETER *is interrupted by* DUSSEL'S *turning on the light.* DUSSEL *stands in the doorway,*

*startled to see* PETER. PETER *advances toward him forbiddingly.* DUSSEL *backs out of the room.* PETER *closes the door on him.*)

ANNE. Do you mean it, Peter? Do you really mean it?

PETER. I said it, didn't I?

ANNE. Thank you, Peter!

(*In the main room* MR. *and* MRS. FRANK *collect the dishes and take them to the sink, washing them.* MARGOT *lies down again on the couch.* DUSSEL, *lost, wanders into* PETER'S *room and takes up a book, starting to read.*)

PETER. (*Looking at the photographs on the wall*) You've got quite a collection.

ANNE. Wouldn't you like some in your room? I could give you some. Heaven knows you spend enough time in there . . . doing heaven knows what . . .

PETER. It's easier. A fight starts, or an argument . . . I duck in there.

ANNE. You're lucky, having a room to go to. His lordship is always here . . . I hardly ever get a minute alone. When they start in on me, I can't duck away. I have to stand there and take it.

PETER. You gave some of it back just now.

ANNE. I get so mad. They've formed their opinions . . . about everything . . . but we . . . we're still trying to find out . . . We have problems here that no other people our age have ever had. And just as you think you've solved them, something comes along and bang! You have to start all over again.

PETER. At least you've got someone you can talk to.

ANNE. Not really. Mother . . . I never discuss anything serious with her. She doesn't understand. Father's all right. We can talk about everything . . . everything but one thing. Mother. He simply won't talk about her. I don't think you can be really intimate with anyone if he holds something back, do you?

PETER. I think your father's fine.

ANNE. Oh, he is, Peter! He is! He's the only one who's ever given me the feeling that I have any sense. But anyway, nothing can take the place of school and play and friends of your own age . . . or near your age . . . can it?

PETER. I suppose you miss your friends and all.

ANNE. It isn't just . . . (*She breaks off, staring up at him for a second*) Isn't it funny, you and I? Here we've been seeing each other every minute for almost a year and a half, and this is the first time we've ever really talked. It helps a lot to have someone to talk to, don't you think? It helps you to let off steam.

PETER. (*Going to the door*) Well, any time you want to let off steam, you can come into my room.

ANNE. (*Following him*) I can get up an awful lot of steam. You'll have to be careful how you say that.

PETER. It's all right with me.

ANNE. Do you mean it?

PETER. I said it, didn't I?

(*He goes out. ANNE stands in her doorway looking after him. As PETER gets to his door he stands for a minute looking back at her. Then he goes into his room. DUSSEL rises as he comes in, and quickly passes him, going out. He starts across for his room. ANNE sees him coming, and pulls her door shut. DUSSEL turns back toward PETER's room. PETER pulls his door shut. DUSSEL stands there, bewildered, forlorn.*

*The scene slowly dims out. The curtain falls on the scene. ANNE's voice comes over in the darkness . . . faintly at first, and then with growing strength.*)

ANNE'S VOICE. We've had bad news. The people from whom Miep got our ration books have been arrested. So we have had to cut down on our food. Our stomachs are so empty that they rumble and make strange noises, all in different keys. Mr. Van Daan's is deep and low, like a bass fiddle. Mine is high, whistling like a flute. As we all sit around waiting for supper, it's like an orchestra tuning up. It only needs Toscanini to raise his baton and we'd be off in the Ride of the Valkyries.[3] Monday, the sixth of March, nineteen forty-four. Mr. Kraler is in the hospital. It seems he has ulcers. Pim says we are his ulcers. Miep has to run the business and us too. The Americans have landed on the southern tip of Italy. Father looks for a quick finish to the war. Mr. Dussel is waiting every day for the warehouse man to demand more money. Have I been skipping too much from one subject to another? I can't help it. I feel that spring is coming. I feel it in my whole body and soul. I feel utterly confused. I am longing . . . so longing . . . for everything . . . for friends . . . for someone to talk to . . . someone who understands . . . someone young, who feels as I do . . .

(*As these last lines are being said, the curtain rises on the scene. The lights dim on. ANNE's voice fades out.*)

SCENE II

*It is evening, after supper. From outside we hear the sound of children playing. The "grownups," with the exception of MR. VAN DAAN, are all in the main room. MRS. FRANK is doing some mending, MRS. VAN DAAN is reading a fashion magazine. MR. FRANK is going over business accounts. DUSSEL, in his dentist's jacket, is pacing up and down, impatient to get into his bedroom. MR. VAN DAAN is upstairs working on a piece of embroidery in an embroidery frame.*

*In his room PETER is sitting before the mirror, smoothing his hair. As the scene goes on, he puts on his tie, brushes his coat and puts it on, preparing himself meticulously for a visit from ANNE. On his wall are now hung some of ANNE's motion picture stars.*

*In her room ANNE too is getting dressed. She stands before the mirror in her slip, trying various ways of dressing her hair. MARGOT*

---

3. Arturo **Toscanini**\tŏs·kə ▲nē·nē\ (1867–1957), a famous conductor. "**The Ride of the Valkyries**," a composition, both fast and loud, from Wagner's *Die Walküre.*

*is seated on the sofa, hemming a skirt for* ANNE *to wear.*

*In the main room* DUSSEL *can stand it no longer. He comes over, rapping sharply on the door of his and* ANNE'S *bedroom.*

ANNE. (*Calling to him*) No, no, Mr. Dussel! I am not dressed yet. (DUSSEL *walks away, furious, sitting down and burying his head in his hands.* ANNE *turns to* MARGOT) How is that? How does that look?

MARGOT. (*Glancing at her briefly*) Fine.

ANNE. You didn't even look.

MARGOT. Of course I did. It's fine.

ANNE. Margot, tell me, am I terribly ugly?

MARGOT. Oh, stop fishing.

ANNE. No. No. Tell me.

MARGOT. Of course you're not. You've got nice eyes . . . and a lot of animation, and . . .

ANNE. A little vague, aren't you?

(*She reaches over and takes a brassière out of* MARGOT'S *sewing basket. She holds it up to herself, studying the effect in the mirror. Outside,* MRS. FRANK, *feeling sorry for* DUSSEL, *comes over, knocking at the girls' door.*)

MRS. FRANK. (*Outside*) May I come in?

MARGOT. Come in, Mother.

MRS. FRANK. (*Shutting the door behind her*) Mr. Dussel's impatient to get in here.

ANNE. (*Still with the brassière*) Heavens, he takes the room for himself the entire day.

MRS. FRANK. (*Gently*) Anne, dear, you're not going in again tonight to see Peter?

ANNE. (*Dignified*) That is my intention.

MRS. FRANK. But you've already spent a great deal of time in there today.

ANNE. I was in there exactly twice. Once to get the dictionary, and then three-quarters of an hour before supper.

MRS. FRANK. Aren't you afraid you're disturbing him?

ANNE. Mother, I have some intuition.

MRS. FRANK. Then may I ask you this much, Anne. Please don't shut the door when you go in.

ANNE. You sound like Mrs. Van Daan!

(*She throws the brassière back in* MAR-GOT'S *sewing basket and picks up her blouse, putting it on.*)

MRS. FRANK. No. No. I don't mean to suggest anything wrong. I only wish that you wouldn't expose yourself to criticism . . . that you wouldn't give Mrs. Van Daan the opportunity to be unpleasant.

ANNE. Mrs. Van Daan doesn't need an opportunity to be unpleasant!

MRS. FRANK. Everyone's on edge, worried about Mr. Kraler. This is one more thing . . .

ANNE. I'm sorry, Mother. I'm going to Peter's room. I'm not going to let Petronella Van Daan spoil our friendship.

(MRS. FRANK *hesitates for a second, then goes out, closing the door after her. She gets a pack of playing cards and sits at the center table, playing solitaire. In* ANNE'S *room* MARGOT *hands the finished skirt to* ANNE. *As* ANNE *is putting it on,* MARGOT *takes off her high-heeled shoes and stuffs paper in the toes so that* ANNE *can wear them.*)

MARGOT (*To* ANNE) Why don't you two talk in the main room? It'd save a lot of trouble. It's hard on Mother, having to listen to those remarks from Mrs. Van Daan and not say a word.

ANNE. Why doesn't she say a word? I think it's ridiculous to take it and take it.

MARGOT. You don't understand Mother at all, do you? She can't talk back. She's not like you. It's just not in her nature to fight back.

ANNE. Anyway . . . the only one I worry about is you. I feel awfully guilty about you.

(*She sits on the stool near* MARGOT, *putting on* MARGOT'S *high-heeled shoes.*)

MARGOT. What about?

ANNE. I mean, every time I go into Peter's room, I have a feeling I may be hurting you. (MARGOT *shakes her head*) I know if it were me, I'd be wild. I'd be desperately jealous, if it were me.

MARGOT. Well, I'm not.

ANNE. You don't feel badly? Really? Truly? You're not jealous?

MARGOT. Of course I'm jealous . . . jealous that you've got something to get up in the morning for . . . But jealous of you and Peter? No.

(ANNE *goes back to the mirror.*)

ANNE. Maybe there's nothing to be jealous of. Maybe he doesn't really like me. Maybe I'm just taking the place of his cat . . . (*She picks up a pair of short white gloves, putting them on*) Wouldn't you like to come in with us?

MARGOT. I have a book.

(*The sound of the children playing outside fades out. In the main room* DUSSEL *can stand it no longer. He jumps up, going to the bedroom door and knocking sharply.*)

DUSSEL. Will you please let me in my room!

ANNE. Just a minute, dear, dear Mr. Dussel. (*She picks up her Mother's pink stole and adjusts it elegantly over her shoulders, then gives a last look in the mirror*) Well, here I go . . . to run the gauntlet.

(*She starts out, followed by* MARGOT.)

DUSSEL. (*As she appears—sarcastic*) Thank you so much.

(DUSSEL *goes into his room.* ANNE *goes toward* PETER's *room, passing* MRS. VAN DAAN *and her parents at the center table.*)

MRS. VAN DAAN. Look at her! (ANNE *pays no attention. She knocks at* PETER's *door*) I don't know what good it is to have a son. I never see him. He wouldn't care if I killed myself. (PETER *opens the door and stands aside for* ANNE *to come in*) Just a minute, Anne. (*She goes to them at the door*) I'd like to say a few words to my son. Do you mind? (PETER *and* ANNE *stand waiting*) Peter, I don't want you staying up till all hours tonight. You've got to have your sleep. You're a growing boy. You hear?

MRS. FRANK. Anne won't stay late. She's going to bed promptly at nine. Aren't you, Anne?

ANNE. Yes, Mother . . . (*To* MRS. VAN DAAN) May we go now?

MRS. VAN DAAN. Are you asking me? I didn't know I had anything to say about it.

MRS. FRANK. Listen for the chimes, Anne dear.

(*The two young people go off into* PETER's *room, shutting the door after them.*)

MRS. VAN DAAN. (*To* MRS. FRANK) In my day it was the boys who called on the girls. Not the girls on the boys.

MRS. FRANK. You know how young people like to feel that they have secrets. Peter's room is the only place where they can talk.

MRS. VAN DAAN. Talk! That's not what they called it when I was young.

(MRS. VAN DAAN *goes off to the bathroom.* MARGOT *settles down to read her book.* MR. FRANK *puts his papers away and brings a chess game to the center table. He and* MRS. FRANK *start to play. In* PETER's *room,* ANNE *speaks to* PETER, *indignant, humiliated.*)

ANNE. Aren't they awful? Aren't they impossible? Treating us as if we were still in the nursery.

(*She sits on the cot.* PETER *gets a bottle of pop and two glasses.*)

PETER. Don't let it bother you. It doesn't bother me.

ANNE. I suppose you can't really blame them . . . they think back to what *they* were like at our age. They don't realize how much more advanced we are . . . When you think what wonderful discussions we've had! . . . Oh, I forgot. I was going to bring you some more pictures.

PETER. Oh, these are fine, thanks.

ANNE. Don't you want some more? Miep just brought me some new ones.

PETER. Maybe later.

(*He gives her a glass of pop and, taking some for himself, sits down facing her.*)

ANNE. (*Looking up at one of the photographs*) I remember when I got that . . . I won it. I bet Jopie that I could eat five ice-cream cones. We'd all been playing ping-pong . . . We used to have heavenly times . . . we'd finish up with

*Peter and Anne visiting in Peter's room. With crosscurrents among the inmates of the hideout intensified by the unnatural confinement, Peter and Anne found much needed understanding in each other.*

ice cream at the Delphi, or the Oasis, where Jews were allowed . . . there'd always be a lot of boys . . . we'd laugh and joke . . . I'd like to go back to it for a few days or a week. But after that I know I'd be bored to death. I think more seriously about life now. I want to be a journalist . . . or something. I love to write. What do you want to do?

PETER. I thought I might go off some place . . . work on a farm or something . . . some job that doesn't take much brains.

ANNE. You shouldn't talk that way. You've got the most awful inferiority complex.

PETER. I know I'm not smart.

ANNE. That isn't true. You're much better than I am in dozens of things . . . arithmetic and algebra and . . . well, you're a million times better than I am in algebra. (*With sudden di-*rectness*) You like Margot, don't you? Right from the start you liked her, liked her much better than me.

PETER. (*Uncomfortably*) Oh, I don't know.

(*In the main room* MRS. VAN DAAN *comes from the bathroom and goes over to the sink, polishing a coffee pot.*)

ANNE. It's all right. Everyone feels that way. Margot's so good. She's sweet and bright and beautiful and I'm not.

PETER. I wouldn't say that.

ANNE. Oh, no, I'm not. I know that. I know quite well that I'm not a beauty. I never have been and never shall be.

PETER. I don't agree at all. I think you're pretty.

ANNE. That's not true!

PETER. And another thing. You've changed . . . from at first, I mean.

ANNE. I have?

PETER. I used to think you were awful noisy.

ANNE. And what do you think now, Peter? How have I changed?

PETER. Well . . . er . . . you're . . . quieter.

(*In his room* DUSSEL *takes his pajamas and toilet articles and goes into the bathroom to change.*)

ANNE. I'm glad you don't just hate me.

PETER. I never said that.

ANNE. I bet when you get out of here you'll never think of me again.

PETER. That's crazy.

ANNE. When you get back with all of your friends, you're going to say . . . now what did I ever see in that Mrs. Quack Quack.

PETER. I haven't got any friends.

ANNE. Oh, Peter, of course you have. Everyone has friends.

PETER. Not me. I don't want any. I get along all right without them.

ANNE. Does that mean you can get along without me? I think of myself as your friend.

PETER. No. If they were all like you, it'd be different.

(*He takes the glasses and the bottle and puts them away. There is a second's silence and then* ANNE *speaks, hesitantly, shyly.*)

ANNE. Peter, did you ever kiss a girl?

PETER. Yes. Once.

ANNE. (*To cover her feelings*) That picture's crooked. (PETER *goes over, straightening the photograph*) Was she pretty?

PETER. Huh?

ANNE. The girl that you kissed.

PETER. I don't know. I was blindfolded. (*He comes back and sits down again*) It was at a party. One of those kissing games.

ANNE. (*Relieved*) Oh. I don't suppose that really counts, does it?

PETER. It didn't with me.

ANNE. I've been kissed twice. Once a man I'd never seen before kissed me on the cheek when he picked me up off the ice and I was crying. And the other was Mr. Koophuis, a friend of Father's who kissed my hand. You wouldn't say those counted would you?

PETER. I wouldn't say so.

ANNE. I know almost for certain that Margot would never kiss anyone unless she was engaged to them. And I'm sure too that Mother never touched a man before Pim. But I don't know . . . things are so different now . . . What do you think? Do you think a girl shouldn't kiss anyone except if she's engaged or something? It's so hard to try to think what to do, when here we are with the whole world falling around our ears and you think . . . well . . . you don't know what's going to happen tomorrow and . . . What do you think?

PETER. I suppose it'd depend on the girl. Some girls, anything they do's wrong. But others . . . well . . . it wouldn't necessarily be wrong with them. (*The carillon starts to strike nine o'clock*) I've always thought that when two people . . .

ANNE. Nine o'clock. I have to go.

PETER. That's right.

ANNE (*Without moving*) Good night.

(*There is a second's pause, then* PETER *gets up and moves toward the door.*)

PETER. You won't let them stop you coming?

ANNE. No. (*She rises and starts for the door*) Sometime I might bring my diary. There are so many things in it that I want to talk over with you. There's a lot about you.

PETER. What kind of things?

ANNE. I wouldn't want you to see some of it. I thought you were a nothing, just the way you thought about me.

PETER. Did you change your mind, the way I changed my mind about you?

ANNE. Well . . . You'll see . . .

(*For a second* ANNE *stands looking up at* PETER, *longing for him to kiss her. As he makes no move she turns away. Then suddenly* PETER *grabs her awkwardly in his arms, kissing her on the cheek.* ANNE *walks out dazed. She stands for a minute, her back to the people in the main room. As she regains her poise she goes to her mother and father and* MARGOT, *silently kissing them. They murmur their good nights to her. As she is about to open her bedroom door, she catches sight of* MRS. VAN DAAN. *She goes quickly to her, taking her face in her hands and kissing her first on one cheek and then on the other. Then she hurries off into her room.* MRS. VAN DAAN *looks after her, and then looks over at* PETER'S *room. Her suspicions are confirmed.*)

MRS. VAN DAAN. (*She knows*) Ah hah!

(*The lights dim out. The curtain falls on the scene. In the darkness* ANNE'S *voice comes faintly at first and then with growing strength.*)

ANNE'S VOICE. By this time we all know each other so well that if anyone starts to tell a story, the rest can finish it for him. We're having to cut down still further on our meals. What makes it worse, the rats have been at work again. They've carried off some of our precious food. Even Mr. Dussel wishes now that Mouschi was here. Thursday, the twentieth of April, nineteen forty-four. Invasion fever is mounting every day. Miep tells us that people outside talk of nothing else. For myself, life has become much more pleasant. I often go to Peter's room after supper. Oh, don't think I'm in love, because I'm not. But it does make life more bearable to have someone with whom you can exchange views. No more tonight. P.S. . . . I must be honest. I must confess that I actually live for the next meeting. Is there anything lovelier than to sit under the skylight and feel the sun on your cheeks and have a darling boy in your arms? I admit now that I'm glad the Van Daans had a son and not a daughter. I've outgrown another dress. That's the third. I'm having to wear Margot's clothes after all. I'm working hard on my French and am now reading *La Belle Nivernaise.*

(*As she is saying the last lines—the curtain rises on the scene. The lights dim on, as* ANNE'S *voice fades out.*)

SCENE III

*It is night, a few weeks later. Everyone is in bed. There is complete quiet. In the* VAN DAANS' *room a match flares up for a moment and then is quickly put out.* MR. VAN DAAN, *in bare feet, dressed in underwear and trousers, is dimly seen coming stealthily down the stairs and into the main room, where* MR. *and* MRS. FRANK *and* MARGOT *are sleeping. He goes to the food safe and again lights a match. Then he cautiously opens the safe, taking out a half-loaf of bread. As he closes the safe, it creaks. He stands rigid.* MRS. FRANK *sits up in bed. She sees him.*

MRS. FRANK. (*Screaming*) Otto! Otto! *Komme schnell!*

(*The rest of the people wake, hurriedly getting up.*)

MR. FRANK. *Was ist los? Was ist passiert?*

(DUSSEL, *followed by* ANNE, *comes from his room.*)

MRS. FRANK. (*As she rushes over to* MR. VAN DAAN) *Er stiehlt das Essen!*[1]

DUSSEL. (*Grabbing* MR. VAN DAAN) You! You! Give me that.

MRS. VAN DAAN. (*Coming down the stairs*) Putti . . . Putti . . . what is it?

DUSSEL. (*His hands on* VAN DAAN'S *neck*) You dirty thief . . . stealing food . . . you good-for-nothing . . .

MR. FRANK. Mr. Dussel! In the name of heaven! Help me, Peter!

(PETER *comes over, trying, with* MR. FRANK, *to separate the two struggling men.*)

PETER. Let him go! Let go!

---

1. The German may be translated as follows: "Otto! Otto! Come right away." "What's up? What is happening?" "He is stealing the food!"

(DUSSEL *drops* MR. VAN DAAN, *pushing him away. He shows them the end of a loaf of bread that he has taken from* VAN DAAN.)

DUSSEL. You greedy, selfish . . . !

(MARGOT *turns on the lights.*)

MRS. VAN DAAN. Putti . . . what is it?

(*All of* MRS. FRANK's *gentleness, her self-control, is gone. She is outraged, in a frenzy of indignation.*)

MRS. FRANK. The bread! He was stealing the bread!

DUSSEL. It was you, and all the time we thought it was the rats!

MR. FRANK. Mr. Van Daan, how could you!

MR. VAN DAAN. I'm hungry.

MRS. FRANK. We're all of us hungry! I see the children getting thinner and thinner. Your own son Peter . . . I've heard him moan in his sleep, he's so hungry. And you come in the night and steal food that should go to them . . . to the children!

MRS. VAN DAAN. (*Going to* MR. VAN DAAN *protectively*) He needs more food than the rest of us. He's used to more. He's a big man.

(MR. VAN DAAN *breaks away, going over and sitting on the couch.*)

MRS. FRANK. (*Turning on* MRS. VAN DAAN) And you . . . you're worse than he is! You're a mother, and yet you sacrifice your child to this man . . . this . . . this . . .

MR. FRANK. Edith! Edith!

(MARGOT *picks up the pink woolen stole, putting it over her mother's shoulders.*)

MRS. FRANK. (*Paying no attention, going on to* MRS. VAN DAAN) Don't think I haven't seen you! Always saving the choicest bits for him! I've watched you day after day and I've held my tongue. But not any longer! Not after this! Now I want him to go! I want him to get out of here!

MR. FRANK. Edith! ⎫
MR. VAN DAAN. Get out of here? ⎬ *Together*
MRS. VAN DAAN. What do you mean? ⎭

MRS. FRANK. Just that! Take your things and get out!

MR. FRANK. (*To* MRS. FRANK) You're speaking in anger. You cannot mean what you are saying.

MRS. FRANK. I mean exactly that!

(MRS. VAN DAAN *takes a cover from the* FRANKS' *bed, pulling it about her.*)

MR. FRANK. For two long years we have lived here, side by side. We have respected each other's rights . . . we have managed to live in peace. Are we now going to throw it all away? I know this will never happen again, will it, Mr. Van Daan?

MR. VAN DAAN. No. No.

MRS. FRANK. He steals once! He'll steal again!

(MR. VAN DAAN, *holding his stomach, starts for the bathroom.* ANNE *puts her arms around him, helping him up the step.*)

MR. FRANK. Edith, please. Let us be calm. We'll all go to our rooms . . . and afterwards we'll sit down quietly and talk this out . . . we'll find some way . . .

MRS. FRANK. No! No! No more talk! I want them to leave!

MRS. VAN DAAN. You'd put us out, on the streets?

MRS. FRANK. There are other hiding places.

MRS. VAN DAAN. A cellar . . . a closet. I know. And we have no money left even to pay for that.

MRS. FRANK. I'll give you money. Out of my own pocket I'll give it gladly.

(*She gets her purse from a shelf and comes back with it.*)

MRS. VAN DAAN. Mr. Frank, you told Putti you'd never forget what he'd done for you when you came to Amsterdam. You said you could never repay him, that you . . .

MRS. FRANK. (*Counting out money*) If my husband had any obligation to you, he's paid it, over and over.

MR. FRANK. Edith, I've never seen you like this before. I don't know you.

MRS. FRANK. I should have spoken out long ago.

DUSSEL. You can't be nice to some people.

MRS. VAN DAAN. (*Turning on* DUSSEL) There would have been plenty for all of us, if *you* hadn't come in here!

MR. FRANK. We don't need the Nazis to destroy us. We're destroying ourselves.

(*He sits down, with his head in his hands.* MRS. FRANK *goes to* MRS. VAN DAAN.)

MRS. FRANK. (*Giving* MRS. VAN DAAN *some money*) Give this to Miep. She'll find you a place.

ANNE. Mother, you're not putting *Peter* out. Peter hasn't done anything.

MRS. FRANK. He'll stay, of course. When I say I must protect the children, I mean Peter too.

(PETER *rises from the steps where he has been sitting.*)

PETER. I'd have to go if Father goes.

(MR. VAN DAAN *comes from the bathroom.* MRS. VAN DAAN *hurries to him and takes him to the couch. Then she gets water from the sink to bathe his face.*)

MRS. FRANK. (*While this is going on*) He's no father to you . . .that man! He doesn't know what it is to be a father!

PETER (*Starting for his room*) I wouldn't feel right. I couldn't stay.

MRS. FRANK. Very well, then. I'm sorry.

ANNE. (*Rushing over to* PETER) No, Peter! No! (PETER *goes into his room, closing the door after him.* ANNE *turns back to her mother, crying*) I don't care about the food. They can have mine! I don't want it! Only don't send them away. It'll be daylight soon. They'll be caught . . .

MARGOT. (*Putting her arms comfortingly around* ANNE) Please, Mother!

MRS. FRANK. They're not going now. They'll stay here until Miep finds them a place. (*To* MRS. VAN DAAN) But one thing I insist on! He must never come down here again! He must never come to this room where the food is stored! We'll divide what we have . . . an equal share for each! (DUSSEL *hurries over to get a sack of potatoes from the food safe.* MRS.

FRANK *goes on, to* MRS. VAN DAAN) You can cook it here and take it up to him.

(DUSSEL *brings the sack of potatoes back to the center table.*)

MARGOT. Oh, no. No. We haven't sunk so far that we're going to fight over a handful of rotten potatoes.

DUSSEL. (*Dividing the potatoes into piles*) Mrs. Frank, Mr. Frank, Margot, Anne, Peter, Mrs. Van Daan, Mr. Van Daan, myself . . . Mrs. Frank . . .

(*The buzzer sounds in* MIEP's *signal.*)

MR. FRANK. It's Miep.

(*He hurries over, getting his overcoat and putting it on.*)

MARGOT. At this hour?

MRS. FRANK. It is trouble.

MR. FRANK. (*As he starts down to unbolt the door*) I beg you, don't let her see a thing like this!

MR. DUSSEL (*Counting without stopping*) . . . Anne, Peter, Mrs. Van Daan, Mr. Van Daan, myself . . .

MARGOT (*To* DUSSEL) Stop it! Stop it!

DUSSEL. . . . Mr. Frank, Margot, Anne, Peter, Mrs. Van Daan, Mr. Van Daan, myself, Mrs. Frank . . .

MRS. VAN DAAN. You're keeping the big ones for yourself! All the big ones . . . Look at the size of that! . . . And that! . . .

(DUSSEL *continues on with his dividing.* PETER, *with his shirt and trousers on, comes from his room.*)

MARGOT. Stop it! Stop it!

(*We hear* MIEP's *excited voice speaking to* MR. FRANK *below.*)

MIEP. Mr. Frank . . . the most wonderful news! . . . The invasion has begun!

MR. FRANK. Go on, tell them! Tell them!

(MIEP *comes running up the steps, ahead of* MR. FRANK. *She has a man's raincoat on over her nightclothes and a bunch of orange-colored flowers in her hand.*)

MIEP. Did you hear that, everybody? Did you hear what I said? The invasion has begun! The invasion!

(*They all stare at* MIEP, *unable to grasp what she is telling them.* PETER *is the first to recover his wits.*)

PETER. Where?

MRS. VAN DAAN. When? When, Miep?

MIEP. It began early this morning . . .

(*As she talks on, the realization of what she has said begins to dawn on them. Everyone goes crazy. A wild demonstration takes place.* MRS. FRANK *hugs* MR. VAN DAAN.)

MRS. FRANK. Oh, Mr. Van Daan, did you hear that?

(DUSSEL *embraces* MRS. VAN DAAN. PETER *grabs a frying pan and parades around the room, beating on it, singing the Dutch National Anthem.* ANNE *and* MARGOT *follow him, singing, weaving in and out among the excited grown-ups.* MARGOT *breaks away to take the flowers from* MIEP *and distribute them to everyone. While this pandemonium is going on* MRS. FRANK *tries to make herself heard above the excitement.*)

MRS. FRANK. (*To* MIEP) How do you know?

MIEP. The radio . . . The B.B.C.![2] They said they landed on the coast of Normandy!

PETER. The British?

MIEP. British, Americans, French, Dutch, Poles, Norwegians . . . all of them. More than four thousand ships! Churchill spoke, and General Eisenhower![3] D-Day they call it!

MR. FRANK. Thank God, it's come!

MRS. VAN DAAN. At last!

MIEP. (*Starting out*) I'm going to tell Mr. Kraler. This'll be better than any blood transfusion.

MR. FRANK. (*Stopping her*) What part of Normandy did they land, did they say?

MIEP. Normandy . . . that's all I know now . . . I'll be up the minute I hear some more!

(*She goes hurriedly out.*)

MR. FRANK. (*To* MRS. FRANK) What did I tell you? What did I tell you?

(MRS. FRANK *indicates that he has forgotten to bolt the door after* MIEP. *He hurries down the steps.* MR. VAN DAAN, *sitting on the couch, suddenly breaks into a convulsive sob. Everybody looks at him, bewildered.*)

MRS. VAN DAAN. (*Hurrying to him*) Putti! Putti! What is it? What happened?

MR. VAN DAAN. Please. I'm so ashamed.

(MR. FRANK *comes back up the steps.*)

DUSSEL. Oh, for God's sake!

MRS. VAN DAAN. Don't, Putti.

MARGOT. It doesn't matter now!

MR. FRANK. (*Going to* MR. VAN DAAN) Didn't you hear what Miep said? The invasion has come! We're going to be liberated! This is a time to celebrate!

(*He embraces* MRS. FRANK *and then hurries to the cupboard and gets the cognac and a glass.*)

MR. VAN DAAN. To steal bread from children!

MRS. FRANK. We've all done things that we're ashamed of.

ANNE. Look at me, the way I've treated Mother . . . so mean and horrid to her.

MRS. FRANK. No, Anneke, no.

(ANNE *runs to her mother, putting her arms around her.*)

ANNE. Oh, Mother, I was. I was awful.

MR. VAN DAAN. Not like me. No one is as bad as me!

DUSSEL. (*To* MR. VAN DAAN) Stop it now! Let's be happy!

MR. FRANK. (*Giving* MR. VAN DAAN *a glass of cognac*) Here! Here! *Schnapps!*[4] *Locheim!*

(VAN DAAN *takes the cognac. They all watch him. He gives them a feeble smile.* ANNE

---

2. **B.B.C.,** the British Broadcasting Corporation.
3. Sir Winston **Churchill,** Prime Minister of Britain. General Dwight D. **Eisenhower,** commander of Allied Forces.
4. **Schnapps**\shnaps\ German brandy.

*In the midst of celebrating the news of the Allied invasion, Mr. Van Daan (left) weeps at betraying the Frank's trust; Anne "makes up" with her mother.*

*puts up her fingers in a V-for-Victory sign. As* van daan *gives an answering V-sign, they are startled to hear a loud sob from behind them. It is* mrs. frank, *stricken with remorse. She is sitting on the other side of the room.*)

mrs. frank. (*Through her sobs*) When I think of the terrible things I said . . .

(mr. frank, anne *and* margot *hurry to her, trying to comfort her.* mr. van daan *brings her his glass of cognac.*)

mr. van daan. No! No! You were right!

mrs. frank. That I should speak that way to you! . . . Our friends! . . . Our guests!

(*She starts to cry again.*)

dussel. Stop it, you're spoiling the whole invasion!

(*As they are comforting her, the lights dim out. The curtain falls.*)

anne's voice. (*Faintly at first and then with growing strength*) We're all in much better spirits these days. There's still excellent news of the invasion. The best part about it is that I have a feeling that friends are coming. Who knows? Maybe I'll be back in school by fall. Ha, ha! The joke is on us! The warehouse man doesn't know a thing and we are paying him all that money! . . . Wednesday, the second of July, nineteen forty-four. The invasion seems temporarily to be bogged down. Mr. Kraler has to have an operation, which looks bad. The Gestapo have found the radio that was stolen. Mr. Dussel says they'll trace it back and back to the thief, and then, it's just a matter of time till they get to us. Everyone is low. Even poor Pim can't raise their spirits. I have often been downcast myself . . . but never in despair. I can shake off everything if I write. But . . . and that is the great question . . . will I ever be able to write well? I want to so much. I want to go on living even after my death. Another birthday has gone by, so now I am fifteen. Already I know what I want. I have a goal, an opinion.

(*As this is being said—the curtain rises on the scene, the lights dim on, and* ANNE's *voice fades out.*)


SCENE IV

*It is an afternoon a few weeks later . . . Everyone but* MARGOT *is in the main room. There is a sense of great tension.*

*Both* MRS. FRANK *and* MR. VAN DAAN *are nervously pacing back and forth,* DUSSEL *is standing at the window, looking down fixedly at the street below.* PETER *is at the center table, trying to do his lessons.* ANNE *sits opposite him, writing in her diary.* MRS. VAN DAAN *is seated on the couch, her eyes on* MR. FRANK *as he sits reading.*

*The sound of a telephone ringing comes from the office below. They all are rigid, listening tensely.* MR. DUSSEL *rushes down to* MR. FRANK.

DUSSEL. There it goes again, the telephone! Mr. Frank, do you hear?

MR. FRANK. (*Quietly*) Yes. I hear.

DUSSEL. (*Pleading, insistent*) But this is the third time, Mr. Frank! The third time in quick succession! It's a signal! I tell you it's Miep, trying to get us! For some reason she can't come to us and she's trying to warn us of something!

MR. FRANK. Please. Please.

MR. VAN DAAN. (*To* DUSSEL) You're wasting your breath.

DUSSEL. Something has happened, Mr. Frank. For three days now Miep hasn't been to see us! And today not a man has come to work. There hasn't been a sound in the building!

MRS. FRANK. Perhaps it's Sunday. We may have lost track of the days.

MR. VAN DAAN. (*To* ANNE) You with the diary there. What day is it?

DUSSEL. (*Going to* MRS. FRANK) I don't lose track of the days! I know exactly what day it is! It's Friday, the fourth of August. Friday, and not a man at work. (*He rushes back to* MR. FRANK, *pleading with him, almost in tears*) I tell you Mr. Kraler's dead. That's the only explanation. He's dead and they've closed down the building, and Miep's trying to tell us!

MR. FRANK. She'd never telephone us.

DUSSEL. (*Frantic*) Mr. Frank, answer that! I beg you, answer it!

MR. FRANK. No.

MR. VAN DAAN. Just pick it up and listen. You don't have to speak. Just listen and see if it's Miep.

DUSSEL. (*Speaking at the same time*) For God's sake . . . I ask you.

MR. FRANK. No. I've told you, no. I'll do nothing that might let anyone know we're in the building.

PETER. Mr. Frank's right.

MR. VAN DAAN. There's no need to tell us what side you're on.

MR. FRANK. If we wait patiently, quietly, I believe that help will come.

(*There is silence for a minute as they all listen to the telephone ringing.*)

DUSSEL. I'm going down. (*He rushes down the steps.* MR. FRANK *tries ineffectually to hold him.* DUSSEL *runs to the lower door, unbolting it. The telephone stops ringing.* DUSSEL *bolts the door and comes slowly back up the steps.*) Too late. (MR. FRANK *goes to* MARGOT *in* ANNE's *bedroom.*)

MR. VAN DAAN. So we just wait here until we die.

MRS. VAN DAAN. (*Hysterically*) I can't stand it! I'll kill myself! I'll kill myself!

MR. VAN DAAN. For God's sake, stop it!

(*In the distance, a German military band is heard playing a Viennese waltz.*)

MRS. VAN DAAN. I think you'd be glad if I did! I think you want me to die!

MR. VAN DAAN. Whose fault is it we're here? (MRS. VAN DAAN *starts for her room. He follows, talking at her*) We could've been safe somewhere . . . in America or Switzerland. But no! No! You wouldn't leave when I wanted to. You couldn't leave your things. You couldn't leave your precious furniture.

MRS. VAN DAAN. Don't touch me!

(*She hurries up the stairs, followed by* MR. VAN DAAN. PETER, *unable to bear it, goes to his room.* ANNE *looks after him, deeply concerned.* DUSSEL *returns to his post at the window.* MR. FRANK *comes back into the main room and takes a book, trying to read.* MRS. FRANK *sits near the sink, starting to peel some potatoes.* ANNE *quietly goes to* PETER'S *room, closing the door after her.* PETER *is lying face down on the cot.* ANNE *leans over him, holding him in her arms, trying to bring him out of his despair.*)

ANNE. Look, Peter, the sky. (*She looks up through the skylight*) What a lovely, lovely day! Aren't the clouds beautiful? You know what I do when it seems as if I couldn't stand being cooped up for one more minute? I *think* myself out. I think myself on a walk in the park where I used to go with Pim. Where the jonquils and the crocus and the violets grow down the slopes. You know the most wonderful part about *thinking* yourself out? You can have it any way you like. You can have roses and violets and chrysanthemums all blooming at the same time . . . It's funny . . . I used to take it all for granted . . . and now I've gone crazy about everything to do with nature. Haven't you?

PETER. I've just gone crazy. I think if something doesn't happen soon . . . if we don't get out of here . . . I can't stand much more of it!

ANNE. (*Softly*) I wish you had a religion, Peter.

PETER. No, thanks! Not me!

ANNE. Oh, I don't mean you have to be Orthodox . . . or believe in heaven and hell and purgatory and things . . . I just mean some religion . . . it doesn't matter what. Just to believe in something! When I think of all that's out there . . . the trees . . . and flowers . . . and seagulls . . . when I think of the dearness of you, Peter . . . and the goodness of the people we know . . . Mr. Kraler, Miep, Dirk, the vegetable man, all risking their lives for us every day . . . When I think of these good things, I'm not afraid any more . . . I find myself, and God, and I . . .

(PETER *interrupts, getting up and walking away.*)

PETER. That's fine! But when I begin to think, I get mad! Look at us, hiding out for two years. Not able to move! Caught here like . . . waiting for them to come and get us . . . and all for what?

ANNE. We're not the only people that've had to suffer. There've always been people that've had to . . . sometimes one race . . . sometimes another . . . and yet . . .

PETER. That doesn't make me feel any better!

ANNE. (*Going to him*) I know it's terrible, trying to have any faith . . . when people are doing such horrible . . . But you know what I sometimes think? I think the world may be going through a phase, the way I was with Mother. It'll pass, maybe not for hundreds of years, but some day . . . I still believe, in spite of everything, that people are really good at heart.

PETER. I want to see something now . . . Not a thousand years from now!

(*He goes over, sitting down again on the cot.*)

ANNE. But, Peter, if you'd only look at it as part of a great pattern . . . that we're just a little minute in the life . . . (*She breaks off*) Listen to us, going at each other like a couple of stupid grownups! Look at the sky now. Isn't it lovely? (*She holds out her hand to him.*

Anne: "In spite of everything, I still believe that people are really good at heart."

PETER *takes it and rises, standing with her at the window looking out, his arms around her)* Some day, when we're outside again, I'm going to . . .

(*She breaks off as she hears the sound of a car, its brakes squealing as it comes to a sudden stop. The people in the other rooms also become aware of the sound. They listen tensely. Another car roars up to a screeching stop.* ANNE *and* PETER *come from* PETER'S *room.* MR. *and* MRS. VAN DAAN *creep down the stairs.* DUSSEL *comes out from his room. Everyone is listening, hardly breathing. A doorbell clangs again and again in the building below.* MR. FRANK *starts quietly down the steps to the door.* DUSSEL *and* PETER *follow him. The others stand rigid, waiting, terrified.*

*In a few seconds* DUSSEL *comes stumbling back up the steps. He shakes off* PETER'S *help and goes to his room.* MR. FRANK *bolts the door below, and comes slowly back up the steps. Their eyes are all on him as he stands there for a minute. They realize that what they feared has happened.* MRS. VAN DAAN *starts to whimper.* MR. VAN DAAN *puts her gently in a chair, and then hurries off up the stairs to their room to collect their things.* PETER *goes to comfort his mother. There is a sound of violent pounding on a door below.*)

MR. FRANK. (*Quietly*) For the past two years we have lived in fear. Now we can live in hope.

(*The pounding below becomes more insistent. There are muffled sounds of voices, shouting commands.*)

MEN'S VOICES. *Auf machen! Da drinnen! Auf machen! Schnell! Schnell! etc., etc.*[1]

(*The street door below is forced open. We hear the heavy tread of footsteps coming up.* MR. FRANK *gets two school bags from the shelves, and gives one to* ANNE, *and the other to* MARGOT. *He goes to get a bag for* MRS. FRANK. *The sound of feet coming up grows louder.* PETER *comes to* ANNE, *kissing her good-bye, then he goes to his room to collect his things. The buzzer of their door starts to ring.* MR. FRANK *brings* MRS. FRANK *a bag. They stand together, waiting. We hear the thud of gun butts on the door, trying to break it down.*)

ANNE *stands, holding her school satchel,*

---

1. The German may be translated as "Open up, you there inside! Open up! Fast! Fast! Fast!" Use of German indicates that this is a Gestapo raid.

*looking over at her father and mother with a soft, reassuring smile. She is no longer a child, but a woman with courage to meet whatever lies ahead.*

*The lights dim out. The curtain falls on the scene. We hear a mighty crash as the door is shattered. After a second* ANNE'S *voice is heard.*)

ANNE'S VOICE. And so it seems our stay here is over. They are waiting for us now. They've allowed us five minutes to get our things. We can each take a bag and whatever it will hold of clothing. Nothing else. So, dear Diary, that means I must leave you behind. Good-bye for a while. P.S. Please, please, Miep, or Mr. Kraler, or anyone else. If you should find this diary, will you please keep it safe for me, because some day I hope . . .

(*Her voice stops abruptly. There is silence. After a second the curtain rises.*)

SCENE V

*It is again the afternoon in November, 1945. The rooms are as we saw them in the first scene.* MR. KRALER *has joined* MIEP *and* MR. FRANK. *There are coffee cups on the table. We see a great change in* MR. FRANK. *He is calm now. His bitterness is gone. He slowly turns a few pages of the diary. They are blank.*

MR. FRANK. No more.

(*He closes the diary and puts it down on the couch beside him.*)

MIEP. I'd gone to the country to find food. When I got back the block was surrounded by police . . .

MR. KRALER. We made it our business to learn how they knew. It was the thief . . . the thief who told them.

(MIEP *goes up to the gas burner, bringing back a pot of coffee.*)

MR. FRANK. (*After a pause*) It seems strange to say this, that anyone could be happy in a concentration camp. But Anne was happy in the camp in Holland where they first took us. After two years of being shut up in these rooms, she could be out . . . out in the sunshine and the fresh air that she loved.

MIEP. (*Offering the coffee to* MR. FRANK) A little more?

MR. FRANK. (*Holding out his cup to her*) The news of the war was good. The British and Americans were sweeping through France. We felt sure that they would get to us in time. In September we were told that we were to be shipped to Poland . . . The men to one camp. The women to another. I was sent to Auschwitz. They went to Belsen. In January we were freed, the few of us who were left. The war wasn't yet over, so it took us a long time to get home. We'd be sent here and there behind the lines where we'd be safe. Each time our train would stop . . . at a siding, or a crossing . . . we'd all get out and go from group to group . . . Where were you? Were you at Belsen? At Buchenwald? At Mauthausen?[1] Is it possible that you knew my wife? Did you ever see my husband? My son? My daughter? That's how I found out about my wife's death . . . of Margot, the Van Daans . . . Dussel. But Anne . . . I still hoped . . . Yesterday I went to Rotterdam. I'd heard of a woman there . . . She'd been in Belsen with Anne . . . I know now.

(*He picks up the diary again, and turns the pages back to find a certain passage. As he finds it we hear* ANNE'S *voice.*)

ANNE'S VOICE. In spite of everything, I still believe that people are really good at heart.

(MR. FRANK *slowly closes the diary.*)

MR. FRANK. She puts me to shame.

(*They are silent.*)

*The Curtain Falls*

---

1. The places named are notorious concentration camps at which Jews were killed: **Auschwitz**\▲aush-vĭts\ in southern Poland; **Belsen**\▲bĕl·sən\ in southern Germany; **Buchenwald**\▲bū·kən 'vald\ in central Germany; **Mauthausen**\▲maut 'hau·zən\ in Austria.

## I

### THE AFTERMATH

From Mr. Frank's words, we know that only he survived the horror of the concentration camp. Slowly the stories of the others came to light. Mrs. Frank gradually lost her mind, and near the end often hid bits of bread under her blanket to give to her husband. She died in January, 1945. Margot became increasingly frail, slipped into a coma, and in February died by falling out of bed. Anne became ill with typhus and died peacefully soon after Margot. Even at the end she felt that nothing bad was happening to her. Mr. Van Daan was gassed and his wife also died, though no details are known of her death. Peter was marched away by Hitler's troups as they fled before the Russian invasion and was never heard of again. Mr. Dussel died in another camp. And Mr. Frank survived because, just by chance, he was in the hospital when Auschwitz was captured by the Russians.

After the book was put into play form by Frances Goodrich and Albert Hackett, it was translated into German and opened simultaneously in seven German theaters. The impact on the German audience is described by Kenneth Tynan, a British theater critic:

"And at the Schlosspark last Monday I survived the most drastic emotional experience the theatre has ever given me. It had little to do with art, for the play was not a great one; yet its effect, in Berlin, at that moment of history, transcended anything that art has yet learned to achieve. It invaded the privacy of the whole audience: I tried hard to stay detached, but the general catharsis engulfed me. Like all great theatrical occasions, this was not only a theatrical occasion: it involved the world outside. The first page of the programme prepared one: a short, stark essay on collective guilt. Turn over for the title: *The Diary of Anne Frank*, directed by Boleslaw Barlog, *premiere* performance. It is not a vengeful dramatization. Quietly, often gaily, it re-creates the daily life of eight Jews who hid for two years in an Amsterdam attic before the Gestapo broke in. Otto Frank was the sole survivor: Anne was killed in Belsen.

"When I saw the play in New York, it vaguely perturbed me. There seemed no *need* to do it: it smacked of exploitation. The Berlin actors (especially Johanna von Koczian and Walter Franck) were better, on the whole, and devouter than the Americans, but I do not think that was why the play seemed so much more urgent and necessary on Monday night. After the interval the man in front of me put his head in his hands and did not afterwards look at the stage. He was not, I believe, Jewish. It was not until the end that one fully appreciated Barlog's wisdom and valour in using an entirely non-Jewish cast. Having read the last lines of the diary, which affirm, movingly and irrationally, Anne Frank's unshattered trust in human goodness, Otto Frank closes the book and says, very slowly: 'She puts me to shame.'

"Thus the play ended. The house-lights went up on an audience that sat drained and ashen, some staring straight ahead, others staring at the ground, for a full half-minute. Then, as if awakening from a nightmare, they rose and filed out in total silence, not looking at each other, avoiding even the customary nods of recognition with which friend greets friend. There was no applause, and there were no curtain-calls.

"All of this, I am well aware, is not drama criticism. In the shadow of an event so desperate and traumatic, criticism would be an irrelevance. I can only record an emotion that I felt, would not have missed, and pray never to feel again."

## II

### IMPLICATIONS

**A.** Look at the second scene where the group is coming together for the first time. Also look at the end of scene three where Mr. Dussel first arrives. At these moments, what is the attitude of one person toward another? What are their intentions toward one another? How do these intentions change in subsequent actions? What are the things over which they argue? Are they important or unimportant?

**B.** Read the following quotations carefully. Try and put in your own words the attitude of young people toward their parents which is expressed in each of the remarks. How typical are they of family life and your own reactions?

**1.** "Mother is unbearable. She insists on treating me like a baby which I loathe." (I,2, p. 202)

From "Curtains" by Kenneth Tynan. Copyright © 1961 by Kenneth Tynan. Reprinted by permission of Atheneum Publishers.

**2.** MR. VAN DAAN. "Haven't you finished yet?"
PETER. "No."
MR. VAN DAAN. "You ought to be ashamed of yourself."
PETER. "All right. All right. I'm a dunce. I'm a hopeless case. Why do I go on?"
(I,3, p. 206)

**3.** "Now, Peter, you listen to Mr. Frank." (I,3, p. 206)

**4.** "Margot! Margot! Margot! That's all I hear from everyone . . . how wonderful Margot is . . . 'Why aren't you like Margot?' " (I,3, p. 208)

**5.** "Everything I do is wrong! I'm the goat around here!" . . . (I,3, p. 208)

**6.** "Whenever I try to explain my views on life to her she asks me if I'm constipated." (I,4, p. 215)

**7.** "You grownups have had your chance! But look at us. . . . It isn't our fault that the world is in such a mess! We weren't around when all this started! So don't try to take it out on us!" (II,1, p. 226)

**8.** "I suppose you can't really blame them . . . they think back to what they were like at our age. They don't realize how much more advanced we are. . . ." (II,2, p. 230)

**C.** Now read the following lines and decide what points of view the parents hold about their children. Once again try to express the parents' reactions in your own words. Do you think your own parents may share some of these feelings toward you?

**1.** "You complain that I don't treat you like a grownup. But when I do, you resent it." (I,3, p. 203)

**2.** "Don't you ever get tired of talking? Suppose you try keeping still for five minutes. Just five minutes." (I,3, p. 207)

**3.** "The trouble with you is, you've been spoiled." (I,3, p. 207)

**4.** "Watch Margot. She's always courteous with them. Never familiar. She keeps her distance. And they respect her for it. Try to be like Margot." (I,3, p. 208)

**5.** "She wants nothing of me. She pulled away when I leaned down to kiss her." (I,4, p. 215)

**6.** "There is so little that we parents can do to help our children. We can only try to set a good example . . . point the way. The rest you must do yourself." (I,4, p. 215)

**7.** "I only wish that you wouldn't expose yourself to criticism." (II,2, p. 229)

**8.** "I don't know what good it is to have a son. I never see him." (II,2, p. 230)

**D.** The remarks that characters make in a play often cause the readers to think about themselves and their own values. Thus, lines may do two jobs: They help the progress of the immediate action on the stage; they force the reader to do some thinking on her or his own.

Select one of the following quotations and be prepared to present your opinion of the ideas presented in the lines. You may agree or disagree.

**1.** "There are no walls, there are no bolts, no locks that anyone can put on your mind." (I,2, p. 200)

**2.** "I can stand off and look at myself doing it and know it's cruel and yet I can't stop doing it. What's the matter with me?" (I,4, p. 215)

**3.** "If we begin thinking of all the horror in the world, we're lost! We're trying to hold onto some kind of ideals." (II,1, p. 226)

**4.** "It's easier. A fight starts, or an argument . . . I duck in here." (II,1, p. 227)

**5.** "We don't need the Nazis to destroy us. We're destroying ourselves." (II,3, p. 235)

**6.** "I think the world may be going through a phase, the way I was with Mother. It'll pass, maybe not for hundreds of years, but some day. . . ." (II,4, p. 239)

**7.** "In spite of everything, I still believe that people are really good at heart." (II,5, p. 241)

### III
### TECHNIQUES

*Characterization*

**A.** You have learned that characters are revealed to the reader through what they do, what they say, and what others say about them. What specific lines or incidents show the following traits about the characters:

**1.** That Mrs. Van Daan is vain.
That she is shallow.
That she is selfish.

**2.** Anne:
That she is talkative.
That she is sentimental
That she is bright.
That she is sensitive.

That she is a tease.

That she is enthusiastic.

3. Peter:

That he is unsocial.

That he is easily embarrassed.

That he is an average student.

That he is lonely.

**B.** If you were to rate the general strength of character of Mr. Frank, Mrs. Frank, Mr. Van Daan, Mrs. Van Daan, and Dussel, how would you rank them? What is the evidence for your ranking?

**C.** If you were to judge the relative intelligence of the three children, Peter, Anne, and Margot, how would you rank them? What in the play did you use as the basis for your judgment?

**D.** In real life, Mrs. Frank became insane after being sent to the concentration camp. Are there any indications in the play that this could happen to her? In actual life, Margot became increasingly frail and sickly. She died falling out of bed. What details in the play indicate this possibility?

*Plot*

**A.** Discuss whether you feel the first and last scenes are basically necessary to the impact of the play on the audience.

**B.** What devices are used to let the audience know the passage of time in the play? How effective would it have been if the dates of the scenes had simply been printed in the programs as is done in most dramas?

**C.** This play consists mainly of isolated happenings that occur over a period of two years. What is the thread that holds these isolated incidents together like beads of a necklace? In other words, how has the author made a plot out of a series of incidents?

**D.** Louis Kronenberger's review of the play said that it was a "weird blend of the brightly ordinary, the hideously abnormal, of comic fault finding, and heroic adjustment." Take these four aspects and list under each one the incidents that illustrate it.

*Symbol*

**A.** Sometimes an object may be a very personal symbol to an individual; that is, it takes on a greater significance than it normally merits. What does:

**1.** The fur coat mean to Mrs. Van Daan?

**2.** The cat mean to Peter?

**3.** The diary mean to Anne?

**B.** A whole work of literature may stand as a symbol of a truth in human life. This is particularly true with *The Diary of Anne Frank*. You have read of the impact it had on the German audience. What do you think the play symbolized to the Germans sitting in the theater that night? In what way might it have meant something different to an American audience?

## IV
### WORDS

**A.** The environment of a word, what is said before and after an unfamiliar word, helps to suggest a general meaning. Grammatical construction—coordination, subordination, parallelism, apposition—further aids in determining meaning. Word analysis is yet another tool. Determine as much as you can of the meaning of the following words. Which clue helped the most: connection of the word to the context, grammatical construction, modifiers, word analysis?

*carillon* (p. 193), *compassionate* (p. 194), *capitulation* (p. 195), *conspicuous* (p. 195), *unabashed* (p. 199), *intolerable* (p. 204), *subjunctive* (p. 205), *meticulous* (p. 210), *humiliated* (p. 211), *fatalist* (p. 216), *improvised* (p. 217), *jubilation* (p. 219), *appalled silence* (p. 221), *foreboding* (p. 225), *intuition* (p. 229), *indignant* (p. 230), *pandemonium* (p. 236), *convulsive* (p. 236).

**B.** **1.** Three-form roots also include *-leg-*, as in *legible* or *legend; -lig-*, as in *eligible* or *negligent;* and *-lect-*, as in *select* or *elect.* This root means "choose, choose to read, read." Similar is the three-form root *-reg-*, as in *regent* or *regal; -rig-*, as in *incorrigible;* and *-rect-*, as in *correct* or *rectangle.* It means "to rule," "to rule rightly," "right, straight, correct." The root meaning "to look, view, see" also appears in English in three forms: *-spec-*, as in *specimen; -spic-*, as in *conspicuous* ("compelling one to look at"); and *-spect-*, as in *inspect* or *suspect.*

**2.** There is no fixed number of forms a given Latin root may eventually show in English. There are two important Latin roots showing four forms in English. One is the Latin root meaning "to make, accomplish, perform, or do," which we sometimes have as *-fac-*, as in *facile; -fact-*, as in *factory* or manufacture; *-fect-*, as in *effective* or *defective;* and *-fic-*, as in *deficient* or *efficiency.* A great many English words employ this root. Make a list of as many as you can find. Another root with four forms in English is one meaning "to take, seize, capture": *-cap-*, as in *capacity; -capt-*, as in *captive; -cept-*, as in *reception;* and *-cip-*, as in *recipient.* Like the root for "to make or do," this root yields a great many words in English. Make up a list of as many as you can think of.

---

## BIOGRAPHICAL NOTES

### Gina Berriault

Gina Berriault has published several novels, among them *The Son, The Descent* (1960), and *Conference of Victims* (1962). Her stories have won the Aga Khan Fiction Award and three O'Henry Awards. They have appeared in periodicals such as *Esquire, Harper's Bazaar, Saturday Evening Post* and *Contact.*

### D. H. Lawrence

D. H. Lawrence (1885–1930) is considered by some critics as one of the most powerful of modern English novelists. He was born in Nottinghamshire and educated at both the high school and the University of Nottingham. He published his first book in 1911. His writing is sometimes classified as psychological, but he showed spiritual insight and great artistic power in his descriptions, both of scenery and people. *Sons and Lovers* and *Lady Chatterley's Lover* are two of his best known works.

### Helen Cresswell

Helen Cresswell (1934–    ), born in Nottinghamshire, England, has had a varied career. Her positions have ranged from literary assistant to foreign author to fashion buyer to jobs with the British Broadcasting Company. Today she writes mainly for children. She says she cannot remember not writing. Cresswell feels that fantasy is an extension of poetry and that rhythm is the single most important factor in writing. One of Cresswell's passions is for "words for their own sake. "I love words and am often terribly tempted to do pages and pages of self-indulgent wallowings in description." A second passion is her love for the English countryside. "Quite often I begin a book soon after a visit to places that have affected me strongly." When asked for whom she writes, she replied, "I have no idea whom I am trying to 'reach.' Everyone, probably."

### Mary Lavin

Mary Lavin (1912–    ), born in the United States, was transplanted to Ireland as a young girl and has lived there ever since. Her early schooling was in East Walpole, Massachusetts, but in Ireland she studied at Loreto Convent and received an M.A. with first-class honors from the National University of Ireland. About her own writing she has said: "It is in the short story that a writer distills the essence of his thought. I believe this because the short story, shape as well as matter, is determined by the writer's own character. Both are one. Short-story writing—for me—is only looking closer than normal into the human heart." Says Jean Stubbs of *Books*, "Miss Lavin invites us to contemplate with her the infinite sadness and beauty of the world, the divine inconsequence of life. . . . She will not allow us to stand by and marvel, but insists that we become participants." Today Mary Lavin is considered not only a great Irish writer of short stories but among the greatest of European short story writers.

### Nicholasa Mohr

Nicholasa Mohr (1935–    ) was born in New York City, the daughter of Pedro and Nicholasa Golpe. She attended several art schools, and her careers have included fine arts painting and printmaking in New York, California, Mexico, and Puerto Rico plus writing and illustrating books and teaching art.

### Stephen Spender

Stephen Spender (1909–    ), born in London, England, supported himself in his teens by printing labels on his hand press, later going on to print entire books for friends. While attending Oxford University from 1928–1930, Spender, along with W. H. Auden, Louis MacNeice, and C. Day Lewis, formed the Oxford Group, which had a tremendous influence on poetry and poetics. Spender was probably the most romantic and lyrical of the group. Supporting himself by editing, teaching, and lecturing, Spender wrote not only poems but also autobiographies, dramas, and critical essays. He recently told an American audience that American poetry today is more interesting than contemporary Britist poetry.

## Robert Hayden

Robert Hayden (1913–    ), rejecting the label "Negro poet," attempts in his poetry, through his direct observations and responses, to capture common human experiences, not necessarily only the black experience. But his works cannot escape the history and folklore of his race which filter through his works. Born in Detroit, Michigan, Hayden graduated from Wayne State University and then went on to the University of Michigan, where he received an M.A. and taught from 1944–1946. Since then he has been a Professor of English at Fisk University and has not only won honors and awards for his poetry, but has also written plays and radio scripts.

## Ray Bradbury

Ray Bradbury (1920–    ), born in Waukegan, Illinois, moved with his family to California when he was in his early teens. While still in high school he wrote science-fiction stories for his own magazine, *Futuria Fantasia*, which ran for four issues. One of his favorite subjects is the clash between society and the individual in an overdeveloped civilization. Bradbury states that "Science fiction is really sociological studies of the future; things that the writer believes are going to happen by putting two and two together. Fantasy fiction is the improbable. If you had a leprechaun or a dinosaur appearing in the streets of New York—that's highly improbable. But science fiction is a logical mathematical projection of reality." Since 1947, he has written almost two dozen books. Some of his most popular works are: *Martian Chronicles* (1950), *Fahrenheit 451* (1953), *Switch on the Night* (1955), *A Medicine for Melancholy* (1959), *Something Wicked This Way Comes* (1962).

# PRIVATE MOODS

For everything there is a season, and a time for everything under heaven:
 a time to be born, and a time to die;
 a time to plant, and a time to pluck up what is planted;
 a time to kill, and a time to bear;
 a time to break down, and a time to build up;
 a time to weep, and a time to laugh;
 a time to mourn, and a time to dance;
 a time to cast away stones, and a time to gather stones together;
 a time to embrace, and a time to refrain from embracing;
 a time to seek, and a time to lose;
 a time to keep, and a time to cast away;
 a time to rend, and a time to sew;
 a time to keep silence, and a time to speak;
 a time to love, and a time to hate;
 a time for war, and a time for peace.
ECCLESIASTES 3:1–8 (Revised Standard Version of the Bible)

An ancient Hebrew writer saw the diversity of experiences and complexity of feelings that all people undergo. He saw that life is not only a matter of actions, but it is also a matter of feelings that no person can escape. Sorrow and delight, hatred and love, desire and regret—each in its own time sweeps over a person.

Private and personal because they are experienced inwardly, moods are like transparent color flooding the mind. They color the picture of the world that the senses transmit. Sometimes they may last for a long time; sometimes they are momentary flashes; but they are never long absent. The poetry in this unit examines and evokes many of peoples' most characteristic moods.

Of all the kinds of writing, lyric poetry is especially concerned with a person's personal emotions—his or her private moods. Like all people, the poet experiences the sights, sounds, smells, tastes, and touches common to all—train whistles, waves slapping the shore, houses at night, oak trees, freshly ground coffee, sharp winds, the ping of an ice cream vendor's bell. But unlike most people's, the poet's reactions to such common experiences are extraordinary, often profound, always intense. The poet sees far deeper and her or his experiences mean far more than similar experiences mean to most people.

Through vivid language the lyric poet attempts to recreate personal experience. The poet crystallizes little bits of life that are exciting, beautiful, or memorable. The reader, by sharing these moments of the poet, adds to his or her own fund of experiences and broadens her or his sense of life. In their peculiar way poets remind us of things we know but did not realize we knew. They make us say, "Yes, I have felt that way, but I did not understand the meaning or depth of that feeling." Or, "I have seen that, but now I really understand what I saw." In this way poetry adds to the richness of our own private moods.

To begin to grasp even a portion of this richness, you must read more intently than when skimming a newspaper or studying a textbook, for the poet compresses experience into a unique fusion of words, images, and rhythms. In order to share the experience the reader must follow closely the meaning of words, hear their sounds, imagine the sensations and comparisons, and feel the rhythm of the lines. The study notes in PRIVATE MOODS help you take up these important considerations systematically. These aids, if followed, give you a method of reading that will increase your understanding and hence your enjoyment of private moods.

The Cry
*Edvard Munch.*
*National Gallery of Art,*
*Washington, D.C.,*
*Rosenwald Collection.*
*The emotional impact of*
The Cry *vividly states the*
*power of private moods.*

**RESTLESSNESS** No one is ever quite content. The worlds beyond the horizon always seem to promise something strange, new, exotic. Jet streams across the sky lead the imagination. Magazine pictures of foreign countries suggest a more exciting life than one knows. Maps lure the mind and make people discontent with their present state. Restlessness is a confusing, cloudy emotion that people are never really without.

Have you ever yearned to be free
from cares, duties, and social restrictions
and yet could not follow the restless urgings of your heart?
If you have, perhaps you too know
"what the caged bird feels."

## Sympathy

I know what the caged bird feels, alas!
  When the sun is bright on the upland slopes;
When the wind stirs soft through the springing grass,
And the river flows like a stream of glass;
  When the first bird sings and the first bud opes,     5
And the faint perfume from its chalice steals—
I know what the caged bird feels!

I know why the caged bird beats his wing
  Till its blood is red on the cruel bars;
For he must fly back to his perch and cling     10
When he fain would be on the bough a-swing;
  And a pain still throbs in the old, old scars
And they pulse again with a keener sting—
I know why he beats his wing!

I know why the caged bird sings, ah me,     15
  When his wing is bruised and his bosom sore,—
When he beats his bars and he would be free;
It is not a carol of joy or glee,
  But a prayer that he sends from his heart's deep core,
But a plea, that upward to Heaven he flings—     20
I know why the caged bird sings!

PAUL LAURENCE DUNBAR

Reprinted by permission of Dodd, Mead & Company from *The Complete Poems of Paul Laurence Dunbar.*

Restlessness begins with a sickness of the heart,
a yearning to break with the old patterns.

# Spring

I said in my heart, "I am sick of four walls and a ceiling.
I have need of the sky.
I have business with the grass.
I will up and get me away where the hawk is wheeling,
Lone and high,
And the slow clouds go by . . ."

RICHARD HOVEY

 The restless heart often turns to travel
as the best means for easing its discontent.

# Travel

The railroad track is miles away,
   And the day is loud with voices speaking,
Yet there isn't a train goes by all day
   But I hear its whistle shrieking.

All night there isn't a train goes by,         5
   Though the night is still for sleep and dreaming,
But I see its cinders red on the sky,
   And hear its engine steaming.[1]

My heart is warm with the friends I make,
   And better friends I'll not be knowing,      10
Yet there isn't a train I wouldn't take,
   No matter where it's going.

EDNA ST. VINCENT MILLAY

Reprinted by permission of Dodd, Mead & Company from *Poems* by Richard Hovey.

Copyright 1917, 1921, 1945, 1948 by Edna St. Vincent Millay. Reprinted by permission of Norma Millay Ellis.

1. The reference is to the old coal-burning, steam-driven locomotive.

For centuries the sea has called many people.
In Masefields "Sea Fever"
the longing for the sea is tinged with melancholy
and loneliness.

# Sea Fever

I must go down to the seas again, to the lonely sea and the sky,
And all I ask is a tall ship and a star to steer her by,
And the wheel's kick and the wind's song and the white sail's shaking,
And a gray mist on the sea's face and a gray dawn breaking.

I must down to the seas again, for the call of the running tide          5
Is a wild call and a clear call that may not be denied;
And all I ask is a windy day with the white clouds flying,
And the flung spray and the blown spume,[1] and the seagulls crying.

I must down to the seas again to the vagrant gypsy life.
To the gull's way and the whale's way where the wind's like a whetted[2] knife: 10
And all I ask is a merry yarn from a laughing fellow rover,
And quiet sleep and a sweet dream when the long trick's[3] over.

JOHN MASEFIELD

Reprinted with permission of The Macmillan Company from POEMS by John Masefield. Copyright 1912 by The Macmillan Company, renewed 1940 by John Masefield.

Should one fight against
the inner restlessness
that makes one dissatisfied?

# Ride
## a Wild Horse

Ride a wild horse
with purple wings
striped yellow and black
except his head
which must be red.          5

Ride a wild horse
against the sky—
hold tight to his wings

before you die
whatever else you leave undone—    10
once ride a wild horse
into the sun.

HANNAH KAHN

"Into the Sun" by Hannah Kahn, reprinted from Saturday Review, March 21, 1953. Copyright 1953 Saturday Review, Inc.

1. **spume**\spyūm\ ocean foam or spray.
2. **whet**\wĕt\ sharpen.
3. **trick**, tour of duty.

When you are caught in heavy traffic there is little you can do to speed your way home. Yet what is the need that compels you to fight this situation?

# *Highway: Michigan*

Here from the field's edge we survey
The progress of the jaded. Mile
On mile of traffic from the town
Rides by, for at the end of day
The time of workers is their own.                    5

They jockey for position on
The strip reserved for passing only.
The drivers from production lines
Hold to advantage dearly won.
They toy with death and traffic fines.              10

Acceleration is their need:
A mania keeps them on the move
Until the toughest nerves are frayed.
They are the prisoners of speed
Who flee in what their hands have made.             15

The pavement smokes when two cars meet
And steel rips through conflicting steel.
We shiver at the siren's blast.
One driver, pinned beneath the seat,
Escapes from the machine at last.                   20

THEODORE ROETHKE

"Highway: Michigan" by Theodore Roethke. Copyright 1940 by Theodore Roethke. From the book COL-LECTED POEMS OF THEODORE ROETHKE by Theodore Roethke. Reprinted by permission of Double-day & Company, Inc.

Feeling restless, with a need to be doing something?
A parked car can be an invitation to excitement and
the ultimate in danger.

# Death Is a Beautiful Car Parked Only

*For Emmett*

Death is a beautiful car parked only
to be stolen on a street lined with trees
whose branches are like the intestines
    of an emerald.

You hotwire death, get in, and drive away          5
like a flag made from a thousand burning
    funeral parlors.

You have stolen death because you're bored.
There's nothing good playing at the movies
    in San Francisco.                              10

You joyride around for a while listening
to the radio, and then abandon death, walk
away, and leave death for the police
    to find.

RICHARD BRAUTIGAN

From THE PILL VERSUS THE SPRINGHILL MINE
DISASTER by Richard Brautigan. Copyright © 1968 by
Richard Brautigan. A Seymour Lawrence Book/Delacorte
Press. Reprinted by permission of the publisher.

There are many dreams that lure people
from the beaten track. All of these dreams have been given
the generalized name of "Eldorado," a city or country
that is beautiful and elusive.

# *Eldorado*

Gaily bedight,[1]
A gallant knight,
In sunshine and in shadow,
Had journeyed long,
Singing a song,                                    5
In search of Eldorado.[2]

But he grew old—
This knight so bold—
And o'er his heart a shadow
Fell as he found                                   10
No spot of ground
That looked like Eldorado.

And, as his strength
Failed him at length,
He met a pilgrim shadow—          15
"Shadow," said he,
"Where can it be—
This land of Eldorado?"

"Over the Mountains
Of the Moon,                                       20
Down the Valley of the Shadow,
Ride, boldly, ride,"
The Shade replied—
"If you seek for Eldorado!"

EDGAR ALLAN POE

———————

1. **bedight**\bē ˄dait\ costumed and equipped.
2. **Eldorado** may be translated as "the golden land."
In other uses, the pronunciation \'ĕl·də ˄rā·dō\ may be
found, but Poe's rhyme calls for \'ĕl·də ˄rā·dō\.

---

### UNDERSTANDING POETRY
*Titles Are Important*

A well-chosen title is often an important key to
understanding a piece of writing, and it is especially useful for reading poetry. A title usually tells
the reader what the poem is about by naming the
poem's subject. This John Masefield does with the
title "Sea Fever." His title tells that the poem is
about a kind of sickness, an abnormal state, caused
by or somehow related to the sea. Often, too, a title
suggests the poem's theme, or meaning. In the
title "Eldorado," Poe not only tells the reader that,
in some fashion, his poem deals with the subject
of impossible dreams but at the same time partly
suggests the theme or meaning of the poem: the
attitude that, in spite of the futility of chasing
"pipe dreams," people cannot resist the hopeless
pursuit.

Titles are so obvious that one often overlooks
them. Always ask yourself how the title is related
to the subject matter and theme of the poem.

### TECHNIQUES
*Rhythm*

In normal English speech, some words and syllables are stressed and some are not (to-mór-row).
This fact makes it possible to establish a beat with
the sounds of words. As in music, recurrent beat
forms a rhythm (tomórrow and tomórrow and
tomórrow). In poetry the basic rhythms (measures,
or meters) result from the repetition of regular
patterns of accented and unaccented syllables.

Rhythm is not something artificially imposed
upon a poem; it grows out of the ideas and feelings
expressed in the poem and, ideally, complements
them perfectly. Indeed, rhythm is one of the poet's
chief means for intensifying a mood and reinforc-

ing the reader's emotions. And just as the background music of a movie or a TV play changes as the action shifts from a gun battle to a love scene, so the rhythm of a poem fits the mood: now slow and sad, now fast and gay, now strong and triumphant.

The most natural and hence most frequently used rhythmic pattern in English poetry is the iambic. An iambic *foot* (a foot is the single unit of the stress pattern which when repeated forms a pattern—the rhythm) is composed of an unaccented followed by an accented syllable (dĕ-líght). Of the poems included in this section of the unit, "Travel" and "Ride a Wild Horse" are basically iambic. But a quick reading of these poems reveals that even within a single poem poets rarely use just one type of foot. Frequently, they substitute other feet for the sake of variety, emphasis, or feeling. A most common substitution is the trochaic foot—an accented syllable followed by an unaccented (óx ĕn). Note that Hanna Kahn's trochee which opens "Ride a Wild Horse" emphasizes the forceful call to action. Used by itself, the trochaic rhythm suits light, gay poems and songs. When used to excess, however, its strong rocking rhythm becomes "singsong" and hence more appropriate for nursery rhymes than for serious poetry. The spondee and the pyrrhic are two other substitutes for the iambic, although unlike the trochee, neither is often sustained for more than a few syllables. The spondee is composed of two accented syllables (gréat háll). It tends to be slow and heavy and therefore gives greater force, importance or solemnity to the rhythm. The pyrrhic, on the other hand, is composed of two unaccented syllables (ănd ă) and hence is quick and light. In an unusual piling up of alternating pyrrhics and spondees, John Masefield reproduces the relentless, forceful surging of wave on wave.

And thĕ / wheel's kíck / ănd thĕ / wind's sóng /
   ănd thĕ / white sáil's / shák ĭng,
And ă / gray míst / ŏn thĕ / sea's fáce / ănd thĕ
   / gray dáwn / breák ĭng

Two other basic feet are the anapest and the dactyl. Although both may be used alone (like the iambic and the trochaic), they occur infrequently in English poetry. The anapest (two unaccented,

one accented—"tŏ thĕ hílls") gives swiftness and emphasizes the last word in the line.

Lĭke ă chíld / frŏm thĕ wómb, / lĭke ă ghóst /
   frŏm thĕ tómb,
Ĭ aríse / ănd unbuíld / ĭt agáin.
                          "The Cloud" . . . Shelley

The dactyl (one accented, two unaccented) has a stately, even grand, movement but is seldom consistently written because it becomes monotonous.

Yé whŏ bĕ/líeve ĭn ăf/féctiŏn thăt / hópes, ănd
   en/dúres, ănd ĭs / pátient,
Yé whŏ bĕ/líeve ĭn thĕ / beáuty ănd / stréngth
   ŏf / wóman's dĕ/vótion.
                    "Evangeline" . . . Longfellow

The quantity, or length, of a line is also an important factor in determining the rhythm of a poem. The line is measured by the number of feet it contains. A line with one foot is called *monometer;* two feet, *dimeter;* three feet, *trimeter;* four feet, *tetrameter;* five feet, *pentameter;* six feet, *hexameter.* The basic rhythm of a poem is described in terms of the predominant foot and the number of feet per line.

To discover the rhythm of a poem, read the poem aloud several times. Let your ear rather than your eye determine the pattern.

In this section, what kind of basic rhythm does each poem have? Can you explain why poems about restlessness should frequently employ unusual rhythms?

*Rhyme*

A poet may use many devices to vary the basic rhythm. The one most people associate exclusively with poetry is rhyme: the patterned repetition and variation of similar sounds. Rhyme serves two purposes: it delights the ear and it emphasizes the rhythm of a stanza. In this way rhyme identifies and sets off individual stanzas as separate sound and thought units.

Masculine rhymes are those that rhyme the final accented syllable of two or more lines, as "sky" and "by" in lines 1 and 2 of "Sea Fever." Feminine rhymes are those in which the last two syllables of two or more lines rhyme; the first syllable is accented and the second is unaccented, as "shrieking" and "squeaking." Masculine rhymes end a line with force, giving a feeling of completeness. Feminine rhymes leave the rhythm "hanging," wanting to move on, and give a feeling of incompleteness. How many of the poems in this section use feminine rhymes? Can you show why poems about restlessness should use such rhymes?

## Sympathy

**1.** What specific experiences awaken the bird's restlessness? Why should they be so provocative?

**2.** Why does the caged bird sing? What perhaps has the poet experienced to give him such sympathy for the bird?

## Spring

**1.** What does the title "Spring" have to do with the poet's sickness?

**2.** Why are the lines so uneven in length?

**3.** Why does the pace of the poem slow down in the last two lines?

## Travel

**1.** What is the progression of restlessness that the poet develops in each stanza?

**2.** What aspect of the train is suggested by the use of feminine rhymes such as *squeaking* and *shrieking*?

**3.** Does the poet ever reveal the source of her discontent?

## Sea Fever

**1.** What unpleasant memories do the details of sea life suggest? What pleasant memories? Can people long for things physically difficult and unpleasant?

**2.** What quality of sound do the long line and the use of many long vowel sounds give the poem?

**3.** To what effect does the poet use masculine and feminine rhymes?

## Ride a Wild Horse

**1.** Here the poet has used a symbol to suggest her meaning. She is thinking of Pegasus, the winged horse of mythology, that has long represented the human flight of fancy. Why does she color him so startlingly?

**2.** What does she imply that people's reactions should be to their inner desires?

## Highway: Michigan

**1.** Do you agree with Roethke that the riders in the cars are jaded . . . that they jockey for position on the highway . . . that they toy with death . . . that speed satisfies a need?

**2.** Describe the incident in the last stanza.

## Death Is a Beautiful Car Parked Only

**1.** What does the title mean to you?

**2.** Why is the car stolen? Is this a usual reason for this act?

**3.** Contemporary poetry often startles the reader by strange combinations of ideas. Pick out one such combination from the poem.

## Eldorado

**1.** Does the poet consider the search for Eldorado rewarding or futile?

**2.** What does the rhythm and the haunting repetition of the word *Eldorado* suggest?

### IMPLICATIONS

**A.** In terms of the different ideas presented about human restlessness in this group of poems, what is your reaction to the following statements:

**1.** No person is ever completely content with her or his own present situation.

**2.** Without restlessness, people would never progress.

**3.** When people feel restless, they never really know exactly what it is that would satisfy their longing.

**B.** Skim back over the group of poems and answer the following questions:

**1.** What kinds of experiences are mentioned that bring on restlessness?

**2.** What seems to be the attitude toward giving in to restlessness and following a whim? Do you agree or disagree?

**3.** Do the poems suggest that people ever find the things they seek?

**4.** Which poems suggest, and how do they suggest, that the search is almost more important than the goal?

**FEAR** People hide some emotions in secret places, ashamed to admit
that they possess them. Fear is such a black sheep. Still, fear is often basic
to life itself, clueing one to retreat from danger; yet, at other times,
fear is foolish . . . the result of ignorance and superstition. Babies are afraid
of loud noises and of falling. Children may fear water, snakes, strangers, the dark.
Adolescents may fear being alone, being different, or being ridiculed. And adults
may fear marrying unhappily, bungling their jobs, losing their youth.

The sensations of fear, ill-founded,
come slowly and mount in intensity.

## *Country Night*

She lived in terror of the country night;
As soon as afternoon began to fade
She went about the house, lit every light,
Bolted the doors, and drew every window-shade.

The house was like a ship that slowly listed,[1]    5
The night was water, and it seemed to her
It rose relentlessly and unresisted,
Inevitable, black, and sinister.

The little liquid noises that she heard
Were friendly and familiar things by day:    10
Tree and insect, flower and grass and bird,
Nothing at all to frighten her this way—
But still the night rose higher, till it found
Her tense and quivering and almost drowned.

SELMA ROBINSON

---

1. **list,** to lean to one side.

Reprinted by permission; Copr. © 1931, 1959 The New Yorker
Magazine, Inc.

Often there is nothing reasonable about fear.
What one does to escape it
is usually ridiculous and irrational.

# House Fear

Always—I tell you this they learned—
Always at night when they returned
To the lonely house from far away,
To lamps unlighted and fire gone gray,
They learned to rattle the lock and key     5
To give whatever might chance to be,
Warning and time to be off in flight:
And preferring the out- to the indoor night,
They learned to leave the house door wide
Until they had lit the lamp inside.     10

ROBERT FROST

Sometimes the openness of the out-of-doors
seems to offer escape . . . a feeling
that makes indoor darkness even more terrifying.
And sometimes the indoors seems a haven
into which mysterious and frightening things
try to force their way.

# The Oft-Repeated Dream

She had no saying dark enough
For the dark pine that kept
Forever trying the window-latch
Of the room where they slept.

The tireless but ineffectual hands     5
That with every futile pass
Made the great tree seem as a little bird
Before the mystery of glass!

It never had been inside the room,
And only one of the two     10
Was afraid in an oft-repeated dream
Of what the tree might do.

ROBERT FROST

What are the defenses against fear?
When it finally pushes one into a corner,
when it has to be faced, how does one react?

# The Lady

The candle is out,
it has crashed to the floor,
she follows the wall
to find the door.

Her petticoats hiss     5
with a hiss of fear,
a path of sound
for a sensitive ear.

When she puts out her hand,
her breath gives a catch,     10
fingers are there
instead of a latch!

When she reaches back
lest she should fall,
a body is there     15
instead of a wall!

What use to scream
so sole alone,
what use to struggle
against the unknown?     20

"Very well," she said
imperiously,
"Pray light the sconces[1]
so we may see.

"Here are my pearls,     25
And here are my rings.
And take off your hats,
you filthy things!"

ELIZABETH COATSWORTH

HOUSE FEAR and THE OFT-REPEATED DREAM from THE POETRY OF ROBERT FROST edited by Edward Connery Lathem. Copyright 1916, 1934, © 1969 by Holt, Rinehart and Winston, Inc. Copyright 1944, © 1962 by Robert Frost. Reprinted by permission of Holt, Rinehart and Winston, Inc.

1. sconce\skŏns\ a candle holder, a candle in its holder.

Copyright © Elizabeth Coatsworth. By kind permission of Mark Paterson on behalf of Elizabeth Coatsworth.

The compression of poetry
makes it possible to suggest
more than is actually said. A few words,
well selected and arranged, can produce
a sudden, inexplicable shudder of fear.

# The Warning

Just now,
Out of the strange
Still dusk . . . as strange, as still . . .
A white moth flew. Why am I grown
So cold?

ADELAIDE CRAPSEY

From VERSE, by Adelaide Crapsey. Copyright
1922 by Algernon S. Crapsey and renewed
1950 by The Adelaide Crapsey Foundation.

# When I Have Fears That I May Cease To Be

Fear may be
a more diffuse emotion
as well, not just a sudden
physical response
to an immediate situation.
It may be a haunting,
continuing thing.

When I have fears that I may cease to be
Before my pen has gleaned my teeming brain,
Before high-pilèd books, in charact'ry,[1]
Hold like rich garners the full-ripened grain;
When I behold, upon the night's starred face,   5
Huge cloudy symbols of a high romance,
And think that I may never live to trace
Their shadows, with the magic hand of chance;
And when I feel, fair creature of an hour!
That I shall never look upon thee more   10
Never have relish in the faery[2] power
Of unreflecting love—then on the shore
Of the wide world I stand alone, and think,
Till Love and Fame to nothingness do sink.

JOHN KEATS

1. **charact'ry**\\ˈkă·rək·trē\\ **charactery,** writing, written
characters.
2. **faery**\\ˈfā·rē\\ a by-form of **fairy,** but the word here
as in other older writing is stronger than its modern
meanings. It may be interpreted as meaning "showing
awesome supernatural strength."

When imagined fear runs out of control . . .

# *The Panther Possible*

The old man's words (Something has skittered the cattle
    or else it's to rain hard—storm—tonight)
That, and the tale of someone coming upon
    a Mexican lion that didn't take fright
but looked up from the calf it ate                 5
    and made a horrible rosin-rub
        of sound in its throat, laid its ears flat,
        and walked off stiffly in the scrub.

And the man who got his tractor to see what that was
    of heavy shape and sound in the prickly pear—     10
who found huge prints and suffered the white fangs
    of a hidden explodable stare—
who hurried back to mount
    the tractor, found it wouldn't start,
        and had to walk five miles in dark     15
        with padding steps timed to his heart—

Was it a wonder the boy heard the panther scream
    in the chaparral[1] (how do you tell for certain?)
a wonder his nose began to itch and his right eye water
    (it always did when he was scared)? What's the hurt in  20
achieving a fear of panthers, pure
    or imaginary? Wasn't his nose
        made itchable? What's a dry eye worth
        compared with one that, stricken, glows?

WILLIAM D. BARNEY

---

1. chaparral\ˈchăp·ə·răl\ a dense thicket of shrubs or dwarf trees.

---

By permission of August Derleth.

It almost seems that people enjoy having their fears
stimulated by strange, eerie places.

# Suicide Pond

It lay, dark in the corner of the field,
Deep and unclouded, like a devil's well,
The dank fern gathered round it in great clumps;
All the wild air was heavy with the smell
Of tansy;[1] and it had the awful look                    5
Of hidden and forbidden water. When
The seasons changed and winter dropped its cloud,
It did not dream in silver, but this fen
Remained a black hole gaping in the snow.
No stream led out of it, no stream led in;               10
No stars reflected in it; rumor said
Men plunged into its cold and took their sin,
Downing it with clenched hands and blinded eyes,
Far down the pitted water; and, alone
And trembling, we, when young, looked down and saw  15
Grim suicides in bottom-rock and stone.

KATHY McLAUGHLIN

---

1. **tansy**\ˈtăn·zē\ an herb with an aromatic odor and a bitter
taste.

---

"Suicide Pond" by Kathy McLaughlin first appeared in POETRY. Copyright 1952 by The Modern Poetry Association. Reprinted by permission
of the Editor of POETRY.

## UNDERSTANDING POETRY
### Locating the Subject

The meaning of a poem often hinges upon the accurate perception of the poem's subject matter. As noted previously, titles usually help to define what a poet is talking about. Still, there are times when the title simply names the thing, person, memory, or idea which caused the poet to ponder some deeper subject. In the set of poems here, what is the real subject of Keats' poem? Is it really about fear, or is fear only part of the universal problem concerning the conflict between peoples' desire for fulfillment and permanence and the world's frustration and brevity?

## TECHNIQUES
### Simile, the Stated Comparison

In the second stanza of "Country Night," Selma Robinson states, "The house was like a ship that slowly listed." Through this comparison the reader can share the woman's fear-caused sensations. The house takes on the qualities of a ship on a rolling sea. The woman is so upset mentally and physically that the house seems to rock beneath her just as a ship at sea rises and falls with each swell. Poets often make statements and convey ideas and sensations through comparison. Stated comparisons indicated by *like* or *as* are called "similes." They are essential to poetry, for through them the poet is able to convey what is unfamiliar to the reader in terms of something familiar. The study questions (below) call your attention to several more similes.

### Country Night

**1.** What precautions did the woman take against the night? Explain why they were rational or irrational.

**2.** How does the simile in the second stanza show the extent and nature of her fear?

### House Fear

**1.** Is Frost's poem humorous or serious?

**2.** Are the actions described familiar or strange?

### The Oft-Repeated Dream

**1.** How is the title related to the subject and meaning of the poem?

**2.** How does the simile in the second stanza point up the foolishness of her fear?

### The Lady

**1.** In what ways does the poem show the woman to be "a lady"?

**2.** What effect is achieved by the short lines?

### The Warning

**1.** The poem is a "cinquain," a name for a five-line poem. Notice that the first line has one stress; the second, two; the third, three; the fourth, four; and the last line, one. What effect does this rhythm have on the reader?

**2.** What reaction to fear is suggested in these few lines?

### When I Have Fears
### That I May Cease To Be

**1.** How are Keats' fears similar to those that most people have about life?

**2.** Explain the simile in line four; how does it make his fears more urgent?

### The Panther Possible

**1.** What are the stories told about the mountain lion?

**2.** Is the panther that frightens the boy real or imagined?

### Suicide Pond

**1.** How important is the title to the poem?

**2.** What qualities about the pond make it seem a fearful place?

## IMPLICATIONS

The following statements are matters of opinion. Think back over the poems that present people and their fears. What then are your reactions to the following propositions?

**1.** The earlier poems in this section deal with the unreasoning, panicky fear triggered by a moment. Keats is speaking of a fear that comes from unsureness of life in general. The second kind of fear is less dramatic but a more devastating fear to have.

**2.** People fear their "unknowns." The things with which they are familiar hold no fears.

**3.** The real roots of fear lie deep in each person's insecurities.

**4.** Fear is an emotion that eventually kills the adventurous spirit.

# PRIVATE MOODS

To explore the depths of our deepest emotions and to understand their intensity are the unfailing challenges accepted by storyteller and poet, theologian and psychologist, sculptor and painter. Painters, like writers, make their statements about the mysteries of private moods in several ways: They may record every detail that they can to hold the mood in place for you to see it too; they may put down only those details that contribute to a particular view so that you see through their eyes some quality that might otherwise be overlooked; or they may speak in a kind of cryptograph, putting together bits and pieces that seem very unrelated so that you must work with them in solving the problem of a highly individual view of life.

In this gallery there is a wide range of private moods and artists' statements about them. The notes will guide you somewhat, but the real work of understanding is a private task you must do alone.

Van Gogh knew much about despair, and this painting is edged with the strong line of his intense sympathy.

DESPAIR
*Vincent Van Gogh*

264

THE FOLLY OF FEAR
*Francisco Goya*
*National Gallery of Art, Washington, D.C.,*
*Rosenwald Collection*

The magnificent Spanish printmaker
Goya explored many human emotions,
both public and private,
and was often disgusted
with what he saw. In his prints
the cruelty, the pettiness,
the utter stupidity of mankind
is thoroughly exposed.
Notice the small face at the end
of the specter's arm. Could it suggest
the unreality of the great figure
which has terrified the foolish men?

The modern painter Vickrey
deals in symbols. What private mood
is indicated by a child's game played
over a tension-filled pattern
on an empty road leading nowhere?

HOPSCOTCH   *Robert Vickrey*

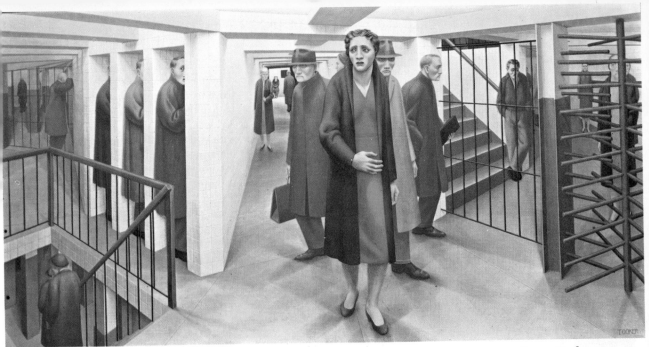

THE SUBWAY   *George Tooker*
*1950, Egg Tempera on composition*
*board, Collection of the Whitney*
*Museum of American Art, New York*

The cold efficiency of a city subway disturbs many observers.
But few have made as pointed a statement about it
as the painter Tooker. His is a lonely crowd
with completely uncommunicating private moods.

This view of the moon
over harbor waters
not only tells its own story
but records the romantic
ideas about moods enjoyed
by the nineteenth century.

PAST AND PRESENT, NO. 3
*Augustus Egg*
*Reproduced by courtesy*
*of The Tate Gallery, London*

One of the most serene occupations of the civilized world
is that of watching fish swim in an aquarium. The fine modern French
painter Henri Matisse has caught this private mood in depth.

WOMAN BEFORE AN AQUARIUM
*Henri Matisse*

AN APRIL MOOD
*Charles Burchfield*
*1946/55, Watercolor,*
*Collection of the Whitney Museum*
*of American Art, New York,*
*gift of Mr. and Mrs. Lawrence A. Fleischman*

What is the mood of April?
For Burchfield it is life awakening
out of winter bareness
and the restlessness of spring.
The coming storm will nourish
new life and new dreams.

A rare and lovely private mood
has been captured by Chapin
as he shows Ruby Green singing.
The contentment and poise
of the figure
contrast with the surging spirit
of the young singer's
uplifted head.

RUBY GREEN SINGING
*James Chapin*

CHAMBERED NAUTILUS
*Andrew Wyeth*

Quietness and morning, contentment serenely contained
within the canopied bed; the artist compares the moment
to the perfection of the sea's chambered nautilus,
with its graceful spiral.

# ANGER AND HATRED

Anger is probably the most vivid and easily recognized of the emotions. It may burst suddenly, blocking out love, understanding, and reason. Or like a long-burning coal it may steadily burn and slowly consume the individual's soul.

What is the nature of anger?
What can it do to body and soul?
If anger became incarnate,
what would it be?

## The Black Panther

There is a panther caged within my breast;
But what his name, there is no breast shall know
Save mine, nor what it is that drives him so,
Backward and forward, in relentless quest—
That silent rage, baffled but unsuppressed,          5
The soft pad of those stealthy feet that go
Over my body's prison to and fro,
Trying the walls forever without rest.
All day I feed him with my living heart;
But when the night puts forth her dreams and stars   10
The inexorable Frenzy reawakes:
His wrath is hurled upon the trembling bars,
The eternal passion stretches me apart,
And I lie silent—but my body shakes.

JOHN HALL WHEELOCK
as printed in *Home Book of Modern Verse*

"The Black Panther" is reprinted by permission of Charles Scribner's Sons from THE BLACK PANTHER by John Hall Wheelock. Copyright 1922 Charles Scribner's Sons; renewal copyright 1950 John Hall Wheelock.

Not many people can keep anger shut up within themselves. Anger calls for action. What do you wish to happen to those who have upset you?

## The Traveler's Curse After Misdirection

May they wander stage by stage
On the same vain pilgrimage,
Stumbling on, age after age,
Night and day, mile after mile,
At each and every step, a stile;[1]          5
At each and every stile, withal,
May they catch their feet and fall;
At each and every fall they take,
May a bone within them break;
And may the bones that break within          10
Not be, for variation's sake,
Now rib, now thigh, now arm, now shin,
But always, without fail, THE NECK.

ROBERT GRAVES
from the Welsh

From *Collected Poems* by Robert Graves. Published by Doubleday & Company, Inc. and Cassell & Company, Ltd. Reprinted by permission of A. P. Watt & Son and International Authors N. V.

1. **stile**\stäil\ a set of steps for crossing over a fence.

Anger may explode so suddenly and violently that it shatters momentarily one's deepest principles. Here the poet fears what one day may happen if he loses control of his feelings.

## Mood

I think an impulse stronger than my mind
May some day grasp a knife, unloose a vial,
Or with a little leaden ball unbind
The cords that tie me to the rank and file.
My hands grow quarrelsome with bitterness,          5
And darkly bent upon the final fray;
Night with its stars upon a grave seems less
Indecent than the too complacent day.

God knows I would be kind, let live, speak fair,
Requite an honest debt with more than just,          10
And love for Christ's dear sake these shapes that wear
A pride that had its genesis in dust,—
The meek are promised much in a book I know
But one grows weary turning cheek to blow.

COUNTÉE CULLEN

"Mood" from *On These I Stand* by Countee Cullen. Copyright 1929 by Harper & Row, Publishers, Inc. Renewed © 1957 by Ida M. Cullen.

Poets not only deal with the anatomy of anger, but they also show the depths of submerged anger, the kind people feel toward unexplained evil and suffering.

## Does It Matter

Does it matter?—losing your leg? . . .
For people will always be kind;
And you need not show that you mind
When the others come in after hunting
To gobble their muffins and eggs.                    5

Does it matter?—losing your sight? . . .
There's such splendid work for the blind;
And people will always be kind,
As you sit on the terrace remembering
And turning your face to the light.                    10

Do they matter?—those dreams from the pit? . . .
You can drink and forget and be glad;
And people won't say that you're mad;
For they know that you've fought for your country,
And no one will worry a bit!                    15

SIEGFRIED SASSOON

From *Collected Poems* by Siegfried Sassoon.
All Rights Reserved. Reprinted by permission
of The Viking Press, Inc.

Anger is, of course,
the soil in which the seed of hatred grows.

## Hate

My enemy came nigh,
And I
Stared fiercely in his face.
My lips went writhing back in a grimace,
And stern I watched him with a narrow eye.                    5
Then, as I turned away, my enemy,
That bitter heart and savage, said to me:
"Some day, when this is past,
When all the arrows that we have are cast,
We may ask one another why we hate,                    10
And fail to find a story to relate.
It may seem to us then a mystery
That we could hate each other."

Thus said he,                    15
And did not turn away,
Waiting to hear what I might have to say.
But I fled quickly, fearing if I stayed
I might have kissed him as I would a maid.

JAMES STEPHENS

What is it like to be a black person in a "white" world?

# The White House

Your door is shut against my tightened face,
And I am sharp as steel with discontent;
But I possess the courage and the grace
To bear my anger proudly and unbent.
The pavement slabs burn loose beneath my feet,     5
A chafing savage, down the decent street;
And passion rends my vitals as I pass,
Where boldly shines your shuttered door of glass.
Oh, I must search for wisdom every hour,
Deep in my wrathful bosom sore and raw,     10
And find in it the superhuman power
To hold me to the letter of your law!
Oh, I must keep my heart inviolate[1]
Against the potent poison of your hate.

CLAUDE MCKAY

---

1. **inviolate**\ĭn ▲vai·ə·lat\ untouched; undisturbed.

---

Reprinted with the permission of Twayne Publishers, a division of G. K. Hall & Company, Boston.

A frustrating experience—striking out in anger at things about you and connecting only with air.

# *Waves Against a Dog*

Had I had the power I would have stretched
that wave on this rock and bitten it. But now
I have to thrust a jaw at this foam. Salting
my teeth, adultering[1] my saliva. And my teeth
get hold of just nothing, just whiteness and sun.          5

Afraid? Not I. Not of this salty anger. I have
killed a lot in my life. Not frightened. Not I.
But nothing to my teeth, just touch and goes
this big blue wave. Afraid of me. Circles my feet.
Vanishes. Must catch before it breaks on the rock. 10

Dive. What strength! I'm hurled back to the rock,
whirling round, looking at the hill, not the sea.
Dive again. A large blue tongue shows me
the pattern of the rocks, puts me on my feet,
there. Soaked. If only I had teeth. If only.               15

To bite this blueness to pieces, to pierce this
blue big belly, take my revenge, bite—If.
But now I cannot even touch: the salt teases me.
I look around: always the white foam. And I bark.
I bark while the rock ducks under another wave.  20

TANER BAYBARS

---

1. **adultering**\ə ˈdəl·tər·iŋ\ shortened from *adulterating;*
making impure by adding a foreign or inferior substance.

---

"Waves Against a Dog" reprinted by permission of Taner Baybars.
Copyright 1964.

Even in anger's rich soil, hatred will wither.
It must be watered and nourished faithfully.

What price hatred?
Haters, clothed in self-righteousness,
isolate themselves from other people.
Is hatred worth it?

# A Poison Tree

I was angry with my friend:
I told my wrath, my wrath did end.
I was angry with my foe:
I told it not, my wrath did grow.

And I watered it in fears          5
Night and morning with my tears,
And I sunned it with smiles
And with soft deceitful wiles.

And it grew both day and night,
Till it bore an apple bright,          10
And my foe beheld it shine,
And he knew that it was mine.

And into my garden stole
When the night had veiled the pole;
In the morning, glad I see          15
My foe outstretched beneath the tree.

WILLIAM BLAKE

# Without a Cloak

Hate has a fashionable cut.
    It is the garment man agrees on,
Snug, colorful, the proper weight
    For comfort in an icy season.

And it is weatherproof, they say—          5
    Becoming, also, to the spirit.
I fetched Hate homeward yesterday,
    But there it hangs. I cannot wear it.

It is a dress that suits me ill,
    However much the mode sustains me          10
At once too ample and too small,
    It trips, bewilders, and confines me.

And in my blood do fevers flow,
    Corruptive, where the fabric presses,
Till I must pluck it off as though          15
    It were the burning shirt of Nessus.[1]

Proud walk the people folded warm
    In Hate. They need not pray for spring.
But threadbare do I face the storm
    Or hug my hearthstone, shivering.          20

PHYLLIS MC GINLEY

---

1. Putting on a magic shirt soaked in the blood of
the centaur **Nessus**\\*nĕ•səs\\, the Greek hero Hercules
was burned to death by it. Hence, a "shirt of Nessus"
is a garment that might produce a similar result.

From *Times Three* by Phyllis McGinley. Copyright 1947 by
Phyllis McGinley. Originally appeared in *The New Yorker.* Reprinted by permission of The Viking Press, Inc.

🕊 Stephen Crane creates a ghastly image
of the results of prolonged, bitter, and terrible emotion.

## The Heart

In the desert
I saw a creature, naked, bestial,
Who, squatting upon the ground,
Held his heart in his hands,
And ate of it.                                                     5
I said, "Is it good, friend?"
"It is bitter—bitter," he answered;
"But I like it
Because it is bitter,
And because it is my heart."                                      10

STEPHEN CRANE

---

### UNDERSTANDING POETRY
*Finding the Theme*

Lyric poets not only recreate their experience, but they also tell or imply what the experience means to them. Wheelock, for example, does not merely recreate the experience of being greatly angered; he tells, in a general way, that his unexpressed anger torments him mentally and physically:

> The eternal passion stretched me apart,
> And I lie silent but my body shakes.

Here is an example of a poet explicitly stating the *theme, the idea or attitude expressed in a poem.* But poets do not always state their themes openly. Sometimes they are implied in the key words, in the images—similes and metaphors— and in the rhythm of the poem. Find one other poem in this section in which the theme seems to be definitely stated by a phrase or line in the poem.

### TECHNIQUES
*Metaphor, the Implied Comparison*

Specific poems in this section compare anger and hatred to a black panther, a poison tree, and a very modish coat. These comparisons differ from similes primarily in that they are not announced by *like* or *as.* In each case they imply that the two objects compared are identical with each other. The poet *implies* that anger and hatred share some action(s) or quality(ies), or both in common with a panther, a tree, a coat. Such implied comparisons are called "metaphors." Metaphor is the only way we have of expressing inner reactions for which we have no meaningful words. They demand that the reader take his knowledge of familiar things and apply it to his understanding of unfamiliar things.

Discuss some of the metaphors you find vivid and appropriate.

*The Black Panther*

1. Why is the title a good one? Does it define the true subject?

2. What details about the panther are mentioned in the poem? How do they make the nature of anger clearer?

*The Traveler's Curse After Misdirection*

1. How important is the poem's title to the meaning?

2. Why does Graves withhold the full extent of his anger until the last line?

3. Why is the accelerating pace of the rhythm, line by line, appropriate to the meaning of the lines?

*Mood*

1. What two forces does the poet feel in conflict within himself? Point out and explain the lines in which he makes this tension clear.

2. What does he mean when he says "a little leaden ball" may "unbind the cords that tie me to the rank and file"?

*Does It Matter*

1. How does the poet answer the question in his title? Why does he repeat it three times?

2. What actually happened to him?

3. Why aren't the people's kindnesses enough?

4. What is the poet implying about war?

*Hate*

1. Contrast the picture the poet gives of himself in the first seven lines with the calm, good reason of his enemy in the next six lines.

2. What strange thing does Stephens observe about hatred? Can you state it in one sentence?

*The White House*

1. How does the interpretation of the poem change if you know that the poet is a black American?

2. What is the speaker afraid that his anger may do to him?

*Waves Against a Dog*

1. Who is the speaker? What is he describing?

2. What situations in human life are comparable to this one?

*A Poison Tree*

1. Explain the contrast in the first stanza.

2. Why is the metaphor announced in the title a good one for the quality of hatred Blake is portraying?

3. Blake starts seven lines with *and;* what quality does this repetition give the poem?

4. What kind of rhythm is Blake using? What is its effect?

*Without a Cloak*

1. Compare the two subjects of the central metaphor as they progress point by point throughout the poem.

2. What reasons does the poet give for rejecting the cloak?

3. In several stanzas, the second and the fourth lines do not rhyme precisely. Such rhymes are called *slant* rhymes. What quality do they give the poem?

*The Heart*

1. What does the title tell about the subject matter and theme of the poem?

2. What is Crane saying about human nature?

## IMPLICATIONS

Consider the poems you have just read on anger. Would you agree or disagree with the following statements in light of what the poets have presented?

1. Anger is an emotion that wells up inside people until they feel they must spew it out.

2. Anger tends to make people irrational in what they say and do.

3. People enjoy being angry and tend to want to nourish their hatred rather than overcome it.

4. Anger may be constructive as well as destructive.

5. Anger serves no useful purpose in human life, destroying the person who harbors it.

6. Poetry portraying anger makes readers see their own moments of anger in a new light.

## WORDS

All nouns may be classified either as *abstract* nouns—things that cannot be touched, smelled, tasted, heard, or seen; or as *concrete* nouns—words that label things observable through the senses. The moods of *restlessness, fear, anger,* and *hatred* are abstractions, and the words which label them are abstract nouns. The words *wheel, wind, sea, train* are concrete nouns which refer to something tangible. When writers use such words as *sea* and *wind,* they depend upon readers to see, feel, and hear the sea and wind.

Concrete nouns, then, because they label something observable, evoke an image. Part of the value of the image is the associations the reader makes. Look up the word *sea* in the dictionary. A dictionary definition generally gives first the specific, or denotative, meaning of a word. What is the denotative meaning of *sea?* But the word *sea* also suggests, or connotes, travel, vastness, freedom, the unknown. The specific meaning, literal meaning, is the *denotation* of a word. The additional associations, the emotional colorings, are the *connotations* of a word. Although words have generally the same denotative meanings for most people, words may not produce the same connotations. From the group of poems you have just read, make a list of nouns which suggest restlessness, fear, anger, and hatred. What connotations does each word produce?

**SORROW** Pain, disillusionment, and death are ever with people. Life is tinged with sorrow. Even in moments of greatest happiness it is not far away but lies like an undercurrent ready to break forth. Much of peoples' greatest music, painting, and poetry is shot through with sorrow for the sufferings of humankind. Some of the great music of the world, such as Tchaikovsky's *Pathétique* Symphony, throbs darkly, mournfully. The Renaissance painters turned to the intimate, frequent incidents of sorrowing people found in the Bible stories. And much of the world's greatest poetry evokes beauty through peoples' sorrows.

Sorrow and beauty
are inevitably mixed,
as Frost shows.

## My November Guest

My Sorrow, when she's here with me,
  Thinks these dark days of autumn rain
Are beautiful as days can be;
She loves the bare, the withered tree;
  She walks the sodden[1] pasture lane.    5

Her pleasure will not let me stay.
  She talks and I am fain to list:[2]
She's glad the birds are gone away,
She's glad her simple worsted grey
  Is silver now with clinging mist.    10

The desolate, deserted trees,
  The faded earth, the heavy sky,
The beauties she so truly sees,
She thinks I have no eye for these,
  And vexes me for reason why.    15

Not yesterday I learned to know
  The love of bare November days
Before the coming of the snow,
But it were vain to tell her so,
  And they are better for her praise.    20

ROBERT FROST

From THE POETRY OF ROBERT FROST edited by Edward Connery Lathem. Copyright 1916, 1934, © 1969 by Holt, Rinehart and Winston, Inc. Copyright 1944, © 1962 by Robert Frost. Reprinted by permission of Holt, Rinehart and Winston, Inc.

1. **sodden**\ˈsŏ·dən\ rain-soaked and muddy.
2. **fain**\fān\ pleased and eager. **list,** listen.

The sea has many faces, many moods.
The sounds of wind and wave in never-ending ebb and flow
chill Joyce with sadness.

## The Noise of Waters

All day I hear the noise of waters
   Making moan,
Sad as the sea-bird is, when, going
   Forth alone,
He hears the winds cry to the waters'     5
   Monotone.

The grey winds, the cold winds are blowing
   Where I go.
I hear the noise of many waters
   Far below.     10
All day, all night, I hear them flowing
   To and fro.

JAMES JOYCE

From *Collected Poems* by James Joyce. Copyright 1918 by B. W. Huebsch, 1946 by Nora Joyce. Reprinted by permission of The Viking Press, Inc.

The loss of loved ones through death
has long been a sorrow explored in poetry.

## Music I Heard

Music I heard with you was more than music,
And bread I broke with you was more than bread.
Now that I am without you, all is desolate,
All that was once so beautiful is dead.

Your hands once touched this table and this silver,     5
And I have seen your fingers hold this glass.
These things do not remember you, beloved:
And yet your touch upon them will not pass.

For it was in my heart you moved among them,
And blessed them with your hands and with your eyes.   10
And in my heart they will remember always:
They knew you once, O beautiful and wise!

CONRAD AIKEN

From *Collected Poems* by Conrad Aiken. Copyright 1953, © 1970 by Conrad Aiken. Reprinted by permission of Oxford University Press, Inc.

Coarse imagery in the following poem provides
a jarring impression of the funeral ritual.

# *The Widow*

The Hammond Organ lubricates the air.
The kind mortician conducts her to her place
of honor. A man with a painted puppet's face
they say is her husband's face is obviously there

in front of her. She would have the casket                    5
closed, but his sister would not. The minister cries
how gloriously the man is dead who lies
before him daily with a face like plastic,

prays that God who took him out of order
will keep his soul from torment, will adorn him          10
with a crown of stars, will hold with those that mourn him.
It is not hard, she thinks, but it will be harder.

The wail of the Hammond weakens, her mind goes black,
turning quickly out of the moment meanders
on curious ways. She looks at his nose. She wonders      15
if they went and slit the good blue suit in the back

and if his shoes are tied, if he has on
the socks they didn't ask for but she sent,
if they still use pennies, decides of course they don't,
hopes they will have their fill and be done with him soon.     20

It would not be fair to say she is not grieving.
She did not want to come, but she is aware
how there will be silence, there will be pleasures to bear
in silence, and dark creatures unbehaving.

She did not want to come. She will not be taken          25
to tears. But she is aware some moment will crush
the brain suddenly, that she will go home and wish
burglars had come there and the blind windows were broken.

MILLER WILLIAMS

From SO LONG AT THE FAIR by Miller Williams. Copyright © 1968, 1967,
1966, 1965, 1964, 1963, 1960, 1958 by Miller Williams. Published by E. P.
Dutton & Co., Inc. and reprinted with their permission.

The mind will absorb just so much sorrow, and then something must happen.
The next two poems tell something about the effect of deep grief on a person.

## After Great Pain a Formal Feeling Comes

After great pain a formal feeling comes—
The nerves sit ceremonious like tombs;
The stiff heart questions—was it He that bore?
And yesterday—or centuries before?

The feet mechanical                                    5
Go round a wooden way
Of ground or air or Ought, regardless grown,
A quartz contentment like a stone.

This is the hour of lead
Remembered if outlived,                               10
As freezing persons recollect the snow—
First chill, then stupor, then the letting go.

EMILY DICKINSON

Copyright, 1929, by Martha Dickinson Bianchi. Copyright, ©
1957, by Mary L. Hampson. From *The Poems of Emily Dickinson* by Emily Dickinson by permission of Little, Brown & Co.

## The Woodspurge

The wind flapped loose, the wind was still,
Shaken out dead from tree and hill:
I had walked on at the wind's will,
I sat now, for the wind was still.

Between my knees my forehead was,—             5
My lips, drawn in, said not Alas!
My hair was over in the grass,
My naked ears heard the day pass.

My eyes, wide open, had the run
Of some ten weeds to fix upon;                      10
Among those few, out of the sun,
The woodspurge[1] flowered, three cups in one.

From perfect grief there need not be
Wisdom or even memory:
One thing that learnt remains to me,—            15
The woodspurge has a cup of three.

DANTE ROSSETTI

1. **woodspurge**\ˈwu̇d ˌspərj\ a European plant with
greenish-yellow flowers in clusters of three.

At times all of nature
seems to mirror a person's grief.
To Shelley, sorrow is stark and violent.

# A Dirge

Rough wind, that moanest loud
   Grief too sad for song;
Wild wind, when sullen cloud
   Knells[1] all the night long;
Sad storm, whose tears are vain,
   Bare woods, whose branches strain,
Deep caves and dreary main,[2]—
   Wail, for the world's wrong!

PERCY BYSSHE SHELLEY

----

1. **knell**\něl\ to sound a death bell to make
a similar mournful sound or sign.
2. **main,** sea or ocean.

## UNDERSTANDING POETRY

*Structure*

The structure of a poem is the way its topics, scenes, statements, and ideas are arranged. To see how these parts are related to form one dominant impression and meaning adds greatly to one's enjoyment of poetry. Most poems are composed of stanzas which are easily recognized because of their fixed pattern of lines and rhymes. In many poems the stanzas also show the thought divisions of the poem, each stanza developing some different aspect of the poet's subject and theme.

An awareness of structure can help you in two ways. On the one hand, if you are not sure of a poem's subject and theme after several readings, examine each part or stanza individually, because it is sometimes much easier to work up from a knowledge of the parts to a grasp of the whole. On the other hand, if you believe that you grasp the meaning of the poem after a reading or two, you may test your belief by asking yourself how (and sometimes *if*) each stanza contributed to the meaning you have found.

## TECHNIQUES

*Rhythm and Sound Effects*

As noted earlier, the poet varies the basic rhythm of a poem by substituting other *feet* and by using rhyme, principally *end-rhyme*. But poets often make use of other devices, such as alliteration, assonance, and consonance, in place of actual rhyme within poems. These devices not only may delight the ear but also may add interesting sub-rhythms to highlight an action, emotion, or key word. Alliteration may be defined as the repetition of similar initial consonant sounds ("Making moan"); assonance as the repetition of identical vowel sounds ("Monotone"); consonance as the repetition of the same consonants but not the same vowels, such as *"try"* and *"tree."*

Find examples of alliteration in "The Noise of Waters," "The Dirge," "After Great Pain a Formal Feeling Comes," and "The Woodspurge." Find examples of assonance in "The Noise of Waters."

## My November Guest

1. What does the title have to do with the poem?

2. What reward does sorrow bring to Frost?

3. What images carry the feeling of November?

## The Noise of Waters

1. What kind of "seascape" is Joyce describing?

2. What is the basic sound quality of the rhyming words in the poem?

3. How does the rhythm affect the mood? Especially what is the rhythmic effect of the short lines?

## Music I Heard

1. What are the intimate details that the poet remembers which bring to him an awareness of his loss?

2. Is the language conversational or elevated, natural or unnatural, strained or easy?

## The Widow

1. How does the tone of this poem compare with the tone of "Music I Heard"?

2. What details give the reader a concrete impression of the funeral service and of the widow's thoughts?

## After Great Pain a Formal Feeling Comes

1. According to the poem, what effects do sorrow and pain have upon one's mind? upon one's actions? How do the similes in lines 2 and 8 help or hinder the meaning?

2. Pick out examples of Dickinson's use of slant rhymes, assonance, and consonance in the poem.

## The Woodspurge

1. What does the mind do when it is overwhelmed with grief?

2. What is the memory that is left from grief?

## A Dirge

1. What does the title mean in relation to the poem?

2. What kind of night is Shelley describing?

3. What particular sounds are emphasized in the poem? What effect do they have?

4. Why does Shelley use so many spondees?

## IMPLICATIONS

In light of the poems you have just read, consider your reactions to the following statements. Do you accept them or reject them?

1. Sorrow can be transmitted through a series of sound qualities and images of nature without the poet's directly mentioning it.

2. Sorrow, in spite of its unpleasantness, has the ability to make the individual see beauty where he could not see it before.

3. Sorrow makes people seek certain kinds of sights and sounds to harmonize with their moods.

4. After a certain amount of sorrow the human mind rebels and refuses to react.

5. Intense sorrow may intensify one's reactions to seemingly trivial things around one.

6. In moods of depression or melancholy, we tend to remind ourselves of all the defects we have and all the unpleasant things that have happened to us.

**NOSTALGIA** People are able to compare and to contrast
the "here and now" with the "there and then." They can think back to childhood,
remember the places they have been, recall the people they used to know.
When peoples' memories cause them to yearn wistfully to return to the past,
they are moved by a mixture of joy and sadness called nostalgia. Nostalgia is perhaps
composed of regret, desire, and sorrow at the realization of the inevitability
of change. Poets have delighted in summoning nostalgia,
perhaps because poetry itself so often grows out of the vision
of "what might be" against the background of "what is."

Did you ever see an old house and wonder
about the people who lived and loved
and worked and died there?

## The House
## on the Hill

They are all gone away,
  The House is shut and still,
There is nothing more to say.

Through broken walls and gray
  The winds blow bleak and shrill;    5
They are all gone away.

Nor is there only one today
  To speak them good or ill:
There is nothing more to say.

Why is it then we stray      10
  Around that sunken sill?
They are all gone away,

And our poor fancy-play
  For them is wasted skill:
There is nothing more to say.      15

There is ruin and decay
  In the House on the Hill:
They are all gone away,
There is nothing more to say.

E. A. ROBINSON

**They Are All Gone Away** *by Stanford W. Williamson.*
*He was inspired by the poem "The House on the Hill."*

The quality of a particular kind of day
can make a person long for a way of life
he or she formerly knew.

# The West Wind

It's a warm wind, the west wind, full of birds' cries;
I never hear the west wind but tears are in my eyes.
For it comes from the west lands, the old brown hills,
And April's in the west wind, and daffodils.

It's a fine land, the west land, for hearts as tired as mine,     5
Apple orchards blossom there, and the air's like wine.
There is cool green grass there, where men may lie at rest,
And the thrushes are in song there, fluting[1] from the nest.

"Will ye not come home brother: Ye have been long away,
It's April, and blossom time, and white is the May;     10
And bright is the sun, brother, and warm is the rain—
Will ye not come home, brother, home to us again?

"The young corn is green, brother, where the rabbits run,
It's blue sky, and white clouds, and warm rain and sun.
It's song to a man's soul, brother, fire to a man's brain,     15
To hear the wild bees and see the merry spring again.

"Larks are singing in the west, brother, above the green wheat,
So will ye not come home, brother, and rest your tired feet?
I've balm for bruised hearts, brother, sleep for aching eyes,"
Says the warm wind, the west wind, full of birds' cries.     20

It's the white road westwards is the road I must tread
To the green grass, the cool grass, and rest for heart and head,
To violets and the brown brooks and the thrushes' song,
In the fine land, the west land, the land where I belong.

JOHN MASEFIELD

---

1. **flute**\flūt\ to sing with an effect like the sound of a flute.

---

Reprinted with permission of the publisher from *Collected Poems*
by John Masefield. Copyright 1912 by The Macmillan Company,
Renewed 1940 by John Masefield.

In spring, Browning's thoughts turn from Italy
where he is to memories of spring in England.

## Home Thoughts from Abroad

Oh, to be in England now that April's there,
And whoever wakes in England sees, some morning, unaware,
That the lowest boughs and the brushwood sheaf
Round the elm-tree bole[1] are in tiny leaf,
While the chaffinch[2] sings on the orchard bough                5
In England—now!

And after April, when May follows,
And the white throat[3] builds, and all the swallows!
Hark, where my blossomed pear-tree in the hedge
Leans to the fields and scatters on the clover              10
Blossoms and dewdrops—at the bent-spray's[4] edge—
That's the wise thrush; he sings each song twice over,
Lest you should think he never could recapture
The first fine careless rapture!
And, though the fields look rough with hoary[5] dew,          15
All will be gay when noontide wakes anew
The buttercups, the little children's dower,[6]
—Far brighter than this gaudy melon-flower!

**ROBERT BROWNING**

---

1. **bole**\bōl\ a tree trunk.
2. **chaffinch**\ˈchǎ·fǐnch\ a colorful European finch
with a pleasing song.
3. **white throat**, a European gray and blue warbler.
4. **bent-spray**, grass clump or cluster.
5. **hoary**\ˈhō·rē\ white, gray
6. **dower**\daʊr\ gift given by nature.

 Edna St. Vincent Millay never outgrew her passion for the seacoast of New England
where she grew up. In this poem she succeeds in communicating that deep, almost unbearable anguish
that nostalgia can become when something one desires desperately is unobtainable.

## Inland

People that build their houses inland,
    People that buy a plot of ground
Shaped like a house, and build a house there,
    Far from the sea-board, far from the sound

Of water sucking the hollow ledges,          5
    Tons of water striking the shore,—
What do they long for, as I long for
    One salt smell of the sea once more?

People the waves have not awakened,
    Spanking the boats at the harbour's head,   10

What do they long for, as I long for,
    Starting up in my inland bed,

Beating the narrow walls, and finding
    Neither a window nor a door,
Screaming to God for death by drowning,—  15
    One salt taste of the sea once more?

**EDNA ST. VINCENT MILLAY**

---

From *Collected Poems*, Harper & Row. Copyright 1921, 1949
by Edna St. Vincent Millay.

When young, people look forward to maturity.
When mature, they often look back wistfully, remembering the youthful times
that are past. This kind of nostalgia is well expressed
by one of America's favorite nineteenth-century poets.

# My Lost Youth

Often I think of the beautiful town
    That is seated by the sea;
Often in thought go up and down
The pleasant streets of that dear old town,
      And my youth comes back to me.          5
        And a verse of a Lapland[1] song
        Is haunting my memory still:
        "A boy's will is the wind's will,
And the thoughts of youth are long, long thoughts."

I can see the shadowy lines of its trees,        10
    And catch, in sudden gleams,
The sheen of the far-surrounding seas,
And islands that were the Hesperides[2]
    Of all my boyish dreams.
        And the burden of that old song,      15
        It murmurs and whispers still:
        "A boy's will is the wind's will,
And the thoughts of youth are long, long thoughts."

I remember the black wharves and the slips,
    And the sea tides tossing free;      20
And Spanish sailors with bearded lips,
And the beauty and mystery of the ships,
    And the magic of the sea.
        And the voice of that wayward song
        Is singing and saying still:      25
        "A boy's will is the wind's will,
And the thoughts of youth are long, long thoughts."

I remember the bulwarks by the shore,
    And the fort upon the hill;
The sunrise gun, with its hollow roar,      30
The drumbeat repeated o'er and o'er,
    And the bugle wild and shrill.

---

1. **Lapland**\ˈlăp·lănd\ the region of the Scandinavian
peninsula above the Arctic Circle.
2. **Hesperides**\hĕs ˈpā·rĭ ˈdēz\ the mythical blessed
islands far to the west in early Greek and Latin story.

And the music of that old song
    Throbs in my memory still:
    "A boy's will is the wind's will,                                   35
And the thoughts of youth are long, long thoughts."

I remember the sea fight far away,
    How it thundered o'er the tide!
And the dead captains, as they lay
In their graves, o'erlooking the tranquil bay              40
    Where they in battle died.
        And the sound of that mournful song
        Goes through me with a thrill:
        "A boy's will is the wind's will,
And the thoughts of youth are long, long thoughts."   45

I can see the breezy dome of groves,
    The shadows of Deering's Woods;[3]
And the friendships old and the early loves
Come back with a Sabbath sound, as of doves
    In quiet neighborhoods.                                        50
        And the verse of that sweet old song,
        It flutters and murmurs still:
        "A boy's will is the wind's will,
And the thoughts of youth are long, long thoughts."

I remember the gleams and glooms that dart         55
    Across the schoolboy's brain;
The song and the silence in the heart,
That in part are prophecies, and in part
    Are longings wild and vain.
        And the voice of that fitful song                       60
        Sings on, and is never still:
        "A boy's will is the wind's will,
And the thoughts of youth are long, long thoughts."

There are things of which I may not speak;
    There are dreams that cannot die;                       65
There are thoughts that make the strong heart weak,
And bring a pallor into the cheek,
    And a mist before the eye.
        And the words of that fatal song
        Come over me like a chill:                               70
        "A boy's will is the wind's will,
And the thoughts of youth are long, long thoughts."

Strange to me now are the forms I meet
    When I visit the dear old town;

---

3. **Deering's Woods,** a woods near Portland, Maine.

But the native air is pure and sweet, 75
And the trees that o'ershadow each well-known street,
  As they balance up and down,
    Are singing the beautiful song,
    Are sighing and whispering still:
    "A boy's will is the wind's will, 80
And the thoughts of youth are long, long thoughts."

And Deering's Woods are fresh and fair,
  And with joy that is almost pain
My heart goes back to wander there,
And among the dreams of the days that were, 85
  I find my lost youth again.
    And the strange and beautiful song,
    The groves are repeating it still:
    "A boy's will is the wind's will,
And the thoughts of youth are long, long thoughts." 90

HENRY WADSWORTH LONGFELLOW

Similar in theme,
but not quite so gentle as "My Lost Youth,"
is Tennyson's "Break, Break, Break."

# *Break, Break, Break*

Break, break, break
  On thy cold gray stones, O Sea!
And I would that my tongue could utter
  The thoughts that arise in me.

O well for the fisherman's boy, 5
  That he shouts with his sister at play!
O well for the sailor lad,
  That he sings in his boat on the bay!

And the stately ships go on
  To their haven under the hill; 10
But O for the touch of a vanished hand,
  And the sound of a voice that is still!

Break, break, break,
  At the foot of thy crags, O Sea!
But the tender grace of a day that is dead 15
  Will never come back to me.

ALFRED, LORD TENNYSON

🜋 Sometimes the significance of certain acts is
understood only in retrospect.

# *Those Winter Sundays*

Sundays too my father got up early
and put his clothes on in the blueblack cold,
then with cracked hands that ached
from labor in the weekday weather made
banked fires blaze. No one ever thanked him.     5

I'd wake and hear the cold splintering, breaking.
When the rooms were warm, he'd call,
and slowly I would rise and dress,
fearing the chronic[1] angers of that house,

Speaking indifferently to him,     10
who had driven out the cold
and polished my good shoes as well.
What did I know, what did I know
of love's austere[2] and lonely offices?[3]

ROBERT HAYDEN

---

1. **chronic**\ˈkrŏn·ĭk\ ever present; always continuing.
2. **austere**\ŏ ˈstē(ə)r\ forbidding.
3. **offices**, duties.

---

"Those Winter Sundays" by Robert Hayden from SELECTED
POEMS. Copyright © 1966 by Robert Hayden. Reprinted by
permission of October House Inc.

## UNDERSTANDING POETRY

*Tone*

One of the oldest complaints in the world is,
"It's not what was said; it's the way it was said."
Such statements attest to an important truth verified every day: the tone of voice is an important ingredient in shaping human communication. But when language is written, the audible voice of the writer disappears. Does "no" on the printed page signify delight, dismay, resoluteness, anger, insolence, or ignorance? One no longer has the inflections and volume of the voice, facial expressions, and body gestures to help. The reader must depend upon the clues in the printed context in order to grasp the writer's tone—*her or his emotional attitude toward the subject.*

Even though these poems deal with nostalgia in general, each has its own unique attitude and emotional intensity. Sometimes poets will say that they are gay or sad; but more often they embody their tone in the rhythm (see page 171), choice of words, and images in the poem. Be alert to catch these clues as you read these poems and answer the study questions. (The term—tone—is also used to mean the poet's attitude toward his audience.)

## TECHNIQUES

### Diction and Imagery

Poetry, because it is so compressed, demands that poets choose their diction (their words) most carefully. Sometimes words strike the reader because they summon up vivid sense impressions: "Bleak and shrill"; "brown hills . . . cool green grass . . . white clouds, and warm rain and sun"; "chaffinch sings on the orchard bough"; "water sucking the hollow ledges . . . one salt smell"; "black wharves"; "cold gray stones." Sometimes poets surprise readers by using precise language in unusual ways: "waves . . . spanking the boats," "peace comes dropping slow," and "noon a purple glow." Such words and phrases that appeal to the senses and imagination are called imagery. (Because similes and metaphors appeal to the senses and imagination, they are images, too.) Poets who wish to share scenes and actions and feelings with readers use imagery that is sharp and definite. They select the right noun, adjective, verb, or adverb for the precise impression they desire.

### The House on the Hill

1. What effect does Robinson achieve by weaving the two melancholy refrains back and forth?

2. Why are so few rhymes used?

3. What specific images are especially appropriate for the mood?

### The West Wind

1. The poet suggests a whole series of pictures. Which are most picturesque and haunting? Which appeal to sight and which to sound?

2. How do the rhythm and the rhyme scheme affect the tone? What use does Masefield make of alliteration? assonance?

### Home Thoughts from Abroad

1. One memory seems to ignite another as the poet rushes onward to get them all down. What images call up specific sights and sounds? Are they pleasant or unpleasant?

2. What is the rhyme scheme? What variation in it makes it somewhat irregular?

### Inland

1. How does the title fit the poem?

2. What is the tone? Is nostalgia a pleasant or an unpleasant emotion in this poem? How many sentences are there and what is the dominant sound in the last line of each? What qualities of the sea are suggested?

### My Lost Youth

1. What are the sensations and thoughts that the poet remembers?

2. Does Longfellow state his theme? How? Where?

3. How does the tone of this poem differ from "Inland"?

4. Longfellow clearly illustrates the combination of repetition with variation which is so essential to keeping poetry from becoming monotonous. Lines 6–9 form a refrain. Why isn't it always the same?

### Break, Break, Break

1. What relation does the title have to the poem?

2. What pleasant things are mentioned?

3. What unpleasant images does Tennyson use and how do they affect the tone? What harsh sounds does he use and how do they affect the tone?

### Those Winter Sundays

1. As he thinks back to Sunday mornings, what does the speaker now understand about his father that he did not understand as a child?

2. What kind of feeling comes to your mind from the words "blueblack cold"?

## IMPLICATIONS

Reflect on the truth or falsity of the following statements in terms of the group of poems you have read in this mood.

1. Nostalgia is an enjoyable emotion.

2. Nostalgia is different from homesickness.

3. Nostalgia is usually a mood of older people. It seldom affects the young.

4. Without experiencing nostalgia occasionally, most people would be somewhat hard.

5. Things out of sight tend to be remembered in an idealized way.

**DELIGHT** is a sudden intensification of a sensation, an experience, or a relationship. A sniff of frying bacon, a crisp May morning, a loved one may unexpectedly evoke the feeling of delight. In expressing their delight, poets depend upon rich imagery and the lilting quality of sounds and rhythm. Poets often find their delight in a particular time of day. The first three poems are expressions of delight in different times of the day.

With fresh images, Housman exhorts the reader to share the delight of the morning.

### Reveille

Wake: the silver dusk returning
Up the beach of darkness brims,
And the ship of sunrise burning
Strands upon the eastern rims.[1]

Wake: the vaulted shadow shatters,          5
Trampled to the floor it spanned,
And the tent of night in tatters
Straws the sky-pavillioned land.

Up, lad, up, 'tis late for lying:
Hear the drums of morning play;          10
Hark, the empty highways crying
"Who'll beyond the hills away?"

Towns and countries woo together,
Forelands beacon, belfries call;
Never lad that trod on leather          15
Lived to feast his heart with all.

Up, lad, thews that lie and cumber[2]
Sunlit pallets[3] never thrive;
Morns abed and daylight slumber
Were not meant for man alive.          20

Clay lies still, but blood's a rover;
Breath's a ware that will not keep.
Up, lad: when the journey's over
There'll be time enough to sleep.

A. E. HOUSMAN

From "A Shropshire Lad"—Authorized Edition—from THE COLLECTED POEMS OF A. E. HOUSMAN. Copyright 1939, 1940, © 1959 by Holt, Rinehart and Winston, Inc. Copyright © 1967, 1968, by Robert E. Symons. Reprinted by permission of Holt, Rinehart and Winston, Inc.

1. The ship of sunrise appears as though stranded.
2. **thews**\thūz\ muscles, sinews. **cumber**\ˈkəm·bər\ clutter.
3. **pallet**\ˈpă·lət\ a thin straw mattress.

292

Like afternoon itself,
there is the slightest suggestion of drowsiness
about Millay's delight.

## Afternoon on a Hill

I will be the gladdest thing
    Under the sun!
I will touch a hundred flowers
    And not pick one.

I will look at cliffs and clouds     5
    With quiet eyes,
Watch the wind blow down the grass,
    And the grass rise.

And when lights begin to show
    Up from the town,
I will mark which must be mine,     10
    And then start down.

EDNA ST. VINCENT MILLAY

From COLLECTED POEMS, Harper & Row. Copyright 1917, 1921, 1934, 1945, 1948, 1962, by Edna St. Vincent Millay and Norma Millay Ellis.

In folklore and literature
the magic of the moon and its light
has long been celebrated
more than any other aspect of the night.

## Silver

Slowly, silently, now the moon
Walks the night in her silver shoon;[1]
This way, and that, she peers and sees
Silver fruit upon silver trees;
One by one the casements catch     5
Her beams beneath the silvery thatch;
Couched in his kennel, like a log,
With paws of silver sleeps the dog;
From their shadowy cote the white breasts peep
Of doves in silver-feathered sleep     10
A harvest mouse goes scampering by,
With silver claws and a silver eye;
And moveless fish in the water gleam,
By silver reeds in a silver stream.

WALTER DE LA MARE

1. shoon\shūn\ shoes.

Reprinted by permission of the Literary Trustees of Walter de la Mare and the Society of Authors as their representative.

Not only does each time of day have its particular joys, but each season of the year also brings a special delight if one has the vision to see it. Here follow five poems of delight, each praising a season.

A modern poet suggests the joy of spring through unusual phrases and words and through the unexpected arrangement and length of lines.

## in Just-spring

in Just-
spring      when the world is mud-
luscious the little
lame balloonman

whistles      far      and wee      5

and eddieandbill come
running for marbles and
piracies and it's
spring

when the world is puddle-wonderful      10

the queer
old balloonman whistles
far      and      wee
and bettyandisbel come dancing

from hopscotch and jump-rope and      15

it's
spring
and
     the

         goat-footed      20

balloonMan      whistles
far
and
wee

E. E. CUMMINGS

The utter softness of "Velvet Shoes" has caught the essence of the poet's delight in a snowstorm.

## Velvet Shoes

Let us walk in the white snow
   In a soundless space;
With footsteps quiet and slow,
   At a tranquil pace,
   Under veils of white lace.      5

I shall go shod in silk,
   And you in wool,
White as a white cow's milk,
   More beautiful
   Than the breast of a gull.      10

We shall walk through the still town
   In a windless peace;
We shall step upon white down,
   Upon silver fleece,
   Upon softer than these.      15

We shall walk in velvet shoes:
   Wherever we go
Silence will fall like dews
   On white silence below.
   We shall walk in the snow.      20

ELINOR WYLIE

Copyright 1921 by Alfred A. Knopf, Inc. and renewed 1949 by William Rose Benet. Reprinted from COLLECTED POEMS OF ELINOR WYLIE by permission of Alfred A. Knopf, Inc.

Copyright, 1923, 1951, by E. E. Cummings. Reprinted from his volume, POEMS 1923–1954 by permission of Harcourt Brace Jovanovich, Inc.

## *Wild Blackberries*

Summer in the country?
For the city dweller its joys may be remote,
but Frances McConnel helps us share her delight
through an unusual symbol for summer.

We dressed for December then,
When the heat crawled on our skin:
Not an inch open to the thorns
Except our mouths, necessary to tongue
The berries from our bruised fingers.                  5
My father put socks on our hands
And with old strong hat pulled to his ears
He led us into the thickest thorns.

That bright July heart above us
Beat its anguish to our heavy bones.                   10
Our juices fermented from the pores
Became blood with the berries' smears.
Yet we plucked the fruit lightly;
Stifled in our protection while
Thorns clawed at our hair                              15
But fell away. Gladly the hot berries,
July berries, melted our quick tongues.

There were creatures at odds with us.
Chiggers so sly and small
The pungent oil filtered none away.                    20
If there were a way to revoke them
My father would have known it.
Even fat ticks are known
To bury in the picker's skin:
Our harehound pup came home                            25
Dalmatiated with the black bulbs.

Also the yellow-banded bees,
The ones that bumble into your legs,
Attack your sneakered feet,
Defied our protection.                                 30
Those bees nest near the briars,
Under the lame grass we trampled,
Are easily shaken to erupt
From the earth in lava bubbles.

And so then, run home                                  35
To the scrubbed kitchen; wash
The green spiders from the harvest;
Husk your hot bodies;
Shower away the afternoon;
And in white dress and shirt                           40
Taste the blackberry, absorbed
Summer in fragrant cream, black suns
Dancing in the white, white summer sky.

Reprinted by permission of Frances McConnel.   FRANCES MCCONNEL

What is summer in the city?
Phyllis McGinley shows her joy in summer through a completely contemporary symbol.

## Good Humor Man

Listen! It is the summer's self that ambles
   Through the green lanes with such a coaxing tongue.
Not birds or daisy fields were ever symbols
   More proper to the time than this bell rung
   With casual insistence—no, not swallow         5
   Circling the roof or bee in hollyhock.
His is the season's voice, and children follow,
   Panting, from every doorway down the block.

So, long ago, in some such shrill procession
   Perhaps the Hamelin[1] children gave pursuit      10
To one who wore a red-and-yellow fashion
   Instead of white, but made upon his flute
The self-same promise plain to every comer:
Unending sweets, imperishable summer.

**PHYLLIS MC GINLEY**

From *Times Three* by Phyllis McGinley. Copyright 1947 by Phyllis McGinley. Originally appeared in *The New Yorker*. Reprinted by permission of The Viking Press, Inc.

1. The author is referring to the story of the Pied Piper of **Hamelin,** who played such bewitching music with his pipes that all the children of the town followed him.

Gone are the youthful songs of spring
and the languid airs of summer. But autumn, too, has its delights.

## A Vagabond Song

There is something in the Autumn that is native to my blood,
Touch of manner, hint of mood;
And my heart is like a rhyme,
With the yellow and the purple and the crimson keeping time.

The scarlet of the maples can shake me like a cry      5
Of bugles going by.
And my lonely spirit thrills
To see the frosty asters like smoke upon the hills.

There is something in October sets the gypsy blood astir;
We must rise and follow her,          10
When from every hill a flame
She calls and calls each vagabond by name.

**BLISS CARMAN**

Reprinted by permission of Dodd, Mead & Company from *Bliss Carman's Poems*. Copyright, 1929, by Bliss Carman.

All manner of things may bring delight to a
person: sights . . . sounds . . . smells . . . objects.
The next group of poems deals with delights
inspired by these kinds of things.

Whitman's great, gusty enthusiasm
for life often flows out in catalogs,
listing item after item.

# *Miracles*

Why, who makes much of a miracle?
As to me I know of nothing else but miracles,
Whether I walk the streets of Manhattan,
Or dart my sight over the roofs of houses toward the sky,
Or wade with naked feet along the beach just in the edge of the water,     5
Or stand under trees in the woods,
Or talk by day with any one I love,
Or sit at table at dinner with the rest,
Or look at strangers opposite me riding in the car,
Or watch honey-bees busy around the hive of a summer forenoon,     10
Or animals feeding in the fields,
Or birds, or the wonderfulness of insects in the air,
Or the wonderfulness of the sundown, or of stars shining so quiet and bright,
Or the exquisite delicate thin curve of the new moon in spring;
These with the rest, one and all, are to me miracles,     15
The whole referring, yet each distinct and in its place.
To me every hour of the light and dark is a miracle,
Every cubic inch of space is a miracle,
Every square yard of the surface of the earth is spread with the same,
Every foot of the interior swarms with the same.     20

To me the sea is a continual miracle,
The fishes that swim—the rocks—the motion of the waves—the ships
    with men in them,
What stranger miracles are there?

WALT WHITMAN

This poem is also a catalog, one of delight in *pied* things, that is,
in things having two or more colors in blotches. To many people such objects may seem imperfect,
indeed blemished, but Hopkins finds them both beautiful and charged with meaning.

## Pied Beauty

Glory be to God for dappled[1] things—
    For skies of couple-color as a brinded[2] cow;
      For rose-moles[3] all in stipple upon trout that swim;
Fresh-firecoal chestnut-falls; finches' wings;
    Landscapes plotted and pieced—fold, fallow, and plow;[4]    5
      And all trades, their gear and tackle and trim.
All things counter, original, spare, strange;
    Whatever is fickle,[5] freckled (who knows how?)
      With swift, slow; sweet, sour; adazzle, dim;
He fathers-forth whose beauty is past change:    10
    Praise him.

GERARD MANLEY HOPKINS

---

1. **dappled**\ˈdă·pəld\ marked or variegated with small spots.
2. **brinded** (or **brindled**)\ˈbrĭn·dəld\ marked with dark streaks or spots.
3. **rose-mole**\ˈrōz 'mōl\ a distinctive spot on a fish.
4. **fold**, an enclosed pasture. **fallow**\ˈfă·lō\ land left uncultivated for a time. **plow**, plowed land.
5. **fickle**\ˈfĭ·kəl\ readily changeable and showing much variety.

How seldom we examine smells
or even become conscious of their effect on our moods.
Morley gives a whole catalog of them
for us to consider.

## Smells

Why is it that the poets tell
So little of the sense of smell?
These are the odors I love well:

The smell of coffee freshly ground;
Or rich plum pudding, holly-crowned;    5
Or onions fried and deeply browned.

The fragrance of a fumy pipe;
The smell of apples, newly ripe
And printers' ink on leaden type.

Woods by moonlight in September    10
Breathe most sweet; and I remember
Many a smoky camp-fire ember.

Camphor, turpentine, and tea,
The balsam[1] of a Christmas tree,
These are whiffs of gramarye[2] . . .    15
*A ship smells best of all to me!*

CHRISTOPHER MORLEY

---

1. **balsam**\ˈbɔl·səm\ an aromatic resin.
2. **gramarye**\ˈgră·mə 'rē\ magic, enchantment. (This word comes from the old French word *grammaire*, and so does the word *grammar*.)

From the book POEMS by Christopher Morley. Copyright, 1929, ©, 1957 by Christopher Morley. Reprinted by permission of J. B. Lippincott Company.

Emily Dickinson takes a simple thing,
joy in books, and tells of her delight.

## Precious Words

He ate and drank the precious words.
His spirit grew robust;
He knew no more that he was poor,
Nor that his frame was dust.
He danced along the dingy days,
And this bequest[1] of wings
Was but a book. What liberty
A loosened spirit brings!

EMILY DICKINSON

1. **bequest**\\'bē ▲kwĕst\\ a legacy, something willed and to be inherited.

Reprinted by permission of the publishers and trustees of Amherst College from *The Poems of Emily Dickinson*, edited by Thomas H. Johnson, Harvard University Press, copyright 1951, 1955 by the president and fellows of Harvard University.

Shakespeare's sonnets often deal with the praise of his loved one or a friend.
Here is a famous one that shows his utter joy in the beauty of his beloved.

## Sonnet CVI

When in the chronicle of wasted time
I see descriptions of the fairest wights,[1]
And beauty making beautiful old rhyme,
In praise of ladies dead and lovely knights,
Then, in the blazon[2] of sweet beauty's best,     5
Of hand, of foot, of lip, of eye, of brow,
I see their antique pen would have express'd
Even such a beauty as you master now.
So all their praises are but prophecies
Of this our time, all you prefiguring,     10
And, for they look'd but with divining eyes,
They had not still enough your worth to sing:
    For we, which now behold these present days,
    Have eyes to wonder, but lack tongues to praise.

WILLIAM SHAKESPEARE

1. **wight**\\waĭt\\ creature, person.
2. **blazon**\\▲blā·zən\\ flowery description or display.

The joy of complete abandon . . .

# Fast Run in the Junkyard

That junkyard fell down the side of the hill
like a river: baby buggy, black leather
cracked car back seat, sofa wind-siphoned
by a clutch of tangled wire hangers hanging on
like spiders. We stood and fell as momentum told us          5
toward somebody's sodden Sealey[1] dying of galloping miasma,[2]
jumped on bedsprings sprung to pogos, and leaped
for king-of-the-mountain where boxes and cans fountained
up the hill's other side. Sailing saucers, we rode
back down, flinging hat racks, burlap sacks, chairs cropped          10
of backs and flotsam crockery,[3] breezed in league boots[4]
back out of everybody's past hazards, up to the road
to break tar bubbles all-the-way-home where things
were wearing out as fast as we were growing up.

JEANNETTE NICHOLS

---

1. **sodden Sealey,** a thoroughly soaked Sealy mattress.
2. **miasma\mē·ᵃaz·mə\** a vapor formerly believed to cause disease.
3. **flotsam crockery,** discarded earthenware such as pots, jars, dishes,
made of baked clay.
4. **league boots,** making giant strides.

---

From *Mostly People* by Jeannette Nichols. Copyright © 1966
by Rutgers, The State University. Reprinted by permission of
Rutgers University Press.

---

## UNDERSTANDING POETRY

*The Whole Poem—Experience and Meaning*

One of the finest shortcuts for widening and deepening one's experience of life and the world is lyric poetry. No other type of literature offers more intense and compressed expressions of truths about human life. The lyric poet widens readers' visions by revealing to them experiences they have never had before. Poets take the landlubber to surfs and seas, the city dweller to the forlorn farmhouse lost in deep night or to the blackberry patch under a July sun, the Midwesterner to New England in November and to England "when April's there"; they take their readers swiftly to strange streets, hills, skies, moonlight nights . . . foreign shores . . . other centuries. But more than this, they may lead the reader beneath the surface of the reader's own everyday experiences—to give new meaning to familiar feelings, ideas, and thoughts.

Mature, experienced readers may grasp, almost spontaneously, the full impact of the poet's broad deep vision the first time they read a poem. But because poets' experiences are so intense and because poets usually see more than readers are accustomed to seeing on their own, most readers must reach a little. Consequently, if one sincerely wishes to share and enjoy the poet's vision, one should consciously develop what has become natural and even subconscious to the good reader. That is, the reader should cultivate the habit of asking the few simple questions about the title, subject matter, theme, tone, structure, rhythm, imagery, and diction taken up throughout PRIVATE MOODS. These elements are not important in themselves but only as they contribute to the total effect of the poem. They should never be studied as ends in themselves but as parts of a whole. It is by coming to know each part better that the reader climbs toward a deeper, more enjoyable realization of the experience and meaning communicated in the whole poem. In this way, readers test their own emotions and thoughts against those of the poet, and they discover that what they thought was purely personal is a universal experience.

### Reveille

1. What is the theme? Where and how is it stated?

2. What is the tone? How do the imagery and rhythm affect it?

3. What are the vivid metaphors Housman uses in the first three stanzas?

### Afternoon on a Hill

1. What do Millay's proposed actions reveal about her?

2. What things are contrasted in the poem?

3. What is the effect of the alternating long and short lines?

### Silver

1. How many things are "besilvered" in the poem?

2. The first two words, "Slowly, silently," state the movement and sound quality carried out in the rest of the poem. Show how the poet, through the imagery and rhythm, maintains the almost motionless silence.

### Velvet Shoes

1. How is the title related to the poem?

2. What images are especially appropriate for suggesting softness, slowness, quietness?

3. The poet uses many *l*'s, *m*'s, *n*'s, *s*'s, *w*'s, and *wh*'s. What effect do they have on the sound in the poem?

### in Just-spring

1. What does the title mean?

2. What elements of spring delight the poet?

3. What is the significance of the balloonman?

4. What words characterize the tone of the poem?

### Wild Blackberries

1. What elements of the July afternoon are "at odds" with the pickers? What is the poet's attitude toward these elements?

2. To which sense does the poet appeal most often?

3. Select four images that are vivid and unusual.

### Good Humor Man

1. What are the images of a country summer? Why is the Good Humor man a more fitting symbol for the city? What other symbols might represent summer to the city dweller?

2. What kind of sonnet has the poet used?

### A Vagabond Song

1. What is the quality of autumn that the poet communicates: its somberness? its quiet? its melancholy? its brilliance?

2. What specific delights compose autumn's song?

### Miracles

1. Classify Whitman's miracles: are they predominantly sights, sounds, places, actions, people, ideas?

2. Some people claim that while Whitman's lines are uneven in length, they are intended to be equal in ideas and to be read with an equal amount of time. Therefore, a long line is to be read relatively fast and a short line slowly, so that each is given the same duration of time. Try reading "Miracles" aloud, and see if you think this contention is a valid one.

*Pied Beauty*

1. What is Hopkins' theme? How and where does he state it?

2. Make a list of the things he praises. What is unusual about the images he uses to describe each?

3. How does the poem move—quickly or slowly? How does Hopkins control his rhythm? What use does he make of alliteration?

*Smells*

Notice the mixture of pleasant and unpleasant, sweet and acrid smells. If only one kind had been used, would the poem have had the same appeal?

*Precious Words*

1. The idea of the poem is fairly trite. State it in a single sentence.

2. What are the elements about the poem that have made it fresh and alive?

*Sonnet CVI*

1. How does each quatrain advance Shakespeare's theme?

2. What is the basic comparison he uses throughout the sonnet to praise his loved one? Is this fresh or trite?

*Fast Run in the Junkyard*

1. Why do children like junkyards?

2. How is a sense of speed conveyed in the poem?

### IMPLICATIONS

Poets try to transmit their feelings of delight more frequently than any other single mood. What you have read is a sampling of the art they have made from it. Consider your own reactions to the following statements:

1. Delight takes a special set of circumstances to set it in motion.

2. Delight comes from inside a person rather than from the external world.

3. Delight is a mood whose depths are increased by being expressed.

4. Delight is usually tinged with a shadow of melancholy.

5. Delight is a momentary thing that quickly fades.

## Private Moods

Moods are reflections of strange and wonderful emotions flooding a person's consciousness. If experiences are the framework on which life is structured, moods give the color and texture and depth to that framework. When one is caught in the meshes of a mood, life becomes more intense.

Take spring, when restlessness seizes your soul and you yearn to be off to a far place. Then your everyday world takes on different dimensions, a different meaning. Or if fear strikes, you are caught by a dark mood that almost strangles your initiative. Once filled with anger or hatred, your mood becomes one of violent and blinding action that may disrupt your pattern of living momentarily or forever. And the dark, agonizing mood of sorrow can almost drown you in its depths and leaves a melancholy thread of color dimming the vividness of today. Nostalgia is a gentle mood, seldom bitter, leading to dreams and memories. But delight heightens joy in the essence of the moment and sends one dancing toward tomorrow.

Poets have written of many subjects, many themes, but nowhere have they found a more satisfying subject than that of private moods: violent or quiet, sad or happy, dreamy or full of action, a mood lends itself to the poetic arts. Like mustard and hot dogs, a child and a dog, a teacher and a book, poetry and moods go together. Happy, indeed, are the readers who can respond to these lyric poems and thus increase their own understanding and enjoyment.

### IMPLICATIONS

A. Consider the following statements in relation to the poetry you have just read. Would you agree with the propositions?

1. Though many of the moods dealt with are unpleasant, they nevertheless become deeply moving as experiences when described in poetry.

2. The poetry in this group of selections explores the world inside the individual's mind, a world that it is difficult to talk about.

3. Often poems such as these help you to understand things about yourself that you didn't completely understand before.

**4.** Part of the satisfaction in reading poetry such as this is the revelation that other people have the same feelings and reactions that you do.

**5.** Beauty is created only out of beautiful things. The dark and ugly moods proved unsuitable for poetry.

**6.** An individual's deepest and most meaningful moods should never be revealed to another. For poets to describe their deep emotions is embarrassing and often dull.

**7.** The only positive mood studied in PRIVATE MOODS was delight. The rest are negative or destructive moods, indicating that poets are negative in their approach to life.

**8.** It is necessary to be a moody person if one is to be a poet.

**9.** The poets are not urging people to steep themselves in moods. Instead they have almost a scientific approach of carefully examining a mood, probing its full meaning, and then moving on to something else.

**B.** In the light of the poems you have read, evaluate the following well-known definitions of poetry:

**1.** "Poetry is the silence and speech between a wet struggling root of a flower and a sunlit blossom of that flower."—Sandburg

**2.** "Poetry is the imaginative expression of strong feeling, usually rhythmical . . . the spontaneous overflow of powerful feelings . . . recollected in tranquillity."—Wordsworth

**3.** "By poetry we mean the art of employing words in such a manner as to produce an illusion of the imagination, the art of doing by means of words what the painter does by means of colors."—Macaulay

**4.** "Poetry, therefore, we will call musical thought."—Carlyle

**5.** "Poetry is the record of the best and happiest moments of the happiest and best minds."—Shelley

**6.** "Poetry is language that tells us, through a more or less emotional reaction, something that cannot be said. All poetry, great or small, does this."—Robinson

### TECHNIQUES

**A.** Poets use different devices to express different moods. Look back at the different sections. In which mood poems were:

**1.** Images stressed?

**2.** Catalogs a favorite device?

**3.** Rhythm important to convey the mood?

**4.** Sound quality of words used to increase mood?

**5.** Rhyme patterns important for the mood?

**B.** Agree or disagree with the following statements regarding literary devices:

**1.** The images (including figures of speech) that poets use to describe the moods are fantastically accurate in expressing an emotion exactly. Cite examples that you felt were either good or bad.

**2.** Rhythm seems to have little importance in mood poetry.

**3.** The way a word sounds can convey as much toward the description of a mood as the meaning of the word itself.

**4.** Rhyme has less and less importance in poetry because it makes it so trite and singsongy. This is why modern poets have abandoned rhyme.

**5.** Shakespeare is one of the greatest of poets because he can combine rhythm, sound, and rhyme and produce new understandings or catch a familiar meaning.

**6.** The real skill of poets is mirrored by their ability to take familiar words and combine them in new patterns that catch the essence of a mood or image: "puddle wonderful," "couple-color," "a quartz contentment." Can you find examples that appealed to you or repelled you?

### WORDS

**A.** *Personification,* a subclass of metaphor, is the figure of speech which endows ideas, nature, animals, inanimate objects with human qualities. Words which label ideas are generally abstract nouns, but nouns referring to animals and inanimate objects are generally concrete nouns. Concrete nouns may be further divided into *animate,* things endowed with life and the ability to reproduce; and *inanimate,* things which occupy space but are lifeless, such as water, pastures. Animate nouns may be divided again into those which refer to people and those which refer to nonhumans, animals or plants. Frequently we attribute to abstract nouns human emotions, human form, human characters. Expressions such as "night's starred face," "magic hand of chance," and "the sea's face" are examples of personification. What other examples of personification do you find in the poems you have just read?

**B.** In the poem "Music I Heard" the poet writes "And bread I broke with you." The word *bread* stands for a whole, all things edible. The figure of speech in which a basic part stands for the whole is called *synecdoche* \sĭ ᐩnĕk·də 'kē\. In the poem "Spring" the poet says "I have need of the *sky*." The word *sky* has been substituted for another word which it suggests *space*. *Metonymy* \mə ᐩtŏ·nə 'mē\ is the substitution of one word for another which it suggests. An expression like "I have read Shakespeare" is a metonymy since what you probably read was the poem by Shakespeare. Metonymy and synecdoche, because a comparison is implied, are subclasses of metaphor.

**C.1.** Joyce writes of "the waters' monotone." What does *monotone* mean and what are its roots?

**2.** Aiken says "all is desolate"; what is the relationship between *desolate, sole,* and *solitaire*?

**3.** In "My November Guest," Frost writes of the "sodden pasture lane." What connection is there between *pasture* and *pastor*?

**4.** Dickinson asks a question about "centuries before" in "After Great Pain a Formal Feeling Comes." What is the connection between *cent, century,* and *percentage*?

**5.** In "Home Thoughts from Abroad," Browning talks of "the first fine careless rapture." Is there a relationship between *rapture* and *rapacious*?

**6.** Shakespeare's "Sonnet CVI" refers to "the chronicle of wasted time." What is the connection between *chronicle* and *chronic,* as in "a chronic disease"?

---

### BIOGRAPHICAL NOTES

## Paul Laurence Dunbar

Paul Laurence Dunbar (1872–1906), American poet, was born in Dayton, Ohio, the son of an escaped Negro slave. He gained a reputation with *Lyrics* (1896), a collection of poems, many of which were in dialect. His complete poems appeared posthumously in 1913.

## Richard Hovey

Richard Hovey (1864–1900), a dark and bearded, romantic-looking American poet, was born in Normal, Illinois. He began to write poetry early, publishing his first small volume when only sixteen. After graduating from Dartmouth, he became in succession an art student, theological student, journalist, actor, and lecturer. His early writing attempts were poetic dramas and an elegy, *Seaward*. Collaborating with Bliss Carman, he produced *Songs of Vagabondia* (1884, 1896, 1901), celebrating the joys of the open road, youth, and companionship.

## Edna St. Vincent Millay

Edna St. Vincent Millay, American poet, was born in Rockland, Maine, 1892. The most popular poet of her time, Miss Millay was still a student when her first major published poem, "Renascence," appeared in *The Lyric Year* in 1912. While at Vassar, she won the Intercollegiate Poetry Prize; and, in 1917, she published her first volume of poetry. In 1923, she received the Pulitzer Prize for "The Harp-Weaver." She died in 1950.

## John Masefield

John Masefield (1878–1967), the Poet Laureate of England, went to sea as a cabin boy when he was fourteen, and his wanderings continued for several years. In 1895, he worked as third assistant barkeeper in a saloon in New York City. He returned to England in 1897, where he lived for a while with the Irish poet and playwright, Synge. He attributed his decision to become a poet to his reading of Chaucer's *The Parlement of Foules.* In his early works, based on his wanderings, Masefield's poetry tended to overemphasize passion and brutality, but he managed to capture a feeling of reality. When he turned to narrative verse his poetry seemed to bloom, though some critics said they were somewhat overwhelmed by his blending the rough physical with the exalted spiritual. He was made Poet Laureate in 1930.

## Hannah Kahn

Hannah Kahn (1911–   ) was born in New York City, the daughter of David and Sarah Abrahams. She married Frank Kahn in 1941 and had three children. Her poems have been published in national magazines and she has won many prizes, including an award by the Poetry Society of Great

Britain and the American Parsons' Sonnet Award, both in 1957. In 1958 she became the poetry review editor for the *Miami* (Florida) *Herald.*

## Theodore Roethke

Theodore Roethke (1908–1963), born in Saginaw, Michigan, was both an educator and a poet. He taught at the University of Washington's English department from 1947 until his death. His first book of verse was *Open House* (1941). A volume of his collected poems was brought out in 1958.

## Richard Brautigan

Richard Brautigan (1935–        ) was born in Tacoma, Washington. He now lives in San Francisco where he writes haunting, very contemporary, mind-jolting poems and novels. A book of verse, *The Pill vs. the Springhill Mine Disaster,* presented a collection of his poems written between 1957 and 1968. His three novels *In Watermelon Sugar* (1969), *A Confederate General from Big Sur* (1967), and *Trout Fishing in America* (1967) have had an enthusiastic reception by college students.

## Edgar Allan Poe

Edgar Allan Poe (1809–1849) led a tragic life, which has made him a romantic figure in American literary history. He felt himself set apart from the spring of ordinary joys and sorrows and so became what he thought he was: "haunted, self-doomed, a weary wayworn traveler." Raised by foster parents, he entered the University of Virginia where he drank too much, ran into debt, and left after a year. He quarreled with his foster-father, tried the army for two years, took a stab at West Point, drifted in and out of editorships. His life was marked by brief successes and dreary, long defeats. He considered the death of a beautiful woman as the most poetic of all subjects and it seems but a natural step to his specializing in horror tales. In addition to horror tales, he wrote many "mystery" stories which have since set the standard for the modern detective story.

## Selma Robinson

Selma Robinson (1902–        ), a Brooklyn-born writer, was educated in public schools and trained in New York University's School of Journalism. She married Howard Markel but continued her writing for *Harper's, New Yorker, Harper's Bazaar, McCalls, Colliers,* and has even tried her hand at television plays. She has also served as staff feature writer for several New York newspapers.

## Robert Frost

Robert Frost (1874–1963), though born in California, is most often called the poet of New England. He went to Massachusetts when he was 10 years old because his mother honored her husband's request to be buried in the family plot in the East. With no money for the return trip. Mrs. Frost settled down in New Hampshire and supported the family by teaching. Frost himself later tried teaching, then farming and journalism, but he really wanted to write poetry. He kept writing poetry even though no one would buy his work. In 20 years of writing he averaged only $10 a year from his poetry. Feeling rejected by America, he moved his family to England and there published his first two volumes of poetry, *A Boy's Will* (1913) and *North of Boston* (1914). The English readers applauded his ability to use common, almost conversational, language in the established forms of poetry. When his two books were published in the United States, Frost returned (1915). His poetry has a regional locale, but its meaning is universal. Frost himself said that poetry must begin in delight and end in wisdom. In 1960, when he was eighty-six years old, he was asked by John F. Kennedy to read a poem at Kennedy's inauguration . . . the first time any poet was thus honored in America.

## Elizabeth Coatsworth

Elizabeth Coatsworth (1893–        ) began her writing career as a poet. Although she has written some 50 children's books and several novels, she still prefers to express herself in poetry rather than in prose. She was born in Buffalo, New York, but since her marriage to Henry Beston in 1929 has made her home in New England. Educated at Vassar College and at Columbia University, she traveled widely for many years in the Orient, North Africa, and Europe. "Sometimes," she says, "in my books I return to these memories. But, in general, I have written about New England, and for everyone from children four or five years old through the late teens into the adult field."

## Adelaide Crapsey

Adelaide Crapsey (1878–1914) was the author of a slender volume of verse written in the last year of her life and published in 1915, a year after her death. Of her refined, sensitive verse, her *cinquains* are best known. The *cinquain*, a plain, almost stark, five-line stanza, was her own invention.

## John Keats

John Keats (1795–1821) one of the finest of the English romantic poets, wrote for only a few years before dying of tuberculosis. Son of a London stablekeeper, he was short and stocky, enjoying athletics and fighting as a boy. Orphaned in his teens, Keats was apprenticed as a surgeon; but when he was twenty-one he shocked his guardian by announcing he did not wish to follow this profession and intended to write instead. His first book of poems was published in 1817. It was at this time he wrote, "I find I cannot exist without poetry. Half the day will not do . . . the whole of it." Many critics feel that Keats' skill in transmitting the experiences of the senses is unsurpassed in English poetry. His great odes, "On a Grecian Urn," "To a Nightingale," "To Autumn," and "On Melancholy" are among the greatest lyrics in the English Language. Like his mother and brother before him, he contracted tuberculosis. He died in Rome, barely twenty-five.

## John Hall Wheelock

John Hall Wheelock (1886–    ) was born at Far Rockaway, Long Island. He graduated from Harvard, studied in Germany, and returned to New York City to become a publisher. His early poetry (1911–1912) was distinguished by its exuberance. His later verse is less vigorous, reflecting his shift from athletic to philosophical poetry. His poetry had now gained greater dignity and his philosophy might be expressed by one of his own lines—"Life, the dreadful, the magnificent."

## Robert Graves

Robert Graves (1895–    ) is an English poet, the son of an Irish songwriter. He was educated at Charterhouse School and St. John's College, Cambridge. He was severely wounded while serving with the Welsh fusiliers in World War I. Since 1922 he has lived in Majorca, Spain. Despite his statement that "I decided to be a poet at the age of fifteen and have since denied priority to all my other activities," he has produced an astonishing

amount of literature in addition to his poetry: two dozen historical novels (1925–1957), more than thirty nonfiction books (1922–1962), thirty volumes of poetry (1916–1963), and ten translations (1937–1959). In his poetry he says that he strives for the pure, the unpretentious, the essential, the vigorous, and the "nonliterary." In his novels and other prose works, he displays a lucid style and far-ranging scholarship.

## Countée Cullen

Countée Cullen (1903–1946), American Negro poet, was born in New York City and educated at New York University and Harvard. He began his literary career with *Color* (1925), a book of poems in which classical models such as the sonnet are used with considerable effect. He published several volumes of verse and a novel, *One Way to Heaven* (1932); he also collaborated with Arna Bontemps in the play *St. Louis Woman* (1946).

## Siegfried Sassoon

Siegfried Sassoon (1886–1967), an English poet, descended from Persian Jews on his father's side and traditional English country people on his mother's side. Hence, he spent his boyhood alternating between rugged activities like fox-hunting and literary endeavors like rhyme-making. When Sassoon published a book of poems in 1917 called *The Old Huntsman,* he was called a "brilliant rising star" by some critics. Some of these poems were violent protests against the glorification of war. *Counter-Attack* (1918) and *Picture Show* (1920), with the first book, form a devastating record of men in World War I. Sassoon once said: "Were there even anything to say for it [war], it should not be said; for its spiritual disasters far outweigh any of its advantages . . . war is hell." *Memoirs of a Fox-Hunting Man* (1928), published anonymously, won the two most coveted literary prizes in England for that year.

## James Stephens

James Stephens (1882–1950) was an Irish poet and storyteller whose fairy tales set in the Dublin slums and his gentle poems about animals reveal his philosophy that nature and God are one. *The Crock of Gold,* with its Celtic theme, established his reputation in 1912. Actively working in the Irish nationalist movement, he moved to London in 1940 and there discovered he had a natural talent for broadcasting, a medium in which he worked until his death.

## Claude McKay

Claude McKay (1891–1948) was born the son of a farmer on the island of Jamaica. He was already known as "the Bobby Burns of Jamaica" when he came to the United States in 1912 to study at Tuskegee Institute and at Kansas State University. Moving to Harlem, McKay supported himself with menial jobs while he wrote poetry. In 1919 he moved to Europe and while living in London published *Spring in New Hampshire* (1920), a collection of his poems. Returning to New York in 1921, he became editor of two radical publications and the next year published what is often considered his finest collection of verse, *Harlem Shadows. Home to Harlem* (1928) was his first novel and the most popular of the three he wrote. This work, along with a collection of short stories, an autobiography, and a sociological study, indicate McKay's writing versatility. But he is best known for his poetry, especially his sonnets. McKay's militancy may be explained by a legend in his family which claimed that his ancestors, brought from Madagascar in chains, avoided having their family separated by vowing publicly that they would kill themselves if sold to separate owners.

## Taner Baybars

Taner Baybars (1936–    ) was born in Nicosia, Cyprus, and was first educated privately and then at the Turkish Lycea, Nicosia. But he feels that his chief educational influences were "life itself and many ordinary people." He has lived in London since 1955 and now works for the British Council in their Books Division. His publications include *To Catch a Falling Man* (1963), *A Trap for the Burglar* (1965), and *Plucked in a Far-off Land* (1970). He has also translated and edited three collections of poems from Turkish.

## William Blake

William Blake (1757–1827) was born in London, England, the second son of a hosiery merchant. He demonstrated visionary leanings at the age of four, when he screamed because God put his forehead

against the window pane. In later years he commented that Heaven pressed close—he could touch it with his walking stick. Recognizing his artistic abilities, his father (unusual for his time) sent him to drawing school at age ten, and when he was twelve apprenticed him to an engraver. His achievement as an artist was remarkable, but equally remarkable were his efforts as a poet. His first poems, created before he was fourteen, are astonishing, for they show a child's delight in his visible world and yet somehow manage to imply far more than they say. This symbolism, suggested in his early works, dominates his later writing, as Blake sought to show his own spiritual struggle.

## Phyllis McGinley

Phyllis McGinley (1905–    ) is a suburban wife and mother who has become well known for her light, satirical verse and her children's books. In 1960 she received the Pulitzer Prize for her volume of poems, *Times Three*. Born in Ontario, Oregon, she reports that the nearest town, six miles away, looked like a scene from a TV Western. Her father died when she was twelve and her mother took the family to her native Ogden, Utah. Phyllis McGinley began selling poetry to national publications while still at the University of Utah. She spent a year teaching, then went to New York. After the *New Yorker* began publishing her poems, she moved to Manhattan, married, and began writing regularly, until by 1960 she had published 20 volumes of prose and verse. Many feel Miss McGinley has helped break down the line between light verse and serious poetry. She has been characterized as both kitten and tiger—she uses language laced with wit to point out men's foibles, the amazing fluctuation in emotional fashions, the humor in the commonplace.

## Stephen Crane

Stephen Crane (1871–1900) was the last of 14 children born to a Methodist minister. He spent two uninspired semesters in college, but during this time he wrote the first draft of *Maggie, a Girl of the Streets*, a book that was to influence greatly the naturalistic writers of the twentieth century. Crane's first popular success was *The Red Badge of Courage*, a story of the Civil War, which he wrote without ever having been in battle. Later, a tour of the Far West and Mexico inspired some of his finest stories, such as "The Blue Hotel" and

"The Bride Comes to Yellow Sky." Then, while covering the gunrunning activities of the men supplying equipment to the rebels in Cuba, he was shipwrecked. From this experience he wrote a classic story, "The Open Boat." He moved to England to escape the criticism of the press, which gave the impression that he was as bizarre in character as Poe and Byron. From there he wrote his brother: "Your little brother . . . knows that he is going on steadily to make his simple little place and he can't be stopped, he can't even be retarded. He is coming." But just three years later, when he was only twenty-nine, he died of tuberculosis.

## James Joyce

James Joyce (1882–1941), an Irish writer, spent most of his adult life in France, though he used Dublin as the setting for his works. He was a gifted tenor with a fantastic knowledge of music. At various times in his life, he began the study of medicine, considered beginning a great Irish daily newspaper, ran a motion-picture theater in Dublin, and took part in the legitimate theater in Zurich. Perhaps this very extraordinary range of interests and abilities led to his experimentation in his writings. In his novel, *Ulysses* (the record of one day), and in *Finnegan's Wake* (the record of one night), he tried to show the stream of thoughts and impressions moving through his characters' minds. Some readers find his work tremendously difficult to understand for he piles one meaning on another until, like a prism, one can find so many interpretations that confusion results. Hence, some call him the master of "extreme obscurity." Yet the poet T. S. Eliot says Joyce is the greatest master of the English language since Milton.

## Conrad Aiken

Conrad Aiken (1889–    ) was born in 1889 in Savannah, Georgia, and was orphaned at ten when his father killed Conrad's mother and then himself. A great-great-aunt took the boy to Massachusetts, where, except for residence abroad, he has lived ever since. After being educated at Harvard he turned to writing. His first three books of poetry tended to be imitative, but his next publications were "symphonies of poetry," in which he tried to write lyrics that resembled music. Though Aiken's prose has never received the same acclaim as his

poetry, certain short stories such as "Silent Snow, Secret Snow" and "Mr. Arcularis" have been widely reprinted. His *Collected Poems*, representing some 18 previously printed books of poetry, received the National Book Award in 1953. In 1958, he received the Gold Medal for Poetry from the Institute of Arts and Letters.

## Miller Williams

Miller Williams was born in Arkansas and received a B.S. in biology from Arkansas State College and an M.S. in zoology from the University of Arkansas. His first book of verse, *A Circle of Stone* (1964), received good reviews from the critics and was followed by *Recital* and *So Long at the Fair* (1968), from which the selection in this unit was taken. At present, he teaches at Loyola University in New Orleans and continues to write poetry, critical articles, translations, and short stories for journals in both North and South America.

## Emily Dickinson

Emily Dickinson (1830–1886) lived her entire life in Amherst, Massachusetts. She spent only intermittent periods in formal schooling, and attended Mt. Holyoke Female Seminary for one year in 1847. Apparently she began writing poetry soon after her return from Mt. Holyoke. In 1862, she sent some poems to a critic for comment and his verdict was that her obscurity and fractured grammar stood in the way of public approval. Since she refused to change her methods of expression, she never consented to have her poetry published while she lived. Only three poems were published in her lifetime out of a total of 1,775. Upon Miss Dickinson's death, her sister, Lavinia, was amazed to find hundreds of poems, neatly placed in packets in a locked box. Lavinia persuaded a friend to help her select and publish a group of them. The critics were hostile, but the public demanded more. Emily Dickinson tried always to find new ways of handling words for, she said, "the old words are numb."

## Dante Gabriel Rossetti

Dante Gabriel Rossetti (1828–1882) was a tortured, haunted poet born into an Italian family that had fled to England. Rossetti was also a painter and the acknowledged leader of his talented family, consisting of one brother—who became an art critic, biographer, and editor of *The Germ*—and two sisters: the older, Maria Francesca, became a nun; the younger, Christina, became a lyricist of note. The Rossetti family had a great impact upon the arts and letters of Victorian England. Trying in his poetry to capture the sensuous imagery of Keats, Rossetti's work often has an unbodied, almost unearthly, quality. When his wife Elizabeth died, he ordered all his unpublished love poems placed in her casket and 9 years later had the body exhumed to retrieve his manuscript. He wrote "The Blessed Damozel" as a companion piece to Poe's "The Raven." Poe had shown the grief of a lover on earth; Rossetti showed the yearnings of the dead woman in heaven. His dependence on drugs led to his increased melancholy and ultimately to his death, which occurred as his finest book, *Ballads and Sonnets,* was being printed.

## Percy Bysshe Shelley

Percy Bysshe Shelley (1792–1822), one of the best-known English romantic poets, was a political, ideological, and moral rebel of his day. At Oxford University, he published *The Necessity of Atheism,* which resulted in his being expelled. His elopement with Harriet Westbrook, the fifteen-year-old daughter of a tavernkeeper, almost brought his father to disinherit him. Later, as he traveled about Europe with Mary Godwin, his deserted wife drowned herself when she was just twenty. When he went to court to gain control of his two children by Harriet, the court awarded the children to Harriet's sister. Plagued by a lung ailment, Mary and he, now legally married, went to Italy, where Clara and William, their two children died. Shelley's poetry efforts were received with the same public reactions that greeted his social life. "Queen Mab" was used in court to prevent his getting the control of his children. "Prometheus Unbound," "Adonais," and "Ode to the West Wind" had cold receptions. In his works some say there are two Shelleys . . . the thinker and the pure poet. His reputation has gone from complete rejection to near sanctification. Most would agree that Shelley can catch in words . . . a sheer, "Unbodied joy." He was drowned in a boating accident off Italy and his ashes were buried in Rome.

## E. A. Robinson

E. A. Robinson (1869–1935), the son of a grain merchant in Gardiner, Maine, entered Harvard determined to write, but his poems were rejected by the *Harvard Monthly* and he left after two years when the family fortune vanished. He kept writing and sending his work out and it kept coming back unpublished. A now famous poem, "The House on the Hill," was printed in a little quarterly with no payment. At twenty-eight he left home for New York without money and without influential friends, determined to live by poetry alone. When Theodore Roosevelt befriended him by getting him a job with the New York custom house, Robinson confided to a friend that he could now not only write poetry but own two pairs of shoes at one time. Three times he won the Pulitzer Prize for poetry. One of his special abilities was the skill to catch, in light verse, the character of the failure, the discarded, the defeated.

## Robert Browning

Robert Browning (1812–1889) was a famous English poet whose life spanned a period of tremendous change in politics and poetry. Browning had little formal education, but he read broadly in his father's library of 6,000 volumes and was encouraged to follow a literary career. His first book of poetry, *Pauline,* much influenced by the great Romantic poet Shelley, appeared when Browning was twenty-one. He had little interest in nature, as did many of the poets of his time, but instead used men and women as the subject of his writing. He tried his hand at drama and finally turned to dramatic monologues in which he condensed a whole life into a few telling stanzas. He married the poetess Elizabeth Barrett after a romance as exciting as anything to be found in fiction. Her reputation far outstripped his during their lifetime, but in the twentieth century Browning has been recognized as one of the great poets of the English language.

## Henry Wadsworth Longfellow

Henry Wadsworth Longfellow (1807–1882) achieved great popularity during his life both as a poet and a respected professor of Modern European Literature at Harvard. His home was the famous Craigie House, which George Washington used as his headquarters in 1775. His first poem, published when he was thirteen, showed no great promise but did indicate his early eagerness to write. At fourteen he entered Bowdoin College and after graduation was invited by Bowdoin to fill a chair especially created for him, a chair in modern languages and literature. He was only nineteen and felt the need to prepare for this position, so he went abroad where he remained for almost four years. Though he claimed that he never liked teaching, he taught for 24 years. When he was twenty-seven, he became professor of languages and belles-lettres at Harvard. In 1854, he retired to devote full time to his writing. Longfellow's poetry is direct, easy to read, filled with a lilting melody and appealing ideas. At his best he is a fascinating teller of tales. At his worst he is banal and dull. Revered and applauded during his lifetime, Longfellow has been underrated ever since.

## Alfred, Lord Tennyson

Alfred, Lord Tennyson (1809–1892), one of the greatest of the Victorian poets, was for his age at once a living embodiment of Victorian virtues and the perfect "bard." He was born at Somersby Rectory, Lincolnshire. His father was a melancholy man forced into the ministry against his wishes. In 1828, Tennyson entered Cambridge but left without achieving a degree, joined the Spanish insurgents, and when he was twenty-four published a volume of poetry. His efforts were so derided by critics that Tennyson published nothing more for nine years. Having fallen in love with Emily Sellwood, he was rejected by her family because he lacked money to support a wife. Fourteen years later, when he was forty-one and successful, he and Emily were married. Added joys of this year were the enthusiastic public reception of *In Memoriam* and his appointment as Poet Laureate of England. *Idylls of the King*, a collection of verse stories about King Arthur and his knights of the round table, is one of his best-known works. Tennyson was the most popular poet of his time. Almost everyone in England, from professional men to farmers, read and recited his best-loved poems which went through edition after edition and were often illustrated and set to music. Many of his lyrics are unsurpassed in English poetry.

## Robert Hayden

For a biography of Robert Hayden, see page 246.

## A. E. Housman

A. E. Housman (1859–1936) was both a scholar and a poet. For years he was a professor of Latin. In this scholarly post, he was noted not only for his knowledge but for his vigor in critical controversies. As a poet he was best known for his book, *A Shropshire Lad* (1896). The title led many to believe that Housman was born in Shropshire, when in truth he was born in another area and only used the hilly Shropshire country as a background . . . a kind of symbolic setting for his childhood fantasies. As a child, Housman was so small and so very quiet that he was nicknamed "mousie." Both literary critics and the less sophisticated admire Housman's poetry for its use of simple language, the flowing melody, the easily understood ideas, and his flawless execution.

## Walter de la Mare

Walter de la Mare (1879–1956) was a clerk in the English branch of the Standard Oil Co. for 20 years; he escaped the monotony of his job by writing imaginative adventures. It has been said that de la Mare longed to dwell in an enchanted past rather than in the ugly present and his poetry is filled with nostalgic, misty memories. Seemingly, he loved all that was "little and lost." He felt that nature was like a veil over some "further" reality of which one could find evidence only in visionary moments. Hence, his writing lies in these visionary moments when he moves into that area that is just slightly removed from reality. Eventually he was awarded an annual grant from the privy purse, so that he was able to give up his office work and write. Outwardly his life remained uneventful . . . his adventures continued to be on paper.

## Elinor Wylie

Elinor Wylie (1885–1928) spent most of her childhood in Washington, D.C. Her first volume of verse was published anonymously in England in 1912. Upon her return to America she wrote four novels and several collections of poetry: *Nets to Catch the Wind, Black Armour, Trivial Breath,* and *Angels and Earthly Creatures.* When she married William Rose Benét, she joined a family of poets and novelists and a stimulating literary group in New York. After her death in 1928, Benét edited her *Collected Poems* and *Collected Prose.*

## e. e. cummings

e. e. cummings (1894–1962) had the reputation of being the "bad boy" of American letters because of his habit of playing clown, critic, lyricist, and satirist almost in the same breath. He is especially noted for his experiments with typography, punctuation, and verse form. Massachusetts-born, he volunteered for service in World War I upon his graduation from Harvard and spent three months in a French concentration camp on an unfounded charge of treasonable correspondence. From this experience came his first novel, *The Enormous Room* (1922). Shortly thereafter he published his first of several volumes of poetry, *Tulips and Chimneys* (1923).

## Frances McConnel

Frances Ruhlen McConnel (1941–    ) was born in Providence, Rhode Island. She moved with her family to Oak Ridge, Tennessee, at the age of four, and again to Anchorage, Alaska, when she was twelve. At fifteen she published her first poem in *American Girl* magazine. In 1960, with her husband, she moved to Seattle, Washington, where she attended the University of Washington. Her poems have been published in *Atlantic Monthly, Poetry Northwest,* and several university magazines.

## Bliss Carman

Bliss Carman (1861–1929) was a Canadian poet whose family descended from English loyalists who fled to Canada during the American Revolution. For professions he prepared for law, then teaching, and finally civil engineering; but abandoned them all as careers. Poetry had always been his love, especially nature poetry. In 1885, he cut loose from his ties and went to Harvard where he met Richard Hovey. Deciding to devote themselves to writing poetry, they went to New York. Poetry as a career was an invitation to starvation, so Carman kept the two of them going by doing editorial work. The poems he wrote with Hovey (who died in 1900) were light, romantic verse. Carman's real talent lay, however, in vigorous nature poems. Fame and a settled income reduced the color and flamboyancy of his poetry, though technically it improved. In 1928, the Canadian Parliament awarded him the Poet Laureate's medal.

## Walt Whitman

Walt Whitman (1819–1892) is an American poet whose book, *Leaves of Grass,* is considered by many as a landmark in American literature. He was born of simple farm people on Long Island; his father took up carpentry and moved the family to Brooklyn while Walt was still a small child. Here the country boy grew to know the city sounds, to enjoy the warm smells of his father's carpentry work and the excitement of the city streets. He left school when he was eleven, working first as an errand boy and then as a "printer's devil." This led him toward journalism and writing. Losing his job on the *Brooklyn Eagle* after two years as a writer (he was then twenty-nine), he accepted a job in New Orleans as a special writer on the daily *Crescent.* Some biographers feel that this city taught him to slow his tempo and opened to him a whole new world of sights and sounds. At thirty-one, back in New York, he gave up his fashionable clothes to wear those of a common workman and let his beard grow long and loose-flowing. *Leaves of Grass* (1855) was hailed by Ralph Waldo Emerson in these words . . . "I greet you at the beginning of a great career." Whitman continued to publish editions (nine in his own lifetime) of this work and increased the number of poems from the original 12 to the almost 400 that have been reprinted many times in this century. In 1864, friends got him a job in the Indian Bureau which he lost almost instantly because his superior thought his poems immoral. A stroke in 1873 almost incapacitated him. He once said of his poetry: "I depart as air . . . If you want me again, look for me under your boot-soles."

## Gerard Manley Hopkins

Gerard Manley Hopkins (1844–1889) was an English poet who graduated from Balliol College in Oxford when he was nineteen. He was much influenced in his undergraduate years by Matthew Arnold and Walter Pater and became such a good friend of Robert Bridges that when Hopkins lay dying, he entrusted his poetry to Bridges. At twenty-one, seeking answers to the religious problems that troubled him, he was converted to Catholicism and in 1877 was ordained a priest. A superior suggested he write a poem about the sinking of the German steamer, *Deutschland,* in which five exiled Franciscan nuns died. This attempt seemed to open the floodgates of Hopkins' creativity, and he began to write poetry. His work is distinguished by the manner in which he unites the sublime with the seemingly ridiculous and by his use of unusual rhythms, striking images, as well as obscure words. Like Emily Dickinson, Hopkins' poetry was not published until after his death. The first publication of his poems, edited by Robert Bridges, came almost 30 years after Hopkins had died from typhoid fever.

## Christopher Morley

Christopher Morley (1890–1957) was an American writer best known for his novels such as *Kitty Foyle, Where the Blue Begins,* and *Parnassus on Wheels* and for his light-hearted verse and essays. He was born two years after his parents came from England to the United States. His father was a professor of mathematics at Haverford College in Pennsylvania and Morley graduated from there with honors in 1910. He spent the next years at Oxford University in England as a Rhodes scholar and while abroad published his first book of verse. On his return in 1913, he worked for Doubleday, Page and Company, a publishing house, and later wrote a column for the *New York Evening Post.* He then became a contributing editor to the *Saturday Review of Literature.*

## Kathy McLaughlin

Kathy McLaughlin (1926–      ) was born in Yakima, Washington. She began writing poetry early in life, with her first poems published at age sixteen. She was graduated from the University of Washington, where she studied under Theodore Roethke. Now married, she lives with her family in Yelm, Washington.

## William Shakespeare

For a biography of Shakespeare, see page 467.

# DREAMS

## In a Glass
## of Cider

It seemed I was a mite of sediment
That waited for the bottom to ferment
So I could catch a bubble in ascent.
I rode up on one till the bubble burst
And when that left me to sink back reversed
I was no worse off than I was at first.
I'd catch another bubble if I waited.
The thing was to get now and then elated.

**ROBERT FROST**

From THE POETRY OF ROBERT FROST edited by
Edward Connery Lathem. Copyright © 1962 by Robert
Frost. Copyright © 1969 by Holt, Rinehart and Winston,
Inc. Reprinted by permission of Holt, Rinehart and Win-
ston, Inc.

The Architect's Dream, *Thomas Cole.*
*The Toledo Museum of Art, Toledo, Ohio.*
*Gift of Florence Scott Libbey.*
*Pyramids and pillars, arches, domes, and*
*spires crystallize the dreams of the*
*past. The architect, contemplating the*
*glories of the past, dreams of his and*
*civilization's future achievements.*

Robert Frost, through a common, homely observation from daily life, says something universal about our experience on this earth. Watching the bubbles rise in a glass of cider, he imagines himself an infinitesimal speck of sediment that is carried occasionally by a bubble up toward the top of the glass. When the bubble explodes, he sinks; but he knows he will find another bubble and rise again.

The bubbles are peoples' dreams of what they want their lives to become. A dream carries one along until it bursts, but people, being what they are, will construct another dream and another and another, for to be alive and to be human is to imagine a better world, a better way of living, a better personality than we now know. The dreams a person has, even though farfetched, determine the direction in which that person will try to move.

All people live their lives in the world of nature which surrounds them. But they also live in the world that they have rearranged to suit themselves. This is the world of fenced fields, of roads, of buildings, and of machines. In addition, they live in the world of their own imagination, the shadowy world of what they would like to have or become. They have the ability to live a kind of double life in which they are physically in one world and mentally in another. This ability to dream makes it possible for people to hope, to plan, to change. From it comes their willingness to struggle, to undergo hardship, to delay immediate rewards.

The literature in DREAMS examines the interaction between people's physical lives and the dreams they dream for themselves. These works show how dreams grow out of people's basic desires: the desire for social status, for material wealth, for security in a family, for moral betterment; the desire for artistic achievement, for better government, or for gaining power over other people.

Not all dreams are pleasant, nor are all dreams admirable. Some are too big or intangible for a person ever to achieve. Some must necessarily lead to disappointment and frustration, but all are deeply human.

Without examining dreams and their impact on life, no one can understand human nature.

A modern Greek courts a contemporary
Grecian maiden in a heroic fashion.
But the dream of romance, which he actively
sets out to achieve,
meets with an unusual reception.

# The Wooing
## of
## Ariadne

### HARRY MARK PETRAKIS

I knew from the beginning she must accept my love—put aside foolish female protestations. It is the distinction of the male to be the aggressor and the cloak of the female to lend grace to the pursuit. Aha! I am wise to these wiles.

I first saw Ariadne at a dance given by the Spartan brotherhood in the Legion Hall on Laramie Street. The usual assemblage of prune-faced and banana-bodied women smelling of virtuous anemia. They were an outrage to a man such as myself.

Then I saw her! A tall stately woman, perhaps in her early thirties. She had firm and slender arms bare to the shoulders and a graceful neck. Her hair was black and thick and piled in a great bun at the back of her head. That grand abundance of hair attracted me at once. This modern aberration women have of chopping their hair close to the scalp and leaving it in fantastic disarray I find revolting.

I went at once to my friend Vasili, the baker, and asked him who she was.

Reprinted by permission of Quadrangle Books from *Pericles on 31st Street* by Harry Mark Petrakis, copyright © 1965 by Harry Mark Petrakis.

"Ariadne Langos," he said. "Her father is Janco Langos, the grocer."

"Is she engaged or married?"

"No," he said slyly. "They say she frightens off the young men. They say she is very spirited."

"Excellent," I said and marveled at my good fortune in finding her unpledged. "Introduce me at once."

"Marko," Vasili said with some apprehension. "Do not commit anything rash."

I pushed the little man forward. "Do not worry, little friend," I said. "I am a man suddenly possessed by a vision. I must meet her at once."

We walked together across the dance floor to where my beloved stood. The closer we came the more impressive was the majestic swell of her breasts and the fine great sweep of her thighs. She towered over the insignificant apple-core women around her. Her eyes, dark and thoughtful, seemed to be restlessly searching the room.

Be patient, my dove! Marko is coming.

"Miss Ariadne," Vasili said. "This is Mr. Marko Palamas. He desires to have the honor of your acquaintance."

She looked at me for a long and piercing moment. I imagined her gauging my mighty strength by the width of my shoulders and the circumference of my arms. I felt the tips of my mustache bristle with pleasure. Finally she nodded with the barest minimum of courtesy. I was not discouraged.

"Miss Ariadne," I said, "may I have the pleasure of this dance?"

She stared at me again with her fiery eyes. I could imagine more timid men shriveling before her fierce gaze. My heart flamed at the passion her rigid exterior concealed.

"I think not," she said.

"Don't you dance?"

Vasili gasped beside me. An old prune-face standing nearby clucked her toothless gums.

"Yes, I dance," Ariadne said coolly. "I do not wish to dance with you."

"Why?" I asked courteously.

"I do not think you heard me," she said. "I do not wish to dance with you."

Oh, the sly and lovely darling. Her subterfuge so apparent. Trying to conceal her pleasure at my interest.

"Why?" I asked again.

"I am not sure," she said. "It could be your appearance, which bears considerable resemblance to a gorilla, or your manner, which would suggest closer alliance to a pig."

317

"Now that you have met my family," I said engagingly, "let us dance."

"Not now," she said, and her voice rose. "Not this dance or the one after. Not tonight or tomorrow night or next month or next year. Is that clear?"

Sweet, sweet Ariadne. Ancient and eternal game of retreat and pursuit. My pulse beat more quickly.

Vasili pulled at my sleeve. He was my friend, but without the courage of a goat. I shook him off and spoke to Ariadne.

"There is a joy like fire that consumes a man's heart when he first sets eyes on his beloved," I said. "This I felt when I first saw you." My voice trembled under a mighty passion. "I swear before God from this moment that I love you."

She stared shocked out of her deep dark eyes and, beside her, old prune-face staggered as if she had been kicked. Then my beloved did something which proved indisputably that her passion was as intense as mine.

She doubled up her fist and struck me in the eye. A stout blow for a woman that brought a haze to my vision, but I shook my head and moved a step closer.

"I would not care," I said, "if you struck out both my eyes. I would cherish the memory of your beauty forever."

By this time the music had stopped, and the dancers formed a circle of idiot faces about us. I paid them no attention and ignored Vasili, who kept whining and pulling at my sleeve.

"You are crazy!" she said. "You must be mad! Remove yourself from my presence or I will tear out both your eyes and your tongue besides!"

You see! Another woman would have cried, or been frightened into silence. But my Ariadne, worthy and venerable, hurled her spirit into my teeth.

"I would like to call on your father tomorrow," I said. From the assembled dancers who watched there rose a few vagrant whispers and some rude laughter. I stared at them care-

fully and they hushed at once. My temper and strength of arm were well known.

Ariadne did not speak again, but in a magnificent spirit stamped from the floor. The music began, and men and women began again to dance. I permitted Vasili to pull me to a corner.

"You are insane!" he said. He wrung his withered fingers in anguish. "You assaulted her like a Turk! Her relatives will cut out your heart!"

"My intentions were honorable," I said. "I saw her and loved her and told her so." At this point I struck my fist against my chest. Poor Vasili jumped.

"But you do not court a woman that way," he said.

"*You* don't, my anemic friend," I said. "Nor do the rest of these sheep. But I court a woman that way!"

He looked to heaven and helplessly shook his head. I waved good-by and started for my hat and coat.

"Where are you going?" he asked.

"To prepare for tomorrow," I said. "In the morning I will speak to her father."

I left the hall and in the street felt the night wind cold on my flushed cheeks. My blood was inflamed. The memory of her loveliness fed fuel to the fire. For the first time I understood with a terrible clarity the driven heroes of the past performing mighty deeds in love. Paris stealing Helen in passion, and Menelaus pursuing with a great fleet.[1] In that moment if I knew the whole world would be plunged into conflict I would have followed Ariadne to Hades.

I went to my rooms above my tavern. I could not sleep. All night I tossed in restless frenzy. I touched my eye that she had struck with her spirited hand.

---

1. **Paris stealing Helen...fleet.** Paris, the son of Priam, king of Troy, abducted Helen, the wife of Menelaus, brother of Agamemnon. This incident set off the Trojan War, a ten-year war waged by the confederated Greeks under King Agamemnon against the Trojans.

*Ariadne! Ariadne!* my soul cried out.

In the morning I bathed and dressed carefully. I confirmed the address of Langos, the grocer, and started to his store. It was a bright cold November morning, but I walked with spring in my step.

When I opened the door of the Langos grocery, a tiny bell rang shrilly. I stepped into the store piled with fruits and vegetables and smelling of cabbages and greens.

A stooped little old man with white bushy hair and owlish eyes came toward me. He looked as if his veins contained vegetable juice instead of blood, and if he were, in truth, the father of my beloved I marveled at how he could have produced such a paragon of women.

"Are you Mr. Langos?"

"I am," he said and he came closer. "I am."

"I met your daughter last night," I said. "Did she mention I was going to call?"

He shook his head somberly.

"My daughter mentioned you," he said. "In thirty years I have never seen her in such a state of agitation. She was possessed."

"The effect on me was the same," I said. "We met for the first time last night, and I fell passionately in love."

"Incredible," the old man said.

"You wish to know something about me," I said. "My name is Marko Palamas. I am a Spartan[2] emigrated to this country eleven years ago. I am forty-one years old. I have been a wrestler and a sailor and fought with the resistance movement in Greece in the war. For this service I was decorated by the king. I own a small but profitable tavern on Dart Street. I attend church regularly. I love your daughter."

As I finished he stepped back and bumped a rack of fruit. An orange rolled off to the floor. I bent and retrieved it to hand it to him, and he cringed as if he thought I might bounce it off his old head.

"She is a bad-tempered girl," he said. "Stubborn, impatient and spoiled. She has been the cause of considerable concern to me. All the eligible young men have been driven away by her temper and disposition."

"Poor girl," I said. "Subjected to the courting of calves and goats."

The old man blinked his owlish eyes. The front door opened and a battleship of a woman sailed in.

"Three pounds of tomatoes, Mr. Langos," she said. "I am in a hurry. Please to give me good ones. Last week two spoiled before I had a chance to put them into Demetri's salad."

"I am very sorry," Mr. Langos said. He turned to me. "Excuse me, Mr. Poulmas."

"Palamas," I said. "Marko Palamas."

He nodded nervously. He went to wait on the battleship, and I spent a moment examining the store. Neat and small. I would not imagine he did more than hold his own. In the rear of the store there were stairs leading to what appeared to be an apartment above. My heart beat faster.

When he had bagged the tomatoes and given change, he returned to me and said, "She is also a terrible cook. She cannot fry an egg without burning it." His voice shook with woe. "She cannot make pilaf or lamb with squash." He paused. "You like pilaf and lamb with squash?"

"Certainly."

"You see?" he said in triumph. "She is useless in the kitchen. She is thirty years old, and I am resigned she will remain an old maid. In a way I am glad because I know she would drive some poor man to drink."

"Do not deride her to discourage me," I said. "You need have no fear that I will mistreat her or cause her unhappiness. When she is married to me she will cease being a problem to you." I paused. "It is true that I am not pretty by the foppish standards that prevail today. But I am a man. I wrestled Zahundos and pinned him two straight falls in Baltimore. A giant of a man. Afterward he con-

---

2. **Spartan**, suggesting Spartan characteristics—brave, undaunted.

ceded he had met his master. This from Zahundos was a mighty compliment."

"I am sure," the old man said without enthusiasm. "I am sure."

He looked toward the front door as if hoping for another customer.

"Is your daughter upstairs?"

He looked startled and tugged at his apron. "Yes," he said. "I don't know. Maybe she has gone out."

"May I speak to her? Would you kindly tell her I wish to speak with her."

"You are making a mistake," the old man said. "A terrible mistake."

"No mistake," I said firmly.

The old man shuffled toward the stairs. He climbed them slowly. At the top he paused and turned the knob of the door. He rattled it again.

"It is locked," he called down. "It has never been locked before. She has locked the door."

"Knock," I said. "Knock to let her know I am here."

"I think she knows," the old man said. "I think she knows."

He knocked gently.

"Knock harder," I suggested. "Perhaps she does not hear."

"I think she hears," the old man said. "I think she hears."

"Knock again," I said. "Shall I come up and knock for you?"

"No, no," the old man said quickly. He gave the door a sound kick. Then he groaned as if he might have hurt his foot.

"She does not answer," he said in a quavering voice. "I am very sorry she does not answer."

"The coy darling," I said and laughed. "If that is her game." I started for the front door of the store.

I went out and stood on the sidewalk before the store. Above the grocery were the front windows of their apartment. I cupped my hands about my mouth.

"Ariadne!" I shouted. "Ariadne!"

The old man came out the door running disjointedly. He looked frantically down the street.

"Are you mad?" he asked shrilly. "You will cause a riot. The police will come. You must be mad!"

"Ariadne!" I shouted. "Beloved!"

A window slammed open, and the face of Ariadne appeared above me. Her dark hair tumbled about her ears.

"Go away!" she shrieked. "Will you go away!"

"Ariadne," I said loudly. "I have come as I promised. I have spoken to your father. I wish to call on you."

"Go away!" she shrieked. "Madman! Imbecile! Go away!"

By this time a small group of people had assembled around the store and were watching curiously. The old man stood wringing his hands and uttering what sounded like small groans.

"Ariadne," I said. "I wish to call on you. Stop this nonsense and let me in."

She pushed farther out the window and showed me her teeth.

"Be careful, beloved," I said. "You might fall."

She drew her head in quickly, and I turned then to the assembled crowd.

"A misunderstanding," I said. "Please move on."

Suddenly old Mr. Langos shrieked. A moment later something broke on the sidewalk a foot from where I stood. A vase or a plate. I looked up, and Ariadne was preparing to hurl what appeared to be a water pitcher.

"Ariadne!" I shouted. "Stop that!"

The water pitcher landed closer than the vase, and fragments of glass struck my shoes. The crowd scattered, and the old man raised his hands and wailed to heaven.

Ariadne slammed down the window.

The crowd moved in again a little closer, and somewhere among them I heard laughter. I fixed them with a cold stare and waited for some one of them to say something offensive.

I would have tossed him around like sardines, but they slowly dispersed and moved on. In another moment the old man and I were alone.

I followed him into the store. He walked an awkward dance of agitation. He shut the door and peered out through the glass.

"A disgrace," he wailed. "A disgrace. The whole street will know by nightfall. A disgrace."

"A girl of heroic spirit," I said. "Will you speak to her for me? Assure her of the sincerity of my feelings. Tell her I pledge eternal love and devotion."

The old man sat down on an orange crate and weakly made his cross.

"I had hoped to see her myself," I said. "But if you promise to speak to her, I will return this evening."

"That soon?" the old man said.

"If I stayed now," I said, "it would be sooner."

"This evening," the old man said and shook his head in resignation. "This evening."

I went to my tavern for a while and set up the glasses for the evening trade. I made arrangements for Pavlakis to tend bar in my place. Afterward I sat alone in my apartment and read a little of majestic Pindar[3] to ease the agitation of my heart.

Once in the mountains of Greece when I fought with the guerrillas in the last year of the great war, I suffered a wound from which it seemed I would die. For days high fever raged in my body. My friends brought a priest at night secretly from one of the captive villages to read the last rites. I accepted the coming of death and was grateful for many things. For the gentleness and wisdom of my old grandfather, the loyalty of my companions in war, the years I sailed between the wild ports of the seven seas, and the strength that flowed to me from the Spartan earth. For one thing only did I weep when it seemed I would leave life, that I had never set ablaze the world with a burning song of passion for one woman. Women I had known, pockets of pleasure that I tumbled for quick joy, but I had been denied

mighty love for one woman. For that I wept.

In Ariadne I swore before God I had found my woman. I knew by the storm-lashed hurricane that swept within my body. A woman whose majesty was in harmony with the earth, who would be faithful and beloved to me as Penelope had been to Ulysses.[4]

That evening near seven I returned to the grocery. Deep twilight had fallen across the street, and the lights in the window of the store had been dimmed. The apples and oranges and pears had been covered with brown paper for the night.

I tried the door and found it locked. I knocked on the glass, and a moment later the old man came shuffling out of the shadows and let me in.

"Good evening, Mr. Langos."

He muttered some greeting in answer. "Ariadne is not here," he said. "She is at the church. Father Marlas wishes to speak with you."

"A fine young priest," I said. "Let us go at once."

I waited on the sidewalk while the old man locked the store. We started the short walk to the church.

"A clear and ringing night," I said. "Does it not make you feel the wonder and glory of being alive?"

The old man uttered what sounded like a groan, but a truck passed on the street at that moment and I could not be sure.

At the church we entered by a side door leading to the office of Father Marlas. I knocked on the door, and when he called to us to enter we walked in.

Young Father Marlas was sitting at his desk in his black cassock and with his black goatee

---

3. **Pindar,** a Greek poet.
4. **Penelope . . . Ulysses,** Penelope, wife of Ulysses, remained faithful and devoted to her husband while waiting twenty years for him to fight in and return from the Trojan War. Homer's *Odyssey* records Ulysses' experiences while returning home.

trim and imposing beneath his clean-shaven cheeks. Beside the desk, in a dark blue dress sat Ariadne, looking somber and beautiful. A bald-headed, big-nosed old man with flint and fire in his eyes sat in a chair beside her.

"Good evening, Marko," Father Marlas said and smiled.

"Good evening, Father," I said.

"Mr. Langos and his daughter you have met," he said and he cleared his throat. "This is Uncle Paul Langos."

"Good evening, Uncle Paul," I said. He glared at me and did not answer. I smiled warmly at Ariadne in greeting, but she was watching the priest.

"Sit down," Father Marlas said.

I sat down across from Ariadne, and old Mr. Langos took a chair beside Uncle Paul. In this way we were arrayed in battle order as if we were opposing armies.

A long silence prevailed during which Father Marlas cleared his throat several times. I observed Ariadne closely. There were grace and poise even in the way her slim-fingered hands rested in her lap. She was a dark and lovely flower, and my pulse beat more quickly at her nearness.

"Marko," Father Marlas said finally. "Marko, I have known you well for the three years since I assumed duties in this parish. You are most regular in your devotions and very generous at the time of the Christmas and Easter offerings. Therefore, I find it hard to believe this complaint against you."

"My family are not liars!" Uncle Paul said, and he had a voice like hunks of dry hard cheese being grated.

"Of course not," Father Marlas said quickly. He smiled benevolently at Ariadne. "I only mean to say——"

"Tell him to stay away from my niece," Uncle Paul burst out.

"Excuse me, Uncle Paul," I said very politely. "Will you kindly keep out of what is not your business."

Uncle Paul looked shocked. "Not my business?" He looked from Ariadne to Father Marlas and then to his brother. "Not my business?"

"This matter concerns Ariadne and me," I said. "With outside interference it becomes more difficult."

"Not my business!" Uncle Paul said. He couldn't seem to get that through his head.

"Marko," Father Marlas said, and his composure was slightly shaken. "The family feels you are forcing your attention upon this girl. They are concerned."

"I understand, Father," I said. "It is natural for them to be concerned. I respect their concern. It is also natural for me to speak of love to a woman I have chosen for my wife."

"Not my business!" Uncle Paul said again, and shook his head violently.

"My daughter does not wish to become your wife," Mr. Langos said in a squeaky voice.

"That is for your daughter to say," I said courteously.

Ariadne made a sound in her throat, and we all looked at her. Her eyes were deep and cold, and she spoke slowly and carefully as if weighing each word on a scale in her father's grocery.

"I would not marry this madman if he were one of the Twelve Apostles," she said.

"See!" Mr. Langos said in triumph.

"Not my business!" Uncle Paul snarled.

"Marko," Father Marlas said. "Try to understand."

"We will call the police!" Uncle Paul raised his voice. "Put this hoodlum under a bond!"

"Please!" Father Marlas said. "Please!"

"Today he stood on the street outside the store," Mr. Langos said excitedly. "He made me a laughingstock."

"If I were a younger man," Uncle Paul growled, "I would settle this without the police. Zi-ip!" He drew a callused finger violently across his throat.

"Please," Father Marlas said.

"A disgrace!" Mr. Langos said.

"An outrage!" Uncle Paul said.

"He must leave Ariadne alone!" Mr. Langos said.

"We will call the police!" Uncle Paul said.

"Silence!" Father Marlas said loudly.

With everything suddenly quiet he turned to me. His tone softened.

"Marko," he said and he seemed to be pleading a little. "Marko, you must understand."

Suddenly a great bitterness assailed me, and anger at myself, and a terrible sadness that flowed like night through my body because I could not make them understand.

"Father," I said quietly, "I am not a fool. I am Marko Palamas and once I pinned the mighty Zahundos in Baltimore. But this battle, more important to me by far, I have lost. That which has not the grace of God is far better in silence."

I turned to leave and it would have ended there.

"Hoodlum!" Uncle Paul said. "It is time you were silent!"

I swear in that moment if he had been a younger man I would have flung him to the dome of the church. Instead I turned and spoke to them all in fire and fury.

"Listen," I said. "I feel no shame for the violence of my feelings. I am a man bred of the Spartan earth and my emotions are violent. Let those who squeak of life feel shame. Nor do I feel shame because I saw this flower and loved her. Or because I spoke at once of my love."

No one moved or made a sound.

"We live in a dark age," I said. "An age where men say one thing and mean another. A time of dwarfs afraid of life. The days are gone when mighty Pindar sang his radiant blossoms of song. When the noble passions of men set ablaze cities, and the heroic deeds of men rang like thunder to every corner of the earth."

I spoke my final words to Ariadne. "I saw you and loved you," I said gently. "I told you of my love. This is my way—the only way I know. If this way has proved offensive to you I apologize to you alone. But understand clearly that for none of this do I feel shame."

I turned then and started to the door. I felt my heart weeping as if waves were breaking within my body.

"Marko Palamas," Ariadne said. I turned slowly. I looked at her. For the first time the warmth I was sure dwelt in her body radiated within the circles of her face. For the first time she did not look at me with her eyes like glaciers.

"Marko Palamas," she said and there was a strange moving softness in the way she spoke my name. "You may call on me tomorrow."

Uncle Paul shot out of his chair. "She is mad too!" he shouted. "He has bewitched her!"

"A disgrace!" Mr. Langos said.

"Call the police!" Uncle Paul shouted. "I'll show him if it's my business!"

"My poor daughter!" Mr. Langos wailed.

"Turk!" Uncle Paul shouted. "Robber!"

"Please!" Father Marlas said. "Please!"

I ignored them all. In that winged and zestful moment I had eyes only for my beloved, for Ariadne, blossom of my heart and black-eyed flower of my soul!

---

### I
### OLD STORIES RETOLD

Literature abounds in story patterns, many of which are found in different cultures. Similar stories may be found in ancient Greek myths, the Bible, children's fairy tales, and American folklore. Often, these old stories carry the accumulated feelings of the common people about the nature of life. In the selection you have just read, there are three familiar patterns: the "sleeping" heroine waiting to be awakened; the ugly duckling that turns into a swan; and the shrew who needs to be tamed. Looking back at the selection, you can see how old patterns can be blended into a thoroughly modern story.

### II
### IMPLICATIONS

Consider the following statements. Do you agree or disagree with the implication suggested?

**1.** "It is the distinction of the male to be the aggressor and the cloak of the female to lend grace to the pursuit."

**2.** Ariadne is basically bad-tempered, stubborn, and spoiled.

**3.** Marko's relationships with people are amusing in a story, but he would be unpleasant to know personally.

**4.** Marko has a dream of a perfect wife which he attempts to superimpose on Ariadne's personality.

### III
### TECHNIQUES

*Irony*

Irony always involves incongruity: incongruity between what one says and what one is understood to say; between what one wants and what one gets; between what one professes and what one actually does; and sometimes between what the reader knows and what the characters know. An example of the first category follows. See if you can explain the irony created in this dialogue between Marko and Ariadne's father.

"My daughter mentioned you," he said. "In thirty years I have never seen her in such a state of agitation. She was possessed."

"The effect on me was the same," I said. "We met for the first time last night and I fell passionately in love."

"Incredible," the old man said.

Sometimes irony is used with humorous effect, as in "The Wooing of Ariadne." Sometimes it creates deeply troubling, disturbing reactions. In both cases, however, irony increases the emotional impact of the story on the reader.

*Organization*

Organization is the writer's patterning of the elements of his story. Suppose that you had a handful of sticks cut to three different lengths. You could organize them in a number of patterns: in known geometrical shapes; from big to little, from little to big; in a contrasting pattern—one size vertically; another, horizontally; the third, diagonally. The writer working with characters, emotions, and events may also move these aspects of a story about to create a variety of patterns and effects.

One of the common patterns of storytelling is the arrangement of a series of trials for a character to meet, often three or four in number. The last is usually successful or somehow significantly different from those leading up to it. This is the pattern in many children's stories, as well as in jokes. For instance, each of the three Billy Goats Gruff tries to cross the river. The first two fail, but the third one makes it across the bridge. "Goldilocks and the Three Bears" uses a similar but more complicated pattern, for it is a three times three pattern. There are *three* objects in each of the *three* trials: the testing of the chairs, the tasting of the porridge, and the selection of the bed. Furthermore, there are *three* bears who have *three* different reactions as they confront the obvious results of the *three* trials.

"The Wooing of Ariadne" is built on this old, old pattern. How many trials are there? What makes the early trials alike? How is the last one different?

## IV

### WORDS

**A.** In "The Wooing of Ariadne," there are references to characters in Greek mythology, such as Menelaus, Penelope, Helen, and Ulysses. The name *Ariadne* itself has a mythic background. Greek mythology has been a wellspring of words and phrases that are now a familiar part of our language. When a person is called a *Cassandra*, it means that she or he is a prophet of calamity. In the Greek myth, Cassandra was given the gift of prophecy by Apollo, who loved her. However, she did not return his love as she had promised. Angered, Apollo decreed that no one would believe her prophecies though she spoke the truth. In ancient Greek literature, Cassandra was a prophet of doom. Thus, anyone who predicts disaster—whether it is believed or not—is called a *Cassandra*.

Also from a mythic origin comes the phrase *Achilles' heel*, referring to a person's weak spot. As an infant, Achilles was dipped in the River Styx by his mother to make him immune to wounds or death in later battles. Unfortunately, she held him by the heel, and that was the one part of his body not covered by the magical water. As fate would have it, Achilles was eventually killed in battle by a poison arrow shot by Paris into his heel. Therefore, a person's "Achilles' heel" is a weakness which makes him or her vulnerable.

Yet another contribution from Greek mythology is *Pandora's box*. According to the myth, Pandora was entrusted with a box containing all the evils that could plague humanity. She was instructed never to open the box, but she did so out of curiosity, letting loose all the ills that afflict us. *Pandora's box*, then, as it is used today, is a source of potential evil.

Now that you know the story behind each of the above mythological references, you may wish to find out more about Ariadne. She is a famous character in Greek mythology. See if you can explain the similarities between the Ariadne of the myth and the one in the story.

**B.** If one source of words in our language is Greek mythology, another source is from idiomatic compounds. These are constructions made up of two or more smaller words. The meaning of the idiomatic compound is not the sum of the two words that make it up, and the meaning cannot be taken literally. *Brainwash*, for instance, does not actually refer to cleansing of the brain; it means the intensive indoctrination of someone. Similarly, the *iron curtain* spoken of in world affairs is not really a curtain of iron; it refers to the political barrier between Western Europe and the Soviet bloc after World War II. And *horseplay* involves no horses, but it does involve rough, noisy play of the kind children engage in. What do the following idiomatic compounds mean: *Molotov cocktail, fourth estate, pen name,* and *red tape?*

# DREAM POEMS

## LANGSTON HUGHES

Although for some forty-five years of writing, Langston Hughes' main purpose
was "to explain and illuminate the Negro condition in America," he came back
again and again to the subject of dreams and their impact on life. The collection
which follows is arranged to show something of the evolution of
his thought on this subject.

## Dream Variation

To fling my arms wide
In some place of the sun,
To whirl and to dance
Till the white day is done.
Then rest at cool evening          5
Beneath a tall tree
While night comes on gently,
    Dark like me—
That is my dream!

To fling my arms wide          10
In the face of the sun,
Dance! Whirl! Whirl!
Till the quick day is done.
Rest at pale evening . . . .
A tall, slim tree . . . .          15
Night coming tenderly
    Black like me.

Copyright 1926 by Alfred A. Knopf,
Inc. and renewed 1954 by Langston
Hughes. Reprinted from SELECTED
POEMS, by Langston Hughes, by per-
mission of Alfred A. Knopf, Inc.

# Daybreak in Alabama

When I get to be a composer
I'm gonna write me some music about
Daybreak in Alabama
And I'm gonna put the purtiest songs in it
Rising out of the ground like a swamp mist          5
And falling out of heaven like soft dew.
I'm gonna put some tall tall trees in it
And the scent of pine needles
And the smell of red clay after rain
And long red necks                                          10
And poppy colored faces
And big brown arms
And the field daisy eyes
Of black and white black white black people.
And I'm gonna put white hands                          15
And black hands and brown and yellow hands
And red clay earth hands in it
Touching everybody with kind fingers
And touching each other natural as dew
In that dawn of music when I                            20
Get to be a composer
And write about daybreak
In Alabama.

Copyright 1948 by Alfred A. Knopf, Inc. Reprinted from
THE PANTHER AND THE LASH, by Langston Hughes, by
permission of Alfred A. Knopf, Inc.

*Youth*

We have tomorrow
Bright before us
Like a flame.

Yesterday
A night-gone thing,                    5
A sun-down name.

And dawn-today
Broad arch above the road we came.

We march!

From THE DREAM KEEPER, by Langston
Hughes. Copyright 1932 by Alfred A. Knopf,
Inc. and renewed 1960 by Langston Hughes, by
permission of Alfred A. Knopf, Inc.

*The Dream Keeper*

Bring me all of your dreams,
You dreamers,
Bring me all of your
Heart melodies
That I may wrap them                    5
In a blue cloud-cloth
Away from the too-rough fingers
Of the world.

From THE DREAM KEEPER, by Langston
Hughes. Copyright 1932 by Alfred A.
Knopf, Inc. and renewed 1960 by Langston
Hughes, by permission of Alfred A. Knopf,
Inc.

*Dreams*

Hold fast to dreams
For if dreams die
Life is a broken-winged bird
That cannot fly.

Hold fast to dreams                    5
For when dreams go
Life is a barren field
Frozen with snow.

From THE DREAM KEEPER, by
Langston Hughes. Copyright 1932 by
Alfred A. Knopf, Inc. and renewed
1960 by Langston Hughes, by permission of Alfred A. Knopf, Inc.

# I, Too

I, too, sing America.

I am the darker brother.
They send me to eat in the kitchen
When company comes,
But I laugh,                                           5
And eat well,
And grow strong.

Tomorrow,
I'll sit at the table
When company comes.                              10
Nobody'll dare
Say to me,
"Eat in the kitchen,"
Then.

Besides,                                                  15
They'll see how beautiful I am
And be ashamed—

I, too, am America.

Copyright 1926 by Alfred A. Knopf, Inc. and renewed 1954 by Langston Hughes. Reprinted from SELECTED POEMS, by Langston Hughes, by permission of Alfred A. Knopf, Inc.

# *As I Grew Older*

It was a long time ago.
I have almost forgotten my dream.
But it was there then,
In front of me,
Bright like a sun—                                    5
My dream.

And then the wall rose,
Rose slowly,
Slowly,
Between me and my dream.                        10
Rose slowly, slowly,
Dimming,
Hiding,
The light of my dream.
Rose until it touched the sky—               15
The wall.

Shadow.
I am black.

I lie down in the shadow.
No longer the light of my dream before me,   20
Above me.
Only the thick wall.
Only the shadow.

My hands!
My dark hands!                                        25
Break through the wall!
Find my dream!
Help me to shatter this darkness,
To smash this night,
To break this shadow                               30
Into a thousand lights of sun,
Into a thousand whirling dreams
Of sun!

Copyright 1926 by Alfred A. Knopf, Inc. and renewed
1954 by Langston Hughes. Reprinted from SELECTED
POEMS, by Langston Hughes, by permission of Alfred A.
Knopf, Inc.

## Let America Be America Again

Let America be America again.
Let it be the dream it used to be.
Let it be the pioneer on the plain
Seeking a home where he himself is free.

(America never was America to me.)

Let America be the dream the dreamers dreamed—
Let it be that great strong land of love
Where never kings connive nor tyrants scheme
That any man be crushed by one above.

(It never was America to me.)

O, let my land be a land where Liberty
Is crowned with no false patriotic wreath,
But opportunity is real, and life is free,
Equality is in the air we breathe.

(There's never been equality for me,
Nor freedom in this "homeland of the free.")

*Say who are you that mumbles in the dark?*
*And who are you that draws your veil across the stars?*

I am the poor white, fooled and pushed apart,
I am the red man driven from the land.
I am the refugee clutching the hope I seek—
But finding only the same old stupid plan
Of dog eat dog, of mighty crush the weak.
I am the Negro, "problem" to you all.
I am the people, humble, hungry, mean—
Hungry yet today despite the dream.
Beaten yet today—O, Pioneers!
I am the man who never got ahead,
The poorest worker bartered through the years.

Yet I'm the one who dreamt our basic dream
In that Old World while still a serf of kings,
Who dreamt a dream so strong, so brave, so true,
That even yet its mighty daring sings
In every brick and stone, in every furrow turned
That's made America the land it has become.
O, I'm the man who sailed those early seas
In search of what I meant to be my home—
For I'm the one who left dark Ireland's shore,
And Poland's plain, and England's grassy lea,
And torn from Black Africa's strand I came
To build a "homeland of the free."

The free?
Who said the free? Not me?
Surely not me? The millions on relief today?
The millions who have nothing for our pay
For all the dreams we've dreamed
And all the songs we've sung
And all the hopes we've held
And all the flags we've hung,
The millions who have nothing for our pay—
Except the dream we keep alive today.

O, let America be America again—
The land that never has been yet—
And yet must be—the land where *every* man is free.
The land that's mine—the poor man's, Indian's, Negro's, ME—
Who made America,
Whose sweat and blood, whose faith and pain,
Whose hand at the foundry, whose plow in the rain,
Must bring back our mighty dream again.

O, yes,
I say it plain,
America never was America to me,
And yet I swear this oath—
America will be!

Reprinted by permission of Harold Ober Associates Incorporated. Copyright 1951 by Langston Hughes.

## Dream Deferred

What happens to a dream deferred?

Does it dry up
like a raisin in the sun?
Or fester like a sore—
And then run?
Does it stink like rotten meat?
Or crust and sugar over—
like a syrupy sweet?

Maybe it just sags
like a heavy load.

*Or does it explode?*

Copyright 1951 by Langston Hughes. Reprinted from THE PANTHER AND THE LASH, by Langston Hughes, by permission of Alfred A. Knopf, Inc.

## THE DREAM DEFERRED

The blending of words with an idea has always had the power to stir people's souls. Pericles in the days of ancient Greece, Lincoln during the Civil War, Roosevelt and Churchill in World War II, and John F. Kennedy—all caught the public's imagination in the web of a phrase. And this is what poetry is really all about. Consider Langston Hughes' phrase "a dream deferred." Why is this ordering of the words so much more effective than "a deferred dream" or "a put-off dream"? Why should the common words "a raisin in the sun" have taken such a hold of Lorraine Hansberry's imagination that she wrote one of the great plays of contemporary black life in America using Hughes' phrase as her title?

## II

### IMPLICATIONS

Hughes, by the way he combines word sounds, movement, and pattern, creates for the reader feelings, perceptions, and intimations about dreams that go far beyond the face value of the individual words used. Reread the group of poems several times until they seem familiar to you. Then respond to the following statements.

### Dream Variation

1. The speaker seems to associate himself with night. This means that day is somehow less congenial to him.

2. The title of the poem has little significance.

### Daybreak in Alabama

1. The poem has a breathless quality like a child imagining one thing after another.

2. There is a vein of bitterness underlying the poem's seemingly joyful mood.

### Youth

The poem is out of keeping with today's mood among young people.

### The Dream Keeper

Speculate about possible definitions of "heart melodies" and the "blue cloud-cloth." Do you agree or disagree that such concepts are important in life, though at a casual glance they seem vague abstractions?

### Dreams

1. To live fully and deeply, one must dream.

2. Every person has some dream.

### I, Too

There is a change in the poem expressed in the difference in the choice of words between the first line, "I . . . sing America," and the last line, "I . . . am America."

### As I Grew Older

This poem expresses anguish? bitterness? despair? hope? frustration?

### Let America Be America Again

1. Who is the speaker of the poem?

2. Why are two lines in italics?

3. Why are some lines in parentheses?

4. Explain the apparent inconsistency between the first lines

Let America be America again.
Let it be the dream it used to be.

and the lines in the next-to-last stanza beginning

O, let America be America again—
The land that never has been yet—
And yet must be—the land where *every* man is free.

Is the poem bitter or hopeful?

### Dream Deferred

A dream too long unrealized injures the dreamer.

## III

### TECHNIQUES

When you studied the poems in the first unit of this book, you looked at the way rhythm is achieved through repetition of certain elements. Reread this material on pages 31 and 33 if you have forgotten it. Choose one of Langston Hughes's poems and be prepared to explain how elements are repeated to make the pattern.

Choose the poem you liked the best in this group of selections. Point out phrases, word arrangements, or word choices that seem unusually apt.

There was a time when it was
a good thing to be an Indian, and old.
But Charley was cheated—almost—of his
honors, because he lived at the wrong time.

# Scars of Honor

## DOROTHY JOHNSON

Charley Lockjaw died last summer on the reservation. He was very old—a hundred years, he had claimed. He still wore his hair in braids, as only the older men do in his tribe, and the braids were thin and white. His fierce old face was like a withered apple. He was bent and frail and trembling, and his voice was like a wailing of the wind across the prairie grass.

Old Charley died in his sleep in the canvas-covered tepee where he lived in warm weather. In the winter he was crowded with the younger ones among his descendants in a two-room log cabin, but in summer they pitched the tepee. Sometimes they left him alone there, and sometimes his great-grandchildren scrambled in with him like a bunch of puppies.

His death was no surprise to anyone. What startled the Indian agent and some of Charley's own people, and the white ranchers when they heard about it, was the fact that some of the young men of the tribe sacrificed a horse on his grave. Charley wasn't buried on holy ground; he never went near the mission. He was buried in a grove of cottonwoods down by the creek that is named for a dead chief. His lame great-grandson, Joe Walking Wolf, and

three other young Indians took this horse out there and shot it. It was a fine sorrel gelding, only seven years old, broke fairly gentle and nothing wrong with it. Young Joe had been offered eighty dollars for that horse.

The mission priest was disturbed about the killing of the horse, justifiably suspecting some dark pagan significance, and he tried to find out the reason the young men killed it. He urged Joe's mother, Mary, to find out, but she never did—or if she did, she never told. Joe only said, with a shrug, "It was my horse."

The white ranchers chuckled indulgently, a little shocked about the horse, but never too much upset about anything Indians did. The rancher who told the story oftenest and with most interest was the one who had made the eighty-dollar offer to Joe Walking Wolf. Joe had said to him, "Ain't my horse." But Joe was the one who shot it on old Charley's grave, and it didn't belong to anyone else.

But the Indian agent guessed what had been going on. He knew more about Indians than the Federal Government required him to know. The horse was not government property nor the tribe's common property; everybody knew it belonged to Joe. The agent did not investigate, figuring it was none of his business.

That was last summer, when old Charley died and the young men took the horse out to where he was buried.

The story about the killing of the horse begins, though, in 1941, before that horse was ever born. The young men were being drafted then, and the agent explained it all, over and over again, through an interpreter, so nobody would have an excuse for not understanding. In the agent's experience, even an Indian who had been clear through high school could fail completely to understand English if he didn't happen to want to.

Some of the white ranchers explained it, too. Some of them were expecting to go, or to have their sons or hired cowboys go, and the draft was a thing they mentioned casually to the Indians who worked for them at two or three

Copyright © 1950 by Dorothy Johnson. Appeared originally in *Argosy*. Reprinted by permission of McIntosh and Otis, Inc.

dollars a day, digging irrigation ditches or hoeing in the kitchen garden or working in the hay fields. So the Indians understood the draft all right, with everybody talking about it.

The agent kept telling them, "In the World War you were not citizens, so you did not have to go in the Army." (He meant the First World War, of course. The United States hadn't got into the second one yet; there was only the draft.) "Many of your fathers enlisted in the Army anyway and they were good fighters. They did not have to go, but they wanted to. Now you are citizens, you can vote, and some of you will have to go in the Army. When the letters come for you, we will talk about it again."

Well, some of the young men didn't want to wait until the letters came. Fighting was part of their tradition. It was in the old men's stories, and the names of their long-dead warriors were in history books, as well as in the stories the old men told around the cabin stoves when snow was deep outside and the cabins were crowded with many people and the air foul with much breathing and not much bathing. (Long ago, before any of these young men were born, their forefathers had bathed every morning in rivers or creeks, even if they had to break the ice, but that custom had passed with their glory.)

The middle-aged men of the tribe remembered the white man's war they had fought in, and some of them still had parts of their old uniforms put away. But the stories they told were of places too distant for understanding, foreign places with no meaning except for the men who had been there. The stories the grandfathers told were better. They were about the stealthy approach through the grass after the men had prayed and painted, the quick, sharp action on riverbanks that were familiar still or in tepee camps where white men now live in brick houses.

The grandfathers' stories were of warriors who never marched or drilled but walked softly in moccasins or rode naked on fleet war ponies. They had no uniforms; they wore mystic painted symbols on face and body. In those battles there was the proud waving of eagle-feathered war bonnets and the strong courage of warriors who dared to carry a sacred buffalo shield, although a man who carried one was pledged not to retreat. They were battles without artillery, but with muzzle-loading rifles and iron-tipped lances and the long feathered arrows hissing out from a horn bow. Killing was not paramount in those old battles; more important was proof of a man's courage in the face of death, and the bravest were those few who dared to carry no weapon at all, but only a whip, for counting coup[1] on a living, unhurt enemy. Nobody was drafted for those battles, and death was often the price of glory.

Only two or three of the old men remembered so far back. One of them was Charley Lockjaw. He was suddenly important. If he had not lived two generations too late, he would have been important simply because he was old. His people would have taken it for granted that he was wise, because his medicine had protected him for so long against death. They would have listened respectfully when he spoke. There was a time when it was a good thing to be an Indian, and old. But Charley was cheated—almost—of his honors, because he lived at the wrong time.

Suddenly he was needed. He was sitting in front of his summer tepee, nodding in the sun, with the good warmth seeping into his joints, when four young men came to him. They were modern Indians, with white men's haircuts. They wore torn blue jeans and faded shirts and white men's boots, because they were all cowboys, even the lame one, his great-grandson, Joe.

Charley looked up, ready to be angry, expecting some disrespectful, hurried greeting, like "Hey, grampa, look here."

They did not say anything for a while. Embarrassed, they shuffled their boots in the dust. Joe Walking Wolf took off his broad-brimmed

---

1. **counting coup,** to touch an enemy in battle, considered the most dangerous test of bravery.

hat, and the other three took their hats off, too, and laid them on the ground.

Joe cleared his throat and said in Cheyenne, "Greetings, my grandfather." It was the way a young man talked to a wise old one in the buffalo years that were gone.

Old Charley blinked and saw that Joe was carrying, with awkward care, an ancient ceremonial pipe of red stone.

Joe asked gravely, "Will you smoke with us, my grandfather?"

Charley was at first indignant, thinking they meant to tease him, because they were atheists who did not believe in the old religion or any of the new ones. He railed at them in English. But they did not go away; they stood there respectfully with their heads bent, accepting what he said and, in the old, courteous way, not interrupting.

He looked at their sober faces and their steady eyes, and he was ashamed for his own lack of courtesy. When he understood that they were sincere, he would have done anything for them, anything they asked. There was not much he could do any more, and nobody had asked him to do anything for a long time.

If he took the pipe and smoked, that said, "I will do whatever you ask." He did not know what they were going to ask, but he would have let them cut him into pieces if that was what they wanted, because his heart was full at being approached in the remembered, ceremonial way, clumsy as these modern Indians were about it. He answered in his reedy voice, "I will smoke with you."

They were going to do it all wrong. One of the young men brought out a sack of tobacco, and that was all right if there was none that had been raised with the right prayers said over it. But Joe pulled out a pocket lighter a white man had given him and another young man brought out some kitchen matches and old Charley could not endure such innovations.

He made them build a fire in the center of his summer tepee, under the fire hole in the peak, and he sat down with a groan of stiffness at the back, in the honor seat, the place of the lodge owner. The young men were patient. They sat where he told them to, on the old ragged carpet his granddaughter had put on the earth floor.

He filled the pipe with pinches of tobacco without touching the bowl and lighted it with a coal from the fire. With slow, remembered ceremony he offered the pipestem to Heammawihic, the Wise One Above, to Ahktunowihic, the power of the earth below, and to the spirits of the four directions—where the sun comes up, where the cold wind goes to, where the sun comes over and where the cold wind comes from.

He spoke reverently to each of these. Then he himself took four puffs and passed the pipe, slowly, carefully, holding the stem upright, to young Yellowbird, who was on his left.

Yellowbird smoked, though awkwardly, in the sacred manner and passed the pipe to Joe Walking Wolf. When Joe had finished, he stood up to take the pipe to the two young men on the other side of Charley, but the old man corrected him patiently. The pipe must not cross the doorway of the lodge; it must be passed back from hand to hand, first to Robert Stands in Water and then on to Tom Little Hand.

The young men were humble when he corrected them. They thanked him when he told them how to do things right.

When he signified that the time had come for them to talk, young Joe, the lame one, said formally in Cheyenne, "My grandfather has told of the old times long ago, and we have listened. He has told how the warriors used to go on a hilltop with a wise old man and stay there and dream before they went on the warpath."

Old Charley said, "I told you those things and they were true. I dreamed on a hilltop when I was young."

Joe Walking Wolf said, "We want to dream that way, my grandfather, because we are going to war."

The old man did not have to promise to help them. He had promised when he took the pipe. He sat for a while with his eyes closed, his head bowed, trying to remember what his instructors had said to him the three times he had gone through the *wu-wun,* the starving. How would anyone know the right way if the old men had forgotten? But he was able to remember, because he remembered his youth better than yesterday.

He remembered the chanted prayers and the hunger and thirst and the long waiting for mystery to be revealed. He remembered the grave warnings, the sympathetic teaching of the wise old men seventy years before.

"It is a hard thing to do," he told the young men. "Some men cannot do it. Alone on a high place for four days and four nights, without food or water. Some men dream good medicine, and some dream bad medicine, and some have no dream. It is good to finish this hard thing, but it is no disgrace not to finish.

"A man lies on a bed of white sage," he told them, "and he is alone after his teacher, his grandfather, has taught him what to do. After four days, his grandfather goes up the hill and gets him—if he has not come back before that time."

Charley Lockjaw remembered something else that was important and added firmly, "The young men bring the grandfather a gift."

And so they went through the *wu-wun,* each of them alone on a high hill, hungering and thirsting for four days and nights. First they brought Charley gifts: four silver dollars from one, new moccasins from another, and two bottles of whiskey. (After the ordeals were over, he spent the four silver dollars for whiskey, too, getting it with difficulty through a man who was going off the reservation and who did not look like an Indian, so he could buy it, though it was against the law. An Indian could vote and be drafted, but he could not buy whiskey.)

The whole thing was secret, so that no one would complain to anybody who might want to interfere. Charley Lockjaw had been inter-fered with so much that he was suspicious. All his long life, white men had been interfering with him and, he thought, his own grand-daughter might go to the priest if she knew what was going on, or the other young men's families might make trouble. No good would come of telling what went on.

Because of the secrecy, the old man had to ride horseback several times. Usually he had to be helped into a saddle because his joints were stiff and his legs hurt, so that if he did not stop himself and remember that now he could be proud again, he might groan.

He took each young man out separately to a hill chosen because of its height, its loneliness and its location. It had to be south or west of a river—that had always been the rule. He had never known the reason, and neither did anyone else. It was one of the things that was right, that was all, and he was very anxious to do everything right.

At the foot of the hill, he and the young man left the horses hobbled. The young man helped Charley up the hill, respectfully and with great patience. He made a bed of white sage, and Charley sang his prayers to the Spirit above.

He added a humble plea that had not been in the ritual when he was young. "If I make a mistake," he cried to the blue sky, "it is be-cause I am old. Do not blame the young man. He wants to do right. If he does wrong, it is my fault. Give him good medicine."

Then he stumbled down the hill and got on the borrowed horse by himself and rode home. If the young man should give up before his time had passed, he could catch up the horse that was left.

None of them gave up, and none of them cheated. Each of them lay alone on the sage bed on the hill, singing the songs Charley Lockjaw had taught him, sometimes watching the sky (and seeing airplanes more often than wheeling eagles) and three times a day smok-ing the sacred pipe.

The first was Joe Walking Wolf. Charley was proud of him when he toiled up the hill with a canteen of water and a chunk of dry bread. He was proud when the boy first splashed water on his face and then drank, unhurriedly, from the canteen.

When Joe's tongue was moistened enough so he could talk, he said briefly, "I dreamed a horse was kicking me."

"I do not know what that means," Charley told him. "Maybe you will know after you think about it."

He was afraid, though, that the dream was bad. The reason Joe limped was that a horse had kicked him when he was three years old.

The second man was Yellowbird. He was impatient. He was standing up, watching, when Charley Lockjaw came in sight on his old bag-of-bones borrowed horse, and he came down the hill to gulp the water the old man had brought. But he had endured the whole four days.

He said in English, "I dreamed I was dead and gone to hell." Then he said it in Cheyenne, except "hell," and Charley knew what that word was. There was no hell for Cheyennes after they were dead, according to the old religion.

Charley said, "That may be good medicine. I do not know."

The third man was Robert Stands in Water. He was sick and he vomited the first water he drank, but he got better in a little while and they went home. He didn't say what his dream was.

The fourth and last was Tom Little Hand, a laughing young man except when there were white people around. He was a proud rider and a dandy; he wore green sunglasses when he went outdoors, and tight shirts like the white cowboys. When Charley brought the water, he was no dandy any more. Naked to the waist, he lay flat on the sage bed, and the old man had to help him sit up so he could drink and eat.

"There was a bright light," he said when he felt like talking. "It floated in the air and I tried to catch it."

Charley didn't know what kind of medicine

that was, but he said Tom Little Hand would probably be able to understand it after a while.

Anyway, they had all done the best they could, the right thing, and they were ready to be warriors. They had endured in the old fashion.

When they got back to the cabin settlement beside the creek that is named for a dead chief, old Charley dug up his whiskey and went into his lodge and drank, and slept, and drank some more. A teacher is worthy of his hire, and Charley Lockjaw was tired out from all that riding and climbing of high hills. For all that time, four days for four men, sixteen days altogether, he had not slept very much. He had been singing in his lodge or in front of it, in his reedy voice like the wailing of the wind across the prairie. The little boys had not bothered him by crowding in to tumble around like puppies. They were afraid of him.

While Charley was having his drunk, the four young men went down to town to enlist in the Army. He did not know that. When he was sober again, two of them had come back —his grandson Joe and Tom Little Hand, the dandy.

Tom said, "They don't want me. I don't see so good."

Joe Walking Wolf didn't say anything. He went around with his bad limp and got a job for a few days on a white man's ranch, sawing branches off some trees in the yard. The cook gave him his meals separate from the white hired hands, but he heard them talking about the draft and joking with each other about being 4F. Some were 4F because cowboys get stove up by bad horses. Joe felt better, knowing he was not the only one.

In the winter the war clouds broke with lightning and thunder, and the Army decided Tom Little Hand could see plenty well enough to go to war. The Army began to take some married men, too, and almost all the single ones except lame Joe Walking Wolf, and a couple who had an eye disease, and six who had tuberculosis and one who was stone-deaf.

Then for a couple of years old Charley Lockjaw wasn't important any more. The people who were important were those who could read the letters that came to the cabin settlement, and those who could write the answers.

Some of the young men came back on furlough, hitchhiking eighty miles from the railroad. In wartime people would pick up a soldier, even if he was an Indian. They strolled around the settlement and rode over to the agency in their uniforms and went to the white men's store, and some of the white ranchers went out of their way to shake hands with them and say, "Well, boy, how goes it?" They were important, the fledgling warriors.

Old Charley, sitting in front of his peaked lodge in the summer, saw them strut, saw the shawl-wrapped, laughing girls hang around them. He saw them walk down the road after dark, and he felt bad about some of the girls. When he was a young man, the Cheyennes took pride in the virtue of their women. His first wife had worn the rope of chastity until he removed it himself, the fourth night after her father had accepted his gift of captured horses.

He was ashamed of the Cheyenne girls, but not of the young warriors. He pitied them a little, remembering the proud nodding eagle-feathered war bonnets and the tall, straight men who wore them. He remembered his own courting; for five years it had gone on. There were many other gallants who had stood in front of the girl's lodge, blanket-wrapped, waiting for her to come out.

One of the letters that came to the reservation had bad news in it. It was in a yellow envelope, and the agent brought it over himself and explained it to the mother of Tom Little Hand.

Tom had been wounded, it said, and was in a hospital.

The next morning Joe Walking Wolf, the lame one, made a ceremonial visit to old Charley, carrying the old stone pipe. He was not embarrassed this time, because he knew how to smoke in the sacred way.

Charley drew in a breath sharply and was ashamed because he trembled.

"The gift for that, to the grandfather," he cautioned, "must be a big gift, because it is a hard ceremony."

"The gift is outside with the pole," Joe said humbly.

And outside was picketed Joe's good sorrel colt.

There was a time when the Cheyennes, the Cut Arm people, could be lordly in their generosity with gifts of captured horses, sometimes bought with their blood. They could be splendid in their charity, giving buffalo meat to the needy and fine robes to the poor. But that time was when Charley Lockjaw was young. He had not owned a horse of his own for thirty years. And this was the only horse his great-grandson had, for the old mare this colt belonged to had died.

Charley blinked at the horse, a beautiful colt without a blemish. He walked over to stroke its neck, and the colt threw its head back and tried to get away. Charley spoke to it sharply, with approval. The colt was no stable pet, but used to running across the prairie with its mane flying in the wind and the snow. It would throw a rider before it was broke, Charley thought.

He nodded and said, "The gift is enough."

When he was a young man, he had paid many fine horses to the old one who taught him the ceremony for swinging at the pole and whose hard, gentle hands had supported him when he fainted. But he had had many horses to give, and plenty of them left. This was a finer present than he had given, because it was all Joe had.

"We will have to wait," Charley said. "We cannot do this thing today. We will wait four days."

He chose four because it was the sacred number and because he needed time to remember. He had been a pupil for this sacrifice, but never a teacher.

"Come back in four days," he said.

In the time while he was remembering and

praying for a return, in some part, of his old strength and steadiness, he fasted for one whole day. His granddaughter fretted and murmured, coming out to the lodge to bring soup because he said he was sick and could not eat.

"I will send one of the children to tell the nurse at the agency," she decided, but he waved her away, promising, "I will be well tomorrow."

He was afraid, not only because he might forget something important or his hand might slip, but because someone might find out and try to stop him. Somebody was always interfering. For years the old religion had been outlawed by the government in Washington. For years no one dared even to make the Medicine Lodge when the grass was tall in summer, so those years passed without the old, careful ceremony of prayer and paint and reverence that brought new life to the tribe and honor to the Lodge Maker.

This was no longer true by the time of the Second World War, though. Every year now the Medicine Lodge was made by some man who could afford it and wanted to give thanks for something. Perhaps his child had been sick and was well again. A man who made the Lodge, who learned the ritual, could teach another man. So that was not lost, though some of it had changed and some was forgotten, and it was very hard to find a buffalo skull to use in the ceremony.

The white ranchers and their guests came to the reservation in July to watch the making of the Lodge and see the prayer cloths waving from the Thunderbird's nest, and Charley took part in those ceremonies. The white people vaguely approved of the Indians keeping their quaint old customs.

But the Medicine Lodge, the Sun Dance, was a public ceremony. Swinging at the pole, as Joe Walking Wolf wanted to do it, was private suffering.

It was a long time since a young man had wished to swing at the pole. There was no one left in the tribe, except Charley Lockjaw, who

could instruct a pupil in the ceremony. No one could teach it except a man who had himself endured it. And only Charley had on his withered breast the knotted scars of that ordeal.

Now that Joe was going to do it, Charley could not keep this great thing to himself. A man who suffered at the pole gained honor—but how could he be credited if no one knew what he had done?

At sunrise on the fourth day, Joe and Charley rode far out to a safe place among the sandstone cliffs.

Then Charley was shaken by terror. He denied his gods. He said, "Do not be too sure about this thing. Maybe the spirits will not hear my voice or yours. Maybe they are all dead and will never hear anything any more. Maybe they starved to death."

Joe Walking Wolf said, "I will do it anyway. Tom Little Hand has a bad wound, and he is my friend. I will make this sacrifice because maybe it will help him get well. Anyway, I will know what it is to be wounded. I did not go to war."

Charley dug a hole to set the pole in. He told Joe how to set up the pole and fasten a lariat to it, and all the time he was thinking about long ago. He could not remember the pain any more. He remembered his strong voice crying out prayers as he jerked against the thong. He had not flinched when the knife cut or when the thong jerked the skewers in the bloody flesh.

He said, "I did this to pay a pledge. My wife, Laughing Woman—my first wife—she was very sick, and I pledged this sacrifice. The baby died, because it was winter and the white soldiers chased our people through the snow in the bitter cold. Lots of people died. But Laughing Woman lived, and in the spring I paid what I had promised."

He had Joe make a bed of white sage. When everything was ready, Joe said, "Fasten it to my back. I don't want to see it."

Charley said, "Kneel on the sage bed."

He made his gnarled hands as steady as he

could and pinched up the skin on Joe's right shoulder. He tunneled through the pinched part with a sharp knife, and the bright blood sprang to the dark skin. Through the tunnel he thrust a wooden skewer three inches long. Joe did not move or murmur. Kneeling on the sage bed, with his head bowed, he was silent as a stone.

Charley put another skewer under the skin on the left shoulder, and over each skewer he put a loop of rawhide, which he tied to the lariat that hung from the pole. The skewers would never be pulled out as they had been put in.

He lifted Joe to his feet and made him lean forward to see that the rope was tight and the pull even. Joe walked a quarter of a circle to the right four times, and back, sagging forward hard on the lariat's pull, trying to tear the skewers through. Then he walked four times to the left, with his blood running down his back.

Charley left the red stone pipe where he could reach it and said, "Three times before the sun goes down, stop and smoke for a little while."

His heart was full of Joe's pain. He ached with tenderness and pride.

"Break away if you can," he urged, "but if you cannot, there is no wrong thing done. If you cannot break away, I will cut you free when the sun goes down. Nobody can take away the honor."

Joe said, "I am not doing it to get honor. I am doing it to make Tom Little Hand get well again."

He kept walking with his bad limp and pulling mightily, but he could not break through the tough flesh that stretched like rubber.

"I will come back when the sun goes down," Charley Lockjaw said.

Back in the settlement he went around and told a few safe, religious men what was happening in the sandstone cliffs. They said their hearts were with Joe, and Charley knew that Joe would have his honor among his people.

When he went back to the pole at sunset, Joe was still walking, still pulling.

Charley asked, "Did you have a dream?"

Joe said, "I saw Tom Little Hand riding a horse."

"What a man dreams when he swings at the pole," Charley told him, "is sure to come true. I saw myself with thin, white braids, and I have lived to be old instead of being killed in battle." He got out his knife and said, "Kneel down."

He cut out a small piece of skin from the right shoulder and the left, freeing the skewers, and laid the bits of bloody skin on the ground as an offering.

He touched Joe's arm and said gently, "It is ended."

Joe stood up, not even giving a deep breath to show he was glad the suffering was over.

Charley did something new then. He bandaged the wounds as well as he could, with clean gauze and tape from the white man's store. These were new things, not part of the ceremony, but he saw that some new things were good as long as there were young men strong enough to keep to the old ones.

"Tonight," he said, "you sleep in my lodge and nobody will bother you." In the sagging bed in the cabin where Joe slept, there were also two or three children who might hurt those wounds.

"Now," Charley said, "I am going to give you something."

He brought from a hiding place, behind a rock, a pint whiskey bottle, still half full, and said, "I am sorry there is not more here."

He told Joe, "Now you can teach the ritual of swinging at the pole. Two men can teach it, you and I, if anyone wants to learn. It will not be forgotten when my shadow walks the Hanging Road across the stars."

The spirits may be dead, he thought, but the strong hearts of the Cheyenne people still beat with courage like the steady sound of drums.

Charley never rode his sorrel horse, but when it was three years old, Joe broke it. The horse threw him two or three times, and the old man cackled, admiring its spirit, while Joe picked himself up from the dust, swearing. Joe used the horse, but he never put a saddle on that sorrel without first asking Charley's permission.

Some of the short-haired young men never did come back from the Army, but Joe's three friends came back, wearing their uniforms and their medals. Tom Little Hand walked on crutches the first time he came home, with a cane the second time, but when he came home to stay he needed only a brace on the leg that had been wounded, and a special shoe on that foot.

The three soldiers went to the agency to show off a little, and to the white man's store off the reservation, to buy tobacco and stand around. The white ranchers, coming in for the mail, shook hands with them and called each one by name and said, "Glad to see you back, boy! Sure glad to see you back!"

The Indian soldiers smiled a little and said, "Yeah."

The ranchers never thought of shaking hands with Joe Walking Wolf. He had been around all the time, and the marks of his honor were not in any medals but in the angry scars under his faded shirt.

After all the girls had had a chance to admire the uniforms, the young men took off their medals, to be put away with the broken-feathered war bonnets and the ancient, unstrung bows. They wore parts of their uniforms to work in, as the white veterans did, and they went back to raising cattle or doing whatever work they could get.

Tom Little Hand, that proud rider, never wore his old cowboy boots again because of the brace on his leg. He could not even wear moccasins, but always the special shoe. But he walked and he rode, and pretty soon he married Joe's sister, Jennie, whose Cheyenne name was Laughing Woman, the same as her great-grandmother's.

That's all there is to the story, except that last summer Charley Lockjaw died. He had thought he was a hundred years old, but his granddaughter told the Indian agent that he had always said he was born the year a certain treaty was made with the white chiefs. The agent knew what year that treaty was, and he figured out that Charley must have been ninety when he died.

The agent was interested in history, and so he asked, "Was Charley in the fight with Yellow Hair at the Little Big Horn?" Charley's granddaughter said she didn't know.

Her son, Joe Walking Wolf, knew but did not say so. Charley Lockjaw had been there, a warrior seventeen years old, and had counted coup five times on blue-coated soldiers of the Seventh Cavalry that June day when General Custer and his men died in the great victory of the Cheyennes and the Sioux. But Joe did not tell everything Charley Lockjaw had told him.

When Charley died, he left his horse to Joe. So Joe wasn't lying when, after he shot the beautiful eighty-dollar sorrel on Charley's grave, he simply said, "It was my horse."

The three other young men were there when Joe killed it. That was the right thing to do, they agreed soberly, because in the old days when a warrior died, his best horse was sacrificed for him. Then he would have it to ride as he went along the Hanging Road to the place where the shadows of the Cheyenne people go. The place is neither heaven nor hell, but just like earth, with plenty of fighting and buffalo and horses, and tall peaked lodges to live in, and everybody there who has gone before. It is just like earth, as Charley Lockjaw remembered earth from his young days.

When Joe had shot the horse, the young men took the sharp knives they had brought along and peeled the hide off. They butchered the carcass and took the great hunks of horse meat home to their families.

Because the buffalo are gone from earth now, and in the dirt-roofed cabins of the Cheyennes, the conquered people, there is not often enough food to get ready a feast.

## I

### DREAMS ARE DIFFERENT THINGS TO DIFFERENT PEOPLE

Dreams in this story are of two different kinds. Each of the young Cheyennes, as he experiences the ceremony of a warrior fasting on a hill before setting out for war, hopes for a prophetic dream, one to point to the direction of his future. A dream here is being used as a tool . . . a voice from the gods. The four young men find interpreting their dreams baffling, confusing, indefinite. Charley Lockjaw knows a different dreaming . . . a yearning in his heart to pass on the old ways and the old ceremonies to the young. He fulfills his dream. But is either kind of dreaming relevant in today's society?

## II

### IMPLICATIONS

A. In this story, many of the white people's attitudes toward the Cheyennes are included. What do the quotations below imply? How valid do you think each idea is?

1. "The white ranchers chuckled indulgently, a little shocked about the horse, but never too much upset about anything Indians did."

2. "In the agent's experience, even an Indian who had been clear through high school could fail completely to understand English if he didn't happen to want to."

3. ". . . some of the young men didn't want to wait until the letters [draft notices] came. Fighting was part of their tradition."

4. "An Indian could vote and be drafted, but he could not buy whiskey."

5. "In wartime people would pick up a soldier, even if he was an Indian."

6. "The white people vaguely approved of the Indians keeping their quaint old customs."

B. What do the following quotations imply about the Cheyennes' feelings about themselves and the white world?

1. "Killing was not paramount in those old battles; more important was proof of a man's courage in the face of death."

2. "How would anyone know the right way if the old men had forgotten?"

3. "Charley Lockjaw had been interfered with so much that he was suspicious."

4. "These were new things, not part of the ceremony, but he saw that some new things were good as long as there were young men strong enough to keep to the old ones."

5. ". . . . the buffalo are gone from earth now, and in the dirt-roofed cabins of the Cheyennes, the conquered people, there is not often enough food to get ready a feast."

6. "But Joe did not tell everything Charley Lockjaw had told him."

## III

### TECHNIQUES

*Irony*

A. This story is filled with ironic touches, not only in the relationships between the old man and the four boys, but between the tribe and the whites. Some of the ironic scenes follow. Explain what the characters expected and what actually happened.

1. Charley Lockjaw's first encounter with Joe Walking Wolf and his friends.

2. The dreams the four boys report and the old man's interpretation of each.

3. Joe and Tom Little Hand's experience with the draft.

B. Look over the first group of quotations in IMPLICATIONS. What is ironic in some of the remarks?

*Organization*

The author begins this short story in the present, but quickly shifts the setting back in time to take the reader through the events that lead up to the present. What advantage do you see in this pattern? How does it emphasize the fulfillment of Charley Lockjaw's dream?

I'm afraid she'll get sore and move away
if she catches me at it, and then I won't
have anyone, because she's my only
real friend, even if she doesn't know it.

# Feels Like Spring

### MILTON KAPLAN

I stop at the corner drugstore for a breakfast of doughnuts and coffee. I eat fast because I'm a little late, and then I race to the subway station and gallop down the steps to catch my usual train. I hold on to the strap and make believe I'm reading my newspaper, but I keep glancing at the people crowded in around me. They're the same ones I see every day. They know me and I know them, but we don't smile. We're strangers thrown together accidentally.

I listen to them talk about their troubles and their friends, and I wish I had someone to talk to, someone to break the monotony of the long subway ride.

As we approach the 175th Street station, I begin to get tense again. She usually gets into the train at this station. She slips in gracefully, not pushing or shoving like the rest, and she squeezes into a little space, clinging to the pole and holding on to an office envelope that probably contains her lunch. She never carries a newspaper or a book; I guess there isn't much sense in trying to read when you're mashed like that.

There's a fresh outdoor look about her, and I figure she must live in New Jersey. The Jersey crowd gets in at that stop. She has a sweet face with that scrubbed look that doesn't need powder or rouge. She never wears make-

up except for lipstick. And her wavy hair is natural, just a nice light brown, like the color of poplar leaves when they turn in the fall. And all she does is hold on to the pole and think her own thoughts, her eyes clear blue and warm.

I always like to watch her, but I have to be careful; I'm afraid she'll get sore and move away if she catches me at it, and then I won't have anyone, because she's my only real friend, even if she doesn't know it. I'm all alone in New York City, and I guess I'm kind of shy and don't make friends easily. The fellows in the bank are all right, but they have their own lives to lead. Besides, I can't ask anyone to come up to a furnished room; so they go their way and I go mine.

The city is getting me. It's too big, and noisy —too many people for a fellow who's all by himself. I can't seem to get used to it. I'm used to the quiet of a small New Hampshire farm, but there isn't any future on a New Hampshire farm any more; so after I was discharged from the Navy, I applied for this position in the bank and got it. I suppose it's a good break, but I'm kind of lonesome.

As I ride along, swaying to the motion of the car, I like to imagine that I'm friends with her. Sometimes I'm even tempted to smile at her, not in a fresh way, but just friendlylike, and say something like "Nice morning, isn't it?" But I'm scared. She might think I'm one of those wise guys and she'd freeze up and look right through me as if I didn't exist, and then the next morning she wouldn't be there any more and I'd have no one to think about. I keep dreaming that maybe someday I'll get to know her. You know, in a casual way.

Like maybe she'd be coming through the door and someone would push her and she'd brush against me and she'd say quickly. "Oh, I beg your pardon," and I'd lift my hat politely and answer, "That's perfectly all right," and I'd smile to show her that I meant it. Then she'd smile back at me and say, "Nice day, isn't it?" and I'd say, "Feels like spring." And we wouldn't say anything more, but when

Copyright 1952 by Milton Kaplan and reprinted by his permission.

she'd be ready to get off at 34th Street, she'd wave her finger a little at me and say, "Good-bye," and I'd tip my hat again.

The next morning when she'd come in, she'd see me and say, "Hello," or maybe "Good morning," and I'd answer and add something like "Violets ought to be coming up soon"—something like that to show her I really knew a little about spring. No wisecracks, because I wouldn't want her to think that I was one of those smooth-talking guys who pick up girls in the subway.

And, after a while, we'd get a little friendlier and start talking about things like the weather or the news, and one day she'd say, "Isn't it funny? Here we are talking every day and we don't even know each other's names." And I'd stand up straight and tip my hat and say, "I'd like you to meet Mr. Thomas Pearse," and she'd say very seriously, "How do you do, Mr. Pearse. I want you to meet Miss Elizabeth Altemose." She'd be wearing those clean white gloves girls wear in the spring, and the other people around us would smile because people in the subway are so close to you that they just can't help sharing a little of your life.

"Thomas," she'd say, as if she were trying out the sound of it.

"What?" I'd ask.

"I can't possibly call you Thomas," she'd say. "It's so formal."

"My friends call me Tommy," I'd tell her.

"And mine call me Betty."

And that's the way it would be. Maybe after a while I'd mention the name of a good movie that was playing at the Music Hall and suggest if she weren't doing anything in particular—

And she would come right out with "Oh, I'd love it." I'd knock off a little earlier and meet her where she worked, and we would go out to dinner somewhere. I'd ask some of the men at the bank for the name of a good restaurant. And I would talk to her and tell her about New Hampshire and maybe mention how lonesome I got, and if it's a really nice place and it's quiet and cozy, maybe I'd tell her how

shy I was, and she'd be listening with shining eyes and she'd clasp her hands and lean over the table until I could smell the fragrance of her hair and she'd whisper, "I'm shy, too." Then we'd both lean back and smile secretly, and we'd eat without saying much because, after all, what's there to say after that?

We'd go to the Music Hall and I'd get reserved seats and we'd sit there, relaxed, enjoying the movie. Some time during the picture, in an exciting part, maybe her hand would brush against mine, or maybe I'd be shifting my position and my hand would touch hers accidentally, but she wouldn't take it away and I'd hold it, and there I'd be in the middle of eight million people, but I wouldn't be alone any more; I'd be out with my girl.

And afterwards I'd take her home. She wouldn't want me to travel all the way out. "I live in New Jersey," she'd say. "It's very nice of you to offer to take me home but I couldn't ask you to make a long trip like that. Don't worry, I'll be all right." But I'd take her arm and say, "Come on. I want to take you home. I like New Jersey." And we'd take the bus across the George Washington Bridge with the Hudson River flowing dark and mysterious below us, and then we'd be in New Jersey and we'd see the lights of small homes and we'd stop in one of those little towns, Englewood, Leonia, Ridgewood—I looked them up on a map, wondering which one was hers—and she'd invite me in but I'd say it was too late and then she'd turn to me and say, "Then you must promise to come for dinner this Sunday," and I'd promise and then—

The train is slowing down and the people are bracing themselves automatically for the stop. It's the 175th Street station. There's a big crowd waiting to get in. I look out anxiously for her, but I don't see her anywhere and my heart sinks, and just then I catch a glimpse of her, way over at the side. She's wearing a new hat with little flowers on it. The door opens and the people start pushing in. She's caught in the rush and there's nothing she can do about it. She bangs into me and she grabs the strap I'm holding and hangs on to it for her life.

"I beg your pardon," she gasps.

My hand is pinned down and I can't tip my hat, but I answer politely, "That's all right."

The doors close and the train begins to move. She has to hold on to my strap; there isn't any other place for her.

"Nice day, isn't it?" she says.

The train swings around a turn and the wheels squealing on the rails sound like the birds singing in New Hampshire. My heart is pounding like mad.

"Feels like spring," I say.

---

*Organization*

The basic elements of the story are:

**1.** A lonely young man regularly rides the subway to work.

**2.** At 175th Street a young woman usually gets on and rides to work.

**3.** One morning, she is shoved and apologizes for bumping him.

**4.** He has daydreamed about how he might meet her.

How are these elements arranged so that the story has an interesting twist to it?

## I
### DAYDREAMS

Everyone indulges in daydreams. The narrator is a quiet, shy kind of person, and his dream is one that fits his personality. Notice that his own behavior is a real factor in his dream. He is imagining how he will act. He wants to be bold and worldly, but he has been taught to be a gentleman and so wants to be sure that the girl does not think him forward or cheap. Do your daydreams tell as much about you?

## II
### IMPLICATIONS

Find support for your opinion about the following statements both in the story and from your own experiences.

**1.** Lonely people tend to be dreamers.

**2.** Mental telepathy made this dream come true.

**3.** The reality is never as good as the dream.

**4.** Though this story may seem like fantasy, dreams like Tommy's can come true.

## III
### TECHNIQUES

*Irony*

What change could be made in the ending of the story to make it deeply ironic?

Who has not dreamed
of finding buried treasure,
receiving a fabulous legacy,
winning a national lottery?
When such an event happens in any area,
the news media interview the lucky person.
And thus the dream of sudden wealth
is kept alive for the rest of us.

# Jug of Silver

## TRUMAN CAPOTE

After school I used to work in the Valhalla drugstore. It was owned by my uncle, Mr. Ed Marshall. I call him Mr. Marshall because everybody, including his wife, called him Mr. Marshall. Nevertheless he was a nice man.

This drugstore was maybe old-fashioned, but it was large and dark and cool: during summer months there was no pleasanter place in town. At the left, as you entered, was a tobacco-magazine counter behind which, as a rule, sat Mr. Marshall: a squat, square-faced, pink-fleshed man with looping, manly, white mustaches. Behind this counter stood the beautiful soda fountain. It was very unique and made of fine, yellowed marble, smooth to the touch but without a trace of cheap glaze. Mr. Marshall bought it at an auction in New Orleans in 1910 and was plainly proud of it. When you sat on the high, delicate stools and looked across the fountain you could see yourself reflected softly, as though by candlelight, in a row of ancient, mahogany-framed mirrors. All general merchandise was displayed in glass-doored, curio-like cabinets that were locked with brass keys. There was always in the air the smell of syrup and nutmeg and other delicacies.

The Valhalla was the gathering place of Wachata County till a certain Rufus McPherson came to town and opened a second drugstore directly across the courthouse square. This old Rufus McPherson was a villain; that is, he took away my uncle's trade. He installed fancy equipment such as electric fans and colored lights, he provided curb service and made grilled-cheese sandwiches to order. Naturally, though some remained devoted to Mr. Marshall, most folks couldn't resist Rufus McPherson.

For a while, Mr. Marshall chose to ignore him: if you were to mention McPherson's name he would sort of snort, finger his mustaches and look the other way. But you could tell he was mad. And getting madder. Then one day toward the middle of October I strolled into the Valhalla to find him sitting at the fountain playing dominoes and drinking wine with Hamurabi.

Hamurabi was an Egyptian and some kind of dentist, though he didn't do much business as the people hereabouts have unusually strong teeth, due to an element in the water. He spent a great deal of his time loafing around the Valhalla and was my uncle's chief buddy. He was a handsome figure of a man, this Hamurabi, being dark-skinned and nearly seven feet tall; the matrons of the town kept their daughters under lock and key and gave him the eye themselves. He had no foreign accent whatsoever, and it was always my opinion that he wasn't any more Egyptian than the man in the moon.

Anyway, there they were swigging red Italian wine from a gallon jug. It was a troubling sight, for Mr. Marshall was a renowned teetotaler. So naturally, I thought: Oh, golly, Rufus McPherson has finally got his goat. That was not the case, however.

"Here, son," said Mr. Marshall, "come have a glass of wine."

"Sure," said Hamurabi, "help us finish it up.

Copyright 1945 and renewed 1973 by Truman Capote. Reprinted from *A Tree of Night and Other Stories* by Truman Capote. By permission of Random House, Inc.

It's store-bought, so we can't waste it."

Much later, when the jug was dry, Mr. Marshall picked it up and said, "Now we shall see!" And with that disappeared out into the afternoon.

"Where's he off to?" I asked.

"Ah," was all Hamurabi would say. He liked to devil me.

A half-hour passed before my uncle returned. He was stooped and grunting under the load he carried. He set the jug atop the fountain and stepped back, smiling and rubbing his hands together. "Well, what do you think?"

"Ah," purred Hamurabi.

"Gee . . ." I said.

It was the same wine jug, God knows, but there was a wonderful difference; for now it was crammed to the brim with nickels and dimes that shone dully through the thick glass.

"Pretty, eh?" said my uncle. "Had it done over at the First National. Couldn't get in anything bigger-sized than a nickel. Still, there's lotsa money in there, let me tell you."

"But what's the point, Mr. Marshall?" I said. "I mean, what's the idea?"

Mr. Marshall's smile deepened to a grin. "This here's a jug of silver, you might say. . . ."

"The pot at the end of the rainbow," interrupted Hamurabi.

". . . and the idea, as you call it, is for folks to guess how much money is in there. For instance, say you buy a quarter's worth of stuff—well, then you get to take a chance. The more you buy, the more chances you get. And I'll keep all guesses in a ledger till Christmas Eve, at which time whoever comes closest to the right amount will get the whole shebang."

Hamurabi nodded solemnly. "He's playing Santa Claus—a mighty crafty Santa Claus," he said. "I'm going home and write a book: *The Skillful Murder of Rufus McPherson*." To tell the truth, he sometimes did write stories and send them out to the magazines. They always came back.

It was surprising, really like a miracle, how Wachata County took to the jug. Why, the Valhalla hadn't done so much business since Station Master Tully, poor soul, went stark raving mad and claimed to have discovered oil back of the depot, causing the town to be overrun with wildcat prospectors. Even the pool-hall bums who never spent a cent on anything not connected with whiskey or women took to investing their spare cash in milk shakes. A few elderly ladies publicly disapproved of Mr. Marshall's enterprise as a kind of gambling, but they didn't start any trouble and some even found occasion to visit us and hazard a guess. The school kids were crazy about the whole thing, and I was very popular because they figured I knew the answer.

"I'll tell you why all this is," said Hamurabi, lighting one of the Egyptian cigarettes he bought by mail from a concern in New York City. "It's not for the reason you may imagine; not, in other words, avidity. No. It's the mystery that's enchanting. Now you look at those nickels and dimes and what do you think: ah, *so* much! No, no. You think: ah, *how* much? And that's a profound question, indeed. It can mean different things to different people. Understand?"

And oh, was Rufus McPherson wild! When you're in trade, you count on Christmas to make up a large share of your yearly profit, and he was hard pressed to find a customer. So he tried to imitate the jug; but being such a stingy man he filled his with pennies. He also wrote a letter to the editor of *The Banner*, our weekly paper, in which he said that Mr. Marshall ought to be "tarred and feathered and strung up for turning innocent little children into confirmed gamblers and sending them down the path to Hell!" You can imagine what kind of laughing stock he was. Nobody had anything for McPherson but scorn. And so by the middle of November he just stood on the sidewalk outside his store and gazed bitterly at the festivities across the square.

At about this time Appleseed and sister made their first appearance.

He was a stranger in town. At least no one could recall ever having seen him before. He said he lived on a farm a mile past Indian Branches; told us his mother weighed only seventy-four pounds and that he had an older brother who would play the fiddle at anybody's wedding for fifty cents. He claimed that Appleseed was the only name he had and that he was twelve years old. But his sister, Middy, said he was eight. His hair was straight and dark yellow. He had a tight, weather tanned little face with mucous green eyes that had a very wise and knowing look. He was small and puny and high-strung; and he wore always the same outfit: a red sweater, blue denim britches and a pair of man-sized boots that went clop-clop with every step.

It was raining that first time he came into the Valhalla: his hat was plastered round his head like a cap and his boots were caked with red mud from the country roads. Middy trailed behind as he swaggered like a cowboy up to the fountain where I was wiping some glasses.

"I hear tell you folks got a bottle fulla money you fixin' to give away," he said, looking me square in the eye. "Seein' as you-all are givin' it away, we'd be obliged iffen you'd give it to us. Name's Appleseed, and this here's my sister, Middy."

Middy was a sad, sad-looking kid. She was a good bit taller and older-looking than her brother: a regular bean pole. She had straw-colored hair that was chopped short, and a pale pitiful little face. She wore a faded cotton dress that came way up above her skinny knees. There was something wrong with her teeth, and she tried to conceal this by keeping her lips pursed like an old lady.

"Sorry," I said, "but you'll have to talk with Mr. Marshall."

So sure enough he did. I could hear my uncle explaining what he would have to do to

win the jug. Appleseed listened attentively, nodding now and then. Presently, he came back and stood in front of the jug and touching it lightly with his hand, said, "Ain't it a pretty thing, Middy?"

Middy said, "Is they gonna give it to us?"

"Naw. What you gotta do, you gotta guess how much money's inside there. And you gotta buy two bits' worth so's even to get a chance."

"Huh, we ain't got no two bits. Where you 'spec we gonna get us two bits?"

Appleseed frowned and rubbed his chin. "That'll be the easy part, just leave it to me. The only worrisome thing is: I can't just take a chance and guess. . . . I gotta know."

Well, a few days later they showed up again. Appleseed perched atop a stool at the fountain and boldly asked for two glasses of water, one for him and one for Middy. It was on this occasion that he gave out the information about his family: ". . . then there's Papa Daddy, that's my mama's papa, who's a Cajun, an' on accounta that he don't speak English good. My brother, the one what plays the fiddle, he's been in jail three times. . . . It's on accounta him we had to pick up and leave Louisiana. He cut a fella bad in a razor fight over a woman ten years older'n him. She had yellow hair."

Middy, lingering in the background, said nervously, "You oughtn't to be tellin' our personal private family business thataway, Appleseed."

"Hush now, Middy," he said, and she hushed. "She's a good little gal," he added, turning to pat her head, "but you can't let her get away with much. You go look at the picture books, honey, and stop frettin' with your teeth. Appleseed here's got some figurin' to do."

This figuring meant staring hard at the jug, as if his eyes were trying to eat it up. With his chin cupped in his hand, he studied it for a long period, not batting his eyelids once. "A lady in Louisiana told me I could see things other folks couldn't see 'cause I was born with a caul[1] on my head."

"It's a cinch you aren't going to see how much there is," I told him. "Why don't you just let a number pop into your head, and maybe that'll be the right one."

"Uh, uh," he said, "too darn risky. Me, I can't take no such a chance. Now, the way I got it figured, there ain't but one sure-fire thing and that's to count every nickel and dime."

"Count!"

"Count what?" asked Hamurabi, who had just moseyed inside and was settling himself at the fountain.

"This kid says he's going to count how much is in the jug," I explained.

Hamurabi looked at Appleseed with interest. "How do you plan to do that, son?"

"Oh, by countin'," said Appleseed matter-of-factly.

Hamurabi laughed. "You better have X-ray eyes, son, that's all I can say."

"Oh, no. All you gotta do is be born with a caul on your head. A lady in Louisiana told me so. She was a witch, she loved me and when my ma wouldn't give me to her she put a hex on her and now my ma don't weigh but seventy-four pounds."

"Ve-ry in-ter-esting," was Hamurabi's comment as he gave Appleseed a queer glance.

Middy sauntered up, clutching a copy of *Screen Secrets*. She pointed out a certain photo to Appleseed and said: "Ain't she the nicest-lookin' lady? Now you see, Appleseed, you see how pretty her teeth are? Not a one outa joint."

"Well, don't you fret none," he said.

After they left Hamurabi ordered a bottle of orange Nehi and drank it slowly, while smoking a cigarette. "Do you think maybe that kid's o.k. upstairs?" he asked presently in a puzzled voice.

Small towns are best for spending Christmas, I think. They catch the mood quicker and change and come alive under its spell. By the first week in December house doors were decorated with wreaths, and store windows were flashy with red paper bells and snowflakes of glittering isinglass.[2] The kids hiked out into the woods and came back dragging spicy evergreen trees. Already the women were busy baking fruitcakes, unsealing jars of mincemeat and opening bottles of blackberry and scuppernong wine. In the courthouse square a huge tree was trimmed with silver tinsel and colored electric bulbs that were lighted up at sunset. Late of an afternoon you could hear the choir in the Presbyterian church practicing carols for their annual pageant. All over town the japonicas were in full bloom.

The only person who appeared not the least touched by this heartwarming atmosphere was Appleseed. He went about his declared business of counting the jug-money with great, persistent care. Every day now he came to the Valhalla and concentrated on the jug, scowling and mumbling to himself. At first we were all fascinated, but after a while it got tiresome and nobody paid him any mind whatsoever. He never bought anything, apparently having never been able to raise the two bits. Sometimes he'd talk to Hamurabi, who had taken a tender interest in him and occasionally stood treat to a jawbreaker or a penny's worth of licorice.

"Do you still think he's nuts?" I asked.

"I'm not so sure," said Hamurabi. "But I'll let you know. He doesn't eat enough. I'm going to take him over to the Rainbow Café and buy him a plate of barbecue."

"He'd appreciate it more if you'd give him a quarter."

"No. A dish of barbecue is what he needs. Besides, it would be better if he never was to make a guess. A high-strung kid like that,

---

1. caul \ˈkȯwl\ the inner membrane surrounding the fetus before birth.

2. isinglass \ˈīz-ən-ˌglăs\ a semitransparent whitish material.

so unusual, I wouldn't want to be the one responsible if he lost. Say, it would be pitiful."

I'll admit that at the time Appleseed struck me as being just funny. Mr. Marshall felt sorry for him, and the kids tried to tease him, but had to give it up when he refused to respond. There you could see him plain as day sitting at the fountain with his forehead puckered and his eyes fixed forever on that jug. Yet he was so withdrawn you sometimes had this awful creepy feeling that, well, maybe he didn't exist. And when you were pretty much convinced of this he'd wake up and say something like, "You know, I hope a 1913 buffalo nickel's in there. A fella was tellin' me he saw where a 1913 buffalo nickel's worth fifty dollars." Or, "Middy's gonna be a big lady in the picture shows. They make lotsa money, the ladies in the picture shows do, and then we ain't gonna never eat another collard green as long as we live. Only Middy says she can't be in the picture shows 'less her teeth look good."

Middy didn't always tag along with her brother. On those occasions when she didn't come, Appleseed wasn't himself; he acted shy and left soon.

Hamurabi kept his promise and stood treat to a dish of barbecue at the café. "Mr. Hamurabi's nice, all right," said Appleseed afterward, "but he's got peculiar notions: has a notion that if he lived in this place named Egypt he'd be a king or somethin'."

And Hamurabi said, "That kid has the most touching faith. It's a beautiful thing to see. But I'm beginning to despise the whole business." He gestured toward the jug. "Hope of this kind is a cruel thing to give anybody, and I'm damned sorry I was ever a party to it."

Around the Valhalla the most popular pastime was deciding what you would buy if you won the jug. Among those who participated were: Solomon Katz, Phoebe Jones, Carl Kuhnhardt, Puly Simmons, Addie Foxcroft, Marvin Finkle, Trudy Edwards and a colored

man named Erskine Washington. And these were some of their answers: a trip to and a permanent wave in Birmingham, a second-hand piano, a Shetland pony, a gold bracelet, a set of *Rover Boys* books and a life insurance policy.

Once Mr. Marshall asked Appleseed what he would get. "It's a secret," was the reply, and no amount of prying could make him tell. We took it for granted that whatever it was, he wanted it real bad.

Honest winter, as a rule, doesn't settle on our part of the country til late January and then is mild, lasting only a short time. But in the year of which I write we were blessed with a singular cold spell the week before Christmas. Some still talk of it, for it was so terrible: water pipes froze solid; many folks had to spend the days in bed snuggled under their quilts, having neglected to lay in enough kindling for the fireplace; the sky turned that strange dull gray as it does just before a storm, and the sun was pale as a waning moon. There was a sharp wind: the old dried-up leaves of last fall fell on the icy ground, and the evergreen tree in the courthouse square was twice stripped of its Christmas finery. When you breathed, your breath made smoky clouds. Down by the silk mill where the very poor people lived, the families huddled together in the dark at night and told tales to keep their minds off the cold. Out in the country the farmers covered their delicate plants with gunny sacks and prayed; some took advantage of the weather to slaughter their hogs and bring the fresh sausage to town. Mr. R. C. Judkins, our town drunk, outfitted himself in a red cheesecloth suit and played Santa Claus at the five'n'dime. Mr. R. C. Judkins was the father of a big family, so everybody was happy to see him sober enough to earn a dollar. There were several church socials, at one of which Mr. Marshall came face to face with Rufus McPherson: bitter words were passed but not a blow was struck.

Now, as has been mentioned, Appleseed

lived on a farm a mile below Indian Branches; this would be approximately three miles from town; a mighty long and lonesome walk. Still, despite the cold, he came every day to the Valhalla and stayed till closing time which, as the days had grown short, was after nightfall. Once in a while he'd catch a ride partway home with the foreman from the silk mill, but not often. He looked tired, and there were worry lines about his mouth. He was always cold and shivered a lot. I don't think he wore any warm drawers underneath his red sweater and blue britches.

It was three days before Christmas when out of the clear sky, he announced: "Well, I'm finished. I mean I know how much is in the bottle." He claimed this with such grave, solemn sureness it was hard to doubt him.

"Why, say now, son, hold on," said Hamurabi, who was present. "You can't know anything of the sort. It's wrong to think so; you're just heading to get yourself hurt."

"You don't need to preach to me, Mr. Hamurabi. I know what I'm up to. A lady in Louisiana, she told me. . . ."

"Yes yes yes—but you got to forget that. If it were me, I'd go home and stay put and forget about this damned jug."

"My brother's gonna play the fiddle at a wedding over in Cherokee City tonight and he's gonna give me the two bits," said Appleseed stubbornly. "Tomorrow I'll take my chance."

So the next day I felt kind of excited when Appleseed and Middy arrived. Sure enough, he had his quarter: it was tied for safekeeping in the corner of a red bandanna.

The two of them wandered hand in hand among the showcases, holding a whispery consultation as to what to purchase. They decided finally on a thimble-sized bottle of gardenia cologne which Middy promptly opened and partly emptied on her hair. "It smells like . . . . Oh, darlin' Mary, I ain't never smelled nothin' as sweet. Here, Apple-

seed, honey, let me douse some on your hair." But he wouldn't let her.

Mr. Marshall got out the ledger in which he kept his records, while Appleseed strolled over to the fountain and cupped the jug between his hands, stroking it gently. His eyes were bright and his cheeks flushed from excitement. Several persons who were in the drugstore at that moment crowded close. Middy stood in the background quietly scratching her leg and smelling the cologne. Hamurabi wasn't there.

Mr. Marshall licked the point of his pencil and smiled. "Okay, son, what do you say?"

Appleseed took a deep breath. "Seventy-seven dollars and thirty-five cents," he blurted.

In picking such an uneven sum he showed originality, for the run-of-the-mill guess was a plain round figure. Mr. Marshall repeated the amount solemnly as he copied it down.

"When'll I know if I won?"

"Christmas Eve," someone said.

"That's tomorrow, huh?"

"Why, so it is," said Mr. Marshall, not surprised. "Come at four o'clock."

During the night the thermometer dropped even lower, and toward dawn there was one of those swift, summerlike rainstorms, so that the following day was bright and frozen. The town was like a picture postcard of a Northern scene, what with icicles sparkling whitely on the trees and frost flowers coating all windowpanes. Mr. R. C. Judkins rose early and, for no clear reason, tramped the streets ringing a supper bell, stopping now and then to take a swig of whiskey from a pint which he kept in his hip pocket. As the day was windless, smoke climbed lazily from various chimneys straightway to the still, frozen sky. By mid-morning the Presbyterian choir was in full swing and the town kids (wearing horror masks, as at Hallowe'en) were chasing one another round and round the square, kicking up an awful fuss.

Hamurabi dropped by at noon to help us fix up the Valhalla. He brought along a fat sack of Satsumas, and together we ate every last one, tossing the hulls into a newly installed potbellied stove (a present from Mr. Marshall to himself) which stood in the middle of the room. Then my uncle took the jug off the fountain, polished and placed it on a prominently situated table. He was no help after that whatsoever, for he squatted in a chair and spent his time tying and retying a tacky green ribbon around the jug. So Hamurabi and I had the rest to do alone: we swept the floor and washed the mirrors and dusted the cabinets and strung streamers of red and green crepe paper from wall to wall. When we were finished it looked very fine and elegant.

But Hamurabi gazed sadly at our work, and said: "Well, I think I better be getting along now."

"Aren't you going to stay?" asked Mr. Marshall, shocked.

"No, oh, no," said Hamurabi, shaking his head slowly. "I don't want to see that kid's face. This is Christmas and I mean to have a rip-roaring time. And I couldn't, not with something like that on my conscience. I wouldn't sleep."

"Suit yourself," said Mr. Marshall. And he shrugged, but you could see he was really hurt. "Life's like that—and besides, who knows, he might win."

Hamurabi sighed gloomily. "What's his guess?"

"Seventy-seven dollars and thirty-five cents," I said.

"Now I ask you, isn't that fantastic?" said Hamurabi. He slumped in a chair next to Mr. Marshall and crossed his legs and lit a cigarette. "If you got any Baby Ruths I think I'd like one; my mouth tastes sour."

As the afternoon wore on, the three of us sat around the table feeling terribly blue. No one said hardly a word and, as the kids had deserted the square, the only sound was the clock tolling the hour in the courthouse steeple.

The Valhalla was closed to business but people kept passing by and peeking in the window. At three o'clock Mr. Marshall told me to unlock the door.

Within twenty minutes the place was jam full; everyone was wearing his Sunday best, and the air smelled sweet, for most of the little silk-mill girls had scented themselves with vanilla flavoring. They scrunched up against the walls, perched on the fountain, squeezed in wherever they could; soon the crowd had spread to the sidewalk and stretched into the road. The square was lined with team-drawn wagons and Model T Fords that had carted farmers and their families into town. There was much laughter and shouting and joking—several outraged ladies complained of the cursing and the rough, shoving ways of the younger men, but nobody left. At the side entrance a gang of colored folks had formed and were having the most fun of all. Everybody was making the best of a good thing. It's usually so quiet around here: nothing much ever happens. It's safe to say that nearly all of Wachata County was present but invalids and Rufus McPherson. I looked around for Appleseed but didn't see him anywhere.

Mr. Marshall harumphed, and clapped for attention. When things quieted down and the atmosphere was properly tense, he raised his voice like an auctioneer, and called: "Now listen, everybody, in this here envelope you see in my hand"—he held a manila envelope above his head—"well, in it's the *answer*— which nobody but God and the First National Bank knows up to now, ha, ha. And in this book"—he held up the ledger with his free hand—"I've got written down what you folks guessed. Are there any questions?" All was silence. "Fine. Now, if we could have a volunteer. . . ."

Not a living soul budged an inch: it was if an awful shyness had overcome the crowd, and even those who were ordinarily natural-born show-offs shuffled their feet, ashamed.

354

Then a voice, Appleseed's, hollered, "Lemme by. . . . Outa the way, please, ma'am." Trotting along behind as he pushed forward were Middy and a lanky, sleepy-eyed fellow who was evidently the fiddling brother. Appleseed was dressed the same as usual, but his face was scrubbed rosy clean, his boots polished and his hair slicked back skin tight with Stacomb. "Did we get here in time?" he panted.

But Mr. Marshall said, "So you want to be our volunteer?"

Appleseed looked bewildered, then nodded vigorously.

"Does anybody have an objection to this young man?"

Still there was dead quiet. Mr. Marshall handed the envelope to Appleseed who accepted it calmly. He chewed his under lip while studying it a moment before ripping the flap.

In all that congregation there was no sound except an occasional cough and the soft tinkling of Mr. R. C. Judkin's supper bell. Hamurabi was leaning against the fountain, staring up at the ceiling; Middy was gazing blankly over her brother's shoulder, and when he started to tear open the envelope she let out a pained little gasp.

Appleseed withdrew a slip of pink paper and, holding it as though it was very fragile, muttered to himself whatever was written there. Suddenly his face paled and tears glistened in his eyes.

"Hey, speak up, boy," someone hollered.

Hamurabi stepped forward and all but snatched the slip away. He cleared his throat and commenced to read when his expression changed most comically, "Well, Mother o' God . . ." he said.

"Louder! Louder!" an angry chorus demanded.

"Buncha crooks!" yelled Mr. R. C. Judkins, who had a snootful by this time. "I smell a rat and he smells to high heaven!" Whereupon a cyclone of catcalls and whistling rent the air.

Appleseed's brother whirled round and shook his fist. "Shuddup, shuddup 'fore I bust every one a your heads together so's you got knots the size of musk melons, hear me?"

"Citizens," cried Mayor Mawes, "citizens— I say, this is Christmas. . . .I say. . . ."

And Mr. Marshall hopped up on a chair and clapped and stamped till a minimum of order was restored. It might as well be noted here that we later found out Rufus McPherson had paid Mr. R. C. Judkins to start the rumpus. Anyway, when the outbreak was quelled, who should be in possession of the slip but me . . . don't ask how.

Without thinking, I shouted. "Seventy-seven dollars and thirty-five cents." Naturally, due to the excitement, I didn't at first catch the meaning; it was just a number. Then Appleseed's brother let forth with his whooping yell, and so I understood. The name of the winner spread quickly, and the awed, murmuring whispers were like a rainstorm.

Oh, Appleseed himself was a sorry sight. He was crying as though he was mortally wounded, but when Hamurabi lifted him onto his shoulders so the crowd could get a gander, he dried his eyes with the cuffs of his sweater and began grinning. Mr. R. C. Judkins yelled, "Gyp! Lousy gyp!" but was drowned out by a deafening round of applause.

Middy grabbed my arm. "My teeth," she squealed. "Now, I'm gonna get my teeth."

"Teeth?" said I, kind of dazed.

"The false kind," says she. "That's what we're gonna get us with the money—a lovely set of white false teeth."

But at that moment my sole interest was in how Appleseed had known. "Hey, tell me," I said desperately, "tell me, how in God's name did he know there was just exactly seventy-seven dollars and thirty-five cents?"

Middy gave me this *look*. "Why, I thought he told you," she said, real serious. "He counted."

"Yes, but how—how?"

"Gee, don't you even know how to count?"

"But is that all he did?"

"Well," she said, following a thoughful pause, "he did do a little praying, too." She started to dart off, then turned back and called, "Besides, he was born with a caul on his head."

And that's the nearest anybody ever came to solving the mystery. Thereafter, if you were to ask Appleseed "How come?" he would smile strangely and change the subject. Many years later he and his family moved to somewhere in Florida and were never heard from again.

But in our town his legend flourishes still; and, till his death a year ago last April, Mr. Marshall was invited each Christmas Day to tell the story of Appleseed to the Baptist Bible class. Hamurabi once typed up an account and mailed it around to various magazines. It was never printed. One editor wrote back and said that "If the little girl really turned out to be a movie star, then there might be something to your story." But that's not what happened, so why should you lie?

---

## I
### BEATING THE ODDS

The mathematical probability that Appleseed could guess the exact amount of money in the jug is so minute that the happening boggles the mind. What do you suppose really happened? Did Mr. Marshall himself write Appleseed's guess on the pink slip or had Hamurabi counted it himself at some time and told the boy? Could it really be possible that Appleseed did have extrasensory perception? But wait . . . does it really make any difference in your reaction to the story that an explanation be given for the lucky guess?

## II
### IMPLICATIONS

1. Appleseed is the kind of person that you [people] like to see win.

2. The fact that Appleseed really expects Mr. Marshall to give him the jug when he asks for it reveals a great deal about him.

3. Appleseed's dream for his sister is as improbable as his dream of winning the jug.

4. If Appleseed's sister had become a movie star, the story would have been unbelievable.

5. Appleseed's dream is what ultimately makes him memorable.

## III
### TECHNIQUES
*Organization*

The story is divided into eight sections. To jog your memory, look back at each one and indicate the content of each in a phrase or sentence. With your notes before you, ask yourself the following questions about the organization.

1. Where does the story really begin? 3
2. Where does Appleseed make his guess? 6
3. Where is the winner determined?
4. What do the other sections do for the story?

## IV
### WORDS

A language is divided into subgroups called dialects. In the United States there are three major geographical dialects called northern, midland, and southern. Appleseed speaks a southern dialect. Sometimes this is indicated by his choice of words and sometimes by his arrangement of words in a phrase or sentence. But there is another division of language which is called edited American English when it is published, and broadcast English when it is spoken. These attempt to transcend the dialects so that all understand what is being said. How might a TV announcer say, or a newspaper print, the following:

1. "I hear tell you fixin' to give away a bottle fulla money."
2. "Seein' as you-all is givin' it away, we'd be obliged iffen you'd give it to us."
3. "This here's my sister, Middy."
4. "What you gotta do, you gotta guess how much money's inside there."
5. "The only worrisome thing is: . . . I gotta know."
6. "You oughtn't to be tellin' our personal private fam'ly business thataway, Appleseed."
7. "Stop frettin' with your teeth, honey."

# *Gallery* | DREAMS

SOARING
*Andrew Wyeth*
*Shelburne Museum, Inc., Shelburne, Vermont*

Dreams are illusions; dreams are ambitions; dreams are escapes; dreams are wishes. Dreams are our private property, to be savored or feared, followed or ignored. This gallery looks at a landscape of dreams— some attainable, some thwarted, some grandiose, some painfully private. Some of them may be yours. Andrew Wyeth has us soaring, as if in a dream, in freedom above the earth with the turkey buzzard. We see the earth dreamily, from a great height; and as the bird—with us above it—suspends itself, we do the impossible, thanks to the artist. We soar, too.

WHIRLWIND
*Pavel Tchelitchew*
Metropolitan Museum of Art,
Arthur H. Hearn Fund, 1950.

In WHIRLWIND Pavel Tchelitchew reveals an inner dreamworld.
Tchelitchew is a surrealist and a Russian American.
And his children swirl like leaves in this view
of children playing. Is his dream such a personal
vision that it "leaves you cold"? Or does
it set you dreaming too?

GIRL IN A WHITE BLOUSE
*Rafael Soyer*
*Metropolitan Museum of Art,*
*George A. Hearn Fund, 1933.*

The immigrant girl in Rafael Soyer's sad but sympathetic painting dreams dreams beyond her stark reality. The eyes tell it; the body reflects it; the artist depicts it. Can you guess what her dreams might be?

NINA SIMONE
*David Wilcox*

Who has not dreamed of fame and fortune and applause? The heroes of our day and age hold worlds and microphones in their hands, and the poster artist captures not only their faces but also their spirit. The poster artist helps the fantasy, promotes the legend, and defines the dream.

ELVIS
*David Edward Byrd*

Our dreams contain our frustrations as well as our wishes. In a surrealistic style, black artist Hughie Lee-Smith sets a young couple in a dream landscape frought with obstacles. They would be as free as the sky, but entanglements, decaying walls, and their own rigid stances prevent it.

IMPEDIMENTS
*Hughie Lee-Smith*
*Parrish Art Museum, The Clark Collection*
*Southhampton, Long Island, New York*

## The Garden

A little garden,
Fragrant and full of roses.
The path is narrow
And a little boy walks along it.

A little boy, a sweet boy,
Like that growing blossom.
When the blossom comes to bloom,
The little boy will be no more.

*Frank Bass*

To be able to dream in the midst of terror is to be able to survive. Because they were Jews, 15,000 children were imprisoned in Terezin by the Nazis during World War II. Only 100 survived. But they left a legacy of art and poetry, preserving their feelings, their visions, their perceptions of the world they had left and the world they were forced to inhabit. Their chronicles of dreams and the shattering of them are a poignant testament to innocence in the midst of horror, dignity in the face of death, dreams that are worth dreaming.

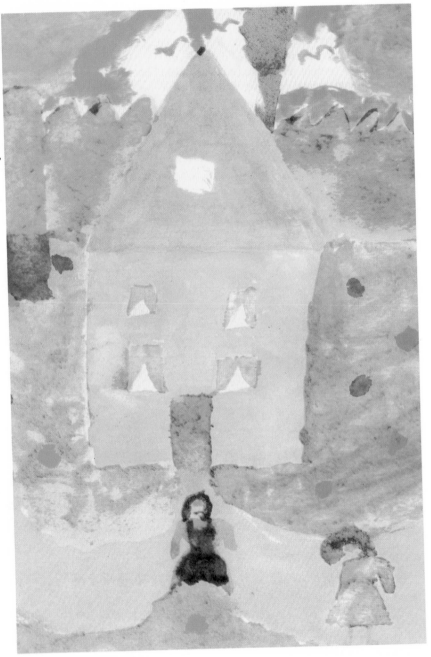

◆ All of us have our dreams
but they seldom dominate and direct
the course of our lives.
How could the conditions
of Paul's life
possibly spawn his particular dreams?
The case of Paul
is a baffling one indeed.

# Paul's Case

## WILLA CATHER

It was Paul's afternoon to appear before the faculty of the Pittsburgh High School to account for his various misdemeanors. He had been suspended a week ago, and his father had called at the Principal's office and confessed his perplexity about his son. Paul entered the faculty room suave and smiling. His clothes were a trifle outgrown, and the tan velvet on the collar of his open overcoat was frayed and worn; but for all that there was something of the dandy about him, and he wore an opal pin in his neatly knotted black four-in-hand,[1] and a red carnation in his buttonhole. This latter adornment the faculty somehow felt was not properly significant of the contrite spirit befitting a boy under the ban of suspension.

Paul was tall for his age and very thin, with high, cramped shoulders and a narrow chest. His eyes were remarkable for a certain hysterical brilliancy, and he continually used them in a conscious, theatrical sort of way, peculiarly offensive in a boy. The pupils were abnormally large, as though he were addicted to belladonna,[2] but there was a glassy glitter about them which that drug does not produce.

When questioned by the Principal as to why he was there, Paul stated, politely enough, that he wanted to come back to school. This was a lie, but Paul was quite accustomed to lying; found it, indeed, indispensable for overcoming friction. His teachers were asked to state their respective charges against him, which they did with such a rancor and aggrievedness as evinced that this was not a usual case. Disorder and impertinence were among the offenses named, yet each of his instructors felt that it was scarcely possible to put into words the real cause of the trouble, which lay in a sort of hysterically defiant manner of the boy's; in the contempt which they all knew he felt for them, and which he seemingly made not the least effort to conceal. Once, when he had been making a synopsis of a paragraph at the blackboard, his English teacher had stepped to his side and attempted to guide his hand. Paul had started back with a shudder and thrust his hands violently behind him. The astonished woman could scarcely have been more hurt and embarrassed had he struck at her. The insult was so involuntary and definitely personal as to be unforgettable. In one way and another, he had made all his teachers, men and women alike, conscious of the same feeling of physical aversion. In one class he habitually sat with his hand shading his eyes; in another he always looked out of the window during the recitation; in another he made a running commentary on the lecture, with humorous intent.

His teachers felt this afternoon that his whole attitude was symbolized by his shrug and his flippantly red carnation flower, and they fell upon him without mercy, his English teacher leading the pack. He stood through it smiling, his pale lips parted over his white teeth. (His lips were continually twitching, and he had a habit of raising his eyebrows that was contemptuous and irritating to the last degree.) Older boys than Paul had broken

---

1. **four-in-hand** necktie, an ordinary necktie that is not a bow tie.
2. **belladonna**\ˈbĕ·lə ˈdŏ·nə\ a poisonous plant, some doses of which dilate the pupils of the eyes.

Reprinted from YOUTH AND THE BRIGHT MEDUSA, by Willa Cather, courtesy of Alfred A. Knopf, Inc.

down and shed tears under that ordeal, but his set smile did not once desert him, and his only sign of discomfort was the nervous trembling of the fingers that toyed with the buttons of his overcoat, and an occasional jerking of the other hand which held his hat. Paul was always smiling, always glancing about him, seeming to feel that people might be watching him and trying to detect something. This conscious expression, since it was as far as possible from boyish mirthfulness, was usually attributed to insolence or "smartness."

As the inquisition proceeded, one of his instructors repeated an impertinent remark of the boy's, and the Principal asked him whether he thought that a courteous speech to make to a woman. Paul shrugged his shoulders slightly and his eyebrows twitched.

"I don't know," he replied. "I didn't mean to be polite or impolite, either. I guess it's a sort of way I have, of saying things regardless."

The Principal asked him whether he didn't think that a way it would be well to get rid of. Paul grinned and said he guessed so. When he was told that he could go, he bowed gracefully and went out. His bow was like a repetition of the scandalous red carnation.

His teachers were in despair, and his drawing-master voiced the feeling of them all when he declared there was something about the boy which none of them understood. He added: "I don't really believe that smile of his comes altogether from insolence; there's something sort of haunted about it. The boy is not strong, for one thing. There is something wrong about the fellow."

The drawing-master had come to realize that, in looking at Paul, one saw only his white teeth and the forced animation of his eyes. One warm afternoon the boy had gone to sleep at his drawing-board, and his master had noted with amazement what a white, blue-veined face it was; drawn and wrinkled like an old man's about the eyes, the lips twitching even in his sleep.

His teachers left the building dissatisfied and unhappy; humiliated to have felt so vin-

dictive toward a mere boy, to have uttered this feeling in cutting terms, and to have set each other on, as it were, in the gruesome game of intemperate reproach. One of them remembered having seen a miserable street cat set at bay by a ring of tormentors.

As for Paul, he ran down the hill whistling the Soldiers' Chorus from *Faust*,[3] looking behind him now and then to see whether some of his teachers were not there to witness his light-heartedness. As it was now late in the afternoon and Paul was on duty that evening as usher at Carnegie Hall,[4] he decided that he would not go home to supper.

When he reached the concert hall, the doors were not yet open. It was chilly outside, and he decided to go up into the picture gallery— always deserted at this hour—where there were some of Raffaelli's[5] gay studies of Paris streets and an airy blue Venetian scene or two that always exhilarated him. He was delighted to find no one in the gallery but the old guard, who sat in the corner, a newspaper on his knee, a black patch over one eye and the other closed. Paul possessed himself of the place and walked confidently up and down, whistling under his breath. After a while he sat down before a blue Rico and lost himself. When he bethought him to look at his watch, it was after seven o'clock, and he rose with a start and ran downstairs, making a face at Augustus Caesar peering out from the east-room, and an evil gesture at the Venus of Milo[6] as he passed her on the stairway.

When Paul reached the ushers' dressing-room, half a dozen boys were there already, and he began excitedly to tumble into his uni-

------

3. **Faust,** an opera by Gounod, of which the soldiers' chorus beginning "Glory and love to the men of old" is well known.
4. **Carnegie**\\'kar ▲nä·gē\\ **Hall,** a music hall in the Oakland district of Pittsburgh.
5. **Jean Raffaelli**\\ra 'fa·ĕ ▲lē\\ (1850–1924), a French painter.
6. He made a face at the cast of the bust of **Augustus Caesar,** the Roman Emperor (63 B.C.–A.D. 14). The **Venus of Milo**\\▲mē·lō\\ (the Greek island better known as Melos) one of the world's most famous statues. Paul makes his gesture at a copy.

*Jean François Raffaelli's painting of the Place St. Germain des Prés, Paris.*

form. It was one of the few that at all approached fitting, and Paul thought it very becoming—though he knew the tight, straight coat accentuated his narrow chest, about which he was exceedingly sensitive. He was always excited while he dressed, twanging all over to the tuning of the strings and the preliminary flourishes of the horns in the music-room; but tonight he seemed quite beside himself, and he teased and plagued the boys until, telling him that he was crazy, they put him down on the floor and sat on him.

Somewhat calmed by his suppression, Paul dashed out to the front of the house to seat the early comers. He was a model usher. Gracious and smiling he ran up and down the aisles. Nothing was too much trouble for him; he carried messages and brought programs as though it were his greatest pleasure in life, and all the people in his section thought him a charming boy, feeling that he remembered and admired them. As the house filled, he grew more and

365

more vivacious and animated, and the color came to his cheeks and lips. It was very much as though this were a great reception and Paul were the host. Just as the musicians came out to take their places, his English teacher arrived with checks for the seats which a prominent manufacturer had taken for the season. She betrayed some embarrassment when she handed Paul the tickets, and a hauteur which subsequently made her feel very foolish. Paul was startled for a moment, and had the feeling of wanting to put her out; what business had she here among all these fine people and gay colors? He looked her over and decided that she was not appropriately dressed and must be a fool to sit downstairs in such togs.[7] The tickets had probably been sent her out of kindness, he reflected, as he put down a seat for her, and she had about as much right to sit there as he had.

When the symphony began, Paul sank into one of the rear seats with a long sigh of relief, and lost himself as he had done before the Rico. It was not that symphonies, as such, meant anything in particular to Paul, but the first sigh of the instruments seemed to free some hilarious spirit within him; something that struggled there like the Genius in the bottle found by the Arab fisherman.[8] He felt a sudden zest of life; the lights danced before his eyes and the concert hall blazed into unimaginable splendor. When the soprano soloist came on, Paul forgot even the nastiness of his teacher's being there, and gave himself up to the peculiar intoxication such personages always had for him. The soloist chanced to be a German woman, by no means in her first youth, and the mother of many children; but she wore a satin gown and a tiara, and she had that indefinable air of achievement, that world-shine upon her, which always blinded Paul to any possible defects.

After a concert was over, Paul was often irritable and wretched until he got to sleep—and tonight he was even more than usually restless. He had the feeling of not being able to let down; of its being impossible to give up

this delicious excitement which was the only thing that could be called living at all. During the last number he withdrew and, after hastily changing his clothes in the dressing-room, slipped out to the side door where the singer's carriage stood. Here he began pacing rapidly up and down the walk, waiting to see her come out.

Over yonder the Schenley,[9] in its vacant stretch, loomed big and square through the fine rain, the windows of its twelve stories glowing like those of a lighted cardboard house under a Christmas tree. All the actors and singers of any importance stayed there when they were in Pittsburgh, and a number of the big manufacturers of the place lived there in the winter. Paul had often hung about the hotel, watching the people go in and out, longing to enter and leave schoolmasters and dull care behind him forever.

At last the singer came out, accompanied by the conductor, who helped her into her carriage and closed the door with a cordial *auf wiedersehen*,[10]—which set Paul to wondering whether she were not an old sweetheart of his. Paul followed the carriage over to the hotel, walking so rapidly as not to be far from the entrance when the singer alighted and disappeared behind the swinging glass doors which were opened by a Negro in a tall hat and a long coat. In the moment that the door was ajar, it seemed to Paul that he, too, entered. He seemed to feel himself go after her up the steps, into the warm, lighted building, into an exotic, a tropical world of shiny, glistening surfaces and basking ease. He reflected upon the mysterious dishes that were brought into the dining-room, the green bottles in buckets of

---

7. **togs**\tŏgz\ informal: clothes.
8. In one of the **Arabian Nights** stories, a fisherman finds a bottle in which a huge and powerful supernatural creature called a jinn or genius has been imprisoned.
9. **Schenley**\ˈshĕn·lē\ a large hotel in the Oakland district of Pittsburgh. The building is now part of the University of Pittsburgh.
10. **auf wiedersehen**\aůf ˈvē·dər ˈsē·ən\ German: "good-bye, until we meet again."

ice, as he had seen them in the supper party pictures of the Sunday supplement.[11] A quick gust of wind brought the rain down with sudden vehemence, and Paul was startled to find that he was still outside in the slush of the gravel driveway; that his boots were letting in the water and his scanty overcoat was clinging wet about him; that the lights in front of the concert hall were out, and that the rain was driving in sheets between him and the orange glow of the windows above him. There it was, what he wanted—tangibly before him, like the fairy world of a Christmas pantomime; as the rain beat in his face, Paul wondered whether he were destined always to shiver in the black night outside, looking up at it.

He turned and walked reluctantly toward the car tracks. The end had to come sometime; his father in his night-clothes at the top of the stairs, explanations that did not explain, hastily improvised fictions that were forever tripping him up, his upstairs room and its horrible yellow wallpaper, the creaking bureau with the greasy plush collar-box, and over his painted wooden bed the pictures of George Washington and John Calvin, and the framed motto, "Feed My Lambs," which had been worked in red worsted by his mother, whom Paul could not remember.[12]

Half an hour later, Paul alighted from the Negley Avenue car and went slowly down one of the side streets off the main thoroughfare. It was a highly respectable street, where all the houses were exactly alike, and where business men of moderate means begot and reared large families of children, all of whom went to Sabbath-school and learned the shorter catechism, and were interested in arithmetic; all of whom were as exactly alike as their homes, and of a piece with the monotony in which they lived. Paul never went up Cordelia Street without a shudder of loathing. His home was next to the house of the Cumberland minister.[13] He approached it tonight with the nerveless sense of defeat, the hopeless feeling of sinking back forever into ugliness and commonness that he had always had when he came home. The mo-

ment he turned into Cordelia Street he felt the waters close above his head. After each of these orgies of living, he experienced all the physical depression which follows a debauch; the loathing of respectable beds, of common food, of a house permeated by kitchen odors; a shuddering repulsion for the flavorless, colorless mass of every-day existence; a morbid desire for cool things and soft lights and fresh flowers.

The nearer he approached the house, the more absolutely unequal Paul felt to the sight of it all: his ugly sleeping chamber; the cold bathroom with the grimy zinc tub, the cracked mirror, the dripping spigots; his father, at the top of the stairs, his hairy legs sticking out from his nightshirt, his feet thrust into carpet slippers. He was so much later than usual that there would certainly be inquiries and reproaches. Paul stopped short before the door. He felt that he could not be accosted by his father tonight; that he could not toss again on that miserable bed. He would not go in. He would tell his father that he had no car-fare, and it was raining so hard he had gone home with one of the boys and stayed all night.

Meanwhile, he was wet and cold. He went around to the back of the house and tried one of the basement windows, found it open, raised it cautiously, and scrambled down the cellar wall to the floor. There he stood, holding his breath, terrified by the noise he had made; but the floor above him was silent, and there was no creak on the stairs. He found a soap-box, and carried it over to the soft ring of light that streamed from the furnace door, and sat down. He was horribly afraid of rats, so he did not try to sleep, but sat looking distrustfully at the dark, still terrified lest he might have awakened his father. In such reactions, after

---

11. **supplement,** in this sense an additional section of a newspaper devoted to special features.
12. **John Calvin** (1509–1564), a French theologian important in the rise of Protestantism. **worsted** \ˈwus·təd\ a heavy woolen fabric.
13. The **Cumberland minister** belonged to a revivalist group in the Presbyterian Church.

one of the experiences which made days and nights out of the dreary blanks of the calendar, when his senses were deadened, Paul's head was always singularly clear. Suppose his father had heard him getting in at the window and had come down and shot him for a burglar? Then, again, suppose his father had come down, pistol in hand, and he had cried out in time to save himself, and his father had been horrified to think how nearly he had killed him? Then, again, suppose a day should come when his father would remember that night, and wish there had been no warning cry to stay his hand? With this last supposition Paul entertained himself until daybreak.

The following Sunday was fine; the sodden November chill was broken by the last flash of autumnal summer. In the morning Paul had to go to church and Sabbath-school, as always. On seasonable Sunday afternoons the burghers[14] of Cordelia Street usually sat out on their front "stoops,"[15] and talked to their neighbors on the next stoop, or called to those across the street in neighborly fashion. The men sat placidly on gay cushions placed upon the steps that led down to the sidewalk, while the women, in their Sunday "waists," sat in rockers on the cramped porches, pretending to be greatly at their ease. The children played in the streets; there were so many of them that the place resembled the recreation grounds of a kindergarten. The men on the steps, all in their shirt-sleeves, their vests unbuttoned, sat with their legs well apart, their stomachs comfortably protruding, and talked of the prices of things, or told anecdotes of the sagacity of their various chiefs and overlords. They occasionally looked over the multitude of squabbling children, listened affectionately to their high-pitched, nasal voices, smiling to see their own proclivities reproduced in their offspring, and interspersed their legends of the iron kings[16] with remarks about their sons' progress at school, their grades in arithmetic, and the amounts they had saved in their toy banks.

On this last Sunday of November, Paul sat all the afternoon on the lowest step of his "stoop," staring into the street, while his sisters, in their rockers, were talking to the minister's daughters next door about how many shirtwaists they had made in the last week, and how many waffles someone had eaten at the last church supper. When the weather was warm, and his father was in a particularly jovial frame of mind, the girls made lemonade, which was always brought out in a red-glass pitcher, ornamented with forget-me-nots in blue enamel. This the girls thought very fine, and the neighbors joked about the suspicious color of the pitcher.

Today Paul's father, on the top step, was talking to a young man who shifted a restless baby from knee to knee. He happened to be the young man who was daily held up to Paul as a model, and after whom it was his father's dearest hope that he would pattern. This young man was of a ruddy complexion, with a compressed, red mouth, and faded, near-sighted eyes, over which he wore thick spectacles, with gold bows that curved about his ears. He was clerk to one of the magnates of a great steel corporation, and was looked upon in Cordelia Street as a young man with a future. There was a story that, some five years ago—he was now barely twenty-six—he had been a trifle "dissipated," but in order to curb his appetites and save the loss of time and strength that a sowing of wild oats might have entailed, he had taken his chief's advice, oft reiterated to his employees, and at twenty-one had married the first woman whom he could persuade to share his fortunes. She happened to be an angular schoolmistress, much older than he, who also wore thick glasses, and who had now borne him four children, all near-sighted like herself.

The young man was relating how his chief, now cruising in the Mediterranean, kept in touch with all the details of the business, arranging his office hours on his yacht just as though he were at home, and "knocking off

---

14. **burgher**\ˈbər·gər\ "townsman" or "citizen," but here suggests stodgy middle-class.
15. **stoop**, a dialect word meaning "small front porch."
16. **iron kings**, leaders in the steel industry.

work enough to keep two stenographers busy." His father told, in turn, the plan his corporation was considering, of putting in an electric railway plant at Cairo. Paul snapped his teeth; he had an awful apprehension that they might spoil it all before he got there. Yet he rather liked to hear these legends of the iron kings, that were told and retold on Sundays and holidays; these stories of palaces in Venice, yachts on the Mediterranean, and high play at Monte Carlo[17] appealed to his fancy, and he was interested in the triumphs of cash-boys[18] who had become famous, though he had no mind for the cash-boy stage.

After supper was over, and he had helped to dry the dishes, Paul nervously asked his father whether he could go to George's to get some help in his geometry, and still more nervously asked for car-fare. This latter request he had to repeat, as his father, on principle, did not like to hear requests for money, whether much or little. He asked Paul whether he could not go to some boy who lived nearer, and told him that he ought not to leave his school work until Sunday; but he gave him the dime. He was not a poor man, but he had a worthy ambition to come up in the world. His only reason for allowing Paul to usher was that he thought a boy ought to be earning a little.

Paul bounded upstairs, scrubbed the greasy odor of the dishwater from his hands with the ill-smelling soap he hated, and then shook over his fingers a few drops of violet water from the bottle he kept hidden in his drawer. He left the house with his geometry conspicuously under his arm, and the moment he got out of Cordelia Street and boarded a downtown car, he shook off the lethargy of two deadening days, and began to live again.

The leading juvenile of the permanent stock company which played at one of the downtown theaters was an acquaintance of Paul's, and the boy had been invited to drop in at the Sunday-night rehearsals whenever he could. For more than a year Paul had spent every available moment loitering about Charley Edwards's dressing-room. He had won a place among Edwards's following not only because the young actor, who could not afford to employ a dresser, often found him useful, but because he recognized in Paul something akin to what churchmen term "vocation."

It was at the theater and at Carnegie Hall that Paul really lived; the rest was but a sleep and a forgetting. This was Paul's fairy tale, and it had for him all the allurement of a secret love. The moment he inhaled the gassy, painty, dusty odor behind the scenes, he breathed like a prisoner set free, and felt within him the possibility of doing or saying splendid, brilliant things. The moment the cracked orchestra beat out the overture from *Martha*, or jerked at the serenade from *Rigoletto*,[19] all stupid and ugly things slid from him, and his senses were deliciously, yet delicately fired.

Perhaps it was because, in Paul's world, the natural nearly always wore the guise of ugliness, that a certain element of artificiality seemed to him necessary in beauty. Perhaps it was because his experience of life elsewhere was so full of Sabbath-school picnics, petty economies, wholesome advice as to how to succeed in life, and the unescapable odors of cooking, that he found this existence so alluring, these smartly clad men and women so attractive, that he was so moved by these starry apple orchards that bloomed perennially under the limelight. It would be difficult to put it strongly enough how convincingly the stage entrance of that theater was for Paul the actual portal of Romance. Certainly none of the company ever suspected it, least of all Charley Edwards. It was very like the old stories that used to float about London of fabulously rich Jews, who had subterranean halls, with palms, and fountains, and soft lamps and richly appareled women who never saw the

---

17. **Monte Carlo**\mŏn ▲tā ▲kar·lō\ a gambling resort in Monaco on the northern Mediterranean coast.
18. **cash-boy,** an errand boy entrusted with the delivery of cash, as to a bank.
19. **Martha,** an opera written in 1847 by Flotow (1812–1883). **Rigoletto**\'rĭ·gə ▲lĕ·tō\ an opera (1851) by Verdi (1813–1901).

disenchanting light of London day. So, in the midst of that smoke-palled city, enamored of figures and grimy toil, Paul had his secret temple, his wishing-carpet, his bit of blue-and-white Mediterranean shore bathed in perpetual sunshine.

Several of Paul's teachers had a theory that his imagination had been perverted by garish fiction; but the truth was, he scarcely ever read at all. The books at home were not such as would either tempt or corrupt a youthful mind, and as for reading the novels that some of his friends urged upon him—well, he got what he wanted much more quickly from music; any sort of music, from an orchestra to a barrel-organ. He needed only the spark, the indescribable thrill that made his imagination master of his senses, and he could make plots and pictures enough of his own. It was equally true that he was not stage-struck—not, at any rate, in the usual acceptation of that expression. He had no desire to become an actor, any more than he had to become a musician. He felt no necessity to do any of these things; what he wanted was to see, to be in the atmosphere, float on the wave of it, to be carried out, blue league after league, away from everything.

After a night behind the scenes, Paul found the schoolroom more than ever repulsive; the bare floors and naked walls; the prosy men who never wore frock coats, or violets in their buttonholes; the women with their dull gowns, shrill voices, and pitiful seriousness about prepositions that govern the dative.[20] He could not bear to have the other pupils think, for a moment, that he took these people seriously; he must convey to them that he considered it all trivial, and was there only by way of a joke, anyway. He had autographed pictures of all the members of the stock company which he showed his class mates, telling them the most incredible stories of his familiarity with these people, of his acquaintance with the soloists who came to Carnegie Hall, his suppers with them and the flowers he sent them. When these stories lost their effect, and his audience grew listless, he would bid all the boys good-bye, announcing that he was going to travel for a while; going to Naples, to California, to Egypt. Then next Monday, he would slip back, conscious and nervously smiling; his sister was ill, and he would have to defer his voyage until spring.

Matters went steadily worse with Paul at school. In the itch to let his instructors know how heartily he despised them, and how thoroughly he was appreciated elsewhere, he mentioned once or twice that he had no time to fool with theorems; adding—with a twitch of the eyebrows and a touch of that nervous bravado which so perplexed them—that he was helping the people down at the stock company; they were old friends of his.

The upshot of the matter was that the Principal went to Paul's father, and Paul was taken out of school and put to work. The manager at Carnegie Hall was told to get another usher in his stead; the doorkeeper at the theater was warned not to admit him to the house; and Charley Edwards remorsefully promised the boy's father not to see him again.

The members of the stock company were vastly amused when some of Paul's stories reached them—especially the women. They were hard-working women, most of them supporting indolent husbands or brothers, and they laughed rather bitterly at having stirred the boy to such fervid and florid inventions. They agreed with the faculty and with his father, that Paul's was a bad case.

The east-bound train was ploughing through a January snowstorm; the dull dawn was beginning to show gray when the engine whistled a mile out of Newark.[21] Paul started up from

---

20. Just as the nominative and objective are "cases" in English grammar, Latin grammar has a *dative* case. It is sometimes preceded by certain prepositions, and Paul's Latin teacher is evidently very intent on such matters.
21. Newark\ˈnū·ərk\ a large city in northern New Jersey on the main line of the Pennsylvania Railroad, on which Paul is traveling.

the seat where he had lain curled in uneasy slumber, rubbed the breath-misted window glass with his hand, and peered out. The snow was whirling in curling eddies above the white bottom lands, and the drifts lay already deep in the fields and along the fences, while here and there the tall dead grass and dried weed stalks protruded black above it. Lights shone from the scattered houses, and a gang of laborers who stood beside the track waved their lanterns.

Paul had slept very little, and he felt grimy and uncomfortable. He had made the all-night journey in a day coach because he was afraid if he took a Pullman[22] he might be seen by some Pittsburgh business man who had noticed him in Denny & Carson's office. When the whistle woke him, he clutched quickly at his breast pocket, glancing about him with an uncertain smile. But the little, clay-bespattered Italians were still sleeping, the slatternly women across the aisle were in open-mouth oblivion, and even the crumby, crying babies were for the time stilled. Paul settled back to struggle with his impatience as best he could.

When he arrived at the Jersey City station, he hurried through his breakfast, manifestly ill at ease and keeping a sharp eye about him. After he reached the Twenty-third Street station, he consulted a cabman, and had himself driven to a men's furnishing establishment which was just opening for the day. He spent upward of two hours there, buying with endless reconsidering and great care. His new street suit he put on in the fitting-room; the frock coat and dress clothes he had bundled into the cab with his new shirts. Then he drove to a hatter's and a shoe house. His next errand was at Tiffany's,[23] where he selected silver-mounted brushes and a scarf-pin. He would not wait to have his silver marked, he said. Lastly, he stopped at a trunk shop on Broadway, and had his purchases packed into various traveling-bags.

It was a little after one o'clock when he drove up to the Waldorf,[24] and after settling with the cabman, went into the office. He registered from Washington; said his mother and father had been abroad, and that he had come down to await the arrival of their steamer. He told his story plausibly and had no trouble, since he offered to pay for them in advance, in engaging his rooms; a sleeping-room, sitting-room, and bath.

Not once, but a hundred times Paul had planned this entry into New York. He had gone over every detail of it with Charley Edwards, and in his scrapbook at home there were pages of description about New York hotels, cut from the Sunday papers.

When he was shown to his sitting-room on the eighth floor, he saw at a glance that everything was as it should be; there was but one detail in his mental picture that the place did not realize, so he rang for the bell-boy and sent him down for flowers. He moved about nervously until the boy returned, putting away his new linen and fingering it delightedly as he did so. When the flowers came, he put them hastily into water, and then tumbled into a hot bath. Presently he came out of his white bathroom, resplendent in his new silk underwear, and playing with the tassels of his red robe. The snow was whirling so fiercely outside his windows that he could scarcely see across the street; but within, the air was deliciously soft and fragrant. He put the violets and jonquils on the taboret beside the couch, and threw himself down with a long sigh, covering himself with a Roman blanket. He was thoroughly tired; he had been in such haste, he had stood up to such a strain, covered so much ground in the last twenty-four hours, that he wanted to think how it had all come about. Lulled by the sound of the wind, the warm air, and the cool fragrance of the flowers, he sank into deep, drowsy retrospection.

---

22. **Pullman**\ˈpʊl·mən\ a railroad car with sleeping berths.
23. **Tiffany's**\ˈtĭ·fə·nēz\ a well-known New York jewelry store.
24. The **Waldorf**\ˈwal ˈdōrf\ an important New York hotel.

*The main entrance of the Waldorf Hotel
as it appeared in 1893.*

It had been wonderfully simple; when they had shut him out of the theater and concert hall, when they had taken away his bone, the whole thing was virtually determined. The rest was a mere matter of opportunity. The only thing that at all surprised him was his own courage—for he realized well enough that he had always been tormented by fear, a sort of apprehensive dread which, of late years, as the meshes of the lies he had told closed about him, had been pulling the muscles of his body tighter and tighter. Until now, he could not remember a time when he had not been dreading something. Even when he was a little boy, it was always there—behind him, or before, or on either side. There had always been the shadowed corner, the dark place into which he dared not look, but from which something seemed always to be watching him—and Paul had done things that were not pretty to watch, he knew.

But now he had a curious sense of relief, as

though he had at last thrown down the gauntlet[25] to the thing in the corner.

Yet it was but a day since he had been sulking in the traces;[26] but yesterday afternoon that he had been sent to the bank with Denny & Carson's deposit, as usual—but this time he was instructed to leave the book to be balanced. There was above two thousand dollars in checks, and nearly a thousand in the banknotes which he had taken from the book and quietly transferred to his pocket. At the bank he had made out a new deposit slip. His nerves had been steady enough to permit his returning to the office, where he had finished his work and asked for a full day's holiday tomorrow, Saturday, giving a perfectly reasonable pretext. The bank book, he knew, would not be returned before Monday or Tuesday, and his father would be out of town for the next week. From the time he slipped the banknotes into his pocket until he boarded the night train for New York, he had not known a moment's hesitation.

How astonishingly easy it had all been; here he was, the thing done; and this time there would be no awakening, no figure at the top of the stairs. He watched the snowflakes whirling by his window until he fell asleep.

When he awoke, it was four o'clock in the afternoon. He bounded up with a start; one of his precious days gone already! He spent nearly an hour in dressing, watching every stage of his toilet carefully in the mirror. Everything was quite perfect; he was exactly the kind of boy he had always wanted to be.

When he went downstairs, Paul took a carriage and drove up Fifth Avenue toward the Park.[27] The snow had somewhat abated; carriages and tradesmen's wagons were hurrying soundlessly to and fro in the winter twilight; boys in woolen mufflers were shoveling off the doorsteps; the avenue stages made fine spots of color against the white street. Here and there on the corners whole flower gardens blooming behind glass windows, against which the snowflakes stuck and melted; violets, roses, carnations, lilies-of-the-valleys—some-how vastly more lovely and alluring that they blossomed thus unnaturally in the snow. The Park itself was a wonderful stage winter-piece.

When he returned, the pause of the twilight had ceased, and the tune of the streets had changed. The snow was falling faster, lights streamed from the hotels that reared their many stories fearlessly up into the storm, defying the raging Atlantic winds. A long, black stream of carriages poured down the avenue, intersected here and there by other streams, tending horizontally. There were a score of cabs about the entrance of his hotel, and his driver had to wait. Boys in livery were running in and out of the awning stretched across the sidewalk, up and down the red velvet carpet laid from the door to the street. Above, about, within it all, was the rumble and roar, the hurry and toss of thousands of human beings as hot for pleasure as himself, and on every side of him towered the glaring affirmation of the omnipotence of wealth.

The boy set his teeth and drew his shoulders together in a spasm of realization; the plot of all dramas, the text of all romances, the nerve-stuff of all sensations was whirling about him like the snowflakes. He burnt like a fagot in a tempest.

When Paul came down to dinner, the music of the orchestra floated up the elevator shaft to greet him. As he stepped into the thronged corridor, he sank back into one of the chairs against the wall to get his breath. The lights, the chatter, the perfumes, the bewildering medley of color—he had, for a moment, the feeling of not being able to stand it. But only for a moment; these were his own people, he told himself. He went slowly about the corridors, through the writing-rooms, smoking-rooms, reception-rooms, as though he were exploring the chambers of an enchanted palace, built and peopled for him alone.

---

25. To throw down the **gauntlet** (\\ˈgɔnt·lət\\ an old word meaning "glove"), to issue a final challenge.
26. He had been acting as a restless horse which might sulk in its harness.
27. **Park,** Central Park.

When he reached the dining-room he sat down at a table near a window. The flowers, the white linen, the many-colored wine-glasses, the gay toilets of the women, the low popping of corks, the undulating repetitions of "The Blue Danube"[28] from the orchestra, all flooded Paul's dream with bewildering radiance. When the roseate tinge of his champagne was added —that cold, precious, bubbling stuff that creamed and foamed in his glass—Paul wondered that there were honest men in the world at all. This was what all the world was fighting for, he reflected; this was what all the struggle was about. He doubted the reality of his past. Had he ever known a place called Cordelia Street, a place where fagged looking business men boarded the early car? Mere rivets in a machine they seemed to Paul—sickening men, with combings of children's hair always hanging to their coats, and the smell of cooking in their clothes. Cordelia Street—Ah, that belonged to another time and country! Had he not always been thus, had he not sat here night after night, from as far back as he could remember, looking pensively over just such shimmering textures, and slowly twirling the stem of a glass like this one between his thumb and middle finger? He rather thought he had.

He was not in the least abashed or lonely. He had no especial desire to meet or to know any of these people; all he demanded was the right to look on and conjecture, to watch the pageant. The mere stage properties were all he contended for. Nor was he lonely later in the evening, in his loge[29] at the Opera. He was entirely rid of his nervous misgivings, of his forced aggressiveness, of the imperative desire to show himself different from his surroundings. He felt now that his surroundings explained him. Nobody questioned the purple;[30] he had only to wear it passively. He had only to glance down at his dress coat to reassure himself that here it would be impossible for anyone to humiliate him.

He found it hard to leave his beautiful sitting-room to go to bed that night, and sat long watching the raging storm from his turret window. When he went to sleep, it was with the lights turned on in his bedroom; partly because of his old timidity, and partly so that, if he should wake in the night, there would be no wretched moment of doubt, no horrible suspicion of yellow wallpaper, or of Washington and Calvin above his bed.

On Sunday morning the city was practically snowbound. Paul breakfasted late, and in the afternoon he fell in with a wild San Francisco boy, a freshman at Yale, who said he had run down for a "little flyer"[31] over Sunday. The young man offered to show Paul the night side of the town, and the two boys went off together after dinner, not returning to the hotel until seven o'clock the next morning. They had started out in the confiding warmth of a champagne friendship, but their parting in the elevator was singularly cool. The freshman pulled himself together to make his train, and Paul went to bed. He awoke at two o'clock in the afternoon, very thirsty and dizzy, and rang for ice-water, coffee, and the Pittsburgh papers.

On the part of the hotel management, Paul excited no suspicion. There was this to be said for him, that he wore his spoils with dignity and in no way made himself conspicuous. His chief greediness lay in his ears and eyes, and his excesses were not offensive ones. His dearest pleasures were the gray winter twilights in his sitting-room; his quiet enjoyment of his flowers, his clothes, his wide divan, his cigarette, and his sense of power. He could not remember a time when he had felt so at peace with himself. The mere release from the necessity of petty lying, lying every day and every day, restored his self-respect. He had never lied for pleasure, even at school; but to make himself noticed and admired, to assert his difference from other Cordelia Street boys; and he felt a good deal

---

28. **The Blue Danube**, a famous waltz by Johann Strauss the younger (1825–1899).
29. **loge**\lōzh\ a booth or box at the theater.
30. **Purple** is associated with kings, Roman Caesars, and aristocrats. The author means that no one questioned Paul's right to the way he was living.
31. **little flyer**, a little weekend vacation trip.

*"Peacock Alley" in the old Waldorf-Astoria Hotel.
The picture was taken shortly after the turn
of the century.*

more manly, more honest, even, now that he had no need for boastful pretensions, now that he could, as his actor friends used to say, "dress the part." It was characteristic that remorse did not occur to him. His golden days went by without a shadow, and he made each as perfect as he could.

On the eighth day after his arrival in New York, he found the whole affair exploited in the Pittsburgh papers, exploited with a wealth of detail which indicated that local news of a sensational nature was at a low ebb. The firm of Denny & Carson announced that the boy's father had refunded the full amount of his theft, and that they had no intention of prosecuting. The Cumberland minister had been interviewed, and expressed his hope of yet reclaiming the motherless lad, and Paul's Sabbath-school teacher declared that she would spare no effort to that end. The rumor had reached Pittsburgh that the boy had been seen in a New York hotel, and his father had gone East to find him and bring him home.

Paul had just come in to dress for dinner; he sank into a chair, weak in the knees, and clasped his head in his hands. It was to be worse than jail, even; the tepid waters of Cordelia Street were to close over him finally and forever. The gray monotony stretched before him in hopeless, unrelieved years; Sabbath-school, Young People's Meeting, the yellow-papered room, the damp dish-towels; it all rushed back upon him with sickening vividness. He had the old feeling that the orchestra had suddenly stopped, the sinking sensation that the play was over. The sweat broke out on his face, and he sprang to his feet, looked about him with his white, conscious smile, and winked at himself in the mirror. With something of the childish belief in miracles with which he had so often gone to class, all his lessons unlearned, Paul dressed and dashed whistling down the corridor to the elevator.

He had no sooner entered the dining-room and caught the measure of the music than his remembrance was lightened by his old elastic power of claiming the moment, mounting with it, and finding it all sufficient. The glare and glitter about him, the mere scenic accessories had again, and for the last time, their old potency. He would show himself that he was game, he would finish the thing splendidly. He doubted, more than ever, the existence of Cordelia Street, and for the first time he drank his wine recklessly. Was he not, after all, one of these fortunate beings: Was he not still himself, and in his own place? He drummed a nervous accompaniment to the music and looked about him, telling himself over and over that it had paid.

He reflected drowsily, to the swell of the violin and the chill sweetness of his wine, that he might have done it more wisely. He might have caught an outbound steamer and been well out of their clutches before now. But the other side of the world had seemed too far away and too uncertain then; he could not have waited for it; his need had been too sharp. If he had to choose over again, he would do the same thing tomorrow. He looked affectionately about the dining-room, now gilded with a soft mist. Ah, it had paid indeed!

Paul was awakened next morning by a painful throbbing in his head and feet. He had thrown himself across the bed without undressing, and had slept with his shoes on. His limbs and hands were lead heavy, and his tongue and throat were parched. There came upon him one of those fateful attacks of clear-headedness that never occurred except when he was physically exhausted and his nerves hung loose. He lay still and closed his eyes and let the tide of realities wash over him.

His father was in New York; "stopping at some joint or other," he told himself. The memory of successive summers on the front stoop fell upon him like a weight of black water. He had not a hundred dollars left; and he knew now, more than ever, that money was everything, the wall that stood between all he loathed and all he wanted. The thing was winding itself up; he had thought of that on his first glorious day in New York, and had even provided a way to snap the thread. It lay on his dressing-table now; he had got it out last night when he came blindly up from dinner—but the shiny metal hurt his eyes, and he disliked the look of it, anyway.

He rose and moved about with a painful effort, succumbing now and again to attacks of nausea. It was the old depression exaggerated; all the world had become Cordelia Street. Yet somehow he was not afraid of anything, was absolutely calm; perhaps because he had looked into the dark corner at last, and knew. It was bad enough, what he saw there; but somehow not so bad as his long fear of it had been. He saw everything clearly now. He had a feeling that he had made the best of it, that he had lived the sort of life he was meant to live, and for half an hour he sat staring at the revolver. But he told himself that was not the way, so he went downstairs and took a cab to the ferry.

When Paul arrived at Newark, he got off the train and took another cab, directing the driver to follow the Pennsylvania tracks out of the town. The snow lay heavy on the roadways and had drifted deep in the open fields. Only here and there the dead grass or dried weed stalks projected, singularly black, above it. Once well into the country, Paul dismissed the carriage and walked, floundering along the tracks, his mind a medley of irrelevant things. He seemed to hold in his brain an actual picture of everything he had seen that morning. He remembered every feature of both his drivers, the toothless old woman from whom he had bought the red flowers in his coat, the agent from whom he had got his ticket, and all of his fellow-passengers on the ferry. His mind, unable to cope with vital matters near at hand, worked feverishly and deftly at sorting and grouping these images. They made for him a part of the ugliness of the world, of the ache in his head, and the bitter burning on his tongue. He stooped and put a handful of snow into his mouth as he walked, but that, too, seemed hot. When he reached a little hillside, where the tracks ran through a cut some twenty feet below him, he stopped and sat down.

The carnations in his coat were drooping with the cold, he noticed; all their red glory over. It occurred to him that all the flowers he had seen in the show windows that first night must have gone the same way, long before this. It was only one splendid breath they had, in spite of their brave mockery at the winter outside the glass. It was a losing game in the end, it seemed, this revolt against the homilies by which the world is run. Paul took one of the blossoms carefully from his coat and scooped a little hole in the snow, where he covered it up. Then he dozed awhile, from his weak condition, seeming insensible to the cold.

The sound of an approaching train woke him, and he started to his feet, remembering only his resolution, and afraid lest he should be too late. He stood watching the approaching locomotive, his teeth chattering, his lips drawn away from them in a frightened smile; once or twice he glanced nervously sidewise, as though he were being watched. When the right moment came, he jumped. As he fell, the folly of his haste occurred to him with merciless clearness, the vastness of what he had left undone.

There flashed through his brain clearer than ever before, the blue of Adriatic[32] water, the yellow of Algerian sands. He felt something strike his chest—his body was being thrown swiftly through the air, on and on, immeasurably far and fast, while his limbs gently relaxed. Then, because the picture-making mechanism was crushed, the disturbing visions flashed into black, and Paul dropped back into the immense design of things.

---

## I
### DREAMS VERSUS REALITY

The title "Paul's Case" suggests that this story may be like the case history a psychologist or social worker would write. Such case histories are completely objective records of the behavior and attitudes of abnormal personalities; the psychologist never indulges in personal feelings about the subject. Paul is, indeed, a bad "case," a thoroughly abnormal boy as far as his teachers, his father, and even his schoolmates are concerned. He seems a fit subject for a case history. But Willa Cather makes us see beyond these judgments. She makes us recognize the poignantly normal quality in Paul's desires and his disgust with his dreary life. But his dreams of escape to an exotic life so hypnotize him that he fails to realize that they are only dreams. Believing them to be the only "real" things in his life, he refuses to deal with the hard and sometimes brutal facts of everyday reality. By doing so, he dooms himself to a desperate awakening and a tragic end.

## II
### IMPLICATIONS

Consider the following questions. In your discussion of them, put yourself as much as you can in Paul's place. Do not be deceived by the attitudes of the other characters toward him.

1. What aspects of Paul's character are revealed in the following scenes in the story?
   a. Paul at the teachers' meeting
   b. Paul at the concert hall
   c. Paul at home with his family

---

32. **Adriatic**\\'ă·drē ʌă·tĭk\\ the sea between Italy and Yugoslavia.

**d.** Paul in New York

**e.** Paul waiting for the train

**2.** What are the elements in Paul's environment that lead to his fantasies? What in his own personality triggers his dreams? How does each work on the other so that Paul gradually loses touch with reality?

**3.** Could Paul have acted differently than he did? Discuss whether or not it was a weakness in him that made him give way to his dreams.

**4.** React to the following statements. Are they true or not?

**a.** It was not Paul's daydreams that were bad but rather the action he took to achieve them.

**b.** People have always escaped from an ugly, impossible situation by daydreaming.

**c.** People who are unhappy with the quality of their lives and work hard to get out of a dreary environment often make real contributions to society.

### III
### TECHNIQUES

*Irony*

See if you can identify the ironic element in each of the following incidents.

**1.** Paul's bowing to the teachers as he leaves the room

**2.** Paul's English teacher appearing at the concert

**3.** Paul's being forbidden to go to the concert hall and the theater as a way of "curing" him

**4.** Paul's having to keep the light on in his hotel room at night

### IV
### WORDS

**A.** From context determine what the italicized words mean. Then check the meaning of each in your dictionary.

**1.** His teachers were asked to state their *respective* charges against him.

**2.** He made a running *commentary* on their lectures.

**3.** He felt that he could not be *accosted* by his father tonight; that he could not toss again on that miserable bed.

**4.** The following Sunday was fine; the *sodden* November chill was broken by the last flash of autumnal summer.

**5.** He wore his spoils with dignity and in no way made himself *conspicuous*.

**B.** Find the root in the word *carnation* ("a red carnation in his buttonhole") in "Paul's Case," and be prepared to tell why the flower is so called. The drug *belladonna* ("as though he were addicted to belladonna") is colorfully named; what do the parts of this word mean? How is intoxication ("the peculiar intoxication such personages always had for him") related to *toxic, toxin*, and *toxicology?*

## SUMMING UP
# *Dreams*

Lord Byron, a famous English poet, epitomized the impact of dreams on men's lives in the following lines. Read them as you recall the individual stories you have read in this section:

And dreams in their development have breath,
And tears, and tortures, and the touch of joy;
They leave a weight upon our waking toils,
They do divide our being; they become
A portion of ourselves as of our time,
And look like heralds of eternity;
They pass like spirits of the past,—they speak
Like sibyls of the future; they have power—
The tyranny of pleasure and of pain:
They make us what we were not—what they will,
And shake us with the vision that is gone by,
The dread of vanished shadows—are they so?
Is not the past all shadow?—What are they?
Creations of the mind?—The mind can make
Substance, and people planets of its own
With beings brighter than have been, and give
A breath to forms which can outlive all flesh. . . .

—from *Dreams*

### IMPLICATIONS

1. Open your book to the table of contents for this unit, DREAMS. Looking at the titles, think back over the stories. Then select one story that illustrates each of the following statements from Byron's poem "Dreams."

a. Dreams bring tears and tortures.

b. Dreams bring a touch of joy.

c. Dreams divide our being.

d. Dreams are heralds of eternity.

e. Dreams make us what we were not.

f. Dreams can create forms that outlive flesh.

2. In each of the selections the basic conflict is between the dream a person has and the real world in which the person lives. With this in mind, examine the selections in the unit. In which of the stories does the individual manage to make a dream come true? In which does the real world seem to win out and crush the dream? In what ways are the people whose dreams were crushed still richer for having had the dream?

### TECHNIQUES
*Irony*

Review the discussion of irony on page 324 and then test your understanding by answering the following questions.

1. Why do stories in which the conflict is between people's dreams and the reality of the world they live in almost inevitably involve irony?

2. Which of the works in DREAMS seemed the most ironic? Back up your choice by pinpointing the ironic aspects of the story.

3. What emotional reactions does irony produce in the reader?

4. Try your hand at using irony in your own writing.

a. Think of some ironic episode from your own life. Try to capture it in a short vignette. It may be sad, amusing, frightening, or anything you wish. Almost all people have had such moments when what they expect and what they get are far apart. A promised surprise gift turns out to be a toolbox instead of a bike, or an auto trip, taken reluctantly, turns out to be the adventure of the year.

b. Write about something you dislike: a food, a sport, a tradition. Describe it with such intense praise that your reader will realize that you really mean the opposite of what you are saying. For example, your first sentence might be: "Spaghetti is really a food for the gods." Go on from there.

c. Write a dialogue between two people in which each misinterprets what the other is saying. You might choose two characters in the unit, such as Paul and his English teacher; Appleseed and the narrator or Mr. Marshall; or the mission priest and Mary, Joe's mother. Or you can use two people you know in your everyday life.

*Organization*

An author takes the elements of a story and arranges them to achieve a definite purpose. He or she may slow down the action to increase suspense, use contrasting details to emphasize a particular point, or change the actual time order of events to intensify a scene. Consider the stories in DREAMS, and select one to illustrate each of the methods of organization given above.

## Robert Frost

Robert Frost (1874–1963), though born in California, is most often called the poet of New England. He went to Massachusetts when he was 10 years old because his mother honored her husband's request to be buried in the family plot in the East. With no money for the return trip, Mrs. Frost settled down in New Hampshire and supported the family by teaching. Frost himself later tried teaching, then farming and journalism, but he really wanted to write poetry. He kept writing poetry even though no one would buy his work. In 20 years of writing he averaged only $10 a year from his poetry. Feeling rejected by America, he moved his family to England and there published his first two volumes of poetry, *A Boy's Will* (1913) and *North of Boston* (1914). The English readers applauded his ability to use common, almost conversational, language in the established forms of poetry. When his two books were published in the United States, Frost returned (1915). His poetry has a regional locale, but its meaning is universal. Frost himself said that poetry must begin in delight and end in wisdom. In 1960, when he was eighty-six years old, he was asked by John F. Kennedy to read a poem at Kennedy's inauguration . . . the first time any poet was thus honored in America.

## Harry Mark Petrakis

Harry Mark Petrakis (1923–    ), son of Greek immigrants, was born in St. Louis, Missouri. He attended the University of Illinois for two years before working as a steelworker, real estate salesman, and speech writer to support himself while writing short stories. In 1957 Petrakis won two awards for his short stories and in 1959 a novel, *Lion at My Heart*, was published. A collection of short stories, *Pericles on 31st Street*, from which the selection in this unit was taken, was one of the final nominees in 1965 for the National Book Award. Recently, another novel, *A Dream of Kings*, was made into a movie. Writing mostly about Greeks, Petrakis credits Nikos Kazantzakis, the creator of *Zorba, the Greek*, as having had the greatest influence on his writing. Readers may indeed see that Marko Palamas shares with Zorba a zest for living that creates an appealing kind of charm.

## Langston Hughes

Langston Hughes (1902–1967), whose parents separated early in his life, had, by the age of twelve, lived in Buffalo; Cleveland; Lawrence and Topeka, Kansas; Colorado Springs; Mexico City; and Lincoln, Illinois. In 1921 Hughes began his publishing career when his famous poem, "The Negro Speaks of Rivers," was published. Abandoning college after an uncongenial year at Columbia University, Hughes held various jobs, finally sailing as a mess boy on a ship touching African ports. When the entire crew was fired, he found a job on a Holland-bound freighter, and during 1924 worked his way about Europe. His experience with the blues as played by top black musicians in Paris nightclubs had a special impact on him. Returning to Harlem, he published several books of poetry in the next few years while supporting himself at odd jobs. At the time of his death in 1967, Hughes had probably written more and longer than any other Negro author, producing thirty-nine volumes of his own, five collaborative adult books, four full-length translated works, and hundreds of uncollected selections of all types. During his forty-five years as a writer, Hughes said that his central purpose was "to explain and illuminate the Negro condition in America."

## Dorothy Johnson

Dorothy Johnson (1905–    ), short story writer and novelist, was born in McGregor, Iowa. After receiving her B.A. from Montana State University, she worked as editor of a magazine in New York. Later she returned to Montana to work as editor of the *Whitefish Pilot*. After this she worked for two years as the secretary and manager of the Montana State Press Association and then became an Assistant Professor of Journalism at Montana State University. Many of Johnson's writings center on Indians, and she is now an honorary member of the Blackfoot tribe of Montana, having been given the name of Kills-Both-Places. Several movies have been made from her stories: *The Hanging Tree, The Man Who Shot Liberty Valence,* and *A Man Called Horse.*

## Truman Capote

Truman Capote (1924–    ) was born in New Orleans to parents of long Southern lineage. He attended six different schools in five different parts of the country. Dropping out of school at seventeen, he worked briefly as a protégé of a fortuneteller and then for *The New Yorker* in various departments. Beginning to write early, Capote won his first prize at the age of eight for a short story. As an adult he has won two O'Henry short story awards. Though he claims writing is an exceedingly slow process for him, Capote insists that nothing else appeals to him. In 1966 he became one of the most-discussed authors in the country when his book *In Cold Blood* was published. Capote claimed that it was a new kind of literature, a nonfiction novel. It was later made into a movie.

## Willa Cather

Willa Cather (1873–1947), born in Winchester, Virginia, moved at age nine with her family to the Nebraska village of Red Cloud. Her friends and neighbors were the immigrants from Europe: Swedes, Bohemians, Russians, and Germans whom she came to know, understand, and respect. Her well-known novels, such as *O Pioneers* and *My Ántonia,* were built on the theme of the pioneers' spirit and courage. Her next group of books depicted the struggle of a talent to emerge from the restricting and stifling prairie life: *Song of the Lark, Youth and the Bright Medusa,* and *Lucy Gayheart.* In her mature years, she again turned to the pioneer spirit, but this time it was the spirit in an earlier pioneer age: *Death Comes for the Archbishop, Shadows on the Rock.* Her stories are honest and direct. They detail the successful conquest of physical and material hardships by people of spirit and determination.

## William Shakespeare

For a biography of William Shakespeare, see page 467.

# JULIUS CAESAR

## Introduction

The dreams you have met so far in this unit, DREAMS, have, for the most part, concentrated on the conflict between the dreams of an individual and the reality of the world. Sometimes, however, when the dreams of individuals come in conflict with those of others, people find themselves locked in a struggle, each trying to impose her or his particular vision of the world upon the others. When such a struggle takes place among powerful people in the state, it affects masses of people and even whole civilizations. William Shakespeare found the rudiments of such a struggle in Plutarch's account of the assassination of Julius Caesar. Using the bare outline of the events as they happened, he fills in the dreams which the participants must have had and recreates the murder and its effects in terms of the conflicts between dreams of power, dreams of freedom, dreams of revenge.

*Pompey, the great general crushed by Caesar.*

### Shakespeare's Audience

To understand fully the background of this grisly murder and its chain of terrible consequences, we need to grasp some of the information and assumptions that were common to Shakespeare's audience. This is not surprising, for during the three and a half centuries that have elapsed since his time, language and customs have changed as radically as clothing and transportation. Shakespeare wrote for his own time and people. He could count on their reactions to certain situations just as today's playwright knows the impact that such references as lynching, teenage gangs, and communism have on the modern audience. Let's consider, then, how an Elizabethan audience would differ from one today.

An audience in Shakespeare's day would be familiar with the words and expressions he used. Though the basic English sentence patterns are the same, some words have changed in spelling, meaning, or usage. Just as an adult may be confused today by teenage slang, so the reader may be confused by Shakespeare's language. The sound is familiar but the meaning sometimes is lost. Footnotes interpret the strange meaning of familiar words, but they also tend to slow down the impact of the dramatic action. Although you may miss some of the details, your first reading should be for the main story; you can return later for careful study of details.

Shakespeare's audience also held a different body of beliefs from today's audience. During

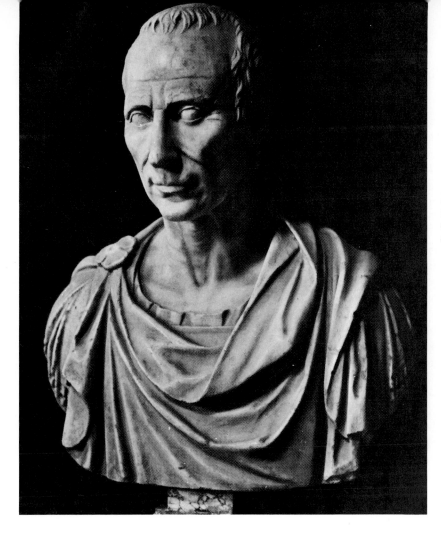

*Julius Caesar. His dreams
of reform, conquest,
and power altered the
course of history.*

Shakespeare's life, England was ruled by Queen Elizabeth I and later by James I, both absolute monarchs who the people believed had been chosen by God and hence were superior to ordinary mortals. In addition, the monarch was held to be the source of order and stability in the state, just as God is the source of law and order in the universe. Therefore, to murder a ruler was not just murder, but a great crime against the order of the universe and consequently against the will of God Himself. In order to feel the full horror of such an act the reader must accept the Elizabethan viewpoint.

The audience also firmly believed in ghosts and took them very seriously. Whether a good or a bad spirit, an apparition was an awesome and terrifying creature. Obviously, the same reaction is not felt by today's audience. The Elizabethans also felt that the moods of nature corresponded to human moods. When horrible acts were put in motion by human agency, then nature responded with darkness, strange sounds, terrible storms, and unnatural events. Although we mentally reject such a theory, we still respond to movies and television shows which heighten a dark, dramatic moment with the eerie sounds of wind and storm.

The Elizabethan audience also differed from today's in their expectations. They expected to be completely familiar with the story of the play, so the plot unfolding on the stage held no surprises for them. What they came to see was the handling of characters and to hear language of great beauty.

## Caesar and Rome

Shakespeare expected his audience to know the history of Rome and the story of Caesar's rise and fall. Even when Caesar was born in approximately 100 B.C., Rome was an old city tracing its history back to 753 B.C. when the legendary Romulus supposedly founded the city and became its first king. About two hundred and fifty years later, in 509 B.C., the last of the cruel and unscrupulous kings of the Tarquin family was expelled from Rome under the leadership of a noble man and great patriot, Lucius Junius Brutus, ancestor of the Brutus you are about to meet in Shakespeare's *Julius Caesar*.

The Tarquins had made the name of king so hated that the nobles (patricians) and the common people (plebeians) enacted a law that anyone expressing a desire for the return of the monarchy should be put to death. Instead, they formed a republic in which, theoretically at least, both the patricians and the plebeians had a share in the government. Over the next four hundred years or so (double the age of our own republic), both factions worked out a balance of power which helped to form the basis of Rome's strength, a strength which made it the leading nation of the Mediterranean world.

By the first century B.C., however, the republic had begun to crumble. Uneasy balances of power exploded sporadically into civil wars in which Rome vacillated between a monarchy, a republic, and a dictatorship. It was in such a world of great political unrest that Caesar rose to power.

Julius Caesar was born of a patrician family but early in his career cast his lot with the common people. As a representative of the popular party he climbed rapidly from one office to another. His eloquence, lavish games, and entertainments for the people, as well as political accomplishments for them, won him a large following in Rome. In 60 B.C., Caesar formed a triumvirate to rule Rome with the wealthy patrician Crassus and a well-known general, Pompey. Two years later Caesar was made governor of Gaul and by brilliant generalship went on to conquer all of Gaul, almost doubling the empire. For almost ten years he served in Gaul, winning the admiration of his legions and the support of the commoners at home. After Crassus was killed in battle, Caesar's growing popularity so frightened the Senators and Pompey that they issued the order for Caesar to disperse his troops and return to Rome.

Caesar took up this challenge to his authority, and in full battle splendor, leading his legions, he crossed the Rubicon, the river separating Gaul from Italy. Pompey fled in fear to Greece. Before pursuing him, Caesar subdued Italy within sixty days . . . then defeated two of Pompey's officers in Spain . . . and then on returning to Rome was elected consul in 48 B.C. Finally turning to Greece, Caesar swiftly crushed Pompey. Three years later he defeated the remnants of Pompey's faction in Spain. During this period of wars, Caesar had been delegated tremendous powers, first being made dictator (customarily a one-year appointment or for the duration of a crisis) in 48 B.C., then dictator for ten years in 46 B.C., and finally dictator for life in 45 B.C. In the full glory of his honors at home and his successes in Spain, Caesar returned to Rome. This is the moment at which Shakespeare begins his drama, *Julius Caesar*.

## Preparing to Read

Watch carefully from the very beginning for the conflicts that will lead to the climax and its repercussions. Note, too, how they are embodied in specific characters whom Shakespeare masterfully reveals through what they say and do, and what others say about them. Watch carefully, too, for Shakespeare's handling of the necessary background details. For just as there is exposition in a short story, so there must be exposition in a drama. It is difficult to make this necessary material seem a part of the action, but Shakespeare does it very

*Marcus Brutus*

*Marc Antony*

# Julius Cæsar

*Cast of Characters*

JULIUS CAESAR.
OCTAVIUS CAESAR,⎫ *triumvirs*
MARCUS ANTONIUS,⎬ *after the death*
M. ÆMILIUS LEPIDUS,⎭ *of Julius Cæsar.*
CICERO,⎫
PUBLIUS,⎬ *senators.*
POPILIUS LENA,⎭
MARCUS BRUTUS,⎫
CASSIUS,⎪
CASCA,⎪ *conspirators*
TREBONIUS,⎬ *against*
LIGARIUS,⎪ *Julius Cæsar.*
DECIUS BRUTUS,⎪
METELLUS CIMBER,⎪
CINNA,⎭
FLAVIUS AND MARULLUS, *tribunes.*
ARTEMIDORUS of Cnidos,
  *a teacher of Rhetoric.*
A Soothsayer.
CINNA, *a poet.* Another Poet.
LUCILIUS,⎫
TITINIUS,⎪ *friends*
MESSALA,⎬ *to Brutus*
Young CATO,⎪ *and Cassius.*
VOLUMNIUS,⎭
VARRO,⎫
CLITUS,⎪
CLAUDIUS,⎬ *servants to Brutus.*
STRATO,⎪
LUCIUS,⎪
DARDANIUS,⎭
PINDARUS, *servant to Cassius.*

CALPURNIA, *wife to Cæsar.*
PORTIA, *wife to Brutus.*

Senators, Citizens, Guards, Attendants, &c.

*Scene:*
*Rome: the neighbourhood of Sardis:*
*the neighbourhood of Philippi.*

cleverly. Notice in the first scenes how carefully he works together the little bits of information that you need for background.

As nearly as scholars can determine, the Elizabethan plays were originally given in two parts. The action played continuously for an hour or so and was interrupted by an intermission which was followed by another period of action. The division of the play into five acts was made at a later date when the plays were printed. *Julius Caesar* breaks neatly into two parts: the first moves through the death of Caesar; the second deals with the results of the murder. If you can, read steadily until you reach the end of the murder scene before going back for a more detailed study of the play. Then start with the funeral oration and read through to the end.

Note that Shakespeare has written most of the play in blank verse. Blank verse is a line of iambic pentameter verse (see page 256). It has five stresses per line, each usually occurring on the second, fourth, sixth, eighth, and tenth syllables of the line. Blank verse has no end rhyme and its rhythm is particularly suited to drama because it so closely resembles the rhythm of normal English speech. In reading blank verse aloud, as you should to sense its grace and power, read it according to the sense of the passage rather than according to the length of individual lines.

# JULIUS CAESAR

## Act I

### SCENE 1

*A street in Rome. The news of* CAESAR's *military victory over the sons of* POMPEY *has spread excitement among the people. A group of tradesmen have quit their shops and have made* CAESAR's *triumph occasion for a holiday. Led by a burly and loud-laughing* COBBLER, *they shout and cheer down the cobbled street and decorate* CAESAR's *statue with garlands of flowers. The tribunes[1]* FLAVIUS *and* MARULLUS *arrive and angrily confront the celebrating tradesmen.*

FLAVIUS. Hence! Home, you idle creatures, get you home!
　Is this a holiday? What! know you not,
　Being mechanical,[2] you ought not walk
　Upon a laboring day[3] without the sign
　Of your profession?[4] (*Points to a man in the group.*)
　　Speak, what trade art thou? 　　　　　　　5
CARPENTER. Why, sir, a carpenter.
MARULLUS. Where is thy leather apron and thy rule?
　What dost thou with thy best apparel on?
　(*Singling out the* COBBLER.) You, sir, what trade are
　　you?
COBBLER. Truly, sir, in respect of a fine workman, I am but, 　10
　as you would say, a cobbler.[5]
MARULLUS. (*Impatiently.*) But what trade art thou? Answer me directly.[6]
COBBLER. (*Smirking and winking at his friends.*) A trade,
　sir, that I hope I may use with a safe conscience; which
　is, indeed, sir, a mender of bad soles.[7] 　　　　15
MARULLUS. What trade, thou knave? thou naughty knave,
　what trade?
COBBLER. Nay, I beseech you, sir, be not out with me;[8]
　yet if you be out, sir, I can mend you.
MARULLUS. (*Indignant.*) What mean'st thou by that?
　Mend me, thou saucy fellow!
COBBLER. Why, sir, cobble you. 　　　　　　20

1. **tribune**\ᐟtrĭ•byūn\ a magistrate originally intended to protect the plebians from oppression by the aristocracy.

2. **mechanical,** artisan, skilled worker.

3. **laboring day,** work day.

4. **without . . . profession,** in Shakespeare's time English craftsmen were required to wear their work clothes and carry the tools of their trade on working days.

5. **cobbler,** (1) a clumsy workman, (2) a mender of shoes. Here Shakespeare uses the word in both senses; such a use of a word in a double sense is called *punning,* a very popular form of word play in Shakespeare's time.
6. **directly,** at once.
7. **soles,** another pun.

8. **be not out,** "do not be angry" in one sense, but in another, he is punning. What is the pun?

FLAVIUS. (*Stepping forward to settle the confusion.*) Thou
  art a cobbler, art thou?

COBBLER. Truly, sir, all that I live by is with the awl.[9] I
  meddle with no tradesman's matters, nor women's matters, but with all. I am, indeed, sir, a surgeon to old
  shoes; when they are in great danger, I recover them. 25
  As proper men as ever trod upon neat's[10] leather have
  gone upon my handiwork.

FLAVIUS. But wherefore art not in thy shop today?
  Why dost thou lead these men about the streets?

COBBLER. Truly, sir, to wear out their shoes, to get myself 30
  into more work. But, indeed, sir, we make holiday, to
  see Caesar and to rejoice in his triumph.

MARULLUS. (*Swelling with anger.*) Wherefore rejoice?
    What conquests brings he home?
  What tributaries[11] follow him to Rome
  To grace in bonds his chariot-wheels? 35
  You blocks, you stones, you worse than senseless things!
  O you hard hearts, you cruel men of Rome,
  Knew you not Pompey? Many a time and oft
  Have you climbed up to walls and battlements,
  To towers and windows, yea, to chimney-tops, 40
  Your infants in your arms, and there have sat
  The live-long day, with patient expectation,
  To see great Pompey pass the streets of Rome;
  And when you saw his chariot but appear
  Have you not made a universal shout, 45
  That Tiber[12] trembled underneath her banks
  To hear the replications[13] of your sounds
  Made on her concave shores?
  And do you now put on your best attire?
  And do you now cull out a holiday? 50
  And do you now strew flowers in his way
  That comes in triumph over Pompey's blood?[14]
  Be gone!
  Run to your houses, fall upon your knees,
  Pray to the gods to intermit[15] the plague 55
  That needs must light on this ingratitude.

FLAVIUS. Go, go, good countrymen, and, for this fault,
  Assemble all the poor men of your sort;
  Draw them to Tiber's banks, and weep your tears
  Into the channel, till the lowest stream 60
  Do kiss the most exalted shores of all.

[*Hesitant and with lowered heads the tradesmen
leave.*]

See, whether their basest metal be not moved;

9. **awl,** shoemaker's tool. The cobbler is
punning.

10. **neat**\nēt\ cow.

11. **tributaries,** conquered leaders forced
into slavery or, if wealthy, sometimes required to pay for their release.

12. **Tiber**\ˈtai·bər\ the river that runs
through Rome.
13. **replications**\ˈrĕ·plĭ ˈkā·shəns\ rever-
berations.

14. **over Pompey's blood,** over the sons
of Pompey.

15. **intermit,** withhold.

They vanish tongue-tied in their guiltiness.
Go you down that way towards the Capitol;
This way will I. Disrobe the images 65
If you do find them decked with ceremonies.[16]

MARULLUS. May we do so?
You know it is the feast of Lupercal.[17]

FLAVIUS. It is no matter; let no images
Be hung with Caesar's trophies. I'll about 70
And drive away the vulgar from the streets.
So do you too, where you perceive them thick.
These growing feathers plucked from Caesar's wing
Will make him fly an ordinary pitch,[18]
Who else would soar above the view of men 75
And keep us all in servile fearfulness.

[*They hurry off in opposite directions.*]

### SCENE 2

*Later the same day in a public square prepared for the ritual
of honoring the god Pan.*[1] CAESAR *enters, attended by* AN-
TONY, *who is dressed for competition in the athletic games.*
DECIUS,[2] CICERO, BRUTUS, CASSIUS, *and* CASCA *follow.* CAL-
PURNIA, *the wife of* CAESAR, *and* PORTIA, *wife of* BRUTUS,
*are in the group with their husbands. A crowd follows*
CAESAR's *train toward the festival to celebrate the Lupercal. A* SOOTHSAYER *in the crowd struggles to attract* CAESAR's
*attention.*

CAESAR. Calpurnia!
CASCA. (*Waving his arms.*)  Peace, ho! Caesar speaks.
CAESAR. Calpurnia!
CALPURNIA.  Here, my lord.
CAESAR. Stand you directly in Antonius' way
   When he doth run his course. Antonius!
ANTONY. Caesar, my lord? 5

16. **Disrobe . . . ceremonies,** take the
decorations (**ceremonies**) from the statues (**images**) of Caesar.
17. **Lupercal**\ˈlü·pər 'kal\ a general
celebration (held annually on February
15) conducted by priests to insure fer-
tility and easy childbirth among women.
The priests, young noblemen, ran a
course through the streets on the Palatine Hill. As they ran they struck people
in their way with a goatskin whip.
Childless women so struck were thought
to be cured of their barrenness.
18. **These growing . . . pitch,** Caesar is
compared to a falcon whose wings must
be clipped to keep it from flying too
high (**pitch**) and out of the Falconer's
control. In other words, Flavius is saying that by depriving Caesar of his popular support now, his lofty political ambitions will be checked in spite of Caesar's wishes.

1. **Pan**\păn\ the classical god of flocks
and pastures honored in the Lupercal.

2. **Decius**\ˈdē·shəs\.  **Cicero**\ˈsĭ·sə 'rō\
(106–43 B.C.) a statesman and orator.
**Brutus**\ˈbrü·təs\.  **Cassius**\ˈkă·shəs\.
**Casca**\ˈkäs·kə\.  **Calpurnia**\ˈkăl ˈpər-
nē·ə\.  **Portia**\ˈpōr·shə\.

CAESAR. Forget not, in your speed, Antonius,
    To touch Calpurnia; for our elders say,
    The barren, touched in this holy chase,[3]
    Shake off their sterile curse.
ANTONY.               I shall remember:
    When Caesar says, "Do this," it is performed.     10
CAESAR. Set on; and leave no ceremony out.

[*Trumpets announce the start of the games.* ANTONY
    *leaves.*]

SOOTHSAYER. (*Crying out from the crowd.*) Caesar!
CAESAR. Ha! Who calls?
CASCA. Bid every noise be still; peace yet again!
CAESAR. Who is it in the press[4] that calls on me?     15
    I hear a tongue shriller than all the music,
    Cry "Caesar!" Speak! Caesar is turned to hear.
SOOTHSAYER. Beware the ides of March.[5]
CAESAR. (*Gazing around to see who has spoken.*) What
    man is that?
BRUTUS. A soothsayer bids you beware the ides of March.
CAESAR. Set him before me! Let me see his face.     20
CASSIUS. Fellow, come from the throng; look upon Caesar.
CAESAR. What say'st thou to me now? Speak once again.
SOOTHSAYER. Beware the ides of March.
CAESAR. He is a dreamer; let us leave him. Pass.

[*Trumpets sound again. The procession and crowd
    move on.* BRUTUS *and* CASSIUS *lag behind.*]

CASSIUS. Will you go see the order of the course?[6]     25
BRUTUS. Not I.
CASSIUS. I pray[7] you, do.
BRUTUS. I am not gamesome;[8] I do lack some part
    Of that quick[9] spirit that is in Antony.
    Let me not hinder, Cassius, your desires.     30
    I'll leave you.
CASSIUS. Brutus, I do observe you now of late;
    I have not from your eyes that gentleness
    And show of love as I was wont[10] to have.
    You bear too stubborn and too strange a hand     35
    Over your friend that loves you.
BRUTUS.               Cassius,
    Be not deceived; if I have veiled my look,
    I turn the trouble of my countenance
    Merely upon myself.[11] Vexed as I am
    Of late with passions of some difference,     40
    Conceptions only proper to myself,
    Which give some soil[12] perhaps to my behaviors;

3. **this holy chase,** this race being run in honor of Pan. **Barren** and **sterile,** unable to bear children; Caesar and Calpurnia were childless.

4. **press,** crowd.

5. **ides**\aidz\ March 15.

6. **see . . . course,** see what happens in the race.

7. **pray,** beg, entreat.

8. **gamesome,** given to play.

9. **quick,** lively.

10. **wont,** accustomed.

11. **I turn . . . myself.** That is, I am turning inwardly, only against myself, whatever troubles, griefs, and worries my countenance seems to show.
12. **soil,** ground or basis and also nurturing element.

But let not therefore my good friends be grieved—
Among which number, Cassius, be you one—
Nor construe any further my neglect,                              45
Than that poor Brutus, with himself at war,
Forgets the shows of love[13] to other men.
CASSIUS. Then, Brutus, I have much mistook your passion;
By means whereof this breast of mine hath buried
Thoughts of great value, worthy cogitations. (*Pauses*)   50
Tell me, good Brutus, can you see your face?
BRUTUS. No, Cassius, for the eye sees not itself
But by reflection, by some other things.
CASSIUS. 'Tis just;
And it is very much lamented, Brutus,                           55
That you have no such mirrors as will turn
Your hidden worthiness into your eye
That you might see your shadow. I have heard
Where many of the best respect in Rome,
Except immortal Caesar, speaking of Brutus                      60
And groaning underneath this age's yoke,
Have wished that noble Brutus had his eyes.
BRUTUS. Into what dangers would you lead me, Cassius,
That you would have me seek into myself
For that which is not in me?                                     65
CASSIUS. Therefore, good Brutus, be prepared to hear;
And since you know you cannot see yourself
So well as by reflection, I, your glass,
Will modestly discover to yourself
That of yourself which you yet know not of.                     70
And be not jealous[14] on me, gentle Brutus.
Were I a common laugher,[15] or did use
To stale with ordinary oaths my love
To every new protester;[16] if you know
That I do fawn on men and hug them hard                         75
And after scandal them, or if you know
That I profess myself in banqueting
To all the rout,[17] then hold me dangerous.

[*Trumpets flourish in the distance, followed by a wave
of cheers.*]

BRUTUS. (*Startled and anxious.*) What means this shout-
ing? I do fear, the people
Choose Caesar for their king.
CASSIUS.                        Ay, do you fear it?             80
Then must I think you would not have it so.
BRUTUS. I would not, Cassius, yet I love him well.
But wherefore do you hold me here so long?
What is it that you would impart to me?

13. **shows of love,** ordinary signs of friendship.

14. **jealous,** suspicious.
15. **laugher,** jester, clown.

16. **protester,** one who professes friendship.

17. **rout,** rabble, worthless crowd.

If it be aught toward the general good,       85
Set honor in one eye and death i' th' other,
And I will look on both indifferently;
For let the gods so speed me as I love
The name of honor more than I fear death.
CASSIUS. I know that virtue to be in you, Brutus,       90
As well as I do know your outward favor.[18]
Well, honor is the subject of my story.
I cannot tell what you and other men
Think of this life; but, for my single self,
I had as lief not be as live to be       95
In awe of such a thing as I myself.
I was born free as Caesar; so were you.
We both have fed as well, and we can both
Endure the winter's cold as well as he;
For once, upon a raw and gusty day,       100
The troubled Tiber chafing with her shores,
Caesar said to me, "Dar'st thou, Cassius, now
Leap in with me into this angry flood
And swim to yonder point?" Upon the word,
Accoutred[19] as I was, I plunged in       105
And bade him follow; so indeed he did.
The torrent roared, and we did buffet it
With lusty sinews, throwing it aside
And stemming it with hearts of controversy;[20]
But ere we could arrive the point proposed,       110
Caesar cried, "Help me, Cassius, or I sink!"
I, as Aeneas,[21] our great ancestor,
Did from the flames of Troy upon his shoulder
The old Anchises bear, so from the waves of Tiber
Did I the tired Caesar. And this man       115
Is now become a god, and Cassius is
A wretched creature, and must bend his body
If Caesar carelessly but nod on him.
He had a fever when he was in Spain,
And when the fit was on him, I did mark       120
How he did shake. 'Tis true, this god did shake.
His coward lips did from their color fly,
And that same eye whose bend[22] doth awe the world
Did lose his luster; I did hear him groan.
Ay, and that tongue of his that bade the Romans       125
Mark him and write his speeches in their books,
Alas, it cried, "Give me some drink, Titinius,"
As a sick girl! Ye gods, it doth amaze me
A man of such a feeble temper should
So get the start[23] of the majestic world       130
And bear the palm[24] alone.

18. **outward favor,** outward appearance.

19. **accoutred**\ə‸kū·tərd\ dressed. Cassius was fully dressed.

20. **and stemming . . . controversy,** overcoming the waves with hearts determined and resolute for the struggle.

21. **Aeneas**\ə ‸nē·əs\ a Trojan leader in the Trojan War, the war between Trojans and Greeks in early Greek history. When the device of the Trojan Horse was successful and the Greeks captured Troy at night, Aeneas, leading his son and taking his elderly father **Anchises** \'ăn ‸kai·sēz\ on his shoulders, escaped from the city. Cassius carried Caesar in the same manner from the Tiber. Virgil tells the story of Aeneas in his **Aeneid** \ə ‸nē·ĭd\. After wandering homeless about the Mediterranean for many years, Aeneas and his Trojan refugees eventually established Rome. This is what Cassius means by calling Aeneas "our great ancestor."
22. **bend,** glance.

23. **get the start,** become leader or commander.
24. **palm,** a token of victory given in athletic contests.

[*More trumpet flourishes in the distance, followed by
general shouting.*]

BRUTUS. (*Distracted by the noise.*) Another general shout!
I do believe that these applauses are
For some new honors that are heaped on Caesar.
CASSIUS. Why, man, he doth bestride the narrow world    135
Like a Colossus,[25] and we petty men
Walk under his huge legs, and peep about
To find ourselves dishonorable graves.
Men at some time are masters of their fates;
The fault, dear Brutus, is not in our stars,    140
But in ourselves, that we are underlings.
Brutus and Caesar: what should be in that "Caesar"?
Why should that name be sounded more than yours?
Write them together; yours is as fair a name.
Sound them; it doth become the mouth as well.    145
Weigh them; it is as heavy; conjure[26] with them;
"Brutus" will start a spirit as soon as "Caesar."
Now, in the names of all the gods at once,
Upon what meat doth this our Caesar feed
That he is grown so great? Age, thou art shamed!    150
Rome, thou hast lost the breed of noble bloods!
When went there by an age, since the great flood,
But it was famed with more than with one man?
When could they say, till now, that talked of Rome,
That her wide walls encompassed but one man?    155
Now is it Rome indeed and room[27] enough,
When there is in it but one only man.
O, you and I have heard our fathers say
There was a Brutus once that would have brooked[28]
The eternal devil to keep his state in Rome    160
As easily as a king.
BRUTUS. That you do love me, I am nothing jealous.
What you would work me to, I have some aim.
How I have thought of this and of these times,
I shall recount hereafter; for this present,    165
I would not, so with love I might entreat you,
Be any further moved. What you have said
I will consider; what you have to say
I will with patience hear, and find a time
Both meet[29] to hear and answer such high things.    170
Till then, my noble friend, chew[30] upon this—
Brutus had rather be a villager
Than to repute himself a son of Rome
Under these hard conditions as this time
Is like to lay upon us.

25. **Colossus**\kə ˄lŏ·səs\ the huge statue
of Rhodes, made in honor of the god
Apollo in the third century B.C. It supposedly straddled the harbor entrance
and ships passed between its legs.

26. **conjure**\kŏn ˄jūr (note the stress)\
to raise spirits of the dead by charms
and incantations.

27. In Elizabethan English the words
**Rome** and **room** were pronounced similarly. Cassius is punning.

28. **brooked,** endured, permitted. This
is a reference to the revolt of Junius
Brutus (see Introduction) against the
early Tarquin Kings of Rome.

29. **meet,** proper.
30. **chew,** think.

CASSIUS.                     I am glad                     175
    That my weak words have struck but thus much show
    Of fire from Brutus.

[*Caesar and his train approach.*]

BRUTUS. The games are done and Caesar is returning.
CASSIUS. (*Whispering.*) As they pass by, pluck Casca by
    the sleeve;
    And he will, after his sour fashion, tell you          180
    What hath proceeded worthy note today.
BRUTUS. I will do so. But, look you, Cassius,
    The angry spot doth glow on Caesar's brow,
    And all the rest look like a chidden[31] train.

> 31. **chidden**, scolded, rebuked.

    Calpurnia's cheek is pale, and Cicero          185
    Looks with such ferret and such fiery eyes[32]

> 32. **ferret . . . eyes,** with eyes red and angry like those of a ferret, a small animal like a weasel.

    As we have seen him in the Capitol,
    Being crossed in conference by some senators.
CASSIUS. Casca will tell us what the matter is.
CAESAR. (*Leaning toward* ANTONY *and glancing in*
    CASSIUS' *direction.*) Antonius.          190
ANTONY. Caesar?
CAESAR. Let me have men about me that are fat,
    Sleek-headed men and such as sleep o' nights.
    Yond Cassius has a lean and hungry look.
    He thinks too much; such men are dangerous.          195
ANTONY. Fear him not, Caesar; he's not dangerous.
    He is a noble Roman and well given.
CAESAR. Would he were fatter! But I fear him not.
    Yet if my name were liable to fear,
    I do not know the man I should avoid          200
    So soon as that spare Cassius. He reads much,
    He is a great observer, and he looks
    Quite through[33] the deeds of men. He loves no plays

> 33. **looks/Quite through,** examines closely, scrutinizes.

    As thou dost, Antony; he hears no music;
    Seldom he smiles, and smiles in such a sort          205
    As if he mocked himself and scorned his spirit
    That could be moved to smile at anything.
    Such men as he be never at heart's ease
    Whiles they behold a greater than themselves,
    And therefore are they very dangerous.          210
    I rather tell thee what is to be feared
    Than what I fear; for always I am Caesar.
    Come on my right hand, for this ear is deaf,
    And tell me truly what thou think'st of him.

[CAESAR *and* ANTONY *walk away talking quietly to-*
*gether. The train follows.* BRUTUS *gently pulls at* CASCA's

*sleeve as he passes.* CASCA *draws aside and speaks to*
BRUTUS.]

CASCA. You pulled me by the cloak. Would you speak
with me?                                                                   215
BRUTUS. Ay, Casca; tell us what hath chanced today
That Caesar looks so sad.
CASCA. Why, you were with him, were you not?
BRUTUS. I should not then ask Casca what had chanced.
CASCA. Why, there was a crown offered him; and being     220
offered him, he put it by with the back of his hand, thus;
and then the people fell a-shouting.
BRUTUS. What was the second noise for?
CASCA. Why, for that too.
CASSIUS. They shouted thrice; what was the last cry for?     225
CASCA. Why, for that too.
BRUTUS. Was the crown offered him thrice?
CASCA. Ay, marry,[34] was't, and he put it by thrice, every
time gentler than other; and at every putting-by mine
honest neighbors shouted.                                              230
CASSIUS. Who offered him the crown?
CASCA. Why, Antony.
BRUTUS. Tell us the manner of it, gentle Casca.
CASCA. I can as well be hanged as tell the manner of it. It
was mere foolery; I did not mark it. I saw Mark Antony     235
offer him a crown—yet 'twas not a crown neither, 'twas
one of these coronets[35]—and, as I told you, he put it by
once; but for all that, to my thinking, he would fain
have had it. Then he offered it to him again; then
he put it by again, but, to my thinking, he was very     240
loath to lay his fingers off it. And then he offered it the
third time; he put it the third time by; and still as he
refused it, the rabblement hooted and clapped their
chapped hands and threw up their sweaty night-caps
and uttered such a deal of stinking breath because     245
Caesar refused the crown, that it had almost choked
Caesar, for he swounded[36] and fell down at it; and for
mine own part, I durst not laugh for fear of opening my
lips and receiving the bad air.
CASSIUS. But, soft, I pray you. What, did Caesar swound?     250
CASCA. He fell down in the market-place, and foamed at
the mouth, and was speechless.
BRUTUS. 'Tis very like; he hath the falling sickness.[37]
CASSIUS. No, Caesar hath it not; but you and I
And honest Casca, we have the falling sickness.     255
CASCA. I know not what you mean by that, but I am sure
Caesar fell down. If the tag-rag people did not clap him

34. **marry,** a light oath in Elizabethan
times. Originally "by Mary," that is, the
mother of Christ (an anachronism here).

35. **coronet**\'kŏ·rə ⁀nĕt\ a small crown,
for one with a rank lower than a king's.

36. **swounded**\⁀swūn·dəd\ fainted.

37. **falling sickness,** epilepsy. It is not
certain historically whether or not Caesar had this affliction.

and hiss him, according as he pleased and displeased them, as they use to do the players in the theater, I am no true man. 260

BRUTUS. What said he when he came unto himself?

CASCA. Marry, before he fell down, when he perceived the common herd was glad he refused the crown, he plucked me ope his doublet[38] and offered them his throat to cut. An[39] I had been a man of any occupa- 265 tion,[40] if I would not have taken him at a word, I would I might go to hell among the rogues. And so he fell. When he came to himself again, he said, if he had done or said anything amiss, he desired their worships to think it was his infirmity. Three or four wenches, where 270 I stood, cried, "Alas, good soul!" and forgave him with all their hearts. But there's no heed to be taken of them. If Caesar had stabbed their mothers, they would have done no less.

BRUTUS. And after that he came, thus sad, away? 275

CASCA. Ay.

CASSIUS. Did Cicero say anything?

CASCA. Ay, he spoke Greek.

CASSIUS. To what effect?

CASCA. Nay, an I tell you that, I'll ne'er look you i' th' face 280 again. But those that understood him smiled at one another and shook their heads; but for mine own part, it was Greek to me. I could tell you more news too. Marullus and Flavius, for pulling scarfs off Caesar's images are put to silence.[41] Fare you well. There was 285 more foolery yet, if I could remember it.

CASSIUS. Will you sup[42] with me tonight, Casca?

CASCA. No, I am promised forth.

CASSIUS. Will you dine with me tomorrow?

CASCA. Ay, if I be alive and your mind hold and your 290 dinner be worth the eating.

CASSIUS. Good! I will expect you.

CASCA. Do so. Farewell, both.

[CASCA *leaves.*]

BRUTUS. What a blunt fellow is this grown to be!
He was quick[43] mettle when he went to school. 295

CASSIUS. So is he now in execution
Of any bold or noble enterprise,
However he puts on this tardy form.[44]
This rudeness is a sauce to his good wit,
Which gives men stomach to digest his words 300
With better appetite.

BRUTUS. And so it is. For this time I will leave you.

38. **doublet,** a tight, colorful jacket worn in Shakespeare's time.

39. **an,** if.

40. **occupation,** self-possession.

41. **put to silence,** either exiled and banished or put to death.

42. **sup,** have dinner.

43. **quick,** lively.

44. **he puts . . . form,** he puts on this appearance of slowness and inactivity.

Tomorrow, if you please to speak with me,
I will come home to you; or, if you will,
Come home to me, and I will wait for you.                    305
CASSIUS. I will do so. Till then, think of the world.

[BRUTUS *turns and leaves.*]

(CASSIUS *watches* BRUTUS *depart and muses to himself.*)
      Well, Brutus, thou art noble; yet, I see,
Thy honorable metal may be wrought
From that it is disposed;⁴⁵ therefore 'tis meet
That noble minds keep ever with their likes;                 310
For who so firm that cannot be seduced?
Caesar doth bear me hard,⁴⁶ but he loves Brutus.
If I were Brutus now and he were Cassius,
He should not humor me. I will this night,
In several hands,⁴⁷ in at his windows throw,                 315
As if they came from several citizens,
Writings all tending to the great opinion
That Rome holds of his name; wherein obscurely
Caesar's ambition shall be glanced⁴⁸ at.
And after this let Caesar seat him sure,                      320
For we will shake him, or worse days endure.

[CASSIUS *leaves slowly.*]

45. **yet, I see, . . . disposed,** despite your fundamentally honorable nature, which would cause you to take one course, you may be swayed to another.
46. **bear me hard,** dislike and suspect me.

47. **In several hands,** in different kinds of handwriting, as though written by many different people.

48. **glanced at,** mentioned.


## SCENE 3

*A street at night. A violent thunderstorm flashes and roars.
The flickering light reveals the blank white walls of houses
and the dark, staring windows. There is no sign of life.*
CASCA *and* CICERO *enter from opposite sides.* CASCA *has
drawn his sword and moves along warily.*

CICERO. Good even,¹ Casca. Brought you Caesar home?
      Why are you breathless? And why stare you so?
CASCA. Are you not moved, when all the sway of earth
      Shakes like a thing unfirm? O Cicero,
      I have seen tempests when the scolding winds            5
      Have rived² the knotty oaks, and I have seen
      The ambitious ocean swell and rage and foam
      To be exalted with the threat'ning clouds;
      But never till tonight, never till now,
      Did I go through a tempest dropping fire.               10
      Either there is a civil strife in heaven,
      Or else the world, too saucy³ with the gods,
      Incenses them to send destruction.
CICERO. Why, saw you anything more wonderful?

1. **even,** evening.

2. **rived\raivd\** split.

3. **saucy,** impudent.

CASCA. A common slave—you know him well by sight— 15
Held up his left hand, which did flame and burn
Like twenty torches joined, and yet his hand,
Not sensible of fire, remained unscorched.
Besides—I have not since put up my sword—
Against[4] the Capitol I met a lion, 20
Who glared upon me, and went surly by
Without annoying me. And there were drawn
Upon a heap a hundred ghastly women,
Transformed with their fear, who swore they saw
Men all in fire walk up and down the streets. 25
And yesterday the bird of night[5] did sit
Even at noonday upon the market-place,
Hooting and shrieking. When these prodigies
Do so conjointly meet, let not men say,
"These are their reasons; they are natural"; 30
For, I believe, they are portentous things
Unto the climate that they point upon.[6]
CICERO. Indeed, it is a strange-disposed time;
But men may construe things after their fashion[7]
Clean from the purpose of the things themselves. 35
Comes Caesar to the Capitol tomorrow?
CASCA. He doth; for he did bid Antonius
Send word to you he would be there tomorrow.
CICERO. Goodnight then, Casca. This disturbed sky
Is not to walk in.
CASCA.              Farewell, Cicero. 40

[*As* CICERO *leaves,* CASSIUS *enters from another direction
and is startled by* CASCA, *who stands in the shadows.*]

CASSIUS. Who's there?
CASCA.              A Roman.
CASSIUS.                    Casca, by your voice.
CASCA. Your ear is good. Cassius, what night is this!
CASSIUS. A very pleasing night to honest men.
CASCA. Who ever knew the heavens menace so?
CASSIUS. Those that have known the earth so full of faults. 45
For my part, I have walked about the streets,
Submitting me unto the perilous night,
And, thus unbraced,[8] Casca, as you see,
Have bared my bosom to the thunder-stone.[9]
And when the cross blue lightning seemed to open 50
The breast of heaven, I did present myself
Even in the aim and very flash of it.
CASCA. But wherefore did you so much tempt the heavens?
It is the part of men to fear and tremble
When the most mighty gods by tokens send 55

4. **against,** by.

5. **bird of night,** owl.

6. **For, I believe . . . point upon.** Casca believes that the unnatural events are omens of impending disaster for Rome.
7. **their fashion,** their (the men) own opinion.

8. **unbraced,** not armored or otherwise protected by heavy clothing.
9. **thunder-stone,** thunder bolt.

Such dreadful heralds to astonish us.

CASSIUS.  You are dull, Casca, and those sparks of life
  That should be in a Roman you do want,
  Or else you use not. You look pale and gaze
  And put on fear and cast yourself in wonder          60
  To see the strange impatience of the heavens.
  But if you would consider the true cause
  Why all these fires, why all these gliding ghosts,
  Why birds and beasts from quality and kind,[10]
  Why old men, fools, and children calculate,          65
  Why all these things change from their ordinance
  Their natures and pre-formed faculties[11]
  To monstrous quality, why, you shall find
  That heaven hath infused them with these spirits,[12]
  To make them instruments of fear and warning        70
  Unto some monstrous state.
  Now could I, Casca, name to thee a man
  Most like this dreadful night,
  That thunders, lightens, opens graves, and roars
  As doth the lion in the Capitol,                      75
  A man no mightier than thyself or me
  In personal action, yet prodigious grown
  And fearful, as these strange eruptions are.

CASCA.  'Tis Caesar that you mean; is it not, Cassius?

CASSIUS.  Let it be who it is; for Romans now          80
  Have thews[13] and limbs like to their ancestors.
  But woe the while! our fathers' minds are dead,
  And we are governed with our mothers' spirits.
  Our yoke and sufferance[14] show us womanish.

CASCA.  Indeed, they say the senators tomorrow         85
  Mean to establish Caesar as a king;
  And he shall wear his crown by sea and land,
  In every place, save here in Italy.[15]

CASSIUS. I know where I will wear this dagger then;
  Cassius from bondage will deliver Cassius.[16]        90
  Therein, ye gods, you make the weak most strong;
  Therein, ye gods, you tyrants do defeat.
  Nor stony tower, nor walls of beaten brass,
  Nor airless dungeon, nor strong links of iron,
  Can be retentive to the strength of spirit;          95
  But life, being weary of these worldly bars,
  Never lacks power to dismiss itself.
  If I know this, know all the world besides,
  That part of tyranny that I do bear
  I can shake off at pleasure.

[*Claps of thunder roar in the sky.*]

10. **from quality and kind,** against their true quality or nature.

11. **pre-formed faculties,** natural powers and functions.

12. **these spirits,** unnatural tendencies.

13. **thews,** sinews.

14. **yoke and sufferance,** our acceptance of oppression.

15. The feelings against a Kingship were stronger in the Italian peninsula than in other parts of the Roman Empire.

16. **Cassius . . . Cassius,** that is, he will commit suicide.

CASCA. (*Inspired by* CASSIUS' *bold statement of
                              rebellion.*) So can I!                    100
    So every bondman in his own hand bears
    The power to cancel his captivity.
CASSIUS. And why should Caesar be a tyrant then?
    Poor man! I know he would not be a wolf,
    But that he sees the Romans are but sheep;        105
    He were no lion, were not Romans hinds.[17]
    Those that with haste will make a mighty fire
    Begin it with weak straws. What trash is Rome,
    What rubbish and what offal, when it serves
    For the base matter to illuminate                 110
    So vile a thing as Caesar! But, O grief,
    Where has thou led me? I perhaps speak this
    Before a willing bondman.[18] Then I know
    My answer must be made. But I am armed,
    And dangers are to me indifferent.                115
CASCA. You speak to Casca, and to such a man
    That is no fleering tell-tale.[19] Hold, my hand.
    Be factious[20] for redress of all these griefs,
    And I will set this foot of mine as far
    As who goes farthest.
CASSIUS.                      There's a bargain made.  120
    Now you know, Casca, I have moved already
    Some certain of the noblest-minded Romans
    To undergo with me an enterprise
    Of honorable-dangerous consequence.
    And I do know, by this they stay[21] for me        125
    In Pompey's Porch;[22] for now, this fearful night,
    There is no stir or walking in the streets.
    And the complexion of the element
    In favor's[23] like the work we have in hand,
    Most bloody, fiery, and most terrible.            130

[CINNA *approaches, hurrying along the street.*]

CASCA. (*Softly to* CASSIUS.) Stand close awhile, for here
    comes one in haste.
CASSIUS. 'Tis Cinna. I do know him by his gait;
    He is a friend. (*Calling out.*) Cinna, where haste you
        so?
CINNA. To find out you. (*Peering at* CASCA.) Who's that?
    Metellus Cimber?[24]
CASSIUS. No, it is Casca: one incorporate[25]          135
    To our attempts. Am I not stayed for, Cinna?
CINNA. I am glad on't. What a fearful night is this!
    There's two or three of us have seen strange sights.
CASSIUS. Am I not stayed for? Tell me.

17. **hinds,** deer.

18. **a willing bondman,** a person willing to be a bondman or slave of Caesar and who might report to him.

19. **fleering tell-tale,** mocking or insincere informer.
20. **be factious,** get together a party, faction, or conspiracy.

21. **stay,** wait.
22. **Pompey's Porch,** the vestibule or entrance to the theater of Pompey.

23. **favor,** appearance.

24. **Metellus Cimber**\mə ˈtĕ·ləs ˈsĭm-bər\.
25. **one incorporate,** one who has joined.

CINNA.                              Yes, you are.
  O Cassius, if you could                                                    140
  But win the noble Brutus to our party—
CASSIUS.  Be you content. Good Cinna, take this paper,
  And look you lay it on the praetor's[26] chair,

26. **praetor**\\\*prē 'tȯr\\   a  high-ranking official with judicial duties.

  Where Brutus may but find it; and throw this
  In at his window; set this up with wax                                     145
  Upon old Brutus' statue. All this done,
  Repair to Pompey's Porch, where you shall find us.
  Is Decius Brutus and Trebonius[27] there?

27. **Trebonius**\\trĕ \*bō·nē·əs\\  formerly a lieutenant of Caesar in Britain.

CINNA.  All but Metellus Cimber, and he's gone
  To seek you at your house. Well, I will hie                                150
  And so bestow these papers as you bade me.
CASSIUS.  That done, repair to Pompey's theater.
  [CINNA *hurries off*.]
  Come, Casca, you and I will yet ere day
  See Brutus at his house. Three parts of him
  Is ours already, and the man entire                                       155
  Upon the next encounter yields him ours.
CASCA.  O, he sits high in all the people's hearts;
  And that which would appear offense in us,
  His countenance, like richest alchemy,[28]

28. **alchemy,** an alchemist could allegedly change baser materials into gold.

  Will change to virtue and to worthiness.                                  160
CASSIUS.  Him and his worth and our great need of him
  You have right well conceited.[29] Let us go,

29. **conceited,** understood.

  For it is after midnight; and ere day
  We will awake him and be sure of him.

  [CASSIUS *and* CASCA *set off together*.]

# ⏹Act II

### SCENE 1

*Rome.* BRUTUS' *garden, a graceful arrangement of trees and shrubbery, fountains and white marble statuary. To the side a gate that leads to the street. It is March 15, shortly before dawn. The dark sky still convulses with periodic flashes of lightning.* BRUTUS *paces nervously. He looks suddenly toward the house, and calls:*

BRUTUS. What, Lucius,[1] ho!
　I cannot by the progress of the stars
　Give guess how near to day. Lucius, I say!
　I would[2] it were my fault to sleep so soundly.
　When, Lucius, when? Awake, I say! What, Lucius!    5
LUCIUS. (*Entering, rubbing his eyes.*) Called you, my
　　lord?
BRUTUS. Get me a taper in my study, Lucius.
　When it is lighted, come and call me here.
LUCIUS. (*Leaving, speaking through a yawn.*) I will,
　　my lord.
BRUTUS. (*Musing to himself.*) It must be by his death;
　　and for my part    10
　I know no personal cause to spurn at him
　But for the general.[3] He would be crowned:
　How that might change his nature; there's the question.
　It is the bright day that brings forth the adder,[4]
　And that craves wary walking. Crown him? That—    15
　And then, I grant, we put a sting in him
　That at his will he may do danger with.
　The abuse of greatness is when it disjoins
　Remorse from power. And, to speak truth of Caesar,
　I have not known when his affections swayed    20
　More than his reason.[5] But 'tis a common proof
　That lowliness is young ambition's ladder,
　Whereto the climber-upward turns his face;
　But when he once attains the utmost rung,
　He then unto the ladder turns his back,    25
　Looks in the clouds, scorning the base degrees
　By which he did ascend. So Caesar may.
　Then, lest he may, prevent.[6] And, since the quarrel
　Will bear no color for the thing he is,
　Fashion it thus—that what he is, augmented,    30
　Would run to these and these extremities;
　And therefore think him as a serpent's egg

1. **Lucius**\ᴧlū·shəs *or* ᴧlū·shi·əs\ Brutus' servant.

2. **I would,** I wish.

3. Brutus knows of no personal reason to object to Caesar, as though kicking at him, but he is concerned about the general good of the Roman state and people.
4. **adder,** snake.

5. He has not known Caesar to be ruled by his emotions and passions rather than his reason.

6. **Then, . . . prevent,** lest Caesar do so, let us anticipate and prevent him.

401

Which, hatched, would, as his kind, grow mischievous,[7]
And kill him in the shell.
LUCIUS. (*Reentering, a folded paper in his hand.*)
The taper burneth in your closet,[8] sir.                                  35
Searching the window for a flint, I found
This paper,[9] thus sealed up. And I am sure
It did not lie there when I went to bed.
BRUTUS. (*Taking the letter.*) Get you to bed again.
It is not day.
Is not tomorrow, boy, the ides of March?                                  40
LUCIUS. I know not, sir.
BRUTUS. Look in the calendar, and bring me word.
LUCIUS. (*Leaving.*) I will, sir.
BRUTUS. The exhalations[10] whizzing in the air
Give so much light that I may read by them.                               45

[*Opening the letter and peering close to read.*]

"Brutus, thou sleep'st. Awake, and see thyself!
Shall Rome, etc. Speak, strike, redress!"

(*Looking up from the letter, frowning.*) "Brutus,
thou sleep'st. Awake!"
Such instigations have been often dropped
Where I have took them up.                                                 50
"Shall Rome, etc." Thus must I piece it out:
Shall Rome stand under one man's awe? What, Rome?
My ancestors did from the streets of Rome
The Tarquin drive when he was called a king.
"Speak, strike, redress!" Am I entreated                                   55
To speak and strike? O Rome, I make thee promise—
If the redress will follow, thou receivest
Thy full petition[11] at the hand of Brutus!
LUCIUS. (*Reentering.*) Sir, March is wasted fifteen days.

[*A knocking comes from the gate.*]

BRUTUS. 'Tis good. Go to the gate. Somebody knocks.                       60

[LUCIUS *leaves.*]

Since Cassius first did whet[12] me against Caesar,
I have not slept.
Between the acting of a dreadful thing
And the first motion,[13] all the interim is
Like a phantasma or a hideous dream.                                       65
The Genius and the mortal instruments[14]
Are then in council; and the state of man,
Like to a little kingdom, suffers then
The nature of an insurrection.

[LUCIUS *reenters.*]

402

7. **mischievous,** injurious, harmful. The word had a stronger meaning in Shakespeare's day than now.

8. **closet,** study.

9. Cinna has been obeying orders. See Act I, Scene 3.

10. **exhalations,** fiery vapors; flashing meteoric lights.

11. **Thy full petition,** all that you ask.

12. **whet,** incite.

13. **the first motion,** the first suggestion.

14. **The Genius and the mortal instruments,** the guiding spirit (personality, soul) of a man and his body (the means for carrying out the deadly purpose of his "Genius").

LUCIUS. Sir, 'tis your brother[15] Cassius at the door,　　　　　70
　Who doth desire to see you.
BRUTUS.　　　　　　　　　　Is he alone?
LUCIUS. No, sir. There are more with him.
BRUTUS.　　　　　　　　　　　Do you know
　them?
LUCIUS. No, sir. Their hats are plucked about their ears,
　And half their faces buried in their cloaks,
　That by no means I may discover them　　　　　75
　By any mark of favor.
BRUTUS.　　　　　　　Let 'em enter.

[LUCIUS *exits toward the gate.*]

They are the faction. O conspiracy,
Shamest thou to show thy dangerous brow by night,
When evils are most free? O, then by day
Where wilt thou find a cavern dark enough　　　　　80
To mask thy monstrous visage? Seek none, conspiracy!
Hide it in smiles and affability;
For if thou path, thy native semblance on,
Not Erebus itself were dim enough
To hide thee from prevention.[16]　　　　　85

[*The conspirators gather quietly. They are:* CASSIUS,
CASCA, DECIUS, CINNA, METELLUS CIMBER, *and* TRE-
BONIUS. CASSIUS *moves to* BRUTUS' *side. The others stand
back.*]

CASSIUS. I think we are too bold upon your rest.
　Good morrow, Brutus. Do we trouble you?
BRUTUS. I have been up this hour, awake all night.
　Know I these men that come along with you?
CASSIUS. Yes, every man of them, and no man here　　　　　90
　But honors you; and every one doth wish
　You had but that opinion of yourself
　Which every noble Roman bears of you.
　This is Trebonius.

[*One by one the conspirators step forward and reveal
themselves to Brutus.*]

BRUTUS.　　　　　　He is welcome hither.
CASSIUS. This, Decius Brutus.
BRUTUS.　　　　　　　　He is welcome too.　　　　　95
CASSIUS. This, Casca. This, Cinna. And this, Metellus
　Cimber.
BRUTUS. They are all welcome.
　What watchful cares do interpose themselves
　Betwixt your eyes and night?
CASSIUS. Shall I entreat a word?　　　　　100

15. **brother,** brother-in-law, Cassius had
married Junia, Brutus' sister.

16. **For if thou . . . prevention. path,**
walk about openly, without disguise.
**thy native semblance on,** in their true
or natural character. **Erebus**\ˈā·rə ˈbəs\
in Roman mythology, the gloomy space
through which souls passed to hell. **prevention,** detection, anticipating, and
forestalling. If they went about openly
indicating their true character, the pas-
sageway to hell itself would not be dark
enough to prevent their being detected
and guarded against.

[*Leads* BRUTUS *aside, and they whisper.*]

DECIUS. Here lies the east. Doth not the day break here?

CASCA. No.

CINNA. O, pardon, sir, it doth. And yon gray lines
That fret[17] the clouds are messengers of day.

CASCA. You shall confess that you are both deceived.          105
Here, as I point my sword, the sun arises,
Which is a great way growing on the south,
Weighing[18] the youthful season of the year.
Some two months hence up higher toward the north
He first presents his fire, and the high east          110
Stands, as the Capitol, directly here.

[BRUTUS *and* CASSIUS *approach the others.*]

BRUTUS. Give me your hands, all over, one by one.

CASSIUS. And let us swear our resolution.

BRUTUS. No, not an oath! If not the face of men,
The sufferance of our souls, the time's abuse,—          115
If these by motives weak, break off betimes,
And every man hence to his idle bed;
So let high-sighted tyranny range on,
Till each man drop by lottery.[19] But if these,
As I am sure they do, bear fire enough          120
To kindle cowards and to steel with valor
The melting spirits of women, then, countrymen,
What need we any spur but our own cause
To prick us to redress? what other bond
Than secret Romans, that have spoke the word          125
And will not palter?[20] and what other oath
Than honesty to honesty engaged
That this shall be, or we will fall for it?
Swear priests and cowards and men cautelous,[21]
Old feeble carrions[22] and such suffering souls          130
That welcome wrongs. Unto bad causes swear
Such creatures as men doubt; but do not stain
The even virtue of our enterprise,
Nor the insuppressive[23] mettle of our spirits,
To think that or[24] our cause or our performance          135
Did need an oath; when every drop of blood
That every Roman bears, and nobly bears,
Is guilty of a several bastardy,[25]
If he do break the smallest particle
Of any promise that hath passed from him.          140

CASSIUS. But what of Cicero? Shall we sound him?
I think he will stand very strong with us.

CASCA. Let us not leave him out.

CINNA.                          No, by no means.

17. **fret**, break up, wear away or consume.

18. **weighing**, taking into consideration. In late winter the sun rises somewhat south of east.

19. **If not the face . . . by lottery. face**, honor or renown; **sufferance**, suffering; **betimes**, at once; **idle**, useless. If honor itself, the suffering our souls undergo, and the abuses of the present times are weak motives for acting, let us break off at once and every one retire uselessly to bed, permitting the arrogant tyrant to continue until every good man is killed at the whim of the tyrant.

20. **palter**, play false.

21. **cautelous**, overcautious.

22. **carrions**, feeble men.

23. **insuppressive**, not to be suppressed.

24. **or**, either.

25. **Is guilty . . . bastardy**, is obviously illegitimate (as unfaithful to his noble ancestors) many times over.

METELLUS. O, let us have him, for his silver hairs
 Will purchase us a good opinion     145
 And buy men's voices to commend our deeds.
 It shall be said his judgment ruled our hands.
 Our youths and wildness shall no whit appear,
 But all be buried in his gravity.
BRUTUS. O, name him not. Let us not break with him,[26] 150
 For he will never follow anything
 That other men begin.
CASSIUS.       Then leave him out.
CASCA. Indeed he is not fit.
DECIUS. Shall no man else be touched but only Caesar?
CASSIUS. Decius, well urged. I think it is not meet, 155
 Mark Antony, so well beloved of Caesar,
 Should outlive Caesar. We shall find of him
 A shrewd contriver. And, you know, his means,
 If he improve them, may well stretch so far
 As to annoy us all; which to prevent,   160
 Let Antony and Caesar fall together.
BRUTUS. Our course will seem too bloody, Caius Cassius,
 To cut the head off and then hack the limbs,
 Like wrath in death and envy afterwards;
 For Antony is but a limb of Caesar.   165
 Let's be sacrificers, but not butchers, Caius.
 We all stand up against the spirit of Caesar,
 And in the spirit of men there is no blood.
 O, that we then could come by Caesar's spirit,
 And not dismember Caesar! But, alas,  170
 Caesar must bleed for it! And, gentle friends,
 Let's kill him boldly, but not wrathfully.
 Let's carve him as a dish fit for the gods,
 Not hew him as a carcass fit for hounds;
 And let our hearts, as subtle masters do, 175
 Stir up their servants to an act of rage,
 And after seem to chide them. This shall make
 Our purpose necessary and not envious;[27]
 Which so appearing to the common eyes,
 We shall be called purgers,[28] not murderers. 180
 And for Mark Antony, think not of him;
 For he can do no more than Caesar's arm
 When Caesar's head is off.
CASSIUS.      Yet I do fear him;
 For in the ingrafted[29] love he bears to Caesar—
BRUTUS. Alas, good Cassius, do not think of him. 185
 If he love Caesar, all that he can do
 Is to himself—take thought and die for Caesar;[30]
 And that were much he should, for he is given

26. **break with him,** tell him the plans under way.

27. **This shall . . . envious,** this procedure will make us seem driven by political necessity but not by hateful envy.
28. **purgers,** persons who purge or clean out an evil from the state.

29. **ingrafted,** grown to be a part of him.

30. **take thought . . . Caesar,** become despondent about Caesar and commit suicide because of his death.

To sports, to wildness, and much company.[31]

TREBONIUS. There is no fear in him.[32] Let him not die;    190
    For he will live and laugh at this hereafter.

[*A clock strikes faintly from within the house.*]

BRUTUS. Peace! Count the clock.

CASSIUS.                     The clock hath stricken three.

TREBONIUS. 'Tis time to part.

CASSIUS.                     But it is doubtful yet
    Whether Caesar will come forth today or no;
    For he is superstitious grown of late,    195
    Quite from the main opinion he held once
    Of fantasy, of dreams, and ceremonies.
    It may be these apparent prodigies,
    The unaccustomed terror of this night,
    And the persuasion of his augurers[33]    200
    May hold him from the Capitol today.

DECIUS. Never fear that. If he be so resolved,
    I can o'ersway him; for he loves to hear
    That unicorns may be betrayed with trees,
    And bears with glasses, elephants with holes,    205
    Lions with toils,[34] and men with flatterers.
    But when I tell him he hates flatterers,
    He says he does, being then most flattered.
    Let me work;
    For I can give his humor the true bent,[35]    210
    And I will bring him to the Capitol.

CASSIUS. Nay, we will all of us be there to fetch him.

BRUTUS. By the eighth hour; is that the uttermost?

CINNA. Be that the uttermost, and fail not then.

METELLUS. Caius Ligarius[36] doth bear Caesar hard,    215
    Who rated him for speaking well of Pompey.
    I wonder none of you have thought of him.

BRUTUS. Now, good Metellus, go along by him.
    He loves me well, and I have given him reasons.
    Send him but hither, and I'll fashion[37] him.    220

CASSIUS. The morning comes upon us. We'll leave you, Brutus,
    And, friends, disperse yourselves; but all remember
    What you have said, and show yourselves true Romans.

BRUTUS. Good gentlemen, look fresh and merrily.
    Let not our looks put on[38] our purposes,    225
    But bear it as our Roman actors do,
    With untired spirits and formal constancy.
    And so good morrow to you every one.

[*The conspirators slip quietly out through the gate, leaving* BRUTUS *alone in the garden.*]

31. Brutus believes that "playboys" like Antony are incapable of serious, purposeful actions.

32. **There is . . . him,** there is nothing to be feared about him.

33. **augurers,** augurs—religious officials —who predicted the future by interpreting omens.

34. **That unicorns . . . toils,** according to the belief, the unicorn might be captured by luring it into driving its horn into a tree and bears might be trapped by luring them on with mirrors. Elephants were trapped in pits and lions by snares or nets (toils).

35. **I can give . . . bent,** I can humor and persuade him in the right way.

36. **Caius**\ˈkā·əs\ **Ligarius**\lĭˈgā·rĭ·əs\.

37. **fashion,** mold (to our will).

38. **put on,** show, betray.

Boy! Lucius! Fast asleep? It is no matter.
Enjoy the honey-heavy dew of slumber.                    230
Thou hast no figures nor no fantasies
Which busy care draws in the brains of men;
Therefore thou sleepest so sound.

[BRUTUS' *wife* PORTIA *enters the garden as
he speaks.*]

PORTIA.                          Brutus, my lord!
BRUTUS. Portia, what mean you? Wherefore rise you now?
　　It is not for your health thus to commit              235
　　Your weak condition to the raw cold morning.
PORTIA. Nor for yours neither. You've ungently, Brutus,
　　Stole from my bed; and yesternight at supper
　　You suddenly arose and walked about,
　　Musing and sighing, with your arms across.            240
　　And when I asked you what the matter was,
　　You stared upon me with ungentle looks.
　　I urged you further. Then you scratched your head
　　And too impatiently stamped with your foot.
　　Yet I insisted; yet you answered not.                 245
　　But with an angry wafture[39] of your hand
　　Gave sign for me to leave you. So I did,
　　Fearing to strengthen that impatience
　　Which seemed too much enkindled, and withal
　　Hoping it was but an effect of humor,[40]             250
　　Which sometime hath its hour with every man.
　　It will not let you eat, nor talk, nor sleep,
　　And could it work so much upon your shape
　　As it hath much prevailed on your condition,
　　I should not know you, Brutus. Dear my lord,          255
　　Make me acquainted with your cause of grief.
BRUTUS. I am not well in health, and that is all.
PORTIA. Brutus is wise, and, were he not in health,
　　He would embrace the means to come by it.
BRUTUS. Why, so I do. Good Portia, go to bed.            260
PORTIA. Is Brutus sick? and is it physical
　　To walk unbraced and suck up the humors
　　Of the dank morning? What, is Brutus sick,
　　And will he steal out of his wholesome bed
　　To dare the vile contagion of the night,             265
　　And tempt the rheumy and unpurged air[41]
　　To add unto his sickness? No, my Brutus;
　　You have some sick offense within your mind,
　　Which, by the right and virtue of my place,
　　I ought to know of; and upon my knees                270
　　I charm you, by my once commended beauty,

39. **wafture,** wave.

40. **humor,** a passing mood.

41. **the rheumy . . . air,** risk the moist air not yet purified by the sun.

By all your vows of love, and that great vow
Which did incorporate and make us one,
That you unfold to me, yourself, your half,
Why you are heavy,[42] and what men tonight      275
Have had resort to you; for here have been
Some six or seven who did hide their faces
Even from darkness.

BRUTUS.             Kneel not, gentle Portia.

PORTIA. I should not need, if you were gentle Brutus.
Within the bond of marriage, tell me, Brutus,      280
Is it excepted I should know no secrets
That appertain to you? Am I yourself
But, as it were, in sort or limitation,
To keep with you at meals, comfort your bed,
And talk to you sometimes? Dwell I but in the suburbs      285
Of your good pleasure? If it be no more,
Portia is Brutus' harlot, not his wife.

BRUTUS. You are my true and honorable wife,
As dear to me as are the ruddy drops
That visit my sad heart.      290

PORTIA. If this were true, then should I know this secret.
I grant I am a woman; but withal[43]
A woman that Lord Brutus took to wife.
I grant I am a woman; but withal
A woman well-reputed, Cato's daughter.      295
Think you I am no stronger than my sex,
Being so fathered[44] and so husbanded?
Tell me your counsels; I will not disclose them.
I have made strong proof of my constancy,
Giving myself a voluntary wound      300
Here, in the thigh. Can I bear that with patience,
And not my husband's secrets?

BRUTUS.             O ye gods!
Render me worthy of this noble wife!

[*A knock comes from the garden gate.* BRUTUS *leads*
PORTIA *toward the house.*]

Hark, hark! One knocks. Portia, go in awhile,
And by and by thy bosom shall partake      305
The secrets of my heart.
All my engagements I will construe[45] to thee;
All the charactery of my sad brows.
Leave me with haste.

[PORTIA *enters the house.* BRUTUS *turns anxiously*
*toward the gate, calling for* LUCIUS.]

         Lucius, who's that knocks?

---

42. **heavy,** sad.

43. **withal,** nevertheless.

44. **fathered,** her father, Cato the younger, had killed himself (46 B.C.) rather than submit to Caesar. He was considered a martyr to the cause of Roman liberty by Caesar's opponents.

45. **construe,** explain fully.

[*Lucius comes from the garden gate, leading* LIGARIUS, *whose head is bandaged with a handkerchief.*]

LUCIUS. Here is a sick man that would speak with you.        310
BRUTUS. Caius Ligarius, that Metellus spake of.
　Boy, stand aside. Caius Ligarius! How?
LIGARIUS. Vouchsafe good morrow from a feeble tongue.
BRUTUS. O, what a time have you chose out, brave Caius,
　To wear a kerchief![46] Would you were not sick!        315
LIGARIUS. I am not sick, if Brutus have in hand
　Any exploit worthy the name of honor.
BRUTUS. Such an exploit have I in hand, Ligarius,
　Had you a healthful ear to hear of it.
LIGARIUS. By all the gods that Romans bow before,        320
　I here discard my sickness! Soul of Rome!
　Brave son derived from honorable loins!
　Thou, like an exorcist, hast conjured up
　My mortified[47] spirit. Now bid me run,
　And I will strive with things impossible;        325
　Yea, get the better of them. What's to do?
BRUTUS. A piece of work that will make sick men whole.
LIGARIUS. But are not some whole that we must make sick?
BRUTUS. That must we also. What it is, my Caius,
　I shall unfold to thee as we are going        330
　To whom it must be done.
LIGARIUS.　　　　　　　　　Set on your foot,
　And with a heart new-fired I follow you,
　To do I know not what; but it sufficeth
　That Brutus leads me on.
BRUTUS.　　　　　　　　　Follow me, then.

[*Thunder rumbles in the distance as they leave.*]


SCENE 2


*Rome.* CAESAR's *house, spacious and decorated with royal magnificence. Outside, thunder rumbles and lightning flickers. The time is shortly before 8 o'clock the same morning.* CAESAR *enters.*

CAESAR. Nor heaven nor earth have been at peace tonight.
　Thrice hath Calpurnia in her sleep cried out,
　"Help! ho! They murder Caesar!" (*Turns quickly.*)
　　Who's within?

[*Servant enters.*]

SERVANT. My lord?

46. **To wear a kerchief,** in Shakespeare's day, if one became sick he wrapped his head in a woman's headcloth for protection against drafts.

47. **mortified,** deadened.

CAESAR. Go bid the priests do present[1] sacrifice
  And bring me their opinions of success.
SERVANT. I will, my lord.

  [SERVANT *leaves.* CALPURNIA *enters and anxiously*
  *approaches* CAESAR.]

CALPURNIA. What mean you, Caesar? Think you to walk
    forth?
  You shall not stir out of your house today.
CAESAR. Caesar shall forth. The things that threatened me   10
  Ne'er looked but on my back; when they shall see
  The face of Caesar, they are vanished.
CALPURNIA. Caesar, I never stood on ceremonies,[2]
  Yet now they fright me. There is one within,
  Besides the things that we have heard and seen,   15
  Recounts most horrid sights seen by the watch.[3]
  A lioness hath whelped in the streets,
  And graves have yawned and yielded up their dead!
  Fierce fiery warriors fought upon the clouds
  In ranks and squadrons and right form of war,   20
  Which drizzled blood upon the Capitol;
  The noise of battle hurtled in the air;
  Horses did neigh, and dying men did groan,
  And ghosts did shriek and squeal about the streets.
  O Caesar! these things are beyond all use,[4]   25
  And I do fear them.
CAESAR.                 What can be avoided
  Whose end is purposed by the mighty gods?
  Yet Caesar shall go forth; for these predictions
  Are to the world in general[5] as to Caesar.

---

5   1. **present,** immediate.

2. **stood on ceremonies,** paid attention
to auguries and predictions.

3. **watch,** watchmen.

4. **use,** ordinary experience.

5. **in general,** they apply as much to
the world in general as to Caesar in particular.

CALPURNIA. When beggars die there are no comets seen.  30
 The heavens themselves blaze forth the death of
  princes.
CAESAR. Cowards die many times before their death;
 The valiant never taste of death but once.
 Of all the wonders that I yet have heard,
 It seems to me most strange that men should fear,  35
 Seeing that death, a necessary end,
 Will come when it will come.

*[Servant returns from the priests.]*

       What say the augurers?
SERVANT. They would not have you to stir forth today.
 Plucking the entrails of an offering forth,
 They could not find a heart within the beast.  40
CAESAR. The gods do this in shame of cowardice!
 Caesar should be a beast without a heart
 If he should stay at home today for fear.
 No, Caesar shall not! Danger knows full well
 That Caesar is more dangerous than he.  45
 We are two lions littered in one day,
 And I the elder and more terrible.
 And Caesar shall go forth!
CALPURNIA.     Alas, my lord,
 Your wisdom is consumed in confidence.
 Do not go forth today. Call it my fear  50
 That keeps you in the house, and not your own.
 We'll send Mark Antony to the Senate House,
 And he shall say you are not well today.
 Let me, upon my knee, prevail in this.
CAESAR. Mark Antony shall say I am not well;  55
 And, for thy humor,[6] I will stay at home.

6. **humor,** disposition at the moment,
whim.

*[DECIUS BRUTUS enters.]*

Here's Decius Brutus; he shall tell them so.
DECIUS. Caesar, all hail! Good morrow, worthy Caesar.
 I come to fetch you to the Senate House.
CAESAR. And you are come in very happy time  60
 To bear my greetings to the Senators
 And tell them that I will not come today.
 Cannot is false, and that I dare not, falser.
 I will not come today. Tell them so, Decius.
CALPURNIA. Say he is sick.
CAESAR.     Shall Caesar send a lie?  65
 Have I in conquest stretched mine arm so far
 To be afraid to tell graybeards the truth?
 Decius, go tell them Caesar will not come.

411

DECIUS. Most mighty Caesar, let me know some cause,
  Lest I be laughed at when I tell them so.                    70
CAESAR. The cause is in my will—I will not come.
  That is enough to satisfy the Senate.
  But for your private satisfaction,
  Because I love you, I will let you know:
  Calpurnia here, my wife, stays me at home.                   75
  She dreamt tonight she saw my statue
  Which, like a fountain with a hundred spouts,
  Did run pure blood; and many lusty Romans
  Came smiling and did bathe their hands in it.
  And these does she apply for warnings and portents          80
  And evils imminent, and on her knee
  Hath begged that I will stay at home today.
DECIUS. This dream is all amiss interpreted!
  It was a vision fair and fortunate.
  Your statue spouting blood in many pipes,                    85
  In which so many smiling Romans bathed,
  Signifies that from you great Rome shall suck
  Reviving blood, and that great men shall press
  For tinctures, stains, relics, and cognizance.
  This by Calpurnia's dream is signified.                      90
CAESAR. And this way have you well expounded it.
DECIUS. I have, when you have heard what I can say;
  And know it now. The Senate have concluded
  To give this day a crown to mighty Caesar.
  If you shall send them word you will not come,               95
  Their minds may change. Besides, it were a mock
  Apt[7] to be rendered, for someone to say,
  "Break up the Senate till another time,
  When Caesar's wife shall meet with better dreams."
  If Caesar hide himself, shall they not whisper,              100
  "Lo, Caesar is afraid"?
  Pardon me, Caesar, for my dear dear love
  To your proceeding bids me tell you this;
  And reason to my love is liable.
CAESAR. How foolish do your fears seem now, Calpurnia!  105
  I am ashamed that I did yield to them.
  Give me my robe, for I will go.

  [*Enter* PUBLIUS, *a stately, elderly Senator, followed
  by the conspirators,* BRUTUS, LACARIUS, METELLUS,
  CASCA, TREBONIUS, *and* CINNA. *They approach*
  CAESAR.]

  And look where Publius is come to fetch me.
PUBLIUS. Good morrow, Caesar.
CAESAR.                          Welcome, Publius.

7. **apt,** ready.

412

What, Brutus, are you stirred so early too?    110
Good morrow, Casca, Caius Ligarius;
Caesar was ne'er so much your enemy[8]
As that same ague which has made you lean.
What is't o'clock?
BRUTUS.                    Caesar, 'tis strucken eight.
CAESAR. I thank you for your pains and courtesy.    115

[*Antony enters.*]

See! Antony, that revels long o' nights,
Is notwithstanding up. Good morrow, Antony.
ANTONY. So to most noble Caesar.
CAESAR.                    Bid them prepare within;
I am to blame to be thus waited for.
Now, Cinna; now, Metellus. What, Trebonius!    120
I have an hour's talk in store for you.
Remember that you call on me today;
Be near me, that I may remember you.
TREBONIUS. Caesar, I will. (*To himself.*) And so near will
    I be,
That your best friends shall wish I had been further.    125
CAESAR. Good friends, go in, and taste some wine with me;
And we, like friends, will straightway go together.
BRUTUS. (*To himself.*) That every like is not the same,
    O Caesar,
The heart of Brutus yearns to think upon![9]

[*Talking quietly together, they all leave.*]

### SCENE 3

*Rome. An empty street near the Capitol. Enter* ARTEMIDORUS,
*a teacher of rhetoric. He strolls hesitantly, preoccupied by
the paper in his hand from which he reads.*

ARTEMIDORUS.    (*Reading aloud.*) *Caesar, beware of
Brutus; take heed of Cassius; come not near Casca;
have an eye to Cinna; trust not Trebonius; mark well
Metellus Cimber; Decius Brutus loves thee not; thou
hast wronged Caius Ligarius. There is but one mind in*    5
*all these men, and it is bent against Caesar. If thou be
not immortal, look about you. Security gives way to conspiracy. The mighty gods defend thee!*
                    *Thy lover,*[1]
                    ARTEMIDORUS    10

[*Clutching the paper to him and looking anxiously up
and down the street.*]

Here will I stand till Caesar pass along,
And as a suitor will I give him this.

8. **your enemy,** Ligarius, recently restored to civil rights, had fought on Pompey's side in the civil war.

9. **That every . . . upon,** Brutus regrets to think that everything is not as it appears, that everyone who seems to be a friend is not a true friend.

1. **lover,** devoted friend.

My heart laments that virtue cannot live
Out of the teeth of emulation.[2]
If thou read this, O Caesar, thou mayst live.
If not, the fates with traitors do contrive.

[*He leaves slowly.*]

2. **that virtue . . . emulation,** that a virtuous man cannot live safe from the teeth (or weapons) of emulation, of envious rivalry.

SCENE 4

*Rome. The same street in front of* BRUTUS' *house.* PORTIA *and* LUCIUS *enter through the gate.* PORTIA *stares in the direction of the Capitol.*

PORTIA. I prithee, boy, run to the Senate House!
　Stay not to answer me, but get thee gone.
　Why dost thou stay?
LUCIUS.　　　　　　　　To know my errand, madam.
PORTIA. I would have had thee there and here again
　Ere I can tell thee what thou should do there.
　O constancy,[1] be strong upon my side;
　Set a huge mountain 'tween my heart and tongue!
　I have a man's mind, but a woman's might.
　How hard it is for women to keep counsel!
　(*Sharply to Lucius.*) Art thou here yet?
LUCIUS.　　　　　　　　Madam, what should I do?
　Run to the Capitol and nothing else?
　And so return to you, and nothing else?
PORTIA. Yes, bring me word, boy, if thy lord look well,
　For he went sickly forth. And take good note
　What Caesar doth, what suitors press to him.
　Hark, boy! What noise is that?
LUCIUS. I hear none, madam.
PORTIA.　　　　　　　　Prithee, listen well!
　I heard a bustling rumor, like a fray,
　And the wind brings it from the Capitol.
LUCIUS. Sooth,[2] madam, I hear nothing.

[*The* SOOTHSAYER *who had warned* CAESAR *to beware the ides of March shuffles by slowly in the direction of the Capitol.*]

PORTIA. Come hither, fellow. Which way hast thou been?
SOOTHSAYER. At mine own house, good lady.
PORTIA. What is it o'clock?
SOOTHSAYER.　　　　　　About the ninth hour, lady.
PORTIA. Is Caesar yet gone to the Capitol?
SOOTHSAYER. Madam, not yet. I go to take my stand
　To see him pass on to the Capitol.
PORTIA. Thou hast some suit to[3] Caesar, hast thou not?

1. **constancy,** self-control.

2. **sooth,** truth—in truth or indeed.

3. **suit to,** request for.

SOOTHSAYER. That I have, lady. If it will please Caesar
  To be so good to Caesar as to hear me,
  I shall beseech him to befriend himself.                           30
PORTIA. Why, know'st thou any harm's intended toward
    him?
SOOTHSAYER. None that I know will be; much that I fear
    may chance.
  Good morrow to you. Here the street is narrow.
  The throng that follows Caesar at the heels,
  Of senators, of praetors, common suitors,                          35
  Will crowd a feeble man almost to death.
  I'll get me to a place more void,[4] and there
  Speak to great Caesar as he comes along.

  [*Moves painfully off.*]

PORTIA. (*Speaking aloud to herself.*) I must go in. Ay me,
    how weak a thing
  The heart of woman is! O Brutus,                                   40
  The heavens speed[5] thee in thine enterprise!
  (*Startled by her revealing words, she glances warily at*
  LUCIUS.) Sure, the boy heard me. (*Addressing* LUCIUS.)
    Brutus hath a suit
  That Caesar will not grant. O, I grow faint!
  Run, Lucius, and commend me to my lord;
  Say I am merry. Come to me again                                   45
  And bring me word what he doth say to thee.

  [LUCIUS *races off toward the Capitol.* PORTIA *slowly
  passes through the gate to the house.*]

4. **more void,** more nearly vacant, less
crowded.

5. **speed,** prosper.

415

# Act III

*Rome. The Capitol. Before the entrance to the Senate Chamber, a large room in the shape of an amphitheater, where tiers of wooden senatorial benches curve before the statue of Pompey. A group of anxious petitioners press close to the marble steps leading up to the chamber.* ARTEMIDORUS *and the* SOOTHSAYER *struggle to take front positions. There is a flourish of trumpets, and* CAESAR *arrives, attended by* BRUTUS, CASSIUS, CASCA, DECIUS, METELLUS, TREBONIUS, CINNA, MARK ANTONY, LEPIDUS, POPILIUS, PUBLIUS, *and others.*

CAESAR. (*Noticing the* SOOTHSAYER *as he mounts the steps.*) The ides of March are come.

SOOTHSAYER. Ay, Caesar, but not gone.

ARTEMIDORUS. (*Waving his message of warning.*) Hail, Caesar! Read this schedule![1]

DECIUS. (*Crowding* ARTEMIDORUS *aside.*) Trebonius doth desire you to o'er-read,

At your best leisure, this his humble suit.                    5

ARTEMIDORUS. O Caesar, read mine first, for mine's a suit

That touches Caesar nearer. Read it, great Caesar!

CAESAR. What touches us ourself shall be last served.

ARTEMIDORUS. Delay not, Caesar! Read it instantly!

CAESAR. What, is the fellow mad?

PUBLIUS. (*Roughly forcing* ARTEMIDORUS *back.*) Sirrah, give place!                    10

CASSIUS. (*Annoyed and impatient.*) What, urge you your petitions in the street?

Come to the Capitol.

[*He mounts the steps to the Senate Chamber. The others follow.* POPILIUS *casually separates himself from* CAESAR's *train and lingers at* CASSIUS' *side.*]

POPILIUS. (*Softly.*) I wish your enterprise today may thrive.

CASSIUS. What enterprise, Popilius?

POPILIUS. (*Winking and smiling.*) Fare you well.

[*Brutus approaches* CASSIUS *with a troubled look on his face.*]

BRUTUS. What said Popilius Lena?[2]                    15

CASSIUS. He wished our enterprise might thrive.

I fear our enterprise is discovered!

BRUTUS. Look, how he makes to Caesar. Mark him.

1. **schedule,** a document, especially one containing a list.

2. **Popilius Lena**\pō ˈpĭ·lĭ·əs ˈLē·nə\.

CASSIUS. (*Over his shoulder to* CASCA.) Casca, be sudden,
    for we fear prevention.
  Brutus, what shall be done? If this be known,    20
  Cassius or Caesar never shall turn back,
  For I will slay myself.
BRUTUS. (*In stern anger*). Cassius, be constant!
  Popilius Lena speaks not of our purposes,
  For, look! He smiles, and Caesar doth not change.
CASSIUS. Trebonius knows his time; for, look you, Brutus.  25
  He draws Mark Antony out of the way.

[ANTONY *and* TREBONIUS *talk quietly together and stroll
out of the Senate Chamber.* DECIUS BRUTUS *slips urgently
over to where* BRUTUS *and* CASSIUS *stand talking.*]

DECIUS. Where is Metellus Cimber? Let him go
  And presently prefer his suit to Caesar.
BRUTUS. (*Nodding toward where* METELLUS *speaks to*
  CAESAR.) He is addressed.[3] Press near and second him.
CINNA. (*Whispering.*) Casca, you are the first that rears
    his hand.    30

[*The conspirators encircle* CAESAR's *chair at the foot of
Pompey's statue. The Senate grows quiet as* CAESAR *begins the session. The senators lean forward on their
benches to listen.*]

CAESAR. Are we all ready? What is now amiss
  That Caesar and his senate must redress?

[METELLUS CIMBER *comes forward and kneels before*
CAESAR.]

METELLUS. Most high, most mighty, and most puissant
    Caesar,
  Metellus Cimber throws before thy seat
  An humble heart—
CAESAR.             I must prevent thee, Cimber.    35
  These couchings[4] and these lowly courtesies
  Might fire the blood of ordinary men,
  And turn pre-ordinance and first decree[5]
  Into the law of children. Be not fond[6]
  To think that Caesar bears such rebel blood    40
  That will be thawed from the true quality
  With that which melteth fools. I mean, sweet words,
  Low-crooked[7] curtsies and base spaniel-fawning.
  Thy brother[8] by decree is banished!
  If thou dost bend and pray and fawn for him,    45
  I spurn thee like a cur out of my way.
  Know, Caesar doth not wrong, nor without cause
  Will he be satisfied.

3. **addressed,** ready.

4. **couchings,** bending down, bowing.

5. **pre-ordinance and first decree,** established laws and decisions already made.
6. **fond,** foolish.

7. **Low-crooked,** bent low.
8. **Thy brother,** Publius Cimber.

417

METELLUS. Is there no voice more worthy than my own,
To sound more sweetly in great Caesar's ear                    50
For the repealing of my banished brother?

[BRUTUS *steps forward and bows.*]

BRUTUS. I kiss thy hand, but not in flattery, Caesar,
Desiring thee that Publius Cimber may
Have an immediate freedom of repeal.
CAESAR. What, Brutus!
CASSIUS. (*On his knees.*) Pardon, Caesar! Caesar, pardon!    55
As low as to thy foot doth Cassius fall
To beg enfranchisement[9] for Publius Cimber.
CAESAR. I could be well moved if I were as you;
If I could pray to move, prayers would move me.
But I am constant as the northern star,                        60
Of whose true-fixed and resting[10] quality
There is no fellow in the firmament.
The skies are painted with unnumbered sparks;
They are all fire and every one doth shine.
But there's but one in all doth hold his place.                65
So in the world; 'tis furnished well with men,
And men are flesh and blood, and apprehensive.[11]
Yet in the number, I do know but one
That unassailable holds on his rank,
Unshaked of motion: and that I am he,                          70
Let me a little show it, even in this—
That I was constant Cimber should be banished,
And constant do remain to keep him so.

[*The conspirators begin to edge closer to* CAESAR, *and
he draws back suspiciously.*]

CINNA. O Caesar—
CAESAR. (*Angered by their persistence.*) Hence! Wilt thou
lift up Olympus?
DECIUS. Great Caesar—
CAESAR.                    Doth not Brutus bootless[12] kneel?  75
CASCA. (*From a position just behind and to the side of*
CAESAR, *where he has slipped unnoticed.*) Speak, hands,
for me!

[*He draws his dagger from the folds of his toga and
strikes at* CAESAR's *back. The conspirators lunge forward, their weapons flashing. They gather about their
victim and drive their daggers into his flesh. There are
cries and shouts, and smears of blood appear on white
togas.* CAESAR, *weaving and faint, sees* BRUTUS' *dagger
poised.*]

CAESAR. *Et tu, Brute!*[13] Then fall, Caesar!

9. **enfranchisement,** the right of citizen-
ship. Here, Cassius begs Caesar to re-
new Cimber's rights as a Roman citizen.

10. **resting,** unchanging.

11. **apprehensive,** perceptive and likely
to be influenced (especially by emotions).

12. **bootless,** without avail, in vain.

13. **Et tu, Brute!**\ĕt tū ⁀brū·tĕ\ And you
too, Brutus!

418

[*He collapses at the foot of Pompey's statue and dies.
A moment of terrified silence follows as the conspirators
stare at their deed. Panic spreads throughout the Senate
Chamber, and the senators murmur in disbelief and
start for the doors.*]

CINNA. Liberty! Freedom! Tyranny is dead!
  Run hence, proclaim. Cry it about the streets!
CASSIUS. Some to the common pulpits,[14] and cry out:      80
  "Liberty, freedom, and enfranchisement!"
BRUTUS. (*To the escaping senators.*) People and senators,
    be not affrighted.
  Fly not; stand still—ambition's debt is paid.
CASCA. Go to the pulpit, Brutus.
DECIUS.                    And Cassius too.
BRUTUS. Where's Publius?                                    85
CINNA. Here, quite confounded with this mutiny.
METELLUS. Stand fast together, lest some friends of
    Caesar's
  Should chance—
BRUTUS. Talk not of standing. Publius, good cheer.
  There is no harm intended to your person,                90
  Nor to no Roman else. So tell them, Publius.
CASSIUS. And leave us, Publius, lest that the people,
  Rushing on us, should do your age some mischief.
BRUTUS. Do so, and let no man abide[15] this deed,
  But we the doers.

[*Dazed with horror and disbelief,* PUBLIUS *leaves, just
as* TREBONIUS *rushes in among the conspirators to learn
of their success.*]

14. **pulpits,** raised places in the Forum
used for public speeches and debates.

15. **abide,** suffer the consequences of.

419

CASSIUS.                    Where is Antony?                                    95
TREBONIUS. Fled to his house amazed.
   Men, wives, and children stare, cry out, and run,
   As it were doomsday.[16]

16. **doomsday,** literally, judgment day.
(An anachronism.)

BRUTUS.                         Fates, we will know your
     pleasures.
   That we shall die, we know. 'Tis but the time
   And drawing days out, that men stand upon.[17]                               100

17. **stand upon,** make a point of.

CASSIUS. Why, he that cuts off twenty years of life
   Cuts off so many years of fearing death.
BRUTUS. Grant that, and then is death a benefit.
   So are we Caesar's friends that have abridged
   His time of fearing death. Stoop, Romans, stoop,                            105
   And let us bathe our hands in Caesar's blood
   Up to the elbows, and besmear our swords.
   Then walk we forth, even to the market-place,
   And, waving our red weapons o'er our heads,
   Let's all cry: "Peace, freedom, and liberty!"                               110
CASSIUS. Stoop, then, and wash. How many ages hence
   Shall this our lofty scene be acted over
   In states unborn and accents yet unknown!

BRUTUS. How many times shall Caesar bleed in sport,[18]
   That now on Pompey's basis lies along                                       115
   No worthier than the dust!

18. **sport,** plays.

CASSIUS.                         So oft as that shall be,
   So often shall the knot of us be called
   The men that gave their country liberty.
DECIUS. What, shall we forth?
CASSIUS.                         Ay, every man away!
   Brutus shall lead, and we will grace his heels[19]                          120
   With the most boldest and best hearts of Rome.

19. **grace his heels,** honor him by following.

   [ANTONY'S SERVANT *arrives and stands in terror at the
   doorway watching the conspirators.*]

BRUTUS. Soft! Who comes here? A friend of Antony's?
SERVANT. (*Approaching fearfully.*) Thus, Brutus, did my
     master bid me kneel;

Thus did Mark Antony bid me fall down.
And, being prostrate, thus he bade me say:     125
Brutus is noble, wise, valiant, and honest;
Caesar was mighty, bold, royal, and loving;
Say I love Brutus, and I honor him;
Say I feared Caesar, honored him, and loved him.
If Brutus will vouchsafe that Antony     130
May safely come to him, and be resolved[20]
How Caesar hath deserved to lie in death,
Mark Antony shall not love Caesar dead
So well as Brutus living; but will follow
The fortunes and affairs of noble Brutus     135
Through all the hazards of this untrod state[21]
With all true faith. So says my master Antony.
BRUTUS. Thy master is a wise and valiant Roman.
    I never thought him worse.
    Tell him, so please him come unto this place,     140
    He shall be satisfied; and, by my honor,
    Depart untouched.
SERVANT.              I'll fetch him presently.

[*Backs off slowly and then races to* ANTONY *to deliver* BRUTUS' *message.*]

BRUTUS. I know that we shall have him well to friend.[22]
CASSIUS. I wish we may; but yet have I a mind
    That fears him much, and my misgiving still     145
    Falls shrewdly to the purpose.[23]

[ANTONY *enters, his stare fixed on the body of fallen* CAESAR.]

BRUTUS. But here comes Antony! Welcome, Mark Antony!

[ANTONY *approaches until he stands directly over* CAESAR.]

ANTONY. O mighty Caesar! Dost thou lie so low?
    Are all thy conquests, glories, triumphs, spoils,
    Shrunk to this little measure? Fare thee well!     150
    (*He looks at each conspirator in turn.*) I know not,
        gentlemen, what you intend;
    Who else must be let blood; who else is rank.[24]
    If I myself, there is no hour so fit
    As Caesar's death hour, nor no instrument     155
    Of half that worth as those your swords, made rich
    With the most noble blood of all this world.
    I do beseech ye, if you bear me hard,
    Now, whilst your purpled hands do reek and smoke,
    Fulfill your pleasure! Live a thousand years,
    I shall not find myself so apt[25] to die.     160

20. **be resolved,** have his questions answered and his doubts dispelled.

21. **untrod state,** new situation.

22. **to friend,** as a friend.

23. **my misgiving . . . purpose,** my doubts always show themselves to be confoundedly near the truth.

24. **rank,** overgrown in power. Hence, to be killed.

25. **apt,** ready.

No place will please me so, no means of death,
As here by Caesar, and by you cut off,
The choice and master spirits of this age.

BRUTUS. O Antony, beg not your death of us.
Though now we must appear bloody and cruel,                    165
As by our hands and this our present act
You see we do; yet see you but our hands
And this the bleeding business they have done.
Our hearts you see not; they are pitiful.
And pity to the general wrong of Rome—                         170
As fire drives out fire, so pity pity[26]—
Hath done this deed on Caesar. For your part,
To you our swords have leaden points, Mark Antony.
Our arms, in strength of malice, and our hearts
Of brothers' temper, do receive you in                         175
With all kind love, good thoughts, and reverence.

CASSIUS. Your voice shall be as strong as any man's
In the disposing of new dignities.

BRUTUS. Only be patient till we have appeased
The multitude, beside themselves with fear.                    180
And then we will deliver you the cause
Why I, that did love Caesar when I struck him,
Have thus proceeded.

ANTONY.                    I doubt not of your wisdom.
Let each man render me his bloody hand.
First, Marcus Brutus, will I shake with you;                   185
Next, Caius Cassius, do I take your hand;
Now, Decius Brutus, yours; now yours, Metellus;
Yours, Cinna; and, my valiant Casca, yours;
Though last, not least in love, yours, good Trebonius.
Gentlemen all! Alas, what shall I say?                         190
My credit now stands on such slippery ground
That one or two bad ways you must conceit me,[27]
Either a coward or a flatterer.
(*Addressing the body of* CAESAR.) That I did love thee,
    Caesar, O, 'tis true!
If then thy spirit look upon us now,                           195
Shall it not grieve thee dearer[28] than thy death
To see thy Antony making his peace,
Shaking the bloody fingers of thy foes,
Most noble! in the presence of thy corpse?
Had I as many eyes as thou hast wounds,                        200
Weeping as fast as they stream forth thy blood,
It would become me better than to close
In terms of friendship with thine enemies.
Pardon me, Julius! Here wast thou bayed, brave hart.[29]
Here didst thou fall; and here thy hunters stand,             205

26. **pity pity,** pity for "the general wrong of Rome" "drives out" pity for Caesar's death.

27. **conceit me,** regard me.

28. **dearer,** more intensely.

29. **bayed, brave hart,** brought to bay, brave stag.

Signed in thy spoil, and crimsoned in thy lethe.[30]
O world, thou wast the forest to this hart;
And this, indeed, O world, the heart of thee.
How like a deer, strucken by many princes,
Dost thou here lie!                                    210

30. lethe\ˈlē·thē\ death. In classical anthology, Lethe was a river in Hades; to drink from its waters caused forgetfulness of previous life.

CASSIUS. (*Showing anger and impatience at* ANTONY's *bold show of allegiance.*) Mark Antony—
ANTONY.                     Pardon me, Caius Cassius!
  The enemies of Caesar shall say this;
  Then, in a friend, it is cold modesty.[31]

31. **cold modesty,** moderate.

CASSIUS. I blame you not for praising Caesar so;
  But what compact mean you to have with us?        215
  Will you be pricked in number of our friends,[32]
  Or shall we on, and not depend on you?

32. **Will you . . . friends,** will your name be counted as among our friends?

ANTONY. Therefore I took your hands, but was, indeed,
  Swayed from the point by looking down on Caesar.
  Friends as I am with you all, and love you all,    220
  Upon this hope: that you shall give me reasons
  Why and wherein Caesar was dangerous.
BRUTUS. Or else were this a savage spectacle.
  Our reasons are so full of good regard[33]

33. **regard,** consideration, thought.

  That were you, Antony, the son of Caesar,          225
  You should be satisfied.
ANTONY.                     That's all I seek;
  And am, moreover, suitor that I may
  Produce his body to the market-place
  And in the pulpit, as becomes a friend,
  Speak in the order of his funeral.                 230
BRUTUS. You shall, Mark Antony.
CASSIUS. (*Frowning, urgently pulling* BRUTUS *aside.*)
  Brutus, a word with you!
  (*Whispering.*) You know not what you do. Do not consent
  That Antony speak in his funeral.

Know you how much the people may be moved
By that which he will utter?
BRUTUS.                    By your pardon.                    235
I will myself into the pulpit first
And show the reason of our Caesar's death.
What Antony shall speak, I will protest[34]
He speaks by leave and by permission,
And that we are contented Caesar shall               240
Have all true rites and lawful ceremonies.
It shall advantage more than do us wrong.
CASSIUS. I know not what may fall. I like it not!
BRUTUS. (*Turning to* ANTONY.) Mark Antony, here, take
    you Caesar's body.
You shall not in your funeral speech blame us,       245
But speak all good you can devise of Caesar,
And say you do it by our permission;
Else shall you not have any hand at all
About his funeral. And you shall speak
In the same pulpit whereto I am going,               250
After my speech is ended.
ANTONY.                    Be it so.
I do desire no more.
BRUTUS. Prepare the body then, and follow us.

[*The conspirators file out of The Senate Chamber after*
BRUTUS, *leaving* ANTONY *alone beside* CAESAR's *body.*]

ANTONY. (*Kneeling.*) O, pardon me, thou bleeding piece
    of earth,
That I am meek and gentle with these butchers!       255
Thou art the ruins of the noblest man
That ever lived in the tide of times.
Woe to the hand that shed this costly blood!
Over thy wounds now do I prophesy,
Which, like dumb mouths, do ope their ruby lips      260
To beg the voice and utterance of my tongue:
A curse shall light upon the limbs of men;
Domestic fury and fierce civil strife
Shall cumber all the parts of Italy;
Blood and destruction shall be so in use             265
And dreadful objects so familiar
That mothers shall but smile when they behold
Their infants quartered with the hands of war;
All pity choked with custom of fell deeds;
And Caesar's spirit ranging for revenge,             270
With Ate[35] by his side, come hot from hell,
Shall in these confines with a monarch's voice
Cry "Havoc!"[36] and let slip the dogs of war,[37]

34. **protest**, assert.

35. Ate\ˈā·tē\ a classical goddess of
revenge.
36. "**Havoc**"\ˈhă·vək\ a direction to
take no prisoners but to kill indiscrim-
inately.
37. **dogs of war**, famine, sword, and fire.

424

That this foul deed shall smell above the earth
With carrion men, groaning for burial. 275

[OCTAVIUS' SERVANT *enters.* ANTONY *turns.*]

You serve Octavius Caesar,[38] do you not?
SERVANT. I do, Mark Antony.
ANTONY. Caesar did write for him to come to Rome.
SERVANT. He did receive his letters, and is coming;
And bid me say to you by word of mouth— 280
(*Recognizes the body of* CAESAR.) O Caesar!—
ANTONY. Thy heart is big. Get thee apart and weep.
Passion,[39] I see, is catching; for mine eyes,
Seeing those beads of sorrow stand in thine,
Began to water. Is thy master coming? 285
SERVANT. He lies tonight within seven leagues of Rome.
ANTONY. Post back with speed and tell him what hath
chanced.
Here is a mourning Rome, a dangerous Rome,
No Rome of safety for Octavius yet.
Hie[40] hence and tell him so. Yet, stay awhile. 290
Thou shalt not back till I have borne this corpse
Into the market-place. There shall I try,
In my oration, how the people take
The cruel issue of these bloody men;
According to the which thou shalt discourse 295
To young Octavius of the state of things.
(*Arranging* CAESAR's *mantle around the body.*) Lend
me your hand.

[*Together they carry* CAESAR *out of the Senate
Chamber.*]

38. **Octavius**\ŏk ᴬtā·vē·əs\ **Caesar,** Caesar's adopted heir, his grand nephew, who later became the emperor Augustus Caesar.

39. **Passion,** suffering, sorrow.

40. **Hie**\haɪ\ hurry.

## CHARACTERIZATION

Shakespeare develops his characters by what others say about them, what they say about themselves, and by their reactions to various situations. Consider and discuss what Shakespeare implies about each of the following characters through the quotations from the characters themselves or from others.

### BRUTUS

*Brutus, Act I, scene 2*
Into what dangers would you lead me, Cassius,
That you would have me seek into myself
For that which is not in me?

*Brutus, Act I, scene 2*
For let the gods so speed me as I love
The name of honor more than I fear death.

*Cassius, Act I, scene 2*
Well, Brutus, thou art noble; yet, I see,
Thy honorable metal may be wrought
From that it is disposed; . . .

*Casca, Act I, scene 3*
O, he sits high in all the people's hearts;
And that which would appear offense in us,
His countenance, like richest alchemy,
Will change to virtue and to worthiness.

*Portia, Act II, scene 1*
Brutus is wise, and, were he not in health,
He would embrace the means to come by it.

*Ligarius, Act II, scene 1*
I am not sick, if Brutus have in hand
Any exploit worthy the name of honor.

*Caesar, Act III, scene 1*
Et tu, Brute! Then fall, Caesar!

*Antony through servant, Act III, scene 1*
Brutus is noble, wise, valiant, and honest; . . .

### CAESAR

*Cassius, Act I, scene 2*
I, as Aeneas, our great ancestor,
Did from the flames of Troy upon his shoulder
The old Anchises bear, so from the waves of Tiber
Did I the tired Caesar.

*Cassius, Act I, scene 2*
Why, man, he doth bestride the narrow world
Like a Colossus, . . .

*Caesar, Act I, scene 2*
I rather tell thee what is to be feared
Than what I fear; for always I am Caesar.

*Casca, Act I, scene 2*
He fell down in the market-place, and foamed at the mouth, and was speechless.

*Brutus, Act II, scene 1*
And, to speak truth of Caesar,
I have not known when his affections swayed
More than his reason.

*Decius, Act II, scene 1*
Never fear that. If he be so resolved,
I can o'ersway him; . . .

*Caesar, Act II, scene 2*
What can be avoided
Whose end is purposed by the mighty gods?

*Caesar, Act II, scene 2*
The valiant never taste of death but once.

*Caesar, Act II, scene 2*
Decius, go tell them Caesar will not come.

*Caesar, Act III, scene 1*
What touches us ourself shall be last served.

*Caesar, Act III, scene 1*
Know, Caesar doth not wrong, . . .

*Antony through servant, Act III, scene 1*
Caesar was mighty, bold, royal, and loving; . . .
Say I feared Caesar, honored him, and loved him.

*Antony, Act III, scene 1*
Thou art the ruins of the noblest man
That ever lived in the tide of times.

### CASSIUS

*Cassius, Act I, scene 2*
I was born free as Caesar; so were you.
We both have fed as well, and we can both
Endure the winter's cold as well as he; . . .

*Caesar, Act I, scene 2*
Yond Cassius has a lean and hungry look.
He thinks too much; such men are dangerous.

*Caesar, Act I, scene 2*
Yet if my name were liable to fear,
I do not know the man I should avoid
So soon as that spare Cassius. He reads much,
He is a great observer, and he looks
Quite through the deeds of men.

*Cassius, Act I, scene 2*
If I were Brutus now and he were Cassius,
He should not humor me.

## ANTONY

*Brutus, Act I, scene 2*
I am not gamesome; I do lack some part
Of that quick spirit that is in Antony.

*Cassius, Act II, scene 1*
We shall find of him
A shrewd contriver; and, you know, his means,
If he improve them, may well stretch so far
As to annoy us all; . . .

*Brutus, Act II, scene 1*
For Antony is but a limb of Caesar.

*Brutus, Act II, scene 1*
For he is given
To sports, to wildness, and much company.

*Caesar, Act II, scene 2*
See! Antony, that revels long o' nights,
Is notwithstanding up.

*Brutus, Act III, scene 1*
Thy master is a wise and valiant Roman.
I never thought him worse.

*Cassius (whispering), Act III, scene 1*
Brutus, a word with you!
You know not what you do. Do not consent
That Antony speak in his funeral.
Know you how much the people may be moved
By that which he will utter?

## IMPLICATIONS

Would you agree or disagree with the following statements? Remember to find support for your opinion in the lines of the play.

**1.** Shakespeare gives characteristics to Caesar which make him obviously a man to be king.

**2.** Caesar was not ambitious.

**3.** Brutus is a stoic, an individual who solves all things by his intellect and rules out emotion in his decisions.

**4.** A good man, like Brutus, is defenseless before evil.

**5.** Portia senses disaster because a woman is sensitive to people instead of events.

**6.** It is not characteristic of Cassius to let Brutus make two fatal decisions: (1) To let Antony live; (2) To let Antony speak at the funeral.

**7.** Caesar is involved in a series of brief encounters in the first part of the play. His handling of them changed his life.

## WORDS

**A.** What do the italicized words mean in the following phrases and clauses: (1) there is no fellow in the *firmament*, (2) till we have *appeased* the multitude, (3) all true *rites* and lawful ceremonies, (4) and none so poor to do him *reverence*, (5) *bequeathing* it as a rich *legacy*, (6) *ingratitude*, more strong than traitors' arms, quite *vanquished* him, (7) *contaminate* our fingers with base bribes, (8) with *meditating* that she must die once, (9) that shapes this monstrous *apparition*, (10) to stay the *providence* of some high powers, (11) alas, thou hast *misconstrued* everything.

**B.** What is the relationship between the following pairs of words: *defer-prefer* ("And presently prefer his suit to Caesar"); *ordinary* ("Might fire the blood of ordinary men")-*pre-ordinance* ("And turn pre-ordinance . . . Into the law of children"); *belligerent-rebel* ("that Caesar bears such rebel blood"); *comprehensive-apprehensive* ("And men are flesh and blood, and apprehensive"); *consistent-persistence* (stage direction—angered by their persistence); *elapse-collapse* (stage direction—He collapses at the foot of Pompey's statue); *acclaim-proclaim* ("Proclaim! Cry it about in the streets!"); *malady-malice* ("in strength of malice"); *suspend-depend* ("or shall we on, and not depend on you?"); *contest-protest* ("I will protest"); *terrestrial-interred* ("The good is oft interred with their bones"); *repel-compel* ("You will compel me, then to read the will?").

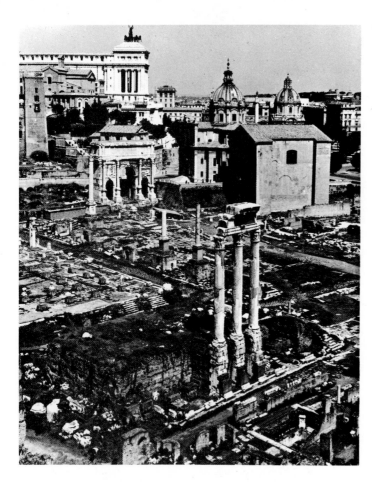

*The Roman forum today as viewed from the Palatine Hill.*

SCENE 2

*Rome. The Forum, the great public square of the city. It is the occasion of* CAESAR's *funeral, and a noisy mob waits nervously near a speaker's platform.*

CROWD. (*Chanting.*) We will be satisfied! Let us be satisfied.

[BRUTUS *and* CASSIUS *appear, followed by a train of anxious citizens.*]

BRUTUS. (*Calling out over the roar.*) Then follow me and give me audience, friends!
(*To* CASSIUS *at his side.*) Cassius, go you into the other street,
And part the numbers.[1]
(*Crying out to the milling crowd.*) Those that will hear me speak, let 'em stay here!    5

1. **part the numbers,** divide the crowds.

428

Those that will follow Cassius, go with him,
And public reasons shall be rendered
Of Caesar's death.

FIRST CITIZEN.       I will hear Brutus speak.

SECOND CITIZEN. I will hear Cassius, and compare their
   reasons

When severally we hear them rendered.      10

[CASSIUS *strides off, followed by those in the crowd who
have chosen to hear him.* BRUTUS *climbs the steps to the
platform and looks out over his eager audience.*]

THIRD CITIZEN. The noble Brutus is ascended! Silence!

BRUTUS. Be patient till the last.

   Romans, countrymen, and lovers! Hear me for my cause,
and be silent that you may hear. Believe me for mine
honor, and have respect to mine honor that you may be-   15
lieve. Censure me in your wisdom, and awake your
senses that you may the better judge. If there be any in
this assembly, any dear friend of Caesar's, to him I say,
that Brutus' love to Caesar was no less than his. If then
that friend demand why Brutus rose against Caesar,   20
this is my answer—Not that I loved Caesar less, but
that I loved Rome more. Had you rather Caesar were
living and die all slaves, than that Caesar were dead, to
live all free men? As Caesar loved me, I weep for him;
as he was fortunate, I rejoice at it; as he was valiant, I   25
honor him; but, as he was ambitious, I slew him. There
is tears for his love; joy for his fortune; honor for his
valor; and death for his ambition. Who is here so base
that would be a bondman? If any, speak; for him I have
offended. Who is here so rude that would not be a   30
Roman? If any, speak; for him have I offended. Who
is here so vile that will not love his country? If any,
speak; for him have I offended. I pause for a reply.

CROWD. (*Roaring enthusiastically.*) None, Brutus, none!

BRUTUS. Then none have I offended. I have done no more   35
to Caesar than you shall do to Brutus. The question of
his death is enrolled[2] in the Capitol; his glory not extenuated,[3] wherein he was worthy, nor his offenses enforced,[4] for which he suffered death.

[ANTONY *appears, solemnly following bearers who carry*
CAESAR's *body on their shoulders.*]

Here comes his body, mourned by Mark Antony; who,   40
though he had no hand in his death, shall receive the
benefit of his dying, a place in the commonwealth; as
which of you shall not? With this I depart, that, as I

2. **The question . . . enrolled,** the matter
of Caesar's death is on record.
3. **his glory not extenuated,** his glory is
not diminished or disparaged.
4. **enforced,** exaggerated.

slew my best lover for the good of Rome, I have the
same dagger for myself, when it shall please my country     45
to need my death.

CROWD. Live, Brutus! Live, live!

FIRST CITIZEN. Bring him with triumph home unto his
house!

SECOND CITIZEN. Give him a statue with his ancestors!

THIRD CITIZEN. Let him be Caesar!

FOURTH CITIZEN.                    Caesar's better parts     50
Shall be crowned in Brutus!

FIRST CITIZEN. We'll bring him to his house with shouts
and clamors!

BRUTUS. My countrymen—

SECOND CITIZEN.               Peace, silence! Brutus speaks!

FIRST CITIZEN. Peace, ho!

BRUTUS. Good countrymen, let me depart alone,            55
And, for my sake, stay here with Antony.
Do grace to Caesar's corpse, and grace his speech
Tending to Caesar's glories; which Mark Antony,
By our permission, is allowed to make.
I do entreat you, not a man depart                       60
Save I alone, till Antony have spoke.

[BRUTUS *descends from the speaking platform, while
the bearers place* CAESAR's *body at the base.* BRUTUS
*leaves amid cheers.* ANTONY *waits.*]

FIRST CITIZEN. Stay, ho! and let us hear Mark Antony.

THIRD CITIZEN. Let him go up into the public chair.
We'll hear him. Noble Antony, go up!

[*Antony climbs the steps of the platform.*]

ANTONY. For Brutus' sake, I am beholding[5] to you.      65     5. **beholding,** obliged.

FOURTH CITIZEN. (*Threateningly.*) What does he say of
Brutus?

THIRD CITIZEN.                    He says, for Brutus' sake
He finds himself beholding to us all.

430

FOURTH CITIZEN. 'Twere best he speak no harm of Brutus here.

FIRST CITIZEN. This Caesar was a tyrant.

THIRD CITIZEN.                              Nay, that's certain.
We are blest that Rome is rid of him.                    70

SECOND CITIZEN. Peace! Let us hear what Antony can say.

ANTONY. You gentle Romans—

CROWD.                              Peace, ho! Let us hear him.

ANTONY. Friends, Romans, countrymen, lend me your ears!

I come to bury Caesar, not to praise him.
The evil that men do lives after them;                    75
The good is oft interred with their bones.
So let it be with Caesar. The noble Brutus
Hath told you Caesar was ambitious.
If it were so, it was a grievous fault,
And grievously hath Caesar answered it.                    80
Here, under leave of Brutus and the rest—
For Brutus is an honorable man;
So are they all, all honorable men—
Come I to speak in Caesar's funeral.
He was my friend, faithful and just to me;                    85
But Brutus says he was ambitious,
And Brutus is an honorable man.
He hath brought many captives home to Rome,
Whose ransoms did the general coffers[6] fill.
Did this in Caesar seem ambitious?                    90
When that the poor have cried, Caesar hath wept;
Ambition should be made of sterner stuff.
Yet Brutus says he was ambitious,
And Brutus is an honorable man.
You all did see that on the Lupercal                    95
I thrice presented him a kingly crown,
Which he did thrice refuse. Was this ambition?
Yet Brutus says he was ambitious,
And, sure, he is an honorable man.
I speak not to disprove what Brutus spoke,                    100
But here I am to speak what I do know.
You all did love him once, and not without cause;
What cause withholds you then to mourn for him?
O judgment! thou art fled to brutish beasts,
And men have lost their reason. Bear with me.                    105
My heart is in the coffin there with Caesar,
And I must pause till it come back to me.

FIRST CITIZEN. Methinks there is much reason in his sayings.

SECOND CITIZEN. If thou consider rightly of the matter,

6. **general coffers**\ˈkŏ·fərz\ the public treasury.

Caesar has had great wrong.

THIRD CITIZEN.                          Has he, masters?          110
    I fear there will a worse come in his place.

FOURTH CITIZEN. Marked ye his words? He would not take
    the crown.
    Therefore 'tis certain he was not ambitious.

FIRST CITIZEN. If it be found so, some will dear abide[7] it.

SECOND CITIZEN. Poor soul! His eyes are red as fire with
    weeping.                                                    115

THIRD CITIZEN. There's not a nobler man in Rome than
    Antony.

FOURTH CITIZEN. Now mark him! He begins again to
    speak.

ANTONY. But yesterday the word of Caesar might
    Have stood against the world. Now lies he there,
    And none so poor to do him reverence.                      120
    O masters, if I were disposed to stir
    Your hearts and minds to mutiny and rage,
    I should do Brutus wrong, and Cassius wrong,
    Who, you all know, are honorable men.
    I will not do them wrong. I rather choose                  125
    To wrong the dead, to wrong myself and you,
    Than I will wrong such honorable men.
    But here's a parchment with the seal of Caesar;
    I found it in his closet. 'Tis his will.
    Let but the commons hear this testament—                   130
    Which, pardon me, I do not mean to read—
    And they would go and kiss dead Caesar's wounds
    And dip their napkins[8] in his sacred blood;
    Yea, beg a hair of him for memory,
    And, dying, mention it within their wills,                 135
    Bequeathing it as a rich legacy
    Unto their issue.

FOURTH CITIZEN. We'll hear the will! Read it, Mark
    Antony!

CROWD. The will, the will! We will hear Caesar's will!

ANTONY. Have patience, gentle friends. I must not read it.     140
    It is not meet[9] you know how Caesar loved you.
    You are not wood; you are not stones, but men;
    And, being men, hearing the will of Caesar,
    It will inflame you. It will make you mad.
    'Tis good you know not that you were his heirs;             145
    For, if you should, O, what would come of it!

FOURTH CITIZEN. Read the will! We'll hear it, Antony.
    You shall read the will, Caesar's will!

ANTONY. Will you be patient? Will you stay awhile?
    I have o'ershot myself to tell you of it.                   150

7. **abide,** pay for, atone for.

8. **napkins,** handkerchiefs.

9. **meet,** suitable.

432

I fear I wrong the honorable men
Whose daggers have stabbed Caesar. I do fear it.
FOURTH CITIZEN. They were traitors! (*Contemptuously.*)
    Honorable men.
CROWD. The will! The testament!
SECOND CITIZEN. They were villains, murderers! The will!
    Read the will!           155
ANTONY. You will compel me, then, to read the will?
    Then make a ring about the corpse of Caesar,
    And let me show you him that made the will.
    Shall I descend? And will you give me leave?
CROWD. Come down!           160
SECOND CITIZEN. Descend!
THIRD CITIZEN. You shall have leave!

[ANTONY *descends from the platform. The crowd
surges forward and encircles him and the body of*
CAESAR. *They are excited and press close.*]

FOURTH CITIZEN. A ring! Stand round!
FIRST CITIZEN. Stand from the hearse![10] Stand from the
    body!

10. **hearse,** here the stand or platform
that supports the body.

SECOND CITIZEN. Room for Antony, most noble Antony!  165
ANTONY. Nay, press not so upon me. Stand far off.
CROWD. Stand back! Room! Bear back!
ANTONY. If you have tears, prepare to shed them now.
    (*Lifting* CAESAR's *bloodstained robe.*) You all do know
      this mantle. I remember
    The first time ever Caesar put it on.      170
    'Twas on a summer's evening, in his tent,
    That day he overcame the Nervii.[11]
    Look, in this place ran Cassius' dagger through!
    See what a rent the envious Casca made!
    Through this the well-beloved Brutus stabbed,  175
    And as he plucked his cursed steel away,
    Mark how the blood of Caesar followed it,
    As rushing out of doors to be resolved
    If Brutus so unkindly knocked or no;
    For Brutus, as you know, was Caesar's angel.[12]  180
    Judge, O you gods, how dearly Caesar loved him!
    This was the most unkindest[13] cut of all;
    For when the noble Caesar saw him stab,
    Ingratitude, more strong than traitors' arms,
    Quite vanquished him. Then burst his mighty heart!  185
    And, in his mantle muffling up his face,
    Even at the base of Pompey's statue,
    Which all the while ran blood, great Caesar fell.
    O, what a fall was there, my countrymen!

11. **Nervii**\ˈnər·vē·ī\ a Celtic tribe in
Gaul, conquered by Caesar.

12. **angel,** dearest friend.

13. **unkindest,** unnatural. (This suggestion is also present in unkindly, line
179.)

Then I, and you, and all of us fell down, 190
Whilst bloody treason flourished over us.
O, now you weep, and I perceive you feel
The dint of pity. These are gracious drops.
Kind souls, what, weep you when you but behold
Our Caesar's vesture wounded? (*Pulling aside* CAESAR'S 195
  *mantle, exposing the body.*) Look you here!
Here is himself, marred, as you see, with traitors!

FIRST CITIZEN. O piteous spectacle!
SECOND CITIZEN. O noble Caesar!
THIRD CITIZEN. O woeful day!
FOURTH CITIZEN. O traitors, villains! 200
FIRST CITIZEN. O most bloody sight!
SECOND CITIZEN. We will be revenged!
CROWD. Revenge! About! Seek! Burn! Fire! Kill! Slay!
  Let not a traitor live!
ANTONY. Stay, countrymen! 205
FIRST CITIZEN. Peace there! Hear the noble Antony!
SECOND CITIZEN. We'll hear him! We'll follow him! We'll
  die with him!
ANTONY. Good friends, sweet friends! Let me not stir
  you up
To such a sudden flood of mutiny.
They that have done this deed are honorable. 210
What private griefs they have, alas, I know not,
That made them do it. They are wise and honorable
And will, no doubt, with reasons answer you.
I come not, friends, to steal away your hearts.
I am no orator, as Brutus is. 215
But, as you know me all, a plain blunt man
That love my friend; and that they know full well
That gave me public leave to speak of him;
For I have neither wit, nor words, nor worth,
Action, nor utterance, nor the power of speech 220
To stir men's blood. I only speak right on.
I tell you that which you yourselves do know;
Show you sweet Caesar's wounds—poor, poor, dumb
  mouths—
And bid them speak for me. But if I were Brutus,
And Brutus Antony, there were an Antony 225
Would ruffle up your spirits, and put a tongue
In every wound of Caesar that should move
The stones of Rome to rise and mutiny.
CROWD. We'll mutiny!
FIRST CITIZEN. We'll burn the house of Brutus! 230
THIRD CITIZEN. Away, then! Come seek the conspirators!
ANTONY. Yet hear me, countrymen! Yet hear me speak!

434

CROWD. Peace, ho! Hear Antony, most noble Antony!

ANTONY. Why, friends, you go to do you know not what.
Wherein hath Caesar thus deserved your loves? 235
Alas, you know not. I must tell you, then.
You have forgot the will I told you of.

CROWD. Most true! The will! Let's stay and hear the will!

ANTONY. (*Holding up the parchment.*) Here is the will,
and under Caesar's seal:
(*Reads.*) To every Roman citizen he gives, 240
To every several[14] man, seventy-five drachmas.[15]

SECOND CITIZEN. Most noble Caesar! We'll revenge his
death!

THIRD CITIZEN. O royal Caesar!

ANTONY. Hear me with patience!

CROWD. Peace, ho! 245

ANTONY. Moreover, he hath left you all his walks,
His private arbors and new-planted orchards,
On this side[16] Tiber. He hath left them you
And to your heirs forever, common pleasures,
To walk abroad and recreate yourselves. 250
Here was a Caesar! When comes such another?

FIRST CITIZEN. Never, never! Come away, away!
We'll burn his body in the holy place,
And with the brands fire the traitors' houses.
Take up the body! 255

SECOND CITIZEN. Go fetch fire!

THIRD CITIZEN. Pluck down benches!

FOURTH CITIZEN. Pluck down forms, windows, anything!

[*Screaming threats of violence, the aroused mob storms
out of the Forum along streets that lead outward in all
directions. They light torches and stampede away in
search of the conspirators. One group bears off the
body of* CAESAR.]

ANTONY. (*Grimly to himself.*) Now, let it work. Mischief,[17] thou art afoot;
Take thou what course thou wilt!

14. **several,** individual.
15. **drachma**\ˈdrăk·mə\ a silver coin, originally Greek. It is usually rated at about nineteen cents, but its real value was considerable since the purchasing power of money in ancient times was great.

16. **side,** side of the

17. **Mischief,** strife, commotion. The meaning of the word was much stronger in Shakespeare's day than now.

[OCTAVIUS' SERVANT *arrives, breathless from running.*]

How now, fellow?                                      260

SERVANT. Sir, Octavius is already come to Rome.

ANTONY. Where is he?

SERVANT. He and Lepidus are at Caesar's house.

ANTONY. And thither will I straight to visit him.
  He comes upon a wish. Fortune is merry,
  And in this mood will give us anything.              265

SERVANT. I heard him say: Brutus and Cassius
  Are rid like madmen through the gates of Rome.

ANTONY. Belike[18] they had some notice of the people,
  How I had moved them. Bring me to Octavius.          270

[*They hurry off together.*]

18. **Belike,** most likely, probably.


SCENE 3

*Rome. A street near the Forum. In the distance shouts of
alarm and noises of rioting. Along the narrow, quiet,
cobbled street, the poet* CINNA *strolls, musing to himself.*

CINNA. I dreamt tonight that I did feast with Caesar,
  And things unluckily charge[1] my fantasy.
  I have no will to wander forth of doors,
  Yet something leads me forth.

1. **charge,** load, weigh down.

[*A group of enraged citizens swarm down the street
and surround* CINNA. *They are armed with torches and
clubs.*]

FIRST CITIZEN. What is your name?                      5

SECOND CITIZEN. Whither are you going?

THIRD CITIZEN. Where do you dwell?

FOURTH CITIZEN. Are you a married man or a bachelor?

SECOND CITIZEN. Answer every man directly.

FIRST CITIZEN. Ay, and briefly.                        10

FOURTH CITIZEN. Ay, and wisely.

THIRD CITIZEN. Ay, and truly, you were best.[2]

CINNA. (*Confused and frightened.*) What is my name?
  Whither am I going? Where do I dwell? Am I a married
  man or a bachelor? Then, to answer every man directly   15
  and briefly, wisely and truly: wisely I say, I am a
  bachelor.

2. **ay . . . best,** and you would be best
advised to do so truly.

SECOND CITIZEN. That's as much as to say: they are fools
  that marry. You'll bear me a bang[3] for that, I fear. Proceed; directly.                                      20

CINNA. Directly, I am going to Caesar's funeral.

FIRST CITIZEN. As a friend or an enemy?

CINNA. As a friend.

3. **bear . . . bang,** get a knock from me.

SECOND CITIZEN. That matter is answered directly.

FOURTH CITIZEN. For your dwelling—briefly. 25

CINNA. Briefly, I dwell by the Capitol.

THIRD CITIZEN. Your name, sir, truly.

CINNA. Truly, my name is Cinna.

[*The crowd closes in on* CINNA, *their weapons raised.*]

FIRST CITIZEN. Tear him to pieces! He's a conspirator!

CINNA. (*Screaming.*) I am Cinna the poet! I am Cinna 30
the poet!

FOURTH CITIZEN. Tear him for his bad verses! Tear him for
his bad verses!

CINNA. I am not Cinna the conspirator!

FOURTH CITIZEN. It is no matter, his name's Cinna. Pluck 35
but his name out of his heart, and turn him going!

[*They leap upon* CINNA *and club him brutally.*]

THIRD CITIZEN. Tear him! Tear him! Come, brands ho! Fire
brands! To Brutus'! To Cassius'! Burn all! Some to
Decius' house, and some to Casca's! Some to Ligarius'! Away, go! 40

[*The crowd runs off shouting, leaving* CINNA's *mangled
body alone on the street.*]

# ⚓ Act IV

*Rome. The interior of* ANTONY's *house. By flickering lamplight* ANTONY, OCTAVIUS, *and* LEPIDUS, *the young ruling Triumvirate[1] since the flight of the conspirators, sit at a table. They study a parchment listing the names of political enemies. It has been some time since the death of* CAESAR, *and Rome has undergone political turmoil. The conspirators have long since fled beyond Italy.*

ANTONY. These many, then, shall die. Their names are
    pricked.[2]
OCTAVIUS. Your brother too must die. Consent you,
    Lepidus?[3]
LEPIDUS. I do consent—
OCTAVIUS.               Prick him down, Antony.
LEPIDUS. Upon condition Publius shall not live,
    Who is your sister's son, Mark Antony.         5
ANTONY. He shall not live. Look, with a spot I damn[4] him!
    But, Lepidus, go you to Caesar's house;
    Fetch the will hither, and we shall determine
    How to cut off some charge[5] in legacies.
LEPIDUS. What, shall I find you here?           10
OCTAVIUS. Or here, or at the Capitol.

[ANTONY *watches carefully to make sure that* LEPIDUS *has left before he speaks.*]

ANTONY. This is a slight unmeritable man,
    Meet to be sent on errands. Is it fit,
    The threefold world divided,[6] he should stand
    One of the three to share it?
OCTAVIUS.             So you thought him;    15
    And took his voice who should be pricked to die,
    In our black sentence and proscription.[7]
ANTONY. Octavius, I have seen more days than you;
    And though we lay these honors on this man
    To ease ourselves of divers sland'rous loads,[8]    20
    He shall but bear them as the ass bears gold—
    To groan and sweat under the business,
    Either led or driven, as we point the way;
    And having brought our treasure where we will,
    Then take we down his load, and turn him off,    25
    Like to the empty ass, to shake his ears
    And graze in commons.[9]

1. **Triumvirate**\ˈtraɪˈəm·və·rət\ a governing coalition of three leaders.

2. **pricked,** marked (on the death list).

3. **Lepidus**\ˈlĕ·pĭ·dəs\.

4. **damn,** condemn.

5. **cut off some charge,** reduce in significance. The Triumvirate wishes to decrease the legacies in Caesar's will (which Antony read to the crowd in the preceding scene).

6. **The threefold world divided,** with the world divided into three spheres of power.

7. **proscription,** list of those condemned.

8. **divers sland'rous loads,** various burdens of shame.

9. **commons,** the public pasture land held by a town or a village. (An anachronism.)

OCTAVIUS.                    You may do your will;
  But he's a tried and valiant soldier.
ANTONY. (*With contempt.*) So is my horse, Octavius, and
    for that
  I do appoint him store of provender.                    30
  It is a creature that I teach to fight,
  To wind, to stop, to run directly on;
  His corporal[10] motion governed by my spirit.
  And, in some taste,[11] is Lepidus but so—
  He must be taught and trained and bid go forth;         35
  A barren-spirited fellow, one that feeds
  On objects, orts,[12] and imitations,
  Which, out of use and staled by other men,
  Begin his fashion.[13] Do not talk of him
  But as a property. And now, Octavius,                    40
  Listen great things—Brutus and Cassius
  Are levying powers.[14] We must straight make head.[15]
  Therefore let our alliance be combined,
  Our best friends made, and our best means stretched
    out;
  And let us presently go sit in council                   45
  How covert matters may be best disclosed
  And open perils surest answered.[16]
OCTAVIUS. Let us do so, for we are at the stake
  And bayed about[17] with many enemies;
  And some that smile have in their hearts, I fear,        50
  Millions of mischiefs.

  [*They leave.*]

10. **corporal**, bodily.
11. **taste**, degree.

12. **objects**, things discarded; **orts**, scraps, bits of refuse.

13. **which . . . fashion**, which, now discarded by others and in fact made stale, are the fashions he takes up as new.

14. **levying powers**, raising armies.
15. **make head**, make headway, proceed (in raising an army).

16. **How covert . . . answered**, how concealed dangers may be discovered and known dangers met.
17. **for we are . . . about**, we are tied to the stake at bay before many enemies. The wording comes from bear-baiting, a recreation in Shakespeare's time in which a bear was tied to a stake and tormented with dogs.

SCENE 2

*Sardis (an ancient city in Asia Minor, capital of
Lydia). A military camp on the outskirts of the city.
It is night. Sentries stand in the shadows. A single light
from inside Brutus' tent dimly illuminates the area. A
roll of drums.* BRUTUS *emerges from the tent with* LU-
CIUS. LUCILIUS, *an officer, approaches with* CASSIUS'
*servant,* PINDARUS.
BRUTUS. Stand, ho!
LUCILIUS. Give the word,[1] ho! and stand.
BRUTUS. What now, Lucilius? Is Cassius near?
LUCILIUS. He is at hand, and Pindarus is come
  To do you salutation from his master.                    5
BRUTUS. He greets me well. Your master, Pindarus,
  In his own change, or by ill officers,[2]
  Hath given me some worthy cause to wish

1. **The word**, the password.

2. **In his own . . . officers**, by some change in his nature or through untrustworthy officers.

Things done undone. But, if he be at hand,
I shall be satisfied.

PINDARUS.　　　　　　　I do not doubt                    10
　But that my noble master will appear
　Such as he is, full of regard and honor.[3]

BRUTUS. He is not doubted. (*Taking* LUCILIUS' *elbow and*
　*leading him off*.) A word, Lucilius—
　How he received you let me be resolved.[4]

LUCILIUS. With courtesy and respect enough;             15
　But not with such familiar instances,[5]
　Nor with such free and friendly conference
　As he hath used of old.

BRUTUS.　　　　　　　Thou hast described
　A hot friend cooling. Ever note, Lucilius,
　When love begins to sicken and decay               20
　It uses an enforced ceremony.
　There are no tricks in plain and simple faith;
　But hollow men, like horses hot at hand,[6]
　Make gallant show and promise of their mettle.
　But when they should endure the bloody spur,        25
　They fall their crests, and, like deceitful jades,[7]
　Sink in the trial.[8]

[*The confused sounds of marching soldiers and shouted*
*orders come from the distance*.]

　　　　　Comes his army on?

3. **full of regard and honor**, that is, for Brutus.

4. **resolved**, informed.

5. **instances**, marks of friendship.

6. **hot at hand**, spirited when held in.

7. **jades**, plugs, nags.
8. **Sink in the trial**, fail when tried.

440

LUCILIUS. They mean this night in Sardis to be quartered.
   The greater part, the horse[9] in general,
   Are come with Cassius.
BRUTUS.                    Hark! He is arrived.        30
   March gently on to meet him.

   [LUCILIUS *salutes and turns to leave.* CASSIUS, *flanked by
   his lieutenants, strides out of the shadows toward*
   BRUTUS.]

CASSIUS. Stand, ho!
BRUTUS. Stand, ho! Speak the word along.

   [CASSIUS' *lieutenants shout, each echoing the other.*]

FIRST LIEUTENANT. Stand!
SECOND LIEUTENANT. Stand!        35
THIRD LIEUTENANT. Stand!

   [CASSIUS *approaches* BRUTUS *with his arms outstretched.*]

CASSIUS. Most noble brother; you have done me wrong.
BRUTUS. (*Severely.*) Judge me, you gods! Wrong I my
      enemies?
   And, if not so, how should I wrong a brother?
CASSIUS. Brutus, this sober form[10] of yours hides wrongs;   40
   And when you do them—
BRUTUS. (*Sharply.*)         Cassius, be content!
   Speak your griefs softly. I do know you well.
   Before the eyes of both our armies here,
   Which should perceive nothing but love from us,
   Let us not wrangle. Bid them move away.        45
   Then, in my tent, Cassius, enlarge your griefs,
   And I will give you audience.
CASSIUS. (*Turning away from* BRUTUS.) Pindarus!
   Bid our commanders lead their charges off
   A little from this ground.
BRUTUS. Lucilius! Do you the like, and let no man        50
   Come to our tent till we have done our conference.
   Lucius and Titinius! Guard our door.

   [BRUTUS *pulls aside the tent flap for* CASSIUS, *and follows
   him inside.* LUCIUS *and* TITINIUS *take up their positions as sentries.*]

SCENE 3

*The same. Inside* BRUTUS' *tent. Armor and weapons are piled
in the corner. A single lamp on a map-strewn table makes
flickering shadows in the dark interior.* CASSIUS *paces.*
BRUTUS *stands watching him.*

9. **the horse,** the cavalry.

10. **sober form,** serious appearance and manner.

CASSIUS. That you have wronged me does appear in this—
  You have condemned and noted[1] Lucius Pella
  For taking bribes here of the Sardinians;
  Wherein my letters, praying on his side,
  Because I knew the man, were slighted off.                    5
BRUTUS. (*His arms folded, looking steadily at* CASSIUS.)
    You wronged yourself to write in such a case.
CASSIUS. In such a time as this it is not meet
  That every nice[2] offense should bear his comment.
BRUTUS. Let me tell you, Cassius, you yourself
  Are much condemned to have an itching palm,                   10
  To sell and mart your offices for gold
  To undeservers.
CASSIUS.          I! An itching palm?
  You know that you are Brutus that speaks this,
  Or, by the gods, this speech were else your last.
BRUTUS. The name of Cassius honors this corruption,            15
  And chastisement does therefore hide his head.[3]
CASSIUS. Chastisement!
BRUTUS. Remember March? The ides of March? Remem-
    ber?
  Did not great Julius bleed for justice' sake?
  What villain touched his body, that did stab                  20
  And not for justice? What, shall one of us,
  That struck the foremost man of all this world
  But for supporting robbers, shall we now
  Contaminate our fingers with base bribes,
  And sell the mighty space of our large honors                 25
  For so much trash as may be grasped thus?
  I had rather be a dog, and bay[4] the moon,
  Than such a Roman.
CASSIUS.                Brutus, bait[5] not me!
  I'll not endure it! You forget yourself
  To hedge me in. I am a soldier; I,                            30
  Older in practice, abler than yourself
  To make conditions.[6]
BRUTUS.                Go to ! You are not, Cassius.
CASSIUS. I am!
BRUTUS. I say you are not!
CASSIUS. Urge me no more! I shall forget myself!               35
  Have mind upon your health. Tempt me no farther!
BRUTUS. Away, slight man.
CASSIUS. Is it possible?
BRUTUS.              Hear me, for I will speak.
  Must I give way and room to your rash choler?[7]
  Shall I be frighted when a madman stares?                     40
CASSIUS. O ye gods! Ye gods! Must I endure all this?

1. **noted,** marked for disgrace or banishment.

2. **nice,** minor.

3. **The name . . . head,** the great name of Cassius makes corruption respectable with the result that wrongdoing goes unpunished.

4. **bay,** bay at.

5. **bait,** torment, as a bull or bear was tormented in Elizabethan entertainments.

6. **conditions,** statements of policy or procedure, decisions.

7. **choler\\ˈkŏ·lər\\** here, anger.

BRUTUS. All this! Ay, more. Fret till your proud heart
   break.
  Go show your slaves how choleric you are,
  And make your bondmen tremble. Must I budge?
  Must I observe you? Must I stand and crouch    45
  Under your testy humor?[8] By the gods,
  You shall digest the venom of your spleen,[9]
  Though it do split you; for, from this day forth,
  I'll use you for my mirth. Yea, for my laughter,
  When you are waspish.

CASSIUS. (*Staring in disbelief.*) Is it come to this?  50

BRUTUS. You say you are a better soldier.
  Let it appear so. Make your vaunting true,
  And it shall please me well. For my own part,
  I shall be glad to learn of noble men.

CASSIUS. You wrong me every way. You wrong me,
   Brutus.    55
  I said an elder soldier, not a better.
  Did I say "better"?

BRUTUS.          If you did, I care not.

CASSIUS. When Caesar lived, he durst not thus have moved
  me.

BRUTUS. Peace, peace! You durst not so have tempted him.

CASSIUS. I durst not!    60

BRUTUS. No!

CASSIUS. What? Durst not tempt him!

BRUTUS.          For your life you durst not.

CASSIUS. Do not presume too much upon my love.
  I may do that I shall be sorry for.    65

BRUTUS. You have done that you should be sorry for.
  There is no terror, Cassius, in your threats,
  For I am armed so strong in honesty
  That they pass by me as the idle wind,
  Which I respect not. I did send to you
  For certain sums of gold, which you denied me;    70
  For I can raise no money by vile means.
  (By heaven! I had rather coin my heart
  And drop my blood for drachmas than to wring
  From the hard hands of peasants their vile trash
  By any indirection.[10]) I did send    75
  To you for gold to pay my legions,
  Which you denied me. Was that done like Cassius?
  Should I have answered Caius Cassius so?
  When Marcus Brutus grows so covetous
  To lock such rascal counters[11] from his friends,    80
  Be ready, gods, with all your thunderbolts!
  Dash him to pieces!

8. **testy humor,** irritable disposition.

9. **You shall . . . spleen,** you shall swallow your anger; you shall control your bad temper. The **spleen** was thought to be the bodily source of anger and jealousy.

10. **indirection,** dishonest means.

11. **rascal counters,** worthless coins.

CASSIUS.                    I denied you not!

BRUTUS. You did!

CASSIUS. I did not! He was but a fool that brought
My answer back. Brutus has rived[12] my heart.                    85
A friend should bear his friend's infirmities,
But Brutus makes mine greater than they are.

BRUTUS. I do not, till you practice them on me.

CASSIUS. You love me not.

BRUTUS.                    I do not like your faults.

CASSIUS. A friendly eye could never see such faults.                    90

BRUTUS. A flatterer's would not, though they do appear
As huge as high Olympus.[13]

CASSIUS. (*Throwing up his arms in despair.*) Come,
Antony, and young Octavius! Come,
Revenge yourselves alone on Cassius,
For Cassius is aweary of the world!                    95
Hated by one he loves; braved by his brother;
Checked like a bondman;[14] all his faults observed,
Set in a notebook, learned and conned by rote[15]
To cast into my teeth. O, I could weep
My spirit from my eyes! (*Offering his knife to* BRUTUS.)
There is my dagger,                    100
And here my naked breast; within, a heart
Dearer than Pluto's mine,[16] richer than gold.
If that thou be'st a Roman, take it forth.
I, that denied thee gold, will give my heart!
Strike, as thou did'st at Caesar; for I know                    105
When thou did'st hate him worst, thou lovedst him
better
Than ever thou lovedst Cassius.

BRUTUS.                    Sheathe your dagger.
Be angry when you will, it shall have scope.
Do what you will, dishonor shall be humor.[17]
O Cassius, you are yoked with a lamb                    110
That carries anger as the flint bears fire:
Who, much enforced,[18] shows a hasty spark,
And straight is cold again.

CASSIUS.                    Hath Cassius lived
To be but mirth and laughter to his Brutus,
When grief and blood ill-tempered vexes him?                    115

BRUTUS. When I spoke that, I was ill-tempered too.

CASSIUS. (*Putting his knife away.*) Do you confess so
much? Give me your hand.

BRUTUS. (*Warmly clasping* CASSIUS' *hand.*) And my heart
too.

CASSIUS.                    O Brutus!

BRUTUS.                    What's the matter?

12. **rived**\raivd\ broken.

13. **Olympus**\ō ˄lĭm·pəs\ a mountain in Greece, the legendary home of the gods of classical mythology.

14. **Checked like a bondman,** scolded like a slave.
15. **learned and conned by rote,** memorized by heart.

16. **Pluto's**\˄plū·tō\ the god of the underworld and hence lord of all mines of precious metals and gems.

17. **humor,** here, a whim or temporary inclination. I will excuse your insults merely as effects of your irritable disposition.
18. **enforced,** provoked.

CASSIUS. Have not you love enough to bear with me,
   When that rash humor which my mother gave me     120
   Makes me forgetful?
BRUTUS.               Yes, Cassius; and from henceforth,
   When you are over-earnest with your Brutus,
   He'll think your mother chides, and leave you so.

[*A violent outburst of angry voices comes from the
door of the tent. An elderly* POET *has tried to force his
way past* LUCIUS *and* TITINIUS *for an audience with*
BRUTUS *and* CASSIUS. LUCILIUS *arrives to assist* LUCIUS
*and* TITINIUS *in restraining the* POET.]

POET. (*From outside the tent.*) Let me go in to see the
     generals!
   There is some grudge between them. 'Tis not meet    125
   They be alone.
LUCILIUS.        You shall not come to them!
POET. Nothing but death shall stay me!

[*The* POET *bursts into the tent.* LUCIUS *and* TITINIUS
*seize his arms.* LUCILIUS, *his sword drawn, follows.*]

CASSIUS. How now! What's the matter?
POET. For shame, you generals! What do you mean?
   Love, and be friends, as two such men should be;    130
   For I have seen more years, I'm sure, than ye.
CASSIUS. Ha, ha! How vilely doth this cynic rhyme!
BRUTUS. Get you hence, sirrah! Saucy[19] fellow, hence!
CASSIUS. Bear with him, Brutus. 'Tis his fashion.
BRUTUS. I'll know his humor, when he knows his time.    135
   What should the wars do with these jigging fools?
   Companion,[20] hence!
CASSIUS.             Away, away! Be gone!

[*Soldiers arrive to drag the* POET *from the tent. He
leaves struggling and protesting.*]

BRUTUS. Lucilius and Titinius, bid the commanders
   Prepare to lodge their companies tonight.
CASSIUS. And come yourselves, and bring Messala with
     you                              140
   Immediately to us.

[LUCILIUS *and* TITINIUS *salute and leave.*]

BRUTUS.         Lucius, a bowl of wine!

[LUCIUS *bows and leaves.*]

CASSIUS. I did not think you could have been so angry.
BRUTUS. O Cassius, I am sick of many griefs!
CASSIUS. Of your philosophy[21] you make no use
   If you give place to accidental evils.    145

19. **Saucy**, impudent. The word was much stronger in Elizabethan times than now.

20. **Companion**, fellow (used contemptuously).

21. **philosophy**, Stoicism. Stoics held that the ideal man directed his life by reason. Hence, he kept his emotions in check and was indifferent to life's sorrows and misfortunes.

BRUTUS. No man bears sorrow better. Portia is dead.

CASSIUS. (*Stiffening with surprise.*) Ha! Portia?

BRUTUS. She is dead.

CASSIUS. How 'scaped I killing when I crossed you so?
   O insupportable and touching loss!           150
   Upon what sickness?

BRUTUS.               Impatient of my absence,
   And grief that young Octavius with Mark Antony
   Have made themselves so strong—for with her death
   That tiding came—with this she fell distract,
   And, her attendants absent, swallowed fire.[22]    155

CASSIUS. And died so?

BRUTUS.         Even so.

CASSIUS.             O ye immortal gods!

[LUCIUS *reenters bearing a bowl of wine and cups.*]

BRUTUS. Speak no more of her. (*To* LUCIUS.) Give me a
   bowl of wine.
   (*He holds up his cup toward* CASSIUS.) In this I bury all
   unkindness, Cassius.

[*Drinks.*]

CASSIUS. My heart is thirsty for that noble pledge.
   Fill, Lucius, till the wine o'erswell the cup;      160
   (*He takes the wine offered him by* LUCIUS.) I cannot
   drink too much of Brutus' love.

[*As he drinks,* TITINIUS *enters the tent and stands near
the door. Beside him stands* MESSALA *in battle dress.*
LUCIUS *quietly slips by the two and out of the tent.*]

BRUTUS. Come in, Titinius! Welcome, good Messala![23]
   Now sit we close about this taper here,
   And call in question our necessities.[24]

CASSIUS. Portia, art thou gone?

BRUTUS. (*To* CASSIUS.)      No more, I pray you.    165
   (*Separating papers on the table.*) Messala, I have here
     received letters
   That young Octavius and Mark Antony
   Come down upon us with a mighty power,
   Bending their expedition toward Philippi.[25]

MESSALA. Myself have letters of the self-same tenor.[26]   170

BRUTUS. With what addition?

MESSALA. That by proscription and bills of outlawry,[27]
   Octavius, Antony, and Lepidus
   Have put to death a hundred senators.

BRUTUS. Therein our letters do not well agree.    175
   Mine speak of seventy senators that died
   By their proscriptions, Cicero[28] being one.

22. **fire,** Plutarch says that Portia committed suicide by swallowing glowing coals.

23. **Messala**\mĕ ˄sā·lə\.

24. **question our necessities,** discuss our problems.

25. **Bending . . . Philippi,** directing their forces toward Philippi\fĭ ˄lĭ·paɪ\, a city in northern Greece.

26. **tenor,** significance.

27. **bills of outlawry,** proscription lists which put certain citizens thereon outside the protection of the law. It was not only legal to kill such citizens but rewards were offered for their deaths.

28. **Cicero,** killed by Antony's orders in 43 B.C.

CASSIUS. Cicero one?

MESSALA.            Cicero is dead,
   And by that order of proscription.
   Had you your letters from your wife, my lord?       180

BRUTUS. No, Messala.

MESSALA. Nor nothing in your letters writ of her?

BRUTUS. Nothing, Messala.

MESSALA.             That, methinks, is strange.

BRUTUS. Why ask you? Heard you aught of her in yours?

MESSALA. (*Confused. Hesitating before he speaks.*) No,
   my lord.       185

BRUTUS. Now, as you are a Roman, tell me true!

MESSALA. Then like a Roman bear the truth I tell—
   For certain she is dead, and by strange manner.

BRUTUS. Why, farewell, Portia. We must die, Messala.
   With meditating that she must die once,       190
   I have the patience to endure it now.

MESSALA. Even so great men great losses should endure.

CASSIUS. I have as much of this in art[29] as you,
   But yet my nature could not bear it so.

BRUTUS. (*Spreading out a map on the table.*) Well, to our
   work alive![30] What do you think       195
   Of marching to Philippi presently?[31]

CASSIUS. I do not think it good.

BRUTUS.                Your reason?

CASSIUS.                    This is it—
   'Tis better that the enemy seek us.
   So shall he waste his means, weary his soldiers,
   Doing himself offense; whilst we, lying still,       200
   Are full of rest, defense, and nimbleness.

BRUTUS. Good reasons must, of force, give place to better.
   The people 'twixt Philippi and this ground
   Do stand but in a forced affection,
   For they have grudged us contributions.       205
   The enemy, marching along by them,
   By them shall make a fuller number up,
   Come on refreshed, new-added, and encouraged;
   From which advantage shall we cut him off
   If at Philippi we do face him there,       210
   These people at our back.

CASSIUS.             Hear me, good brother.

BRUTUS. Under your pardon. You must note beside
   That we have tried the utmost of our friends.
   Our legions are brimful; our cause is ripe.
   The enemy increases every day;       215
   We, at the height, are ready to decline.
   There is a tide in the affairs of men

29. **in art,** in theory. Cassius means that he knows the Stoic philosophy regarding fortitude, yet he could not control his emotions as Brutus does.

30. **to our work alive,** let us take up the work which we living men have to do.

31. **presently,** at once.

Which, taken at the flood, leads on to fortune;
Omitted, all the voyage of their life
Is bound in shallows and in miseries. 220
On such a full sea are we now afloat,
And we must take the current when it serves,
Or lose our ventures.
CASSIUS.                           Then, with your will, go on.
We'll along ourselves, and meet them at Philippi.
BRUTUS. The deep of night is crept upon our talk 225
And nature must obey necessity,
Which we will niggard with a little rest.[32]
There is no more to say?
CASSIUS.                           No more. Good night.
Early tomorrow will we rise and hence.
BRUTUS. (*Calling out.*) Lucius!

[LUCIUS *appears at the door of the tent.*]

                           My gown.
[LUCIUS *goes to the rear of the tent and opens a trunk.*]

                           Farewell,
     good Messala; 230
Good night. Noble, noble Cassius,
Good night, and good repose.
CASSIUS.                           O my dear brother!
This was an ill beginning of the night.
Never come such division 'tween our souls!
Let it not, Brutus.
BRUTUS.                 Everything is well. 235
CASSIUS. Good night, my lord.
BRUTUS.                           Good night, good brother.
MESSALA. Good night, Lord Brutus.
BRUTUS.                           Farewell, everyone.

[CASSIUS *and* MESSALA *leave.* LUCIUS *stands holding*
BRUTUS' *gown.*]

Give me the gown. (*Stands lost in thought for a mo-
     ment.*) Where is thy instrument?[33]
LUCIUS. (*Yawning.*) Here in the tent.
BRUTUS. (*Gently.*)        What, thou speakest drowsily?
Poor knave, I blame thee not; thou art overwatched.[34] 240
Call Claudius and some other of my men.
I'll have them sleep on cushions in my tent.
LUCIUS. (*Calling out.*) Varro and Claudius!

[ VARRO *and* CLAUDIUS *enter.*]

VARRO. Calls my lord?
BRUTUS. I pray you, sirs, lie in my tent and sleep; 245
It may be I shall raise you by and by

32. **which we . . . rest,** which (the
antecedent is "nature") however, we
will slight with only a little rest.

33. **instrument,** lute.

34. **overwatched,** tired out from watching too long.

448

On business to my brother Cassius.

VARRO. So please you, we will stand and watch your
    pleasure.³⁵

35. **Watch your pleasure,** watch out for
whatever wish you may have.

BRUTUS. I will not have it so. Lie down, good sirs.
    It may be I shall otherwise bethink me:           250

[VARRO *and* CLAUDIUS *arrange cushions on the floor and
lie down, covering themselves with their cloaks.* BRUTUS
*takes his gown from* LUCIUS. *He reaches into a pocket.*]

Look, Lucius! Here's the book I sought for so.
    I put it in the pocket of my gown.

LUCIUS. I was sure your lordship did not give it me.

BRUTUS. Bear with me, good boy. I am much forgetful.
    Canst thou hold up thy heavy eyes awhile,        255
    And touch thy instrument a strain or two?

LUCIUS. Ay, my lord, an't³⁶ please you.

36. **an't,** if it.

BRUTUS.                  It does, my boy.
    I trouble thee too much, but thou art willing.

LUCIUS. It is my duty, sir.

BRUTUS. I should not urge thy duty past thy might.    260
    I know young bloods look for a time of rest.

[LUCIUS *sits cross-legged on a floor cushion, and readies
his lute.*]

LUCIUS. I have slept, my lord, already.

BRUTUS. It was well done, and thou shalt sleep again.
    I will not hold thee long. If I do live,
    I will be good to thee.                 265

[LUCIUS *strums his lute and sings softly.*]

This is a sleepy tune.

[LUCIUS' *head nods forward; his hands slide across
the strings of his lute, and he sleeps.*]

             O murderous slumber,
Lay'st thou thy leaden mace³⁷ upon my boy
That plays thee music? Gentle knave, good night.
    I will not do thee so much wrong to wake thee.
    If thou dost nod, thou break'st thy instrument.    270

37. **mace,** here, a staff used by a sheriff's
officer to touch on the shoulder of a
person as a sign that the person is
placed under arrest.

    (*Slides the lute out from* LUCIUS' *hands and lays it
      aside.*) I'll take it from thee; and, good boy, good
      night.
    (*Taking his book to the light on the table.*) Let me see.
      Let me see. Is not the leaf turned down
Where I left reading? Here it is, I think.

[*As he speaks, the glowing ghost of* CAESAR *moves
stealthily out from the shadows and stands watching
in the flickering lamplight.*]

How ill this taper burns! (*Looks up suddenly.*) Ha!
    Who comes here?
I think it is the weakness of my eyes           275
That shapes this monstrous apparition.
It comes upon me! Art thou anything?
Art thou some god, some angel, or some devil,
That makes my blood cold and my hair to stand?
Speak to me what thou art!              280
GHOST. Thy evil spirit, Brutus.
BRUTUS.              Why com'st thou?
GHOST. To tell thee thou shall see me at Philippi.
BRUTUS. Well, then I shall see thee again?
GHOST. Ay, at Philippi.
BRUTUS. Why, I will see thee at Philippi, then.    285

[*The ghost backs toward the shadows in the tent and
fades out of sight.* BRUTUS *advances cautiously, peering
anxiously into the darkness.*]

Now I have taken heart thou vanishest!
Ill spirit, I would hold more talk with thee.
    (*Shouting.*) Boy! Lucius! Varro! Claudius! Sirs, awake!
    Claudius!
LUCIUS. The strings, my lord, are false.        290
BRUTUS. He thinks he still is at his instrument.
    Lucius, awake!
LUCIUS. My lord?
BRUTUS. Did'st thou dream, Lucius, that thou so cried
    out?
LUCIUS. My lord, I do not know that I did cry.    295
BRUTUS. Yes, that thou did'st. Did'st thou see anything?
LUCIUS. Nothing, my lord.
BRUTUS. Sleep again, Lucius. Sirrah, Claudius! Fellow,
    thou! awake!
VARRO. My lord?
CLAUDIUS. My lord?              300
BRUTUS. Why did you so cry out, sirs, in your sleep?
VARRO, CLAUDIUS. Did we, my lord?
BRUTUS.              Ay! Saw you anything?
VARRO. No, my lord. I saw nothing.
CLAUDIUS.             Nor I, my lord.
BRUTUS. Go and commend me to my brother Cassius.
    Bid him set on his powers betimes before,[38]    305
    And we will follow.
VARRO, CLAUDIUS.      It shall be done, my lord.

[*They leave.* BRUTUS *sits at the table and rests his head
on his arms.*]

38. **Bid him . . . before,** order him to
start his forces marching in advance at
once.

450

# Act V

### SCENE 1

*Philippi, a city of ancient Macedon,[1] named after Phillip,*
*father of Alexander the Great. In 168 B.C., the city fell*
*under the power of conquering Romans. On the great*
*plains outside Philippi, the armies of* BRUTUS *and* CASSIUS
*have formed to meet the legions of* ANTONY *and* OCTAVIUS.
*Amid the dust and confusion of cavalry and infantry units*
*hurrying to their positions,* ANTONY *and* OCTAVIUS *stand*
*together looking toward the distant ranks of the enemy.*
*They are dressed for battle. From behind come the sounds*
*of drums and excited barks of command.*

OCTAVIUS. Now, Antony, our hopes are answered.
  You said the enemy would not come down,
  But keep[2] the hills and upper regions.
  It proves not so. Their battles[3] are at hand.
  They mean to warn us at Philippi here,      5
  Answering before we do demand of them.
ANTONY. Tut! I am in their bosoms,[4] and I know
  Wherefore they do it. They could be content
  To visit other places, and come down
  With fearful bravery, thinking by this face[5]      10
  To fasten in our thoughts that they have courage.
  But 'tis not so.

[*A* MESSENGER *runs up to* ANTONY *and* OCTAVIUS.
*He salutes.*]

MESSENGER.        Prepare you, Generals!
  The enemy comes on in gallant show.
  Their bloody sign of battle[6] is hung out,
  And something to be done immediately.      15
ANTONY. (*Looking toward the horizon and pointing.*)
  Octavius, lead your battle softly on
  Upon the left hand of the even field.
OCTAVIUS. (*Stiffening at* ANTONY's *assumption of total*
    *command.*) Upon the right hand I! Keep thou the
    left.
ANTONY. Why do you cross me in this exigent?[7]
OCTAVIUS. I do not cross you, but I will do so.      20

[*They walk off toward their separate commands.*

*At the head of the conspirators' armies* BRUTUS *and* CAS-
SIUS *enter, attended by* LUCILIUS, TITINIUS, MESSALA, *and*
*other officers.*]

1. **Macedon**\ˈmă·sə·dən\ an ancient
kingdom, including northeastern Greece
and adjacent areas.

2. **keep,** keep to.

3. **battles,** battalions, forces.

4. **I am in their bosoms,** I understand
them.

5. **face,** outward show.

6. **sign of battle,** a red flag displayed
outside the general's tent was the battle
sign.

7. **Why do . . . exigent,** why do you oppose me in this urgent occasion?

451

*The famous Appian Way, a portion of it as it appears
today. Over similar roads throughout the empire,
Rome moved her troops and commerce.*

BRUTUS. They stand and would have parley.
CASSIUS. Stand fast, Titinius! We must out and talk.

  [OCTAVIUS *from his position on the field sees* BRUTUS *and*
  CASSIUS *walking forth. He calls to* ANTONY.]

OCTAVIUS. Mark Antony! Shall we give sign of battle?
ANTONY. No, Caesar. We will answer on their charge.[8]
  Make forth! The generals would have some words.    25
OCTAVIUS. (*To his officers.*) Stir not until the signal.

  [BRUTUS *approaches* OCTAVIUS *and* ANTONY, *who now
  stand together.*]

BRUTUS. Words before blows. Is it so, countrymen?
OCTAVIUS. Not that we love words better, as you do.
BRUTUS. Good words are better than bad strokes, Octavius.

8. **charge,** a message indicating bidding
or request.

452

ANTONY. In[9] your bad strokes, Brutus, you give good
    words.                                 30
    Witness the hole you made in Caesar's heart,
    Crying, "Long live! Hail, Caesar!"
CASSIUS.                    Antony,
    The posture[10] of your blows are yet unknown!
    But for your words, they rob the Hybla[11] bees,
    And leave them honeyless.
ANTONY.              Not stingless too?    35
BRUTUS. O, yes, and soundless too,
    For you have stolen their buzzing, Antony;
    And very wisely threat before you sting.
ANTONY. Villains! You did not so when your vile
    daggers
    Hacked one another in the sides of Caesar!    40
    You showed your teeth like apes, and fawned like
    hounds,
    And bowed like bondmen, kissing Caesar's feet;
    Whilst damned Casca, like a cur, behind
    Struck Caesar on the neck. O you flatterers!
CASSIUS. Flatterers! Now, Brutus, thank yourself.    45
    This tongue had not offended so today
    If Cassius might have ruled.
OCTAVIUS. Come, come! The cause?[12] If arguing make us
    sweat,
    The proof of it will turn to redder drops.
    Look!    50
    I draw a sword against conspirators!
    When think you that the sword goes up again?
    Never! till Caesar's three and thirty wounds
    Be well avenged; or till another Caesar[13]
    Have added slaughter to the sword of traitors!    55
BRUTUS. Caesar, thou canst not die by traitors' hands
    Unless thou bring'st them with thee.
OCTAVIUS.               So I hope!
    I was not born to die on Brutus' sword.
BRUTUS. O, if thou wert the noblest of thy strain,
    Young man, thou could'st not die more honorable.    60
CASSIUS. A peevish schoolboy, worthless of such honor,
    Joined with a masker and a reveller!
ANTONY. (*Gripping the hilt of his sword.*) Old Cassius,
    still!
OCTAVIUS. (*Restraining him.*)        Come, Antony, away!
    Defiance, traitors, hurl we in your teeth!
    If you dare fight today, come to the field;    65
    If not, when you have stomachs.

9. **In,** with.

10. **posture,** condition, fashion.

11. **Hybla** \\\`hai·blə\\ a town in Sicily famous for its bees and honey.

12. **come, . . . cause,** come to the point of this meeting.

13. **another Caesar,** Octavius likewise bore the name Caesar.

[ANTONY *and* OCTAVIUS *turn and stride back toward their armies.*]

CASSIUS. Why, now, blow wind, swell billow, and swim bark!

The storm is up, and all is on the hazard.[14]

BRUTUS. (*Calling back.*) Ho, Lucilius! Hark, a word with you.

[LUCILIUS *races from his battle position to* BRUTUS' *side.*]

LUCILIUS. My lord?

[BRUTUS *takes his arm and guides him off to the side, and they talk softly, their heads together, facing away from* CASSIUS.]

CASSIUS. Messala!

[MESSALA *approaches* CASSIUS.]

MESSALA.                 What says my General?

CASSIUS.                              Messala,                70
This is my birthday; as this very day
Was Cassius born. Give me thy hand, Messala.
Be thou my witness that against my will,
As Pompey was, I am compelled to set
Upon one battle all our liberties.                          75
You know that I held Epicurus strong
And his opinion.[15] Now I change my mind,
And partly credit things that do presage.
Coming from Sardis, on our former[16] ensign
Two mighty eagles fell, and there they perched,      80
Gorging and feeding from our soldier's hands,
Who to Philippi here consorted[17] us.
This morning are they fled away and gone;
And in their steads do ravens, crows, and kites
Fly o'er our heads and downward look on us,            85
As we were sickly prey. Their shadows seem
A canopy[18] most fatal, under which
Our army lies, ready to give up the ghost.

MESSALA. Believe not so!

CASSIUS.                          I but believe it partly;
For I am fresh of spirit, and resolved                     90
To meet all perils very constantly.

[BRUTUS *and* LUCILIUS *finish their private talk and return to* CASSIUS.]

BRUTUS. Even so, Lucilius.

CASSIUS.                      Now, most noble Brutus,
The gods today stand friendly, that we may,

14. **all is on the hazard,** everything is hazarded; everything depends on dangerous chances.

15. **You know . . . opinion,** you know that I was a strong believer in the opinions of Epicurus (\'ĕ·pĭ ▲kyū·rəs\ a Greek philosopher of the Fourth and Third Centuries B.C., who disbelieved in omens).

16. **former,** foremost.

17. **consorted,** accompanied.

18. **canopy,** a tapestry hung overhead.

454

Lovers in peace, lead on our days to age![19]
But since the affairs of men rest still uncertain,                    95
Let's reason[20] with the worst that may befall:
If we do lose this battle, then is this
The very last time we shall speak together.
What are you then determined to do?

BRUTUS. Even by the rule of that philosophy                           100
By which I did blame Cato[21] for the death
Which he did give himself—I know not how,
But I do find it cowardly and vile,
For fear of what might fall, so to prevent
The time of life[22]—arming myself with patience                     105
To stay[23] the providence of some high powers
That govern us below.

CASSIUS.                              Then, if we lose this battle,
You are contented to be led in triumph
Through the streets of Rome?

BRUTUS. No, Cassius, no! Think not, thou noble Roman,                 110
That ever Brutus will go bound to Rome.
He bears too great a mind. But this same day
Must end that work the ides of March begun;
And whether we shall meet again I know not;
Therefore our everlasting farewell take.                             115
Forever, and forever, farewell, Cassius!
If we do meet again, why, we shall smile.
If not, why then, this parting was well made.

CASSIUS. Forever, and forever, farewell, Brutus!
If we do meet again, we'll smile indeed.                             120
If not, 'tis true this parting was well made.

BRUTUS. Why, then, lead on! O that a man might know
The end of this day's business ere it come!
But it sufficeth that the day will end,
And then the end is known. Come, ho! Away!                           125

[*They walk back toward their waiting legions.*]


SCENE 2


*The plains beyond Philippi. The battle has begun.* BRUTUS'
*forces hurl themselves on the enemy.* BRUTUS *himself,*
*flushed by the fever of combat, enters with* MESSALA.

BRUTUS. Ride, ride, Messala! Ride, and give these bills[1]
Unto the legions on the other side!
(*Pointing with his sword.*) Let them set on at once,
    for I perceive
But cold demeanor in Octavius' wing,

19. **lead on . . . age,** live to old age.

20. **reason,** consider.

21. **The younger Cato**\ˈkā·tō\ (95–46
B.C.) the father-in-law of Brutus com-
mitted suicide rather than submit to
Caesar.

22. **to prevent . . . life,** to cut short
one's full term of life, to commit suicide.
23. **to stay,** to await.

1. **bills,** written orders.

And sudden push gives them the overthrow.                5
Ride, ride, Messala! Let them all come down!

[MESSALA *runs for his horse.* BRUTUS *heads back toward the fighting.*]


SCENE 3

*The part of the field where* CASSIUS' *forces fall back in disorganized retreat from the powerful thrusts of* ANTONY's
*disciplined legions.* CASSIUS, *furious at the failure of his
men, tries to rally them to resist more fiercely. With one
hand gripping the staff of his ensign and the other clench-
ing the hilt of his sword, he watches the gathering defeat
from the slope of a small hill.* TITINIUS *stands at his side.*

CASSIUS. (*In despair.*) O, look, Titinius, look! The villains
    fly!
Myself have to mine own turned enemy.[1]
This ensign here of mine was turning back.
I slew the coward, and did take it from him.
TITINIUS. O Cassius, Brutus gave the word too early;     5
Who, having some advantage on Octavius,
Took it too eagerly. His soldiers fell to spoil,[2]
Whilst we by Antony are all enclosed.

[PINDARUS *arrives, torn and battered from the fighting.*]

PINDARUS. Fly further off, my lord! Fly further off!
Mark Antony is in your tents, my lord.                  10
Fly, therefore, noble Cassius! Fly far off!
CASSIUS. This hill is far enough. Look, look, Titinius!
Are those my tents where I perceive the fire?
TITINIUS. They are, my lord.
CASSIUS.                        Titinius, if thou lovest me,
Mount thou my horse, and hide thy spurs in him          15
Till he have brought thee up to yonder troops
And here again; that I may rest assured
Whether yon troops are friend or enemy.
TITINIUS. I will be here again, even with a thought.

[*He mounts* CASSIUS' *horse and dashes off.*]

CASSIUS. Go, Pindarus, get higher on that hill.         20
My sight was ever thick.[3] Regard Titinius,
And tell me what thou not'st about the field.

[PINDARUS *turns to climb to the crest of the hill.*]

This day I breathed first. Time is come around,
And where I did begin, there shall I end.
My life has run his compass. (*Calling up to* PINDARUS.)
    Sirrah, what news?                                  25

1. **Myself . . . enemy,** I have turned to
fighting against my own men (who were
deserting).

2. **fell to spoil,** turned to looting and
pillaging.

3. **thick,** bad, indistinct.

456

PINDARUS. (*From above.*) O, my lord!

CASSIUS. (*Anxiously.*) What news!

PINDARUS. Titinius is enclosed round about
  With horsemen, that make to him on the spur;
  Yet he spurs on. Now, they are almost on him.     30
  Now, Titinius! Now some light. O, he lights too!
  He's ta'en!

[*A faint volley of shouts from the distance.*]

          And, hark! They shout for joy.

CASSIUS. Come down. Behold no more.
  O, coward that I am, to live so long
  To see my best friend ta'en before my face!     35

[PINDARUS *climbs down from his lookout position on the
hill and stands waiting at his master's side.*]

(*After a long moment lost in thought.*) Come hither,
  sirrah.
In Parthia[4] did I take thee prisoner,
And then I swore thee, saving of thy life,[5]
That whatsoever I did bid thee do,
Thou should'st attempt it. (*Drawing his sword and
  handing it hilt first to* PINDARUS.) Come now! Keep
  thine oath.     40
Now be a freeman, and with this good sword
That ran through Caesar's bowels, search this bosom.

[PINDARUS *backs away and holds up his hand in
protest.*]

Stand not to answer! Here, take thou the hilt,
And, when my face is covered, as 'tis now,
Guide thou the sword.

[PINDARUS *stands staring at the sword in his hands, as
if he does not know what to do with it.* CASSIUS, *defeated but proudly erect, waits, his face covered with
his cloak.* PINDARUS *grips the sword in both hands and
plunges it into his master.* CASSIUS *staggers backward
from the thrust.*]

          Caesar, thou art revenged,     45
Even with the sword that killed thee.

[*He falls and dies.*]

PINDARUS. (*Looking down at the sword in his hands.*)
  So, I am free; yet would not so have been,
  Durst I have done my will. O Cassius!
  Far from this country Pindarus shall run,
  Where never Romans shall take note of him.     50

4. **Parthia**\ˈpär·thē·ə\ Persia.

5. **And then . . . life,** and then I made
you swear, in return for saving your life.

[*He drops the sword beside* CASSIUS' *body and runs off.* TITINIUS *arrives with* MESSALA *at the hill where* CASSIUS *lies dead.* TITINIUS *looks around anxiously.*]

MESSALA. It is but change,[6] Titinius, for Octavius
    Is overthrown by noble Brutus' power,
    As Cassius' legions are by Antony.
TITINIUS. (*Frowning as he looks about.*) These tidings
    will well comfort Cassius.
MESSALA. Where did you leave him?
TITINIUS.                       All disconsolate,     55
    With Pindarus his bondman, on this hill.
MESSALA. Is not that he that lies upon the ground?
TITINIUS. He lies not like the living. O my heart!
MESSALA. Is not that he?
TITINIUS. (*Kneeling beside* CASSIUS' *body.*) No, this was
    he, Messala,
    But Cassius is no more. O setting sun,     60
    As in thy red rays thou dost sink tonight,
    So in his red blood Cassius' day is set.
    The sun of Rome is set! Our day is gone!
    Clouds, dews, and dangers come; our deeds are done!
    Mistrust of my success hath done this deed.     65
MESSALA. Mistrust of good success hath done this deed.
    O hateful error, Melancholy's child,
    Why dost thou show to the apt[7] thoughts of men
    The things that are not? O error, soon conceived,
    Thou never com'st unto a happy birth,     70
    But kill'st the mother that engendered[8] thee!
TITINIUS. (*Standing over* CASSIUS *and looking from side
    to side.*) What, Pindarus! Where art thou, Pindarus?
MESSALA. Seek him, Titinius, whilst I go to meet
    The noble Brutus, thrusting this report
    Into his ears. I may say "thrusting" it,     75
    For piercing steel and darts envenomed
    Shall be as welcome to the ears of Brutus
    As tidings of this sight.
TITINIUS.                   Hie[9] you, Messala,
    And I will seek for Pindarus the while.

[MESSALA *hurries off to find* BRUTUS. TITINIUS *lifts* CASSIUS' *sword and stares at the bloodstained blade.*]

(*To himself.*) Why did'st thou send me forth, brave
    Cassius?     80
    Did I not meet thy friends? And did not they
    Put on my brows this wreath of victory
    And bid me give it thee? Did'st thou not hear their
    shouts?

6. **change,** an exchange.

7. **apt,** ready.

8. **engendered,** bore.

9. **hie,** hurry.

458

Alas, thou hast misconstrued everything!

[TITINIUS *bends over and puts the laurel wreath on* CASSIUS' *head.*]

But, hold thee, take this garland on thy brow.               85
Thy Brutus bid me give it thee, and I
Will do his bidding. Brutus, come apace[10]
And see how I regarded Caius Cassius.
(*Holding up the sword.*) By your leave, gods! This is
  a Roman's part.
Come, Cassius' sword, and find Titinius' heart!          90

[*He drives the sword into his breast and falls.* MESSALA
*returns, leading* BRUTUS, *young* CATO, STRATO,[11] VO-
LUMNIUS,[12] LUCILIUS, *and other officers.*]

BRUTUS. Where, where, Messala, doth his body lie?
MESSALA. Lo, yonder, and Titinius mourning it.
BRUTUS. Titinius' face is upward.
CATO.                                He is slain!
BRUTUS. O Julius Caesar, thou art mighty yet!
Thy spirit walks abroad, and turns our swords          95
In our own proper entrails.

[*From the distance, shouts and sounds of renewed battle.*]

CATO.                             Brave Titinius!
  Look, whether he have not crowned dead Cassius!
BRUTUS. Are yet two Romans living such as these?
The last of all the Romans, fare thee well!
It is impossible that ever Rome                              100
Should breed thy fellow.[13] Friends, I owe more tears
To this dead man than you shall see me pay.
I shall find time, Cassius! I shall find time.
Come, therefore, and to Thasos[14] send his body;
His funerals shall not be in our camp,                    105
Lest it discomfort[15] us. Lucilius, come;
And come, young Cato; let us to the field.
Labeo and Flavius set our battles on.
'Tis three o'clock; and, Romans, yet ere night
We shall try fortune in a second fight.                   110

[*With drawn swords, they set off toward the noise of fighting.*]

10. **apace,** at once.

11. **Strato\\**strā·tō\\.

12. **Volumnius\\**və **lyŭm 'nē·əs\\.

13. **fellow,** equal, match.

14. **Thasos\\**thā 'sōs\\ an island in the northern Aegean Sea.

15. **discomfort,** discourage.

SCENE 4

*The field of battle.* ANTONY's *forces have begun to overwhelm* BRUTUS' *army. The fighting has broken up into scattered engagements.* BRUTUS *tries desperately to re-form his dis-*

*persed men for an organized attack. He enters, accompanied by* MESSALA, *young* CATO, LUCILIUS, *and* FLAVIUS.

BRUTUS. Yet, countrymen! O, yet hold up your heads!
CATO. What bastard doth not? (*Flourishing his sword.*)
    Who will go with me?
  I will proclaim my name about the field.
  I am the son of Marcus Cato, ho!
  A foe to tyrants, and my country's friend.      5
  I am the son of Marcus Cato, ho!

[*He hurls himself at a roving group of* ANTONY'S *soldiers.*]

BRUTUS. (*Holding his sword aloft and shouting.*) And I
    am Brutus! Marcus Brutus, I!

[*He heads for the fighting in another part of the field.* CATO *falls back from his struggle mortally wounded.*]

LUCILIUS. (*Hurrying over to support* CATO'S *lifeless body.*)
  O young and noble Cato, art thou down?
  Why, now thou diest as bravely as Titinius,
  And may'st be honored, being Cato's son.     10

[ANTONY'S *soldiers surround* LUCILIUS *and threaten him with their swords.*]

FIRST SOLDIER. Yield, or thou diest!
LUCILIUS.                Only I yield to die.
  (*He offers money.*) There is so much that thou wilt
    kill me straight.[1]
  Kill Brutus, and be honored in his death.
FIRST SOLDIER. (*Stepping forward to protect* LUCILIUS.)
  We must not. (*Shouting.*) A noble prisoner!

[ANTONY *withdraws from the fighting and approaches.*]

SECOND SOLDIER. Room, ho! Tell Antony Brutus is ta'en.   15
FIRST SOLDIER. I'll tell the news. Here comes the general.
  Brutus is ta'en! Brutus is ta'en, my lord!
ANTONY. Where is he?
LUCILIUS. (*Laughing bitterly.*) Safe, Antony. Brutus is
  safe enough.
  I dare assure thee that no enemy     20
  Shall ever take alive the noble Brutus.
  The gods defend him from so great a shame!
  When you do find him, or[2] alive or dead,
  He will be found like Brutus, like himself.
ANTONY. (*To the* FIRST SOLDIER.) This is not Brutus,
  friend; but, I assure you,     25
  A prize no less in worth. Keep this man safe.
  Give him all kindness; I had rather have

1. **straight**, straightway.

2. **or**, either.

Such men as friends than enemies. Go on,
And see if Brutus be alive or dead;
And bring us word unto Octavius' tent                    30
How everything is chanced.³

[*He returns to the fighting.*]

SCENE 5

*The field of battle. Night has fallen.* BRUTUS, *weary and hope-less, stands near a cluster of huge boulders. With him are* DARDANIUS,¹ CLITUS, STRATO, *and* VOLUMNIUS.

BRUTUS. Come, poor remains of friends. Rest on this rock.
CLITUS. Statilius² showed the torchlight, but, my lord,
    He came not back. He is or ta'en, or slain.
BRUTUS. Sit thee down, Clitus. Slaying is the word.
    It is a deed in fashion. Hark thee, Clitus.            5

[*He leans over and whipers into* CLITUS' *ear.*]

CLITUS. What, I, my lord? No, not for all the world!
BRUTUS. Peace, then! No words.
CLITUS.                         I'll rather kill myself.
BRUTUS. (*Turning to where* DARDANIUS *sits.*) Hark thee,
    Dardanius.

[*He whispers.*]

DARDANIUS.                  Shall I do such a deed?
CLITUS. O Dardanius!
DARDANIUS. O Clitus!                                       10
CLITUS. What ill request did Brutus make to thee?
DARDANIUS. To kill him, Clitus. Look, he meditates.
CLITUS. Now is that noble vessel full of grief,
    That it runs over even at his eyes.
BRUTUS. Come hither, good Volumnius; list a word.³         15
VOLUMNIUS. What says my lord?
BRUTUS.                         Why, this, Volumnius—
    The ghost of Caesar hath appeared to me
    Two several⁴ times by night; at Sardis once,
    And, this last night, here in Philippi fields.
    I know my hour has come.
VOLUMNIUS.                      Not so, my lord.            20
BRUTUS. Nay, I am sure it is, Volumnius.
    Thou see'st the world, Volumnius, how it goes;
    Our enemies have beat us to the pit.⁵

[*The sounds of scattered fighting come from the darkness.*]

It is more worthy to leap in ourselves

1. **Dardanius**\'dar ᐱdä·nē·əs\.

2. **Statilius**\stə ᐱtĭ·lē·əs\ a scout who was to signal with his torch if all was well.

3. **list a word,** listen to a word or so.

4. **several,** separate.

5. **Our enemies . . . pit,** our enemies have driven us, like encircled animals, backward into a pit (in which we will be taken).

461

Than tarry till they push us. Good Volumnius,  25
Thou know'st that we two went to school together;
Even for that our love of old, I prithee,
Hold thou my sword-hilt, whilst I run on it.
VOLUMNIUS. That's not an office for a friend, my lord.

[*From nearby the shouts and cries of approaching
enemy troops.*]

CLITUS. Fly, fly, my lord! There is no tarrying here!  30
BRUTUS. Farewell to you, and you, and you, Volumnius.
Strato, thou has been all this while asleep;
Farewell to thee, Strato. Countrymen,
My heart doth joy that yet in all my life
I found no man but he was true to me.  35
I shall have glory by this losing day
More than Octavius and Mark Antony
By this vile conquest shall attain unto.
So fare you well at once, for Brutus' tongue
Hath almost ended his life's history.  40
Night hangs upon mine eyes. My bones would rest,
That have but labored to attain this hour.

[*Voices and the excited commands of the searching
enemy.*]

CLITUS. Fly, my lord! Fly!
BRUTUS.                    Hence! I will follow.

[CLITUS, DARDANIUS, *and* VOLUMNIUS *slip away into the
shadows.* BRUTUS *grips* STRATO's *arm as he attempts to
follow.*]

I prithee, Strato, stay thou by thy lord.
Thou art a fellow of a good respect.[6]  45
Thy life hath had some smatch[7] of honor in it.
Hold then my sword, and turn away thy face,
While I do run upon it. Wilt thou, Strato?

[STRATO *turns away in a momentary gesture of refusal.
Then he faces* BRUTUS *and grips his hand firmly.*]

STRATO. Give me your hand first. Fare you well, my lord.
BRUTUS. Farewell, good Strato.

[*He grips* STRATO's *shoulders and pulls himself upon
the blade.*]

                    Caesar, now be still;  50
I killed not thee with half so good a will.

[BRUTUS *falls.* OCTAVIUS *and* ANTONY *and their troops
appear out of the darkness. The captives,* MESSALA *and*
LUCILIUS, *are with them.* OCTAVIUS *points to* STRATO,
*who stands beside* BRUTUS' *body.*]

*Octavius (Augustus) Caesar*

6. **respect,** reputation.
7. **smatch,** hint, suggestion.

OCTAVIUS. What man is that?

MESSALA. My master's man. Strato, where is thy master?

STRATO. Free from the bondage you are in, Messala.
The conquerors can but make a fire of him,                    55
For Brutus only overcame himself,
And no man else hath honor by his death.

LUCILIUS. So Brutus should be found. I thank thee, Brutus,
That thou hast proved Lucilius' saying true.

OCTAVIUS. All that served Brutus, I will entertain[8] them.    60
Fellow, wilt thou bestow[9] thy time with me?

STRATO. Ay, if Messala will prefer[10] me to you.

OCTAVIUS. Do so, good Messala.

MESSALA. How died my master, Strato?

STRATO. I held the sword, and he did run on it.                65

MESSALA. Octavius, then take him to follow thee,
That did the latest service to my master.

ANTONY. (*Walking slowly until he stands over the body
of* BRUTUS.) This was the noblest Roman of them all.
All the conspirators, save only he,
Did that they did in envy of great Caesar.                    70
He only, in a general honest thought
And common good to all, made one of them.
His life was gentle, and the elements
So mixed in him that Nature might stand up
And say to all the world, "This was a man!"                   75

OCTAVIUS. According to his virtue let us use him,
With all respect and rites of burial.
Within my tent his bones tonight shall lie,
Most like a soldier, ordered honorably.
So call the field to rest, and let's away                     80
To part[11] the glories of this happy day.

[*They leave, bearing away the body of* BRUTUS.]

8. **entertain,** receive and maintain without hostility.
9. **bestow,** employ.
10. **prefer,** recommend.

11. **part,** divide.

## CHARACTERIZATION
*How many ages hence*
*Shall this our lofty scene be acted over*
*In states unborn and accents yet unknown*

As a study of politics and political maneuvering among men, *Julius Caesar* is probably the greatest play ever written. Except for Brutus, all the major characters in the play are politicians. The decisions they make are primarily political decisions. It is interesting to note that *Julius Caesar* has been popular during certain periods of history and forgotten during others. It has been extremely popular in the last thirty years in the United States which may indicate the state of political unrest in the world. Of course, political power resides in flesh and blood human beings whose moods, motives, and aspirations are similar to our own. Shakespeare brings his characters alive, vividly and warmly.

**1.** Shakespeare adds new dimensions to the characters in the last half of the play. Study the following quotations. What do they reveal about these men?

### BRUTUS

*Brutus, Act IV, scene 2*
There are no tricks in plain and simple faith; . . .

*Cassius, Act IV, scene 3*
When Caesar lived, he durst not thus have moved me.

*Brutus, Act IV, scene 3*
There is no terror, Cassius, in your threats
For I am armed so strong in honesty
That they pass by me as the idle wind,
Which I respect not.

*Cassius, Act IV, scene 3*
A friendly eye could never see such faults.

*Brutus, Act IV, scene 3*
O Cassius, I am sick of many griefs!

*Brutus, Act IV, scene 3*
Bear with me, good boy. I am much forgetful.

*Brutus, Act V, scene 5*
Caesar, now be still;
I killed thee not with half so good a will.

*Antony, Act V, scene 5*
This was the noblest Roman of them all.
All the conspirators, save only he,

Did that they did in envy of great Caesar.
He only, in a general honest thought
And common good to all, made one of them.
His life was gentle, and the elements
So mixed in him that Nature might stand up
And say to all the world, "This was a man!"

### CASSIUS

*Brutus, Act IV, scene 2*
Your master, Pindarus,
In his own change, or by ill officers,
Hath given me some worthy cause to wish
Things done undone.

*Brutus, Act IV, scene 3*
Let me tell you, Cassius, you yourself
Are much condemned to have an itching palm, . . .

*Cassius, Act IV, scene 3*
Brutus, bait not me!
I'll not endure it!

*Cassius, Act IV, scene 3*
I am a soldier; I,
Older in practice, abler than yourself
To make conditions.

*Brutus, Act IV, scene 3*
Away, slight man.

*Brutus, Act IV, scene 3*
Must I give way and room to your rash choler?
Shall I be frighted when a madman stares?

*Cassius, Act IV, scene 3*
For Cassius is aweary of the world!
Hated by one he loves; braved by his brother;
Checked like a bondman; all his faults observed,
Set in a notebook, learned and conned by rote
To cast into my teeth.

*Cassius, Act V, scene 3*
Caesar, thou art revenged
Even with the sword that killed thee.

*Brutus, Act V, scene 3*
The last of all the Romans, fare thee well!

### ANTONY

*Antony, Act III, scene 2*
But, as you know me all, a plain blunt man
That love my friend; and that they know full well
That gave me public leave to speak of him;
For I have neither wit, nor words, nor worth,

Action, nor utterance, nor the power of speech
To stir men's blood.

**2.** Great tragedy is often built around an individual in high position who is basically an admirable person, but who has a flaw in his character which eventually leads to downfall or death. If you think back through the play, you will realize that Brutus is the one character for whom all the others feel respect, love and affection. But his chief flaw is that he thinks those about him are motivated by the same love of honor that he himself holds. He lets himself be led into a terrible murder and yet in the final act he wins the sympathy of the audience as he stumblingly tries to retrieve his honor.

In addition to Brutus, Cassius and Caesar die and apparently fall in the course of the play. What is Cassius' major flaw? What is Caesar's? Are both tragic figures in the full sense described above?

### IMPLICATIONS

**1.** Does Shakespeare in *Julius Caesar* support or deny the following statements?

**a.** No good can come from an evil beginning.

**b.** Antony's funeral oration is a masterpiece of propaganda.

**c.** When a strong leader dies many factions spring into being, throwing a nation into chaos.

**d.** An idealist is seldom a practical person.

**e.** Fate plays a bigger part in an individual's life than does a person's character.

**f.** Caesar, Cassius and Mark Antony are all politicians.

**2.** Following are some larger implications of the play . . . the meaning goes beyond the lines. What is your opinion?

**a.** What can happen to a country if one person has total power?

**b.** Hitler and Mussolini had much in common with Caesar.

**c.** What are the dangers when people let their ideals run away with their reason?

**d.** What are some of the things that can happen to people if they let jealousy rule their lives?

**e.** Can a person be a dictator and still be a wise, competent leader?

**f.** It has been said that power corrupts and absolute power corrupts absolutely. Do you agree?

**g.** Offering a crown to Caesar would be as repulsive to most Romans of that day as offering a crown to the President of the United States would be to most Americans today.

### TECHNIQUES

*Irony*

*Julius Caesar* is a play that is built largely around the irony of a situation. In addition, it has many examples of irony in specific scenes and speeches.

**1.** What does Brutus hope to accomplish by joining the conspirators? What does he accomplish and why is it ironic?

**2.** When the conspirators are planning the murder, Brutus argues Cassius out of killing Antony along with Caesar. Why is this ironic?

**3.** After the murder Brutus says:

"And let us bathe our hands in Caesar's blood
Up to the elbows, and besmear our swords.
Then walk we forth, even to the market-place,
And waving our red weapons o'er our heads,
Let's all cry: 'Peace, freedom, and liberty!' "

What is ironic about the idea expressed? Why is it particularly ironic that Brutus should suggest such actions?

**4.** Antony's funeral oration speech is one of the greatest examples of the use of irony that has ever been written. Examine it closely to see how Antony makes his words mean almost exactly the opposite of what they seem to be saying.

**5.** What is ironic about Antony's final appraisal of Brutus?

"This was the noblest Roman of them all. . . ."

*Organization*

*Julius Caesar* has often seemed disorganized to people who read it for the first time. It seems to involve two stories instead of one. The murder of Caesar appears to form one neat unit, but the fourth and fifth acts may seem confused and less interesting. Is the play disorganized or has the reader misread Shakespeare's intentions? Think through the answers to the following:

**1.** The Elizabethan audience probably saw the play in two parts. Part one ended with the murder of Caesar. Part two began with the funeral oration.

Shakespeare's audience would, of course, be familiar with the stage of that period. This stage had evolved from the days when plays were presented in the courtyards of inns. A wagon was moved against one side of the yard to support the platform on which the players presented the drama. The audience watched either from the balconies if they could afford it or stood on the ground if they wanted a cheaper point of observation. Shakespeare's theater, the Globe, had departed from the rectangular shape of the inn yard and was built instead in a circle, but still there were balconies around the open space which seated the well to do and an open space on the floor where the groundlings stood. At one end a platform with a partial roof jutted out. On either side of this platform, near the back, a door opened to the actors' dressing rooms. Between these was a small room called the back stage which was the only section to have a curtain. Here scenes in caves, bedrooms, tombs, and the like were played. Above this room a gallery or balcony served for scenes involving high places such as battlements or upper windows. All plays were put on in the afternoon when there was plenty of daylight to illuminate the stage. A flag flying from the tower of the theater indicated that a play would be performed that day.

Supposing you were asked to give a title to each of the two parts separately. What would you entitle them? Do your two titles show a kind of organizational structure?

**2.** Who is the hero, or leading character, of the play? Most works of literature that use the name of a character as the title are named for the major character. Is this true in *Julius Caesar*? If you feel that Caesar is the central character, how is his character important even in the last two acts?

**3.** At the end of the second and fourth acts of his plays, Shakespeare has a habit of causing something to happen or a character to say something which sets up the action for the following acts. What is said and/or what happens at the end of Act II which leads to the action in Acts III and IV? Likewise, what is said and/or what happens at the end of Act IV which brings about the action in Act V?

### WORDS

**A.** What do the italicized words mean in the following phrases and clauses: (1) with thy best *apparel* on, (2) in her *concave* shores, (3) thoughts of great value, worthy *cognitations,* (4) he doth *bestride* the narrow world, (5) her side walls *encompassed* but one man, (6) to *repute* himself a son of Rome, (7) the nature of an *insurrection,* (8) To mask thy monstrous *visage,* (9) Hide it in smiles and *affability,* (10) A shrewd *contriver,* (11) To dare the vile *contagion* of the night, (12) Any *exploit* worthy the name of honor, (13) for warnings and portents, And evils *imminent?*

**B.** In the three hundred and fifty years since Shakespeare's day, some words have changed their meaning. Most obvious illustrations of semantic change have been pointed out in the notes. A number of other words, however, that have not changed so radically are interesting. Examine the denotation and the connotation of the italicized words in the following phrases. How have they changed their meaning somewhat? (1) without the sign of your *profession,* (2) what *trade,* thou knave? (3) thou *saucy* fellow, (4) to rejoice in his *triumph,* (5) for this *fault* assemble all the poor men, (6) who is it in the *press* that calls on me? (7) that *quick* spirit that is in Antony, (8) vexed I am of late with *passions,* (9) will modestly *discover* to yourself, (10) to keep his *state* in Rome.

**C. 1.** Following are a number of words from Act I of *Julius Caesar.* In these words the roots are italicized, and the general meanings of the roots are given in quotes. Indicate what specific sense of the general meaning is used in the play: re*spect* "look, see," 1, 10; di*rect*ly "straight, correct," 1, 12; con*fus*ion "pour, pour out," 1, 21; con*quest* "seek, search, ask," 1, 33; inter*mit* "send," 1, 55; *hes*itant "stick, cling," 1, 62; *vulg*ar "common," 1, 71; per*form* "form," 2, 10, pro*cess*ion "go, move," 2, 24; con*cep*tion "take, seize, catch," 2, 41; pro*pose* "put, place," 2, 110; dis*tract* "draw," 2, 132; con*jure* "swear," 2, 146; *senat*or "old," 2, 188; in*firm*ity "strong," 2, 270; *dig*est "eat, take in," 2, 300; se*duc*ed "lead," 2, 311; e*rupt*ion "break," 3, 78; *fact*ious "make, do," 3, 118.

**2.** Analyze the following italicized words from Act II into affixes and roots. Does the general meaning given for the root always agree with the meaning Shakespeare intended for the word? Then, lest he may, *prevent* 1, 28; what watchful cares do *interpose* themselves 1, 98; giving myself a *voluntary* wound 1, 300; decorated with royal

*magnificence* 2, stage direction; for these *predictions* are to the world as to Caesar 2, 28; your wisdom is consumed in *confidence* 2, 49; from you great Rome shall suck *reviving* blood 2, 88; the Senate have *concluded* 2, 93; Why, know'st thou any harm's *intended* towards him? 4, 31.

---

## Shakespeare— the Artist and the Man

### The Artist

In *Julius Caesar,* Shakespeare demonstrates the many facets of the playwright's craft in which he excelled. You have already examined his minute and intricate development of characters. Even without careful study you were aware of the moving story he unfolds. Short scenes prepare for the long dramatic moments or add emphasis to a scene just past. The change of pace keeps the audience alert, tense, eager. Shakespeare also had a way with language. Not only could he catch an idea with a few telling words and images, but he could put ideas into the flowing rhythm of powerful blank verse.

But the quality that has made Shakespeare survive through the ages is his ability to capture in words and actions the great problems that have always tormented us. Look about you in your school, your town, your state, and you will find people exactly like Brutus and Cassius, Caesar and Antony. They are not just government officials. You can find them in your clubs, your school, your sports. Our stumbling efforts to find our way in life may be reflected by Brutus or Cassius. Perhaps you find comfort in the fact that a strong man like Caesar is also superstitious or worry that you may feel as ruthless as Antony. But all individuals in the audience can find in this play some interpretation of life that makes their own more meaningful.

Other great writers have sometimes succeeded in doing one or two of these things with excellence, but no one else since his time has been able to turn out play after play, year after year with the high degree of excellence that is Shakespeare's. Who then was this man, Shakespeare?

## The Man (1564–1616)

For several hundred years scholars have probed dusty old records, dug through crumbling papers and books trying to find the answer to who Shakespeare was. Lawyers insist that he must have been a lawyer . . . he seems to know so much about the law. Sailors are equally sure that he must have gone to sea, for his knowledge of the sea is so astute. And so it goes. The truth is that no one tried to collect any information about Shakespeare until a hundred years after his death and by that time most of the records had disappeared or been destroyed.

He was born at an agricultural trading center, Stratford-on-Avon, about 90 miles from London. Here his mother and father were both people of some prominence, and it is supposed that he was sent to school. At eighteen he married Anne Hathaway, a girl eight years older than himself. They had a daughter, and two years later, twins, a boy and a girl. For the next eight years there is no tangible record of his activities, but in 1592 he turned up in London, acting and writing plays.

At this time it was common for groups of actors to join together and form a company to produce plays and split the profits. Shakespeare soon became a member of such a group, both writing plays and acting in them. His company was unusually successful and eventually bought its own theater, the Globe. It later became officially connected with the court and was known as The King's Company. During the long middle period of his life, Shakespeare was a rising businessman as well as a writer; and his worldly success can be traced through various pieces of property he purchased at this time. He bought a large tract of land near Stratford and later two large houses, one in Stratford and one in London. With a 10 percent interest in the Globe and a 14 percent interest in the Blackfriar's Theater his financial situation was a secure one.

After 1612 he seems to have retired to Stratford where he supposedly died on his birthday in 1616. Thus the pattern of his life was a kind of circle. He grew up in a small rural town, went to the city where he made a dramatic splash, and returned to the small town to live quietly and die.

# PEOPLE UNDER PRESSURE

## *Boots*

We're foot—slog—slog—slog—sloggin' over Africa
Foot—foot—foot—foot—sloggin' over Africa—
(Boots—boots—boots—boots—movin' up an' down again!)
  There's no discharge in the war!

Seven—six—eleven—five—nine-an'-twenty miles today—
Four—eleven—seventeen—thirty-two the day before—
(Boots—boots—boots—boots—movin' up an' down again!)
  There's no discharge in the war!

Don't—don't—don't—don't—look at what's in front of you.
(Boots—boots—boots—boots—movin' up an' down again!)
Men—men—men—men—men go mad with watchin' 'em,
  An' there's no discharge in the war!

Try—try—try—try—to think o' something different—
Oh—my—God—keep—men from goin' lunatic!
(Boots—boots—boots—boots—movin' up an' down again!)
  There's no discharge in the war!

Count—count—count—count—the bullets in the bandoliers.[1]
If—your—eyes—drop—they will get atop o' you!
(Boots—boots—boots—boots—movin' up an' down again!)
  There's no discharge in the war!

---

Reprinted by permission of Doubleday & Company, Inc.

---

1. **bandolier**\\'băn·də ᴀlēr\\ belts worn over the shoulder and across the chest, used for carrying cartridges.

We—can—stick—out—'unger, thirst, an' weariness,
But—not—not—not—not the chronic sight of 'em—
(Boots—boots—boots—boots—movin' up an' down again!)
    An' there's no discharge in the war!

'Tain't—so—bad—by—day because o' company,
But—night—brings—long—strings—o' forty thousand million
(Boots—boots—boots—boots—movin' up an' down again!)
    There's no discharge in the war!

I—'ave—marched—six—weeks in 'ell an' certify
It—is—not—fire—devils, dark, or anything,
But boots—boots—boots—boots—movin' up an' down again,
    An' there's no discharge in the war!

**RUDYARD KIPLING**

The Gulf Stream
*Winslow Homer*
*The Metropolitan Museum of Art*
*Wolfe Fund, 1906*

*The fisherman fights a lonely
struggle against the perils
of the sea.*

Life is lived in the midst of many kinds of pressures. The pressure of environment, the pressure of nature, the pressure of other people, the pressure of our own emotions: all of these come to bear on each of us. In turn, we seek ways to adjust and to establish a balance between these pressures and ourselves. There is a thrust and counterthrust.

In Kipling's "Boots," the soldiers, under the pressure of great physical strain, are driven close to madness. Their minds become numb, their perceptions distorted, until the only real thing in their world is the endless tramping of their own boots. The only refuge for their sanity is to define their suffering and, by defining it, to save themselves from destruction.

Writers, as you know, take the elements of actual life as their raw material and put these elements together in meaningful patterns. Through the process of recording and arranging their experience, writers not only produce satisfying artistic creations, but also help readers deepen their understanding of themselves and of the life around them. By examining the brief encounters between people, the emotional states of individuals, and the tensions of family life, skillful writers have led you to discover and to interpret experiences which would take many lifetimes to gather by yourself. It is natural that writers should also be fascinated with the moments in living when severe pressures are brought to bear on individuals.

Some of the selections that follow show people under momentary tensions; others show them living for long periods under steady strains. Some of the characters actively fight back, others do not. Some react to seemingly trivial matters, while others require catastrophic events to make them struggle against the oppressive force.

Working with the pressures that bear on human lives, the writers represented in this group of selections have created different kinds of literary experiences. Sometimes they amuse readers with the absurdity of a situation. Sometimes they evoke the despair of hopeless frustration. Sometimes they stir our pride in the dignity of people's ability to fight back. But whatever the mood, each selection will carry readers toward a better understanding of people pushed to the breaking point.

Early in John Milton's great epic
*Paradise Lost*, Satan claims that the mind
can make a heaven of hell
or a hell of heaven. Can the mind be pressured
into seeing perfectly ordinary events
as something horrifying? Saki, an English writer
of bizarre tales, has one answer.
When "The Open Window" begins,
the readers are thrust into the center
of the action and must, from the rush of events,
figure out the situation for themselves.

# The Open Window

## SAKI

My aunt will be down presently, Mr. Nuttel," said a very self-possessed young lady of fifteen. "In the meantime you must try and put up with me."

Framton Nuttel endeavoured to say the correct something which should duly flatter the niece of the moment without unduly discounting the aunt that was to come. Privately he doubted more than ever whether these formal visits on a succession of total strangers would do much towards helping the nerve cure which he was supposed to be undergoing.

"I know how it will be," his sister had said when he was preparing to migrate to this rural retreat; "You will bury yourself down there and not speak to a living soul, and your nerves will be worse than ever from moping. I shall just give you letters of introduction to all the people I know there. Some of them, as far as I can remember, were quite nice."

Framton wondered whether Mrs. Sappleton, the lady to whom he was presenting one of the letters of introduction, came into the nice division.

"Do you know many of the people round here?" asked the niece, when she judged that they had had sufficient silent communion.

"Hardly a soul," said Framton. "My sister was staying here, at the rectory,[1] you know, some four years ago, and she gave me letters of introduction to some of the people here."

He made the last statement in a tone of distinct regret.

"Then you know practically nothing about my aunt?" pursued the self-possessed young lady.

"Only her name and address," admitted the caller. He was wondering whether Mrs. Sappleton was in the married or widowed state. An undefinable something about the room seemed to suggest masculine habitation.

"Her great tragedy happened just three years ago," said the child; "that would be since your sister's time."

"Her tragedy?" asked Framton. Somehow in this restful country spot tragedies seemed out of place.

"You may wonder why we keep that window wide open on an October afternoon," said the niece, indicating a large French window[2] that opened on to a lawn.

"It is quite warm for the time of the year," said Framton; "but has that window got anything to do with the tragedy?"

"Out through that window, three years ago to a day, her husband and her two young brothers went off for their day's shooting. They never came back. In crossing the moor to their favourite snipe-shooting ground they were all three engulfed in a treacherous piece of bog. It had been that dreadful wet summer, you know, and places that were safe in other years gave way suddenly without warning. Their bodies were never recovered. That was the dreadful part of it." Here the child's voice lost its self-possessed note and became falteringly human. "Poor aunt always thinks that they will

---

1. **rectory**\ˈrĕk·tə·rē\ the residence of a parish clergyman.
2. **French window,** a casement window reaching to the floor.

From *The Complete Short Stories of Saki* by H. H. Munro, All Rights Reserved. Reprinted by permission of The Viking Press, Inc.

come back some day, they and the little brown spaniel that was lost with them, and walk in at that window just as they used to do. That is why the window is kept open every evening till it is quite dusk. Poor dear aunt, she has often told me how they went out, her husband with his white waterproof coat over his arm, and Ronnie, her youngest brother, singing, 'Bertie, why do you bound?' as he always did to tease her, because she said it got on her nerves. Do you know, sometimes on still, quiet evenings like this, I almost get a creepy feeling that they will all walk in through that window—"

She broke off with a little shudder. It was a relief to Framton when the aunt bustled into the room with a whirl of apologies for being late in making her appearance.

"I hope Vera has been amusing you?" she said.

"She has been very interesting," said Framton.

"I hope you don't mind the open window," said Mrs. Sappleton briskly. "My husband and brothers will be home directly from shooting, and they always come in this way. They've been out for snipe in the marshes today, so they'll make a fine mess over my poor carpets. So like you menfolk, isn't it?"

She rattled on cheerfully about the shooting and the scarcity of birds, and the prospects for duck in the winter. To Framton it was all purely horrible. He made a desperate but only partially successful effort to turn the talk on to a less ghastly topic. He was conscious that his hostess was giving him only a fragment of her attention, and her eyes were constantly straying past him to the open window and the lawn beyond. It was certainly an unfortunate coincidence that he should have paid his visit on this tragic anniversary.

"The doctors agree in ordering me complete rest, and absence of mental excitement, and avoidance of anything in the nature of violent physical exercise," announced Framton, who laboured under the tolerably widespread delusion that total strangers and chance acquaintances are hungry for the least detail of one's ailments and infirmities, their cause and cure. "On the matter of diet they are not so much in agreement," he continued.

"No?" said Mrs. Sappleton, in a voice which only replaced a yawn at the last moment. Then she suddenly brightened into alert attention—but not to what Framton was saying.

"Here they are at last!" she cried. "Just in time for tea, and don't they look as if they were muddy up to the eyes!"

Framton shivered slightly and turned towards the niece with a look intended to convey sympathetic comprehension. The child was staring out through the open window with dazed horror in her eyes. In a chill shock of nameless fear Framton swung round in his seat and looked in the same direction.

In the deepening twilight three figures were walking across the lawn towards the window. They all carried guns under their arms, and one of them was additionally burdened with a white coat hung over his shoulders. A tired brown spaniel kept close at their heels. Noiselessly they neared the house, and then a hoarse young voice chanted out of the dusk: "I said, Bertie, why do you bound?"

Framton grabbed wildly at his stick and hat. The hall-door, the gravel-drive, and the front gate were dimly noted stages in his headlong retreat. A cyclist[3] coming along the road had to run into the hedge to avoid imminent collision.

"Here we are, my dear," said the bearer of the white mackintosh,[4] coming in through the window; "fairly muddy, but most of it's dry. Who was that who bolted out as we came up?"

"A most extraordinary man, a Mr. Nuttel," said Mrs. Sappleton; "could only talk about his illness, and dashed off without a word of good-by or apology when you arrived. One would think he had seen a ghost."

---

3. **cyclist**\ˈsaɪ·klĭst\ a bicycle rider.
4. **mackintosh**\ˈmă·kən ˈtŏsh\ chiefly British: a light raincoat.

"I expect it was the spaniel," said the niece calmly. "He told me he had a horror of dogs. He was once hunted into a cemetery somewhere on the banks of the Ganges by a pack of pariah[5] dogs, and had to spend the night in a newly-dug grave with the creatures snarling and grinning and foaming just above him. Enough to make any one lose their nerve."

Romance at short notice was her specialty.

---

# I
## CALLING ON THE READER'S IMAGINATION

Part of the charm of "The Open Window" lies in so much story being packed into so little space. Much of the readers' pleasure comes from active participation in the story. They must make connections between the characters and supply a final explanation of the story from their imagination.

# II
## IMPLICATIONS

You have probably used your imagination more than you realize while reading this story. When you have answered the following questions, you will see how skillfully Saki has stimulated and made use of his readers' private responses.

1. What must have been the secret reactions of the following characters to each other? (a) Vera to Mr. Nuttel; (b) Mr. Nuttel to Vera; (c) Mr. Nuttel to Mrs. Sappleton; (d) Mrs. Sappleton to Mr. Nuttel.

2. What pressures were operating on Mr. Nuttel? How did he react to them?

3. Do you think Saki means you to feel sorry for Mr. Nuttel? If not, what evidence is there in the story that Mr. Nuttel at least partly deserves what happens to him?

4. What details of setting, time, and place, add to the pressures on Mr. Nuttel?

# III
## TECHNIQUES

In the creation of a story, a writer must, as you know, solve the problems of exposition, conflict, climax, characterization, plot, and symbol. In these selections you will examine three more elements of the story: theme, style, and identification.

---

5. **pariah**\ˈpă·rē·ə *or* pə ˈrai·ə\ outcast, wild. **Ganges** \ˈgăn ˈjēz\ the great river of northern India.

## Theme

There are two ways of considering themes in literature. The first is best illustrated by the organization of this book. Each group of selections in this anthology is built around a particular theme, that is, an underlying motif or idea. The ten selections which follow, for instance, deal with the behavior of people under pressure. Thus, PEOPLE UNDER PRESSURE is the general theme. There are many other such general themes in literature. "The Struggle for Justice," "People Look to the Future," "Young Love" might be cited as examples.

The other way of looking at themes is more particular. The theme, in this sense, is what a story itself is about. It is the meaning embodied in interplay of setting, plot, and characters in a story. Note that it is not a summary of its plot or a capsule description of its characters. Thus, the theme of "The Open Window" is not "a nervous man frightened by an imaginative young girl." You must look below the surface events of the story to discover the real theme. The surface actions, however, have been carefully arranged by the author to reveal what lies beneath them. If you have read "The Open Window" carefully, you will doubtless agree that the theme of this story is actually the power of suggestion. It is the pressure exerted by the young girl's story on Mr. Nuttel's nervous mind that makes him believe her version of the open window, rather than her aunt's more sensible and realistic explanation.

The particular themes of all the selections that follow will be related to the general theme of the group in a similar way. They will serve as variations on the general theme and will show you instances of specific kinds of pressure on different kinds of people.

## Style

Style is that special handling of language that makes one piece of writing distinct from another. Style is to writing what personality is to the human being—the distinctive, individual quality. A famous French critic once said "Style is the man himself." All writers of talent and originality develop a particular way of writing. It shows in the kinds of words they choose, the figures of speech they invent, and even in the grammatical structure of their sentences.

Some writers pay closer attention than others to the kind of language they use. Searching for exactly the right word or phrase to express their meaning, they try to give their writing the elegance, roughness, or naturalness that they consider appropriate to their story. But in the deepest sense of the word, all good writing reveals a concern with style. Although a distinctive style of writing is as natural to a good writer as a distinctive way of throwing a baseball is to a good pitcher or a way of sewing to a good dressmaker, it has usually been acquired only after years of hard work and diligent practice.

Reread the first few paragraphs of "The Open Window," and decide which adjective in the following pairs best describes Saki's style.

1. restrained      emotional
2. rambling      precise
3. cloudy      sparkling
4. light      heavy
5. informal      formal

In what way would you say the kind of story he is telling influences the kind of language he uses?

## Identification

As a friend recounts to you something that has happened to him, you automatically put yourself in his place and live through his experience with him. Much the same thing happens when you read a story. But there is this difference: A friend can count on your sympathy; writers cannot. Writers must win readers sympathy for their characters. They do this by leading readers to identify with the characters. By giving characters personality traits that are familiar, by placing them in exciting situations, and, most of all, by giving them hopes, fears, and other feelings that readers recognize, writers skillfully draw readers into the characters' lives. Readers soon find themselves sharing the characters' experiences and emotions. Identification is the means by which writers persuade their readers to take a deep interest in the story and in its people.

In "The Open Window," with which character did you identify yourself most strongly? In whose shoes did you put yourself while reading? Name some of the personality traits of this character which you found familiar.

◆
On certain extraordinary occasions,
as in this story, the mind and the body
seem to operate independently of one another.
Which was more real, what Peter Nilson's body
was performing or the way his mind was reacting?
You will note that the pressure on him
comes both from the immediate situation and also
from a deep personal insecurity.

# Going to Run
# All Night

## HARRY SYLVESTER

They brought him in before the commanding officer, a lieutenant colonel, and stood him there, almost as though he were a prisoner, a slight, almost little man, whose face, they now remembered, had been curiously harassed and marked by strain even before this campaign, or any campaign, had begun. He noticed himself that they walked on either side of him, as if guarding him, as if, indeed, he were a prisoner or someone valued. And since he could think of nothing he had done or left undone for which they should make him a prisoner, he was driven to the incredible conclusion that finally and at last he had come to be of value.

He looked at the lieutenant colonel, seeing that the officer's face was hardly less, though newly, harassed than his own. All day, in the midst of the danger which constantly encircled them and intermittently killed some of them, the new legend of the lieutenant colonel's irascibility had grown, so that now, standing before the man, the corporal could wonder that he was not ripped up and down with words as scores of men had been that day.

From ALL YOUR IDOLS by Harry Sylvester. Copyright 1948 by Harry Sylvester. Reprinted by permission of Holt, Rinehart and Winston, Inc.

The lieutenant colonel looked at him, blinking and staring at the same time, as though making some kind of adjustment, as if from rage to a kind of calm. Which it was, perhaps, for to Nilson's amazement, he said rather mildly, "They tell me that you used to be a runner, Corporal?"

"Why, yes," Nilson said. "Yes, sir, I mean."

"You used to run distances? I mean road races and such."

"Yes, sir."

"Ever run in Marathon races or anything like that?"

"Yes, sir," the corporal said, though he was thinking: There is nothing "like" the Marathon. Just the figures alone mean something that no other race means: 26 miles, 385 yards. "I ran seventh one year in the Boston Marathon."[1] Right after he had said it, he could see that the lieutenant colonel was not impressed, that he did not know that running seventh in the Boston Marathon was not the same as running seventh in just another foot race.

"Well," the officer said, as though making the best of a bad bargain, rubbing his eyes tiredly and slowly with the heels of his hands. "Well, as you know, they've sort of got us over a barrel[2] here. The one radio we still have that is working has been damaged so that we cannot vary the wave or frequency enough to keep the enemy from picking it up rather often."

He went on like that, rubbing his eyes, explaining to the corporal as if the corporal were a general—someone who ought to be told of what the situation was. "We think we can break out at dawn, if we can synchronize our attack with some sort of aid coming from our main forces opposite the point of our own attack. Break through the ring," he said

---

1. **marathon**\ˈmă·rə·thŏn\ a long-distance run. The **Boston Marathon,** held yearly on Patriot's Day (April 19, the anniversary of the Battle of Lexington and Concord), is a run from Hopkinton, Massachusetts, to Exeter Street in Boston, a distance of 26 miles, 385 yards.
2. **over a barrel,** in a very difficult or hopeless position.

vaguely. Then: "Look! You think you could run across the hills by dawn and carry them a message?"

Nilson began to think, for some reason, about how his grandmother used to talk so frequently about lightning and how you never knew where or when it was going to strike. It was not fear in him, although for a little while he would think it was fear. He made a silent gasp, so that his mouth was open before he began to speak. He said, "Why, I guess so. I mean, I'm not in very good shape. I—"

"But in no worse shape than anyone else here," the lieutenant colonel said. "And you used to be a runner. How long since you stopped active competition?"

"Oh, I was running all the time. Right up until my induction,[3] and even then, when I was still in the States and could get leave, I was competing some."

The officer nodded. "Well, that's about all. There'll be no written message in case you might be taken. You'll be picked up by one of our own patrols probably. Just tell them that we can't last another day here and that we're going to try to come through at dawn. It's possible they won't believe you. But that's a chance we'll have to take. If they have time, they can send a plane over with a message, to let us know that they understand, although it hasn't been any too healthy here for planes. There won't be much trouble getting you through their lines at night. I'll send a guard with you until you're beyond their lines and then you'll be on your own. Just follow the road. The main idea is to get there before dawn. I figure it's thirty-five or forty miles before they'll pick you up. We won't attack for six hours. You think you could make it in, say, five hours?"

"Why, if I was in shape," Nilson said, "I could, maybe, easy."

"Still," the officer said, "you're the best we have. Good luck."

"Yes, sir," Nilson said, and saluted and turned.

Outside, the two sergeants stood on either side of him, and the tall one said, "Well, what are you gonna need?"

"I dunno," Nilson said, "I guess I won't need anything. Maybe I'll take a canteen, maybe not." He knew that thirst for water and the actual need for water were not necessarily the same thing; he was already weighing, only half-consciously, the weight of the canteen against the necessity for water.

"Well, let's get going, then," the other sergeant said.

The tall sergeant got Nilson a canteen filled with water, and they moved out into the deeper darkness beyond where the tanks and cars stood in a shallow arc like great animals vaguely huddled in the dark.

They were more than halfway across the plain of three or four miles that separated them from the hills that held the enemy, when Nilson said, "Look, this isn't any good for you two, is it? I mean, if they see us, three isn't going to be much better than one?"

"Stop being noble," the tall sergeant said. "Someone's got to show you through the hills."

"I see what you mean," Nilson said.

It was simpler than he had thought it would be. You could neither hear nor see the enemy. They needed no pickets to hear tanks approaching or a plane.

The three moved upward over the dry hills, the soil crumbling under foot as they climbed, so that at the crest, the sergeants were bushed, panting in the heat and the altitude like animals, and even Nilson was sweating. In the moonlight below them and to the west and right, they could see the road.

"I guess this is where we get off," the tall sergeant said. "You better get going."

"All right," Nilson said. "I gotta get ready, though."

He undressed in the cloud-broken dark, until he sat there in his underwear, his socks and

---

3. **induction**\in ᴧdək·shən\ formal enrolling into the armed services.

shoes and his dog tag.[4] The other sergeant handed him the canteen.

"I'll take a drink now," Nilson said, "and that'll have to hold me. The canteen's too heavy—"

"You take that canteen," the tall sergeant said. "You're gonna need it."

"Look," Nilson said, then stopped. He saw that they did not know about water and running or any violent exercise. You could be thirsty for an awfully long time without actually needing water, but this was no time to start explaining that to them. "Well," he said, "I'll go along then."

"Good luck," they said. They watched him move, still walking down the slope toward the road a half-mile away. They thought it was because he couldn't run down a slope that steep, but Nilson was walking until the water he had just drunk was out of his stomach and he could be fairly sure he wouldn't get a stitch when he started to run.

Watching him, the tall sergeant said, "You think he's gonna do any good?"

"No, I don't," the other sergeant said. "Even if he gets through their patrols, he'll drop before he gets to our people—or quit and go hide."

"What do you say that for?" the tall sergeant said.

"Because you're probably thinking the same thing I am!"

In the darkness, the tall sergeant nodded. "We both know we could go along, too, now and hide somewhere until this is over, because they're not going to get through tomorrow morning."

"But we go back, instead," the other sergeant said. "And I don't know why."

"I don't know why, either," the tall sergeant said.

Then they both turned and began to go back the way they had come.

Nearing the road, the sense of great adventure that Nilson had begun to know, started to leave him. Not fear but a sense of futility took him; a sense of his own littleness in the night

and the desert that was also the enemy's country. At the edge of the road he paused, although he could not tell exactly why and so attributed it to fear, long the conventional reason for all unknown hesitations or doubts. It was not fear, though, so much as an unwillingness to undergo one more futility.

He had not been a very good runner, and he was now thirty-one. Like most of the young men of the Scandinavian colonies in Brooklyn, he had run more because it was custom—tradition, among their people. He had liked it, too, although after almost fifteen years of little or no glory, he had unconsciously begun to feel that he was too old to keep losing that often, had begun to realize that, after a while, it did something to a man. Not that it was any fault of his; after all, you'd have to be pretty special to run well Saturdays or Sundays or any other day after being on your feet all day as a post-office clerk.

He still hesitated on the edge of the road; there was in his hesitation a quality that was close to sullenness, a vague, an even shadowy resentment against the long years of defeat.

Without quite knowing what the resentment was, he knew it was, if not wrong, at least inappropriate now and here. He sighed and at the edge of the road did a curious little exercise that relatives of his also had done— oh, say, three hundred years before in Norway. He bent over, touching his toes five or six times and each time straightening up and flinging his arms wide. The idea was to open up his lungs quickly and limber the muscles of his chest and arms. Although he was not a very good runner, he knew all about running; he knew a man ran as much with his arms as with his legs.

Then he stepped onto the road and in a reflective gesture pawed at the crude paving as though it were hard-packed cinders, and the heavy G.I.[5] shoes were the short-spiked ones

---

4. **dog tag**, a soldier's identification tag worn around the neck.

5. **G.I.**, government issue, official army uniform or material.

of the distance runner. He felt sheepish, and in the darkness his mouth twisted into a half-grin. Then he began to run.

Almost immediately he felt easier; felt confidence flow through him as though it were his blood; felt that now, at last, he was in his own country, or, perhaps more accurately, in his own medium. For there are mediums of action that vary with the individual; some people feel best moving in an automobile, others on a horse, a few running or flying.

More or less unconsciously, as he ran, he felt with his feet for the part of the tar-and-gravel road that was best suited to him. The road was slightly crowned in the center and in places pocked lightly by machine-gun bullets from the planes that had gone over it. As on most roads, he found that the shoulder was best suited for running. It was softer, the spike-less shoes slipped less on it, and the slightly more resilient quality of it would keep him from having shin-splints[6] tomorrow. He thought with irony—a new emotion for him—that it was of no importance whether he had

the little pains along the shin from bruising or pulling the tendons there that held the muscle to the bone. Certainly he would run no more tomorrow, come what might; indeed, there might not even be a tomorrow.

This started him thinking of what he called fear—because so many things were called fear —but what was really a saturation in himself of having for so many years done things to no purpose. He wondered if this, too, would be to no purpose; if some burial detail, an indefinite number of days from now, would find his shapeless and twisted body some place along this road.

Then came the thought, also new to him, that it would be worse to get to where he was going and not be believed. There was nothing he could think of to do about that though, so he stopped thinking of it. Like most Scandinavians, he was a fatalist, and the war had not helped him to overcome that.

---

6. **shin-splints,** injuries and inflammations of the feet sometimes experienced by distance runners.

He was running faster, now; too fast, he thought. He was breathing rather hard. It was rather early to be breathing so hard; but he knew that would pass soon, and the thing called second wind would come to him. He slackened his pace a little, feeling more, as he did so, the weight of the shoes and trying to reject the thought that was starting to come in him, before it took too much form; trying not to think of it.

He began to think of the enemy and where the enemy might be; all around him, to be sure, but probably not too near the road, because, by night, planes could see a road. Still, there might always be patrols that would know a man running steadily by night was a strange and perhaps a fearful thing. Still, they might never see him; only hear him and the pounding of his feet on the road. So, deviously, his mind came back to the thought he knew he had been trying to avoid, and now he could not avoid it any longer: there was only one thing to do, take the G.I. shoes off and run without them.

He slowed down gradually until he was walking and then he walked perhaps thirty yards before he stopped. Then he sat on the ground and took his shoes off.

When he stood up he hesitated again. Once, he had lost a shoe in a race and had finished the race, but the cinders hadn't been very good for his bare feet.

The road here was bad, but principally what he feared was stepping on one of the scorpions that they saw every day. He wondered if they were out by night—and then he began to run again.

Without knowing it, he moved at times in a kind of stupor. The nights of little or fitful sleep, the days of too little food and water, were beginning to affect him now, and he began to take refuge from exhaustion and pain in something at times close to unconsciousness.

Twice he passed tanks not far from the road, their crews sleeping, he himself not knowing he passed them. Like a dun ghost, he drifted with the short, more or less effortless stride he had developed over the long years of competi-

tion and training. These little spells of semi-consciousness could no longer occur, though; effort was too much to permit them, too sustained and by now even terrible. So that his senses became acute again, his thoughts long-ranging, sharp and filled with color. It was perhaps this return to full and acute consciousness, induced by pain, that saved him.

Some place there was sound and some place a dull shouting. He could not tell for a moment whether they were in his thoughts or in the reality of the night all around him. Then there came the sound now long familiar to him, but still terrible, of an automatic rifle coughing in the night.

The firing came again, a little farther away, but not near him. He neither heard nor felt bullets. With one of those sudden lifts of speed —but unconscious and desperate now—with which a distance runner sometimes tries to break the hearts of his opponents in the middle of the race, Nilson suddenly started to sprint.

The road ran downhill here, and now through the warm, dark night, the little man cut loose, letting his feet shoot out ahead of him, carrying his legs with the curious sort of controlled abandon of the cross-country runner going downhill.

He ran with an almost incredible lack of sound, although he was not aware of this. The shooting and the sound of guns continued behind him. With a faint pleasure, he realized that it must have been his passing that had alarmed the enemy.

There was, then, a sense of other-worldliness about him as he moved in the night. It made him aware of the strangeness of what he was trying to do. He found a new strength in his body; the legs, the rhythmically moving arms recovered the thing of which, in his boyhood, he and the others trying to be runners had made a fetish—the thing called form.

So, going downhill now, the enemy all around him, he experienced a sense of power, almost as though he were invisible, almost as though he were fleeter and stronger than anything that could seek to kill or hinder him.

Sweat bathed him, so that he glistened as though oiled, and there was a slight froth at his lips.

The road leveled under him, ran flat for perhaps a quarter-mile, then began to mount again. He was aware of this change only gradually. The change he was first aware of was in himself, first the mind, then the body. The sense of power or superhuman ability was gone, almost abruptly; then his lungs began to hurt badly, and the cords in his neck. He was, he suddenly realized, nothing special; he was Pete Nilson from Brooklyn, and he was bushed, he was just about done.

He shook his head, not unlike an animal trapped and bewildered. The desire, the need to stop was extraordinarily strong in him. He tried an old trick, for which he had no name: he tried to analyze his pain, knowing that this sometimes made it disappear. There was the pain in the lungs, in the throat, in the muscles of the eyes, but not yet where his arms went into the shoulders, not yet just above the knees where the thigh muscles overlapped.

His stride had shortened—as it must, uphill—his body leaned forward. He had not been above quitting in a few races in his life, when he was hopelessly outdistanced, when he had not been trained right, when he had not had enough rest the previous week to make him strong.

It seemed to him that he had never been so exhausted as now, and his mind sought for excuses to stop. Oddest and first, there came to him the thought that if he only knew how long he had run, he might endure it. Twenty-six miles, 385 yards—that was the distance of the Marathon, and in Boston, in Toronto[7] you always knew to within a few hundred yards how far you had come, how far you had to go. But now, no one knew or had known, not within four or five miles. The enemy was in the hills, and the hills were all around the lieutenant colonel and his men, and beyond the hills that held the enemy were more of your own men, some place. So late, oh, so very late in his life he learned that it is important to

all men in their various endurings to see an end, to know a little bit about how far off an end is.

He was closer to being blind than he knew. He had started to deviate from a straight line, veering slightly from side to side. Although he did not know it, he was beyond the enemy, and all he had to combat was himself.

Some sort of anger formed in him: he could not tell its nature or its object. He realized it might even be at himself; then that it was at himself. He must have been crazy, he thought; he supposed that, all his life, his efforts had been directed obscurely and even deviously toward trying to achieve a sense of usefulness, corrupted sometimes into what was often called a sense of glory. And now that he was close to it, he had almost rejected it.

Why the change in him had occurred, the sudden insight, he might never know. He was on top of a hill, though, and looking down into a plain full of great shadows, and there was a paleness in the sky over the shadows. He was on top of this hill, but whether he was running or standing still, he might also never know, for it was just as great an effort to stand as to run.

He began to move downhill again, but still veering from side to side. He sensed, if he did not see, that there were no more hills beyond and he knew that his own people must be somewhere near, perhaps at the bottom of the hill he was now descending.

As he staggered, half-blind in the half-light, to the foot of the hill, he thought of the Athenian runner finishing the first Marathon[8] and as he collapsed, crying, "Rejoice, we conquer!" Nilson realized only now how much that image, those words had been with him, influencing him all his life. They heartened him now, sealed the sense of meaning in him.

---

7. **Toronto** also holds a marathon race.
8. **At Marathon,** some twenty-six miles from Athens, the Greeks defeated the Persians in 490 B.C. According to legend, **Pheidippides**\'fai ▴dĭ•pĭ 'dēz\ ran to Athens to bring news of the victory.

A sentry challenged him as the road leveled out into the plains, and Nilson, not knowing the password, figured that this was the place, if there ever was a place, for him to collapse. Pheidippides, finishing the first Marathon, had cried, "Rejoice, we conquer!" but Pete Nilson, thinking this, and finishing his own run, only said in a kind of prayer, "Hey, buddy, don't shoot," and knelt and quietly fell forward in the dust.

He didn't remember exactly what he said to them, but they took him with surprising quickness to another lieutenant colonel. And the miracle was not done yet. He could not believe it then; all the rest of his life, he could hardly believe it. They believed him: they believed him, and some place about him as he sat stupefied on a canvas stool in a tent, he heard all around him, in the first light, the sound of armor beginning to move, the clank and roar of the tanks.

A staff sergeant tried to explain to him. "Look," the sergeant said, "nobody comes down here in the shape you're in to lie to somebody else. You see?" Especially the feet, the sergeant thought.

But all Nilson did was sit on the canvas stool and stare.

"Look," the sergeant said again, "you'll get something big for this. Don't you catch?"

Nilson stared right at him. He was beginning to catch, but it would be a long time, if ever, before he could make anyone understand. The big thing, the most important thing in his life, was that he had come down here, without credentials of any sort, and they had believed him. The citation, the medal, nothing was ever going to mean that much.

"Look," the sergeant said. "They're getting you a doctor. You want anything now, though? Coffee or something?" Don't the guy know about his feet, he thought.

The little froth at his lips still, Nilson shook his head slightly. He looked like a madman, and the sergeant thought that maybe he was mad. But all Nilson was doing was sitting there listening to the roar—the clamor that was the

sound of salvation for a lot of men who couldn't hear it, yet—and thinking that he, Pete Nilson, had actually set it in motion. He didn't want anything right now, only to sit there and listen.

---

## I

### THE CONTINUITY OF EXPERIENCE

Through its reference to the Marathon race, this story suggests a continuity of human experience from Greek times down to the present. The exploit of the Greek runner Pheidippides has become a legend of self-sacrificing heroism. Although the present account of Peter Nilson's ordeal is a fictional one, it suggests that the spirit of such heroism survives in our own day. As long as there are wars, pressures will be brought to bear on individual soldiers, offering them the opportunity to respond with courage or with weakness.

### II

### IMPLICATIONS

A. The outcome of this story is delayed until the last few minutes. The author maintains suspense by raising doubts about Nilson's chances of success. What does each of the following quotations from the story tell you about his chances?

1. " 'Still,' the officer said, 'you're the best we have. Good luck.' "

2. " 'No, I don't,' the other sergeant said. 'Even if he gets through their patrols, he'll drop before he gets to our people—or quit and go hide.' "

3. "Not fear but a sense of futility took him; a sense of his own littleness in the night and the desert that was also the enemy's country."

4. "He wondered if this, too, would be to no purpose; if some burial detail, an indefinite number of days from now, would find his shapeless and twisted body some place along this road."

5. "It seemed to him that he had never been so exhausted as now, and his mind sought for excuses to stop."

6. "Some sort of anger formed in him. . . . He realized it might even be at himself; then that it was at himself. . . . all his life, his efforts had been directed obscurely and even deviously toward trying to achieve a sense of usefulness. . . . And now that he was close to it, he had almost rejected it."

**B.** Three of the quotations above reveal a struggle in Nilson separate from the physical struggles of his ordeal. Understanding what it is will help you form an opinion about the following statements. Give your reasons for supporting or disagreeing with them.

**1.** The real pressure that Nilson is fighting against is not physical but mental. It is his sense of continuous failure.

**2.** People need to know how far they have gone and how far they have yet to go in order to endure fatigue.

**3.** The fact that they believe him when he arrives is more important to Peter than the fact of having got there at all. Their belief restores to him his self-respect.

**4.** When people are under great strain, their bodies dominate their minds.

### III
### TECHNIQUES

*Theme*

The theme of this story might be stated as a man's response to pressures of personal anxiety under conditions of war. Nowhere in the story is it mentioned where the war is taking place, who the enemy are, or even what war it is. What do you think the author is implying about his theme by omitting these specific details?

*Style*

Compare the style of writing in "Going to Run All Night" with the style in "The Open Window." Which is more like a newspaper account of the happenings? Without rereading either of the stories, decide which has left a more vivid impression on your mind. What connection is there between the sharpness of impression and the kind of language in the two stories? Try to explain the effect that the style in each had on your response to the story.

*Identification*

"Going to Run All Night" is the story of an ordeal. Few of its readers ever have or ever will go through a comparable experience, and yet it is almost impossible not to identify with Peter Nilson as he undertakes his task. What reactions did you have to the following elements of his experience, and how did that reaction lead you to identify yourself with him?

**1.** His immediate willingness to try the run.

**2.** His fear of failing.

**3.** His physical suffering.

Most people have a secret desire to perform, just once in their lives, some heroic deed. If you have ever experienced this desire, how do you think it affected your feelings about Peter Nilson?

### IV
### WORDS

**A.** Using words figuratively with originality and appropriateness is basic to vocabulary growth. In "The Open Window" a character assumes that "total strangers are *hungry* for details." What does the word *hungry* suggest? Comment on the effectiveness of the following expressions. What associations do the words convey? What figure, if any, is used?

> whirl of apologies; self-possessed young girl of fifteen; danger which intermittently killed some of them; sweat bathed him; road levelled under him; controlled abandon; shook his head not unlike an animal trapped and bewildered.

**B.** From context determine the meaning of the italicized words:

**1.** flatter the niece without unduly *discounting* the aunt that was to come.

**2.** He was preparing to *migrate* to this retreat.

**3.** It was certainly an unfortunate *coincidence* that he should have paid his visit on this tragic anniversary.

**4.** He was driven to the *incredible* conclusion that finally and at last he had come to be of value. . . . He ran with an almost *incredible* lack of sound.

**5.** We can break at dawn, if we can *synchronize* our attack with some sort of aid coming from our main forces.

**C.** What do the roots in the following pairs of words mean: *progress-succession* ("a succession of total strangers"); *immigrant-migrate* ("to migrate to this rural retreat"); *reduction-introduction* ("letters of introduction"); *geology-apology* ("a whirl of apologies for being late"); *annual-anniversary* ("his visit on this tragic anniversary"); *illusion-delusion* ("the tolerably widespread delusion that total strangers and chance acquaintances are hungry for the least detail of one's ailments"); *elision-collision* ("to avoid imminent collision").

◆
There he hung shivering and past knowing
what more he could ever do.

# The
# Vertical Ladder

### WILLIAM SANSOM

As he felt the first watery eggs of sweat moistening the palms of his hands, as with every rung higher his body seemed to weigh more heavily, this young man, Flegg, regretted in sudden desperation, but still in vain, the irresponsible events that had thrust him into his present precarious climb. Here he was, isolated on a vertical iron ladder flat to the side of a gas tank, and bound now to climb higher and higher until he reached the vertiginous[1] skyward summit.

How could he ever have wished this on himself? How easy it had been to laugh away his cautionary fears on the firm ground! Now he would give the very hands that clung to the ladder for a safe conduct to solid earth.

It had been a strong spring day, abruptly as warm as midsummer. The sun flooded the parks and streets with sudden heat—Flegg and his friends had felt stifled in their thick winter clothes. The green glare of the new leaves everywhere struck the eye too fiercely, the air seemed almost sticky from the exhalations of buds and swelling resins. Cold winter senses were overcome—the girls had complained of headaches, and their thoughts had grown confused and as uncomfortable as the wool underneath against their skins. They had wandered out from the park by a back gate into an area of back streets.

The houses there were small and old, some of them already falling into disrepair; short streets, cobbles,[2] narrow sidewalks, and the only shops a tobacconist or a desolate drugstore to color the gray—it was the outcrop of some industrial undertaking beyond. At first these quiet, almost deserted streets had seemed more restful than the park; but soon a dusty air of peeling plaster and powdering brick, the dark windows and the dry stone steps, the very dryness altogether, had proved more wearying than before, so that when suddenly the houses had ended and the ground had opened to reveal the yards of a disused gasworks, Flegg and his friends had welcomed the green of nettles and milkwort that grew among the scrap iron and broken brick.

They walked out into the wasteland, the two girls and Flegg and the other two boys, and stood presently before the old gas tank itself. Among the ruined sheds this was the only structure still whole; it still predominated over the yards, towering high above other buildings for hundreds of feet around. So they threw bricks against its rusted sides.

The rust flew off in flakes, and the iron rang dully. Flegg, who wished to excel in the eyes of the dark-haired girl, began throwing bricks higher than the others, at the same time lobbing them, to suggest that he knew something of grenade throwing, claiming for himself vicariously the glamour of a uniform. He felt the girl's eyes follow his shoulders; his shoulders broadened. She had black eyes, unshadowed beneath short, wide-awake lids, as bright as a boy's eyes; her lips pouted with difficulty over a scramble of irregular teeth, so that it often looked as if she were laughing; she always frowned, and Flegg liked her earnest, purposeful expression. Altogether she seemed a wide-awake girl, who would be the first to appreciate an active sort of man. Now she frowned and shouted, "Bet you can't climb as high as you can throw!"

Copyright © 1960 by William Sansom. From *The Stories of William Sansom* by William Sansom, by permission of Little, Brown & Company, in association with The Atlantic Monthly Press.

1. **vertiginous**\vər ▲tĭj·ə·nəs\ causing dizziness.
2. **cobbles,** cobblestones with which the streets were paved.

Then there began one of those uneasy jokes, innocent at first, that, taken seriously, can accumulate a hysterical volume of spite. Everyone recognizes this underlying unpleasantness—it is plainly felt. But just because of this, the joke must at all costs be pressed forward; one becomes frightened, one laughs all the louder, pressing to drown the embarrassments of danger and guilt.

The third boy shouted instantly, "Course he can't. He can't climb no higher than himself." Flegg turned round, scoffing, so that the girl shouted again, laughing shrilly and pointing upward. Already all five of them felt uneasy. Then in quick succession, all in a few seconds, the third boy repeated, "Course he can't." Flegg said, "Climb to the top of anything." The other boy said, "Climb to the top of my Aunt Fanny." The girl said, "Climb to the top of the gas tank then."

Flegg said, "That's nothing." And the girl, pressing on then as she had to, suddenly introduced the inevitable detail that made these suppositions into fact: "Go on then, climb it. Here—tie my hanky on the top. Tie my flag on the top."

Even then Flegg had a second's chance. It occurred to him instantly that he could laugh it off; but hysterical emphasis now possessed the girl's face—she was dancing up and down and clapping her hands insistently—and this confused Flegg. He began stuttering after the right words. But the words refused to come. At all costs he had to cover his stuttering. So: "Off we go then!" he said. And he turned to the gas tank.

It was not, after all, so very high. It was hardly a full-sized tank, its trellised[3] iron toprail would have stood level with the roof coping[4] of a five- or six-story tenement. Until then Flegg had seen the gas tank as a rough mass of iron, but now every detail sprang into abrupt definition. He studied it intently, alertly considering its size and every feature of stability: the brown, rusted iron sheeting smeared here and there with red lead; a curious buckling that sometimes deflated its curved bulk,

as though a vacuum were collapsing it from within; the ladders scaling the sides flush with the sheeting; the grid of girders, a complexity of struts,[5] the bolting.

There were two ladders, one Jacob's ladder[6] clamped fast to the side, another that was more of a staircase, zigzagging up the belly of the tank in easy gradients[7] and provided with a safety rail. This must have been erected later as a substitute for the Jacob's ladder, which demanded an unnecessarily stringent climb and was now in fact in disuse, for some twenty feet of its lower rungs had been torn away. However, there was apparently some painting in progress, for a painter's wooden ladder had been propped beneath with its top reaching to the undamaged bottom of the vertical ladder —the ascent was thus serviceable again. Flegg looked quickly at the foot of the wooden ladder—was it well grounded?—and then at its top farther up—was this secure?—and then way to the top, screwing his eyes to note any fault in the iron rungs reaching innumerably and indistinctly to the summit platform.

Flegg, rapidly assessing these structures, never stopped sauntering forward. He was committed, and so while deliberately sauntering to appear thus the more at ease, he knew that he must never hesitate. The two boys and his own girl kept up a chorus of encouraging abuse. "How I climbed Mount Everest," they shouted. "He'll come down quicker'n he went up." "Mind you don't bang your head on a harp, Sir Galahad."[8] But the second girl had remained quiet throughout; she was already frightened, sensing instantly that the guilt for some tragedy was hers alone—although she never had opened her mouth. Now she chewed passionately on gum that kept her jaws firm and circling.

Suddenly the chorus rose shriller. Flegg had

---

3. **trellised**\ˈtrĕl·əst\ having a frame of latticework.
4. **coping**\ˈkō·piŋ\ a finishing cap to a wall.
5. **struts**, bars for bracing.
6. **Jacob's ladder**, a flat ladder with iron rungs.
7. **gradients**\ˈgrād·ē·əntz\ angles of slope.
8. **Sir Galahad**, a knight of King Arthur's Round Table. In this context the name means gentlemanly.

485

veered slightly toward the safer staircase. His eyes naturally had questioned this along with the rest of the gas tank, and almost unconsciously his footsteps had veered in the direction of his eyes. Then this instinct had emerged into full consciousness: perhaps he could use the staircase—no one actually had mentioned the Jacob's ladder; there might yet be a chance. But the quick eyes behind him had seen, and immediately the chorus rose: "No, you don't!" "Not up those sissy stairs!"

Flegg switched his course by only the fraction that turned him again to the perpendicular ladder. "Who's talking about stairs?" he shouted back.

Behind him they still kept up a din, still kept up to pitch, worrying at him viciously. "Look at him, he doesn't know which way to go—he's like a duck's uncle without an aunt."

So that Flegg realized finally there was no alternative. He had to climb the tank by the vertical ladder. And as soon as this was finally settled, the doubt cleared from his mind. He braced his shoulders and suddenly found himself really making light of the job. "After all," he thought, "it isn't so high. Why should I worry? Hundreds of men climb such ladders every day, no one falls, the ladders are clamped as safe as houses." He began to smile within himself at his earlier perturbations.

Added to this, the girl now ran up to him and handed him her handkerchief. As her black eyes frowned a smile at him, he saw that her expression no longer held its vicious, laughing scorn, but had grown softer, with a look of real encouragement and even admiration. "Here's your flag," she said. And then she even added, "Tell you what—you don't really have to go! I'll believe you!" But this came too late. Flegg had accepted the climb—it was fact, and already he felt something of an exhilarating glow of glory. He took the handkerchief, blew the girl a dramatic kiss, and started up the lowest rungs of the wooden ladder at a run.

This painter's ladder was placed at a comfortable slant. Nevertheless, Flegg had climbed only some ten feet—what might correspond to the top of a first-floor window—when he began to slow up; he stopped running and gripped harder at the rungs above and placed his feet more firmly on the unseen bars below. Although he had not yet measured his distance from the ground, somehow he sensed distinctly that he was already unnaturally high, with nothing but air and a precarious skeleton of wooden bars between him and the receding ground. He felt independent of solid support; yet, according to his eyes, which stared straight forward at the iron sheeting, he might have been still standing on the lowest rungs by the ground. The sensation of height infected him strongly; it had become an urgent necessity to maintain a balance; each muscle of his body became unnaturally alert. This was not an unpleasant feeling; he almost enjoyed a new athletic command of every precarious movement. He climbed then methodically until he reached the ladder top and the first of the perpendicular iron rungs.

Here for a moment Flegg paused. He rested his knees against the last three steps of the safely slanting wooden ladder; he grasped the two side supports of the rusted iron that led so straightly upward. His knees then clung to the motherly wood; his hands felt the iron cold and gritty. The rust powdered off and smeared him with its red, and one large scrap flaked off and fell onto his face as he looked upward. He wanted to brush this away from his eye, but the impulse was, to his surprise, much less powerful than the vicelike will that clutched his hand to the iron support. His hand remained firmly gripping the iron; he had to shake off the rust flake with a jerk of his head. Even then, this sharp movement nearly unbalanced him, and his stomach gulped coldly with sudden shock. He settled his knees more firmly against the wood; and though he forced himself to laugh at this sudden fear, so that in some measure his poise did really return, nevertheless he did not alter the awkward knock-kneed position of his legs patently clinging for safety. With all this, he had scarcely paused. Now he pulled at the stanchions[9] of the iron ladder; they were as firm as if they had been driven into rock.

He looked up, following the dizzying rise of the rungs to the skyline. From this angle, flat against the iron sheeting, the gas tank appeared higher than before. The blue sky seemed to descend and almost touch it. The redness of the rust dissolved into a deepening gray shadow; the distant, curved summit loomed black and high. Although it was immensely stable, as seen in rounded perspective from a few yards away, there against the side it appeared top-heavy, so that this huge segment of sheet iron seemed to have lost the support of its invisible complement behind—the support that was now unseen and therefore unfelt—and Flegg imagined despite himself that the entire erection had become unsteady, that quite possibly the gas tank might suddenly blow over like a gigantic, top-heavy sail. He lowered his eyes quickly and concentrated on the hands gripped on the ladder before him. He began to climb.

From below, there still rose a few cries from the boys. But the girl had stopped shouting—probably she was following Flegg's every step with admiring eyes. He imagined again her frown and her peculiarly pouting mouth, and from this image drew new strength with which he clutched the rungs more eagerly. But now he noticed that the cries had begun to ring with an unpleasant new echo, as though they were already far off. And Flegg could not so easily distinguish their words. Even at this height he seemed to have penetrated into a distinct stratum[10] of separate air, for it was certainly cooler, and for the first time that day he felt the light fanning of a wind.

He looked down. His friends appeared shockingly small. Their bodies had disappeared, and he saw only their upturned faces. He wanted to wave to demonstrate in some way a carefree attitude; but then instantly he felt frustrated as his hands refused to unlock their grip. He turned to the rungs again, with the smile dying on his lips.

He swallowed uneasily and continued to tread slowly upward, hand after hand, foot after foot. He had climbed ten rungs of the iron ladder when his hands first began to feel moist; when suddenly, as though a catastrophe had overtaken him not gradually but in one overpowering second, he realized that he was afraid—incontrovertibly. He could conceal it no longer; he admitted it all over his body. His hands gripped with pitiable eagerness; they were now alert to a point of shivering, as though the nerves inside them had been forced taut for so long that now they had burst beyond their strained tegument.[11] His feet no longer trod firmly on the rungs beneath, but first stepped for their place timorously, then glued themselves to the iron. In this way his body lost much of its poise; these nerves and muscles in his two legs and two arms seemed to work independently, no longer integrated with the rhythm of his body, but moving with the dangerous, the unwilled jerk of crippled limbs.

His body hung slack away from the ladder, with nothing beneath it but a thirty-foot drop to the ground; only his hands and feet were fed with the security of an attachment—most of him lay off the ladder, hanging in space. His arms revolted at the strain of their unfamiliar angle, as though they were flies' feet denying all natural laws. For the first time, as the fear took hold of him, he felt that what he had attempted was impossible. He never could achieve the top. If at this height of only thirty feet—as it were, three stories of a building—he felt afraid, what would he feel at sixty feet? Yet he trod heavily up. He was afraid, but not desperate. He dreaded each step, yet forced himself to believe that at some time it would be over; it could not take long.

A memory crossed his mind. It occurred vividly, then flashed away, for his eyes and mind were continually concentrated on the

---

9. **stanchions**\ˈstän·chənz\ upright bars of the ladder.
10. **stratum**\ˈsträt·əm\ a layer.
11. **tegument**\ˈtĕg·yə·mənt\ covering.

487

rusted iron bars and white knuckles of his hands. But for an instant he remembered waking up long ago in the nursery and seeing that the windows were light, as if they reflected a coldness of moonlight. Only they were not so much lit by light as by a sensation of space. The windows seemed to echo with space. He crawled out of bed and climbed onto a chair that stood below the window. It was as he had thought: outside there was space, nothing else—a limitless area of space. Yet this was not unnatural, for soon his logical eyes supplied for what had at first appeared an impossible infinity the later image of a perfectly reasonable flood. A vast plain of still water continued as far as his eyes could see. The tennis courts and the houses beyond had disappeared; they were quite submerged. Motionless water spread out immeasurably to the distant arched horizon all around. It lapped silently at the sides of the house, and in the light of an unseen moon winked and washed darkly, concealing great beasts of mystery beneath its black, calm surface.

This water attracted him; he wished to jump into it from the window and immerse himself in it and allow his head to sink slowly under. However, he was perched too high. He felt, alone at the window, infinitely high, so that the flood seemed to lie in miniature at a great distance below, as later in life when he was ill he saw the objects of his bedroom grow small and infinitely remote in the fevered reflection behind his eyes. Isolated at the little window, he was frightened by the emptiness surrounding him—only the sky and the water and the marooned stone wall of the house. He was terrified, yet drawn down by dread and desire.

Then a battleship sailed by. He awakened, saved by the appearance of the battleship. And now, on the ladder, he had a sudden hope that something as large and stable would intervene again to help him.

But ten rungs farther up he began to sweat more violently than ever. His hands streamed with wet rust, the flesh inside his thighs blenched. Another flake of rust fell on his fore-

head; this time it stuck in the wetness. He felt physically exhausted. Fear was draining all his strength, and the precarious position of his body demanded an awkward physical effort. From his outstretched arms suspended most of the weight of his body. Each stressed muscle ached. His body weighed more heavily at each step upward; it sagged beneath his arms like a leaden sack. His legs no longer provided their adequate support; it seemed as though they needed every pull of their muscles to force themselves, as independent limbs, close to the ladder. The wind blew faster. It dragged now at his coat, it blew its space about him, it echoed silently a lonely spaciousness. "Don't look down," the blood whispered in his temples. "Don't look down, *don't look down.*"

Three quarters up the tank and fifty feet from the ground, Flegg grew desperate. Every other consideration suddenly left him. He wanted only to reach the ground as quickly as possible—only that. Nothing else mattered. He stopped climbing and clung to the ladder panting. Very slowly, lowering his eyes carefully so that he could raise them instantly if he saw too much, he looked down a rung, and another past his armpit, past his waist, and focused on the ground below. He looked quickly up again.

He pressed himself to the ladder. Tears started in his eyes. For a moment they reeled red with giddiness. He closed them, shutting out everything. Then instantly opened them, afraid that something might happen. He must watch his hands, watch the bars, watch the rusted iron sheeting itself; no movement should escape him. The struts might come creaking loose, the whole edifice might sway over. Although a fading reason told him that the gas tank had remained firm for years and was still steady as a cliff, his horrified senses suspected that this was the one moment in the building's life when a wind would blow that was too strong for it, some defective strut would snap, the whole structure would heel over and go crashing to the ground. This image became so clear that he could see the sheets of iron buckling and folding like cloth as the huge weight sank to the earth.

The ground had receded horribly; the drop now appeared terrifying, out of all proportion to this height he had reached. From the ground such a height would have appeared unnoteworthy. But now, looking down, the distance seemed to have doubled. Each object familiar to his everyday eyes—his friends, the lampposts, a brick wall, the sidewalk—all these had grown infinitely small. His senses demanded that these objects should be of a certain accustomed size. Alternatively, the world of chimneys and attic windows and roof copings would grow unpleasantly giant as his sidewalk-bred eyes approached. Even now the iron sheeting that stretched to either side and above and below seemed to have grown; he was lost among such huge, smooth dimensions —grown smaller himself, and clinging now like a child lost on some monstrous desert of red dust.

These unfamiliarities shocked his nerves more than the danger of falling. The sense of isolation was overpowering. All things were suddenly alien. Yet exposed on the iron spaces, with the unending winds blowing round him, among such free things—he felt shut in. Trembling and panting, so that he stifled himself with the shortness of his own breath, he took the first step downward.

A commotion began below. A confusion of cries came drifting up to him. Above all he could hear the single voice of the girl who so far had kept quiet. She was screaming high, a shrill scream that rose in the air incisively, like a gull's shriek. "Put it back, put it back, put it back!" the scream seemed to say. So that Flegg, thinking that these cries were to warn him of some new danger apparent only from the ground, gripped himself onto the ladder and looked down again. He glanced down for only a fraction of a second, but in that time saw enough. He saw that the quiet girl was screaming and pointing to the base of the iron ladder. He saw the others crowding round her, gesticulating. He saw that she really had been

crying, "Put it back!" And he realized now what the words meant. Someone had removed the painter's ladder.

It lay clearly on the ground, outlined like a child's drawing of a ladder. The boys must have seen his first step downward, and then, from fun or from spite, they had removed his only means of retreat. He remembered that from the base of the iron ladder to the ground the drop fell twenty feet. He considered quickly descending and appealing from the bottom of the ladder, but foresaw that for precious minutes they would jeer and argue, refusing to replace the ladder, and he felt then that he never could risk these minutes, unnerved, with his strength failing.

Besides, he already had noticed that the whole group was wandering off. The boys were driving the quiet girl away, now more concerned with her than with Flegg. The quiet girl's sense of guilt had been brought to a head by the removal of the ladder. Now she was hysterically terrified. She was yelling to them to put the ladder back. She—only she, the passive one—sensed the terror that awaited them all. But her screams defeated their own purpose. They had altogether distracted the attention of the others; now it was fun to provoke more screams, to encourage this new distraction—and they forgot about Flegg far up and beyond them. They were wandering away. They were abandoning him, casually unconcerned that he was alone and helpless up in his wide prison of rust. His heart cried out for them to stay. He forgot their scorn in new and terrible torments of self-pity. An uneasy feeling lumped his throat; his eyes smarted with dry tears.

But they were wandering away. There was no retreat. They did not even know he was in difficulties. So Flegg had no option but to climb higher. Desperately he tried to shake off his fear; he actually shook his head. Then he stared hard at the rungs immediately facing his eyes and tried to imagine that he was not high up at all. He lifted himself tentatively by one rung, then by another, and in this way dragged himself higher and higher—until he must have been some ten rungs from the top, over the fifth story of a house, with now perhaps only one more story to climb. He imagined that he might then be approaching the summit platform, and to measure this last distance he looked up.

He looked up and heaved. He felt for the first time panicked beyond desperation, wildly, violently loose. He almost let go. His senses screamed to let go, yet his hands refused to open. He was stretched on a rack[12] made by these hands that would not unlock their grip and by the panic desire to drop. The nerves left his hands, so that they might have been dried bones of fingers gripped round the rungs —hooks of bone fixed perhaps strongly enough to cling on, or perhaps ready at some moment of pressure to uncurl and straighten to a drop. His insteps pricked with cold cramp. The sweat sickened him. He shivered, grew giddy, and flung himself froglike onto the narrow iron ladder.

The sight of the top of the gas tank had proved more frightful than the appearance of the drop beneath. There lay about it a sense, not of material danger, not of the risk of falling, but of something removed and inhuman— a sense of appalling isolation. It echoed its elemental iron aloofness; a wind blew round it that never had known the warmth of flesh or the softness of green fibers. Its blind eyes were raised above the world. It might have been the eyeless iron vizor[13] of an ancient god. It touched against the sky, having risen in awful perpendicular to this isolation, solitary as the gray gannet cliffs[14] that mark the end of the northern world. It was immeasurably old, outside the connotation of time; it was nothing human, only washed by the high weather, echoing with wind, visited never, and silently alone.

And in this summit Flegg measured clearly the full distance of his climb. This close skyline emphasized the whirling space beneath him. He clearly saw a man fall through this space, spread-eagling, to smash with the sick-

ening force of a locomotive on the stone beneath. The man turned slowly in the air, yet his thoughts raced faster than he fell.

Flegg, clutching his body close to the rust, made small weeping sounds through his mouth. Shivering, shuddering, he began to tread up again, working his knees and elbows outward like a frog so that his stomach could feel the firm rungs. Were they firm? His ears filled with a hot roaring; he hurried himself; he began to scramble, wrenching at his last strength, whispering urgent, meaningless words to himself like the swift whispers that close in on a nightmare. A huge weight pulled at him, dragging him to drop.

He climbed higher. He reached the top rung —and found his face staring still at a wall of red rust. He looked, wild with terror. It was the top rung! The ladder had ended! Yet—no platform. The real top rungs were missing. The platform jutted five impassable feet above. Flegg stared dumbly, circling his head like a lost animal. Then he jammed his legs in the lower rungs and his arms past the elbows to the armpits through the top rungs, and there he hung shivering and past knowing what more he could ever do.

---

I

### CHALLENGED BY FRIENDS

Flegg is pressured into an action that he really does not want to take by the dare of the dark-haired girl he admires. Suddenly an innocent game of rock throwing takes an unexpected turn. He feels that his manhood is being challenged. He moves into a situation from which his whole being recoils. Readers may have been involved in similar situations themselves. Why is it so important to individuals to look good in the eyes of other people that they allow themselves to be forced into unpleasant or

---

12. **rack,** an instrument of torture on which the body was stretched.
13. **vizor**\ˈvaɪ·zər\ the front piece of a helmet.
14. **gannet cliffs,** cliffs inhabited by gannets, large fish-eating birds.

untenable positions? Is Sansom saying something about the nature of people or about the society in which they live or both?

## II
### IMPLICATIONS

How do the following quotations relate to the story and to your own experiences?

**1.** "Then there began one of those uneasy jokes, innocent at first, that, taken seriously, can accumulate a hysterical volume of spite."

**2.** "He wanted to brush [the flake] away from his eye, but the impulse was, to his surprise, much less powerful than the vicelike will that clutched his hand to the iron support."

**3.** "He looked up, following the dizzying rise of the rungs to the skyline. From this angle, flat against the iron sheeting, the gas tank appeared higher than before."

**4.** "He was afraid, but not desperate. He dreaded each step, yet forced himself to believe that at some time it would be over . . . ."

**5.** "Fear was draining all his strength . . . ."

**6.** ". . . his horrified senses suspected that this was the one moment in the building's life when a wind would blow that was too strong for it, some defective strut would snap, the whole structure would heel over and go crashing to the ground."

## III
### TECHNIQUES

*Theme*

Most readers live with Flegg as he climbs; some so intensely that they actually have sensations of panic. What were your reactions as you read the story? How would you define the theme? What details from the story support your statement?

*Style*

This story has a rough, uneven, almost harsh quality that you can perhaps feel by rereading a paragraph from it aloud and following it with a paragraph from "Going to Run All Night." In Sylvester's story the language flows smoothly and easily. "The Vertical Ladder" has a hard, staccato quality. Is this appropriate to the subject matter? Can you discover particular uses of language that give it this quality?

## IV
### WORDS

**A.** Some of Flegg's companions shouted teasingly that he would later write about his conquest of Mount Everest. They called him Sir Galahad. Mount Everest is the highest mountain on Earth and is the ultimate challenge to mountain climbers. In Arthurian legend, Sir Galahad was the pure and noble knight who succeeded in his quest for the Holy Grail. A reference to a place or a thing like Mount Everest or to a person like Sir Galahad with which the reader or listener is presumed to be familiar is called an *allusion*. Allusions have their origins in history, folklore, the Bible, and literature, to name a few sources. Our daily language abounds in these familiar references; for example, "solid as the rock of Gibraltar," "poor as Job," "honest Abe," "the wisdom of Solomon," and "the Midas touch." Other allusions appear in the sentences which follow. Can you identify the source of each?

**1.** Like the phoenix, he will rise out of the ashes of defeat.

**2.** Don't be enchanted by her Siren song.

**3.** That doubting Thomas accepts nothing on faith alone.

**4.** This project has been his Golgotha.

**5.** Like Cassius, he has a lean and hungry look.

**6.** Johnny has a Dr. Jekyll and Mr. Hyde personality.

**B.** Though in everyday language we do not speak poetry, we do use *metaphors*, which are often used in poetry. When the author of "The Vertical Ladder" refers to "the belly of the tank," he is using a metaphor. Since strictly speaking, an inanimate object cannot have a belly, the author is implying a comparison between the tank and an animal. Through metaphor, *belly* has come to mean an object or a surface rounded or curved like the human stomach or the undersurface of an animal. Elsewhere in the story, the writer mentions "sheet of iron," meaning thin layers of iron. The comparison here is obvious: the layers are thin like sheets. During the winter, we speak of a "sheet of ice." Here are several other common metaphors: *face of a clock, foot of a mountain, legs of a chair, eye of a hurricane,* and *family tree.* Can you think of others?

Most people have something they cherish
above all else: a pet, another person, their job,
a particular ability. James Thurber creates
a quiet little man who cherishes his job,
a man so meek that he seems incapable
of defending himself. But when his position
is threatened, he rises to the challenge.
Suddenly there is an unexpected struggle to see
who will end up sitting in the catbird seat—
who will end up sitting pretty.

# The Catbird Seat

## JAMES THURBER

Mr. Martin bought the pack of Camels on Monday night in the most crowded cigar store on Broadway. It was theater time and seven or eight men were buying cigarettes. The clerk didn't even glance at Mr. Martin, who put the pack in his overcoat pocket and went out. If any of the staff at F & S had seen him buy the cigarettes, they would have been astonished, for it was generally known that Mr. Martin did not smoke, and never had. No one saw him.

It was just a week to the day since Mr. Martin had decided to rub out Mrs. Ulgine Barrows. The term "rub out" pleased him because it suggested nothing more than the correction of an error—in this case an error of Mr. Fitweiler. Mr. Martin had spent each night of the past week working out his plan and examining it. As he walked home now he went over it again. For the hundredth time he resented the element of imprecision, the margin of guesswork that entered into the business. The project as he had worked it out was casual and bold, the risks were considerable. Something

Copyright 1945 James Thurber. Copyright © 1973 Helen W. Thurber and Rosemary Thurber Sauers. From *The Thurber Carnival*, published by Harper & Row. Originally printed in *The New Yorker*.

might go wrong anywhere along the line. And therein lay the cunning of his scheme. No one would ever see in it the cautious, painstaking hand of Erwin Martin, head of the filing department at F & S, of whom Mr. Fitweiler had once said, "Man is fallible but Martin isn't." No one would see his hand, that is, unless it were caught in the act.

Sitting in his apartment, drinking a glass of milk, Mr. Martin reviewed his case against Mrs. Ulgine Barrows, as he had every night for seven nights. He began at the beginning. Her quacking voice and braying laugh had first profaned the halls of F & S on March 7, 1941 (Mr. Martin had a head for dates). Old Roberts, the personnel chief, had introduced her as the newly appointed special adviser to the president of the firm, Mr. Fitweiler. The woman had appalled Mr. Martin instantly, but he hadn't shown it. He had given her his dry hand, a look of studious concentration, and a faint smile. "Well," she had said, looking at the papers on his desk, "are you lifting the oxcart out of the ditch?" As Mr. Martin recalled that moment, over his milk, he squirmed slightly. He must keep his mind on her crimes as a special adviser, not on her peccadillos as a personality. This he found difficult to do, in spite of entering an objection and sustaining it. The faults of the woman as a woman kept chattering on in his mind like an unruly witness. She had, for almost two years now, baited him. In the halls, in the elevator, even in his own office, into which she romped now and then like a circus horse, she was constantly shouting these silly questions at him. "Are you lifting the oxcart out of the ditch? Are you tearing up the pea patch? Are you hollering down the rain barrel? Are you scraping around the bottom of the pickle barrel? Are you sitting in the catbird seat?"

It was Joey Hart, one of Mr. Martin's two assistants, who had explained what the gibberish meant. "She must be a Dodger fan," he had said. "Red Barber announces the Dodger games over the radio and he uses those expressions

—picked 'em up down South."[1] Joey had gone on to explain one or two. "Tearing up the pea patch" meant going on a rampage; "sitting in the catbird seat" meant sitting pretty, like a batter with three balls and no strikes on him. Mr. Martin dismissed all this with an effort. It had been annoying, it had driven him near to distraction, but he was too solid a man to be moved to murder by anything so childish. It was fortunate, he reflected as he passed on to the important charges against Mrs. Barrows, that he had stood up under it so well. He had maintained always an outward appearance of polite tolerance. "Why, I even believe you like the woman," Miss Paird, his other assistant, had once said to him. He had simply smiled.

A gavel rapped in Mr. Martin's mind and the case proper was resumed. Mrs. Ulgine Barrows stood charged with willful, blatant, and persistent attempts to destroy the efficiency and system of F & S. It was competent, material, and relevant to review her advent and rise to power.[2] Mr. Martin had got the story from Miss Paird, who seemed always able to find things out. According to her, Mrs. Barrows had met Mr. Fitweiler at a party, where she had rescued him from the embraces of a powerfully built drunken man who had mistaken the president of F & S for a famous retired Middle Western football coach. She had led him to a sofa and somehow worked upon him a monstrous magic. The aging gentleman had jumped to the conclusion there and then that this was a woman of singular attainments, equipped to bring out the best in him and in the firm. A week later he had introduced her into F & S as his special adviser. On that day confusion got its foot in the door. After Miss Tyson, Mr. Brundage, and Mr. Bartlett had been fired and Mr. Munson had taken his hat and stalked out, mailing in his resignation later, old Roberts had been emboldened to speak to Mr. Fitweiler. He mentioned that Mr. Munson's department had been "a little disrupted" and hadn't they perhaps better resume the old system there? Mr. Fitweiler had said certainly not. He had the greatest faith in Mrs. Barrows' ideas. "They require

a little seasoning, a little seasoning, is all," he had added. Mr. Roberts had given it up. Mr. Martin reviewed in detail all the changes wrought by Mrs. Barrows. She had begun chipping at the cornices of the firm's edifice and now she was swinging at the foundation stones with a pickaxe.

Mr. Martin came now, in his summing up, to the afternoon of Monday, November 2, 1942—just one week ago. On that day, at 3 P.M., Mrs. Barrows had bounced into his office. "Boo!" she had yelled. "Are you scraping around the bottom of the pickle barrel?" Mr. Martin had looked at her from under his green eyeshade, saying nothing. She had begun to wander about the office, taking it in with her great, popping eyes. "Do you really need *all* these filing cabinets?" she had demanded suddenly, Mr. Martin's heart had jumped. "Each of these files," he had said, keeping his voice even, "plays an indispensable part in the system of F & S." She had brayed at him, "Well, don't tear up the pea patch!" and gone to the door. From there she had bawled, "But you sure have got a lot of fine scrap in here!" Mr. Martin could no longer doubt that the finger was on his beloved department.[3] Her pickaxe was on the upswing, poised for the first blow. It had not come yet; he had received no blue memo from the enchanted Mr. Fitweiler bearing nonsensical instructions deriving from the obscene woman. But there was no doubt in Mr. Martin's mind that one would be forthcoming. He must act quickly. Already a precious week had gone by. Mr. Martin stood up in his living room, still holding his milk glass. "Gentlemen of the jury," he said to himself, "I demand the death penalty for this horrible person."

---

1. The reference is to the Brooklyn Dodger team before the organization was moved to Los Angeles. **Red Barber** announced the Brooklyn Dodger games and had a wide following in New York.
2. In using the phrase "**competent, material, and relevant,**" Mr. Martin is using legalistic terminology.
3. **That the finger was on his beloved department,** that the finger of doom or fate, as personified by Mrs. Barrows, was now pointing at his department.

The next day Mr. Martin followed his routine, as usual. He polished his glasses more often and once sharpened an already sharp pencil, but not even Miss Paird noticed. Only once did he catch sight of his victim; she swept past him in the hall with a patronizing "Hi!" At five-thirty he walked home, as usual, and had a glass of milk, as usual. He had never drunk anything stronger in his life—unless you could count ginger ale. The late Sam Schlosser, the S of F & S, had praised Mr. Martin at a staff meeting several years before for his temperate habits. "Our most efficient worker neither drinks nor smokes," he had said. "The results speak for themselves." Mr. Fitweiler had sat by, nodding approval.

Mr. Martin was still thinking about that red-letter day as he walked over to the Schrafft's on Fifth Avenue near Forty-Sixth Street.[4] He got there, as he always did, at eight o'clock. He finished his dinner and the financial page of the *Sun* at a quarter to nine, as he always did. It was his custom after dinner to take a walk. This time he walked down Fifth Avenue at a casual pace. His gloved hands felt moist and warm, his forehead cold. He transferred the Camels from his overcoat to a jacket pocket. He wondered, as he did so, if they did not represent an unnecessary note of strain. Mrs. Barrows smoked only Luckies. It was his idea to puff a few puffs on a Camel (after the rubbing-out), stub it out in the ashtray holding her lipstick-stained Luckies, and thus drag a small red herring across the trail. Perhaps it was not a good idea. It would take time. He might even choke, too loudly.

Mr. Martin had never seen the house on West Twelfth Street where Mrs. Barrows lived, but he had a clear enough picture of it. Fortunately, she had bragged to everybody about her ducky[5] first-floor apartment in the perfectly darling three-story red-brick. There would be no doorman or other attendants; just the tenants of the second and third floors. As he walked along, Mr. Martin realized that he would get there before nine-thirty. He had considered walking north on Fifth Avenue from

Schrafft's to a point from which it would take him until ten o'clock to reach the house. At that hour people were less likely to be coming in or going out. But the procedure would have made an awkward loop in the straight thread of his casualness, and he had abandoned it. It was impossible to figure when people would be entering or leaving the house, anyway. There was a great risk at any hour. If he ran into anybody, he would simply have to place the rubbing-out of Ulgine Barrows in the inactive file forever. The same thing would hold true if there were someone in her apartment. In that case he would just say that he had been passing by, recognized her charming house, and thought to drop in.

It was eighteen minutes after nine when Mr. Martin turned into Twelfth Street. A man passed him, and a man and a woman, talking. There was no one within fifty paces when he came to the house, halfway down the block. He was up the steps and in the small vestibule in no time, pressing the bell under the card that said "Mrs. Ulgine Barrows." When the clicking in the lock started,[6] he jumped forward against the door. He got inside fast, closing the door behind him. A bulb in a lantern hung from the hall ceiling on a chain seemed to give a monstrously bright light. There was nobody on the stair, which went up ahead of him along the left wall. A door opened down the hall in the wall on the right. He went toward it swiftly, on tiptoe.

"Well, I'll be, look who's here!" bawled Mrs. Barrows, and her braying laugh rang out like the report of a shotgun. He rushed past her like a football tackle, bumping her. "Hey, quit shoving!" she said, closing the door behind them. They were in her living room,

4. **red-letter day**, one marked by great joy and celebration. **Schrafft's**\shrăfts\ a New York restaurant chain. Mr. Martin is in midtown Manhattan.
5. **ducky**, women's slang, "very pleasant."
6. When the tenant's bell was pressed from without, he could press a bell in his own apartment that would release a catch on the front door.

which seemed to Mr. Martin to be lighted by a hundred lamps. "What's after you?" she said. "You're as jumpy as a goat." He found he was unable to speak. His heart was wheezing in his throat. "I—yes," he finally brought out. She was jabbering and laughing as she started to help him off with his coat. "No, no," he said. "I'll put it here." He took it off and put it on a chair near the door. "Your hat and gloves, too," she said. "You're in a lady's house." He put his hat on top of the coat. Mrs. Barrows seemed larger than he had thought. He kept his gloves on. "I was passing by," he said. "I recognized—is there anyone here?" She laughed louder than ever. "No," she said, "we're all alone. You're as white as a sheet, you funny man. Whatever *has* come over you? I'll mix you a toddy."[7] She started toward a door across the room. "Scotch-and-soda be all right? But say, you don't drink, do you?" She turned and gave him her amused look. Mr. Martin pulled himself together. "Scotch-and-soda will be all right," he heard himself say. He could hear her laughing in the kitchen.

Mr. Martin looked quickly around the living room for the weapon. He had counted on finding one there. There were andirons and a poker and something in a corner that looked like an Indian club.[8] None of them would do. It couldn't be that way. He began to pace around. He came to a desk. On it lay a metal paper knife with an ornate handle. Would it be sharp enough? He reached for it and knocked over a small brass jar. Stamps spilled out of it and it fell to the floor with a clatter. "Hey," Mrs. Barrows yelled from the kitchen, "are you tearing up the pea patch?" Mr. Martin gave a strange laugh. Picking up the knife, he tried its point against his left wrist. It was blunt. It wouldn't do.

When Mrs. Barrows reappeared, carrying two highballs, Mr. Martin, standing there with his gloves on, became acutely conscious of the fantasy he had wrought. Cigarettes in his pocket, a drink prepared for him—it was all too grossly improbable. It was more than that; it was impossible. Somewhere in the back of his mind a vague idea stirred, sprouted. "For heaven's sake, take off those gloves," said Mrs. Barrows. "I always wear them in the house," said Mr. Martin. The idea began to bloom, strange and wonderful. She put the glasses on a coffee table in front of a sofa and sat on the sofa. "Come over here, you odd little man," she said. Mr. Martin went over and sat beside her. It was difficult getting a cigarette out of the pack of Camels, but he managed it. She held a match for him, laughing. "Well," she said, handing him his drink, "this is perfectly marvellous. You with a drink and a cigarette."

Mr. Martin puffed, not too awkwardly, and took a gulp of the highball. "I drink and smoke all the time," he said. He clinked his glass against hers. "Here's nuts to that old windbag, Fitweiler," he said, and gulped again. The stuff tasted awful, but he made no grimace. "Really, Mr. Martin," she said, her voice and posture changing, "you are insulting our employer." Mrs. Barrows was now all special adviser to the president. "I am preparing a bomb," said Mr. Martin, "which will blow the old goat higher than heck." He had only had a little of the drink, which was not strong. It couldn't be that. "Do you take dope or something?" Mrs. Barrows asked coldly. "Heroin," said Mr. Martin. "I'll be coked to the gills when I bump that old buzzard off"[9] "Mr. Martin!" she shouted, getting to her feet. "That will be all of that. You must go at once." Mr. Martin took another swallow of his drink. He tapped his cigarette out in the ashtray and put the pack of Camels on the coffee table. Then he got up. She stood glaring at him. He walked over and put on his hat and coat. "Not a word about this," he said, and laid an index finger against his lips. All Mrs. Barrows could bring out was "Really!"

7. **toddy**\ˈtŏ·dē\ an alcoholic drink usually made of whiskey and water.
8. **andirons**\ˈăn ˈdai·rənz\ firedogs or metal objects in fireplaces to insure draft. **Indian club**, a wooden club used in gymnastics and shaped somewhat like a tenpin.
9. **heroin**\ˈhĕ ˈrō·ən\ a powerful narcotic drug made from morphine. **coked to the gills**, entirely under the influence of a narcotic.

Mr. Martin put his hand on the doorknob. "I'm sitting in the catbird seat," he said. He stuck his tongue out at her and left. Nobody saw him go.

Mr. Martin got to his apartment, walking, well before eleven. No one saw him go in. He had two glasses of milk after brushing his teeth, and he felt elated. It wasn't tipsiness, because he hadn't been tipsy.[10] Anyway, the walk had worn off all effects of the whiskey. He got in bed and read a magazine for a while. He was asleep before midnight.

Mr. Martin got to the office at eight-thirty the next morning, as usual. At a quarter to nine, Ulgine Barrows, who had never before arrived at work before ten, swept into his office. "I'm reporting to Mr. Fitweiler now!" she shouted, "if he turns you over to the police, it's no more than you deserve!" Mr. Martin gave her a look of shocked surprise. "I beg your pardon?" he said. Mrs. Barrows snorted and bounced out of the room, leaving Miss Paird and Joey Hart staring after her. "What's the matter with that old devil now?" asked Miss Paird. "I have no idea," said Mr. Martin, resuming his work. The other two looked at him and then at each other. Miss Paird got up and went out. She walked slowly past the closed door of Mr. Fitweiler's office. Mrs. Barrows was yelling inside, but she was not braying. Miss Paird could not hear what the woman was saying. She went back to her desk.

Forty-five minutes later, Mrs. Barrows left the president's office and went into her own, shutting the door. It wasn't until half an hour later that Mr. Fitweiler sent for Mr. Martin. The head of the filing department, neat, quiet, attentive, stood in front of the old man's desk. Mr. Fitweiler was pale and nervous. He took his glasses off and twiddled them. He made a small, bruffing sound in his throat. "Martin," he said, "you have been with us more than twenty years." "Twenty-two, sir," said Mr. Martin. "In that time," pursued the president, "your work and your—uh—manner have been exemplary." "I trust so, sir," said Mr. Martin. "I have under-

stood, Martin," said Mr. Fitweiler, "that you have never taken a drink or smoked." "That is correct, sir," said Mr. Martin. "Ah, yes." Mr. Fitweiler polished his glasses. "You may describe what you did after leaving the office yesterday, Martin," he said. Mr. Martin allowed less than a second for his bewildered pause. "Certainly, sir," he said. "I walked home. Then I went to Schrafft's for dinner. Afterward I walked home again. I went to bed early, sir, and read a magazine for a while. I was asleep before eleven." "Ah, yes," said Mr. Fitweiler again. He was silent for a moment, searching for the proper words to say to the head of the filing department. "Mrs. Barrows," he said finally, "Mrs. Barrows has worked hard, Martin, very hard. It grieves me to report that she has suffered a severe breakdown. It has taken the form of a persecution complex accompanied by distressing hallucinations." "I am very sorry, sir," said Mr. Martin. "Mrs. Barrows is under the delusion," continued Mr. Fitweiler, "that you visited her last evening and behaved yourself in an—uh—unseemly manner." He raised his hand to silence Mr. Martin's little pained outcry. "It is the nature of these psychological diseases," Mr. Fitweiler said, "to fix upon the least likely and most innocent party as the—uh—source of persecution. These matters are not for the lay mind to grasp, Martin. I've just had my psychiatrist, Doctor Fitch, on the phone. He would not, of course, commit himself, but he made enough generalizations to substantiate my suspicions. I suggested to Mrs. Barrows, when she had completed her—uh—story to me this morning, that she visit Doctor Fitch, for I suspected a condition at once. She flew, I regret to say, into a rage, and demanded —uh—requested that I call you on the carpet. You may not know, Martin, but Mrs. Barrows had planned a reorganization of your department—subject to my approval, of course, subject to my approval. This brought you, rather than anyone else, to her mind—but again that is a phenomenon for Doctor Fitch and not for

---

10. **tipsy,** informal: drunk.

us. So, Martin, I am afraid Mrs. Barrows' usefulness here is at an end." "I am dreadfully sorry, sir," said Mr. Martin.

It was at this point that the door to the office blew open with the suddenness of a gas-main explosion and Mrs. Barrows catapulted through it. "Is the little rat denying it?" she screamed. "He can't get away with that!" Mr. Martin got up and moved discreetly to a point beside Mr. Fitweiler's chair. "You drank and smoked at my apartment," she bawled at Mr. Martin, "and you know it! You called Mr. Fitweiler an old windbag and said you were going to blow him up when you got coked to the gills on your heroin!" She stopped yelling to catch her breath and a new glint came into her popping eyes. "If you weren't such a drab, ordinary little man," she said, "I'd think you'd planned it all. Sticking your tongue out, saying you were sitting in the catbird seat, because you thought no one would believe me when I told it! Oh my, it's really too perfect!" She brayed loudly and hysterically, and the fury was on her again. She glared at Mr. Fitweiler. "Can't you see how he has tricked us, you old fool? Can't you see his little game?" But Mr. Fitweiler had been surreptitiously pressing all the buttons under the top of his desk and employees of F & S began pouring into the room. "Stockton," said Mr. Fitweiler, "you and Fishbein will take Mrs. Barrows to her home. Mrs. Powell, you will go with them." Stockton, who had played a little football in high school, blocked Mrs. Barrows as she made for Mr. Martin. It took him and Fishbein together to force her out of the door into the hall, crowded with stenographers and office boys. She was still screaming imprecations at Mr. Martin, tangled and contradictory imprecations. The hubbub finally died down the corridor.

"I regret that this has happened," said Mr. Fitweiler. "I shall ask you to dismiss it from your mind, Martin." "Yes, sir," said Mr. Martin, anticipating his chief's "That will be all" by moving to the door. "I will dismiss it." He went out and shut the door, and his step was light and quick in the hall. When he entered his department he had slowed down to his customary gait, and he walked quietly across the room to the W20 file, wearing a look of studious concentration.

---

## I
### A MODERN FABLE

David and Goliath, Cinderella and the wicked sisters, the tortoise and the hare—this plot of the unlikely hero winning out over a favored adversary is one of the most cherished in literature. Readers like it because they identify themselves with the underdog and are led to hope that they too can find a secret weapon against the bullies of their own world. Since he has neither the strength to overcome her physically nor the influence to dislodge her through office politics, what could be more ingenious than Mr. Martin's psychological warfare against Mrs. Barrows?

## II
### IMPLICATIONS

James Thurber had an almost unequaled skill in exposing the absurdities of human conduct without ridiculing them. His eye was sharp but not cruel. One of his favorite themes was the differences among the way people see themselves, the way others see them, and the way they really are.

**1.** What is the picture that Mr. Martin has of himself? What is the picture that Mrs. Barrows has of herself? What is the picture that each has of the other?

**2.** What kind of executive does Mr. Fitweiler think he is? What kind would you say he really is?

**3.** Is Martin's ingenious plan for getting himself into the catbird seat consistent with his character or not? Give reasons for your opinion.

**4.** No one knows about Martin's success but himself. Does this lead him to take more or less pleasure in it? Why?

## III
### TECHNIQUES

*Theme*

Below are some general statements. In your opinion which comes closest to stating the theme of "The Catbird Seat"? Support your choice with reasons.

1. The weak win out in the long run.

2. Appearances are deceptive.

3. There is more than one way to achieve one's ends.

4. Office regimentation makes direct actions difficult.

5. All people have a point at which they will turn and fight.

*Style*

Humor, as you have already learned, is often the result of the unexpected and the incongruous. Below are five quotations from "The Catbird Seat" that are good examples of Thurber's comic style. What element is it in each that makes it humorous? Is it a word or a phrase? Or the general picture it evokes?

1. ". . . Mrs. Barrows had met Mr. Fitweiler at a party, where she had rescued him from the embraces of a powerfully built drunken man who had mistaken the president of F & S for a famous retired Middle Western football coach. She had led him to a sofa and somehow worked upon him a monstrous magic."

2. "She had begun chipping at the cornices of the firm's edifice and now she was swinging at the foundation stones with a pickaxe."

3. "If he ran into anybody, he would simply have to place the rubbing-out of Ulgine Barrows in the inactive file forever."

4. "He clinked his glass against hers. 'Here's nuts to that old windbag, Fitweiler,' he said, and gulped again."

5. "Mr. Fitweiler was pale and nervous. He took his glasses off and twiddled them. He made a small, bruffing sound in his throat."

*Identification*

To make people laugh is one of the quickest ways to engage their sympathy. Great comic figures like Charlie Chaplin's little tramp are held in universal affection, and when the comic figure is also an underdog, as Mr. Martin is in this story, the reader's sympathy is almost guaranteed. Yet Mrs. Barrows is also a comic figure; but it could hardly be said that she evokes sympathy. What reasons can you give for this difference? How might they be related to identifying with the two characters?

## IV
## WORDS

**A. 1.** In "The Vertical Ladder," Sansom uses a British slang expression to describe the taunts of Flegg's companions:

"Look at him . . . he's like a duck's uncle without an aunt."

What do you think Flegg's companions meant? Can you think of an American slang expression that would convey the same meaning?

**2.** In "The Catbird Seat" James Thurber uses slang in the dialogue and metaphorical expressions which seem slangy. Comment on the effectiveness and appropriateness of the following:

rushed past like a football tackle; as jumpy as a goat; tearing up the pea patch; sitting in the catbird seat.

**B.** Determine from context the meaning of the italicized words.

**1.** clamped down upon the will of *prostrate* peoples.

**2.** It was a very poor quarter, a *labyrinth* of *squalid* huts, winding all over a steep hillside.

**3.** that I first grasped the hollowness, the *futility.*

**4.** an enormous *senility* seemed to have settled upon him. One could have imagined him thousands of years old.

**5.** he resented the element of *imprecision,* the margin of guesswork.

**6.** You have been with us more than twenty years . . . your work and your manner have been *exemplary.*

**7.** he made enough generalizations to *substantiate* my suspicions.

**C. 1.** In "The Open Window," Saki says, "An undefinable something . . . seemed to suggest masculine habitation." Can you trace the construction of *undefinable?* Start by looking up *define* in your dictionary. Another word to look up is *romance.* How is it used in the last sentence, "Romance at short notice was her speciality"?

**2.** In "Going to Run All Night," Sylvester says that the runner Nilson is concerned because he lacks *credentials.* What is the origin of this word? What other English words share this origin? Sylvester also says that Nilson is a *fatalist.* What connection can you see among the words *fatalist, fatal,* and *fatality?*

Jack London saw life as a constant process of "pursuing and being pursued, of hunting and being hunted . . . a chaos . . . ruled over by chance, merciless, planless, endless." He felt that in living one either exerted pressures or resisted the pressures exerted on one. Life was an uninterrupted struggle, always against the odds, in which the strong survived and the weak succumbed.

# To Build a Fire

### JACK LONDON

Day had broken cold and gray, exceedingly cold and gray, when the man turned aside from the main Yukon trail and climbed the high earthbank, where a dim and little-traveled trail led eastward through the fat spruce timberland. It was a steep bank, and he paused for breath at the top, excusing the act to himself by looking at his watch. It was nine o'clock. There was no sun nor hint of sun, though there was not a cloud in the sky. It was a clear day, and yet there seemed an intangible pall over the face of things, a subtle gloom that made the day dark, and that was due to the absence of sun. This fact did not worry the man. He was used to the lack of sun. It had been days since he had seen the sun, and he knew that a few more days must pass before that cheerful orb, due south, would just peep above the sky-line and dip immediately from view.

The man flung a look back along the way he had come. The Yukon lay a mile wide and hidden under three feet of ice. On top of this ice were as many feet of snow. It was all pure white, rolling in gentle undulations where the ice-jams of the freeze-up had formed. North and south, as far as his eye could see, it was un-broken white, save for a dark hair-line that curved and twisted from around the spruce-covered island to the south, and that curved and twisted away into the north, where it disappeared behind another spruce-covered island. This dark hair-line was the trail—the main trail—that led south five hundred miles to the Chilkoot Pass, Dyea, and salt water; and that led north seventy miles to Dawson, and still on to the north a thousand miles to Nulato, and finally to St. Michael on Bering Sea, a thousand miles and half a thousand more.[1]

But all this—the mysterious, far-reaching hair-line trail, the absence of sun from the sky, the tremendous cold, and the strangeness and weirdness of it all—made no impression on the man. It was not because he was long used to it. He was a newcomer in the land, a *chechaquo*,[2] and this was his first winter. The trouble with him was that he was without imagination. He was quick and alert in the things of life, but only in the things, and not in the significances. Fifty degrees below zero meant eighty-odd degrees of frost. Such fact impressed him as being cold and uncomfortable, and that was all. It did not lead him to meditate upon his frailty as a creature of temperature, and upon man's frailty in general, able only to live within certain narrow limits of heat and cold; and from there on it did not lead him to the conjectural field of immortality and man's place in the universe. Fifty degrees below zero stood for a bite of frost that hurt and that must be guarded against by the use of mittens, ear-flaps, warm moccasins, and thick socks. Fifty degrees below zero was to him just precisely fifty degrees below zero. That there should be anything more to it than that was a thought that never entered his head.

---

1. **Chilkoot**\ˈchĭl ˈkūt\ **Pass** is in extreme northwestern British Columbia between Alaska and the Yukon. **Dyea** \ˈdai·ā\ a former Alaska village at which the Chilkoot Pass Trail started. **Dawson** is west central Yukon Territory. **Nulato**\nu ˈla·tō\ is in west central Alaska on the Yukon. **St. Michael** is on the Alaskan coast north of the mouth of the Yukon.
2. **chechaquo**\ˈchē ˈcha·kō\ a newcomer to the Northwest.

---

Reprinted by permission of Mr. Irving Shepard.

As he turned to go on, he spat speculatively. There was a sharp, explosive crackle that startled him. He spat again. And again, in the air, before it could fall to the snow, the spittle crackled. He knew that at fifty below spittle crackled on the snow, but this spittle had crackled in the air. Undoubtedly it was colder than fifty below—how much colder he did not know. But the temperature did not matter. He was bound for the old claim on the left fork of Henderson Creek, where the boys were already. They had come over across the divide from the Indian Creek country, while he had come the roundabout way to take a look at the possibilities of getting out logs in the spring from the islands in the Yukon. He would be in to camp by six o'clock; a bit after dark, it was true, but the boys would be there, a fire would be going, and a hot supper would be ready. As for lunch, he pressed his hand against the protruding bundle under his jacket. It was also under his shirt, wrapped up in a handkerchief and lying against the naked skin. It was the only way to keep the biscuits from freezing. He smiled agreeably to himself as he thought of those biscuits, each cut open and sopped in bacon grease, and each enclosing a generous slice of fried bacon.

He plunged in among the big spruce trees. The trail was faint. A foot of snow had fallen since the last sled had passed over, and he was glad he was without a sled, traveling light. In fact, he carried nothing but the lunch wrapped in the handkerchief. He was surprised, however, at the cold. It certainly was cold, he concluded, as he rubbed his numb nose and cheek-bones with his mittened hand. He was a warm-whiskered man, but the hair on his face did not protect the high cheek-bones and the eager nose that thrust itself aggressively into the frosty air.

At the man's heels trotted a dog, a big native husky, the proper wolf-dog, gray-coated and without any visible or temperamental difference from its brother, the wild wolf. The animal was depressed by the tremendous cold. It knew that it was no time for traveling. Its in-

stinct told it a truer tale than was told to the man by the man's judgment. In reality, it was not merely colder than fifty below zero; it was colder than sixty below, than seventy below. It was seventy-five below zero. Since the freezing-point is thirty-two above zero, it meant that one hundred and seven degrees of frost obtained. The dog did not know anything about thermometers. Possibly in its brain there was no sharp consciousness of a condition of very cold such as was in the man's brain. But the brute had its instinct. It experienced a vague but menacing apprehension that subdued it and made it slink along at the man's heels, and that made it question eagerly every unwonted movement of the man as if expecting him to go into camp or to seek shelter somewhere and build a fire. The dog had learned fire, and it wanted fire, or else to burrow under the snow and cuddle its warmth away from the air.

The frozen moisture of its breathing had settled on its fur in a fine powder of frost, and especially were its jowls, muzzle, and eyelashes whitened by its crystaled breath. The man's red beard and mustache were likewise frosted, but more solidly, the deposit taking the form of ice and increasing with every warm, moist breath he exhaled. Also, the man was chewing tobacco, and the muzzle of ice held his lips so rigidly that he was unable to clear his chin when he expelled the juice. The result was that a crystal beard of the color and solidity of amber was increasing its length on his chin. If he fell down it would shatter itself, like glass, into brittle fragments. But he did not mind the appendage. It was the penalty all tobacco-chewers paid in that country, and he had been out before in two cold snaps. They had not been so cold as this, he knew, but by the spirit thermometer at Sixty Mile he knew they had been registered at fifty below and at fifty-five.

He held on through the level stretch of woods for several miles, crossed a wide flat of nigger-heads,[3] and dropped down a bank to the frozen bed of a small stream. This was

—————

3. **nigger-head,** a clump or mound of plant growth.

Henderson Creek, and he knew he was ten miles from the forks. He looked at his watch. It was ten o'clock. He was making four miles an hour, and he calculated that he would arrive at the forks at half-past twelve. He decided to celebrate that event by eating his lunch there.

The dog dropped in again at his heels, with a tail drooping discouragement, as the man swung along the creek-bed. The furrow of the old sled-trail was plainly visible, but a dozen inches of snow covered the marks of the last runners. In a month no man had come up or down that silent creek. The man held steadily on. He was not much given to thinking, and just then particularly he had nothing to think about save that he would eat lunch at the forks and that at six o'clock he would be in camp with the boys. There was nobody to talk to; and, had there been, speech would have been impossible because of the ice-muzzle on his mouth. So he continued monotonously to chew tobacco and to increase the length of his amber beard.

Once in a while the thought reiterated itself that it was very cold and that he had never experienced such cold. As he walked along he rubbed his cheek-bones and nose with the back of his mittened hand. He did this automatically, now and again changing hands. But rub as he would, the instant he stopped his cheek-bones went numb, and the following instant the end of his nose went numb. He was sure to frost his cheeks; he knew that, and experienced a pang of regret that he had not devised a nose-strap of the sort Bud wore in cold snaps. Such a strap passed across the cheeks, as well, and saved them. But it didn't matter much, after all. What were frosted cheeks? A bit painful, that was all; they were never serious.

Empty as the man's mind was of thoughts, he was keenly observant, and he noticed the changes in the creek, the curves and bends and timber-jams, and always he sharply noted where he placed his feet. Once, coming around a bend, he shied abruptly, like a startled horse, curved away from the place where he had been walking, and retreated several paces back

along the trail. The creek he knew was frozen clear to the bottom,—no creek could contain water in that arctic winter,—but he knew also that there were springs that bubbled out from the hillsides and ran along under the snow and on top the ice of the creek. He knew that the coldest snaps never froze these springs, and he knew likewise their danger. They were traps. They hid pools of water under the snow that might be three inches deep, or three feet. Sometimes a skin of ice half an inch thick covered them, and in turn was covered by the snow. Sometimes there were alternate layers of water and ice-skin, so that when one broke through he kept on breaking through for a while, sometimes wetting himself to the waist.

That was why he had shied in such panic. He had felt the give under his feet and heard the crackle of a snow-hidden ice-skin. And to get his feet wet in such a temperature meant trouble and danger. At the very least it meant delay, for he would be forced to stop and build a fire, and under its protection to bare his feet while he dried his socks and moccasins. He stood and studied the creek-bed and its banks, and decided that the flow of water came from the right. He reflected awhile, rubbing his nose and cheeks, then skirted to the left, stepping gingerly and testing the footing for each step. Once clear of the danger, he took a fresh chew of tobacco and swung along at his four-mile gait.

In the course of the next two hours he came upon several similar traps. Usually the snow above the hidden pools had a sunken, candied appearance that advertised the danger. Once again, however, he had a close call; and once, suspecting danger, he compelled the dog to go on in front. The dog did not want to go. It hung back until the man shoved it forward, and then it went quickly across the white, un-broken surface. Suddenly it broke through; floundered to one side, and got away to firmer footing. It had wet its forefeet and legs, and almost immediately the water that clung to it turned to ice. It made quick efforts to lick the ice off its legs, then dropped down in the snow and began to bite out the ice that had formed between the toes. This was a matter of instinct. To permit the ice to remain would mean sore feet. It did not know this. It merely obeyed the mysterious prompting that rose from the deep crypts of its being. But the man knew, having achieved a judgment on the subject, and he removed the mitten from his right hand and helped tear out the ice-particles. He did not expose his fingers more than a minute, and was astonished at the swift numbness that smote them. It certainly was cold. He pulled on the mitten hastily, and beat the hand savagely across his chest.

At twelve o'clock the day was at its brightest. Yet the sun was too far south on its winter journey to clear the horizon. The bulge of the earth intervened between it and Henderson Creek, where the man walked under a clear sky at noon and cast no shadow. At half-past twelve, to the minute, he arrived at the forks of the creek. He was pleased at the speed he had made. If he kept it up, he would certainly be with the boys by six. He unbuttoned his jacket and shirt and drew forth his lunch. The action consumed no more than a quarter of a minute, yet in that brief moment the numbness laid hold of the exposed fingers. He did not put the mitten on, but, instead, struck the fingers a dozen sharp smashes against his leg. Then he sat down on a snow-covered log to eat. The sting that followed upon the striking of his fingers against his leg ceased so quickly that he was startled. He had had no chance to take a bite of biscuit. He struck the fingers repeatedly and returned them to the mitten, baring the other hand for the purpose of eating. He tried to take a mouthful, but the ice-muzzle prevented. He had forgotten to build a fire and thaw out. He chuckled at his foolishness, and as he chuckled he noted the numbness creeping into the exposed fingers. Also, he noted that the stinging which had first come to his toes when he sat down was already passing away. He wondered whether the toes were warm or numb. He moved them inside the moccasins and decided that they were numb.

He pulled the mitten on hurriedly and stood up. He was a bit frightened. He stamped up and down until the stinging returned into the feet. It certainly was cold, was his thought. That man from Sulphur Creek had spoken the truth when telling how cold it sometimes got in the country. And he had laughed at him at the time! That showed one must not be too sure of things. There was no mistake about it, it *was* cold. He strode up and down, stamping his feet and threshing his arms, until reassured by the returning warmth. Then he got out matches and proceeded to make a fire. From the undergrowth, where high water of the previous spring had lodged a supply of sea-soned twigs, he got his firewood. Working carefully from a small beginning, he soon had a roaring fire, over which he thawed the ice from his face and in the protection of which he ate his biscuits. For the moment the cold of space was outwitted. The dog took satisfaction in the fire, stretching out close enough for warmth and far enough away to escape being singed.

When the man had finished, he filled his pipe and took his comfortable time over a smoke. Then he pulled on his mittens, settled the earflaps of his cap firmly about his ears, and took the creek trail up the left fork. The dog was disappointed and yearned back toward the fire. This man did not know cold. Possibly all the generations of his ancestry had been ignorant of cold, of real cold, of cold one hundred and seven degrees below freezing-point. But the dog knew; all its ancestry knew, and it had inherited the knowledge. And it knew that it was not good to walk abroad in such fearful cold. It was the time to lie snug in a hole in the snow and wait for a curtain of cloud to be drawn across the face of outer space whence this cold came. On the other hand, there was no keen intimacy between the dog and the man. The one was the toil-slave of the other, and the only caresses it had ever received were the caresses of the whiplash and of harsh and menacing throat-sounds that threatened the whiplash. So the dog made no effort to communicate its apprehension to the man. It was not concerned in the welfare of the man; it was for its own sake that it yearned back toward the fire. But the man whistled, and spoke to it with the sound of whiplashes, and the dog swung in at the man's heels and followed after.

The man took a chew of tobacco and proceeded to start a new amber beard. Also, his moist breath quickly powdered with white his mustache, eyebrows, and lashes. There did not seem to be so many springs on the left fork of the Henderson, and for half an hour the man saw no signs of any. And then it happened. At a place where there were no signs, where the soft, unbroken snow seemed to advertise solidity beneath, the man broke through. It was not deep. He wet himself halfway to the knees before he floundered out to the firm crust.

He was angry, and cursed his luck aloud. He had hoped to get into camp with the boys at six o'clock, and this would delay him an hour, for he would have to build a fire and dry out his foot-gear. This was imperative at that low temperature—he knew that much; and he turned aside to the bank, which he climbed. On top, tangled in the underbrush about the trunks of several small spruce trees, was a high-water deposit of dry fire-wood—sticks and twigs, principally, but also larger portions of seasoned branches and fine, dry, last-year's grasses. He threw down several large pieces on top of the snow. This served for a foundation and prevented the young flame from drowning itself in the snow it otherwise would melt. The flame he got by touching a match to a small shred of birch-bark that he took from his pocket. This burned even more readily than paper. Placing it on the foundation, he fed the young flame with wisps of dry grass and with the tiniest dry twigs.

He worked slowly and carefully, keenly aware of his danger. Gradually, as the flame grew stronger, he increased the size of the twigs with which he fed it. He squatted in the snow, pulling the twigs out from their entanglement in the brush and feeding directly to the flame. He knew there must be no failure. When

it is seventy-five below zero, a man must not fail in his first attempt to build a fire—that is, if his feet are wet. If his feet are dry, and he fails, he can run along the trail for half a mile and restore his circulation. But the circulation of wet and freezing feet cannot be restored by running when it is seventy-five below. No matter how fast he runs, the wet feet will freeze the harder.

All this the man knew. The old-timer on Sulphur Creek had told him about it the previous fall, and now he was appreciating the advice. Already all sensation had gone out of his feet. To build the fire he had been forced to remove his mittens, and the fingers had quickly gone numb. His pace of four miles an hour had kept his heart pumping blood to the surface of his body and to all the extremities. But the instant he stopped, the action of the pump eased down. The cold of space smote the unprotected tip of the planet, and he, being on that unprotected tip, received the full force of the blow. The blood of his body recoiled before it. The blood was alive, like the dog, and like the dog it wanted to hide away and cover itself up from the fearful cold. So long as he walked four miles an hour, he pumped that blood, willy-nilly, to the surface; but now it ebbed away and sank down into the recesses of his body. The extremities were the first to feel its absence. His wet feet froze the faster, and his exposed fingers numbed the faster, though they had not yet begun to freeze. Nose and cheeks were already freezing, while the skin of his body chilled as it lost its blood.

But he was safe. Toes and nose and cheeks would be only touched by the frost, for the fire was beginning to burn with strength. He was feeding it with twigs the size of his finger. In another minute he would be able to feed it with branches the size of his wrist, and then he could remove his wet foot-gear, and, while it dried, he could keep his naked feet warm by the fire, rubbing them at first, of course, with snow. The fire was a success. He was safe. He remembered the advice of the old-timer on Sulphur Creek, and smiled. The old-timer had been very serious in laying down the law that no man must travel alone in the Klondike after fifty below. Well, here he was; he had had the accident; he was alone; and he had saved himself. Those old-timers were rather womanish, some of them, he thought. All a man had to do was to keep his head, and he was all right. Any man who was a man could travel alone. But it was surprising, the rapidity with which his cheeks and nose were freezing. And he had not thought his fingers could go lifeless in so short a time. Lifeless they were, for he could scarcely make them move together to grip a twig, and they seemed remote from his body and from him. When he touched a twig, he had to look and see whether or not he had hold of it. The wires were pretty well down between him and his finger-ends.

All of which counted for little. There was the fire, snapping and crackling and promising life with every dancing flame. He started to untie his moccasins. They were coated with ice; the thick German socks were like sheaths of iron halfway to the knees; and the moccasin strings were like rods of steel all twisted and knotted as by some conflagration. For a moment he tugged with his numb fingers, then, realizing the folly of it, he drew his sheath-knife.

But before he could cut the strings, it happened. It was his own fault or, rather, his mistake. He should not have built the fire under the spruce tree. He should have built it in the open. But it had been easier to pull the twigs from the brush and drop them directly on the fire. Now the tree under which he had done this carried a weight of snow on its boughs. No wind had blown for weeks, and each bough was fully freighted. Each time he had pulled a twig he had communicated a slight agitation to the tree—an imperceptible agitation, so far as he was concerned, but an agitation sufficient to bring about the disaster. High up in the tree one bough capsized its load of snow. This fell on the boughs beneath, capsizing them. This process continued, spreading out and involving the whole tree. It grew like an avalanche, and it descended with-

out warning upon the man and the fire, and the fire was blotted out! Where it had burned was a mantel of fresh and disordered snow.

The man was shocked. It was as though he had just heard his own sentence of death. For a moment he sat and stared at the spot where the fire had been. Then he grew very calm. Perhaps the old-timer on Sulphur Creek was right. If he had only had a trail-mate he would have been in no danger now. The trail-mate could have built the fire. Well, it was up to him to build the fire over again, and this second time there must be no failure. Even if he succeeded, he would most likely lose some toes. His feet must be badly frozen by now, and there would be some time before the second fire was ready.

Such were his thoughts, but he did not sit and think them. He was busy all the time they were passing through his mind. He made a new foundation for a fire, this time in the open, where no treacherous tree could blot it out. Next, he gathered dry grasses and tiny twigs from the high-water flotsam. He could not bring his fingers together to pull them out, but he was able to gather them by the handful. In this way he got many rotten twigs and bits of green moss that were undesirable, but it was the best he could do. He worked methodically, even collecting an armful of the larger branches to be used later when the fire gathered strength. And all the while the dog sat and watched him, a certain yearning wistfulness in its eyes, for it looked upon him as the fire-provider, and the fire was slow in coming.

When all was ready, the man reached in his pocket for a second piece of birchbark. He knew the bark was there, and, though he could not feel it with his fingers, he could hear its crisp rustling as he fumbled for it. Try as he would, he could not clutch hold of it. And all the time, in his consciousness, was the knowledge that each instant his feet were freezing. This thought tended to put him in a panic, but he fought against it and kept calm. He pulled on his mittens with his teeth, and threshed his arms back and forth, beating his hands with all his might against his sides. He did this sitting down, and he stood up to do it; and all the while the dog sat in the snow, its wolf-brush of a tail curled around warmly over its forefeet, its sharp wolf-ears pricked forward intently as it watched the man. And the man, as he beat and threshed with his arms and hands, felt a great surge of envy as he regarded the creature that was warm and secure in its natural covering.

After a time he was aware of the first faraway signals of sensation in his beaten fingers. The faint tingling grew stronger till it evolved into a stinging ache that was excruciating, but which the man hailed with satisfaction. He stripped the mitten from his right hand and fetched forth the birchbark. The exposed fingers were quickly going numb again. Next he brought out his bunch of sulphur matches. But the tremendous cold had already driven the life out of his fingers. In his effort to separate one match from the others, the whole bunch fell in the snow. He tried to pick it out of the snow, but failed. The dead fingers could neither touch nor clutch. He was very careful. He drove the thought of his freezing feet, and nose, and cheeks, out of his mind, devoting his whole soul to the matches. He watched, using the sense of vision in place of that of touch, and when he saw his fingers on each side the bunch, he closed them—that is, he willed to close them, for the wires were down, and the fingers did not obey. He pulled the mitten on the right hand, and beat it fiercely against his knee. Then, with both mittened hands, he scooped the bunch of matches, along with much snow, into his lap. Yet he was no better off.

After some manipulation he managed to get the bunch between the heels of his mittened hands. In this fashion he carried it to his mouth. The ice crackled and snapped when by a violent effort he opened his mouth. He drew the lower jaw in, curled the upper lip out of the way, and scraped the bunch with his upper teeth in order to separate a match. He succeeded in getting one, which he dropped on his lap. He was no better off. He could not pick it up. Then he devised a way. He picked it up in his teeth and scratched it on his leg. Twenty times he scratched before he succeeded in lighting it. As it flamed he held it with his teeth to the birchbark. But the burning brimstone went up his nostrils and into his lungs, causing him to cough spasmodically. The match fell into the snow and went out.

The old-timer on Sulphur Creek was right, he thought in the moment of controlled despair that ensued: after fifty below, a man should travel with a partner. He beat his hands, but failed in exciting any sensation. Suddenly he bared both hands, removing the mittens with his teeth. He caught the whole bunch between the heels of his hands. His arm-muscles not being frozen enabled him to press the hand-heels tightly against the matches. Then he scratched the bunch along his leg. It flared into flame, seventy sulphur matches at once! There was no wind to blow them out. He kept his head to one side to escape the strangling fumes, and held the blazing bunch to the birch-bark. As he so held it, he became aware of sensation in his hand. His flesh was burning. He could smell it. Deep down below the surface he could feel it. The sensation developed into pain that grew acute. And still he endured it, holding the flame of the matches clumsily to the bark that would not light readily because his own burning hands were in the way, absorbing most of the flame.

At last, when he could endure no more, he jerked his hands apart. The blazing matches fell sizzling into the snow, but the birch-bark was alight. He began laying dry grasses and the tiniest twigs on the flame. He could not pick and choose, for he had to lift the fuel between the heels of his hands. Small pieces of rotten wood and green moss clung to the twigs, and he bit them off as well as he could with his teeth. He cherished the flame carefully and awkwardly. It meant life, and it must not perish. The withdrawal of blood from the surface of his body now made him begin to shiver, and he grew more awkward. A large piece of green moss fell squarely on the little

*"The sight of the dog put a wild idea into his head."*

fire. He tried to poke it out with his fingers, but his shivering frame made him poke too far, and he disrupted the nucleus of the little fire, the burning grasses and tiny twigs separating and scattering. He tried to poke them together again, but in spite of the tenseness of the effort, his shivering got away with him, and the twigs were hopelessly scattered. Each twig gushed a puff of smoke and went out. The fire-provider had failed. As he looked apathetically about him, his eyes chanced on the dog, sitting across the ruins of the fire from him, in the snow, making restless, hunching movements, slightly lifting one forefoot and then the other, shifting its weight back and forth on them with wistful eagerness.

The sight of the dog put a wild idea into his head. He remembered the tale of the man, caught in a blizzard, who killed a steer and crawled inside the carcass, and so was saved.

He would kill the dog and bury his hands in the warm body until the numbness went out of them. Then he could build another fire. He spoke to the dog, calling it to him; but in his voice was a strange note of fear that frightened the animal, who had never known the man to speak in such way before. Something was the matter, and its suspicious nature sensed danger—it knew not what danger, but somewhere, somehow, in its brain arose an apprehension of the man. It flattened its ears down at the sound of the man's voice, and its restless, hunching movements and the liftings and shiftings of its forefeet became more pronounced; but it would not come to the man. He got on his hands and knees and crawled toward the dog. This unusual posture again excited suspicion, and the animal sidled mincingly away.

The man sat up in the snow for a moment and struggled for calmness. Then he pulled on his mittens, by means of his teeth, and got upon his feet. He glanced down at first in order to assure himself that he was really standing up, for the absence of sensation in his feet left him unrelated to the earth. His erect position in itself started to drive the webs of suspicion from the dog's mind; and when he spoke peremptorily, with the sound of whiplashes in his voice, the dog rendered its customary allegiance and came to him. As it came within reaching distance, the man lost his control. His arms flashed out to the dog, and he experienced genuine surprise when he discovered that his hands could not clutch, that there was neither bend nor feeling in the fingers. He had forgotten for the moment that they were frozen and that they were freezing more and more. All this happened quickly, and before the animal could get away, he encircled its body with his arms. He sat down in the snow, and in this fashion held the dog, while it snarled and whined and struggled.

But it was all he could do, hold its body encircled in his arms and sit there. He realized that he could not kill the dog. There was no way to do it. With his helpless hands he could neither draw nor hold his sheath-knife nor throttle the animal. He released it, and it plunged wildly away, with tail between its legs, and still snarling. It halted forty feet away and surveyed him curiously, with ears sharply pricked forward. The man looked down at his hands in order to locate them, and found them hanging on the ends of his arms. It struck him as curious that one should have to use his eyes in order to find out where his hands were. He began threshing his arms back and forth, beating the mittened hands against his sides. He did this for five minutes, violently, and his heart pumped enough blood up to the surface to put a stop to his shivering. But no sensation was aroused in the hands. He had an impression that they hung like weights on the ends of his arms, but when he tried to run the impression down, he could not find it.

A certain fear of death, dull and oppressive, came to him. This fear quickly became poignant as he realized that it was no longer a mere matter of freezing his fingers and toes, or of losing his hands and feet, but that it was a matter of life and death with the chances against him. This threw him into a panic, and he turned and ran up the creek-bed along the old, dim trail. The dog joined in behind and kept up with him. He ran blindly, without intention, in fear such as he had never known in his life. Slowly, as he ploughed and floundered through the snow, he began to see things again,—the banks of the creek, the old timber-jams, the leafless aspens, and the sky. The running made him feel better. He did not shiver. Maybe, if he ran on, his feet would thaw out; and, anyway, if he ran far enough, he would reach camp and the boys. Without doubt he would lose some fingers and toes and some of his face; but the boys would take care of him, and save the rest of him when he got there. And at the same time there was another thought in his mind that said he would never get to the camp and the boys; that it was too many miles away, that the freezing had too great a start on him, and that he would soon be stiff and dead. This thought he kept in the background and refused to consider. Sometimes it pushed itself forward and demanded to be heard, but he thrust it back and strove to think of other things.

It struck him as curious that he could run at all on feet so frozen that he could not feel them when they struck the earth and took the weight of his body. He seemed to himself to skim along above the surface, and to have no connection with the earth. Somewhere he had once seen a winged Mercury, and he wondered if Mercury[4] felt as he felt when skimming over the earth.

His theory of running until he reached camp and the boys had one flaw in it: he lacked the endurance. Several times he stumbled, and finally he tottered, crumpled up, and fell. When he tried to rise, he failed. He must sit and rest, he decided, and next time he would merely walk and keep on going. As he sat and

---

4. **Mercury**, a Greek and Roman god and messenger for the other gods, was winged.

regained his breath, he noted that he was feeling quite warm and comfortable. He was not shivering, and it even seemed that a warm glow had come to his chest and trunk. And yet, when he touched his nose or cheeks, there was no sensation. Running would not thaw them out. Nor would it thaw out his hands and feet. Then the thought came to him that the frozen portions of his body must be extending. He tried to keep this thought down, to forget it, to think of something else; he was aware of the panicky feeling that it caused, and he was afraid of the panic. But the thought asserted itself, and persisted, until it produced a vision of his body totally frozen. This was too much, and he made another wild run along the trail. Once he slowed down to a walk, but the thought of the freezing extending itself made him run again.

And all the time the dog ran with him, at his heels. When he fell down a second time, it curled its tail over its forefeet and sat in front of him, facing him, curiously eager and intent. The warmth and security of the animal angered him, and he cursed it till it flattened down its ears appeasingly. This time the shivering came more quickly upon the man. He was losing in his battle with the frost. It was creeping into his body from all sides. The thought of it drove him on, but he ran no more than a hundred feet, when he staggered and pitched headlong. It was his last panic. When he had recovered his breath and control, he sat up and entertained in his mind the conception of meeting death with dignity. However, the conception did not come to him in such terms. His idea of it was that he had been making a fool of himself, running around like a chicken with its head cut off—such was the simile that occurred to him. Well, he was bound to freeze anyway, and he might as well take it decently. With this new-found peace of mind came the first glimmerings of drowsiness. A good idea, he thought, to sleep off to death. It was like taking an anesthetic. Freezing was not so bad as people thought. There were lots worse ways to die.

He pictured the boys finding his body next day. Suddenly he found himself with them, coming along the trail and looking for himself. And, still with them, he came around a turn in the trail and found himself lying in the snow. He did not belong with himself any more, for even then he was out of himself, standing with the boys and looking at himself in the snow. It certainly was cold, was his thought. When he got back to the States he could tell the folks what real cold was. He drifted on from this to a vision of the old-timer on Sulphur Creek. He could see him quite clearly, warm and comfortable, and smoking a pipe.

"You were right, old hoss; you were right," the man mumbled to the old-timer of Sulphur Creek.

Then the man drowsed off into what seemed to him the most comfortable and satisfying sleep he had ever known. The dog sat facing him and waiting. The brief day drew to a close in a long, slow twilight. There were no signs of a fire to be made, and, besides, never in the dog's experience had it known a man to sit like that in the snow and make no fire. As the twilight drew on, its eager yearning for the fire mastered it, and with a great lifting and shifting of forefeet, it whined softly, then flattened its ears down in anticipation of being chidden by the man. But the man remained silent. Later, the dog whined loudly. And still later it crept close to the man and caught the scent of death. This made the animal bristle and back away. A little longer it delayed, howling under the stars that leaped and danced and shone brightly in the cold sky. Then it turned and trotted up the trail in the direction of the camp it knew, where were the other food-providers and fire-providers.

---

### I
### DANGER AND FEAR

Jack London introduces the reader to the quiet, subtle, indifferent, and yet ever present pressure of nature on man. The sky is gray, the landscape bleak, but this is usual in the Far North. A man and a dog are alone in the vast expanses of snow. This, too, is usual. But it is seventy-five degrees below zero, and this is unusual. It is also extremely dangerous, but the man is unaware of his danger until it is too late. When he does realize it, he begins to feel that he is being hunted down by nature as surely as if he were being tracked by a wolf. But is this feeling accurate, or is it really a sign of his own panic?

## II
### IMPLICATIONS

**A.** It could be said that the man's real enemy in this story is his own nature, not the cold. Discuss this proposition in the light of the following quotations. What elements in this character, as revealed by the quotations, help the man to cope with the cold? What elements hinder him? How does the balance of these elements create suspense?

**1.** "The trouble with him was that he was without imagination. He was quick and alert in the things of life, but only in the things, and not in the significances."

**2.** "Empty as the man's mind was of thoughts, he was keenly observant, and he noticed the changes in the creek, the curves and bends and timber-jams, and always he sharply noted where he placed his feet."

**3.** "He had forgotten to build a fire and thaw out. He chuckled at his foolishness. . . ."

**4.** "This man did not know cold. Possibly all the generations of his ancestry had been ignorant of cold, of real cold. . . ."

**5.** "He worked slowly and carefully [building the fire], keenly aware of his danger."

**B.** To what extent do you think the following statements are accurate generalities? Discuss them with reference to your own experience as well as to your understanding of "To Build a Fire."

**1.** The man in this story dies because of his own weaknesses.

**2.** Once a person's self-confidence is shaken, it becomes increasingly difficult to act rationally.

**3.** People are more likely to make mistakes when they are frightened than when they are not.

**4.** People are ill-equipped by nature to endure extremes of climate, or even live at all outside of civilization. Whenever they venture into the wilderness, they must therefore survive by their wits.

## III
### TECHNIQUES
*Theme*

If the theme of this story is the disintegration of rationality under the pressure of fear, how does the extreme cold contribute to the theme? How does the man's lack of imagination contribute to it? Where does Jack London show you the man's first sign of fear? What step-by-step incidents reveal its growing power over him?

On what basis could you say that the development of the theme is complex and disguised, or simple and straightforward?

*Style and Identification*

Jack London's manner of telling this story is matter-of-fact and impersonal almost to the point of seeming heartless. This style, however, is deliberate, and is calculated to evoke certain responses in the reader. Recall your feelings while you were reading the story. Did you care about the man from the beginning? For what reasons did you want him to survive? What was your reaction to his behavior as he grew more and more desperate? How did you feel about his death?

Why does London call the central figure simply "the man"? Why doesn't he describe the man's family, friends, ambitions, etc.? On the other hand, choose several passages and show how he describes the physical setting and action with great detail. Why does London emphasize factual rather than personal details? How does this affect your feelings toward the man? What might your response to the action and the man have been if London had told the story in very emotional prose, full of his own feelings about the situation?

Now briefly discuss the following proposition: In telling a tragic event, the more unemotional the style, the greater the impact on the reader.

The moment is intense. The first sentences
picture a man on a bridge. He is
about to be hanged. How does such
pressure affect the mind of the victim?

# An Occurrence
## at
# Owl Creek Bridge

AMBROSE BIERCE

## 1

A man stood upon a railroad bridge in northern Alabama, looking down into the swift water twenty feet below. The man's hands were behind his back, the wrists bound with a cord. A rope loosely encircled his neck. It was attached to a stout cross-timber above his head, and the slack fell to the level of his knees. Some loose boards laid upon the sleepers[1] supporting the metals of the railway supplied a footing for him and his executioners —two private soldiers of the Federal army, directed by a sergeant who in civil life may have been a deputy sheriff. At a short remove upon the same temporary platform was an officer in the uniform of his rank, armed. He was a captain. A sentinel at each end of the bridge stood with his rifle in the position known as "support," that is to say, vertical in front of the left shoulder, the hammer resting on the forearm thrown straight across the chest—a formal and unnatural position, enforcing an erect carriage of the body. It did not appear to be the duty of these two men to know what was occurring at the center of the bridge; they merely blockaded the two ends of the foot plank which traversed it.

Beyond one of the sentinels, nobody was in sight; the railroad ran straight away into a forest for a hundred yards, then, curving, was lost to view. Doubtless there was an outpost farther along. The other bank of the stream was open ground—a gentle acclivity topped with a stockade of vertical tree trunks, loopholed for rifles, with a single embrasure through which protruded the muzzle of a brass cannon commanding the bridge. Midway of the slope between bridge and fort were the spectators—a single company of infantry in line, at "parade rest," the butts of the rifles on the ground, the barrels inclining slightly backward against the right shoulder, the hands crossed upon the stock. A lieutenant stood at the right of the line, the point of his sword upon the ground, his left hand resting upon his right. Excepting the group of four at the center of the bridge, not a man moved. The company faced the bridge, staring stonily, motionless. The sentinels, facing the banks of the stream, might have been statues to adorn the bridge. The captain stood with folded arms, silent, observing the work of his subordinates, but making no sign. Death is a dignitary who when he comes announced is to be received with formal manifestations of respect, even by those most familiar with him. In the code of military etiquette silence and fixity are forms of deference.

The man who was engaged in being hanged was apparently about thirty-five years of age. He was a civilian, if one might judge from his habit, which was that of a planter. His features were good—a straight nose, firm mouth, broad forehead, from which his long, dark hair was combed straight back, falling behind his ears to the collar of his well-fitting frock coat. He wore a mustache and pointed beard, but no whiskers; his eyes were large and dark gray, and had a kindly expression which one would hardly have expected in one whose

---

reprinted from THE COLLECTED WRITINGS OF AM-
BROSE BIERCE, Citadel Press, Inc., New York, N.Y.

1. **sleepers,** timbers to keep rails in place.

510

neck was in the hemp.² Evidently this was no vulgar assassin. The liberal military code makes provision for hanging many kinds of persons, and gentlemen are not excluded.

The preparations being complete, the two private soldiers stepped aside and each drew away the plank upon which he had been standing. The sergeant turned to the captain, saluted, and placed himself immediately behind that officer, who in turn moved apart one pace. These movements left the condemned man and the sergeant standing on the two ends of the same plank, which spanned three of the crossties of the bridge. The end upon which the civilian stood almost, but not quite, reached a fourth. This plank had been held in place by the weight of the captain; it was now held by that of the sergeant. At a signal from the former, the latter would step aside, the plank would tilt, and the condemned man go down between two ties. The arrangement commended itself to his judgment as simple and effective. His face had not been covered nor his eyes bandaged. He looked a moment at his "unsteadfast footing," then let his gaze wander to the swirling water of the stream racing madly beneath his feet. A piece of dancing driftwood caught his attention and his eyes followed it down the current. How slowly it appeared to move! What a sluggish stream!

He closed his eyes in order to fix his last thoughts upon his wife and children. The water, touched to gold by the early sun, the brooding mists under the banks at some distance down the stream, the fort, the soldiers, the piece of drift—all had distracted him. And now he became conscious of a new disturbance. Striking through the thought of his dear ones was a sound which he could neither ignore nor understand, a sharp, distinct, metallic percussion like the stroke of a blacksmith's hammer upon the anvil; it had the same ringing quality. He wondered what it was, and whether immeasurably distant or near by—it seemed both. Its recurrence was regular, but as slow as the tolling of a death knell. He

awaited each stroke with impatience and—he knew not why—apprehension. The intervals of silence grew progressively longer; the delays became maddening. With their greater infrequency the sounds increased in strength and sharpness. They hurt his ear like the thrust of a knife; he feared he would shriek. What he heard was the ticking of his watch.

He unclosed his eyes and saw again the water below him. "If I could free my hands," he thought, "I might throw off the noose and spring into the stream. By diving I could evade the bullets and, swimming vigorously, reach the bank, take to the woods, and get away home. My home, thank God, is as yet outside their lines; my wife and little ones are still beyond the invader's farthest advance."

As these thoughts, which have here to be set down in words, were flashed into the doomed man's brain rather than evolved from it, the captain nodded to the sergeant. The sergeant stepped aside.

## 2

Peyton Farquhar was a well-to-do planter of an old and highly respected Alabama family. Being a slave owner and like other slave owners a politician, he was naturally an original secessionist and ardently devoted to the Southern cause. Circumstances of an imperious nature, which it is unnecessary to relate here, had prevented him from taking service with the gallant army which had fought the disastrous campaigns ending with the fall of Corinth, and he chafed under the inglorious restraint, longing for the release of his energies, the larger life of the soldier, the opportunity for distinction. That opportunity, he felt, would come, as it comes to all in war time. Meanwhile he did what he could. No service was too humble for him to perform in aid of the South, no adventure too perilous for him to undertake if consistent with the character of a civilian who was at heart a soldier, and who in good faith and without too

___
2. **hemp,** rope; the noose.

much qualification assented to at least a part of the frankly villainous dictum[3] that all is fair in love and war.

One evening while Farquhar and his wife were sitting on a rustic bench near the entrance to his grounds, a gray-clad soldier rode up to the gate and asked for a drink of water. Mrs. Farquhar was only too happy to serve him with her own white hands. While she was fetching the water her husband approached the dusty horseman and inquired eagerly for news from the front.

"The Yanks are repairing the railroads," said the man, "and are getting ready for another advance. They have reached the Owl Creek bridge, put it in order, and built a stockade on the north bank. The commandant has issued an order, which is posted everywhere, declaring that any civilian caught interfering with the railroad, its bridges, tunnels, or trains will be summarily hanged. I saw the order."

"How far is it to the Owl Creek bridge?" Farquhar asked.

"About thirty miles."

"Is there no force on this side the creek?"

"Only a picket post half a mile out, on the railroad, and a single sentinel at this end of the bridge."

"Suppose a man—a civilian and student of hanging—should elude the picket post and perhaps get the better of the sentinel," said Farquhar, smiling, "what could he accomplish?"

The soldier reflected. "I was there a month ago," he replied. "I observed that the flood of last winter had lodged a great quantity of driftwood against the wooden pier at this end of the bridge. It is now dry and would burn like tow."

The lady had now brought the water, which the soldier drank. He thanked her ceremoniously, bowed to her husband, and rode away. An hour later, after nightfall, he repassed the plantation, going northward in the direction from which he had come. He was a Federal scout.

## 3

As Peyton Farquhar fell straight downward through the bridge he lost consciousness and was as one already dead. From this state he was awakened—ages later, it seemed to him—by the pain of a sharp pressure upon his throat, followed by a sense of suffocation. Keen, poignant agonies seemed to shoot from his neck downward through every fiber of his body and limbs. These pains appeared to flash along well-defined lines of ramification and to beat with an inconceivably rapid periodicity. They seemed like streams of pulsating fire heating him to an intolerable temperature. As to his head, he was conscious of nothing but a feeling of fullness—of congestion. These sensations were unaccompanied by thought. The intellectual part of his nature was already effaced; he had power only to feel, and feeling was torment. He was conscious of motion. Encompassed in a luminous cloud, of which he was now merely the fiery heart, without material substance, he swung through unthinkable arcs of oscillation,[4] like a vast pendulum. Then all at once, with terrible suddenness, the light about him shot upward with the noise of a loud plash; a frightful roaring was in his ears, and all was cold and dark. The power of thought was restored; he knew that the rope had broken and he had fallen into the stream. There was no additional strangulation; the noose about his neck was already suffocating him and kept the water from his lungs. To die of hanging at the bottom of a river!—the idea seemed to him ludicrous. He opened his eyes in the darkness and saw above him a gleam of light, but how distant, how inaccessible! He was still sinking, for the light became fainter and fainter until it was a mere glimmer. Then it began to grow and brighten, and he knew that he was rising toward the surface—knew it with reluctance, for he was now very comfortable. "To be hanged and

---

3. **dictum,** pronouncement.
4. **oscillation**\\'äs•ə **▲**lā•shən\\ swinging back and forth.

drowned," he thought, "that is not so bad; but I do not wish to be shot. No; I will not be shot; that is not fair."

He was not conscious of an effort, but a sharp pain in his wrist apprised him that he was trying to free his hands. He gave the struggle his attention, as an idler might observe the feat of a juggler, without interest in the outcome. What splendid effort!—what magnificent, what superhuman strength! Ah, that was a fine endeavor! Bravo! The cord fell away; his arms parted and floated upward, the hands dimly seen on each side in the growing light. He watched them with a new interest as first one and then the other pounced upon the noose at his neck. They tore it away and thrust it fiercely aside, its undulations resembling those of a water snake. "Put it back, put it back!" He thought he shouted these words to his hands, for the undoing of the noose had been succeeded by the direst pang that he had yet experienced. His neck ached horribly; his brain was on fire; his heart, which had been fluttering faintly, gave a great leap, trying to force itself out at his mouth. His whole body was racked and wrenched with an insupportable anguish! But his disobedient hands gave no heed to the command. They beat the water vigorously with quick, downward strokes, forcing him to the surface. He felt his head emerge; his eyes were blinded by the sunlight; his chest expanded convulsively, and with a supreme and crowning agony his lungs engulfed a great draught of air, which instantly he expelled in a shriek!

He was now in full possession of his physical senses. They were, indeed, preternaturally keen and alert. Something in the awful disturbance of his organic system had so exalted and refined them that they made record of things never before perceived. He felt the ripples upon his face and heard their separate sounds as they struck. He looked at the forest on the bank of the stream, saw the individual trees, the leaves and the veining of each leaf— saw the very insects upon them: the locusts, the brilliant-bodied flies, the gray spiders stretching their webs from twig to twig. He noted the prismatic colors in all the dewdrops upon a million blades of grass. The humming of the gnats that danced above the eddies of the stream, the beating of the dragonflies' wings, the strokes of the water spiders' legs, like oars which had lifted their boat—all these made audible music. A fish slid along beneath his eyes and he heard the rush of its body parting the water.

He had come to the surface facing down the stream; in a moment the visible world seemed to wheel slowly round, himself the pivotal point, and he saw the bridge, the fort, the soldiers upon the bridge, the captain, the sergeant, the two privates, his executioners. They were in silhouette against the blue sky. They shouted and gesticulated, pointing at him. The captain had drawn his pistol, but did not fire; the others were unarmed. Their movements were grotesque and horrible, their forms gigantic.

Suddenly he heard a sharp report and something struck the water smartly within a few inches of his head, spattering his face with spray. He heard a second report, and saw one of the sentinels with his rifle at his shoulder, a light cloud of blue smoke rising from the muzzle. The man in the water saw the eye of the man on the bridge gazing into his own through the sights of the rifle. He observed that it was a gray eye and remembered having read that gray eyes were keenest, and that all famous marksmen had them. Nevertheless, this one had missed.

A counterswirl had caught Farquhar and turned him half round; he was again looking into the forest on the bank opposite the fort. The sound of a clear, high voice in a monotonous singsong now rang out behind him and came across the water with a distinctness that pierced and subdued all other sounds, even the beating of the ripples in his ears. Although no soldier, he had frequented camps enough to know the dread significance of that deliberate, drawling, aspirated chant; the lieutenant on shore was taking a part in the morning's work.

How coldly and pitilessly—with what an even, calm intonation, presaging and enforcing tranquillity in the men—with what accurately measured intervals fell those cruel words:

"Attention, company! . . . Shoulder arms! . . . Ready! . . . Aim! . . . Fire!"

Farquhar dived—dived as deeply as he could. The water roared in his ears like the voice of Niagara, yet he heard the dulled thunder of the volley and, rising again toward the surface, met shining bits of metal, singularly flattened, oscillating slowly downward. Some of them touched him on the face and hands, then fell away, continuing their descent. One lodged between his collar and neck; it was uncomfortably warm and he snatched it out.

As he rose to the surface, gasping for breath, he saw that he had been a long time under water; he was perceptibly farther downstream —nearer to safety. The soldiers had almost finished reloading; the metal ramrods flashed all at once in the sunshine as they were drawn from the barrels, turned in the air, and thrust into their sockets. The two sentinels fired again, independently and ineffectually.

The hunted man saw all this over his shoulder; he was now swimming vigorously with the current. His brain was as energetic as his arms and legs; he thought with the rapidity of lightning.

"The officer," he reasoned, "will not make that martinet's error a second time. It is as easy to dodge a volley as a single shot. He has probably already given the command to fire at will. God help me, I cannot dodge them all!"

An appalling plash within two yards of him was followed by a loud, rushing sound, *diminuendo,*[5] which seemed to travel back through the air to the fort and died in an explosion which stirred the very river to its deeps! A rising sheet of water, which curved over him, fell down upon him, blinded him, strangled him! The cannon had taken a hand in the game. As he shook his head free from the commotion of the smitten water, he heard the deflected shot humming through the air ahead, and in an instant it was cracking and smashing the branches in the forest beyond.

"They will not do that again," he thought; "the next time they will use a charge of grape. I must keep my eye upon the gun; the smoke will apprise me—the report arrives too late; it lags behind the missile. That is a good gun."

Suddenly he felt himself whirled round and round—spinning like a top. The water, the banks, the forests, the now distant bridge, fort, and men—all were commingled and blurred. Objects were represented by their colors only; circular horizontal streaks of color—that was all he saw. He had been caught in a vortex and was being whirled on with a velocity of advance and gyration which made him giddy and sick. In a few moments he was flung upon the gravel at the foot of the left bank of the stream—the southern bank—and behind a projecting point which concealed him from his enemies. The sudden arrest of his motion, the abrasion of one of his hands on the gravel, restored him, and he wept with delight. He dug his fingers into the sand, threw it over himself in handfuls, and audibly blessed it. It looked like diamonds, rubies, emeralds; he could think of nothing beautiful which it did not resemble. The trees upon the bank were giant garden plants; he noted a definite order in their arrangement, inhaled the fragrance of their blooms. A strange, roseate light shone through the spaces among their trunks and the wind made in their branches the music of aeolian harps. He had no wish to perfect his escape—was content to remain in that enchanting spot until retaken.

A whiz and rattle of grapeshot among the branches high above his head roused him from his dream. The baffled cannoneer had fired him a random farewell. He sprang to his feet, rushed up the sloping bank, and plunged into the forest.

All that day he traveled, laying his course by the rounding sun. The forest seemed interminable; nowhere did he discover a break in

---

5. **diminuendo**\də 'mĭn·yə ▲wĕn·dō\ diminishing.

it, not even a woodman's road. He had not known that he lived in so wild a region. There was something uncanny in the revelation.

By nightfall he was fatigued, footsore, famishing. The thought of his wife and children urged him on. At last he found a road which led him in what he knew to be the right direction. It was as wide and straight as a city street, yet it seemed untraveled. No fields bordered it, no dwelling anywhere. Not so much as the barking of a dog suggested human habitation. The black bodies of the trees formed a straight wall on both sides, terminating on the horizon in a point, like a diagram in a lesson in perspective. Overhead, as he looked up through this rift in the wood, shone great golden stars looking unfamiliar and grouped in strange constellations. He was sure they were arranged in some order which had a secret and malign significance. The wood on either side was full of singular noises, among which—once, twice, and again—he distinctly heard whispers in an unknown tongue.

His neck was in pain and lifting his hand to it he found it horribly swollen. He knew that it had a circle of black where the rope had bruised it. His eyes felt congested; he could no longer close them. His tongue was swollen with thirst; he relieved its fever by thrusting it forward from between his teeth into the cold air. How softly the turf had carpeted the untraveled avenue—he could no longer feel the roadway beneath his feet!

Doubtless, despite his suffering, he had fallen asleep while walking, for now he sees another scene—perhaps he has merely recovered from a delirium. He stands at the gate of his own home. All is as he left it, and all bright and beautiful in the morning sunshine. He must have traveled the entire night. As he pushes open the gate and passes up the wide white walk, he sees a flutter of female garments; his wife, looking fresh and cool and sweet, steps down from the veranda to meet him. At the bottom of the steps she stands waiting, with a smile of ineffable joy, an attitude of matchless grace and dignity. Ah, how

beautiful she is! He springs forward with extended arms. As he is about to clasp her, he feels a stunning blow upon the back of the neck; a blinding white light blazes all about him with a sound like the shock of a cannon— then all is darkness and silence!

Peyton Farquhar was dead; his body, with a broken neck, swung gently from side to side beneath the timbers of the Owl Creek bridge.

---

I

## THE PRESSURE OF CRISIS

People report that in moments of extreme crisis a person's whole life flashes before her or his eyes. Psychologists estimate that the mind works about ten times as rapidly as the voice can speak. Therefore, we can think a great deal more rapidly, even mentally putting the ideas into words, than we can possibly express out loud. This story is built upon that premise. Notice how the story is structured in three sections: The first is the actual hanging, the second backs up and tells us how Farquhar got himself into the situation, and the third deals with his imaginary escape. Through this structure the readers are led by their emotions to believe that Farquhar's escape is real. Thus, the last paragraph hits with sudden, unexpected force.

II

## IMPLICATIONS

Consider the following statements. From what you learned through reading the story and from your own experiences, do you agree or disagree?

**1.** The reader hopes that Farquhar escapes.

**2.** As Farquhar waits, the ticking of his watch sounds like a loud bell in the distance. There are several instances in the story of intensified sensory reactions. In times of great stress, one's sensory responses are heightened.

**3.** Since the escape happens only in Farquhar's mind, it is not reasonable that he would imagine himself experiencing such ordeals as being shot at in the water or having his tongue swell from thirst.

**4.** There are clues in the description of the escape tipping off the reader that Farquhar is not experiencing reality.

**5.** What people experience in their minds (their imaginings) has as much reality as what happens to them physically.

### III
### TECHNIQUES

*Theme*

The theme of the story is fairly obvious. Are you more concerned with the external events or with the internal reactions? What, then, does Bierce seem to be exploring?

*Style*

When people have read a good deal of literature, they come to recognize that styles of writing are related to the historical period in which a work was written as well as to the peculiarities of the individual writer. Shakespeare's language does not sound like present-day English. Hemingway would not have written as he did if he had lived in the eighteenth century. Bierce first published this story in 1881. Reread sentence three of Part 2. It begins, "Circumstances of an imperious nature . . . ." What are the details of phrasing or of the arrangement of words which make this sentence different from the way a contemporary author would write it? If you cannot pick out specific details, try to rewrite the sentence as a writer might do it today.

### IV
### WORDS

**A.** Military titles such as those used in "An Occurrence at Owl Creek Bridge" have come into the language from a variety of sources. A *private* is "deprived" of status or rank. This title is derived from the Latin word *privare*, meaning "to deprive." It is related—and you can easily see the resemblance—to *privation*, which means "a lack of what is needed for existence." A *captain* is the "head" of his troop, battery, or company. This title comes from *caput*, meaning in Latin "head." Based on the same Latin word are *capital*, the "head" city of a state or a country, and *decapitate*, which means the severing of the head from the body as was done by the infamous French guillo-

tine. Another military title, *lieutenant*, has its origin in two French words, *lieu*, "place," and *tenant*, "holding." A lieutenant, then, is "holding" the "place" of another, probably that of a higher officer who is relieved of the duties the lieutenant performs. *Lieutenant* has obvious kinship with the common phrase *in lieu of*, meaning "in place of." It is also related to *tenant*, the name given a person who "holds" or rents an apartment or house. Using your dictionary, see whether you can determine the source of these military titles: *major, sergeant, colonel, general, corporal,* and *admiral*.

**B.** In the story, the bridge crosses over a fairly shallow body of water called a *creek*. In Louisiana, a similar body of water is called a *bayou*. In still other parts of the country, it is referred to as *stream, brook, fork, burn, gulf, rivulet, riverlet,* and *branch*. Another word in the story, *veranda*, also has a different name in other sections of the country. A veranda is the extended platform, usually roofed, at the entrance to a building. Among its other names are *porch, portico, gallery,* and *piazza*. Another example of vocabulary difference is reflected in the various names given to what some speakers call *eaves troughs: gutters, canals, spouts, water troughs,* and *spouting*. When you travel from one part of the country to another, you will discover that vocabulary is often one aspect of regional differences. What other names, if any, do you know for each of the following: *cottage cheese, string beans, faucet, paper bag, shed, weather boards, seesaw, peanuts, sofa,* and *window shades*?

**C.** While awaiting execution, Peyton Farquhar hears the *recurrence* of "a sharp, distinct, metallic percussion." The word *recurrence* shares a common Latin root, *-curr-*, with the word *occurrence* in the title of the story. The root means "to run." A *recurrence* of anything is a repetition or "rerunning" of it. An *occurrence* is the taking place of an action or an event; for it to come about, some movement or "running" is necessary. Also based on *-curr-* is the word *current*, referring to the swiftest "running" part of a stream, river, or other body of water. Keeping the meaning of *-curr-* and its variant, *curs*, in mind, try to answer the following questions: Would a good doctor be likely to give an ill patient a cursory examination? What is a cursive style of writing? In what sense was John the Baptist a precursor of Christ? What is an excursion?

## PEOPLE UNDER PRESSURE

People under pressure is a major theme
in modern art and literature. Fortunately,
many of the modern statements on this theme
seem to spring from a humanitarian urgency
to discover trouble and bring help.
However, the long history of torture and
deliberate cruelty in the world reminds us that this
theme is an ancient one and our preoccupation
with it springs from a dark well.

MIGRATION
*William Gropper*
*Oliver B. James Collection of American Art,*
*Arizona State University, Tempe*

Nature has many ways of putting
people under pressure. A dust-bowl
family has been forced to move on
in search of greener pastures.

TORNADO OVER KANSAS
*John Steuart Curry*

A storm funnel threatens a Kansas farm family
in the action-filled painting
by the contemporary painter Curry.
Luckier than some, these people are able to respond
to the pressure by evacuating to a storm cellar.

The pressures that war imposes upon people
are all too well known. This sketch
of the occupants of an invasion craft
points out the pressures of waiting
to be landed in battle.

FRAIL CRAFT
*Lieut. Mitchell Jamieson,* USNR

The atmosphere
of death hangs
over the blue
painting of tragedy.
The pressure of loss
and its damage
to the spirit
are movingly
recorded.

THE TRAGEDY
*Pablo Picasso*
*National Gallery of Art,*
*Washington, D.C.,*
*Chester Dale Collection*

520

**COURTYARD
OF A PRISON**
*Vincent*

Confinement, real or imagined, is one of humankind's most destructive pressures. The unhappy circle of defeated men revolving within the high confining prison walls is Van Gogh's stirring statement of their bitter pressure.

TERROR IN BROOKLYN
*Louis Guglielmi*
*1941, Oil, Collection*
*of the Whitney Museum of*
*American Art, New York*

The terrified women in Guglielmi's painting are trapped
in a confining glass, and the horrors that they fear are indicated
by the painter's symbols. You must decide
whether the threats are real or imagined.

The Biblical hero Samson,
like all epic heroes,
often found himself
under great pressure.
Here, blinded,
he is tied to a mill wheel
and tormented by slave drivers.
This painting is an early work
of the modern French painter
Rouault whose later style
was much less detailed
than what you see.

SAMSON AT THE MILLSTONE
*Georges Rouault*
*Los Angeles County Museum of Art,*
*Museum Purchase with De Sylva Funds*

THE PIT AND THE PENDULUM
*Alphonse Legros*
*Philadelphia Museum of Art*

In his etching
for Edgar Allan Poe's story
of the same name,
Legros depicts
the unendurable pressures
on the prisoner in the
rat-infested pit waiting for
the descending blade swinging
closer on the pendulum.

You are sixty-one years old, living comfortably, or so you think, a life of quiet contentment. Can it be that even so, you are under pressures from your subconscious which cause you to lose your grip on reality?

# Miriam

### TRUMAN CAPOTE

For several years Mrs. H. T. Miller had lived alone in a pleasant apartment (two rooms with kitchenette) in a remodeled brownstone[1] near the East River. She was a widow: Mr. H. T. Miller had left a reasonable amount of insurance. Her interests were narrow, she had no friends to speak of, and she rarely journeyed farther than the corner grocery. The other people in the house never seemed to notice her: her clothes were matter of fact, her hair iron-gray, clipped, and casually waved; she did not use cosmetics, her features were plain and inconspicuous, and on her last birthday she was sixty-one. Her activities were seldom spontaneous: she kept the two rooms immaculate, smoked an occasional cigarette, prepared her own meals, and tended a canary.

Then she met Miriam. It was snowing that night. Mrs. Miller had finished drying the supper dishes and was thumbing through an afternoon paper when she saw an advertisement of a picture playing at a neighborhood theater. The title sounded good, so she struggled into her beaver coat, laced her galoshes, and left the apartment, leaving one light burning in the foyer—she found nothing more disturbing than a sensation of darkness.

The snow was fine, falling gently, not yet making an impression on the pavement. The wind from the river cut only at street crossings. Mrs. Miller hurried, her head bowed, oblivious as a mole burrowing a blind path. She stopped at a drugstore and bought a package of peppermints.

A long line stretched in front of the box office; she took her place at the end. There would be (a tired voice groaned) a short wait for all seats. Mrs. Miller rummaged in her leather handbag till she collected exactly the correct change for admission. The line seemed to be taking its own time and, looking around for some distraction, she suddenly became conscious of a little girl standing under the edge of the marquee.

Her hair was the longest and strangest Mrs. Miller had ever seen: absolutely silver-white, like an albino's. It flowed waist-length in smooth, loose lines. She was thin and fragilely constructed. There was a simple, special elegance in the way she stood with her thumbs in the pockets of a tailored plum velvet coat.

Mrs. Miller felt oddly excited, and when the little girl glanced toward her, she smiled warmly. The little girl walked over and said, "Would you care to do me a favor?"

"I'd be glad to, if I can," said Mrs. Miller.

"Oh, it's quite easy. I merely want you to buy a ticket for me; they won't let me in otherwise. Here, I have the money." And gracefully she handed Mrs. Miller two dimes and a nickel.

They went into the theater together. An usherette directed them to a lounge; in twenty minutes the picture would be over.

"I feel just like a genuine criminal," said Mrs. Miller gaily, as she sat down. "I mean that sort of thing's against the law, isn't it? I do hope I haven't done the wrong thing. Your mother knows where you are, dear? I mean she does, doesn't she?"

The little girl said nothing. She unbuttoned

Copyright 1945 by Truman Capote. Reprinted from SELECTED WRITINGS OF TRUMAN CAPOTE by permission of Random House, Inc.

1. **brownstone**, a house faced with reddish-brown sandstone, once very popular.

525

her coat and folded it across her lap. Her dress underneath was prim and dark blue. A gold chain dangled about her neck and her fingers, sensitive and musical-looking, toyed with it. Examining her more attentively, Mrs. Miller decided the truly distinctive feature was not her hair, but her eyes; they were hazel, steady, lacking any childlike quality whatsoever and, because of their size, seemed to consume her small face.

Mrs. Miller offered a peppermint. "What's your name, dear?"

"Miriam," she said, as though, in some curious way, it were information already familiar.

"Why, isn't that funny? My name's Miriam too. And it's not a terribly common name either. Now, don't tell me your last name's Miller!"

"Just Miriam."

"But isn't that funny?"

"Moderately," said Miriam, and rolled the peppermint on her tongue.

Mrs. Miller flushed and shifted uncomfortably. "You have such a large vocabulary for such a little girl."

"Do I?"

"Well, yes," said Mrs. Miller, hastily changing the topic to: "Do you like the movies?"

"I really wouldn't know," said Miriam. "I've never been before."

Women began filling the lounge; the rumble of the newsreel bombs exploded in the distance. Mrs. Miller rose, tucking her purse under her arm. "I guess I'd better be running now if I want to get a seat," she said. "It was nice to have met you."

Miriam nodded ever so slightly.

It snowed all week. Wheels and footsteps moved soundlessly on the street, as if the business of living continued secretly behind a pale but impenetrable curtain. In the falling quiet there was no sky or earth, only snow lifting in the wind, frosting the window glass, chilling the rooms, deadening and hushing the city. At all hours it was necessary to keep a lamp lighted, and Mrs. Miller lost track of the days:

Friday was no different from Saturday and on Sunday she went to the grocery: closed, of course.

That evening she scrambled eggs and fixed a bowl of tomato soup. Then, after putting on a flannel robe and cold-creaming her face, she propped herself up in bed with a hot-water bottle under her feet. She was reading the *Times* when the doorbell rang. At first she thought it must be a mistake and whoever it was would go away. But it rang and rang and settled to a persistent buzz. She looked at the clock: a little after eleven; it did not seem possible, she was always asleep by ten.

Climbing out of bed, she trotted barefoot across the living room. "I'm coming; please be patient." The latch was caught; she turned it this way and that way and the bell never paused an instant. "Stop it!" she cried. The bolt gave way and she opened the door an inch. "What in heaven's name?"

"Hello," said Miriam.

"Oh . . . why, hello," said Mrs. Miller, stepping hesitantly into the hall. "You're that little girl."

"I thought you'd never answer, but I kept my finger on the button; I knew you were home. Aren't you glad to see me?"

Mrs. Miller did not know what to say. Miriam, she saw, wore she same plum velvet coat and now she had also a beret to match; her white hair was braided in two shining plaits and looped at the ends with enormous white ribbons.

"Since I've waited so long, you could at least let me in," she said.

"It's awfully late."

Miriam regarded her blankly. "What difference does that make? Let me in. It's cold out here and I have on a silk dress." Then, with a gentle gesture, she urged Mrs. Miller aside and passed into the apartment.

She dropped her coat and beret on a chair. She was indeed wearing a silk dress. White silk. White silk in February. The skirt was beautifully pleated and the sleeves long; it made a faint rustle as she strolled about the room. "I like your place," she said. "I like the rug; blue's my favorite color." She touched a paper rose in a vase on the coffee table. "Imitation," she commented wanly. "How sad. Aren't imitations sad?" She seated herself on the sofa, daintily spreading her skirt.

"What do you want?" asked Mrs. Miller.

"Sit down," said Miriam. "It makes me nervous to see people stand."

Mrs. Miller sank to a hassock. "What do you want?" she repeated.

"You know, I don't think you're glad I came."

For a second time Mrs. Miller was without an answer; her hand motioned vaguely. Miriam giggled and pressed back on a mound of chintz pillows. Mrs. Miller observed that the girl was less pale than she remembered; her cheeks were flushed.

"How did you know where I lived?"

Miriam frowned. "That's no question at all. What's your name? What's mine?"

"But I'm not listed in the phone book."

"Oh, let's talk about something else."

Mrs. Miller said, "Your mother must be insane to let a child like you wander around at all hours of the night . . . and in such ridiculous clothes. She must be out of her mind."

Miriam got up and moved to a corner where a covered bird cage hung from a ceiling chain. She peeked beneath the cover. "It's a canary," she said. "Would you mind if I woke him? I'd like to hear him sing."

"Leave Tommy alone," said Mrs. Miller anxiously. "Don't you dare wake him."

"Certainly," said Miriam. "But I don't see why I can't hear him sing." And then, "Have you anything to eat? I'm starving! Even milk and a jam sandwich would be fine."

"Look," said Mrs. Miller, arising from the hassock, "look, if I make some nice sandwiches will you be a good child and run along home? It's past midnight, I'm sure."

"It's snowing," reproached Miriam. "And cold and dark."

"Well, you shouldn't have come here to begin with," said Mrs. Miller, struggling to control her voice. "I can't help the weather. If you want anything to eat you'll have to promise to leave."

Miriam brushed a braid against her cheek. Her eyes were thoughtful, as if weighing the proposition. She turned toward the bird cage. "Very well," she said, "I promise."

*How old is she? Ten? Eleven?* Mrs. Miller, in the kitchen, unsealed a jar of strawberry preserves and cut four slices of bread. She poured a glass of milk and paused to light a cigarette. *And why has she come?* Her hand shook as she held the match, fascinated, till it burned her finger. The canary was singing— singing as he did in the morning and at no other time. "Miriam," she called, "Miriam, I told you not to disturb Tommy." There was no answer. She called again; all she heard was the canary. She inhaled the cigarette and discovered she had lighted the cork-tip end and . . . oh, really, she mustn't lose her temper.

She carried the food in on a tray and set it on the coffee table. She saw first that the bird cage still wore its night cover. And Tommy was singing. It gave her a queer sensation. And no one was in the room. Mrs. Miller went through an alcove leading to her bedroom; at the door she caught her breath.

"What are you doing?" she asked.

Miriam glanced up, and in her eyes there was a look that was not ordinary. She was standing by the bureau, a jewel case opened before her. For a minute she studied Mrs. Miller, forcing their eyes to meet, and she smiled. "There's nothing good here," she said. "But I like this." Her hand held a cameo brooch. "It's charming."

"Suppose—perhaps you'd better put it back," said Mrs. Miller, feeling suddenly the need of some support. She leaned against the doorframe; her head was unbearably heavy; a pressure weighted the rhythm of her heartbeat. The light seemed to flutter defectively. "Please, child—a gift from my husband . . . ."

"But it's beautiful and I want it," said Miriam. *"Give it to me."*

As she stood, striving to shape a sentence

which would somehow save the brooch, it came to Mrs. Miller there was no one to whom she might turn; she was alone; a fact that had not been among her thoughts for a long time. Its sheer emphasis was stunning. But here in her own room in the hushed snow city were evidences she could not ignore or, she knew with startling clarity, resist.

Miriam ate ravenously, and when the sandwiches and milk were gone, her fingers made cobweb movements over the plate, gathering crumbs. The cameo gleamed on her blouse, the blond profile like a trick reflection of its wearer. "That was very nice," she sighed, "though now an almond cake or a cherry would be ideal. Sweets are lovely, don't you think?"

Mrs. Miller was perched precariously on the hassock, smoking a cigarette. Her hair net had slipped lopsided and loose strands straggled down her face. Her eyes were stupidly concentrated on nothing, and her cheeks were mottled in red patches, as though a fierce slap had left permanent marks.

"Is there a candy . . . a cake?"

Mrs. Miller tapped ash on the rug. Her head swayed slightly as she tried to focus her eyes. "You promised to leave if I made the sandwiches," she said.

"Dear me, did I?"

"It was a promise and I'm tired and I don't feel well at all."

"Mustn't fret," said Miriam. "I'm only teasing."

She picked up her coat, slung it over her arm, and arranged her beret in front of a mirror. Presently she bent close to Mrs. Miller and whispered, "Kiss me good night."

"Please . . . I'd rather not," said Mrs. Miller.

Miriam lifted a shoulder, arched an eyebrow. "As you like," she said, and went directly to the coffee table, seized the vase containing the paper roses, carried it to where the hard surface of the floor lay bare, and hurled it downward. Glass sprayed in all directions and she stamped her foot on the bouquet.

Then slowly she walked to the door, but before closing it she looked back at Mrs. Miller with a slyly innocent curiosity.

Mrs. Miller spent the next day in bed, rising once to feed the canary and drink a cup of tea; she took her temperature and had none, yet her dreams were feverishly agitated; their unbalanced mood lingered even as she lay staring wide-eyed at the ceiling. One dream threaded through the others like an elusively mysterious theme in a complicated symphony, and the scenes it depicted were sharply outlined, as though sketched by a hand of gifted intensity: a small girl, wearing a bridal gown and a wreath of leaves, led a gray procession down a mountain path, and among them there was unusual silence till a woman at the rear asked, "Where is she taking us?" "No one knows," said an old man marching in front. "But isn't she pretty?" volunteered a third voice. "Isn't she like a frost flower—so shining and white?"

Tuesday morning she woke up feeling better; harsh slats of sunlight, slanting through Venetian blinds, shed a disrupting light on her unwholesome fancies. She opened the window to discover a thawed, mild-as-spring day; a sweep of clean new clouds crumpled against a vastly blue, out-of-season sky; and across the low line of rooftops she could see the river and smoke curving from tugboat stacks in a warm wind. A great silver truck plowed the snow-banked street, its machine sound humming on the air.

After straightening the apartment, she went to the grocer's, cashed a check, and continued to Schrafft's, where she ate breakfast and chatted happily with the waitress. Oh, it was a wonderful day . . . more like a holiday . . . and it would be so foolish to go home.

She boarded a Lexington Avenue bus and rode up to Eighty-sixth Street; it was here that she had decided to do a little shopping.

She had no idea what she wanted or needed, but she idled along, intent only upon the passers-by, brisk and preoccupied, who gave her a disturbing sense of separateness.

It was while waiting at the corner of Third Avenue that she saw the man: an old man, bowlegged and stooped under an armload of bulging packages; he wore a shabby brown coat and a checkered cap. Suddenly she realized they were exchanging a smile; there was nothing friendly about this smile, it was merely two cold flickers of recognition. But she was certain she had never seen him before.

He was standing next to an el[2] pillar, and as she crossed the street he turned and followed. He kept quite close; from the corner of her eye she watched his reflection wavering on the shopwindows.

Then in the middle of the block she stopped and faced him. He stopped also and cocked his head, grinning. But what could she say? Do? Here, in broad daylight, on Eighty-sixth Street? It was useless and, despising her own helplessness, she quickened her steps.

Now Second Avenue is a dismal street, made from scraps and ends; part cobblestone, part asphalt, part cement; and its atmosphere of desertion is permanent. Mrs. Miller walked five blocks without meeting anyone, and all the while the steady crunch of his footfalls in the snow stayed near. And when she came to a florist's shop, the sound was still with her. She hurried inside and watched through the glass door as the old man passed; he kept his eyes straight ahead and didn't slow his pace, but he did one strange, telling thing: he tipped his cap.

"Six white ones, did you say?" asked the florist. "Yes," she told him, "white roses."

From there she went to a glassware store and selected a vase, presumably a replacement for the one Miriam had broken, though the price was intolerable and the vase itself (she thought) grotesquely vulgar. But a series of unaccountable purchases had begun, as if by prearranged plan—a plan of which she had not the least knowledge or control.

She bought a bag of glazed cherries, and at a place called the Knickerbocker Bakery she paid forty cents for six almond cakes.

Within the last hour the weather had turned cold again; like blurred lenses, winter clouds cast a shade over the sun, and the skeleton of an early dusk colored the sky; a damp mist mixed with the wind and the voices of a few children who romped high on mountains of gutter snow seemed lonely and cheerless. Soon the first flake fell, and when Mrs. Miller reached the brownstone house, snow was falling in a swift screen and foot tracks vanished as they were printed.

The white roses were arranged decoratively in the vase. The glazed cherries shone on a ceramic plate. The almond cakes, dusted with sugar, awaited a hand. The canary fluttered on its swing and picked at a bar of seed.

At precisely five the doorbell rang. Mrs. Miller *knew* who it was. The hem of her house coat trailed as she crossed the floor. "Is that you?" she called.

"Naturally," said Miriam, the word resounding shrilly from the hall. "Open this door."

"Go away," said Mrs. Miller.

"Please hurry—I have a heavy package."

"Go away," said Mrs. Miller. She returned to the living room, lighted a cigarette, sat down and calmly listened to the buzzer; on and on and on. "You might as well leave. I have no intention of letting you in."

Shortly the bell stopped. For possibly ten minutes Mrs. Miller did not move. Then, hearing no sound, she concluded Miriam had gone. She tiptoed to the door and opened it a sliver; Miriam was half reclining atop a cardboard box with a beautiful French doll cradled in her arms.

"Really, I thought you were never coming," she said peevishly. "Here, help me get this in, it's awfully heavy."

It was not spell-like compulsion that Mrs. Miller felt, but rather a curious passivity; she brought in the box, Miriam the doll. Miriam curled up on the sofa, not troubling to remove her coat or beret, and watched disinterestedly as Mrs. Miller dropped the box and stood trembling, trying to catch her breath.

---

2. **el**, elevated railway.

"Thank you," she said. In the daylight she looked pinched and drawn, her hair less luminous. The French doll she was loving wore an exquisite powdered wig and its idiot glass eyes sought solace in Miriam's. "I have a surprise," she continued. "Look into my box."

Kneeling, Mrs. Miller parted the flaps and lifted out another doll; then a blue dress which she recalled as the one Miriam had worn that first night at the theater; and of the remainder she said, "It's all clothes. Why?"

"Because I've come to live with you," said Miriam, twisting a cherry stem. "Wasn't it nice of you to buy me the cherries——"

"But you can't! For God's sake go away— go away and leave me alone!"

"——and the roses and the almond cakes? How really wonderfully generous. You know, these cherries are delicious. The last place I lived was with an old man; he was terribly poor and we never had good things to eat. But I think I'll be happy here." She paused to snuggle her doll closer. "Now, if you'll just show me where to put my things . . . ."

Mrs. Miller's face dissolved into a mask of ugly red lines; she began to cry, and it was an unnatural, tearless sort of weeping, as though, not having wept for a long time, she had forgotten how. Carefully she edged backward till she touched the door.

She fumbled through the hall and down the stairs to a landing below. She pounded frantically on the door of the first apartment she came to; a short, redheaded man answered and she pushed past him. "Say, what is this?" he said. "Anything wrong, lover?" asked a young woman who appeared from the kitchen, drying her hands. And it was to her that Mrs. Miller turned.

"Listen," she cried, "I'm ashamed behaving this way, but—well, I'm Mrs. H. T. Miller and I live upstairs and"—she pressed her hands over her face—"it sounds so absurd . . . ."

The woman guided her to a chair, while the man excitedly rattled pocket change. "Yeah?"

"I live upstairs and there's a little girl visiting me, and I suppose that I'm afraid of her. She won't leave and I can't make her and— she's going to do something terrible. She's already stolen my cameo, but she's about to do something worse—something terrible!"

The man asked, "Is she a relative, huh?"

Mrs. Miller shook her head. "I don't know who she is. Her name's Miriam, but I don't know for certain who she is."

"You gotta calm down, honey," said the woman, stroking Mrs. Miller's arm. "Harry here'll tend to this kid. Go on, lover." And Mrs. Miller said, "The door's open—5A."

After the man left, the woman brought a towel and bathed Mrs. Miller's face. "You're very kind," Mrs. Miller said. "I'm sorry to act like such a fool, only this wicked child . . . ."

"Sure, honey," consoled the woman. "Now, you better take it easy."

Mrs. Miller rested her head in the crook of her arm; she was quiet enough to be asleep. The woman turned a radio dial; a piano and a husky voice filled the silence and the woman, tapping her foot, kept excellent time. "Maybe we oughta go up too," she said.

"I don't want to see her again. I don't want to be anywhere near her."

"Uh huh, but what you shoulda done, you shoulda called a cop."

Presently they heard the man on the stairs. He strode into the room frowning and scratching the back of his neck. "Nobody there," he said, honestly embarrassed. "She musta beat it."

"Harry, you're a jerk," announced the woman. "We been sitting here the whole time and we woulda seen . . ." She stopped abruptly, for the man's glance was sharp.

"I looked all over," he said, "and there just ain't nobody there. Nobody, understand?"

"Tell me," said Mrs. Miller, rising, "tell me, did you see a large box? Or a doll?"

"No, ma'am, I didn't."

And the woman, as if delivering a verdict, said, "Well, for cryinoutloud . . . ."

Mrs. Miller entered her apartment softly; she walked to the center of the room and stood quite still. No, in a sense it had not changed: the roses, the cakes, and the cherries were in place. But this was an empty room, emptier than if the furnishings and familiars were not present, lifeless and petrified as a funeral parlor. The sofa loomed before her with a new strangeness: its vacancy had a meaning that would have been less penetrating and terrible had Miriam been curled on it. She gazed fixedly at the space where she remembered setting the box and for a moment the hassock spun desperately. And she looked through the window; surely the river was real, surely snow was falling. But then one could not be certain witness to anything: Miriam, so vividly *there* . . . and yet, where was she? Where, where?

As though moving in a dream, she sank to a chair. The room was losing shape; it was dark and getting darker and there was nothing to be done about it: she could not lift her hand to light a lamp.

Suddenly, closing her eyes, she felt an upward surge, like a diver emerging from some deeper, greener depth. In times of terror or immense distress there are moments when the mind waits, as though for a revelation, while a skein of calm is woven over thought; it is like sleep, or a supernatural trance; and during this lull one is aware of a force of quiet reasoning: well, what if she had never really known a girl named Miriam? That she had been foolishly frightened on the street? In the end, like everything else, it was of no importance. For the only thing she had lost to Miriam was her identity, but now she knew she had found again the person who lived in this room, who cooked her own meals, who owned a canary, who was someone she could trust and believe in: Mrs. H. T. Miller.

Listening in contentment, she became aware of a double sound: a bureau drawer opening and closing; she seemed to hear it long after completion—opening and closing. Then gradually the harshness of it was replaced by the murmur of a silk dress and this, delicately faint, was moving nearer and swelling in intensity till the walls trembled with the vibration and the room was caving under a wave of whispers. Mrs. Miller stiffened and opened her eyes to a dull, direct stare.

"Hello," said Miriam.

## I

### A QUIET DESPERATION

Everyone experiences times when things that are real seem to take on an unreal quality: the ordinary is extraordinary; the known is unknown. This distortion of the familiar may take place in a heavy fog that changes our perspective or during a heat wave accompanied by an oppressive wind that brings on irrational emotions. In times of illness, pain and fever may distort a room or make faces strangely weird. Capote's story has this same quality. Notice that it takes place during a prolonged snowstorm when the life of the city has momentarily stopped. The reader slowly comes to feel the strangely disoriented feelings that Mrs. Miller herself is experiencing, which produce a kind of quiet desperation.

## II

### IMPLICATIONS

**A.** The following statements were generated by the story you have read. They are not necessarily right or wrong. What do your own experiences lead you to believe is the truth about these implications?

**1.** Loneliness is a terrible pressure. Mrs. Miller only imagines Miriam.

**2.** Miriam is trying to take over Mrs. Miller's personality.

**3.** In legend, the Snow Queen is often portrayed as Death. Many details in the story tie Miriam to this legend.

**4.** Mrs. Miller's strange passivity when Miriam arrives to stay is a stage of dying.

**5.** Mrs. Miller is trying to withstand two pressures at one time: that of her moral obligation to help a child and her feeling that she is being used.

**B.** Discuss the following quotations. How valid are the ideas presented? What do they imply about life?

**1.** " 'Imitation,' she commented wanly. 'How sad. Aren't imitations sad?' "

**2.** "But a series of unaccountable purchases had begun, as if by prearranged plan—a plan of which she had not the least knowledge or control."

**3.** "In the end, like everything else, it was of no importance. For the only thing she had lost to Miriam was her identity. . . ."

## III

### TECHNIQUES

*Theme*

What happens to Mrs. Miller's personality as the story progresses? Considering this, how would you express the theme?

*Style*

How does the language reflect Mrs. Miller's personality? How does this style contrast with the events?

## IV

### WORDS

**A.** Words often spring from seemingly unlikely backgrounds. It appears improbable, for example, that Mrs. Miller's canary could be related to the canine (dog) family. Yet, in an etymological sense, it is. (*Etymology* is the study of the origin and development of words.) The canary is a native of the Canary Islands from which it gets its name. When the Romans landed on the islands, they were astonished to find many huge dogs. They were so impressed by these wild animals that they named the islands "*Canariae Insulae*," that is, "The Canary Islands," meaning "The Isles of Dogs." *Canariae* is derived from *canis*, "dog." The little bird was later named after the islands.

**B.** The English lexical (word) stockpile has been greatly enriched, as you have seen elsewhere in this book, by borrowings from French. The following words from "Miriam" are all French contributions: *beret, bouquet, alcove, marquee, foyer,* and *bureau.* A dictionary ordinarily indicates, usually within brackets, the derivation of a word. If the word originated from French, the abbreviation, when used, is *F.* When *O* or *M* precedes the *F*, it means Old French or Middle French. Frequently, a French loan-word is traceable to yet another language. *Alcove,* for example, goes back to Spanish *alcoba,* from Arabic *al-qubbah,* "the vault." Using a dictionary, look up the meaning as well as the background of each of these words borrowed from French: *sacrament, vestige, chaperone, brochure, encore, liaison, melee, rapport, surveillance,* and *protégé.*

He would have liked a few more minutes in which to turn things around in his head. As it was, with Jennie chiding him about being afraid, he had to keep going.

# A Summer Tragedy

### ARNA BONTEMPS

Old Jeff Patton, the black share farmer, fumbled with his bow tie. His fingers trembled and the high, stiff collar pinched his throat. A fellow loses his hand for such vanities after thirty or forty years of simple life. Once a year, or maybe twice if there's a wedding among his kinfolks, he may spruce up; but generally fancy clothes do nothing but adorn the wall of the big room and feed the moths. That had been Jeff Patton's experience. He had not worn his stiff-bosomed shirt more than a dozen times in all his married life. His swallow-tailed coat lay on the bed beside him, freshly brushed and pressed, but it was as full of holes as the overalls in which he worked on weekdays. The moths had used it badly. Jeff twisted his mouth into a hideous toothless grimace as he contended with the obstinate bow. He stamped his good foot and decided to give up the struggle.

"Jennie," he called.

"What's that, Jeff?" His wife's shrunken voice came out of the adjoining room like an echo. It was hardly bigger than a whisper.

"I reckon you'll have to he'p me wid this heah bow tie, baby," he said meekly. "Dog if I can hitch it up."

Her answer was not strong enough to reach him, but presently the old woman came to the door, feeling her way with a stick. She had a wasted, dead-leaf appearance. Her body, as scrawny and gnarled as a string bean, seemed less than nothing in the ocean of frayed and faded petticoats that surrounded her. These hung an inch or two above the tops of her heavy unlaced shoes and showed little grotesque piles where the stockings had fallen down from her negligible legs.

"You oughta could do a heap mo' wid a thing like that'n me—beingst as you got yo' good sight."

"Looks like I oughta could," he admitted. "But my fingers is gone democrat on me. I get all mixed up in the looking glass an' can't tell wicha way to twist the devilish thing."

Jennie sat on the side of the bed, and old Jeff Patton got down on one knee while she tied the bow knot. It was a slow and painful ordeal for each of them in this position. Jeff's bones cracked, his knee ached, and it was only after a half dozen attempts that Jennie worked a semblance of a bow into the tie.

"I got to dress maself now," the old woman whispered. "These is ma old shoes an' stockings, and I ain't so much as unwrapped ma dress."

"Well, don't worry 'bout me no mo', baby," Jeff said. "That 'bout finishes me. All I gotta do now is slip on that old coat 'n ves' an' I'll be fixed to leave."

Jennie disappeared again through the dim passage into the shed room. Being blind was no handicap to her in that black hole. Jeff heard the cane placed against the wall beside the door and knew that his wife was on easy ground. He put on his coat, took a battered top hat from the bed post, and hobbled to the front door. He was ready to travel. As soon as Jennie could get on her Sunday shoes and her old black silk dress, they would start.

Outside the tiny log house, the day was warm and mellow with sunshine. A host of wasps were humming with busy excitement in the trunk of a dead sycamore. Gray squirrels were searching through the grass for hickory nuts, and blue jays were in the trees, hopping

Reprinted by permission of HAROLD OBER ASSOCIATES INCORPORATED. Copyright 1933 by Arna Bontemps.

from branch to branch. Pine woods stretched away to the left like a black sea. Among them were scattered scores of log houses like Jeff's, houses of black share farmers. Cows and pigs wandered freely among the trees. There was no danger of loss. Each farmer knew his own stock and knew his neighbor's as well as he knew his neighbor's children.

Down the slope to the right were the cultivated acres on which the colored folks worked. They extended to the river, more than two miles away, and they were today green with the unmade cotton crop. A tiny thread of a road, which passed directly in front of Jeff's place, ran through these green fields like a pencil mark.

Jeff, standing outside the door, with his absurd hat in his left hand, surveyed the wide scene tenderly. He had been forty-five years on these acres. He loved them with the unexplained affection that others have for the countries to which they belong.

The sun was hot on his head, his collar still pinched his throat, and the Sunday clothes were intolerably hot. Jeff transferred the hat to his right hand and began fanning with it. Suddenly the whisper that was Jennie's voice came out of the shed room.

"You can bring the car round front whilst you's waitin'," it said feebly. There was a tired pause; then it added, "I'll soon be fixed to go."

"A'right, baby," Jeff answered. "I'll get it in a minute."

But he didn't move. A thought struck him that made his mouth fall open. The mention of the car brought to his mind, with new intensity, the trip he and Jennie were about to take. Fear came into his eyes; excitement took his breath. Lord, Jesus!

"Jeff . . . . O Jeff," the old woman's whisper called.

He awakened with a jolt. "Hunh, baby?"

"What you doin'?"

"Nuthin. Jes studyin'. I jes been turnin' things round 'n round in ma mind."

"You could be gettin' the car," she said.

"Oh yes, right away, baby."

He started round to the shed, limping heavily on his bad leg. There were three frizzly chickens in the yard. All his other chickens had been killed or stolen recently. But the frizzly chickens had been saved somehow. That was fortunate indeed, for these curious creatures had a way of devouring "poison"[1] from the yard and in that way protecting against conjure[2] and black luck and spells. But even the frizzly chickens seemed now to be in a stupor. Jeff thought they had some ailment; he expected all three of them to die shortly.

The shed in which the old T-model Ford stood was only a grass roof held up by four corner poles. It had been built by tremulous hands at a time when the little rattletrap car had been regarded as a peculiar treasure. And, miraculously, despite wind and downpour, it still stood.

Jeff adjusted the crank and put his weight upon it. The engine came to life with a sputter and bang that rattled the old car from radiator to tail light. Jeff hopped into the seat and put his foot on the accelerator. The sputtering and banging increased. The rattling became more violent. That was good. It was good banging, good sputtering and rattling, and it meant that the aged car was still in running condition. She could be depended on for this trip.

Again Jeff's thought halted as if paralyzed. The suggestion of the trip fell into the machinery of his mind like a wrench. He felt dazed and weak. He swung the car out into the yard, made a half turn, and drove around to the front door. When he took his hands off the wheel, he noticed that he was trembling violently. He cut off the motor and climbed to the ground to wait for Jennie.

A few minutes later she was at the window, her voice rattling against the pane like a broken shutter.

"I'm ready, Jeff."

---

1. **poison,** something left in the yard to cast spells on the occupants of the house.
2. **conjure**\ˈkən·jər\ harmful magic or spells.

He did not answer, but limped into the house and took her by the arm. He led her slowly through the big room, down the step, and across the yard.

"You reckon I'd oughta lock the do'?" he asked softly.

They stopped and Jennie weighed the question. Finally she shook her head.

"Ne' mind the do'," she said. "I don't see no cause to lock up things."

"You right," Jeff agreed. "No cause to lock up."

Jeff opened the door and helped his wife into the car. A quick shudder passed over him. Jesus! Again he trembled.

"How come you shaking so?" Jennie whispered.

"I don't know," he said.

"You mus' be scairt, Jeff."

"No, baby, I ain't scairt."

He slammed the door after her and went around to crank up again. The motor started easily. Jeff wished that it had not been so responsive. He would have liked a few more minutes in which to turn things around in his head. As it was, with Jennie chiding him about being afraid, he had to keep going. He swung the car into the little pencil-mark road and started off toward the river, driving very slowly, very cautiously.

Chugging across the green countryside, the small battered Ford seemed tiny indeed. Jeff felt a familiar excitement, a thrill, as they came down the first slope to the immense levels on which the cotton was growing. He could not help reflecting that the crops were good. He knew what that meant, too; he had made forty-five of them with his own hands. It was true that he had worn out nearly a dozen mules, but that was the fault of old man Stevenson, the owner of the land. Major Stevenson had the odd notion that one mule was all a share farmer needed to work a thirty-acre plot. It was an expensive notion, the way it killed mules from overwork, but the old man held to it. Jeff thought it killed a good many share farmers as well as mules, but he had no sympathy for them. He had always been strong, and he had been taught to have no patience with weakness in men. Women or children

535

might be tolerated if they were puny, but a weak man was a curse. Of course, his own children—

Jeff's thought halted there. He and Jennie never mentioned their dead children any more. And naturally, he did not wish to dwell upon them in his mind. Before he knew it, some remark would slip out of his mouth and that would make Jennie feel blue. Perhaps she would cry. A woman like Jennie could not easily throw off the grief that comes from losing five grown children within two years. Even Jeff was still staggered by the blow. His memory had not been much good recently. He frequently talked to himself. And, although he had kept it a secret, he knew that his courage had left him. He was terrified by the least unfamiliar sound at night. He was reluctant to venture far from home in the daytime. And that habit of trembling when he felt fearful was now far beyond his control. Sometimes he became afraid and trembled without knowing what had frightened him. The feeling would just come over him like a chill.

The car rattled slowly over the dusty road. Jennie sat erect and silent with a little absurd hat pinned to her hair. Her useless eyes seemed very large, very white in their deep sockets. Suddenly Jeff heard her voice, and he inclined his head to catch the words.

"Is we passed Delia Moore's house yet?" she asked.

"Not yet," he said.

"You must be drivin' mighty slow, Jeff."

"We just as well take our time, baby."

There was a pause. A little puff of steam was coming out of the radiator of the car. Heat wavered above the hood. Delia Moore's house was nearly half a mile away. After a moment Jennie spoke again.

"You ain't really scairt, is you, Jeff?"

"Nah, baby, I ain't scairt."

"You know how we agreed—we gotta keep on goin'."

Jewels of perspiration appeared on Jeff's forehead. His eyes rounded, blinked, became fixed on the road.

"I don't know," he said with a shiver, "I reckon it's the only thing to do."

"Hm."

A flock of guinea fowls, pecking in the road, were scattered by the passing car. Some of them took to their wings; others hid under bushes. A blue jay, swaying on a leafy twig, was annoying a roadside squirrel. Jeff held an even speed till he came near Delia's place. Then he slowed down noticeably.

Delia's house was really no house at all, but an abandoned store building converted into a dwelling. It sat near a crossroads, beneath a single black cedar tree. There Delia, a cattish old creature of Jennie's age, lived alone. She had been there more years than anybody could remember, and long ago had won the disfavor of such women as Jennie. For in her young days Delia had been gayer, yellower, and saucier than seemed proper in those parts. Her ways with menfolks had been dark and suspicious. And the fact that she had had as many husbands as children did not help her reputation.

"Yonder's old Delia," Jeff said as they passed.

"What she doin'?"

"Jes sittin' in the do'," he said.

"She see us?"

"Hm," Jeff said. "Musta did."

That relieved Jennie. It strengthened her to know that her old enemy had seen her pass in her best clothes. That would give the old she-devil something to chew her gums and fret about, Jennie thought. Wouldn't she have a fit if she didn't find out? Old evil Delia! This would be just the thing for her. It would pay her back for being so evil. It would also pay her, Jennie thought, for the way she used to grin at Jeff—long ago, when her teeth were good.

The road became smooth and red,[3] and Jeff could tell by the smell of the air that they were nearing the river. He could see the rise where the road turned and ran along parallel to the

_____
3. **red,** the color of a clay road.

stream. The car chugged on monotonously. After a long silent spell, Jennie leaned against Jeff and spoke.

"How many bale o' cotton you think we got standin'?" she said.

Jeff wrinkled his forehead as he calculated.

" 'Bout twenty-five, I reckon."

"How many you make las' year?"

"Twenty-eight," he said. "How come you ask that?"

"I's jes thinkin'," Jennie said quietly.

"It don't make a speck o' difference though," Jeff reflected. "If we get much or if we get little, we still gonna be in debt to old man Stevenson when he gets through counting up agin us. It's took us a long time to learn that."

Jennie was not listening to these words. She had fallen into a trance-like meditation. Her lips twitched. She chewed her gums and rubbed her gnarled hands nervously. Suddenly, she leaned forward, buried her face in the nervous hands, and burst into tears. She cried aloud in a dry, cracked voice that suggested the rattle of fodder on dead stalks. She cried aloud like a child, for she had never learned to suppress a genuine sob. Her slight old frame shook heavily and seemed hardly able to sustain such violent grief.

"What's the matter, baby?" Jeff asked awkwardly. "Why you cryin' like all that?"

"I's jes thinkin'," she said.

"So you the one what's scairt now, hunh?"

"I ain't scairt, Jeff. I's jes thinkin' 'bout leavin' eve'thing like this—eve'thing we been used to. It's right sad-like."

Jeff did not answer, and presently Jennie buried her face again and cried.

The sun was almost overhead. It beat down furiously on the dusty wagon-path road, on the parched roadside grass and the tiny battered car. Jeff's hands, gripping the wheel, became wet with perspiration; his forehead sparkled. Jeff's lips parted. His mouth shaped a hideous grimace. His face suggested the face of a man being burned. But the torture passed and his expression softened again.

"You mustn't cry, baby," he said to his wife.

"We gotta be strong. We can't break down."

Jennie waited a few seconds, then said, "You reckon we oughta do it, Jeff? You reckon we oughta go 'head an' do it, really?"

Jeff's voice choked; his eyes blurred. He was terrified to hear Jennie say the thing that had been in his mind all morning. She had egged him on when he had wanted more than anything in the world to wait, to reconsider, to think things over a little longer. Now she was getting cold feet. Actually, there was no need of thinking the question through again. It would only end in making the same painful decision once more. Jeff knew that. There was no need of fooling around longer.

"We jes as well to do like we planned," he said. "They ain't nothin' else for us now—it's the bes' thing."

Jeff thought of the handicaps, the near impossibility, of making another crop with his leg bothering him more and more each week. Then there was always the chance that he would have another stroke, like the one that had made him lame. Another one might kill him. The least it could do would be to leave him helpless. Jeff gasped—Lord, Jesus! He could not bear to think of being helpless, like a baby, on Jennie's hands. Frail, blind Jennie.

The little pounding motor of the car worked harder and harder. The puff of steam from the cracked radiator became larger. Jeff realized that they were climbing a little rise. A moment later the road turned abruptly, and he looked down upon the face of the river.

"Jeff."

"Hunh?"

"Is that the water I hear?"

"Hm. Tha's it."

"Well, which way you goin' now?"

"Down this-a way," he said. "The road runs 'long 'side o' the water a lil piece."

She waited a while calmly. Then she said, "Drive faster."

"A'right, baby," Jeff said.

The water roared in the bed of the river. It was fifty or sixty feet below the level of the road. Between the road and the water there was a long smooth slope, sharply inclined. The slope was dry, the clay hardened by prolonged summer heat. The water below, roaring in a narrow channel, was noisy and wild.

"Jeff."

"Hunh?"

"How far you goin'?"

"Jes a lil piece down the road."

"You ain't scairt, is you, Jeff?"

"Nah, baby," he said trembling. "I ain't scairt."

"Remember how we planned it, Jeff. We gotta do it like we said. Brave-like."

"Hm."

Jeff's brain darkened. Things suddenly seemed unreal, like figures in a dream. Thoughts swam in his mind foolishly, hysterically, like little blind fish in a pool within a dense cave. They rushed again. Jeff soon became dizzy. He shuddered violently and turned to his wife.

"Jennie, I can't do it. I can't." His voice broke pitifully.

She did not appear to be listening. All the grief had gone from her face. She sat erect, her unseeing eyes wide open, strained and frightful. Her glossy black skin had become dull. She seemed as thin, as sharp and bony, as a starved bird. Now, having suffered and endured the sadness of tearing herself away from beloved things, she showed no anguish. She was absorbed with her own thoughts, and she didn't even hear Jeff's voice shouting in her ear.

Jeff said nothing more. For an instant there was light in his cavernous brain. The great chamber was, for less than a second, peopled by characters he knew and loved. They were simple, healthy creatures, and they behaved in a manner that he could understand. They had quality. But since he had already taken leave of them long ago, the remembrance did not break his heart again. Young Jeff Patton was among them, the Jeff Patton of fifty years ago who went down to New Orleans with a crowd of country boys to the Mardi Gras[4] doings. The gay young crowd, boys with candy-striped shirts and rouged brown girls in noisy silks, was like a picture in his head. Yet it did not make him sad. On that very trip Slim Burns had killed Joe Beasley—the crowd had been broken up. Since then Jeff Patton's world had been the Greenbriar Plantation. If there had been other Mardi Gras carnivals, he had not heard of them. Since then there had been no time; the years had fallen on him like waves. Now he was old, worn out. Another paralytic stroke (like the one he had already suffered) would put him on his back for keeps. In that condition, with a frail blind woman to look after him, he would be worse off than if he were dead.

Suddenly Jeff's hands became steady. He actually felt brave. He slowed down the motor of the car and carefully pulled off the road. Below, the water of the stream boomed, a soft thunder in the deep channel. Jeff ran the car onto the clay slope, pointed it directly toward the stream, and put his foot heavily on the accelerator. The little car leaped furiously down the steep incline toward the water. The movement was nearly as swift and direct as a fall. The two old black folks, sitting quietly side by side, showed no excitement. In another instant the car hit the water and dropped immediately out of sight.

A little later it lodged in the mud of a shallow place. One wheel of the crushed and upturned little Ford became visible above the rushing water.

---

I

THE END OF THE ROPE

What do people do when they come to the end of their rope? The old couple in this story, having reached this point in their lives, obviously must have talked things over before reaching a decision. They approach their last day almost as if it were

---

4. **Mardi Gras**\\'mar·dē ▲gra\\ a carnival period celebrated before Lent, especially in New Orleans.

a holiday. They put on their best clothes, set their house in order, and climb into their old car. There is something almost creative about the way they have chosen to take their own lives. The very intensity of the story is heightened because these are simple people, acting with great dignity from some inner sense of destiny.

## II
### IMPLICATIONS

What does the story indicate about the following statements? Do you have any facts to support your opinion?

**1.** It takes great courage to commit suicide.

**2.** The way the two old people end their lives says a great deal about the kind of people they have been.

**3.** Readers are caught by surprise at the very end when they realize that Jeff and Jennie are committing suicide.

## III
### TECHNIQUES

*Theme*

List the pressures accumulating on Jeff and Jennie. Are there other alternatives open to them? What is the real "tragedy" of the story? How would you state the theme?

*Style*

The story has great pathos which grows steadily throughout the tale. Yet there is no use of emotional language. Actions and words are quiet and simple. What everyday activities do the couple perform that give a quality of simple dignity to their behavior?

## IV
### WORDS

**A.** To make his characters believable, Arna Bontemps has Jennie and Jeff Patton speak the variety of American English that poor share-farmers in real life might use. Their language pattern, with its own rules of pronunciation, vocabulary, and grammar, is called a *dialect*. Language scholars regard all dialects as being equal rather than one being superior or inferior to another. Each variety of American English, they maintain, serves its speakers equally well. However, they do acknowledge that, for one reason or another, a speaker of one dialect may wish to learn another one for use in different situations. In "A Summer Tragedy" the writer has faithfully reproduced the dialectal features common to speakers like the Pattons. Examples are: pronunciation—*scairt* (scared) and *do'* (door); vocabulary—*reckon* (suppose) and *poison* (evil substance); and grammar—*I'se* (I am) and *What she doin'?* (What is she doing?). What other identifying features can you find?

**B.** At one point in the story, Jennie is described as being "as scrawny and gnarled as a string bean." At another point, she is pictured as being "as thin, as sharp and bony, as a starved bird." In yet another place, her "shrunken" voice is said to sound "like an echo." By comparing Jennie's body to a string bean and to a starved bird and her voice to an echo, Arna Bontemps is attempting to sensitize the reader to the corrosive effects of poverty. Comparisons like the examples above, in which *like* or *as* are used, are called similes. The purpose of a simile is to paint a vivid picture in the reader's mind. The success of this figure of speech depends largely upon how striking and how original the comparison is. Note how these similes sparkle: "eyes like burning anthracite, "small and deadly as an asp," and "as ever-present as sin." On a scale of *poor to excellent,* how would you rate each of the following similes: "as fierce as a tigress protecting her young," "as spry and mean as a woodchuck," "like a gazelle, the picture of fluid motion," "tough as tungsten," and "as calm as the eye of a hurricane"?

**C.** Making use of context clues, try to determine the meaning of the italicized word in each of the following sentences from "A Summer Tragedy":

**1.** "Jeff twisted his mouth into a hideous toothless *grimace* as he contended with the obstinate bow."

**2.** "But even the frizzly chickens seemed now to be in a *stupor.* Jeff thought they had some ailment . . . ."

**3.** "As it was, with Jennie *chiding* him about being afraid, he had to keep going."

**4.** "The car chugged on *monotonously.*"

**5.** "Her slight old frame shook heavily and seemed hardly able to *sustain* such violent grief."

The narrator of this story
has already felt strangely dissatisfied
with his walk through the English countryside.
And then the rain begins.
While told in a completely realistic way,
the action takes on the quality of a nightmare.
Even the title brings dreamlike images
to the mind—what is a rain horse?

# The Rain Horse

### TED HUGHES

As the young man came over the hill the first thin blowing of rain met him. He turned his coat-collar up and stood on top of the shelving rabbit-riddled hedgebank, looking down into the valley.

He had come too far. What had set out as a walk along pleasantly remembered tarmac lanes had turned dreamily by gate and path and hedge-gap into a cross-ploughland trek, his shoes ruined, the dark mud of the lower fields inching up the trouser legs of his grey suit where they rubbed against each other. And now there was a raw, flapping wetness in the air that would be downpour again at any minute. He shivered, holding himself tense against the cold.

This was the view he had been thinking of. Vaguely, without really directing his walk, he had felt he would get the whole thing from this point. For twelve years, whenever he had recalled this sense, he had imagined it as it looked from here. Now the valley lay sunken in front of him, utterly deserted, shallow, bare fields, black and sodden as the bed of an ancient lake after the weeks of rain.

Nothing happened. Not that he had looked forward to any very transfiguring experience. But he had expected something, some pleasure, some meaningful sensation, he didn't quite know what.

So he waited, trying to nudge the right feelings alive with the details—the surprisingly familiar curve of the hedges, the stone gate-pillar and iron gatehook let into it that he had used as a target, the long bank of the rabbit-warren on which he stood and which had been the first thing he ever noticed about the hill when twenty years ago, from the distance of the village, he had said to himself "That looks like rabbits."

Twelve years had changed him. This land no longer recognized him, and he looked back at it coldly, as at a finally visited home-country, known only through the stories of a grandfather; felt nothing but the dullness of feeling nothing. Boredom. Then, suddenly, impatience, with a whole exasperated swarm of little anxieties about his shoes and the spitting rain and his new suit and that sky and the two-mile trudge through the mud back to the road.

It would be quicker to go straight forward to the farm a mile away in the valley and behind which the road looped. But the thought of meeting the farmer—to be embarrassingly remembered or shouted at as a trespasser—deterred him. He saw the rain pulling up out of the distance, dragging its grey broken columns, smudging the trees and the farms.

A wave of anger went over him: anger against himself for blundering into this mud-trap and anger against the land that made him feel so outcast, so old and stiff and stupid. He wanted nothing but to get away from it as quickly as possible. But as he turned, something moved in his eye-corner. All his senses started alert. He stopped.

Over to his right a thin, black horse was running across the ploughland towards the hill, its head down, neck stretched out. It seemed to be running on its toes like a cat,

"The Rain Horse" from *Wodwo* by Ted Hughes. Copyright © 1959 by Ted Hughes.

like a dog up to no good.

For the high point on which he stood the hill dipped slightly and rose to another crested point fringed with the tops of trees, three hundred yards to his right. As he watched it, the horse ran up that crest, showed against the sky—for a moment like a nightmarish leopard —and disappeared over the other side.

For several seconds he stared at the skyline, stunned by the unpleasantly strange impression the horse had made on him. Then the plastering beat of icy rain on his bare skull brought him to himself. The distance had vanished in a wall of grey. All around him the fields were jumping and streaming.

Holding his collar close and tucking his chin down into it he ran back over the hilltop towards the town-side, the lee-side, his feet sucking and splashing, at every stride plunging to the ankle.

This hill was shaped like a wave, a gently rounded back lifting out of the valley to a sharply crested, almost concave front hanging over the river meadows towards the town. Down this front, from the crest, hung two small woods separated by a fallow field. The near wood was nothing more than a quarry, circular, full of stones and bracken, with a few thorns and nondescript saplings, foxholes and rabbit holes. The other was rectangular, mainly a planting of scrub oak trees. Beyond the river smouldered the town like a great heap of blue cinders.

He ran along the top of the first wood and finding no shelter but the thin, leafless thorns of the hedge, dipped below the crest out of the wind and jogged along through thick grass to the wood of oaks. In blinding rain he lunged through the barricade of brambles at the wood's edge. The little crippled trees were small choice in the way of shelter, but at a sudden fierce thickening of the rain he took one at random and crouched down under the leaning trunk.

Still panting from his run, drawing his knees up tightly, he watched the bleak lines of rain, grey as hail, slanting through the boughs into the clumps of bracken and bramble. He felt hidden and safe. The sound of the rain as it rushed and lulled in the wood seemed to seal him in. Soon the chilly sheet lead of his suit became a tight, warm mold, and gradually he sank into a state of comfort that was all but trance, though the rain beat steadily on his exposed shoulders and trickled down the oak trunk on to his neck.

All around him the boughs angled down, glistening, black as iron. From their tips and elbows the drops hurried steadily, and the channels of the bark pulsed and gleamed. For a time he amused himself calculating the variation in the rainfall by the variations in a dribble of water from a trembling twig-end two feet in front of his nose. He studied the twig, bringing dwarfs and continents and animals out of its scurfy bark. Beyond the boughs the blue shoal of the town was rising and falling, and darkening and fading again, in the pale, swaying backdrop of rain.

He wanted this rain to go on forever. Whenever it seemed to be drawing off he listened anxiously until it closed in again. As long as it lasted he was suspended from life and time. He didn't want to return to his sodden shoes and his possibly ruined suit and the walk back over that land of mud.

All at once he shivered. He hugged his knees to squeeze out the cold and found himself thinking of the horse. The hair on the nape of his neck pricked slightly. He remembered how it had run up to the crest and showed against the sky.

He tried to dismiss the thought. Horses wander about the countryside often enough. But the image of the horse as it had appeared against the sky stuck in his mind. It must have come over the crest just above the wood in which he was now sitting. To clear his mind, he twisted around and looked up the wood between the tree stems, to his left.

At the wood top, with the silvered grey light coming in behind it, the black horse was standing under the oaks, its head high and alert, its ears pricked, watching him.

A horse sheltering from the rain generally goes into a sort of stupor, tilts a hind hoof and hangs its head and lets its eyelids droop, and so it stays as long as the rain lasts. This horse was nothing like that. It was watching him intently, standing perfectly still, its soaked neck and flank shining in the hard light.

He turned back. His scalp went icy and he shivered. What was he to do? Ridiculous to try driving it away. And to leave the wood, with the rain still coming down full pelt was out of the question. Meanwhile the idea of being watched became more and more unsettling until at last he had to twist around again, to see if the horse had moved. It stood exactly as before.

This was absurd. He took control of himself and turned back deliberately, determined not to give the horse one more thought. If it wanted to share the wood with him, let it. If it wanted to stare at him, let it. He was nestling firmly into these resolutions when the ground shook and he heard the crash of a heavy body coming down the wood. Like lightning his legs bounded him upright and about face. The horse was almost on top of him, its head stretching forward, ears flattened and lips lifted back from the long yellow teeth. He got one snapshot glimpse of the red-veined eyeball as he flung himself backwards around the tree. Then he was away up the slope, whipped by oak twigs as he leapt the brambles and bushwood, twisting between the close trees till he tripped and sprawled. As he fell the warning flashed through his head that he must at all costs keep his suit out of the leaf-mold, but a more urgent instinct was already rolling him violently sideways. He spun around, sat up and looked back, ready to scramble off in a flash to one side. He was panting from the sudden excitement and effort. The horse had disappeared. The wood was empty except for the drumming, slant grey rain, dancing the bracken and glittering from the branches.

He got up, furious. Knocking the dirt and leaves from his suit as well as he could he looked around for a weapon. The horse was evidently mad, had an abscess on its brain or something of the sort. Or maybe it was just spiteful. Rain sometimes puts creatures into queer states. Whatever it was, he was going to get away from the wood as quickly as possible, rain or no rain.

Since the horse seemed to have gone on down the wood, his way to the farm over the hill was clear. As he went, he broke a yard length of wrist-thick dead branch from one of the oaks, but immediately threw it aside and wiped the slime of rotten wet bark from his hands with his soaked handkerchief. Already he was thinking it incredible that the horse could have meant to attack him. Most likely it was just going down the wood for better shelter and had made a feint at him in passing —as much out of curiosity or playfulness as anything. He recalled the way horses menace each other when they are galloping round in a paddock.

The wood rose to a steep bank topped by the hawthorn hedge that ran along the whole ridge of the hill. He was pulling himself up to a thin place in the hedge by the bare stem of one of the hawthorns when he ducked and shrank down again. The swelling gradient of fields lay in front of him, smoking in the slowly crossing rain. Out in the middle of the first field, tall as a statue, and a ghostly silver in the undercloud light, stood the horse, watching the wood.

He lowered his head slowly, slithered back down the bank and crouched. An awful feeling of helplessness came over him. He felt certain the horse had been looking straight at him. Waiting for him? Was it clairvoyant? Maybe a mad animal can be clairvoyant. At the same time he was ashamed to find himself acting so inanely, ducking and creeping about in this way just to keep out of sight of a horse. He tried to imagine how anybody in their senses would just walk off home. This cooled him a little, and he retreated farther down the wood. He would go back the way he had come, along under the hill crest, without any more nonsense.

The wood hummed and the rain was a cold weight, but he observed this rather than felt it. The water ran down inside his clothes and squelched in his shoes as he eased his way carefully over the bedded twigs and leaves. At every instant he expected to see the prick-eared black head looking down at him from the hedge above.

At the woodside he paused, close against a tree. The success of this last maneuver was restoring his confidence, but he didn't want to venture out into the open field without making sure that the horse was just where he had left it. The perfect move would be to withdraw quietly and leave the horse standing out there in the rain. He crept up again among the trees to the crest and peered through the hedge.

The grey field and the whole slope were empty. He searched the distance. The horse was quite likely to have forgotten him altogether and wandered off. Then he raised himself and leaned out to see if it had come in close to the hedge. Before he was aware of anything the ground shook. He twisted around wildly to see how he had been caught. The black shape was above him, right across the light. It whinnying snort and the spattering whack of its hooves seemed to be actually inside his head as he fell backwards down the bank, and leapt again like a madman, dodging among the oaks, imagining how the buffet would come and how he would be knocked headlong. Half-way down the wood the oaks gave way to bracken and old roots and stony rabbit diggings. He was well out into the middle of this before he realized that he was running alone.

Gasping for breath now and cursing mechanically, without a thought for his suit he sat down on the ground to rest his shaking legs, letting the rain plaster the hair down over his forehead and watching the dense flashing lines disappear abruptly into the soil all around him as if he were watching through thick plate glass. He took deep breaths in the effort to steady his heart and regain control of himself. His right trouser turn-up was ripped at the seam and his suit jacket was splashed with the yellow mud of the top field.

Obviously the horse had been farther along the hedge above the steep field, waiting for him to come out at the woodside just as he had intended. He must have peeped through the hedge—peeping the wrong way—within yards of it.

However, this last attack had cleared up one thing. He need no longer act like a fool out of mere uncertainty as to whether the horse was simply being playful or not. It was definitely after him. He picked two stones about the size of goose eggs and set off towards the bottom of the wood, striding carelessly.

A loop of the river bordered all this farmland. If he crossed the little level meadow at the bottom of the wood, he could follow the three-mile circuit, back to the road. There were deep hollows in the river bank, shoaled with pebbles, as he remembered, perfect places to defend himself from if the horse followed him out there.

The hawthorns that choked the bottom of the wood—some of them good-sized trees— knitted into an almost impassable barrier. He had found a place where the growth thinned slightly and had begun to lift aside the long spiny stems, pushing himself forward, when he stopped. Through the bluish veil of bare

544

twigs he saw the familiar shape out in the field below the wood.

But it seemed not to have noticed him yet. It was looking out across the field towards the river. Quietly, he released himself from the thorns and climbed back across the clearing toward the one side of the wood he had not yet tried. If the horse would only stay down there he could follow his first and easiest plan, up the wood and over the hilltop to the farm.

Now he noticed that the sky had grown much darker. The rain was heavier every second, pressing down as if the earth had to be flooded before nightfall. The oaks ahead blurred and the ground drummed. He began to run. And as he ran he heard a deeper sound running with him. He whirled around. The horse was in the middle of the clearing. It might have been running to get out of the terrific rain except that it was coming straight for him, scattering clay and stones, with an immensely supple and powerful motion. He let out a tearing roar and threw the stone in his right hand. The result was instantaneous. Whether at the roar or the stone the horse reared as if against a wall and shied to the left. As it dropped back on to its forefeet he flung his second stone, at ten yards' range, and saw a bright mud blotch suddenly appear on the glistening black flank. The horse surged down the wood, splashing the earth like water, tossing its long tail as it plunged out of sight among the hawthorns.

He looked around for stones. The encounter had set the blood beating in his head and given him a savage energy. He could have killed the horse at that moment. That this brute should pick him and play with him in this malevolent fashion was more than he could bear. Whoever owned it, he thought, deserved to have its neck broken for letting the dangerous thing loose.

He came out at the woodside, in open battle won, still searching for the right stones. There were plenty here, piled and scattered where they had been ploughed out of the field. He selected two, than straightened and saw the horse twenty yards off in the middle of the steep field, watching him calmly. They looked at each other.

"Out of it!" he shouted, brandishing his arm. "Out of it! Go on!" The horse twitched its pricked ears. With all his force he threw. The stone soared and landed beyond with a soft thud. He re-armed and threw again. For several minutes he kept up his bombardment without a single hit, working himself up into a despair and throwing more and more wildly, till his arm began to ache with the unaccustomed exercise. Throughout the performance the horse watched him fixedly. Finally he had to stop and ease his shoulder muscles. As if the horse had been waiting for just this, it dipped its head twice and came at him.

He snatched up two stones and roaring with all his strength flung the one in his right hand. He was astonished at the crack of the impact. It was as if he had struck a tile—and the horse actually stumbled. With another roar he jumped forward and hurled his other stone. His aim seemed to be under superior guidance. The stone struck and rebounded straight up into the air, spinning fiercely, as the horse swirled away and went careering down towards the far bottom corner of the field, at first with great, swinging leaps, then at a canter, leaving deep churned holes in the soil.

It turned up the far side of the field, climbing till it was level with him. He felt a little surprise of pity to see it shaking its head, and once it paused to lower its head and paw over its ear with its forehoof as a cat does.

"You stay there!" he shouted. "Keep your distance and you'll not get hurt."

And indeed the horse did stop at that moment, almost obediently. It watched him as he climbed to the crest.

The rain swept into his face and he realized that he was freezing, as if his very flesh were sodden. The farm seemed miles away over the dreary fields. Without another glance at the horse—he felt too exhausted to care now

what it did—he loaded the crook of his left arm with stones and plunged out on to the waste of mud.

He was half-way to the first hedge before the horse appeared, silhouetted against the sky at the corner of the wood, head high and attentive, watching his laborious retreat over the three fields.

The ankle-deep clay dragged at him. Every stride was a separate, deliberate effort, forcing him up and out of the sucking earth, burdened as he was by his sogged clothes and load of stones and limbs that seemed themselves to be turning to mud. He fought to keep his breathing even, two strides in, two strides out, the air ripping his lungs. In the middle of the last field he stopped and looked around. The horse, tiny on the skyline, had not moved.

At the corner of the field he unlocked his clasped arms and dumped the stones by the gatepost, then leaned on the gate. The farm was in front of him. He became conscious of the rain again and suddenly longed to stretch out full-length under it, to take the cooling, healing drops all over his body and forget himself in the last wretchedness of the mud. Making an effort, he heaved his weight over the gate-top. He leaned again, looking up at the hill.

Rain was dissolving land and sky together like a wet watercolor as the afternoon darkened. He concentrated, raising his head, searching the skyline from end to end. The horse had vanished. The hill looked lifeless and desolate, an island lifting out of the sea, awash with every tide.

Under the long shed where the tractors, plough, binders and the rest were drawn up, waiting for their seasons, he sat on a sack thrown over a petrol drum, trembling, his lungs heaving. The mingled smell of paraffin, creosote, fertilizer, dust—all was exactly as he had left it twelve years ago. The ragged swallows' nests were still there tucked in the angles of the rafters. He remembered three dead foxes hanging in a row from one of the beams, their teeth bloody.

The ordeal with the horse had already sunk from reality. It hung under the surface of his mind, an obscure confusion of fright and shame, as after a narrowly escaped street accident. There was a solid pain in his chest, like a spike of bone stabbing, that made him wonder if he had strained his heart on that last stupid burdened run. Piece by piece he began to take off his clothes, wringing the grey water out of them, but soon he stopped that and just sat staring at the ground, as if some important part had been cut out of his brain.

---

## I

### REALITY VERSUS THE IMAGINED

The man in the story is unnamed, giving him a vague, faceless quality. He has returned to this particular spot because it has lain in his memory for twelve years like a dream. Now he stands at the top of the hill waiting for some feeling, some reaction to tell him why he has remembered this landscape. Nothing happens. Did you notice his vague dissatisfaction with the jaunt even before the rain started? What kind of person sets out for a cross-country walk wearing a brand new suit and good shoes when there is a promise of a storm in the air? Notice how these same clothes become a major concern once the rain begins. Note, too, that when the man crouches down under the protection of the trees, he goes into a trancelike state, wishing that the rain would never stop so that he could float in this limbo with no decisions to be faced. Why do you suppose he works so hard to convince himself that the horse has no evil intentions toward him? Could it be that all these details are suggesting important facts about the man's character? A very real pressure on both the man and the reader is the drumming, penetrating rain. What happens to a person when his or her clothes are wet through to the skin and discomfort becomes all-pervasive? Could it be that the rain horse is not real at all, that the nightmare pressure is all in the man's mind—or is it?

## II

### IMPLICATIONS

There are no clear-cut answers in the story to the statements that follow. They are intended to challenge both your perceptions and your thinking.

**1.** Consider how each of the following exerts pressure on the man:

**a.** His feelings about the day

**b.** The rain

**c.** His concern about his clothes

**d.** His indecision about which route he should follow to the road—toward the farm or toward the town

**e.** The fear generated by the horse's strange, hostile behavior

**2.** Consider the following generalizations about pressure implied by the story.

**a.** People try to find a logical explanation for what is happening in order to reassure themselves.

**b.** When pressure reaches a certain point, a person no longer cares what happens.

**c.** The release from pressure produces a kind of numbness.

## III

### TECHNIQUES

*Theme*

Against a background of misty shadows and soggy ground, the horse's vicious attacks become terrifyingly real. One feels that one has been dropped into a nightmare. The story is baffling and yet is one most people cannot forget. When you think back on the tale, what is the first thing that comes to your mind: the man himself, the rain, the action, the rising fear?

From your central impression can you state a theme?

*Style*

If "style is the *person*" what do you surmise about the man who wrote this story. Is he living? Has he lived in the country? Does he know animals? Is he an aristocrat or from the laboring class? Is he an exact man or a careless one? What other things are suggested by his language? Now turn to his biographical sketch to see how close your guesses come to the author's life. Has his style revealed him correctly?

*Identification*

The reader obviously identifies with the man in the story. This is interesting because you know almost nothing about him. Why then do you care what happens to him? What has the author done to elicit our fellow feeling for him?

SUMMING UP

# *People under Pressure*

This group of selections has been focused on the effects that various kinds of pressure can create in the lives of human beings. Some individuals respond to pressure with an angry surge of resistance. Others quietly pit their ingenuity against the force. And some give way until their spirits are destroyed. Continuing pressure distorts, compresses, and shifts the focus of a person's life. It changes the pattern, but whether the change is for the better or worse depends on the individual's character and strength. Though pressures vary in kind and in degree, every one must face them, for they are as natural to living as the air we breathe. It is the response to those pressures that determines what a person may be.

It is also natural that writers should frequently choose the theme of people under pressure as the subject matter of their writing. Pressure provides a natural kind of conflict, and by dealing with peoples' reactions to it, the writer is able to explore and evolve new understandings of life.

## IMPLICATIONS

Recall the selections you have just read, and use illustrations from them to support your evaluation of each of the following statements. Wherever possible, make comparisons between the stories and your own experience.

**1.** The way people react to pressure reveals their personalities.

**2.** Pressure on an individual tends to distort normal reactions.

**3.** External pressures often bring out submerged internal ones.

**4.** Internal pressures are more devastating than external pressures.

**5.** Pressure may be unintentionally applied.

**6.** A crushing pressure builds up from inconsequential things, none of which are very important in themselves.

## TECHNIQUES

### *Theme*

Think back on the selections and decide what particular pressure or pressures were brought to bear on the principal character in each selection. Make a list of these pressures, and using it as a reference, consider the following questions.

**1.** Which story did you like best? Did this selection have only one pressure or more than one?

**2.** Do you feel a story which piles many pressures on an individual makes a more telling impression than one with a single pressure?

**3.** There were two humorous stories in this group, "The Open Window" and "The Catbird Seat." Do you think this theme is a good one for a humorous treatment?

### *Style*

Style reflects the personality of a writer as well as giving a piece of writing a distinctive quality. From the way he or she writes, as much as from what is written about, you often learn a great deal about an author: whether she or he sees life as tragic or comic or neither; whether he or she is compassionate, emotional, reserved, intellectual, detached, involved, angry, or calm. In a few sentences, describe the personality of two of the following authors as you feel it must have been from reading their works. How are they different? What have they in common?

    **1.** Saki
    **2.** James Thurber
    **3.** Jack London
    **4.** William Sansom
    **5.** Truman Capote

### *Identification*

You have met a wide variety of characters in the preceding selections. To which central characters did you feel yourself most drawn?

Which of the following reasons helped you identify with them:

**1.** Did they have character traits similar to your friends'? to your own?

**2.** Were they involved in actions you have never had but frequently wanted to experience?

**3.** Did they have feelings you have known yourself?

**4.** Were they confronted by problems similar to ones you have faced?

## Introduction to The Pearl

Some years ago while traveling in Mexico, John Steinbeck came across a moving story about an Indian boy who found and attempted to sell a wondrous pearl. The story of the boy's subsequent suffering and loss of the pearl so haunted Steinbeck that in *Sea of Cortez* he wrote:

> This seems to be a true story, but it is so much like a parable that it almost can't be. This Indian boy is too heroic, too wise. He knows too much and acts on his knowledge. In every way he goes contrary to human direction. The story is probably true, but we can't believe it; it is far too reasonable to be true.

In *The Pearl,* he has recast this "true" story and enlarged its meaning. The Indian boy has become Kino, the fisherman, and Kino has a young wife, Juana, and first baby, Coyotito. Through this young family Steinbeck ponders many of the questions which trouble all people. In exploring Kino's and Juana's reactions to the terrible pressure of poverty and ignorance, wealth and power, ambition and hope, love and hate, he leads the reader in a parable-like way to search beyond the apparently simple action of the story to the lessons it embodies. To do this Steinbeck says of *The Pearl,* "I tried to write it as folklore, to give it that set-aside, raised-up feeling that all folk stories have."

One of the chief means Steinbeck uses to give Kino's story that "raised-up feeling" is to present the characters, events, and objects in the story in such a way that they become symbols of timeless truths about God, humans, and the world. We feel the power of the "boundless" sea and the "eternal" mountains. We sense a certain universal fear in the shadows of night. When we know that Kino is named after a great seventeenth-century missionary-explorer, we have a sense of our heroic effort to overcome nature. When we consider that the name *Juana* simply means "woman," we sense that she in some ways is meant to represent all women.

But most symbolic of all is the pearl itself, especially when we recall its long history in literature and symbolism. In the Bible it is most often a symbol of earthly riches—riches that can be either good or bad. As good, the pearl is a symbol of physical beauty and goodness through which we are able, in a small way, to value spiritual truths; as bad, the pearl represents the wealth and worldly pleasures which lead to our destruction. But on two significant occasions the pearl represents spiritual truths. Jesus uses the pearl to symbolize the word of God, heavenly wisdom. "Do not throw your pearls before swine, lest they trample them underfoot and turn to attack you" (Matthew 7:6). Later (Matthew 13:45–46), Jesus uses the pearl to represent both the kingdom of heaven and the committed soul which sells all and dedicates all of its talents and energies to one end—acquiring a share in the kingdom. "Again, the kingdom of heaven is like a merchant in search of fine pearls, who, finding one pearl of great value, went and sold all that he had and bought it."

In the rich symbolism of the Middle Ages the pearl represents integrity and purity. In a very famous and beautiful fifteenth-century poem entitled "The Pearl," an unknown poet laments the loss of his girl child "who lived upon the earth two years." To the poet, the pearl becomes both the symbol of his little daughter's innocence and the daughter herself, for she had been his riches, his most valued possession. To Kino and to Juana, too, their pearl becomes a symbol . . . one that takes on new dimensions and new meanings as the story unfolds.

Steinbeck also uses a simple, subdued, straightforward style to give *The Pearl* the flavor of a folk story or parable. His sentences are plain and uncomplicated. His words are common and even folksy. Scenes are drawn with cameralike clarity and objectivity. The story moves directly from one incident to another. In stark simplicity Steinbeck records the internal and external pressures which beset man in search of his soul.

550

# THE PEARL

### JOHN STEINBECK

In the town they tell the story of the great pearl—how it was found and how it was lost again. They tell of Kino, the fisherman, and of his wife, Juana, and of the baby, Coyotito.[1] And because the story has been told so often, it has taken root in every man's mind. And, as with all retold tales that are in people's hearts, there are only good and bad things and black and white things and good and evil things and no in-between anywhere.

"If this story is a parable, perhaps everyone takes his own meaning from it and reads his own life into it. In any case, they say in the town that . . ."

## 1

Kino awakened in the near dark. The stars still shone, and the day had drawn only a pale wash of light in the lower sky to the east. The roosters had been crowing for some time, and the early pigs were already beginning their ceaseless turning of twigs and bits of wood to see whether anything to eat had been overlooked. Outside the brush house in the tuna clump, a covey[2] of little birds chittered and flurried with their wings.

Kino's eyes opened, and he looked first at the lightening square which was the door, and then he looked at the hanging box where Coyotito slept. And last he turned his head to Juana, his wife, who lay beside him on the mat, her blue head shawl over her nose and over her breasts and around the small of her back.

Juana's eyes were open too. Kino could never remember seeing them closed when he awakened. Her dark eyes made little reflected stars. She was looking at him as she was always looking at him when he awakened.

Kino heard the little splash of morning waves on the beach. It was very good—Kino closed his eyes again to listen to his music. Perhaps he alone did this, and perhaps all of his people did it. His people had once been great makers of songs so that everything they saw or thought or did or heard became a song. That was very long ago. The songs remained; Kino knew them, but no new songs were added. That does not mean that there were no personal songs. In Kino's head there was a song now, clear and soft; and if he had been able to speak it, he would have called it the Song of the Family.

His blanket was over his nose to protect him from the dank air. His eyes flicked to a rustle beside him. It was Juana arising, almost soundlessly. On her hard bare feet she went to the hanging box where Coyotito slept, and she leaned over and said a little reassuring word. Coyotito looked up for a moment and closed his eyes and slept again. Juana went to the fire pit and uncovered a coal and fanned it alive while she broke little pieces of brush over it.

Now Kino got up and wrapped his blanket about his head and nose and shoulders. He slipped his feet into his sandals and went outside to watch the dawn.

Outside the door he squatted down and gathered the blanket ends about his knees. He saw the specks of Gulf clouds flame high in the air. And a goat came near and sniffed at him and stared with its cold, yellow eyes. Behind him Juana's fire leaped into flame and threw spears of light through the chinks of the brush-house wall and threw a wavering square of light out the door. A late moth blustered in to

---

1. **Kino**\ᵏkē·nō\. **Juana**\ᵏhwa·na\. **Coyotito**\kɔi·ō ᵏtē-tō\.
2. **tuna**\ᵏtū·na\ a common tropical prickly pear. **covey** \ᵏkə·vē\a group of young birds.

*The Pearl* by John Steinbeck. Copyright 1945 by John Steinbeck. Reprinted by permission of The Viking Press, Inc.

*The poverty of Kino and Juana is reflected in this scene taken from a motion picture of* The Pearl.

find the fire. The Song of the Family came now from behind Kino. And the rhythm of the family song was the grinding stone where Juana worked the corn for the morning cakes.

The dawn came quickly now, a wash, a glow, a lightness, and then an explosion of fire as the sun arose out of the Gulf. Kino looked down to cover his eyes from the glare. He could hear the pat of the corncakes in the house and the rich smell of them on the cooking plate. The ants were busy on the ground, big black ones with shiny bodies, and little dusty, quick ants. Kino watched with the detachment of God while a dusty ant frantically tried to es-

cape the sand trap an ant lion[3] had dug for him. A thin, timid dog came close and, at a soft word from Kino, curled up, arranged its tail neatly over its feet, and laid its chin delicately on the pile. It was a black dog with yellow-gold spots where its eyebrows should have been. It was a morning like other mornings and yet perfect among mornings.

Kino heard the creak of the rope when Juana took Coyotito out of his hanging box and cleaned him and hammocked him in her shawl, in a loop that placed him close to her breast. Kino could see these things without looking at

3. **ant lion,** an insect the larva of which traps ants in pits.

552

them. Juana sang softly an ancient song that had only three notes and yet endless variety of interval. And this was part of the family song too. It was all part. Sometimes it rose to an aching chord that caught the throat, saying this is safety, this is warmth, this is the *Whole*.

Across the brush fence were other brush houses, and the smoke came from them too, and the sound of breakfast; but those were other songs, their pigs were other pigs, their wives were not Juana. Kino was young and strong, and his black hair hung over his brown forehead. His eyes were warm and fierce and bright, and his mustache was thin and coarse. He lowered his blanket from his nose now; for the dark poisonous air was gone, and the yellow sunlight fell on the house. Near the brush fence, two roosters bowed and feinted at each other with squared wings and neck feathers ruffed out. It would be a clumsy fight. They were not game chickens. Kino watched them for a moment, and then his eyes went up to a flight of wild doves twinkling inland to the hills. The world was awake now, and Kino arose and went into his brush house.

As he came through the door, Juana stood up from the glowing fire pit. She put Coyotito back in his hanging box, and then she combed her black hair and braided it in two braids and tied the ends with thin green ribbon. Kino squatted by the fire pit and rolled a hot corn-cake and dipped it in sauce and ate it. And he drank a little pulque,[4] and that was breakfast. That was the only breakfast he had ever known, outside of feast days and one incredible fiesta on cookies that had nearly killed him. When Kino had finished, Juana came back to the fire and ate her breakfast. They had spoken once, but there is not need for speech if it is only a habit anyway. Kino sighed with satisfaction—and that was conversation.

The sun was warming the brush house, breaking through its crevices in long streaks. And one of the streaks fell on the hanging box where Coyotito lay and on the ropes that held it.

It was a tiny movement that drew their eyes to the hanging box. Kino and Juana froze in their positions. Down the rope that hung the baby's box from the roof support, a scorpion moved slowly. His stinging tail was straight out behind him, but he could whip it up in a flash of time.

Kino's breath whistled in his nostrils, and he opened his mouth to stop it. And then the startled look was gone from him and the rigidity from his body. In his mind a new song had come, the Song of Evil, the music of the enemy, of any foe of the family, a savage, secret, dangerous melody; and underneath, the Song of the Family cried plaintively.

The scorpion moved delicately down the rope toward the box. Under her breath Juana repeated an ancient magic to guard against such evil, and on top of that she muttered a Hail Mary[5] between clenched teeth. But Kino was in motion. His body glided quietly across the room, noiselessly and smoothly. His hands were in front of him, palms down; and his eyes were on the scorpion. Beneath it, in the hanging box, Coyotito laughed and reached up his hand toward it. It sensed danger when Kino was almost within reach of it. It stopped; and its tail rose up over its back in little jerks, and the curved thorn on the tail's end glistened.

Kino stood perfectly still. He could hear Juana whispering the old magic again, and he could hear the evil music of the enemy. He could not move until the scorpion moved, and it felt for the source of the death that was coming to it. Kino's hand went forward very slowly, very smoothly. The thorned tail jerked upright. And at that moment the laughing Coyotito shook the rope, and the scorpion fell.

Kino's hand leaped to catch it; but it fell past his fingers, fell on the baby's shoulder, landed and struck. Then, snarling, Kino had it, had it in his fingers, rubbing it to a paste in his hands. He threw it down and beat it into the earth floor with his fist, and Coyotito screamed

---

4. **pulque**\ˈpül ˈkā\ a fermented drink made from the juice of the agave plant in Mexico.
5. **Hail Mary,** a brief prayer to the Virgin Mary.

with pain in his box. But Kino beat and stamped the enemy, until it was only a fragment and a moist place in the dirt. His teeth were bared, and fury flared in his eyes, and the Song of the Enemy roared in his ears.

But Juana had the baby in her arms now. She found the puncture with redness starting from it already. She put her lips down over the puncture and sucked hard and spat and sucked again, while Coyotito screamed.

Kino hovered; he was helpless; he was in the way.

The screams of the baby brought the neighbors. Out of their brush houses they poured—Kino's brother Juan Tomás and his fat wife Apolonia and their four children crowded in the door and blocked the entrance, while behind them others tried to look in, and one small boy crawled among legs to have a look. And those in front passed the word back to those behind—"Scorpion. The baby has been stung."

Juana stopped sucking the puncture for a moment. The little hole was slightly enlarged and its edges whitened from the sucking, but the red swelling extended farther around it in a hard lymphatic mound.[6] And all of these people knew about the scorpion. An adult might be very ill from the sting, but a baby could easily die from the poison. First, they knew, would come swelling and fever and tightened throat, and then cramps in the stomach, and then Coyotito might die if enough of the poison had gone in. But the stinging pain of the bite was going away. Coyotito's screams turned to moans.

Kino had wondered often at the iron in his patient, fragile wife. She, who was obedient and respectful and cheerful and patient, she could arch her back in child pain with hardly a cry. She could stand fatigue and hunger almost better than Kino himself. In the canoe she was like a strong man. And now she did a most surprising thing.

"The doctor," she said. "Go to get the doctor."

The word was passed out among the neighbors where they stood close-packed in the little yard behind the brush fence. And they repeated among themselves, "Juana wants the doctor." A wonderful thing, a memorable thing, to want the doctor. To get him would be a remarkable thing. The doctor never came to the cluster of brush houses. Why should he, when he had more than he could do to take care of the rich people who lived in the stone and plaster houses of the town.

"He would not come," the people in the yard said.

"He would not come," the people in the door said, and the thought got into Kino.

"The doctor would not come," Kino said to Juana.

She looked up at him, her eyes as cold as the eyes of a lioness. This was Juana's first baby—this was nearly everything there was in Juana's world. And Kino saw her determination, and the music of the family sounded in his head with a steely tone.

"Then we will go to him," Juana said, and with one hand she arranged her dark blue shawl over her head and made of one end of it a sling to hold the moaning baby and made of the other end of it a shade over his eyes to protect him from the light. The people in the door pushed against those behind to let her through. Kino followed her. They went out of the gate to the rutted path and the neighbors followed them.

The thing had become a neighborhood affair. They made a quick soft-footed procession into the center of the town, first Juana and Kino, and behind them Juan Tomás and Apolonia, her big stomach jiggling with the strenuous pace, then all the neighbors with the children trotting on the flanks. And the yellow sun threw their black shadows ahead of them so that they walked on their own shadows.

They came to the place where the brush houses stopped and the city of stone and plaster began, the city of harsh outer walls and inner cool gardens, where a little water played

---

6. **lymphatic mound,** a swelling caused mostly by accumulation of lymph and white corpuscles.

and the bougainvillaea crusted the walls with purple and brick-red and white. They heard from the secret gardens the singing of caged birds and heard the splash of cooling water on hot flagstones.[7] The procession crossed the blinding plaza and passed in front of the church. It had grown now, and on the outskirts the hurrying newcomers were being softly informed how the baby had been stung by a scorpion, how the father and mother were taking it to the doctor.

And the newcomers, particularly the beggars from the front of the church who were great experts in financial analysis, looked quickly at Juana's old blue skirt, saw the tears in her shawl, appraised the green ribbons on her braids, read the age of Kino's blanket and the thousand washings of his clothes, and set them down as poverty people and went along to see what kind of drama might develop. The four beggars in front of the church knew everything in the town. They were students of the expressions of young women as they went into confession, and they saw them as they came out and read the nature of the sin. They knew every little scandal and some very big crimes. They slept at their posts in the shadow of the church so that no one crept in for consolation without their knowledge. And they knew the doctor. They knew his ignorance, his cruelty, his avarice, his appetites, his sins. They knew his clumsy operations and the little brown pennies he gave sparingly for alms. They had seen his corpses go into the church. And, since early Mass was over and business was slow, they followed the procession, these endless searchers after perfect knowledge of their fellow men, to see what the fat, lazy doctor would do about an indigent baby with a scorpion bite.

The scurrying procession came at last to the big gate in the wall of the doctor's house. They could hear the splashing water and the singing of caged birds and the sweep of the long brooms on the flagstones. And they could smell the frying of good bacon from the doctor's house.

Kino hesitated a moment. This doctor was not of his people. This doctor was of a race which for nearly four hundred years had beaten and starved and robbed and despised Kino's race, and frightened it, too, so that the indigene[8] came humbly to the door. And as always when he came near to one of this race, Kino felt weak and afraid and angry at the same time. Rage and terror went together. He could kill the doctor more easily than he could talk to him, for all of the doctor's race spoke to all of Kino's race as though they were simple animals. And as Kino raised his right hand to the iron ring knocker in the gate, rage swelled in him, and the pounding music of the enemy beat in his ears, and his lips drew tight against his teeth—but with his left hand he reached to take off his hat. The iron ring pounded against the gate. Kino took off his hat and stood waiting. Coyotito moaned a little in Juana's arms, and she spoke softly to him. The procession crowded close the better to see and hear.

After a moment the big gate opened a few inches. Kino could see the green coolness of the garden and little splashing fountains through the opening. The man who looked out at him was one of his own race. Kino spoke to him in the old language. "The little one—the first born—has been poisoned by the scorpion," Kino said. "He requires the skill of the healer."

The gate closed a little, and the servant refused to speak in the old language. "A little moment," he said. "I go to inform myself," and he closed the gate and slid the bolt home. The glaring sun threw the bunched shadows of the people blackly on the white wall.

In his chamber the doctor sat up in his high bed. He had on his dressing gown of red watered silk that had come from Paris, a little tight over the chest now if it was buttoned. On his lap was a silver tray with a silver chocolate pot and a tiny cup of eggshell china, so delicate that it looked silly when he lifted it with his big hand, lifted it with the tips of thumb and forefinger and spread the other three fingers

---

7. **flagstone,** a large flat paving stone.
8. **indigene**\ˈĭn·dĭ·jĕn\ a native, aborigine.

wide to get them out of the way. His eyes rested in puffy little hammocks of flesh, and his mouth drooped with discontent. He was growing very stout, and his voice was hoarse with the fat that pressed on his throat. Beside him on a table was a small Oriental gong and a bowl of cigarettes. The furnishings of the room were heavy and dark and gloomy. The pictures were religious, even the large tinted photograph of his dead wife, who, if Masses willed and paid for out of her own estate could do it, was in Heaven. The doctor had once for a short time been a part of the great world, and his whole subsequent life was memory and longing for France. "That," he said, "was civilized living"—by which he meant that on a small income he had been able to keep a mistress and eat in restaurants. He poured his second cup of chocolate and crumbled a sweet biscuit in his fingers. The servant from the gate came to the open door and stood waiting to be noticed.

"Yes?" the doctor asked.

"It is a little Indian with a baby. He says a scorpion stung it."

The doctor put his cup down gently before he let his anger rise.

"Have I nothing better to do than cure insect bites for 'little Indians'? I am a doctor, not a veterinary."

"Yes, Patron,"[9] said the servant.

"Has he any money?" the doctor demanded. "No, they never have any money. I, I alone in the world am supposed to work for nothing—and I am tired of it. See if he has any money!"

At the gate the servant opened the door a trifle and looked out at the waiting people. And this time he spoke in the old language.

"Have you money to pay for the treatment?"

Now Kino reached into a secret place somewhere under his blanket. He brought out a paper folded many times. Crease by crease he unfolded it, until at last there came to view eight small, misshapen seed pearls,[10] as ugly and gray as little ulcers, flattened and almost valueless. The servant took the paper and closed the gate again, but this time he was not

gone long. He opened the gate just wide enough to pass the paper back.

"The doctor has gone out," he said. "He was called to a serious case." And he shut the gate quickly out of shame.

And now a wave of shame went over the whole procession. They melted away. The beggars went back to the church steps; the stragglers moved off; and the neighbors departed so that the public shaming of Kino would not be in their eyes.

For a long time Kino stood in front of the gate with Juana beside him. Slowly he put his suppliant hat on his head. Then, without warning, he struck the gate a crushing blow with his fist. He looked down in wonder at his split knuckles and at the blood that flowed down between his fingers.

*[handwritten margin notes: feels hopeless, powerless — angry at the injustice — can't do anything to help his baby]*

## 2

The town lay on a broad estuary, its old yellow plastered buildings hugging the beach. And on the beach the white and blue canoes that came from Nayarit[1] were drawn up, canoes preserved for generations by a hard, shell-like water-proof plaster whose making was a secret of the fishing people. They were high and graceful canoes with curving bow and stern and a braced section midships where a mast could be stepped to carry a small lateen sail.[2]

The beach was yellow sand, but at the water's edge a rubble of shell and algae took its place. Fiddler crabs bubbled and sputtered in their holes in the sand, and in the shallows little lobsters popped in and out of their tiny homes in the rubble and sand. The sea bottom was rich with crawling and swimming and

---

9. **Patron**\English pro. ˄pā·trən\ here means "sir, master, lord."
10. **seed pearl**, a quite small and often irregular pearl.

---

1. **Nayarit**\˄na·ya·rēt\ a small state in western Mexico northwest of Mexico City.
2. **lateen**\lă ˄tēn\ **sail,** one hung from a long spar attached to a short mast.

growing things. The brown algae waved in the gentle currents, and the green eel grass swayed, and little sea horses clung to its stems. Spotted botete,[3] the poison fish, lay on the bottom in the eel-grass beds; and the bright-colored swimming crabs scampered over them.

On the beach, the hungry dogs and the hungry pigs of the town searched endlessly for any dead fish or sea bird that might have floated in on a rising tide.

Although the morning was young, the hazy mirage was up. The uncertain air that magnified some things and blotted out others hung over the whole Gulf so that all sights were unreal and vision could not be trusted; so that sea and land had the sharp clarities and the vagueness of a dream. Thus it might be that the people of the Gulf trust things of the spirit and things of the imagination, but they do not trust their eyes to show them distance or clear outline or any optical exactness. Across the estuary from the town, one section of mangroves stood clear and telescopically defined, while another mangrove clump was a hazy black-green blob. Part of the far shore disappeared into a shimmer that looked like water. There was no certainty in seeing, no proof that what you saw was there or was not there. And the people of the Gulf expected all places were that way, and it was not strange to them. A copper haze hung over the water, and the hot morning sun beat on it and made it vibrate blindingly.

The brush houses of the fishing people were back from the beach on the right-hand side of the town, and the canoes were drawn up in front of this area.

Kino and Juana came slowly down to the beach and to Kino's canoe, which was the one thing of value he owned in the world. It was very old. Kino's grandfather had brought it from Nayarit; and he had given it to Kino's father, and so it had come to Kino. It was at once property and source of food, for a man with a boat can guarantee a woman that she will eat something. It is the bulwark against starvation. And every year Kino refinished his canoe with the hard, shell-like plaster by the secret method that had also come to him from his father. Now he came to the canoe and touched the bow tenderly as he always did. He laid his diving rock and his basket and the two ropes in the sand by the canoe. And he folded his blanket and laid it in the bow.

Juana laid Coyotito on the blanket, and she placed her shawl over him so that the hot sun could not shine on him. He was quiet now, but the swelling on his shoulder had continued up his neck and under his ear and his face was puffed and feverish. Juana went to the water and waded in. She gathered some brown seaweed and made a flat, damp poultice of it; and this she applied to the baby's swollen shoulder, which was as good a remedy as any and probably better than the doctor could have done. But the remedy lacked his authority because it was simple and didn't cost anything. The stomach cramps had not come to Coyotito. Perhaps Juana had sucked out the poison in time, but she had not sucked out her worry over her first-born. She had not prayed directly for the recovery of the baby—she had prayed that they might find a pearl with which to hire the doctor to cure the baby, for the minds of people are as unsubstantial as the mirage of the Gulf.

Now Kino and Juana slid the canoe down the beach to the water; and when the bow floated, Juana climbed in, while Kino pushed the stern in and waded beside it until it floated lightly and trembled on the little breaking waves. Then, in co-ordination, Juana and Kino drove their double-bladed paddles into the sea; and the canoe creased the water and hissed with speed. The other pearlers were gone out long since. In a few moments Kino could see them clustered in the haze, riding over the oyster bed.

Light filtered down through the water to the bed where the frilly pearl oysters lay fastened to the rubbly bottom, a bottom strewn with shells of broken, opened oysters. This was the

---

3. **botete**\\'bō ▲tä·tĕ\\.

bed that had raised the King of Spain to be a great power in Europe in past years, had helped to pay for his wars, and had decorated the churches for his soul's sake. The gray oysters with ruffles like skirts on the shells, the barnacle-crusted oysters with little bits of weed clinging to the skirts and small crabs climbing over them. An accident could happen to these oysters; a grain of sand could lie in the folds of muscle and irritate the flesh until, in self-protection, the flesh coated the grain with a layer of smooth cement. But once started, the flesh continued to coat the foreign body until it fell free in some tidal flurry or until the oyster was destroyed. For centuries men had dived down and torn the oysters from the beds and ripped them open, looking for the coated grains of sand. Swarms of fish lived near the bed to live near the oysters thrown back by the searching men and to nibble at the shining inner shells. But the pearls were accidents; and the finding of one was luck, a little pat on the back by God or the gods or both.

Kino had two ropes, one tied to a heavy stone and one to a basket. He stripped off his shirt and trousers and laid his hat in the bottom of the canoe. The water was oily smooth. He took his rock in one hand and his basket in the other, and he slipped feet first over the side, and the rock carried him to the bottom. The bubbles rose behind him until the water cleared and he could see. Above, the surface of the water was an undulating mirror of brightness, and he could see the bottoms of the canoes sticking through it.

Kino moved cautiously so that the water would not be obscured with mud or sand. He hooked his foot in the loop on his rock; and his hands worked quickly, tearing the oysters loose, some singly, other in clusters. He laid them in his basket. In some places the oysters clung to one another so that they came free in lumps.

Now, Kino's people had sung of everything that happened or existed. They had made songs to the fishes, to the sea in anger and to the sea in calm, to the light and the dark and the sun and the moon; and the songs were all in Kino and in his people—every song that had ever been made, even the ones forgotten. And as he filled his basket, the song was in Kino; and the beat of the song was his pounding heart as it ate the oxygen from his held breath; and the melody of the song was the gray-green water and the little scuttling animals and the clouds of fish that flitted by and were gone. But in the song there was a secret little inner song, hardly perceptible, but always there, sweet and secret and clinging, almost hiding in the counter-melody; and this was the Song of the Pearl That Might Be, for every shell thrown in the basket might contain a pearl. Chance was against it, but luck and the gods might be for it. And in the canoe above him, Kino knew that Juana was making the magic of prayer, her face set rigid and her muscles hard to force the luck, to tear the luck out of the god's hands, for she needed the luck for the swollen shoulder of Coyotito. And because the need was great and the desire was great, the little secret melody of the pearl that might be was stronger this morning. Whole phrases of it came clearly and softly into the Song of the Undersea.

Kino, in his pride and youth and strength, could remain down over two minutes without strain, so that he worked deliberately, selecting the largest shells. Because they were disturbed, the oyster shells were tightly closed. A little to his right a hummock of rubbly rock stuck up, covered with young oysters not ready to take. Kino moved next to the hummock; and then, beside it, under a little overhang, he saw a very large oyster lying by itself, not covered with its clinging brothers. The shell was partly open, for the overhang protected this ancient oyster, and in the liplike muscle Kino saw a ghostly gleam, and then the shell closed down. His heart beat out a heavy rhythm, and the melody of the maybe pearl shrilled in his ears. Slowly he forced the oyster loose and held it tightly against his breast. He kicked his foot free from the rock loop, and his body rose to the surface, and his black hair gleamed in the sunlight. He reached over the side of the canoe and laid the oyster in the bottom.

Then Juana steadied the boat while he climbed in. His eyes were shining with excitement, but in decency he pulled up his rock, and then he pulled up his basket of oysters and lifted them in. Juana sensed his excitement, and she pretended to look away. It is not good to want a thing too much. It sometimes drives the luck away. You must want it just enough, and you must be very tactful with God or the gods. But Juana stopped breathing. Very deliberately Kino opened his short, strong knife. He looked speculatively at the basket. Perhaps it would be better to open *the* oyster last. He took a small oyster from the basket, cut the muscle, searched the folds of flesh, and threw it in the water. Then he seemed to see the great oyster for the first time. He squatted in the bottom of the canoe, picked up the shell, and examined it. The flutes were shining black to brown, and only a few small barnacles adhered to the shell. Now Kino was reluctant to open it. What he had seen, he knew, might be a reflection, a piece of flat shell accidentally drifted in, or a complete illusion. In this Gulf of uncertain light there were more illusions than realities.

But Juana's eyes were on him, and she could not wait. She put her hand on Coyotito's covered head. "Open it," she said softly.

Kino deftly slipped his knife into the edge of the shell. Through the knife he could feel the muscle tighten hard. He worked the blade leverwise, and the closing muscle parted, and the shell fell apart. The liplike flesh writhed up and then subsided. Kino lifted the flesh; and there it lay, the great pearl, perfect as the moon. It captured the light and refined it and gave it back in silver incandescence. It was as large as a sea gull's egg. It was the greatest pearl in the world.

Juana caught her breath and moaned a little. And to Kino the secret melody of the maybe pearl broke clear and beautiful, rich and warm and lovely, glowing and gloating and triumphant. In the surface of the great pearl he could see dream forms. He picked the pearl from the dying flesh and held it in his palm, and he turned it over and saw that its curve was perfect. Juana came near to stare at it in his hand, and it was the hand he had smashed against the doctor's gate, and the torn flesh of the knuckles was turned grayish-white by the sea water.

Instinctively Juana went to Coyotito where he lay on his father's blanket. She lifted the poultice of seaweed and looked at the shoulder. "Kino," she cried shrilly.

He looked past his pearl, and he saw that the swelling was going out of the baby's shoulder, the poison was receding from its body. Then Kino's fist closed over the pearl, and his emotion broke over him. He put back his head and howled. His eyes rolled up, and he screamed, and his body was rigid. The men in the other canoes looked up, startled; and then they dug their paddles into the sea and raced toward Kino's canoe.

## ❧ 3

A town is a thing like a colonial animal. A town has a nervous system and a head and shoulders and feet. A town is a thing separate from all other towns, so that there are no two towns alike. And a town has a whole emotion. How news travels through a town is a mystery not easily to be solved. News seems to move faster than small boys can scramble and dart to tell it, faster than women can call it over the fences.

Before Kino and Juana and the other fishers had come to Kino's brush house, the nerves of the town were pulsing and vibrating with the news—Kino found the Pearl of the World. Before panting little boys could strangle out the words, their mothers knew it. The news swept on past the brush houses, and it washed in a foaming wave into the town of stone and plaster. It came to the priest walking in his garden, and it put a thoughtful look in his eyes and a memory of certain repairs necessary to the church. He wondered what the pearl would be worth. And he wondered whether he had baptized Kino's baby, or married him for that matter. The news came to the shopkeepers, and they looked at men's clothes that had not sold so well.

The news came to the doctor where he sat with a woman whose illness was age, though neither she nor the doctor would admit it. And when it was made plain who Kino was, the doctor grew stern and judicious at the same time. "He is a client of mine," the doctor said. "I'm treating his child for a scorpion sting." And the doctor's eyes rolled up a little in their fat hammocks, and he thought of Paris. He remembered the room he had lived in there as a great and luxurious place; and he remembered the hard-faced woman who had lived with him as a beautiful and kind girl, although she had been none of these three. The doctor looked past his aged patient and saw himself sitting in a restaurant in Paris and a waiter was just opening a bottle of wine.

The news came early to the beggars in front of the church, and it made them giggle a little with pleasure, for they knew that there is no almsgiver in the world like a poor man who is suddenly lucky.

Kino had found the Pearl of the World. In the town, in little offices, sat the men who bought pearls from the fishers. They waited in their chairs until the pearls came in, and then they cackled and fought and shouted and threatened until they reached the lowest price the fishermen would stand. But there was a price below which they dared not go, for it had happened that a fisherman in despair had given his pearls to the church. And when the buying was over, these buyers sat alone; and their fingers played restlessly with the pearls; and they wished they owned the pearls. For there were not many buyers really—there was only one, and he kept these agents in separate offices to give a semblance of competition. The news came to these men, and their eyes squinted and their fingertips burned a little, and each one

thought how the patron could not live forever and someone had to take his place. And each one thought how with some capital he could get a new start.

All manner of people grew interested in Kino—people with things to sell and people with favors to ask. Kino had found the Pearl of the World. The essence of pearl mixed with essence of men and a curious, dark residue was precipitated. Every man suddenly became related to Kino's pearl; and Kino's pearl went into the dreams, the speculations, the schemes, the plans, the futures, the wishes, the needs, the lusts, the hungers, of everyone; and only one person stood in the way, and that was Kino; so that he became curiously every man's enemy. The news stirred up something infinitely black and evil in the town; the black distillate was like the scorpion, or like hunger in the smell of food, or like loneliness when love is withheld. The poison sacs of the town began to manufacture venom, and the town swelled and puffed with the pressure of it.

But Kino and Juana did not know these things. Because they were happy and excited, they thought everyone shared their joy. Juan Tomás and Apolonia did, and they were the world too. In the afternoon, when the sun had gone over the mountains of the Peninsula to sink in the outward sea, Kino squatted in his house with Juana beside him. And the brush house was crowded with neighbors. Kino held the great pearl in his hand, and it was warm and alive in his hand. And the music of the pearl had merged with the music of the family, so that one beautified the other. The neighbors looked at the pearl in Kino's hand, and they wondered how such luck could come to any man.

And Juan Tomás, who squatted on Kino's right hand because he was his brother, asked, "What will you do now that you have become a rich man?"

Kino looked into his pearl, and Juana cast her eyelashes down and arranged her shawl to cover her face so that her excitement could not be seen. And in the incandescence of the pearl, the pictures formed of the things Kino's mind had considered in the past and had given up as impossible. In the pearl he saw Juana and Coyotito and himself standing and kneeling at the high altar, and they were being married now that they could pay. He spoke softly, "We will be married—in the church."

In the pearl he saw how they were dressed—Juana in a shawl stiff with newness and a new skirt, and from under the long skirt Kino could see that she wore shoes. It was in the pearl—the picture glowing there. He himself was dressed in new white clothes, and he carried a new hat—not of straw but of fine black felt—and he too wore shoes—not sandals but shoes that laced. But Coyotito—he was the one—he wore a blue sailor suit from the United States and a little yachting cap such as Kino had seen once when a pleasure boat put into the estuary. All of these things Kino saw in the lucent pearl and he said, "We will have new clothes."

And the music of the pearl rose like a chorus of trumpets in his ears.

Then to the lovely gray surface of the pearl came the little things Kino wanted: a harpoon to take the place of one lost a year ago, a new harpoon of iron with a ring in the end of the shaft; and—his mind could hardly make the leap—a rifle—but why not, since he was so rich. And Kino saw Kino in the pearl, Kino holding a Winchester carbine. It was the wildest daydreaming and very pleasant. His lips moved hesitantly over this—"A rifle," he said. "Perhaps a rifle."

It was the rifle that broke down the barriers. This was an impossibility; and if he could think of having a rifle, whole horizons were burst; and he could rush on. For it is said that humans are never satisfied, that you give them one thing and they want something more. And this is said in disparagement, whereas it is one of the greatest talents the species has and one that has made it superior to animals that are satisfied with what they have.

The neighbors, close pressed and silent in the house, nodded their heads at his wild imaginings. And a man in the rear murmured, "A rifle. He will have a rifle."

But the music of the pearl was shrilling with triumph in Kino. Juana looked up, and her eyes were wide at Kino's courage and at his imagination. And electric strength had come to him now the horizons were kicked out. In the pearl he saw Coyotito sitting at a little desk in a school, just as Kino had once seen it through an open door. And Coyotito was dressed in a jacket and he had on a white collar and a broad silken tie. Moreover, Coyotito was writing on a big piece of paper. Kino looked at his neighbors fiercely. "My son will go to school," he said, and the neighbors were hushed. Juana caught her breath sharply. Her eyes were bright as she watched him, and she looked quickly down at Coyotito in her arms to see whether this might be possible.

But Kino's face shone with prophecy. "My son will read and open the books, and my son will write and will know writing. And my son will make numbers, and these things will make us free because he will know—he will know, and through him we will know." And in the pearl Kino saw himself and Juana squatting by the little fire in the brush hut while Coyotito read from a great book. "This is what the pearl will do," said Kino. And he had never said so many words together in his life. And suddenly he was afraid of his talking. His hand closed down over the pearl and cut the light away from it. Kino was afraid as a man is afraid who says, "I will," without knowing.

Now the neighbors knew they had witnessed a great marvel. They knew that time would now date from Kino's pearl and that they would discuss this moment for many years to come. If these things came to pass, they would recount how Kino looked and what he said and how his eyes shone; and they would say, "He was a man transfigured. Some power was given to him, and there it started. You see what a great man he has become, starting from that moment. And I myself saw it."

And if Kino's planning came to nothing, those same neighbors would say, "There it started. A foolish madness came over him so that he spoke foolish words. God keep us from such things. Yes, God punished Kino because he rebelled against the way things are. You see what has become of him. And I myself saw the moment when his reason left him."

Kino looked down at his closed hand, and the knuckles were scabbed over and tight where he had struck the gate.

Now the dusk was coming. And Juana looped her shawl under the baby so that he hung against her hip, and she went to the fire hole and dug a coal from the ashes and broke a few twigs over it and fanned a flame alive. The little flames danced on the faces of the neighbors. They knew they should go to their own dinners, but they were reluctant to leave.

The dark was almost in, and Juana's fire threw shadows on the brush walls when the whisper came in, passed from mouth to mouth. "The Father is coming—the priest is coming." The men uncovered their heads and stepped back from the door, and the women gathered their shawls about their faces and cast down their eyes. Kino and Juan Tomás, his brother, stood up. The priest came in—a graying, aging man with an old skin and a young sharp eye. Children he considered these people, and he treated them like children.

"Kino," he said softly, "thou art named after a great man—and a great Father of the Church." He made it sound like a benediction. "Thy namesake tamed the desert and sweetened the minds of thy people, didst thou know that? It is in the books."

Kino looked quickly down at Coyotito's head, where he hung on Juana's hip. Someday, his mind said, that boy would know what things were in the books and what things were not. The music had gone out of Kino's head; but now, thinly, slowly, the melody of the morning, the music of evil, of the enemy sounded; but it was faint and weak. And Kino looked at his neighbors to see who might have brought this song in.

But the priest was speaking again. "It has come to me that thou hast found a great fortune, a great pearl."

Kino opened his hand and held it out, and the priest gasped a little at the size and beauty of the pearl. And then he said, "I hope thou wilt remember to give thanks, my son, to Him who has given thee this treasure and to pray for guidance in the future."

Kino nodded dumbly, and it was Juana who spoke softly. "We will, Father. And we will be married now. Kino has said so." She looked at the neighbors for confirmation, and they nodded their heads solemnly.

The priest said, "It is pleasant to see that your first thoughts are good thoughts. God bless you, my children." He turned and left quietly, and the people let him through.

But Kino's hand had closed tightly on the pearl again; and he was glancing about suspiciously; for the evil song was in his ears, shrilling against the music of the pearl.

The neighbors slipped away to go to their houses, and Juana squatted by the fire and set her clay pot of boiled beans over the little flame. Kino stepped to the doorway and looked out. As always, he could smell the smoke from many fires, and he could see the hazy stars and feel the damp of the night air so that he covered his nose from it. The thin dog came to him and threshed itself in greeting like a wind-blown flag, and Kino looked down at it and didn't see it. He had broken through the horizons into a cold and lonely outside. He felt alone and unprotected, and scraping crickets and shrilling tree frogs and croaking toads seemed to be carrying the melody of evil. Kino shivered a little and drew his blanket more tightly against his nose. He carried the pearl still in his hand, tightly closed in his palm, and it was warm and smooth against his skin.

Behind him he heard Juana patting the cakes before she put them down on the clay cooking sheet. Kino felt all the warmth and security of his family behind him, and the Song of the Family came from behind him like the purring of a kitten. But now, by saying what his future was going to be like, he had created it. A plan

562

is a real thing, and things projected are experienced. A plan, once made and visualized, becomes a reality along with other realities—never to be destroyed but easily to be attacked. Thus Kino's future was real; but having set it up, other forces were set up to destroy it; and this he knew, so that he had to prepare to meet the attack. And this Kino knew also—that the gods do not love men's plans and the gods do not love success unless it comes by accident. He knew that the gods take their revenge on a man if he be successful through his own efforts. Consequently Kino was afraid of plans; but having made one, he could never destroy it. And to meet the attack, Kino was already making a hard skin for himself against the world. His eyes and his mind probed for danger before it appeared.

Standing in the door, he saw two men approach; and one of them carried a lantern which lighted the ground and the legs of the men. They turned in through the opening of Kino's brush fence and came to his door. And Kino saw that one was the doctor and the other the servant who had opened the gate in the morning. The split knuckles on Kino's right hand burned when he saw who they were.

The doctor said, "I was not in when you came this morning. But now, at the first chance, I have come to see the baby."

Kino stood in the door, filling it, and hatred raged and flamed in back of his eyes, and fear too; for the hundreds of years of subjugation were cut deep in him.

"The baby is nearly well now," he said curtly.

The doctor smiled, but his eyes in their little lymph-lined hammocks did not smile.

He said, "Sometimes, my friend, the scorpion sting has a curious effect. There will be apparent improvement, and then without warning—pouf!" He pursed his lips and made a little explosion to show how quick it could be, and he shifted his small black doctor's bag about so that the light of the lamp fell upon it, for he knew that Kino's race love the tools of any craft and trust them. "Sometimes," the doctor went on in a liquid tone, "sometimes there will

be a withered leg or a blind eye or a crumpled back. Oh, I know the sting of the scorpion, my friend; and I can cure it."

Kino felt the rage and hatred melting toward fear. He did not know, and perhaps this doctor did. And he could not take the chance of putting his certain ignorance against this man's possible knowledge. He was trapped as his people were always trapped, and would be until, as he had said, they could be sure that the things in the books were really in the books. He could not take a chance—not with the life or with the straightness of Coyotito. He stood aside and let the doctor and his man enter the brush hut.

Juana stood up from the fire and backed away as he entered, and she covered the baby's face with the fringe of her shawl. And when the doctor went to her and held out his hand, she clutched the baby tight and looked at Kino where he stood with the fire shadows leaping on his face.

Kino nodded, and only then did she let the doctor take the baby.

"Hold the light," the doctor said, and when the servant held the lantern high, the doctor looked for a moment at the wound on the baby's shoulder. He was thoughtful for a moment, and then he rolled back the baby's eyelid and looked at the eyeball. He nodded his head while Coyotito struggled against him.

"It is as I thought," he said. "The poison has gone inward, and it will strike soon. Come look!" He held the eyelid down. "See—it is blue. And Kino, looking anxiously, saw that indeed it was a little blue. And he didn't know whether or not it was always a little blue. But the trap was set. He couldn't take the chance.

The doctor's eyes watered in their little hammocks. "I will give him something to try to turn the poison aside," he said. And he handed the baby to Kino.

Then from his bag he took a little bottle of white powder and a capsule of gelatine. He filled the capsule with the powder and closed it, and then around the first capsule he fitted a second capsule and closed it. Then he worked very deftly. He took the baby and pinched its lower lip until it opened its mouth. His fat fingers placed the capsule far back on the baby's tongue, back of the point where he could spit it out, and then from the floor he picked up the little pitcher of pulque and gave Coyotito a drink, and it was done. He looked again at the baby's eyeball and he pursed his lips and seemed to think.

At last he handed the baby back to Juana, and he turned to Kino. "I think the poison will attack within the hour," he said. "The medicine may save the baby from hurt, but I will come back in an hour. Perhaps I am in time to save him." He took a deep breath and went out of the hut, and his servant followed him with the lantern.

Now Juana had the baby under her shawl, and she stared at it with anxiety and fear. Kino came to her, and he lifted the shawl and stared at the baby. He moved his hand to look under the eyelid, and only then saw that the pearl was still in his hand. Then he went to a box by the wall, and from it he brought a piece of rag. He wrapped the pearl in the rag, then went to the corner of the brush house and dug a little hole with his fingers in the dirt floor, and he put the pearl in the hole and covered it up and concealed the place. And then he went to the fire where Juana was squatting, watching the baby's face.

The doctor, back in his house, settled into his chair and looked at his watch. His people brought him a little supper of chocolate and sweet cakes and fruit, and he stared at the food discontentedly.

In the houses of the neighbors, the subject that would lead all conversations for a long time to come was aired for the first time to see how it would go. The neighbors showed one another with their thumbs how big the pearl was, and they made little caressing gestures to show how lovely it was. From now on they would watch Kino and Juana very closely to see whether riches turned their heads, as riches turn all people's heads. Everyone knew why the doctor had come. He was not good at dissembling, and he was very well understood.

Out in the estuary a tight-woven school of small fishes glittered and broke water to escape a school of great fishes that drove in to eat them. And in the houses the people could hear the swish of the small ones and the bouncing splash of the great ones as the slaughter went on. The dampness arose out of the Gulf and was deposited on bushes and cacti and on little trees in salty drops. And the night mice crept about on the ground, and the little night hawks hunted them silently.

The skinny black puppy with flame spots over his eyes came to Kino's door and looked in. He nearly shook his hind quarters loose when Kino glanced up at him, and he subsided when Kino looked away. The puppy did not enter the house, but he watched with frantic interest while Kino ate his beans from the little pottery dish and wiped it clean with a corncake and ate the cake and washed the whole down with a drink of pulque.

Kino was finished and was rolling a cigarette when Juana spoke sharply. "Kino." He glanced at her and then got up and went quickly to her for he saw fright in her eyes. He stood over her, looking down, but the light was very dim. He kicked a pile of twigs into the fire hole to make a blaze, and then he could see the face of Coyotito. The baby's face was flushed and his throat was working and a little thick drool of saliva issued from his lips. The spasm of the stomach muscles began, and the baby was very sick.

Kino knelt beside his wife. "So the doctor knew," he said; but he said it for himself as well as for his wife; for his mind was hard and suspicious, and he was remembering the white powder. Juana rocked from side to side and moaned out the little Song of the Family as though it could ward off the danger, and the baby vomited and writhed in her arms. Now uncertainty was in Kino, and the music of evil throbbed in his head and nearly drove out Juana's song.

The doctor finished his chocolate and nibbled the little fallen pieces of sweet cake. He brushed his fingers on a napkin, looked at his watch, arose, and took up his little bag.

The news of the baby's illness traveled quickly among the brush houses, for sickness is second only to hunger as the enemy of poor people. And some said softly, "Luck, you see, brings bitter friends." And they nodded and got up to go to Kino's house. The neighbors scuttled with covered noses through the dark until they crowded into Kino's house again. They stood and gazed, and they made little comments on the sadness that this should happen at a time of joy; and they said, "All things are in God's hands." The old women squatted down beside Juana to try to give her aid if they could and comfort if they could not.

Then the doctor hurried in, followed by his man. He scattered the old women like chickens. He took the baby and examined it and felt its head. "The poison it has worked," he said. "I think I can defeat it. I will try my best." He asked for water, and in the cup of it he put three drops of ammonia, and he pried open the baby's mouth and poured it down. The baby spluttered and screeched under the treatment, and Juana watched him with haunted eyes. The doctor spoke a little as he worked. "It is lucky that I know about the poison of the scorpion, otherwise—" and he shrugged to show what could have happened.

But Kino was suspicious, and he could not take his eyes from the doctor's open bag and from the bottle of white powder there. Gradually the spasms subsided, and the baby relaxed under the doctor's hands. And then Coyotito sighed deeply and went to sleep, for he was very tired with vomiting.

The doctor put the baby in Juana's arms. "He will get well now," he said. "I have won the fight." And Juana looked at him with adoration.

The doctor was closing his bag now. He said, "When do you think you can pay this bill?" He said it even kindly.

"When I have sold my pearl, I will pay you," Kino said.

"You have a pearl? A good pearl?" the doctor asked with interest.

And then the chorus of the neighbors broke in. "He has found the Pearl of the World," they cried, and they joined forefinger with thumb to show how great the pearl was.

"Kino will be a rich man," they clamored. "It is a pearl such as one has never seen."

The doctor looked surprised. "I had not heard of it. Do you keep this pearl in a safe place? Perhaps you would like me to put it in my safe?"

Kino's eyes were hooded now, his cheeks were drawn taut. "I have it secure," he said. "Tomorrow I will sell it, and then I will pay you."

The doctor shrugged and his wet eyes never left Kino's eyes. He knew the pearl would be buried in the house, and he thought Kino might look toward the place where it was buried. "It would be a shame to have it stolen before you could sell it," the doctor said, and he saw Kino's eyes flick involuntarily to the floor near the side post of the brush house.

When the doctor had gone and all the neighbors had reluctantly returned to their houses, Kino squatted beside the little glowing coals in the fire hole and listened to the night sound: the soft sweep of the little waves on the shore and the distant barking of dogs, the creeping of the breeze through the brush-house roof and the soft speech of his neighbors in their houses in the village. For these people do not sleep soundly all night; they awaken at intervals and talk a little and then go to sleep again. And after a while, Kino got up and went to the door of his house.

He smelled the breeze and he listened for any foreign sound of secrecy or creeping, and his eyes searched the darkness, for the music of evil was sounding in his head, and he was fierce and afraid. After he had probed the night with his senses, he went to the place by the side post where the pearl was buried; and he dug it up and brought it to his sleeping mat, and under his sleeping mat he dug another little hole in the dirt floor and buried his pearl and covered it up again.

And Juana, sitting by the fire hole, watched him with questioning eyes; and when he had buried his pearl, she asked, "Who do you fear?"

Kino searched for a true answer, and at last he said, "Everyone." And he could feel a shell of hardness drawing over him.

After a while they lay down together on the sleeping mat, and Juana did not put the baby in his box tonight, but cradled him on her arms and covered his face with her head shawl. And the last light went out of the embers in the fire hole.

But Kino's brain burned, even during his sleep, and he dreamed that Coyotito could read, that one of his own people could tell him the truth of things. And in his dream, Coyotito was reading from a book as large as a house with letters as big as dogs, and the words galloped and played on the book. And then darkness spread over the page, and with the darkness came the music of evil again, and Kino stirred in his sleep; and when he stirred, Juana's eyes opened in the darkness. And then Kino awakened with the evil music pulsing in him, and he lay in the darkness with his ears alert.

Then from the corner of the house came a sound so soft that it might have been simply a thought, a little furtive movement, a touch of a foot on earth, the almost inaudible purr of controlled breathing. Kino held his breath to listen, and he knew that whatever dark thing was in his house was holding its breath too, to listen. For a time no sound at all came from the corner of the brush house. Then Kino might have thought he had imagined the sound. But Juana's hand came creeping over to him in warning, and then the sound came again! the whisper of a foot on dry earth and the scratch of fingers in the soil.

And now a wild fear surged in Kino's breast, and on the fear came rage, as it always did. Kino's hand crept into his breast where his knife hung on a string, and then he sprang like an angry cat, leaped striking and spitting for the dark thing he knew was in the corner of the house. He felt cloth, struck at it with his knife and missed, and struck again and felt the knife go through cloth; and then his head crashed with lightning and exploded with pain. There was a soft scurry in the doorway and running steps for a moment, and then silence.

Kino could feel warm blood running down from his forehead, and he could hear Juana calling to him. "Kino! Kino!" And there was terror in her voice. Then coldness came over him as quickly as the rage had, and he said, "I am all right. The thing has gone."

He groped his way back to the sleeping mat. Already Juana was working at the fire. She uncovered an ember from the ashes and shredded little pieces of cornhusk over it and blew a little flame into the cornhusks so that a tiny light danced through the hut. And then from a secret place Juana brought a little piece of consecrated candle and lighted it at the flame and set it upright on a fireplace stone. She worked quickly, crooning as she moved about. She dipped the end of her head shawl in water and swabbed the blood from Kino's bruised forehead. "It is nothing," Kino said; but his eyes and his voice were hard and cold, and a brooding hate was growing in him.

Now the tension which had been growing in Juana boiled up to the surface, and her lips were thin. "This thing is evil," she cried harshly. "This pearl is like a sin! It will destroy us," and her voice rose shrilly. "Throw it away, Kino. Let us break it between stones. Let us bury it and forget the place. Let us throw it back into the sea. It has brought evil. Kino, my husband, it will destroy us." And in the firelight her lips and her eyes were alive with her fear.

But Kino's face was set, and his mind and his will were set. "This is our one chance," he said. "Our son must go to school. He must break out of the pot that holds us in."

"It will destroy us all," Juana cried. "Even our son."

"Hush," said Kino. "Do not speak any more. In the morning we will sell the pearl, and then the evil will be gone and only the good remain. Now hush, my wife." His dark eyes scowled into the little fire, and for the first time he knew that his knife was still in his hands, and he raised the blade and looked at it and saw a little line of blood on the steel. For a moment he seemed about to wipe the blade on his trousers, but then he plunged the knife into the earth and so cleansed it.

The distant roosters began to crow, and the air changed, and the dawn was coming. The wind of the morning ruffled the water of the estuary and whispered through the mangroves, and the little waves beat on the rubbly beach with an increased tempo. Kino raised the sleeping mat and dug up his pearl and put it in front of him and stared at it.

And the beauty of the pearl, winking and glimmering in the light of the little candle, cozened his brain with its beauty. So lovely it was, so soft; and its own music came from it —its music of promise and delight, its guarantee of the future, of comfort, of security. Its warm lucence promised a poultice against illness and a wall against insult. It closed a door on hunger. And as he stared at it, Kino's eyes softened and his face relaxed. He could see the little image of the consecrated candle reflected in the soft surface of the pearl, and he heard again in his ears the lovely music of the undersea, the tone of the diffused, green light of the sea bottom. Juana, glancing secretly at him, saw him smile. And because they were in some way one thing and one purpose, she smiled with him.

And they began this day with hope.

## 4

It is wonderful the way a little town keeps track of itself and of all its units. If every single man and woman, child and baby, acts and conducts itself in a known pattern and breaks no walls and differs with no one and experiments in no way and is not sick and does not endanger the ease and peace of mind or steady unbroken flow of the town, then that unit can disappear and never be heard of. But let one man step out of the regular thought or the known and trusted pattern, and the nerves of the townspeople ring with nervousness and communication travels over the nerve lines of the town. Then every unit communicates to the whole.

Thus, in La Paz,[1] it was known in the early morning through the whole town that Kino was going to sell his pearl that day. It was known among the neighbors in the brush huts, among the pearl fishermen; it was known among the Chinese grocery-store owners; it was known in the church, for the altar boys whispered about it. Word of it crept in among the nuns; the beggars in front of the church spoke of it, for they would be there to take the tithe[2] of the first fruits of the luck. The little boys knew about it with excitement, but most of all the pearl buyers knew about it; and when the day had come, in the offices of the pearl buyers, each man sat alone with his little black velvet tray; and each man rolled the pearls about with his fingertips and considered his part in the picture.

It was supposed that the pearl buyers were individuals acting alone, bidding against one another for the pearls the fishermen brought in. And once it had been so. But this was a wasteful method, for often, in the excitement of bidding for a fine pearl, too great a price had been paid to the fishermen. This was extravagant and not to be countenanced. Now there was only one pearl buyer with many hands; and the men who sat in their offices and waited for Kino knew what price they would offer, how high they would bid, and what method each one would use. And although these men would not profit beyond their salaries, there was excitement among the pearl buyers; for there was excitement in the hunt; and if it be a man's function to break down a price, then he must take joy and satisfaction in breaking it as far down

---

1. **La Paz**\English pro. la paz\ a Mexican town near the tip of lower California on La Paz Bay in the Gulf of California.
2. **tithe**\taith\ technically a tenth, but loosely any portion given to charity.

as possible. For every man in the world functions to the best of his ability, and no one does less than his best, no matter what he may think about it. Quite apart from any reward they might get, from any word of praise, from any promotion, a pearl buyer was a pearl buyer, and the best and happiest pearl buyer was he who bought for the lowest prices.

The sun was hot yellow that morning, and it drew the moisture from the estuary and from the Gulf and hung it in shimmering scarves in the air, so that the air vibrated and vision was insubstantial. A vision hung in the air to the north of the city—the vision of a mountain that was over two hundred miles away, and the high slopes of this mountain were swaddled with pines, and a great stone peak arose above the timber line.

And the morning of this day the canoes lay lined up on the beach; the fishermen did not go out to dive for pearls, for there would be too much happening, too many things to see when Kino went to sell the great pearl.

In the brush houses by the shore, Kino's neighbors sat long over their breakfasts; and they spoke of what they would do if they had found the pearl. And one man said that he would give it as a present to the Holy Father in Rome. Another said that he would buy Masses for the souls of his family for a thousand years. Another thought he might take the money and distribute it among the poor of La Paz; and a fourth thought of all the good things one could do with the money from the pearl, of all the charities, benefits, of all the rescues one could perform if one had money. All of the neighbors hoped that sudden wealth would not turn Kino's head, would not make a rich man of him, would not graft onto him the evil limbs of greed and hatred and coldness. For Kino was a well-liked man; it would be a shame if the pearl destroyed him. "That good wife Juana," they said, "and the beautiful baby Coyotito, and the others to come. What a pity it would be if the pearl should destroy them all."

For Kino and Juana this was the morning of mornings of their lives, comparable only to the day when the baby was born. This was to be the day from which all other days would take their arrangement. Thus they would say, "It was two years before we sold the pearl," or, "It was six weeks after we sold the pearl." Juana, considering the matter, threw caution to the winds; and she dressed Coyotito in the clothes she had prepared for his baptism, when there would be money for his baptism. And Juana combed and braided her hair and tied the ends with two little bows of red ribbon, and she put on her marriage skirt and waist. The sun was quarter high when they were ready. Kino's ragged white clothes were clean at least, and this was the last day of his raggedness. For tomorrow, or even this afternoon, he would have new clothes.

The neighbors, watching Kino's door through the crevices in their brush houses, were dressed and ready too. There was no self-consciousness about their joining Kino and Juana to go pearl selling. It was expected, it was an historic moment, they would be crazy if they didn't go. It would be almost a sign of unfriendship.

Juana put on her head shawl carefully; and she draped one end under her right elbow and gathered it with her right hand so that a hammock hung under her arm; and in this little hammock she placed Coyotito, propped up against the head shawl so that he could see everything and perhaps remember. Kino put on his large straw hat and felt it with his hand to see that it was properly placed, not on the back or side of his head, like a rash, unmarried, irresponsible man, and not flat as an elder would wear it, but tilted a little forward to show aggressiveness and seriousness and vigor. There is a great deal to be seen in the tilt of a hat on a man. Kino slipped his feet into his sandals and pulled the thongs up over his heels. The great pearl was wrapped in an old soft piece of deerskin and placed in a little leather bag, and the leather bag was in a pocket in Kino's shirt. He folded his blanket carefully and draped it in a narrow strip over his left shoulder, and now they were ready.

Kino stepped with dignity out of the house;

568

foreshadowing

and Juana followed him, carrying Coyotito. And as they marched up the freshet-washed alley toward the town, the neighbors joined them. The houses belched people; the doorways spewed out children. But because of the seriousness of the occasion, only one man walked with Kino, and that was his brother Juan Tomás.

Juan Tomás cautioned his brother. "You must be careful to see they do not cheat you," he said.

And, "Very careful," Kino agreed.

"We do not know what prices are paid in other places," said Juan Tomás. "How can we know what is a fair price, if we do not know what the pearl buyer gets for the pearl in another place."

"That is true," said Kino, "but how can we know? We are here, we are not there."

As they walked up toward the city, the crowd grew behind them; and Juan Tomás, in pure nervousness, went on speaking.

"Before you were born, Kino," he said, "the old ones thought of a way to get more money for their pearls. They thought it would be better if they had an agent who took all the pearls to the capital and sold them there and kept only his share of the profit."

Kino nodded his head. "I know," he said. "It was a good thought."

"And so they got such a man," said Juan Tomás, "and they pooled the pearls, and they started him off. And he was never heard of again, and the pearls were lost. Then they got another man, and they started him off, and he was never heard of again. And so they gave the whole thing up and went back to the old way."

"I know," said Kino. "I have heard our father tell of it. It was a good idea, but it was against religion, and the Father made that very clear. The loss of the pearl was a punishment visited on those who tried to leave their station. And the Father made it clear that each man and woman is like a soldier sent by God to guard some part of the castle of the Universe. And some are in the ramparts and some far deep in the darkness of the walls. But each one must remain faithful to his post and must not go running about, else the castle is in danger from the assaults of Hell."

"I have heard him make that sermon," said Juan Tomás. "He makes it every year."

The brothers, as they walked along, squinted their eyes a little, as they and their grandfathers and their great-grandfathers had done for four hundred years, since first the strangers came with arguments and authority and gunpowder to back up both. And in the four hundred years Kino's people had learned only one defense—a slight slitting of the eyes and a slight tightening of the lips and a retirement. Nothing could break down this wall, and they could remain whole within the wall.

The gathering procession was solemn, for they sensed the importance of this day, and any children who showed a tendency to scuffle, to scream, to cry out, to steal hats and rumple hair, were hissed to silence by their elders. So important was this day that an old man came to see, riding on the stalwart shoulders of his nephew. The procession left the brush huts and entered the stone and plaster city, where the streets were a little wider and there were narrow pavements beside the buildings. And as before, the beggars joined them as they passed the church; the grocers looked out at them as they went by; the little saloons lost their customers, and the owners closed up shop and went along. And the sun beat down on the streets of the city, and even tiny stones threw shadows on the ground.

The news of the approach of the procession ran ahead of it, and in their little dark offices the pearl buyers stiffened and grew alert. They got out papers so that they could be at work when Kino appeared, and they put their pearls in the desks, for it is not good to let an inferior pearl be seen beside a beauty. And word of the loveliness of Kino's pearl had come to them. The pearl buyers' offices were clustered together in one narrow street, and they were barred at the windows, and wooden slats cut out the light so that only a soft gloom entered the offices.

A stout, slow man sat in an office waiting. His face was fatherly and benign, and his eyes twinkled with friendship. He was a caller of good mornings, a ceremonious shaker of hands, a jolly man who knew all jokes and yet who hovered close to sadness, for in the midst of a laugh he could remember the death of your aunt, and his eyes could become wet with sorrow for your loss. This morning he had placed a flower in a vase on his desk, a single scarlet hibiscus,[3] and the vase sat beside the black, velvet-lined pearl tray in front of him. He was shaved close to the blue roots of his beard, and his hands were clean and his nails polished. His door stood open to the morning, and he hummed under his breath while his right hand practiced legerdemain.[4] He rolled a coin back and forth over his knuckles and made it appear and disappear, made it spin and sparkle. The coin winked into sight and as quickly slipped out of sight, and the man did not even watch his own performance. The fingers did it all mechanically, precisely, while the man hummed to himself and peered out the door. Then he heard the tramp of feet of the approaching crowd, and the fingers of his right hand worked faster and faster until, as the figure of Kino filled the doorway, the coin flashed and disappeared.

"Good morning, my friend," the stout man said. "What can I do for you?"

Kino stared into the dimness of the little office, for his eyes were squeezed from the outside glare. But the buyer's eyes had become as steady and cruel and unwinking as a hawk's eyes, while the rest of his face smiled in greeting. And secretly, behind his desk, his right hand practiced with the coin.

"I have a pearl," said Kino. And Juan Tomás stood beside him and snorted a little at the understatement. The neighbors peered around the doorway, and a line of little boys clambered on the window bars and looked through. Several little boys, on their hands and knees, watched the scene around Kino's legs.

"You have a pearl," the dealer said. "Sometimes a man brings in a dozen. Well, let us see your pearl. We will value it and give you the best price." And his fingers worked furiously with the coin.

Now Kino instinctively knew his own dramatic effects. Slowly he brought out the leather bag, slowly took from it the soft and dirty piece of deerskin; and then he let the great pearl roll into the black velvet tray, and instantly his eyes went to the buyer's face. But there was no sign, no movement; the face did not change, but the secret hand behind the desk missed in its precision. The coin stumbled over a knuckle and slipped silently into the dealer's lap. And the fingers behind the desk curled into a fist. When the right hand came out of hiding, the forefinger touched the great pearl, rolled it on the black velvet; thumb and forefinger picked it up and brought it near to the dealer's eyes and twirled it in the air.

Kino held his breath, and the neighbors held their breath, and the whispering went back through the crowd. "He is inspecting it—No price has been mentioned yet—They have not come to a price."

Now the dealer's hand had become a personality. The hand tossed the great pearl back to the tray, the forefinger poked and insulted it, and on the dealer's face there came a sad and contemptuous smile.

"I am sorry, my friend," he said, and his shoulders rose a little to indicate that the misfortune was no fault of his.

"It is a pearl of great value," Kino said.

The dealer's fingers spurned the pearl so that it bounced and rebounded softly from the sides of velvet tray.

"You have heard of fool's gold," the dealer said. "This pearl is like fool's gold. It is too large. Who would buy it? There is no market for such things. It is a curiosity only. I am sorry. You thought it was a thing of value, and it is only a curiosity."

---

3. **hibiscus**\hĭ ˄bĭs·kəs\ a southern shrub or small tree with a large colorful flower.
4. **legerdemain**\˄lĕ·jər·də ′mān\ magic, conjuring, or extreme skill at card tricks.

*"I am cheated," Kino cried fiercely.*
*"My pearl is not for sale here."*

Now Kino's face was perplexed and worried. "It is the Pearl of the World," he cried. "No one has ever seen such a pearl."

"On the contrary," said the dealer, "it is large and clumsy. As a curiosity it has interest; some museum might perhaps take it to place in a collection of seashells. I can give you, say, a thousand pesos."

Kino's face grew dark and dangerous. "It is worth fifty thousand," he said. "You know it. You want to cheat me."

And the dealer heard a little grumble go through the crowd as they heard his price. And the dealer felt a little tremor of fear.

"Do not blame me," he said quickly. "I am only an appraiser. Ask the others. Go to their offices and show your pearl—or better let them come here, so that you can see there is no collusion. Boy," he called. And when his servant looked through the rear door, "Boy, go to such a one, and such another one and such a third one. Ask them to step in here and do not tell them why. Just say that I will be pleased to see them." And his right hand went behind the desk and pulled another coin from his pocket, and the coin rolled back and forth over his knuckles.

Kino's neighbors whispered together. They had been afraid of something like this. The pearl was large, but it had a strange color.

They had been suspicious of it from the first. And after all, a thousand pesos was not to be thrown away. It was comparative wealth to a man who was not wealthy. And suppose Kino took a thousand pesos. Only yesterday he had nothing.

But Kino had grown tight and hard. He felt the creeping of fate, the circling of wolves, the hover of vultures. He felt the evil coagulating about him, and he was helpless to protect himself. He heard in his ears the evil music. And on the black velvet the great pearl glistened, so that the dealer could not keep his eyes from it.

The crowd in the doorway wavered and broke and let the three pearl dealers through. The crowd was silent now, fearing to miss a word, to fail to see a gesture of an expression. Kino was silent and watchful. He felt a little tugging at his back, and he turned and looked in Juana's eyes; and when he looked away, he had renewed strength.

The dealers did not glance at one another nor at the pearl. The man behind the desk said, "I have put a value on this pearl. The owner here does not think it fair. I will ask you to examine this—this thing and make an offer. Notice," he said to Kino, "I have not mentioned what I have offered."

The first dealer, dry and stringy, seemed now to see the pearl for the first time. He took it up, rolled it quickly between thumb and forefinger, and then cast it contemptuously back into the tray.

"Do not include me in the discussion," he said dryly. "I will make no offer at all. I do not want it. This is not a pearl—it is a monstrosity." His thin lips curled.

Now the second dealer, a little man with a shy soft voice, took up the pearl, and he examined it carefully. He took a glass from his pocket and inspected it under magnification. Then he laughed softly.

"Better pearls are made of paste," he said. "I know these things. This is soft and chalky, it will lose its color and die in a few months. Look—" He offered the glass to Kino, showed

him how to use it; and Kino, who had never seen a pearl's surface magnified, was shocked at the strange-looking surface.

The third dealer took the pearl from Kino's hands. "One of my clients likes such things," he said. "I will offer five hundred pesos, and perhaps I can sell it to my client for six hundred."

Kino reached quickly and snatched the pearl from his hand. He wrapped it in the deerskin and thrust it inside his shirt.

The man behind the desk said, "I'm a fool, I know, but my first offer stands. I still offer one thousand. What are you doing?" he asked, as Kino thrust the pearl out of sight.

"I am cheated," Kino cried fiercely. "My pearl is not for sale here. I will go, perhaps, even to the capital."

Now the dealers glanced quickly at one another. They knew they had played too hard; they knew they would be disciplined for their failure; and the man at the desk said quickly, "I might go to fifteen hundred."

But Kino was pushing his way through the crowd. The hum of talk came to him dimly, his rage blood pounded in his ears, and he burst through and strode away. Juana followed, trotting after him.

When the evening came, the neighbors in the brush houses sat eating their corncakes and beans, and they discussed the great theme of the morning. They did not know; it seemed a fine pearl to them, but they had never seen such a pearl before, and surely the dealers knew more about the value of pearls than they. "And mark this," they said. "Those dealers did not discuss these things. Each of the three knew the pearl was valueless."

"But suppose they had arranged it before?"

"If that is so, then all of us have been cheated all of our lives."

Perhaps, some argued, perhaps it would have been better if Kino took the one thousand five hundred pesos. That is a great deal of money, more than he has ever seen. Maybe Kino is being a pigheaded fool. Suppose he should really go to the capital and find no buyer for his pearl. He would never live that down.

And now, said other fearful ones, now that he had defied them, those buyers will not want to deal with him at all. Maybe Kino has cut off his own head and destroyed himself.

And others said, Kino is a brave man and a fierce man; he is right. From his courage we may all profit. These were proud of Kino.

In his house Kino squatted on his sleeping mat, brooding. He had buried his pearl under a stone of the fire hole in his house, and he stared at the woven tules[5] of his sleeping mat until the crossed design danced in his head. He had lost one world and had not gained another. And Kino was afraid. Never in his life had he been far from home. He was afraid of strangers and of strange places. He was terrified of that monster of strangeness they called the capital. It lay over the water and through the mountains, over a thousand miles; and every strange, terrible mile was frightening. But Kino had lost his old world, and he must clamber on to a new one. For his dream of the future was real and never to be destroyed; and he had said "I will go," and that made a real thing, too. To determine to go and to say it was to be halfway there.

Juana watched him while he buried his pearl, and she watched him while she cleaned Coyotito and nursed him, and Juana made the corncakes for supper.

Juan Tomás came in and squatted down beside Kino and remained silent for a long time, until at last Kino demanded, "What else could I do? They are cheats."

Juan Tomás nodded gravely. He was the elder, and Kino looked to him for wisdom. "It is hard to know," he said. "We do know that we are cheated from birth to the overcharge on our coffins. But we survive. You have defied not the pearl buyers, but the whole structure, the whole way of life; and I am afraid for you."

"What have I to fear but starvation?" Kino asked.

But Juan Tomás shook his head slowly. "That we must all fear. But suppose you are correct—

suppose your pearl is of great value—do you think then the game is over?"

"What do you mean?"

"I don't know," said Juan Tomás, "but I am afraid for you. It is new ground you are walking on, you do not know the way."

"I will go. I will go soon," said Kino.

"Yes," Juan Tomás agreed. "That you must do. But I wonder if you will find it any different in the capital. Here, you have friends and me, your brother. There, you will have no one."

"What can I do?" Kino cried. "Some deep outrage is here. My son must have a chance. That is what they are striking at. My friends will protect me."

"Only so long as they are not in danger or discomfort from it," said Juan Tomás. He arose, saying, "Go with God."

And Kino said, "Go with God," and did not even look up; for the words had a strange chill in them.

Long after Juan Tomás had gone, Kino sat brooding on his sleeping mat. A lethargy had settled on him and a little gray hopelessness. Every road seemed blocked against him. In his head he heard only the dark music of the enemy. His senses were burningly alive; but his mind went back to the deep participation with all things, the gift he had from his people. He heard every little sound of the gathering night: the sleepy complaint of settling birds, the love agony of cats, the strike and withdrawal of little waves on the beach, and the simple hiss of distance. And he could smell the sharp odor of exposed kelp from the receding tide. The little flare of the twig fire made the design on his sleeping mat jump before his entranced eyes.

Juana watched him with worry, but she knew him, and she knew she could help him best by being silent and by being near. And as though she too could hear the Song of Evil, she fought it, singing softly the melody of the family, of the safety and warmth and wholeness of the family. She held Coyotito in her arms

---

5. **tule**\ˈtū·lē\ a tropical reed or rush.

and sang the song to him, to keep the evil out; and her voice was brave against the threat of the dark music.

Kino did not move nor ask for his supper. She knew he would ask when he wanted it. His eyes were entranced; and he could sense the wary, watchful evil outside the brush house; he could feel the dark, creeping things waiting for him to go out into the night. It was shadowy and dreadful, and yet it called to him and threatened him and challenged him. His right hand went into his shirt and felt his knife; his eyes were wide; he stood up and walked to the doorway.

Juana willed to stop him; she raised her hand to stop him, and her mouth opened with terror. For a long moment Kino looked out into the darkness, and then he stepped outside. Juana heard the little rush, the grunting struggle, the blow. She froze with terror for a moment, and then her lips drew back from her teeth like a cat's lips. She set Coyotito down on the ground. She seized a stone from the fireplace and rushed outside, but it was over by then. Kino lay on the ground, struggling to rise; and there was no one near him. Only the shadows and the strike and rush of waves and the hiss of distance. But the evil was all about, hidden behind the brush fence, crouched beside the house in the shadow, hovering in the air.

Juana dropped her stone, and she put her arms around Kino and helped him to his feet and supported him into the house. Blood oozed down from his scalp, and there was a long, deep cut in his cheek from ear to chin, a deep, bleeding slash. And Kino was only half conscious. He shook his head from side to side. His shirt was torn open and his clothes half pulled off. Juana sat him down on his sleeping mat, and she wiped the thickening blood from his face with her skirt. She brought him pulque to drink in a little pitcher, and still he shook his head to clear out the darkness.

"Who?" Juana asked.

"I don't know," Kino said. "I didn't see."

Now Juana brought her clay pot of water, and she washed the cut on his face while he stared dazed ahead of him.

"Kino, my husband," she cried, and his eyes stared past her. "Kino, can you hear me?"

"I hear you," he said dully.

"Kino, this pearl is evil. Let us destroy it before it destroys us. Let us crush it between two stones. Let us—let us throw it back in the sea where it belongs. Kino, it is evil; it is evil!"

And as she spoke, the light came back in Kino's eyes so that they glowed fiercely; and his muscles hardened, and his will hardened.

"No," he said. "I will fight this thing. I will win over it. We will have our chance." His fist pounded the sleeping mat. "No one shall take our good fortune from us," he said. His eyes softened then, and he raised a gentle hand to Juana's shoulder. "Believe me," he said. "I am a man." And his face grew crafty.

"In the morning we will take our canoe, and we will go over the sea and over the mountains to the capital, you and I. We will not be cheated. I am a man." *→ determination*

"Kino," she said huskily. "I am afraid. A man can be killed. Let us throw the pearl back into the sea."

"Hush," he said fiercely. "I am a man. Hush." And she was silent, for his voice was command. "Let us sleep a little," he said. "In the first light we will start. You are not afraid to go with me?"

"No, my husband."

His eyes were soft and warm on her then; his hand touched her cheek. "Let us sleep a little," he said.

## 5

The late moon arose before the first rooster crowed. Kino opened his eyes in the darkness, for he sensed movement near him, but he did not move. Only his eyes searched the darkness; and in the pale light of the moon that crept through the holes in the brush house, Kino saw Juana arise silently from beside him. He saw her move toward the fireplace. So carefully did she work that he heard only the lightest sound when she moved the fireplace stone. And then like a shadow she glided toward the door. She paused for a moment beside the hanging box where Coyotito lay, then for a second she was back in the doorway, and then she was gone.

And rage surged in Kino. He rolled up to his feet and followed her as silently as she had gone, and he could hear her quick footsteps going toward the shore. Quietly he tracked her, and his brain was red with anger. She burst clear of the brush line and stumbled over the little boulders toward the water, and then she heard him coming, and she broke into a run. Her arm was up to throw when he leaped at her and caught her arm and wrenched the pearl from her. He struck her in the face with his clenched fist, and she fell among the boulders, and he kicked her in the side. In the pale light he could see the little waves break over her, and her skirt floated about and clung to her legs as the water receded.

Kino looked down at her, and his teeth were bared. He hissed at her like a snake; and Juana stared at him with wide, unfrightened eyes, like a sheep before the butcher. She knew there was murder in him, and it was all right; she had accepted it, and she would not resist or even protest. And then the rage left him, and a sick disgust took its place. He turned away from her and walked up the beach and through the brush line. His senses were dulled by his emotion.

He heard the rush, got his knife out and lunged at one dark figure and felt his knife go home; and then he was swept to his knees and swept again to the ground. Greedy fingers went through his clothes; frantic fingers searched him; and the pearl, knocked from his hand, lay winking behind a little stone in the pathway. It glinted in the soft moonlight.

Juana dragged herself up from the rocks on the edge of the water. Her face was a dull pain, and her side ached. She steadied herself on her knees for a while, and her wet skirt clung to her. There was no anger in her for Kino. He had said, "I am a man," and that meant certain things to Juana. It meant that he was half insane and half god. It meant that Kino would drive his strength against a mountain and plunge his strength against the sea. Juana, in her woman's soul, knew that the mountain would stand while the man broke himself, that the sea would surge while the man drowned in it. And yet it was the thing that made him a man, half insane and half god; and Juana had need of a man; she could not live without a man. Although she might be puzzled by these differences between man and woman, she knew them and accepted them and needed them. Of course she would follow him; there was no question of that. Sometimes the quality of women, the reason, the caution, the sense of preservation, could cut through Kino's manness and save them all. She climbed painfully to her feet, and she dipped her cupped palms in the little waves and washed her bruised face with the stinging salt water, and then she went creeping up the beach after Kino.

A flight of herring clouds[1] had moved over the sky from the south. The pale moon dipped in and out of the strands of clouds, so that Juana walked in darkness for a moment and in light the next. Her back was bent with pain and her head was low. She went through the line of brush when the moon was covered; and when it looked through, she saw the glimmer of the great pearl in the path behind the rock. She sank to her knees and picked it up, and the moon went into the darkness of the clouds again. Juana remained on her knees while she considered whether to go back to the sea and finish her job; and as she considered, the light came again; and she saw two dark figures lying in the path ahead of her. She leaped forward and saw that one was Kino and the other a stranger, with dark shiny fluid leaking from his throat.

Kino moved sluggishly; arms and legs stirred like those of a crushed bug; and a thick muttering came from his mouth. Now, in an instant, Juana knew that the old life was gone forever.

---

1. **herring clouds,** formations that show a strongly marked streaked effect.

A dead man in the path and Kino's knife, dark-bladed beside him, convinced her. All of the time Juana had been trying to rescue something of the old peace, of the time before the pearl. But now it was gone, and there was no retrieving it. And knowing this, she abandoned the past instantly. There was nothing to do but to save themselves.

Her pain was gone now, her slowness. Quickly she dragged the dead man from the pathway into the shelter of the brush. She went to Kino and sponged his face with her wet skirt. His senses were coming back, and he moaned.

"They have taken the pearl. I have lost it. Now it is over," he said. "The pearl is gone."

Juana quieted him as she would quiet a sick child. "Hush," she said. "Here is your pearl. I found it in the path. Can you hear me now? Here is your pearl. Can you understand? You have killed a man. We must go away. They will come for us; can you understand? We must be gone before the daylight comes."

"I was attacked," Kino said uneasily. "I struck to save my life."

"Do you remember yesterday?" Juana asked. "Do you think that will matter? Do you remember the men of the city? Do you think your explanation will help?"

Kino drew a great breath and fought off his weakness. "No," he said. "You are right." And his will hardened, and he was a man again.

"Go to our house and bring Coyotito," he said, "and bring all the corn we have. I will drag the canoe into the water, and we will go."

He took his knife and left her. He stumbled toward the beach, and he came to his canoe. And when the light broke through again, he saw that a great hole had been knocked in the bottom. And a searing rage came to him and gave him strength. Now the darkness was closing in on his family; now the evil music filled the night, hung over the mangroves, skirled in the wave beat. The canoe of his grandfather, plastered over and over, and a splintered hole broken in it. This was an evil beyond thinking. The killing of a man was not so evil as the killing of a boat. For a boat does not have sons, and a boat cannot protect itself, and a wounded boat does not heal. There was sorrow in Kino's rage, but this last thing had tightened him beyond breaking. He was an animal now, for hiding, for attacking; and he lived only to preserve himself and his family. He was not conscious of the pain in his head. He leaped up the beach, through the brush line toward his brush house; and it did not occur to him to take one of the canoes of his neighbors. Never once did the thought enter his head, any more than he could have conceived breaking a boat.

The roosters were crowing, and the dawn was not far off. Smoke of the first fires seeped out through the walls of the brush houses, and the first smell of cooking corncakes was in the air. Already the dawn birds were scampering in the bushes. The weak moon was losing its light, and the clouds thickened and curdled to the southward. The wind blew freshly into the estuary, a nervous, restless wind with the smell of storm on its breath; and there was change and uneasiness in the air.

Kino, hurrying toward his house, felt a surge of exhilaration. Now he was not confused, for there was only one thing to do, and Kino's hand went first to the great pearl in his shirt and then to his knife hanging under his shirt.

He saw a little glow ahead of him, and then without interval a tall flame leaped up in the dark with a crackling roar, and a tall edifice of fire lighted the pathway. Kino broke into a run; it was his brush house, he knew. And he knew that these houses could burn down in a very few moments. And as he ran, a scuttling figure ran toward him—Juana, with Coyotito in her arms and Kino's shoulder blanket clutched in her hand. The baby moaned with fright, and Juana's eyes were wide and terrified. Kino could see the house was gone, and he did not question Juana. He knew; but she said, "It was torn up and the floor dug—even the baby's box turned out; and as I looked, they put the fire to the outside."

The fierce light of the burning house lighted Kino's face strongly. "Who?" he demanded.

"I don't know," she said. "The dark ones."

The neighbors were tumbling from their houses now, and they watched the falling sparks and stamped them out to save their own houses. Suddenly Kino was afraid. The light made him afraid. He remembered the man lying dead in the brush beside the path, and he took Juana by the arm and drew her into the shadow of a house away from the light, for light was danger to him. For a moment he considered, and then he worked among the shadows until he came to the house of Juan Tomás, his brother; and he slipped into the doorway and drew Juana after him. Outside, he could hear the squeal of children and the shouts of the neighbors, for his friends thought he might be inside the burning house.

The house of Juan Tomás was almost exactly like Kino's house; nearly all the brush houses were alike, and all leaked light and air; so that Juana and Kino, sitting in the corner of the brother's house, could see the leaping flames through the wall. They saw the flames tall and furious; they saw the roof fall and watched the fire die down as quickly as a twig fire dies. They heard the cries of warning of their friends, and the shrill, keening cry of Apolonia, wife of Juan Tomás. She, being the nearest woman relative, raised a formal lament for the dead of the family.

Apolonia realized that she was wearing her second-best head shawl, and she rushed to her house to get her fine new one. As she rummaged in a box by the wall, Kino's voice said quietly, "Apolonia, do not cry out. We are not hurt."

"How do you come here?" she demanded.

"Do not question," he said. "Go now to Juan Tomás and bring him here and tell no one else. This is important to us, Apolonia."

She paused, her hands helpless in front of her; and then, "Yes, my brother-in-law," she said.

In a few moments Juan Tomás came back with her. He lighted a candle and came to them where they crouched in a corner, and he said, "Apolonia, see to the door, and do not let any-one enter." He was older, Juan Tomás, and he assumed the authority. "Now, my brother," he said.

"I was attacked in the dark," said Kino. "And in the fight I have killed a man."

"Who?" asked Juan Tomás quickly.

"I do not know. It is all darkness—all darkness and shape of darkness."

"It is the pearl," said Juan Tomás. "There is a devil in this pearl. You should have sold it and passed on the devil. Perhaps you can still sell it and buy peace for yourself."

And Kino said, "Oh, my brother, an insult has been put on me that is deeper than my life. For on the beach my canoe is broken, my house is burned, and in the brush a dead man lies. Every escape is cut off. You must hide us, my brother."

And Kino, looking closely, saw deep worry come into his brother's eyes; and he forestalled him in a possible refusal. "Not for long," he said quickly. "Only until a day has passed and the new night has come. Then we will go."

"I will hide you," said Juan Tomás.

"I do not want to bring danger to you," Kino said. "I know I am like a leprosy. I will go tonight, and then you will be safe."

"I will protect you," said Juan Tomás, and he called, "Apolonia, close up the door. Do not even whisper that Kino is here."

They sat silently all day in the darkness of the house, and they could hear the neighbors speaking of them. Through the walls of the house, they could watch their neighbors raking the ashes to find the bones. Crouching in the house of Juan Tomás, they heard the shock go into their neighbors' minds at the news of the broken boat. Juan Tomás went out among the neighbors to divert their suspicions, and he gave them theories and ideas of what had happened to Kino and to Juana and to the baby. To one he said, "I think they have gone south along the coast to escape the evil that was on them." And to another, "Kino would never leave the sea. Perhaps he found another boat." And he said, "Apolonia is ill with grief."

And in that day the wind rose up to beat the Gulf and tore the kelps[2] and weeds that lined the shore, and the wind cried through the brush houses, and no boat was safe on the water. Then Juan Tomás told among the neighbors, "Kino is gone. If he went to the sea, he is drowned by now." And after each trip among the neighbors Juan Tomás came back with something borrowed. He brought a little woven straw bag of red beans and a gourd full of rice. He borrowed a cup of dried peppers and a block of salt, and he brought in a long working knife, eighteen inches long and heavy, as a small ax, a tool, and a weapon. And when Kino saw this knife his eyes lighted up; and he fondled the blade, and his thumb tested the edge.

The wind screamed over the Gulf and turned the water white, and the mangroves plunged like frightened cattle, and a fine sandy dust arose from the land and hung in a stifling cloud over the sea. The wind drove off the clouds and skimmed the sky clean and drifted the sand of the country like snow.

Then Juan Tomás, when the evening approached, talked long with his brother. "Where will you go?"

"To the north," said Kino. "I have heard that there are cities in the north."

"Avoid the shore," said Juan Tomás. "They are making a party to search the shore. The men in the city will look for you. Do you still have the pearl?"

"I have it," said Kino. "And I will keep it. I might have given it as a gift, but now it is my misfortune and my life, and I will keep it." His eyes were hard and cruel and bitter.

Coyotito whimpered, and Juana muttered little magics over him to make him silent.

"The wind is good," said Juan Tomás. "There will be no tracks."

They left quietly in the dark before the moon had risen. The family stood formally in the house of Juan Tomás. Juana carried Coyotito on her back, covered and held in by her head shawl; and the baby slept, cheek turned sideways against her shoulder. The head shawl covered the baby, and one end of it came across Juana's nose to protect her from the evil night air. Juan Tomás embraced his brother with the double embrace and kissed him on both cheeks. "Go with God," he said, and it was like a death. "You will not give up the pearl?"

"This pearl has become my soul," said Kino. "If I give it up, I shall lose my soul. Go thou also with God."

## 6

The wind blew fierce and strong; and it pelted them with bits of sticks, sand, and little rocks. Juana and Kino gathered their clothing tighter about them and covered their noses and went out into the world. The sky was brushed clean by the wind, and the stars were cold in a black sky. The two walked carefully, and they avoided the center of town where some sleeper in a doorway might see them pass. For the town closed itself in against the night, and anyone who moved about in the darkness would be noticeable. Kino threaded his way around the edge of the city and turned north, north by the stars, and found the rutted sandy road that led through the brushy country toward Loreto where the miraculous Virgin has her station.[1]

Kino could feel the blown sand against his ankles, and he was glad, for he knew there would be no tracks. The little light from the stars made out for him the narrow road through the brushy country. And Kino could hear the pad of Juana's feet behind him. He went quickly and quietly, and Juana trotted behind him to keep up.

Some ancient thing stirred in Kino. Through his fear of dark and the devils that haunt the night, there came a rush of exhilaration; some animal thing was moving in him so that he was cautious and wary and dangerous; some an-

---

2. **kelp**\kĕlp\ seaweed.

---

1. **Loreto**\lō ᴬrä·tō\. **station**, established place for religious observance.

*maybe Song of Family*

578

cient thing out of the past of his people was alive in him. The wind was at his back, and the stars guided him. The wind cried and whisked in the brush; and the family went on monotonously, hour after hour. They passed no one and saw no one. At last, to their right, the waning moon arose; and when it came up, the wind died down; and the land was still.

Now they could see the little road ahead of them, deep-cut with sand-drifted wheel tracks. With the wind gone there would be footprints, but they were a good distance from the town, and perhaps their tracks might not be noticed.

*"Come," he said. "We will go into the mountains. Maybe we can lose them in the mountains."*

Kino walked carefully in a wheel rut, and Juana followed in his path. One big cart, going to the town in the morning, could wipe out every trace of their passage.

All night they walked and never changed their pace. Once Coyotito awakened, and Juana shifted him in front of her and soothed him until he went to sleep again. And the evils of the night were about them. The coyotes cried and laughed in the brush, and the owls screeched and hissed over their heads. And once some large animal lumbered away, crackling the undergrowth as it went. And Kino gripped the handle of the big working knife and took a sense of protection from it.

The music of the pearl was triumphant in Kino's head, and the quiet melody of the family underlay it, and they wove themselves into the soft padding of sandaled feet in the dusk. All night they walked, and in the first dawn Kino searched the roadside for a covert to lie in during the day. He found his place near to the road, a little clearing where deer might have lain; and it was curtained thickly with the dry, brittle trees that lined the road. And when Juana had seated herself and had settled to nurse the baby, Kino went back to the road. He broke a branch and carefully swept the footprints where they had turned from the roadway. And then, in the first light, he heard the creak of a wagon; and he crouched beside the road and watched a heavy two-wheeled cart go by, drawn by slouching oxen. And when it had passed out of sight, he went back to the roadway and looked at the rut and found that the footprints were gone. And again he swept out his traces and went back to Juana.

She gave him the soft corncakes Apolonia had packed for them, and after a while she slept a little. But Kino sat on the ground and stared at the earth in front of him. He watched the ants moving, a little column of them near to his foot, and he put his foot in their path. Then the column climbed over his instep and continued on its way, and Kino left his foot there and watched them move over it.

The sun arose hotly. They were not near the Gulf now; and the air was dry and hot, so that the brush cricked[2] with heat, and a good resinous[3] smell came from it. And when Juana awakened, when the sun was high, Kino told her things she knew already.

"Beware of that kind of tree there," he said, pointing. "Do not touch it, for if you do and then touch your eyes, it will blind you. And beware of the tree that bleeds. See, that one over there. For if you break it, the red blood will flow from it; and it is evil luck." And she nodded and smiled a little at him, for she knew these things.

"Will they follow us?" she asked. "Do you think they will try to find us?"

"They will try," said Kino. "Whoever finds us will take the pearl. Oh, they will try."

And Juana said, "Perhaps the dealers were right and the pearl has no value. Perhaps this has all been an illusion."

Kino reached into his clothes and brought out the pearl. He let the sun play on it until it burned in his eyes. "No," he said, "they would not have tried to steal it if it had been valueless."

"Do you know who attacked you? Was it the dealers?"

"I do not know," he said. "I didn't see them."

He looked into his pearl to find his vision.

"When we sell it at last, I will have a rifle," he said; and he looked into the shining surface for his rifle, but he saw only a huddled dark body on the ground with shining blood dripping from its throat. And he said quickly, "We will be married in a great church." And in the pearl he saw Juana with her beaten face, crawling home through the night. "Our son must learn to read," he said frantically. And there in the pearl Coyotito's face, thick and feverish from the medicine.

And Kino thrust the pearl back into his clothing, and the music of the pearl had become sinister in his ears, and it was interwoven with the music of evil.

The hot sun beat on the earth, so that Kino and Juana moved into the lacy shade of the brush; and small, gray birds scampered on the ground in the shade. In the heat of the day, Kino relaxed and covered his eyes with his hat and wrapped his blanket about his face to keep the flies off; and he slept.

But Juana did not sleep. She sat quiet as a stone, and her face was quiet. Her mouth was

---

2. **crick**\krĭk\ to turn or twist.
3. **resinous**\ˈrĕ-zĭ-nəs\ of or pertaining to resin, an insoluble thick plant substance like pine tar.

still swollen where Kino had struck her, and big flies buzzed around the cut on her chin. But she sat as still as a sentinel; and when Coyotito awakened, she placed him on the ground in front of her and watched him wave his arms and kick his feet; and he smiled and gurgled at her, until she smiled too. She picked up a little twig from the ground and tickled him, and she gave him water from the gourd she carried in her bundle.

Kino stirred in a dream, and he cried out in a guttural voice, and his hand moved in symbolic fighting. And then he moaned and sat up suddenly, his eyes wide and his nostrils flaring. He listened and heard only the cricking heat and the hiss of distance.

"What is it?" Juana asked.

"Hush," he said.

"You were dreaming."

"Perhaps." But he was restless; and when she gave him a corncake from her store, he paused in his chewing to listen. He was uneasy and nervous; he glanced over his shoulder; he lifted the big knife and felt its edge. When Coyotito gurgled on the ground, Kino said, "Keep him quiet."

"What is the matter?" Juana asked.

"I don't know."

He listened again, an animal light in his eyes. He stood up then, silently; and crouched low, he threaded his way through the brush toward the road. But he did not step into the road; he crept into the cover of a thorny tree and peered out along the way he had come.

And then he saw them moving along. His body stiffened, and he drew down his head and peeked out from under a fallen branch. In the distance he could see three figures, two on foot and one on horseback. But he knew what they were, and a chill of fear went through him. Even in the distance he could see the two on foot moving slowly along, bent low to the ground. Here, one would pause and look at the earth, while the other joined him. They were the trackers; they could follow the trail of a bighorn sheep in the stone mountains. They were as sensitive as hounds. Here, he and

Juana might have stepped out of the wheel rut; and these people from the inland, these hunters, could follow, could read a broken straw or a little tumbled pile of dust. Behind them, on a horse, was a dark man, his nose covered with a blanket; and across his saddle a rifle gleamed in the sun.

Kino lay as rigid as the tree limb. He barely breathed, and his eyes went to the place where he had swept out the track. Even the sweeping might be a message to the trackers. He knew these inland hunters. In a country where there is little game, they managed to live because of their ability to hunt; and they were hunting him. They scuttled over the ground like animals and found a sign and crouched over it while the horseman waited.

The trackers whined a little, like excited dogs on a warming trail. Kino slowly drew his big knife to his hand and made it ready. He knew what he must do. If the trackers found the swept place, he must leap for the horseman, kill him quickly, and take the rifle. That was his only chance in the world. And as the three drew nearer on the road, Kino dug little pits with his sandaled toes, so that he could leap without warning, so that his feet would not slip. He had only a little vision under the fallen limb.

Now Juana, back in her hidden place, heard the pad of the horse's hoofs; and Coyotito gurgled. She took him up quickly and put him under her shawl and gave him her breast, and he was silent.

When the trackers came near, Kino could see only their legs and only the legs of the horse from under the fallen branch. He saw the dark, horny feet of the men and their ragged white clothes, and he heard the creak of leather of the saddle and the clink of spurs. The trackers stopped at the swept place and studied it, and the horseman stopped. The horse flung his head up against the bit, and the bit-roller[4] clicked under his tongue, and the

---

4. **bit-roller,** the roller or round bar to which the bit of a horse's bridle is attached.

horse snorted. Then the dark trackers turned and studied the horse and watched his ears.

Kino was not breathing, but his back arched a little, and the muscles of his arms and legs stood out with tension, and a line of sweat formed on his upper lip. For a long moment the trackers bent over the road; and then they moved on slowly, studying the ground ahead of them; and the horseman moved after them. The trackers scuttled along, stopping, looking, and hurrying on. They would be back, Kino knew. They would be circling and searching, peeping, stooping; and they would come back sooner or later to his covered track.

He slid backward and did not bother to cover his tracks. He could not; too many little signs were there, too many broken twigs and scuffed places and displaced stones. And there was a panic in Kino now, a panic of flight. The trackers would find his trail; he knew it. There was no escape, except in flight. He edged away from the road and went quickly and silently to the hidden place where Juana was. She looked up at him in question.

"Trackers," he said. "Come!"

And then a helplessness and a hopelessness swept over him, and his face went black, and his eyes were sad. "Perhaps I should let them take me."

Instantly Juana was on her feet, and her hand lay on his arm. "You have the pearl," she cried hoarsely. "Do you think they would take you back alive to say they had stolen it?"

His hand strayed limply to the place where the pearl was hidden under his clothes. "They will find it," he said weakly.

"Come," she said. "Come!"

And when he did not respond, "Do you think they would let me live? Do you think they would let the little one here live?"

Her goading struck into his brain; his lips snarled and his eyes were fierce again. "Come," he said. "We will go into the mountains. Maybe we can lose them in the mountains."

Frantically he gathered the gourds and the little bags that were their property. Kino carried a bundle in his left hand, but the big knife swung free in his right hand. He parted the brush for Juana; and they hurried to the west, toward the high stone mountains. They trotted quickly through the tangle of the undergrowth. This was panic flight. Kino did not try to conceal his passages; he trotted, kicking the stones, knocking the telltale leaves from the little trees. The high sun streamed down on the dry, creaking earth, so that even vegetation ticked in protest. But ahead were the naked granite mountains, rising out of erosion rubble and standing monolithic against the sky. And Kino ran for the high place, as nearly all animals do when they are pursued.

This land was waterless, furred with the cacti which could store water and with the great-rooted brush, which could reach deep into the earth for a little moisture and get along on very little. And underfoot was not soil but broken rock, split into small cubes, great slabs, but none of it water-rounded. Little tufts of sad, dry grass grew between the stones, grass that had sprouted with one single rain and headed, dropped its seed, and died. Horned toads watched the family go by and turned their little pivoting dragon heads. And now and then a great jackrabbit, disturbed in his shade, bumped away and hid behind the nearest rock. The singing heat lay over this desert country, and ahead the stone mountains looked cool and welcoming.

And Kino fled. He knew what would happen. A little way along the road the trackers would become aware that they had missed the path, and they would come back, searching and judging; and in a little while they would find the place where Kino and Juana had rested. From there it would be easy for them—these little stones, the fallen leaves and the whipped branches, the scuffed places where a foot had slipped. Kino could see them in his mind, slipping along the track, whining a little with eagerness, and behind them, dark and half disinterested, the horseman with the rifle. His work would come last, for he would not take them back. Oh, the music of evil sang loud in Kino's head now; it sang with the whine of heat and with the dry ringing of snake rattles. It was not large and overwhelming now, but secret and poisonous; and the pounding of his heart gave it undertone and rhythm.

The way began to rise; and as it did, the rocks grew larger. But now Kino had put a little distance between his family and the trackers. Now, on the first rise, he rested. He climbed a great boulder and looked back over the shimmering country, but he could not see his enemies, not even the tall horseman riding through the brush. Juana had squatted in the shade of the boulder. She raised her bottle of water to Coyotito's lips; his little dried tongue sucked greedily at it. She looked up at Kino when he came back; she saw him examine her ankles, cut and scratched from the stones and brush; and she covered them quickly with her skirt. Then she handed the bottle to him, but he shook his head. Her eyes were bright in her tired face. Kino moistened his cracked lips with his tongue.

"Juana," he said, "I will go on, and you will hide. I will lead them into the mountains, and when they have gone past, you will go north to Loreto or to Santa Rosalia.[5] Then, if I can escape them, I will come to you. It is the only safe way."

She looked full into his eyes for a moment. "No," she said. "We go with you."

"I can go faster alone," he said harshly. "You will put the little one in more danger if you go with me."

"No," said Juana.

"You must. It is the wise thing, and it is my wish," he said.

"No," said Juana.

He looked then for weakness in her face, for fear or irresolution; and there was none. Her eyes were very bright. He shrugged his shoulders helplessly then, but he had taken strength from her. When they moved on, it was no longer panic flight.

The country, as it rose toward the mountains, changed rapidly. Now there were long outcroppings of granite with deep crevices between, and Kino walked on bare unmarkable stone when he could and leaped from ledge to ledge. He knew that wherever the trackers lost his path they must circle and lose time before they found it again. And so he did not go straight for the mountains any more; he moved in zigzags, and sometimes he cut back to the south and left a sign and then went toward the mountains over bare stone again. And the path rose steeply now, so that he panted a little as he went.

The sun moved downward toward the bare stone teeth of the mountains, and Kino set his direction for a dark and shadowy cleft in the range. If there were any water at all, it would be there where he could see, even in the distance, a hint of foliage. And if there were any passage through the smooth stone range, it would be by this same deep cleft. It had its danger, for the trackers would think of it too, but the empty water bottle did not let that consideration enter. And as the sun lowered, Kino and Juana struggled wearily up the steep slope toward the cleft.

High in the gray stone mountains, under a frowning peak, a little spring bubbled out of a rupture in the stone. It was fed by shade-preserved snow in the summer, and now and then it died completely, and bare rocks and dry algae were on its bottom. But nearly always it gushed out, cold and clean and lovely. In the times when the quick rains fell, it might become a freshet and send its column of white water crashing down the mountain cleft, but nearly always it was a lean little spring. It bubbled out into a pool and then fell a hundred feet to another pool, and this one, overflowing, dropped again, so that it continued, down and down, until it came to the rubble of the upland; and there it disappeared altogether. There wasn't much left of it then anyway; for every time it fell over an escarpment,[6] the thirsty air drank it; and it splashed from the pools to the dry vegetation. The animals

---

5. **Santa Rosalia**\ˈsan·ta ˈrō ˈza·lē·a\ a town on the west coast of lower California. Other places in the story have been on the east coast.
6. **escarpment**\ĕ ˈskarp·mĭnt\ a long sheer cliff.

from miles around came to drink from the little pools; and the wild sheep and the deer, the pumas and raccoons, and the mice—all came to drink. And the birds which spent the day in the brushland came at night to the little pools, that were like steps in the mountain cleft. Beside this tiny stream, wherever enough earth collected for roothold, colonies of plants grew, wild grape and little palms, maidenhair fern, hibiscus, and tall pampas[7] grass with feathery rods raised above the spike leaves. And in the pool lived frogs and waterskaters,[8] and waterworms crawled on the bottom of the pool. Everything that loved water came to these few shallow places. The cats took their prey there and strewed feathers and lapped water through their bloody teeth. The little pools were places of life because of the water, and places of killing because of the water, too.

The lowest step, where the stream collected before it tumbled down a hundred feet and disappeared into the rubbly desert, was a little platform of stone and sand. Only a pencil of water fell into the pool, but it was enough to keep the pool full and to keep the ferns green in the underhang of the cliff, and wild grape climbed the stone mountain, and all manner of little plants found comfort here. The freshets had made a small sandy beach through which the pool flowed, and bright green watercress grew in the damp sand. The beach was cut and scarred and padded by the feet of animals that had come to drink and to hunt.

The sun had passed over the stone mountains when Kino and Juana struggled up the steep, broken slope and came at last to the water. From this step they could look out over the sunbeaten desert to the blue Gulf in the distance. They came utterly weary to the pool, and Juana slumped to her knees and first washed Coyotito's face and then filled her bottle and gave him a drink. And the baby was weary and petulant, and he cried softly until Juana gave him her breast, and then he gurgled and clucked against her. Kino drank long and thirstily at the pool. For a moment, then, he

stretched out beside the water and relaxed all his muscles and watched Juana feeding the baby, and then he got to his feet and went to the edge of the step where the water slipped over, and he searched the distance carefully. His eyes set on a point and he became rigid. Far down the slope he could see the two trackers; they were little more than dots or scurrying ants and behind them a larger ant.

Juana had turned to look at him, and she saw his back stiffen.

"How far?" she asked quietly.

"They will be here by evening," said Kino. He looked up the long, steep chimney of the cleft where the water came down. "We must go west," he said, and his eyes searched the stone shoulder behind the cleft. And thirty feet up on the gray shoulder he saw a series of little erosion caves. He slipped off his sandals and clambered up to them, gripping the bare stone with his toes, and he looked into the shallow caves. They were only a few feet deep, wind-hollowed scoops, but they sloped slightly downward and back. Kino crawled into the largest one and lay down and knew that he could not be seen from the outside. Quickly he went back to Juana.

"You must go up there. Perhaps they will not find us there," he said.

Without question she filled her water bottle to the top, and then Kino helped her up to the shallow cave and brought up the packages of food and passed them to her. And Juana sat in the cave entrance and watched him. She saw that he did not try to erase their tracks in the sand. Instead, he climbed up the brush cliff beside the water, clawing and tearing at the ferns and wild grape as he went. And when he had climbed a hundred feet to the next bench, he came down again. He looked carefully at the smooth rock shoulder toward the cave to see that there was no trace of passage,

_____
7. **pampas**\\ᵊpăm·pəs\\ **grass,** a South and Central American grass that grows in tall stalks from thick clumps.
8. **waterskater,** an insect that skims on the surface of the water.

and last he climbed up and crept into the cave beside Juana.

"When they go up," he said, "we will slip away, down to the lowlands again. I am afraid only that the baby may cry. You must see that he does not cry."

"He will not cry," she said, and she raised the baby's face to her own and looked into his eyes, and he stared solemnly back at her.

"He knows," said Juana.

Now Kino lay in the cave entrance, his chin braced on his crossed arms, and he watched the blue shadow of the mountain move out across the brushy desert below until it reached the Gulf, and the long twilight of the shadow was over the land.

The trackers were long in coming, as though they had trouble with the trail Kino had left. It was dusk when they came at last to the little pool. And all three were on foot now, for a horse could not climb the last steep slope. From above they were thin figures in the evening. The two trackers scurried about on the little beach, and they saw Kino's progress up the cliff before they drank. The man with the rifle sat down and rested himself, and the trackers squatted near him, and in the evening the points of their cigarettes glowed and receded. And then Kino could see that they were eating, and the soft murmur of their voices came to him.

Then darkness fell, deep and black in the mountain cleft. The animals that used the pool came near and smelled men there and drifted away again into the darkness.

He heard a murmur behind him. Juana was whispering, "Coyotito." She was begging him to be quiet. Kino heard the baby whimper, and he knew from the muffled sounds that Juana had covered his head with her shawl.

Down on the beach a match flared; and in its momentary light Kino saw that two of the men were sleeping, curled up like dogs, while the third watched; and he saw the glint of the rifle in the match light. And then the match died, but it left a picture on Kino's eyes. He could see it, just how each man was, two sleep-

ing curled and the third squatting in the sand with the rifle between his knees.

Kino moved silently back into the cave. Juana's eyes were two sparks reflecting a low star. Kino crawled quietly close to her, and he put his lips near to her cheek.

"There is a way," he said.

"But they will kill you."

"If I get first to the one with the rifle," Kino said, "I must get to him first, then I will be all right. Two are sleeping."

Her hand crept out from under her shawl and gripped his arm. "They will see your white clothes in the starlight."

"No," he said. "And I must go before moonrise."

He searched for a soft word and then gave it up. "If they kill me," he said, "lie quietly. And when they are gone away, go to Loreto."

Her hand shook a little, holding his wrist.

"There is no choice," he said. "It is the only way. They will find us in the morning."

Her voice trembled a little. "Go with God," she said.

He peered closely at her, and he could see her large eyes. His hand fumbled out and found the baby, and for a moment his palm lay on Coyotito's head. And then Kino raised his hand and touched Juana's cheek, and she held her breath.

Against the sky in the cave entrance Juana could see that Kino was taking off his white clothes; for dirty and ragged though they were, they would show up against the dark night. His own brown skin was a better protection for him. And then she saw how he hooked his amulet[9] neck-string about the horn handle of his great knife, so that it hung down in front of him and left both hands free. He did not come back to her. For a moment his body was black in the cave entrance, crouched and silent; and then he was gone.

Juana moved to the entrance and looked out. She peered like an owl from the hole in the mountain; and the baby slept under the

---

9. **amulet**\ˈăm•yʊ 'lĕt\ a charm, a magic ornament.

blanket on her back, his face turned sideways against her neck and shoulder. She could feel his warm breath against her skin; and Juana whispered her combination of prayer and magic, her Hail Marys and her ancient intercession, against the black, unhuman things.

The night seemed a little less dark when she looked out; and to the east there was a lightening in the sky, down near the horizon where the moon would show. And, looking down, she could see the cigarette of the man on watch.

Kino edged like a slow lizard down the smooth rock shoulder. He had turned his neck-string so that the great knife hung down from his back and could not clash against the stone. His spread fingers gripped the mountain, and his bare toes found support through contact, and even his chest lay against the stone, so that he would not slip. For any sound, a rolling pebble or a sigh, a little slip of flesh on rock, would rouse the watchers below. Any sound that was not germane to the night would make them alert. But the night was not silent: the little tree frogs that lived near the stream twittered like birds, and the high metallic ringing of the cicadas[10] filled the mountain cleft. And Kino's own music was in his head, the music of the enemy, low and pulsing, nearly asleep. But the Song of the Family had become as fierce and sharp and feline as the snarl of a female puma. The family song was alive now and driving him down on the dark enemy. The harsh cicada seemed to take up its melody, and the twittering tree frogs called little phrases of it.

And Kino crept silently as a shadow down the smooth mountain face. One bare foot moved a few inches, and the toes touched the stone and gripped, and the other foot a few inches, and then the palm of one hand a little downward, and then the other hand, until the whole body, without seeming to move, had moved. Kino's mouth was open so that even his breath would make no sound, for he knew that he was not invisible. If the watcher, sensing movement, looked at the dark place against the stone which was his body, he could see

him. Kino must move so slowly he would not draw the watcher's eyes. It took him a long time to reach the bottom and to crouch behind a little dwarf palm. His heart thundered in his chest, and his hands and face were wet with sweat. He crouched and took slow long breaths to calm himself.

Only twenty feet separated him from the enemy now, and he tried to remember the ground between. Was there any stone which might trip him in his rush? He kneaded his legs against cramp and found that his muscles were jerking after their long tension. And then he looked apprehensively to the east. The moon would rise in a few moments now, and he must attack before it rose. He could see the outline of the watcher, but the sleeping men were below his vision. It was the watcher Kino must find—must find quickly and without hesitation. Silently he drew the amulet string over his shoulder and loosened the loop from the horn handle of his great knife.

He was too late; for as he rose from his crouch, the silver edge of the moon slipped above the eastern horizon; and Kino sank back behind his bush.

It was an old and ragged moon, but it threw hard light and hard shadow into the mountain cleft, and now Kino could see the seated figure of the watcher on the little beach beside the pool. The watcher gazed full at the moon, and then he lighted another cigarette, and the match illumined his dark face for a moment. There could be no waiting now; when the watcher turned his head, Kino must leap. His legs were as tight as wound springs.

And then from above came a little murmuring cry. The watcher turned his head to listen, and then he stood up, and one of the sleepers stirred on the ground and awakened and asked quietly, "What is it?"

"I don't know," said the watcher. "It sounded like a cry, almost like a human—like a baby."

The man who had been sleeping said, "You

10. **cicada**\sĭ ᵊkā·də\ an insect with a stout body and wide wings whose vibrations make a distinctive sound.

can't tell. Some coyote bitch with a litter. I've heard a coyote pup cry like a baby."

The sweat rolled in drops down Kino's forehead and fell into his eyes and burned them. The little cry came again, and the watcher looked up the side of the hill to the dark cave.

"Coyote maybe," he said, and Kino heard the harsh click as he cocked the rifle.

"If it's a coyote, this will stop it," the watcher said as he raised the gun.

Kino was in mid-leap when the gun crashed, and the barrel-flash made a picture on his eyes. The great knife swung and crunched hollowly. It bit through neck and deep into chest, and Kino was a terrible machine now. He grasped the rifle even as he wrenched free his knife. His strength and his movement and his speed were a machine. He whirled and struck the head of the seated man like a melon. The third man scrabbled away like a crab, slipped into the pool; and then he began to climb frantically, to climb up the cliff where the water penciled down. His hands and feet threshed in the tangle of the wild grapevine, and he whimpered and gibbered as he tried to get up. But Kino had become as cold and deadly as steel. Deliberately he threw the lever of the rifle, and then he raised the gun and aimed deliberately and fired. He saw his enemy tumble backward into the pool, and Kino strode to the water. In the moonlight he could see the frantic frightened eyes, and Kino aimed and fired between the eyes.

And then Kino stood uncertainly. Something was wrong; some signal was trying to get through to his brain. Tree frogs and cicadas were silent now. And then Kino's brain cleared from its red concentration, and he knew the sound—the keening,[11] moaning, rising hysterical cry from the little cave in the side of the stone mountain, the cry of death.

Everyone in La Paz remembers the return of the family; there may be some old ones who saw it, but those whose fathers and whose grandfathers told it to them remember it nevertheless. It is an event that happened to everyone.

It was late in the golden afternoon when the first little boys ran hysterically in the town and spread the word that Kino and Juana were coming back. And everyone hurried to see them. The sun was settling toward the western mountains, and the shadows on the ground were long. And perhaps that was what left the deep impression on those who saw them.

The two came from the rutted country road into the city, and they were not walking in single file, Kino ahead and Juana behind, as usual, but side by side. The sun was behind them, and their long shadows stalked ahead, and they seemed to carry two towers of darkness with them. Kino had a rifle across his arm, and Juana carried her shawl like a sack over her shoulder. And in it was a small, limp, heavy bundle. The shawl was crusted with dried blood, and the bundle swayed a little as she walked. Her face was hard and lined and leathery with fatigue and with the tightness with which she fought fatigue. And her wide eyes stared inward on herself. She was as remote and as removed as Heaven. Kino's lips were thin and his jaws tight, and the people say that he carried fear with him, that he was as dangerous as a rising storm. The people say that the two seemed to be removed from human experience, that they had gone through pain and had come out on the other side, that there was almost a magical protection about them. And those people who had rushed to see them crowded back and let them pass and did not speak to them.

Kino and Juana walked through the city as though it were not there. Their eyes glanced neither right nor left nor up nor down, but stared only straight ahead. Their legs moved a little jerkily, like well-made wooden dolls, and they carried pillars of black fear about them. And as they walked through the stone and plaster city, brokers peered at them from barred windows, and servants put one eye to a

---

11. **keen,** to lament a death with loud outcry.

slitted gate, and mothers turned the faces of their youngest children inward against their skirts. Kino and Juana strode side by side through the stone and plaster city and down among the brush houses, and the neighbors stood back and let them pass. Juan Tomás raised his hand in greeting and did not say the greeting and left his hand in the air for a moment uncertainly.

In Kino's ears the Song of the Family was as fierce as a cry. He was immune and terrible, and his song had become a battle cry. They trudged past the burned square where their house had been without even looking at it. They cleared the brush that edged the beach and picked their way down the shore toward the water. And they did not look toward Kino's broken canoe.

And when they came to the water's edge, they stopped and stared out over the Gulf. And then Kino laid the rifle down, and he dug among his clothes, and then he held the great pearl in his hand. He looked into its surface, and it was gray and ulcerous. Evil faces peered from it into his eyes, and he saw the light of burning. And in the surface of the pearl he saw the frantic eyes of the man in the pool. And in the surface of the pearl he saw Coyotito lying in the little cave with the top of his head shot away. And the pearl was ugly; it was gray, like a malignant growth. And Kino heard the music of the pearl, distorted and insane. Kino's hand shook a little, and he turned slowly to Juana and held the pearl out to her. She stood beside him, still holding her dead bundle over her shoulder. She looked at the pearl in his hand for a moment, and then she looked into Kino's eyes and said softly, "No, you."

And Kino drew back his arm and flung the pearl with all his might. Kino and Juana watched it go, winking and glimmering under the setting sun. They saw the little splash in the distance, and they stood side by side watching the place for a long time.

And the pearl settled into the lovely green water and dropped toward the bottom. The waving branches of the algae called to it and

beckoned to it. The lights on its surface were green and lovely. It settled down to the sand bottom among the fernlike plants. Above, the surface of the water was a green mirror. And the pearl lay on the floor of the sea. A crab scampering over the bottom raised a little cloud of sand; and when it settled, the pearl was gone.

And the music of the pearl drifted to a whisper and disappeared.

---

## I
### THE MEANING OF LIFE

Steinbeck has cast the story in the form of a folk legend, but the reader quickly realizes that though the story is seemingly following this simple pattern, it is far more complicated in all its elements than the usual folk story. Steinbeck presents the reader with two people and their child, but they are involved in events and a situation that is intended to demonstrate the complicated relationship of man and his society. The language is carefully controlled and detailed by the writer . . . it appears simple but is really a triumph of artistry. What the writer is saying about life escapes a simple formula . . . it is no mere moral lesson . . . it is a delicate judgment on man, far-reaching and intricate. To help you isolate the complex parts of the story, carefully think through the following considerations.

## II
### IMPLICATIONS

**A.** Consider the implications of the following quotations in relationship to: (1) plot development, (2) revelation of character, (3) theme, (4) life in general.

**1.** "Perhaps he alone did this [activities in getting up in the morning], and perhaps all of his people did it."

**2.** "They had spoken once, but there is not need for speech if it is only a habit anyway. Kino sighed with satisfaction—and that was conversation."

**3.** "But the remedy lacked his authority [that of the doctor] because it was simple and didn't cost anything."

**4.** "It is not good to want a thing too much. It sometimes drives the luck away."

**5.** "For it is said that humans are never satisfied, that you give them one thing and they want something more. And this is said in disparagement, whereas it is one of the greatest talents the species has and one that has made it superior to animals that are satisfied with what they have."

**6.** "A plan, once made and visualized, becomes a reality along with other realities—never to be destroyed but easily to be attacked."

**7.** " 'Luck, you see, brings bitter friends.' "

**8.** "But let one man step out of the regular thought or the known and trusted pattern, and the nerves of the townspeople ring with nervousness. . . ."

**9.** "He had said, 'I am a man,' and that meant certain things to Juana. It meant that he was half insane and half god."

**10.** "The killing of a man was not so evil as the killing of a boat."

**11.** " 'This pearl has become my soul. . . . If I give up I shall lose my soul.' "

**12.** "The people say that the two seemed to be removed from human experience, that they had gone through pain and had come out on the other side, that there was almost a magical protection about them."

**B.** Examine the following statements. Are they true? untrue? partly true? Assemble evidence from the story to support your opinion.

**1.** The pressures in this story were twofold: the inner pressure of Kino's dream and the external pressures of greedy men.

**2.** No one knows what she or he is capable of until put under great pressure.

**3.** The Pearl of the World is basically an evil thing.

**4.** In the world that Steinbeck pictures there was absolutely no hope of Kino's dream becoming a reality.

**5.** There is something of greatness in every human being, no matter how stupid, uneducated, or poverty-stricken that person may be.

**6.** When Kino kills the thief, the reader knows that the story must end tragically.

**7.** To accept one's lot in life is a more admirable human trait than the desire to change it.

**8.** The desires of men and those of women tend to be quite different.

### III
### TECHNIQUES

*Theme*

The theme of *The Pearl*, like that of the other selections in this section, is the impact of pressures, both external and internal. But more specifically, Steinbeck is concerned with the effect these pressures have on man's search for his soul. This theme is embedded in the entire fabric of the story. Consider the following:

**1.** What is the sequence of pressures that come to bear on Kino? How is each a natural outgrowth of the one that comes before?

**2.** Throughout the story Steinbeck mentions certain things again and again, and with each recurrence they gather additional meaning. Where and how are the following used? How is each related to Kino's search?

   **a.** The various songs . . . of the family . . . of the pearl . . . of evil

   **b.** Kino's injured hand

   **c.** Kino's boat

   **d.** Coyotito

**3.** Reread the last three paragraphs of the story. What is Kino admitting to Juana when he offers her the pearl? What does her refusal mean to Kino? Amid the pressures of shifting personal values and the confused forces of a mad society, what is the value that yet endures?

*Style*

Steinbeck has given *The Pearl* the flavor of a folk story by using a simple, straightforward pattern of sentences. For example, how many sentences in the first four paragraphs of Chapter 1 are simple sentences? How many are compound sentences with short clauses joined by *and*? How many clauses follow the most common English word order of subject-predicate-(complement)? In general, are these first paragraphs characteristic of the rest of the story?

Steinbeck also develops the folklike flavor by rendering the scenes, actions, and emotions of the story objectively, like a camera. He paints La Paz and the mountains as they are without interjecting his personal feelings about them. Nor does he describe the characters' emotions directly. How do the various songs reveal Kino's emotions? How are others' emotions revealed? For instance, how can you tell that the first pearl buyer in Chapter 4 is nervous? Does Steinbeck say so?

## Identification

With which character did you identify yourself most strongly? How did Steinbeck win your sympathy for Kino and Juana? Which pressures suffered by Kino and Juana are shared, in your opinion, by all human beings?

### IV
### WORDS

**A.** The force of a narrative depends upon the impressions formed through words. To recreate an experience a writer may use figurative or concrete representations. What do the phrases and clauses below suggest?

> a late moth blustered in to find the fire; his mouth drooped with discontent; electric strength; flames danced on the faces of the neighbors; inaudible purr of controlled breathing; hissed to silence; coin stumbled over a knuckle; he felt the evil coagulating about him; senses were burningly alive; the bare stone teeth of the mountains.

**B.** From context determine the meaning of the italicized words.

**1.** A *covey* of little birds chittered and flurried with their wings.

**2.** The surface of the water was an *undulating* mirror of brightness.

**3.** What he had seen might be a reflection, a piece of flat shell accidentally drifted in, or a complete *illusion*.

**4.** She looked at the neighbors for *confirmation* and they nodded their heads solemnly.

**5.** The hundreds of years of *subjugation* were cut deep in him.

**6.** High slopes of the mountain were *swaddled* with pines.

**7.** Gradually the spasms *subsided* and the baby relaxed.

**C. 1.** Steinbeck tells us that Kino was attentive to inner music of various kinds. What does the root of the word *music* mean? Is it related to the word *museum?*

**2.** When the baby is bitten by the scorpion, Juana tries to find the puncture. What does the root of *puncture* mean? Is it related to *punctuate, punctilious, pungent?*

**3.** The appetites of the doctor were known to the people. Is the word *appetite* related to the word *petition?* In what way has the word *appetite* undergone specialization?

**4.** The pearl "captured the light and refined it and gave it back in silver incandescence." The root in *incandescence* is -*cand*-, meaning "white, glowing." Does the same root appear in the word *candidate?*

**5.** The root of *patron* ("each one thought how the patron could not live forever") is -*patr*-, originally meaning "father." How are *patron* and *patronize* related to this same root? What has happened to these words? What words in English illustrate the form -*pater*- with its original meaning?

**6.** What are the roots in the following words and what do they mean: *explosion* ("an explosion of fire"); *detachment* ("the detachment of God"); *incredible* ("one incredible fiesta on cookies"); *fragment* ("a fragment and a moist place in the dirt"); *subsequent* ("his whole subsequent life was memory and longing for France"); *magnified* ("the uncertain air that magnified some things"); *undulating* ("an undulating mirror of brightness"); *subsided* ("the flesh writhed up and then subsided"); *semblance* ("a semblance of competition"); *rebelled* ("he rebelled against the way things are"); *consecrated* ("a little piece of consecrated candle")?

---

### BIOGRAPHICAL NOTES

### Saki

Saki (1870–1916) was the pseudonym for Hector Hugo Munro, who delighted in spoofing British Victorian society. Born in Burma of British parents, he was educated in England by two strict aunts. Later he returned to Burma to serve with the military police. But seven fevers in 13 months forced his return to Britain. In London he discovered he could earn a living by writing. His first popular successes were political satires for the *Westminster Gazette.* Later he wrote short stories satirizing British society and, especially, aunts. He was killed by a sniper's bullet in France during World War I.

## Harry Sylvester

Harry Sylvester (1908–      ) was born in Brooklyn and attended Notre Dame University, graduating in 1930. He sold his first short story when he was a senior at Notre Dame, and within 10 years had published more than 100, mainly sports stories in various magazines such as *Colliers, Scribners, Story,* and *Pictorial Review.* He has had some of his works reprinted in England and Scandinavia, showing the universal appeal of a good sports story. *A Boxer Old* was published in the *O. Henry Memorial Award Prize Stories* of 1934. At different times he worked for both the *New York Evening Post* and the *New York Herald Tribune,* and in 1943 published his first novel, *Dearly Beloved,* set in a small southern town.

## William Sansom

William Sansom (1912–      ), British novelist and short story writer, reports of his beginnings: "I was born, and soon began writing. The pattern is familiar. The worried baby, the shy child, schooldays spent avoiding the ball, the first rungs of the commercial ladder—indeed, in a bank— and then the revolt that ended not in a garret but an advertising agency." World War II extracted him from advertising, and during the blitz of London he learned to write seriously. Instead of trying to write what he imagined people wanted, Sansom wrote what he himself really thought. And suddenly he was published. Eudora Welty says: "He makes you see, hear, taste, touch, and smell to his order—Mr. Sansom's descriptive power is a steady fireworks."

## James Thurber

James Thurber (1894–1961) is considered by many as the best American humorist since Mark Twain. His books are illustrated with his own drawings of shapeless but determined women; droopy-eared, sad dogs; and worried-looking men. Many of his prose sketches concern the same kind of characters: little people unable to cope with their world. His fables are a blend of nonsense and fact, showing how well Thurber knew people and their foibles. His last years were a struggle against blindness.

## Jack London

Jack London (1876–1916) was an American novelist and short-story writer who used many of his own adventures as the basis for his work. Although he attended the University of California for one year, his real education came from his experiences as a longshoreman, sailor, gold hunter in the Klondike, and as a war correspondent during the Russo-Japanese War. Although physically he appeared as a rough character, he was unusually sensitive, especially to social injustices. Some feel his careless, rough life was an outward expression of his revolt against society. Unfortunately, his health was damaged by his way of life and he died a relatively young man. In 16 years he wrote some 50 books, the first of which, *The Son of the Wolf,* was published in 1900. His best known books are *Call of the Wild* (1903), *The Sea Wolf* (1904), and *White Fang* (1906).

## Ambrose Bierce

Ambrose Bierce (1842–1914?), born in Ohio, fought in the Civil War and then moved west to become a successful journalist in San Francisco. He also lived several years in England and there published three books. In California he was the dominant literary figure in the 1890s, but a series of unhappy personal experiences made him an increasingly bitter man. Primarily a short story writer, his best collections are *Tales of Soldiers and Civilians* and *Can Such Things Be?* both published in the nineties. In 1913 he went to Mexico to join the civil war there and disappeared.

## Truman Capote

Truman Capote (1924–      ) was born in New Orleans to parents of long Southern lineage. He attended six different schools in five different parts of the country. Dropping out of school at seventeen, he worked briefly as a protégé of a fortune-teller and then for *The New Yorker* in various departments. Beginning to write early, Capote won his first prize at the age of eight for a short story. As an adult he has won two O'Henry short story awards. Though he claims writing is an exceedingly slow process for him, Capote insists that nothing else appeals to him. In 1966 he became one of the most-discussed authors in the country when his book *In Cold Blood* was published. Capote claimed that it was a new kind of literature, a nonfiction novel. It was later made into a movie.

## Arna Bontemps

Arna Bontemps (1902–    ) was reared in California, graduating in 1923 from Pacific Union College. The following year he headed for Harlem, abandoning his plan to be a doctor for the challenge and excitement of writing. He won several poetry prizes while teaching in private schools. In the 1930s, while teaching in Alabama and Chicago, Bontemps found time to write three novels and two children's books. After studying at both Columbia University and the University of Chicago, Bontemps became Head Librarian at Fisk University, a position he held for twenty-two years. But he never gave up his own writing or the anthologizing of other black writers' works. His forty-five years of writing, teaching, and inspiring black writers has made him one of the best-known contributors to the field of black literature.

## Ted Hughes

Ted Hughes (1930–    ) was born in the West Riding district of Yorkshire, England. Here he attended Mexborough Grammar School and later went to Cambridge's Pembrooke College, where he received a B.A. and M.A. He served in the Royal Air Force for two years and in 1956 married Sylvia Plath, the poet, who died in 1967 leaving him with two children. Earlier he had been a night guard, a rose gardener, and a reader for a publisher. But since 1965, along with David Weissbort, Hughes has been editor of *Modern Poetry in Translation*. His awards for his writing have been numerous, and his fellowships, many.

Hughes has often been classified as a mature poet and rightly so. Much of his work centers on animals: sometimes noble like the horse, but more often the predators of nature, such as hawks, wolves, rats, and foxes. Edwin Muir, writing of Hughes's first book, *The Hawk in the Rain*, said: "His images have an admirable violence . . . the violence of nature red in tooth and claw." Even his humans are seen in terms of brute physical activity. Hughes constantly calls on his childhood background as the settings for his works. The country where he was raised is rural and lonely, and though factories and mills have attempted to encroach on the countryside, they have made little impact on it. Hughes draws on his memories of this land and evokes it so powerfully in his stories that the place somehow becomes "realer" than anywhere else.

## John Steinbeck

John Steinbeck (1902–1968) is an American fiction writer whose book *Grapes of Wrath*, a story of the dispossessed Oklahoma farmers and their trek to California, has been called the "Uncle Tom" of the migrant workers. Born in California, Steinbeck went intermittently to Stanford University, but never achieved his degree. He had published several books before his story *The Red Pony*, published in the *North American Review*, attracted an interested group of readers. His first real success was *Tortilla Flat*, which was followed by *Of Mice and Men*. *Grapes of Wrath*, for which Steinbeck was awarded the Pulitzer Prize, was both attacked and praised. Lewis Gannett, a critic, wrote that there was something Emersonian about the book, because it was Emerson who wrote that "in the mud and scum of things there always, always, something sings." "Steinbeck," says Gannet, "almost alone among all the modern writers who write of mud and scum, invariably hears, and communicates, the song." In 1962, Steinbeck received the Nobel Prize for Literature.

# LIFE'S IRONIES

## We Real Cool

We real cool. We
Left school. We

Lurk late. We
Strike straight. We

Sing sin. We
Thin gin. We

Jazz June. We
die soon.

GWENDOLYN BROOKS

"We Real Cool: The Pool Players. Seven at the Golden Shovel" from *The World of Gwendolyn Brooks* (1971) by Gwendolyn Brooks. Copyright © 1959 by Gwendolyn Brooks.

Gwendolyn Brooks's poem hits hard with the unexpectedness of the last line. Life (or death) has a way of striking back at us no matter how self-confident we may be. This is life's irony.

Just to be alive is to be subject to life's ironies. Whether rich or poor, ambitious or lazy, talented or not talented, a person cannot escape the strange incongruities that arise at times between what is expected and what actually happens. These are life's ironies: a person extends himself to catch an earlier flight and rides to sudden death in a crash; a health faddist insists on jogging two miles a day and drops dead of a heart attack after a workout; a contractor cuts back a hill to build a client's garage and loses it in a landslide.

Ironies that arise in life are not all generated by the same forces. Sometimes nature triggers the unexpected; sometimes society forces the surprise; and sometimes something within a person springs the ironic trap.

Writers have always turned to life's ironies as a rich theme for their storytelling. Usually, such writing leaves an indelible impression on readers, hitting them with all the force of a blow to the stomach. At times, readers, upon finishing such a story, may want to argue that such a thing could not happen . . . wish it hadn't happened . . . are emotionally shaken by its unexpected ending. And yet, as readers think about the selection they are often aware that the outcome, though unexpected, is peculiarly right, peculiarly just. Because of this emotional impact, stories centering on life's ironies are long remembered.

*The arrogance*
*and pride of the wealthy*
*is satirized in this deeply*
*ironical painting by Georges Rouault.*
The Society Lady Fancies
She Has a Reserved Seat in Heaven.
*Collection, The Museum of Modern Art,*
*New York. Gift of the artist.*

Life may startle us by the ironic
twist of permitting us to achieve a desired
goal but demanding an unexpected
forfeit in return.

# The Wrath of the Raped

## MacKINLAY KANTOR

I arranged to spend the weekend with Aunt Thesnelda in Eagle Falls—to eat the bacon gravy and plum preserves which were always on her table, to sleep in the too-short walnut bed where I had slept so many times before, to stroll with her around the tiny garden, and hear lamentations concerning the elm which shaded her nasturtium plot, and the dog from next door who carried on sundry excavations amid her moss-roses.

All of these events took place according to schedule, and as I hadn't intended driving on until Tuesday morning, I took a solitary jaunt in my car on Monday afternoon, driving over forgotten hill roads along the Eagle River.

The hill roads were not as forgotten as I had thought. I remembered them as cart paths, clustered with brier bushes and crab trees, where the grass switched high enough between the wheel ruts to kiss a wagon axle. Now one of the lanes had been made into a primary road, with embankments chopped away, raw culverts lifting their concrete ridges on either side. Taut fences of rustproof wire stretched beside the fields, and several times I

"The Wrath of the Raped" by MacKinlay Kantor. Copyright 1929 by the Isaak Walton League of America. From STORY TELLER by MacKinlay Kantor. Reprinted by permission of Doubleday & Company, Inc.

caught a sparkling flash from the roadside which could mean only one thing—an empty bottle. A new race had inhabited the valley of the Eagle, and I felt my kinship dwindling.

But when I had parked the car near the old Burgess farm, and wandered down across the hill pasture, something of ancient lure and contentment sang in my ears again. This was the same field—the creek had cut a little deeper, roadside trees had been chopped down—but undeniably it was the same field. Scrub red cattle grazing near the river cottonwoods were doubtless the legitimate descendants of the cows that wandered there so long before. And overhead was the same sky, washed to a porcelain blue and filmed with puffing clouds that broke from the prairie beyond the river.

One stubborn smokestack emerged from green haze at an upper bend of the river. There had been no smokestack there twenty years before, but I felt that no one should begrudge Eagle Falls whatever bustling institution was giving birth to that thin strand of black smoke.

Once along the river, I wandered in a daze. A fallen cottonwood, holding a dry drift of polished sticks, should have been there. I should have observed a gaping hole in the high bank opposite the first bend, and there should have been a muskrat rippling doggedly among the quiet shadows . . . . Drift, hole and muskrat—all were gone. The bank had caved alarmingly, and the huge pink boulder which used to bulge in the center of the narrows was high and dry on the opposite shore. Even the river had moved itself during twenty years.

I strolled north through the thin fringe of undergrowth; a distant crow squawled peevishly, and I smiled as I remembered how Georgie Terrell and I had lain in wait for hours, concealed near a bait of corn and hoping with futile confidence to club marauding crows.

Georgie Terrell, I recalled, had been able to stay under water longer than anyone else. He could plunge from an arching elm branch, and go down, down in the glassy greenness, until only bubbles broke the sheer surface and you'd think he was gone for good . . . . Sadly enough, this accomplishment had availed him little when the *Tuscania* rolled beneath wintry waters. The Irish Sea was not like Howard's Hole on the Eagle River.

Somewhere in the woods ahead of me I heard a shrill wavering cry that brought a sudden ripple under my skin. It might have been the naked ghost of Georgie Terrell, calling to me that the water was over his head and hand . . . . And then I smiled ruefully, and with sudden thanksgiving. Georgie's name was on a bronze tablet in the courthouse, but still there were boys to splash the dim waters of Howard's Hole, and scramble up the bank in wet pink skins.

Little boys. Noisy boys. I could hear them now, singing and whooping, talking with the blasphemous assurance of boys who are alone.

"Duck him, Gorsey!" one of them was yelling, and "Sit on him, Skeet!" shrilled another.

Their damp bedlam was suddenly stilled when I came out on the bank above their heads. Yes, the boys were still swimming in Howard's Hole. The broad pool had shrunk to a narrow ribbon, and areas of greasy mud clotted along the opposite shore, but the same trees still swung above the dark mirror. Somehow the mirror did not seem so freshly green as I remembered it.

The boys watched me; four of them, their slick wet heads bobbing quietly on the surface.

"How's the water?" I asked.

"All right." They watched me with suspicion; they seemed to feel that I might interfere with their splashing riot. I could not help knowing that they wished I hadn't come.

But I clung fiercely to those vestiges of a quiet past which were lifting in my mind. "How deep?"

To my surprise, one of the boys suddenly emerged from the water to a point at his nipples, and remained mutely standing for my delectation.[1]

"Do you mean to tell me that it's only rib deep in there?"

They stared, wide-eyed. "Why, this is pretty deep, ain't it?" one of them asked cautiously. "Last summer it was only up to my belly, sometimes."

I sat down stupidly on the bank. "It's tough, to see that," I told them. "When I used to go swimming here it was always over my head and hand, in the deep hole."

It was a fairy story to them. "Gosh!" they exploded. "When was that?"

"Oh, twenty years ago," I had to tell them in confusion. "Don't mind me, boys. Go ahead and swim. I'm just going to sit here and smoke awhile."

They began to move about, cautiously and reluctantly, but gaining in freedom as they observed that my thoughts were evidently far removed from them. Before long they were tumbling about—swimming a few strokes, dog-paddling, wrestling in the water like a troop of maudlin puppies.

I bit down fiercely on my pipe, but was unable to see where I could have improved matters. The river was there; the farmers owned the land; if they wanted to cut down trees until the banks caved, if they wanted to drain their corn-bottom silt into the stream and clog the channel, there was little I could do about it.

One of the boys stepped on a piece of glass and came clambering up the bank to examine his wound. It was not a bad cut, and he sat there hugging his glistening knees while we talked together.

"What's that stuff on your shoulder?" I asked curiously.

He turned, and with a careless gesture brushed off a string of matted filth. "It's in the water. See, there's some more just going by." He pointed to another putrescent[2] object slowly turning in the sluggish current.

---

1. **delectation**\\'dē 'lĕk ᵃtā·shən\\ pleasure, enjoyment.
2. **putrescent**\\pyū ᵃtrĕs·ənt\\ decomposing, rotting.

I sniffed. There was a sickening odor. "Where does it come from?"

"Rendering plant.[3] It's up the river a ways."

"And is this stuff in the river all the time?"

"Sure." He looked at me indignantly. "Wasn't there any rendering plant when you lived here?"

"No," I replied fervently. "I don't see how you can swim in that filth. I don't think you ought to."

"Where'd we swim, then?" he countered belligerently.

That was right. "Nowhere, I guess," I admitted.

He forgave me kindly. "Aw, we don't mind it so much. It isn't real bad unless you get it in your mouth . . . . We can all swim fine."

"Can you?"—absently.

"Sure. Gorsey"—he pointed to a yellow head between two brown ones in the water—"he can swim better'n any of the other guys. He can stay under water the longest, too."

So Georgie Terrell's laurels were endangered by the advance of a new champion. "What's his name?"

"Gorsey. Joe Gorse. He can swim good!"

My companion began to pull on his shirt. I put my pipe in my pocket, called a goodbye to the swimmers, and picked my way through the undergrowth back to the open pasture. I broke off a maple sprout and flicked my leg as I walked . . . . Once in a while I forgot myself and became an unconscious masochist;[4] the skin was black and blue when I removed my clothes that night.

Two weeks in Omaha, Sioux Falls, Minneapolis, and Mason City. Two weeks of customers and order-blanks and restaurant fare. Then I swung back to Eagle Falls for another night at Aunt Thesnelda's before I returned to the main office in Chicago. But misfortune lay in wait for me.

Aunt Nelda has no garage, or need for one, unless it would be as quarters for her tomcat, and who ever kept a tomcat in a garage? . . . I parked my car in front of the old house that night, and long before morning some son of

Satan, driving without lights, smashed into the front of it. Dawn showed a shattered wheel, a bent axle and a twisted radiator. Also a great deal of broken glass which proved that the malefactor had not escaped undamaged.

There was nothing for it but to leave the car in a local garage for repairs, and take the afternoon train to Chicago.

Thirty seconds after I had seated myself in the observation car of the Limited, a fat, beaming-eyed gentleman puffed into a chair beside me. He was the only other parlor-car passenger from Eagle Falls.

"Going far?" he inquired.

"Chicago."

"Waterloo's my home," he offered expansively. "Name's Madger. Julius R. Madger."

Wearily enough, I told him my name. I had hoped for a drowsy afternoon, filled with relaxation from the strain of driving, but this was not to be.

He spouted effusively as the train sped across the bridge and up the long grade.

"Eagle Falls . . . nice little burg . . . good, live town. Things going good, now."

"They are?"

"Sure. Banking slump hit them rather hard but they're making things hum again. Not your home, huh?"

"I've been visiting a relative," I said.

"Oh, I see. Don't know many people there, huh? Know Gorse?"

Gorse, Gorse. The name lodged in my mind . . . . Then I remembered: the boy, the golden-head, the contender for George Terrell's forgotten honors. "I met a boy—" I began, but he was already giving me the history of the Gorse fortunes.

". . . Didn't do so well at Waterloo. Came out there from Chicago; used to be with a soap company; company went broke and he was out. Tried one thing and then another.

---

3. **rendering plant,** a plant treating dead animals so as to convert them into industrial oils and fats and fertilizers.

4. **masochist** \ˈmăs·ə·kəst\ a person who takes delight in hurting himself.

Finally his wife's old man died and that gave him a little capital."

He waggled his cigar with emphatic punctuation.

"Now, here's the point I'd like to bring out. My friend Gorse took advantage of an opportunity which no one else had touched. He went to Eagle Falls and established his business. Virgin territory. Chance for anybody with the guts to do it." He chuckled suddenly. "That was a pun, by golly—guts!"

"What was it?" I asked.

"Dead animals! Dead animals, that people burn or bury or drag away to let them rot. Always wasted before. You wouldn't think of that, see?"

I agreed. "No, I wouldn't."

"Well, that's the kind of a fellow Gorse is. He's got a man-size plant there at Eagle Falls, now. A lot of employees. Drive around in trucks —cover more than a thousand square miles of territory. Dead cows, pigs, horses, sheep—even down to dogs and cats. No, sir, Gorse doesn't miss an opportunity. Even a dog or cat's got a little grease in it."

He rumbled at his own humor.

"Where is this plant—on the river?" I was beginning to remember an odor; the sight of floating scum; the black smokestack that reared itself above the river trees . . . .

"Yes, sir, on the river, mile and a half below town. That way the smell (it's rather a smelly process, see?) doesn't bother folks. Oh, a few of 'em kick now and then. But Gorse can tell 'em to go to hell if they don't like it. He's got a legitimate business, and he's making a darn good thing out of it."

I asked, automatically and not because of any interest: "I suppose you've been over to Eagle Falls to see your friend Gorse?"

"Sure. Didn't I tell you?" His face was suddenly very sober. "Tough on Gorse—awful tough on him. I've been back there to a funeral. His kid died. His boy."

"Died?" was all I could say.

"Yes. Died on Tuesday night. It was his only son, too. Gorse had the best doctors in the State, but no use. The kid died of a—a— what you call it—Mastoid infection, I think. Infection in his ear. It was a funny thing; nobody could figure out how he ever got it."

---

## I

### THE PROPHECY OF LITERATURE

"The Wrath of the Raped" was first published in 1929. Yet it probably has a greater impact and meaning for today's reader than it did when it was written because the prophecies in the story have proved increasingly true. Note the number of details throughout the selection that indicate that people are destroying the very environment that nurtures them. In addition to the obvious detail that the rendering plant is dumping raw sewage into the stream, the narrator notes that the stream-bed has moved and is narrower than it used to be, the topsoil has silted into the pool lowering the water's depth, the very water has changed color, the muskrats and their dam have vanished, and the stream has cut deeper into the earth. A smokestack pours black waste into the formerly clear sky. Empty bottles litter the roadside. All of these details are startling to readers when they realize that this is a description written forty years ago. Ironically, even the attitudes of the people are unchanged and very familiar.

## II

### IMPLICATIONS

Opinions may be based on both the materials given in the stories and on students' own experiences. There is no clear-cut right or wrong answer.

**1.** Owners of a piece of property should be able to do anything they want with it.

**2.** The good the plant does for the people in the town makes up for the pollution it causes.

**3.** There are two ironic happenings in the story: (1) Joe Gorse dies from the pollution caused by his father's plant and (2) Joe Gorse's father is unaware that he has caused his son's death. The first is more ironic than the second.

## III

### TECHNIQUES

As you read stories centering on life's ironies, your attention will be directed to two more qualities that enhance the impact of a piece of literature. These are atmosphere and suspense.

## Atmosphere

The atmosphere is the prevailing mood a story creates in the reader's mind. If it is well done, it establishes certain expectations about the story: that it will be down-to-earth or lighthearted or somber or melancholy. Atmosphere might be likened to color tonality. Some stories seem to be bright yellow and orange; some ooze mysterious deep red or purple; others seem dark brown or drab gray.

In "The Wrath of the Raped" the story centers on a man's return to the small Iowa town he had known as a boy. He feels a kind of despair at the passing of the good things he had known and the devastating changes people are inflicting on their environment. Even the conversation with the stranger on the train is written so that the reader feels the narrator's disgust at the sentiments being expressed. The single effect is that of overwhelming despair and disgust.

## Suspense

Suspense is one of the most common ways of holding readers' interest. Their curiosity is aroused by a problem, a situation, or a question. But writers, instead of satisfying the readers' curiosity, hold back the answer. They may, instead, elaborate the problem by adding complications, by taking characters through a sequence of trials and failures; or they may extend the waiting by philosophical reflections on the situation. Suspense is usually the ingredient that makes a plot "go."

In "The Wrath of the Raped" the suspense is unusual. The reader is not involved with the narrator, nor is there any specific problem set forth. The details do not take on real significance until the very end of the story. The reader's curiosity is tantalized by the sheer puzzle about where the story is going. It is a little like the game children play in which a person must tell a story about a group of unrelated items: a snake, a handkerchief, a pizza, and a chess set. So in this story you assemble a group of seemingly unrelated pieces: a traveling salesman revisiting his childhood town, a group of boys in a swimming hole, a rendering plant, an accidentally damaged car, a ride on a train. . . . The reader keeps wondering—well, what is this all about?

## IV

## WORDS

**A.** As you have learned elsewhere in this book, words are often traceable to proper names. Refering to some youngsters swimming in Howard's Hole, the narrator in "The Wrath of the Raped" speaks of their "damp bedlam." The word *bedlam* is actually a dialectal pronunciation of the word *Bethlehem*. In the dialect of London in the thirteenth century, the last word in the name St. Mary's of Bethlehem was pronounced *bedlam*. In the fifteenth century, St. Mary's, a priory, was converted into an insane asylum. In time, *bedlam* became associated with the uproar and confusion common in such an institution. As used in the story, *bedlam* refers to the noisy, unrestrained fun the boys were having in their swimming hole. Like *bedlam*, the word *maudlin* is derived from a proper name, in this case, Mary Magdalene. In the Bible, Mary Magdalene is the sinner from whom Christ cast out seven devils. In classical art, she is portrayed quite often as a weeping, repentant figure. Thus, anyone, who is given to weeping, especially an overly sentimental person, is said to be *maudlin*. Comparing the water to tears, the narrator says that the boys were "dog-paddling, wrestling in the water like a troop of maudlin puppies." From what proper names are these words derived: *dunce, shrapnel, hooligan, limerick, academy, maverick, mausoleum, cologne, braille,* and *cardigan?*

**B.** Many an American place name has its origin in an Indian language. For instance, *Sioux Falls, Omaha,* and *Minneapolis,* all of which are mentioned in "The Wrath of the Raped," originated in an American Indian language. *Sioux Falls* (in South Dakota) is derived from *Sioux,* which is traceable to a Chippewa Indian word meaning "little snake." The Sioux peoples were North American Indians who formerly occupied parts of the Great Plains in the Dakotas, Minnesota, and Nebraska. *Minneapolis* (Minnesota) is obviously related to *Minnesota,* which in the Dakotan language is *minisota,* "clear water." The last part, *polis,* is Greek for "city." From Dhegiha, a Siouan language, comes *umāhā,* "upstream," or *Omaha* (Nebraska). Using your dictionary, try to find out the Indian language and the original meaning behind each of these place names: *Nebraska, Wichita, Milwaukee, South Dakota, Mississippi, Delaware,* and *Connecticut.*

and smile placed the stranger on a footing of innocent familiarity with the eldest daughter.

"Ah, this fire is the right thing!" cried he; "especially when there is such a pleasant circle round it. I am quite benumbed; for the Notch is just like the pipe of a great pair of bellows; it has blown a terrible blast in my face all the way from Bartlett."

"Then you are going towards Vermont?" said the master of the house, as he helped to take a light knapsack off the young man's shoulders.

"Yes; to Burlington, and far enough beyond," replied he. "I meant to have been at Ethan Crawford's to-night; but a pedestrian lingers along such a road as this. It is no matter; for, when I saw this good fire, and all your cheerful faces, I felt as if you had kindled it on purpose for me, and were waiting my arrival. So I shall sit down among you, and make myself at home."

The frank-hearted stranger had just drawn his chair to the fire when something like a heavy footstep was heard without, rushing down the steep side of the mountain, as with long and rapid strides, and taking such a leap in passing the cottage as to strike the opposite precipice. The family held their breath, because they knew the sound, and their guest held his by instinct.

"The old mountain has thrown a stone at us, for fear we should forget him," said the landlord, recovering himself. "He sometimes nods his head and threatens to come down; but we are old neighbors, and agree together pretty well upon the whole. Besides we have a sure place of refuge hard by if he should be coming in good earnest."

Let us now suppose the stranger to have finished his supper of bear's meat; and, by his natural felicity[2] of manner, to have placed himself on a footing of kindness with the whole family, so that they talked as freely together as if he belonged to their mountain brood. He was of a proud, yet gentle spirit—haughty and reserved among the rich and great; but ever ready to stoop his head to the lowly cottage door, and be like a brother or a son at the poor man's fireside. In the household of the Notch he found warmth and simplicity of feeling, the pervading intelligence of New England, and a poetry of native growth, which they had gathered when they little thought of it from the mountain peaks and chasms, and at the very threshold of their romantic and dangerous abode. He had travelled far and alone; his whole life, indeed, had been a solitary path; for, with the lofty caution of his nature, he had kept himself apart from those who might otherwise have been his companions. The family, too, though so kind and hospitable, had that consciousness of unity among themselves, and separation from the world at large, which, in every domestic circle, should still keep a holy place where no stranger may intrude. But this evening a prophetic sympathy impelled the refined and educated youth to pour out his heart before the simple mountaineers, and constrained them to answer him with the same free confidence. And thus it should have been. Is not the kindred of a common fate a closer tie than that of birth?

The secret of the young man's character was a high and abstracted ambition. He could have borne to live an undistinguished life, but not to be forgotten in the grave. Yearning desire had been transformed to hope; and hope, long cherished, had become like certainty, that, obscurely as he journeyed now, a glory was to beam on all his pathway,—though not, perhaps, while he was treading it. But when posterity should gaze back into the gloom of what was now the present, they would trace the brightness of his footsteps, brightening as meaner glories faded, and confess that a gifted one had passed from his cradle to his tomb with none to recognize him.

"As yet," cried the stranger—his cheek glowing and his eyes flashing with enthusiasm—"as yet, I have done nothing. Were I to vanish from the earth to-morrow, none would know so much of me as you: that a nameless youth

---

2. felicity\fə ᴬlĭ•sə•tē\ happiness; here, charm of manner.

came up at nightfall from the valley of the Saco, and opened his heart to you in the evening, and passed through the Notch by sunrise, and was seen no more. Not a soul would ask, 'Who was he? Whither did the wanderer go?' But I cannot die till I have achieved my destiny. Then, let Death come! I shall have built my monument!"

There was a continual flow of natural emotion, gushing forth amid abstracted reverie, which enabled the family to understand this young man's sentiments, though so foreign from their own. With quick sensibility of the ludicrous, he blushed at the ardor into which he had been betrayed.

"You laugh at me," said he, taking the eldest daughter's hand, and laughing himself. "You think my ambition as nonsensical as if I were to freeze myself to death on the top of Mount Washington, only that people might spy at me from the country round about. And, truly, that would be a noble pedestal for a man's statue!"

"It is better to sit here by this fire," answered the girl, blushing, "and be comfortable and contented, though nobody thinks about us."

"I suppose," said her father, after a fit of musing, "there is something natural in what the young man says; and if my mind had been turned that way, I might have felt just the same. It is strange, wife, how his talk has set my head running on things that are pretty certain never to come to pass."

"Perhaps they may," observed the wife. "Is the man thinking what he will do when he is a widower?"

"No, no!" cried he, repelling the idea with reproachful kindness. "When I think of your death, Esther, I think of mine, too. But I was wishing we had a good farm in Bartlett, or Bethlehem, or Littleton, or some other township round the White Mountains; but not where they could tumble on our heads. I should want to stand well with my neighbors and be called Squire,[3] and sent to General Court for a term or two; for a plain, honest man may do as much good there as a lawyer. And when I

*The Maine Central Railroad crosses Willey Brook in a picturesque section of Crawford Notch, N.H. This notch, one of four in the White Mountains, is believed to be the one Hawthorne had in mind when he wrote "The Ambitious Guest."*

should be grown quite an old man, and you an old woman, so as not to be long apart, I might die happy enough in my bed, and leave you all crying around me. A slate gravestone would suit me as well as a marble one—with just my name and age, and a verse of a hymn, and something to let people know that I lived an honest man and died a Christian."

"There now!" exclaimed the stranger; "it is our nature to desire a monument, be it slate or

---

3. **Squire**\skwair\ *U.S.* a title used in certain small towns and country districts and applied to a justice of the peace, a local judge, or other local dignitary.

marble, or a pillar of granite, or a glorious memory in the universal heart of man."

"We're in a strange way, to-night," said the wife, with tears in her eyes. "They say it's a sign of something, when folks' minds go a wandering so. Hark to the children!"

They listened accordingly. The younger children had been put to bed in another room, but with an open door between, so that they could be heard talking busily among themselves. One and all seemed to have caught the infection from the fireside circle, and were outvying[4] each other in wild wishes, and childish projects of what they would do when they came to be men and women. At length a little boy, instead of addressing his brothers and sisters, called out to his mother.

"I'll tell you what I wish, mother," cried he. "I want you and father and grandma'm, and all of us, and the stranger too, to start right away, and go and take a drink out of the basin of the Flume!"

Nobody could help laughing at the child's notion of leaving a warm bed, and dragging them from a cheerful fire, to visit the basin of the Flume,—a brook, which tumbles over the precipice, deep within the Notch. The boy had hardly spoken when a wagon rattled along the road, and stopped a moment before the door. It appeared to contain two or three men, who were cheering their hearts with the rough chorus of a song, which resounded, in broken notes, between the cliffs, while the singers hesitated whether to continue their journey or put up here for the night."

"Father," said the girl, "they are calling you by name."

But the good man doubted whether they had really called him, and was unwilling to show himself too solicitous of gain by inviting people to patronize his house. He therefore did not hurry to the door; and the lash being soon applied, the travellers plunged into the Notch, still singing and laughing, though their music and mirth came back drearily from the heart of the mountain.

"There, mother!" cried the boy, again. "They'd have given us a ride to the Flume."

Again they laughed at the child's pertinacious[5] fancy for a night ramble. But it happened that a light cloud passed over the daughter's spirit; she looked gravely into the fire, and drew a breath that was almost a sigh. It forced its way, in spite of a little struggle to repress it. Then starting and blushing, she looked quickly round the circle, as if they had caught a glimpse into her bosom. The stranger asked what she had been thinking of.

"Nothing," answered she, with a downcast smile. "Only I felt lonesome just then."

"Oh, I have always had a gift of feeling what is in other people's hearts," said he, half seriously. "Shall I tell the secrets of yours? For I know what to think when a young girl shivers by a warm hearth, and complains of lonesomeness at her mother's side. Shall I put these feelings into words?"

"They would not be a girl's feelings any longer if they could be put into words," replied the mountain nymph, laughing, but avoiding his eye.

All this was said apart. Perhaps a germ of love was springing in their hearts, so pure that it might blossom in Paradise, since it could not be matured on earth; for women worship such gentle dignity as his; and the proud, contemplative, yet kindly soul is oftenest captivated by simplicity like hers. But while they spoke softly, and he was watching the happy sadness, the lightsome shadows, the shy yearnings of a maiden's nature, the wind through the Notch took a deeper and drearier sound. It seemed, as the fanciful stranger said, like the choral strain of the spirits of the blast, who in old Indian times had their dwelling among these mountains, and made their heights and recesses a sacred region. There was a wail along the road, as if a funeral were passing. To chase away the gloom, the family threw pine

---

4. **outvying**\aut ▲vai·ĭŋ\ outdoing each other, competing.
5. **pertinacious**\pər·tən ▲ā·shəs\ stubborn, obstinate.

branches on their fire, till the dry leaves crackled and the flame arose, discovering once again a scene of peace and humble happiness. The light hovered about them fondly, and caressed them all. There were the little faces of the children, peeping from their bed apart, and here the father's frame of strength, the mother's subdued and careful mien,[6] the high-browed youth, the budding girl, and the good old grandam, still knitting in the warmest place. The aged woman looked up from her task, and, with fingers ever busy, was the next to speak.

"Old folks have their notions," said she, "as well as young ones. You've been wishing and planning; and letting your heads run on one thing and another, till you've set my mind a wandering too. Now what should an old woman wish for, when she can go but a step or two before she comes to her grave? Children, it will haunt me night and day till I tell you."

"What is it, mother?" cried the husband and wife at once.

Then the old woman, with an air of mystery which drew a circle closer round the fire, informed them that she had provided her grave-clothes some years before,—a nice linen shroud, a cap with a muslin ruff, and everything of a finer sort than she had worn since her wedding day. But this evening an old superstition had strangely recurred to her. It used to be said, in her younger days, that if anything were amiss with a corpse, if only the ruff were not smooth, or the cap did not set right, the corpse in the coffin and beneath the clods would strive to put up its cold hands and arrange it. The bare thought made her nervous.

"Don't talk so, grandmother!" said the girl, shuddering.

"Now,"—continued the old woman, with singular earnestness, yet smiling strangely at her own folly,—"I want one of you, my children—when your mother is dressed and in the coffin—I want one of you to hold a looking-glass over my face. Who knows but I may take a glimpse at myself, and see whether all's right?"

"Old and young, we dream of graves and monuments," murmured the stranger youth. "I wonder how mariners feel when the ship is sinking, and they, unknown and undistinguished, are to be buried together in the ocean—that wide and nameless sepulchre?"

For a moment, the old woman's ghastly conception so engrossed the minds of her hearers that a sound abroad in the night, rising like the roar of a blast, had grown broad, deep, and terrible, before the fated group were conscious of it. The house and all within it trembled; the foundations of the earth seemed to be shaken, as if this awful sound were the peal of the last trump.[7] Young and old exchanged one wild glance, and remained an instant, pale, affrighted, without utterance, or power to move. Then the same shriek burst simultaneously from all their lips.

"The Slide! The Slide!"

The simplest words must intimate, but not portray,[8] the unutterable horror of the catastrophe. The victims rushed from their cottage, and sought refuge in what they deemed a safer spot—where, in contemplation of such an emergency, a sort of barrier had been reared. Alas! they had quitted their security, and fled right into the pathway of destruction. Down came the whole side of the mountain, in a cataract of ruin. Just before it reached the house, the stream broke into two branches—shivered not a window there, but overwhelmed the whole vicinity, blocked up the road, and annihilated everything in its dreadful course. Long ere the thunder of the great Slide had ceased to roar among the mountains, the mortal agony had been endured, and the victims were at peace. Their bodies were never found.

The next morning, the light smoke was seen stealing from the cottage chimney up the

---

6. mien\mēn\ air or bearing.
7. **the last trump,** the last trumpet. See Revelation 8:6, "And the seven angels which had the seven trumpets prepared themselves to sound."
8. intimate\ˈĭn·tə ˈmāt\, **but not portray,** suggest but not describe.

mountain side. Within, the fire was yet smouldering on the hearth, and the chairs in a circle round it, as if the inhabitants had but gone forth to view the devastation of the Slide, and would shortly return, to thank Heaven for their miraculous escape. All had left separate tokens, by which those who had known the family were made to shed a tear for each. Who has not heard their name? The story has been told far and wide, and will forever be a legend of these mountains. Poets have sung their fate.

There were circumstances which led some to suppose that a stranger had been received into the cottage on this awful night, and had shared the catastrophe of all its inmates. Others denied that there were sufficient grounds for such a conjecture. Woe for the high-souled youth, with his dream of Earthly Immortality! His name and person utterly unknown; his history, his way of life, his plans, a mystery never to be solved, his death and his existence equally a doubt! Whose was the agony of that death moment?

---

## I
### WHOSE WAS THE AGONY OF THAT DEATH MOMENT?

Thus ends Hawthorne's story, underlining the terrible irony of the guest's fate: he who wanted nothing more from life than to be remembered is irrevocably forgotten, and those who were content to be forgotten are immortalized forever in legend. There is an added note of irony to the story: if the people had stayed in the cottage, they would have been spared; in attempting to save themselves, they rushed to their destruction.

## II
### IMPLICATIONS

Consider these statements from the story. Why have they become ironic at the story's end? Do they also expand to say something about life itself?

**1.** "They had found the 'herb, heart's-ease,' in the bleakest spot of all New England."

**2.** "Is not the kindred of a common fate a closer tie than that of birth?"

**3.** " '. . . it is our nature to desire a monument, be it slate or marble, or a pillar of granite, or a glorious memory in the universal heart of man.' "

**4.** "Alas! they had quitted their security, and fled right into the pathway of destruction."

**5.** "The story has been told far and wide, and will forever be a legend of these mountains."

## III
### TECHNIQUES

*Atmosphere*

List the things you saw, the sounds you heard, and the feelings you had as you read the story. Can you find a word or two to express the atmosphere that Hawthorne created?

*Suspense*

What hints does Hawthorne give the reader that this night is not quite usual . . . that a mysterious force seems to be working?

## IV
### WORDS

From the number of words of Latin derivation you have studied so far, it should be clear that Latin has contributed significantly to the vocabulary of English. "The Ambitious Guest" has many words of Latin origin; for example, *lamentation, solitude, transformed, precipice,* and *felicity.* The infusion of Latin into English began in the middle of the first century with the conquest of Britain by the Romans, who remained there until A.D. 410. Even after the departure of the Romans, Latin words still flowed into English and were in varying degrees anglicized; that is, made into English-sounding words. During the Old English period (449–1100), *alter, demon, martyr, rule,* and *port* (which are not long and unfamiliar) came into English. Borrowed from Latin during the Middle English period (1100–1500) were such words as *subpoena, library, medicine, client,* and *recipe.* The great influx of Latin words, however, occurred during the Modern period (after 1500) when such words as *abdomen, urban, penetrate, lapse,* and *notorious* entered English.

# LIFE'S IRONIES

The public world provides for an endless harvest of ironic circumstances in which pretense and dishonesty hide under a mask of smiling virtue. The political cartoonist loves to show the wolf grinning under its lambskin costume.

**FOR DISCOVERING THE MOTION OF THE EARTH**
*Francisco Goya*

**SHADOWS**
*Grandville*

BREADLINE—NO ONE HAS STARVED
*Reginald Marsh*

México se transforma en una gran ciudad. . . .

MEXICO TRANSFORMS ITSELF INTO A GREAT CITY
*Alfredo Zalce*
*The Metropolitan Museum of Art*
*Whittelsey Fund, 1946*

**M**arsh's *Breadline—No One Has Starved*, winding endlessly, speaks of hopelessness during the Great Depression and "too little, too late" methods of dealing with social crises.

The pillaged, starving inner city overwhelms the signs of progress in *Mexico Transforms Itself Into a Great City*. Zalce's comment could apply to many cities in the world today.

The startling symbolism of *The Cog*, 1905, protests the destruction of man in favor of machinery.

THE COG  *Franz Kupka*

609

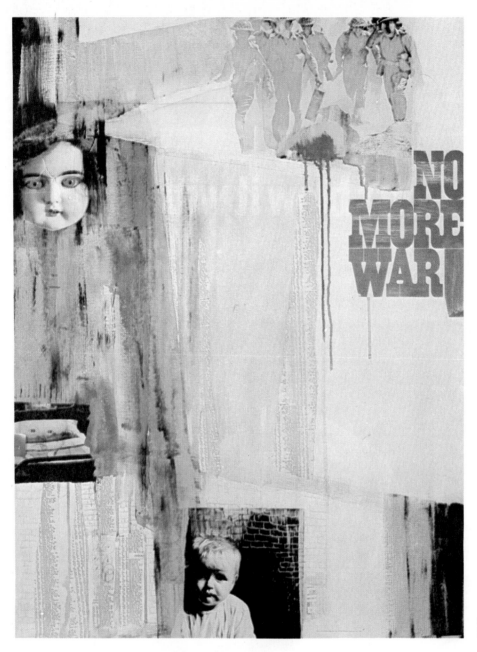

NO MORE WAR
*Marilyn Kaplan*

Posters are among this age's most dramatic commentaries. Marilyn Kaplan uses the collage—an arrangement of images and splashes of color—to make a scathing comment upon war and its effect upon the people it professes to save. The placement of child and doll and their facial expressions leave us in no doubt about Ms. Kaplan's point of view. Thomas Nast's cartoon MILITARY GLORY, 1870, makes a similar protest. Robinson reflects antiwar convictions during World War I.

MILITARY GLORY
*Thomas Nast*

VICTORY, 1916
*Boardman Robinson*
Reproduced from The Masses, Oct. 1916
*Columbia University Library, New York*

PUCK.

LOOKING BACKWARD.
THEY WOULD CLOSE TO THE NEW-COMER THE BRIDGE THAT CARRIED THEM AND THEIR FATHERS OVER.

LOOKING BACKWARD
*Joseph Keppler*
*New York Public Library*

Above, Joseph Keppler uses an approach similar to that used by Grandville in SHADOWS, on page 607. Through the shadow technique, Keppler shows the ironic contrast between the present situation of the five "successful" men and what they were when they first arrived in this country. What point is Keppler making? Below, Warhol takes a stab at a more contemporary target. Facial reconstruction has become a sort of mania for middle-aged, affluent people, and Warhol satirizes this nicely.

BEFORE AND AFTER, 3.
*Andy Warhol*
*Collection of Whitney Museum of American Art.*
*Gift of Charles Simon (and purchase).*

"Each year in the past," says the chairman
of the Board of Directors as he opens
the annual meeting, "Mr. Kovac has been the
object of a cruel and criminal action
by the members of this Board. Each year
in the past, it has been our decision
to repeat this crime." Now the group
once again must face the decision.

# The
# Cold, Cold Box

## HOWARD FAST

As always, the annual meeting of the Board of Directors convened at nine o'clock in the morning, on the 10th of December. Nine o'clock in the morning was a sensible and reasonable hour to begin a day's work, and long ago, the 10th of December had been chosen as a guarantee against the seduction of words.[1] Every one of the directors would have to be home for the Christmas holiday—or its equivalent—and therefore the agenda was timed for precisely two weeks and not an hour more.

In the beginning, this had caused many late sessions, sometimes two or three days when the directors met the clock round, with no break for sleep or rest. But in time, as things fell into the proper place and orderly management replaced improvisation, each day's meeting was able to adjourn by four o'clock in the afternoon—and there were even years when the general meeting finished its work a day or two early.

By now, the meeting of the Board of Directors was very matter-of-fact and routine. The

big clock on the wall of the charming and spacious meeting room was just sounding nine, its voice low and musical, as the last of the directors found their seats. They nodded pleasantly to each other, and if they were seated close to old friends, they exchanged greetings. They were completely relaxed, neither tense nor uneasy at the thought of the long meeting that lay ahead of them.

There were exactly three hundred of these directors, and they sat in a comfortable circle of many tiers of seats—in a room not unlike a small amphitheatre. Two aisles cut through to a center circle or stage about twenty feet in diameter, and there a podium was placed which allowed the speaker to turn in any direction as he spoke. Since the number of three hundred was an arbitrary one, agreed upon after a good deal of trial and error, and maintained as an excellent working size, half the seats in the meeting room were always empty. There was some talk now and then of redesigning the meeting room, but nobody ever got down to doing it and by now the empty seats were a normal part of the decor.

The membership of the Board was about equally divided between men and women. No one could serve under the age of thirty, but retirement was a matter of personal decision, and a reasonable number of members were over seventy. Two-thirds of them were in their fifties. Since the Board was responsible for an international management, it was only natural that all nations and races should be represented, black men and white men and brown men and yellow men—and all the shadings and gradations in between. Like the United Nations—they were too modest to make such a comparison themselves—they had a number of official languages and a system of simultaneous translation; but as with the United Nations, English was most frequently used.

As a matter of fact, the Chairman of the Board, who had been born in Indochina,

Copyright © 1960 by Howard Fast. Reprinted by permission of Paul R. Reynolds, Inc., 12 East 41st Street, New York, NY 10017.

1. **seduction of words**\sə ˄dək·shən\ the temptation to talk too long.

opened this meeting in English, which he spoke very well and with ease, and after he had welcomed them and announced the total attendance—all members present—he said, "At the beginning of our annual meeting—and this is an established procedure, I may say—we deal with a moral and legal point, the question of Mr. Steve Kovac. We undertake this before the reading of the agenda, for we have felt that the question of Mr. Kovac is not a matter of agenda or business, but of conscience. Of our conscience, I must add, and not without humility; for Mr. Kovac is the only secret of this meeting. All else that the Board discusses, votes upon and decides or rejects will be made public, as you know. But of Mr. Steve Kovac, the world knows nothing; and each year in the past, our decision has been that the world should continue to know nothing about Mr. Kovac. Each year in the past, Mr. Kovac has been the object of a cruel and criminal action by the members of this Board. Each year in the past, it has been our decision to repeat this crime."

To these words, most of the members of the Board did not react at all—but here and there young men and women showed their surprise, bewilderment and unease, either by the expression on their faces or by low protestations of disbelief. The members of the Board were not insensitive people.

"This year, as in the past, we make this question of Mr. Kovac our first piece of business—because we cannot go on to our other business until it is decided. As in the past, we will decide whether to engage in a criminal conspiracy or not."

A young woman, a new member of the Board, her face flushed and angry, rose and asked the Chairman if he would yield for a question. He replied that he would.

"Am I to understand that you are serious, Mr. Chairman, or is this some sophomoric prank for the edification of new members?"

"This Board is not used to such descriptive terms as sophomoric, as you should know, Mrs. Ramu," he answer mildly. "I am quite serious."

The young woman sat down. She bit her lower lip and stared at her lap. A young man arose.

"Yes, Mr. Steffanson?" the Chairman said pleasantly.

The young man sat down again. The older members were gravely attentive, thoughtful without impatience.

"I do not intend to choke off any discussion, and I will gladly yield to any questions," said the Chairman, "but perhaps a little more about this troublesome matter first. There are two reasons why we consider this problem each year. Firstly, because the kind of crime we have committed in the past is hardly anything to which we should grow indifferent; we need to be reminded; premeditated crime is a deadly threat to basic decency, and God help us if we should ever become complacent! Secondly, each year, there are new members on this Board, and it is necessary that they should hear all the facts in the case of Mr. Kovac. This year, we have seven new members. I address myself to them, but not only to them; I include all of my fellow members of this Board."

"Steve Kovac," the Chairman of the Board began, "was born in Pittsburgh in the year 1913. He was one of eleven children, four of whom survived to adulthood. This was not too unusual in those days of poverty, ignorance and primitive medicine.

"John Kovac, Steve Kovac's father, was a steelworker. When Steve Kovac was six years old, there was a long strike—an attempt on the part of the steelworkers to increase their wages. I am sure you are all familiar with the method of the strike, and therefore I will not elaborate.

"During this strike, Steve Kovac's mother died; a year later, John Kovac fell into a vat of molten steel. The mother died of tuberculosis, a disease then incurable. The father's body was dissolved in the molten steel. I mention these things in terms of their very deep and lasting effect on the mind and character of Steve

Kovac. Orphaned at the age of seven, he grew up like an animal in the jungle. Placed in a county home for orphan children, he was marked as a bad and intractable boy, beaten daily, deprived of food, punished in every way the ignorance and insensitivity of the authorities could devise. After two years of this, he ran away.

"This is a very brief background to the childhood of a most remarkable man, a man of brilliance, character and determination, a man of high inventive genius and grim determination. Unfortunately, the mind and personality of this man had been scarred and traumatized[2] beyond redemption. A psychiatric analysis of this process has been prepared, and each of you will find a copy in your portfolio. It also itemizes the trials and suffering of Steve Kovac between the ages of nine and twenty—the years during which he fought to survive and to grow to adulthood.

"It also gives a great many details of this time of his life—details I cannot go into. You must understand that while the question before us is related to this background, there are many other features I will deal with."

At this point, the Chairman of the Board paused to take a drink of water and to glance through his notes. The younger members of the Board glanced hurriedly at the psychiatric report; the older members remained contemplative, absorbed in their own thoughts. As many times as they had been through this, somehow it was never dull.

"At the age of twenty," the Chairman resumed, "Steve Kovac was working in a steel mill outside of Pittsburgh. He was friendly then with a man named Emery. This man, Emery, was alone, without family or means of support. A former coal miner, he suffered from a disease of the lungs, common to his trade. All he had in the world was a five-thousand-dollar insurance policy. Steve Kovac agreed to support him, and in return he made Kovac the beneficiary of the insurance policy. In those

days, insurance policies were frequently the only means by which a family could survive the death of the breadwinner.

"Four months later, Emery died. Years afterward, it was rumored that Kovac had hastened his death, but there is no evidence for the rumor. The five thousand dollars became the basis for Steve Kovac's subsequent fortune. Twenty-five years later, the net worth of Steve Kovac was almost three billion dollars. As an individual, he was possibly the wealthiest man in the United States of America. He was a tycoon in the steel and aluminum industries, and he controlled chemical plants, copper mines, railroads, oil refineries and dozens of associated industries. He was then forty-six years old. The year was 1959.

"The story of his climb to power and wealth is unique for the generations he lived through. He was a strong, powerful, handsome man— tortured within himself, driven by an insatiable lust to avenge himself, and his father and mother too, for the poverty and suffering of his childhood. Given the traumatic factors of his childhood, his craving for power turned psychopathic and paranoid,[3] and he built this structure of power securely in his own hands. He owned newspapers as well as airlines, television stations and publishing houses, and much more than he owned, he controlled. Thereby, he was able to keep himself out of the public eye. In any year of the fifties, you can find no more than an occasional passing reference to him in the press.

"How an individual achieved this in a time of the public corporation and the 'corporation man' is a singular tale of drive and ambition. Steve Kovac was ambitious, ruthless, merciless and utterly without compassion or pity. His policy was to destroy what stood in his way, if he could; if he could not, he bent to his will in one way or another. He wrecked lives and

---

2. **traumatized**\ˈtrau·mə ˈtaizd\ wounded in spirit.
3. **psychopathic**\ˈsai·kə ˈpăth·ĭk\ mentally ill or unstable, **paranoid**\ˈpar·ə ˈnoid\ characterized by suspiciousness, feelings of persecution, and belief in one's superiority to others.

fortunes. He framed and entrapped his competitors; he used violence when he had to—when he could not buy or bribe what he wanted. He corrupted individuals and bribed parliaments and bought governments. He erected a structure of power and wealth and control that reached out to every corner of the globe.

"And then, in his forty-sixth year, at the height of his wealth and power, he discovered that he had cancer."

The Chairman of the Board paused to allow the impact of the words to settle and tell. He took another drink of water. He rearranged the papers in front of him.

"At this time," he said, "I propose to read to you a short extract from the diary of Dr. Jacob Frederick. I think that most of you are familiar with the work of Dr. Frederick. In any case, you know that he was elected a member of our Board. Naturally, that was a long time ago. I need only mention that Dr. Frederick was one of the many wise and patient pioneers in the work of cancer research—not only a great physician, but a great scientist. The first entry I propose to read is dated January 12, 1959."

"I had an unusual visitor today," the Chairman of the Board read, "Steve Kovac, the industrial tycoon. I had heard rumors to the effect of the wealth and power of this man. In himself, he is a striking individual, tall, muscular, handsome with a broad strong face and a great mane of prematurely white hair. He has blue eyes, a ruddy complexion and appears to be in the prime of life and health. Of course, he is not. I examined him thoroughly. There is no hope for the man.

" 'Doctor,' he said to me, 'I want the truth. I know it already. You are not the first physician I have seen. But I also want it from you, plainly and bluntly.'

"I would have told him in any case. He is not the kind of a man you can lie to easily. 'Very well,' I said to him, 'you have cancer. There is no cure for your cancer. You are going to die.'

" 'How long?'

" 'We can't say. Perhaps a year.'

" 'And if I undergo operative procedure?'

" 'That could prolong your life—perhaps a year or two longer if the operation is successful. But it will mean pain and incapacity.'

" 'And there is no cure?' His surface was calm, his voice controlled; he must have labored for years to achieve that kind of surface calm and control; but underneath, I could see a very frightened and desperate man.

" 'None as yet.'

" 'And the quacks and diet men and the rest—they promise cures.'

" 'It's easy to promise,' I said. 'But there isn't any cure.'

" 'Doc,' he said to me, 'I don't want to die and I don't intend to die. I have worked twenty-five years to be where I am now. The tree is planted. I'm going to eat the fruit. I am young and strong—and the best years of my life are ahead of me.'

"When Kovac talked like that, he was convincing, even to me. It is his quality, not simply to demand of life, but to take. He denies the inevitable. But the fact remained.

" 'I can't help you, Mr. Kovac,' I told him.

" 'But you're going to help me,' he said calmly. 'I came to you because you know more about cancer than any man in the world. Or so I am told.'

" 'You have been misinformed,' I said shortly. 'No one man knows more than anyone else. Such knowledge and work is a collective thing.'

" 'I believe in men, not mobs. I believe in you. Therefore, I am ready to pay you a fee of one million dollars if you can make it possible for me to beat this thing and live a full lifespan.' He then reached into his coat for his wallet and took out a certified check for one million dollars. 'It is yours—if I live.'

"I told him to return the following day—that is, tomorrow. And now I have been sitting here for hours, thinking of what one million dollars would mean to my work, my hopes—indeed, through them, to all people. I have been thinking with desperation and with small result. Only one thought occurs to me. It is fantastic, but then Steve Kovac is a fantastic man."

Again, the Chairman of the Board paused and looked inquiringly at some of the younger members. They had been listening with what appeared to be hypnotic concentration. There were no questions and no comments.

"Then I will continue with the diary of Dr. Frederick," the Chairman nodded.

"*January 13.* Steve Kovac returned at 2:00, as we had arranged. He greeted me with a confident smile.

" 'Doc, if you are ready to sell, I am ready to buy.'

" 'And you really believe that you can buy life?'

" 'I can buy anything. It's a question of price.'

" 'Can you buy the future?' I asked him. 'Because that is where the cure for cancer lies. Do you want to buy it?'

" 'I'll buy it because you have decided to sell,' he said flatly. 'I know with whom I am dealing. Make your offer, Dr. Frederick.'

"I made it, as fantastic as it was. I told him about my experiments with the effect of intense cold upon cancer cells. I explained that though, as yet, the experiments had not produced any cure, I had made enormous strides in the intense and speedy application of extreme cold—or, to put it more scientifically, my success in removing heat from living objects. I detailed my experiments—how I had begun with frogs and snakes, freezing them, and then removing the cold and resuming the life process at a later date, how I had experimented with mice, cats, dogs—and most recently, monkeys.

"He followed me and anticipated me. 'How do you restore life?' he wanted to know.

"I don't restore it. The life never dies. In the absence of heat, what might be called the ripening or aging process of life is suspended, but the life remains. Time and motion are closely related; and under intense cold, motion slows and theoretically could cease—all motion, even within the atomic structure. When the motion ceases, time ceases.'

" 'Is it painful?'

" 'As far as I know, it isn't. The transition is too quick.'

" 'I would like to see an experiment myself.'

"I told him that I had in my laboratory a spider monkey that had been frozen seven weeks ago. My assistants could attest to that. He went into the laboratory with me and watched me as we successfully restored the monkey. Seemingly, it was none the worse.

" 'And the mind?' he asked me.

"I shrugged. 'I don't know. I have never attempted it with a human being.'

" 'But you think it would work?'

"I am almost certain that it would work. I would need better and larger equipment. With some money to spend, I can improve the process—well, considerably.'

"He nodded and took the certified check out of his wallet. 'Here is your retainer—apart from what you have to spend. Buy whatever you need, and charge it to me. Spend whatever you have to spend and buy the best. No ceiling, no limit. And when I wake up, after a cure has been discovered, there will be a second million to add to your fee. I am not a generous man, but neither am I niggardly when I buy what I want. When will you be ready, Doctor?'

" 'Considering the prognosis[4] of your disease,' I said, 'we should not delay more than five weeks. I will be ready then. Will you?'

"Steve Kovac nodded. 'I will be ready. There are a good many technical and legal details to work out. I have many and large interests, as you may know, and this is a journey of uncertain duration. I will also take care of your own legal responsibilities.'

---

4. **prognosis**\prŏg ˄nō·səs\ prospect for recovery.

"Then he left, and it was done—possibly the strangest agreement ever entered into by a doctor and his patient. I try to think only of one thing—that I now have a million dollars to put into my work and research."

The Chairman of the Board wore pince-nez,[5] and now he paused to wipe them. He cleared his throat, rearranged the papers on the lectern once again, and explained, "You see, the plan was a simple one and a sensible one, too. Since Mr. Kovac's condition could not be cured, here was a means of preserving his life and arresting the disease until science had found a cure. Timidity was never one of Mr. Kovac's qualities. He analyzed the situation, faced it and accepted the only possible escape offered to him. So he went about placing his affairs in such order as to guarantee the success and prosperity of his enterprises while he slept—and also their return to his bidding and ownership when he awoke.

"In brief, he formed a single holding company for all of his many interests. He gathered together a Board of Directors to manage that holding company in his absence, making himself president in absentia,[6] with a substitute Chairman to preside while he was gone. He made a set of qualifying bylaws, that no Chairman could hold office for more than two years, that the Board was to be enlarged each year and a number of other details, each of them aimed at the single goal of retaining all power for himself. And because he was not dead, but merely absent, he created a unique situation, one unprecedented in all the history of finance.

"This holding company was exempted from all the traditional brakes and tolls placed upon previous companies through the mechanism of death. Until Mr. Kovac returned, the holding company was immortal. Naturally, Dr. Frederick was placed upon the Board of Directors. In other words," the Chairman of the Board concluded, "that is how this Board of Directors came into being."

He allowed himself his first smile then. "Are there any questions at this point?" he asked mildly.

A new member from Japan rose and wanted to know why, if this was the case, the whole world should be taught otherwise?

"We thought it best," said the Chairman. "Just as we, on this Board, have great powers for progress and construction, so do we have no inconsiderable powers of concealment and alternation. The people of the United States and the United Kingdom might have accepted the knowledge that Steve Kovac brought this Board of Directors into being, but certainly in the Soviet Union and China, such knowledge might have been most disconcerting and destructive. Remember that once we had established an open trade area in the Soviet Union and had brought three of her leading government people onto our Board of Directors, our situation changed radically. We were enabled then, through a seizure of all fuel supplies on earth, to prevent the imminent outbreak of World War III.

"At that point, neither the extent of our holdings nor the amount of our profits could be further concealed. I say we," the Chairman deferred modestly, "but of course, it was our predecessors who faced these problems. Our cash balance was larger than that of the United States Treasury, our industrial potential greater than that of any major power. Believe me, without planned intent or purpose, this Board of Directors suddenly found itself the dominant force on earth. At that point, it became desperately necessary for us to explain ourselves, who we were and what we represented."

A new member from Australia rose and asked, "How long was that, Mr. Chairman, if I may inquire, after the visit of Mr. Kovac to Dr. Frederick?"

The Chairman nodded. "It was the year

5. **pince-nez**\pă(n) ▲snā\ eyeglasses pinched to the nose by a spring.
6. **in absentia,** in his absence.

618

Dr. Frederick died—twenty-two years after the treatment began. By then, five types of cancer had already surrendered their secrets to science. But there was not yet any cure for Mr. Kovac's disease."

"And all the time, the treatment had remained secret?"

"All the time," the Chairman nodded.

"You see," he went on, "at that time, the Board felt that the peoples of earth had reached a moment of crisis and decision. A moment, I say, for the power was only momentarily in the hands of this Board. We had no armies, navies or air-fleets—all we had were a major portion of the tools of production. We knew we had not prevented war but simply staved it off. This was a Board of Directors for management, not for power, and any day the installations and plants we owned and controlled could have been torn from our grasp. That was when our very thoughtful and wise predecessors decided to embark on a vast, global propaganda campaign to convince the world that we represented a secret parliament of the wisest and best forces of mankind—that we were in effect a Board of Directors for the complex of mankind.

"And in this we succeeded, for the television stations, the newspapers, the radio networks, the film industry and the theatre—all these were ours. And in that brief, fortunate moment, we launched our attack. We used the weapons of Steve Kovac—let us be honest and admit that. We acted as he would have acted, but out of different motives entirely.

"We bought and bribed and framed. We infiltrated the parliaments of all mankind. We bought the military commanders. We dissolved the armies and navies in the name of super-weapons, and then we destroyed the super-weapons in the name of mankind. Where leaders could not be bought or bribed, we brought them into our Board. And above all, we bought control—control of every manufacturing, farming or mining unit of any consequence upon the face of the earth.

"It took the Board of Directors twenty-nine years more to accomplish this; and at the end of that twenty-nine years, our earth was a single complex of production for use and happiness—and if I may say so, for mankind. A semblance of national structure remained, but it was even then as ritualistic and limited as any commonwealth among the old states of the United States. Wars, armies, navies, atom bombs—all of these were only ugly memories. The era of reason and sanity began, the era of production for use and life under the single legal code of man. Thus, we have become creatures of law, equal under the law, and abiding by the law. This Board of Directors was never a government, nor is it now. It is what it purports to be, a group management for the holding company. Only today, the holding company and the means of mankind are inseparable. Thereby, our very great responsibility, which of course you understand . . . ."

The Chairman of the Board wiped his face and took a few more sips of water. A new member from the United States rose and said, "But, Mr. Chairman, the cure for all types of cancer was discovered sixty-two years ago."

"So it was," the Chairman agreed.

"Then, Steve Kovac—" The new member paused. She was a beautiful, sensitive woman in her middle thirties, a physicist of note and also an accomplished musician.

"You see, my dear," the Chairman said, lapsing into a most informal mode of address, pardonable only because of his years and dignity, "it faced us. When we make a law for mankind and submit to it, we must honor it. Sixty-two years ago, Steve Kovac owned the world and all its wealth and industry, a dictator beyond the dream of any dictator, a tyrant above all tyrants, a king and emperor to dwarf all other kings and emperors—"

As he spoke, two of the older members left the meeting room. Minutes later, they returned, wheeling into the room and up to the podium a rectangular object, five feet high, seven feet long and three feet wide, the whole of it covered with a white cloth. They left it there and returned to their seats.

"—yes, and he owned the world. Think of it—for the first time in history, a just peace governed the nations of mankind. Cities were being rebuilt, deserts turned into gardens, jungles cleared, poverty and crime a thing of the past. Man was standing erect, flexing his muscles, reaching out to the planets and the stars—and all of this belonged to a single savage, merciless, despotic paranoid, Steve

Kovac. Then, as now, my dear associates, this Board of Directors was faced with the problem of the man to whom we owed our existence, the man who all unwittingly unified mankind and ushered in the new age of man —yes, the man who gave us the right and authority to hold and manage, the man whose property we manage. Then as now, we were faced with Steve Kovac!"

Almost theatrical in his conclusion and gestures, the Chairman stepped down from the podium and with one motion swept the cloth aside. The entire Board fixed their eyes on the cabinet where, under a glass cover, in a cold beyond all concept of cold, a man lay sleeping in what was neither life nor death, but a subjective pause[7] in the passage of time. He was a handsome man, big and broad, ruddy of face and with a fine mane of white hair. He seemed to sleep lightly, expectantly, confidently—as if he were dreaming hungrily but pleasantly of what he would awaken to.

"Steve Kovac," the Chairman said. "So he sleeps, from year to year, no difference, no changes. So he appeared to our predecessors sixty-two years ago, when they first had the means to cure him and the obligation to awaken him. They committed the first of sixty-two crimes; they took no action in the face of a promise, a duty, a legality and an almost sacred obligation. Can we understand them? Can we forgive them? Can we forgive the Board of Directors that voted this same decision again and again? Above all, can we forgive ourselves if we stain our honor, break the law, and ignore our own inheritance of an obligation?

"I am not here to argue the question. It is never argued. The facts are presented, and then we vote. Therefore, will all those in favor of awakening Mr. Kovac raise their right hands?"

The Chairman waited. Long moments became minutes, but no hands were raised. The two older members covered the cold, cold box and wheeled it out. The Chairman of the Board took a sip of water and announced, "We will now have the reading of the agenda."

---

I

THE ULTIMATE IRONY—
A MAN'S MASTERPIECE DESTROYS HIM

Steve Kovac, in making his decision to be frozen so that he can await a cure for his particular type of cancer, never dreams that the corporation he created to handle his affairs while he is absent will one day own the world. Nor does he dream that his Board of Directors, having produced a prosperous and peaceful society where men live together in harmony, cannot justify reactivating him, even though legally he owns it all. Thus, Steve Kovac is the victim of the masterpiece he created.

II

IMPLICATIONS

In your opinion, considering both the selection and your experiences, are the following statements right, wrong, or somewhere in between?

**1.** The Board of Directors should have eliminated Steve Kovac long ago, since reactivating him could destroy the new order.

**2.** The Chairman claims that the peoples of the world have now become creatures of law, yet the society had been founded on illegal actions. Ultimately, right cannot exist founded on a wrong.

**3.** The irony in this story is that the peoples of the world are ignorant of Steve Kovac's part in creating the peaceful new order.

III

TECHNIQUES

*Atmosphere*

The atmosphere of the story is one of quiet, matter-of-fact dignity. How does this contrast with the content of the story itself?

*Suspense*

The reader is startled by the opening words of the Chairman, who speaks of Mr. Steve Kovac about whom the world knows nothing. One wonders why. And what is the crime committed against him each year? The Board members are obviously going to vote on the question again. How will the vote go this time? All these questions tease the readers' curiosity and lead them to continue reading in order to find the answers.

When the chairman's final word of explanation is given and the vote called for, what was your reaction? Did you want it to be for restoring the man or for letting him sleep? How then did you react to the Board's vote?

---

7. **subjective pause,** a pause in all mental and sensory functions.

This piece of raw irony under the
Chicago El shows a society doing
what it bitterly condemns others for doing
in the rest of the world.

# Prelude

### ALBERT HALPER

I was coming home from school, carrying
my books by a strap, when I passed Gavin's
poolroom and saw the big guys hanging
around. They were standing in front near the
windows, looking across the street. Gavin's has
a kind of thick window curtain up to eye
level, so all I saw was their heads. The guys
were looking at Mrs. Oliver, who lately has
started to get talked about. Standing in her
window across the street, Mrs. Oliver was
doing her nails. Her nice red hair was hanging
loose down her back. She certainly is a nice-
looking woman. She comes to my father's
newspaper stand on the corner and buys five
or six movie magazines a week, also the afternoon papers. Once she felt me under the chin,
and laughed. My father laughed, too, stamping about in his old worn leather jacket to
keep warm. My old man stamps a lot because
he has leg pains and he's always complaining
about a heavy cold in his head.

When I passed the poolroom one or two
guys came out. "Hey, Ike, how's your good-
looking sister?" they called, but I didn't turn
around. The guys are eighteen or nineteen and
haven't ever had a job in their life. "What they
need is work," my father is always saying
when they bother him too much. "They're not
bad; they get that way because there's nothing
to do," and he tries to explain the meanness

of their ways. But I can't see it like my father.
I hate those fellas and I hope every one of
them dies under a truck. Every time I come
home from school past Lake Street they jab
me, and every time my sister Syl comes along
they say things. So when one of them, Fred
Gooley, calls, "Hey, Ike, how's your sister?"
I don't answer. Besides, Ike isn't my name
anyway. It's Harry.

I passed along the sidewalk, keeping close
to the curb. Someone threw half an apple but
it went over my head. When I went a little
farther someone threw a stone. It hit me in
the back of the leg and stung me but it didn't
hurt much. I kept a little toward the middle
of the sidewalk because I saw a woman coming the other way and I knew they wouldn't
throw.

When I reached the corner under the Elevated two big news trucks were standing with
their motors going, giving my father the latest
editions. The drivers threw the papers onto
the sidewalk with a nice easy roll so the
papers wouldn't get hurt. The papers are
bound with that heavy yellow cord which my
father saves and sells to the junkyard when he
fills up a bag. "All right, Silverstein," a driver
called out. "We'll give you a five-star[1] at six,"
and both trucks drove off.

The drivers are nice fellas and when they
take back the old papers they like to kid my
old man. They say, "Hey, you old banker,
when are you gonna retire?" or, "Let's roll
him, boys, he's got bags of gold in his socks."
Of course they know my old man isn't wealthy
and that the bags in the inside of the newsstand hold only copper pennies. But they like
to kid him and they know he likes it. Sometimes the guys from Gavin's pitch in, but the
truck drivers would flatten them if they ever
got rough with my old man.

I came up to the newsstand and put my
school books inside. "Well, Pa," I said, "you
can go to Florida now." So my Pa went to
"Florida," that is, a chair near the radiator

"Prelude," by Albert Halper: Copyright 1938, 1966 by Albert Halper. Reprinted by permission of the Author. First
published in *Harper's* magazine.

1. **five-star,** a late edition of the newspaper.

that Nick Pappas lets him use in his restaurant. He has to use Nick's place because our own flat is too far away, almost a quarter-mile off.

While my father was in Nick's place another truck came to a stop. They dropped off a big load of early sport editions and yelled, "Hey, there, Harry, how's the old man?" I checked off the papers, yelling back, "He's okay, he's in Nick's." Then the truck drove away and the two helpers waved.

I stood around, putting the papers on the stand and making a few sales. The first ten minutes after coming home from school and taking care of the newsstand always excites me. Maybe it's the traffic. The trucks and cars pound along like anything and of course there's the Elevated right up above you which thunders to beat the band. We have our newsstand right up against a big El post and the stand is a kind of cabin which you enter from the side. But we hardly use it, only in the late morning and around two P.M., when business isn't very rushing. Customers like to see you stand outside over the papers ready for business and not hidden inside where they can't get a look at you at all. Besides, you have to poke your head out and stretch your arm to get the pennies, and kids can swipe magazines from the sides, if you don't watch. So we most always stand outside the newsstand, my father, and me, and my sister. Anyhow, I like it. I like everything about selling papers for my father. The fresh air gets me and I like to talk to customers and see the rush when people are let out from work. And the way the news trucks bring all the new editions so we can see the latest headlines, like a bank got held up on the South Side on Sixty-third Street, or the Cubs are winning their tenth straight and have a good chance to cop the pennant, is exciting.

The only thing I don't like is those guys from Gavin's. But since my father went to the police station to complain they don't come around so often. My father went to the station a month ago and said the gang was bothering

him, and Mr. Fenway, he's the desk sergeant there, said, "Don't worry any more about it, Mr. Silverstein, we'll take care of it. You're a respectable citizen and taxpayer and you're entitled to protection. We'll take care of it." And the next day they sent over a patrolman who stood around almost two hours. The gang from Gavin's saw him and started to go away, but the cop hollered, "Now listen, don't bother this old fella. If you bother him any I'll have to run some of you in."

And then one of the guys recognized that the cop was Butch, Fred Gooley's cousin. "Listen who's talkin'," he yells back. "Hey, Fred, they got your cousin Butch takin' care of the Yid." They said a lot of other things until the cop got mad and started after them. They ran faster than lightning, separating into alleys. The cop came back empty-handed and said to my father, "It'll blow over, Mr. Silverstein; they won't give you any more trouble." Then he went up the street, turning into Steuben's bar.

Well, all this happened three or four weeks ago and so far the gang has let us alone. They stopped pulling my sixteen-year-old sister by her sweater and when they pass the stand going home to supper all they give us is dirty looks. During the last three or four days, however, they passed by and kinda muttered, calling my father a communist banker and me and my sister reds. My father says they really don't mean it, it's the hard times and bad feelings, and they got to put the blame on somebody, so they put the blame on us. It's certain speeches on the radio and the pieces in some of the papers, my father told us. "Something is happening to some of the people and we got to watch our step," he says.

I am standing there hearing the traffic and thinking it over when my little fat old man comes out from Nick's looking like he liked the warm air in Nick's place. My old man's cheeks looked rosy, but his cheeks are that way from high blood pressure and not from good health. "Well, colonel," he says smiling, "I am back on the job." So we stand around, the two of us, taking care of the trade. I hand out change snappy and say thank you after each sale. My old man starts to stamp around in a little while and, though he says nothing, I know he's got pains in his legs again. I look at the weather forecast in all the papers and some of them say flurries of snow and the rest of them say just snow. "Well, Pa," I tell my old man, "maybe I can go skating tomorrow if it gets cold again."

Then I see my sister coming from high school carrying her briefcase and heading this way. Why the heck doesn't she cross over so she won't have to pass the poolroom, I say to myself; why don't she walk on the other side of the street? But that's not like Sylvia; she's a girl with a hot temper, and when she thinks she is right you can't tell her a thing. I knew she wouldn't cross the street and then cross back, because according to her, why, that's giving in. That's telling those hoodlums that you're afraid of their guts. So she doesn't cross over but walks straight on. When she comes by the pool hall two guys come out and say something to her. She just holds herself tight and goes right on past them both. When she finally comes up she gives me a poke in the side. "Hello, you mickey mouse, what mark did you get in your algebra exam?" I told her I got A, but the truth is I got a C.

"I'll check up on you later," she says to me. "Pa, if he's lying to us we'll fine him ten years!"

My father started to smile and said, "No, Harry is a good boy, two years is enough."

So we stand around kidding and pretty soon, because the wind is coming so sharp up the street, my old man has to "go to Florida" for a while once more. He went into Nick's for some "sunshine," he said, but me and Syl could tell he had the pains again. Anyway, when he was gone we didn't say anything for a while. Then Hartman's furniture factory, which lately has been checking out early, let out and we were busy making sales to the men. They came up the sidewalk, a couple of hundred, all anxious to get home, so we had

to work snappy. But Syl is a fast worker, faster than me, and we took care of the rush all right. Then we stood waiting for the next rush from the Hillman's cocoa factory up the block to start.

We were standing around when something hit me in the head, a half of a rotten apple. It hurt a little. I turned quick but didn't see anybody, but Syl started yelling. She was pointing to a big El post across the street behind which a guy was hiding.

"Come on, show your face," my sister was saying. "Come on, you hero, show your yellow face!" But the guy sneaked away, keeping the post between. Syl turned to me and her face was boiling. "The rats! It's not enough with all the trouble over in Europe; they have to start it here."

Just then our old man came out of Nick's and when he saw Syl's face he asked what was the matter.

"Nothing," she says. "Nothing, I'm just thinking."

But my old man saw the half of a rotten apple on the sidewalk, and at first he didn't say anything but I could see he was worried. "We just have to stand it," he said, like he was speaking to himself, "we just have to stand it. If we give up the newsstand where else can we go?"

"Why do we have to stand it?" I exploded, almost yelling. "Why do we—"

But Mrs. Oliver just then came up to the stand, so I had to wait on her. Besides, she's a good customer and there's more profit on two or three magazines than from a dozen papers.

"I'll have a copy of *Film Fan,* a copy of *Breezy Stories,* and a copy of *Movie Stars on Parade,*" she says. I go and reach for the copies.

"Harry is a nice boy," Mrs. Oliver told my father, patting my arm. "I'm very fond of him."

"Yes, he's not bad," my father answered smiling. "Only he has a hot temper once in a while."

But who wouldn't have one, that's what I

wanted to say! Who wouldn't? Here we stand around minding our own business and the guys won't let us alone. I tell you sometimes it almost drives me crazy. We don't hurt anybody and we're trying to make a living, but they're always picking on us and won't let us alone. It's been going on for a couple of years now, and though my old man says it'll pass with the hard times, I know he's worried because he doesn't believe what he says. He reads the papers as soon as he gets them from the delivery trucks and lately the news about Europe is all headlines and I can see that it makes him sick. My old man has a soft heart and every time he sees in the papers that something bad in Europe has happened again he seems to grow older and he stands near the papers kind of small and all alone. I tell you, sometimes it almost drives me crazy. My old man should be down in Florida, where he can get healthy, not in Nick Pappas' "Florida," but down in real Florida where you have to go by train. That's where he should be. Then maybe his legs would be all right and he wouldn't have that funny color in his cheeks. Since our mother died last year it seems the doctor's treatments don't make him any better, and he has to skip a treatment once in a while because he says it costs too much. But when he stands there with a customer chuckling you think he's healthy and hasn't got any worries and you feel maybe he has a couple thousand in the bank.

And another thing, what did he mean when he said something two days ago when the fellas from Gavin's passed by and threw a stone at the stand? What did he mean, that's what I want to know. Gooley had a paper rolled up with some headlines about Europe on it and he wiggled it at us and my father looked scared. When they were gone my father said something to me, which I been thinking and thinking about. My Pa said we got to watch our step extra careful now because there's no other place besides this country where we can go. We've always been picked on, he said, but we're up against the

last wall now, he told me, and we got to be calm because if they start going after us here there's no other place where we can go. I been thinking and thinking about that, especially the part about the wall. When he said that, his voice sounded funny and I felt like our newsstand was a kind of island and if that went we'd be under the waves.

"Harry, what are you thinking of?" Mrs. Oliver asked me. "Don't I get any change?" She was laughing.

And then I came down from the clouds and found she had given me two quarters. I gave her a nickel change. She laughed again. "When he looks moody and kind of sore like that, Mr. Silverstein, I think he's cute."

My old man crinkled up his eyes and smiled. "Who can say, Mrs. Oliver. He should only grow up to be a nice young man and a good citizen and a credit to his country. That's all I want."

"I'm sure Harry will," Mrs. Oliver answered, then talked to Syl a while and admired Syl's new sweater and was about to go away. But another half of a rotten apple came over and splashed against the stand. Some of it splashed against my old man's coat sleeve. Mrs. Oliver turned around and got mad.

"Now you boys leave Mr. Silverstein alone! You've been pestering him long enough! He's a good American citizen who doesn't hurt anybody! You leave him alone!"

"Yah!" yelled Gooley, who ducked behind an El post with two other guys. "Yah! Sez you!"

"You leave him alone!" hollered Mrs. Oliver.

"Aw, go peddle your papers," Gooley answered. "Go run up a rope."

"Don't pay any attention to them," Syl told Mrs. Oliver. "They think they're heroes, but to most people they're just yellow rats."

I could tell by my old man's eyes that he was nervous and wanted to smooth things over, but Syl didn't give him a chance. When she gets started and knows she's in the right not even the Governor of the State could make her keep quiet.

"Don't pay any attention to them," she said in a cutting voice while my old man looked anxious. "When men hide behind Elevated posts and throw rotten apples at women you know they're not men but just things that wear pants. In Europe they put brown shirts on them and call them saviors of civilization. Here they haven't got the shirts yet and hang around poolrooms."

Every word cut like a knife and the guys ducked away. If I or my father would have said it we would have been nailed with some rotten fruit, but the way Syl has of getting back at those guys makes them feel like yellow dogs. I guess that's why they respect her even though they hate her, and I guess that's why Gooley and one or two of his friends are always trying to get next to her and date her up.

Mrs. Oliver took Syl's side and was about to say something more when Hillman's cocoa factory up the block let out and the men started coming up the street. The 4:45 rush was on and we didn't have time for anything, so Mrs. Oliver left, saying she'd be back when the blue-streak edition of the *News* would arrive. Me and Syl were busy handing out the papers and making change and our Pa helped us while the men took their papers and hurried for the El. It started to get darker and colder and the traffic grew heavier along the street.

Then the *Times* truck, which was a little late, roared up and dropped a load we were waiting for. I cut the strings and stacked the papers and when my father came over and read the first page he suddenly looked scared. In his eyes there was that hunted look I had noticed a couple of days ago. I started to look at the first page of the paper while my old man didn't say a word. Nick came to the window and lit his new neon light and waved to us. Then the light started flashing on and off, flashing on the new headlines. It was all about Austria and how people were fleeing toward the borders and trying to get out of the country before it was too late. My old man grew

sick and looked kind of funny and just stood there. Sylvia, who is active in the high-school social science club, began to read the *Times* out loud and started analyzing the news to us; but our Pa didn't need her analysis and kept standing there kind of small with that hunted look on his face. He looked sick all right. It almost drove me crazy.

"For Pete's sake," I yelled at Syl. "Shut up, shut up!"

Then she saw our Pa's face, looked at me, and didn't say anything more.

In a little while it was after five and Syl had to go home and make supper. "I'll be back in an hour," she told me. "Then Pa can go home and rest a bit and me and you can take care of the stand." I said all right.

After she was gone it seemed kind of lonesome. I couldn't stop thinking about what my father had said about this being our last wall. It got me feeling funny and I didn't want to read the papers any more. I stood there feeling queer, like me and my old man were standing on a little island and the waves were coming up. There was still a lot of traffic and a few people came up for papers, but from my old man's face I could tell he felt the same as me.

But pretty soon some more editions began coming and we had to check and stack them up. More men came out from factories on Walnut Street and we were busy making sales. It got colder than ever and my old man began to stamp again. "Go into Nick's, Pa," I told him. "I can handle it out here." But he wouldn't do it because just then another factory let out and we were swamped for a while. "Hi, there, Silverstein," some of the men called to him, "what's the latest news, you king of the press?" They took the papers, kidding him, and hurried up the stairs to the Elevated, reading all about Austria and going home to eat. My father kept staring at the headlines and couldn't take his eyes off the print where it said that soldiers were pouring across the border and mobs were robbing people they hated and spitting on them and making them go down on their hands and knees to scrub the streets. My old man's eyes grew small, like he had the toothache and he shook his head like he was sick. "Pa, go into Nick's," I told him. He just stood there, sick over what he read.

Then the guys from Gavin's poolroom began passing the stand on their way home to supper after a day of just killing time. At first they looked as if they wouldn't bother us. One or two of them said something mean to us, but my old man and me didn't answer. If you don't answer hoodlums, my father once told me, sometimes they let you alone.

But then it started. The guys who passed by came back and one of them said: "Let's have a little fun with the Yids." That's how it began. A couple of them took some magazines from the rack and said they wanted to buy a copy and started reading.

In a flash I realized it was all planned out. My father looked kind of worried but stood quiet. There were about eight or nine of them, all big boys around eighteen and nineteen, and for the first time I got scared. It was just after six o'clock and they had picked a time when the newspaper trucks had delivered the five-star and when all the factories had let out their help and there weren't many people about. Finally one of them smiled at Gooley and said, "Well, this physical culture magazine is mighty instructive, but don't you think we ought to have some of the exercises demonstrated?" Gooley said, "Sure, why not?"

So the first fella pointed to some pictures in the magazine and wanted me to squat on the sidewalk and do the first exercise. I wouldn't do it. My father put his hand on the fella's arm and said, "Please, please." But the guy pushed my father's hand away.

"We're interested in your son, not you. Go on, squat."

"I won't," I told him.

"Go on," he said. "Do the first exercise so that the boys can learn how to keep fit."

"I won't," I said.

"Go on," he said, "do it."

"I won't."

Then he came over to me smiling, but his face looked nasty. "Do it. Do it if you know what's good for you."

"Please, boys," said my Pa. "Please go home and eat and don't make trouble. I don't want to have to call a policeman—"

But before I knew it someone got behind me and tripped me so that I fell on one knee. Then another of them pushed me, trying to make me squat. I shoved someone and then someone hit me, and then I heard someone trying to make them stop. While they held me down on the sidewalk I wiggled and looked up. Mrs. Oliver, who had come for the blue-flash edition, was bawling them out.

"You let him alone! You tramps, you hoodlums, you let him alone!" She came over and tried to help me, but they pushed her away. Then Mrs. Oliver began to yell as two guys twisted my arm and told me to squat.

By this time a few people were passing and Mrs. Oliver called at them to interfere. But the gang were big fellows and there were eight or nine of them, and the people were afraid.

Then while they had me down on the sidewalk Syl came running up the street. When she saw what was happening she began kicking them and yelling and trying to make them let me up. But they didn't pay any attention to her.

"Please," my Pa kept saying. "Please let him up; he didn't hurt you. I don't want to have to call the police—"

Then Syl turned to the people who were watching and yelled at them. "Why don't you help us? What are you standing there for?" But none of them moved. Then Syl began to scream:

"Listen, why don't you help us? Why don't you make them stop picking on us? We're human beings the same as you!"

But the people just stood there afraid to do a thing. Then while a few guys held me, Gooley and about four others went for the stand, turning it over and mussing and stamping on all the newspapers they could find. Syl started to scratch them, so they hit her, then

I broke away to help her, and then they started socking me too. My father tried to reach me, but three guys kept him away. Four guys got me down and started kicking me and all the time my father was begging them to let me up and Syl was screaming at the people to help. And while I was down, my face was squeezed against some papers on the sidewalk telling about Austria and I guess I went nuts while they kept hitting me, and I kept seeing the headlines against my nose.

Then someone yelled, "Jiggers, the cops!" and they got off of me right away. Nick had looked out the window and had called the station, and the guys let me up and beat it away fast.

But when the cops came it was too late; the stand was a wreck. The newspapers and magazines were all over the sidewalk and the rack that holds the *Argosy* and *Western Aces* was all twisted up. My Pa, who looked sicker than ever, stood there crying and pretty soon I began to bawl. People were standing looking at us like we were some kind of fish, and I just couldn't help it, I started to bawl.

Then the cops came through the crowd and began asking questions right and left. In the end they wanted to take us to the station to enter a complaint, but Syl wouldn't go. She looked at the crowd watching and she said, "What's the use? All those people standing around and none of them would help!" They were standing all the way to the second El post, and when the cops asked for witnesses none of them except Mrs. Oliver offered to give their names. Then Syl looked at Pa and me and saw our faces and turned to the crowd and began to scream.

"In another few years, you wait! Some of you are working people and they'll be marching through the streets and going after you too! They pick on us Jews because we're weak and haven't any country; but after they get us down they'll go after you! And it'll be your fault; you're all cowards, you're afraid to fight back!"

"Listen," one of the cops told my sister, "are you coming to the station or not? We can't hang around here all evening."

Then Syl broke down and began to bawl as hard as me. "Oh, leave us alone," she told them and began wailing her heart out. "Leave us alone. What good would it do?"

By this time the crowd was bigger, so the cops started telling people to break it up and move on. Nick came out and took my father by the arm into the lunchroom for a drink of hot tea. The people went away slowly and then, as the crowd began to dwindle, it started to snow. When she saw that, Syl started bawling harder than ever and turned her face to me. But I was down on my hands and knees with Mrs. Oliver, trying to save some of the magazines. There was no use going after the newspapers, which were smeared up, torn, and dirty from the gang's feet. But I thought I could save a few, so I picked a couple of them up.

"Oh, leave them be," Syl wept at me. "Leave them be, leave them be!"

---

### I

THE IRONY OF FRANTIC DESPERATION

Syl and Harry, born and brought up in the United States, are confident that the persecution of the Jews taking place in Nazi Germany can never happen in America. Mr. Silverstein's long experience has not offered him much hope, yet he continues to feel that the United States is the last country open to Jews. They approach the tormenting poolroom gang in their own ways: Syl defies them; Harry avoids them; Mr. Silverstein treats them as mischievous boys. When the gang attacks, life underlines the irony for all three family members, for none of their attitudes produce the hoped-for result. As their livelihood is destroyed, people stand around and stare; the only person who attempts to help is a woman little respected in the neighborhood.

### II

IMPLICATIONS

Following are a group of quotations from the story. Consider the persons who are speaking.

What do their words say about them? How would you feel and talk in similar situations? Is there an ironic element in the remark?

**1.** "What they need is work . . . . They're [the gang] not bad; they get that way because there's nothing to do." (Mr. Silverstein)

**2.** "I knew she [Sylvia] wouldn't cross the street and then cross back, because according to her, why, that's giving in. That's telling those hoodlums that you're afraid of their guts." (Harry)

**3.** "We've always been picked on, he said, but we're up against the last wall now, he told me, and we got to be calm because if they start going after us here there's no other place where we can go." (Mr. Silverstein)

**4.** " 'We just have to stand it,' he said . . . 'we just have to stand it.' " " 'Why do we have to stand it?' I exploded." (Harry)

**5.** "Don't pay any attention to them," Syl [said]. "They think they're heroes, but to most people they're just yellow rats." (Sylvia)

**6.** ". . . Why don't you help us? Why don't you make them stop picking on us? We're human beings the same as you!" (Sylvia)

**7.** "Oh, leave us alone [to the police] . . . . Leave us alone. What good would it do?" (Sylvia)

### III
### TECHNIQUES

*Atmosphere*

The mood of this selection is one of desperation and despair. What details of setting contribute to the dark, dreary atmosphere?

*Suspense*

What are the brief actions before the final confrontation between the boys and the Silversteins?

Did the boys' attack come as a surprise or did you expect it? How did this add to the suspense?

After five years of rebellion against England, Ireland was offered dominion status. De Valera's Republicans refused to sign the treaty, holding out for complete independence. But other Sinn Fein leaders did sign, and the Irish Free State became official in 1922, setting off guerrilla warfare between the dissident Republicans and the Free Staters. The next story is set in the Ireland of the 1920s when civil war enveloped the small country.

# The Sniper

### LIAM O'FLAHERTY

The long June twilight faded into night. Dublin lay enveloped in darkness, but for the dim light of the moon, that shone through fleecy clouds, casting a pale light as of approaching dawn over the streets and the dark waters of the Liffey. Around the beleaguered Four Courts the heavy guns roared. Here and there through the city, machine guns and rifles broke the silence of the night, spasmodically, like dogs barking on lone farms. Republicans and Free Staters were waging civil war.

On a roof-top near O'Connell Bridge, a Republican sniper lay watching. Beside him lay his rifle and over his shoulders were slung a pair of field-glasses. His face was the face of a student—thin and ascetic,[1] but his eyes had the cold gleam of the fanatic. They were deep and thoughtful, the eyes of a man who is used to looking at death.

He was eating a sandwich hungrily. He had eaten nothing since morning. He had been

---

1. **ascetic**\ə ▲sĕt•ĭk\ as if practicing strict self-denial.

---

From SPRING SOWING by Liam O'Flaherty. Reprinted by permission of Harcourt Brace Jovanovich, Inc.

too excited to eat. He finished the sandwich, and taking a flask of whiskey from his pocket, he took a short draught.[2] Then he returned the flask to his pocket. He paused for a moment, considering whether he should risk a smoke. It was dangerous. The flash might be seen in the darkness and there were enemies watching. He decided to take the risk. Placing a cigarette between his lips, he struck a match, inhaled the smoke hurriedly and put out the light. Almost immediately, a bullet flattened itself against the parapet of the roof. The sniper took another whiff and put out the cigarette. Then he swore softly and crawled away to the left.

Cautiously he raised himself and peered over the parapet. There was a flash and a bullet whizzed over his head. He dropped immediately. He had seen the flash. It came from the opposite side of the street.

He rolled over the roof to a chimney stack in the rear, and slowly drew himself up behind it, until his eyes were level with the top of the parapet. There was nothing to be seen —just the dim outline of the opposite house-top against the blue sky. His enemy was under cover.

Just then an armoured car came across the bridge and advanced slowly up the street. It stopped on the opposite side of the street fifty yards ahead. The sniper could hear the dull panting of the motor. His heart beat faster. It was an enemy car. He wanted to fire, but he knew it was useless. His bullets would never pierce the steel that covered the grey monster.

Then round the corner of a side street came an old woman, her head covered by a tattered shawl. She began to talk to the man in the turret of the car. She was pointing to the roof where the sniper lay. An informer.

The turret opened. A man's head and shoulders appeared, looking towards the sniper. The sniper raised his rifle and fired. The head fell heavily on the turret wall. The woman darted toward the side street. The sniper fired again. The woman whirled round and fell with a shriek into the gutter.

Suddenly from the opposite roof a shot rang out and the sniper dropped his rifle with a curse. The rifle clattered to the roof. The sniper thought the noise would wake the dead. He stopped to pick the rifle up. He couldn't lift it. His fore-arm was dead.

Dropping flat on to the roof, he crawled back to the parapet. With his left hand he felt the injured right fore-arm. The blood was oozing through the sleeve of his coat. There was no pain—just a deadened sensation, as if the arm had been cut off.

Quickly he drew his knife from his pocket, opened it on the breastwork of the parapet and ripped open the sleeve. There was a small hole where the bullet had entered. On the other side there was no hole. The bullet had lodged in the bone. It must have fractured it. He bent the arm below the wound. The arm bent back easily. He ground his teeth to overcome the pain.

Then, taking out his field dressing, he ripped open the packet with his knife. He broke the neck of the iodine bottle and let the bitter fluid drip into the wound. A paroxysm of pain swept through him. He placed the cotton wadding over the wound and wrapped the dressing over it. He tied the end with his teeth.

Then he lay still against the parapet, and closing his eyes, he made an effort of will to overcome the pain.

In the street beneath all was still. The armoured car had retired speedily over the bridge, with the machine gunner's head hanging lifeless over the turret. The woman's corpse lay still in the gutter.

The sniper lay for a long time nursing his wounded arm and planning escape. Morning must not find him wounded on the roof. The enemy on the opposite roof covered his escape. He must kill that enemy and he could not use his rifle. He had only a revolver to do it. Then he thought of a plan.

Taking off his cap, he placed it over the muzzle of his rifle. Then he pushed the rifle

2. **draught**\dråft\ British spelling of draft.

slowly upwards over the parapet, until the cap was visible from the opposite side of the street. Almost immediately there was a report, and a bullet pierced the centre of the cap. The sniper slanted the rifle forward. The cap slipped down into the street. Then, catching the rifle in the middle, the sniper dropped his left hand over the roof and let it hang, lifelessly. After a few moments he let the rifle drop to the street. Then he sank to the roof, dragging his hand with him.

Crawling quickly to the left, he peered up at the corner of the roof. His ruse had succeeded. The other sniper, seeing the cap and rifle fall, thought that he had killed his man. He was now standing before a row of chimney pots, looking across, with his head clearly silhouetted against the western sky.

The Republican sniper smiled and lifted his revolver above the edge of the parapet. The distance was about fifty yards—a hard shot in the dim light, and his right arm was paining him like a thousand devils. He took a steady aim. His hand trembled with eagerness. Pressing his lips together, he took a deep breath through his nostrils and fired. He was almost deafened with the report and his arm shook with the recoil.

Then, when the smoke cleared, he peered across and uttered a cry of joy. His enemy had been hit. He was reeling over the parapet in his death agony. He struggled to keep his feet, but he was slowly falling forward, as if in a dream. The rifle fell from his grasp, hit the parapet, fell over, bounded off the pole of a barber's shop beneath and then cluttered on to the pavement.

Then the dying man on the roof crumpled up and fell forward. The body turned over and over in space and hit the ground with a dull thud. Then it lay still.

The sniper looked at his enemy falling and he shuddered. The lust of battle died in him. He became bitten by remorse. The sweat stood out in beads on his forehead. Weakened by his wound and the long summer day of fasting and watching on the roof, he revolted from the sight of the shattered mass of his dead enemy. His teeth chattered. He began to gibber to himself, cursing the war, cursing himself, cursing everybody.

He looked at the smoking revolver in his hand and with an oath he hurled it to the roof at his feet. The revolver went off with the concussion, and the bullet whizzed past the sniper's head. He was frightened back to his senses by the shock. His nerves steadied. The cloud of fear scattered from his mind and he laughed.

Taking the whiskey flask from his pocket, he emptied it at a draught. He felt reckless under the influence of the spirits. He decided to leave the roof and look for his company commander to report. Everywhere around was quiet. There was not much danger in going through the streets. He picked up his revolver and put it in his pocket. Then he crawled down through the sky-light to the house underneath.

When the sniper reached the laneway on the street level, he felt a sudden curiosity as to the identity of the enemy sniper whom he had killed. He decided that he was a good shot whoever he was. He wondered if he knew him. Perhaps he had been in his own company before the split in the army. He decided to risk going over to have a look at him. He peered around the corner into O'Connell Street. In the upper part of the street there was heavy firing, but around here all was quiet.

The sniper darted across the street. A machine gun tore up the ground around him with a hail of bullets, but he escaped. He threw himself face downwards beside the corpse. The machine gun stopped.

Then the sniper turned over the dead body and looked into his brother's face.

## TRAGIC IRONY

The two opponents are evenly matched, but the writer centers his attention on the one he calls "the sniper." The man's calculating brutality is vividly demonstrated by his almost mechanical killing of the gunner in the armored car and the old woman informer. After the sniper is wounded, the duel between him and his opponent is intensified. To survive, the wounded man executes a plan which deceives his enemy, whom he kills. Only then does the sniper feel remorse. But how much deeper must this remorse be when he turns over the body of the dead man and sees his brother's face. Again, Fate gives a tragic ironic twist to an encounter.

## II

### IMPLICATIONS

What is your reaction to the following statements? Use the selection and your own experiences to form your opinion.

**1.** If both snipers had known who their enemy was, they could not have shot at each other.

**2.** It is worse to kill one's brother than to kill an unknown person.

**3.** In this story, people are only enemies to be slain.

## III

### TECHNIQUES

*Atmosphere*

Reread the first three paragraphs. What kind of sentences are used: simple or complex? long or short? direct or involved? What atmosphere or expectancy is created by these sentence patterns?

*Suspense*

There are five vivid actions described in the story. How does each add to the story's suspense?

## IV

### WORDS

**A.** Some words sound very much like the sounds they name. The bullet that "whizzed" over the sniper's head made a hissing sound. When you say the word *whizzed,* you can hear a similar sound. Another word that imitates the sound it names is *thud.* The pronunciation of this word comes fairly close to the dull, heavy sound to which it refers. No doubt, this sound is permanently etched in the sniper's mind, for his brother's body "hit the ground with a thud." Words such as *whizzed* and *thud* are called *onomatopoetic* words. Other words in this category are: *buzz, rattle, crunch, meow, hiss, crackle, roar, clank, zoom,* and *crack.* Can you think of others?

**B.** At one point in the story, the sniper "struck a match, inhaled the smoke hurriedly and *put out* the light." At another point, having dropped it a few minutes earlier, he "stopped to *pick* the rifle *up.*" In the two quotations just given, the words *put* and *out* as well as *pick* and *up* are so closely related that they function as one word. In other words, they form a verb-adverb combination that serves the same purpose as a single verb. *Put out* means "to extinguish," and *pick up* means "to lift." The use of *out* or *up* with a verb does not always result in a verb-adverb unit, however. For example, in the sentence "John put out the cat," the word *out* functions in its normal way, telling the reader where John put the cat. By contrast, *out* in the first quotation above does not tell where the light is. Two-word verbs like *put out* and *pick up* abound in English; for example, *check up, fill in, set up, slow down,* and *hand out.* Can you add others? Here are some to get you started: *pick up, speed up,* and *check out.*

When leaving home, there is comfort
in having a round-trip ticket.
It is a "security blanket."
But tickets become outdated.
When, in the course of life, do we arrive
at a similar point of no return?
Do we fool ourselves
about our freedom to choose?

# Louisa, Please Come Home

### SHIRLEY JACKSON

"Louisa," my mother's voice came over
the radio; it frightened me badly for a minute.
"Louisa," she said, "please come home. It's
been three long years since we saw you last;
Louisa, I promise you that everything will be
all right. We all miss you so. We want you
back again. Louisa, please come home."

Once a year. On the anniversary of the day
I ran away. Each time I heard it I was
frightened again, because between one year
and the next I would forget what my mother's
voice sounded like, so soft and yet strange
with that pleading note. I listened every year.
I read the stories in the newspapers—"Louisa
Tether vanished one year ago"—or two years
ago, or three; I used to wait for the twentieth
of June as though it were my birthday. I kept
all the clippings at first, but secretly; with my
picture on all the front pages I would have
looked kind of strange if anyone had seen me

From *Come Along with Me* by Shirley Jackson. Copyright ©
1960 by Shirley Jackson. Reprinted by permission of the
Viking Press.

cutting it out. Chandler, where I was hiding,
was close enough to my old home so that the
papers made a big fuss about all of it, but of
course the reason I picked Chandler in the
first place was because it was a big enough
city for me to hide in.

I didn't just up and leave on the spur of
the moment, you know. I always knew that I
was going to run away sooner or later, and I
had made plans ahead of time, for whenever
I decided to go. Everything had to go right
the first time, because they don't usually give
you a second chance on that kind of thing and
anyway if it had gone wrong I would have
looked like an awful fool, and my sister Carol
was never one for letting people forget it
when they made fools of themselves. I admit
I planned it for the day before Carol's wedding on purpose, and for a long time afterward I used to try and imagine Carol's face
when she finally realized that my running
away was going to leave her one bridesmaid
short. The papers said that the wedding went
ahead as scheduled, though, and Carol told
one newspaper reporter that her sister Louisa
would have wanted it that way; "She would
never have meant to spoil my wedding," Carol
said, knowing perfectly well that that would
be exactly what I'd meant. I'm pretty sure that
the first thing Carol did when they knew I
was missing was go and count the wedding
presents to see what I'd taken with me.

Anyway, Carol's wedding may have been
fouled up, but *my* plans went fine—better, as
a matter of fact, than I had ever expected.
Everyone was hurrying around the house putting up flowers and asking each other if the
wedding gown had been delivered, and opening up cases of champagne and wondering
what they were going to do if it rained and
they couldn't use the garden, and I just closed
the front door behind me and started off.
There was only one bad minute when Paul
saw me; Paul has always lived next door and
Carol hates him worse than she does me. My
mother always used to say that every time I

did something to make the family ashamed of me Paul was sure to be in it somewhere. For a long time they thought he had someto do with my running away, even though he told over and over again how hard I tried to duck away from him that afternoon when he met me going down the driveway. The papers kept calling him "a close friend of the family," which must have overjoyed my mother, and saying that he was being questioned about possible clues to my whereabouts. Of course he never even knew that I was running away; I told him just what I told my mother before I left—that I was going to get away from all the confusion and excitement for a while; I was going downtown and would probably have a sandwich somewhere for supper and go to a movie. He bothered me for a minute there, because of course he wanted to come too. I hadn't meant to take the bus right there on the corner but with Paul tagging after me and wanting me to wait while he got the car so we could drive out and have dinner at the Inn, I had to get away fast on the first thing that came along, so I just ran for the bus and left Paul standing there; that was the only part of my plan I had to change.

I took the bus all the way downtown, although my first plan had been to walk. It turned out much better, actually, since it didn't matter at all if anyone saw me on the bus going downtown in my own home town, and I managed to get an earlier train out. I bought a round-trip ticket; that was important, because it would make them think I was coming back; that was always the way they thought about things. If you did something you had to have a reason for it, because my mother and my father and Carol never did anything unless *they* had a reason for it, so if I bought a round-trip ticket the only possible reason would be that I was coming back. Besides, if they thought I was coming back they would not be frightened so quickly and I might have more time to hide before they came looking for me. As it happened, Carol found out I was gone that same night when she couldn't sleep and came into my room for some aspirin, so all the time I had less of a head start than I thought.

I knew that they would find out about my buying the ticket; I was not silly enough to suppose that I could steal off and not leave any traces. All my plans were based on the fact that the people who get caught are the ones who attract attention by doing something strange or noticeable, and what I intended all along was to fade into some background where they would never see me. I knew they would find out about the round-trip ticket, because it was an odd thing to do in a town where you've lived all your life, but it was the last unusual thing I did. I thought when I bought it that knowing about that round-trip ticket would be some consolation to my mother and father. They would know that no matter how long I stayed away at least I always had a ticket home. I did keep the return-trip ticket quite a while, as a matter of fact. I used to carry it in my wallet as a kind of lucky charm.

I followed everything in the papers. Mrs. Peacock and I used to read them at the breakfast table over our second cup of coffee before I went off to work.

"What do you think about this girl disappeared over in Rockville?" Mrs. Peacock would say to me, and I'd shake my head sorrowfully and say that a girl must be really crazy to leave a handsome, luxurious home like that, or that I had kind of a notion that maybe she didn't leave at all—maybe the family had her locked up somewhere because she was a homicidal maniac. Mrs. Peacock always loved anything about homicidal maniacs.

Once I picked up the paper and looked hard at the picture. "Do you think she looks something like me?" I asked Mrs. Peacock, and Mrs. Peacock leaned back and looked at me and then at the picture and then at me again and finally shook her head and said, "No. If you wore your hair longer, and curlier, and your face was maybe a little fuller, there

might be a little resemblance, but then if you looked like a homicidal maniac I wouldn't ever of let you in my house."

"I think she kind of looks like me," I said.

"You get along to work and stop being vain," Mrs. Peacock told me.

Of course when I got on the train with my round-trip ticket I had no idea how soon they'd be following me, and I suppose it was just as well, because it might have made me nervous and I might have done something wrong and spoiled everything. I knew that as soon as they gave up the notion that I was coming back to Rockville with my round-trip ticket they would think of Crain, which is the largest city that train went to, so I only stayed in Crain part of one day. I went to a big department store where they were having a store-wide sale; I figured that would land me in a crowd of shoppers and I was right; for a while there was a good chance that I'd never get any farther away from home than the ground floor of that department store in Crain. I had to fight my way through the crowd until I found the counter where they were having a sale of raincoats, and then I had to push and elbow down the counter and finally grab the raincoat I wanted right out of the hands of some old monster who couldn't have used it anyway because she was much too fat. You would have thought she had already paid for it, the way she howled. I was smart enough to have the exact change, all six dollars and eighty-nine cents, right in my hand, and I gave it to the salesgirl, grabbed the raincoat and the bag she wanted to put it in, and fought my way out again before I got crushed to death.

That raincoat was worth every cent of the six dollars and eighty-nine cents; I wore it right through until winter that year and not even a button ever came off it. I finally lost it the next spring when I left it somewhere and never got it back. It was tan, and the minute I put it on in the ladies' room of the store I began thinking of it as my "old" raincoat; that was good. I had never before owned a raincoat like that and my mother would have fainted dead away. One thing I did that I thought was kind of clever. I had left home wearing a light short coat; almost a jacket, and when I put on the raincoat of course I took off my light coat. Then all I had to do was empty the pockets of the light coat into the raincoat and carry the light coat casually over to a counter where they were having a sale of jackets and drop it on the counter as though I'd taken it off a little way to look at it and had decided against it. As far as I ever knew no one paid the slightest attention to me, and before I left the counter I saw a woman pick up my jacket and look it over; I could have told her she was getting a bargain for three ninety-eight.

It made me feel good to know that I had gotten rid of the light coat. My mother picked it out for me and even though I liked it and it was expensive it was also recognizable and I had to change it somehow. I was sure that if I put it in a bag and dropped it into a river or into a garbage truck or something like that sooner or later it would be found and even if no one saw me doing it, it would almost certainly be found, and then they would know I had changed my clothes in Crain.

That light coat never turned up. The last they ever found of me was someone in Rockville who caught a glimpse of me in the train station in Crain, and she recognized me by the light coat. They never found out where I went after that; it was partly luck and partly my clever planning. Two or three days later the papers were still reporting that I was in Crain; people thought they saw me on the streets and one girl who went into a store to buy a dress was picked up by the police and held until she could get someone to identify her. They were really looking, but they were looking for Louisa Tether, and I had stopped being Louisa Tether the minute I got rid of that light coat my mother bought me.

One thing I was relying on: there must be

thousands of girls in the country on any given day who are nineteen years old, fair-haired, five feet four inches tall, and weighing one hundred and twenty-six pounds. And if there are thousands of girls like that, there must be, among those thousands, a good number who are wearing shapeless tan raincoats; I started counting tan raincoats in Crain after I left the department store and I passed four in one block, so I felt well hidden. After that I made myself even more invisible by doing just what I told my mother I was going to—I stopped in and had a sandwich in a little coffee shop, and then I went to a movie. I wasn't in any hurry at all, and rather than try to find a place to sleep that night I thought I would sleep on the train.

It's funny how no one pays any attention to you at all. There were hundreds of people who saw me that day, and even a sailor who tried to pick me up in the movie, and yet no one one really *saw* me. If I had tried to check into a hotel the desk clerk might have noticed me, if I had tried to get dinner in some fancy restaurant in that cheap raincoat I would have been conspicuous, but I was doing what any other girl looking like me and dressed like me might be doing that day. The only person who might be apt to remember me would be the man selling tickets in the railroad station, because girls looking like me in old raincoats didn't buy train tickets, usually, at eleven at night, but I had thought of that, too, of course; I bought a ticket to Amityville, sixty miles away, and what made Amityville a perfectly reasonable disguise is that at Amityville there is a college, not a little fancy place like the one I had left so recently with nobody's blessing, but a big sprawling friendly affair, where my raincoat would look perfectly at home. I told myself I was a student coming back to the college after a weekend at home. We got to Amityville after midnight, but it still didn't look odd when I left the train and went into the station, because while I was in the station, having a cup of coffee and killing time, seven other girls—I counted—wearing raincoats like mine came in or went out, not seeming to think it the least bit odd to be getting on or off trains at that hour of the night. Some of them had suitcases, and I wished that I had had some way of getting a suitcase in Crain, but it would have made me noticeable in the movie, and college girls going home for weekends often don't bother; they have pajamas and an extra pair of stockings at home, and they drop a toothbrush into one of the pockets of those invaluable raincoats. So I didn't worry about the suitcase then, although I knew I would need one soon. While I was having my coffee I made my own mind change from the idea that I was a college girl coming back after a weekend at home to the idea that I was a college girl who was on her way home for a few days; all the time I tried to think as much as possible like what I was pretending to be, and after all, I *had* been a college girl for a while. I was thinking that even now the letter was in the mail, traveling as fast as the U.S. Government could make it go, right to my father to tell him why I wasn't a college student any more; I suppose that was what finally decided me to run away, the thought of what my father would think and say and do when he got that letter from the college.

That was in the paper, too. They decided that the college business was the reason for my running away, but if that had been all, I don't think I would have left. No, I had been wanting to leave for so long, ever since I can remember, making plans till I was sure they were foolproof, and that's the way they turned out to be.

Sitting there in the station at Amityville, I tried to think myself into a good reason why I was leaving college to go home on a Monday night late, when I would hardly be going home for the weekend. As I say, I always tried to think as hard as I could the way that suited whatever I wanted to be, and I liked to have a good reason for what I was doing. Nobody ever asked me, but it was good to know that I could answer them if they did. I finally decided that my sister was getting married the next day and I was going home at the beginning of the week to be one of her bridesmaids. I thought that was funny. I didn't want to be going home for any sad or frightening reason, like my mother being sick, or my father being hurt in a car accident, because I would have to look sad, and that might attract attention. So I was going home for my sister's wedding. I wandered around the station as though I had nothing to do, and just happened to pass the door when another girl was going out; she had on a raincoat just like mine and anyone who happened to notice would have thought that it was me who went out. Before I bought my ticket I went into the ladies' room and got another twenty dollars out of my shoe. I had nearly three hundred dollars left of the money I had taken from my father's desk and I had most of it in my shoes because I honestly couldn't think of another safe place to carry it. All I kept in my pocketbook was just enough for whatever I had to spend next. It's uncomfortable walking around all day on a wad of bills in your shoe, but they were good solid shoes, the kind of comfortable old shoes you wear whenever you don't really care how you look, and I had put new shoelaces in them before I left home so I could tie them good and tight. You can see, I planned pretty carefully, and no little detail got left out. If they had let me plan my sister's wedding there would have been a lot less of that running around and screaming and hysterics.

I bought a ticket to Chandler, which is the biggest city in this part of the state, and the place I'd been heading for all along. It was a good place to hide because people from Rockville tended to bypass it unless they had some special reason for going there—if they couldn't find the doctors or orthodontists or psychoanalysts or dress material they wanted in Rockville or Crain, they went directly to one of the really big cities, like the state

capital; Chandler was big enough to hide in, but not big enough to look like a metropolis to people from Rockville. The ticket seller in the Amityville station must have seen a good many college girls buying tickets for Chandler at all hours of the day or night because he took my money and shoved the ticket at me without even looking up.

Funny. They must have come looking for me in Chandler at some time or other, because it's not likely they would have neglected any possible place I might be, but maybe Rockville people never seriously believed anyone would go to Chandler from choice, because I never felt for a minute that anyone was looking for me there. My picture was in the Chandler papers, of course, but as far as I ever knew no one ever looked at me twice, and I got up every morning and went to work and went shopping in the stores and went to movies with Mrs. Peacock and went out to the beach all that summer without ever being afraid of being recognized. I behaved just like everyone else, and dressed just like everyone else, and even *thought* just like everyone else, and the only person I ever saw from Rockville in three years was a friend of my mother's, and I knew *she* only came to Chandler to get her poodle bred at the kennels there. She didn't look as if she was in a state to recognize anybody but another poodle-fancier, anyway, and all I had to do was step into a doorway as she went by, and she never looked at me.

Two other college girls got on the train to Chandler when I did; maybe both of them were going home for their sisters' weddings. Neither of them was wearing a tan raincoat, but one of them had on an old blue jacket that gave the same general effect. I fell asleep as soon as the train started, and once I woke up and for a minute I wondered where I was and then I realized that I was doing it, I was actually carrying out my careful plan and had gotten better than halfway with it, and I almost laughed, there in the train with everyone asleep around me. Then I went back to sleep and didn't wake up until we got into Chandler about seven in the morning.

So there I was. I had left home just after lunch the day before, and now at seven in the morning of my sister's wedding day I was so far away, in every sense, that I *knew* they would never find me. I had all day to get myself settled in Chandler, so I started off by having breakfast in a restaurant near the station, and then went off to find a place to live, and a job. The first thing I did was buy a suitcase, and it's funny how people don't really notice you if you're buying a suitcase near a railroad station. Suitcases look *natural* near railroad stations, and I picked out one of those stores that sell a little bit of everything, and bought a cheap suitcase and a pair of stockings and some handkerchiefs and a little traveling clock, and I put everything into the suitcase and carried that. Nothing is hard to do unless you get upset or excited about it.

Later on, when Mrs. Peacock and I used to read in the papers about my disappearing, I asked her once if she thought that Louisa Tether had gotten as far as Chandler and she didn't.

"They're saying now she was kidnapped," Mrs. Peacock told me, "and that's what *I* think happened. Kidnapped, and murdered, and they do *terrible* things to young girls they kidnap."

"But the papers say there wasn't any ransom note."

"That's what they *say*." Mrs. Peacock shook her head at me. "How do we know what the family is keeping secret? Or if she was kidnapped by a homicidal maniac, why should *he* send a ransom note? Young girls like you don't know a lot of the things that go on. *I* can tell you."

"I feel kind of sorry for the girl," I said.

"You can't ever tell," Mrs. Peacock said. "Maybe she went with him willingly."

I didn't know, that first morning in Chand-

ler, that Mrs. Peacock was going to turn up that first day, the luckiest thing that ever happened to me. I decided while I was having breakfast that I was going to be a nineteen-year-old from upstate with a nice family and good background who had been saving money to come to Chandler and take a secretarial course in the business school there. I was going to have to find some kind of a job to keep on earning money while I went to school; courses at the business school wouldn't start until fall, so I would have the summer to work and save money and decide if I really wanted to take secretarial training. If I decided not to stay in Chandler I could easily go somewhere else after the fuss about my running away had died down. The raincoat looked wrong for the kind of conscientious young girl I was going to be, so I took it off and carried it over my arm. I think I did a pretty good job on my clothes, altogether. Before I left home I decided that I would have to wear a suit, as quiet and unobtrusive as I could find, and I picked out a gray suit, with a white blouse, so with just one or two small changes like a different blouse or some kind of a pin on the lapel, I could look like whoever I decided to be. Now the suit looked absolutely right for a young girl planning to take a secretarial course, and I looked like a thousand other people when I walked down the street carrying my suitcase and my raincoat over my arm; people get off trains every minute looking just like that. I bought a morning paper and stopped in a drugstore for a cup of coffee and a look to see the rooms for rent. It was all so usual—suitcase, coat, rooms for rent—that when I asked the soda clerk how to get to Primrose Street he never even looked at me. He certainly didn't care whether I ever got to Primrose Street or not, but he told me very politely where it was and what bus to take. I didn't really need to take the bus for economy, but it would have looked funny for a girl who was saving money to arrive in a taxi.

"I'll never forget how you looked that first morning," Mrs. Peacock told me once, much later. "I knew right away you were the kind of girl I like to rent rooms to—quiet, and well-mannered. But you looked almighty scared of the big city."

"I wasn't scared," I said. "I was worried about finding a nice room. My mother told me so many things to be careful about I was afraid I'd never find anything to suit her."

"*Any*body's mother could come into my house at any time and know that her daughter was in good hands," Mrs. Peacock said, a little huffy.

But it was true. When I walked into Mrs. Peacock's rooming house on Primrose Street, and met Mrs. Peacock, I knew that I couldn't have done this part better if I'd been able to plan it. The house was old, and comfortable, and my room was nice, and Mrs. Peacock and I hit it off right away. She was very pleased with me when she heard that my mother had told me to be sure the room I found was clean and that the neighborhood was good, with no chance of rowdies following a girl if she came home after dark, and she was even more pleased when she heard that I wanted to save money and take a secretarial course so I could get a really good job and earn enough to be able to send a little home every week; Mrs. Peacock believed that children owed it to their parents to pay back some of what had been spent on them while they were growing up. By the time I had been in the house an hour Mrs. Peacock knew all about my imaginary family upstate: my mother, who was a widow, and my sister, who had just gotten married and still lived at my mother's home with her husband, and my young brother Paul, who worried my mother a good deal because he didn't seem to want to settle down. My name was Lois Taylor, I told her. By that time, I think I could have told her my real name and she would never have connected it with the girl in the paper, because by then she was feeling that she almost knew my fam-

ily, and she wanted me to be sure and tell my mother when I wrote home that Mrs. Peacock would make herself personally responsible for me while I was in the city and take as good care of me as my own mother would. On top of everything else, she told me that a stationery store in the neighborhood was looking for a girl assistant, and there I was. Before I had been away from home for twenty-four hours I was an entirely new person. I was a girl named Lois Taylor who lived on Primrose Street and worked down at the stationery store.

I read in the papers one day about how a famous fortuneteller wrote to my father offering to find me and said that astral signs had convinced him that I would be found near flowers. That gave me a jolt, because of Primrose Street, but my father and Mrs. Peacock and the rest of the world thought that it meant that my body was buried somewhere. They dug up a vacant lot near the railroad station where I was last seen, and Mrs. Peacock was very disappointed when nothing turned up. Mrs. Peacock and I could not decide whether I had run away with a gangster to be a gun moll, or whether my body had been cut up and sent somewhere in a trunk. After a while they stopped looking for me, except for an occasional false clue that would turn up in a small story on the back pages of the paper, and Mrs. Peacock and I got interested in the stories about a daring daylight bank robbery in Chicago. When the anniversary of my running away came around, and I realized that I had really been gone for a year, I treated myself to a new hat and dinner downtown, and came home just in time for the evening news broadcast and my mother's voice over the radio.

"Louisa," she was saying, "please come home."

"That poor poor woman," Mrs. Peacock said. "Imagine how she must feel. They say she's never given up hope of finding her little girl alive someday."

"Do you like my new hat?" I asked her.

I had given up all idea of the secretarial course because the stationery store had decided to expand and include a lending library and a gift shop, and I was now the manager of the gift shop and if things kept on well would someday be running the whole thing; Mrs. Peacock and I talked it over, just as if she had been my mother, and we decided that I would be foolish to leave a good job to start over somewhere else. The money that I had been saving was in the bank, and Mrs. Peacock and I thought that one of these days we might pool our savings and buy a little car, or go on a trip somewhere, or even a cruise.

What I am saying is that I was free, and getting along fine, with never a thought that I knew about ever going back. It was just plain rotten bad luck that I had to meet Paul. I had gotten so I hardly ever thought about any of them any more, and never wondered what they were doing unless I happened to see some item in the papers, but there must have been something in the back of my mind remembering them all the time because I never even stopped to think; I just stood there on the street with my mouth open, and said *Paul!* He turned around and then of course I realized what I had done, but it was too late. He stared at me for a minute, and then frowned, and then looked puzzled; I could see him first trying to remember, and then trying to believe what he remembered: at last he said, "Is it possible?"

He said I had to go back. He said if I didn't go back he would tell them where to come and get me. He also patted me on the head and told me that there was still a reward waiting there in the bank for anyone who turned up with conclusive news of me, and he said that after he had collected the reward I was perfectly welcome to run away again, as far and as often as I liked.

Maybe I did want to go home. Maybe all that time I had been secretly waiting for a chance to get back; maybe that's why I

recognized Paul on the street, in a coincidence that wouldn't have happened once in a million years—he had never even *been* to Chandler before, and was only there for a few minutes between trains; he had stepped out of the station for a minute, and found me. If I had not been passing at that minute, if he had stayed in the station where he belonged, I would never have gone back. I told Mrs. Peacock I was going home to visit my family upstate. I thought that was funny.

Paul sent a telegram to my mother and father, saying that he had found me, and we took a plane back; Paul said he was still afraid that I'd try to get away again and the safest place for me was high up in the air where he knew I couldn't get off and run.

I began to get nervous, looking out the taxi window on the way from the Rockville airport; I would have sworn that for three years I hadn't given a thought to that town, to those streets and stores and houses I used to know so well, but here I found that I remembered it all, as though I hadn't ever seen Chandler and *its* houses and streets; it was almost as though I had never been away at all. When the taxi finally turned the corner into my own street, and I saw the big old house again, I almost cried.

"Of course I wanted to come back," I said, and Paul laughed. I thought of the return-trip ticket I had kept as a lucky charm for so long, and how I had thrown it away one day when I was emptying my pocketbook; I wondered when I threw it away whether I would ever want to go back and regret throwing away my ticket. "Everything looks just the same," I said. "I caught the bus right there on the corner; I came down the driveway that day and met you."

"If I had managed to stop you that day," Paul said, "you would probably never have tried again."

Then the taxi stopped in front of the house and my knees were shaking when I got out. I grabbed Paul's arm and said, "Paul . . . wait a minute," and he gave me a look I used to know very well, a look that said "If you back out on me now I'll see that you never forget it," and put his arm around me because I was shivering and we went up the walk to the front door.

I wondered if they were watching us from the window. It was hard for me to imagine how my mother and father would behave in a situation like this, because they always made such a point of being quiet and dignified and proper; I thought that Mrs. Peacock would have been halfway down the walk to meet us, but here the front door ahead was still tight shut. I wondered if we would have to ring the doorbell; I had never had to ring this doorbell before. I was still wondering when Carol opened the door for us. "Carol!" I said. I was shocked because she looked so old, and then I thought that of course it had been three years since I had seen her and she probably thought that *I* looked older, too. "Carol," I said, "Oh, Carol!" I was honestly glad to see her.

She looked at me hard and then stepped back and my mother and father were standing there, waiting for me to come in. If I had not stopped to think I would have run to them, but I hesitated, not quite sure what to do, or whether they were angry with me, or hurt, or only just happy that I was back, and of course once I stopped to think about it all I could find to do was just stand there and say "Mother?" kind of uncertainly.

She came over to me and put her hands on my shoulders and looked into my face for a long time. There were tears running down her cheeks and I thought that before, when it didn't matter, I had been ready enough to cry, but now, when crying would make me look better, all I wanted to do was giggle. She looked old, and sad, and I felt simply foolish. Then she turned to Paul and said, "Oh, *Paul*— how can you do this to me again?"

Paul was frightened; I could see it. "Mrs. Tether—" he said.

"What is your name, dear?" my mother asked me.

"Louisa Tether," I said stupidly.

"No, dear," she said, very gently, "your *real* name?"

Now I could cry, but now I did not think it was going to help matters any. "Louisa Tether," I said. "That's my name."

"Why don't you people leave us alone?" Carol said; she was white, and shaking, and almost screaming because she was so angry. "We've spent years and years trying to find my lost sister and all people like you see in it is a chance to cheat us out of the reward— doesn't it mean *any*thing to you that *you* may think you have a chance for some easy money, but *we* just get hurt and heartbroken all over again? Why don't you leave us *alone?*"

"Carol," my father said, "you're frightening the poor child. Young lady," he said to me, "I honestly believe that you did not realize the cruelty of what you tried to do. You look like a nice girl; try to imagine your own mother—"

I tried to imagine my own mother; I looked straight at her.

"—if someone took advantage of her like this. I am sure you were not told that twice before, this young man—" I stopped looking at my mother and looked at Paul— "has brought us young girls who pretended to be our lost daughter; each time he protested that he had been genuinely deceived and had no thought of profit, and each time we hoped desperately that it would be the right girl. The first time we were taken in for several days. The girl *looked* like our Louisa, she *acted* like our Louisa, she knew all kinds of small family jokes and happenings it seemed impossible that anyone *but* Louisa could know, and yet she was an imposter. And the girl's mother—my wife—has suffered each time her hopes have been raised." He put his arm around my mother—his wife—and with Carol they stood all together looking at me.

"Look," Paul said wildly, "give her a *chance* —she *knows* she's Louisa. At least give her a chance to *prove* it."

"How?" Carol asked. "I'm sure if I asked her something like—well—like what was the color of the dress she was supposed to wear at my wedding—"

"It was pink," I said. "I wanted blue but you said it had to be pink."

"I'm sure she'd know the answer," Carol went on as though I hadn't said anything. "The other girls you brought here, Paul—*they* both knew."

It wasn't going to be any good. I ought to have known it. Maybe they were so used to looking for me by now that they would rather keep on looking than have me home; maybe once my mother had looked in my face and seen there nothing of Louisa, but only the long careful concentration I had put into being Lois Taylor, there was never any chance of my looking like Louisa again.

I felt kind of sorry for Paul; he had never understood them as well as I did and he clearly felt there was still some chance of talking them into opening their arms and crying out "Louisa! Our long-lost daughter!" and then turning around and handing him the reward; after that, we could all live happily ever after. While Paul was still trying to argue with my father I walked over a little way and looked into the living room again; I figured I wasn't going to have much time to look around and I wanted one last glimpse to take away with me; sister Carol kept a good eye on me all the time, too. I wondered what the two girls before me had tried to steal, and I wanted to tell her that if *I* ever planned to steal anything from that house I was three years too late; I could have taken whatever I wanted when I left the first time. There was nothing there I could take now, any more than there had been before. I realized that all I wanted was to stay—I wanted to stay so much that I felt like hanging onto the stair rail and screaming, but even though a temper tantrum might bring them some fleeting recollection of their dear lost Louisa I hardly

thought it would persuade them to invite me to stay. I could just picture myself being dragged kicking and screaming out of my own house.

"Such a lovely old house," I said politely to my sister Carol, who was hovering around me.

"Our family has lived here for generations," she said, just as politely.

"Such beautiful furniture," I said.

"My mother is fond of antiques."

"Fingerprints," Paul was shouting. We were going to get a lawyer, I gathered, or at least Paul thought we were going to get a lawyer and I wondered how he was going to feel when he found out that we weren't. I couldn't imagine any lawyer in the world who could get my mother and my father and my sister Carol to take me back when they had made up their minds that I was not Louisa; could the law make my mother look into my face and recognize me?

I thought that there ought to be some way I could make Paul see that there was nothing we could do, and I came over and stood next to him. "Paul," I said, "can't you see that you're only making Mr. Tether angry?"

"Correct, young woman," my father said, and nodded at me to show that he thought I was being a sensible creature. "He's not doing himself any good by threatening me."

"Paul," I said, "these people don't want us here."

Paul started to say something and then for the first time in his life thought better of it and stamped off toward the door. When I turned to follow him—thinking that we'd never gotten past the front hall in my great homecoming—my father—excuse me, Mr. Tether—came up behind me and took my hand. "My daughter was younger than you are," he said to me very kindly, "but I'm sure you have a family somewhere who love you and want you to be happy. Go back to them, young lady. Let me advise you as though I were really your father—stay away from that fellow, he's wicked and he's worthless. Go back home where you belong."

"We know what it's like for a family to worry and wonder about a daughter," my mother said. "Go back to the people who love you."

That meant Mrs. Peacock, I guess.

"Just to make sure you get there," my father said, "let us help toward your fare." I tried to take my hand away, but he put a folded bill into it and I had to take it. "I hope someday," he said, "that someone will do as much for our Louisa."

"Good-by, my dear," my mother said, and she reached up and patted my cheek. "Very good luck to you."

"I hope your daughter comes back someday," I told them. "Good-by."

The bill was a twenty, and I gave it to Paul. It seemed little enough for all the trouble he had taken and, after all, I could go back to my job in the stationery store. My mother still talks to me on the radio, once a year, on the anniversary of the day I ran away.

"Louisa," she says, "please come home. We all want our dear girl back, and we need you and miss you so much. Your mother and father love you and will never forget you. Louisa, please come home."

---

## I
### OUTSMARTING ONESELF

Louisa is smugly sure of herself. She is delighted by the cleverness of her plan. And she congratulates herself on her careful attention to details: the purchase of the round-trip ticket; the tan raincoat; her choice of a rooming house; her conversations with Mrs. Peacock about the Rockville girl's disappearance. When she runs into Paul unexpectedly and he insists on taking her home, she finds she really wants to go there. But her family simply assumes that she is an imposter. Louisa has played a role for so long that she has lost her real identity. She has outfoxed herself.

## II
### IMPLICATIONS

Express your opinion about the statements that follow. There is not always a right or wrong opinion.

**1.** There are multiple reasons for Louisa's running away.

**2.** By playing a role too well, you can lose your real identity and become the person you are pretending to be.

**3.** Basically we are pleased that Louisa's parents fail to recognize her.

**4.** Part of the irony of this story is the family's name of Tether.

## III
### TECHNIQUES

*Atmosphere*

Notice that in the first sentence Louisa is momentarily frightened. And near the very end, when Paul is described as frightened, Louisa's father orders Carol to "stop frightening the child." These moments of high emotion are in contrast to the atmosphere of the rest of the story. What words might you select to describe the atmosphere of the story?

*Suspense*

**1.** What are the questions set up in the reader's mind?

**2.** The story has a surprise ending. Were you deliberately misled?

Emerson said, "People are too good
for banning and too bad for blessing."
An unimpressive middle-aged professor
finds out the truth of the statement
when he sets out to save the world.

# Report on the Barnhouse Effect

### KURT VONNEGUT, JR.

Let me begin by saying that I don't know any more about where Professor Arthur Barnhouse is hiding than anyone else does. Save for one short, enigmatic message left in my mailbox on Christmas Eve, I have not heard from him since his disappearance a year and a half ago.

What's more, readers of this article will be disappointed if they expect to learn how *they* can bring about the so-called "Barnhouse Effect." If I were able and willing to give away that secret, I would certainly be something more important than a psychology instructor.

I have been urged to write this report because I did research under the professor's direction and because I was the first to learn of his astonishing discovery. But while I was his student I was never entrusted with knowledge of how the mental forces could be released and directed. He was unwilling to trust anyone with that information.

I would like to point out that the term "Barnhouse Effect" is a creation of the popular press, and was never used by Professor Barnhouse. The name he chose for the phenomenon was *dynamopsychism,* or *force of the mind.*

I cannot believe that there is a civilized person yet to be convinced that such a force exists, what with its destructive effects on display in every national capital. I think humanity has always had an inkling that this sort of force does exist. It has been common knowledge that some people are luckier than others with inanimate objects like dice. What Professor Barnhouse did was to show that such "luck" was a measurable force, which in his case could be enormous.

By my calculations, the professor was about fifty-five times more powerful than a Nagasaki-type atomic bomb at the time he went into hiding. He was not bluffing when, on the eve of "Operation Brainstorm," he told General Honus Barker: "Sitting here at the dinner table, I'm pretty sure I can flatten anything on earth—from Joe Louis to the Great Wall of China."

There is an understandable tendency to look upon Professor Barnhouse as a supernatural visitation. The First Church of Barnhouse in Los Angeles has a congregation numbering in the thousands. He is godlike in neither appearance nor intellect. The man who disarms the world is single, shorter than the average American male, stout, and averse to exercise. His I.Q. is 143, which is good but certainly not sensational. He is quite mortal, about to celebrate his fortieth birthday, and in good health. If he is alone now, the isolation won't bother him too much. He was quiet and shy when I knew him, and seemed to find more companionship in books and music than in his associations at the college.

Neither he nor his powers fall outside the sphere of Nature. His dynamopsychic radiations are subject to many known physical laws that apply in the field of radio. Hardly a person has not now heard the snarl of "Barnhouse static" on his home receiver. The

"Report on the Barnhouse Effect" excerpted from *Welcome to the Monkey House* by Kurt Vonnegut, Jr. Copyright 1950 by Kurt Vonnegut, Jr. Originally published in *Collier's*. Reprinted by permission of Delacorte Press/Seymour Lawrence.

radiations are affected by sunspots and variation in the ionosphere.

However, they differ from ordinary broadcast waves in several important ways. Their total energy can be brought to bear on any single point the professor chooses, and that energy is undiminished by distance. As a weapon, then, dynamopsychism has an impressive advantage over bacteria and atomic bombs, beyond the fact that it costs nothing to use: it enables the professor to single out critical individuals and objects instead of slaughtering whole populations in the process of maintaining international equilibrium.

As General Honus Barker told the House Military Affairs Committee: "Until someone finds Barnhouse, there is no defense against the Barnhouse Effect." Efforts to "jam" or block the radiations have failed. Premier Slezak could have saved himself the fantastic expense of his "Barnhouse-proof" shelter. Despite the shelter's twelve-foot-thick lead armor, the premier has been floored twice while in it.

There is talk of screening the population for men potentially as powerful dynamopsychically as the professor. Senator Warren Foust demanded funds for this purpose last month, with the passionate declaration: "He who rules the Barnhouse Effect rules the world!" Commissar Kropotnik said much the same thing, so another costly armaments race, with a new twist, has begun.

This race at least has its comical aspects. The world's best gamblers are being coddled by governments like so many nuclear physicists. There may be several hundred persons with dynamopsychic talent on earth, myself included. But, without knowledge of the professor's technique, they can never be anything but dice-table despots. With the secret, it would probably take them ten years to become dangerous weapons. It took the professor that long. He who rules the Barnhouse Effect is Barnhouse and will be for some time.

Popularly, the "Age of Barnhouse" is said to have begun a year and a half ago, on the day of Operation Brainstorm. That was when dynamopsychism became significant politically. Actually, the phenomenon was discovered in May 1942, shortly after the professor turned down a direct commission in the Army and enlisted as an artillery private. Like X rays and vulcanized rubber, dynamopsychism was discovered by accident.

From time to time Private Barnhouse was invited to take part in games of chance by his barrack mates. He knew nothing about the games, and usually begged off. But one evening, out of social grace, he agreed to shoot craps. It was terrible or wonderful that he played, depending upon whether or not you like the world as it now is.

"Shoot sevens, Pop," someone said.

So "Pop" shot sevens—ten in a row to bankrupt the barracks. He retired to his bunk and, as a mathematical exercise, calculated the odds against his feat on the back of a laundry slip. His chances of doing it, he found, were one in almost ten million! Bewildered, he borrowed a pair of dice from the man in the bunk next to his. He tried to roll sevens again, but got only the usual assortment of numbers. He lay back for a moment, then resumed his toying with the dice. He rolled ten more sevens in a row.

He might have dismissed the phenomenon with a low whistle. But the professor instead mulled over the circumstances surrounding his two lucky streaks. There was one single factor in common: on both occasions, *the same thought train had flashed through his mind just before he threw the dice.* It was that thought train which aligned the professor's brain cells into what has since become the most powerful weapon on earth.

The soldier in the next bunk gave dynamopsychism its first token of respect. In an understatement certain to bring wry smiles to the faces of the world's dejected demagogues, the soldier said, "You're hotter'n a two-dollar pistol, Pop." Professor Barnhouse was all of that. The dice that did his bidding weighed but a few grams, so the forces involved were minute; but the unmistakable fact that there were such forces was earthshaking.

Professional caution kept him from revealing his discovery immediately. He wanted more facts and a body of theory to go with them. Later, when the atomic bomb was dropped in Hiroshima, it was fear that made him hold his peace. At no time were his experiments, as Premier Slezak called them, "a bourgeois plot to shackle the true democracies of the world." The professor didn't know where they were leading.

In time, he came to recognize another startling feature of dynamopsychism: *its strength increased with use.* Within six months, he was able to govern dice thrown by men the length of a barracks distant. By the time of his discharge in 1945, he could knock bricks loose from chimneys three miles away.

Charges that Professor Barnhouse could have won the last war in a minute, but did not care to do so, are perfectly senseless. When the war ended, he had the range and power of a 37-millimeter cannon, perhaps—certainly no more. His dynamopsychic powers graduated from the small-arms class only after his discharge and return to Wyandotte College.

I enrolled in the Wyandotte Graduate School two years after the professor had rejoined the faculty. By chance, he was assigned as my thesis adviser. I was unhappy about the assignment, for the professor was, in the eyes of both colleagues and students, a somewhat ridiculous figure. He missed classes or had lapses of memory during lectures. When I arrived, in fact, his shortcomings had passed from the ridiculous to the intolerable.

"We're assigning you to Barnhouse as a sort of temporary thing," the dean of social studies told me. He looked apologetic and perplexed. "Brilliant man, Barnhouse, I guess. Difficult to know since his return, perhaps, but his work before the war brought a great deal of credit to our little school."

When I reported to the professor's laboratory for the first time, what I saw was more distressing than the gossip. Every surface in the room was covered with dust; books and apparatus had not been disturbed for months. The professor sat napping at his desk when I entered. The only signs of recent activity were three overflowing ashtrays, a pair of scissors, and a morning paper with several items clipped from its front page.

As he raised his head to look at me, I saw that his eyes were clouded with fatigue. "Hi," he said, "just can't seem to get my sleeping done at night." He lighted a cigarette, his hands trembling slightly. "You the young man I'm supposed to help with a thesis?"

"Yes, sir," I said. In minutes he converted my misgivings to alarm.

"You an overseas veteran?" he asked.

"Yes, sir."

"Not much left over there, is there?" He frowned. "Enjoy the last war?"

"No, sir."

"Look like another war to you?"

"Kind of, sir."

"What can be done about it?"

I shrugged. "Looks pretty hopeless."

He peered at me intently. "Know anything about international law, the U.N., and all that?"

"Only what I pick up from the papers."

"Same here," he sighed. He showed me a fat scrapbook packed with newspaper clippings. "Never used to pay any attention to international politics. Now I study them the way I used to study rats in mazes. Everybody tells me the same thing—'Looks hopeless.'"

"Nothing short of a miracle———" I began.

"Believe in magic?" he asked sharply. The professor fished two dice from his vest pocket. "I will try to roll twos," he said. He rolled twos three times in a row. "One chance in about 47,000 of that happening. There's a miracle for you." He beamed for an instant, then brought the interview to an end, remarking that he had a class which had begun ten minutes ago.

He was not quick to take me into his confidence, and he said no more about his trick with the dice. I assumed they were loaded, and forgot about them. He set me the task of watching male rats cross electrified metal strips to get to food or female rats—an experiment that had been done to everyone's satisfaction in the 1930's. As though the pointlessness of my work were not bad enough, the professor annoyed me further with irrelevant questions. His favorites were: "Think we should have dropped the atomic bomb on Hiroshima?" and "Think every new piece of scientific information is a good thing for humanity?"

However, I did not feel put upon for long. "Give those poor animals a holiday," he said one morning, after I had been with him only a month. "I wish you'd help me look into a more interesting problem—namely, my sanity."

I returned the rats to their cages.

"What you must do is simple," he said, speaking softly. "Watch the inkwell on my desk. If you see nothing happen to it, say so, and I'll go quietly—relieved, I might add— to the nearest sanitarium."

I nodded uncertainly.

He locked the laboratory door and drew the blinds, so that we were in twilight for a moment. "I'm odd, I know," he said. "It's fear of myself that's made me odd."

"I've found you somewhat eccentric, perhaps, but certainly not———"

"If nothing happens to that inkwell, 'crazy as a bedbug' is the only description of me that will do," he interrupted, turning on the overhead lights. His eyes narrowed. "To give you an idea of how crazy, I'll tell you what's been running through my mind when I should have been sleeping. I think maybe I can save the world. I think maybe I can make every

nation a *have* nation, and do away with war for good. I think maybe I can clear roads through jungles, irrigate deserts, build dams overnight."

"Yes, sir."

"Watch the inkwell!"

Dutifully and fearfully I watched. A high-pitched humming seemed to come from the inkwell; then it began to vibrate alarmingly, and finally to bound about the top of the desk, making two noisy circuits. It stopped, hummed again, glowed red, then popped in splinters with a blue-green flash.

Perhaps my hair stood on end. The professor laughed gently. "Magnets?" I managed to say at last.

"Wish to heaven it were magnets," he murmured. It was then that he told me of dynamopsychism. He knew only that there was such a force; he could not explain it. "It's me and me alone—and it's awful."

"I'd say it was amazing and wonderful!" I cried.

"If all I could do was make inkwells dance, I'd be tickled silly with the whole business." He shrugged disconsolately. "But I'm no toy, my boy. If you like, we can drive around the neighborhood, and I'll show you what I mean." He told me about pulverized boulders, shattered oaks, and abandoned farm buildings demolished within a fifty-mile radius of the campus. "Did every bit of it sitting right here, just thinking—not even thinking hard."

He scratched his head nervously. "I have never dared to concentrate as hard as I can for fear of the damage I might do. I'm to the point where a mere whim is a blockbuster." There was a depressing pause. "Up until a few days ago, I've thought it best to keep my secret for fear of what use it might be put to," he continued. "Now I realize that I haven't any more right to it than a man has a right to own an atomic bomb." He fumbled through a heap of papers. "This says about all that needs to be said, I think." He handed me a draft of a letter to the Secretary of State.

*Dear Sir:*

*I have discovered a new force which costs nothing to use, and which is probably more important than atomic energy. I should like to see it used most effectively in the cause of peace, and am, therefore, requesting your advice as to how this might best be done.*

*Yours truly,*
*A. Barnhouse.*

"I have no idea what will happen next," said the professor.

There followed three months of perpetual nightmare, wherein the nation's political and military great came at all hours to watch the professor's tricks.

We were quartered in an old mansion near Charlottesville, Virginia, to which we had been whisked five days after the letter was mailed. Surrounded by barbed wire and twenty guards, we were labeled "Project Wishing Well," and were classified as Top Secret.

For companionship we had General Honus Barker and the State Department's William K. Cuthrell. For the professor's talk of peace-through-plenty they had indulgent smiles and much discourse on practical measures and realistic thinking. So treated, the professor, who had at first been almost meek, progressed in a matter of weeks toward stubbornness.

He had agreed to reveal the thought train by means of which he aligned his mind into a dynamopsychic transmitter. But, under Cuthrell's and Barker's nagging to do so, he began to hedge. At first he declared that the information could be passed on simply by word of mouth. Later he said that it would have to be written up in a long report. Finally, at dinner one night, just after General Barker had read the secret orders for Operation Brainstorm, the professor announced, "The report may take as long as five years to write." He looked fiercely at the general. "Maybe twenty."

The dismay occasioned by this flat an-

nouncement was offset somewhat by the exciting anticipation of Operation Brainstorm. The general was in a holiday mood. "The target ships are on their way to the Caroline Islands at this very moment," he declared ecstatically. "One hundred and twenty of them! At the same time, ten V-2s are being readied for firing in New Mexico, and fifty radio-controlled jet bombers are being equipped for a mock attack on the Aleutians. Just think of it!" Happily he reviewed his orders. "At exactly 1100 hours next Wednesday, I will give you the order to *concentrate;* and you, professor, will think as hard as you can about sinking the target ships, destroying the V-2s before they hit the ground, and knocking down the bombers before they reach the Aleutians! Think you can handle it?"

The professor turned gray and closed his eyes. "As I told you before, my friend, I don't know what I can do." He added bitterly, "As for this Operation Brainstorm, I was never consulted about it, and it strikes me as childish and insanely expensive."

General Barker bridled. "Sir," he said, "your field is psychology, and I wouldn't presume to give you advice in that field. Mine is national defense. I have had thirty years of experience and success, Professor, and I'll ask you not to criticize my judgment."

The professor appealed to Mr. Cuthrell. "Look," he pleaded, "isn't it war and military matters we're all trying to get rid of? Wouldn't it be a whole lot more significant and lots cheaper for me to try moving cloud masses into drought areas, and things like that? I admit I know next to nothing about international politics, but it seems reasonable to suppose that nobody would want to fight wars if there were enough of everything to go around. Mr. Cuthrell, I'd like to try running generators where there isn't any coal or water power, irrigating deserts, and so on. Why, you could figure out what each country needs to make the most of its resources, and I could give it to them without costing American taxpayers a penny."

"Eternal vigilance is the price of freedom," said the general heavily.

Mr. Cuthrell threw the general a look of mild distaste. "Unfortunately, the general is right in his own way," he said. "I wish to heaven the world were ready for ideals like yours, but it simply isn't. We aren't surrounded by brothers, but by enemies. It isn't a lack of food or resources that has us on the brink of war—it's a struggle for power. Who's going to be in charge of the world, our kind of people or theirs?"

The professor nodded in reluctant agreement and arose from the table. "I beg your pardon, gentlemen. You are, after all, better qualified to judge what is best for the country. I'll do whatever you say." He turned to me. "Don't forget to wind the restricted clock and put the confidential cat out," he said gloomily, and ascended the stairs of his bedroom.

For reasons of national security, Operation Brainstorm was carried on without the knowledge of the American citizenry which was paying the bill. The observers, technicians, and military men involved in the activity knew that a test was under way—a test of what, they had no idea. Only thirty-seven key men, myself included, knew what was afoot.

In Virginia, the day for Operation Brainstorm was unseasonably cool. Inside, a log fire crackled in the fireplace, and the flames were reflected in the polished metal cabinets that lined the living room. All that remained of the room's lovely old furniture was a Victorian love seat, set squarely in the center of the floor, facing three television receivers. One long bench had been brought in for the ten of us privileged to watch. The television screens showed, from left to right, the stretch of desert which was the rocket target, the guinea-pig fleet, and a section of the Aleutian sky through which the radio-controlled bomber formation would roar.

Ninety minutes before H-hour the radios announced that the rockets were ready, that the observation ships had backed away to what was thought to be a safe distance, and that the bombers were on their way. The small Virginia audience lined up on the bench in order of rank, smoked a great deal, and said little. Professor Barnhouse was in his bedroom. General Barker bustled about the house like a woman preparing Thanksgiving dinner for twenty.

At ten minutes before H-hour the general came in, shepherding the professor before him. The professor was comfortably attired in sneakers, gray flannels, a blue sweater, and a white shirt open at the neck. The two of them sat side by side on the love seat. The general was rigid and perspiring; the professor was cheerful. He looked at each of the screens, lighted a cigarette and settled back.

"Bombers sighted!" cried the Aleutian observers.

"Rockets away!" barked the New Mexico radio operator.

All of us looked quickly at the big electric clock over the mantel, while the professor, a half-smile on his face, continued to watch the television sets. In hollow tones, the general counted away the seconds remaining. "Five . . . four . . . three . . . two . . . one . . . *Concentrate!*"

Professor Barnhouse closed his eyes, pursed his lips, and stroked his temples. He held the position for a minute. The television images were scrambled, and the radio signals were drowned in the din of Barnhouse static. The professor sighed, opened his eyes, and smiled confidently.

"Did you give it everything you had?" asked the general dubiously.

"I was wide open," the professor replied.

The television images pulled themselves together, and mingled cries of amazement came over the radios tuned to the observers. The Aleutian sky was streaked with the smoke trails of bombers screaming down in flames. Simultaneously, there appeared high over the rocket target a cluster of white puffs, followed by faint thunder.

General Barker shook his head happily. "By George!" he crowed. "Well, sir, by George, by George, by George!"

"Look!" shouted the admiral seated next to me. "The fleet—it wasn't touched!"

"The guns seem to be drooping," said Mr. Cuthrell.

We left the bench and clustered about the television sets to examine the damage more closely. What Mr. Cuthrell had said was true. The ships' guns curved downward, their muzzles resting on the steel decks. We in Virginia were making such a hullabaloo that it was impossible to hear the radio reports. We were so engrossed, in fact, that we didn't miss the professor until two short snarls of Barnhouse static shocked us into sudden silence. The radios went dead.

We looked around apprehensively. The professor was gone. A harassed guard threw open the front door from the outside to yell that the professor had escaped. He brandished his pistol in the direction of the gates, which hung open, limp and twisted. In the distance, a speeding government station wagon topped a ridge and dropped from sight into the valley beyond. The air was filled with choking smoke, for every vehicle on the grounds was ablaze. Pursuit was impossible.

"What in God's name got into him?" bellowed the general.

Mr. Cuthrell, who had rushed out onto the front porch, now slouched back into the room, reading a penciled note as he came. He thrust the note into my hands. "The good man left this *billet-doux*[1] under the door knocker. Perhaps our young friend here will be kind enough to read it to you gentlemen, while I take a restful walk through the woods."

"*Gentlemen.*" I read aloud, "*As the first superweapon with a conscience, I am removing myself from your national defense*

*stockpile. Setting a new precedent in the behavior of ordnance, I have humane reasons for going off. A. Barnhouse.*"

Since that day, of course, the professor has been systematically destroying the world's armaments, until there is now little with which to equip an army other than rocks and sharp sticks. His activities haven't exactly resulted in peace, but have, rather, precipitated a bloodless and entertaining sort of war that might be called the "War of the Tattletales." Every nation is flooded with enemy agents whose sole mission is to locate military equipment, which is promptly wrecked when it is brought to the professor's attention in the press.

Just as every day brings news of more armaments pulverized by dynamopsychism, so has it brought rumors of the professor's whereabouts. During last week alone, three publications carried articles proving variously that he was hiding in an Inca ruin in the Andes, in the sewers of Paris, and in the unexplored lower chambers of Carlsbad Caverns. Knowing the man, I am inclined to regard such hiding places as unnecessarily romantic and uncomfortable. While there are numerous persons eager to kill him, there must be millions who would care for him and hide him. I like to think that he is in the home of such a person.

One thing is certain: at this writing, Professor Barnhouse is not dead. Barnhouse satic jammed broadcasts not ten minutes ago. In the eighteen months since his disappearance, he has been reported dead some half-dozen times. Each report has stemmed from the death of an unidentified man resembling the professor, during a period free of the static. The first three reports were followed at once by renewed talk of rearmament and recourse to war. The saber-rattlers have learned how imprudent premature celebrations of the professor's demise can be.

Many a stouthearted patriot has found himself prone in the tangled bunting and timbers

---

1. **billet-doux** \bil-ᵃā-dü\ French for love letter.

of a smashed reviewing stand, seconds after having announced that the arch-tyranny of Barnhouse was at an end. But those who would make war if they could, in every country in the world, wait in sullen silence for what must come—the passing of Professor Barnhouse.

To ask how much longer the professor will live is to ask how much longer we must wait for the blessing of another world war. He is of short-lived stock: his mother lived to be fifty-three, his father to be forty-nine; and the life spans of his grandparents on both sides were of the same order. He might be expected to live, then, for perhaps fifteen years more, if he can remain hidden from his enemies. When one considers the number and vigor of these enemies, however, fifteen years seems an extraordinary length of time, which might better be revised to fifteen days, hours, or minutes.

The professor knows that he cannot live much longer. I say this because of the message left in my mailbox on Christmas Eve. Unsigned, typewritten on a soiled scrap of paper, the note consisted of ten sentences. The first nine of these, each a bewildering tangle of psychological jargon and references to obscure texts, made no sense to me at first reading. The tenth, unlike the rest, was simply constructed and contained no large words— but its irrational content made it the most puzzling and bizarre sentence of all. I nearly threw the note away, thinking it a colleague's warped notion of a practical joke. For some reason, though, I added it to the clutter on top of my desk, which included, among other mementos, the professor's dice.

It took me several weeks to realize that the message really meant something, that the first nine sentences, when unsnarled, could be taken as instructions. The tenth still told me nothing. It was only last night that I discovered how it fitted in with the rest. The sentence appeared in my thoughts last night, while I was toying absently with the professor's dice.

I promised to have this report on its way to the publishers today. In view of what has happened, I am obliged to break that promise, or release the report incomplete. The delay will not be a long one, for one of the few blessings accorded a bachelor like myself is the ability to move quickly from one abode to another, or from one way of life to another. What property I want to take with me can be packed in a few hours. Fortunately, I am not without substantial private means, which may take as long as a week to realize in liquid and anonymous form. When this is done, I shall mail the report.

I have just returned from a visit to my doctor, who tells me my health is excellent. I am young, and, with any luck at all, I shall live to a ripe old age indeed, for my family on both sides is noted for longevity.

Briefly, I propose to vanish.

Sooner or later, Professor Barnhouse must die. But long before then I shall be ready. So, to the saber-rattlers of today—and even, I hope, of tomorrow—I say: Be advised. Barnhouse will die. But not the Barnhouse Effect.

Last night, I tried once more to follow the oblique instructions on the scrap of paper. I took the professor's dice, and then, with the last, nightmarish sentence flitting through my mind, I rolled fifty consecutive sevens.

Good-by.

I

PROJECT WISHING WELL

After his letter to the Secretary of State, Barnhouse is rushed to a top security installation in Virginia. It is given the ironic label above. Here the antagonistic forces for war and peace are bound together by the Barnhouse Effect. No matter what Professor Barnhouse does to try to convince the government to use his powers for peace, they see him only as a weapon for war. The situation is almost as impossible as solving one's problems by throwing pennies in a wishing well.

## II
### IMPLICATIONS

Base your opinion of the following on both the story and your own experience. There may not always be a right or wrong answer.

**1.** Professor Barnhouse is incredibly naïve about the nature of governments and people.

**2.** In describing the dice game, the narrator says, "It was terrible or wonderful that he played, depending upon whether or not you like the world as it now is." At the end of the story, is the world pictured as terrible or wonderful?

**3.** The story makes fun both of human foibles and of institutions.

**4.** The following are echoes of familiar cliches. What is ironic about their use here?

**a.** "He who rules the Barnhouse Effect rules the world."

**b.** "Eternal vigilance is the price of freedom."

**c.** "The world is not ready for ideals like yours."

## III
### TECHNIQUES

*Atmosphere*

**1.** What do you know about the narrator of the story?

**2.** Under what circumstances is he writing this story?

**3.** Knowing these circumstances, what is the atmosphere created?

## IV
### WORDS

At times new scientific discoveries are named after their discoverer, such as the Van Allen Rings or the Barnhouse Effect. But often new discoveries are labeled by creating a name from Greek words and roots. The custom has evolved because the ancient Greeks are generally conceded to be the first experimental scientists.

The Barnhouse Effect is called dynamopsychism which the narrator describes as force of the mind. Dyna in Greek means power. Psyche was a beautiful girl in Greek myth who was loved by Eros, the God of Love. She personifies the soul or spirit of the mind. So dynamopsychism is the power of the soul.

If only ordinary English words had been used, what might Barnhouse's discovery have been called?

Mark Twain thrived on poking fun
at people's pretensions.
By exaggerating these to ridiculous size,
he makes us
laugh at ourselves and
our own pretensions.

# The Story of the Good Little Boy

## MARK TWAIN

Once there was a good little boy by the name of Jacob Blivens. He always obeyed his parents, no matter how absurd and unreasonable their demands were; and he always learned his book, and never was late at Sabbath-school. He would not play hookey, even when his sober judgment told him it was the most profitable thing he could do. None of the other boys could ever make that boy out, he acted so strangely. He wouldn't lie, no matter how convenient it was. He just said it was wrong to lie, and that was sufficient for him. And he was so honest that he was simply ridiculous. The curious ways that that Jacob had, surpassed everything. He wouldn't play marbles on Sunday, he wouldn't rob birds' nests, he wouldn't give hot pennies to organ-grinders' monkeys; he didn't seem to take any interest in any kind of rational amusement. So the other boys used to try to reason it out and come to an understanding of him, but they couldn't arrive at any satisfactory conclusion. As I said before, they could only figure out a sort of vague idea that he was "afflicted," and so they took him under their protection, and never allowed any harm to come to him.

This good little boy read all the Sunday-school books; they were his greatest delight. This was the whole secret of it. He believed in the good little boys they put in the Sunday-school books; he had every confidence in them. He longed to come across one of them alive once; but he never did. They all died before his time, maybe. Whenever he read about a particularly good one he turned over quickly to the end to see what became of him, because he wanted to travel thousands of miles and gaze on him; but it wasn't any use; that good little boy always died in the last chapter, and there was a picture of the funeral, with all his relations and the Sunday-school children standing around the grave in pantaloons[1] that were too short, and bonnets that were too large, and everybody crying into handkerchiefs that had as much as a yard and a half of stuff in them. He was always headed off in this way. He never could see one of those good little boys on account of his always dying in the last chapter.

Jacob had a noble ambition to be put in a Sunday-school book. He wanted to be put in, with pictures representing him gloriously declining to lie to his mother, and her weeping for joy about it; and pictures representing him standing on the doorstep giving a penny to a poor beggar-woman with six children, and telling her to spend it freely, but not to be extravagant, because extravagance is a sin; and pictures of him magnanimously refusing to tell on the bad boy who always lay in wait for him around the corner as he came from school, and welted him over the head with a lath, and then chased him home, saying, "Hi! hi!" as he proceeded. That was the ambition of young Jacob Blivens. He wished to be put in a Sunday-school book. It made him feel a little uncomfortable sometimes when he reflected that the good little boys always died. He loved to live, you know, and this was the most unpleasant feature about being a Sunday-school-book boy. He knew it was not healthy to be good. He knew it was more fatal than consumption to be so supernaturally good as the boys in the books were; he knew that none of them had ever been

able to stand it long, and it pained him to think that if they put him in a book he wouldn't ever see it, or even if they did get the book out before he died it wouldn't be popular without any picture of his funeral in the back part of it. It couldn't be much of a Sunday-school book that couldn't tell about the advice he gave to the community when he was dying. So at last, of course, he had to make up his mind to do the best he could under the circumstances— to live right, and hang on as long as he could, and have his dying speech all ready when his time came.

But somehow nothing ever went right with this good little boy; nothing ever turned out with him the way it turned out with the good little boys in the books. They always had a good time, and the bad boys had the broken legs; but in his case there was a screw loose somewhere, and it all happened just the other way. When he found Jim Blake stealing apples, and went under the tree to read to him about the bad little boy who fell out of a neighbor's apple tree and broke his arm, Jim fell out of the tree, too, but he fell on *him* and broke *his* arm, and Jim wasn't hurt at all. Jacob couldn't understand that. There wasn't anything in the books like it.

And once, when some bad boys pushed a blind man over in the mud, and Jacob ran to help him up and receive his blessing, the blind man did not give him any blessing at all, but whacked him over the head with his stick and said he would like to catch him shoving *him* again, and then pretending to help him up. This was not in accordance with any of the books. Jacob looked them all over to see.

One thing that Jacob wanted to do was to find a lame dog that hadn't any place to stay, and was hungry and persecuted, and bring him home and pet him and have that dog's imperishable gratitude. And at last he found one and was happy; and he brought him home and fed him, but when he was going to pet him the dog flew at him and tore all the clothes off him ex-

_____
1. **pantaloons**\păn·tə ⁴lūnz\ trousers.

654

cept those that were in front, and made a spectacle of him that was astonishing. He examined authorities, but he could not understand the matter. It was of the same breed of dogs that was in the books, but it acted very differently. Whatever this boy did he got into trouble. The very things the boys in the books got rewarded for turned out to be about the most unprofitable things he could invest in.

Once, when he was on his way to Sunday-school, he saw some bad boys starting off pleasuring in a sailboat. He was filled with consternation, because he knew from his reading that boys who went sailing on Sunday invariably got drowned. So he ran out on a raft to warn them, but a log turned with him and slid him into the river. A man got him out pretty soon, and the doctor pumped the water out of him, and gave him a fresh start with his bellows, but he caught cold and lay sick abed nine weeks. But the most unaccountable thing about it was that the bad boys in the boat had a good time all day, and then reached home alive and well in the most surprising manner. Jacob Blivens said there was nothing like these things in the books. He was perfectly dumfounded.

When he got well he was a little discouraged, but he resolved to keep on trying anyhow. He knew that so far his experiences wouldn't do to go in a book, but he hadn't yet reached the allotted term of life for good little boys, and he hoped to be able to make a record yet if he could hold on till his time was fully up. If everything else failed he had his dying speech to fall back on.

He examined his authorities, and found that it was now time for him to go to sea as a cabin-boy. He called on a ship-captain and made his application, and when the captain asked for his recommendations he proudly drew out a tract[2] and pointed to the word, "To Jacob Blivens, from his affectionate teacher." But the captain was a coarse, vulgar man, and he said, "Oh, that be blowed! *that* wasn't any proof that he knew how to wash dishes or handle a slush-bucket,[3] and he guessed he didn't want him." This was altogether the most extraordinary thing that ever happened to Jacob in all his life. A compliment from a teacher, on a tract, had never failed to move the tenderest emotions of ship-captains, and open the way to all offices of honor and profit in their gift—it never had in any book that ever *he* had read. He could hardly believe his senses.

This boy always had a hard time of it. Nothing ever came out according to the authorities with him. At last, one day, when he was around hunting up bad little boys to admonish,[4] he found a lot of them in the old iron-foundry fixing up a little joke on fourteen or fifteen dogs, which they had tied together in long procession, and were going to ornament with empty nitroglycerin cans made fast to their tails. Jacob's heart was touched. He sat down on one of those cans (for he never minded grease when duty was before him), and he took hold of the foremost dog by the collar, and turned his reproving eye upon wicked Tom Jones. But just at that moment Alderman Mc-Welter, full of wrath, stepped in. All the bad boys ran away, but Jacob Blivens rose in conscious innocence and began one of those stately little Sunday-school-book speeches which always commence with "Oh, sir!" in dead opposition to the fact that no boy, good or bad, ever starts a remark with "Oh, sir." But the alderman never waited to hear the rest. He took Jacob Blivens by the ear and turned him around, and hit him a whack in the rear with the flat of his hand; and in an instant that good little boy shot out through the roof and soared away toward the sun, with the fragments of those fifteen dogs stringing after him like the tail of a kite. And there wasn't a sign of that alderman or that old iron-foundry left on the face of the earth; and, as for young Jacob Blivens, he never got a chance to make his last dying speech after all his trouble fixing it up,

---

2. **tract**\trăkt\ a booklet or leaflet on some moral or religious subject.
3. **slush-bucket**, a bucket used in washing the decks of a ship.
4. **to admonish**\ăd ᷓmŏ•nĭsh\ to warn, to advise.

unless he made it to the birds; because, although the bulk of him came down all right in a tree-top in an adjoining county, the rest of him was apportioned[5] around among four townships, and so they had to hold five inquests[6] on him to find out whether he was dead or not, and how it occurred. You never saw a boy scattered so.

Thus perished the good little boy who did the best he could, but didn't come out according to the books. Every boy who ever did as he did prospered except him. His case is truly remarkable. It will probably never be accounted for.

## I
### TONGUE IN CHEEK

The reader knows almost immediately that Twain meant his picture to be ridiculous. Certainly by the end of the first paragraph readers are sure that Twain is pulling their leg. But how do they know it? For every sentence by itself is perfectly straightforward: The words seem to mean exactly what they say. But subtly Twain somehow suggests an interpretation different from the apparent one. Skim through paragraph one and see if you can discover any particular words and techniques that tell you Twain has his "tongue in his cheek."

## II
### IMPLICATIONS

What is your opinion of the following statements?

**1.** Twain is a realist making fun of idealists.

**2.** Twain does not believe in "goodness."

**3.** It would be difficult to like Jacob Bliven.

**4.** The story makes us aware of our own tendencies toward self-deceit.

## III
### TECHNIQUES

*Atmosphere*

You know that this story is told tongue in cheek—that it gives the impression of saying one thing while really it is saying another. The surface quality differs from the underneath one. Pick adjectives to describe its surface quality.

*Suspense*

This selection creates suspense by using a principle of organization commonly used in expository essays. Twain uses this principle of *illustration* (or multiple examples, as it is sometimes called). According to this principle, writers state their thesis, then explain what it means, and then "prove" it by a series of examples often ending with a climactic one that demonstrates the thesis beyond a doubt. Taking as Twain's thesis statement, "nothing ever turned out with him the way it turned out with the good little boys in the books," what are the examples used to prove the point?

## IV
### WORDS

Analyze the following words into affixes and roots, giving the general meanings of the latter. In each case determine how the original meaning of the root is related to the current meaning of the word: *arrogant, lethargically, hazard, elation, preposterous, precarious, eccentricity, transcend, affluence, proposition.*

---

5. **apportioned**\ə ˈpōr·shənd\ distributed in proper shares.

6. **inquests**\ˈin·kwĕsts\ investigations by a coroner and a coroner's jury of any death not clearly due to natural causes.

## SUMMING UP
## *Life's Ironies*

Like brief encounters, life's ironies hold a peculiar fascination for people. Do they result from sheer accident or are they evidence that our lives are controlled by something outside ourselves? Since individuals who experience irony receive the opposite of their expectations, one may sense the operation of a malicious, insensitive force. And yet, after further thought, one sees that the character's fate is singularly appropriate. A young stranger who stumbles into a mountain inn and reveals that more than anything else he wants to be remembered is buried by an avalanche and no one even knows he is among the dead. A soldier carefully sets a trap to kill an unknown enemy only to find out later that he has killed his own brother. A young girl who runs away from home and takes on a new personality goes unrecognized by her parents and sister when she finally returns.

Because human beings are fascinated with people and their actions which produce irony, storytellers delight in using this element. As you have seen, the ironic story is one in which the impact is saved until the very end. Suddenly everything that has gone before is seen in a new light. This adds to the emotional shock. The pollution of a stream by a rendering plant becomes a tragic personal matter, not just a part of a larger problem. The new world order of peace, progress, and harmonious living is the unwitting gift of a ruthless man who spawned the organization to conserve his own business interests. A professor who has discovered how to convert brain waves into a powerful force finds himself unable to use his discovery to improve the world. Instead he hides away and uses all his force to destroy the world's stockpiles of weapons. Therefore, in the stories in LIFE'S IRONIES, it is the "afterburn" that provides the real thrust.

### IMPLICATIONS

1. In the stories you have read, irony springs from a number of different kinds of situations and operates in various ways.

a. In which stories does the irony seem to be almost a payment for a character's faults?

b. In which stories does the irony develop because of social problems?

c. In which stories does the irony seem to result from sheer accident?

d. In which stories does nature contribute to the ironic fate?

2. The statements that follow are designed to help you sum up your new and old ideas about life's ironies. Use the selections as well as your own experiences to support your opinions.

a. Ironic twists are always unexpected, but not all unexpected events are ironic.

b. The possibility of ironic results makes human endeavors seem useless.

c. Everyone experiences ironic twists fairly frequently.

d. It takes a sensitive person to perceive the irony in a situation.

### TECHNIQUES
*Atmosphere*

1. Is the atmosphere more often created by the tone and rhythm of language or by the choice of details? Use selections to support your contention.

2. If the atmosphere is at variance with the content of the story, what is the effect?

3. Once established, should the atmosphere be consistent throughout a story?

4. Turn to the Table of Contents for this unit. As you look at the title of each selection, try to pin down in one or two words the mood you felt after you had finished the story.

*Suspense*

1. In which of the selections is there a deliberate slowing down of answers to the questions in the reader's mind in order to create suspense?

2. Can a good story be told and still have little suspense?

3. Which of the stories in this unit best held your attention? How did the author create suspense?

4. Give titles of stories either in comic strips or in other reading which depend entirely on suspense. How do they rate in literary quality?

## Introduction to
## I Heard the Owl Call My Name

"We die soon!" So runs the last line of the poem that introduced this unit on LIFE'S IRONIES. Yet most of us live our days as if there were no end. Only now and then do we feel a cold breath from the grave. Perhaps then one may wonder—"If I die tomorrow, what might I wish I had done?" Only those in our society who are diagnosed as terminally ill are suddenly and terribly aware of the timetable for death's arrival. Faced with such knowledge, what would one elect to do? How would it affect one's list of priorities for living? Strange, isn't it, that the well and strong seldom stop to ponder these values?

This deep concern with the real meaning of life lies at the heart of the novel you are about to read. As you will discover on the first page, the hero, a young priest, is terminally ill. But the young man does not know of his illness. The reader's knowing something that the character himself is unaware of heightens the poignancy of the young man's experiences. Surprisingly, the Bishop sends him to the hardest parish in his district, that of the Kwakiutl Indians in the wilderness of British Columbia. "So short a time to learn so much? It leaves me no choice," says the Bishop.

A puzzling statement perhaps, echoing many other ironic and enigmatic injunctions that spring from our Western culture. Who has not heard such prescriptions for the good life as to gain one's life, one must lose it; to find self, one must forget self; to grow, one must diminish; to gain wealth, one must give it away. Each of these contradictory and ironic statements is saying a similar thing. Human beings have a tendency to choose the wrong route to their goals. Human nature seems to emphasize the unimportant details and push the important ones to the fringes of consciousness.

To better understand *I Heard the Owl Call My Name* it may help to know that the priest in this story belongs to the Anglican, and not the Roman Catholic, Church. The Anglican Church is a part of the Church of England. It came into being in the sixteenth century when Henry the VIII broke with the Pope and the church in Rome because of his eagerness to divorce Catherine of Aragon, who had not produced a male heir. Many of the practices of the Anglican Church are almost identical to those of the Roman Catholic Church, but it differs in not recognizing the Pope as its spiritual leader. Instead, the Anglican Church is headed by the Archbishop of Canterbury, who is mentioned in the story as knowing about the work at Kingcome. The clergy of the Anglican Church are permitted to marry. Their titles are similar to those in the Roman church: bishop, priest, curate. And the priests are often addressed as "father."

Your enjoyment of the story may be greater if you have a clear picture of the setting. Look at the map of British Columbia to get yourself oriented. The place-names used in *I Heard the Owl Call My Name* are all actual names of real locations that can be found on the map. The story begins with the initial journey of the young priest to his new parish. Follow his route to Kingcome on the map. This is the same trip that Margaret Craven, the author, made in 1965 in a small boat from Vancouver into the Queen Charlotte Straits of British Columbia. She was in search of adventure and material for her writing. And when she reached the Kwakiutl Indian village at the top of Kingcome Inlet, she knew she had reached her destination. It was a beautiful spot with its icy, clear waters, deep inlets dotted with islands, fir trees lining the shore, and cedar forests crowding back against the mountains behind. At times the deep silences were

*I Heard the Owl Call My Name* by Margaret Craven. Copyright © 1973 by Margaret Craven. Reprinted by special arrangement with Doubleday & Company, Inc.

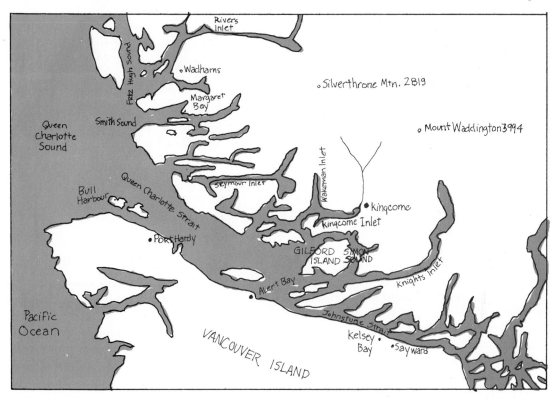

punctuated by the sounds of the splashing of salmon as they came home from the sea to spawn or the sound of the owl's call echoing in the night.

Miss Craven does not fit one's picture of the usual adventurer. At the time of her journey she was in her sixties, wore stout, sensible shoes as befitted her age, and a skirt, because she'd been told Canadians disliked women in slacks. With her white hair, glasses, and slightly plump figure she looked more like someone's grandmother than a writer who could and did put up with primitive conditions in order to get her story.

She lived in Kingcome for weeks, listening to and interviewing the Indians, taking careful notes. And at the same time she soaked up the fantastic beauty of the spot and the terrible sadness of the Indians. In her story she blends fact and fancy. What she learned bit by bit

about the customs and life of these people are the same things that Mark learns bit by bit in his stay. Perhaps this is what makes the experiences come alive and illumines the picture of the Kwakiutls.

This particular group of Indians once spread in a narrow band along the whole coast of the Pacific from Alaska to Puget Sound. They were a vigorous group whose civilization was built upon an abundant food supply from the sea and wood from the forests for housing, blankets, and canoes. The mountainous, heavily wooded land beyond the beaches made canoes and water their only means of transportation. And they were a gregarious group who went visiting often.

Among the Indian tribes they were considered wealthy, counting among their possessions the inherited rights to particular land spots for berry hunting and clam digging as well as rights to hunt and fish in a particular territory. Note in the story how T. P., Gordon's grandfather, first bequeaths his fishing rights to Gordon and later to Jim. If a group moved away, they had to return long distances to their own inherited territories for food.

The women in the tribe made quantities of mats, baskets, and blankets from the cedar trees, and these—along with the canoes, copper, and valuable boxes made by the men—comprised their tangible wealth. But the most important possessions of all were intangible things: myths, names, and privileges that were owned by a family but, during a particular time, belonged to a member of that family. Only the owner could sing a song or perform that dance. Sometimes an outsider might kill the owner of a song, and then the song became the killer's. The dances and celebrations in the story are traditional ones of the Kwakiutls.

These Indians saw life as a ladder of which the rungs were the titles they had gained and the privileges that went with those titles. Each step up this ladder had to be celebrated by potlatches, which were great feasts highlighted by an economic contest. Each participant tried to outdo opponents in giving gifts. Sometimes this ended in bankruptcy. Suicide was often the only exit from such a humiliating encounter.

Now only remnants of the Kwakiutls remain. The young are reluctant to leave their own culture with its customs to enter the "outside world." Yet they know their old ways are dying. It is ironic, indeed, that a dying white man finds his answers to what living and dying are all about among a group of Indians whose own way of life is gradually becoming extinct.

# I
# Heard the Owl
# Call My Name

## MARGARET CRAVEN

# Part 1
### Yes, My Lord—No, My Lord

The doctor said to the Bishop, "So you see, my lord, your young ordinand can live no more than three years and doesn't know it. Will you tell him, and what will you do with him?"

The Bishop said to the doctor, "Yes, I'll tell him, but not yet. If I tell him now, he'll try too hard. How much time has he for an active life?"

"A little less than two years if he's lucky."

"So short a time to learn so much? It leaves me no choice. I shall send him to my hardest parish. I shall send him to Kingcome on patrol of the Indian Villages."

"Then I hope you'll pray for him, my lord."

But the Bishop only answered gently that it was where he would wish to go if he were young again, and in the ordinand's place.

## 1

He stood at the wheel, watching the current stream, and the bald eagles fishing for herring that waited until the boat was almost upon them to lift, to drop the instant it had passed. The tops of the islands were wreathed in cloud, the sides fell steeply, and the firs that covered them grew so precisely to the high tide line that now, at slack, the upcoast of

British Columbia showed its bones in a straight selvage[1] of wet, dark rock.

"There's the sign of an old village," said the Indian boy who was his deckhand.

His eyes sought a beach which, long ago, the big stones had been removed so that the war canoes could be pulled up stern first. But there was no beach. There was nothing but clean, straight selvage, and a scattered mound of something broken and white in the gray of rain against the green of spruce, and he remembered the words Caleb had quoted him, and he repeated them now.

" 'When you see clam shells, know it is Indian country. Leave it alone.' "

"Queen Victoria," the Indian boy said quickly. "Some people didn't hear her."

Caleb had prepared him for this one, the first he was to know: "He's been working for a year in a mill town and is eager to return to his village. You'll not take the boat out without him until you get your papers. He could handle a boat when the was ten, and he knows more about the coast than you will ever learn. You'll think he's shy, and you'll be wrong. When you shake his hand, you'll know at once it's a gesture he's learned which has no meaning. In his eyes you'll see a look that is in the eyes of all of them, and it will be your job to figure out what it means, and what you are going to do about it. And he will watch you—they will all watch you—and in his own time he will accept or reject you."

Caleb, the old canon, had come out of retirement to acquaint him with all the endearing —and exasperating—little ways of the forty-foot diesel launch upon which his life would depend.

Back up. Go forward. Up and down the straits. In and out the lower inlets in a mild chop, in a moderate chop, in a gale. The tide-book open by the compass because you came with the tide, you went with the tide, you waited for the tide, and sometimes you prayed for the tide. Check the oil pressure and the shaft bearings. Pump the bilge. Watch for the drift logs. Count the lights on the masts of the tug boats that showed the size of their booms.

Because Caleb was old, the young man had thought, of course, he would be garrulous and full of reminiscence, but he was wrong. The talk had been entirely nautical. Even in the galley, over meals which the young man cooked, Caleb had occasionally dropped what surely could not, yet must be, godly counsel.

"Be sure to use the Victorian 'we,' lad."

"When you bury anybody, remember to look in the box the very last minute. Forty years ago up at Fort Rupert I buried the wrong man, and even now the RCMP has not forgotten it."

"Don't call them cannibals. It was never true literally. No one alive has seen the famous dance in which the young man, maddened by the cannibal spirit, returns to his village crying for flesh and carrying a body taken from a grave tree."

Then one evening they had tied up at the marina of Powell River where the Indian boy had been working, and Caleb lived.

"He'll be here early in the morning, and he'll help you load the organ the local church is sending to Kingcome Village. Don't be sorry for yourself because you are going to so remote a parish. Be sorry for the Indians. You know nothing and they must teach you," and Caleb had blessed him and ambled off, bare-headed in the rain, a man whose work on the coast was so legendary that it was said the Archbishop of Canterbury greeted him by his first name and a joke old between them, "Tell me, Caleb, how's your trap line? Any poaching?"

Then he was alone in the galley and sure of the look he would see in the Indian's eyes. The tribes of the villages which would form his patrol belonged to a people that had never been at war with the white man. They lived

---

1.  **selvage** \\ˈsël-vij\\ an outer or peripheral part.

where they had always lived. They fished as they had always fished, known for their intelligence and a culture that was perhaps the most highly developed of any native band on the continent. In the old days when a chief had given a great feast for his rivals, he let the fire that burned in the center of his ceremonial house catch the roof beams until the red embers fell, knowing that until he gave the sign, no guest dared move lest he admit the host's fire had conquered him. When he served his guests from the great ceremonial dishes, he spilt hot grease on their bare arms to see if he could make them wince. And sometimes he broke his own copper—big as a shield, it buying power as great as three thousand of the white man's dollars—broke it to show to his guests his disdain for his own wealth. Surely the look would be one of arrogance.

In the morning he awakened early, dressed, put the coffee on to boil, and went up the ladder into the wheelhouse and out onto the deck. On the float waited the first one.

He waited patiently as if he had waited all his life, as if he were part of time itself. He was twenty-seven, perhaps, which was the age of the young vicar. He wore a fisherman's dark trousers and jacket; a pair of gum boots hung over one shoulder. Beside him were his belongings in a heavy cardboard box, tied with string.

The young vicar jumped down on the float.

"Welcome aboard. I'm Mark—Mark Brian," and he held out his hand.

"I'm Jim Wallace," the Indian said shyly, and he took the hand with no answering pressure.

There was pride in his eyes without arrogance. Behind the pride was a sadness so deep it seemed to stretch back into ancient mysteries Mark could not even imagine, and he felt that small thrill of fear, of anticipation, which a man knows if he's lucky enough to meet and recognize his challenge.

He led the way aboard. Eager to be off,

the two of them worked hard, loading the organ onto the aft deck, covering it with a canvas, and lashing it tight.

Then they started north in a moderate swell and a driving rain, past the fishing village of Lund, past Cortes and Redonda, through the Yuculta Rapids, with Jim, the Indian, fighting the tide for the wheel. Just before dark they came to a lonely float in Shoal Bay.

"Shall we spend the night here?" Mark asked carefully. "Shall we have supper? I'll get it."

Now, on the second afternoon in the twentieth hour of passage, he stood at the wheel, approaching the first village which was to be part of his patrol.

"How soon now?"

"Very soon now. First you will see Ghost Island. It is where the Indians of Gilford village once buried their dead."

"In the ground?"

"No—in low sheds. Most of them have fallen and broken. If you go there now, you stumble over skulls green with moss."

He saw the small island, lovely as a jade jewel, and he slowed the boat and passed the village with its rare beach, white with clam shells, its stretch of cedar houses facing the water, and four great cedar posts standing in in the rain—all that was left of some ancient ceremonial house.

"This is the same tribe as yours at Kingcome?"

"No, but we're close relatives. Each February we come here to clam. Once the Indian agent asked us to live here because he could step easily onto the big float without getting his feet wet."

"And you refused?"

"No. Our old people said, 'We are going to Hollywood,' and we came. We had some fine dancing, the air filled with duck down. We saw the famous blanket trimmed with a thousand eagle beaks, and because we are not permitted to buy liquor to serve in our own homes, the boys traded two masks for three cases of beer, and we drank it very fast and got very drunk."

"And then?"

"Then we returned to our own village."

Beyond the village, inches above the high tide mark, Mark saw two carved killer whales, topped by a full moon.

"It's only the grave of Johnny Ray who was drowned," Jim told him. "When you come here to marry, to bury, to hold church in the school house, they will say to you, 'Johnny's hiding in the bush, and he steals things and scares our women. What'll we do?' "

In Cramer Pass a school of porpoise refused to move out of the boat's way, and watched the boat, heads up, headed straight for the boat and, at the last moment, leapt aside. And in the late afternoon they stopped to take on oil and water at the last point of contact with the outside world, a store where the loggers and Indians came for mail and supplies, built on a float, cabled to the steep island side.

The young vicar introduced himself to the oil agent and handed him a list of groceries he wished filled.

"Biggest order I'll fill this week. Newcomers don't buy here. They fill up south where things are cheaper."

"I know. Caleb told me," and the man's wife filled the order while he helped Jim with the oil. Two small raccoons, making a strange whirring sound, begged Mark for bread and took it gently in their strange little hands. When they were leaving, the wife of the oil agent gave Mark a bundle.

"One of your pals left his duds here," she said, "Caleb, probably," and Mark opened the bundle to find a cassock, its hem thick with dried mud.

Then they went on, the young vicar preparing supper in the galley, handing up plates of food and mugs of coffee. The Indian ate standing at the wheel; Mark perched on the high stool beside him.

No tug boat passed now; no huge boom of mixed logs. There was nothing but a lonely magnificence of sea and islands. When they went through Pamphrey's Pass and into King-come Inlet, which was the last, Mark saw the dorsal fine of a killer whale cruising slowly down the far side.

"Sometimes they rub against the boat," the Indian told him. "Sometimes they jump out of the water and come down flat with a terrific smash to knock off the barnacles that grow on the underside of their bodies."

"Why are we slowing?"

"Because we're passing the float house of Calamity Bill, the hand-logger. See his shack there and his A-frame? If we go too fast the wake of our boat will knock the nails out of his float, and he'll come out shaking his fist and swearing. He wears two sets of long-legged underwear and he changes one."

"The inside one, I hope."

"No—the outside one. The other's part of his skin, and when she knows you better, the wife of oil agent at the float store will ask you to help her get it off him and into ther washing machine."

"Oh, no, she won't."

They slipped through a pass so narrow Mark was sure the boat would scrape on a huge rock shaped like a whale and covered with brown seaweed.

"My people call it 'Whale Pass' because long ago the gods turned a whale into that rock."

Now they could see the great mountains lifting into the sky. On the far side of the inlet was a strip of bare granite, like the ragged scar of some huge grizzly, where a slide had peeled off every tree, every bit of soil. They could see the little falls that cascaded down cliffs, green with moss. The young vicar said to himself, "If man were to vanish from this planet tomorrow, here he would leave no trace that he ever was."

They moved up the twenty-mile inlet with the dusk deepening into dark, the raindrops glistening, falling slowly in the searchlight, an occasional little fish darting through the white, spumy wake off the bow. And they came at last to the government float, a third of a mile from the inlet's end and three and one-half miles from the village of Kingcome. They tied up on the inside of the float where the boat would not roll.

"In the morning how will we manage?"

"In the morning we will lower the speed boat and I will go first with your gear and food. I will return with boys from the village and two of the thirty-foot canoes, and they will help load the organ and take it to the village."

"Up the river?"

"Yes. On the cliffs before you reach the river, you will see paintings of cattle, sheep, goats and coppers that mark the gifts given in a great tribal potlatch. There were so many that, put end to end, it is said they would have reached from the village three miles down the inlet."

"The paintings are very old?"

"Less than thirty years. The potlatch was in 1936."

In the cabin under the bow the young vicar awakened in the night. The rain had stopped. Through the open porthole he could hear the wind murmuring in the firs, and the distant mewing of the gulls.

Somewhere in the dark night beyond the inlet and up the river waited the village, and he lay still, remembering all the Bishop had told him of the village when he had first asked him to come:

"It is an old village—nobody knows how old. According to the myth, after the great flood two brothers were the only human beings left alive in the world, and they heard a voice speak and it said, 'Come, Wolf, lend them your skin that they may go fleetly and find themselves a home.' And in the wolf's skin the brothers moved south until they came to a small lovely valley on a river's edge, surrounded by high mountains, and here they returned the skin to their friend, the wolf,

and they threw a magic stone to see which one would build his village here, and Quelele, the younger, moved on, and Khawadelugha, the elder, built his house, and in his dances he moved right as even now the dancers move right because the wolf moved right, and on his totem he carved a wolf as one of the crests of his tribe.

"The Indian name of the village is Quee which means 'inside place,' and according to the tribal history its site was chosen wisely because the river, its access, is treacherous and easily defended. But the enemy was wise also, and in the great tribal wars it came through a mountain pass and down the river, and the spirit that lives in Whoop-Szo, the Noisy Mountain, that is across the river and towers over the village, heard the enemy coming and set down a slide and buried it.

"Now Kingcome is known as a compact, Christian village, and this means that to run smoothly the elected chief, the vicar and the agent from the Indian Affairs Department must be co-operative and wise, and though I am sure the Lord could pass a small miracle and manage this, He seldom does. Once there was a chief who agreed with anyone on anything. Once there was an agent who said there was no use educating the Indian because if you did, you'd have to find him a job, and he was bound to die off anyway. And once the church sent a man to Kingcome who had never worked out well anywhere because it was sure here he could do no harm. All were wrong, and the village survived them.

"The Indian knows his village and feels for his village as no white man for his country, his town, or even for his own bit of land. His village is not the strip of land four miles long and three miles wide that is his as long as the sun rises and the moon sets. The myths are the village and the winds and the rains. The river is the village, and the black and white killer whales that herd fish to the end of the inlet the better to gobble them. The village is the salmon who comes up the river to spawn, the seal who follows the salmon and bites off his head, the bluejay whose name is like the sound he makes—'Kwiss-kwiss.' The village is the talking bird, the owl, who calls the name of the man who is going to die, and the silver-tipped grizzly who ambles into the village, and the little white speck that is the mountain goat on Whoop-Szo.

"The fifty-foot totem by the church is the village, and the Cedar-man who stands at the bottom holding up the eagle, the wolf and the raven! And a voice said the great cedar tree in Bond Square, 'Come forth, Tzakamayi and be a man,' and he came forth to be the Cedar-man, the first man-god of the people and more powerful than all others."

And the Bishop had been silent for a moment before he added slowly, "This is the village. If you go there, from the time you tie up at the float in the inlet, the village is you. But there is one thing you must understand. They will not thank you. Even if you should leave a broken man, they will not thank you. There is no word for thank you in Kwákwala."

## 2

The next morning the young vicar and his Indian deckhand were up at daylight. After a hurried breakfast in the galley, they went up on deck and jumped down onto the float to survey the day.

The rain had stopped, the wind had softened, and the sky was blue, flecked with cloud.

They swung out and lowered the small boat, and they stowed in it the young vicar's gear and everything that was to go to the village except the organ. Then Jim put on his gum boots, undid the line, climbed into the boat and started the outboard motor, and he was off to the mouth of the river without a word.

While he was gone, the young vicar worked on the boat. Already he had begun to think of the boat as he thought of his own arms and legs, an extension of himself. Caleb had told him how frequently a fisherman lost a boat because he was too busy with the catch to check its bilge.

"There is no more beautiful sight than a boat burning in the night," Caleb had said dryly."

Mark went over the engine room slowly, double-checking everything. He washed the dishes in the galley, placing them carefully behind the little racks that held them tight in a gale. He checked the log, put away the charts, made up the berths, cleaned the refrigerator, and closed the portholes. When he was done, the sun was high in the sky, and he went out on deck to await the canoes.

He heard them coming far down the inlet, the outboard motors sharp in the cedar air, and then he saw them, one black, one green, each thirty feet long, and narrow.

Jim had brought with him four young men of the village, and to Mark they looked strangely alike, with the same watchful, waiting eyes. Jim spoke to them in their own language, and when they had maneuvered the canoes to the stern of the boat, they lashed them together, while he and Mark untied the organ and removed the canvas that covered it.

Now it occurred to Mark that every single thing that went to Kingcome had to be taken up the river and for the first time he knew the stolid, stubborn indifference of the inanimate.

They moved the organ onto the gunwale of the aft deck. They tugged, pulled, shoved and lifted—the young vicar trying awkwardly to help, afraid the canoes would tip over and the organ end in the salt chuck. At last the organ was balanced on the canoes. Mark locked the boat, put on his gum boots, and took his place on the narrow crosspiece which was the seat, and they started up the inlet.

Even on this, one of the last good days of fall, it was cold, the water calm, and deep green from the shadow of the cedars. The falls slipped down the mossy cliffs. The mountains were snow-tipped above the timber line. When they passed the potlatch paintings and reached the muskeg[2] near the mouth of the river, the hand of the Welcome totem rose above the trees, and hundreds of small birds, of ducks and geese, rose at their passing.

They entered the river, passed the snags and the log jam, slowing now to seek the channels, to avoid the sandbars where the water was shallow. And up the river on the left Mark saw Whoop-Szo, the Noisy Mountain, and the white barked alders that edged the bank, and flying over them the sleek black ravens. But on the right he saw only one thing, the little white church of Saint Geroge.

The Indians took the canoes close to the shore and stepped out into the icy river. As carefully as they had placed the organ onto the canoes, they lifted it and carried it onto the black sands of Kingcome and up the little path that led past the old vicarage to the church.

They carried it up the steps to the porch, through the door, and set it down inside the church. Jim pulled over a bench, sat down and pedaled vigorously. Mark poked a key. Nothing happened.

"Oh, no!"

"It's a little damp. It will dry out in time."

Then Mark walked down the center aisle toward the hand-carved altar and the great, carved, golden eagle which was the lectern, its talons close together, its head turned so that it looked most smugly down its beak, its wings slightly parted to hold the Bible. He saw the carved chair where the Bishop must sit when he came here, and the life-sized Indian painting of Christ holding a little lamb. His face was the Indian's face, His eyes the Indian's eyes, and in them the depth of sadness.

He turned away slowly; he was alone in the church. He walked down the aisle to the door

and saw Jim waiting on the steps. No one else was visible, not even a child or a dog.

"Shall we go to the vicarage?" Jim asked.

They walked back to the old vicarage on the little path through the trees, and as they drew near, Mark heard a strange sound.

On the broken step of the vicarage sat an old Indian woman, her face scratched and bleeding. She was wailing loudly.

"One of the professional mourners," Jim told him. "There are three. When somebody dies they take turns wailing day and night."

"I did not see her when we passed the vicarage carrying the organ to the church."

"She saw you, and was afraid. She hid."

"And why here? Why does she wail at the vicarage?"

"Because the bodies are kept in the vicarage until burial."

As they approached the steps the old Indian woman scuttled into the trees. Jim opened the door and they stepped inside. On boards laid across two trestles was a small body covered with a plastic sheet. Mark lifted the sheet and drew it back, and he looked at what lay under it, and put the sheet down carefully.

"Who is he?"

"The weesa-bedó—the little, small boy. He had a birth defect injury and did not grow like the others. He was sailing a paper boat at the river's edge and fell in. When they saw him floating on the water, the other children thought he was a doll."

"And why—why hasn't he been buried?"

"Because no burial permit has been given. The chief councillor went at once to the nearest radio-telephone and summoned the RCMP, but no one has come yet."

"Then we had better call again."

"The constable will come today. The old men say so."

"How do they know?"

"How did they know you were coming today? They almost always know. Besides it is the first good day and he will come soon now. It is a five hour trip from Alert Bay,

---

2. muskeg \ˈməs keg\ a bog.

and he will want to get back before night, and he will be young, and he will be hard."

"How do you know he will be young?"

"An older man would not wait ten days."

"Will you take me to the mother?"

But when they had walked up the path through the trees and up the steps of one of the little cedar houses, and knocked on the door and entered, Mark did not know what to say to the woman who waited.

She waited as if she had waited all her life, as if she were part of time itself, gently and patiently. Did she remember that in the old days the Indian mother of the Kwakiutl band who lost a child kicked the small body three times and said to it, "Do not look back. Do not turn your head. Walk straight on. You are going to the land of the owl"?

He took her hands and spoke to her. "The old men say the constable will come soon. Then we shall bury him, and you can rest," but in her soft dark eyes found no response at all. When he returned to the vicarage to wait, he saw Jim and an older Indian, no doubt the chief councillor, walk down the path to the river, and he heard the motor of a speed boat, and watched it come and stop close to the beach.

The RCMP officer was young, and it was obvious why he had been long in coming. He had been waiting for a fair day, because with him he had brought his girl. He picked her up and carried her to the sands and Mark was sure he knew the words he spoke to her. "Look around as much as you want. Don't go into any of the houses except the church. This won't take long."

Then the RCMP officer talked to the chief councillor, both voices loud and angry.

"You had no business to move him. You know the rules. In an accident the body must not be moved."

"We were not sure he was dead. We thought we could revive him."

"And when you couldn't, you should have covered him and left him there."

"On the edge of the river with the tide coming in? In the rain?"

"Where is the body now?"

"It is in the vicarage."

They came toward Mark, followed by several Indian men.

"I'm Constable Pearson. Who are you?"

"Mark Brian. I am the new vicar-in-residence."

"And what do you know of this?"

"Nothing, I have just arrived."

"Let's go in. I'll want an autopsy."

"I'm afraid it is a little late for that?"

They entered the vicarage. Constable Pearson plucked the sheet from the small body and leaned toward it. Then he bolted from the room, down the rickety steps, and into the bush where he was very sick. The Indians were delighted. Laughter rose in their eyes, higher and higher, filling them, and hovering there in tremulous balance. Not a drop overflowed. When Constable Pearson emerged from the bush, all the eyes were sad again, and all the faces solemn.

"May I offer you a cup of tea?" asked the vicar, his voice expressively polite. "I notice there is smoke coming from the chimneys of several of the houses. I think we could manage a cup of tea."

Constable Pearson did not wish a cup of tea. He wanted to give the burial permit and leave. The forms must be filled out. Was there a table somewhere? Mark led him to the church, and on the top of the organ that wouldn't play they made out the forms, and the constable left.

"Now," said Jim, "we can hold the service for the boy."

"In the church?"

"No—in the open air. We have a new burial ground, but it is a mile from the village, and each time anyone dies the path must be cleared. The chief wishes the weesa-bedó to be buried in the old burial ground just beyond the end of the village, and the box is made, and the grave is dug, and already my

667

people are gathering there."

"I'll get my things."

"I'll help you," and they scrambled through Mark's gear that had been piled on the porch of the vicarage until they found a cassock and his Book of Common Prayer.

Then for the first time Mark walked the main path from one end of the village to the other, past the cedar houses that faced the path, the ceremonial house, the battered eagle poised on a slender shaft. One totem pole was so old he could discern only the top figure, a bear wearing at a most jaunty angle the lid of a garbage can to keep him from weathering further.

Beyond the village they entered the deep woods, Jim walked quickly, Mark holding his cassock out of the mud, and trying not to slip off the small saplings that made a bridge across one swampy place where the trees were so thick the sun never penetrated. At last they came into a glade and stopped, and stared.

"It is only the grave trees. In the old days each family had its own trees. The lower limbs were cut off as protection against the animals, and the boxes were hoisted by ropes and tied one above another in the tops. Many have fallen as you can see, and the grave sheds that were built later have fallen and most of the old carvings."

Later Mark could never remember the details of his first burial. Only parts remained clear. The faces of the tribe, which all looked alike, lifted and waiting in the brooding woods.

But the words were the same simple words that have been said for the weesa-bedós of all men, and it was as if they had been written for this place and this time. When he spoke, "I will lift up mine eyes unto the hills," there were the mountains rising above the great trees, and when he read that small and lovely prayer, ". . . protect him all day long until the shadows lengthen and the evening comes . . ." the sun had slipped beneath the mountain

tops, and the shadows were lengthening on the small grave at his feet. When it was done, he managed to find among all the faces the mother, and this time it was she who touched his sleeve gently and thanked him with her eyes.

But the tribe did not disperse, and he sensed there was something yet unfinished of which he had no part, and he said, "I will go back to the village now, Jim."

"I'll go with you."

On the way back Mark could hear an old man's voice speaking loudly in the burial glade, almost shouting.

"It is the eldest. He is speaking the ancient Elizabethan Kwákwala which the young no longer know. Where there is no written language, anything which must be remembered must be said."

When they reached vicarage, the trestle was gone. Someone had made a fire in the old wood stove and let the vicarage fill with the smoke of green cedar and let the breeze clear it. Two places were set on the tattered oil-cloth of the kitchen table, a plate and a fork, and in the center of the table was a board holding an unappetizing mess of something black and steaming.

"We have had nothing to eat since breakfast. Shall we have dinner?" Jim asked. "It is probably old Marta who brought it."

"What is it?"

"Seaweed and corn. It is called gluckaston. Try it. You'll like it," and the young vicar tried it and found it excellent.

"I will not need you tomorrow. I'll be busy here in the vicarage."

"Then I'll go fishing. Maybe I'll get drunk. Do you want to know why I'll get drunk?

"Because the weesa-bedó was my relative. When I was five, which was his age, my uncle gave a feast for me and I was given my third name and I danced. I had practiced the steps in play."

After the meal Jim helped carry the gear into the vicarage, and when he left, Mark walked with him onto the porch and watched him go up the path into the dark trees. Then he went inside by himself, into the sweet and spicy smell of death.

# 3

When dark came to the village there was a gentle, cautious confabulation[3] about the young vicar who had come from the great outside world. The young women found an imminent need to exchange crochet patterns, and they met like a huddle of young hens and whispered about his looks, his manners, even his clean fingernails.

Chief Eddy, on his way to the social hall, met Jim on the path and he asked, "How does he seem to you?"

"He will be no good at hunting or fishing. He knows little of boats. All the time he says we. 'Shall we have dinner now? Shall we tie up here?' Pretty soon he will say, 'Shall we build a new vicarage?' He will say we and he will mean us," and they both smiled.

In the social hall Chief Eddy found the old men waiting to play the ancient guessing game of La-hell, the benches in place, the bones on the floor. He sat down and the game began, all the players waiting for T. P. Wallace, the elder, the orator of the tribe, to mention the young vicar first.

T. P. was the only one alive now whose broad brow showed that as an infant it had been tightly bound with cedar bands. In his white shirt, tie and best jacket, he was as impressive as any Montreal executive, and cast in bronze his head would have been out of place in that museum room reserved for the busts of the ancient Romans. He was slow to speak.

"Did you notice that at the graveside he left quietly and asked no questions?" They all nodded. "He respected our customs. And what will he say when he knows we are losing our sons, and that our young no longer understand the meaning of totems?"

"When the constable was sick in the bushes," said Chief Eddy, "how well he held his laughter."

In one of the best houses of the village Mrs. Hudson, and matriarch, was pleased that a vicar was again in residence. The Bishop would surely come more frequently, perhaps even with a boatload of landlubber clergy to be fed and housed, and the young wives would gather here in her house to defer to her judgment, speaking softly in Kwákwala.

"What meat shall we have?"

"Roast beef." Or salmon. Or wild goose. Or duck.

"And what vegetable shall we have?" Mrs. Hudson's answer was always the same, and her small revenge on the white man, the intruder.

"Mashed turnips." No white man liked mashed turnips.

In a small neat house off the main path, Marta Stephens prepared to knit a toque to keep the new vicar's head warm when he came up the river in the winter. Marta was one of the grandmothers of the tribe. Her hair was white, which, in an Indian, means she was very old. Her face was finely wrinkled and of obvious gentility. She was the daughter of an hereditary chief, the wife of a chief, the mother of a chief. At the tribal feasts held for the Bishop, it was she who always slipped him a little dish of peas from her garden because he detested mashed turnips, and when he had first come to the village years before, cowering in a canoe under a tarpaulin in a heavy rain, it had been she who held a cup of coffee to his lips because his hands were so cold he could not hold it.

"And how did you like our river?" And the Bishop had answered dryly that getting into heaven could be no harder than reaching this

---

3. **confabulation** \kən-ˈfab-ū-lā-shən\ a discussion.

village, and didn't Mrs. Stephens agree it was bound to be warmer?

In the poorest house Sam, the unlucky one, considered how best to approach the new vicar for a loan. Soon, of course, while he was green and before the Bishop had a chance to warn him. Sam was descended from slaves and in the old days to be a slave was to be worse than a nothing. He had no pride. His boats burned under him. When he reached the fishing grounds, the fish had not come yet, or they had seen him and fled. Sam wanted only two things in life, liquor and sex, and when he had no money for liquor, he beat his wife and Ellie, his daughter.

In the night Jim awakened and asked himself, "Will he know that here I am free?"

In the night Keetah, Mrs. Hudson's grand-daughter, awakened also, the only one of the tribe who had no English proper name, and she asked herself, "Will he know that my Gordon feels himself trapped here?"

In the night in the last house next to the old burial ground old Peter, the carver, heard a flight of wild geese pass over the village, honking loudly, and he counted the seconds of their passing as was his custom. But it was not a huge migration. No more than a mile long. "How long will he be here before he knows that I live among the dead?"

In the teacher's house the only other white man in the village did not think of the vicar at all. He didn't even know he had arrived; he didn't even know he was coming. This was the teacher's second year in the village. He did not like the Indians and they did not like him. When he had returned from his summer holiday, a seaplane had deposited him at flood tide under the alders on the far side of the river, and he had stood there in the rain yelling loudly, "Come and get me," and T. P. had announced, "If he cannot be more polite, let him stay there." It was old Marta who finally poled across the river and plucked him from the bank. The teacher had come to the village solely for the isolation pay which

would permit him a year in Greece studying the civilization he adored.

At star-fall a young buck walked through the village to drink at the river. He was unafraid of guns. The Indian hunted for food, not for fun, and when he found it necessary to kill a deer, he did not shoot him. If possible, he knocked him over the head with a club.

Just before dawn when day and night were locked in their tug-of-war, and day began slowly to push away the dark, Ellie, the little lost one, returned to the house of Sam, her father. Ellie went willingly to the bed of any man who beckoned her, and since, at thirteen years, brutality was all she knew of masculine attention, she liked best the man who mistreated her the most.

4

In the morning when the young vicar stepped onto the rickety porch, it was as if the funeral of the weesa-bedó had never happened. The village was quiet, and utterly at peace. In the river he could see a long, black canoe moored, and as he watched, an older Indian woman waded out into the icy water, climbed into the canoe, poled into the center of the stream and dumped her garbage, and he knew that was what he would do—in the sun, in the sleet, in the rain, and the snow.

When he tried to start a fire in the kitchen stove, the wood was wet and the stovepipe smoked, and when he went to open a can of coffee, there was no can opener, and he finally extracted sufficient coffee for two cups by hammering a hole in the top of the can with a nail. For the first time it occurred to him that just to stay alive, fed, and clean here was going to occupy many hours a day.

After breakfast, he went to the church, and for the first time noticed that the tower was broken, that there were no altar hangings and no candles. When he approached the altar, he saw that the frontal piece—no doubt given by some small town church that had acquired a new one—was propped up on old crates. And, more important, on this fine day of early fall, the little church was dank and cold. He knew that unless he wanted to stand by the golden eagle on a winter Sunday and watch his congregation freeze between the "dearly beloved brethren" and the blessing, he must manage somehow to nail plywood over the bare studding and insulation behind it. He knew also that even if he managed it, he would be up at dawn every Sunday hurrying along the little path from the vicarage, a coat hastily flung over his pajamas, on his way to rattle up a fire in the big, round, black stove.

Then he returned to the vicarage and went over it carefully—all two rooms of it. There was no plumbing. The paper hung in shreds from the walls. The walls were discolored and warped where the rain had entered. When he tried to open a window, the whole sill came loose in his hand, and the floor sagged under him. There was no doubt about it. The vicarage was falling down.

He had come to give and he was going to begin where every man is apt to begin who is sent to hold some lonely outpost. He was going to begin by begging. "I want this. I need that. I need paint. I need plywood. I would appreciate a couple of hundred pounds of insulation, and if it isn't too much trouble, send me a new vicarage complete with plumbing."

It was all wrong and he knew it. In desperation he shot an arrow prayer into the air: "Oh, dear Lord, what am I going to do about this vicarage?" He sent it aloft at ten in the morning and the Lord answered him promptly at twelve. Chief Eddy came to the door with a letter from the Bishop which had been brought in the mail bag by one of the fishermen some days previously, and forgotten in the confusion of yesterday's funeral.

The young vicar sat down at the kitchen table and opened it slowly. He knew it must have been written before he and Jim had started north, and he was afraid to read it.

"I am sure," wrote the Bishop, "that when you receive this, you will be aware that the old vicarage must be replaced. When you are ready, I shall make arrangements to have a pre-fabricated two-bedroom house delivered at the float at the end of the inlet. I can, of course, send no one to help you put it up. You must begin by working with your hands. The Indians work with their hands. This is the way they will respect you and this is your ministry."

Mark read it twice and had a sudden and appalling vision of hundreds of boards, kegs of nails, bolts and shingles, perhaps even a bathtub, all heavy, stubborn and totally inanimate, piled high on the float, waiting to be carried up the river by canoe.

He scurried through his luggage for paper and pencil, and he seated himself at the kitchen table and wrote to the Bishop.

"Please, my lord, do not send me a vicarage. At least, not yet. I do not even know how to get it up the river, much less put it up. I am going to begin today by cleaning the church. When I finish, I shall patch up the vicarage. It's strange, but since receiving your letter, I do not seem to find the sweet smell of death too oppressive."

He sealed the letter and gave it to Chief Eddy to go out by the first boat. Then he returned to the church, and in the tiny vestry in back he found an ancient broom, and he swept the church carefully. He made a fire in the big round stove and heated water. Then he scrubbed the strip of red linoleum that covered the center aisle.

"There is a bear loose in the church," said Mrs. Hudson, the matriarch, to T. P., the elder. "What a clatter he is making!"

"By evening he will be quieter," T. P. told her. "By evening the bear will have blistered both paws."

The Indians were polite. They were not unfriendly. When he had cleaned the church, he worked on the vicarage with the broom and the scrub brush, and when he wearied and ambled to the river's edge where the women were smoking and drying fish, they smiled at him shyly. When he stopped in the door of the ceremonial house and looked beyond the dirt floor to the carved posts and the two-headed serpent painted on the rear wall, old Peter, the carver, who was working on a canoe, answered his questions.

"How are you going to widen it?" the vicar asked, and Peter told him he was going to fill the canoe with water and drop into it hot rocks to make the wood expand to the cedar stretchers, and when this was done, he would singe the bottom.

They were polite and this was all. When Jim returned from fishing, they went again down the river to the float and by the boat to the other villages which were part of his patrol, and in each he arranged to hold church in a schoolhouse or a private home once a month. It was always the same. The sad eyes. The shy smiles. The cautious waiting.

But for what? How must he prove himself? What was it they wished to know of him? And what did he know of himself here where loneliness was an unavoidable element of life, and a man must rely solely on himself?

On the river on the way back to Kingcome in the little speed boat, the young vicar knew that the Indians belonged here as the birds and fish belonged, that they were as much a part of the land as the mountains themselves. He was a guest in their house, and he knew, also, that this might never change, and he told himself what does it matter if a man is lonely? One does not die of it.

When they reached the village, he hoed out the wild grass that had grown rank around the vicarage. When this was done, he visited the sick. On his way back to the vicarage, he passed a small, weathered cedar house, its owner out in the yard trying to start an ancient washing machine hitched up to a small gasoline engine, and he stopped to help him.

The next morning he removed the broken board of the vicarage steps and the Indian he had helped came by to offer him a saw and found him a board for a new step.

In the afternoon he climbed up on the roof to see if he could stop the leaks, and Chief Eddy walked by to watch him.

"Aren't you afraid you'll fall through?" And Mark answered that he considered it not only possible, but likely.

"I'd rather come down on top of the vicarage than have the vicarage come down on me," and for a moment he saw humor rise in the sad eyes and hold.

He did not mention the Bishop's offer to send him a new vicarage. He had made up his mind that he would not ask help in getting it up the river, or putting it up. He would wait until they offered help, or do without it.

Sam, the ne'er-do-well, came over to watch him work, shedding large tears and shamelessly begging money, and Mark turned him down.

Also, the teacher accosted him on the path, asking that he intervene with the authorities that he be given proper supplies. Even the smallest villages were given more pencils and pads. Also, he was expected to pay for the paper tissues which he dropped so generously for the sniffling noses of his pupils. Furthermore, his house had no electricity, and its tiny bathroom was so small that when he sat upon the throne-of-thought he could not shut the door without hitting his knees, which was an outrage.

The young vicar suggested the teacher cut two round holes for his knees to stick through, and offered to trade his outhouse for the teacher's bathroom, but the teacher was not amused. There was one more thing he felt it his duty to inform the vicar. The vicar might as well know right now that as for himself, he was an atheist; he considered Christianity a calamity. He believed that any man who professed it must be incredibly naïve.

The young vicar grinned and agreed. There were two kinds of *naïveté*, he said, quoting

Schweitzer; one not even aware of the problems, and another which has knocked on all the doors of knowledge and knows man can explain little, and is still willing to follow his convictions into the unknown.

"This takes courage," he said, and he thanked the teacher and returned to the vicarage.

When he closed the door, he sensed he was not alone, and when he turned slowly, he welcomed his first visitors.

They were six years old perhaps—a little girl and boy. They had entered without knocking—never would he be able to teach them to knock—and they stood like fawns—too small to be afraid. They stood absolutely still, and they smiled, slowly and gently. When he asked their names, they did not answer, watching him from their soft, dark, sad eyes, as their ancestors must have watched the first white man in the days of innocence.

"I think," he said, "I shall go for a little walk," and the little boy said, "We will go with you." When they went out the door, the boy ran ahead to the grease pole that stood in front of the church, and up it, hand over hand.

Mark held out his hand, and the little girl took it, and they stood a moment, staring up at Whoop-Szo, the Noisy Mountain, towering beyond the river, and she said, as if it were very important, "I love the snow on the mountains."

Thus, the children were his first friends, and for love of their laughter he always kept his door ajar. One day, when Chief Eddy stopped to see if he had fallen yet through the roof of the vicarage, the young vicar stopped his patching and descended the ladder.

"Chief Eddy," he said earnestly, "there is something I have been meaning to ask you. How do you pronounce the name of your tribe?" It is spelled Tsawataineuk.

"Jowedaino."

There was a silence.

"Would you mind saying it again?"

"Jowedaino," and Mark listened more carefully than he had ever listened to any word in his entire life and could not tell if the word was Zowodaino or Chowudaino.

"And the name of the band to which your tribe belongs?" which in the books of anthropology is written Kwakiutl.

"Kwacutal," and Mark listened and could not tell if the word was Kwagootle, Kwakeetal or Kwakweetul.

"And the name of the cannibal who lived at the north end of the world?"

"Bakbakwalanuksiwae," and it came from the chief's lips like a ripple.

"What chance did he have with a name like that? And what chance have I? I shall never be able to spell or pronounce even the name of this tribe."

"I can't spell it myself," said the chief. "Begin with something easier. Try saying how do you do. Weeksas—weeksas."

After that when Mark passed the Indians on the path, he said "Weaksauce," exactly as the chief had said it, and saw the humor take their eyes.

On the first Sunday morning he tolled the church bell half an hour before the service. He was sure no one would come. He stayed in the tiny vestry behind the altar and waited.

He was wrong. Everyone came except the teacher, Sam, the sick and the very young. On the very first hymn he found he must never for an instant let go of a high note because if he did, his congregation would sink an octave and never come up again. He was young enough to be a little proud of his first sermon, to which he had given considerable thought: "It is better to be a small shrimp in the sea of faith than a dead whale on the beach."

When the service was over, he stood at the door, trying desperately to learn what the Indians called their English nicknames and to affix each to the right face. Marta Stephens was last, and it was now she presented the toque.

"To keep your head warm on the river," she explained, and the young vicar thanked her, and put it on.

"How do I look?"

"Like an egg. Exactly like an egg."

He walked down the steps with her, sensing somehow that she was to mean much to him.

"Mrs. Stephens, tell me something. Do you remember the first man who came here for the church?"

"Yes. He had a long white beard. He had to learn our language so he could teach us his. He said, 'What is this? What is that?' and sometimes we told him the wrong word to tease him. I am ashamed of it now. He was so patient. He was patient even with the children who pulled his beard."

"How do you know?"

"Because," Marta said, "I was one of them."

## 5

Often in the first weeks, Mark was beset by a sense of futility, and always he was lonely. On the patrol to the other villages, which somehow he must bind together into a parish, hour passed hour and neither he nor Jim spoke a word. He gave up trying to know Jim, even hoping to understand him, and learned to wait, clinging staunchly to Caleb's Victorian we. In his turn Jim served him well and dutifully, the cautious waiting still in his eyes.

Then one late afternoon there was a change. They had been to the float store to pick up a load of plywood to cover the bare studdings in the church, and when they reached the government float at the end of the inlet, they left the load to bring up the river by canoe the next day, and started for the village in the speed boat. When they neared the river mouth on a rising tide, Jim stopped the engine and motioned Mark to be still.

They sat quietly, the boat drifting slowly, Jim watching a ripple line on the clear and sunless water. Then they saw it. A run of humpback salmon was entering the river to spawn in the Clearwater. Two or three feet beneath the surface Mark could see hundreds of silvery fish, pressed tight, moving secretly, almost stealthily, with a kind of desperate urgency, as an army moves to hold an outpost which must be reached at any cost. He watched, fascinated, until they had passed, and for a moment he was not sure that it had happened at all.

" 'Come, swimmer,' " he said. " 'I am glad to be alive now that you have come to this good place where we can play together. Take this sweet food. Hold it tight, younger brother.' "

Then, for the first time, the watchful waiting left the Indian's eyes and he said eagerly, "How did you know that? Where did you hear it?"

"It's a prayer your people once said to the salmon, and I read it in a book written long ago. The hook was called 'younger brother.' The halibut was called 'old woman.' When your people pulled a halibut into a canoe, they said 'Go, old flabby mouth, and tell your uncles, and your cousins, and your aunts how lucky you were to come here.' But they spoke with respect of the salmon and they called him 'swimmer.' "

"The salmon is still the swimmer in our language, and I can remember my grandfather speaking to him as you do now. I had forgotten."

"Do you see him enter the river often?"

"No, not often. He enters usually at night."

"And in the end, does he always die?"

"Always. Both the males and the females die. On the way up the river the swimmer will pass the fingerlings of his kind coming down to the sea. They want to go and are afraid to go. They still swim upstream, but gently, letting the river carry them downstream tail first, and the birds and the larger fish prey upon them to devour them, and pretty soon they turn to face their dangers."

"And when they reach the open sea?"

"Then they are free. Nobody knows how far they go or where. When the time comes to return, their bodies tell them, and those hatched in the same stream separate from all the others and come home together. And in the end the swimmer dies, and the river takes him downstream, tail first, as he started."

"Could we see the end?"

"Easily."

On one of the last lovely days of September Mark packed a lunch and he and Jim went up-river in one of the smaller outboard canoes to seek the end of the swimmer. Above the village where the river curved left into rapids, they stopped at a pool at the foot of Che-kwa-lá, the falls, on a stream that fell into the river. Here it was cool and misty, the spruce and the hemlock hanging with moss, one huge cottonwood standing guard. They stood for a long time watching the troubled restless water of the falls coming to rest in the deep quiet pool, and neither spoke.

Then they went on up the rapids of the river, and a bear, fishing for the swimmer, saw them come and scrambled into the trees, and the two deer that had come to the river to drink saw them also, and were gone in one lovely fluid leap.

Well up the river they passed cedar shake cabins, smoke coming from the holes in their roofs, and Mark could see some of the children of the tribe playing under the trees.

"They have come to smoke fish," Jim told him. "Each fall, families come to do this. It is a time everyone likes. The children run wild and the women talk. And at night the men sit by the fire and tell the old myths, and when they return, they are as well smoked as the fish."

When they came to the Clearwater where the swimmer spawned, they turned off the motor and paddled through deep quiet pools, overhung with thick brush, to the little falls at the end of the stream and pulled the canoe up on a small, rocky beach of a little island, and they saw they were not alone. Old Marta was there and the girl called Keetah, and the two small children who were his friends, come from the shake cabins to pick blueberries.

At lunch, which they shared, Mark felt at ease for the first time. It was a picnic like any picnic. The day was fair on the small and lovely island. The children played as all children play, and the girl called Keetah, in the faded blue denim slacks and jacket, was a pretty girl anywhere.

"Mark wants to see the end of the swimmer," Jim announced after lunch, and Marta smiled and said she was too old to hang over the pool's edge flat on her middle; she would stay with the children and pick the rest of the blueberries. Jim found a place where an old maple grew over the stream and the under-brush cast deep shadows. There the three of them crept carefully to the stream's edge and looked down.

Under the clear water they saw the female swimmer digging the seed beds with her torn tail, her sides deep red and blue, her fins battered and torn.

"When she has laid her eggs and the wait-ing males have covered them with milt, she will linger, guarding them for several days," Jim said. "Let's try another pool." They moved again and saw the end of the swimmer. They watched her last valiant fight for life, her struggle to right herself when the gentle stream turned her, and they watched the water force open her gilles and draw her slowly downstream, tail first, as she had started to the sea as a fingerling. Then they crept away from the pool's edge and returned to Marta, and Mark saw that in Keetah's eyes there were tears.

"It is always the same," she said. "The end of the swimmer is sad."

"But, Keetah, it isn't. The whole life of the swimmer is one of courage and adventure. All of it builds to the climax and the end. When the swimmer dies he has spent himself com-pletely for the end for which he was made, and this is not sadness. It is triumph."

"Mark is right, Keetah," Marta said. "It is not sad. It is natural. When I was a child and a sea-hunter died, we believed he went to the land of the killer whale, and a land-hunter to the home of the wolves, and a slave to the home of the owls. But when twins were born in the village, we did not think they were children at all. They were swimmers."

"I have a twin sister," Mark said. "She is my only close relative," and they all laughed, and Marta said, "The swimmer is your relative. You belong to the salmon people."

On the way back to the village Mark and Jim spoke little. When they had moored the canoe, waded ashore, and were walking up the path to the vicarage, Mark said slowly, "Keetah is a beautiful girl. Do you not think so?"

"Yes. When she was at the government school in Alert Bay she was called the 'little princess.' She was homesick. When the children stood in line to receive the cod-liver oil, she went to the end of the line for another dosage because the oil tastes like the gleena in which we dip our food."

"She is married?"

"No—she is to marry Gordon. Her grandmother has arranged it. He is at the government school in Alert Bay. He is older than the others there because he stayed out of school to help his uncle with the fishing. But she will not marry him. She will marry me."

"What makes you so sure?"

"Because I am the only other man in the village she can marry. She is too closely related to the others. She will marry me, keep my house, and have my children, and I will leave her and go off to fish."

"She does not like Gordon?"

"She likes him."

"Then what is the matter with him?"

"Gordon is che-kwa-lá, which means fast moving water," Jim said slowly, "and Keetah is the pool."

Whenever they came up the river from the float, Mark watched for the swimmer, the pressed silver forms moving secretly beneath the surface. He did not see him again.

## 6

In late October the fishing days grew fewer, lessening slowly to an end. Now there were more men in the village. Sometimes Mark would see one setting off into the woods to hunt, his rifle held so easily it seemed part of the man himself. And sometimes he saw two starting off together, one man's arm over the shoulder of the other, and he knew this was no indication of homosexuality; it was the warrior-to-warrior relationship, centuries old. But never did he see groups of men talking loudly of the hunt that was planned, and this also was rooted in the past. If a man said aloud, "I will pursue the deer here; I will seek the bear there," some woman would hear him, and ten minutes later all the wives of the tribe would be promising each other venison and bear steaks, and discussing how to cook them, and the spirits that lived in the bear and the deer would hear them, and the game would hide.

One day in the vicarage over lunch, Mark questioned Jim about the hunting, and Jim asked if he'd like to go along, and Mark said he would—to watch, that is, since he was no hunter himself and had never shot anything larger than a rabbit or a duck.

"Have you had sufficient sustenance to suffice?" he asked when the meal was done, and Jim said, "What is this word *suffice*?" and Mark told him it meant "Have you had enough to eat?"

Early one morning, they went again upriver with three other men from the village, and after an hour on a mountain called Quanade, they followed a bear. However hard Mark tried to keep up, he was always last, breaking through the underbrush with a frightful clatter, snagged on the devil's club, slipping on the shale. When he was sure he could not take another step, one of the Indians whirled and a shot sounded, and a large brown form dropped. They approached it carefully.

*A Kwakiutl with bounty from the sea.*

"I thought we were following the bear," Mark said to Jim.

"We were until he circled. He's been following us for an hour."

"But there's no bullet hole."

"It is hidden by the fur and rolls of fat," and Mark saw the laughter rise and hold in all the dark eyes.

"This bear did not die of a bullet," one of the Indians told him gravely. "He died of shock. It's the first time he's ever seen a vicar so far up on the mountain."

In mid-afternoon one of the men shot a gray timber wolf that weighed at least a hundred and thirty pounds, its big mouth full of what semed to Mark an overabundance of very large teeth, and he and Jim took leave of the others and walked through the woods back to the shake cabins to start supper and prepare the bough beds upon which the blankets would be spread.

They trudged in silence for at least an hour.

"You know something, Jim?"

"What?"

"I think we're being followed."

"It's only the mate of the wolf that was

killed. When we move, she moves. When we stop, she stops. Let's rest."

They rested, and Mark got out his pipe, filled, tamped and lighted it, trying very hard not to look back, trying not to show by squirming that he wished to go on. Finally Jim spoke. He spoke slowly and carefully.

"Have we had sufficient to suffice? Have we had enough?"

"Did you say we?"

"Yes."

"I don't know about you, but I have," and they went on quickly, leaving behind them the widow wolf and Caleb's splendid Victorian we that had served Mark well and that he would not use again.

That night, in the largest of the shake cabins, they lay close together on their bough beds in their clothes and their wool caps, the fire burning on the dirt floor, and the Indians talked so long of the man-god who lived in the sea and controlled the fishes that Mark went to sleep before he ever learned what the killer whale said to the swimmer, and the swimmer to the halibut. When he awoke the shake cabin was filled with smoke, his face was grimy with soot, his eyes stung, the bough bed had grown hard, and even with his head under the blankets, he could not stop coughing. He pulled on his boots—the only thing he'd taken off—and, plucking the top blanket, he crept for the door and out. He put the blanket around his shoulder and his back against a big cedar, and stood in the cool dark. Presently Jim joined him.

"What are you doing here? We thought we'd lost you."

"I couldn't stop coughing. I was afraid I'd awaken the others. Jim, don't ask me to creep behind a deer and wham him over the head with a club."

"I won't."

"And I'll never fish as well as the Indians. Sometimes I'm not even sure I'll learn to handle the boat."

"You are doing well with the boat. In an-

other six months you will be almost as good as an Indian boy by the time he is ten."

They stood under the cedar in the rain until daybreak. Both knew there was friendship between them now, forged without words and needing none.

In November the rain fell in a slow and patient drizzle. Already the rain had become an element of life like the air Mark breathed, and when it stopped, he missed it somehow, and found himself listening for the drip, drip, drip that seemed now a necessary and comforting component of his life.

## 7

In November the hospital ship of the tiny Anglican fleet tied up at the float as it did every six weeks, and the doctor was brought up the river by canoe, and turned the old vicarage into a clinic. The doctor was new on the ship and had never pulled a tooth in his life. He could not hypnotize the Indians during the process as had his predecessor. When he did not wait long enough for the novocaine to take hold, Sam, his first patient, let out such horrific moans that little Ethel, one of the two children who had come first to the vicarage, hid in the woods. When the doctor had gone, Mark found her among the trees, and he took her to the vicarage, sat her in a chair, tied one end of a string around her wobbly baby tooth and the other to a doorknob, and he said, "Now, Ethel, I'll count ten, and then I'll kick the door shut."

"One-two-three," he counted, and he slammed the door on five and out flew the tooth.

"Nothing to it," he said, and while he picked up the swabs, the lint, and the bandages, little Ethel swept up the teeth from the vicarage floor.

A week later one of the boys of the village was very ill in the night with what Mark was sure was acute appendicitis. The hospital ship was in Seymour Inlet, too far to come quickly, and a bush plane, if he could manage to summon one by the radio-telephone on the boat, could not land on the river at night. He and Jim packed the boy in blankets, took him by canoe to the boat, packed his side in crushed ice and took him to Alert Bay.

When they had delivered the patient safely to the hospital and started back to the village, they found the straits shrouded in a thick fog, and the boat rolling heavily in the swell that came down Queen Charlotte Sound. But Jim knew the way, sounding the whistle to catch an echo from an island or an inlet side. They crept up the inlet to the float, and they crept up the river past the log jams and the snags, the water gurgling around them, Mark, who had forgotten his Kingcome slippers, trying to hold his feet out of the rain water in the bottom of the canoe.

When they reached the vicarage, Marta had started a fire, and set a pot of soup on the back of the stove and a loaf of homemade bread on the table, and they ate ravenously.

With December all the things in the village —the stubborn, inanimate things—revolted at once. The church stove smoked. The wet wood refused to burn. The hot water boiler in the house of Chief Eddy burst its seams. The mended roof of the old vicarage developed sundry leaks, the rain hitting the waiting buckets with a rhythmic plop. The boat developed gasket trouble, and the generator that operated the lights in the church—the only one in the village—refused to start fifteen minutes before the Sunday Evensong. Mark took off his surplice, put on his heavy Indian sweater. Out came the wrenches, off came the fuel line. He drained the fuel tank. He bled the air from the fuel line, then connected it all up again. He cranked, talking steadily to himself, "Yes, my lord. No, my lord. Yes, my lord. No, my lord."

"Who are you talking to?" Jim asked.

"The Bishop."

"But he isn't here."

"And a good thing too—" and he gave a violent kick to the generator which responded with a surprised wheeze and a chug-chug. Then he hurried to the vicarage, washed the grease from his hands and face, got into his surplice and went to the church where the congregation was waiting. "And God said, let there be light, and there was light."

In the last week of the month Mark neglected his boat and paid for it heavily. He and Jim had returned from patrol and had just tied up at the float when the radio-telephone began to beep, and they were summoned back to one of the other villages, where three children, left alone in their cedar house for a few moments, had tipped over a kerosene lamp and been burned to death.

On the way back from the funeral on a rainless night, the wind blowing and the tide running, the engine died. Frantically Jim worked on the filter while Mark tried to keep the boat from the rocks, and when the filter was cleaned and the engine caught, he knew that curious change of tempo—one moment every breath a prayer and the next moment, the tension gone, and the two of them joking. The next day he knew also the exhaustion which is the price of courage.

When the weather turned cold, the trip upriver became torment. One afternoon a violent wind caught them in the open boat, the sleet blown vertically across the mountain sides. It cut their faces and blew an empty oil drum and the mail sack from the boat. When they reached the vicarage, they sat with their feet propped in the oven door of the old stove, sure that they would never know what it was to be warm again.

Mark wrote to the Bishop: "I have learned little of the Indians as yet. I know only what they are not. They are none of the things one has been led to believe. They are not simple, or emotional, they are not primitive." The Bishop wrote back: "Wait—you will come to know them."

But his acquaintance had widened now. He knew the young hand-logger who took his

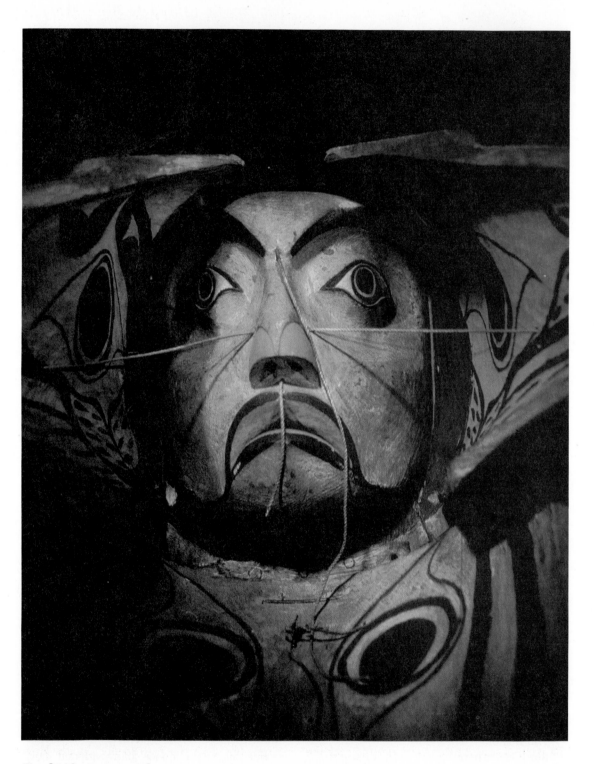

*Kwakiutl warrior mask.*

four children in a little open boat to the school at Echo Bay each morning and home again each afternoon, and sometimes he shared dinner with him and his fine brood at their float house on the edge of the chuck. He had visited the logging camp, and never did he pass the float house of Calamity Bill without looking to see if smoke was coming from his chimney and his ancient donkey engine was wheezing in the spruce. At sixty-five, Calamity climbed four thousand feet each day straight up the mountain side to cut his timber, and three times he had ridden his gear down into the chuck. When Mark stopped to ask how things were, the reply never varied, "Calamitous," and when Calamity Bill asked if he might come aboard, Mark's reply never varied either, "Yes, if you take off your cork boots."

One day in the church he remembered the organ, and he sat down and pumped the pedals and very tentatively, as if he didn't care at all, he pulled out a stop and poked a key and was rewarded by a fine, round tone. That night, one of the Indian women who had studied music at the school of Alert Bay, practiced the hymns which were to be sung at Christmas, and an old brown bear, hibernating under the church, awoke, and the Indian hounds heard him and began to worry him. In the night the village suddenly exploded into sound, and Mark put on his slippers, threw a robe over his pajamas and dashed out to collide with a huge dark shape. He made two complete circles of the vicarage.

The next morning Chief Eddy stopped him on the path.

"I don't believe the Bishop would want you chasing bears around the vicarage in your pajamas."

"But I wasn't. You have it all wrong. The bear was chasing me."

Christmas was a busy time in the village. The churches in Vancouver sent toys which the women sorted into packs, not only for the village children, but for those at the logging camps, the isolated float houses on Mark's patrol. Ten days before Christmas Mark and Jim delivered the gifts, visiting the other villages, and each lonely float, in and out the inlets, traveling usually by compass, often with the bow awash, and always with the mountains thick with snow. Wherever there were children Jim wore the ancient Santa Claus suit and lifted the pack of toys on his back while the children waited on the float to welcome them, to rearrange the boats so they could tie up. And after the carols were sung, and the gifts given, always Mark set up the portable altar for the simple service, and when they were pulling away, always he looked back to see some little girl clutching the rag doll to be cherished all year long.

They returned to the village Christmas Eve, with no time for dinner, and a hundred details to be checked before the midnight service. At eleven Mark was still trying to extract a little more heat from the fat round stove in the church. Hurrying back to the vicarage, he washed the soot from his hands, put on his vestments, and returned to the church to check the wine and the chalice, to toll the bell, to light the candles.

Then all was ready. He was alone, waiting in the hushed silence with the candlelight shining on the golden eagle and on the sad eyes of Christ holding the little lamb, and it seemed to him the little church waited also.

He walked slowly down the center aisle, and not wanting to open the door until the very last minute for fear of losing the precious heat, he walked to the window at the left of the door and stepped without expectation into one of those moments that is suspended between time and space and lingers in the mind.

The snow lay thick on the shoulders of the Cedar-man; the limbs of the young spruce bent beneath its weight. He saw the lights of houses go out, one by one, and the lanterns begin to flicker as the tribe came slowly, single file along the path to the church. How many times had they traveled thus through the mountain passes down from the Bering Sea?

He went to the door and opened it, and he stepped out into the soft white night, the snow whispering now under the footfalls. For the first time he knew them for what they were, the people of his hand and the sheep of his pasture, and he knew how deep was his commitment to them. When the first of the tribe reached the steps, he held out his hand to greet each by name. But first he spoke to himself, and he said, "Yes, my Lord."

---

DISCUSSION FOR UNDERSTANDING
Consider the following questions.

1. What is the time period covered by Part One?

2. The chapters are given no names. Look back and see how each one deals with a single subject. What would you name each one?

3. What is Jim's first appraisal of Mark?

4. Does Mark change Jim's opinion of him?

5. Why is Mark labeled a "swimmer"?

6. What does the reader know that makes this name even more appropriate?

7. Why is the section called "Yes, My Lord—No, My Lord."

# Part 2
## The Depth of Sadness

### 8

Now for the first time since Mark's coming, the whole tribe was in residence and all the men were home from the fishing. Three days before Christmas, one of the seiners[4] had brought the young people—those in their teens—from the church residential school at Alert Bay, and two of the largest canoes had met them at the float and brought them upriver. They had arrived at slack tide before the snowfall, the canoes grounding on the sandbars, the men climbing out into the icy water to shove, and push, to carry the girls to the bank, everyone laughing and the girls clutching the presents they had made at school for their parents. Mark had thought he had never seen such a joyous burst of bright-eyed youth.

But after Christmas, when the snow turned to slush and the rain fell, the children were kept inside and the men played La-hell in the social hall long into the night, Mark felt a strange little wind of dissent which seemed to whisper in the firs, to precede him, to follow him wherever he went.

He spoke of it to old Peter, the carver, who was down with a cold.

"Peter, what is it? What is this unease that is now in the village?" and the old man looked at him long and carefully before answering.

"It is always so when the young come back from the school. My people are proud of them, and resent them. They come from a far country. They speak English all the time, and forget the words of Kwákwala. They are ashamed to dip their food in the oil of the óolachon[5] which we call gleena. They say to their parents, 'Don't do it that way. The white man does it this way.' They do not remember the myths, and the meaning of the totems. They want to choose their own wives and husbands."

He faltered as if what he was going to say was too painful to utter.

"Here in the village my people are at home as the fish in the sea, as the eagle in the sky. When the young leave, the world takes them, and damages them. They no longer listen when the elders speak. They go, and soon the village will go also."

---

4. **seiners** \ˈsān-nər\ a fishing boat that uses large nets that hang vertically in the water to catch fish.

5. **o'olachon** \ˈū-lä-shăn\ a food fish of the North Pacific, related to the smelt. Also called candlefish.

"Kingcome will be one of the last to go, Peter."

"Yes, but in the end it will be deserted, the totems will fall, and the green will cover them. And when I think of it, I am glad I will not be here to see."

On the little organ in the church Mark had left a carton of books his sister had sent for Christmas. One day he noticed the lid of the carton was up and a book was missing. The next day the book was back and another gone, and when he went into the church on the third, one of the boys who was home from school was sitting on the bench by the organ reading.

It was Gordon, whose father had been lost in a heavy sea in the Queen Charlotte Straits. He looked up. He stood up and came forward with the book. He was not embarrassed. He had even forgotten to be shy.

"This word," he said eagerly, "what does it mean?" and Mark explained the meaning and he said, "I have some other new books you might enjoy seeing. I'll leave them here for you."

He took over the books the next afternoon and found the boy waiting. On the pew beside him was a mask.

"It's the giant mask," Gordon said. "The thong that ties it on is broken. Peter is going to mend it for me. They will need it in the dancing."

"May I see it?"

The boy held it up.

"Yes. See how thin it is. The modern ones are thick." He added, shyly, "It is my great-grandmother's hair."

The mask was black with red lips and abalone eyes. When Mark took it into his hands, he felt almost as if he held a strong,

*The children were the first to befriend Mark.*

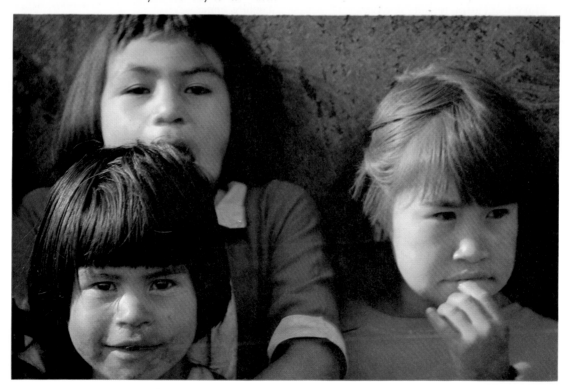

proud, living face, so beautifully was it carved."

"My father was offered three thousand dollars for it," Gordon said, "but we do not want to sell it."

"No—only to a museum where the world can see it—only then."

Just before the end of the holiday, Mark heard in the village the first sound from the world outside. A jet plane broke the sound barrier. At first he thought it was a slide on Whoop-Szo, and he ran out of the vicarage. The sound caught in the inlets, tossed from one steep mountain side to another, echoing and reverberating, and receding slowly to echo and re-echo far, far away. It lasted several minutes, and he looked around to see a curious sight.

None of the older Indians had come out, only the young, the children, running excitedly up and down the path, the young people in a group by themselves. And Gordon.

Gordon stood motionless, head up.

Mark went over to him slowly.

"When I was a small boy I used to visit my grandmother in one of the little prairie towns in the midcontinent," he said. "And the sound I listened for was the long, shaky whistle of the freight train in the night. It was the eeriest sound I ever heard, and it seemed to call to me from the big world, and even then I knew I would answer it. I would go. Is this not the way you feel now?"

The depth of sadness in the boy's eyes deepened, as Peter's had deepened when he spoke of his village, and he said, "Yes." That was all.

On Sunday after church the young people returned to school. Many of the tribe went to the river's edge to see them off in the canoes. And the young people regretted going and wanted to go, and the elders wanted to keep them and were relieved when they went. The little dissent went with them, and the village was at peace.

But not for long. When the January storms tempered a little, Mark managed to reach the other villages for the first time in a month, and he stopped at the float store to pick up the mail sack for the village.

On the evening of the day he returned, Keetah knocked at the vicarage to tell him that Mrs. Hudson, her grandmother, was ill.

He found the old matriarch sitting very straight by her fire, her breath coming in short gasps, and he knew her well enough by now to guess that Mrs. Hudson was more upset than ill. He asked how she was. She was bad. It was her heart again. She was sure of it— she was determined she was not long for this world.

"And what is it that has upset you?" he asked her, and Mrs. Hudson shook her head, making a strange little aye-aye-aye sound that must have come down through the centuries in a chant of sorrow, and she told him sadly that her granddaughter, Keetah's sister, had written (and he himself had brought the letter in the mail sack) that she was going to marry a white man.

"But this happens often and frequently very successfully. There are even white women who have married Indians and been asked to sit on the councils."

Mrs. Hudson lifted her fine old head.

"She will no longer be an Indian. Legally she will be white. She will have no right to come here, except as a visitor."

"But you can go and visit her."

"Yes. And when we go, she will say, 'Not today, Grandmother. Come tomorrow. My husband is home today.' And her husband will say, 'Do not ask your grandmother tomorrow. I do not want my aunt to see her.'"

"No," Keetah said. "No. My sister will not leave us. My sister is not like that. I know her. She will never, never be ashamed of us."

Mrs. Hudson lifted her fine old head.

"Of this I'm not afraid," she said simply. "What I fear is that we will be ashamed of her," and she was silent.

Mark sat beside her. When her breathing

*And the mountains tower beyond the river.*

 9

had eased and quieted, he told her of the Navaho, one of the great, proud tribes who lived in the southwest of the United States, so many hundreds of miles distant.

"One of the great chiefs of the Navaho said to his tribe, 'We can hear the white man talking, but we cannot reach him. Education is the ladder. Take it.'"

Mrs. Hudson said, "You do not understand. My granddaughter goes to a world of which she knows nothing. It will destroy her and I cannot help her. To watch her go is to die a little."

And Keetah took the old hands in hers and said, "She will come to us. I know she will come, and she will not change. You will see."

This was the time of year when the deepest beliefs of the tribe were relived in the dances; no stranger asked, no potographs permitted. When Mark walked along the path past the long house, he could see masks in readiness, but he asked no questions and was told nothing.

In January the men of the tribe went to Gilford village to dig clams, and returned to Kingcome each weekend. Now the tide dominated all life. When the tide was out, clamming was on. When clamming was on, all else waited, even church.

One late afternoon when Mark and Jim were going to the most remote of the villages, they were passed by seiners headed for Gilford, and Mark was asked by radio-telephone if he would hold Evensong in the long house before a dance-potlatch to be given that evening by an elder in preparation for his own death.

When they reached Gilford village, many boats were tied up at the float, and when they entered the long house, more than three hundred Indians were waiting, the old carved house posts casting their shadows by lantern light, and by the light of the fire burning on the dirt floor in the center of the great room. And when Evensong was over and coffee was served, Mark saw that almost all of the tribe from Kingcome was here. With Keetah was her sister.

She was a pretty girl, her hair carefully cut and waved, her fingernails red, the heels of her slippers very high, and on her face that radiance of fulfillment, of all the wonders of the new life she was about to enter.

The two sat apart, talking earnestly, and though Mark could not hear the words, he was sure he knew them:

"Nothing will change. Tell me—tell me you don't feel I have deserted you."

"Of course not. You know that. I want you to go."

He watched their faces, and he knew each meant desperately what she said because they loved each other, and deep inside surely each knew the words were false, that the true words were those unspoken. Which was the braver, the one who left, or the one who stayed?

He said to Jim, "Which is the man Keetah's sister is going to marry? Is he here? I want to meet him."

"There is only one stranger. He is with the men from the forestry boat who are friends of the tribe." But in the flickering light of the fire and the lanterns Mark could not see clearly the face.

Then the potlatch began. In the back of the room was the orchestra—the hollow log with the painted ends which was the drum,

propped on a wheel barrow, and the older men with the carved batons and the ancient rattles. The elder pounded on the ground with his long talking stick and welcomed the guests in Kwákwala and the orchestra began its rhythmic beat.

The women danced first, dressed alike in their red and black ceremonial blankets, with the two-headed serpent on the back or the fir tree outlined in handmade buttons. They turned right because the wolf turned right. When they shook their head-dresses, the air was filled with duck down, and the light caught on the blankets, the ermine-tailed robes and the spread aprons.

Then came the Grouse Dance, brought to the tribe by marriage from River's Inlet. When the elder introduced it, Jim translated his words:

"A little boy went to the woods to snare grouse and he was sure he had caught one because he could feel it pulling and jerking. But each time he lost it, and thought someone had taken it. The little boy lay down under a fir and went to sleep, and he could hear the grouse still drumming in the snare. This dance is his dream.

"Now watch carefully. The first character wears the door mask, and when it opens the grouse will enter calling softly. If you were an Indian walking beside a stream in the woods, knowing the woods as only an Indian knows them, everything you saw would come to life in this dance with all its meaning and its beauty."

The dance lasted three hours, and there were twenty-six characters, each with his masks, his songs and his dances. In came the old stump looking for its trunk, a little green spruce growing from its top. In came the mossy log, the fish swimming upstream, the long face, the laughing face, the giant and the skull of the man lost in the woods. Through it all the Indians sat without sound or movement, utterly attentive.

Last was the Moon Dance, performed in

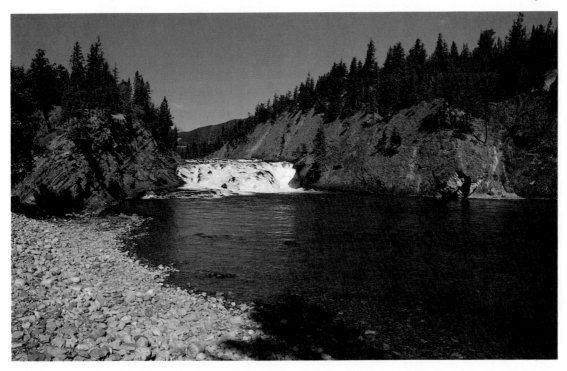

*One of the many streams where the "swimmer" returns every year to spawn and die.*

pantomime by two men, the Full Moon and the Half Moon. Which would come out tonight? "I will come out tonight. I am more powerful than you." "But I will stay out longer." They taunted each other, fingers to noses, and this time the audience shrieked with laughter, taunting each in turn, and applauding the favorite.

When the dance was over there were refreshments and gifts of china, linen and cutlery, and a fifty-cent piece for each guest except the family of the host.

"Where is the man Keetah's sister is to marry? I cannot find him," Mark asked Jim.

"He is gone. Keetah's sister is taking him to Kingcome tomorrow. You can meet him there."

They walked down the wet, dark path to the float, climbing over the railing and the deck of a seiner to reach their boat, and in the galley they discussed the potlatch. Was it true that in the old days the gifts had been so lavish they had beggared whole families and tribes, and made others rich?

Jim agreed it was true. "Even when I was a small boy stoves, refrigerators and washing machines were given as gifts. It is true that families gave all they had. But when the government forbade the great dance-potlatches, it gave us nothing to take their place, and changed the deepest purpose of our being. Once they were like the coronations of a king, or the inauguration of a president. They were the great rituals of my people, solemn and important. Now the meaning is gone."

"But Jim, isn't it true they were based on a chief's desire to shame his rival, even if it meant his tribe and his children went hungry?"

"Yes, and it was based also on generosity. My people have forgotten how to give. You do not understand how it was once. When I

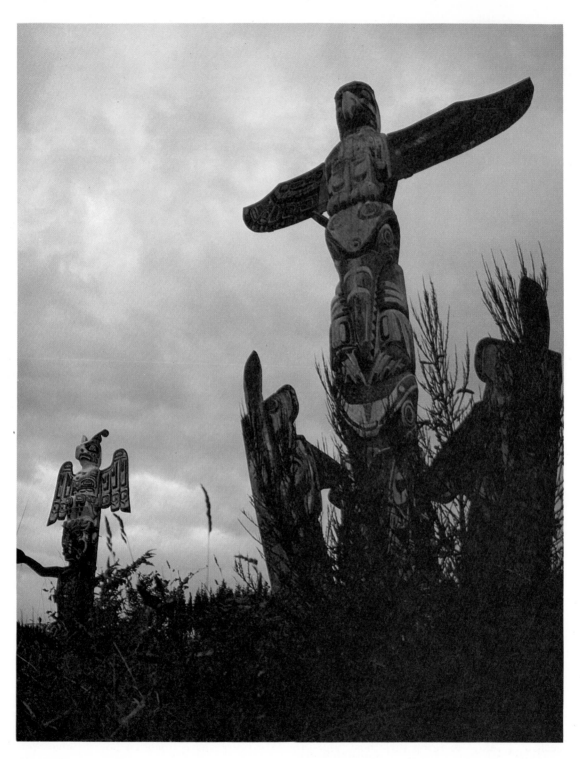

*A Kwakiutl cemetery.*

was seven my grandfather taught me my family's dances, and he gave a dance-potlatch in my honor, and asked the tribes of the other villages. Whether they came was not important. It would have been discourteous not to ask them.

"The guests were billeted in the houses of Kingcome, twenty or thirty to each house, to be fed, to be cared for, and boats came up the inlet, and the canoes brought the guests up the river. Each night one of my relatives gave a great feast of seal, duck or salmon, and a tremendous quantity of gifts was brought from Alert Bay. Each night in the big house there was dancing."

"Did you dance the Grouse Dance?"

"No, I danced the hamatsa. I remember that for three days my mother kept me shut in my room because the young man bewitched by the cannibal spirit must not be seen until he returns from the woods. I did not understand this and I resented it. On the night of the dance my family hid me in the woods, and when it was dark, I returned to the village calling the hamatsa cry. I have never forgotten it. It was the greatest moment of my life."

At dawn with the tide, the forestry boat and the seiners of the guests from the other villages left Gilford. At eight, Mark was summoned by radio-telephone to Turnour Island to transport a sick child to the hospital at Alert Bay, and when this was done, a gale was blowing, and it was too rough to return to Kingcome, so they tied up at the dock, the boat rolling in the swell.

The next morning after breakfast they started home, the wind still strong, the sky leaden, the snow thick on the mountains. When they came up the inlet they knew that the tribe had returned for the weekend; the float was thickly moored with boats.

It was very cold on the river, as it was always bitterly cold on the river in the winter. Mark could feel the wind biting through his parka, and because the tide was wrong, they grounded and had to pull the boat over a sandbar. When at last they waded ashore in front of the vicarage, they knew at once something was wrong.

Farther down the river's bank they saw a group of the oldsters packing one of the larger canoes with great bundles of clothing as if for a long trek. Mrs. Hudson was one of them and when she saw them, she did not speak.

The village was very quiet, as it had been the day Mark had arrived. But its silence lacked peace. Although this was a Saturday and the children were out of school, not a child showed, no Indian hound came running to greet them.

Mark motioned to Jim that he was going on to the vicarage, and Jim nodded, and said, softly, "I will find out. I will come and tell you," but when he came to the vicarage, it was a long time before he spoke.

"Keetah's sister brought her man to the village the morning after the potlatch. He had his own boat, and her family was proud she had come, and welcomed him. While she showed the women her red fingernails and her new clothes, and told them of her new life, her man was with the men of the family."

"Yes. And what did he do, Jim?"

"He gave them liquor. When Gordon's uncle was very drunk, he sold the giant mask. The white man paid fifty dollars for it, and the uncle wrote him a bill of sale. In the morning before it was light, the white man left, and the girl with him."

"It is possible she did not know of it."

"Her family does not think so. The old of her family are leaving. They are leaving in shame and sadness. They are going to a deserted village."

"But how will they live?"

"As my people have always lived. They will live on fish, and clams, and seaweed. Later they will pick berries."

"I must stop them."

"You can't stop them."

"Then I must go to them. I must talk to them."

"It won't help."

When Mark walked along the bank to the place where the canoe waited, he knew it was useless. They were ready to go—the old of Keetah's family, warmly wrapped against the cold, and sitting very straight on the narrow wooden seats. As he approached, Keetah and Mrs. Hudson came slowly through the black sands, stopped, and Mrs. Hudson lifted her proud old face and spoke to him slowly.

"What have you done to us? What has the white man done to our young?" and they waded into the icy water and climbed into the canoe, and because, to keep them here, someone had removed the outboard motor, one of the old men poled into the center of the river where the current took them, the paddles lifting and falling. Not even Keetah looked back.

They were larger than themselves. They belonged to the great and small hegiras[6] of the self-exiles of this earth, clinging fiercely to a way that is almost gone, as the last leaves fall at last gently and with great pride.

*What have you done to us?*

The words lingered in the wind, in the spruce, in the drizzle that had begun to fall, and Mark turned from them in pain and saw old Marta. He said, "Marta, what can I do?" And she said, "You can wait," and he stumbled past her and up the path and into the church.

That evening he wrote the Bishop and when the answer came two weeks later, he took it to the church, afraid to open it. Had he failed? Was it his fault?

The letter was short: "I think it is time you knew of Tagoona, the Eskimo. Last year one of our white men said to him, 'We are glad you have been ordained as the first priest of your people. Now you can help us with their problem.' Tagoona asked, 'What is a problem?' and the white man said, 'Tagoona, if I held you by your heels from a third-story window, you would have a problem.' Tagoona considered long and carefully. Then he said, 'I do not think so. If you saved me, all would be well. If you dropped me, nothing would matter. It is you who would have the problem.'"

## 10

In the cold, blustery days of February and March, when the men could not pursue the fish and the game, the life of the tribe turned in upon itself. The faces, once so much the same, grew clearly defined. Even Mark's ear had begun its attunement to the strange tongue. One weekday when the men were away clamming, and the younger matrons gathered at Marta's house to make new altar cloths, he dropped in to find them, heads bent to their work, talking softly in Kwákwala, and he realized, with almost a sense of shock, that words no longer sounded like the click of knitting needles, and that they were speaking of him.

"Wait a minute," he said. "I didn't say that at all," and they looked startled, then burst out laughing, and never, never again did they discuss him in Kwákwala in his presence.

When Ellie, the lost one, slipped home to her father's house before daylight, Mark knew now from whence she came, and when Ellie's mother sat sewing with the other women, totally unresponsive, in her vague, sweet way, Mark knew also that she was probably in a drunken stupor because Sam had beat her again.

Twice, when Mark did not need him on the boat, Jim left the village, and though he did not say so, Mark knew he had gone to see Keetah and the oldsters of her family.

"And how is Keetah?" he asked him.

---

6. **hegiras** \\▲hej-ə-rəs\\ a journey, especially when undertaken to escape something unpleasant or dangerous.

"I told her that someday she would marry me, and that I would build her a fine house with a pink bathtub. No woman in the tribe has seen a pink bathtub."

"And what did she say?"

"She said I had no manners. She said when I want coffee, I bang on the table. She said I want a wife only to keep my house," and he laughed, then sobered.

"She is worried about her sister. All the time she is worried. It is more than two months and there is no word of her. There is no word at all."

"I'm going to Alert Bay to see if there is any way I can get Ellie away from her parents and into the residential school. We will ask the RCMP there to find the sister."

In Alert Bay Mark visited the residential school and saw Gordon and the older children from the village who were there. At the headquarters of the RCMP Mark discussed the problem of Ellie with the sergeant in charge of the detachment, a man past middle age and wise, and from him Mark learned that to take Ellie from her parents without their consent was not easy. Then Mark told the sergeant about Keetah's sister, the older man listening carefully and without interruption.

"It is possible the man learned of the giant mask from some dealer who had tried to buy it," he said. "The dealers have a genius at knowing when the fishing is poor, which family is needy. With the Indians it is easy come, easy go. This goes back to the days of the great potlatches. They do not budget what they have, and even when times are

*To the Kwakiutl, the sea is a highway—the sea is life.*

excellent, they get into debt. It is then the dealers pick up their best carvings."

"I cannot believe the girl had any part of it. Her family is one of the finest in the village."

"Then there was trouble when she found out about it. I'll watch for her. I doubt if the man has married her. When he tires of her, she will be alone in a world for which she has no preparation. I'll find her."

In late March the tribe prepared for the coming of the óolachon, the candlefish, a season so deep in the tradition of the people that all the taboos and superstitions were remembered, and followed. No pregnant woman must cross the river. No body must be transported upon it. The chief of the tribe must catch the first fish.

On the night before the run began, there was a great feast in the social hall to which everyone came—except the school teacher, of course—and when the meal was done, the chief related the first myth of the óolachon:

"And Khawadelugha, the older brother, built his house here in Kingcome and carved its house posts with human figures, and one day when he walked to the river's edge he saw many small fish in the river and he was afraid. But the man who came from the moon said to him, 'Fear not. This fish will come year after year, and it will be the great wealth of your tribe,' and the fish was the óolachon, and the older brother called his tribe the Tsawataineuk, which means the people of the óolachon country."

T. P., the elder, related the second myth:

"And one year the óolachon did not come, and the young laughed, and cared not. One of the old men painted his canoe red, and he paddled toward Knight's Inlet until he came to Twin Falls where the óolachon were living. 'What do you want?' asked the óolachon.

'Come back to the river. Treat the young as they have treated me.' And the óolachon said, 'Have you brought eagle feathers and goat fat?' 'Yes, I have them here.' 'Then return to your river and prepare your nets,' and the old man did so, and the good members of the tribe filled their nets with óolachon, but the nets of the bad ones broke."

The next day the men placed their nets in the river, gathering them in by canoe, and the brailing[7] began, shoulders lifting and falling, and the air filled with the mewing of thousands of gulls, and the little children leaning over the bank to catch the fish in tins.

The males who came up the shallow side of the river were dried on V-frames, smoked and canned. But the females, richer in fat, who came up the far, deep side of the river were rendered into gleena in huge wooden vats over a slow fire. Day after day after day it lasted, and when Mark escaped on the boat to another village, he found the odor had permeated his clothes and went with him, and when he returned and the rendering was over, it lingered.

One day the RCMP sergeant came unexpectedly up the river in a small boat, and Mark saw him from the vicarage and went to the river's edge to meet him.

"I've been dreading that smell all day," said the RCMP officer cheerfully. "It's just as bad as I remembered it. You know, when I was younger—and considerably more stupid—I came once to take pictures of the óolachon fishing. I knew the Indians did not permit pictures, but I figured they couldn't stop me."

"And did they?"

"Oh, no, they were polite. They welcomed me. They helped me back to my boat. But you know, in doing so, one of the young men managed to drop my camera in the river. All the way down the path to the float I was sure

I could hear them laughing, and when I got home I found I had to bury my uniform and pay for a new one myself."

Mark led him to the vicarage, put on the coffee pot and prepared sandwiches, and when they had finished lunch at the kitchen table—the rain pattering on the roof—the sergeant took a photograph from his pocket.

"Is this the girl? Look at it carefully."

Mark did so.

"Yes. There's no doubt about it. This is Keetah's sister."

"The man didn't marry her. When she found out about the mask, she objected, I suppose. He left her in Vancouver, penniless, and he disappeared. I don't suppose she'd ever seen a paved street, or a train, or a telephone. There was no place for her to go, no work she was trained to do. She drifted to the only place where she was welcome."

"A beer parlour?"

"Yes. The money men paid her kept her alive. No one knew to what tribe she belonged. Even if she'd had the money to charter a plane, I suppose she would have been ashamed to return to her village. Soon she was taking dope—it's what is apt to happen—and one night she took too much, deliberately, probably, though we'll never know. You're sure of the identification?"

"Yes, I'm sure, but I'd like Jim to see the picture also. He's not here today."

"Dead in three months—well, it doesn't take long. You'll tell the family?"

"I'll have Jim tell them."

Mark went with the sergeant to the river's edge and watched his boat head downstream to the inlet. He did not know that when he turned back in his own eyes was the depth of sadness which he had begun to understand.

---

7. **brailing** \ˈbrā(z)l-ĭng\ hoisting fish by means of a net.

 **11**

With spring the leaden skies broke, the

winds lightened, the rains softened, and the eagles and the robins returned to the village. High in the skyways wild geese called exultantly on their first early passages back from the south, the wise old crow cawed over the river, his wings flapping loosely and slowly, and the sleek black raven, who stayed all year, nested in the tall alders.

With spring the first buds began to swell, and the fresh green needles of the spruce. The bracken and the fern reached out the tips of tender fronds, the devil's club put out small new leaves for the deer to nibble, and the bears emerged from their dens, thin, blinking in the light.

In May all the men readied the boats for the fishing, and the banks were piled with gill-nets to be mended, their white and green floats fresh with paint.

In May the boats left to gig for halibut, Mark and Jim accompanying them for two days' fishing in Knight's Inlet, a wild, lovely and lonely land, the boat rolling in the tidal sweep, the seals disputing each fish. When Mark and Jim returned to the village, they brought with them an orphaned baby seal, who repaid his bottle feedings by dusting the floors of the vicarage carefully with his flippers. When he was old enough, Mark taught him to swim in the river and let him go.

In June the men of the tribe went north to gill-net for salmon in River's Inlet. Now Mark was busier in the village than he had ever been, picking up the freight, the mail, the supplies; handling any accident or emergency that occurred in the village.

One night in early June he awakened to the sound of feet running on the path, to the calling of his name and fists pounding on the door.

"Come quickly—come quickly."

He pulled on his pants and his shoes in the dark, and snatched his jacket, and followed the Indian who had come to summon him into the night to the house of Gordon's mother, up the steps and in the door.

All the relatives waited in the front room,

the dark eyes of the children big with wonder. Mark pushed past them and went into the bedroom.

On the blood-soaked bed lay Gordon's mother. At forty-six she had borne her sixth child, which Marta held wrapped in a blanket. All the other births had been normal, and although the native mid-wife was absent from the village, no difficulty had been expected. But this was a breech birth. This was abnormal and even Marta was afraid to have anything to do with the abnormal because of the RCMP.

"She is bleeding to death," Marta said, "and there is no time to get help."

Mark took the woman's cold hand. The nails were white, the face ashen, and the eyes fixed on his face. He bent to her.

"Help Gordon get an education," she whispered. "He will need it."

"I will."

He held her hand until she died, and she died quietly and quickly. Then Marta cleared the front room of the relatives, and gathered the woman's children to the bedside where Mark said the Lord's Prayer.

Then they closed the bedroom door, because nothing could be done until the RCMP came, and they undressed the children and put them to bed. In the early dawn Mark and Jim went down the river to the boat to summon the police by radio-telephone and to send word of the death to the fishing boats in River's Inlet, so that the male relatives would come, stopping first at Alert Bay for the box in which to bury her.

When Mark returned to the village he noticed there were no professional wailers with scratched faces and he asked Marta why.

"She did not want them."

The RCMP came in the late afternoon by boat. He was the constable who had come for the weesa-bedó, as cold as the first time. Mark showed him the body and called the relatives that he might take the statement of each. When the questions were all asked and the

694

statements signed, the constable issued the burial permit and left.

Then he and Marta were alone in the bedroom with the ugliness of death.

"Marta, what do we do now?" and she told him.

Mark closed the eyes, straightened the limbs and packed the orifices of the body against further seepage. He and the men of the family carried the body into the tiny vestry of the church, and Marta and the women bathed it, powdered it, and dressed it in its best clothes, and when the box came from Alert Bay, they put the body in it, closed it, and they placed it by the golden eagle, by the Christ with the dark, sad eyes holding the little lamb.

Everyone in the village shared the death. Here death could not be hidden or pushed aside. Here death was normal. The women were busy in their kitchens preparing food for the relatives and the guests who would come from the other villages. Two canoes, spliced together, bore the coffin carefully up the river. The older men went to the new burial ground, a mile from the village, to dig the grave, and the older boys followed them, cutting away the bracken, the devil's club, that had grown over the narrow path. Even the small children went into the woods to seek wild flowers and green fern fronds which the younger women needed for the wreaths. The older women swept and dusted the church. And Jim and Peter, the carver, made the long trip to the residential school to bring Gordon.

On the morning of the funeral Mark tolled the bell, and the tribe gathered in the church for the service. When it was over, he left the church first, leading the way down the aisle, down the steps, to the path that led through the deep woods to the new burial ground. Behind him six men carried the burial box, another six following to take their places when they tired. Behind them, single file, came the tribe.

Sometimes the path was so narrow that the men who carried the box had to tilt it, man-euvering it carefully through the trees, and in the deep shadowy woods there were puddles that never dried, and here Mark held up his cassock and felt on his bare head the wet drops that fell from the dark firs from the last rain.

An eagle accompanied them, soaring and returning in great, wide arcs, and once they surprised a doe and her little fawn. The doe carefully nudged the fawn off the path, keeping herself between it and them. When the path made a turn, Mark looked back and saw the tribe stretched through the cedar and the hemlock, coming slowly and silently, except for the footfalls on the soft duff.

Thus he went, the air fresh from rain and filled with the sweet smell of fir, the sky blue and white with cloud. On the top of Whoop-Szo above the timber line, snow lay waiting for the warm suns of July to send it sliding downward with a rumble that would fill the village. And it seemed to Mark that death belonged here as the mountains belonged, as the eagle belonged, and the little scurrying squirrels that peered at him from the fir boughs. And it seemed to him that the ugliness of death was as unimportant here as the fir needles which made the path soft beneath his feet, or last year's windfall in the thick underbrush.

When Mark led the way into the glade of the new burial ground, the six men set down the box, the tribe gathering quietly in a circle around it. The committal was brief, and when Mark had said the last words, "Rest eternal grant unto her, O Lord, and let light perpetual shine upon her," each man of the tribe helped fill the grave with a spade of earth while the women sang in Kwákwala the first hymns the tribe had been taught sixty-five years before.

Then the wreaths were placed on the grave. T. P., the elder, stepped forward. He spoke in the ancient Elizabethan Kwákwala and the children, tugging at their parents, asked, "What does he say?" and though Mark did not ask him, Jim translated.

"He says she was a mother of the tribe. She spoke little and only when asked, and the men listened to her counsel. He says she was one of the first to choose her own husband—and he says that her husband, as a boy, was the first to have shoes, and that he hung them on a tree for all to see but did not wear them. And he says she was good."

Mark walked back to the village with Gordon and when the path widened enough that they could walk side by side, they talked briefly.

"Now I will have to come home and care for my brothers and sisters, and for the new one."

"No—I have given this much thought. The older ones will go to the residential school where you can be with them. The younger children we will care for here, and the new one also. Your mother wanted you to get an education. I told her I would help you."

The next morning Mark stepped from the vicarage into the first lovely day of summer. Sitting on a log near the river's edge was Marta, the small boy and girl who had been his first friends kneeling at her feet. As he approached he could hear her singing to them in Kwákwala.

> Wake up, small daughter, wake up.
> The sun is high and the tide is out.
> All the other children are playing in the
>     water.
> You will be the last.

The small boy cried in English. "My turn— my turn," and Marta sang the next song for him.

> I want to pursue the swimmer like my
>     father.
> I want to hunt the bear like my father.
> When I am grown, my father will lack
>     nothing.

Then Marta saw Mark standing there, the weariness plain on his face. She shooed the children away with a gesture, and Mark sat down on the log beside her.

"You are tired," she said.
"Yes."

They sat then without talking, listening to the mewing of the gulls, watching two sleek black ravens in the alders across the river. Presently Mark saw a sight he could not at first believe—he saw Mrs. Hudson come to the beach, wade into the water, climb into a canoe, and pole into the middle of the river to dump her garbage.

"The old have returned," he said cautiously, "I did not see them at the funeral."

"You did not see them because there were so many."

"They are leaving again?"

"No, they have returned to stay."

He was so grateful he did not trust himself to speak. Then Chief Eddy came along the beach by the river's edge, and saw them sitting there on the log and drew close.

"Mark," he said, "the men have asked me to tell you that when you are ready to build a new vicarage, they will help you. It would be wise to get it up before the rains come."

"I will write the Bishop today. Will you tell the men I am grateful?"

Then they were alone. But there was a difference now. The cautious waiting was over. That night Mark wrote to the Bishop and the Bishop's answer affirmed it. "You suffered with them, and now you are theirs, and nothing will ever be the same again."

---

DISCUSSION FOR UNDERSTANDING
Note that this section is called "The Depth of Sadness."

1. What period of time does this section cover?
2. How many things happen? What are they?
3. What is going on in the tribe as these things take place?
4. What seems to be happening to the tribe?
5. What is the change that takes place in Mark's relationship with the tribe? What is the symbol of this change?

# Part 3
## Che-kwa-la

### 12

The men of the village tore down the vicarage. The old boards were cut and shared with all for firewood. The foundation for the new house was prepared according to the blueprints which the Bishop sent, and Mark went to live at Marta's house where she spoiled him with Indian delicacies, berry sprouts cooked with alder and salal, and salmon eggs baked with milkweed, topped with fern. Usually Jim dined with them, and often Keetah, and the times Mark liked the best were the long summer twilights when the elders dropped in to speak of the old culture.

They were all alike, the old, tied by a common bond. "We are the only ones left who remember the old ways and if we do not speak now, they will be forgotten."

Sometimes Mark was appalled at how much was gone, how little they remembered from their past, and he encouraged Keetah to write down the small treasures that floated up in the old minds:

"And the little girl of the family took the bones of the first halibut to the water's edge, and gave them back to the sea, and she said, 'Come again, Mr. Halibu-u-u-t, come again next year.'"

"And the young men strolled through the village singing the old love songs, and the songs were always of absence and of sorrow, and they spoke from the heart."

"I went with my mother to strip the bark from the young cedar and I remember that she spoke to the tree. She said, 'Forgive me because I seek your dress. I will not leave you naked,' and she told the tree what she would make from the bark—a blanket, and a pillow for her baby's head."

"I was afraid of the hamatsa dance. I was afraid of the men who looked so fierce with their heads wreathed with hemlock, and their bearskins tied with cedar rope."

"We went in the sixty-foot canoe to buy gifts for my uncle's potlatch, and we spent all we had, and gave away all our blankets. That winter we were cold and the children cried."

The first weekend Gordon was home from fishing with his uncle, he came to Marta's house, bringing three boys who had been with him at the Indian school and who wished also to board with a white family and go to school in a white man's town.

When Gordon was there, Jim did not come or the elders. Gordon was not interested in the past. His mind reached only ahead with that urgent intensity which makes youth seem selfish, and is so necessary to difficult accomplishment.

"Do you think I can do it?" he would ask Keetah. "What do you think?" and she would answer, "I know you can. Of course you can."

When Gordon returned to the fishing, the elders returned, Keetah's dark head bent again to her notebook, and Jim reasserting the old role of the tribal male, pounding on the table when he wished coffee, and Keetah, putting down her pen to wait on him without a look, without a word.

When the freight boat deposited the new pre-fabricated vicarage on the float at the end of the inlet, those men of the tribe who were not off fishing went by canoe to see and consult. There waited the vicarage—every beam, every shingle, every nail, to be carried up the willful river. Even Calamity Bill came in his ancient rowboat with its ancient outboard motor, and the younger hand-logger, the summer sun shining on his hard hat, and all of them nodded their heads and agreed that the easiest and the quickest way to get the makings of the vicarage to the village was to hire a forestry barge at a prodigious thirty dollars a day.

It took two days and two nights to transfer the lumber to the barge, to maneuver it carefully up the river, past the snags and the sand-bars, and to unload it. Sometimes, at night, Mark would stop working a moment to watch. The whole tribe helped. Even some of the women waded into the cold water to help carry the larger pieces, while the small boys bent their backs to the kegs, and in the flickering lantern light Keetah's dark head bent to the coffee pot as she filled cups, and carried them to the river's edge. On the third morning the forestry barge was returned and the new vicarage lay on the green grass of the meadow.

"Now," said Chief Eddy, proudly, "we will put up the house."

For six weeks the village was filled with a constant activity. Every available man—and even some of the women—helped put up the new vicarage. It must be done before the heavy rains of August, and for another reason of which no one spoke. In August, for the first time, the Indian was to be permitted to buy liquor.

All day long and into the long twilight the sound of hammering continued, accompanied by laughter and the shouts of the men, and by the shuffling of feet under the loads of timber.

One July night the inlet became a small and lovely city of lights. The gill-netters—a hundred and fifty of them—were fishing for salmon, drifting slowly with the will of wind and tide, their nets extended to the full twelve hundred feet, and the three lights on each ship rising and falling with the tidal sweep. And the villagers went by canoe to watch and marvel.

Now when Mark and Jim moved up and down the inlet in the little speed boat on patrol, they had to take care lest they foul the lines. Often men on the gill-netters yelled loudly and boisterously, "Watch where you're going, you fools. Look out for that net—" the finest words Mark had heard here because they could be said only by one friend to another which meant he was one of them.

When the gill-netting in the inlet was over,

the little city of lights went out in the summer night, and the smaller children asked anxiously, "Where has it gone? Will it come again?" and the inlet was empty as the room is empty when the Yule tree is stripped and carried out into the rain.

These were the lovely days of summer; the water of the inlet deep green from the shadows of the spruce, the children in and out of the river all day long, agile as seals, and the village full of laughter.

When the new vicarage was done at last there was a brief respite until the new furniture, chosen by the wife of the Archdeacon at the Bishop's request, was delivered to the float to be carried upriver.

Mark and Jim took Marta, and the two children who had been his first friends, on a picnic. In a cove where there was a small sandy beach they spread their supper on a driftwood log, and in the long twilight, because it was a time of much phosphorescence, they lingered to watch the fish jump and fall back into pools of golden light. And the barefoot children ran backwards to watch their small footprints glowing in the dark sand.

When they returned up the river in the soft quiet night and reached the village, Mark carried the little girl ashore and Jim the boy, and when they delivered them to their parents, Mark walked alone by the river's edge, clinging to the lovely day. "Don't go—not yet—not yet—" but the day slipped away as fast as any other.

The freight boat dumped the new furniture on the float. The men brought it up the river and set it in place. The women pressed the new curtains and hung them, and the little children crept inside the new doors to touch nothing, to stand big-eyed and marvel, and the Bishop was asked to come bless the vicarage, a tribal feast planned in his honor.

The younger wives went at once to the house of Mrs. Hudson, sitting before her in a respectable circle, and they said in Kwákwala, "What shall we serve?"

"Barbecued salmon."

"How many?" and Mrs. Hudson considered it carefully and said, "Twenty."

"What vegetable?"

"Mashed turnips."

"How many?"

"Forty pounds."

The Bishop sent word that he would arrive on the hospital ship early on Sunday morning, and that he had asked six city rectors to join him in a retreat in the village, and that they would be deposited at Gilford Island by seaplane Saturday noon.

Mark and Jim met the clergy at Gilford village. On the way to Kingcome, near Whale Pass, they saw a huge black bear swimming across the narrow channel, and stopped the boat and drew alongside. On an impulse, Jim picked up a line from the deck and tossed the noose neatly over the bear's head. Up came two huge claws and a furiously shaking black head, full of teeth, and emitting loud growls, and the town rectors began to laugh and yell, while Mark grabbed the axe, cut the rope, and the bear headed shoreward.

When they reached the home float and transferred to the canoes a heavy mist hung over the river. The land-lubber clergy tried desperately to find a comfortable way to perch on the one-by-four crosspieces that formed the seats, the water gurgling ominously, Jim's torch seeking the log jams and the snags. When they reached the vicarage, Keetah and old Marta were waiting at the door of the new vicarage to ask, "And how did you like coming up our river?"

Two of the clergy stayed with Mark in the vicarage, sleeping on the sofa, the big bed in the spare bedroom reserved, of course, for the Bishop, and the remaining four of the visitors were lodged in the homes of the Indians. In mid-morning of the next day, the hospital ship tied up at the float, and when the canoe came up-river with the Bishop, Caleb was with him, wading ashore in his ancient hip boots. But the Bishop had no Kingcome slippers and was carried piggyback to the bank.

For the service the church was filled. Caleb baptized two babies. The Bishop confirmed three of the younger Indians, and gave the sermon and blessed the vicarage. When it was done, he said to Marta, "Where was Mrs. Hudson?" and when Marta replied that Mrs. Hudson was ill, he said, "Then I must take her communion."

The Bishop went first up the path through the woods carrying his staff, Mark followed with the chalice and the paten. They found Mrs. Hudson propped on pillows, her breath coming in small, short gasps, and Mark, who had cherished the unchristian idea that Mrs. Hudson's old nose was badly out of place because the Bishop was housed in the new vicarage instead of her house, as had long been his custom, was ashamed of himself and sure she was about to die.

When they left, the Bishop stood a moment outside the door and he said loudly, "What a pity Mrs. Hudson will not be able to dance tomorrow after the tribal dinner. No one dances as well as Mrs. Hudson. No one."

That night the combined clergy prepared dinner in the new vicarage kitchen, and Mark told Caleb about the four boys who were going out to school.

"Have you found homes for them?" Caleb asked. "If not, I will help you. You don't want them with families who will say, 'Are they dirty? Do they steal?' I'll make the arrangements and you bring them to me."

In the morning the kitchen was turned into a clinic, busy with the doctor treating all assorted aches and pains. At noon one of the Indians broke his arm when the kicker on his canoe acted up, and he had to be taken to the hospital ship to have it X-rayed and set. In the afternoon the village was filled with the fragrance of the salmon barbecuing on the alder fires. The community feast was held in the social hall, and when it was over the visitors and the tribe moved to the ceremonial house. When the women began the dancing, there was Mrs. Hudson, turning right because the wolf turns right, the sequins of her ceremonial blanket shining in the firelight, her face pink with pleasure. And the Bishop leaned to Mark and said gently, "I have seen it happen many times. I cannot explain it."

Caleb and the clergy left the hospital ship at six the next morning, the sky leaden, the breeze cool. When the Bishop left at nine, an hour more suitable to his station, the rain was heavy. As he and Mark climbed into the speed boat, another passenger appeared. Dolores, one of the young Indian women, whose first baby was not due for a month, had started labor and asked to be taken to the hospital at Alert Bay.

They went downriver in a torrential rain, the young wife and the Bishop cowering under a polyethelene sheet. When they reached the boat at the float, they had to wait only moments before the tiny seaplane came, as ordered, to carry the Bishop to Vancouver Island.

The young bush pilot was properly appalled by the imminent prospect of birth.

"What'll I do?" he said to Mark. Mark said, "Nonsense. Just loop the loop—it'll all come out. Get going now." And he said softly to Dolores, "Hang on to it. Do you hear me?"

"Oh, I will, I will—."

"You are worrying because day after tomorrow the tribe will be able to buy liquor?" the Bishop asked Mark as he climbed on the plane.

"A little, my lord; I am afraid some of my best parishioners will end up in the gutter."

"The church belongs in the gutter. It is where it does some of its best work."

Then the little seaplane skittered across the water like a bug, lifted and turned. Mark saw Dolores' small determined smile. The young pilot waved. The Bishop lifted his hand, as if in blessing. He was alone on the float there in the wilderness, a drop of something wet on his cheek that was not rain.

 13

August began with floods. For days the rain poured down and the river rose until it lapped at the top step of the new vicarage, covering the path and the meadow, the villagers paddling from house to house by canoe. When the river went down, a small slide damaged the dam, and while the women carried water in pots and pails, Mark and the older men repaired the dam. In the night Mark could hear the footfalls of the men checking the moorings of the canoes, and he could hear the drip-drip of the rain, which had become a part of life itself, so that when it ceased, the world was filled suddenly with a strange, unnatural silence. Then the skies cleared, the sun shone, the weather turned suddenly warm, and the mosquitoes and the "no-seeums" emerged in hungry swarms.

August was a month of worry and waiting. Every time Mark went on patrol to the other villages, he returned filled with anxiety. At Gilford the captain of the freight boat told him the fishermen of the tribe had spent at least two thousand dollars on liquor in one week at Alert Bay. They had met other tribes with whom they had never been friendly, and there had been fights, even fights with knives, and it was said several Indians had gambled away their boats.

Coming home from Gilford one warm afternoon, Mark found a splendid, large American yacht tied at the float in the inlet. There was no one aboard, and when he and Jim moored their own boat and climbed into the speed boat, they could see through the portholes the rich polished helm, the gleaming mahogany of the main cabin with its elaborate bar.

When they came up the river to the village, a shabby speed boat was pulled up on the beach and a young logger in a plaid shirt perched on the bank, who explained that the yacht owner had paid him to bring his party here.

There were three women and four men, and as he walked up the path to the vicarage, Mark could hear chatter and gay laughter, and when he passed the vicarage, he could see them—the women in their tailored slacks and cashmere sweaters, the yacht owner in his white jacket and gold braided cap.

They were swatting mosquitoes and horse flies, gawking in the windows of the church, and the voices of the women had a shrill quality he had almost forgotten.

"Look—look at the funny man at the bottom of the totem."

When he approached and introduced himself, they were most affable.

"What are you doing here?" asked the yacht owner, and Mark said he belonged here; he lived here. And one of the women said, "How do you tell the Indians apart?" and Mark said, the same way she told her friends apart, because she knew them.

He showed them the village and he answered their questions, and, when they were ready to go, he went with them to the river bank. When the yacht owner saw his speed boat, he said, "I wonder if you would take us to the yacht in your boat? The mosquitoes are eating us alive, and the logger's tub is too slow. It would mean a little money in your collection plate." And Mark said, no, they would have to return the way they had come, and he noticed that Jim had picked up a stick and was drawing on the sands the picture of a dollar bill.

"If you come to southern California, you must look us up," said the wife of the yacht owner. "We will show you our big parish," and he knew he would never see it, and that she knew it also.

They climbed into the logger's boat and pushed off, and the river took them. They were on their way back to a life he no longer knew, as distant as another planet, and he was glad to see them go—and a little ashamed of it.

He looked at the picture in the sand.

"What does it mean?" he asked, and Jim answered, "It means an American stood here."

That weekend for the first time there was much drunkenness in the village. Three of the fishermen came home, reeling up the dark path. From Sam's house in the night came sounds Mark had never heard here, a woman's voice in a high, drunken giggle, and in the moonlight he saw Mrs. Hudson march down the path like a thunderhead and up the steps. Instantly the laughter stopped.

In the latter third of the month, an English woman anthropologist came to visit the village, housed, by arrangement of the Indian Agent with a couple who were among the very few of the tribe who were not Christians and did not attend church. When Mark went to call on her and offer any help he could, he was at once rebuked.

She was a large, mannish, gray-haired woman who informed him that her visit was a fulfillment of a wish of many years standing.

"Since I was a girl," she announced, "I have been interested in the culture of the Quackadoodles."

Mark said hastily, "I had trouble with that word too. It took me a month to learn it. The Indians pronounce it Kwacutals."

"Young man, for the past century in England this band has been known as the Quackadoodles and as the Quackadoodles, it will be known forever."

"I beg your pardon."

Mark asked if she would like to see the church, and when they entered, she saw at once the new insulated sidings which had caused him so many blisters.

"How much better it would have been to have left the rude studding," she said sadly, and he told her that even with the plywood the flowers on the altar at Christmas had frozen solid in the water that held them.

She did not hear him. What a shame that Christianity had come here! If the white man had not intruded where he was not wanted, where he did not belong, even now, protected by the mountains and the river, the village would have remained a last stronghold of a culture which was almost gone.

Mark tried to say that no village, no culture, can remain static.

"I have often thought that if this lovely and magnificent land belongs to anyone, it is to the birds and the fish. They were here long before the first Indian, and when the last man is gone from the earth, it will be theirs again."

After this encounter Mark left the lady anthropologist alone. But he could see her sometimes, going around the village in her brogues and tweeds, with her notebooks and her pencils, asking innumerable questions of everyone. At the end of ten days, she knocked at the vicarage.

"I have completed my work except for one thing. The raven."

"What about the raven?" Mark asked.

"That's just it. There is a mystery about the raven they will not tell me. If I ask one of the Indians, he says he knows but he can't translate it. When I ask the chief, he says he knows, but the older Indians know better and I must ask them. And when I ask the older Indians, they say they knew it once and cannot remember."

Mark promised to help her, and went straight to Mrs. Hudson with his problem, who said she would arrange it.

"It is a long myth," said Mrs. Hudson, "and T. P. Wallace knows it well. He is going on a five-hour trip tomorrow on his son's seiner, and if the lady anthropologist cares to go along, the time should be ample."

The Englishwoman never mentioned the trip, and Mark did not question her, but late on the night of the day it was made, old T. P. came to the vicarage to apologize.

"We had bad luck. We went into Knight's Inlet and on the way back we hit a very strong tidal sweep."

"You told her the myth?"

"Certainly. I started the minute we left the float and I didn't reach the end until we returned. But you know, boss, she was so seasick, she didn't hear me. All she could say was, 'Oh, ghastly, ghastly.' "

On the afternoon the lady anthropologist left, the tide was out and the seaplane could not put down on the river, so Mark and Jim took her to the float in one of the canoes.

"The water's lower than it has been for some time," he explained. "Now, if we get stuck on a sandbar, you stay in the canoe. We'll get out and push."

The anthropologist said she would do her part. She wanted no favors.

"No, no—the water's very cold."

And, sure enough, the boat grounded and Mark climbed out in his rubber boots and Jim, also.

"Now?" asked the anthropologist, rolling up her slacks, and out she stepped—into a hole and up to her armpits.

When the seaplane arrived and took her, she did not wave, and they watched the plane disappearing into the blue sky.

"Oh, ghastly," Jim said with an exaggerated English accent. "Ghastly—ghastly."

But the vicar had a new word also.

"Quackadoodle, let's go home."

At the end of August, Mark received a letter from the Bishop who wrote that he had been informed by the RCMP that the tribe had spent now a total of $6,000.00 on liquor at Alert Bay.

"When you bring the first four boys out to school, plan on at least three week's vacation. This will give the fishermen a chance to make their own peace with the old people. And when you return and the first man knocks at the vicarage to say he has no money to feed his family or to repair the outboard motor of his canoe, you will say, 'You will fish and hunt to feed your family. You were born with a paddle and a fish hook in your hand. Use them.' "

## 14

In the late summer Mark and Jim took the boat for its annual overhauling on the long journey to Vancouver. With them went the four boys who were to be the first of the tribe to attend the white man's school in a world of which they knew nothing and which knew nothing of them.

Chief Eddy took them in the largest canoe with all their assorted bundles and boxes, and the tribe gathered on the black sands by the river's edge to see them off.

"You will write. You will come home at Christmas," Keetah said to Gordon, and he answered, "I promise you. I will write. I will come on the seaplane," and his eyes were bright with eagerness, like the eyes of the three younger boys, and none knew that when the canoe left the shallows and the current took it, he was leaving his boyhood behind and would not find it again.

But the old knew it. The old knew this was another bit of the slow dying of all they held dear in their own race. And because he could not bear to see the look in the old eyes, Mark hurried the boys into the canoe, easing the tension with small jokes. Jim started the outboard motor, and they were off.

One afternoon on the trip down-coast they hid out a gale in a deserted village, the boys pitching horseshoes in a clearing white with broken clam shells. At night the boys slept on the floor, and at meals in the galley Mark drilled them in the little amenities of the big wide world: "May I have another glass of milk, please?—Would you pass the bread, please?—Excuse me.—I beg your pardon.—How do you do?—And when you shake hands, press a little." And he remembered that none of them had ever seen a shower, and drew a picture of one, explaining it carefully. "This is the hot water faucet, and when you turn it on, be careful not to scald yourself," and Gordon asked, "But how do you wash your hands and face in this little box without getting your clothes wet?"

When they had finished the small amenities, it was Jim who introduced them to the larger ones.

"When somebody calls you a dirty Siwash, what will you do?" When one of the younger boys answered him, Mark said quickly, "No, you won't. None of that. You will make a joke of it. You'll laugh and you'll say, 'What's the matter, paleface?' and remember something: that in sports at school you'll be as good as any white boy and far better than most, and they will respect it."

The trip down was full of laughter and anticipation, and when at last they entered the lovely harbor of Vancouver, there stretched before them was the first large city.

They slept on the boat, and by day, while the work was being done on the engine, Jim and Mark introduced them to the parks, the pavements strangely hard to their feet, the noise to their ears.

Once Mark took them out to dinner to their first large restaurant, and Gordon said to him, "They are staring at us," and Mark answered, "Nonsense, they are staring at me and my clerical collar." On the way back to the boat they passed three young Indians, loud spoken, ill-kempt and slovenly, and he felt the boys stiffen with enmity.

"What's the matter?"

"They belong to a southern tribe. We do not know them. We have never had anything to do with them."

Mark took his examinations to handle the boat alone. His sister, who was his only close relative, came from Victoria to meet him and they had a fine luncheon in one of the finest hotels. Mark's talk was almost entirely of the village, of the Indians, of the little amusing happenings. Since he was used to it, he did not heed, consciously at least, the sadness she could not keep back from her eyes.

When he looked up some of the friends with whom he had attended college, he realized with a shock that he no longer talked the same language. They spoke freely of their problems and assumed they were his also. Had he noticed how many young people there were now who seemed to find in life no challenge? And how did he handle the growing materialism in which so many people feel no need of faith and consider the church almost an anachronism? And Mark answered that in an Indian village the challenge was obvious to all, to stay alive men had to depend on each other, and that everyone came to church, even the agnostics and the atheists. They came out of respect for the church itself and for the man who served it, and because there were few settlers in a six thousand square mile area who had not been done kindness by the church, its hospital ship, its men, and repaid it.

On the last evening Mark had dinner with a professor under whom he had studied, the older man asking him many questions of his life in the village.

"You're growing more and more like Caleb," he told Mark. "You've dropped yourself overboard in some quiet inlet, too busy living your faith to think of yourself at all. We'll have to watch you, Mark. You'll be wearing a white stole at Yuletide."

"With mud on my cassock? That's one place where you failed me. There was nothing in my training that told me how to remove mud from cassocks."

"I'll put it in the curriculum. Caleb spoke to the students last winter. The week before he came, we'd had a famous theologian whose words sent the students scurrying to their rooms to hassle half the night. But Caleb was like a cool wind from the north, or the smell of fir in the sun. No great theological problems. No debatable tenets. He spoke simply of his life on the up-coast, and often humorously. I remember watching the faces of the students as they listened, and I was sure I knew the look on the faces of the first ones who met long ago in some little hidden room in Antioch."

When the holiday was over, they started up-coast to Powell River. Now the boys had seen enough of the world to sense the size of the battle ahead, and they were like Jim the first night Mark had met him—quiet, poised, and proud. Even at dinner in the galley there was no joking, and when on the second day they tied up at the float at the marina, old Caleb was waiting.

"I hate good-bys," Caleb said to Mark. "Let's make this fast," and Mark agreed.

"I've found fine homes for you," Caleb told the boys. "A doctor and his wife are going to take Gordon. They have a son of their own and the doctor has a small cruiser he uses for weekends. He can use a good hand. And as for you three—a widow's going to make room for you so you'll all be together. She has a big, old house and two grown children of her own. This morning she called to ask me what she could prepare for dinner that you would especially like. Nothing like a familiar dish to make a man feel at home. And when I said you'd like seaweed and óolachon, she laughed, and said she didn't have an óolachon in the house but did I think you'd settle for apple pie?"

When the boys had all their belongings moved to the float, there was one bad moment. Mark held out his hand to Gordon and he said, "You will be lonely, and you will be afraid sometimes. I was lonely, and I was afraid when I went to your village. Both are an inescapable part of every life." He shook hands with each of the boys very formally. He watched them pick up their luggage and follow Caleb up the ramp, like a small, proud army. Then he was in the cabin, starting the engine, while Jim coiled the lines. They were off. Neither looked back.

On the second day when they drew near the area of his patrol, Mark felt the quickening, the growing eagerness of one who comes home after an absence that seemed very long. How well he had come to know the landmarks; the turn at Broken Island. The last of the lights at Chatham Sound. The rock that was always covered with cormorants where he never failed to blow the whistle to watch them lift as one—and settle. He knew the pass where the porpoise was, and if he were blindfolded, surely he would know the place in the Johnstone Straits where the sea begins to roughen when the wind is against the tide. He knew the rocks that were marked on no chart as the Indian knew them, because he had scraped his keel on them on some dark night.

When they came to Kingcome Inlet and approached the float, he was like the man who comes to the door of his house, feels the weight of the day lift from his shoulders, and thinks, "Thank God, I'm home."

Then they were in the small boat going up the inlet into the river, past the log jams and the snags, toward the white-barked alders across from the village.

How had the drinking gone? In the entire holiday the question had been lying in his mind waiting an answer. But the village seemed utterly at peace. No one reeled down the path. No one lay inert, sleeping it off in the bushes. And Chief Eddy, who was painting his canoe on the bank, waved and came forward.

"How is it, Ed?"

"Okay, boss. Everybody's broke, but no one's dead. You might say it's steeled down, and it's all due to Sam."

To Sam, who had never done anything right in his life? Mark could not believe it.

"He collided with some fish. He made a lot of money. He spent most of it on liquor, and with what he had left he bought a washing machine, and brought it up the river in his canoe. But he was so drunk he hit the snags, tipped over, and lost it."

"I'm sorry to hear that."

"Did wonders for his wife, boss. You'd never know her. She beat him over the head with a skillet and locked him out of the house, and she wouldn't let him in until he agreed

to let Ellie go out to school. I expect they'll be over to see you tonight."

"I'll be here, Ed."

When Mark entered the vicarage he saw that it had been freshly cleaned and dusted. On the kitchen table was a loaf of bread, still warm from the oven. The Indians had known somehow he would return this day.

 15

On the second night of Mark's return from his holiday, Marta asked him to dinner, and she did not ask Jim also, which was unusual.

"After the dinner the old will come," she told him. "They have something to request."

"You don't suppose they are still grieving about the drinking, or the boys going out to school," Mark asked Jim. "You don't suppose they are going to leave the village again?"

Jim did not think so.

"If this were it, I am sure I would be told. It is something which concerns only the old."

At dinner Marta did not mention what it was the elders wished. She asked of the holiday in Vancouver and she asked of Gordon and the boys.

"The younger ones will adjust more easily," Mark told her. "For Gordon it will be harder. He is much older than the boys he will meet at school. But he will endure, Marta, and he will win his battle."

After dinner there was a knock at the door and the elders entered: Mrs. Hudson, T. P., Peter the carver, and several others whom Mark did not know well, who still thought in Kwákwala, dreamed in Kwákwala, and spoke little English.

When they were seated there was a long silence, as the old watched Mark intently and soberly. It was not the drinking that had brought them here. It was not even the loss of the young. It was something that led back into the deepest beliefs of the tribe, and Mark sensed it and waited.

T. P. spoke for them.

"We have come about the ancient burial ground," he said. "Except for the weesa-bedó, it has not been used for many years."

"And you want the body of the weesa-bedó moved to the new graveyard. Is that it, T. P.?"

"No—he is well where he is. In the early days we buried our dead in a square box and we placed the box about a third of the way up a large tree, and we cut off the limbs below the box so the animals could not reach it, and later, other boxes were hauled up by ropes and each family had its own burial tree."

"I have seen them."

"Later we cut down a large tree ten feet from the ground and on its stump we built a house, and in the house we placed ten boxes and sometimes more."

"I have seen them also."

"But now many boxes have fallen from the trees and other trees have fallen on the grave houses built on the stumps. The bones of our ancestors lie scattered on the ground, and the old totems and the carvings are broken and beyond repair."

"If this disturbs you," Mark said, choosing his words carefully, "we can build a large communal grave and in it we can place all the boxes and the broken carvings. And if you wish in the morning I will go with you and the older men to start the clearing."

The old people rose.

"It is well," T. P. said. "I will stop by for you in the morning."

The next day the fine weather holding, Mark went with the elder men of the tribe, and what had seemed so reasonable a project became suddenly huge and macabre.

The little path that led to the ancient burial ground was overgrown. When they had cut their way through it, they saw that the year's windfall had been severe and that the old grave houses and the boxes that had fallen

from the trees were covered with brush and branches.

For five days the men of the tribe worked at the clearing, and when this was done, Jim and other younger men went up the huge spruce trees with ropes to lower the grave boxes that were still intact. Where any box had fallen and touched the ground, only bones were left, but where the boxes had remained in the air, the bodies were partially mummified, the wrists still holding the copper bracelets, green now and paper-thin; and beside the heads were ancient water vessels placed there in case the soul of the dead thirsted on his journey.

When the huge grave was dug and ready, forty boxes were placed in it, and all the broken bones and bits of ancient grave posts and carvings. The men who had done the work buried also the clothes they had worn. Then on a sunny, clear morning, Mark held a brief service and the grave was covered. When it was over, he saw relief in the eyes of the old, and again T. P. spoke for them.

"At last a man has come to us who has seen to it that our dead can rest in peace."

When he returned along the little path to the village, Mark stopped at the house of Peter, the carver, and sat a moment on the steps to chat.

"When spring comes, grass will grow over the huge new grave," Peter said. "The air will be sweet smelling again from the wild flowers, and the old people will walk there often."

"Why will they go there, Peter?" Mark asked slowly.

"To be sure that at last our dead are safe from the hamatsa."

"I do not know the myth of the hamatsa."

"The myth is a story. There is no harm in the myth, and I will tell it to you.

"A young man was ready to dance and he did not know what dance to do. He stood up in his red cedar bark dress, and he threw off his blankets, and he walked up a mountain until he came to a lake and saw a loon. The loon said, 'I know why you have come and I will help you,' and he led him to a house from which smoke came and told him to enter. The doorkeeper let him in and asked him to sit, and the second man, who was the cannibal man, asked why he had come, and the young man answered, 'Because I want to be as you are.' "

"And then?" Mark asked.

"And then the cannibal man went behind a screen and came out with a body, and he gobbled up one, and he gobbled two, and he gobbled up four, because that is the ceremonial number, and a lady followed him around and put the bones in a basket. Then he danced four times around the house and disappeared up a pole, and he put into the young man the whistle which makes the cannibal cry, and he tied hemlock branches to his wrists and ankles to protect him, and the young man did the dance as he had been shown, and returned to his village.

"And one night his people decided to give a dance. They lighted a pitch pole and sent four of the villagers to bring water, but none came back. They heard the hamatsa cry and recognized the young man, and they knew he had been bewitched by the cannibal man and had eaten the four people.

"They sang their songs and piled food boxes to the ceremonial house roof and the roof opened, and they heard a skull roll down its side, and were afraid.

"The next night his people tried to get the young man into the house to tame him, and he came four times on four nights, and they thought he was safely cured because he had fallen in love with a maiden. On the last night they knew he was not cured, so they killed him with magic, and he returned to the wood and was not seen again. And this is the myth which the old men tell and it is harmless."

"And the dance was based on the myth?"

"Yes. In the winter ceremonials, the hamatsa dance was the last and it took four nights. The young man who did it disappeared from the village and he lived beyond the old burial ground in a little cedar house hidden in the deep woods. I know, because when I was a young boy, my father's house was the last in the village, and I was the one who took him food.

"My friend, you cannot imagine what it was like—the tribe waiting on the first night of the dance, and the hamatsa coming at last, crying in the woods. In my father's day if anyone laughed, if he made a mistake in the dances, he was killed. In my father's day when the hamatsa entered on the second night of the dance carrying a real body taken from the old burial ground, the women were afraid, and they said, 'Is the body from my family's tree? Is it one of ours?' When I was a boy the hamatsa carried no body because the government forbade it, and he only pretended to bite people, holding a piece of seal liver in his mouth. As a boy I saw the scars on the arms of the old men, and I heard the tales."

Then Peter was silent, and Mark left him and walked along down the path through the woods.

How had it been in the old days when the magic, and supernatural spirits, and the cannibal man who lived at the north end of the world had dominated life here in this village? How had it been when the hamatsa had come in the night through the great trees, crying his soft and terrible call? He would never know. No man would ever know. But Mark had seen the light of the old, old ways reflected on our faces like the glow from a dying campfire, and he knew that it was the hamatsa who had been freed at last from his holy madness, and was at peace in the deep woods.

## 16

Fall came gently with the second blooming of the dogwood. No wind blew, the clouds hung low over the village, and the rains were soft. When Mark and Jim came home from patrol, Keetah was always waiting on the black sands, and Gordon's uncle also.

Had Caleb written? And how did it go with Gordon? Did he miss his village?

"Caleb had written and it does not go well. Gordon can't eat. He can't sleep. He is losing weight," and in the evening in the cedar houses along the path the old ones spoke the same words, softly and with hope. "He will come back to us as Jim came back. He is still an Indian."

Then Caleb's letters brightened. Gordon was studying hard and well. He planned to do two years' work in one. In the little cedar houses along the path, the old nodded their heads. "And by the end of the year, he will be cured of his madness and he will return to his people."

Slowly, as the needles fell, the waters of the inlet grew less clear, and on the river floated the first green leaves of the alders. When the nights cooled, the little berry bush burned crimson under the great, dark cedar, and on one deep green island side, a single cottonwood turned gold.

Now the land belonged to the wild fowl. Coming up the inlet, Mark would stop the engine of the little boat to hear the loud calling of the first immense flocks of snow geese on their way from Siberia to the Sacramento Valley. He knew the white fronts that came from Bristol Bay, and watched for the white markings on the dark necks of the Canada geese. He knew the black brants that fed late on the eel grass of Izemberg Bay, passing high over the village like a long whisper, like a sigh, on their way to Baja California.

Here every bird and fish knew its course. Every tree had its own place upon this earth. Only man had lost his way. Then, when the geese had passed, and the bear and the little hibernating animals had hidden themselves for their long sleep, the white trunks of the alders stood stripped and stark across the river, and man began to emerge, to prove

again his capacity for endurance and faithfulness. It was in loneliness the Indians had lived through all the centuries, and it was in loneliness Mark came to know them best.

He relied on Jim as he had never relied on anyone, yet their friendship was forged in the long hours on the boat in which neither spoke an unnecessary word. And always there was the trip in the little open boat up the cold river, and the vicarage waiting with the warm food on the back of the stove that Marta had placed there, the clothes Keetah had washed and ironed, the wood old Peter had cut and stacked, the piece of fish or game set aside from each and every hunt. And there were the Indians who dropped by in the evening to offer help or ask it, and the children who entered without knocking to stand, motionless, watching him from their big, soft eyes, smiling shyly.

Thus fall flowed past the village like the river, and again Mark stood in the small hushed church on Christmas Eve with the candlelight glowing on the golden eagle, watching the lights go out, and his people coming down the path through the trees. When he opened the door to meet them, he saw that Gordon had come home to his village.

He saw Gordon with a surge of pride and a twinge of anguish. Gone was the shy and eager boy in the fisherman's trousers and jacket, the dark hair a little long on the neck. How much he had changed and how fast—a handsome young man in his city suit, his white shirt and tie, and on his face the discipline that marked the size of his battle.

When he came up the steps with Keetah, Mark held out his hand and said, "Welcome home, Gordon. And how does it go with you?" and Gordon answered gravely, "It goes well, Mark. Thank you," and he shook hands as does the white man.

Now the wind of unease was again in the village—even here in the church. When T. P., Gordon's grandfather, came to the rail and held up his hands for the bread from the paten, Mark saw that the fine old man could not keep them from trembling.

Each day Mark and Jim set out early to take Christmas to the hand-logger and his family, to Calamity Bill, and the remote camps, and to the other villages. Each time they returned, the village was full of mutterings:

"Gordon does not even look like an Indian. Have you not noticed?"

"He does not dip his fish into the gleena. He speaks down to us. He is critical of ways he has known all his life."

"That is natural. One must expect it. He will finish his year at school and return to stay. He will return as Jim came back to us, and he will let his hair grow and put on his old clothes, and he will be one of us, and free."

One evening there was a knock at the vicarage and when Mark answered the door, Gordon's grandfather and uncle waited in the dark. He asked them to come in and to be seated. When they had done so, it was the grandfather who spoke.

"We are having a family dinner for Gordon. Since we know that on the night it is to be held you will be on patrol, we have come to tell your of our plans for him."

"I can tell you some of the plans, T. P. I have seen the change in him as you have seen it, and I have tried to stand in your shoes. When he returns in the summer you will give a great potlatch and at it you will give him the ceremonial rites of your family, and the dances that have come down in it."

"Yes, that is part of it. When the rains have ceased, the men of the family will build his house, and when he and Keetah are married, we will give them a fine wedding with the canoes moving up and down the river bringing the guests, and all the houses of the village filled, and a great wedding feast."

And the uncle said quickly, "And next year I shall remain in the village during the fishing. Gordon will be in charge of the gill-netter.

When the run is good, he will make as much as four thousand dollars in the season. No young man in the village will have so fine a future."

The old man leaned forward.

"Mark, will you urge him to agree?"

"No, I will not. This is something he must decide. I am sure he knows it now, because he is avoiding me. If he comes back to stay, I shall be proud of him. If he decides to remain outside, although it breaks your hearts, in the end you will be proud of him also."

Mark and Jim were at another village on the night the dinner was given for Gordon. Neither mentioned it, nor forgot it. In his mind Mark could see them, the old and middle-aged of the family clan, gathered in T. P.'s old cedar house beneath the dark trees, and he could see T. P. making his appeal in the ancient Kwákwala, the others listening, waiting for Gordon's answer.

A gale delayed their return. When at last they came up the river in the gray rain, the village was still. Not an Indan was visible. When they entered the vicarage, no child came to welcome them. They knew now Gordon's answer.

He came after dark. With him was Keetah.

"You have decided?" Mark asked.

"Yes. I asked time to consider, and for two days and nights I have thought of nothing else. But that is not why I have come. I have come to ask if you will take me to Alert Bay in the morning where I can get the plane?"

"Of course. You know I will."

"Then I will go now and tell my grandfather I want to remain outside, that I want to go to the university. I want to be the first of my people to enter a profession. When I left here it was like taking a knife and cutting a piece out of myself, but to tell my grandfather I do not wish to come back to stay—this is to take a knife and cut through the flesh of my own people."

"I know."

"Mark, I cannot come home again. I have

changed too much. It is my mind that has changed. I can never come home again."

"Someday you will be able to live in both worlds. And I will tell you something, Gordon, as I told your grandfather. You will represent your people in the outside world and they will be proud of you. And even if you cannot return, you will find that the work you do, the kind of man you are, all that is deepest and best in you will be based on what you have learned here. And one more thing. Tell me—what of Keetah?"

"She will go with me. I can't leave her. She will go with me. She does not promise to stay, but she will try."

Early the next morning before dawn the four went down the river to the float. When they left on the larger boat, Gordon remained on the aft deck in the cold rain, looking up at the mountains and the steep green sides of the inlet. Keetah said good-by to nothing. She made coffee and carried the mugs into the cabin for Mark and Jim. Not once did she look directly at either.

When they reached Alert Bay, there was only time to catch the seaplane and for a hasty handshake. When Mark and Jim returned to the boat to start home, it was Jim who spoke first.

"Keetah will come back. She knows it now."

"Gordon will do well, and in the end he will be able to live in both worlds," Mark said. "But if Keetah is not strong enough to return by choice and not by failure, she will never again be able to live in either."

## 17

Shortly after Christmas the hospital ship arrived on patrol. When Mark heard the put-put of the small boat bringing the doctor and the captain to the village, he went to the river's edge to meet them and saw to his delight that Caleb had come also.

"I invited myself," announced Caleb. "I hitched a ride, and do you know what these sinners did? They passed a resolution behind my back that any guest who complained about the food should be automatically elected cook. Then they served me the worst lunch I ever ate in my life. Lad, save me. I have peeled spuds up the Johnstone Straits," and Mark said he could stay as long as he wished and not a spud in sight.

Again the kitchen was turned into a clinic. When the pills had been dispensed, the children given their shots, and the teeth pulled, word came from Village Island that an Indian had broken his leg, and the doctor and captain left hastily. Mark cleaned up the kitchen and put on the coffee pot. He told Caleb of Gordon and Keetah, but the old priest made no comment, and Mark sensed he had come for some specific reason. But for what? Did he think Mark had not done well? Was that it?

Outside dusk was coming, and a cold rain fell.

"I like the rain, lad. Surely it was on the bleak and rainy nights that the coastal Indians began to create an identity for themselves. There were perhaps eighty thousand in all, speaking many dialects, belonging to many tribes, scattered in many small villages over a very long and intricate coast line. Yet they began in the same way, as we began."

"With the myths, Caleb?"

"Yes. They hunted the sea, and the sea teemed with fish, the woods were full of game and berries, and the air with fowl. Food was easy to find. This gave them time to create, and they shared one splendid friend."

"What?"

"The cedar tree. It had a thick brown pelt from which they could make clothes and blankets. It split readily under their first stone axes and wooden wedges. They made their houses and canoes from the cedar. They carved masks and totems from its wood. In gratitude they turned it into a myth, and if you look out the window into the rain, you will see the Cedar-man at the bottom of the great totem holding up the crests of this tribe."

Mark refilled the coffee cups.

"Three summers ago I flew to the Queen Charlottes," Caleb said slowly. "An old Haida friend met me with his boat, and we spent several days visiting the ancient deserted Haida villages, even Tanu, the most famous of them all.

"The one I remember best had no name. It did not even exist in memory. No one knew how long it had been deserted or why. We moored the boat and rowed ashore. One totem faced the beach, gray and simple as a Greek column. But in the deep woods we found what was left of several others, badly broken and covered with moss, new trees growing from their ruin. They had come from the forest, and the forest had reclaimed them.

"And suddenly the place became eerie, as if eyes were watching us, the silence filled with voices we felt but couldn't hear. We were intruders and we knew it, and walked quickly to the beach and rowed to the boat, and we did not look back."

"Caleb, why are you telling me this?"

"Because it is going to happen to Kingcome and sooner than we think. The long trek down the lonely coast is not yet over. The young will follow Gordon. Very soon only the old will be left and a very few others, and when the old die, the others will leave. The tribe is going to trade its simplicity for the shiny gadgetry of our complex world, and it will not be so content, because there is one thing it does not anticipate. The outside world will not accept it easily."

There was a long silence.

"And now it's my turn, Caleb," said Mark. "You're right. In the end they will all leave, and the wrong people will use them for the wrong reasons. For publicity, for politics, for egotism, even for greed. But you have forgotten something. They have one splendid

friend who understands them and will stand by them. They have men like you, Caleb. Don't you know yet that in life you have been to this tribe what the Cedar-man was to them in the myth?"

The old priest looked abashed.

"I hope it's a little true, Mark," he said humbly. "And if it is true of me, it is true of you also."

---

DISCUSSION FOR UNDERSTANDING

**1.** How does Mark react to the strangers who visit the tribe and to his own trip outside? How has he changed?

**2.** This section deals with Gordon. What is happening to Gordon, and how is his experience symbolic?

**3.** What has Caleb come to tell Mark?

**4.** The section is called "Che-kwa-lá," the Indian word for fast-running water. In Chapter 5 (p. 674) Jim and Mark stand for a long time watching the troubled, restless water of the falls coming to rest in the deep, quiet pool. Why is is this section called Che-kwa-lá?

# Part 4
## Come Wolf, Come Swimmer

### 18

One afternoon in January the weather turned very cold, and on the river in any little protected spot where the current was not so swift, ice began to form. For two days all the able men of the tribe broke ice in a desperate attempt to keep the river free that the boats might move, but on the third night Mark, who had taken his turn, awoke to the sound of the canoes being dragged up on the bank, and he arose and made a huge pot of coffee to take to them.

The next morning the children were walking gleefully across the river on the firm ice, and by afternoon the men were walking across also to drag back any wood that would burn, because now the village was ice-bound and no boat could go for oil, or propane.

To keep fed, to keep warm, to keep alive. No woman said, "I am sorry. I have only enough fuel for my own family," and no man said, "It is true that I have shot a deer. I am freezing what I do not need now. I cannot share with you, friend."

Then huge wet flakes fell in place of the dry snow and ice began to break in the river, and Mark and Jim reached the float by canoe, and went by boat to the float store to bring back food and forty-five gallon drums of oil and one-hundred pound tanks of propane.

Men of the tribe met them at the float to help load the canoes, the snow falling heavily, the mountains and the sides of the inlet ghostly white in the night. And it seemed to Mark that the river was life itself, flowing by the village with all its wonder and its agony.

When the cold rain replaced the snow, there was illness in the village. Twice the hospital ship reached the float, and Jim and Mark brought the doctor by canoe to the village. The kitchen of the vicarage became a clinic, and the doctor trudged down the wet soggy paths visiting those too old, or too sick to come to him. And twice an elder was wrapped in blankets, and carried in the bottom of a canoe in a heavy rain to the hospital boat and on to Alert Bay. But nobody died.

In February the clamming at Gilford began, and for the first time in six weeks Mark reached the other villages of his patrol. In the log book he wrote; "full gale" again and again, hiding out the storms in some little cove on the leeward side of an island. And when he reached the small villages, the little portable altar was set up in the school house or a private dwelling, a hymn or two sung with someone playing the accordion, or the

banjo. It was always the same. It was not fine sermons they sought now in the long cruel winter. It was communion.

Mark and Jim spent five days in the other villages and on the way home, when they went through Whale Pass and could see the white Kingcome Mountains, they passed the A-frame on Calamity's float, and, as he always did, Mark looked to see if smoke was coming from Calamity's little shack. None was.

"He's probably away," Jim said. "All the big camps are still closed because of snow. Nothing but a skeleton crew left anywhere. I expect some logging boat stopped and took him out."

"Pull up alongside, Jim. I'd better check."

How many times he had stopped to hide out a gale or to chat, and always Calamity had taken out the carved walrus tusk which was the cribbage board, and always he had said, "Just one game, Mark, while I put on a mite of supper."

But this time when he knocked at the door, no rough voice answered him, and he opened the door and stepped in. There was the table with its ancient oil cloth cover, and the coffee pot, doubtless half full of grounds, waiting for Calamity to toss in a handful of coffee and boil it up again. There was the broken easy chair, and on the cot in the corner lay Calamity.

Mark pulled the chair close to the cot and sat down, and he reached over and touched the shoulder.

"What's the matter, old-timer? Did you get hit by a window-maker?"

"I knew you'd come, lad. I been waiting. I went upside to check the snow and damned if I didn't slip off the cliff and wake up with the tide lickin' at my boots. Had to drag myself to the shack."

"How long have you been here?"

"Four days, maybe. All I need is some food within reach and the stove going, and I'd take it kindly if you'd move the cot so I can put in a stick now and then."

Mark went over him carefully.

"I think you've broken a hip, Calamity. What you need is a trip to Alert Bay. If the hospital ship's close enough, she'll take you, and if she's too far to get here, I'll take you."

"Damn waste of money. First thing they'd do is take off my red long-johns and I'd die of pneumonia." And Mark asked of himself, "And what do you think you're doing now?"

While Mark built the fire, Jim sent out an emergency on the radio-telephone, but the hospital ship was too far away to come and the gale warnings were out and the straits too rough to cross. But it didn't matter. It was too late for help and Mark knew it, and Calamity knew it also.

Mark sat beside the cot.

"I ain't much of a church man, Mark. Guess you might say I'm an agnostic. I don't know."

"There's a good bit of agnostic in all of us, Calamity. None of us knows much—only enough to trust to reach out a hand in the dark."

"Under my pillow there's a map of Knight's Inlet. I put a cross on the place where I cut trees once. I always thought that when it was my time to conk out, I'd kind of like my ashes—"

"I'll do it, Calamity. It's a promise."

"Don't say no fine words about me; we'll both know they're lies. Do it in the spring, on some fine day."

Mark sat by Calamity through the deep night, until the hand he held slipped from his, and the period between breaths grew longer and longer. At dawn the old handlogger sighed deeply and was done. Then Mark covered the body with a blanket and returned to the boat to catch the first weather report, which promised that by noon the straits might be navigable. By radio-telephone he managed at last to reach his friend, the sergeant, and tell him what had happened, and ask permission to bring the body of Calamity for cremation, and this he was given. Then he lay down for a few hours' sleep.

When he awakened and went out on deck to check, the weather had improved somewhat. He stepped again into one of those small unforgettable events he had come to expect. The skeletal crew in the nearest camp had picked up the news of Calamity's death on the radio-telephone and, feeling it unseemly that he go on his last journey tied in an old tarpaulin, they had put together a proper box to hold him.

Three were six men in all in two small boats, and a third boat bringing the couple from the float store, who had picked up the news also and come to help, the wife with an old suit of her husband's folded over the arm because she was sure that at last she was going to part Calamity from his red long-johns and send him to his Maker suitably garbed. But when Mark and Jim had caught the lines and she held out the suit without a word, Mark shook his head.

"Calamity wouldn't be separated from them in life," he said gently, "and I don't think he'd want to change now," and for an instant a bit of laughter rose in the solemen eyes beneath the knit caps in all the toughened faces, and was instantly squelched.

Two of the loggers helped put Calamity in the box, and carry it to the aft of the boat, and lash it down. Then Mark put on his cassock and said for Calamity a few very simple prayers. After the blessing Jim struck eight bells to mark the end of the watch and loosed the line, and Calamity started his last rough journey to what he had always called the happy logging country.

When they had moved well out from the float where the last of a southwesterly funneled up the inlet, Mark looked back to see the small group still standing on the little float on the snowy inlet side.

He never passed the float on patrol that he did not say a small prayer for the old-timer and remember his promise.

"In the spring, Calamity. On the first fine day."

In the long winter no one asked, "How does it go with Keetah?" One afternoon when Mark stopped at Marta's house on some small errand, he found her sitting by her fire, knitting a heavy gray Indian sweater, a polar bear in white on the black, and he asked, "Is it for me?" and Marta answered, "Not this time. It is for Keetah."

"You think she will return?"

"Yes."

"By choice, and not by defeat?"

"Yes, Mark, by choice," and Marta's soft dark eyes searched his long and carefully, and she said no more.

Keetah returned on a windy, bleak March day. She flew to Gilford village and one of the tribe, returning to Kingcome for the weekend from the clamming, brought her to the float.

She came up the river sitting very straight on the narrow crosspiece of the canoe, and when it reached the beach in front of the vicarage, she did not let the men carry her to the bank. She took off her city shoes, stepped out into the cold water and waded ashore, standing motionless on the black sands of her village, turning slowly to look at Whoop-Szo rising across the river, at Kingcome Mountains back of the village.

From the vicarage, Mark heard the smaller children run to greet her, and Marta also, and he went to the window to watch, and he knew Keetah was no longer the shy, sweet, young girl who had wept at the end of the swimmer. Keetah had returned a woman.

That evening Mark waited in the vicarage for Keetah's knock, sure she would come to tell him of Gordon, of Caleb, of all that had happened to her in the great outside world. She did not come; no one knocked on the vicarage door, and the next day he saw her only at a distance.

On Sunday morning Keetah was in her usual place, but when the service was over and Mark stood at the door shaking each hand, "And how was the clamming at Gilford?"—"And has the part for your boat come yet, Sam?"—she slipped away without a word.

He waited and asked no questions, not even of Jim. For the first time since the death of the woman by breech birth, it seemed to him that again the dark eyes watched him cautiously. Keetah had returned to her people, and they knew why and accepted her as if she had not been away, but would he? It was Mark they doubted and he realized, suddenly, even yet he did not know them—perhaps no white man would ever know them—and he knew they knew him better than he did himself.

On Saturday morning two weeks after Keetah's return, Mark carried a load of firewood to the church as was his custom, and when he had placed it in the wood box, he turned to see Keetah standing quietly by the golden eagle, and he went to her slowly and held out his hands.

"I knew you'd come. You have been afraid I would not approve because you have returned to the village. Is that not it? Oh, Keetah, do you trust me so little?" And he sat down in the first pew and she beside him, but it was a long time before she spoke.

Caleb had been kind to her. Everyone had been kind to her. Caleb found her a place to live, and work for her board and room while she went to school. The woman of the house had been afraid at first because she had never known an Indian girl, and she had asked, "Is she dirty? Will she steal?" and the woman had spoken to her as if she were a child. "You must take two baths a week. You must be in the house every night by half-past seven," though the woman had never helped with birth or death, and would have been afraid to do so. At school she had not belonged. She was older than the others, and the two younger Indian girls had said of her, "What is this old one doing here?"

Keetah spoke haltingly, never once lifting

her eyes. Then she stood up slowly, and Mark also.

"I could not sleep. I could not eat. I missed my village. I missed my gleena and my fish dishes. At night I dreamed of the black sands of Kingcome and of the mountains. The world swallowed me, and I knew I could not stay there because my village is the only place I know myself."

"The world is here also, Keetah."

"Each day I saw my Gordon grow more and more like the white man until even in church the white girls said, 'Who is that good-looking boy?' I am too Indian for Gordon now and I know it and he knows it. He will marry a white girl who can do more for him than I can do, or he will marry an Indian girl who has lived outside since she was very small. I lost my sister to death. I have lost Gordon to life, and this is harder. But there is something harder yet."

"To come home, Keetah?"

"Yes, to come home to the village I love. It is the same. I am not. I have seen how the white man treats his woman. He shares his pleasures and even his work. He does not marry her and leave her to fish. Now I know what Gordon knew long ago. To be an Indian in my own village is to be free as no white man is ever free, and it is to live behind a wall. I did not tell Gordon I was returning, but I think he knew. Sometimes, when he was not working at his books, we walked away from the town through the trees and into the woods. I stayed until I was sure that when I came home I would bear his child."

"To hold him—to make him marry you— to force him to return?"

"No! He does not know. He will not return for many years, and when he does, no one will tell him. Not to hold him. To let him go. To keep a part of him here in his village with his own people so they can last, so I too, can live."

Then she waited, her eyes fixed on his.

What she had done was logical to her, and

if he told her it was wrong, he would destroy her.

"What you have done is strange to me, but I think I understand it. You will grow over the wall. You will remain as long as the village lasts, and someday you will take Marta's place and become one of the great women of your tribe, and I shall always be proud of you."

That night, over supper, Mark said to Jim, "Keetah is going to have Gordon's child. Did you know?"

"Yes."

"And does this change you?"

"A child is always welcome," Jim said. "When I marry her, her child be mine."

## 20

On a Sunday in late March there occurred another of those small unforgettable happenings. Mark had grown to expect. The snow was gone. Day after day the rain had fallen patiently. When Mark shook up the fire in the big round stove and rang the church bell, he noticed that the leaden sky, which had overhung the village all winter long, seemed less dark and gloomy. During the communion service, just as he spoke the old, old words, "Therefore, with Angels and Archangels and with all the company of heaven," bright light suddenly filled the church and all the bowed heads lifted to see the sun glistening on the snows that crowned Whoop-Szo, and it seemed to Mark that he felt the burden of the winter lift as from a common shoulder, and heard the sigh of gratitude rise from a common heart.

When the service was over, the tribe poured slowly from the church, lingering in little groups on the path by the Cedar-man at the foot of the great totem.

"How thin we are," said old Peter. "We are like the bear when he leaves his den, and stands blinking in the light."

They all agreed, nodding that the cruel winter had been hard on them all. Then T. P., the elder, grandfather of Gordon, went up the steps of the church, lifted his arm and cried, "Quiet. Be still. I have something to say of importance. When the clamming is done, and the fishing has not yet begun, while we are waiting for the óolachon, I am giving a dance-potlatch for Jim, my grand-nephew, to pass to him the rights, the ceremonies of my family. All our tribe is invited and our relatives in the other villages, and there will be a feast and gifts for all."

One of the older men, distantly related, climbed the steps also to stand beside the old man, and he said to T. P.: "If it is pleasing to you, my branch of the family will give a feast also in honor of your family, and we will dance in honor of your nephew."

"It will please me."

Now everyone began to laugh and to talk in Kwákwala, the young women drawing around Mrs. Hudson, who would undoubtedly be asked to estimate the food which must be brought in by boat and to help choose the gifts. The younger men formed another group, and the older men a third.

"We will have at least three hundred people in the village. How will we feed them . . . ?"

"Let us do the Dog Dance. Let us do dances that were created here in our own village."

"Then we must check the masks. We must make sure the strings work properly so the fins of the fish can move and the mouths open."

Under a green spruce Marta stood by herself, her eyes on the young vicar. How thin and white he was! How long had it been there—that look on his face she had seen many times in her long life and knew well? It was not the hard winter that had placed it there. It was death reaching out his hand, touching the face gently, even before the owl had called the name.

While the others were still talking of the potlatch, Marta returned to her house and slowly, and with much care, she wrote a letter to the Bishop:

"My lord, it is your friend, Marta Stephens, who keeps her promise now. When T. P., the elder, gives a potlatch for Jim Wallace you come. It is time you come then. God bless you."

For three weeks the village was busier than Mark had ever seen it, except during the building of the new vicarage. At night in the social hall the older men checked the masks. After school the children practiced the dance steps at their play. The younger men cleaned the big house, built plank seats for the visitors who had been asked, and gathered wood for the great fire which would burn in the middle of the dirt floor.

Mrs. Hudson checked the ceremonial robes to be sure the abalone shells and the ancient buttons were still sewed tight, and she and the women of Jim and Gordon's families made two trips to Alert Bay for the gifts and food.

At last all was ready. The gill-netters and the seiners began to arrive at the float from the other villages, and hour after hour the canoes moved up and down the river bringing the guests. When the last canoe arrived two of the Indians stepped into the cold water in their Kingcome slippers and carried the Bishop ashore and a little whisper of excitement ran through the spruce, as the children spread the news. "The Bissop is here. The Bissop has come."

That night there was a great feast in the social hall. Then the tribe walked to the big house where T. P. and his family greeted the guests and seated them. Then there was nothing in all the world but the shadows of the carved house posts, the swirling ermine-tailed robes, the flickering of the great fire; no sound but the beat of the drums, the rhythm of the rattles, the chanting of the songs. Mark and the Bishop sat to the right of the fire in the place of honor, and saw the dance of the fish and the dog dance. They saw Jim do the dance of the angry man lost in the woods; his bird mask was so big that another dancer had to guide him lest he fall in the fire. It was all that was left of the famous hamatsa.

At dawn when the dancing was done and the guests served refreshments, gifts of linen, towels and shirts were distributed, and at the end as the guests left, each was handed a bright silver dollar.

On the second day there was another great feast and more dancing, and on the third morning the exodus began. When the canoes had taken the last guests down the river, the Bishop lingered in the quiet village. Once Mark saw him talking to Marta by the river's edge. When he walked to the end of the village on an errand, he saw the Bishop sitting with Peter, the carver, on the porch of the last house. In the late afternoon he saw him go into the church by himself.

"Something worries him. He has taken his problem into the church as I have done so many times, and put it down at the altar."

At dinner in the vicarage, the Bishop spoke little, and early the next morning the two of them left the village in the speed boat to go to the float.

When they entered the inlet, the Bishop motioned Mark to stop the engine.

"Let's not hurry," he said. "It's so seldom I have a few hours to myself."

The breeze was gentle with the first promise of spring. They could see the float moored to the inlet side and beyond it they could see the jagged scar of the great slide.

"Always when I leave the village," the Bishop said slowly, "I try to define what it means to me, why it sends me back to the world refreshed and confident. Always I fail. It is so simple, it is difficult. When I try to put it into words, it comes out one of those unctuous, over-pious platitudes at which Bishops are expected to excel."

They both laughed.

"But when I reach here and see the great scar where the inlet side shows its bones, for a moment I know."

"What, my lord?"

"That for me it has always been easier here, where only the fundamentals count, to learn what every man must learn in this world."

"And that, my lord?"

"Enough of the meaning of life to be ready to die," and the Bishop motioned Mark to start the motor, and they went on.

On the three-hour trip to the float store, they took turns at the wheel. Once the Bishop left the cabin and Mark could hear him in the galley banging the pots and pans. When he returned he carried a plate of sandwiches and two mugs of coffee. When they came at last to the store, the two raccoons greeted them with their strange whirring sound, and the Bishop fed them the crusts.

It was not until the seaplane set down on the water that the Bishop spoke.

"I will begin at once to seek a replacement for you, Mark. Your work in the village is almost done. When I have found the right man to take your place, I shall write you, and when you come out, you will come to me."

"Yes, my lord."

 21

When the little seaplane lifted and was gone, Mark turned back to his boat, checked the oil and water, and started to Knight's Inlet to keep his promise to Calamity Bill. Already nothing looked the same because it was going to end, because he was going to leave it, and the thought filled him with a twinge of sudden anguish and the little, unexpected fear that precedes any big change, sad or joyous.

How would he live again in the old world he had almost forgotten, where men throw up smoke screens between themselves and the fundamentals whose existence they fear but seldom admit? Here, where death waited behind each tree, he had made friends with loneliness, with death and deprivation, and, solidly against his back had stood the wall of his faith.

How much had he accomplished? If he asked him, he knew what the Bishop's answer would be: "You may never know, or perhaps something you have done will reveal itself in Keetah's child, in Gordon's life. You have done your small bit."

And what had he learned? Surely not the truth of the Indian. There was no one truth. He had learned a little of the truth of one tribe in one village. He had seen the sadness, the richness, the tragic poignancy of a way of life that each year, bit by bit, slipped beyond memory and was gone. For a time he had been part of it, one of the small unknown men who take their stand in some remote place, and fight out their battle in a quiet way.

When Mark was well into Knight's Inlet, he came on a strange sight. Two loggers were moving their float camp to a new location. The dwelling houses, the machine shop, the garden and the loading floats, made a double row, all enclosed by boom-sticks, joined end to end with chains. A tug boat had attached its towing cable to the gill-poke at the end of the A-frame float, and was pulling valiantly.

But the tide was running, and when Mark slowed his boat and drew as close to the tug as he dared, he was sure that the little community was scarcely moving at all, and he opened the cabin door and hailed them.

"How're you doing?" and the tugboat captain yelled back they'd made twenty-five miles in twenty-three hours, and four more to go, and Mark yelled back that he'd help with the tow.

He stayed with the haul for six hours, sometimes at the wheel of his own boat, when a man from the tug relieved him, in one of the dwelling houses on the floats. The Scottish granny of the two brothers who owned the camp made sandwiches and a pot of tea. The three children showed him the tiny schoolroom where, every morning, Granny taught them. The two wives showed him the light

plant, the washing machine, the refrigerator.

The smaller girl put in his lap Robert Burns, the tomcat, respected by all because last summer when a large brown bear had walked a boom log into the dwelling float, he had greeted him with such an outraged screech that the bear had fallen off the log and into the chuck.

The float camp seemed to stand still, while the green sides of the inlet moved by, slowly and majestically. When the new site was reached and the boats stopped, the two loggers discussed with him for a bit the new logging methods, the greater number of logs, the higher costs. When he left them, these staunch kindly people, he felt somehow that he had known them all his life.

Now, beside the compass, he placed the map he had taken from under Calamity's pillow, watching for the narrow finger of the sea on the left side of the inlet, found and entered it, slowing the boat until it barely moved, seeking the cove Calamity had marked with a cross. When he saw it, he stopped the engine and let the boat drift slowly in.

At flood tide no eddy moved, no ripple marred the surface. On the water Mark saw reflected the cliffs that rose above the narrow fingerling, the green spruce and cedar, and one huge hemlock that must have been growing when Christ was a little lad. Here he gave the ashes of Calamity to the sea, and when he came to the last words of the committal, "Rest eternal grant unto him, O Lord," he heard the echo of the words come back to him from across the narrow channel, softly and eerily, as if from another world. Then there was no sound but the soft mewing of the gulls nesting in the cliffs.

"Calamity, my friend," he thought, "you have had a funeral finer than a king's and this is the way it ought to be, and I have seen it once," and he started the engine and went on up the fingerling to its end and anchored there for the night.

In the morning after breakfast, he started

back to the village, and when he passed the site where he had left the float camp, he sounded the whistle and the Scottish granny and the children rushed out of the house to wave and call to him. After that he saw no one; he passed no boat.

All day long he moved down the longest, the loveliest of all the inlets, and it seemed to him that something strange had happened to time. When he had first come to the village, it was the future that loomed huge. So much to plan. So much to learn. Then it was the present that had consumed him—each day with all its chores and never enough hours to do them. Now time had lost its contours. He seemed to see it as the raven or the bald eagle, flying high over the village, must see the part of the river that had passed the village, that had not yet reached the village, one and the same.

All day long, on his way back to Kingcome, because he was alone and receptive, the little questions, the observations he had pushed deep within him, began to rise slowly toward the door of the conscious mind which was almost ready to open, to receive them, and give them words: "You are tired. You have told yourself that it was due to the winter which was hard on everyone. Deep inside haven't you known it was more than this? When the Bishop came to the potlatch and lingered after the others had gone, and went into the church by himself, didn't you guess then it had something to do with you? And your sister? When you took the boys down and lunched with her, did you not see the sadness in her eyes? And in the hospital, don't you remember the doctor's face, the look of quiet resignation upon it, and the way he hesitated an instant before answering your questions? And when the Bishop first told you of the village, how carefully he did so. Did you not think, "He is anxious I go there. Why?"

It was dusk when he entered Kingcome Inlet and moored the boat at the float, and climbed into the speed boat. When he entered

the river, the stars were shining, the moon bright also, and he went slowly.

Soon the huge flights of snow geese would fly over the river on their way back to the nesting place, the spring swimmer would come up the river to the Clearwater, and on the river pairs of cocky, small, red-necked sawbills would rest, the father flying off when Mark passed and the mother pretending she had broken a wing to lead him away from her little ones. And each would feel the pull of the earth and know his small place upon it, as did the Indian in his village.

He went slowly up the river. In front of the vicarage he anchored the boat and waded ashore. He trudged up the black sands to the path and stopped. From the dark spruce he heard an owl call—once, and again—and the questions that had been rising all day long reached the door of his mind and opened it.

He went up the path and the steps, through the living room and into the kitchen. The lights were on. At the stove Marta was preparing his dinner.

"Marta, something strange happened tonight. On the bank of the river I heard the owl call my name," and it was a question he asked, an answer he sought.

She did not say, "Nonsense, it was my name the owl called, and I am old and with me it does not matter." She did not say, "It's true you're thin and white, but who is not? It has no importance."

She turned, spoon still in her hand, lifting her sweet, kind face with its network of tiny wrinkles, and she answered his question as she would have answered any other.

She said, "Yes, my son."

## 22

In the night the heaviest of the spring rains fell in torrents as the young vicar struggled with the one fact of his life about which no man has doubt and yet is never ready to meet. One of the thoughts that comforted him was from his life here on the up-coast, the simple memory of the many times on the boat when he and Jim had seemed to be heading straight into a cliff or a steep island side only to find at the last moment some little finger of the sea waiting to lead them on. But almost as big as the fact of death was the thought of leaving. How could he return now to that far country he no longer knew, where, while awaiting death, he would be a stranger?

In the morning the rain had stopped, and the gray sky was broken by sun shining through soft white clouds. In the alders called the ravens, high over the river flew a flock of small birds he had come to know. As yearlings they had passed over the village in the fall, crossing lands they had never seen and with no older bird to guide them. Yet they had known their way to the southern valley where their kind had wintered for untold centuries, as now they knew their way back to the nesting place.

He walked slowly to the river bank. All was the same. The children too small to be in school came running to greet him. The older men were emptying rain water from the canoes, and Mrs. Hudson was poling out into the current to dump her garbage. The dark eyes held their usual sadness, the voices gentle, the mouths quick to smile, the hands lifting in the usual greeting.

"Good morning, Mark."

"What a rain we had. Did you hear it?"

"The village has become a sponge."

"But the morning will be splendid."

"It will not last. We will have another storm by night."

They did not know, and how could he tell them? How could he face the pity that would come to the sad eyes? And he tried desperately to speak as usual, and he turned slowly away and walked past the vicarage, and the church, past the Cedar-man at the foot of the great totem, following the main path through the quiet village. When he had passed the last house, which was that of Peter, the carver, he took the little narrow path through the deep wet woods, fragrant from rain, to the glade that was once the old burial ground.

There he stood alone in a world that had become a waiting room, and when he turned at last, he saw Keetah watching him. She came to him slowly and put her hands on his shoulders.

"I have come to speak for my people, Mark. There is something we wish you to do for us."

"But of course, Keetah. Anything I am able to do, I will do gladly."

"Stay with us. Marta has told us. We have written the Bishop and asked that he let you remain here to the end, because this is your village and we are your family. You are the swimmer who came to us from the great sea," and he put his arms around her and held her close, finding no words to say thank you for the sudden, unexpected gift of peace which they had offered him in their quiet, perceptive way.

In the late afternoon of this day there occurred one of those minor emergencies typical of Mark's life in the village. A young logger, long in the woods, reached the beer parlor at a float store, drank too much, too fast, stole a small motor boat, and headed happily for the straits, despite gale warnings, and predictions of a storm by nightfall. Since his boat was the fastest, Mark was summoned to aid in the search.

Jim received the message by radio-telephone on the boat and came for Mark at once, and together they went downriver, past the snags and the log jam, and transferred to the larger boat at the float. They went out the inlet, Jim at the wheel, Mark perched on the stool, binoculars in hand, ready to search the rocks, the reefs, the hidden coves.

In two hours they had not found the drunken

logger. When they reached the place where the boat began to pitch in the tidal sweap that came down from Queen Charlotte Sound, they received word by the radio-telephone that the young logger had been found peacefully sleeping it off, his boat neatly stuck between two rocks not three miles from the float store from which he had started.

"And here we are in the cold, wasting oil, and supperless," Jim said. "I hope he has the good grace to drown himself."

"He won't even have a sniffle in his nose. I'll make us some coffee."

They went back in silence, as they had so many times. When they entered Kingcome Inlet, Mark was at the wheel, Jim beside him watching for drift logs in the searchlight.

"Jim."

"Yes."

"When I am no longer in the village, take care of Keetah. When you want coffee, don't bang on the table. Say *please* and when she hands you the cup, say *thank you*. You'll find it most efficacious."

"What is this *efficacious*?"

"It means it works. And when you build Keetah a house, let her plan it with you. And don't leave her alone in the village too long. Take her and the children with you sometimes on the fishing, and each year take her outside until it is familiar to her. Someday, when the village is no more, you too must cross the bridge."

"You ask me to do this for Keetah? Why?"

"Because I care for her also—and for you."

Then neither spoke, the wake from the bow white in the night. As they neared the float thunder sounded overhead, and lightening cut the sky and struck a tree at the top of the inlet forty yards ahead of the boat and high above them. The tree fell upon the trees below and, weakened by the heavy rains, they fell also, slowly at first, then faster and faster, end over end, until a long jagged strip peeled from the inlet side, and the whole world exploded into sound.

## 23

In the village the tribe heard the roar of the slide, prolonged and intensified as it was tossed from one steep inlet side to another until, even after the last of the trees had fallen and the waters begun to calm, the echoes still rumbled in the far distance, growing slowly fainter until they too were gone.

The tribe heard it and knew what it meant as had their ancestors. The sound lay in the oldest, deepest memories and in the myths. The sound was in the name of Whoop-Szo; "and the gods that lived on Noisy Mountain saw the enemy coming down the river and sent a huge slide to destroy it."

In the little cedar houses the men did not wait to light the lamps, but pulled on their shirts and trousers, their jackets and gum boots, seeking their tools and their lanterns. Footfalls sounded softly on the path that led past the dark vicarage to the river bank in a night suddenly starkly still. The water splashed as the men waded to the boats, a woman's voice following them, "Be careful—be careful," and the outboard motors sputtered and caught.

Then they were gone. The women were alone with the young, the old, the sick, as women have been left to wait through all the ages everywhere.

All night long the women waited. In the morning of the next day one of the men returned to bring news and take back food. The boat of the vicar had been caught in the slide and its wreckage sighted, and from the wreckage they had heard a voice call but they could not draw close enough to identify it. The RCMP had been summoned, the Bishop notified. The logging camps had sent men and boats to help.

All day long the women waited. But Keetah could not wait quietly with the others. When the bluejay called its name. "Kwiss-kwiss-kwiss-kwiss," it seemed to ask, "Which one? Which one?" and Keetah went through the village, through the dark, wet trees to the slope of the mountain that rose back of the village, and she climbed to the farseeing spot from which it was possible to see down the river to the inlet.

She did not know that her great-great-grandmother had come long ago to this same spot. No one in the tribe remembered now that in the days of the great tribal conflicts, before taking his place in the war canoe each man had blown his breath into a strip of dried kelp, tied the strip into a ring, and placed the ring around the neck of his wife saying, "Guard well my breath." Keetah's great-great-grandmother had hung the ring at the head of her bed and when she had returned to the house to check it, and found the kelp ring flabby, she had come to this spot to watch for the returning canoes, to see if her husband was in his accustomed place. And she had called loudly upon all the gods, the guardian spirits of the tribe, to help her. "Come wolf, come swimmer. Come raven, come eagle"; even upon the cannibal who lived at the north end of the world.

But Keetah could not choose between Mark and Jim. She prayed for both, waiting hour after hour. When she saw the canoe enter the river and the blanket-wrapped figure who sat on the center crosspiece, she could not tell which he was, and she started back to the village, down the smooth shale, through the dark trees, the devil's club scratching at her arms.

When she entered the village, she saw the old men gathered by the ceremonial house, and as she passed them, she heard their voices.

"We must plan carefully. There is much to do."

"But the Bishop will not come for two days. This gives us time."

"Yes, but others will come with him. There will be visitors from all the villages and many guests to be housed and fed."

"We have time. The RCMP has not yet given the permit, and the boat has not yet brought the box from Alert Bay. It will be late tomorrow before they bring the body and by then all the searchers and the fishermen will be home to help us."

Keetah walked slowly to the vicarage and up the steps to the door, afraid to open it, dreading whichever truth waited her. Then she went in.

At the kitchen table sat Jim, his head buried in his arms. He lifted it slowly.

"You have been crying."

"It is the salt water that stung my eyes. I have not cried since I was eight and made a mistake in the dance, and my mother scolded me."

"You have been crying because you loved him also. What will you do now?"

"I will fish on my uncle's boat. In the fall when the fishing days are almost over, I will put up the sides and roof of my house, and in the winter I will finish the inside of the house, and I will ask you to plan it as you wish."

"And then?"

"Once I would have sent my sisters to bring you to my house, and thus you would be my wife. Now I will wait. When you come I will not bang on the table when I want coffee. I will not leave you too much alone in the village, and each year I will take you out and show you the big world, because Mark said that when the village is gone, we too must be able to walk across the bridge."

"When the house is ready, I will marry you."

In the evening every house in the village was lighted and there was much talk.

"Who will dig the grave? Who will cut away the underbrush from the path?" And the young men answered, "We will do it."

"And who will cut the cedar for the wreaths? Who will search the woods for the new green ferns?" And the children answered, "We will go."

In the house of Mrs. Hudson the young matrons said to her in Kwákwala, "There will be many guests. What meat shall we prepare for them?"

"Roast beef."

"And how much?"

"A hundred and fifty pounds."

"And what vegetable?"

"Carrots," and tears trickled down the cheeks of the matriarch. "He never liked mashed turnips and I made him eat them. I am a stubborn woman who wants her own way." And the young matrons moved closer to her like chicks to an old hen, "Oh, no—no—no."

By late afternoon of the next day, all was ready. The path was cleared. The grave was dug. The wreaths were made. The church was swept and cleaned. The beds in the vicarage were made up with fresh linen. The village was waiting and listening, and it was the children who heard first the canoes coming up the river, and they ran down the path calling, "They come now. They bring him now."

In his tiny house the teacher heard the running footfalls on the path to the river bank, and he went quickly to the door and could not open it. To join the others was to care, and to care was to live and to suffer.

The tribe waited on the bank, and when the canoes came around the bend in the river, the old people began a chant of sorrow in the ancient language which the young no longer knew. "Aie-aie-aie—he has left us—aie-aie-aie," until even the breeze seemed to whisper it, and the trees to sigh of it.

Then the men of the tribe waded into the icy water to meet the canoes, each man taking his turn carrying the body of the young vicar to the black sands of Kingcome, while the women sang an ancient hymn to a Supreme Being whose existence had been sensed before the white man had ever come to this land. And when the body had been prepared for burial, six men carried the box into the church, the tribe waiting there. They placed it on trestles before the altar, and T.P., the elder, took his place at the lectern which was the golden eagle and spoke the Lord's Prayer, the tribe joining him:

Kunuh Umpa Laka ike Mayauntla Hyis
Glikum us: gak la hyis gikasa us;

· · · · · · · · · · · · · · ·

Au uma gagila gakunuh
Laka yaksami.

In the night the only light in the village was that from the lantern which Jim had placed in the little church of Saint George. The village was quiet and at peace.

In her house old Marta lay awake in the dark, and she said softly, "Walk straight on, my son. Do not look back. Do not turn your head. You are going to the land of our Lord."

In the last house of the village, Peter, the carver, lay awake also, and he remembered that in the old days when a great chief died, his soul came straight back to the village in the sleek body of a raven, and the soul of a lesser man returned in his own body no higher than an inch or as a ha-moo-moo, a butterfly. Peter did not believe this literally. Yet it seemed likely to him that the soul of the young vicar would return to the village he had loved, as would his own, and surely it would be most inhospitable if no one was awake and waiting. Thus he dressed and sat on the top step of his house in the dark night, and hearing the rustle of some small night creature he, too, spoke softly, "It is only old Peter, the carver, who waits here, friend."

Past the village flowed the river, like time, like life itself, waiting for the swimmer to come again on his way to the climax of his adventurous life, and to the end for which he had been made.

Wa Laum
(That is all)

1. What are the author's reasons for relating the incidents dealing with Calamity's death?

2. Earlier in the book, Jim has said that Gordon is "moving rapids" and Keetah is a pool of "still water." How do her actions bear this out?

3. Why does T. P. give a dance potlatch for Jim? How does the Bishop happen to attend?

4. What is Mark's reaction to the Bishop's statement that he is going to seek a replacement for Mark, that his work in the village is almost done?

5. Why does the author introduce the incident of the float family at this point?

6. How do the villagers learn that Mark is to leave them? What is their reaction?

7. What emergency takes Jim and Mark out in the boat? Would you have preferred Mark's death to have been from his disease rather than an accident?

---

# I
## A JOURNEY TOWARD DEATH

Mark is terminally ill. He has at most two or three years to live. You know that he is moving away from life toward death. The book begins with an actual physical journey in which Mark threads his way through ever-narrowing waterways toward a village that can be reached only by canoe. But at this place, where the Bishop says "only fundamentals count," Mark is also taking a journey into himself to the inevitable destination of death: overcoming self, passing through loneliness, testing his physical and emotional endurance.

The Indians call Mark a "swimmer" because he is a twin. This is also the name given to the salmon. Early in his stay, Mark goes to see the salmon coming back to their spawning grounds in a mountain stream. Here he watches as the female swimmer digs her nest with her battered tail, lays her eggs, and then, exhausted, is drowned in the turbulent waters. Keetah finds this terribly sad. Mark sees it as a triumph that the salmon spends itself completely in doing the thing for which it is made. It is the climax of its life. Is Mark's death also the climax of his life? The Bishop says everyone must learn enough of the meaning of life to be ready to die. Has Mark come to this understanding?

# II
## IMPLICATIONS

A. Consider the following and tell what your reactions to them are.

1. Had you been the Bishop, would you have chosen a different way for Mark to spend the last days of his life?

2. If you had been Mark, would you have wanted to be told that you had little time left for living?

3. If the Kwakiutls had known that Mark was dying, would they have treated him differently?

4. Would the story have been just as effective if you had not known that Mark was terminally ill?

5. The basic irony in this story is the best way to move toward an objective is to move away from it.

B. There are many quotations in the story that are provocative. How do you feel about the ones that follow?

1. "Don't be sorry for yourself. . . . Be sorry for the Indians. You know nothing and they must teach you."

2. "They will not thank you. Even if you should leave a broken man, they will not thank you."

3. "And the young people regretted going and wanted to go, and the elders wanted to keep them and were relieved when they went."

4. "And the young men strolled through the village singing the old love songs, and the songs were always of absence and of sorrow, and they spoke from the heart."

# III
## TECHNIQUES
*Atmosphere*

Aside from Mark's story, there are two predominant impressions that the story leaves. One is that the tribe of Kwakiutls. Although individuals in the tribe are portrayed, it is the tribe as a whole that is characterized. What are the words that come to mind when you think of this group of Kwakiutls? The second impression is of the natural setting. What words come to mind to describe it? The atmosphere of the story is a combination of these two.

*Suspense*

1. Throughout the story, there are questions set up in the reader's mind. The most obvious one is the question of what is going to happen to Mark, how is he going to die. What are some of the others?

2. The highest moment of suspense comes near the very end after the slide has caught Mark's boat. How is the action manipulated so that you do not find out immediately what has happened?

---

BIOGRAPHICAL NOTES

## MacKinlay Kantor

MacKinlay Kantor (1904–    ) was born in Webster City, Iowa, and grew up under the shadow of his father's escapades as an international confidence man. Determined to show everybody that he could succeed in spite of his father's reputation, he started out upon graduation from high school working on a newspaper, then plunged into free-lance writing. His first novel was published when he was twenty-four, but success did not come until 1934 with the publication of an epic novel centered on the Battle of Gettysburg. By 1967 he had published 36 books, one of which, *Andersonville*, won him the Pulitzer Prize.

## Nathaniel Hawthorne

Son of a New England sea captain, Nathaniel Hawthorne (1804–1864) was born in New Salem, Massachusetts. When he was four, his father died and his mother became a recluse even from her children. Little effort was made to give Hawthorne an early education, but during his lonely childhood he developed a taste for reading. At his uncle's expense he attended Bowdoin College. After graduating he returned to Salem and secluded himself in his mother's house; for the next twelve years he worked at becoming a writer. In 1837 he published his first collection of tales and sketches, *Twice-Told Tales*. In 1842 he married Sophia Peabody and moved for a while to the Old Manse at Concord where they were often visited by Thoreau, Emerson, Bronson Alcott, and Margaret Fuller. Here Hawthorne wrote a second collection of stories, *Mosses from an Old Manse;* but his income was still so small that he took a job as surveyor for the Customs House in Salem. Dismissed after three years for political reasons, he devoted full time to writing, and in seven months created his masterpiece, *The Scarlet Letter*. This success was followed shortly by two more novels. *The House of the Seven Gables* and *The Blithedale Romance*. When Franklin Pierce became president of the United States, he sent Hawthorne, a college chum, to Liverpool as consul. He remained abroad until 1860.

## Howard Fast

Howard Fast (1914–    ), a novelist, short story writer, editor, and lecturer, attended the National Academy of Design for a short time after graduating from high school. Working at several odd jobs and as a page in the New York Public Library to support himself, he published his first novel when he was eighteen. "In the years since," he has said, "I have lectured, preached, exhorted, and agitated on platforms, in the classroom, on radio and television more times than I care to recall." Commenting on *April Morning*, considered by many a teen-age classic, Fast said: "*April Morning* is as good a book as I have ever written, as nearly perfect a book as I could hope to write." He indicates that the writer owes nothing to his material or to the public. "His only obligation is to the truth." His thinking on this point is similar to that of Bernard Malamud.

## Albert Halper

Albert Halper (1904–    ) was born in Chicago and educated at Northwestern University, attending classes there in 1924–1925. His short stories and articles have appeared in *The New Yorker*, *Harpers*, and *The Atlantic*. He has also written novels and plays.

## Liam O'Flaherty

Liam O'Flaherty (1897–    ), an Irish novelist born in the Aran Islands, was educated by the Holy Ghost Fathers as a postulant for the priesthood. After studying in Dublin at Holy Cross College he gave up the idea of taking religious orders and entered the University College of Dublin. Soon after, he joined the Irish Guard and was shell-shocked in France during World War I. After his recovery, he worked his way almost around the world. Returning to Ireland in 1922, he headed a group of unemployed workers who seized a public building in Dublin. After this action, the government drove him out of the country. At this point he began writing, publishing two novels, *Thy Neighbor's Wife* and *The Black Soul*, and a collection of short stories; *Spring Sowing*, from which the selection in this unit was taken. In 1925 his novel, *The Informer*, took the world by storm. O'Flaherty's main concern in his writing is with the perpetual struggle of the mass of humanity for bread, freedom, and civilization.

## Shirley Jackson

Shirley Jackson (1919–1965), novelist and short story writer, graduated from Syracuse University in 1940. One of her short stories, "The Lottery," which appeared in *The New Yorker,* established her as the master of the Gothic horror tale. Her works center on two types of writing: the humorous, in which the delights and turmoils of ordinary home life are made hilarious, and the horror story, in which abnormal behavior is made perilously ordinary. *Raising Demons* (1957) and *Life Among the Savages* (1953) represent the first type, and *We Have Always Lived in the Castle* (1962) is an example of the second. She once said she wrote because "it's the only chance I get to sit down," and that writing "gives me an excuse not to clean out closets."

## Kurt Vonnegut, Jr.

Kurt Vonnegut, Jr., (1922–    ), was born in Indianapolis, Indiana. He married Jane Cox in 1945, and they had three children: Mark, Edith, and Nanette. He also raised his deceased sister's three boys. His jobs have ranged from police reporter to public relations man to lecturer at the University of Iowa Writer's Workshop. Since 1950 his main occupation has been as a free-lance writer. Richard Schickel, the critic, has said: "The trouble with Kurt Vonnegut, Jr., is that he fits

too easily into superficial literary categories, thus sparing critics from thinking very hard or well about his work." Vonnegut was first classified as a science fiction writer, next as a writer of black comedy, and today as a satirist of today's society. He believes all ideologies and elaborate programs for mass progress are only frauds that men perpetrate on themselves. Schickel believes that Vonnegut feels no self-pity but only purifying laughter, which is a sign of maturity. He even suggests that Vonnegut is an exorcist using comedy to remove temporarily the pain caused by today's society.

## Mark Twain

Mark Twain (1835–1910) was born Samuel Langhorne Clemens in Florida, Missouri, but lived as a child in Hannibal, Missouri, on the Mississippi River. He took the pen name, Mark Twain, from the call of the pilots on the river steamers. This call indicated that the water was 12 feet deep, a safe depth for a steamer. Leaving school when he was 12, he served as a printer's apprentice, a riverboat pilot, a Confederate soldier, a prospector, and a reporter. After a junket to Hawaii, he hit the lecture trail and became famous as a platform speaker. In 1869 *Innocents Abroad* established him as an American humorist, but it was *Tom Sawyer* and *The Adventures of Huckleberry Finn,* both set in his hometown, that made his reputation as one of the greatest of American writers. Financial disaster and personal unhappiness marred his last years. Only his daughter, Clara, survived Twain, who died as he had prophesied he would—when Halley's comet returned in 1910.

## Margaret Craven

For biographical information see the introduction to *I Heard the Owl Call My Name,* page 658.

# Glossary of Literary Terms

The definitions that follow cover the literary terms found in *Encounters,* as well as a number of others commonly used that do not appear in the text.

**Alliteration:** A sequence of words that have the same initial sound: tall trembling trees.

**Allusion:** An indirect or unspecified but pointed reference to something with which the reader is presumed to be familiar, such as *the Midas touch, a Goliath, a glass slipper.*

**Anapest:** A foot of poetry consisting of two unaccented and one accented syllable: *lĭke ă chíld.*

**Assonance:** A sequence of words having the same vowel sounds: counting mountains.

**Atmosphere:** The mood a piece of literature creates in the reader's mind, such as happiness, melancholy, despair, nostalgia.

**Blank Verse:** A characteristic English form of poetry having five iambic feet without end rhymes. See *Julius Caesar* for examples.

**Characterization:** The word portrait of a person in literature created by (1) direct description, (2) what the person does and says, (3) what others say about the person.

**Climax:** The point in a piece of literature at which the conflicting issues are resolved toward one possible ending.

**Consonance:** Correspondence of consonant sounds within words which may or may not be in sequence: trembling tumble.

**Dactyl:** A foot of poetry consisting of one accented and two unaccented syllables: */Thĭs ĭs thĕ/fórĕst prĭm/évăl."*

**Dialect:** A regional variety of a language distinguished from others by slight variations in pronunciation, grammar, and vocabulary.

**Dialogue:** Conversation between two or more characters.

**Diction:** Choice and use of words in speech or writing.

**Dimeter:** A line of poetry consisting of only two metrical feet: *I saw a man.*

**End Rhyme:** A term usually applying to drama in which the end of a scene is indicated by the use of a series of rhyming lines. Look at the last four lines of *Julius Caesar* (p. 463) as an example.

**Essay:** A short, nonfiction prose piece relating an experience, reflecting about life, or presenting a point of view.

**Etymology:** The origin and history of a word.

**Exposition:** The background information a reader needs about characters, setting, time, and prior happenings to understand the action of a story.

**Feminine Rhyme:** Sometimes called weak rhyme. Rhyming words that end in unaccented syllables such as *moáning, gróaning.*

**Flashback:** An interlude in a story in which something is told that took place at an earlier time than the present action.

**Foot:** A single unit in poetry consisting of a stressed or unstressed syllable. When repeated in a pattern, rhythm is produced.

**Hexameter:** A line of poetry consisting of six feet.

**Humor:** Something designed to induce laughter or amusement.

**Iambic Foot:** A foot of poetry with one unaccented and one accented syllable. English falls naturally into iambic patterns. *Thĕ ráil/rŏad tráck /ĭs míles/ ăwáy.*

**Iambic Pentameter:** A line of poetry consisting of five iambic feet.

**Identification:** The process by which the reader gets "into the skin" of a character and shares the character's emotions and thoughts.

**Idiomatic Compound:** A combination of two or more smaller words whose meaning is different from the literal definition of the words: *iron curtain, brainwash, red tape.*

**Imagery:** The use of figures of speech or vivid words to produce a mental picture: *"Ghost Lake's a dark lake, a deep lake and cold/Ice black as ebony, frostily scrolled."*

**Irony:** *Verbal irony* is the use of words in such a way that they mean the opposite of their literal meaning. "How lucky can you get?" is ironic when said to someone who has just fallen and sprained an ankle.

*Dramatic irony* occurs when the action produces exactly the opposite result from what is expected, as when a health-food fanatic dies from eating infected honey.

**Lyric Poetry:** Poetry that explores emotions and sensations rather than telling a story. Its sound patterns come closest to sounding like music.

**Masculine Rhyme:** Sometimes called strong rhyme. The rhyming words end with an accented syllable such as *deríde* and *decíde.*

**Metaphor:** An implied comparison between two unlike objects. (See p. 276.)

**Metonymy:** A figure of speech in which a part of an object is used to designate the whole, as: She saw a *sail* on the horizon.

**Monometer:** A line of poetry with a single foot. See "The Warning" (p. 260). The first and last lines are monometers.

**Narrative:** A story or description of actual or fictional events.

**Onomatopoeia:** A word so formed that it sounds like the thing to which it refers, such as *moo, buzz, snap.*

**Organization:** In literature this refers to the conscious pattern formed by the placement of elements in relation to one another.

**Parable:** A simple story illustrating a moral or religious lesson.

**Pentameter:** A line of poetry composed of five feet: *"When I/have fears/that I/may cease/to be."*

**Personal Narrative:** An account of an experience encountered by the author.

**Personification:** The endowment of inanimate objects or abstractions with human qualities, as in *the dancing flowers* or *the shivering stone.*

**Plot:** The outline or pattern of the events making up a narrative.

**Poetry:** A composition designed to convey a vivid and imaginative sense of life in language chosen for its sound and rhythms as well as for its meaning.

**Prose:** The ordinary kind of language used in speech or writing as contrasted to that used in verse. Meaning is dominant over other qualities of language.

**Pyrrhic:** A foot of poetry consisting of two unaccented syllables: *"And thĕ/*whéel's kićk/*and thĕ/*wind's sóng."*

**Rhyme:** Two words with differing initial sounds but with identical final sounds. In poetry this correspondence of sounds usually occurs at the ends of lines: "The wind was a torrent of darkness among the gusty *trees,/*The moon was a ghostly galleon tossed upon cloudy *seas.*

**Rhythm:** In language, rhythm is created by a repetitive pattern of stressed and unstressed syllables.

**Root:** A word or word element from which other words are formed. Often the base word is to be found in German, Greek, or Latin.

**Short Story:** A short fictional narrative using a limited number of characters and built around a single incident or issue designed to produce a single effect.

**Simile:** An expressed comparison between two unlike things, usually using the words "like" or "as": *"My Love is like a red, red rose"* or *Her biscuits were light as feathers.*

**Slang:** A current, non-standard expression that only rarely continues in the language. Examples of outdated slang are *23 skidoo, dullsville, square, trucking, keeno.*

**Spondee:** A metric foot of poetry consisting of two accented syllables. See *pyrrhic* for an example of a pyrrhic foot followed by a spondee foot.

**Stanza:** A unit in poetry of two or more lines comparable to a paragraph in prose and marked off by blank space after it. Usually it uses a common pattern of meter, rhyme, and number of lines.

**Structure:** In a poem this concerns the arrangement of topics, scenes, statements, and ideas to produce one dominant impression.

**Style:** The way something is said or written as distinguished from its meaning. By a combination of language, sentence structure, figures of speech, and even grammar, a writer achieves a certain individual quality of writing. Style may be the trademark of a particular writer, a school, an era, or a culture, as the style of Hemingway, the style of the Romantics, the style of the twenties, or the style of Indian literature.

**Suspense:** The technique in writing of keeping the reader uncertain, anxious, or apprehensive about what is going to happen in a story.

**Symbol:** Something that is used or regarded as representing something else. Symbols are like signs pointing to meanings. There are some common symbols that are easily recognized, such as the cross representing the Christian religion and the flag representing a particular nation. But writers may create their own symbols.

**Synecdoche:** A figure of speech (the opposite of metonymy) in which a larger classification is used to designate one of its subparts: the law is used to designate a police officer or silver is used for a knife, fork, and spoon.

**Tetrameter:** A line of poetry containing four metrical feet: *Thĕ ráil/road tráck/ĭs míles/ăway.*

**Theme:** The idea, perception, or impression that a work of literature conveys.

**Tone:** The tone of voice in which the reader imagines the writer to be speaking, such as rapid, slow, loud, soft, happy, sad. The writer conveys tone by rhythm, choice of words, images, length of sentences, and even punctuation. Tone may also be used to describe the writer's attitude toward the reader.

**Trimeter:** A line of poetry consisting of three feet: *"Thĕ hóuse/ĭs shút/and still."*

**Trochee:** A foot of poetry consisting of an accented syllable followed by an unaccented one. This is often used for emphasis in, say, a poem using mostly iambic feet. Its rhythm is best suited to light, gay poems and songs and hence is often found in nursery rhymes: *"Máry/hád ă/little/lámb."*

# Glossary

This glossary contains difficult words which are not in the vocabularies of average tenth-grade students. The definitions apply to the uses of the words in this text. For more complete study of the range of meanings for these words, the student must consult his dictionary. Many other specific and uncommon terms have been footnoted with the selections.

## Pronunciation Guide

A key to the pronunciation symbols is given at the bottom of every other page. By consulting the most recent dictionaries, the student may notice that the symbols here represent a series of compromises between current scholarly interpretations of sounds and less precise symbols which continue to have wide acceptance. A few minutes' study of the pronunciation key before using this glossary will make it possible for the student to use the pronunciation transcriptions with the greatest ease and efficiency.

The same key is used for pronunciations given here and in the footnotes. Foreign terms and names are transcribed so as to be acceptable in standard American speech rather than precise in terms of their original languages.

*Accent* marks precede the stressed syllables. The mark ▲ indicates the heaviest stress and the mark ' indicates intermediate stress.

*Abbreviations* indicate parts of speech and special spellings. The following are used:

|       |           |
|-------|-----------|
| n.    | noun      |
| v.    | verb      |
| adj.  | adjective |
| adv.  | adverb    |
| pl.   | plural    |

**abash**\ə ▲băsh\ v. To make bashful, cause to lose confidence or composure.

**abate**\ə ▲bāt\ v. To die down, subside, diminish.

**ab·er·ra·tion**\ ˈăb·ə ▲rā·shən\ n. Departure from the normal or natural way or manner.

**ab·hor**\əb ▲hōr\ v., -red, -ring. To hate, abominate.

**ab·ject**\▲ăb 'jĕkt\ adj. Hopeless, dispirited, downcast.

**ab·ne·ga·tion**\'ăb·nə ▲gā·shən\ n. Self-denial, rejection of egoism.

**ab·sorp·tion**\əb ▲sōrp·shən\ n. Complete occupation of one's mind and thoughts with one thing, ignoring all others.

**ac·cen·tu·ate**\ăk ▲sĕn·chʊ 'āt\ v. To emphasize, stress.

**ac·cep·ta·tion**\'ăk·sĕp ▲tā·shən\ n. Meaning or interpretation commonly connected with a word.

**ac·ces·si·ble**\ək ▲sĕ·sĭ·bəl\ adj. Capable of being reached, possible or convenient to come to.

**ac·cliv·i·ty**\ə ▲klĭv·ət·ē\ n. A slope that ascends.

**ac·cord**\ə ▲kō(ə)rd\ v. To grant, allow as proper.

**ac·cost**\ə ▲kŏst\ v. To stop and speak to by way of challenge or inquiry.

**ac·qui·si·tion**\'ăk·wə ▲zĭsh·ən\ n. Something acquired or gained. (Also v. The act of acquiring or gaining.)

**ad·a·mant**\▲ă·də·mənt\ adj. Absolutely resolute and not to be deterred by any argument or appeal.

**ad·dict**\ə ▲dĭkt\ v. To bring about habitual compulsive use. (Also n. \▲ă·dĭkt\)

**adieu**\ə ▲dū\ n. Good-bye, farewell.

**ad·ja·cent**\ə ▲jā·sənt\ adj. Touching along one side, neighboring, nearby.

**ad·ju·tant**\▲a·jə·tənt\ n. A minor military or police officer.

**ad·mon·ish**\ăd ▲mŏ·nĭsh\ v. To warn, reprimand.

**ad·o·les·cence**\'ă·də ▲lĕ·səns\ n. Youth, the period between boyhood or girlhood and maturity.

**ad·o·ra·tion**\'ă·də ▲rā·shən\ n. Love, great respect, veneration.

**ad·vent**\▲ăd 'vĕnt\ n. Coming, arrival.

**af·fa·ble**\▲ă·fə·bəl\ adj. Good natured, politely friendly.

**af·fir·ma·tion**\'ă·fər ▲mā·shən\ n. Assertion, confirming statement.

**ag·gres·sive**\ə ▲grĕ·sĭv\ adj. 1. Showing fight or determination. 2. Bold, confident, and forward; not at all shy or afraid. (Adv. -ly, n. -ness)

**aghast**\ə ▲găst\ adj. Extremely afraid, stunned with fear.

**agil·i·ty**\ə ▲jĭ·lĭ·tē\ n. Nimbleness, spryness.

**ag·o·nize**\▲ă·gə 'naiz\ v. To cause agony or great pain.

**ague**\āg *or* ▲ā 'gyū\ n. Sickness, fever.

**ail·ment**\▲āl·mənt\ n. Illness, malady.

**airy**\▲ā·rē\ adj. Carefree, nonchalant. (Adv. -ily)

**al·che·mist**\▲ăl·kə·mĭst\ n. The medieval forerunner of the modern chemist, one who tried to find ways of changing other substances into gold.

**al·ga**\▲ăl·gə\ n., pl. -ae. A small sea plant giving the effect of scum in the water.

**al·le·giance**\ə ▲lē·jəns\ n. Loyalty.

**al·ler·gy**\▲ă·lər·jē\ n., pl. -ies. A physical condition in which certain substances or situations, normally harmless, are very irritating.

**al·lure**\ə ▲lūr\ v. To attract, charm, enchant. (Also n.)

---

ă bad, ā bake, a father, ĕ sell, ē equal, ai mile, ĭ sit, ŏ cot, ō note, ɔ law, ū boom, ʊ wood, yū you, yʊ fury, aʊ cow, ɔi boy. The schwa is used for both stressed and unstressed sounds: ə mud, word, even; ch chase, itch; sh shell, wish; th path, thin; th the, either; ŋ wing; w wet, wheat; zh pleasure.

729

**alms·giv·er**\\ᴬamz 'gĭ·vər\\ n. One who gives alms; especially, one who gives money to beggars.

**al·tim·e·ter**\\ăl ᴬtĭ·mə·tər\\ n. A device for measuring altitude.

**am·ber**\\ᴬăm·bər\\ n. A dark-orange fossil resin.

**am·big·u·ous**\\ăm ᴬbĭg·yū·əs\\ adj. Subject to more than one meaning or interpretation.

**am·bi·va·lent**\\ăm ᴬbĭv·ə·lənt\\ adj. Simultaneously attracted toward and turned against an object, person, or action.

**am·ble**\\ᴬăm·bəl\\ v. To walk slowly, saunter, stroll.

**am·bus·cade**\\ᴬăm·bəs ˈkād\\ n. Ambush. (Also v.)

**amend**\\ə ˈmĕnd\\ v. To correct, adjust.

**ame·ni·ty**\\ə ᴬmē·nĭ·tē or ə ᴬmĕ·nĭ·tē\\ n., pl. -ies. Civilized and pleasant comfort.

**ami·a·ble**\\ᴬā·mē·ə·bəl\\ adj. Showing pleasing friendliness. (Adv. -ly)

**am·i·ca·ble**\\ᴬăm·ĭ·kə·bəl\\ adj. Characterized by friendship and goodwill.

**amiss**\\ə ᴬmĭs\\ adj. Wrong, bad. (Also adv.)

**am·phi·the·ater**\\ᴬăm·fĭ ˈthē·ə·tər\\ n. A natural outdoor theater with rising rows of seats (as on a hillside).

**am·pu·tate**\\ᴬăm·pyu ˈtat\\ v. To cut off surgically.

**anal·o·gy**\\ə ᴬnă·lə·jē\\ n., pl. -ies. A sustained similarity discovered between seemingly unlike things or conditions, a comparison or resemblance sustained between unlike things.

**an·es·thet·ic**\\ˈă·nĕs ᴬthĕ·tĭk\\ n. A drug that eliminates pain.

**an·guish**\\ᴬăŋ·gwĭsh\\ n. Pain and extreme distress, discomfort, sorrow.

**an·gu·lar**\\ᴬăŋ·gyu·lər\\ adj. 1. Showing distinct angles, as a rectangle, pentagon, or other straight-line figure. 2. Thin, bony, and unattractive.

**an·i·mate**\\ᴬă·nĭ·mət\\ adj. Alive, having life. (Also v. \\ᴬa·nĭ·māt\\ To inspire, give zest or enthusiasm to.)

**an·i·ma·tion**\\ˈă·nĭ ᴬmā·shən\\ n. High-spirited activity, liveliness, vivacity.

**an·ni·hi·la·tion**\\ə ᴬnai·hĭ ˈlā·shən\\ n. Complete destruction, reduction to nothingness.

**an·ti·quat·ed**\\ᴬăn·tĭ ˈkwā·təd\\ adj. Very old and very much out of date.

**an·tiq·ui·ty**\\ăn ᴬtĭ·kwĭ·tē\\ n. 1. Very old times. 2. An old object.

**ap·a·thet·ic**\\ˈă·pə ᴬthĕ·tĭk\\ adj. Showing apathy, marked by dull lack of feeling. (Adv. -ally)

**a·pex**\\ᴬa ˈpĕks\\ n. The highest point of something.

**apol·o·get·ic**\\ə ˈpŏ·lə ᴬjĕ·tĭk\\ adj. As though expressing an apology, not expressed with full confidence.

**ap·pal**\\ə ᴬpɔl\\ v., -led, -ling. To shock with dislike or fear, stun with fear.

**ap·par·el**\\ə ᴬpă·rəl\\ n. Clothing.

**ap·pa·ri·tion**\\ˈă·pə ᴬrĭ·shən\\ n. Phantasm, ghost.

**ap·pease**\\ə ᴬpēz\\ v. To calm, placate, seek to dispel anger or dislike. (Adv. -ingly)

**ap·pen·dage**\\ə ᴬpĕn·dĭj\\ n. A limb or similar feature of the body.

**ap·per·tain**\\ˈă·pər ᴬtān\\ v. To pertain, be connected or related to.

**ap·praise**\\ə ᴬprāz\\ v. To note and estimate the value or status of.

**ap·pre·hen·sion**\\ˈă·prĕ ᴬhĕn·shən\\ n. Fear, misgiving,

worry, foreboding about the future.

**aprise**\\ə ᴬpraiz\\ v. To give notice, inform.

**ap·ti·tude**\\ᴬăp·tĭ ˈtūd\\ n. Natural inclination or bent.

**aq·ui·line**\\ᴬă·kwĭ ˈlain\\ adj. Prominent and suggesting an eagle's beak.

**arc**\\ark\\ n. A section of a circle.

**arch·an·gel**\\ark ˈān·jəl\\ n. An angel of high rank in the heavenly order.

**ar·dent**\\ᴬar·dənt\\ adj. With much feeling, passionate.

**ar·ma·da**\\ar ᴬma·də\\ n. A fleet, especially of armed sailing vessels.

**ar·mi·stice**\\ᴬar·mĭ·stĭs\\ n. A period in which warfare is halted by mutual agreement between the warring powers.

**ar·rears**\\ə ᴬrērz\\ n. *plural*. Indebtedness on overdue payments.

**ar·tic·u·late**\\ar ᴬtĭk·yə·lət\\ adj. Able to speak. (Also v. \\ar ᴬtĭk·yə·lāt\\ To give clear and effective utterance to.)

**as·cen·sion**\\ə ᴬsĕn·shən\\ n. Ascent, rise.

**as·pi·ra·tion**\\ˈăs·pə ᴬrā·shən\\ n. Eventual hope or ambition, a goal that one cherishes.

**as·sail**\\ə ᴬsāl\\ v. To attack violently.

**as·sid·u·ous**\\ə ᴬsĭ·dyu·əs\\ adj. With careful and persistent attention. (Adv. -ly)

**as·suage**\\ə ᴬswaj\\ v. To soothe, comfort, relieve from pain.

**as·sump·tion**\\ə ᴬsəm·shən\\ n. 1. Something assumed, believed, or presumed. 2. The act of taking a command, office, or privilege.

**as·ter·oid**\\ᴬăs·tə ᴬrɔid\\ n. A small starlike body or planet fragment.

**asth·ma**\\ᴬăz·mə\\ n. A disease marked by great difficulty in breathing.

**as·tro·nau·tics**\\ˈăs·trə ᴬnɔ·tĭks\\ n. The study of space navigation.

**as·tron·o·mer**\\ə ᴬstrŏ·nə·mər\\ n. An expert at or student of the stars.

**as·tute**\\əs ᴬtūt\\ adj. Shrewd, wise, perceptive. (Adv. -ly)

**asy·lum**\\ə ᴬsai·ləm\\ n. A place of security, refuge.

**athwart**\\ə ᴬthwɔrt\\ adv. Across diagonally.

**atro·cious**\\ə ᴬtrō·shəs\\ adj. Awful, shocking.

**at·tire**\\ə ᴬtair\\ n. Garments. (Also v.)

**at·tri·bute**\\ə ᴬtrĭ ˈbyūt\\ v. 1. To accredit, acknowledge as source or author, report as from or of. 2. To explain, assign as a cause or origin. (Also n. \\ᴬă·trĭ ˈbyūt\\ Characteristic, accomplishment.)

**au·dac·i·ty**\\ɔ ᴬdă·sĭ·tē\\ n. Daring bravery against superior odds.

**au·di·ble**\\ᴬɔ·dĭ·bəl\\ adj. Capable of being heard.

**aug·ment**\\ˈɔg ᴬmĕnt\\ v. To add to or increase, increase in force or power.

**aus·tere**\\ɔ ᴬstĭr\\ adj. Severe, stern, strict.

**au·then·tic**\\ɔ ᴬthĕn·tĭk\\ adj. Real, genuine, without any suggestion of being imitation.

**au·to·ma·tic·i·ty**\\ˈɔ·tə·mə ᴬtĭ·sĭ·tē\\ n. Automatic operation or nature.

**av·a·rice**\\ᴬă·və·rəs\\ n. Greed for wealth or possessions.

**aver·sion**\\ə ᴬvər·zhən\\ n. Dislike, hatred, loathing.

**avert**\\ə ᴬvərt\\ v. To turn down, aside, or away.

**azure**\\ᴬă·zhər\\ adj. Clear sky-blue.

**bac·cha·nal**\\'băk·ə ▲năl\ n. Any drunken or riotous celebration.

**bait**\bāt\ v. To tease, heckle, haze, mistreat.

**bale·ful**\▲bāl·fəl\ adj. Ominous, menacing, sinister.

**balm**\bam *or* balm\ n. Soothing ointment, comfort from pain or sorrow.

**bal·sa**\▲bɔl·sə\ n. A tropical tree whose wood is quite light and easy to carve.

**bap·tism**\băp·tĭzm\ n. Initiation.

**bar·bi·tu·rate**\bar ▲bich·ər·īt\ n. Any of a group of barbituric acid derivatives used as sedatives.

**bask**\băsk\ v. To recline at rest.

**bat·tle·ment**\▲bă·təl·mənt\ n. A fortified protruding section on top of a walk, superimposed defensive wall at the top of a building.

**beach·comb·er**\▲bēch 'kō·mər\ n. One who spends much time loafing on a beach.

**be·fud·dle**\bē ▲fə·dəl\ v. To confuse, becloud.

**beg·gar·ly**\▲bĕ·gər·lē\ adj. Mean, trivial.

**be·hold·en**\bē ▲hōl·dən\ adj. Obliged, indebted.

**bel·lig·er·ent**\bə ▲lĭj·(ə)rənt\ adj. Inclined to or showing a tendency to fight, quarrelsome. (Adv. -ly)

**bel·low**\▲bĕ·lō\ v. To yell very loud. (Also n.)

**bene·dic·tion**\'bĕ·nə ▲dĭk·shən\ n. Blessing.

**be·nev·o·lent**\bə ▲nĕ·və·lənt\ adj. Well-wishing, kindly, and gentle. (Adv. -ly)

**be·nign**\bə ▲naɪn\ adj. Kindly, well-wishing, and charitable.

**be·queath**\bē· ▲kwēth\ v. To leave a legacy in one's will.

**be·rate**\bē ▲rāt\ v. To scold, rebuke forcefully.

**be·seech**\bē ▲sēch\ irreg. v., besought. To beg, implore.

**bes·tial**\▲bĕst·chəl\ adj. Beastlike, inhuman.

**bil·let**\▲bĭ·lət\ n. Quarters, a temporary place to stay.

**bland**\blănd\ adj. Soft, mild, very easy to eat and digest.

**blas·phe·mous**\▲blăs·fə·məs\ adj. Irreverent, profane statements about God.

**bla·tant**\▲blā·tənt\ adj. Loudly and coarsely demonstrative.

**bleak**\blēk\ adj. Dark and cheerless.

**blench**\blĕnch\ v. To draw back from lack of courage, flinch.

**blithe**\blaɪth\ adj. Very happy, carefree. (Adv. -ly)

**bloat·ed**\▲blō·təd\ adj. Abnormally swollen.

**bond·age**\▲bŏn·dəj\ n. Complete subjection to another, servitude, slavery.

**bond·man**\▲bŏnd·mən\ n. Slave, unfree man.

**bour·geois**\▲burzh 'wa\ adj. Middle-class.

**bra·va·do**\brə ▲va·dō\ n. An extreme show of rash daring.

**bray**\brā\ v. To make the loud sound of a mule.

**bra·zen**\▲brā·zən\ v. To act with self-confident and defiant insolence.

**bris·tle**\▲brĭ·səl\ v. To threaten.

**bro·ker**\▲brō·kər\ n. Dealer, one who buys and sells.

**brusque**\brəsk\ adj. So brief, quick, and firm as to approach rudeness.

**buf·fet**\▲bə·fət\ n. A heavy blow. (Also v. To hit, strike, beat against.)

**bul·wark**\▲bul·wərk\ n. Defense; fortification, especially of earth; rampart.

**bur·ble**\▲bər·bəl\ v. To speak in a rapid, enthusiastic, and not very sensible way.

**bur·ly**\▲bər·lē\ adj. Large, strong, and brawny.

**bur·nish**\▲bər·nĭsh\ v. To polish brightly, give a pleasing metallic lustre to. (Also n.)

**but·tocks**\▲bə·təks\ n. *plural.* The lower part of the back, the part on which one sits.

**cab·a·lis·tic**\'kă·bə ▲lĭs·tĭk\ adj. Suggesting some secret rite or ritual. (Adv. -ally)

**ca·dence**\▲kā·dəns\ n. A regular sequence of sound, often a falling one; a measured rhythm.

**cal·o·rie**\▲kă·lə·rē\ n. A unit of food value expressed in terms of heat and energy production.

**can·o·py**\▲kă·nə·pē\ n., pl. -ies. The hinged covering fitted over the cockpit of a plane.

**ca·pit·u·la·tion**\kə 'pĭ·chə ▲lā·shən\ n. Yielding, surrender.

**ca·price**\kə ▲prēs\ n. Whim, unguided chance inclination.

**cap·sule**\▲kăp·səl\ n. A medicine-containing shell that dissolves readily.

**cap·tion**\▲kăp·shən\ n. A heading, title. (Also v.)

**car·bine**\▲kar·bain\ n. A light and short rifle.

**car·di·nal**\▲kar·dĭ·nəl\ adj. Main, major.

**ca·reer**\kə ▲rēr\ v. To run or dash along madly.

**car·il·lon**\▲kă·rĭ 'lŏn\ n. A set of bells on which tunes can be played.

**car·niv·o·rous**\'kar ▲nĭ·və·rəs\ adj. Flesh-eating, existing on a diet of flesh alone.

**car·ol**\▲kă·rəl\ n. A joyful song. (Also v.)

**case·ment**\▲kās·mənt\ n. A window mounted on hinges at the side.

**caste**\kăst\ n. An inflexible and changeless social class based on birth.

**cat·a·clys·mic**\'kă·tə ▲klĭz·mĭk\ adj. Momentous, having overwhelming and disastrous results.

**cat·a·pult**\▲kă·tə 'pəlt\ v. To shoot forward as though hurled by a catapult. (Also n.)

**ca·tas·tro·phe**\kə ▲tăs·trə 'fē\ n. Calamity, great misfortune.

**cat·e·chism**\▲kă·tə 'kĭzm\ n. A list of questions and answers setting forth elementary religious beliefs.

**ca·thar·sis**\kə ▲thar·səs\ n. A cleansing of the emotions through the arts or other means that bring about release from tension.

**caul·dron**\▲kɔl·drən\ n. A large kettle for boiling or stewing.

**ce·ler·i·ty**\sə ▲lĕr·ə·tē\ n. Swiftness, quickness, speed.

**ce·les·tial**\sə ▲lĕs·chəl\ adj. Pertaining to the heavens or skies (often as viewed by a pilot).

---

ă b*a*d, ā b*a*ke, a f*a*ther, ĕ s*e*ll, ē *e*qual, ai m*i*le, ĭ s*i*t, ŏ c*o*t, ō n*o*te, ɔ l*a*w, ū b*oo*m, ʊ w*oo*d, yū *you*, yʊ f*u*ry, aʊ c*ow*, ɔi b*oy*. The schwa is used for both stressed and unstressed sounds: ə m*u*d, w*o*rd, *e*ven; ch *ch*ase, it*ch*; sh *sh*ell, wi*sh*; th p*ath*, *th*in; th *the*, ei*ther*; ŋ wi*ng*; w *w*et, *wh*eat; zh plea*sure*.

**cer·e·mo·ni·ous**\'sā·rə ᐱmō·nē·əs\ adj. 1. Showing ceremony, marked by slow orderly arrangements. 2. Engaging in much ceremony or stiff formal politeness. (Adv. -ly)

**ces·sa·tion**\sĕ ᐱsā·shən\ n. Stopping, ceasing.

**champ**\chămp\ v. To make biting or chewing motions.

**cha·os**\kā 'ōs\ n. A complete confusion of things jumbled together in disorder, disturbed utter confusion and disorder.

**chas·ten**\chā·sən\ v. To subdue by rebuke or punishment.

**chas·tise·ment**\'chăs ᐱtaiz·mənt\ n. Humbling punishment.

**chide**\chaid\ v., -ed or chid or chidden. To scold, rebuke.

**chip·per**\chĭ·pər\ adj. Healthy, active, happy.

**cho·ler·ic**\kŏ·lə·rĭk\ adj. Ill-tempered, angry, quick to take offense.

**chord**\kōrd\ n. A harmonious combination of tones.

**chron·ic**\krŏ·nĭk\ adj. Ever-present, always continuing.

**chron·i·cle**\krŏ·nĭ·kəl\ n. A history; record, especially a daily record. (Also v.)

**cir·cum·scribe**\sər·kəm 'skraib\ v. To encircle narrowly, be confined to a limited area.

**ci·ta·tion**\sai ᐱtā·shən\ n. A written official notice of special merit or distinction, a formal statement of praise.

**clam·or**\klă·mər\ n. Noise, uproar, commotion. (Also v. To speak out noisily, continuously, and incoherently.)

**cli·ent**\klai·ənt\ n. One who uses another's services or buys another's wares.

**clin·i·cal**\klĭ·nĭ·kəl\ adj. As though produced by a scientific clinic, most exact.

**clois·tered**\klɔis·tərd\ adj. Closed, sealed off, secluded from life around.

**co·ag·u·late**\kō ᐱă·gyʊ 'lāt\ v. To thicken and congeal as from a liquid to a semisolid state.

**cog·i·ta·tion**\'kŏ·jĭ ᐱtā·shən\ n. Thought, consideration, reflection.

**cog·ni·zant**\kɔg·nə·zənt\ adj. Aware, knowing.

**col·lu·sion**\kə ᐱlū·zhən\ n. Unethical cooperation, secret deceitful working together.

**comb·er**\kō·mər\ n. A long or high wave.

**com·mis·er·ate**\kə ᐱmĭ·zə 'rāt\ v. To extend sympathy to, condole with.

**com·mo·di·ous**\kə ᐱmō·dē·əs\ adj. Spacious, roomy, able to accommodate much or many.

**com·mon**\kŏ·mən\ n. Land to be used by all people of a community for grazing their animals.

**com·pact**\kŏm·păkt\ n. Accord, agreement.

**com·pas·sion·ate**\kəm ᐱpă·shə·nət\ adj. Sympathetic, merciful.

**cam·pat·i·ble**\kəm ᐱpă·tĭ·bəl\ adj. In accordance, fitting in well.

**com·pen·sate**\kŏm·pən 'sāt\ v. To make up for, make amends for.

**com·pla·cent**\kəm ᐱplăs·ənt\ adj. Satisfied; especially, self-satisfied.

**com·plex**\kŏm·plĕks\ n. An abnormally compulsive series of notions.

**com·pli·ance**\kəm ᐱplai·əns\ n. Accord, inclination to fit in with.

**com·pre·hend**\'kŏm·prē ᐱhĕnd\ v. To understand.

**com·pre·hen·sive**\'kŏm·prē ᐱhĕn·sĭv\ adj. Inclusive, all-embracing.

**com·punc·tion**\kəm ᐱpəŋ(k)·shən\ n. Anxiety arising from guilt, an uneasy twinge.

**com·pute**\kəm ᐱpyūt\ v. To reckon, calculate.

**con·cep·tion**\kən ᐱsĕp·shən\ n. Idea, notion.

**con·cise**\kən ᐱsais\ adj. Sharp and dexterous without waste motion.

**con·clu·sive**\kən ᐱklū·sĭv\ adj. Marked by (or as if by) a final decision shutting off discussion.

**con·fi·den·tial**\'kŏn·fĭ ᐱdĕn·shəl\ adj. In confidence or secrecy, not to be told to another. (Adv. -ly)

**con·fir·ma·tion**\'kŏn·fər ᐱmā·shən\ n. Agreement, supporting statement, claim.

**con·fla·gra·tion**\'kăn·flə ᐱgrā·shən\ n. A great or very destructive fire, a very hot fire.

**con·found**\kən ᐱfaund\ v. To confuse, bewilder.

**con·front**\kən ᐱfrənt\ v. To oppose and challenge.

**con·i·cal**\kan·ĭ·kəl\ adj. Like a cone in shape.

**con·jec·ture**\kən ᐱjĕk·chər\ v. To make guesses, speculate. (Also n.)

**con·joint**\kən ᐱjɔint\ adj. Together, joined, occurring at the same time or place.

**con·junc·tion**\kən ᐱjəŋ·shən\ n. Joining, juncture.

**con·se·crate**\kŏn·sə 'krāt\ v. To bless, sanctify, treat as holy.

**con·sen·sus**\kən ᐱsĕn·səs\ n. Generality, majority expression or opinion.

**con·sign**\kən ᐱsain\ v. To deliver, assign.

**con·sole**\kən ᐱsōl\ v. To comfort, sympathize with.

**con·spic·u·ous**\kən ᐱspĭk·yū·əs\ adj. Very noticeable, demanding attention, hard or impossible to overlook. (Adv. -ly)

**con·ster·na·tion**\'kŏn·stər ᐱnā·shən\ n. Amazed and agitated dismay, panic.

**con·sti·tute**\kŏn·stĭ 'tūt\ v. To make up, compose.

**con·sti·tu·tion·al**\'kŏn·stĭ ᐱtū·shə·nəl\ n. A short walk taken for health's sake.

**con·strue**\kən ᐱstrū\ v. To explain, interpret, understand.

**con·sum·mate**\kɔan ᐱsəm·ət\ adj. Complete in every detail, of highest excellence.

**con·ta·gious**\kən ᐱtā·jəs\ adj. Readily communicable, spreading readily from one person to another.

**con·tam·i·nate**\kən ᐱtă·mĭ 'nāt\ v. To make unclean, infect, sully, defile with impurity.

**con·tem·plate**\kŏn·tĕm 'plāt\ v. To look at or think about thoughtfully.

**con·temp·tu·ous**\kən ᐱtĕm·chu·əs\ adj. Showing contempt and mocking scorn.

**con·tort**\kən ᐱtōrt\ v. To twist or writhe out of a normal position or appearance.

**con·trite**\kən ᐱtrait\ adj. Regretful or sorrowful for one's misconduct or offenses.

**con·triv·er**\kən ᐱtrai·vər\ n. One who plans and schemes.

**con·ven·tion·al·ize**\kən ᐱvĕn·shə·nə 'laiz\ v. To make or form according to certain conventions or conventional notions.

**con·verge**\kən ˄vərj\ v. To come together and join.

**con·vulse**\kən ˄vəls\ v. To be agitated, shaken.

**con·vul·sive**\kən ˄vəl·sĭv\ adj. Marked by strong physical agitation or wild motion.

**cor·don**\˄kôr·dən\ v. To isolate and treat as a closed-off area.

**cor·nice**\˄kôr·nĭs\ n. An overhanging structure projecting from the top of a building or wall.

**cor·ol·lary**\˄kô·rə 'lā·rē\ n., pl. -ies. An accompanying effect, a necessarily connected or related notion.

**cor·o·net**\˄kô·rə 'nĕt\ n. A small or plain crown showing a rank below a king's.

**cor·po·ral**\˄kôr·pə·rəl\ adj. Bodily, physical.

**cor·rode**\kə ˄rōd\ v. To eat away as in the action of an acid.

**cor·rup·tive**\kə ˄rəp·tĭv\ adj. Bringing about corruption and infection.

**cos·mic**\˄kŏz·mĭk\ adj. Pertaining to the whole world, solar system, or universe; hence, extremely important.

**cos·mol·o·gy**\kŏz ˄mŏ·lə·jē\ n., pl. -ies. A conception or scheme of the relationships of the heavenly bodies.

**cote**\kōt\ n. A bird house or shelter.

**coun·te·nance**\˄kaun·tə·nəns\ v. To tolerate or sanction. (Also n. Facial appearance.)

**court**\kôrt\ v. To seek, ask for.

**co·vert**\˄kə·vərt\ n. A concealed or secret place, a hiding place that an animal might use. (Also adj.)

**cov·et·ous**\˄kə·və·təs\ adj. Greedy, grasping.

**cow·er**\kau·ər\ v. To flinch down as in fear or fright.

**coz·en**\˄kə·zən\ v. To deceive, beguile, ensnare.

**cra·ni·um**\˄krā·nē·əm\ n. Skull.

**cre·den·tial**\krĕ ˄dĕn·shəl\ n. A certification or official document to back up a person's claims.

**cre·ma·tion**\'krē ˄mā·shən\ n. Disposal of dead bodies by reducing to ashes through fire.

**cren·el·late** or **cren·el·ate**\˄krĕ·nə 'lāt\ v. To furnish with protective or defensive ramparts on the top of the walls of.

**crev·ice**\˄krĕ·vĭs\ n. A split, chink.

**crit·i·cal**\˄krĭ·tĭ·kəl\ adj. Criticizing, evaluating, expressing criticism.

**cru·ci·ble**\˄krū·sĭ·bəl\ n. A vessel for melting down solid substances.

**cru·ci·fy**\˄krū·sĭ 'fai\ v., -ies, -ied. To torture or kill by nailing or binding the hands and feet to a cross with the arms outstretched to the sides.

**crypt**\krĭpt\ n. Innermost secret recess.

**crys·tal**\˄krĭs·təl\ v. To form into crystals, turn to crystals. (Also n.)

**cull**\kəl\ v. To pick, choose.

**cul·mi·nate**\˄kəl·mĭ 'nāt\ v. To attain to a climax, reach to a height or an outcome.

**cum·ber**\˄kəm·bər\ v. To harass, trouble.

**cu·mu·lus**\˄kyū·myu·ləs\ n., pl. -i. A cloud formation suggesting heaping or piling up.

**cur·dle**\˄kər·dəl\ v. To thicken or congeal as milk does when it sours.

**curt**\kərt\ adj. So brief and sparing of words as to be rude and demanding. (Adv. -ly)

**cur·tail**\kər ˄tāl\ v. To cut down, diminish.

**cyn·ic**\˄sĭ·nĭk\ n. One given to suspecting evil whenever possible, one suspicious of good motives.

**dam**\dăm\ n. Mother (especially as used of an animal).

**dan·dy**\˄dăn·dē\ n., pl. -ies. A stylishly dressed person.

**dank**\dăŋk\ adj. Damp and chill.

**daunt**\dônt\ v. To cause fear or loss of resolution.

**dearth**\'dərth\ n. Scarcity.

**de·bauch**\dē ˄bôch\ n. An intemperate indulgence in sensual pleasure.

**de·bris**\də ˄brē\ n. Rock fragments.

**dec·a·dence**\˄dĕ·kə·dəns\ n. Decay, deterioration, loss of strength and virtue.

**de·ci·sive**\dē ˄sai·sĭv\ adj. Having a definitive result, finally deciding a conflict or question.

**de·fer**\də ˄fər\ v., -red, -ring. To postpone.

**def·er·ence**\˄dĕf·ə·rən(t)s\ n. Courteous and respectful regard for another.

**deft**\dĕft\ adj. Showing graceful or clever skill in handling.

**de·hy·drate**\'dē ˄hai·drāt\ v. To remove water or liquid from.

**de·lib·er·ate**\də ˄lĭ·bə·rət\ adj. Marked by slow cautious motion. (Adv. -ly)

**de·lir·i·ous**\də ˄lē·rē·əs\ adj. Suffering from loss of sense and rationality and experiencing delusions; out of one's mind, as with fever or madness.

**del·uge**\˄dĕl 'yūj\ n. Flood. (Also v.)

**de·lu·sion**\dē ˄lū·zhən\ n. A mistaken or totally false notion or belief.

**de·luxe**\də ˄luks\ adj. Luxurious, elegant.

**de·mur**\də ˄mər\ v., -red, -ring. To hesitate and withhold assent or agreement.

**de·mure**\də ˄myūr\ adj. Modest, quiet, and prim.

**de·plete**\dē ˄plēt\ v. To diminish by using up.

**de·plor·a·ble**\dĭ ˄plôr·ə·bəl\ adj. Strongly regretted, considered unfortunate or wretched.

**de·port**\dē ˄pôrt\ v. To send out of a country, exile.

**de·pre·cate**\˄dĕ·prə 'kāt\ v. To suggest lack of worth or significance.

**de·pres·sur·ize**\dē ˄prē·shə 'raiz\ v. To reverse pressurizing devices.

**der·e·lict**\˄dĕ·rə 'lĭkt\ n. Something left abandoned and purposeless, a now meaningless relic of past life.

**der·e·lic·tion**\'dĕ·rə 'lĭk·shən\ n. Neglect or omission of duty.

**de·ri·sion**\də ˄rĭ·zhən\ n. Mocking ridicule.

**de·rog·a·to·ry**\dĭ ˄rag·ə·tôr·ē\ adj. Expressive of a low opinion.

**des·o·late**\˄dĕ·sə·lət\ adj. Lonely, forlorn, and hopeless. (Also v.)

---

ă b*a*d, ā b*a*ke, a f*a*ther, ĕ s*e*ll, ē *e*qual, ai m*i*le, ĭ s*i*t, ŏ c*o*t, ō n*o*te, ɔ- l*aw*, ū b*oo*m, ʊ w*oo*d, yū *you*, yʊ f*u*ry, au c*ow*, ɔi b*oy*. The schwa is used for both stressed and unstressed sounds: ə m*u*d, w*o*rd, ev*e*n; ch *ch*ase, i*tch*; sh *sh*ell, wi*sh*; th pa*th*, *th*in; th *the*, ei*th*er; ŋ wi*ng*; w *w*et, *wh*eat; zh plea*s*ure.

**de·spon·dent**\dĭ ᴧspon·dənt\ adj. Disheartened, dejected.

**des·pot·ic**\dĕs ᴧpŏ·tĭk\ adj. Oppressive, tyrannical.

**des·ti·ny**\ᴧdĕs·tĭ·nē\ n., pl. -ies. Fate, that which is planned by a supernatural power.

**de·tach·ment**\dĭ ᴧtăch·mənt\ n. Aloofness, indifference.

**de·vi·ate**\ᴧdē·vē·āt\ v. To twist or bend away from a straightforward course.

**de·vi·ous**\ᴧdē·vē·əs\ adj. Roundabout, indirect, not straightforward. (Adv. -ly)

**de·vise**\də ᴧvaiz\ v. To think of, find, invent.

**de·void**\də ᴧvɔid\ adj. Lacking, missing, without.

**de·vout**\də ᴧvaut\ adj. Reverent, showing marked solemnity.

**di·a·bol·i·cal**\ᴧdī·ə ˈbŏl·ĭ·kəl\ adj. Extremely wicked, fiendishly cruel.

**di·aph·a·nous**\ˈdai ᴧă·fə·nəs\ adj. Sheer, light, and virtually transparent.

**dif·fuse**\dĭ ᴧfyūz\ v. To spread out (or through) softly and evenly.

**di·lap·i·dat·ed**\dĭ ᴧlă·pĭ ˈdā·təd\ adj. Thoroughly worn out; thin, torn, and frayed.

**di·late**\ˈdai ᴧlāt\ v. To widen, expand, swell abnormally.

**dil·i·gent**\ᴧdĭ·lĭ·jənt\ adj. Marked by steady, careful, conscientious work. (Adv. -ly)

**di·min·u·tive**\dĭ ᴧmĭn·yu·tĭv\ adj. Very small, tiny.

**dis·cern**\dĭ ᴧsərn\ v. To perceive, comprehend.

**dis·ci·plin·ary**\ᴧdĭ·sĭ·plĭ ˈnă·rē\ adj. Of the nature of discipline, applying discipline for some error or omission.

**dis·com·fit**\dĭs ᴧkəm·fĭt\ n. *archaic.* Discomfort, concern.

**dis·con·cert**\ˈdĭs·kən ᴧsərt\ v. To throw into confusion, disturb the composure of, embarrass.

**dis·con·so·late**\dĭs ᴧkŏn·sə·lət\ adj. Cheerless and discouraged.

**dis·course**\ᴧdĭs ˈkɔrs\ n. Conversation.

**dis·creet**\dĭs ᴧkrēt\ adj. 1. With an eye to safety, calculated to protect oneself. 2. Showing restraint and careful moderation. 3. Quiet, well-trained, and maintaining suitable reserve in speech.

**dis·dain**\dĭz ᴧdān\ n. Lofty and haughty scorn and disapproval. (Also v. To shun or scorn, let alone as through pride or taste.)

**dis·em·bar·rass**\ˈdĭs·əm ᴧbă·rəs\ v. To rid, eliminate.

**dis·en·chant·ing**\ˈdĭs·ən ᴧchăn·tĭŋ\ adj. Dispelling any enchantment, charm, or appeal.

**dis·en·gage**\ˈdĭs·ən ᴧgāj\ v. To free from encumbrance, take out or away.

**dis·shev·eled**\dĭ ᴧshĕ·vəld\ adj. Wrinkled, mussed up.

**dis·par·age·ment**\dĭs ᴧpă·rəj·mənt\ n. Belittling, lowering of reputation or worth.

**dis·pense**\dĭs ᴧpĕns\ v. To do without.

**dis·sem·ble**\dĭ ᴧsĕm·bəl\ v. To pretend, conceal one's true thoughts or motives.

**dis·si·pat·ed**\ᴧdĭ·sĭ ˈpā·təd\ adj. Given to drinking and other sensual pleasures.

**dis·so·lu·tion**\ˈdĭ·sə ᴧlū·shən\ n. Destruction by breaking up into component parts.

**dis·til·late**\ᴧdĭs·tĭ ˈlāt\ n. A product of distilling, a condensed essence.

**dis·tort**\dĭs ᴧtōrt\ v. To twist or wrench from normal (often grotesquely).

**dis·trac·tion**\dĭs ᴧtrăk·shən\ n. Madness, inability to focus one's mind or think rationally.

**di·ur·nal**\ˈdai ᴧər·nəl\ adj. Daily.

**di·vers**\ᴧdai·vərz\ adj. Various.

**di·vert**\dĭ ᴧvərt\ v. To turn aside, deflect, turn to another course.

**di·vine**\dĭ ᴧvɑin\ v. To foretell, record and estimate accurately.

**di·vin·i·ty**\dĭ ᴧvĭ·nĭ·tē\ n., pl. -ies. God, deity.

**di·vulge**\dĭ ᴧvəlj\ v. To give out, tell.

**dog·ged**\ᴧdŏ·gəd\ adj. Resolute, stubborn, determined not to yield. (Adv. -ly)

**do·mi·cile**\ᴧdŏ·mĭ ˈsail\ v. To house, quarter. (Also n.)

**dom·i·nate**\ᴧdŏ·mĭ ˈnāt\ v. To possess a commanding or superior position.

**do·min·ion**\də ᴧmĭn·yən\ n. Governmental control, rulership.

**dooms·day**\ᴧdūmz ˈdā\ n. Judgment Day.

**dor·sal**\ᴧdōr·səl\ adj. Joined to or projecting from the back.

**dow·er**\daur\ n. Gift; especially, a dowry (a gift to the husband from the bride's family at marriage).

**dreg**\drĕg\ n. Waste remnant left in a container.

**dross**\drŏs\ n. Scum, waste, impurity.

**du·bi·ous**\ᴧdū·bē·əs\ adj. Showing worry or suspicion, doubtful.

**dun**\dən\ adj. Dark gray.

**du·pli·cate**\ᴧdū·plĭ·kət\ n. An exact copy. (Also v.)

**ea·sel**\ᴧē·zəl\ n. A support for an artist's canvas while he is painting.

**ec·sta·sy**\ᴧĕk·stə·sē\ n., pl. -ies. Extreme joy or happiness.

**ed·i·fi·ca·tion**\ˈĕd·ə·fə ᴧkā·shən\ n. Act or process of instructing or improving.

**ed·i·fice**\ᴧĕ·dĭ·fĭs\ n. Building, construction.

**ef·face**\ə ᴧfās\ v. To wipe out, erase.

**ef·fu·sion**\ə ᴧfyū·zhən\ n. Noisy, showy display of emotion.

**ef·fu·sive**\ĭ ᴧfyū·sĭv\ adj. Excessively demonstrative, gushing. (Adv. -ly)

**ego·ism**\ᴧē·gō·ĭzm\ n. An inclination to think too much of oneself, to be too self-centered or self-interested.

**elat·ed**\ē ᴧlā·təd\ adj. Extremely joyful and triumphant.

**el·e·gant**\ᴧĕ·lə·gənt\ adj. 1. With meticulous fineness. 2. Very attractive and appetizing.

**el·o·quent**\ᴧĕ·lə·kwənt\ adj. Smooth-spoken and glib; speaking easily, fluently, and persuasively; showing well and clearly.

**e·lude**\ĭ ᴧlūd\ v. To avoid adroitly, escape the notice of.

**elu·sive**\ē ᴧlū·sĭv\ adj. 1. Hard to settle or fix in place. 2. Constantly going away or disappearing. 3. Hard to catch or place in a difficult position.

**em·a·na·tion**\ˈĕ·mə ᴧnā·shən\ n. An intangible flowing or issuing outward.

**eman·ci·pate**\ē ᴧmăn·sĭ ˈpāt\ v. To free, release from the supervision of.

**em·bold·en**\ĕm ˄bōl·dən\ v. To give courage, brace up, inspire.

**em·bra·sure**\ĭm ˄brā·zhər\ n. Wall opening with sides flaring outward in order to allow greater angles when firing weapons.

**em·u·late**\˄ĕm·yʊ 'lāt\ v. To imitate, attempt to be like.

**en·am·ored** or **en·am·oured**\ĕ ˄nă·mərd\ adj. In love, loving, entranced.

**en·com·pass**\ĕn ˄kəm·pəs\ v. To surround completely.

**en·gen·der**\ĕn ˄jĕn·dər\ v. To give birth to.

**en·hance**\ĕn ˄hăns\ v. To augment, increase.

**en masse**\ĕn ˄măs\ adv. In one group or body.

**en·sue**\ĕn ˄sū\ v. To follow next, happen in order.

**en·tail**\ĕn ˄tāl\ v. To involve or include necessarily.

**en·thrall** or **en·thral**\ĕn ˄thrɔl\ v. To please, delight, and entrance; command blended joy and interest.

**en·trails**\˄ĕn·trəlz\ n. plural. Intestines, along with adjacent inner organs.

**en·trance**\ĕn ˄trăns\ v. To enchant, delight, charm, enrapture.

**en·ven·om**\ĕn ˄vĕ·nəm\ v. To poison.

**en·vis·age**\ĕn ˄vĭz·əj\ v. To picture in one's mind, visualize, imagine.

**e·pit·o·me**\ĭ ˄pĭt·ə·mē\ n. Embodiment or ideal expression of.

**er·rat·ic**\ə ˄ră·tĭk\ adj. Unpredictable, uneven, variable, inconsistent.

**erup·tion**\ə ˄rəp·shən\ n. A violent breaking out.

**es·sence**\˄ĕ·səns\ n. Real inner nature or significance, genuine inner individualizing quality.

**es·trange**\ĕ ˄strănj\ v. To make unfamiliar, strange, hostile.

**es·tu·ary**\˄ĕs·chʊ 'ă·rē\ n., pl. -ies. A river mouth area where river current and ocean tides meet.

**ether**\˄ē·thər\ n. Upper air, the part of the air that transmits radio waves.

**evince**\ē ˄vĭns\ v. To show, demonstrate.

**evo·lu·tion**\'ĕ·və ˄lū·shən\ n. The process of evolving, of progressing from one stage to another.

**ex·alt·ed**\ĕg ˄zɔl·təd\ adj. Raised, elevated.

**ex·cru·ci·ating**\ĕks ˄krū·shē 'ā·tĭŋ\ adj. Extremely painful.

**ex·em·pla·ry**\ĕg ˄zĕm·plə·rē\ adj. Faultless, perfect, fit to serve as an example.

**ex·hil·a·rate**\ĕg ˄zĭ·lə 'rāt\ v. To inspire with extreme joy or happiness.

**ex·or·cist**\ĕk ˄sōr·sĭst\ n. One who exorcises or commands and drives out devils and evil spirits.

**ex·ot·ic**\ĕg ˄zŏ·tĭk\ adj. Far-off, strange, romantic, and interesting.

**ex·pan·sive**\ĕks ˄păn·sĭv\ adj. 1. Swelling, expanding, tending to grow and become stronger. 2. Extrovertive; outgoing; given to conversation, gaiety, and companionship.

**ex·ploit**\ĕks ˄plɔit\ v. To make use of, take advantage of, utilize.

**ex·pound**\ĕks ˄paʊnd\ v. To explain, lecture on and clarify some detail.

**ex·punge**\ĭk ˄spənj\ v. To obliterate, erase.

**ex·qui·site**\˄ĕks·kwĭ·zĭt\ adj. Beautiful, compelling wonder and admiration for superb craftsmanship and delicate perfection; showing finest, most delicate performance.

**ex·trav·a·gant**\ĕks ˄tră·və·gənt\ adj. Elaborate, excessive.

**ex·u·ber·ant**\ĕk ˄sū·bə·rənt\ adj. Gaily happy.

**ex·ul·tant**\ĕg ˄zəl·tənt\ adj. Feeling wild joy and triumphant happiness.

**fab·u·lous**\˄fă·byʊ·ləs\ adj. As though in or from a fable or myth, incredible, extreme. (Adv. -ly)

**fa·ce·tious**\fə ˄sē·shəs\ adj. Humorous, light, completely lacking in seriousness. (Adv. -ly)

**fa·cil·i·tate**\fə ˄sĭl·ə 'tāt\ v. To make a procedure easier and faster to perform.

**fac·tion**\˄făk·shən\ n. A group linked together for some political purpose.

**fag·ot** or **fag·got**\˄fă·gət\ n. A torch, a stick or bundle to be burned for light, a bundle of firewood.

**fal·li·ble**\˄fă·lĭ·bəl\ adj. Likely to make mistakes.

**fa·tal·ist**\˄fă·tə·lĭst\ n. One inclined to accept without protest what fate brings.

**feint**\fānt\ v. To fake, pretend to make an aggressive gesture.

**fe·line**\˄fē 'lain\ adj. Catlike, of or pertaining to the cat family.

**fer·ment**\fər ˄mĕnt\ v. To seethe, bubble. (Also n.)

**fer·vid**\˄fər·vĭd\ adj. Marked by strong feeling or enthusiastic expression.

**fer·vor**\˄fər·vər\ n. Ardent or intense feeling.

**fe·tish**\˄fĕ·tĭsh\ n. A thing or characteristic to be highly valued (perhaps without logical reasons).

**fet·ter**\˄fĕ·tər\ n. Chain.

**fi·del·i·ty**\fə ˄dĕ·lĭ·tē\ n. Faithfulness.

**fid·gety**\˄fĭ·jə·tē\ adj. Nervous, edgy.

**fi·es·ta**\'fĕ ˄ĕs·tə\ n. A celebration and feast (especially in a Latin American country).

**fin·icky**\˄fĭ·nĭ·kē\ adj. Fussy about details.

**fir·ma·ment**\˄fər·mə·mənt\ n. The heavens, especially as viewed as background for the stars.

**fit·ful**\˄fĭt·fəl\ adj. Erratic, marked by stops and starts.

**flax·en**\˄flăk·sən\ adj. Of the color of flax, blonde, yellowish.

**flip·pant**\˄flĭ·pənt\ adj. Disrespectfully humorous in a situation calling for sober obedience.

**flor·id**\˄flŏ·rĭd\ adj. Flowery, elaborate, ornate.

**flot·sam**\˄flŏt·səm\ n. Material floating around in a sea, lake, or river.

**flu·ent**\˄flū·ənt\ adj. Marked by ready, easy, and graceful motion.

**fol·ly**\˄fŏ·lē\ n., pl. -ies. An act of foolishness, instance of stupidity or lack of wisdom.

**fon·dle**\˄fŏn·dəl\ v. To caress, handle affectionately.

---

ă bad, ā bake, a father, ĕ sell, ē equal, ai mile, ĭ sit, ŏ cot, ō note, ɔ law, ū boom, ʊ wood, yū you, yʊ fury, aʊ cow, ɔi boy. The schwa is used for both stressed and unstressed sounds: ə mud, word, even; ch chase, itch; sh shell, wish; th path, thin; th the, either; ŋ wing; w wet, wheat; zh pleasure.

**for·ay**\ˈfō 'rā\ n. A raid, sally, expedition.

**fore·bod·ing**\fər ˈbō·dĭŋ\ n. Anxious worry; a vague intuitive feeling of coming disappointment, difficulty, evil, or tragedy.

**fore·land**\ˈfōr·lănd\ n. A cape, promontory.

**fore·stall**\fər ˈstal\ v. To anticipate, prevent possible opposition by using prior measures.

**for·mu·late**\ˈfōr·myʊ 'lāt\ v. To put into a customary form, especially to find conventional wording for.

**for·sak·en**\fər ˈsā·kən\ adj. Abandoned, left alone.

**for·ti·fy**\ˈfōr·tĭ 'fai\ v., -ies, -ied. To prepare with additional calories and other food values.

**for·ti·tude**\ˈfōr·tĭ 'tūd\ n. Blended bravery and resolution.

**fort·night**\ˈfōrt 'nait\ n. A two-week period.

**for·tu·itous**\fōr ˈtū·ĭ·təs\ adj. Accidental, chance.

**foun·der**\ˈfaʊn·dər\ v. To fail utterly, break down.

**found·ling**\ˈfaʊnd·lĭŋ\ n. Baby or child abandoned to be found (as at an orphanage or church door).

**frail·ty**\ˈfrā·əl·tē\ n., pl. -ies. Weakness, delicateness, lack of real endurance.

**fraught**\frɔt\ adj. Freighted, packed.

**fresh·et**\ˈfrĕ·shət\ n. A stream in flood, the overflow of a stream caused by melting snow.

**fur·tive**\ˈfər·tĭv\ adj. As though done or made by a thief; with stealthy, quiet concealment.

**fu·tile**\ˈfyū·tĭl\ adj. Useless, vain, ineffectual, serving no purpose.

**gab·ar·dine**\ˈgă·bər 'dēn\ n. A firm, hard-finished, durable, ribbed fabric.

**gad**\găd\ v. To stroll and mill about.

**gait**\gāt\ n. Way of walking.

**gal·lant·ry**\ˈgă·lən·trē\ n., pl. -ies. Chivalrous courtesy, showy courtesy to ladies.

**gar·gan·tu·an**\'gar ˈgăn·chu·ən\ adj. Huge, immense.

**gar·ish**\ˈgă·rĭsh\ adj. Brightly or outlandishly colorful, marked by tasteless or untrue flashiness.

**gar·land**\ˈgăr·lənd\ n. A wreath or other similar flower arrangement.

**gar·ner**\ˈgăr·nər\ v. To gather, harvest. (Also n. A granary, storehouse.)

**gauche**\gōsh\ adj. Crude, awkward, unsophisticated.

**gaudy**\ˈgɔ·dē\ adj. Marked by overly bright color or ornament.

**gaunt**\gɔnt\ adj. Very thin and worn (as from hunger or illness).

**ge·nial**\ˈjē·nē·əl\ adj. Friendly, companionable, pleasant.

**ger·mane**\jər ˈmān\ adj. Suitable, appropriate, relevant.

**ges·tic·u·late**\jĕs ˈtĭk·yu 'lāt\ v. To motion with the hands to express or emphasize meaning, make demonstrative gestures with hands and facial features.

**ges·ture**\ˈjĕs·chər\ n. A motion, as with hands or facial features; communicate. (Also v.)

**ghast·ly**\ˈgăst·lē\ adj. Frightful, terrible, deathly.

**ghoul·ish**\ˈgū·lĭsh\ adj. Like a ghoul (a person given to robbing graves).

**gib·ber·ish**\ˈjĭ·bə·rĭsh\ n. Nonsense.

**gid·dy**\ˈgĭ·dē\ adj. Dizzy. (Adv. -ily)

**gist**\jĭst\ n. Meaning, significance separated out from items unimportant or nonessential.

**glean**\glēn\ v. To gather or harvest the fruits or products of.

**glob·al**\ˈglō·bəl\ adj. Pertaining to or affecting the whole earth.

**gnash**\năsh\ v. To grind the teeth together.

**goad**\gōd\ v. To urge; spur on, as with a sharp pointed stick. (Also n.)

**gran·deur**\ˈgrăn·dyʊr\ n. Grandness, splendid or impressive majesty.

**grat·i·fy**\ˈgrăt·ə·fai\ v. To give or be a source of pleasure or satisfaction to, confer a favor on.

**grat·i·tude**\ˈgră·tĭ 'tūd\ n. Gratefulness, extreme sense of thankfulness.

**gri·mace**\ˈgrĭ·məs\ v. To contort one's face, make odd facial expressions. (Also n.)

**gris·ly**\ˈgrĭz·lē\ adj. Fearful, dreadful.

**gross·ly**\ˈgrōs·lē\ adv. Utterly, obviously.

**grue·some**\ˈgrū·səm\ adj. Frightful, grisly. (Adv. -ly)

**guile**\gail\ n. Deception, fraud, dishonesty.

**guise**\gaiz\ n. Aspect, semblance, appearance.

**gut·tur·al**\ˈgə·tə·rəl\ adj. Thick, harsh, throaty.

**gy·ra·tion**\jai ˈrā·shən\ n. A revolving around a point, spiral motion.

**hab·i·tat**\ˈhă·bĭ 'tăt\ n. Dwelling area, place in which one lives.

**ha·bit·u·ate**\hə ˈbĭ·chu 'āt\ v. To accustom, make used to.

**hag·gard**\ˈhă·gərd\ adj. Wan, thin, and wasted (as by hunger or disease).

**hal·lo**\hă ˈlō\ v. To call, shout.

**hal·loo**\hă ˈlū\ n. A shout, loud call. (Also v.)

**hand·i·work**\ˈhăn·di·wərk\ n. Craftsmanship.

**ha·rass**\hə ˈrăs\ v. To worry, oppress, wear down.

**har·lot**\ˈhar·lət\ n. Mistress, prostitute.

**har·row·ing**\ˈhă·rə·wĭŋ\ adj. Trying, disturbing.

**haunt**\hɔnt\ v. To visit continually, as a ghost does. (Also n. Place, locale.)

**hau·teur**\hō ˈtyər\ n. Lofty and chilling pride and haughtiness, aloof extreme pride and disdain.

**her·ald**\ˈhĕ·rəld\ n. A messenger.

**her·mit·age**\ˈhər·mĭ·təj\ n. A hermit's quarters, a place where one lives alone.

**hes·i·tant**\ˈhĕ·zĭ·tənt\ adj. Hesitating, uncertain.

**hid·eous**\ˈhĭ·dē·əs\ adj. Most ugly and loathsome.

**hil·lock**\ˈhĭ·lək\ n. A little hill.

**hind**\haind\ n. Deer.

**hom·i·ly**\ˈhŏ·mĭ·lē\ n., pl. -ies. A sermon, a moralistic lesson or preaching.

**hulk**\həlk\ n. 1. A large, awkward, looming form. 2. The frame of an abandoned boat or ship.

**hu·mane**\hyū ˈmān\ adj. Merciful and kindly, not cruel or oppressive.

**id·i·o·mat·ic**\'ĭd·ē·ə ˈmăt·ĭk\ adj. Characteristic of and natural to a given language.

**id·io·syn·cra·sy**\'ĭ·dē·ō ˈsĭŋ·krə·sē\ n. pl. -ies. Peculiarity, individual and unusual mannerism or trait.

**ig·no·ble**\ĭg ˈnō·bəl\ adj. Low, mean. (Adv. -ly)

**il·lu·mine**\ĭ ˈlū·mĭn\ v. To light up, illuminate.

il·lu·sion\ĭ ▴lū·zhən\ n. A false appearance; a false semblance of reality; an ill-based or false vision, perception, notion, or belief.

im·men·si·ty\ĭ ▴měn·sĭ·tē\ n. Enormity, hugeness.

im·merse\ĭ ▴mərs\ v. To dip, submerge.

im·mi·nent\ˈĭ·mĭ·nənt\ adj. About to happen, very likely to happen.

im·mo·bile\ĭ ▴mō·bĭl\ adj. Unable to move.

im·mune\ĭ ▴myūn\ adj. Not receptive or responsive, detached and safe from.

im·pal·pa·ble\ĭm ▴păl·pə·bəl\ adj. Incapable or practically incapable of being touched or otherwise sensed.

im·pas·sive\ĭm ▴păs·ĭv\ adj. Showing no emotion, expressionless.

im·pec·ca·ble\ˈĭm ▴pěk·ə·bəl\ adj. Flawless.

im·per·a·tive\ĭm ▴pā·rə·tĭv\ adj. 1. Absolutely necessary. 2. Commanding, not to be denied or withstood.

im·per·cep·ti·ble\ˈĭm·pər ˈsěp·tĭ·bəl\ adj. Impossible or very difficult to perceive, incapable or barely capable of being perceived. (Adv. -ly)

im·pe·ri·al·ism\ĭm ▴pē·rē·ə ˈlĭzm\ n. The policy, procedure, or tendency of the worlds' great powers to bring other areas under their control and dominate and subjugate them.

im·pe·ri·ous\ĭm ▴pē·rē·əs\ adj. Lordly, with haughty command, with command as by an emperor.

im·per·ish·able\ĭm ▴pě·rĭsh·ə·bəl\ adj. Undying, lasting forever.

im·per·ti·nence\ĭm ▴pər·tĭ·nəns\ n. Impudence, lack of obedience, insolence.

im·per·turb·able\ˈĭm·pər ▴tər·bə·bəl\ adj. Incapable of being agitated, ruffled, or concerned; calm and composed.

im·plic·it·ly\ĭm ▴plĭs·ət·lē\ adv. 1. Unquestioningly. 2. In a manner unexpressed but implied.

im·po·tence\ˈĭm·pə·təns\ n. Powerlessness, utter lack of strength and force.

im·pre·ca·tion\ˈĭm·prē ˈkā·shən\ n. An oath, curse.

im·pre·ci·sion\ˈĭm·prē ▴sĭ·zhən\ n. Inexactness, uncertainty.

im·preg·na·tion\ĭm·prěg ▴nā·shən\ n. The act of filling, spreading through, or permeating a substance.

im·pro·vise\ˈĭm·prə 'vaiz\ v. To make up at the moment, make up or contrive out of whatever is available, fabricate.

im·pul·sive\ĭm ▴pəl·sĭv\ adj. Acting quickly without measured thought.

in·ad·ver·tent\ˈĭn·əd ▴vər·tənt\ adj. Accidental, usually through lack of observation or notice. (Adv. -ly)

inane\ĭ ▴nān\ adj. Empty of meaning or point. (Adv. -ly)

in·an·i·mate\ĭn ▴ă·nĭ·mət\ adj. Lifeless.

in·ar·tic·u·late\ĭn·ar ▴tĭk·yu·lət\ adj. 1. Unable to speak coherently because of extreme emotion. 2. Spoken without clear adequate division between words and hence hard to understand.

in·au·di·ble\ĭn ▴ɔ·dĭ·bəl\ adj. Impossible to hear.

in·can·des·cence\ĭn·kən ▴dě·səns\ n. 1. Brilliant whiteness. 2. Beautiful shining brilliance.

in·car·nate\ĭn ▴kar·nət\ adj. In the flesh, bodily, not existing as a detached spirit.

in·cense\ĭn ▴sěns\ v. To irritate, anger.

in·ci·sion\ĭn ▴sĭ·zhən\ n. A cutting in or into, as in surgery; a slit.

in·co·her·ent\ĭn·kō ▴hē·rənt\ adj. Without coherence, not logically or clearly thought out or expressed. (Adv. -ly)

in·con·gru·ous\ĭn ▴kŏŋ·gru·əs\ adj. Strikingly out of place, quite discordant with the surroundings.

in·con·se·quent\ĭn ▴kŏn·sə·kwənt\ adj. Unimportant, not worth paying attention to.

in·cred·i·ble\ĭn ▴krě·dĭ·bəl\ adj. Unbelievable.

in·cre·du·li·ty\ĭn·krě ▴dū·lĭ·tē\ n. Disbelief, disinclination or disability to believe or accept.

in·de·fin·able\ĭn·də ▴fai·nə·bəl\ adj. Defying definition, description, or explanation.

in·dif·fer·ent\ĭn ▴dĭ·fə·rənt\ adj. Neither good nor bad, decidedly not superior.

in·di·gent\ˈĭn·dĭ·jənt\ adj. Quite poor and needy.

in·dis·pens·able\ĭn·dĭs ▴pěn·sə·bəl\ adj. Completely necessary, impossible to dispense with.

in·do·lent\ˈĭn·də·lənt\ adj. Disinclined to any activity; inert, lazy, and inactive.

in·duct\ĭn ▴dəkt\ v. To install, initiate formally, make part of.

in·due\ĭn ▴dū\ v. To imbue, tinge, or color throughout.

in·dulge\ĭn ▴dəlj\ v. To give free rein or play to, permit free range to.

in·ed·i·ble\ĭn ▴ě·dĭ·bəl\ adj. Uneatable, incapable of being digested.

in·ef·fa·ble\ĭn ▴ě·fə·bəl\ adj. Indescribable; not to be narrated, described, or explained in ordinary ways.

in·ef·fec·tu·al\ĭn·ə ▴fěk· chəl\ adj. Ineffective; unavailing, weak, and forceless; futile and vain.

in·ert\ĭ ▴nərt\ adj. Unmoving, motionless.

in·ev·i·ta·ble\ĭn ▴ěv·ət·ə·bəl\ adj. Impossible to avoid, bound to come.

in·ex·o·ra·ble\ĭn ▴ěk·sə·rə·bəl\ adj. 1. Unbending, not to be moved or touched by any plea. 2. Unavoidable, inevitably continuing or operating.

in·ex·press·ible\ĭn·əks ▴prě·sĭ·bəl\ adj. Defying expression, incapable of being expressed.

in·ex·tri·ca·ble\ĭn ▴ěk·strĭ·kə·bəl\ adj. Incapable of being disentangled.

in·fal·li·ble\ĭn ▴fă·lĭ·bəl\ adj. Perfect, never showing failure or mistake.

in·fer·ence\ˈĭn·f(ə)r·ən(t)s\ n. A conclusion, guess, or surmise drawn from facts; an outcome of thought.

in·fer·nal\ĭn ▴fər·nəl\ adj. Hellishly unpleasant, hellish, damnable, awful.

---

ă bad, ā bake, a father, ě sell, ē equal, ai mile, ĭ sit, ŏ cot, ō note, ɔ law, ū boom, ʊ wood, yū you, yʊ fury, aʊ cow, ɔi boy. The schwa is used for both stressed and unstressed sounds: ə mud, word, even; ch chase, itch; sh shell, wish; th path, thin; th the, either; ŋ wing; w wet, wheat; zh pleasure.

**in·fer·no**\in ´fər·nō\ n. Hell or a similar subterranean region.

**in·fi·nite**\´ĭn·fĭ·nĭt\ adj. Endless, measureless, unceasing. (Adv. -ly)

**in·fin·i·tes·i·mal**\ĭn ´fĭ·nĭ ´tĕ·zĭ·məl\ adj. Very tiny.

**in·fir·mi·ty**\ĭn ´fər·mĭ·tē\ n., pl. -ies. Illness, sickness, or weakness.

**in·fuse**\ĭn ´fyūz\ v. To instill, mix in.

**in·ge·nious**\ĭn ´jē·nē·əs\ adj. Clever, able to improvise crafty plans or devices.

**in·hib·it**\ĭn ´hĭb·ət\ v. To hold in check, to repress.

**in·i·ti·a·tive**\ĭn ´ĭsh·ət·ĭv\ n. Energy or aptitude displayed in setting up action, enterprise.

**in·noc·u·ous**\ĭ ´nŏ·kyu·əs\ adj. Innocent, harmless, and seemingly unimportant.

**in·no·va·tor**\´ĭ·nə ´vā·tər\ n. One who introduces or practices something new.

**in·nu·mer·a·ble**\ĭ ´nū·mə·rə·bəl\ adj. Numberless.

**im·pec·ca·ble**\ĭm ´pĕk·ə bəl\ adj. Without fault, blemish, or flaw.

**in·qui·si·tion**\ĭn·kwĭ ´zĭ·shən\ n. A prying, sustained series of questions; a series of searching and embarrassing questions to ferret out misconduct.

**in·quis·i·tive**\ĭn ´kwĭ·zĭ·tĭv\ adj. Curious, questioning, investigative.

**in·sa·tia·ble**\ĭn ´sā·shə·bəl\ adj. Incapable of being satisfied.

**in·sid·i·ous**\ĭn ´sĭ·dē·əs\ adj. Not easily perceived or recognized and likely to mislead, endanger, or entrap. (Adv. -ly)

**in·so·lence**\´ĭn·sə·ləns\ n. Impudent disregard of or opposition to authority.

**in·sou·ci·ance**\ĭn ´sū·sē·əns\ n. Carefree nonchalance.

**in·sti·ga·tion**\´ĭn·stĭ ´gā·shən\ n. Incitement, encouragement to action.

**in·suf·fer·able**\ĭn ´sə·fər·ə·bəl\ adj. Most unpleasant and difficult to be with.

**in·sur·rec·tion**\´ĭn·sə ´rĕk·shən\ n. Rebellion, revolt.

**in·tact**\ĭn ´tăkt\ adj. Whole, entire, undamaged.

**in·tan·gi·ble**\ĭn ´tăn·jĭ·bəl\ adj. Impossible or hard to perceive clearly or to analyze. (Adv. -ly)

**in·tem·per·ate**\ĭn ´tĕm·pə·rət\ adj. Immoderate, extreme.

**in·ter·cede**\ĭn ´tər ´sēd\ v. To plead in another's behalf.

**in·ter·ces·sion**\´ĭn·tər ´sĕ·shən\ n. A prayer to a superior power to intercede and protect.

**in·ter·dict**\´ĭn·tər ´dĭkt\ n. A strict legal prohibition or ban.

**in·ter·im**\´ĭn·tə·rĭm\ n. Intervening space or time.

**in·ter·mi·na·ble**\ĭn ´tər·mĭ·nə·bəl\ adj. Endless, unceasing, lasting forever or as if forever. (Adv. -ly)

**in·ter·mit·tent**\´ĭn·tər ´mĭ·tənt\ adj. Not continuous, occurring or operating at intervals from time to time, starting and stopping.

**in·ter·pose**\ĭn·tər ´pōz\ v. To place or come between.

**in·ter·sperse**\´ĭn·tər ´spərs\ v. To intermix, insert into at intervals from time to time, scatter about here and there.

**in·ti·mate**\´ĭn·tĭ·mət\ adj. Near, very close, marked by close and understanding relationship. (Adv. -ly, v. \´ĭn·tĭ ´māt\ To hint, suggest.)

**in·tol·er·a·ble**\ĭn ´tŏ·lə·rə·bəl\ adj. Very hard to tolerate or put up with.

**in·tri·cate**\´ĭn·trĭ·kət\ adj. Complicated, delicate, having many interrelations and interconnections.

**in·trude**\ĭn ´trūd\ v. To thrust or press forward or inward without invitation or welcome.

**in·tu·ition**\´ĭn·tū ´ĭ·shən\ n. A sense of inner perception and quick understanding.

**in·ure**\ĭn ´yūr\ v. To accustom.

**in·vin·ci·ble**\ĭn ´vĭn( t)·sə·bəl\ adj. Unconquerable.

**in·vi·o·la·ble**\ĭn ´vai·əl·ə·bəl\ adj. Not to be violated, interrupted, or profaned; to be treated as sacred; kept from violation; of a secret, never told or divulged.

**in·voice**\´ĭn·vɔis\ n. An itemized statement of goods sold or consigned.

**iras·ci·bil·i·ty**\ĭ ´ră·sĭ ´bĭ·lĭ·tē\ n. Bad temper, anger.

**ir·i·des·cent**\´ĭ·rĭ ´dĕ·sənt\ adj. Showing a sheen of many colors with a rainbowlike effect.

**iron·c**\ai ´rŏ·nĭk\ adj. Pertaining to or showing a situation opposed to what would be expected from forethought, plans, or probabilities.

**ir·ra·di·ate**\ĭr ´ād·ē·āt\ v. To cast rays of light upon, enlighten, shine.

**ir·re·deem·a·ble**\´ĭ·rə ´dēm·ə·bəl\ adj. Impossible to redeem, bring back, or compensate for.

**ir·rel·e·vant**\ĭ ´rĕ·lə·vənt\ adj. Unrelated, immaterial.

**ir·res·o·lu·tion**\ĭ ´rĕ·zə ´lū·shən\ n. Uncertainty, doubt, indecision.

**ir·re·vo·ca·ble**\ĭ ´rĕ·və·kə·bəl\ adj. Impossible to revoke, take back, change, or alter.

**item·ize**\´ai·tə ´maiz\ v. To list or record mentioning each individual item.

**jab·ber**\´jă·bər\ v. To speak excitedly and incoherently.

**ja·ded**\´jā·dĭd\ adj. Tired, made spiritless by fatigue.

**jaun·ty**\´jɔn·tē\ adj. Happy, lighthearted, and carefree; good-humored, gay, and self-confident. (Adv. -ily)

**jet·ti·son**\´jĕ·tĭ·sən\ v. To throw out, pour out, or otherwise get rid of.

**jounce**\jaʊns\ v. To pitch or sway as in a rough ride.

**jowls**\jaʊlz\ n. *plural*. The slack flesh around the lower jaw or neck.

**ju·bi·la·tion**\´jū·bĭ ´lā·shən\ n. Extreme demonstrative joy, celebration of extreme joy and happiness.

**ju·di·cious**\jū ´dĭ·shəs\ adj. Marked by careful judgment, attempting to judge and calculate.

**ju·ve·nile**\´jū·və·nĭl\ n. An actor or actress who plays children's or adolescents' parts.

**ka·lei·do·scope**\kə ´lai·də ´skōp\ n. A device in which bits of colored stone produce innumerable colorful patterns.

**kin·dred**\´kĭn·drəd\ adj. Similar; having the same inclinations, ideas, or emotions.

**lab·y·rinth**\´lă·bĭ ´rĭnth\ n. A confusing maze or tangle.

**la·con·ic**\lə ´kŏ·nĭk\ adj. Speaking little, using as few words as possible.

**lag·gard**\ˈlă·gərd\ n. One who lags behind, slowpoke, loiterer.

**la·goon**\lə ˈgūn\ n. A section of quiet water ringed about by a coral reef or similar formation.

**lam·en·ta·tion**\ˈlăm·ən ˈtā·shən\ n. Act of expressing sorrow or regret for, mourning for.

**lan·guid**\ˈlăŋ·gwĭd\ adj. Marked by very little energy or force. ( Adv. -ly)

**lan·guor**\ˈlăŋ·gər\ n. Tired drowsiness and disinclination to activity.

**lar·va**\ˈlar·və\ n., pl. -ae. An immature form of an insect.

**las·si·tude**\ˈlă·sĭ ˈtūd\ n. Tiredness (often during convalescence ) and disinclination to move or act.

**lath**\lăth\ n. A narrow strip of wood used in building a wall.

**lave**\lāv\ v. To wash, bathe.

**lay**\lā\ n. A poem, song, story. ( Also adj. Untrained, inexperienced, uneducated in a particular area. )

**lay·man**\ˈlā·mən\ n., pl. -men. A person not trained in or familiar with some profession.

**league**\lēg\ n. Any of various units of distance from about 2.4 to 4.6 statute miles.

**leav·en**\ˈlĕ·vən\ v. To cause dough to rise by using a fermenting substance like yeast.

**leg·a·cy**\ˈlĕ·gə·sē\ n., pl. -ies. What is willed to a survivor.

**leg·en·dary**\ˈlĕ·jən ˈdā·rē\ adj. Known in a legend, fictitious, mythical.

**leth·ar·gy**\ˈlĕ·thər·jē\ n. A sense of tired, sleepy, and listless inactivity; disinclination· or inability to move or act.

**levy**\ˈlĕ·vē\ v. To enlist troops for army service ( usually by drafting).

**li·ai·son**\ˈlē ˈa·zŏn\ n. Communication, contact.

**lin·tel**\ˈlĭn·təl\ n. Threshold.

**liq·ui·date**\ˈlĭ·kwĭ ˈdāt\ v. To get rid of, end, engage in self-destruction.

**list·less**\ˈlĭst·ləs\ adj. Inattentive, indifferent, and bored.

**lit·a·ny**\ˈlĭ·tə·nē\ n., pl. -ies. A long prayer with invocations and responses.

**lit·ter**\ˈlĭ·tər\ v. To give birth (used of animals).

**liv·ery**\ˈlĭ·və·rē\ n., pl. -ies. The sort of uniform worn by a driver, coachman, doorman, or the like.

**liv·id**\ˈlĭ·vĭd\ adj. Unwholesomely pale.

**loath**\lōth\ adj. Unwilling, reluctant.

**lo·cust**\ˈlō·kəst\ n. A tall spiny tree with very hard wood and twisted seed pods.

**lo·gis·ti·cal**\ˈlō ˈjĭs·tĭ·kəl\ adj. Involving the problem of supplies and materials, conditioned by supplies and material.

**lope**\lōp\ n. A running stride marked by strong steps.

**lu·cent**\ˈlū·sənt\ adj. Clear and gleaming.

**lu·cre**\ˈlū·kər\ n. Money, profit in money.

**lu·di·crous**\ˈlū·dĭ·krəs\ adj. Ridiculous, laughable.

**lum·ber**\ˈləm·bər\ v. To walk or lurch along heavily or clumsily.

**lus·ter**\ˈləs·tər\ n. Gleaming brightness.

**lux·u·ri·ous**\lək ˈshu·rē·əs\ adj. With full enjoyment and relaxation. ( Adv. -ly)

**lym·phat·ic**\lĭm ˈfă·tĭk\ adj. Pertaining to lymph ( the bodily fluid containing white blood cells).

**ma·ca·bre**\mə ˈka·bər\ adj. Grim, ghastly, suggestive of death.

**mace**\mās\ n. A heavy club or staff carried as a symbol of authority.

**mael·strom**\ˈmāl·strəm\ n. A whirlpool, eddy.

**mag·a·zine**\ˈmă·gə ˈzēn\ n. A gun chamber designed to hold cartridges to be fed into the firing mechanism.

**mag·na·nim·i·ty**\ˈmăg·nə ˈnĭ·mĭ·tē\ n. Great soul or spirit showing extreme generosity.

**mag·nate**\ˈmăg·nət\ n. A man of great wealth and financial power.

**male·dic·tion**\ˈmă·lə ˈdĭk·shən\ n. A curse, imprecation.

**mal·e·fac·tor**\ˈmăl·ə·făk·tər\ n. One who commits an offence against the law, evildoer.

**mal·ice**\ˈmă·lĭs\ n. Ill-will, hatred.

**ma·lign**\mə ˈlain\ adj. Evil in nature or· effect, injurious.

**ma·lig·nant**\mə ˈlĭg·nənt\ adj. Utterly evil in nature or effect, producing evil and death.

**ma·ni·a**\ˈmā·nĭ·ə\ n. An extremely intense desire for something, excessive enthusiasm for something.

**man·i·fest**\ˈmă·nĭ·fĕst\ adj. Clear, obvious, plain. ( Adv. -ly)

**man·i·fes·ta·tion**\ˈmăn·ə·fə ˈstā·shən\ n. Demonstration or showing of.

**ma·nip·u·late**\mə ˈnĭ·pyə ˈlāt\ v. To operate or manage skillfully with the hands.

**man·tle**\ˈmăn·təel\ v. To coat, cloak.

**mar·a·thon**\ˈmă·rə ˈthŏn\ n. Any activity that is sustained over a remarkably long period.

**ma·raud**\mə ˈrŏd\ v. To raid, harry, pillage.

**mar·i·time**\ˈmă·rĭ ˈtaim\ adj. Marine, oceanic.

**ma·roon**\mə ˈrūn\ v. To leave, abandon, cause abandonment.

**mar·ti·net**\ˈmar·tə ˈnĕt\ n. A strict disciplinarian.

**mas·sive**\ˈmă·sĭv\ adj. Extreme and severe.

**mas·ti·cate**\ˈmăs·tĭ ˈkāt\ v. To chew and intermix with saliva.

**maud·lin**\ˈmŏd·lən\ adj. Over-sentimental, drunk enough to be emotionally silly, fuddled.

**max·im**\ˈmăk·sĭm\ n. A proverbial rule or principle.

**med·i·tate**\ˈmĕ·dĭ ˈtāt\ v. To think and consider, especially quietly and for a long time.

**med·ley**\ˈmĕd·lē\ n. Miscellany, mixture.

**mel·an·choly**\ˈmĕ·lən ˈkŏ·lē\ adj. Sad, pensively plaintive.

---

ă bad, ā bake, a father, ĕ sell, ē equal, ai mile, ĭ sit, ŏ cot, ō note, ɔ law, ū boom, ʊ wood, yū you, yʊ fury, aʊ cow, ɔi boy. The schwa is used for both stressed and unstressed sounds: ə mud, word, even; ~~ch~~ chase, itch; ~~sh~~ shell, wish; ~~th~~ path, thin; <u>th</u> the, either; ŋ wing; w wet, ~~wh~~eat; ~~zh~~ pleasure.

**men·ace**\ˈmĕ·nəs\ v. To threaten. (Also n. A threat.)

**me·nial**\ˈmēn·yəl\ n. A servant, especially one serving in a very low capacity.

**mer·ce·nary**\ˈmər·sə 'nā·rē\ adj. Motivated only or mainly by money and not by emotions.

**mer·cu·ri·al**\mər ˈkyu·rē·əl\ adj. Showing very quick changes in mood, often volatile and demonstrative.

**me·tic·u·lous**\mə ˈtĭk·yu·ləs\ adj. Most careful, neat, precise, and exact; marked by extreme care about details. (Adv. -ly)

**met·tle**\ˈmĕ·təl\ n. Marked force, strength, and worth; resolution, bravery.

**mi·cro·wave**\ˈmai·krō 'wāv\ n. A short electromagnetic wave.

**mid·dy**\ˈmĭ·dē\ n., pl. -ies. A loose-fitting informal blouse with a collar like a sailor's.

**mi·gra·tion**\'mai ˈgrā·shən\ n. Moving or changing habitation, especially by many people to new lands.

**min·i·mum**\ˈmĭ·nĭ·məm\ n. Least possible point or degree.

**mi·rage**\mĭ ˈrazh\ n. A false vision, an illusion.

**mis·con·strue**\mĭs·kən ˈstrū\ v. To misinterpret, misunderstand.

**mis·de·mean·or**\mĭs·də ˈmē·nər\ n. An instance of misconduct calling for punishment but less serious than a crime.

**mo·bile**\ˈmō·bĭl\ adj. Suggesting or expressing motion and freedom to move.

**mock·ery**\ˈmŏ·kə·rē\ n., pl. -ies. 1. Ridicule and scorn; mocking and defying; a thing, gesture, or statement that mocks. 2. An imitation or substitute ridiculously inadequate.

**mo·men·tous**\mō ˈmĕn·təs\ adj. Of greatest importance and significance.

**mo·men·tum**\mō ˈmĕn·təm\ n. Impetus, the force that keeps a moving body in motion.

**mo·nas·tic**\mə ˈnăs·tĭk\ adj. Characteristic of monks and their self-denying way of life.

**mon·grel**\ˈməŋ·grəl\ n. A crossbred cur.

**mon·i·tor**\ˈmŏ·nĭ·tər\ n. One who constantly observes, checks, and records.

**mo·no·lith·ic**\'mŏ·nə ˈlĭ·thĭk\ adj. Huge, tall, and made (or as though made) of one single stone.

**mono·tone**\ˈmŏ·nə 'tōn\ n. A single tone or sound endlessly repeated.

**mo·not·o·nous**\mə ˈnŏ·tə·nəs\ adj. Entirely without variation, boresomely changeless. (Adv. -ly)

**mope**\mōp\ v. To brood in solitude.

**mor·bid**\ˈmôr·bĭd\ adj. Unwholesome, unhealthy, abnormal.

**mo·rose**\mə ˈrōs\ adj. Gloomy, ill-tempered, sullen.

**mor·ti·fy**\ˈmôr·tĭ 'fai\ v., -ies, -ied. 1. To kill, bring near to death. 2. To shame and embarrass.

**mote**\mōt\ n. A particle in the eye that interferes with vision.

**mul·ish**\ˈmyū·lĭsh\ adj. Stubborn, contrary. (Also n. -ness)

**mute**\myūt\ v. To still, decrease very much in volume or intensity.

**my·o·pic**\'mai ˈōp·ək\ adj. Nearsighted.

**mys·tic**\ˈmĭs·tĭk\ n. One who gains perception or knowledge without direct uses of senses and ration-ality, one whose knowledge or beliefs come from intuition and insight rather than rational factual observation.

**mys·ti·fy**\ˈmĭs·tĭ 'fai\ v., -ies, -ied. To puzzle, perplex.

**name·sake**\ˈnām 'sāk\ n. A person or figure for whom one is named.

**nau·sea**\ˈnɔ·zē·ə\ n. Sickness at the stomach, tendency to vomit.

**neg·li·gence**\ˈnĕg·lĭ·jəns\ n. Neglect.

**neg·li·gi·ble**\ˈnĕg·lĭ·jĭ·bəl\ adj. So trivial as to be neglected or overlooked completely.

**neu·ro·sis**\nū ˈrō·səs\ n. A nervous or emotional disorder.

**neu·rot·ic**\nū ˈrŏ·tĭk\ adj. Suffering from or pertaining to a functional nervous disorder.

**nil**\nĭl\ adj. Zero, nonexistent.

**noc·tur·nal**\'nŏk ˈtər·nəl\ adj. Occurring at night, nightly.

**nod·ule**\ˈnŏ·jəl\ n. A small rounded particle, a bit.

**no·mad**\ˈnō·măd\ n. A wanderer, especially one of a people without a fixed permanent place of residence.

**non·sen·si·cal**\nŏn ˈsĕn·sĭ·kəl\ adj. Stupid, ridiculous, composed only of nonsense.

**nos·tal·gia**\nə ˈstăl·jə\ n. A yearning for something familiar in the past, especially for a home that one has left; a pleasure at such yearning and recollection.

**no·ta·tion**\'nō ˈtā·shən\ n. A note, memorandum.

**nov·ice**\ˈnŏ·vĭs\ n. A person (especially a woman) in the first stages of becoming a member of a convent or other religious establishment.

**nu·cle·us**\ˈnū·klē·əs\ n., pl. -ei or -es. Center, core.

**nug·get**\ˈnə·gət\ n. A little lump (often of gold or other precious mineral).

**obliv·i·on**\əb ˈlĭ·vē·ən\ n. Forgetfulness in sleep.

**obliv·i·ous**\əb ˈlĭ·vē·əs\ adj. Entirely unobservant and unaware, not perceiving or noticing, forgetful.

**ob·scene**\əb ˈsēn\ adj. Vile, loathsome.

**ob·scu·ri·ty**\əb ˈskū·rĭ·tē\ n. Darkness, blackness.

**ob·ses·sion**\əb ˈsĕ·shən\ n. An idea or thought (often false) that completely dominates the mind to the exclusion of all else.

**ob·sti·nate**\ˈŏb·stĭ·nət\ adj. Stubbornly determined not to yield or concede; persistent, determined, and impossible to change.

**ocean·og·ra·phy**\'ō·shə ˈnŏg·rə·fē\ n. The science or study of the ocean.

**oc·tave**\ˈŏk·təv\ n. One group of eight (as of eight colors) set in order within a number of other groups.

**o·di·ous**\ˈō·dĭ·əs\ adj. Deserving of or exciting hatred, hateful, detestable.

**of·fal**\ˈɔ·fəl\ n. Trash, rubbish, garbage.

**omen**\ˈō·mən\ n. A sign or indication of future developments.

**on·i·nous**\ˈŏ·mĭ·nəs\ adj. Sinister, suggesting or threatening evil developments to come.

**om·nip·o·tence**\ŏm ˈnĭ·pə təns\ n. Unlimited power.

**om·ni·pres·ent**\'ŏm·nĭ ˈprĕ·zənt\ adj. Always present.

**on·slaught**\ˈŏn 'slɔt\ n. Fierce or determined attack.

**op·ti·cal**\\ˇŏp·tĭ·kəl\ adj. Pertaining to the eyes or vision.

**orb**\ōrb\ n. *poetic.* The sun.

**or·ches·tra·tion**\'ōr·kə ˄strä·shən\ n. An arranging and combining for best artistic or forceful effect.

**or·dain**\ōr ˄dān\ v. To establish and follow strictly (as a religious usage).

**or·deal**\ōr ˄dēl\ n. A period of severe trouble, distress, trial, worry, pain, or danger.

**or·gy**\ˈōr·jē\ n., pl. -ies. An excessive indulgence in any pleasure.

**or·nate**\ōr ˄nāt\ adj. Elaborately decorated.

**os·se·ous**\ˇŏ·sē·əs\ adj. Composed of bone, like bone.

**os·ten·si·ble**\ə ˄stĕn·sĭ·bəl\ adj. Seeming, apparent. (Adv. -ly)

**os·ten·ta·tious**\'ŏs·tən ˄tā·shəs\ adj. Showy, accomplished or done in such a way as to demand attention.

**over·ture**\ˈō·vər·chur\ n. An instrumental introduction or prelude to an opera.

**over·wrought**\'ō·vər ˄rɔt\ adj. Agitated and unnerved.

**pag·eant**\˄pă·jənt\ n. A procession of colorfully costumed romantic figures.

**pal·ate**\˄pă·lət\ n. Technically, the roof of the mouth; loosely, those parts of the mouth containing the taste buds.

**pal·ette**\˄pă·lət\ n. A thin board with a thumb hole on which an artist mixes paints.

**pall**\pɔl\ n. Something that covers or conceals, often producing an effect of gloom.

**pal·lor**\˄pă·lər\ n. Paleness, lack of color.

**pal·pi·tate**\˄păl·pə·tāt\ v. To beat rapidly and strongly, throb.

**pal·ter**\˄pɔl·tər\ v. To be insincere, treacherous, cowardly.

**pal·try**\˄pɔl·trē\ adj. Puny, weak, slight. (Also n. -ness)

**pan·de·mo·ni·um**\'păn·də ˄mō·nē·əm\ n. Extreme confused noise preventing rational speech or thought.

**pan·to·mime**\˄păn·tə 'maim\ n. 1. Expression of meaning or emotion by gesture alone and entirely without use of words, a series of gestures communicating meaning without words. 2. A dramatic production in which words are not used but gestures and actions express the message involved.

**par·a·ble**\˄pă·rə·bəl\ n. A story with a moral or lesson.

**par·a·gon**\˄pă·rə·gən\ n. A pattern of excellence, a model of superlative characteristics.

**par·a·mount**\˄păr·maunt\ adj. Superior to all others.

**para·noia**\'pă·rə ˄nɔi·ə\ n. A form of madness featuring delusions that one is being persecuted.

**par·a·site**\˄pă·rə 'sait\ n. An animal or fish that depends on another and clings to that creature.

**parch·ment**\˄parch·mənt\ n. A document on parchment.

**pa·ro·chi·al**\pə ˄rō·kē·əl\ adj. Pertaining to or restricted to a very small area; narrow, provincial, local.

**par·ry**\˄pă·rē\ v., -ies, -ied. To turn aside or withstand, as an onset, attack, rebuke, or question.

**par·ti·san**\˄par·tə·zən\ n. A staunch supporter of a cause or a party.

**pas·sive**\˄pă·sĭv\ adj. Without necessary force or action. (Adv. -ly)

**pas·to·ral**\˄păs·tə·rəl\ adj. Of or pertaining to a pastor, churchly, religious.

**pa·tent·ly**\˄păt·ənt·lē\ adv. Obviously, openly.

**pa·thos**\˄pā 'thōs\ n. 1. Deep and genuine feeling for the sad or tragic. 2. Sadness or sorrow that calls forth pity or sympathy.

**pa·tron**\˄pā·trən\ n. A wealthy or influential person in control of some enterprise.

**pa·tron·age**\˄pā·trə·nəj\ n. Financial assistance, especially given grudgingly and with condescension.

**pa·tron·ize**\˄pā·trə 'naiz\ v. To condescend, act in a lofty or haughty way toward.

**paunchy**\˄pɔn·chē\ adj. Having a noticeable paunch, stout.

**pa·vil·ion**\pə ˄vĭl·yən\ n. A large spacious tent.

**pec·ca·dil·lo**\'pĕ·kə ˄dĭ·lō\ n. A minor and readily forgivable transgression, sin, or omission.

**pee·vish**\˄pē·vĭsh\ adj. Fretful, complaining.

**pen·sive**\˄pĕn·sĭv\ adj. Thoughtful, contemplative.

**per·cep·ti·ble**\pər ˄sĕp·tĭ·bəl\ adj. Capable of being perceived.

**pe·remp·to·ry**\pə ˄rĕm·tə·rē\ adj. Commandingly, with sharp and postive orders. (Adv. -ily)

**pe·ren·ni·al**\pə ˄rĕ·nē·əl\ adj. Year after year, not dying yearly.

**per·me·ate**\˄pər·mē 'āt\ v. To seep, spread, or diffuse through thoroughly.

**per·pen·dic·u·lar**\'pər·pən ˄dĭk·yə·lər\ adj. Straight up and down.

**per·plex**\pər ˄plĕks\ v. To puzzle, confuse.

**per·sist**\pər ˄sĭst\ v. To continue despite causes for stopping.

**per·son·age**\˄pər·sə·nəj\ n. An important personality.

**per·son·i·fy**\pər ˄sə·nĭ 'fai\ v., -ies, -ied. To typify or represent by a particular person.

**per·son·nel**\'pər·sə ˄nĕl\ n. The sum total of persons employed by a company or engaged in an enterprise.

**per·ti·nent**\˄pər·tĭ·nənt\ adj. Relevant, having a connection.

**per·tur·ba·tion**\'pərt·ər ˄bā·shən\ n. Confusion, disturbance of the mind.

**per·vade**\pər ˄vād\ v. To become diffused through every part.

**per·vert**\'pər ˄vərt\ v. To turn from the normal, usual, or true.

**pe·ti·tion**\pə ˄tĭ·shən\ n. Prayer, what is asked or sought for.

**pet·ri·fy**\˄pĕt·rĭ 'fai\ v., -ies, -ied. To turn (usually

---

ă *b*ad, ā *b*ake, a *f*ather, ĕ *s*ell, ē *e*qual, ai *m*ile, ĭ *s*it, ŏ *c*ot, ō *n*ote, ɔ *l*aw, ū *b*oom, ʊ *w*ood, yū *you*, yʊ *fury*, au *c*ow, ɔi *b*oy. The schwa is used for both stressed and unstressed sounds: ə *m*ud, *word*, *even*; ch *ch*ase, it*ch*; sh *sh*ell, wi*sh*; th *p*ath, *thin*; th *the*, *either*; ŋ wi*ng*; w *w*et, *wh*eat; zh plea*sure*.

from wood or other vegetable matter) to stone.

**pet·tish**\ˇpĕ·tĭsh\ adj. Mildly contradictory and fretful.

**pet·ty**\ˇpĕ·tē\ adj. Attaching undue significance to very minor matters.

**pet·u·lant**\ˇpĕ·chə·lənt\ adj. Fretful; inclined to cry, whimper, or protest.

**phe·nom·e·non**\fə ˇnŏ·mə·nŏn\ n., pl. -a. A set of circumstances, a happening.

**phil·an·throp·ic**\ˈfĭl·ən ˆthrŏp·ĭk\ adj. Deeds that reflect love of mankind, benevolent.

**phos·pho·res·cence**\ˈfŏs·fə ˆrĕ·səns\ n. Glowing light, often luminous light without heat, light without heat that comes from forms of marine life.

**pick·et**\ˇpĭ·kət\ n. A guard or sentinel stationed far outside a main base or encampment. (Also v. To attach an animal to a stake with a rope or chain.)

**pine**\pain\ v. To regret in futile sorrow and helplessness.

**pi·ous**\ˇpai·əs\ adj. Showing religious devoutness.

**pi·rat·i·cal**\pə ˆră·tĭ·kəl\ adj. Of or pertaining to pirates.

**pit·e·ous**\ˇpĭ·tē·əs\ adj. Arousing pity. (Adv. -ly)

**piv·ot**\ˇpĭ·vət\ v. To turn the body or head without moving the feet.

**plac·id**\ˇplă·sĭd\ adj. Entirely calm and peaceful, at peace and free from concern.

**pla·gi·a·rism**\ˇplā·jĭ·ə ˈriz·əm\ n. Copying or imitating the language, ideas, and thoughts of another author and passing off the same as one's original work.

**plain·tive**\ˇplān·tĭv\ adj. Sad, mournful, lamenting, marked by sad complaint.

**plait**\plāt\ v. To interweave.

**plat·i·tude**\ˇplăt·ə ˈtūd\ n. A flat, dull, or commonplace remark.

**plau·si·ble**\ˇplɔ·zĭ·bəl\ adj. Readily believable, without cause for disbelief. (Adv. -ly)

**pla·za**\ˇplă·zə\ n. A central open square (particularly in an Italian, Spanish, or Latin American town).

**pleas·ant·ry**\ˇplĕ·zən·trē\ n., pl. -ies. An amiable or good-natured conversational touch, an unimportant conversational bit intended to be pleasing.

**plumb**\pləm\ n. A vertical position.

**plu·ral·i·ty**\plʊ ˆră·lĭ·tē\ n., pl. -ies. Manifold nature, multiplicity, great number.

**plush**\pləsh\ n. A fabric like velvet.

**poach·er**\ˇpō·chər\ n. A trespasser who hunts or traps in areas forbidden to him.

**poi·gnant**\ˇpɔin·yənt\ adj. Marked by keen feeling, especially by sadness or pity.

**pom·mel**\ˇpəm·əl\ v. To beat.

**pon·der·ous**\ˇpŏn·də·rəs\ adj. Large, heavy, and awkward.

**pon·iard**\ˇpŏn·yərd\ n. A dagger.

**por·tend**\ˈpŏr ˆtĕnd\ v. To indicate for the future.

**por·tent**\ˇpŏr·tĕnt\ n. A sign or omen of evil to come, the feeling brought about by a threatening sign.

**port·fo·lio**\ˈpŏrt ˆfō·lē·ō\ n. A case or folder for carrying drawings, paintings, or papers.

**port·ly**\ˇpŏrt·lē\ adj. Stout.

**por·tray·al**\pər ˆtrā·əl\ n. A depiction, picturing, description.

**pos·sessed**\pə ˆzĕst\ adj. Obsessed, dominated.

**post·hu·mous**\ˇpŏs·chu·məs\ adj. After one's death.

**pos·ture**\ˇpŏs·chər\ n. Bodily pose or set.

**po·ten·cy**\ˇpō·tən·sē\ n., pl. -ies. Force, effectiveness.

**po·ten·ti·al·i·ty**\pə ˈtĕn·chē ˆă·lĭ·tē\ n., pl. -ies. Possibility, ability to occur.

**poul·tice**\ˇpōl·tĭs\ n. A soft dressing or similar mass applied to a sore or injury.

**pre·car·i·ous**\prē ˆkă·rē·əs\ adj. Dangerous, risky, insecure, likely to lead to a fall or other injury.

**pre·cau·tion**\ˈprē ˆkɔ·shən\ n. An advance safety measure, a cautious measure taken in advance.

**pre·ced·ence**\prĭ ˆsē·dəns\ n. The right to come before in rank or order.

**pre·cept**\prē ˈsĕpt\ n. A command or principle intended as a general rule of behavior.

**pre·cinct**\prē ˈsĭŋkt\ n. Area, space enclosed or included.

**pre·cip·i·tate**\prē ˆsĭ·pĭ ˈtāt\ v. To separate and fall or sink out.

**pre·cip·i·tous**\prē ˆsĭ·pĭ·təs\ adj. Most steep and sheer.

**pre·ci·sion**\prē ˆsĭ·zhən\ n. Exact careful and methodical motion.

**pred·a·to·ry**\ˇprĕ·də ˈtŏ·rē\ adj. Preying on others, living by killing others.

**pre·dic·a·ment**\prē ˆdĭ·kə·mənt\ n. Difficult or dangerous situation, plight.

**pre·dom·i·nate**\prē ˆdŏm·ə·nāt\ v. To stand out.

**prej·u·dice**\ˇprĕ·jə·dĭs\ n. Unreasonable disliking, liking not based on facts.

**prem·is·es**\ˇprĕ·mĭ·səs\ n. *plural*. A property; especially, a house, its adhering buildings, and its land.

**pre·oc·cu·pied**\prē ˆŏk·yʊ ˈpaid\ adj. Abstracted, intent on only one thing so that others are not noticed.

**pre·pos·ter·ous**\prē ˆpŏs·tə·rəs\ adj. Absurd, ridiculous.

**pre·sage**\prə ˆsaj\ v. To foretell, predict.

**pre·ten·sion**\prē ˆtĕn·shən\ n. A vain or showy pretending at being more than one is.

**pre·ter·na·tu·ral**\ˈprēt·ər ˆnăch·ə·rəl\ adj. Beyond what is natural. (Adv. -ly)

**pre·text**\ˇprē ˈtĕkst\ n. A fictitious or made-up reason.

**prev·a·lence**\ˇprĕ·və·ləns\ n. Commonness, frequency.

**prim**\prĭm\ adj. Neat, quiet, and polite.

**pri·mal**\ˇprai·məl\ adj. Going back to the original or primitive, showing primitive simplicity.

**pri·me·val**\ˈprai ˆmē·vəl\ adj. Most primitive, earliest and quite without invention or culture.

**pro·ba·tion**\prō ˆbā·shən\ n. A testing period before fully joining or becoming a member.

**probe**\prōb\ v. To examine deeply and carefully.

**pro·claim**\prō ˆklām\ v. To announce openly and publicly.

**pro·cliv·i·ty**\prə ˆklĭ·vĭ·tē\ n., pl. -ies. Mental or tempermental liking or inclination.

**pro·di·gious**\prə ˆdĭ·jəs\ adj. Of the nature of a prodigy, uncommonly great, huge and remarkable.

**pro·fane**\prō ˆfān\ v. To desecrate, treat with disrespect what should be regarded as sacred.

**pro·fess**\prə ˆfĕs\ v. To declare by words or conduct (often without full honesty).

**pro·jec·tile**\prə ˆjĕk·tĭl\ n. An object (especially a weapon) that is shot or hurled.

**pro·lon·ga·tion**\'prō 'lŏŋ ▲gā·shən\ n. Something that lengthens.

**pro·pel·lant**\prə ▲pĕl·lənt\ n. Fuel used in high-speed aircraft.

**pros·trate**\▲prŏs·trāt\ adj. Prone on the ground as a defenseless support; powerless, weak, and unable to assert independence.

**prosy**\▲prō·zē\ adj. Dull, commonplace, trite, and unimaginative.

**pro·trude**\prə ▲trūd\ v. To stick or jut up or out.

**prov·en·der**\▲prŏ·vən·dər\ n. Food (often for animals), supplies.

**pro·vi·sion·al**\prə ▲vĭ·zhə·nəl\ adj. By way of temporary decision or for temporary expediency. (Adv. -ly)

**pro·voc·a·tive**\prə ▲vŏ·kə·tĭv\ adj. Stimulating, arousing new thoughts and discussions.

**prow·ess**\▲prau·ĭs\ n. Valor, bravery, daring, and skill.

**prox·im·i·ty**\prŏk ▲sĭ·mĭ·tē\ n. Nearness, closeness, adjacency.

**pru·dent**\▲prū·dənt\ adj. Wise, showing forethought and care.

**psy·chi·a·trist**\'sai ▲kai·ə·trĭst\ n. A doctor who treats mental patients.

**psy·chol·o·gy**\sai ▲kŏl·ə·jē\ n. 1. The science of mind and behavior. 2. The mental behavior and characteristics of an individual or group.

**pug·nac·i·ty**\pəg ▲nă·sĭ·tē\ n. Aggressiveness, quarrelsomeness, tendency to fight.

**puis·sant**\▲pwĭ·sənt\ adj. Powerful.

**pul·sa·tion**\pəl ▲sā·shən\ n. Regular throbbing, like the beating of a heart.

**pul·ver·ize**\▲pəl·və 'raiz\ v. To reduce to dust, demolish as by grinding or breaking.

**pun·gent**\▲pən·jənt\ adj. Showing a sharp stinging or biting taste or smell.

**pur·ga·to·ry**\▲pər·gə 'tō·rē\ n., pl. -ies. A division of the afterlife in which souls are purged of their sins before rising to heaven.

**pyre**\pair\ n. Fire; often, a funeral or cremation fire.

**quartz**\kwartz\ n. A mineral commonly found in crystals or crystalline masses.

**quer·u·lous**\▲kwĕr·yə·ləs\ adj. Fretful, whining, always complaining. (Adv. -ly)

**quin·tes·sence**\kwĭn ▲tĕ·səns\ n. Completely pure essence, most genuine nature.

**quip**\kwĭp\ n. Jest, witticism.

**quiz·zi·cal**\▲kwĭ·zĭ·kəl\ adj. Questioning, uncertain, speculative.

**rai·ment**\▲rā·mənt\ n. Clothing, garment.

**ram·i·fi·ca·tion**\'răm·ə·fə ▲kā·shən\ n. A branching out, outgrowth.

**ram·part**\▲răm·pərt\ n. A defensive wall, an outer fortification, an embankment or parapet likely to be attacked.

**ram·shack·le**\▲răm 'shă·kəl\ adj. Most carelessly and haphazardly made and ready to collapse.

**ran·cor** or **ran·cour**\▲răŋ·kər\ n. Ill will, malice, bitterness.

**ran·kle**\▲răŋ·kəl\ v. 1. To irritate, vex, serve as a cause of soreness. 2. To feel bitter, show irritation or anger.

**rasp**\răsp\ v. To grate or scrape with or as with a file.

**rau·cous**\▲rɔ·kəs\ adj. Rough, harsh, and crude.

**rav·age**\▲ră·vəj\ v. To lay waste to, destroy and ruin.

**re·cep·ta·cle**\rə ▲sĕp·tə·kəl\ n. A container, vessel.

**re·cip·ro·cal**\rə ▲sĭp·rə·kəl\ adj. Working or acting with equal motion and return.

**re·coil**\rē ▲kɔil\ v. To pull or spring back.

**re·con·noi·ter**\'rĕ·kə ▲nɔi·tər\ v. To scout, venture out or forward and observe.

**rec·ti·fy**\▲rĕk·tĭ·fai\ v., -ies, -ied. To remedy, correct.

**rec·ti·tude**\▲rĕk·tə·tūd\ n. Moral integrity, correctness of judgment or procedure, righteousness.

**re·doubt·able**\rə ▲dau·tə·bəl\ adj. Formidable and dangerous to oppose.

**re·dress**\rē ▲drĕs\ n. Remedy, correction, compensation. (Also v. To remedy, compensate.)

**re·flex**\▲rē·flĕks\ n. Reaction to a stimulus accomplished without thought or analysis.

**re·fute**\rĭ·fyūt\ v. To overthrow by argument, evidence, or proof; show to be false or wrong.

**re·it·er·ate**\'rē ▲ĭ·tə 'rāt\ v. To repeat (often emphatically).

**rel·e·vant**\▲rĕl·ə·vənt\ adj. Suitable, related, appropriate.

**rel·ish**\▲rĕ·lĭsh\ n. Pleasure and appreciation, especially in eating.

**re·luc·tant**\rē ▲lək·tənt\ adj. Showing unwillingness or aversion. (Adv. -ly)

**re·mon·strate**\rē ▲mŏn·strāt\ v. To argue against with reasoning and pleading.

**re·morse·ful**\rē ▲mōrs·fəl\ adj. Showing genuine regret and contriteness.

**rend**\rĕnd\ v. to tear, tear apart.

**re·nun·ci·a·tion**\rē 'nən·sē ▲ā·shən\ n. Denial; especially, self-denial.

**re·pel·lent**\rə ▲pĕ·lənt\ adj. Repulsive, loathsome.

**re·plen·ish**\rē ▲plĕ·nĭsh\ v. To resupply, stock up.

**re·ple·tion**\rə ▲plē·shən\ n. Complete fullness and entire satisfaction of all desire to eat.

**re·pose**\rē ▲pōz\ n. Rest, inactivity.

**re·prieve**\rē ▲prēv\ n. A delay in punishment; specifically, a postponement of a death sentence.

**rep·ri·mand**\▲rĕp·rĭ·mănd\ v. To scold, rebuke.

**re·proach·ful**\rē ▲prōch·fəl\ adj. Expressing reproach or hurt rebuke to another.

**re·pu·di·ate**\rĭ ▲pyūd·ē 'āt\ v. To refuse to have anything to do with, refuse to accept, reject as untrue or unjust.

**re·pug·nant**\rĭ ▲pəg·nənt\ adj. Exciting distaste, strong dislike, or antagonism.

---

ă b*a*d, ā b*a*ke, a f*a*ther, ĕ s*e*ll, ē *e*qual, ai m*i*le, ĭ s*i*t, ŏ c*o*t, ō n*o*te, ɔ l*a*w, ū b*oo*m, ʊ w*oo*d, yū *you*, yʊ f*u*ry, aʊ c*ow*, ɔi b*oy*. The schwa is used for both stressed and unstressed sounds: ə m*u*d, w*o*rd, ev*e*n; ch *ch*ase, i*tch*; sh *sh*ell, wi*sh*; th p*a*th, *thin*; th *the*, ei*ther*; ŋ wi*ng*; w *w*et, *wh*eat; zh plea*s*ure.

**re·pul·sion**\rə ‸pəl·shən\ n. Aversion, repugnance.

**re·pute**\rē ‸pyūt\ v. To consider or think of as.

**re·sent·ment**\rə ‸zĕnt·mənt\ n. A feeling of irritated displeasure and bitterness as for some injury or slight.

**res·i·due**\‸rĕ·zĭ 'dū\ n. Remainder, substance falling from or filtered from a solution.

**res·ig·na·tion**\'rĕ·zĭg ‸nā·shən\ n. Inclination to accept fate without protest, struggle, or regret.

**re·signed**\rē ‸zaind\ adj. Without emotion and with acceptance as of something inevitable.

**re·sil·ient**\rə ‸zĭl·yənt\ adj. Springy.

**re·sound·ing**\rə ‸zaund·ĭŋ\ adj. Seemingly of major importance and promising much.

**re·spec·tive**\rē ‸spĕk·tĭv\ adj. Different, individual, each for each.

**res·pite**\‸rĕs·pət\ n. A temporary interval of rest or relief.

**res·tive**\‸rĕ·stĭv\ adj. Moving uneasily, fidgety.

**retch**\rĕch\ v. To gag, vomit.

**ret·i·cent**\‸rĕt·ə·sənt\ adj. Inclined to be silent or secretive, uncommunicative.

**re·trieve**\rē ‸trēv\ v. To find and bring back again, restore.

**re·tro·spec·tion**\'rĕ·trə ‸spĕk·shən\ n. Recollection, remembrance.

**rev·eil·le**\‸rĕ·və 'lĭ\ n. A bugle call to wake up and get up.

**rev·el**\‸rĕ·vəl\ v. To exult, take great joy.

**rev·e·la·tion**\'rĕ·və ‸lā·shən\ n. Some enlightening or revealing fact.

**re·ver·ber·ate**\rē ‸vər·bə 'rāt\ v. To reecho, resound back and forth.

**rhet·o·ric**\‸rĕ·tə·rĭk\ n. The study of the principles of effective composition.

**rhyth·mic**\‸rĭth·mĭk\ adj. Showing rhythm, graceful regularity, and coordination of motion.

**ric·o·chet**\‸rĭ·kə 'shā\ v. To rebound from surface to surface.

**rift**\rĭft\ n. A clear space between clouds.

**ri·gid·i·ty**\rĭ ‸jĭ·dĭ·tē\ n. Stiffness, unbendingness.

**rig·or·ous**\‸rĭ·gə·rəs\ adj. Strict and demanding.

**rite**\rait\ n. A ritual or ceremony, a form prescribed by etiquette.

**rit·u·al**\‸rĭ·chəl\ n. An act customarily performed through or as though through religious reasons.

**rive**\raiv\ v. To split, rend.

**ro·bot**\‸rō·bət\ n. A mechanical man, an automaton.

**ro·bust**\rō ‸bəst\ adj. Strong, sturdy, and healthy. (Also n. -ness)

**ro·manc·er**\rō ‸măn·sər\ n. One who daydreams and makes up stories.

**ro·se·ate**\‸rō·zē·ət\ adj. Like or suggestive of roses.

**rote**\rōt\ n. Memory; especially, memory not accompanied by thoughts or evaluations.

**rout**\raut\ n. A group or crowd; especially, a mixed, disorderly, noisy crowd.

**rub·ble**\‸rə·bəl\ n. Broken rock and stone, a fragment of broken stone.

**rue·ful**\‸rū·fəl\ adj. Sorrowful, sad. (Adv. -ly)

**ru·mi·nate**\‸rū·mĭ 'nāt\ v. To think over slowly and repeatedly.

**run·nel**\‸rə·nəl\ n. A brook, small stream.

**rup·ture**\‸rəp·chər\ n. A break, split.

**rus·tic**\‸rəs·tĭk\ adj. Rural, countrified.

**ruth·less**\‸rūth·ləs\ adj. Merciless.

**sac**\săk\ n. A pouch; often, the pouch containing the poison of a poisonous snake.

**sa·gac·i·ty**\sə ‸gă·sĭ·tē\ n. Wisdom, shrewdness.

**sa·lient**\‸sā·lyĕnt\ adj. Conspicuous.

**sa·line**\‸sā 'lĭn\ adj. Salt, salty.

**sal·low**\‸să·lō\ adj. Unwholesomely colorless and pale, gray.

**sal·vage**\‸săl·vəj\ n. The action of saving anything of value from a wrecked or disabled ship.

**sanc·ti·fy**\‸săŋk·tĭ 'fai\ v., -ies, -ied. To bless, hallow.

**sanc·tu·ary**\‸săn·chu 'ā·rē\ n., pl. -ies. A place of refuge in which one may be secure, a place of known certain safety.

**sar·don·ic**\sar ‸dan·ĭk\ adj. Bitter, mocking.

**sa·ti·e·ty**\sə ‸tai·ə·tē\ n. A feeling of overfullness from eating too much.

**sat·u·rate**\‸să·chə 'rāt\ v. To soak, wet completely.

**saun·ter**\‸sɔn·tər\ v. To stroll along slowly and unconcernedly.

**sa·vor**\‸sā·vər\ n. Taste; especially, a distinctive taste to be relished.

**scape·grace**\‸skāp 'grās\ n. Rascal, imp.

**scin·til·late**\‸sĭnt·əl 'āt\ v. To sparkle, throw off quick flashes like sparks.

**score**\skōr\ v. To dig, grave, cut.

**scourge**\skərj or skōrj\ v. To whip severely as in punishment, compel as by whipping.

**scrab·ble**\‸skră·bəl\ v. To crawl as rapidly as possible.

**scru·pu·lous**\‸skrū·pyə·ləs\ adj. Strictly honest, upright, and careful. (Adv. -ly)

**scru·ti·nize**\‸skrū·tĭ 'naiz\ v. To examine closely, minutely, and searchingly.

**scut·tle**\‸skə·təl\ v. 1. To sink by opening holes in the hull. 2. To run rapidly but awkwardly, run hastily. 3. To run or scurry, as a small animal or as a crab.

**se·date**\sə ‸dāt\ adj. Marked by slow, serious, or sober dignity. (Adv. -ly)

**sed·u·lous**\‸sĕ·jə·ləs\ adj. Constantly showing painstaking care and industry. (Adv. -ly)

**sem·blance**\‸sĕm·bləns\ n. Resemblance, appearance.

**sen·a·to·ri·al**\'sĕ·nə ‸tō·rē·əl\ adj. Pertaining to or intended for a senator.

**se·nil·i·ty**\sə ‸nĭ·lĭ·tē\ n. Weakened old age without good control of mind or body.

**sen·su·ous**\‸sĕn·shu·əs\ adj. Having a pleasing appeal to the senses.

**sen·ti·men·tal·i·ty**\'sĕn·tĭ 'mĕn ‸tă·lĭ·tē\ n. Artificially played-up feeling, emotion for emotion's sake.

**se·quence**\‸sē·kwĕns\ n. Succession in order.

**se·quin**\‸sē·kwĭn\ n. A colorful thin metal plate used as a dress adornment.

**ser·e·nade**\'sĕ·rə ‸nād\ n. A musical compliment to a woman (usually to be performed outdoors at night).

**ser·vile**\‸sər·vĭl\ adj. Menial, befitting a slave or servant of the lowest sort. (Adv. -ly)

**set·tee**\sĕ ‸tē\ n. A straight seat with a back for two or three persons.

**sev·er**\\ˇsĕ·vər\ v. To cut.

**shack·le**\\ˇshă·kəl\ n. Chain.

**sheen**\shēn\ n. Gleam, colorful reflection.

**shy**\shai\ v., -ies, -ied. To rear back, retreat abruptly.

**si·dle**\ˇsai·dəl\ v. To proceed sideways.

**sim·i·le**\ˇsĭ·mĭ ˈlē\ n. Comparison; technically, a comparison worded with *like* or *as*.

**sin·ewy**\ˇsĭn·yu·wē\ adj. Wiry and strong.

**sin·is·ter**\ˇsĭ·nĭs·tər\ adj. Ominous; threatening, promising, or suggesting extreme evil.

**sire**\sair\ n. Father.

**slan·der**\ˇslan·dər\ n. A malicious, false, defamatory statement.

**slat·tern·ly**\ˇslă·tərn·lē\ adj. Quite untidy and careless about one's appearance, dirty and disorderly.

**sod·den**\ˇsŏ·dən\ adj. Rain-soaked.

**so·journ**\ˇsō·jərn\ n. Stay.

**so·lace**\ˇsō·ləs\ n. Consolation and comfort, comfort and soothing of embarrassment or grief.

**sole**\sōl\ adj. Solitary, alone.

**so·lic·i·tude**\sə ˈlĭ·sĭ·tūd\ n. Anxious care and concern.

**sol·i·tude**\ˇsŏ·lĭ ˈtūd\ n. Condition of being alone without necessarily being lonesome.

**som·ber**\ˇsŏm·bər\ adj. Dark, colorless, and gloomy; dark, gloomy, and reproachful.

**som·bre·ro**\səm ˈbrĕ·rō\ n. A large straw hat with a wide curving brim (worn in Mexico).

**som·nam·bu·list**\səm ˈnăm·byu·lĭst\ n. A person who walks in his sleep.

**som·no·lence**\ˇsŏm·nə·ləns\ n. Sleepiness, lethargy.

**son·ics**\ˇsŏ·nĭks\ n. The study or the manipulation of sounds.

**sooth**\sūth\ n. *archaic.* Truth.

**soph·o·mor·ic**\ˇsof·ə ˈmor·ĭk\ adj. Suggestive of the traditional sophomore, as in intellectual pretensions and self-assurance.

**spare**\spăr\ adj. Thin, lanky.

**spas·mod·ic**\ˇspăz ˈmŏ·dĭk\ adj. Marked by spasms, by uneven convulsive fits. (Adv. -ally)

**spe·cif·ic**\spə ˈsĭ·fĭk\ adj. Definite; not vague, general, or uncertain.

**spec·ter**\ˇspĕk·tər\ n. A grim supernatural repulsive or deathly figure.

**spec·trum**\ˇspĕk·trəm\ n. A range of all the colors in order, the orderly arrangement of colors.

**spec·u·late**\ˇspĕk·yu ˈlāt\ v. To guess, conjecture.

**spec·u·la·tion**\ˇspĕk·yu ˈlā·shən\ n. A surmise, guess.

**spi·ral**\ˇspai·rəl\ v. To go up or down in a twisting course.

**spoor**\spūr *or* spōr\ n. The track of an animal.

**squal·id**\ˇskwa·lĭd\ adj. Very dirty, mean, and sordid.

**squan·der**\ˇskwan·dər\ v. To waste, dissipate, throw away.

**squea·mish**\ˇskwē·mĭsh\ adj. Particular and fussy, given to nice objections and scruples.

**stag·nant**\ˇstăg·nənt\ adj. Motionless and fostering decay or rot.

**staid**\stād\ adj. Sober, quiet, and dignified.

**stalk**\stɔk\ v. To stride angrily.

**stal·wart**\ˇstɔl·wərt\ adj. Strong and robust.

**stam·i·na**\ˇstă·mĭ·nə\ n. Strength, energy, vitality.

**stanch**\stɔnch *or* stanch\ v. To stop or abate the flow of.

**stan·chion**\ˇstăn·shən\ n. An upright pole, post, or support.

**state·ly**\ˇstāt·lē\ adj. Orderly, dignified, and impressive.

**stat·u·ary**\ˇstă·chu·wĕ·rē\ n. Statues (collectively).

**stave**\stāv\ v. Repel, fend off.

**stealth**\stĕlth\ n. Cautious, quiet, fearful conduct like a thief's.

**steep**\stēp\ v. To saturate in, instill with.

**stew·ard**\ˇstū·ərd\ n. An officer in charge of meals and food supplies on a ship.

**sti·fle**\ˇstai·fəl\ v. To suffocate, deprive of, or cut the supply of breathable air.

**sti·let·to**\stĭ ˈlĕ·tō\ n. A short dagger.

**stole**\stōl\ n. A fur (or cloth) neck or shoulder piece.

**stol·id**\ˇstŏ·lĭd\ adj. Expressionless and unemotional.

**stra·te·gic**\strə ˈtē·jĭk\ adj. Affording best use of resources and forces in combat or war.

**stra·tum**\ˇstrā·təm\ n., pl. -a. Layer.

**stretch·er**\ˇstrĕ·chər\ n. A device on which an artist's canvas can be stretched.

**stu·pe·fy**\ˇstū·pə ˈfai\ v., -ies, -ied. To cause to lose one's senses or one's ability to think or perceive cleary; shock or stun so that talk and thought are impossible.

**stu·por**\ˇstū·pər\ n. 1. Loss of one's senses and feeling, daze. 2. Deep unconsciousness, as from drugs or injury.

**suave**\swav\ adj. Smooth, urbane, and unruffled.

**sub·ju·ga·tion**\ˇsəb·jə ˈgā·shən\ n. A state of affairs in which one is controlled or dominated by another.

**sub·junc·tive**\səb ˈjəŋ·tĭv\ n. A verb form used to express uncertainty or condition contrary to fact.

**sub·lime**\ˇsə ˈblaim\ adj. Wonderful, lofty, and exalted.

**sub·side**\səb ˈsaid\ v. To recede, diminish, grow less.

**sub·sist**\səb ˈsĭst\ v. To exist, continue to live.

**sub·stan·ti·ate**\səb ˈstăn·chē·āt\ v. To verify, confirm.

**sub·ter·fuge**\ˇsəb·tər·fyūj\ n. A deception by a stratagem or ruse.

**sub·ter·ra·nean**\ˇsəb·tə ˈrā·nē·ən\ adj. Underground.

**suc·ces·sive**\sək ˈsĕ·sĭv\ adj. Succeeding or following in order or sequence.

**suc·cor**\ˇsə·kər\ n. Aid or assistance from another.

**suc·cumb**\sə ˈkəm\ v. To give way, yield.

**suf·fer·ance**\ˇsə·fə·rəns\ n. Suffering.

**suf·fice**\sə ˈfais\ v. To be enough or adequate.

**suf·fo·cate**\ˇsə·fə ˈkāt\ v. To stifle, die from lack of air.

**sul·len**\ˇsə·lən\ adj. Quiet, grim, gloomy, and lonesome.

**su·perb**\sū ˈpərb\ adj. Wonderful, excellent.

---

ă bad, ā bake, a father, ĕ sell, ē equal, ai mile, ĭ sit, ŏ cot, ō note, ɔ law, ū boom, ʊ wood, yū you, yʊ fury, aʊ cow, ɔi boy. The schwa is used for both stressed and unstressed sounds: ə mud, word, even; ch chase, itch; sh shell, wish; th path, thin; th the, either; ŋ wing; w wet, wheat; zh pleasure.

**su·per·cil·ious**\\'sū·pər ˆsĭ·lē·əs\ adj. Proud, haughty, and aloof.

**su·per·fi·cial**\\'sū·pər ˆfĭ·shəl\ adj. On the surface, not deep or dangerous.

**sup·plant**\sə ˆplănt\ v. To take the place of.

**sup·pli·ant**\\'sə·plē·ənt\ adj. In a begging or beseeching manner.

**sup·po·si·tion**\\'sə·pə ˆzĭ·shən\ n. That which is supposed, idea, notion.

**sur·plus**\\'sər·pləs\ adj. Extra, additional.

**ser·rep·ti·tious**\sə·rəp ˆtĭ·shəs\ adj. Secret, covert, stealthy, and quick; so as not to be noticed.

**sur·veil·lance**\sər ˆvā·ləns\ n. Vigilant watch; observation to prevent danger, crime, or escape.

**sus·tain**\sə ˆstān\ v. To maintain, keep on, support.

**sus·te·nance**\\'səs·tə·nəns\ n. Food, nourishment necessary to life, provision, material to eat.

**swad·dle**\\'swa·dəl\ v. To cover over as with a protective blanket of cloth.

**swank**\swănk\ adj. Luxurious and upper-class, showing prestige values.

**swarthy**\\'swar·thē\ adj. Dark complexioned.

**swath**\swath or swoth\ n. A row like that made by a mower in long grass.

**sym·bol·ic**\sĭm ˆbŏ·lĭk\ adj. Imaginary, figurative.

**sym·bol·ize**\\'sĭm·bə 'laiz\ v. To typify, express.

**syn·chro·nize**\\'sĭn·krə 'naiz\ v. To time so as to occur exactly when something else does.

**syn·op·sis**\sə ˆnŏp·sĭs\ n., pl. -es. Résumé, shortened version.

**tac·it**\\'tă·sĭt\ adj. Unstated and undeclared, but accepted and understood.

**tac·i·tur·ni·ty**\\'tăs·ə·tər·nət·ē\ n. State of being disinclined to talk, be silent.

**tack**\tăk\ v. To proceed in a diagonal course.

**tan·gen·tial**\tăn ˆjĕn·chəl\ adj. Following a tangent, a diverging curving or diagonal course. (Adv. -ly)

**tan·gi·ble**\\'tăŋ·jĭ·bəl\ adj. Readily perceptible by the senses; especially, easily touched or felt. (Adv: -ly)

**tan·trum**\\'tăn·trəm\ n. A childish display of wild ungoverned temper.

**ta·per**\\'tā·pər\ n. Candle.

**tar·ry**\\'tă·rē\ v. To delay, linger.

**taut**\tot\ adj. Tight, with the skin stretched close.

**tech·no·log·i·cal**\\'tĕk·nə ˆlŏ·jĭ·kəl\ adj. Pertaining to applied technical knowledge.

**teem**\tēm\ v. To be full, replete, packed.

**tele·path·ic**\\'tĕ·lə ˆpă·thĭk\ adj. Of or pertaining to communication without visible or other explicable procedures.

**tele·vise**\\'tĕ·lə 'vaiz\ v. To communicate with by a telephone with an additional visual feature.

**tem·per·a·men·tal**\\'tĕm·pə·rə ˆmĕn·təl\ adj. 1. Pertaining to disposition, attitude, or personality. 2. Showing individual temperament, such as whims, odd desires, or fickle changes of mind. (Adv. -ly)

**tem·per·ate**\\'tĕm·pə·rət\ adj. Showing no excesses.

**ten·dril**\\'tĕn·drĭl\ n. A slender and sensitive shoot or leaf growing out from a plant.

**te·net**\\'tĕ·nət\ n. Belief, idea, ideal.

**ten·or**\\'tĕ·nər\ n. Gist, meaning, significance.

**ten·sion**\\'tĕn·shən\ n. Nervous strain and anxiety, an inner feeling of nervous discomfort.

**ten·ta·cle**\\'tĕn·tə·kəl\ n. A long flexible member like the arm of an octopus.

**ten·ta·tive**\\'tĕn·tə·tĭv\ adj. 1. Doubtfully slow and experimental. 2. Hesitant and uncertain. (Adv. -ly)

**ten·u·ous**\\'tĕn·yu·əs\ adj. 1. Very thin, easily interrupted or broken. 2. Thin and airy, not concentrated or firm.

**tep·id**\\'tĕ·pĭd\ adj. Lukewarm.

**ter·res·tri·al**\tə ˆrĕs·trē·əl\ adj. Earthly, of the earth in contrast to planets and stars.

**terse**\tərs\ adj. Brief, expressed without wasting words.

**teth·er**\\'teth·ər\ v. To restrain or bind an animal with or as with a halter, rope, or chain.

**texture**\\'tĕks·chər\ n. Composition of woven cloth.

**the·o·rem**\\'thē·ə·rəm\ n. A mathematical formula or proposition.

**the·o·ret·i·cal**\\'thē·ə ˆrĕ·tĭ·kəl\ adj. Based on more or less abstract and detached thought rather than on realities.

**thew**\thū\ n. Muscle, sinew.

**thread·bare**\\'thrĕd 'băr\ adj. Shabby and practically worn out.

**thresh·old**\\'thrĕ·shəld\ n. Door sill.

**throt·tle**\\'thrŏ·təl\ v. To choke.

**ti·ara**\tē ˆa·rə\ n. A jeweled band across the forehead.

**tim·o·rous**\\'tĭ·mə·rəs\ adj. Shy, diffident, and afraid. (Also n. -ness)

**to·ga**\\'tō·gə\ n. The Roman citizen's loose gownlike outer garment.

**tol·er·a·bly**\\'tŏ·lə·rə·blē\ adv. Rather, generally, more-or-less, reasonably.

**tol·er·ance**\\'tŏ·lə·rəns\ n. Kindly acceptance of another, despite his faults or despite one's differences with him.

**tor·e·ador**\\'tŏ·rē·ə 'dŏr\ n. A bullfighter.

**tor·pid**\\'tŏr·pĭd\ adj. Sluggish, inactive, lethargic.

**tor·por**\\'tŏr·pər\ n. Sleepy or lethargic inactivity.

**tor·so**\\'tŏr·sō\ n. Trunk, body.

**tor·tu·ous**\\'tŏr·chu·əs\ adj. Winding, twisting.

**tran·quil**\\'trăn·kwĭl\ adj. Entirely peaceful and unworried; calm, peaceful, and quiet. (Adv. -ly)

**trans·ac·tion**\\'trăns ˆăk·shən\ n. Sale, purchase.

**tran·scen·dent**\\'trăn ˆsĕn·dənt\ adj. Superlative, surpassing anything comparable.

**trans·fig·ure**\\'trăns ˆfĭg·yər\ v. To beautify and illuminate, as by a god's action.

**tran·sient**\\'trăn·shənt\ adj. Temporary, short-lived, not permanent or lasting.

**tran·si·to·ry**\\'trăn(t)s·ə ˆtŏr·ē\ adj. Of brief duration, temporary.

**trans·par·en·cy**\\'trăns ˆpă·rən·sē\ n. The quality of permitting seeing through.

**trans·port**\\'trăns 'pŏrt\ n. Extreme joy.

**tra·vail**\trə 'văl\ n. Labor performed with some difficulty and struggle.

**trav·el·ogue**\\'tră·və 'lŏg\ n. A movie showing travels in a strange land.

**tra·verse**\trə ˆvərs\ n. A gap or passage affording a safe crossing.

**trem·or**\\'trĕ·mər\ n. A quiver, tremble, or shiver.

**trem·u·lous**\ˈtrĕm·yu·ləs\ adj. Fluttering in an erratic course like that of a butterfly's.

**trep·i·da·tion**\ˈtrĕp·ə ˈdā·shən\ n. Tremulous alarm or agitation.

**triv·i·al·i·ty**\ˈtrĭ·vē ˈă·lĭ·tē\ n., pl. -ies. 1. Unimportance, lack of significance. 2. Something utterly unimportant or minor.

**truss**\trəs\ v. To tie, bind, confine.

**tu·mult**\ˈtū·məlt\ n. Noisy confused uproar.

**tur·bu·lence**\ˈtər·byu·ləns\ n. Agitated commotion, swift uneven confused motion.

**tur·gid**\ˈtər·jĭd\ adj. Cloudy and murky.

**tur·moil**\ˈtər ˈmoil\ n. Confused turbulent agitation.

**ul·cer**\ˈəl·sər\ n. A festering sore.

**ul·te·ri·or**\əl ˈtē·rē·ər\ adj. Extending further or deeper than appears at first.

**ul·ti·mate**\ˈəl·tĭ·mət\ adj. 1. Final, last in a series or sequence. 2. Last and most extreme.

**um·ber**\ˈəm·bər\ n. A brownish painting pigment.

**um·bil·i·cal**\əm ˈbĭ·lĭ·kəl\ adj. Pertaining to the cord that binds an unborn child to its mother.

**un·abashed**\ˈən·ə ˈbăsht\ adj. Not embarrassed, confused, or checked.

**un·as·sail·able**\ˈən·ə ˈsā·lə·bəl\ adj. Incapable of being attacked or defeated.

**un·can·ny**\ən ˈkă·nē\ adj. Weird or supernatural, not to be readily understood or appreciated, strange.

**un·com·pre·hend·ing**\ən ˈkŏm·prə ˈhĕnd·ĭŋ\ adj. Not understanding. (Adv. -ly)

**un·de·fin·able**\ən·də ˈfai·nə·bəl\ adj. Impossible or difficult to define and analyze.

**un·der·ling**\ˈən·dər ˈlĭŋ\ n. Inferior, follower, one who takes orders from another.

**un·du·la·tion**\ən·də ˈlā·shən\ n. 1. A land contour giving a wavy, up-and-down effect. 2. Arrangement in waves, wavy effect.

**un·en·cum·bered**\ˈən·ən ˈkəm·bərd\ adj. Free of hindrances, weights, and inconveniences.

**uni·son**\ˈyū·nĭ·sən\ n. Concord, exact agreement in content and time, uniformity.

**un·per·turbed**\ən·pər ˈtərbd\ adj. Calm, not agitated or concerned.

**un·prec·e·dent·ed**\ən ˈprĕ·sə ˈdĕnt·əd\ adj. Not having happened or been experienced before.

**un·seem·ly**\ən ˈsēm·lē\ adj. Improper, discourteous, ungentlemanly.

**un·so·lic·it·ed**\ən·sə ˈlĭ·sĭ·təd\ adj. Unsought, not actively looked for.

**un·sub·stan·tial**\ən·səb ˈstăn·chəl\ adj. Unreal, nonexistent.

**un·time·ly**\ən ˈtaim·lē\ adj. Extremely unfortunate, touched too young or too soon by death or disaster.

**un·wont·ed**\ən ˈwŏnt·əd\ adj. Unaccustomed, unusual.

**up·surg·ing**\əp ˈsərj·ĭŋ\ adj. Rapidly rising.

**ur·chin**\ˈər·chĭn\ n. A street child, typically one noisy and dirty.

**ur·gen·cy**\ˈər·jən·sē\ n. An insistent force.

**ur·gent**\ˈər·jənt\ adj. 1. Important and demanding attention, very important and necessary to prevent failure or catastrophe. 2. Expressing a pressing appeal as though dealing with a most serious or important matter. (Adv. -ly)

**ut·ter·most**\ˈə·tər ˈmōst\ adj. Latest, last.

**vac·u·ous**\ˈvăk·yu·əs\ adj. Inane, empty of sense or significance.

**vag·a·bond**\ˈvă·gə ˈbŏnd\ n. Tramp, wanderer, vagrant.

**va·grant**\ˈvā·grənt\ adj. Homeless, wandering.

**vale**\vāl\ n. Valley.

**val·id**\ˈvă·lĭd\ adj. Worthwhile, true and important.

**va·lid·i·ty**\və ˈlĭ·dĭ·tē\ n. Value, worth.

**vari·ance**\ˈvă·rē·əns\ n. Opposition, dissension, disagreement.

**var·ie·gat·ed**\ˈvă·rē·ə ˈgāt·əd\ adj. Varied, interspersed with contrasting elements.

**vaunt**\vont\ v. To brag or boast. (Also n. Brag or boast of triumph.)

**ve·he·mence**\ˈvē·ə·məns\ n. Notable force or intensity.

**ve·loc·i·ty**\və ˈlŏ·sĭ·tē\ n. Speed, rapidity.

**ven·er·a·ble**\ˈvĕn·ər·ə·bəl\ adj. Calling forth respect through age, character, and attainments; impressive by reason of age.

**ven·om**\ˈvĕ·nəm\ n. Poison.

**ver·dict**\ˈvər·dĭkt\ n. Statement of decision.

**ver·dure**\ˈvər·dər\ n. The greenness of plant growth.

**ver·i·ta·ble**\ˈvĕ·rĭ·tə·bəl\ adj. True, real, genuine. (Adv. -ly)

**ver·ti·go**\ˈvər·tĭ ˈgō\ n. Dizziness, usually accompanied by faintness.

**ves·tige**\ˈvĕs·tĭj\ n. A trace or visible sign left by something vanished or lost, a minute remaining amount.

**vest·ment**\ˈvĕst·mənt\ n. Garment, clothing.

**vet·er·i·nary**\ˈvĕ·tə·rĭ ˈnā·rē\ n., pl. -ies. A veterinarian, a doctor who treats the ailments of animals.

**vi·brant**\ˈvai·brənt\ adj. Pulsating with life, vigor, or activity.

**vi·brate**\ˈvai·brāt\ v. To swing to and fro or back and forth regularly.

**vile**\vail\ adj. Loathsome, mean.

**vi n·dic·tive**\vĭn ˈdĭk·tĭv\ adj. Vengeful and savagely determined to hurt or wound.

**vir·ile**\ˈvĕ·rĭl\ adj. Showing manly force and strength.

**vir·tu·al·ly**\ˈvər·chə·lē\ adv. Practically.

**vir·tu·ous**\ˈvər·chu·əs\ adj. With show of prim virtue and morality. (Adv. -ly)

**vis·cous**\ˈvĭs·kəs\ adj. Thick and sticky.

**vis·i·tant**\ˈvĭ·zĭ·tənt\ n. Visitor.

**vis·ta**\ˈvĭs·tə\ n. View; vision, especially of large scope or pleasing nature.

**vi·su·al·ize**\ˈvĭ·zhə ˈlaiz\ v. To form a mental picture of.

---

ă b*a*d, ā b*a*ke, a f*a*ther, ĕ s*e*ll, ē *e*qual, ai m*i*le, ĭ s*i*t, ŏ c*o*t, ō n*o*te, ɔ l*aw*, ū b*oo*m, ʊ w*oo*d, yū *you*, yʊ f*u*ry, aʊ c*ow*, ɔi b*oy*. The schwa is used for both stressed and unstressed sounds: ə m*u*d, w*o*rd, *e*ven; ch *ch*ase, it*ch*; sh *sh*ell, wi*sh*; th p*a*th, *th*in; th *th*e, ei*th*er; ŋ wi*ng*; w *w*et, *wh*eat; zh plea*s*ure.

**vi·tal·i·ty**\vai ᴧtă·lǐ·tē\ n. 1. Active liveliness. 2. Stamina and vigor to endure.

**vit·ri·fy**\ᴧvǐ·trǐ 'fai\ v., -ies, -ied. To turn to glass or a glasslike substance.

**vi·va·cious**\vǐ ᴧvā·shəs\ adj. Lively and spirited.

**viv·id**\ᴧvǐ·vǐd\ adj. Bright, colorful, showing high intensity.

**vo·ca·tion**\vō ᴧkā·shən\ n. Calling, profession.

**vol·a·tile**\ᴧvŏ·lə·tǐl\ adj. Readily vaporizing or changing from liquid to gas.

**vol·u·ble**\ᴧvŏl·yʊ·bəl\ adj. Talkative, constantly chattering and never silent.

**vo·ra·cious**\və ᴧrā·shəs\ adj. Showing extreme hunger and haste and greed in eating.

**vouch·safe**\'vaʊch ᴧsāf\ v. To grant and guarantee.

**vul·gar**\ᴧvəl·gər\ adj. Common, crude.

**wad·dle**\ᴧwa·dəl\ n. An ungainly walk like that of a duck.

**wake**\wāk\ n. Literally, a trail of wave and foam after a boat or ship; loosely, a trail or track.

**wan**\wan\ adj. Lacking in normal expression and interest. (Adv. -ly)

**wane**\wān\ v. To lessen or diminish, as in size or aspect, as a waning moon; dwindle, die out.

**wan·ton**\ᴧwan·tən\ v. To play sportively.

**wary**\ᴧwā·rē\ adj. Cautious and very watchful for possible danger, suspicious.

**wat·tle**\ᴧwa·təl\ n. *usually plural.* A construction employing twigs or reeds sometimes daubed with mud.

**way·lay**\'wā 'lā\ v., waylaid. To stop after lying in wait for.

**way·ward**\ᴧwā·wərd\ adj. Marked by unpredictable originality or difference.

**wench**\wěnch\ n. A low coarse woman or girl.

**whelp**\wělp\ v. To give birth (usually used of dogs and other animals).

**where·abouts**\ᴧwā·rə 'baʊts\ n. *plural.* Location.

**whet**\wět\ v. To incite.

**wile**\wail\ n. Treacherous or hypocritical action or suggestion.

**wil·ly-nil·ly**\'wǐ·lē- 'nǐ·lē\ adv. Whether desired or not, regardless of a person's wishes.

**wist·ful·ness**\ᴧwǐst·fəl·nəs\ n. Yearning desire.

**wor·sted**\ᴧwʊ·stəd\ n. A heavy wool cloth.

**writhe**\raith\ v. To twist or contort one's body violently as in pain or distress.

**wry**\rai\ adj. Sarcastic, ironic. (Adv. -ly)

**yon**\yŏn\ adj. Yonder.

# General Index

# Literary Types Index

## Dramas

*The Diary of Anne Frank,* 189, Frances Goodrich and Albert Hackett

*Julius Caesar,* 382, William Shakespeare

*The Pen of My Aunt,* 52, Gordon Daviot

## Essays and Personal Accounts

*Stopover in Querétaro,* 4, Jerrold Beim

*The Story of the Good Little Boy,* 653, Mark Twain

## Novellas

*His Enemy, His Friend,* 66, John Tunis

*The Pearl,* 550, John Steinbeck

## Parables

*The Parable of the Good Samaritan,* 1, Luke 10:30–37

*The Parable of the Prodigal Son,* 130, Luke 15:11–24

## Poetry—Lyric

*After Great Pain a Formal Feeling Comes,* 281, Emily Dickinson

*Afternoon on a Hill,* 293, Walter de la Mare

*The Alarm Clock,* 33, Mari Evans

*As I Grew Older,* 331 Langston Hughes

*The Black Panther,* 270, John Hall Wheelock

*Boots,* 469, Rudyard Kipling

*Break, Break, Break,* 289 Alfred, Lord Tennyson

*Corner,* 34, Ralph Pomeroy

*Country Night,* 258, Selma Robinson

*Daybreak in Alabama,* 328, Langston Hughes

*Death Is a Beautiful Car Parked Only,* 254, Richard Brautigan

*A Dirge,* 282, Percy Bysshe Shelley

*Does It Matter,* 272, Siegfried Sassoon

*Dream Deferred,* 333, Langston Hughes

*The Dream Keeper,* 329, Langston Hughes

*Dream Variation,* 327, Langston Hughes

*Dreams,* 329, Langston Hughes

*Eldorado,* 255, Edgar Allan Poe

*Faces,* 37, Sara Teasdale

*Fast Run in the Junkyard,* 300, Jeannette Nichols

*For Everything There Is a Season,* 247, Ecclesiastes 3:1–8

*Good Humor Man,* 296, Phyllis McGinley

*Hate,* 272, James Stephens

*The Heart,* 276, Stephen Crane

*Highway: Michigan,* 253, Theodore Roethke

*Home Thoughts from Abroad,* 286, Robert Browning

*House Fear,* 259, Robert Frost

*The House on the Hill,* 284, E. A. Robinson

*I, Too,* 330, Langston Hughes

*In a Glass of Cider,* 313, Robert Frost

*in Just-spring,* 294, e. e. cummings

*Inland,* 286, Edna St. Vincent Millay

*The Lady,* 259, Elizabeth Coatsworth

*Let America Be America Again,* 332, Langston Hughes

*The Man He Killed,* 31, Thomas Hardy

*Miracles,* 297, Walt Whitman

*Mood,* 271, Countée Cullen

*Music I Heard,* 279, Conrad Aiken

*My Lost Youth,* 287, Henry Wadsworth Longfellow

*My November Guest,* 278, Robert Frost

*The Noise of Waters,* 279, James Joyce

*The Oft-Repeated Dream,* 259, Robert Frost

*The Panther Possible,* 261, William D. Barney

*Pied Beauty,* 298, Gerald Manley Hopkins

*A Poison Tree,* 275, William Blake

*Precious Words,* 299, Emily Dickinson

*Reveille,* 292, A. E. Housman

*Ride a Wild Horse,* 252, Hannah Kahn

*Sea Fever,* 252, John Masefield

*Silver,* 293, Walter de la Mare

*Smells,* 298, Christopher Morley

*Sonnet CVI,* 299, William Shakespeare

*Souvenir de Londres,* 170, Stephen Spender

*Spring,* 251, Richard Hovey

*Suicide Pond,* 262, Kathy McLaughlin

*Sympathy,* 250, Paul Laurence Dunbar

*Those Winter Sundays,* 290, Robert Hayden

*To a Beautiful Girl Whose Name I Don't Know,* 36, Audrey Brooks

*Travel,* 251, Edna St. Vincent Millay

*The Traveler's Curse After Misdirection,* 271, Robert Graves

*A Vagabond Song,* 296, Bliss Carman

*Velvet Shoes,* 294, Elinor Wylie

*The Warning,* 260, Adelaide Crapsey

*Waves Against a Dog,* 274, Taner Baybars

*We Real Cool,* 593, Gwendolyn Brooks

*The West Wind,* 285, John Masefield

*When I Have Fears That I May Cease to Be,* 260, John Keats

*The Whipping,* 171, Robert Hayden

*The White House,* 273, Claude McKay

*The Widow,* 280, Miller Williams

*Wild Blackberries,* 295, Frances McConnel

*Without a Cloak,* 275, Phyllis McGinley

*The Woodspurge,* 281, Dante Gabriel Rossetti

*Youth,* 329, Langston Hughes

## Short Stories

*The Ambitious Guest,* 601, Nathaniel Hawthorne

*The Catbird Seat,* 492, James Thurber

*The Cold, Cold Box,* 613, Howard Fast

*Feels Like Spring,* 345, Milton Kaplan

*Going to Run All Night,* 476, Harry Sylvester

*The Grains of Paradise,* 10, James Street

*Jug of Silver,* 348, Truman Capote

*Louisa, Please Come Home,* 633, Shirley Jackson

# Fine Art
# Index

# Illustration Sources

Alinari Collection: 382, 383, 385, 462

Art Institute of Chicago: Friends of American Art Collection, 43; Gift of Kate L. Brewster, 187; Helen Birch Bartlett Memorial Collection, 267.

Art Reference Bureau: Kröller Müller Museum, Otterlo, 2, 264; National Gallery, Oslo, 184B; Staatliche Museum, Berlin, 186B.

Bibliotheque Nationale, Paris: 607B, 610

Mrs. Sara d'Harnoncourt: 16

Editorial Projects, Inc. 610, from Les Temps Nouveaux. Reprinted from *The Indignant Eye* by Ralph E. Shikes. Published by Beacon Press, 1969

Fred Fehl: 197, 201, 231, 237, 240

Collection of Mr. & Mrs. Lawrence Fleischman: 265B

Folger Library, model by John Cranford Adams and Irwin Smith: 466

French Government Tourist Office: 24

Giraudon, Paris: 183T, 521

The Hackley Art Gallery: 557

I.B.M. Art Collection: 579

The Image Bank: Larry Dale Gordon, 697; Toby Molenaar, 677, 680, 683, 688, 696; A. Seiden, 693; John Lewis Stage, 685

Magnum Photos: 326

Maine Central Railroad: 603

Metropolitan Museum of Art: 40T, Mrs. Frank B. Porter, 1922

Collection of Mr. & Mrs. Robert Montgomery: 269B

Museo del Prado, Madrid: 607TR

Museum of Fine Arts, Houston: Hogg Brothers Collection, 42T

Museum of Modern Art Film Library: 552, 571

Netherlands Information Service: 190, 191, 192

The New York Public Library: General Research and Humanities Division, Astor, Lenox and Tilden Foundations, 611T; Prints Division, Astor, Lenox and Tilden Foundations, 506, 608T

Norton Gallery and School of Art: 269T

Philadelphia Museum of Art: The Pilling Fund Exchange, 523B; Collection of the John and Mabel Ringling Museum of Art, 38TL

Sara Roby Foundation Collection: 183B

South African Information Service: 174

Trans World Airlines: 452, 482

U.S. Navy Combat Art Collection: 519BL

Universal Pictures: 144

Waldorf-Astoria: 372, 375

Orson Welles and Roger Hill: 386–463

Stanford W. Williamson: 284

11 12 KPKP 87 86 85